# ANTIQUES
## PRICE GUIDE 2006

# ANTIQUES

## PRICE GUIDE 2006

### Judith Miller

DK

LONDON, NEW YORK,
MELBOURNE, MUNICH, DELHI

A joint production from DORLING KINDERSLEY
and THE PRICE GUIDE COMPANY

## THE PRICE GUIDE COMPANY LIMITED

**Publisher** Judith Miller

**Publishing Manager** Julie Brooke

**Senior Managing Editor** Carolyn Madden

**European Consultants** Martina Franke,
Nicolas Tricaud de Montonnière

**Sub-editors** Jessica Bishop, Dan Dunlavey,
Sandra Lange

**Digital Image Co-ordinator** Ellen Spalek

**Editorial Assistant** Alexandra Barr

**Design & DTP** Tim & Ali Scrivens, TJ Graphics

**Photographers** Graham Rae, Bruce Boyajian, John
McKenzie, Andy Johnson, Byron Slater, Heike
Löwenstein, Adam Gault, Ellen McDermott

**Indexer** Hilary Bird

**Workflow Consultant** Bob Bousfield

**Publishing Advisor** Nick Croydon

## DORLING KINDERSLEY LIMITED

**Publishing Director** Jackie Douglas

**Managing Art Editor** Heather McCarry

**Managing Editor** Julie Oughton

**DTP Designer** Adam Walker

**Production** Melanie Dowland

**Production Manager** Sarah Coltman

While every care has been taken in the compilation of this guide, neither the authors
nor the publishers accept any liability for any financial or other loss incurred by
reliance placed on the information contained in *Antiques Price Guide 2006*

First American edition, 2005
00 01 02 03 04 05 06 07 08 09 10 9 8 7 6 5 4 3 2 1

Published in the United States by
DK Publishing, Inc.
375 Hudson Street
New York, New York 10014

The Price Guide Company Ltd
info@thepriceguidecompany.com

A CIP catalog record for this book is available from the Library of Congress.

ISBN: 0-7566-1336-1

Color reproduction by Colourscan, Singapore
Printed and bound by MOHN media and Mohndruck GmbH, Germany

Discover more at
**www.dk.com**

# CONTENTS

# INTRODUCTION

Yes, the doom and gloom merchants are at it again. How many times over the last 30 years have I heard that antiques have had their day? And yet good specialist dealers and auctioneers adapt and their businesses continue to grow. Many are taking advantage of the Internet boom and trading online where they can reach a thriving global marketplace.

A full-color annual price guide such as this one is an indispensable companion to online trading. My team travels the globe photographing antiques to ensure that all of the items featured are new each year. The prices featured are a guide – and nothing more – to the antiques pictured and tell you what you should expect to pay for a similar item in a similar condition.

My 'CARD' philosophy, that value is dependent on condition, age, rarity, and desirability, has never been more true. I would also add to this the 'Two Ps' – provenance and prettiness. You may think prettiness is subjective, but in a climate where buyers are more discriminating, looks are vital. And when faced with a nervous and discerning market more people want to be absolutely assured of an item's authenticity.

The items that have shown the greatest growth in recent months are pieces designed by the greats of the 20thC such as Le Corbusier, Marcel Breuer, and Charles and Ray Eames. These visionaries are beginning to rise to the same dizzy heights as Chippendale and Hepplewhite.

Tribal Art remains a growing market, as does American Folk Art. Pieces from the Arts and Crafts movement in America and Europe are enjoying renewed popularity thanks to recent international exhibitions. The market for fine and unusual furniture is also extremely buoyant.

I think this is a great time to buy, with prices for good quality pieces, particularly from the 19thC, offering superb value. They will last you a lot longer than mass-produced tat from the superstores – and you could become the auctioneer's best friend.

Trust me – this is the time to buy and I for one am doing just that. Just please don't tell my husband!

Sincerely,

Judith Miller.

# LIST OF CONSULTANTS

## Americana

**Tom Flanagan**
Pook & Pook
463 East Lancaster Avenue
Downingtown, PA 19335

**Gail Lettick**
Pantry & Hearth
994 Main Street South
Woodbury, CT 06798

## Canadiana

**Cynthia Findlay**
The Toronto Antique Center
276 King Street West
Toronto, Ontario M5V 1J2

## Ceramics

**Jill Fenichell**
By appointment only
Tel: 718 237 2490

## Clocks

**Bob Schmitt**
R.O. Schmitt Fine Arts
PO Box 1941
Salem, NH 03079

## Costume Jewelry

**Roxanne Stuart**
gemfairy@aol.com

**Bonny Yankauer**
bonnyy@aol.com

## Decorative Arts

**David Rago**
Rago Arts & Auction Center
333 North Main Street
Lambertville, NJ 08530

**Macklowe Gallery**
667 Madison Avenue
New York, NY 10021

## Furniture

**Lee Young**
Freeman's
1808 Chestnut Street
Philadelphia, PA 19103

**Ronald Bourgeault**
Northeast Auctions
93 Pleasant Street
Portsmouth, NH 03801

**Burden & Izett**
180 Duane Street
New York, NY 10013

## Glass

**Dudley Brown**
James D Julia
PO Box 830
Fairfield, ME 04937

## Lalique

**Nicholas Dawes**
Rago Arts & Auction Center
333 North Main Street
Lambertville, NJ 08530

## Modern Classics

**John Sollo**
Rago Arts & Auction Center
333 North Main Street
Lambertville, NJ 08530

## Oriental

**Robert McPherson**
R & G McPherson Antiques
40 Kensington Church Street
London W8 4BX, UK

## Paintings

**Alasdair Nichol**
Freeman's
1808 Chestnut Street
Philadelphia, PA 19103

## Posters

**Nicholas D. Lowry**
Swann Galleries
104 East 25th Street
New York, NY 10010

## Toys

**Barbara Lauver**
Harper General Store
10482 Jonestown Road
Annville, PA 17003

## Tribal Art

**Philip Keith**

# HOW TO USE THIS BOOK

**Page tab** – This device appears on every spread and identifies the main category heading as indicated in the Contents List on pp.5–6.

**The introduction** – The key facts about a factory, maker, or style are given, along with stylistic identification points, value tips, and advice on fakes.

**The caption** – The description of the item illustrated, including, when relevant, the period, the maker or factory, medium, the year it was made, dimensions, and condition. Many captions have **footnotes** which explain terminology or give identification or valuation information.

**The price guide** – The price ranges in the Guide are there to give a ball-park figure of what you should pay for a similar item. The great joy of antiques is that there is not a recommended retail price. These prices guides are based on actual prices, either what a dealer will take or the full auction price. They are expressed in US$ (even for the Canadian antiques shown). Canadian readers should refer to the latest currency conversion rates at http://finance.yahoo.com/currency/.

**Running head** – Indicates the sub-category of the main heading.

**A closer look at** – Does exactly that. This is where we show identifying aspects of a factory or maker, point out rare colors or shapes, and explain why a particular piece is so desirable.

**The object** – The antiques are shown in full color. This is a vital aid to identification and valuation. With many objects, a slight color variation can signify a large price differential.

**The source code** – Every item in *Antiques Price Guide 2006* has been specially photographed at an auction house, a dealer, an antiques market, or a private collection. These are credited by the code at the end of the caption, and can be checked against the Key to Illustrations on pages 724–8.

## THE PORCELAIN MARKET

Excitement rippled through European porcelain enthusiasts early last year as a number of very significant lots went under the hammer. A pair of mid-18thC tawny owls by Bow secured a record price of more than $215,000 at Sotheby's in New York. In the UK, a seated Chinaman found in a box of bric-a-brac turned out to be the first ever recorded example of a figure by Limehouse, the short-lived and almost mythical London factory.

Demand for Welsh porcelain continues unabated. Further afield, buyers from ex-Soviet states such as Russia, Latvia and Estonia have buoyed up demand for early Russian porcelain by factories such as St Petersburg and Gardner.

Continued economic uncertainty in the US has kept prices at the highest end of the market slightly lower than they might otherwise have been. Antique American porcelain is as scarce as ever. Good examples of wares by Tucker and Hemphill will always find a ready market, as will any quality American porcelain with a recognized name. The middle and lower end of the markets are undoubtedly suffering from a lack of younger collectors, but the best pieces continue to achieve good prices. The market still awaits with bated breath the discovery of dinner services by the 18thC American China Manufactory.

*– John Axford, Woolley & Wallis*

## BELLEEK

A Belleek oval covered basket, with three-strand center and double-looped rim, applied with roses, thistles and shamrocks, impressed mark "Belleek Co Fermanagh", some damage and repair.

*c1875*          5.5in (14cm) high

**$400-600**          **HAMG**

A Belleek circular basket, the rim applied with roses, shamrocks and rose stems forming the handles, with impressed "Belleek" on a strap.

9.25in (23cm) wide

**$800-1,200**          **WW**

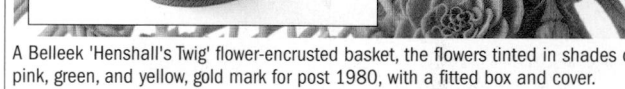

A Belleek 'Henshall's Twig' flower-encrusted basket, the flowers tinted in shades of pink, green, and yellow, gold mark for post 1980, with a fitted box and cover.

11in (28cm) wide

**$300-500**          **DN**

A late 19thC Belleek teapot and cover, molded as a sea-urchin, the handle, spout and foot molded as coral, with an impressed and molded mark.

6.5in (16.5cm) wide

**$400-600**          **WW**

### BELLEEK

- Founded in 1857 in County Fermanagh, Northern Ireland, by David McBirney and Robert Armstrong, Belleek initially produced earthenware.
- In 1863, a number of Stoke-on-Trent craftsmen joined the firm and it began to produce parian porcelain.
- The factory made a wide variety of vases, flower-pots, and centerpieces, often decorated with flowers or marine motifs.
- Teaware is Belleek's most extensive product. Common colors are white, green, and pink. Blue and butterscotch are rare.
- William Henshall originated the openwork baskets, with applied flowers, for which Belleek is famous.
- The earliest baskets were 'Convolvulus', 'Sydenham', 'Twig', and 'Shamrock'. The finest is thought to be 'Rathmore'.
- The history of the factory has been divided into a number of periods and the marks change accordingly.
- The factory is still in operation today.

A Belleek First Period globular teapot and cover, with basket molded loop handle and bird mask spout, molded with wheatsheaves, berries, and leaves, picked out in enamels and gilt, printed mark in black, short crack to spout.

*c1875*          6in (15cm) high

**$500-800**          **LFA**

A late 19thC Belleek glazed parian planter, applied with flowers to the shoulders, below the wavy rim, the lobed body molded with four sprays of prunus, on a petal-shaped foot, black hound, harp and Belleek mark.

9.75in (25cm) diam

**$400-600**          **CHEF**

A Bow chinoiserie octagonal plate, painted with a mythical dragon and flaming pearl, painter's no. "13".

c1755     8.5in (21.5cm) diam

**$1,500-2,000**     DN

A Bow powder-blue ground plate, typically painted with circular and fan-shaped chinoiserie panels around a central river landscape, with painted Chinese-style marks, slight surface wear.

c1760     8.25in (21cm) diam

**$500-800**     DN

A Bow blue and white plate, painted with the 'Caddy' pattern of figures in a landscape, slight damage.

c1760     9.5in (24cm) diam

**$500-800**     WW

A Bow blue and white chinoiserie plate or stand, painted with flowers and shrubs issuing from rockwork, within a floral panel and diaper band border, rim chips and manufacturing faults.

c1760     9.25in (23.5cm) long

**$280-320**     DN

A Bow dish, of lobed lozenge form painted in underglaze blue with a chinoiserie scene of a pagoda.

c1760     11.25in (28.5cm) wide

**$280-320**     SWO

A rare Bow dish, in the form of two overlapping cabbage leaves, picked out in underglaze blue and painted with berries, within a feuille-de-choix border, Chinese style four character mark in blue.

c1770     11.5in (29cm) wide

**$1,500-2,000**     LFA

A documentary Bow blue and white cup, with a molded flared top, the inner rim decorated with peony and lotus on a ground of dots and circles, the exterior painted with peony and willow, the base inscribed "Eliz.th Mackly. 1764", broken and re-glued and a large rim chip.

*Despite the extensive damage, this cup is valuable because it is inscribed and dated. This is rare in a piece of Bow.*

2.75in (7cm) high

**$3,200-3,800**     WW

A small Bow blue and white butter boat, with three feet and looped handle, decorated with flowers.

c1760     2.75in (7cm) wide

**$1,000-1,500**     JN

A Bow blue and white sauceboat, molded in low relief with flowers and painted with floral panels, the interior with a diaper band border, small chips.

7in (18cm) wide

**$500-700**     DN

One of a pair of Caughley blue and white plates, printed with figures in a landscape, unmarked, small chips.

*c1780*          7.75in (20cm) diam

**$220-280 pair**          **WW**

A Caughley blue and white plate, printed with the 'Nankin' pattern, rim chip.

*c1790*          8in (20.5cm) high

**$100-150**          **DN**

A Caughley Low Chelsea ewer, molded with acanthus leaves and painted with flowers, faint rim crack.

*c1770*          4.25in (11cm) long

**$400-600**          **WW**

A Caughley blue and white molded bowl, printed with Chinese figures on a bridge, in a pagoda landscape, "S" mark, the gilt rim rubbed.

*c1780*          6in (15cm) diam

**$180-220**          **WW**

## A CLOSER LOOK AT A CAUGHLEY DISH

The well-controlled printing in dark blue and the light straw colored glaze is typical of Caughley. When held to a light, the body looks slightly orange, compared to the greenish tint found on Worcester.

Both Caughley and Worcester made versions of this design. They can be distinguished by the fact that the fisherman in the Worcester version has a larger fish and longer wiggly line.

Finely powdered black cobalt oxide is mixed with oil and painted onto the surface. When fired, it reacts with a lead glaze and turns blue.

Pieces are often marked with an "S" or an "S+" for the county of Salop, although a "C" was used between c1775-1795.

A Caughley blue and white water basin, printed with the 'Fisherman and Cormorant' pattern.

*c1790*          11.5in (29cm) diam

**$1,200-1,800**          **DN**

A rare Caughley lobed oval sauce tureen, cover, stand and ladle, with a loop knop, painted in underglaze blue with Chinese river landscapes within key fret and diaper paneled borders, gilded detail, the stand with a blue "X" inside the footrim, slight damage.

*c1790*          9in (23cm) wide

**$2,200-2,800**          **LFA**

A Caughley porcelain jug, molded with cabbage leaves and a mask spout, transfer-printed blue floral decoration, underglaze blue crescent mark.

*c1785*          8.5in (21cm) high

**$700-1,000**          **S&K**

A Chelsea raised anchor deep fluted dish, painted with a central circular reserve of a wolf and a heron from Aesop's Fables.

*c1750*　　　　4.5in (11.5cm) wide

**$18,000-22,000**　　　**SHF**

A Chelsea raised anchor deep fluted dish, painted with a central circular reserve of two tigers playing on a rock.

*c1750*　　　　5in (13cm) wide

**$18,000-22,000**　　　**SHF**

A Chelsea lobed plate, with fluted cavetto, painted in a Kakiemon palette with the 'Hob in the Well' pattern within a scrolling border, red anchor mark.

*c1750*　　　9.5in (24cm) diam

**$7,000-10,000**　　　**LFA**

A Chelsea lobed plate, painted in colored enamels with flowers, the rim with wave molded panels and painted exotic birds, red anchor mark.

*c1755*　　　8.5in (21.5cm) diam

**$300-500**　　　**LFA**

A Chelsea plate, painted with sprays of flowers, red anchor mark, some surface scratches.

*c1755*　　　8in (20.5cm) diam

**$400-600**　　　**DN**

A Chelsea Hans Sloane botanical plate, of faceted form, painted with branches from the Arbutus tree and scattered insects, chocolate line rims, red anchor mark.

*c1755*　　　8in (20.5cm) wide

**$12,000-18,000**　　　**SHF**

A Chelsea plate, boldly painted in colored enamels with an exotic bird perched on rockwork within a brown line rim, brown anchor mark, restored rim.

*c1760*　　　8.75in (22cm) diam

**$800-1,200**　　　**LFA**

A Chelsea figure of a dancing man, gold anchor mark.

*c1760*　　　7.75in (20cm) high

**$10,000-15,000**　　　**AA**

A Chelsea blue and white soup plate, painted with a pair of long-tailed fowl in a landscape, with a diaper and floral panel band and shaped rim, blue anchor mark.

*c1755*　　　8.75in (22.5cm) diam

**$28,000-32,000**　　　**DN**

A large pair of Chelsea masqueraders, modeled as a lady and gentleman in Turkish dress, he wears a turban, she with an ermine lined cloak, each raised on a gilded scrolling base applied with flowers, gold anchor marks.

*c1760*　　　13in (32.5cm) high

**$10,000-15,000**　　　**WW**

A 'Girl-in-a-Swing' factory porcelain scent bottle.

*3in (7.5cm) high*

**$4,000-6,000**     **AA**

A small 'Girl-in-a-Swing' factory fob seal, modeled and painted as a standing figure of Punchinello, the cornelian seal cut with a dove and a motto, the mounts of yellow metal.

*'Girl-in-a-Swing' is the name attributed to a London factory established by Charles Gouyn in 1749. The name was inspired by a white figure of a girl, currently in the Victoria & Albert Museum, London, thought to be from Gouyn's factory.*

*1.25in (3cm) high*

**$300-500**     **CHEF**

A Chelsea raised anchor tall beaker, of molded faceted form, painted with a Ho Ho bird in blossoming branches on glaze enamel, the Phoenix bird to the reverse, small rim chip, unmarked.

*c1750*     *3in (7.5cm) high*

**$12,000-18,000**     **SHF**

---

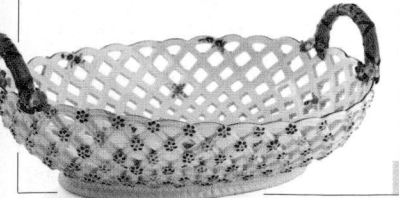

Rear: A small Chelsea red anchor ashet, painted with Deutsche Blumen, the border relief decorated with scroll and diaper panel, painted red anchor mark.

*13in (33cm) wide*

**$1,000-1,500**     **L&T**

Front: A Chelsea red anchor circular pierced basket, painted with a central panel of Deutsche Blumen including roses and lilies, the exterior embossed with yellow flowerheads, exterior decoration of leaves and forget-me-not, faint painted red anchor mark, crack to rim.

*16.75in (17cm) diam*

**$1,000-1,500**     **L&T**

A Chelsea pierced oval two-handled basket, painted with floral bouquets and sprays, loop handles with flowerhead terminals, red anchor mark, repair to handles.

*c1755*     *11.25in (29cm) long*

**$500-800**     **DN**

---

## A CLOSER LOOK AT A CHELSEA CREAMBOAT

Chelsea was founded by silversmith Nicholas Sprimont. Many early shapes, like this cream boat, were influenced by British silverware.

Jefferyes Hammett O'Neale enjoyed success at Chelsea, where he specialized in fable decoration and figures, as well as at Worcester. A named and highly regarded designer add to this piece's value.

Pieces from this period often feature Chelsea 'moons' – bubbles trapped in the body that appear as lighter spots when held to a strong light.

This cream boat dates from the 'Red Anchor' period (1752-56) when Chelsea was influenced by Meissen.

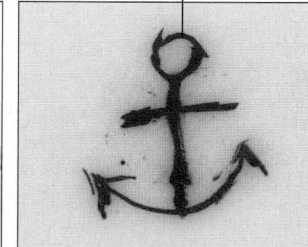

A Chelsea leaf-shaped creamboat, of fluted form, by Jefferyes Hammett O'Neale, with a solid loop handle, the reserve painted with birds in foliate and a landscape scene, red anchor mark, small cracks to rim.

*c1780*     *4in (10cm) wide*

**$40,000-45,000**     **SHF**

## DERBY

- The Derby factory produced porcelain from c1750. From 1787 it operated under William Duesbury the younger.
- Early wares, including tea sets, tureens, and baskets, aimed at the London market, were influenced by the designs of Meissen.
- During the Regency period, patterns were copied from Chinese and Japanese wares. The 'Old Witches', 'Tree of Life' and 'Kings' patterns from the Imari range were popular.
- The factory also produced many figures, often portraying pastoral scenes or Chinese and allegorical figures.
- Derby also produced a large range of ornamental pieces for display. The creamy white glaze gave pieces a unique, soft finish, making it popular today.
- Derby porcelain is sometimes called 'dry edge' because the glaze was removed from the base before firing to prevent pooling.
- Pieces were unmarked before 1770. After this, a model number was often added to the base.
- The company went into decline after Duesbury died in 1797.
- In 1870, the factory became home to Derby Crown Porcelain Co., which became Royal Crown Derby. It is still in operation today.

A Derby shepherd boy, with appliqué details, sitting on a wicker basket and holding flowers in a bow-shaped felt hat, unglazed, the flowers with blue glaze, the base impressed with "N 36".

c1770       6in (15.5cm) high

**$600-900**     **SHF**

A pair of Derby cupids, with appliqué details, one holding a falcon by a string and the other sitting under a tree with a dog, originally part of a four-piece sporting series, unglazed.

c1785       5in (13cm) high

**$500-800**     **SHF**

A Derby 'The Gardener' figure, with appliqué details, depicting a country gentleman leaning on a tree stump and holding a posy of flowers, on a Greek key base.

c1785       8in (20.5cm) high

**$500-800**     **SHF**

A Duesbury Derby group of two child musicians, with appliqué flowers, on a scroll molded base, from a Tournai original by Nicholas Gauron, patch marks, incised number "140", glazed.

c1770       10in (25.5cm) high

**$3,000-4,000**     **SHF**

A pair of Derby models of the 'Welsh Tailor and his Wife', from the King Street Works, in the white, each astride a goat, on shell and scroll molded oval mound base, painted marks in blue, some damage.

6.5in (16.5cm) high

**$400-600**     **LFA**

A Derby Longton Hall figure of a seated harlequin playing a set of bagpipes, decorated in polychrome enamels, on a scroll molded base, slight damage and restoration, unmarked.

c1755       5.5in (14cm) high

**$6,000-9,000**     **SHF**

A Derby allegorical figure of Ceres, with appliqué details, holding a sickle and sheaves of wheat in her right arm, with a prancing infant by her side, on a scroll molded base.

c1755       7in (18cm) high

**$2,800-3,200**     **SHF**

A Derby figure of a boy as Summer, his coat finely painted with sprays of flowers, on a scroll molded base, once part of a four-piece set depicting the seasons.

c1755       5in (12.5cm) high

**$3,000-4,000**     **SHF**

A pair of Derby figures, with appliqué details, the lady holding a posy of flowers, the man with a floral-patterned vest, on scroll molded bases.

c1755       man 5.5in (14cm) high

**$3,000-4,000**     **SHF**

A pair of early 19thC Derby porcelain vases, each with gilt pierced border and grotesque masks, above a floral painted band, on quatriform base, red painted marks, covers missing.

*4in (10cm) high*

**$320-380** HAMG

A garniture of three Derby Imari campana, each with two gilt snake handles, iron-red script marks, minor damage and wear.

*c1820*       *largest 8in (20.5cm) high*

**$700-1,000** DN

A pair of Derby porcelain twin-handled vases and covers, each of compressed circular shape with a domed cover and strap handles with gilt masks, printed marks including date code.

*1884*       *5in (13cm) high*

**$400-600** SWO

A Victorian Derby inkstand decorated in Imari palette with pattern number 80, comprising a two handled tray, inkwell and cover, cylindrical box and cover, and a taper stick, damaged.

**$350-400** CHEF

A garniture of three Derby bough pots, painted with a still life of fruit, probably by Steele, in a rectangular panel on a green and gilt ground, raised on scroll feet, red printed marks.

*c1820*       *8.5in (21cm) high*

**$4,000-6,000** WW

Part of an extensive composite Derby tea and coffee service, decorated in the Imari palette, rust-painted factory mark, comprising teapot, cover and stand, sucrier and cover, cake plate, four bread plates, 24 tea cups, 16 coffee cans, 16 saucers, and a slop bowl.

**$1,500-2,000 set** L&T

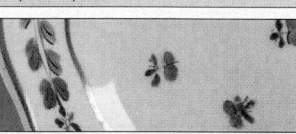

Two pieces from a part Derby fruit service, painted with cornflower sprays and a leaf and flower repeat border, rust painted factory marks, comprising five heart-shaped serving dishes with scroll handles, three plainer heart-shaped dishes, three lozenge-shaped dishes, two lozenge-shaped stands, sauce tureen and cover, and a large twin-handled serving bowl.

**$400-600 set** L&T

## A CLOSER LOOK AT A DERBY CUP & SAUCER

*Trembleuses, saucers with a circular pierced gallery in the center to hold the cup and prevent it from 'trembling' and spilling, were created in the early 18thC for drinking chocolate.*

*William Duesbury took over control of the factory from his father in 1786 and oversaw a period in which finely decorated display wares were produced for the higher end of the market.*

*This mark was used c1782-1825. Earlier Derby is generally unmarked. Since the introduction of marks, around 30 different versions have been used.*

*James Banford (1758--1798) worked at Derby from 1789 to about 1797. He specialized in fine quality figure subjects.*

A rare Derby cabinet cup and trembleuse saucer, probably by James Banford, the cup with entwined handle, finely painted in colored enamels with two female figures garlanding a bust of Pan, with inscription "Olim truncus eram ticulnus inutile lignum" ("once upon a time I was a trunk, a useless log from a fig tree"), crowned crossed baton marks in blue and titled beneath, saucer with restored rim chip.

*This design is taken from an engraving by William Wynne Ryland, after Angelica Kauffman, 'Olim Truncus Elim', published by Ryland in 1776.*

*c1790*

**$8,000-12,000** LFA

15

A pair of Richard Chaffers & Co. Liverpool teabowls and matching saucers, painted in underglaze blue with a scene of deer in a park, picked out in brown, red, green, and gilt enamels, diaper border to the interior.

*c1760*     *bowl 2in (5cm) high*

**$350-400**     **H&L**

A Liverpool finely potted bowl, probably by Philip Christian's factory, painted in underglaze blue with a crane in a Chinese river landscape of a fence, flowering branches and rockwork, the interior with a stylized leaf scroll within a diaper band.

*c1760*

**$1,000-1,500**     **LFA**

An 18thC Pennington's Liverpool blue and white coffee pot and cover painted with flowers on the lid and baluster body, the rims with alternating flower vignette, cell and coral diaper bands.

*9.75in (25cm) high*

**$180-220**     **CHEF**

A Pennington's Liverpool porcelain sparrow-beak jug, printed in blue with sprays of flowers.

*c1785*     *3.75in (9.5cm) high*

**$280-320**     **DN**

A rare Liverpool small cylindrical can, with notched loop handle, painted in underglaze blue with a Chinese angler in a river landscape, with a boat in full sail, tiny rim chip.

*c1755*     *2.5in (6.5cm) high*

**$1,800-2,200**     **LFA**

A Pennington's Liverpool porcelain sparrow-beak jug, printed in blue with sprays of flowers.

*c1785*     *3.75in (9.5cm) high*

**$280-320**     **DN**

## LIVERPOOL

- In the 1750s a number of porcelain factories operated in Liverpool in close proximity.
- The key companies were: Richard Chaffers 1754-65, Philip Christian 1765-76, Samuel Gilbody c1754-61, William Reid and others c1755-70, John and James Pennington c1770-94 and Seth Pennington and John Part 1778-1803.
- Chaffers and Christian were leading makers. They produced blue and white porcelain tea wares, inspired by Chinese designs, which can be difficult to distinguish from Worcester.
- Liverpool porcelain is variable in quality and is often 'peppered' with small speckles on the glaze.
- Pieces were decorated in blue and white, colored enamels or a harsh famille-rose palette.
- Pieces were left unmarked, making identification difficult today.
- Coffee services are popular today and figures are rare.

A Liverpool cylindrical mug, probably Richard Chaffers & Co., with a flattened loop handle, brightly painted in colored enamels with flowering branches, a fence and rockwork, in Chinese famille rose palette.

*c1760*     *4.5in (11.5cm) high*

**$3,200-3,800**     **LFA**

A Richard Chaffers & Co. Liverpool coffee can, with a Chinese landscape painted in underglaze blue, iron red, and gilt, interior with a diaper band.

*c1760*     *2.5in (6.5cm) high*

**$1,200-1,800**     **LFA**

A Liverpool coffee cup, with notched loop handle, painted in famille rose palette with Chinese figures, the interior with an iron red spearhead band.

*c1760*     *2.5in (6.5cm) high*

**$700-1,000**     **LFA**

A William Ball sparrow beak jug, enameled in colors with fence and flowers, slight chip to rim.

*An advertisement appeared for William Reid's porcelain in the Liverpool Advertiser of November 12th 1756. By June 1761, the company was bankrupt. It continued under William Ball until it was leased to James Pennington & Co. in 1763.*

*c1760*     *3in (7.5cm) high*

**$1,500-2,000**     **JN**

A rare Longton Hall slender baluster milk jug, with a sparrow beak and loop handle, painted in underglaze blue with a Chinese river landscape of two buildings beneath a tree.

*c1755*                    *3.5in (9cm) high*

**$3,000-4,000**                        **LFA**

A Longton Hall blue and white bowl, painted with a Chinese landscape, small foot rim chip.

*c1755*          *4.5in (11.5cm) diam*

**$700-1,000**                      **WW**

A Longton Hall 'Folly' pattern spoon tray, of modified leaf form, depicting an obelisk and figure with a walking stick.

*1755*          *6.75in (17cm) long*

**$8,000-12,000**                  **RTC**

A pair of Longton Hall Strawberry leaf plates, painted with exotic birds in foliage, within a molded border of strawberry leaves and fruit, tiny chip to rim, unmarked.

*c1755*          *10in (25.5cm) wide*

**$4,000-6,000**                  **SHF**

A Longton Hall melon tureen and cover, of naturalistic form with a twig finial, on a triangular leaf-shaped foot, decorated in yellows and greens, painter's mark in black.

*c1760*          *4in (12cm) high*

**$10,000-15,000**                **SHF**

## LOWESTOFT

A very rare Lowestoft blue and white cup, painted with a three-turret bridge and flowers.

*c1760*

**$600-900**                        **JN**

A Lowestoft cylindrical mug, with an S-scroll handle, printed in underglaze blue, interior with a diaper band, chips.

*c1785*          *5.5in (14cm) high*

**$400-600**                        **LFA**

A Lowestoft teabowl and saucer, painted in underglaze blue, teabowl with decorator's mark "X" and cracks.

*c1780*

**$500-800**                        **LFA**

A large Lowestoft blue and white bowl, the exterior decorated with a Chinese figure, bird and two boats in a pagoda landscape, the center with a flower spray, marked "5", hairline crack.

*c1765*          *9.5in (24.5cm) diam*

**$2,000-3,000**                    **WW**

### LOWESTOFT

- Robert Brown and partners founded the Lowestoft porcelain factory in Suffolk, England in 1757. It closed in 1802.
- The shapes of early underglaze blue ware tended to be based on salt-glaze stoneware.
- Foot-rims were usually marked with a numeral.
- After 1765, overglaze colors were used.
- Worcester became a major influence on designs, although the porcelain used at Lowestoft was coarser and prone to staining.
- The quality of the porcelain declined after 1770, when shapes and patterns were simplified and marks were seldom used.
- Rare Lowestoft birth tablets, painted with a baby's name, and pieces inscribed for the local market, are popular with collectors.
- Identification of Lowestoft largely relies on knowledge of patterns and shapes.

A Lowestoft bowl, painted in underglaze blue with two horses in a Chinese river landscape, the interior with a diaper band, short rim crack.

*c1780*          *6.25in (16cm) diam*

**$300-500**                        **LFA**

A Lowestoft teapot cover, with ball knop, painted in underglaze blue with a Chinese river landscapes within a flower diaper band.

*c1780*          *3.25in (8.5cm) diam*

**$180-220**                        **LFA**

A rare Lowestoft blue and white circular plate, decorated with a Chinese woman standing in a garden with a two-handled urn, flowers to the border.

*c1770*                    8.75in (22cm) diam

**$5,000-8,000**                          JN

A Lowestoft creamboat, of Low Chelsea ewer form, with a scroll handle, painted in underglaze blue with trailing flowers and leaves.

*c1780*              4in (10cm) long

**$1,200-1,800**              LFA

A Lowestoft globular teapot and cover, painted in colors and gilt with Chinese figures in a garden at various pursuits.

*c1770*

**$1,000-1,500**              JN

A Lowestoft baluster milk jug, with a sparrow beak and S-scroll handle, painted in colored enamels.

*c1785*         3.25in (8.5cm) high

**$1,200-1,800**              LFA

A Lowestoft butter boat, of Low Chelsea ewer form, painted in colored enamels with flowers and leaves beneath a brown line rim, crack, some discoloration.

*c1785*              4in (10cm) long

**$300-500**              LFA

## MINTON

A pair of Minton biscuit porcelain figures, 'Flower-Seller' and 'Fruit-Seller', a country maiden carrying flowers in the apron of her dress, damage, and a youth carrying a basket of fruit, both on spiral molded bases, unglazed.

*c1810*              7in (18cm) high

**$800-1,200**              SHF

A Minton bowl, part of a rare set comprised of two large plates, three side plates and three bowls, with illustrations of a chick and a wasp, the illustrations attributed to the Frenchman Pierre Mallet (1836-1898).

*c1870*         9.75in (25cm) diam

**$500-700 set**              TCS

A mid-Victorian inkwell and cover, possibly Minton, modeled as a bunch of flowers, the handle formed of the stalks tied by a pink ribbon, daisy head cover with morning glory tendril knop.

8.75in (22cm) wide

**$400-600**              CHEF

An unusual Minton Parian bust of Princess Mary of Teck, later Queen Mary, after H. Tyler, on a titled cylindrical socle and square base, impressed mark and incised "H. Tyler Sc. 1898".

10.75in (27cm) high

**$700-1,000**              LFA

A pair of Minton's china ewers, of Neo-Classical design, the loop handles with laurel leaf decoration and satyr mask terminals, with royal blue ground and oval beaded portrait medallions of Lady Hamilton (Romney) and Mrs Fitzherbert (Romney), both signed "F.N. Sutton", and with gilt printed mark.

*c1900*         11.5in (28.5cm) high

**$1,800-2,200**              L&T

## A CLOSER LOOK AT A MINTON BOTTLE

*Marc-Louis Solon (1835-1912) worked with the technique of pâte-sur-pâte whilst at Sèvres before introducing it to Minton, when he joined the company, in 1871. The importance of this artist makes this signed piece extremely valuable.*

*The high quality porcelain of Minton is some of the finest produced in England during the 18th and 19thC.*

*The decoration is inspired by Classicism and Renaissance styles. White slip is built up in layers against a dark background, to give the effect of depth.*

A fine Minton pâte-sur-pâte olive green pilgrim bottle, the sides finely painted and hand-tooled in white slip with a seated nymph holding a cupid amongst stars, gold crowned globe mark, impressed "Mintons, N-Y, shape 1343", signed "L. Solon".

*c1880*                    *10.5in (26cm) high*

**$28,000-32,000**                    **FRE**

A pair of Minton blanc-de-chine four-light candelabra, with leaf-molded sconces and scroll branches held aloft by a male and female figure, each with a torch bearing putto and seated on a column, impressed mark and puce printed retailer's mark, some restoration.

*c1885*          *23.5in (59.5cm) high*

**$500-800**                    **HAMG**

## SPODE

A Spode perfume bottle, the mazarin blue ground enriched with gilt florate patterns.

*c1805*          *4in (10cm) wide*

**$2,800-3,200**                    **SHF**

An early Victorian Spode scent bottle and stopper, the broad rim of the baluster shape in gilt, above applied flowers and shells on a pea green body, gilt mark.

*5in (13cm) high*

**$500-800**                    **CHEF**

A Spode scent bottle and cover, the mazarin blue ground overlaid with cisele figures of exotic birds in foliage, pattern number "4051".

*Cisele is a technique where patterns are tooled into thickly applied gilding to create intricate decoration.*

*c1805*          *4in (10cm) high*

**$500-800**                    **SHF**

An early Victorian scent bottle and stopper, possibly Spode, the downswept neck and shoulders applied with flowers between gilt handles, gilt bands to the dished rim, rim of the body and the socle foot, marked "1664" in mauve.

*6.35in (16cm) high*

**$300-500**                    **CHEF**

A Spode spill vase, the pale blue mazarin ground enriched with with gilt scrolls and florate sprays, pattern number "4298".

*c1810*          *3in (8cm) high*

**$280-320**                    **SHF**

A Spode potpourri vase and cover, with gilt crocodile handles, painted with applied white slip with figures of cherubs, on an aubergine ground.

*c1805*          *3in (8cm) high*

**$600-900**                    **SHF**

A Spode teapot and cover, of swept-neck form, the mazarin blue ground painted in gilt enriched with Chantilly spray patterns and gilt line rims.

*c1805*          *7in (18cm) wide*

**$400-600**                    **SHF**

A Spode porcelain campana-shaped pastille burner and cover, painted with sprays of flowers reserved on a blue and gilt scale ground, the pierced cover with flamiform finial, iron-red mark and pattern number "1166".

c1820                          4.75in (12cm) high

**$4,000-6,000**                                    **DN**

A Spode trio, comprising a teacup, coffee cup and saucer, with shaped handles, the mazarin blue ground enriched with gilt decoration and line rims, pattern "1166".

c1805          saucer 5.5in (14cm) diam

**$4,000-6,000**                                   **SHF**

A Spode chamberstick with snuffer, the mazarin blue ground enriched with gilt decoration, pattern "1166".

c1805                          5in (13cm) wide

**$3,500-4,000**                                   **SHF**

A Spode watering can, with two handles, the mazarin blue ground with raised florate sprays and chrysanthemum sprigs, pattern "3153".

c1805                            4in (10cm) high

**$1,800-2,200**                                   **SHF**

An early 19thC Spode inkwell, decorated with the 3993 pattern of birds and foliage on a claret ground, two quill holders and an inkwell within the oval rim.

4.75in (12cm) wide

**$120-180**                                       **CHEF**

## STAFFORDSHIRE

A Staffordshire porcelain ovoid jug, the leaf-molded scroll handle picked out in blue, painted in colored enamels with flowers and leaves, and inscribed in gilt "F/R Lees, 1816".

5.5in (14cm) high

**$320-380**                                        **LFA**

A Staffordshire porcelain cottage-shaped pastille burner and stand, with a thatched roof and an oriel window to one end, painted in colored enamels with climbing flowers and leaves, picked out in gilt, shallow chip.

c1820                          5in (13cm) high

**$1,000-1,500**                                    **LFA**

A 20thC Staffordshire porcelain stirrup cup, modeled as a fox with a red coat and black eyes, the collar dressed with holly.

4.75in (12cm) long

**$280-320**                                        **S&K**

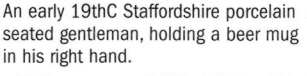

An early 19thC Staffordshire porcelain seated gentleman, holding a beer mug in his right hand.

c1840          5.25in (13.5cm) high

**$220-280**                                        **KGO**

An early 20thC Staffordshire porcelaineous elephant group of a leopard hunter, of William Kent type, modeled with a leopard slung over the elephant's withers and the mahout seated next to it in Eastern dress, tusks restored.

8in (20.5cm) high

**$300-500**                                         **DN**

A Swansea 'Carnation' or 'Peony Rose' pattern dinner plate, printed in blue with the floral center and chinoiserie-type border, impressed "SWANSEA".

*c1810*      *9.5in (24.5cm) diam*

**$800-1,200**      **DN**

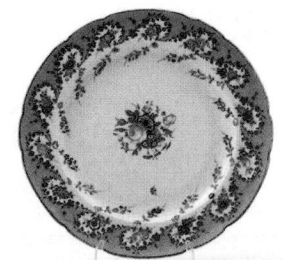

A Swansea plate, decorated in London, with flowers in colored enamels, the border with a blue dot ground and trailing flowers within tooled gilt flower and leaf scroll loops, star crack.

*c1815*      *7.25in (18.5cm) diam*

**$700-1,000**      **LFA**

A good Swansea plate, painted in the manner of William Billingsley, in brightly colored enamels with a loose garland of flowers, the rim gilded, red painted 'Swansea' mark.

*c1820*      *8.5in (21.5cm) diam*

**$7,000-10,000**      **WW**

A pair of Swansea porcelain dessert plates, the centers painted with a floral bouquet within a floral band ring, the pale-green-ground borders with C-scroll panels of flower sprays, iron-red "SWANSEA", slight wear.

*c1820*      *8.25in (21cm) diam*

**$5,000-7,000**      **DN**

A Swansea two-handled shaped rectangular serving dish, painted with scattered floral sprays, iron-red mark, cracked.

*c1820*      *12.5in (32cm) wide*

**$500-800**      **DN**

A Swansea porcelain plate, sparsely painted in green and gilt with scattered floral sprigs within a band of urns suspending husk swags and a gilt-line rim, gilt script mark, some wear.

*c1820*      *8.25in (21cm) diam*

**$280-320**      **DN**

One of a rare pair of porcelain candlesticks, possibly Swansea, with a ribbed stem picked out in gilt, the base painted in colored enamels.

*c1820*

**$5,000-8,000 pair**      **LFA**

## WORCESTER

An 18thC Worcester blue and white sparrow beak jug, the baluster sides with sprays of flowers, the interior with foliate rim band with diaper vignettes.

*3.5in (8.5cm) high*

**$120-180**      **CHEF**

An 18thC Worcester blue and white jug and cover, the baluster sides painted with sprays of flowers below diaper vignettes, crescent mark.

*5in (13cm) high*

**$280-320**      **CHEF**

A Worcester blue and white sparrow beak jug, printed with the so-called 'Three Flowers' pattern, blue crescent mark.

*c1775*      *4in (10.5cm) high*

**$500-700**      **DN**

A Worcester porcelain cabbage leaf jug, with a mask spout and floral decoration.

*c1770*      *8.25in (21cm) high*

**$180-220**      **SWO**

A Worcester blue and white sparrow beak jug, painted with the 'Cannonball' pattern.

*c1775*      *3.75in (9.5cm) high*

**$300-500**      **DN**

A Worcester white porcelain sparrow beak jug and cover, with a flower finial, molded in low relief with the 'Chrysanthemum' pattern.

*c1765*      *5.5in (14cm) high*

**$600-900**      **DN**

An 18thC Worcester blue and white sauceboat, molded with cartouches and fluted decoration and painted with scenes of fishermen in a boat.

*5in (13cm) wide*

**$700-1,000**      **GORL**

## WORCESTER

■ The first factory in Worcester was established in 1751. The major shareholder, Dr John Wall, acquired the stock and closely guarded steatite recipe of Lund's failed Bristol porcelain works.

■ In 1783, Thomas Flight bought the factory to be run by Joseph and John Flight, his sons.

■ The 'Flight' period was between 1783 and 1792.

■ The 'Flight & Barr' period lasted from 1792 to 1804. The new, simpler forms of this period were characterized by fine painting.

■ The 'Barr Flight & Barr' period was between 1804 and 1813.

■ The 'Flight Barr & Barr' period lasted from 1813 to 1840.

■ In 1840 the company was amalgamated with Chamberlain's, another Worcester porcelain firm.

■ In 1862 the conglomerate became Royal Worcester Porcelain.

■ The final amalgamation of the porcelain manufacturers in the area took place in 1889 when Grainger's was brought under the umbrella of the Royal Worcester Porcelain Company.

An 18thC Worcester blue and white chocolate cup and saucer, painted with the 'Fence' pattern within shaped rims, with ogee-handled cup.

*5.5in (14cm) wide*

**$700-1,000**      **GORL**

An 18thC Worcester teabowl and saucer, painted with a willow tree and a fence.

*3.5in (8cm) wide*

**$700-1,000**      **GORL**

An early 18thC Worcester blue and white teacup, painted with the 'Warbler' pattern.

*2.5in (6cm) high*

**$500-700**      **GORL**

One of a pair of Worcester blue and white butter boats, the painted inside with gooseberries and flowers, the exteriors molded with three tiers of leaves about the stalk handles, one with crescent mark.

*c1765*      *3.5in (9cm) wide*

**$800-1,200 pair**      **CHEF**

A Worcester blue and white butter boat, painted on the interior with four sprays of flowers and a butterfly, the exterior molded with three tiers of leaves, the stem handle continuing into the center of the foot-rim, crescent mark.

*c1765*      *3.5in (9cm) wide*

**$400-600**      **CHEF**

A Worcester globular teapot, with loop handle, painted in underglaze blue with the 'Canonball' pattern, beneath a diaper band, script "W" mark, no cover.

*c1770*      *4.75in (12cm) high*

**$280-320**      **LFA**

A Worcester globular teapot and cover, with loop handle and flower knop, printed in underglaze blue with the 'Fruit and Wreath' pattern, within leaf and C-scroll bands, hatched crescent mark, small chip to tip of spout.

*c1775*      *6in (15cm) high*

**$500-800**      **LFA**

A Worcester flared basket, printed in underglaze blue with the 'Pine Cone' pattern, within a flower, scroll and diaper border, the exterior applied with flowerheads, picked out in blue, hatched crescent mark.

*c1770*      *7.25in (18.5cm) diam*

**$700-1,000**      **LFA**

A rare Worcester round chamberpot, with loop handle and turned over rim, printed in underglaze blue with the 'Three Flowers' pattern, the interior with Auriculas, beneath a cell diaper band, hatched crescent mark.

*c1770*      *5.25in (13.5cm) high*

**$2,200-2,800**      **LFA**

A Worcester dish, of naturalistic form, molded in the shape of a lettuce leaf, with overlapping handles, penciled in lilac with a chinoiserie scene of two Chinamen outside a pavilion, slight rubbing to highlights, unmarked.

c1760     10.5in (26.5cm) wide

**$2,200-2,800**     **SHF**

A Worcester teapot stand, of hexagonal form, decorated with polychrome enamels depicting a Chinese family fishing in a lake, all within a scale red border and vignette of lakeside scenes, slight rubbing, unmarked.

c1765     5.5in (14cm) wide

**$3,200-3,800**     **SHF**

## A CLOSER LOOK AT A WORCESTER DISH

*This piece dates from the very first years of porcelain production at Worcester, making it of great interest to the collector.*

*James Rogers' painting is particularly celebrated. He is known to have specialized in the depiction of birds, but any decoration that can be attributed to his hand is very desirable.*

*The molded edge of this dish is very vulnerable to chipping. This piece is remarkable in that it has survived intact.*

*Depictions of ruins are typical of the Neo-Classical period, during which the arts were suffused with the Graeco-Roman culture.*

A Worcester dish, by James Rogers, of naturalistic form, molded in the shape of a leaf with a short stalk, painted monochrome handles, decorated with a European landscape of ruins, and bouquets of flowers in a scrolled reserve edged with yellow, all within sprays and bouquets of flowers, unmarked.

c1755     8in (20cm) long

**$12,000-18,000**     **SHF**

A Worcester deep sauce dish, possibly by James Giles, painted in the chinoiserie style, with a central circular reserve depicting a Chinaman and a horse in a wooded Chinese garden, within a border enriched with gilt scrolls, unmarked, mint condition.

c1770     7.5in (19cm) wide

**$4,000-6,000**     **SHF**

A Worcester plate, with indented border, painted in colored enamels in the London atelier of James Giles.

c1770     9in (23cm) diam

**$800-1,200**     **LFA**

A Worcester plate, with fluted border, painted in colored enamels in the London atelier of James Giles.

c1770     8.25in (21cm) diam

**$1,000-1,500**     **LFA**

A Worcester scallop-edged plate, decorated in the Giles workshop, in gilt and colored enamels with two cranes, peony, prunus, and bamboo to an Arita design, no marks.

**Provenance:** *Raby Castle, Durham, North England, UK.*

c1770     8in (20.5cm) diam

**$1,500-2,000**     **WW**

A First Period Worcester cornucopia-shaped wall picket, with spiral molding, painted on glaze, with bouquets of flowers and scattered insects, originally one of a pair.

*c1755*      *9.5in (24cm) high*

**$6,000-9,000**      **SHF**

A Worcester faceted circular bowl, painted in the Chinese style and depicting a corpulent monk holding a fan by a screen and three girls seated at a table, the interior with foliate sprays and gilt enriched dot border, unmarked.

*c1765*      *6in (15cm) wide*

**$1,800-2,200**      **SHF**

A Worcester cabbage leaf molded sauceboat, with stalk loop handle, painted in colored enamels.

*c1755*      *8.75in (22cm) long*

**$280-320**      **LFA**

A Worcester sweetmeat basket, of pierced and circular form, the exterior with molded florets, the interior interlaced with circlets, painted with bouquets of English flowers and insects.

*c1770*      *8in (20.5cm) wide*

**$1,800-2,200**      **SHF**

## BARR, FLIGHT & BARR

An early 19thC Barr period Worcester teacup and saucer, from a trio, each piece finely decorated with a Japanese pattern, the cup and saucer Barr, Flight & Barr, the coffee can Barr period.

*5.5in (14cm) diam*

**$500-700 trio**      **GORL**

A Flight, Barr & Barr Worcester plate, painted in colored enamels with an exotic bird, the shaped pale blue ground with butterflies and insects, within a gilt gadrooned rim, impressed mark and printed mark in brown.

*c1815*      *8.5in (21.5cm) diam*

**$500-700**      **LFA**

### A CLOSER LOOK AT A BARR, FLIGHT & BARR WORCESTER DESSERT PLATE

As a result of Worcester's good standing and reputation at the time, members of the aristocracy commissioned services from the firm. This piece bears the crest of John Prendergast-Smythe, First Viscount Gort.

High quality gold adorned the factory's wares from the end of the 18thC. Following a visit by the king in 1788, Worcester abandoned its blue and white output to focus on higher-end pieces.

The landscape scene is well executed. Worcester was known for its fine hand-painted decoration during the Barr, Flight & Barr period.

The piece is marked BFB for the Barr, Flight & Barr period of 1804-1813.

A Barr, Flight & Barr Worcester dessert plate, made for John Prendergast, First Viscount, depicting a landscape scene, probably by Thomas Rogers, of the Wye near Goodrich Castle, within a border of gilt arabesques and line rims, with the crest of Viscount Gort, including Prince of Wales plumes, fine condition.

*c1810*      *9in (23cm) wide*

**$5,000-8,000**      **SHF**

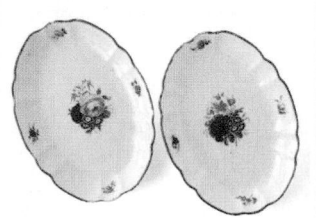

A pair of Nantgarw oval dishes, each painted with a central bouquet within four small scattered floral sprays and a gilt dentil rim, one impressed "Nantgarw C.W.", wear to gilding.

*c1820*          *11.5in (29.5cm) wide*

**$2,200-2,800**          **DN**

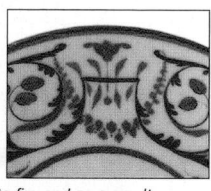

A Nantgarw teacup and saucer, decorated in shades of iron-red, green and gilt with scrolling foliage, saucer fritted to underside.

*Nantgarw porcelain is fine and translucent. It was difficult to fire and as a result, teaware is especially scarce. Many pieces were sent to London to be decorated in the fashions of the time, but this piece was decorated locally.*

*c1820*          *55in (14cm) wide*

**$1,200-1,800**          **DN**

A Nantgarw shaped oval dish, with a gilt shell handle and painted in blue with scattered floral sprays, impressed "Nantgarw C.W."

*c1820*          *8in (20.5cm) wide*

**$400-600**          **DN**

A New Hall cream jug, of tapered form with fluted lower section and conical foot, painted in the Chinese export style with pattern N173, small foot rim chip, slight fritting.

*c1800*          *5in (12.5cm) high*

**$150-200**          **DN**

A New Hall plate, brightly printed and painted with three sprays of flowers and leaves, molded border with black and green bands, pattern number 1749.

*New Hall was the first factory to assign pattern numbers to its designs, helping collectors to identify and date pieces.*

*c1815*          *8.25in (21cm) diam*

**$220-280**          **LFA**

A Wedgwood porcelain potpourri vase and cover, painted in polychrome enamels, with a long-tailed tit, dartford warbler and a group of bathers, with gilt ring handles and faceted rims, marked "Wedgwood" in script and titles in black.

*c1820*          *3.5in (9cm) wide*

**$1,800-2,200**          **SHF**

One of a set of seven early 20thC Wedgwood fish plates, painted by A. Holland with the W2582 pattern of named freshwater fish swimming within powder blue and gilt rim bands, printed marks.

*8.75in (22.5cm) diam*

**$700-1,000 set**          **CHEF**

A 20thC Wedgwood porcelain part dinner service, each piece with rich gilt foliate decoration on a deep red ground, comprising of 18 dinner plates, 18 side plates, 18 bread and butter plates, 18 cups, 18 saucers and four small dishes, printed brown and green marks.

*dinner plate 11in (27.5cm) diam*

**$3,000-5,000**          **FRE**

A mid-19thC Wedgwood glazed parian figure of a lady reclining, with a blue drape over her knee and an anchor in her left hand, impressed mark.

*9.5in (24cm) high*

**$300-500**          **CHEF**

A Samuel Alcock Parian model of Arthur Wellesley, first Duke of Wellington, the base with a wreath surmounted with a ducal coronet and molded with monogram "WW", the underside printed "Published by Saml. Alcock & Co., June 18 1852, Alfred Crowquill Designavit. G. Abbott. Sculpit", hands repaired, crack and blisters.

*11in (28cm) high*

**$300-500** DN

A Copeland Parian bust of Napoleon Bonaparte, on a socle base, after an original by William Theed (1804-91), the reverse impressed "Copeland", small chips and cracks.

*c1865* *11in (28cm) high*

**$800-1,200** DN

A Copeland Parian bust of Enid, modeled after the original by F.M. Miller, with gilt highlights, on a column plinth base, the reverse with printed and impressed marks.

*c1860* *16.5in (41cm) high*

**$1,000-1,500** DN

A Parian bust of Ned Hanlan, the professional rowing world champion, raised on a socle base.

*c1880* *11.75in (30cm) high*

**$2,800-3,200** RTC

## COMMEMORATIVE CERAMICS

A circular footed punch bowl, the oak leaf and acorn painted border with a pair of opposing swags, inscribed with "Nelson 22 April", the interior painted with central panel depicting the "Armorials of Vice Admiral Horatio, Viscount Nelson of the Nile, K B".

*The armorial bearings allude to incidents in Nelson's life and the honors accorded him. This illustration of Nelson's arms is accurate and complete, in the highest late-Hanoverian artistic style.*

*9in (23cm) diam*

**$2,800-3,200** L&T

A cylindrical tyg, the oak leaf and acorn painted border with a pair of opposing swags, inscribed with "Nelson 22 April", the front painted with a panel depicting the "Armorials of Vice Admiral Horatio, Viscount Nelson of the Nile, K B".

*5.25in (13.5cm) high*

**$2,800-3,200** L&T

An early 19thC Masonic Sunderland luster jug, with black printed decoration, the Masonic print inscribed "Dixon & Austin Sunderland Pottery", a view of the cast Ironbridge verso and a monogram "WM".

**$800-1,200** SWO

A black basalt rectangular commemorative teapot and cover, with everted rim, serpent loop handle and a lion mask spout modeled with Britannia garlanding a bust of Wellington, the reverse inscribed "India, Portugal and Spain, Vittoria 21st June 1813", rim chip to cover.

*c1815* *5.75in (14.5cm) high*

**$500-800** LFA

An 1825 Reform commemorative jug, of ornate Rococo shape printed in mulberry with the figure of Britannia and flags titled "UNION" and "REFORM", with union sprays around and inside the neck titled "COMMERCE AND FREEDOM" and "UNITY AND LIBERTY", unmarked.

*1825* *7in (18cm) high*

**$300-500** DN

An unusual earthenware cylindrical mug, with angular loop handle, printed in underglaze blue with "The Immortal Shakespeare", "Shakspeare's Mulberry Tree" and a figure of fame, beneath a band of figures.

*c1830* *5.75in (14.5cm) high*

**$700-1,000** LFA

A rare pearlware lobed plate commemorating "Our Amiable Queen Adelaide", printed in purple with a portrait and titled beneath, the gadrooned border with sprays of flowers and leaves, printed lion and crown mark, small chip to underside of rim.

c1830                8.5in (21.5cm) diam

**$700-1,000**                **LFA**

A nursery plate commemorating the wedding of Victoria and Albert, of octagonal shape with a portrait of the couple printed in black and enameled in red, blue and green, the daisy molded rim lined with pink luster, unmarked.

c1840                6in (15cm) wide

**$400-600**                **DN**

A Sunderland luster jug commemorating the Crimea, of typical Dutch shape with pink luster lining and highlights, printed in black and enameled in colors, one side with a pseudo coat-of-arms titled "Crimea", the other with a print titled "The Flag that Braved a Thousand Years", the front with a verse "England, England, Glorious Name ... ", unmarked, minor chip to spout.

c1855                7in (18cm) high

**$600-900**                **DN**

## A CLOSER LOOK AT A COMMEMORATIVE BEAKER

*Commemorative wares have crossover interest as they appeal to porcelain aficionados as well as people with an interest in history. This increases the desirability and value of an item.*

*Edward VII's coronation was postponed due to his appendicitis. Although this piece is not dated, many commemorative items on the market are incorrectly dated June 24th 1902. Pieces bearing the correct date – August 9th – are far harder to find.*

*This piece sold at auction for a sum considerably higher than estimated. In a highly specialized field such as commemorative ceramics, prices can fluctuate wildly, particularly if two collectors are interested in the same rare piece.*

*There is little if any evidence of rubbing to the attractive gilt decoration on this beaker, enhancing the value.*

A Minton & Hollins paperweight commemorating the golden jubilee of Queen Victoria, covered with green glaze and molded with a portrait of the Queen, with monogram and "JUBILEE 1887", detailed impressed mark with maker's name and address, "Rd.68207", minor edge chipping.

1887                5in (12cm) high

**$180-220**                **DN**

A Copeland souvenir Edward VII loving cup, with flaring rim and gilt handles, printed shield mark to base "Souvenir Edward VII. 1910, Subscribers copy, T Goode & Co, South Audley St, London".

7in (18cm) high

**$1,000-1,500**                **SWO**

A Royal Doulton beaker commemorating the coronation of Edward VII, with an oval portrait and raised gilt foliage on a red ground.

1902                4in (10cm) high

**$1,200-1,800**                **WW**

## CHANTILLY

- The Chantilly factory was founded in 1725 by Louis-Henri of Bourbon, Prince of Condé. The factory started making soft-paste porcelain in the 1730s.
- Many of the early wares were decorated in the Kakiemon style or in designs copied from Chinese originals.
- Kakiemon style figures were a speciality before c1750.

- During the second half of the 18thC, pieces were decorated with scattered European flowers. Designs were typically painted in simple blue or colored enamels following the 1753 edict limiting the use of gilded decoration to Vincennes.
- Pieces are marked with a hunting horn and sometimes with the word "Chantilly". The factory closed c1800.

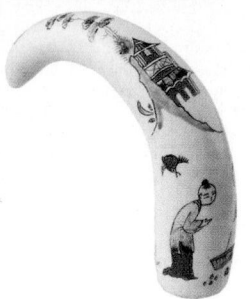

A Chantilly cane handle, decorated in the Kakiemon style with figures and buildings.

c1740     3in (8cm) high

**$1,200-1,800**    **HFG**

### A CLOSER LOOK AT A CHANTILLY BOX & COVER

*Before 1740, pieces had a yellowish body and an opaque tin glaze. After this time a transparent lead glaze was used.*

*The decoration on early Chantilly may have been inspired by pieces in the Prince of Condé's extensive Oriental ceramic collection.*

*The Kakiemon style became popular throughout Europe, but no other factory rivaled Chantilly for the quality of its imitation Kakiemon pieces.*

A Chantilly magot figure, depicting a reclining Chinese figure, decorated with flowers in the Kakiemon style, gilt-bronze mounts.

c1740     12.5in (32cm) wide

**$80,000-100,000**    **GV**

A Chantilly oval box and cover, polychrome decorated in the Kakiemon style.

c1745     2.5in (6.5cm) wide

**$1,800-2,200**    **PIA**

A Chantilly bowl, decorated with flowers and insects in the Kakiemon style, with red hunting horn mark.

c1740

**$2,800-3,200**    **GV**

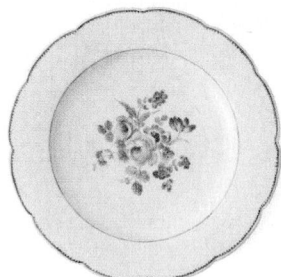

A Chantilly plate, polychrome decorated with floral bouquets, hunting horn mark.

c1760     9.5in (24cm) diam

**$400-600**    **HFG**

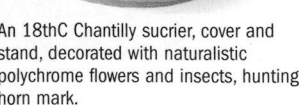

An 18thC Chantilly sucrier, cover and stand, decorated with naturalistic polychrome flowers and insects, hunting horn mark.

9in (23cm) wide

**$3,500-4,000**    **HFG**

An 18thC Chantilly plate, decorated with flowering sprigs, hunting horn mark.

9.5in (24cm) diam

**$180-220**    **HFG**

An 18thC Chantilly cream pot and cover, decorated with flowering sprigs, hunting horn mark.

3in (8cm) high

**$300-500**    **HFG**

A Chantilly square fruit dish, with 'à la brindille' decoration of flowering sprigs in monochrome blue.

c1770     8.75in (22cm) wide

**$280-320**    **GV**

A late 19thC set of four Samson figures of the gods, after Meissen, depicting 'Diana', 'Vulcan', 'Jupiter' and 'Apollo', marks in blue.

*6in (15cm) high*

**$300-500** | **CHEF**

A late 19thC Samson figure modeled as a lady playing a hurdy-gurdy, in a chinoiserie style.

*11.5in (29cm) high*

**$280-320** | **CHEF**

## A CLOSER LOOK AT A PAIR OF SAMSON 'MEISSEN' FIGURES

*Edmé Samson (1810-1891) specialized in reproductions and copies of other popular ceramic manufacturers, such as Meissen, Worcester, Bow, Derby, and Chelsea. This pair is modeled on a Meissen original. They were also copied by Derby in the 18thC.*

*Distinctions between an original and a Samson piece are evident. A grayish hard paste was used to copy creamy soft paste originals and the reproductions tended to be less sharply modeled.*

*Johann Joachim Kändler, on whose work this pair is based, was the most famous Meissen modeler. He produced a wide range of lively and flamboyant figures including a tailor – thought to be tailor to Count Brühl, the director of the factory, who had many clothes – and his wife.*

*Despite being copies, Samson pieces are sought after today because they are highly decorative and were popular at the time.*

A pair of 19thC Samson goat groups, in the Meissen style, the subjects based upon the 'Tailor and Tailor's Wife' models by Kändler and Eberlein, on oval bases with mock Derby marks.

*7in (18cm) high*

**GORL**

A late 19thC Samson shaped box and hinged cover, painted with a Watteauesque vignette and sprays of flowers, blue cross mark, glued mount.

*2.5in (9cm) wide*

**$120-180** | **DN**

A late 19thC Samson pill box and hinged cover modeled as a mouse, the cover painted with a cat chasing a mouse.

*2.5in (6cm) wide*

**$80-120** | **DN**

## SÈVRES

One of a pair of Sèvres plates, painted with polychrome flower sprays within blue leaf scroll borders, marked with interlaced "L"s enclosing a "G".

*c1760*    *10.25in (25.5cm) wide*

**$800-1,200 pair** | **WW**

A late 18thC Sèvres dessert dish molded as a flowerhead, painted with colorful flower sprays, marked with interlaced "L"s enclosing "M".

*8.5in (21cm) wide*

**$700-1,000** | **WW**

One of a set of twelve Sèvres porcelain portrait plates, retailed by Davis Collamore & Co., New York, each plate painted with portraits of 'Roi de Rome', several Bonaparte ladies and other French dignitaries, within apple green borders, enhanced with gilt lattice and jeweled decoration, printed marks "Chateau Des Tuileries" and "Sèvres 1844", signed "Morin".

*9.5in (24cm) diam*

**$10,000-15,000 set** | **FRE**

A pair of 19thC Sèvres porcelain plates, painted with swags of summer flowers within gilt borders.

*8.35in (21cm) diam*

**$300-500** | **ROS**

## BERLIN

- The Royal Porcelain Factory in Berlin (est. 1752) is highly regarded for its late 18thC and early 19thC Neo-Classical wares.
- During the early 19thC, the company specialized in producing fine gilt wares. Dinner wares and vases were meticulously painted with scenes framed with an opulent gilt border.
- Topographical views of well-known buildings, Classical scenes and portraits were popular subjects.
- Berlin successfully adapted to the expanding middle class market by producing ornate display wares, particularly 'cabinet cups'.
- Vases, usually based on urns and kraters, and decorated with Classical motifs, formed a major part of the output from c1830.
- From c1840 the factory began to produce porcelain plaques enclosed in gilt frames. Blanks would be sent to decorators who would paint copies of Old Masters or sentimental subjects.
- Pieces are marked "KPM" (Königliche Porzellan-Manufaktur).
- The Berlin factory is still in operation today.

A large Berlin plaque, painted with the 'Penitent Magdalene', after Correggio, draped in blue velvet, lying in a wooded grotto reading a book, impressed scepter and "KPM" marks.

c1860    22.25in (55.5cm) wide

**$10,000-15,000**    FRE

A large Berlin rectangular plaque, painted with a young girl sitting beside a river with a classical building in the distance, impressed "KPM" and scepter marks, incised "13 1/4 - 11 1/4".

c1870    13.5in (34cm) wide

**$10,000-15,000**    WW

A good Berlin porcelain plaque, painted with a gypsy girl standing beside a tree with a tambourine at her feet, impressed "KPM" and scepter mark.

c1880    13in (32.5cm) high

**$7,000-10,000**    FRE

A Berlin porcelain plaque, painted with a Pre-Raphaelite beauty wearing a Grecian gown, in a rose draped interior with mosaic floor, with an ornate carved gilt-wood rococo scroll frame, impressed "KPM" and scepter mark.

c1880    13in (32.5cm) high

**$7,000-10,000**    FRE

### A CLOSER LOOK AT A KPM PORCELAIN PLAQUE

Berlin was known for treating porcelain vases and plates as a medium for painted images. Plaques allowed further experimentation with painting.

Many plaques were copied from well-known paintings. This is after the work of the French religious artist Charles Landelle (1821-1908).

Berlin plaques had elaborately scrolling gilt frames. This intricate frame adds to the value.

Unmarked plaques can be worth up to 50 percent less.

A good Berlin porcelain plaque, depicting 'Ruth' after Landelle, holding a wheatsheaf under one arm, in an ornate carved gilt wood rococo scroll frame, impressed "KPM" and scepter mark.

c1880    13in (32.5cm) high

**$7,000-10,000**    FRE

A good Berlin porcelain plaque, painted with young gypsy girl leaning against a brick wall and holding a lute, impressed "KPM" and scepter mark.

c1880    13in (32.5cm) high

**$8,000-12,000**    FRE

A late 19thC Berlin porcelain plaque, depicting Madonna reading, framed, impressed "KPM" and scepter mark.

17.5in (44cm) high

**$3,000-5,000**    FRE

A Dresden rectangular box, with polychrome flower decoration and a gilt edge, blue mark.

*3.5in (9cm) wide*

**$180-220** | BMN

A late 19thC Dresden flower-encrusted oval wall mirror, mounted with putti and musical motifs, blue cross mark, some small chips and repairs.

*17.75in (45cm) high*

**$800-1,200** | DN

A Dresden-style miniature salon suite, decorated with painted floral sprays in relief, the table with an impressed crossed swords mark and initials "DKE".

*chair 5in (12.5cm) high*

**$400-600** | H&L

A Dresden porcelain figure of the Pied Piper of Hamlin, modeled dancing and playing his pipe.

*8in (20cm) high*

**$150-200** | DN

## FRANKENTHAL

A Frankenthal pug bowl, with naturalistic painting and engraved gilded brass mounting with hinge and cambered thumb rest, blue crowned "CT" mark.

*c1770*     *2.5in (6.5cm) high*

**$1,500-2,000** | BMN

A Frankenthal porcelain figure of a seated pug, on a raised base, naturalistic design and decoration, impressed "PH", incised mark.

*c1760*     *3.5in (8.8cm) high*

**$2,800-3,200** | MTZ

A mid-18thC Frankenthal figure of a lady playing a mandolin, blue lion rampant mark and impressed marks.

*4in (10cm) high*

**$500-800** | WW

A Frankenthal figure of a country woman, model by Johann Wilhelm Lanz, standing on a gilded rocaille socle, holding a wheatsheaf with both arms and wearing a hat, a white blouse and a red and green striped skirt, blue "CT" mark, the hat restored.

*c1760*     *6in (15cm) high*

**$1,800-2,200** | LPZ

A Frankenthal porcelain tea caddy, with rounded shoulders and painted birds, blue lion mark and interlaced "JAH", incised mark with three dots.

*c1760*

**$800-1,200** | MTZ

A Frankenthal porcelain coffeepot, on three scrolled feet, the domed lid with a pear knop, gilt-scroll borders, with painted scenes, blue underglaze lion mark, four dots in a square, letter "I".

*This piece is part of a service originally made for the Court of Kurpfalz.*

*c1760*     *10in (25cm) high*

**$42,000-48,000** | MTZ

A large Frankenthal plate, with 'Altozier' relief decoration, gilding, Indianische Blumen and rocks, blue lion mark.

*c1760*     *13in (32.5cm) diam*

**$1,200-1,800** | BMN

A Frankenthal plate, painted with flowers, the gold slightly rubbed, blue lion mark.

*c1760*     *8.5in (21cm) diam*

**$220-280** | BMN

A Fürstenberg bullet-shaped teapot and cover, painted with colored enamels and gilt, script "F" mark, chips.

*c1770*

**$800-1,200**     DN

A pair of Fürstenberg cups and saucers, decorated with floral paintings and scattered flowers, gilding, blue "F" mark.

*c1800*

**$280-320**     BMN

A Louis XVI Fürstenberg lidded vase, gilded and decorated with Camaieu-Sepia paintings of parkscapes, the lid partly restored, blue mark "A.B."

*c1785*     *16.75in (42cm) high*

**$1,500-2,000**     BMN

An early 19thC Fürstenberg 'Berliner Stummel' shape pipe bowl, with polychrome painted scene in a gold reserve, blue F-mark to inside.

*4.5in (11cm) long*

**$500-800**     BMN

A Fürstenberg porcelain oval snuff box, with gilt-metal mounts, the exterior with scroll and floral reliefs painted in purple, the inside lid and reserves painted with putti in landscape, unmarked.

*c1770*     *3.25in (8cm) wide*

**$3,000-5,000**     MTZ

An early 19thC Fürstenberg group of the drunken Silenus on a barrel, the putto with a flask at his feet, the barrel painted with panels of harbor scenes in the Meissen style, on a scroll-molded base, partially colored and with gilt, script "F" mark, some damage and restoration.

*9.75in (25cm) high*

**$2,800-3,200**     DN

## HÖCHST

- In 1746, the elector of Mainz granted a privilege to Adam Friedrich von Löwenfinck (1746-58), a porcelain decorator who had once worked at Meissen, to establish a faience factory in Höchst. The factory produced porcelain from 1750.
- The factory became known for its figures, modeled by talented craftsmen including Simon Feilner (1726–98), who produced a range inspired by the Commedia dell'Arte, and Johann Peter Melchior (1742-1825), who created finely detailed figures on mound bases.
- Wares were painted with landscapes and figures, especially rustic scenes, or scattered flowers.
- Modeled details, such as scrollwork spouts, small animals details and wishbone handles, decorated many of the factory's wares, including trembleuse cups and saucers.
- From c1750, a blue wheel mark was used.
- The firm suffered from financial difficulties and political upheavals in the region, finally closing in 1796. The molds were sold to the Damm Pottery (est. 1827) in Aschaffenburg, and original Höchst pieces were reproduced in faience from c1830. These reproductions are also widely collected today.
- In 1946, the Höchst porcelain factory reopened at its original location in Höchst.

A Höchst porcelain group of three putti.

*c1770*     *6.5in (16.5cm) high*

**$4,000-6,000**     BMN

A Höchst porcelain jug, decorated with a landscape of buildings and a figure, restored, blue wheel mark.

*c1770*     *5.5in (14cm) high*

**$1,500-2,000**     BMN

A Höchst cup and saucer, decorated with rural scenes, the rims gilded, blue wheel mark.

*c1770*

**$2,200-2,800**     LPZ

A Höchst candlestick, ornately modeled as a couple kissing, minor restorations.

*c1755*     *10.5in (26cm) high*

**$22,000-28,000**     LPZ

A Meissen tea cup and saucer, painted with rural vignettes of cowherds and cows within ozier-molded borders, blue crossed swords marks.

*c1760*

**$500-800** DN

A late 19thC Meissen flower-encrusted cabinet cup and saucer, painted with scattered floral sprigs, blue crossed swords marks.

**$500-800** DN

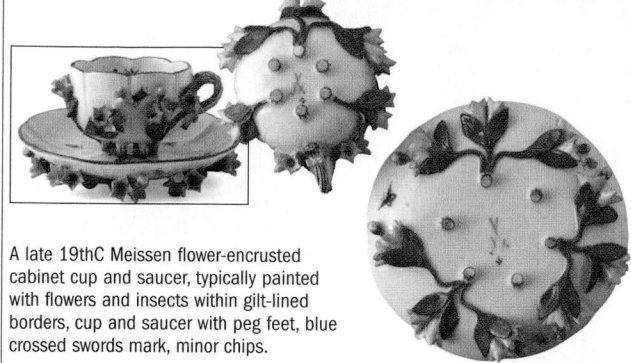

A late 19thC Meissen flower-encrusted cabinet cup and saucer, typically painted with flowers and insects within gilt-lined borders, cup and saucer with peg feet, blue crossed swords mark, minor chips.

*4.5in (11.5cm) wide*

**$500-800** DN

A Meissen blue ground saucer, painted with a quatrefoil panel of a rural scene, within an elaborate gilt diaper panel cartouche surmounted with shells, within a gilt border, blue crossed swords mark, rubbed.

*c1740*     *5in (12.5cm) diam*

**$500-800** DN

A Meissen Kakiemon plate, painted with the 'Lowe' pattern, within a 'Sulkowski' ozier border with insects and sprays of Indianische Blumen, blue crossed swords and dot mark, riveted repair to rim.

*c1740*     *9in (23cm) diam*

**$300-500** DN

A mid-18thC Meissen quatrefoil ozier-molded tureen stand, painted with scattered Deutsche Blumen, gilt-line rims, blue crossed swords mark and dot mark, rubbing to gilt.

*11in (28cm) wide*

**$400-600** DN

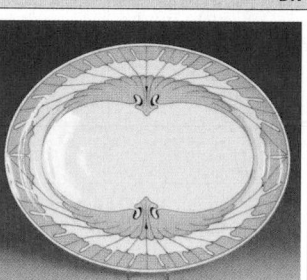

A Meissen large oval porcelain serving dish, from the 'Flügelmuster' service, blue underglazed swords mark and model number.

*c1900*     *19.12in (47.8cm) wide*

**$500-800** MTZ

An important Meissen porcelain coffee and tea service, comprising of 25 pieces in the original wooden case, with coffee pot, milk jug, teapot, waste bowl, spoon cup, sucrier, twelve teacups, six coffee cups, 18 saucers, all with blue and coral red scrolling decoration and a central crested coat-of-arms, blue underglazed swords mark and "8".

*c1740*

**$80,000-100,000** MTZ

A Meissen porcelain bowl and cover, with a button knop, with gilt and coral-framed cartouches of trading and equestrian scenes, gold to rims, blue swords mark, number in gold.

*c1735*     *4.28in (10.7cm) diam*

**$3,000-5,000** MTZ

A Marcolini Meissen porcelain tureen, with molded ram-head handles, painted panels and gold staffage, the cover with berry knop, blue underglazed swords mark with a star, painter's mark.

*c1775*     *10.5in (26cm) wide*

**$1,800-2,200** MTZ

A Meissen porcelain tureen and cover with stand, with a baluster-shaped body and two weaved loop handles, heavily embossed with flower trails and painted with birds and insects, gold rims, blue underglazed swords mark.

*c1745*

**$3,000-5,000** MTZ

A Marcolini Meissen porcelain tureen and stand, with a baluster-shaped body and a pine-cone knop, painted in rose and coral-red with colorful reserves, gilt-scroll borders, blue underglazed swords mark with star.

*c1775*

**$5,000-7,000**     **MTZ**

An Augustus Rex two-handled bowl, cover and stand, painted with panels of birds and butterflies, "A.R." mark in blue.

*9.5in (24cm) wide*

**$1,500-2,000**     **JN**

A Meissen sucrier and cover, with flower knop, decorated in colored enamels with figures and panels of flowers, gilt scroll borders, canceled mark in blue.

*4.25in (10.5cm) high*

**$400-600**     **LFA**

A 19thC Meissen sugar bowl and cover, with a matching milk jug, the bowl painted with a view of Bastei, the jug with a view of Wesenstein and further panels of colorful flowers and rich, gilt scrollwork, crossed swords mark and titled to bases.

*4.5in (11.5cm) wide*

**$2,200-2,800**     **WW**

A 19thC Meissen porcelain breakfast set, comprising an oval tray, teapot, milk jug, sucrier, and a pair of cups and saucers, all with quatrefoil gold reserves painted with scenes and figures on a yellow ground, blue underglazed swords mark.

**$2,800-3,200**     **MTZ**

An early Meissen teapot, in white Böttger porcelain, of baluster shape with a domed lid and pointed finial, the slim curved spout with gilt and a mask, gilt-crested oval reserves of painted chinoiserie scenes in iron-red and purple.

*c1725*     *5.5in (14cm) high*

**$8,000-12,000**     **MTZ**

A Meissen coffee pot, in white Böttger porcelain, with a domed lid and pine-cone knop, decorated with quatrelobe reserves of landscape scenes in gilt-edged cartouches, gold cipher, blue underglazed swords mark, purple triangle and cross.

*c1730*     *8in (20cm) high*

**$10,000-15,000**     **MTZ**

A Meissen porcelain coffee pot, decorated with gilt-edged reserves of painted figural scenes and rich Böttger luster, blue underglazed swords mark, gold cipher, turner's mark.

*c1730*     *7.75in (19.5cm) high*

**$5,000-8,000**     **MTZ**

A Meissen porcelain coffee pot, with a rocaille spout and domed lid with gilt pine-cone knop, gilt-scroll border and continuous painting of a river landscape, blue underglazed swords mark, gold cipher.

*c1745*     *9.25in (23cm) high*

**$5,000-7,000**     **MTZ**

One of a pair of 19thC Meissen porcelain 'Element' ewers, representing 'Air and Water', with an S-shape handle, richly decorated with putti, Neptune and a peacock, blue underglazed swords mark, damage and restoration.

*26.5in (66cm) high*

**$10,000-15,000 pair**     **MTZ**

A 19thC Meissen porcelain vase, designed by H.A. Leuteritz, with scroll handles and a gilt-edged pâte-sur-pâte reserve of a woman holding a mirror, cobalt-blue ground, underglazed blue swords mark.

*14.75in (37cm) high*

**$7,000-10,000**     **MTZ**

A Meissen porcelain figure of a seated harlequin holding a bagpipe, by Johann Joachim Kändler, the rocaille base encrusted with flowers and leaves.

c1740          5.5in (13.5cm) high

**$1,500-2,000**                    **MTZ**

A Meissen porcelain figure of a female gardener holding a wicker basket, modeled by Johann Joachim Kändler, the base with flowers and leaves, blue underglazed swords mark.

c1745          7.8in (19.5cm) high

**$2,200-2,800**                    **MTZ**

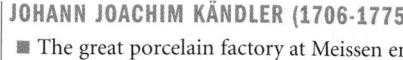

## JOHANN JOACHIM KÄNDLER (1706-1775)

- The great porcelain factory at Meissen employed Johann Joachim Kändler to revitalize its modeling section in 1731.
- He became chief modeler two years later when Kirchner, his predecessor, left the firm.
- This position meant that he was responsible for sculpting original models out of wax or clay from which molds were made.
- Kändler produced figures ranging from tinkers to lords, as well as more idiosyncratic ranges of harlequins and monkey bandsmen.
- His signature was complicated yet refined detailing in the Baroque style. He had an eye for fluid, naturalistic movement
- His most prestigious commission was to create a large collection of porcelain animals for Augustus the Strong – the most ambitious ceramic project ever attempted in Europe at the time.
- Kändler's work was much imitated by his contemporaries. If unsure about the authenticity of a piece, it is always best to examine it against one that is known to be genuine to compare the quality of the modeling and the colors.
- Groups, especially those that combine human figures with animals, are invariably more valuable than single figures.
- Kändler worked at the factory for 44 years.

A Meissen model of a baker, after a model by Johann Joachim Kändler, holding a baking bat, crossed swords mark to base, rubbing to gilt, restoration.

c1745          7in (17.5cm) high

**$5,000-7,000**                    **WW**

A pair of Meissen figures of trinket sellers, after models by Johann Joachim Kändler from drawings by Edmé Bouchardon, unmarked, lacking box lids, some repairs.

c1745          7.25in (18.5cm) high

**$5,000-8,000**                    **WW**

An 18thC Meissen 'Street Chef with Turkey' porcelain, modeled by Peter Reinicke and Johann Joachim Kändler, model no. 31, painted and gilded, blue crossed swords mark, restored.

5.5in (14cm) high

**$1,200-1,800**                    **BMN**

An 18thC Meissen two-faced mythological porcelain figure, wearing a long robe, crown and bayleaf wreath, polychrome painted, gilded, unglazed base, blue crossed swords mark.

5in (12.5cm) high

**$1,200-1,800**                    **BMN**

A Meissen porcelain 'Violinist' figure, modeled by Friedrich Elias Meyer, model no. 10, from the series 'Gallant Band', gilded, blue crossed swords mark, damage and restoration.

c1750          5.5in (13.5cm) high

**$1,000-1,500**                    **BMN**

A Meissen 'Winter' putto figure, modeled seated on a plinth base and wearing an ermine-lined cloak and holding a small brazier, figure and base probably glued.

c1750          5in (12.5cm) high

**$500-700**                    **DN**

A Meissen porcelain 'The Earth' putto figure, after an original by Johann Joachim Kändler, model no. C100, from the series 'The Four Elements', blue crossed swords mark, restored.

c1860          4.5in (11.5cm) high

**$500-800**                    **BMN**

A Meissen porcelain figure of a gardening child, after an original by Johann Joachim Kändler, model no. 7x, painted and gilded, blue crossed swords mark, arms and hat restored.

c1860          5in (13cm) high

**$700-1,000**                    **BMN**

A late 19thC Meissen rustic group, of a gentleman and two companions, one modeled seated with a birdcage on her knee, the other standing with a bird in one hand and a basket of flowers in the other, gilt, blue crossed swords mark and incised "F94", damage and losses.

*8.75in (22cm) high*

**$1,000-1,500**    **DN**

A late 19thC Meissen group, of a boy escorting a maid with apples, a third figure, probably the boy's tutor, holding a book, the boy's books and a cane in a pile at their feet, painted with colored enamels and gilt, on an oval base with a gilt ovolo band frieze, blue crossed swords mark and incised "J. 61", chips.

*7.75in (21cm) high*

**$2,200-2,800**    **DN**

A late 19thC Meissen group, of a seated lady holding a heart, with a male courtier, a female attendant offering manicure and a young male attendant with a tray, crossed swords mark, incised mark and incised numeral "100".

*10.5in (27cm) wide*

**$1,200-1,800**    **GORL**

A late 19thC Meissen allegorical group, modeled as a rocky mound base surmounted with figures wearing 18thC dress, sparsely colored and with gilt, blue crossed swords mark, incised "D.93", damage, losses and restoration.

*11.5in (29cm) high*

**$800-1,200**    **DN**

---

A late 19thC Meissen model of a winged putto, probably Cupid, tied to a tree trunk with roses, blue crossed swords mark, "R123", restored.

*7in (18cm) high*

**$700-1,000**    **DN**

A late 19thC Meissen group, of dancing lovers, on a scroll-molded base, blue crossed swords mark, incised "C.75", restored.

*5in (14cm) high*

**$700-1,000**    **DN**

A late 19thC Meissen group, of a shepherdess playing a lute and a companion with a bunch of flowers, blue crossed swords mark, "447", restored.

*5.5in (14cm) high*

**$1,200-1,800**    **DN**

A late 19thC Meissen Bacchic model, of a man wearing 18thC dress, with a flower-encrusted wine ewer, blue crossed swords mark, incised "907".

*8in (20cm) high*

**$700-1,000**    **DN**

A late 19thC Meissen figure of a woman, emblematic of 'Sight' from a series of 'The Senses', blue crossed swords mark, small chips to lace frills.

*6in (15cm) high*

**$1,500-2,000**    **DN**

---

A late 19thC Meissen group of three children, amongst ruined columns, on an oval mound base, blue crossed swords and cancelation marks, incised "G 32", numbered, restored.

*8.5in (22cm) high*

**$800-1,200**    **DN**

A Meissen porcelain figural group, of a faun caught by two nymphs, designed by Paul Helmig, polychrome painted and gilded, decorated with reeds, waterlilies and shells, model number Q 191, blue crossed swords mark.

*c1900*    *15in (37.5cm) high*

**$2,800-3,200**    **BMN**

A Meissen porcelain figure of a putto, 'The Summer', after an original by Johann Joachim Kändler, from 'The Seasons' series, blue jubilee crossed swords mark, "A 67", restored.

*c1910*    *5in (13cm) high*

**$500-800**    **BMN**

An early 20thC Meissen group of children, modeled holding hands dancing around a central tree, blue crossed swords mark, numbered and incised "2728", chips, losses.

*13in (33cm) high*

**$1,800-2,200**    **DN**

A late 19thC Vienna porcelain portrait plate, depicting a woman with flowing hair, blue, brown and gilded border, titled "Innocence" and signed "Wagner".

*10in (25cm) diam*

**$2,200-2,800**                                    **FRE**

A late 19thC Vienna porcelain portrait plate, painted with a woman's bust, signed "Weigel", frame restored.

*10in (25cm) diam*

**$1,500-2,000**                                    **FRE**

A Vienna porcelain 'The Secret' plate, painted with a scene of two small boys, with gold to border, blue swords mark, signed "Storch", numbered.

*9.75in (24.5cm) diam*

**$800-1,200**                                    **L&T**

A lidded Vienna porcelain urn, with two handles, painted with scenes of "The Three Graces" and "Achilles and Agamemnon", signed "K Weh", red "Austria" mark, restored.

*10.5in (26.5cm) high*

**$500-700**                                    **FRE**

A Vienna porcelain model of a codfish seller, standing on a round base with green stripes and holding a fish basket under her left arm, a fish in her right hand, wearing a lilac dress with a darker flounce, blue mark, shield mark to glazed base, embossed "0", engraved "5", a finger restored.

*c1755*                                    *8in (20cm) high*

**$2,200-2,800**                                    **LPZ**

A Vienna porcelain wall plate, printed with mythological scenes, blue and gold rim.

*c1900*                                    *13.5in (33.5cm) diam*

**$80-120**                                    **LFA**

A pair of 20thC Vienna porcelain plates, in white, blue, and red, with open-work gilded rims.

*9.5in (23.5cm) diam*

**$120-180**                                    **FRE**

A Vienna porcelain 'Mother and Child at the Breakfast Table' group, the lady wearing a crinoline skirt and supporting a child on her knee, a coffee service and parrot on the table, on a colorfully painted base with gold decoration and flowers, blue shield mark, parrot reglued.

*7.5in (19cm) high*

**$500-700**                                    **BMN**

A Vienna porcelain 'The Music' allegorical putti group, the two amorettes with a lyre, book, and sheet of music, an eagle at their feet, reticulated rocaille-flower base, gilt decoration, blue shield mark, partially restored.

*c1760*                                    *10.75in (27cm) high*

**$700-1,000**                                    **BMN**

A Doccia plate, painted in colored enamels and gilt with stylized flowers, the ozier-molded border with scattered floral sprays, some surface wear.

*c1760*          *9in (22.5cm) wide*

**$400-600**          **DN**

A Doccia teapot and cover, decorated 'con basso relievo istoriato' with classical subjects including the goddess Diana, with richly gilt borders, some small losses, extensive damage and old repairs.

*c1770*          *6in (15cm) high*

**$400-600**          **DN**

One of a good pair of Naples Monteiths of rare form, the rims applied with six birds divided by short pillars, the bodies and interiors painted with flowers in colored enamels above bands of flutes, each raised on three paw feet, incised marks.

*These Monteiths are of the same form as the celebrated 'Servizio dell'Oca' made for the Bourbon court between 1793 and 1795, much of which is on display in the Capodimonte museum in Naples.*

*c1795*          *11.25in (28cm) diam*

**$12,000-18,000**          **WW**

A pair of Russian Imperial platters, each decorated with a central rosette surrounded by a black ground roundel with green scrolling vines and radiating leaves with stems on a gilt ground, within a beaded border, painted and printed marks.

*14.25in (35.5cm) diam*

**$5,000-7,000**          **L&T**

A set of five porcelain plates from St. Petersburg, each with a raised border and gilt-scrolled rim, the polychrome Asiatic floral decoration with butterflies on a turquoise ground, blue-gray interlaced mark, press mark.

*c1850*          *9.25in (23.5cm) diam*

**$280-320**          **MTZ**

## A CLOSER LOOK AT A TUCKER & HEMPHILL BASKET

*Tucker porcelain is fairly rare and can be difficult to identify. A letter from the Philadelphia Art Museum, attributing the piece to Tucker, accompanies it.*

*The shape is classical. The company drew inspiration from the styles of high quality European porcelain of the time.*

A late 19thC Samson shaped box and hinged cover painted with a Watteauesque vignette and sprays of flowers, blue cross mark, glued mount.

*The gold bands found on this piece were a typical decorative feature. Tucker Porcelain produced prior to 1831 was usually decorated with transfer-printed landscapes or floral motifs. Later pieces were often overglaze painted in the Sèvres style.*

*Pieces were in hard-paste porcelain and often had a greenish translucent tint to the body when held to the light.*

*2.5in (9cm) wide*

$80-100          **DN**

A 19thC gilt-decorated porcelain footed basket, by the Tucker and Hemphill factory, the flaring reticulated basket on reel-turned and square base, chips, gilt wear.

*William Ellis Tucker and his brother Thomas established his porcelain factory in Philadelphia in 1826. Judge Joseph Hemphill provided finance from c1832. Tucker is generally considered to be the first truly successful American porcelain maker.*

*c1830*          *8.5in (21.5cm) high*

**$2,200-2,800**          **FRE**

## THE POTTERY MARKET

The demand for pottery at the middle and lower end of the market has slowed as buyers seek out high quality, unusual and rare pieces at the higher end of the market.

As far as Staffordshire figures are concerned, groups with historical themes – depicting military, political, religious and royal subjects – have fallen out of favor. Collectors specializing in these areas are predominantly British and are becoming fewer in number. They favor unusual, rare examples over easier to find pieces. Staffordshire animal groups, however, continue to sell well, largely because the US market for these is very strong.

New life has been injected into the market by buyers, such as professional interior designers, looking for pottery to enhance the décor of their homes. Staffordshire dogs and hens on nests, as well as a wide variety of other subjects, have proved popular.

In the pre-1830 pottery market, the top end is holding up well. Creamware, lusterware and Delft – which is currently undervalued and becoming harder to find – remain popular. Walton, Obadiah Sherrat and Thomas Parr figures are also desirable.

In general, pottery that offers something extra is currently commanding the best prices. High quality pieces with appealing subjects or attractive coloring tend to perform well.

*– John Howard, Woodstock, Oxfordshire*

## CREAMWARE

A large baluster-shaped creamware jug, with female mask spout, the reeded entwined loop handle with applied flower and leaf terminals, printed in black with 'The Tithe Pig', the couple and parson above the verse, old restoration.

*c1780*      9.5in (24cm) high

**$700-1,000**      **LFA**

A Liverpool double transfer-printed creamware jug.

*c1790*      7in (18cm) high

**$2,200-2,800**      **JHOR**

A large creamware jug, printed in black with two fat men en route to the tavern.

*c1800*      9.75in (24.5cm) high

**$1,000-1,500**      **WW**

A creamware jug, printed in black with an armorial titled "The Weaver's Arms".

*c1800*      7.25in (18cm) wide

**$800-1,200**      **WW**

### A CLOSER LOOK AT A TRANSFER-PRINTED JUG

*This jug is made from Queensware, a refined version of creamware introduced by Josiah Wedgwood in 1765 and named for Queen Charlotte, consort of George III.*

*Liverpool was among the first towns to apply transfer decoration to ceramics and remained the center of this niche industry for years. Designs like this one were produced c1780-1830, making this jug one of the earliest examples.*

*The scene depicts the death of James Wolfe, a British general who enjoyed great success against the French in Canada. He died from wounds sustained in battle in 1759.*

*The encampment scene on the reverse of this jug is rare, adding to its value.*

A Liverpool double transfer-printed creamware jug.

*c1780*      7in (18cm) high

**$6,000-9,000**      **JHOR**

A creamware jug, transfer-printed in black, with a village scene titled "The Church Militant", the reverse inscribed with a verse.

c1800     7.25in (18cm) high

**$1,000-1,500**     WW

A late 18thC creamware jug, double transfer-printed in black with a Classical lady and a verse "How Hard to Avoid Censure How Soon Get Applause".

11in (28cm) wide

**$800-1,200**     CHEF

A green glazed creamware jug, with floral motif finials, probably Yorkshire.

c1770     7in (18cm) high

**$6,000-9,000**     JHOR

A creamware teapot and cover, with a molded handle and spout, one side printed with a rural couple and their child, the reverse with a beggar woman and a young lady holding a rake, good restoration.

c1765     7.25in (18.5cm) long

**$500-800**     WW

A rare William Greatbatch cylindrical creamware teapot and cover, with a cross-over handle and flower knop, brightly painted with Aurora in her chariot, the reverse with a rising sun, minor faults.

c1775     7.5in (19cm) high

**$2,800-3,200**     WW

A Staffordshire or Yorkshire bullet-shaped creamware teapot and cover, painted in colored enamels with a rose spray and other flowers, the strap handle with flowerhead terminals, minor wear.

c1790     8in (20.5cm) wide

**$300-500**     DN

A creamware coffee pot and cover, printed with Thomas Rothwell-type prints of 'The Shepherd' and 'Tea Party No.1', the spout reduced.

c1790     9.75in (25cm) high

**$500-700**     DN

A late 18thC blue and white creamware jug painted with six foliage panels below pale green glazed leaves molded on the rim.

c1780     3.75in (9.5cm) high

**$300-500**     CHEF

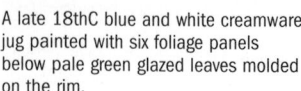

A creamware Toby jug, modeled in a seated position and holding a foaming jug of ale, painted in blue, brown, and green colored glazes, restored hat, lacks cover.

*Toby jugs are modeled to show the full body, in contrast to character jugs which depict just the head and shoulders of a subject.*

c1780     9.5in (24cm) high

**$1,800-2,200**     DN

A Pratt-type creamware Toby jug, 'Hearty Good Fellow', typically modeled and painted, hat repaired.

*c1800*        9.75in (25cm) high

**$1,000-1,500**        **DN**

## CREAMWARE

■ Staffordshire potters, led by Josiah Wedgwood, developed creamware c1750.

■ By the late 18thC it had become the standard household pottery throughout Europe, undermining tin-glazed wares.

■ The clay was mixed with flint to produce a fine, lightweight, close-grained surface that was then thinly glazed with a smooth, ivory-tinted lead solution.

■ Production centered around Staffordshire and Yorkshire.

■ Wedgwood coined the name 'Queensware' after Queen Charlotte granted him a Royal Warrant for his creamware in 1765.

■ Creamware was versatile and could be finely molded and printed or painted either under or over the glaze.

An early 19thC Dawson cylindrical creamware mug, printed and painted in polychrome with a view of the Iron Bridge at Sunderland, Lowford Pottery mark.

5.5in (14cm) high

**$1,200-1,800**        **WW**

A late 18thC cylindrical creamware mug, printed in brown with 'The Tea Party'.

4.75in (12cm) high

**$300-500**        **WW**

A late 18thC cylindrical creamware mug, printed in black with a scene depicting "The Tithe Pig" above a verse.

5.5in (14cm) high

**$1,200-1,800**        **WW**

A late 18thC cylindrical creamware mug, transfer-printed in black with "The Triple Plea" illustrating a priest, a doctor and a lawyer discussing their fees above a verse attacking the hypocrisy of their vows.

4.75in (12cm) high

**$1,500-2,000**        **WW**

A cylindrical creamware jug, printed in black with a view of the Iron Bridge over the River Wear.

*c1800*        5.75in (14.5cm) high

**$800-1,200**        **WW**

A cylindrical creamware mug, printed in black with a parson and a clerk above a verse.

*c1800*        6.25in (15.5cm) high

**$800-1,200**        **WW**

A cylindrical creamware mug, printed in black with the shipwrights' arms of a shield surmounted by an ark, flanked by two figures above a motto.

*c1800*        5.75in (14.5cm) high

**$1,500-2,000**        **WW**

A cylindrical creamware mug, printed in black with a view of the "Iron Bridge in Sunderland", the print signed "Barker".

*c1815*        4.75in (12cm) wide

**$500-700**        **WW**

An early 19thC cylindrical creamware mug, transfer-printed in dark brown with 'The Gypsy Fortune Teller'.

*4.75in (12cm) wide*

$300-500    WW

An early 19thC cylindrical creamware mug, printed in black with a ship in full sail flying the American flag.

*6in (15cm) high*

$1,500-2,000    WW

An early 19thC cylindrical creamware mug, printed in black with the verse "A little Health, A little Wealth, A little House and Freedom, And at the end a little Friend, And little cause to need Him", signed "Johnson Hanley".

*3.5in (9cm) wide*

$500-800    WW

A Liverpool creamware bowl, printed in black by Sadler & Green, the interior decorated with a gypsy woman telling the fortune of a young lady, the exterior with four further vignettes of figures.

*c1770*    *9.25in (23cm) high*

$700-1,000    WW

A round creamware bowl, the interior printed in black with "A First Rate Ship of War With Rigging etc At Anchor", and titled on a scroll beneath, the exterior with a family and young lovers seated on a bench, beneath a green line rim, slight damage.

*c1800*    *9in (23cm) diam*

$500-800    LFA

A Staffordshire or Yorkshire creamware slop bowl, extensively cracked and repaired.

*c1790*    *6in (15cm) wide*

$150-200    DN

A circular creamware sugar bowl and cover, probably Staffordshire or Yorkshire, painted with a spray of roses and other flowers, the cover with flower finial, the bowl with strap handles and flowerhead terminals, minor chips.

*c1790*    *5.5in (12.5cm) wide*

$600-900    DN

A flared oval two-handled creamware basket and stand, probably Yorkshire, of pierced form with winged masks suspending swags.

*c1780*    *11.25in (28cm) wide*

$700-1,000    DN

An English pierced oval creamware chestnut basket and stand, both parts ozier-molded central section, the stand with rim chips.

*c1790*    *stand 10in (25.5cm) wide*

$300-500    DN

A pair of creamware ice pails with liners, the domed covers with mauve detailed bud knops, the shallow lobed bodies painted with bands of green-leaved brown vines and mauve lines.

*c1810*    *9in (23cm) high*

$1,800-2,200    CHEF

A cylindrical creamware tea canister and domed cover, probably Staffordshire or Yorkshire, painted in colored enamels with a spray of roses and other flowers, small foot rim chip.

*c1790*    *5.5in (12.5cm) high*

$700-1,000    DN

A cylindrical creamware tea canister, printed in black with figures in an interior, and titled "Conjugal Felicity", the reverse with figures and a book, in a river landscape, lacks lid, rim chips.

*c1800*    *9.75in (9.5cm) high*

$180-220    LFA

A Leeds creamware ewer and basin, pattern number 188, restored hairlines, bowl has chip.

c1780                                                    14.5in (36.5cm) high

**$7,000-10,000**                                                    **JHD**

A pair of Wedgwood Queensware navette-shaped cruet bottle stands, with shaped rims, impressed marks.

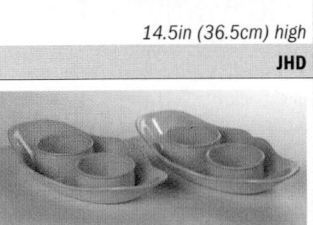

c1790                    10.25in (26cm) wide

**$600-900**                                    **DN**

A late 18thC Leeds plate, decorated with a scalloped blue rim and blue, yellow and orange spotted peafowl.

8in (20cm) diam

**$500-700**                                    **POOK**

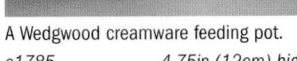

A Wedgwood creamware feeding pot.

c1785                    4.75in (12cm) high

**$800-1,200**                                    **JHD**

A Wedgwood creamware teapot and cover, with a leaf-molded handle and spout, each side printed in black with hunting scenes, impressed "Wedgwood" mark.

c1765                    7.5in (18.5cm) high

**$1,200-1,800**                                    **WW**

A Wedgwood Queensware ozier-molded oval basket and stand, with pierced rims, the interior of the basket painted in colored enamels with a band of flowers, impressed marks, painted pattern number N899, some wear to stand.

*Wedgwood's creamware was renamed 'Queensware' after Queen Charlotte's patronage was given to the line.*

c1810                    stand 10in (25.5cm) diam

**$300-500**                                    **DN**

## BRISTOL DELFT

A Bristol delft plate, chip to rim.

c1740                    10in (25.5cm) diam

**$800-1,200**                                    **AS**

A Bristol pancake-shaped delft plate, with a pale manganese border and a central blue swan.

c1740                    9in (23cm) diam

**$1,200-1,800**                                    **AS**

A mid-18thC Bristol delft plate, repaired chip and associated crack.

13.25in (33.5cm) diam

**$1,200-1,800**                                    **AS**

A Bristol delft charger, with an Oriental harbor scene.

c1760                    13in (33cm) diam

**$1,200-1,800**                                    **JHOR**

A Bristol delft plate, with a portrait of Frederick the Great of Prussia, inscribed "KP".

c1755                    8.75in (22cm) diam

**$7,000-10,000**                                    **AS**

A pair of Bristol bianco sopra bianco delft plates.

*Bianco sopra bianco refers to the use of white enamel decoration on the white tin glaze.*

c1760                    9in (23cm) diam

**$1,800-2,200**                                    **AS**

A mid-18thC Bristol delft bowl, with crimped edge, decorated with foliage.

*c1740*                                    *8in (20.5cm) diam*

**$1,800-2,200**                                              **AS**

An English delft jar, with handles, probably Bristol.

*c1705*                        *6in (15cm) high*

**$1,200-1,800**                            **JHOR**

An English blue and white delft posset pot, probably Bristol, of baluster form, painted with stylized plants.

*c1720*                    *5.5in (14cm) high*

**$600-900**                              **ROS**

A Bristol delft tulip charger, with blue dash border.

*c1700*                    *13in (33cm) diam*

**$6,000-9,000**                        **JHOR**

A Bristol delft charger, with an Oriental figure on a lake.

*c1730*                    *13in (33cm) diam*

**$5,000-7,000**                        **JHOR**

A Bristol delft dish, chipped.

*c1740*                *11.75in (30cm) diam*

**$1,800-2,200**                          **AS**

A Bristol delft charger, painted with Oriental figures on a bridge.

*c1740*                    *14in (36cm) diam*

**$7,000-10,000**                        **JHOR**

A Bristol delft charger.

*c1740*                    *13in (33cm) diam*

**$2,200-2,800**                        **JHOR**

A Bristol delft charger.

*c1760*                  *13in (39.5cm) diam*

**$3,000-5,000**                        **JHOR**

## A CLOSER LOOK AT A PAIR OF ENGLISH DELFT PLATES

*The body of English delft tends to be harder and coarser than that of the Dutch equivalent. Glazes are smoother and more prone to chipping. Small glaze chips do not therefore have a particularly detrimental effect on value.*

*The decoration on 18thC delft tended to be less formal than earlier pieces, which were influenced initially by Dutch and Italian and later by Chinese design. The cockerel image makes this pair of plates quirky and appealing.*

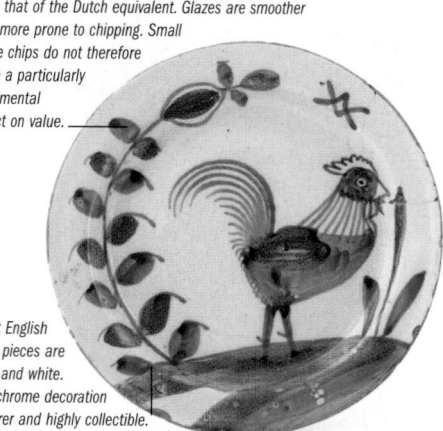

*Most English delft pieces are blue and white. Polychrome decoration is rarer and highly collectible.*

*This pair was probably made in Bristol, where delft was made between c1685-1770.*

A pair of mid-18thC English delft plates, probably Bristol, each with painted design of a cockerel and a stylized flower in blue, green, and orange.

                                              *9in (23cm) diam*

**$15,000-20,000**                                          **B&H**

An English blue and white delft punch bowl, probably London, painted with Chinoiserie landscapes, the interior with an 'oxo' band border, minor chips and cracks.

c1760 — 10.5in (27cm) diam

**$320-380** — DN

A mid-18thC London or Glasgow delft barber's bowl.

12in (30cm) diam

**$2,800-3,200** — JHOR

An early 17thC delft apothecary jar, probably Southwark.

6in (15cm) wide

**$1,800-2,200** — JHOR

An early 18thC English delft apothecary wet jar, probably London, inscribed "S. Croci".

7in (18cm) high

**$300-500** — JHOR

An early 18thC London delft apothecary wet jar, with a spout, inscribed "S Rubi Idaei".

7.5in (19cm) high

**$3,000-5,000** — JHOR

## A CLOSER LOOK AT A DELFT CISTERN

This cistern, used for dispensing spirits or wine, may well have been used in a public house. The 18thC England saw a huge growth in drinking establishments following a rise in gin consumption. The number of alehouses rose as brewers fought to maintain their share of the market.

The back of the cistern is flat so that it can be pushed against a wall.

This is a fairly late piece of delft. Production virtually ceased at the end of the 18thC due to the competition from creamware.

This piece was made to perform a practical function, making it surprising that it has survived in such good condition. Delftware is brittle and prone to damage.

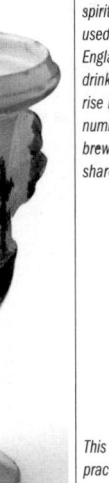
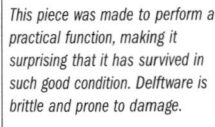

A mid-18thC London delft campana vase, with a landscape scene of a row of buildings with trees in the foreground.

6in (15cm) high

**$3,200-3,800** — JHOR

An English delft cistern, probably London, with a tap for wine or spirits with a bone handle, three cracks to rim.

c1780 — 11in (28cm) high

**$10,000-15,000** — JHOR

A Liverpool delft plate, inscribed "Admiral Keppel Forever", cracked.

*At the Battle of Quiberon Bay on 20 November 1759, Admiral Keppel commanded the 74 gun 'Torbay' and sank the French ship 'Thesée'.*

*c1760*     9in (23cm) diam

**$6,000-9,000**     **AS**

A Liverpool delft plate, with Fazackerley colors.

*c1760*     8.75in (22cm) diam

**$1,200-1,800**     **AS**

A Liverpool polychrome delft plate.

*c1760*     8.75in (22cm) diam

**$1,200-1,800**     **AS**

A Liverpool octagonal delft ship's plate, the border decorated with flowers and four cherubs representing the four winds, inscribed "Vertrouwen" above the ship and "Pieter Pieters Eisen" below, dated.

*1765*     8.75in (22cm) diam

**$8,000-12,000**     **AS**

A Liverpool delft plate, with Fazackerley colors.

*c1760*     10.75in (27.5cm) diam

**$1,200-1,800**     **AS**

*c1760*

**$1,200-1,800**

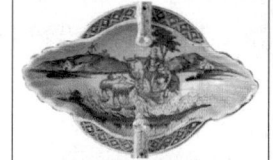

A rare double-ended delft sauceboat, after a Chinese shape with animal head handles, the interior well painted with a farmer and his wife feeding three goats and a cow in a field with buildings and a windmill beyond, probably Liverpool, some restoration.

    8.25in (21cm) wide

    **WW**

A rare delft sweetmeat dish, with six compartments and a scalloped edge, painted in blue with flowers and foliage within a hatched border, all raised upon five stump feet, probably Liverpool.

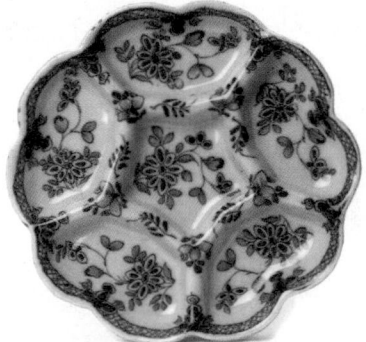

*c1765*     8in (20.5cm) high

**$1,800-2,200**     **WW**

A mid-18thC Liverpool delft flower brick, decorated in blue and white.

    6in (15cm) wide

**$800-1,200**     **AS**

A Liverpool delft tile by Sadler, printed in brown with a sleeping shepherd, the print signed "J. Sadler Liverp".

*c1770*     5in (12.5cm) wide

**$400-600**     **WW**

An English delft flower brick, decorated with sprigs of flowers.

c1740     6in (15.5cm) wide

**$1,500-2,000**     **JHOR**

An English delft flower brick, decorated with birds and flowers.

c1750     6in (16cm) wide

**$1,500-2,000**     **JHOR**

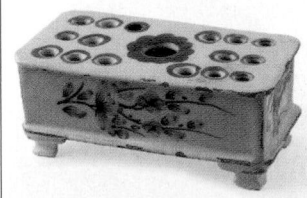

A delft flower brick with floral decoration to the sides, on raised bracket feet.

c1750     5in (13cm) wide

**$2,200-2,800**     **JHOR**

An English delft jar, with handles and polychrome flowers.

c1705     6.5in (16.5cm) wide

**$3,000-4,000**     **JHOR**

An English delft tankard, with polychrome landscape decoration.

c1760     5in (13cm) high

**$5,000-7,000**     **JHOR**

An English delft fuddling cup.

*Fuddling cups were designed as a tavern joke. The drinker was 'befuddled' as to which of the three mouthpieces to drink from. Examples from the 17th and 18thC are particularly sought after.*

c1640     4in (11.5cm) wide

**$7,000-10,000**     **JHOR**

An English delft stand, with foliate decoration and raised scroll feet.

c1725     5.25in (13.5cm) diam

**$4,000-6,000**     **JHOR**

## IRISH DELFT

One of a pair of large blue and white delft meat plates, of chamfered rectangular form, possibly Irish, painted with a pine tree and building on a rocky island, a few small rim chips.

c1765     16.5in (42.5cm) wide

**$2,200-2,800 pair**     **WW**

An Irish delft plate.

c1750     9in (23cm) diam

**$500-800**     **AS**

An Irish delft plate, with a scalloped edge, painted with floral decoration.

c1750     9in (23cm) wide

**$800-1,200**     **AS**

A mid-18thC delft sauceboat, possibly Irish, with two handles and floral decoration, minor crack.

8in (20cm) wide

**$8,000-12,000**     **JHOR**

A delft posset pot, probably Irish, with double handles.

c1720   9.5in (29cm) wide

**$5,000-7,000**     **JHOR**

**POTTERY**

A blue and white Delft charger, painted in the Kraak style with Chinese figures seated beneath an arbor, within a border of figures and flowers.

*c1700*          *12.5in (24.5cm) diam*

**$500-800**                              **DN**

One of a pair of Delft Chinese-style dishes.

*c1720*          *13.25in (33.5cm) diam*

**$1,200-1,800 pair**              **R&GM**

A blue and white lobed Delft dish, with a raised central boss painted with a stylized plant, within a dash border, minor rim chips.

*c1700*          *8.75in (22cm) diam*

**$300-500**                              **DN**

An 18thC molded Delft dish, decorated with a blue, yellow and ocher bird within a foliate band, rim section re-glued.

*11.75in (30cm) diam*

**$300-500**                              **WW**

One of a pair of 18thC Delft plates, painted in polychrome with flowers, foliage and blue rockwork, small glaze chips to the rims.

*12in (30.5cm) diam*

**$800-1,200 pair**                      **WW**

An 18thC ovoid Delft vase, inscribed "Rappe" in an elaborate floral cartouche, the base marked "Honl 9", minor faults.

*10.5in (26.5cm) high*

**$1,500-2,000**                          **WW**

A ribbed hexagonal Delft vase and cover, with an animal finial, the body painted with a Chinese figure, animals, birds, insects and flowers.

*c1750*          *13.25in (33cm) high*

**$500-800**                              **WW**

An 18thC blue and white Delft vase, the hexagonal molded body decorated with flowers and fabulous beasts.

*10.5in (26cm) high*

**$500-800**                              **WW**

An octagonal section Delft vase, painted with a peacock and other birds amidst chrysanthemum, the neck and the foot modeled with flutes, probably 18thC.

*11in (27.5cm) high*

**$700-1,000**                            **WW**

A pair of early 18thC Delft drug jars, each painted with a cartouche surmounted by pheasants and a basket of flowers in blue, inscribed "Violarum" and "Nervinum".

*7in (18cm) high*

**$1,800-2,200**                        **GORL**

An 18thC blue and white Delft drug jar, with a flared foot, the ovoid body inscribed "E. Catholicum" in a Baroque cartouche with cherub surmounts.

*8.75in (22cm) high*

**$800-1,200**                            **WW**

An 18thC blue and white Delft tobacco jar, inscribed "No.5 Tonca" within a Baroque panel flanked by native Indians smoking pipes.

*10.75in (27cm) high*

**$700-1,000**                            **WW**

## MASON'S PATENT IRONSTONE

- The first earthenware to be patented was produced by William and John Turner in 1800.
- Charles James Mason developed his successful 'Patent Ironstone China' c1810, as an alternative to imported porcelain.
- His recipe, patented in 1813, included ironstone slag and cobalt oxide, which gave the finished product a faint blue tinge.
- Mason's Ironstone was so strong that it was used to make fireplaces and even furniture, including four-poster beds.
- Mason's Ironstone was very successful and was exported in bulk to Europe and America.
- Ironstone was decorated with colors and patterns derived from Oriental designs, particularly the colors of Imari ceramics.
- A great deal of Mason's Ironstone bears a crown mark with the inscription "Mason's Patent Ironstone China".
- When Mason's patent expired in 1827 a number of rival firms began manufacturing similar wares.

A Mason's Patent Ironstone China two-handled vase, of ribbed form with a flared rim, richly decorated with the 'Old School House' pattern, impressed "Mason's Patent Ironstone China" mark.

*c1820*      8.25in (21cm) high

**$700-1,000**    **WW**

A Mason's Patent Ironstone China octagonal jug, with a winged dragon handle, decorated with the 'Japan Fence' pattern, impressed "Mason's Patent Ironstone China" mark, minor faults.

*c1820*      8.25in (21cm) high

**$700-1,000**    **WW**

A very large Mason's Patent Ironstone China jug, surmounted by two cherubs, rich gilt decoration with scrolled sides and mask mounts, on a black square base.

*26in (66cm) high*

**$7,000-10,000**    **JN**

Three Mason's Patent Ironstone China octagonal hydra-shape jugs, with molded serpent handles, decorated with a typical Japanese pattern in blue and iron-red with green on the handles, two with peach luster rims, the largest with impressed mark "Mason's Patent Ironstone China", the others with blue-printed crown and drape marks.

*c1830*      9in (22cm) high

**$1,000-1,500**    **DN**

A pair of Mason's Patent Ironstone China wine coolers, of tapered shape with flared feet and blue-molded leaf handles, rims molded with flowers and leafy scrolls, decorated with a typical Japanese pattern in blue and iron-red, unmarked.

*c1825*      8.75in (22cm) high

**$700-1,000**    **DN**

A good pair of Mason's Patent Ironstone China dessert plates, of lobed form with gilt foliate decorated rims, the centers well painted with landscape views of Orford, Suffolk and Niton, Isle of Wight by Samuel Borne, impressed mark and titled in red.

*c1820*    9.25in (23.5cm) diam

**$2,800-3,200**    **WW**

A Mason's Patent Ironstone China covered sauce tureen with matching stand, of octagonal form with pedestal foot and molded handles.

*c1830*      8in (20cm) wide

**$500-800**    **DN**

A large Mason's Patent Ironstone China mug, of octagonal form with a hydra handle, decorated with Chinoiserie scenes, black printed mark.

*c1825*      7.75in (20cm) wide

**$500-800**    **WW**

A Mason's Patent Ironstone China footbath, of twelve-sided shape with dog's head handles, decorated with the 'Table and Flower Pot' pattern.

*c1825*      19.5in (49cm) wide

**$1,500-2,000**    **DN**

A rare Mason's Patent Ironstone China orange ground vase, with gilt wreath handles, painted with two figures in a landscape, rare circular mark.

*c1815*      6in (15cm) wide

**$1,200-1,800**    **WW**

An early 15thC Italian earthenware bowl with handles.

5.5in (14cm) wide

**$800-1,200**                                    **JHOR**

A 15thC Italian earthenware bowl with handles, probably for drinking.

4.5in (11cm) diam

**$800-1,200**                                    **JHOR**

An unusual earthenware mug, with lion loop handle, applied relief of Wellington on horseback and soldiers, inscribed "Plunder".

c1815                                    4in (10cm) high

**$700-1,000**                                    **LFA**

A rare canaryware child's mug, depicting sheep, with luster rim.

c1800                        1.75in (4.5cm) diam

**$500-700**                                    **PST**

A German blue glazed cylindrical earthenware mug, decorated in gilt, red and black with foliage, the hinged pewter cover with bird thumbpiece.

c1760                        10in (25.5cm) high

**$500-700**                                    **LFA**

A Sussex puzzle jug, the green splashed ocher sides with two birds and flowers in sgraffito, inscribed "God Save The King", initialled "Jn B" and dated.

1833                        8in (20.5cm) high

**$1,800-2,200**                                    **CHEF**

An early 19thC bear jug and cover, possibly Nottingham, modeled standing holding a ring, the textured fur covered in a treacle brown glaze.

7.75in (20cm) high

**$300-500**                                    **CHEF**

A Swansea-type cow creamer and cover, standing on a rectangular base.

c1820                        5.75in (14.5cm) high

**$700-1,000**                                    **AD**

An earthenware cow creamer, standing on a rectangular base, painted with brown and blue patches, lacks cover, some losses and damage.

5.5in (14cm) high

**$400-600**                                    **HAMG**

A 19thC country earthenware tobacco jar and cover, modeled as a young bear sitting holding a stick, the removable head with white details to the eyes and teeth.

6in (15.5cm) high

**$500-800**                                    **WW**

A black basalt rectangular teapot and cover, with loop handle and flower knop, applied with a putto, a young boy and a dog, within oval panels and stiff leaf borders.

c1815                        5.5in (14cm) high

**$280-320**                                    **LFA**

A rare pair of yellow slip-glazed lions, minor chips repaired.

c1820                        10.75in (27.5cm) wide

**$6,000-9,000**                                    **AS**

## FAIENCE

- Tin-glazed pottery first arrived in Europe during the Middle Ages, after invading Arabs introduced the technology to Andalusian Spain.
- Faience is a general term referring to earthenware products covered with a tin-enameled, or stanniferous, glaze which became popular in Europe in the 16thC.
- Faience is made from a mixture of different clays, which are beaten and filtered to remove impurities, mixed with water and then sieved before drying.
- The tin glaze is prepared by combining molten siliceous sand and potash salt from wine sediment with lead and tin ashes. The resultant white enamel is applied to the prepared clay, painted and fired.

- Some pieces were glazed, fired at high temperature, then painted and fired again at a lower temperature. This method helps to seal the decoration more permanently.
- During the glaze firing the tin oxide creates a uniform white surface, which is more opaque and less glossy than a lead glaze, providing a superior foundation for colored paints and enamels.
- The pigments used to decorate early tin-glazed ceramics were oxides of metals such as iron, which fired red, and manganese, which produced a purple color.
- Faience reached the height of its popularity in France during the 18thC, when whimsical forms and decoration captured the imagination of the middle classes.

## LUNÉVILLE

- The Chambrette family of Lunéville developed the art of tin-glazed earthenware during the 18thC under the patronage of the Dukes of Lorraine.
- They also manufactured 'faience fine' lead-glazed earthenwares in the English manner.
- In 1750 the Chambrettes adopted the 'petit feu' technique, which allowed a greater range of color than the 'grand feu' method.
- Painted ornamentation consisted of flowers, birds, rustic scenes, and decoration in the Chinese style.

A late 18thC Lunéville faience plate, with petit feu polychrome decoration of a bouquet of flowers outlined in the Strasbourg style in the center, and pea pods and leeks in relief around a Rococo rim outlined in purple.

*Pea pods and leeks in relief are typical of the first period of 'petit feu' decoration at Lunéville.*

9.75in (25cm) diam

**$700-1,000**    **HFG**

A pair of late 18thC Lunéville faience oval wine coolers with Rococo handles, wavy rims outlined in purple and petit feu polychrome decoration of Chinese figures.

4.25in (11cm) high

**$1,800-2,200**    **HFG**

A late 18thC Lunéville faience cup and saucer, with petit feu polychrome decoration of flowers and forget-me-not buds, the rim outlined with purple.

4.75in (12cm) diam

**$150-200**    **HFG**

A late 18thC Lunéville faience plate, decorated with a bouquet of assorted flowers in the center and florets scattered around the lobed rim.

9.5in (24cm) diam

**$150-200**    **HFG**

A late 18thC Lunéville oval faience wine glass cooler, with Rococo handles, undulating rim and petit feu polychrome Chinoiserie decoration.

14.5in (37cm) long

**$1,500-2,000**    **HFG**

A late 18thC Lunéville faience plate, with a molded wavy rim outlined in green and petit feu polychrome decoration of a Chinese figure.

*As Lunéville faience was not marked, pieces can be confused with those from neighboring factories, notably Saint-Clément, which was also managed by the Chambrette family.*

8.75in (22cm) diam

**$220-280**    **HFG**

A mid-18thC Sceaux faience covered sugar bowl and stand, with petit feu polychrome decoration of outlined bouquets of assorted flowers and branches, the undulating border outlined in purple.

*8.75in (22cm) long*

**$1,500-2,000**          **HFG**

A Sceaux faience covered tureen with Rococo handles, the cover with a lemon finial, with petit feu polychrome decoration of delicate outlined flowers and bouquets.

*11in (28cm) high*   *c1780*

**$1,500-2,000**          **HFG**

A Sceaux half-moon faience wall jardinière, feathered with purple, blue and green petit feu polychrome decoration, with three rectangular panels of Chinese figures in landscapes.

*c1780*   *7.5in (19cm) long*

**$2,800-3,200**          **HFG**

A Sceaux faience wall jardinière, feathered with purple, blue and green petit feu polychrome decoration, with three rectangular panels depicting scenes from 'les Fables de La Fontaine'.

*Jacques Chapelle took control of the Sceaux factory in 1759 after working there for a decade. The Duchesse du Maine, who held court nearby, was an early patron.*

*c1780*   *7.75in (20cm) long*

**$2,200-2,800**          **HFG**

A Chapelle period Sceaux faience silver shape plate, painted with the 'Indian Flowers' pattern of scattered flower sprigs with a black outline, the rim outlined in manganese-purple.

*9.5in (24cm) wide*

**$500-700**          **HFG**

A Sceaux faience cabbage leaf tureen stand, painted with scattered flower sprays within a cabbage leaf-molded border picked out in shades of green with yellow veins, fleur de lys mark in brown.

*c1755*   *14.25in (36cm) wide*

**$2,200-2,800**          **HFG**

A Sceaux faience plate with petit feu polychrome decoration of figures in a landscape, the molded and scalloped rim feathered in blue.

*c1760*   *9in (23cm) wide*

**$1,500-2,000**          **HFG**

A Sceaux faience plate with petit feu polychrome decoration of an outlined bouquet of assorted flowers, the trompe l'oeil rim molded with leaves.

*c1770*   *9.5in (24cm) wide*

**$800-1,200**          **HFG**

A Sceaux faience plate with petit feu polychrome decoration of naturalistic birds in imitation of Sèvres porcelain, inspired by the prints of Buffon.

*c1770*   *9in (23cm) wide*

**$1,800-2,200**          **GV**

## MAIOLICA

- Maiolica has its origins in the 14thC, when Italians began to manufacture their own version of the ceramics made by the Spanish Moors.
- The Moors exported cargoes of pottery to Pisa via Majorca. The European misconception that the pottery came from Majorca resulted in its name.
- From the start of the Renaissance, Italian maiolica entered a more decorative phase. The tin glaze gives the pottery a glassy white finish, which is an ideal base for painted decoration.
- The technique spread into northern Europe after Italian potters set up business in the Low Countries.
- Albarelli, or drug jars, are among the most prized maiolica forms. Plaques, tiles, and plates were also produced in quantity.

A pair of Italian polychrome albarelli, with oak leaf decoration.

*Albarelli were pharmacy jars, often made in sets for monasteries. The groove around the neck allowed a parchment lid to be tied on.*

c1600                    10in (26cm) high

**$3,000-5,000**                    **JHOR**

A Sicilian polychrome albarello, with a Turk's head design.

c1600                    12in (35cm) high

**$4,000-6,000**                    **JHOR**

A pair of 17thC Sicilian blue and white albarelli, of waisted cylindrical form, titled across the body, one painted with a portrait and a bird picking berries, the other with a deer amidst foliage.

10in (25.5cm) high

**$3,000-5,000**                    **ROS**

A garniture of three 17thC Sicilian blue and white albarelli, each titled diagonally across the body, the larger example decorated with a stylized lion amidst foliage.

largest 10.25in (26cm) high

**$2,800-3,200**                    **ROS**

A small Italian waisted albarello, inscribed in blue "Grand Citri" amidst a figure and buildings in a landscape, painted Savona mark.

4.25in (11cm) high

**$280-320**                    **LFA**

A pair of 20thC Italian albarelli, of cylindrical form with narrow flared neck, portrait medallion on orange ground, trophy decoration and inscription, unmarked.

14.75in (37.5cm) high

**$700-1,000**                    **MTZ**

A late 19thC Cantagalli waisted albarello in the Urbino style, painted with a figure of a Roman soldier in a landscape, cockerel mark, foot rim chip.

11.5in (29cm) high

**$180-220**                    **DN**

An Italian rectangular maiolica plaque, probably 18thC, molded in relief with the Madonna and child and decorated in blue, green, yellow, and manganese.

15.25in (38cm) wide

**$1,500-2,000**                    **WW**

An 18thC Savona maiolica tazza, painted in shades of green, ocher, manganese and blue with birds, trees and ruins, Genoa beacon-light mark, minor damage.

13.5in (34cm) diam

**$1,000-1,500**                    **DN**

A 19thC Urbino-style maiolica crespina, painted in shades of ocher, green and blue in the Istoriato manner depicting Apollo with a lyre, surrounded by a centaur and figures from Classical mythology, rim chips.

11.5in (29cm) diam

**$300-500**                    **DN**

A pearlware Toby jug, modeled seated, holding a jug of ale, painted in pale shades of ocher and manganese glazes, slight damage, lacks cover.

*c1800*     10.25in (26cm) high

**$1,800-2,200**     **DN**

A pearlware Toby jug, modeled seated, holding a foaming jug of ale, painted with colored enamels, hat restored, lacks cover.

*c1800*     9.75in (25cm) high

**$1,000-1,500**     **DN**

A pearlware 'Hearty Good Fellow' Toby jug, modeled with mug and pipe and painted in Pratt colors, restored.

*c1810*     6.75in (17.5cm) high

**$500-800**     **DN**

A Yorkshire pearlware standing Toby jug, modeled holding a flask and beaker, painted in Pratt colors, damaged.

*c1825*     7.75in (20cm) high

**$800-1,200**     **DN**

A rare pair of English pearlware candlestick groups, possibly by Ralph Wood, one with a boy playing a pipe, a girl, and animals against bocage, the other with a boy by a stream holding a birdcage, a girl and animals, impressed numbers "89" and "90", restored.

*c1790*     11in (28cm) high

**$4,000-6,000**     **JN**

A rare pair of early 19thC Staffordshire pearlware groups, in the manner of Obadiah Sherratt, depicting the 'Flight into Egypt' and the 'Return from Egypt', well colored and raised on rectangular bases molded with blue, red, and yellow panels, minor repairs.

7.75in (20cm) high

**$3,000-5,000**     **WW**

## A CLOSER LOOK AT A TOBY JUG

*Toby jugs were first made by Ralph Wood in the 1760s and were imitated throughout Staffordshire and other parts of England.*

*The name 'Toby' comes from a famous engraving of a seated drinker holding a pipe and a mug of ale which was itself inspired by a popular song about one 'Sir Toby Philpott'.*

*Although Toby jugs in good condition are more desirable, some minor chipping and cracks are usually acceptable on older examples, like this one, because they were functional objects, well-used in the alehouses of their day.*

*A corner of the tricorn hat forms a spout for pouring. There would originally have been a cover, which sometimes doubled as a measure or cup, but these are missing from all but a very few Toby jugs on the market today.*

A pearlware Toby jug, probably Yorkshire, typically modeled seated with a jug in one hand and a beaker in the other, painted in colored glazes, restored, lacks cover.

*c1825*     9.75in (24cm) high

**$2,200-2,800**     **DN**

A Staffordshire pearlware model of a girl with a dove and a basket, partially painted with colored enamels, minor flaking.

*c1820*                7.25in (18.5cm) high

**$280-320**                          **DN**

A Staffordshire pearlware girl and sheep group, modeled before bocage, the sheep jumping up to her, painted with colored enamels, chipped.

*c1820*                5in (13cm) high

**$280-320**                          **DN**

A Staffordshire pearlware model of a gardener, modeled standing and preparing to graft a tree, painted with colored enamels.

*c1820*                7in (17.5cm) high

**$400-600**                          **DN**

An early 19thC pearlware figure of Elijah, seated beneath a tree with birds perched in the boughs, on a naturalistic mound base, some losses.

10.5in (26.5cm) high

**$280-320**                          **HAMG**

A small pearlware model of a bird on a nest, sponged in brown, yellow, ocher, and green, restored.

*c1800*                3.5in (9cm) wide

**$280-320**                          **LFA**

A pearlware cow creamer, sponged in black and ocher, a seated milkmaid at its side, impressed number "13".

*c1815*                5.5in (14cm) high

**$800-1,200**                          **LFA**

A small early 19thC pearlware model of a sheep, sitting on a grassy bank, decorated in gray and green.

3.25in (8cm) wide

**$500-700**                          **WW**

A pair of Staffordshire pearlware recumbent sheep, modeled facing left and right with sponged puce patches and green bases, the ram with curly horns, the ewe with restored ears.

*c1830*                5.5in (14cm) wide

**$700-1,000**                          **DN**

A pair of Staffordshire pearlware recumbent sheep, modeled facing left and right with sponged black patches and green bases, the ram with curly horns, restored.

*c1830*                6.25in (16cm) wide

**$700-1,000**                          **DN**

An octagonal pearlware teapot and cover, perhaps Yorkshire, molded with bands of acanthus leaves and painted with flower sprays in the famille rose style, restored.

*c1790*                9.25in (23.5cm) high

**$180-220**                          **WW**

A rare pearlware jug, possibly Welsh, the spiral-fluted body printed in underglaze blue depicting an Oriental landscape, painted asterisk mark.

*c1800*                7.25in (18.5cm) high

**$300-500**                          **ROW**

An ovoid pearlware jug, with angular loop handle, the diamond-molded ground picked out in yellow and iron red, beneath a band of flowers.

*c1810*                4in (10cm) high

**$80-120**                          **LFA**

An unusual ovoid pearlware jug, with angular loop handle, decorated in silver resist with a flower and leaf scroll band, within silver luster line borders, small rim chip.

*c1815*                5.5in (14cm) high

**$280-320**                          **LFA**

A Swansea baluster-shaped pearlware puzzle jug, with loop handle, the diamond- and roundel-pierced neck with three nozzles, painted with foliage within brown line borders, rim chip, one nozzle glued.

*c1815*                                    6.75in (17cm) high

**$3,000-5,000**                                          **LFA**

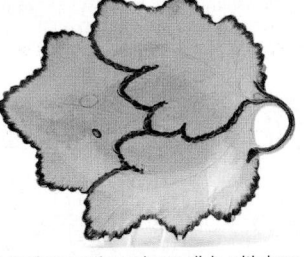

A 19thC transfer-printed and enameled pearlware jug, the ovoid form printed on one side with "The Farmer's Arms – In God We Trust".

8in (20cm) high

**$500-700**                    **FRE**

An unusual ovoid pearlware jug, with loop handle and straight neck, decorated in silver resist with vines, on a pale purple ground.

*c1900*          4.5in (11.5cm) high

**$320-380**                    **LFA**

## PEARLWARE & PRATTWARE

- Josiah Wedgwood is generally credited with the invention of pearlware, although a number of factories developed similar products from c1780. The name at least is derived from Wedgwood's version, which he called 'Pearl White'.
- Pearlware differs from factory to factory, but it is essentially an earthenware made with china clay to produce a white body, covered with a cobalt glaze which gives it a slight blue color.
- Plain shell-edged pearlware was very affordable and purchased in quantity by those on lower incomes. Pearlware might also be decorated with transfer-printed designs.
- Prattware is a colored and relief-molded version of pearlware. Common forms include plaques, figures, and pipes.
- The blue, yellow, brown and green pigments that could withstand high firing temperatures came to be known as 'Pratt colors'.
- Although named for William Pratt of Lane Delph in the Potteries, Prattware was made by a number of factories.

An early 18thC Staffordshire pearlware ladle, with a scalloped finial.

11in (30.5cm) long

**$1,800-2,200**          **JHOR**

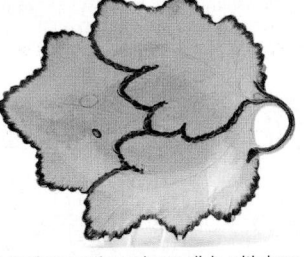

A leaf-shaped pearlware dish, with loop handle, picked out in underglaze blue, on three short tapering feet.

*c1790*          7.5in (19cm) long

**$150-200**                    **LFA**

A pair of pearlware teabowls and saucers, each printed with Chinese figures in landscapes, colored in enamels.

*c1800*

**$400-600**                                          **LFA**

A small pearlware plaque, modeled in relief with a putto riding a dolphin, picked out in yellow, brown, and green within a reeded border.

*c1800*          4.5in (11.5cm) diam

**$700-1,000**                    **LFA**

An unusual pearlware supper set, each piece printed in underglaze blue with a flower and fruit band, on an iron red vermicelli ground with brown rim, comprising four square dishes and a rectangular tray with two scroll and loop handles, rim chip.

*c1815*          11in (28cm) wide

**$700-1,000**                    **LFA**

A Bristol pearlware spirit barrel, decorated in the manner of William Fifield, painted in colored enamels with a central band of flowers between horizontal brown and green bands.

*c1830*          5in (12.5cm) high

**$300-500**                    **DN**

A Bristol pearlware spirit barrel, decorated in the manner of William Fifield, painted in enamels with a band of flowers and the monogram "FAW" between colored bands.

*c1830*          5in (12.5cm) high

**$300-500**                    **DN**

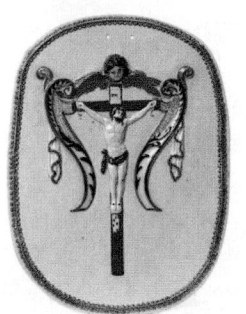

A large Prattware plaque, molded with a scene of the crucifixion, the border molded with bands of small flower heads, decorated in blue, yellow, brown, and ocher.

c1800            13.5in (34cm) high

**$3,000-4,000**            **WW**

An early 19thC Prattware money box, formed as a cottage flanked by two figures, with two children's faces at the bedroom windows, the sides molded with trees.

5.25in (13cm) high

**$300-400**            **WW**

A small early 19thC Prattware figure of a man, possibly a Rabbi, standing holding a prayer book, on a green circular base.

3.75in (9.5cm) high

**$300-500**            **WW**

An early 19thC Prattware plaque, of arched form and molded with a hunting scene, figures and trees, decorated in green, brown, yellow, blue, and ocher.

9in (23cm) wide

**$3,000-4,000**            **WW**

## STAFFORDSHIRE FIGURES

A pair of Alcock and Co. Staffordshire spaniels on yellow bases.

c1840            5in (13cm) high

**$2,200-2,800**            **JHD**

A pair of Staffordshire spaniel and pup groups, minor flaking.

c1845            5.25in (13.5cm) high

**$4,000-6,000**            **JHD**

A Staffordshire spaniel, on black base.

c1845            5.5in (14cm) high

**$1,500-2,000**            **AD**

A pair of mid-19thC Staffordshire pottery models of spaniels, facing left and right, seated on their haunches, painted with iron red patches, some chips and flaking.

8.25in (21cm) high

**$300-500**            **DN**

A pair of brown and white Staffordshire spaniels.

c1850            5.5in (14cm) high

**$1,000-1,500**            **AD**

A pair of recumbent Staffordshire spaniels with gold chains.

9.75in (25cm) wide

**$4,000-6,000**            **JHD**

A pair of Staffordshire spaniels on cobalt blue bases, well modeled with finely detailed faces, restored seam stresses.

*Cobalt blue was the only color able to withstand 'glost' firing and is a sign of quality.*

c1850            8.25in (21cm) high

**$3,000-5,000**            **JHD**

An unusual Staffordshire pottery window rest, in the form of a spaniel's head, picked out in brown, and wearing a black collar, chipped.

c1850            4.5in (11.5cm) high

**$1,200-1,800**            **LFA**

One of a pair of mid-19thC Staffordshire penholders modeled as recumbent spaniels on cushion bases, partially painted with iron red patches and ocher collars, one damaged.

*5.5in (14cm) long*

**$800-1,200 pair** DN

A mid-19thC Staffordshire model of a spaniel with a pipe, modeled seated on its haunches on a turquoise base with a scrolling frieze, with black patches and pink muzzle, pipe missing.

*9in (22cm) high*

**$1,000-1,500** DN

A pair of Staffordshire spaniels with children sitting on their backs.

*c1855* *6.75in (17cm) high*

**$3,000-4,000** JHD

A small pair of Staffordshire spaniels, restored.

*c1855* *4.5in (11.5cm) high*

**$500-700** JHD

A Staffordshire pen holder with three spaniels on a cobalt blue base.

*c1855* *6.25in (16cm) high*

**$500-800** JHD

A rare pair of Staffordshire spaniels on colored bases, restored hairline crack.

*c1855* *8.25in (21cm) high*

**$3,000-4,000** JHD

A pair of Staffordshire spaniels with puppies, painted black and brown detail.

*c1860* *6in (15cm) high*

**$800-1,200** AD

A Staffordshire pottery clock group, the painted dial flanked by seated spaniels, picked out in black on brown, and surmounted by a standing poodle, the oval mound base with a gilt band.

*c1860* *9.5in (24cm) high*

**$500-800** LFA

A Staffordshire spaniel jug with black and white detail.

*c1860* *10in (25.5cm) high*

**$1,500-2,000** JHD

One of a pair of Staffordshire spaniels.

*c1860* *9.5in (24cm) high*

**$800-1,200 pair** JHD

One of a pair of Staffordshire sporting spaniels.

*c1860* *8.75in (22.5cm) high*

**$2,200-2,800 pair** JHD

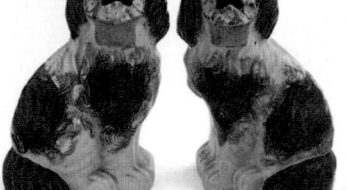

A pair of Staffordshire spaniels with baskets of flowers in their mouths.

*c1860* *8in (20.5cm) high*

**$2,200-2,800** JHD

A pair of Staffordshire seated spaniels, sitting up and decorated with yellow eyes and chains and black patches.

*c1875* *12.25in (31cm) high*

**$500-800** WW

A pair of Staffordshire spaniel jugs, modeled seated on their haunches and painted with iron red patches.

*7.5in (19cm) high*

**$300-500** DN

A pair of Staffordshire poodles with baskets.

*c1840*          3.25in (8.5cm) high

**$300-500**          AD

A pair of Staffordshire poodles on cushions.

*c1860*          3.5in (9cm) high

**$500-700**          RDER

## STAFFORDSHIRE FIGURES

- The first Staffordshire figures were made c1740 and were intended to be budget versions of the fine porcelain models offered by European factories such as Meissen and Sèvres.
- The most popular animal figures were dogs, especially spaniels. Depictions of famous people were also popular – modelers copied likenesses from paintings and newspapers.
- From the 1840s many Staffordshire figures were produced with unmolded and unpainted backs, designed to rest against walls.
- Staffordshire figures were made in plaster molds, and painted over the glaze. More than 100 separate Staffordshire factories produced figures and very few bear maker's marks.

A pair of late 19thC Staffordshire poodle groups, each depicting a seated mother with her two pups, on blue rounded rectangular plinths.

5.5in (14cm) high

**$1,200-1,800**          L&T

A Staffordshire poodle trio clock group, restored.

7.75in (20cm) high

**$800-1,200**          JHD

A Staffordshire brown and white dog.

*c1800*          4.5in (11.5cm) high

**$3,000-4,000**          JHOR

A Staffordshire dog with bocage.

*c1820*          6in (15.5cm) high

**$2,200-2,800**          JHOR

A pair of Staffordshire dalmations, with free-standing legs and original gilding.

*The spear marks on the base are probably a gilder's signature.*

*c1840*          5.25in (13.5cm) high

**$1,800-2,200**          RDER

A Staffordshire standing dog with leaf on a base.

*c1850*          6in (15cm) high

**$1,500-2,000**          JHD

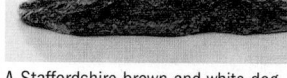

A pair of Staffordshire pottery dalmations on cobalt blue bases with spear decoration.

*c1855*          5in (13cm) high

**$1,200-1,800**          JHD

A pair of Staffordshire lion dogs with baskets, restoration to one leg.

10.5in (26.5cm) high

**$4,000-6,000**          JHD

A mid-19thC Staffordshire dog trio on a pink base, whippet's head restored.

7in (18cm) high

**$3,000-4,000**          JHD

# STAFFORDSHIRE FIGURES

A pair of Staffordshire greyhounds, seated on their haunches, painted with iron red coats and on blue gilt-lined bases, one with hairline cracks.

*c1860* — *6in (15cm) high*

**$300-500** — **DN**

A Staffordshire child with Afghan hound.

*c1860* — *11.75in (30cm) high*

**$2,200-2,800** — **JHD**

A pair of Staffordshire St Bernards.

*c1860* — *5in (13cm) high*

**$1,200-1,800** — **JHD**

A pair of Staffordshire dogs with baskets, ridden by children.

*c1860* — *9.75in (25cm) high*

**$4,000-6,000** — **JHD**

A pair of late 19thC Staffordshire recumbent dalmatian pen holders, modeled facing left and right, on blue gilt lined bases.

*6.25in (16cm) long*

**$400-600** — **DN**

A pair of Staffordshire pottery models of hounds, each standing with mouth open, painted with liver markings, on white oval mound bases.

*3.5in (9cm) high*

**$280-320** — **HAMG**

■ The Staffordshire ceramics trade developed around the six towns of the Potteries in the mid-17thC, when local farmers developed a sideline manufacturing butter pots.
- The rich natural resources in the area include good seams of coal and red clay, close enough to the surface in some areas as to be dug from the road. White clays were brought to north Staffordshire from Dorset, Devon, and Cornwall.
- The industry developed steadily throughout the 18thC, with literally hundreds of firms producing pottery in the area at various times. By 1800, the Potteries were home to the most prolific collection of ceramic factories in the world.
- It is very hard to ascribe a particular Staffordshire figure to any one factory. Pieces are rarely marked, and smaller factories often sold their molds to rival firms when they went out of business.
- The ceramics industry has declined in more recent years, but a number of companies continue to thrive around Stoke-on-Trent.

A Staffordshire figure of a dog with a basket, ridden by a child.

*c1860* — *9.75in (25cm) high*

**$800-1,200** — **JHD**

One of a pair of Staffordshire models of dogs, possibly collies, seated on its haunches on a pink gilt-lined base, sparsely colored and gilt, slight damage.

*c1860* — *6in (15cm) high*

**$1,800-2,200 pair** — **DN**

A Ralph Wood-type Staffordshire lion and cub group spill vase.

*Ralph Wood, active 1781-1801, was from a family of Staffordshire potters. He became well known for his fine modeling and colored glazes, and his work was much imitated. Some of his work is marked "RA. Wood Burlsem".*

*c1790  5.5in (14cm) high*

**$5,000-7,000** — **JHOR**

A Staffordshire lion spill vase.

*c1855* — *6.25in (16cm) high*

**$800-1,200** — **JHD**

A Staffordshire lion spill vase.

*c1855* — *6.25in (16cm) high*

**$800-1,200** — **JHD**

A Staffordshire standing lion.

c1850 · 4.25in (11cm) high

$1,000-1,500 · JHD

A Staffordshire lion and leopard pair.

c1855 · 6in (15cm) high

$3,000-4,000 · JHD

A pair of Staffordshire models of standing lions.

c1860 · 6.75in (17cm) high

$2,800-3,200 · HAMG

A pair of Staffordshire English lions overcoming Napoleon III.

c1860 · 9.75in (25cm) high

$3,000-4,000 · JHD

A Staffordshire swan, by Alcock and Co.

c1840 · 4.75in (12cm) high

$1,200-1,800 · JHD

A Staffordshire spill vase depicting hens fighting over a worm.

c1860 · 6in (15.5cm) high

$1,200-1,800 · JHD

A pair of Staffordshire pigeon tureens and covers, modeled as nesting birds and painted in iron red, restored.

c1860 · 9in (22cm) long

$700-1,000 · DN

A Staffordshire parrot.

c1855 · 9.25in (23.5cm) high

$700-1,000 · AD

A pair of Staffordshire roosters.

c1860 · 4in (10.5cm) high

$800-1,200 · JHD

A rare Staffordshire spill vase group, inscribed "The Milkmaid".

c1830 · 5.25in (13.5cm) high

$500-700 · GCL

A rare Staffordshire seated monkey, on an inkwell base.

c1840 · 5.5in (14cm) high

$1,000-1,500 · AD

A Staffordshire prancing fox, with restored ear.

c1850 · 6.5in (16.5cm) high

$800-1,200 · JHD

A Staffordshire fox vase.

c1850 · 5in (13cm) high

$700-1,000 · JHD

**POTTERY**

A Staffordshire pony on a textured base.

c1860      6.75in (17cm) high

**$700-1,000**      AD

A Staffordshire spill vase group with a zebra in flight chased by a fox, mostly colored, on an oval gilt-lined base.

c1860      11in (28cm) high

**$300-500**      DN

A Staffordshire horse and foal spill vase.

c1860      11.5in (29.5cm) high

**$1,500-2,000**      JHD

A Staffordshire figure of a cow.

c1860      4.5in (11.5cm) high

**$500-700**      AD

One of a pair of Staffordshire lambs with flags.

c1860      3in (7.5cm) high

**$700-1,000 pair**      JHD

A pair of Staffordshire sheep and ram spill vases with some flaking paint, retouched on bases.

c1880      7.5in (19cm) high

**$1,500-2,000**      JHD

A pair of Staffordshire rabbits.

c1860      3.5in (9cm) long

**$1,200-1,800**      JHD

## HUMAN FIGURES

A figure of a lady with a basket, probably Staffordshire.

c1800      10.75in (27.5cm) high

**$4,000-6,000**      JHOR

An early 19thC Staffordshire figure representative of Winter.

c1810      7.5in (19cm) high

**$300-500**      AD

An unusual Staffordshire buff earthenware figure of a man in Turkish costume, decorated in colored enamels, and flanked by a gun and a game bird, on a mound base.

c1820      6in (15.5cm) high

**$300-500**      LFA

A Staffordshire group of children with their nanny and dog, before a flowering tree.

c1815     9in (23cm) high

**$8,000-12,000**     **JHOR**

An early 19thC Staffordshire figure of a man holding a book.

7in (18cm) high

**$800-1,200**     **AD**

An early 19thC Staffordshire figure inscribed "Autum", on a square base.

6.75in (17.5cm) high

**$100-150**     **CHEF**

An early 19thC Staffordshire figure of a trumpeter, modeled in Walton style.

6in (15.5cm) high

**$500-700**     **CHEF**

A pair of early 19thC Staffordshire figures of Elijah and the widow, both seated on rocks by streams and with square marbled bases, he with a raven and she with her arm around her child.

10in (25.5cm) high

**$280-320**     **CHEF**

A Staffordshire model of a man and a woman on a bench.

c1820     8.5in (21.5cm) high

**$5,000-7,000**     **JHOR**

A Staffordshire family group sitting on a bench, with bocage.

c1825

**$7,000-10,000**     **JHOR**

A Staffordshire figural group of a woman with children, bocage missing.

c1830

**$220-280**     **AD**

An unusual Staffordshire figure of a country woman.

c1850     11.5in (29cm) high

**$500-800**     **JHD**

A Staffordshire figure of Sir Robert Peel, modeled standing, holding a scroll in his right hand, decorated in colored enamels, the rectangular base titled in gilt "S.R. Peel", restored.

c1850     7.5in (19cm) high

**$400-600**     **LFA**

A mid-19thC Staffordshire group of a man and companion, modeled wearing Jacobean dress, dancing.

*7.5in (19cm) high*

**$220-280**     **DN**

A 19thC Staffordshire model of the jockey Fred Archer, wearing an orange cap and a pink jacket.

*9in (23cm) high*

**$280-320**     **WW**

A mid-19thC Staffordshire group of a fisherman with wife and child, modeled seated in a boat with nets.

*11in (28cm) high*

**$280-320**     **DN**

A mid-19thC Staffordshire figure of a Highlander.

*16.5in (42cm) high*

**$600-900**     **SWO**

A 19thC Staffordshire flatback figural group of Samson and the lion, on an oval plinth base.

*9in (23cm) high*

**$280-320**     **SWO**

A Staffordshire pottery figure of a young woman, standing, wearing a plumed hat and holding a riding crop.

*c1865*     *12in (30.5cm) high*

**$150-200**     **GAL**

## A CLOSER LOOK AT A LATE STAFFORDSHIRE GROUP

During the mid-19thC there was a demand for figures of famous people such as politicians, criminals, sportsmen, and actors. Prior to this, Staffordshire groups had typically depicted allegorical figures, children, or lovers.

The resemblance to the person portrayed was often poor as well-known personalities were modeled from drawings and prints rather than from life. Factories also used the same molds for different characters.

Styles were generally copied from grand figures in stately homes, transferred to subjects that appealed to the working classes.

There are many fakes of Staffordshire figures on the market. Look out for artificially stained white porcelain, poor modeling and over-pronounced crazing.

Charlotte Cushman (1816-1876) was a famous American actress and patron who was particularly well known for playing male roles, including Romeo.

A late Staffordshire pottery group by Thomas Parr, depicting Charlotte Cushman as Romeo and Susan Cushman as Juliet, standing with arms entwined, the base with gilt painted title.

*c1850*     *10.5in (25.5cm) high*

**$300-500**     **HAMG**

A Staffordshire flatback watch stand group, the male standing beside a seated lady with a guitar.

*12in (30.5cm) high*

**$50-80** GORL

A Staffordshire arbor group, of two lovers under a vine with Cupid to one side.

*c1870* *12in (30.5cm) high*

**$280-320** SWO

A Staffordshire figure of a huntsman and his dog.

*18.5in (47cm) high*

**$700-1,000** SWO

A Staffordshire figure of Napoleon, his right arm resting on a cannon.

*c1875* *16.25in (41cm) high*

**$280-320** SWO

## WHIELDON

A rare Whieldon-type model of a seated cat, decorated with a runny green and mottled brown glaze, small chip to one ear.

*c1750* *4.5in (11.5cm) high*

**$2,800-3,200** WW

A rare Whieldon-type commemorative box, the cover applied with a portrait bust, a canon, an eagle, an axe and the initials "K.P." for the King of Prussia.

*c1755* *3.25in (8cm) high*

**$700-1,000** WW

A rare Whieldon-type creamware coffeepot and cover, with a molded spout and strap handle.

*c1760* *10.75in (27cm) high*

**$1,000-1,500** WW

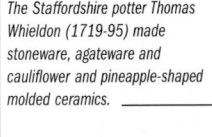

A Whieldon-type tortoiseshell glazed teapot and cover, with a bird knop and a crabstock handle and spout, raised on three mask-capped paw feet, some restoration.

*c1765* *8in (20.5cm) high*

**$1,500-2,000** WW

A Whieldon school teapot, restored finial.

*c1765* *8.5in (21.5cm) long*

**$1,500-2,000** AS

### A CLOSER LOOK AT A WHIELDON FIGURE

*The Staffordshire potter Thomas Whieldon (1719-95) made stoneware, agateware and cauliflower and pineapple-shaped molded ceramics.*

*The earliest Staffordshire figures, made by Astbury or Whieldon, are scarce and valuable.*

*Whieldon created this mottled decoration by kneading together clays of various colors, or by applying splashes of colored slip to the body.*

*These early figures are naively modeled compared to later examples. Figures became more refined during the second half of the 18thC.*

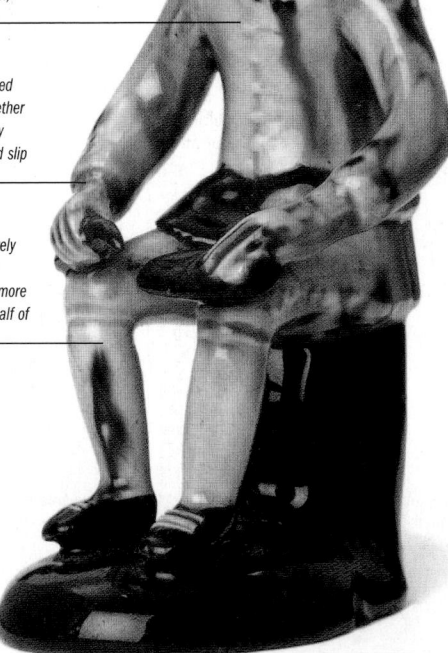

A rare Whieldon-type figure of a cobbler, seated mending a shoe on his knee and wearing an apron, raised on an oval base, the blade of his knife restored.

*c1750* *4.5in (11.5cm) high*

**$5,000-7,000** WW

**POTTERY**

## THOMAS WHIELDON

- Thomas Whieldon (1719-95) worked from the Fenton Vivian potworks in Fenton, one of the Pottery towns in Staffordshire.
- He employed Josiah Spode from 1749 and went into partnership with Josiah Wedgwood c1755.
- Whieldon is associated most closely with the production of tortoiseshell ware, but he also produced agateware.
- Many Staffordshire potteries also produced tortoiseshell pieces, sometimes known as 'Whieldon-type' wares.
- Translucent colored glazes, usually in manganese brown, copper green and cobalt blue, were applied to produce a mottled effect.
- Teaware forms in cream-colored earthenware dominate the range, often with applied motifs.

A Whieldon-type miniature teapot with molded decoration.

c1780    5.5in (14cm) long

**$800-1,200**    **AS**

A Whieldon-type lead-glazed earthenware tea canister, decorated with a figure of Flora, cover missing.

c1765    7in (18cm) high

**$6,000-9,000**    **JHOR**

A Whieldon-type 'Domino' caddy.

c1770    5in (12.5cm) high

**$1,800-2,200**    **AS**

## AGATEWARE

A solid agateware teapot and cover, modeled as a shell, the handle modeled as a serpent, the knop as a lion, restored.

c1745    7.25in (18.5cm) high

**$3,000-5,000**    **WW**

A mid-18thC agateware teapot, with lion knop, restored.

6in (15cm) high

**$5,000-8,000**    **AS**

A shell-shaped agateware teapot, with lion knop.

c1755    5in (12.5cm) high

**$5,000-8,000**    **JHOR**

A Staffordshire agateware teapot, with applied chain and tripod feet.

c1755    8in (20.5cm) wide

**$6,000-9,000**    **JHOR**

An agateware cream jug, with three legs molded as lion heads and claws.

c1755    3.5in (9cm) high

**$3,000-5,000**    **JHOR**

An agateware cat, salt-glazed with blue splashes, the eyes picked out in brown.

c1750    5in (13cm) high

**$3,000-5,000**    **JHOR**

A solid agateware model of a seated cat, marbled in cream and brown, on an oval mound base, chips to ears.

8in (20.5cm) high

**$600-900**    **LFA**

A 19thC solid agateware tobacco jar, the finial mounted lid above a cylindrical body applied with a panel incised "Major W.O. Wade".

1889    8.75in (22cm) high

**$280-320**    **ROW**

An agateware bowl.

c1750    4.25in (11cm) high

**$5,000-7,000**    **AS**

A Staffordshire salt-glazed stoneware teapot and cover, the branch handle issuing applied leafy branches, grapes and a squirrel, painted in polychrome with a bird chasing insects, restored.

c1760      7.5in (19cm) long

**$500-700**      **WW**

An English polychrome salt-glazed teapot with Chinoiserie decoration, restored chips to lid.

c1760      4.5in (11.5cm) high

**$7,000-10,000**      **AS**

A rare Staffordshire blue ground salt-glazed teapot and cover, painted in polychrome with two large and three small panels of flowers, restored.

c1765      7in (18cm) long

**$2,200-2,800**      **WW**

A polychrome salt-glazed inkwell and inner, inscribed "EM".

c1760      2.75in (7cm) diam

**$4,000-6,000**      **AS**

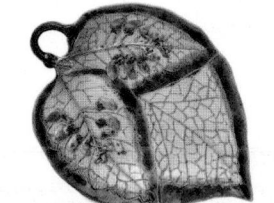

A Staffordshire salt-glazed stoneware leaf-molded dish, with a green stalk handle, molded with pink pea flowers and painted green, yellow, and pink, restored.

c1760      7in (18cm) wide

**$500-700**      **WW**

A Staffordshire salt-glazed teapot.

c1750      6.5in (16cm) high

**$4,000-6,000**      **JHOR**

## A CLOSER LOOK AT A SALT-GLAZED TEAPOT

*Small Staffordshire teapots of this period are very scarce. This example features a rare faceted spout with molded decoration, making it even more unusual.*

*This rose, with pink fading to white leaves, may have had Jacobite significance. This teapot was made around the time of the last great Jacobite Rebellion in 1745.*

*This teapot is exceptionally well modeled. It is of regular shape, is well proportioned, and the lid fits snugly onto the body.*

*The enamels on this teapot remain extremely vibrant and attractive despite its age. Aside from a small patch of restoration to the spout, this piece is in perfect condition.*

A mid-18thC English blue salt-glazed midget teapot, enamel rose decoration, restored spout.

7.5in (19cm) long

**$15,000-20,000**      **AS**

A Staffordshire salt-glazed teapot, on three lion feet.

c1750      3in (8cm) high

**$1,200-1,800**      **JHOR**

A Staffordshire salt-glazed stoneware sauceboat, of silver shape, molded with scrolls on a diaper ground, a few faint hairlines.

c1750      6in (15cm) long

**$300-400**      **WW**

A Staffordshire salt-glazed stoneware butter tub, restored.

c1750      5in (13cm) wide

**$2,200-2,800**      **JHOR**

A pair of salt-glazed potpourri containers, probably Leeds.

c1780      5in (13cm) high

**$6,000-9,000**      **JHOR**

An early 19thC mochaware pitcher, of ovoid form with molded green bands at the neck and base, the mid-section banded in taupe and tan with blue and brown earthworming, some roughness at spout.

*7in (17.5cm) high*

**$5,000-7,000**     **FRE**

An early 19thC mochaware jug, decorated with concentric blue and brown bands with root designs.

*8in (20cm) wide*

**$1,200-1,800**     **WW**

A Staffordshire mochaware jug, of baluster form, painted with a sponged band of stylized trees.

*c1840*     *7.5in (19cm) high*

**$500-700**     **DN**

## MOCHAWARE

- Mochaware was produced by William Adams of Tunstall in Staffordshire during the late 18thC.
- Its popularity was such that production spread throughout Europe and America during the 19thC. The technique is still used today.
- The name is derived from the moss agate stone, which has thin, branching striations of color. Many of these stones were shipped across the world from the port of Mocha in Yemen.
- The process involves dripping a 'tea' of tobacco and a coloring agent, such as iron oxide, onto a ground of slip clay. The acidic tea reacts with the alkaline ground and causes a tree-like pattern to grow across the surface of the pot.
- Mochaware is sometimes slip-decorated with designs known as 'cat's-eye', 'earthworm', and 'tobacco leaf'.
- Popular and inexpensive at the time it was made, a wide variety of mochaware is available on today's market. However, its popularity means that prices are usually high and exceptional pieces are becoming more scarce.
- Mugs and jugs are the most common forms, although other types of vessel such as canisters and pots can also be found.
- Mochaware is not usually marked, making attribution to a specific factory, or even an area, difficult.

A mochaware pitcher with green, ocher and brown banding.

*4.25in (11cm) high*

**$1,200-1,800**     **POOK**

A mochaware pitcher with green, black, ocher, blue, and white banding and spotted decoration.

*6in (15cm) high*

**$4,000-6,000**     **POOK**

An early 19thC English mochaware cup, of baluster form with brick-red body decorated with brown and blue fans and brown stripe at neck, restored.

*3.25in (8cm) high*

**$1,500-2,000**     **FRE**

A 19thC mochaware mustard pot and cover, decorated with six blue designs within buff borders.

*3.75in (9.5cm) wide*

**$180-220**     **WW**

A large mochaware mug with earthworming on tan ground and green and black banding.

*6.25in (16cm) high*

**$2,800-3,200**     **POOK**

A mochaware canister with green band and multicolor mottled glazing.

*5in (12.5cm) high*

**$700-1,000**     **POOK**

An early 19thC Staffordshire money box, modeled as a house.

*5in (13cm) high*

**$280-320**  **ROS**

A Staffordshire triple house pastille burner, by Alcock, with restored finials.

*c1830*  *6in (15.5cm) wide*

**$1,500-2,000**  **JHD**

A Staffordshire model of Stanfield Hall, partially colored in gilt, restored turret.

*c1850*  *6.25in (16cm) wide*

**$500-700**  **DN**

A 19thC Staffordshire model of a lighthouse beside a cottage, with a shepherd and his dog and four sheep.

*7.25in (18.5cm) high*

**$320-380**  **WW**

A Staffordshire Fair Hebe jug, modeled after John Voyez with three figures and a dog around a tree stump, inscriptions.

*c1790*  *10.5in (26cm) wide*

**$700-1,000**  **WW**

A Staffordshire basaltware teapot, with lion head spout and Duke of Wellington relief.

*1813*  *12in (30.5cm) high*

**$1,200-1,800**  **JHOR**

A Staffordshire frog mug, the interior modeled with a brown and black spotted frog perched on the base of the side, the exterior with rustic figures drinking.

*c1850*  *4.75in (12cm) high*

**$80-120**  **H&L**

A small late 18thC Staffordshire lead-glazed green leaf dish.

*8.5in (22cm) wide*

**$700-1,000**  **JHOR**

## STONEWARE

A rare Waldenburg salt-glazed stoneware beaker, with tin mounts on a molded brown body, the lid with relief border and ball-shaped knop.

*10.5in (26.5cm) high*

**$7,000-10,000**  **WKA**

A Creussen dark brown salt-glazed stoneware bottle, with short neck, floral relief between four oval fields, tin mounting and screw cap.

*c1680*  *7.75in (19.5cm) high*

**$500-800**  **BMN**

A late 17thC Westerwald salt-glazed stoneware jug, painted in blue, decorated with five stamped angels' heads, the tin mounting with flat lid and oak handle.

*11.5in (29cm) high*

**$700-1,000**  **BMN**

An early 18thC Westerwald salt-glazed stoneware tankard, painted in blue, the inside with a scale, tin mounting.

*8.5in (21.5cm) high*

**$180-220**  **BMN**

A 19thC Muskau salt-glazed stoneware jug, painted in blue, the tin mounting with flat lid and oak handle, engraved monogram and indistinct mark.

*7.5in (18.5cm) high*

**$150-200**  **BMN**

**POTTERY**

A small Ralph & James Clews "Romantic Ruins" pattern dish, printed in blue with a Classical scene and foliage border, impressed crown mark with "GR" and "Clews Warranted Staffordshire", small chip.

*c1820*     *11in (28cm) wide*

**$180-220**     **DN**

A small Ralph & James Clews 'Indian Sporting' series tea plate, printed in blue with "Groom Leading Out" within a strip border of animals, impressed circular crown mark.

*c1820*     *8in (20.5cm) diam*

**$180-220**     **DN**

A Ralph & James Clews blue and white decorated plate, printed with "Doctor Syntax Taking Possession of his Living", with impressed and printed marks.

*c1820*     *10.25in (25.5cm) diam*

**$180-220**     **SWO**

A Ralph & James Clews 'Foliage and Scroll Border' series dessert plate, printed in dark blue with a scene identified as St. Catherine's Hill near Guildford, within irregular foliage border.

*c1825*     *8.75in (22.5cm) diam*

**$180-220**     **DN**

A 'Donovan' pattern pierced dessert plate, attributed to Davenport, the basketweave rim edged in blue, printed in blue with a Chinoiserie scene of fishermen by a temple, unmarked.

*c1805*     *8in (20.5cm) diam*

**$220-280**     **DN**

A Davenport 'Tudor Mansion' pattern well-and-tree meat dish, printed in blue with a country house scene and a border of running branches, impressed lower-case anchor mark.

*c1815*     *18.5in (47cm) wide*

**$300-500**     **DN**

A pair of Davenport 'Chinese River Scene' pattern dinner plates, printed in blue with a view identified as the Imperial Park at Gehol, impressed maker's name, one with cracked rim.

*c1815*     *10in (25.5cm) diam*

**$150-200**     **DN**

A Davenport 'Rustic Scenes' series dinner plate, printed in blue with the "Thatched Farmshed" scene within the usual floral border, impressed lower-case anchor mark.

*c1820*     *9.75in (25cm) diam*

**$180-220**     **DN**

A Davenport 'Fisherman' series dinner plate, printed in blue with the 'Fisherman's Tale' or 'Fisherman and Woman with Basket' scene within a geometric border, impressed anchor mark.

*c1820*     *9.75in (25cm) diam*

**$80-120**     **DN**

A rare Ridgway 'Net' pattern dinner plate, printed in blue with a Chinoiserie pattern and border, impressed "Ridgway" mark.

*c1810*     *9.75in (25cm) diam*

**$180-220**     **DN**

A Ridgway 'Angus Seats' series arcaded tea plate, printed in blue with Tong Castle in Shropshire, within a square frame and border, unmarked.

*c1815*     *7.75in (19.5cm) diam*

**$180-220**     **DN**

A Ridgway 'Christ Church, Oxford' pattern dinner plate from the 'Oxford and Cambridge College' series, printed in blue with the titled view within an octagonal frame and border of cherub vignettes, printed mark.

*c1820*     *9.75in (25cm) diam*

**$180-220**     **DN**

A Francis Morley & Co. armorial well-and-tree meat dish, printed in green with the border from the 'Caledonian' pattern and a central crest of a rising sun with the motto "Quis Separabit", impressed mark "Real Ironstone China F. Morley & Co.", further printed marks with pattern title, maker's initials "RMW & Co." and registration diamond for 21 July 1846.

1846    19in (48.5cm) wide

**$280-320**    **DN**

A Ridgway stone china dinner plate, printed in blue with an Oriental-style pattern of a vase of flowers within a paneled border of flowers and other symbols, printed marks.

c1815    10in (25.5cm) diam

**$150-200**    **DN**

A pair of 'British Scenery' series dinner plates attributed to Ridgway, printed in blue with the scene known as 'Cottages and Castle' within flower and leaf border, printed series title mark.

c1820    10in (25.5cm) diam

**$280-320**    **DN**

A Ridgway 'Oxford and Cambridge College' series dinner plate, printed in blue with "Christ Church, Oxford" within an octagonal frame, printed mark.

c1820    10in (25.5cm) diam

**$280-320**    **DN**

A Ridgway 'Giraffe' pattern dinner plate, printed in blue with an animal group and open floral border, printed mark with title and maker's name.

c1830    10in (25.5cm) wide

**$300-400**    **DN**

A Ridgway blue and white 'Clare Hall' pattern dessert dish, of shell shape, with fruiting vine handle.

c1820    9.25in (23.5cm) wide

**$180-220**    **HAMG**

One of a pair of early 19thC Rogers' blue and white platters printed with the 'Monopteros' pattern of a buffalo being driven past towers and ancient ruins, impressed marks.

16.75in (42.5cm) wide

**$220-280 pair**    **CHEF**

A Spode 'Caramanian' series dinner plate, printed in blue with "Sarcophagi and Sepulchres at the Head of the Harbor of Cacamo", impressed mark.

c1815    10in (25.5cm) diam

**$280-320**    **DN**

## A CLOSER LOOK AT A TRANSFER-PRINTED PLATE

Joseph Spode's 'Indian Sporting' series is one of the most famous patterns.

The illustrations are based on colored engravings taken from Samuel Howitt's drawings in Thomas Williamson's 'Oriental Field Sports', published in 1807.

This blue and white meat dish displays the pattern to its best advantage. Dishes should not be hung using sprung metal grips as these can scratch or even crack the rim.

The pattern on this dish has been transfer printed via the application of a sheet of paper bearing a wet ink image from an engraved copper plate. The design is under the glaze.

A Spode 'Indian Sporting' series meat dish, printed in blue with "Shooting a Leopard", printed title and printed and impressed marks.

c1820    20.25in (51.5cm) wide

**$3,000-5,000**    **DN**

**POTTERY**

A Spode 'Indian Sporting' series dinner plate, printed in blue with the "Death of the Bear", printed title and printed and impressed marks.

c1820      9.75in (25cm) diam

**$300-400**      **DN**

A Spode 'Indian Sporting' series meat dish, printed in blue with "Dooreahs Leading Out Dogs", printed title and printed and impressed marks.

c1820      18.75in (47.5cm) wide

**$3,000-4,000**      **DN**

A Spode 'Indian Sporting' series meat dish, printed in blue with "Driving a Bear out of Sugar Canes", printed title and printed and impressed marks.

c1820      16.5in (42cm) wide

**$1,500-2,000**      **DN**

A 'Greek' series dish of Spode type, with ocher rim, printed in blue with a central scene known as 'Artemis Drawn by a Griffin and a Lynx' within a border.

c1820      18in (46cm) wide

**$280-320**      **DN**

A 'Greek' series well-and-tree dish, attributed to Spode, printed in blue with a central scene known as 'Cynisca Winning the Chariot Race' within a border of vases and Classical figure panels, unmarked.

c1830      20.75in (52.5cm) wide

**$180-220**      **DN**

A Spode printed and enameled earthenware oval drainer, printed in blue with the 'Trophies-Etruscan' or 'Hundred Antiques' pattern within the 'Cracked Ice and Prunus' border, with details picked out in ocher enamel, printed and impressed upper-case marks.

c1825      12in (22cm) wide

**$700-1,000**      **DN**

A Copeland 'Aesop's Fables' series meat dish, printed in blue with a scene identified as 'The Dog in the Manger' within flower and scroll border, printed "Copeland Late Spode" mark and impressed crown.

c1855      18.5in (47cm) wide

**$500-700**      **DN**

A 'Beehive and Vases' pattern dinner plate, attributed to Ralph Stevenson & Williams, printed in dark blue with a central still life scene and border.

c1825      10in (25.5cm) diam

**$150-200**      **DN**

A Stevenson 'Acorn and Oak Leaf Border' series cake or cheese stand, printed in blue with a scene identified as Windsor Castle, unmarked.

c1825      10.75in (27cm) diam

**$500-700**      **DN**

An Andrew Stevenson 'Culford Hall, Suffolk' pattern dinner plate from the 'Rose Border' series, printed in dark blue with the titled view and border.

c1825      10.25in (26cm) diam

**$180-220**      **DN**

A 'Beehive and Vases' pattern dinner plate, attributed to Stevenson & Williams, printed in dark blue with a central still life scene and a border.

c1825      10in (25.5cm) diam

**$100-150**      **DN**

A Stevenson 'Fig Tree' pattern mug, with ocher rim, printed with a Chinoiserie scene with a pavilion-like building and a fig tree with hanging lanterns.

c1800      5in (12cm) high

**$150-200**      **DN**

An Enoch Wood & Sons 'Gunton Hall, Norfolk' pattern tea plate from the 'Grapevine Border' series, printed in blue with the titled scene and border.

c1825      7.5in (19cm) diam

**$220-280**      **DN**

A 'Lady with Parasol' pattern soup plate, of octagonal shape, printed in blue with a Chinoiserie scene and running floral border, unmarked.

c1795          8.75in (22.5cm) wide

**$80-120**                    **DN**

A Bovey Tracey 'Pagoda and Swan' pattern dessert plate, printed in dark blue with a Chinoiserie scene and a narrow geometric border.

c1800          8in (20.5cm) diam

**$120-180**                   **DN**

A Wedgwood & Co. 'Elephant' pattern dessert plate, printed in blue with a Chinoiserie scene including an elephant and other figures, impressed marks.

c1800          8in (20.5cm) diam

**$150-200**                   **DN**

A Leeds Pottery 'Great Wall of China' pattern dessert plate, printed in blue with a Chinoiserie scene and border, impressed mark.

c1810          8.5in (21.5cm) diam

**$100-150**                   **DN**

A pearlware plate, printed in underglaze blue with the 'Grazing Rabbits' pattern, within a broad band of flowers and leaves.

c1815          8.5in (21.5cm) diam

**$500-700**                   **LFA**

A Hartley Greens & Co. 'Scene After Claude Lorraine' pattern dinner plate, printed in blue with a European-style scene and strip border.

c1815          9.5in (24cm) diam

**$80-120**                    **DN**

A Tams 'Floral City' series dinner plate, decorated in dark blue with an unidentified central scene framed by the usual irregular foliage border.

c1820          10in (25.5cm) diam

**$80-120**                    **DN**

A 'Pashkov Palace' pattern soup plate, printed in blue with a Moscow scene and floral border, unmarked.

c1820          9.5in (24cm) diam

**$220-280**                   **DN**

A pair of 'Parrot Border' series dinner plates, printed in blue with the "Mausoleum of Kausim Solemanee at Chunar Gur", printed title marks, one also with retailer's mark for "King's Warehouse Dundee", glaze crack.

c1820          10in (25.5cm) diam

**$280-320**                   **DN**

An 'Audley End Essex' pattern dinner plate, possibly by Carey's, printed in blue with the identified country house scene and floral border, unmarked.

c1825          9.75in (25cm) diam

**$280-320**                   **DN**

A John Denton Bagster 'Vignette' series dinner plate, printed with a scene depicting a Scottish shepherd, flowers and scroll and ribbon framing.

c1825          10in (25.5cm) diam

**$80-120**                    **DN**

A Copeland & Garrett 'Caramanian' series dessert plate, printed in blue with the 'Necropolis' or 'Cemetery of Cacamo' pattern within series border.

c1840          8.5in (21.5cm) diam

**$150-200**                   **DN**

A 'Gleaners' pattern soup plate, printed in blue with the genre scene and fruit and flower border, unmarked except for impressed date code "10/23".

               9.75in (25cm) diam

**$80-120**                    **DN**

A set of eight English transfer-printed soup plates, each printed in brown with a romantic river landscape of pavilions, castles, and a bridge.

c1825          9.5in (24cm) diam

**$300-500**                   **FRE**

An early 19thC pearlware bowl, printed in blue with "The Ghost", a specter appearing before four cowering characters, crack to border.

10in (25.5cm) wide

**$300-500**     **GORL**

A Minton 'English Scenery' series meat dish, printed in blue with the scene identified as Windsor Castle within the usual floral scroll border, printed series title mark.

c1825    20.75in (53cm) wide

**$700-1,000**     **DN**

A 'Swiss Scenery' pattern well-and-tree meat dish, with molded wavy rim, printed in brown with a typical Swiss-style romantic scene and open floral border, printed title cartouche mark.

c1830    20in (51cm) wide

**$400-600**     **DN**

A 'Temple with Panel' pattern meat dish, probably by Barker, printed in blue with a Chinoiserie scene and border, unmarked, damaged.

c1790    19in (48cm) wide

**$280-320**     **DN**

A 'Tall Pagoda' pattern dish, attributed to Lakin & Poole, printed in blue with a Chinoiserie scene featuring a tall pagoda, buildings and three junks.

c1795    12in (22.5cm) wide

**$150-200**     **DN**

A pair of oval pearlware dishes, each printed in underglaze blue with the 'Willow' pattern, the reeded pierced basketwork borders picked out in blue.

c1810    10.5in (26.5cm) wide

**$280-320**     **LFA**

A 'View of Brecknock' pattern dish from the 'Diorama' series, printed in dark blue with the titled view within the usual foliage border, printed title mark.

c1825    13.5in (34.5cm) wide

**$500-700**     **DN**

An early Victorian blue and white platter printed with fishermen on and about a toll bridge with castle ruins in the distance, the rim with flowering vines over cherry leaves.

c1840    21.25in (54cm) wide

**$280-320**     **CHEF**

A 'Conversation' pattern teapot, of circular form with distinct shoulder and acorn knop to cover, printed in dark blue with a line-engraved Chinoiserie scene, unmarked, some restoration.

c1790    9in (22cm) long

**$300-400**     **DN**

A 'Chinaman with Rocket' pattern teapot, of spherical shape with flower-molded knop to the cover, printed in blue with a Chinoiserie scene, unmarked, restored.

c1805    10in (25.5cm) long

**$280-320**     **DN**

A centerpiece from a supper set attributed to the Herculaneum Pottery, of oval shape with domed cover and internal pierced egg tray, printed in blue with an Italianate scene.

c1815    10in (25.5cm) wide

**$300-400**     **DN**

A Don Pottery 'Named Italian Views' series sauce tureen and cover, with a blue lion knop to the cover, printed with scenes and floral border, with flying putti beneath the handles, unmarked.

c1820    6in (15.5cm) wide

**$180-220**     **DN**

A 'Castle and Bridge' pattern tea plate with matching soup tureen stand, each printed in blue with a scene representing St. Albans and border of buildings and foliage, unmarked.

c1815    stand 14.5in (37cm) wide

**$280-320**     **DN**

A printed blue and white pottery tureen, printed with the 'Piping Shepherd' pattern, damaged.

c1820    14in (35.5cm) wide

**$500-800**     **SWO**

A William Smith & Co. 'Select Views' series covered vegetable dish, of ornate oval shape, printed with romantic scenes and border of flowers, printed vignette mark with title and maker's name and impressed "Wedgwood" mark.

c1830          12.5in (24.5cm) long

**$150-200**          **DN**

A 'May Queen' pattern mug, with turned rim, foot and central band and simple strap handle, printed with a genre scene of the May Queen, a companion and a piper playing to dancers.

c1820          6in (15.5cm) high

**$400-600**          **DN**

A mid-19thC blue and white transfer-printed vomit pot or child's chamber pot, with strap handle, decorated with a Chinoiserie pattern beneath an elaborate floral border, unmarked.

5.5in (14cm) diam

**$180-220**          **H&L**

A Victorian blue and white 'Willow' pattern scent flask, of flat circular form, the silver lid marked "London 1886, Samson & Mordan" with printed number "29260".

2.25in (5.75cm) high

**$280-320**          **HAMG**

## WEDGWOOD

A decorated Wedgwood vase, of twin-handled ovoid form, the encaustic decoration depicting two Classical figures within Greek key and laurel leaf borders.

c1790          9.5in (24cm) high

**$2,200-2,800**          **ROS**

A Wedgwood black basalt amphora, painted in Etruscan enamels with Classical figures between Greek key and anthemion band borders, impressed "Wedgwood" mark.

c1800          12.25in (31cm) high

**$2,200-2,800**          **DN**

A 19thC Wedgwood black basalt 'Bacchus' ewer, modeled with a strap handle with a satyr enveloping the neck and clutching the horns of a goat's mask, suspending swags of fruiting vine, on a pedestal stem and plinth foot, impressed "Wedgwood" mark, restored.

15.25in (39cm) high

**$1,500-2,000**          **DN**

An early 19thC Wedgwood black basalt bust of Shakespeare, the bearded bard wearing a buttoned jerkin and open-collared shirt, supported on a socle plinth.

12.5in (32cm) high

**$800-1,200**          **CHEF**

A large Wedgwood black basalt teapot or punch-pot, the frieze sprigged in relief with dancing Classical maidens, the cover with a finial of fruit, impressed mark, restored spout.

c1800

**$280-320**          **DN**

A rare Wedgwood black basalt model of a raven, modeled by E.W. Light, with glass eyes, on a shaped base, impressed mark.

c1915          8in (20.5cm) long

**$500-800**          **LFA**

A Wedgwood blue jasper dip canopic vase and cover, the cover molded as a pharaoh's head, the body applied with Egyptian motifs, impressed "Wedgwood" mark and incised date.

1796          9.75in (24.5cm) high

**$1,000-1,500**          **WW**

A Wedgwood lidded jasperware jug, with relief decoration in white.

c1880          7.25in (18.5cm) high

**$280-320**          **GCL**

A late 19thC Wedgwood black jasper two-handled urn and cover, impressed mark.

9in (23cm) high

**$400-600**          **DN**

A 19thC Wedgwood black basalt bust of Mercury, the reverse impressed "Mercury" and "Wedgwood", on a socle base.

18in (46cm) high

**$1,800-2,200**          **DN**

A Wedgwood white ware teapot and cover, molded with two bands of foliate scrolls, the cover with a spaniel finial.

c1820          7in (18cm) long

**$300-400**          **ROS**

## THE FOLK ART MARKET

At present, Folk Art collectors are seeking out exceptional and rare pieces at the higher end of the market. Ceramics, and especially Redware, have attracted a great deal of attention. Jugs and bowls with exquisite decoration are very collectible and are probably a good investment. Early pieces and those with graphic decoration proved very popular at this year's auctions.

The bestseller at an auction at Pook & Pook, who are well-known in the US for folk art sales, was a miniature yellow-painted blanket chest that sold for $80,500 (see page 245). The bright color and excellent condition of this piece appealed to many folk art enthusiasts.

The top end of the horn and scrimshaw field is also doing well. Rare pieces are commanding high prices, such as a narwhal skull with two tusks that reached $57,000 at auction.

Fraktur is always a popular area. Highly sought after, rare and colorful pieces reach six-figure prices easily. Condition is extremely important with Fraktur, as is proven provenance. A famous Fraktur collection by Dr. & Mrs. Donald Shelley sold for $780,000 at Pook & Pook. The top end of the market is doing extremely well, where as the lower end is stagnating at the moment.

The quilt market has seen a bit of a rebound recently for better 19thC examples, some selling for the high hundreds of dollars instead of the low hundreds.

Collectors must look out for fakes. Contacting auction houses and specialist dealers will help to assure the authenticity of a piece.

*– Thomas Flanagan, Vice President, Pook & Pook Inc.*

## REDWARE

A glazed redware jar with cover, the cover of tapering circular form with strap handle on a tapering ovoid base, chips at rim of cover.

*14.5in (37cm) diam*

$300-500      FRE

A 19thC glazed redware jar with handle, flared mouth on ovoid form decorated with sprays of blue, yellow and brown tulips, repair at mouth, glaze and enamel wear.

*8.5in (21.5cm) high*

$400-600      FRE

A 19thC Pennsylvania redware suppressed ovoid lidded bean pot, with sgraffito decoration with birds sitting on tulip tree arising from a basket, with overall orange and black manganese glazing.

*6.5in (16.5cm) high*

$2,800-3,200      POOK

A 19thC Pennsylvania redware charger, with yellow four-line slip decoration, damaged.

*12in (30cm) diam*

$300-500      POOK

A glazed slip and sgraffito-decorated redware dish, shallow, circular-form decorated with incised German inscription and date, floral sprays at concave rim, losses.

*1855*      *10.5in (26cm) diam*

$400-600      FRE

A glazed redware figure of a pelican, modeled in the full-round on a circular base, incised details heightened with green glaze, inscription at base, dated, loss and repairs.

*1797*      *7in (18cm) high*

$1,800-2,200      FRE

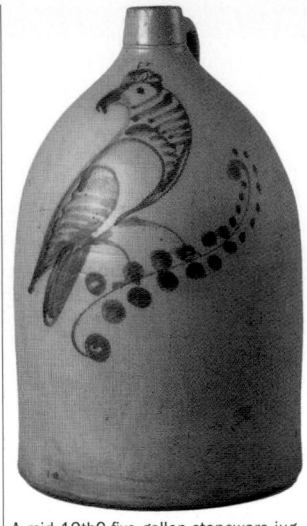

A mid-19thC five-gallon stoneware jug, with large vibrant blue parrot perched on a branch with fruit, repair to handle.

*19in (48cm) high*

**$1,800-2,200**     **POOK**

A 19thC stoneware presentation pitcher, inscribed "Miss Emma L.E. Hard my sister, manufactory Nov. 5, 189_ remember these words on here buy your brother John E.F. Zellers, Reading, Pa. take care on this pitcher and think of me when you take it in your hands...", restorations to handle.

*8.25in (20.5cm) high*

**$8,000-10,000**     **POOK**

## A CLOSER LOOK AT A STONEWARE CROCK

*The basic forms of everyday storage jugs such as this crock have been interpreted by generations of rural potters in response to the needs and traditions of their communities.*

*The appeal for collectors in this crock lies in its very unusual subject matter.*

*Unpainted examples of storage pottery are rarely of interest to collectors. Depicting a Civil War scene is extremely rare.*

*Minor damage may lower the value but also speaks for authenticity. This crock is in good condition with normal traces of usage.*

A rare 19thC three-gallon stoneware crock, with cobalt decoration of a civil war soldier and his wife, the man holding a regimental flag.

*13in (32.5cm) high*

**$28,000-30,000**     **POOK**

A stoneware presentation jug, with cobalt floral decoration, inscribed "Emma L. Hard West Leesport PA John E.F. Zellers Schuylkill Ave. No 155 Reading PA, D_P Shenfelder Pottery Manufactory in Reading PA 1885 Harry Zerby Reading PA 1885", handle restored.

*1885*     *9.5in (24cm) high*

**$6,000-9,000**     **POOK**

A pair of three-gallon matching stoneware crocks, with cobalt bird on a basket decoration, impressed "Evan R. Jones, Pittston, Pa".

**$3,000-4,000**     **POOK**

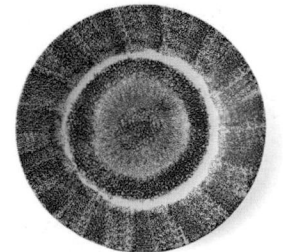

A six-gallon stoneware lidded butter churn, with cobalt bird perched on a leafy branch, impressed "N.A. White & Son Utica NY".

*19in (48cm) high*

**$1,800-2,200**     **POOK**

## OTHER AMERICAN CERAMICS

A red, blue, and green rainbow spatter striped plate.

*9.5in (24cm) diam*

**$5,000-8,000**     **POOK**

A green and red rainbow spatter bullseye plate.

*7.5in (19cm) diam*

**$1,200-1,800**     **POOK**

A massive 19thC chalkware bull, with overall ivory polychrome surface with black mottling, red ears and mouth, and black tipped horns.

*19in (48cm) long*

**$10,000-12,000**     **POOK**

A 19thC molasses jug stamped "Paris CW".

*6.5in (16.5cm) high*

**$500-700** BP

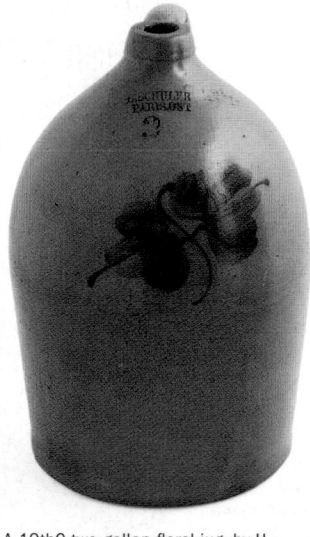

A 19thC two gallon floral jug, by H. Schuler of Paris, Ontario.

*14in (35.5cm) high*

**$400-600** BP

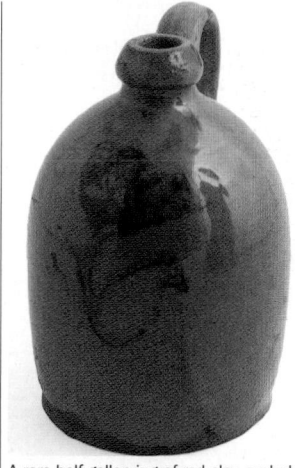

A rare half-gallon jug of red clay, probably by Wagner of Kitchener in Ontario, green slip floral design on buff base, dated.

**Provenance**: *From the 'Schlomb' collection.*

*1867* *8.25in (21cm) high*

**$1,800-2,200** BP

A stoneware crock, marked "Porter & Wilde, Galton Ontario 1912".

*1912* *10.5in (26.5cm) high*

**$300-500** BP

A rare 'Cape Rouge' redware bowl from Quebec City.

*c1820* *16.5in (42cm) diam*

**$300-400** BP

A vessel or paint dish created by and belonging to Emily Carr, signed on the base "Klee Wyck".

*c1925* *2.5in (5.5cm) diam*

**$300-500** BP

A vessel or paint dish created by and belonging to Emily Carr, signed on the base "Klee Wyck".

*'Klee Wyck' was Carr's Indian name, meaning 'Laughing One'.*

*c1925* *2.5in (5cm) diam*

**$300-500** BP

A vessel or paint dish created by and belonging to Emily Carr, signed on the base "Klee Wyck".

*c1925* *3.25in (8.5cm) diam*

**$300-500** BP

A vessel or paint dish created by and belonging to Emily Carr, signed on the base "Klee Wyck".

*c1925* *2.5in (6.5cm) diam*

**$300-500** BP

An early 20thC handpainted unglazed pottery candlestick, signed "KLEE WYCK", by Emily Carr.

*A famed Canadian, Emily Carr started making clay objects c1924, most of which were decorated with Indian style motifs and sold to the tourist trade.*

*2.75in (7cm) high*

**$3,000-5,000** BP

A spittoon from Waterloo County in Ontario, cylindrical form with brown and yellow spattered glaze.

*5.5In (14cm) diam*

**$300-500** BP

Prices in this section are shown in US dollars, using the conversion rate CAN$1 = US$0.75.

A late 18thC carved and gilded spread wing eagle, resting on top of a rock form plinth.

*47.5in (119cm) wide*

**$7,000-10,000**     **POOK**

An early 19thC American pine carved giltwood eagle, with one leg resting on a green orb.

*24.75in (62cm) wide*

**$8,000-10,000**     **POOK**

A carved and painted spread-winged eagle, by John Haley Bellamy (1836-1914), Kittery Point, Maine, perched atop a blue orb and red painted turned round plinth, retains its original gold and green decorated surface.

*23.25in (59cm) wide*

**$50,000-55,000**     **POOK**

An early 20thC carved and painted pine eagle, Harrisburg, PA, with the richly carved figure in the three-quarter round.

*56.5in (143.5cm) wide*

**$3,000-5,000**     **FRE**

A rare carved plaque of a gilded wooden eagle, by George Stapf (1862-1958), Harrisburg and Lancaster, Pennsylvania, surmounted by an American flag, a shield and olive branch in one talon and three arrows in the other.

*George Stapf worked in Harrisburg and Lancaster, carving eagles for government buildings including GAR posts (one is still on display in Philadelphia, Post No 2), A Pennsylvania State Capital, and others. Similar examples include one from The River Queen, President Lincoln's barge, on display at the U.S. Naval Academy, and one sold from the Garbisch Collection, Sotheby's, 1980. Photographs and history supplied by Stapf's great grandson accompany this piece.*

*38in (96.5cm) wide*

**$60,000-65,000**     **POOK**

A carved and painted spread winged eagle plaque, by George Stapf, the arched top with applied stars flanked by American flags, the eagle holding a laurel branch and bundle of arrows in his talons.

*29.5in (75cm) wide*

**$19,000-21,000**     **POOK**

An American carved and polychromed pine eagle plaque, inscribed "Don't Give Up The Ship", retains its original red and black painted surface.

*c1900*     *27in (68.5cm) long*

**$2,800-3,200**     **POOK**

A carved and painted eagle in the manner of John Haley Bellamy, spread-winged with banner inscribed "Live And Let Live", signed on top of wing "GED 1938."

*c1938*     *41.5in (105.5cm) wide*

**$3,000-3,500**     **POOK**

A Massachusetts carved mahogany bust of Benjamin Franklin, possibly by Samuel McIntyre.

*c1810*     *14in (35.5cm) high*

**$4,000-6,000**     **POOK**

A late 19thC American folk art carved wood wall mounted stick rack, modeled as Caesar holding a snake.

*24in (61cm) diam*

**$800-1,200**     **SWO**

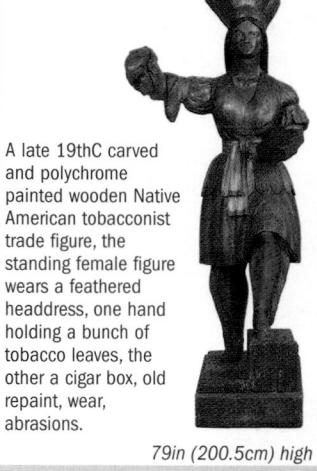

A late 19thC carved and polychrome painted wooden Native American tobacconist trade figure, the standing female figure wears a feathered headdress, one hand holding a bunch of tobacco leaves, the other a cigar box, old repaint, wear, abrasions.

*79in (200.5cm) high*

**$30,000-35,000**     **SK**

A carved wood folk art doll, the male figure standing on a round base, possibly depicting a South American Indian, remnant paint on the loincloth and headband, articulated arms, cracks.

*23.5in (59.5cm) high*

**$400-600**     **SK**

A 19thC carved and painted figure of a spaniel, with typical crosshatch carving and old brown painted surface.

**Provenance**: *Dittmar Collection.*

*23.5in (59cm) long*

**$3,000-5,000**     **POOK**

A Pennsylvania Federal mahogany watch safe, the arched top above rising sun and urn inlay, above a base with single drawer, over a scalloped base resting on ball feet.

*c1815*     *14.5in (37cm) high*

**$2,200-2,800**     **POOK**

Three Victorian architectural whimseys, the first, a watch hutch, composed of painted fret-work elements in the form of a church painted red and gold, the second, a chip-carved gothic-style structure, and the third, a display case, painted red, white, and blue.

*c1900*     *tallest 33in (84cm) high*

**$2,200-2,800**     **FRE**

A late 19thC painted wood and tin doll's house, in the form of a two-story brick with a mansard roof.

*33in (84cm) high*

**$1,800-2,200**     **FRE**

A mid-19thC miniature decorated bench, the top with red and gilt floral decoration on a yellow ground within a salmon bordered cartouche, the sides and legs with leaf decoration.

*9in (23cm) wide*

**$5,000-7,000**     **POOK**

A rare miniature wooden yellow cup and bowl, by Joseph Long Lehn, with strawberry decoration and black trim.

*Joseph Long Lehn, American, 1792-1898.*

*bowl 3in (7.5cm) diam*

**$7,000-9,000**     **POOK**

A mid-18thC overmantel pine panel, depicting leaping stags in a landscape silhouetted against a skyline, minor paint loss.

*Leaping stags in a landscape setting were frequently used as a design in 18thC samplers, chimney pieces, wallpapers, and paintings.*

*61in (154cm) wide*

**$90,000-95,000**     **SK**

A late 19thC carved and painted panel, scrolling spandrels enclose oval reserve with berry border and profile figure of a gentleman in 18thC dress, polychrome painted, some restoration.

*15.25in (39cm) wide*

**$2,200-2,800**     **FRE**

An early 20thC trade sign for a ship's chandler, New England, a painted wood dinghy hangs from a wrought iron bracket incorporating an anchor and chain, labeled with brass plaque, "Wall & Co. Boston", weathered surface.

*56in (142cm) wide*

**$4,000-6,000**     **FRE**

A pine box, from Quebec, with square nails and rimework on hinge.

*c1820*                          *10in (25.5cm) wide*

$300-500                          BP

A 19thC wooden salt box, with hinged lid.

$300-400          BP

A 19thC paint decorated red and black geometric tough box.

**Provenance:** *From the Hastings County collection.*

*25in (63.5cm) high*

$1,200-1,800          BP

A primitive mid-19thC knife sharpening box, with original paint and square nails, missing flint.

*12.5in (32cm) long*

$300-500          BP

A pine salt and candle box, with square nails from the Eastern Townships of Quebec.

*There is an identical box in the Musée des Civilizations in Quebec City.*

*c1880          18in (45.5cm) high*

$700-1,000          BP

A rare wooden sugar mold, from Isle d'Orleans in Quebec, with a cross, three hearts and square nails.

*c1850          16in (40.5cm) high*

$1,200-1,800          BP

A late 19thC butter press.

*6.5in (16.5cm) wide*

$120-180          BP

A large 19thC storage basket form Waterloo County in Ontario.

*20in (51cm) diam*

$300-500          BP

An early 18thC kettle stand with adjustable height.

*26in (66cm) high*

**$1,200-1,800** | **BP**

A late 19thC wooden centerpiece bowl, possibly originating from Ontario.

**Provenance**: *From the collection of Concordia University, Montreal, Quebec.*

*11.5in (29cm) diam*

**$30-50** | **TSG**

A 19thC wooden axe, with red painted blade, possibly used as a trade sign.

*36.5in (92.5cm) high*

**$120-180** | **BP**

A 20thC folk art bust carved from wood, with snakes for hair.

*17in (43cm) high*

**$400-600** | **TJL**

A Mergausen duck decoy, from Nova Scotia.

*14in (35.5cm) long*

**$300-500** | **BP**

A red-painted wooden door stop, in the form of a shoe.

*6.75in (17cm) long*

**$180-220** | **BP**

A handmade pine toy plane, finished with polychromatic paint surface, from Verigin in Saskatchewan, in the Doukhobor vernacular.

*It is very rare to find wooden toys from the Doukhobor culture, who were a group of extreme Christian pacifist Dutch and German immigrants.*

c1935

*10in (25.5cm) long*

**$300-400** | **BP**

A Quebec checkerboard, from the Montreal area, in perfect condition.

*32in (81.5cm) wide*

**$700-1,000** | **BP**

An old gameboard, with yellow and red checker design.

*27in (68.5cm) wide*

**$120-180** | **BP**

*Prices in this section are shown in US dollars, using the conversion rate CAN$1 = US$0.75.*

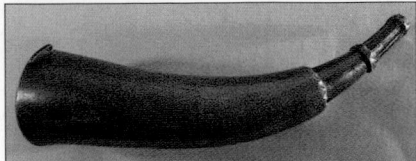

An American powder horn, with scenes of Skanakady, Albany, Fort Jon, Long Island, and Amboy, an elaborate mermaid, dragon, bird, and flowers, inscribed "Abner Robinson's Horn Dated Crown Point Octr.__1759".

| 1759 | 11.5in (29.5cm) long |
|---|---|
| **$8,000-10,000** | **POOK** |

An important American powder horn, adorned with scenes of Philadelphia, Bristo, Burlinton, Albeney, Town, New City, New York, inscribed "David Egleston's Horn Made Decr. 17 AD 1777 In the Army".

| 1777 | 10in (25.5cm) long |
|---|---|
| **$9,000-11,000** | **POOK** |

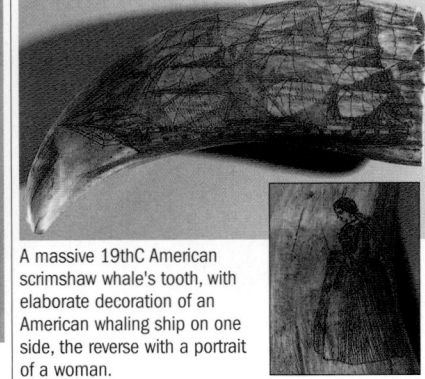

A massive 19thC American scrimshaw whale's tooth, with elaborate decoration of an American whaling ship on one side, the reverse with a portrait of a woman.

*Accompanying this lot is an old typed history of this tooth which identifies it as having been removed from a whale captured by Capt. Edward's whaling ship.*

| | 8.25in (21cm) long |
|---|---|
| **$6,000-9,000** | **POOK** |

A 19thC American polychrome scrimshaw whale's tooth, decorated with an eagle flanked by an American flag and banner inscribed "E Pluribus Unum", the reverse with a cherub holding a garland, above a sawtooth and checkerboard decorated base.

| | 5.75in (14.5cm) long |
|---|---|
| **$1,800-2,200** | **POOK** |

A 19thC American scrimshaw whale's tooth, with decoration of a spread winged eagle, an American flag and cannon, above a circular cartouche inscribed "Peace Independence and Plenty".

| | 5.5in (14cm) high |
|---|---|
| **$5,000-7,000** | **POOK** |

A mid-19thC engraved whale's tooth commemorating patriot Joseph Warren, the obverse with engraving depicting the Bunker Hill Monument and a portrait bust of Joseph Warren, a banner inscribed "Warren", the reverse with a stylized American flag and a small seated figure, a female allegorical figure, her hand on a globe surmounting an American shield, heightened with red pigment.

*Joseph Warren, a leader in the cause of liberty, became a doctor and surgeon. He was an officer in the Colonial Militia, and at the outbreak of the Revolutionary War he was in official command of the forces at the Battle of Bunker Hill. He was killed early on, and was the first officer to lose his life in that war.*

| | 6in (15cm) high |
|---|---|
| | **SK** |

A 19thC American scrimshaw baleen busk, with decoration of a ship with an American flag, fort, cottage, and hearts, all within a sawtooth border, the reverse inscribed "LLH/L".

| | 13.75in (35cm) long |
|---|---|
| **$1,800-2,200** | **POOK** |

A 19thC American scrimshaw whale bone busk, with detailed scene of New Bedford with five frigates and three sailing ships, lighthouse, and houses.

| | 14.5in (37cm) high |
|---|---|
| **$4,000-6,000** | **POOK** |

An American scrimshaw walrus tusk love token, with a cartouche inscribed "H.C. Allin", above an American star and flag, flanked by a profile of a lady and a heart with crossed anchor and cross, above a cod, the reverse with a sailing ship, dated.

| 1884 | 4in (10cm) long |
|---|---|
| **$280-320** | **POOK** |

## FRAKTUR

- Fraktur is a term used to describe highly artistic 18th and 19th century illuminated folk art drawings.
- They were created by the Pennsylvania Germans, and executed in ink or watercolor. A Fraktur can be Vorschriften (writing samples), Taufscheine (birth and baptismal certificates), or marriage or house blessings. Birds, hearts, and tulips are common artistic motifs in Fraktur.
- Appreciation for the aesthetic, moral, devotional, genealogical, and sentimental values associated with Fraktur art has increased markedly in recent decades in the US, as is evident from the development of personal and church-related collections.
- Look for early examples executed entirely by hand. Rare handwritten documents can fetch six-figure prices at auction.
- Later examples with printed text are not as valuable. However, interesting provenance or handwritten notes, usually stuck to the back of a Fraktur, can make a piece of high personal interest.

A Fraktur, depicting "A Verse from a Hymn to the Nightingale", Reverend George Geistweit (c1761-1831), Centre County, Pennsylvania, ink on paper, framed, some discoloration, signed and dated "Gr Geistweit, 5 June 1801".

*As a circuit-riding Reformed minister and schoolmaster, Reverend George Geistweit was a well-known personality in Centre County from 1794-1804. His body of work is small. Only two writing models are known by him, which he turned out in 1801 and 1802. They are among the grandest of all Fraktur.*

**Provenance:** *The backboard inscribed "Originally this belonged to Grandpa Bower. It was made by his day school teacher Jacob Geisewite in the year 1801. After Grandma Bower's death Aunt Polly Keen had it in her possession. After Aunt Polly died Sister Alice brought it home for mother. My father framed it. C.G. Bright Dec. 5 1901. The Fraktur probably came to the Bright family with the marriage of Jane Bower to William H. Bright Sunbury, Pa. in 1855".*

1801

**$360,000-400,000** FRE

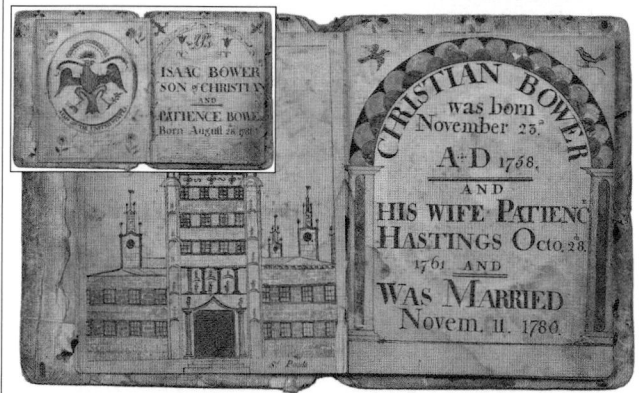

A family record book, by John Barnard, watercolor and ink on paper, probably from Pennsylvania, consisting of 30 pages with the birth records for Christian Bower, his wife, and 14 children, each record page with typical decorations, including a cathedral inscribed "St Paul's", the frontpiece inscribed "An Age Book – Made by John Barnard May 1805".

16in (40.5cm) open

**$6,000-9,000** POOK

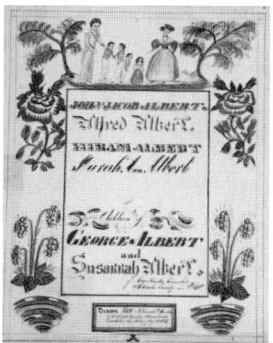

A watercolor and ink on paper family register of George and Susannah Albert of Huntington Township, Adams County, signed "Drawn by Nathaniel P. Buckley of Huntington Township, Adams County. Teacher – this 12th day of August 1834", unframed.

1834 15.25in (39cm) high

**$11,000-13,000** FRE

A birth record of "Mary Hoyt Born May 6, 1807," by Moses Conner Jr., watercolor and ink on paper, decorated with two birds in ovals on the front and signed on the reverse "Henniker May 7, 1829 by Moses Conner".

*Moses Conner Jr. was born in Wolfeboro, New Hampshire and was a teacher there beginning in 1808.*

1829 9in (23cm) high

**$9,000-11,000** SK

A watercolor on paper Schwenkfelder Fraktur drawing, by Abraham W. Heebner, (Worcester Township, Montgomery County, PA, 1802-77), with night-time and daytime cityscapes.

8.25in (21cm) high

**$4,000-6,000** POOK

A Taufschein, by Johann Jacob Friedrich Krebs, printed and hand-drawn watercolor and ink on paper, from Cocalico Township in Lancaster County, Pennsylvania, with central heart enclosing script surrounded by parrots, stars with faces, printed by Jungmann of Reading.

*Johann Jacob Friederich Krebs, Southeastern Pennsylvania, active 1784-1812.*

16in (40.5cm) wide

**$3,000-4,000** POOK

A Pennsylvania watercolor and ink on paper Fraktur, depicting a bird perched on a branch, inscribed "Jacob Leith, 1818".

*4in (10cm) high*

**$12,000-14,000**    **POOK**

A Pennsylvania watercolor and ink on paper Fraktur, depicting a spread winged eagle with heart-shaped body, holding flowers in its talons, inscribed faintly lower right "Leith".

*The Fraktur bears elements associated with some of the prominent Fraktur artists of that time period, such as Martin Gottschall, Durs Rudy, and Johann Eyer.*

*c1820*    *4in (10cm) wide*

**$2,200-2,800**    **POOK**

A Pennsylvania watercolor and ink on paper Fraktur, depicting a bird perched on an urn with lowering branches, inscribed "Jacob Leith".

*c1820*    *4in (10cm) high*

**$3,000-5,000**    **POOK**

A Pennsylvania watercolor and ink on paper Fraktur, of a bird perched on a flowering tulip branch arising from an urn, inscribed "Jacob Leith".

*c1820*    *4in (10cm) high*

**$2,800-3,200**    **POOK**

A Pennsylvania watercolor and ink on paper Fraktur, with two panels, the lower panel with a heart enclosing "Jacob Leith" and additional script, with birds and flowers, and an upper panel with angel, all surrounded by intricate border, dated.

*1824*    *8in (20cm) high*

**$32,000-34,000**    **POOK**

A Pennsylvania watercolor and ink on paper Fraktur, with soldier in elaborate uniform with raised sword on horseback, dated, inscribed "Jacob Leith".

*1821*    *4in (10cm) high*

**$35,000-40,000**    **POOK**

A Pennsylvania watercolor and ink on paper Fraktur, depicting a dog in an elaborate border, inscribed "Jacob Leith" in upper panel and "Mastiff AD1822" in archway.

*1822*    *3.5in (9cm) wide*

**$25,000-28,000**    **POOK**

An early 19thC Pennsylvania family record for the Ivens and Hendrick family, watercolor and ink on paper in the manner of John Van Minion, with center panel including script flanked by panels with birds, geometric designs and trailing floral vines over panels with birth, marriage, and death records.

*15in (38cm) high*

**$2,800-3,200**    **POOK**

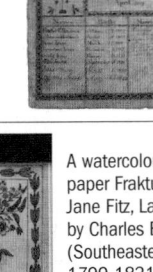

A watercolor and ink on paper Fraktur birth record for Jane Fitz, Lancaster County, by Charles E. Munch (Southeastern, PA, active 1799-1831), with typical beribboned wreaths enclosing script, signed "Charles E. Munch A.D. 1822".

*1822*    *15.25in (38cm) wide*

**$20,000-25,000**    **POOK**

A printed and watercolor Fraktur, printer Johann Henrich Otto, artist Arnold Hoevelmann, watercolor and ink on watermarked paper, foliate swag and birds enclose the printed Taufschein form.

*c1766*                                    *16.5in (42cm) wide*

**$3,000-5,000**                                    **FRE**

A Taufschein by Johann Henrich Otto, printed and hand-drawn watercolor and ink on paper, for Johann Jacob Ranninger, with heart enclosing script, surrounded by parrots, tulips, crowns, and stylized flowers, printed by Barton and Jungmann of Reading.

*Johann Henrich Otto, Lancaster and Northumberland Counties, Pennsylvania, active 1762-1797.*

*1792*                                    *16in (40.5cm) wide*

**$1,800-2,200**                                    **POOK**

A watercolor on paper Fraktur drawing, by Daniel Otto, birth certificate for Georg Stober of Centre County, with heart and script flanked by six parrots, paper label verso from American Folk Art Gallery.

*Daniel Otto, Centre County, Pennsylvania, active 1792-1822.*

*1808*                                    *12.75in (32.5cm) wide*

**$4,000-6,000**                                    **POOK**

A watercolor and ink on paper Fraktur, by Daniel Peterman, for John Koller of York County, Pennsylvania, with script flanked by two ladies, each holding a branch with birds and stylized flowers, inscribed "Made by Daniel Peterman Shrewsbury Township, York County" and "John Koller".

*Daniel Peterman, York County, Pennsylvania, active 1819-1864.*

*1809*                                    *16in (40.5cm) wide*

**$8,000-12,000**                                    **POOK**

A Bucks County, Pennsylvania watercolor Fraktur bookplate and Bible, attributed to the 'Rockhill Artist', with vibrant bird and flowers above a heart with script, dated.

*Provenance: Dittmar Collection.*

*1835*                                    *7in (17.5cm) high*

**$3,000-5,000**                                    **POOK**

A late 18thC printed, watercolor and ink on paper Fraktur, by J. Schneider and Co., and Friedrich Krebs, the birth and baptism certificate for Johannes Albert, Huntington Township, with parrots, suns, and flowers enclosing printed form, unframed.

*16in (40cm) wide*

**$3,000-5,000**                                    **FRE**

A Pennsylvania Fraktur birth certificate, watercolor and ink on paper, possibly from Berks County, for Anna Maria Kaufman, with heart enclosing script flanked by tulip trees.

*1782*        *13in (33cm) wide*

**$2,800-3,200**        **POOK**

A Fraktur watercolor and ink on paper birth record, by a Leacock Township artist, for Catharina Roland, with typical central elaborate script intertwined with stylized flowers.

*1792*                    *10in (25.5cm) wide*

**$6,000-8,000**                    **POOK**

A Pennsylvania watercolor and ink on paper Fraktur, with stylized flowers, bird, and face arising from an urn.

*c1820*                    *5.5in (14cm) high*

**$8,000-10,000**                    **POOK**

A Pennsylvania Fraktur bookplate, with hand-drawn watercolor and Ink on paper, for Sarah Fordin, script with flourishes over a stylized flower.

*6.75in (17cm) high*

**$1,200-1,800**                    **POOK**

An early 19thC stenciled and stamp decorated woven cotton bedspread, three-piece spread, central field composed of rows of sunburst and floral motifs surrounded by grapevine and weeping willow borders, light stains.

*A handwritten note accompanying the spread describes the provenance of this bedspread.*

92in (233.5cm) long

**$4,000-6,000** SK

A mid-19thC pieced and appliquéd cotton album quilt, with 24 blocks of calico floral motifs, on white muslin ground, three blocks are signed, printed calico border, intricately quilted around the motifs, with feather and herringbone borders.

c1840 106.5in (270.5cm) long

**$12,000-14,000** SK

An appliquéd cotton Baltimore album quilt with birds, 25 blocks with floral, wreath, bird, and leaf motifs, one corner with applied fabric strip with ink inscription "Annie D. Morrison".

c1845 104in (264cm) square

**$20,000-30,000** SK

A mid-19thC appliqué floral quilt, nine blocks, red sashing, conforming border on three sides with similar serrated leaves, wear.

82in (205cm) long

**$300-500** BRU

A mid-19thC pieced quilt, 30 blocks with radiating tulip corners, triple red and beige sashing, scalloped borders, quilt skewed, wear.

82in (205cm) long

**$500-800** BRU

A 19thC pieced compass quilt, 25 blocks of brown and blue compasses on white quilted field, small blue binding, Kentucky family history, stains.

97in (242.5cm) long

**$500-800** BRU

A mid-19thC large summer-weight appliqué quilt, 25 blocks with peony or Carolina lily variant, applied Indian-style printed border, 'broderie perse' style, losses and wear.

102.5in (256cm) long

**$700-1,000** BRU

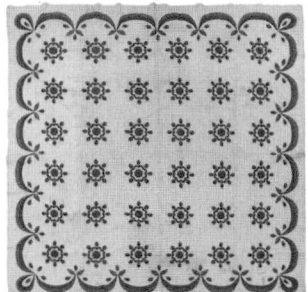

A mid-19thC large pieced quilt, Kentucky family history, roses and rosebuds with swag borders and embroidered highlights, detailed quilting with floral and stippled blocks.

115in (287.5cm) long

**$400-600** BRU

A 19thC wool and cotton jacquard coverlet, Pennsylvania, a large flower-filled urn flanked by peacocks enclosed by floral swags on a blue ground, fringe loss, scattered wool loss.

108in (270cm) long

**$280-320** FRE

A 19thC pieced cotton 'eagle with baton' quilt, worked with solid cotton patches arranged with four eagles enclosing a scrolling floral center within a sawtooth border, heightened with diamond, conforming and rope quilting, some fading.

80in (203cm) square

**$1,200-1,800** FRE

A 19thC pieced, appliquéd and embroidered friendship quilt, comprised of 16 squares within a berry and vine border, each square embroidered with signature of maker, heightened with embroidery and diamond, conforming and feather and flowerhead quilting.

94in (239cm) long

**$2,800-3,200** FRE

A 19thC pieced and appliquéd 'nine patch' quilt, comprised of variously printed cotton patches, enclosed by border with appliquéd leaves and stars, heightened by conforming and shamrock, and geometric device quilting, some fading.

*110in (279.5cm) long*

**$500-800**     **FRE**

A 19thC woven wool candlewick spread, comprised of two panels woven with wool and patterned with central medallion enclosed by flowers and leafy devices within tree, star and cable border, slight damage.

*80in (203cm) long*

**$1,200-1,800**     **FRE**

A red, white, and blue pieced Civil War quilt, with central star pattern with American flags in the corners and shields between the star points.

*Worked by Martha Moore Baker for her daughter, Eliza Baker Holcomb, exhibited at the Connecticut Fair in 1915, receiving a blue ribbon.*

*c1860*

**$12,000-14,000**     **POOK**

An appliquéd cotton Civil War era quilt, made by Margaret Hazzard, with 20 blocks depicting several buildings and figures, embroidered details.

*The history of the quilt, verified through the Berrien County Historical Society, relates that the quilt was made by Margaret Hazzard for her husband Philetus when he joined the Union army in February 1864. Philetus died soon after, and the quilt was returned to Margaret. It features buildings that were familiar to Philetus. Most of them were in Barrien County, as was the schoolhouse which is still standing. The house with a water pump beside it is stitched on both sides of the quilt and may have been Philetus' own home.*

*c1864*               *74in (188cm) long*

**$90,000-95,000**     **SK**

An appliquéd cotton Baltimore album 'heart-in-hand' quilt, the 25 blocks depicting album quilt designs including cornucopia of flowers, heart-in-hand, and hearts and arrows, with appliqué, some accented with cotton embroidery, ground, some blocks with stitched names, one name "Mary Boyd" is dated "1850".

*c1850*     *102in (259cm) square*

**$6,000-9,000**     **SK**

An appliquéd cotton peacock quilt, southeastern Pennsylvania, central bouquet of flowers and berries issuing from an urn-like device, topped with a stylized peacock, the peacock and berries are stuffed.

*c1865*     *82.5in (209.5cm) long*

**$18,000-20,000**     **SK**

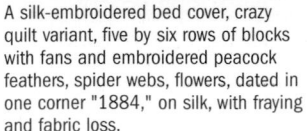

A silk-embroidered bed cover, crazy quilt variant, five by six rows of blocks with fans and embroidered peacock feathers, spider webs, flowers, dated in one corner "1884," on silk, with fraying and fabric loss.

*1884*     *72in (180cm) long*

**$5,000-8,000**     **BRU**

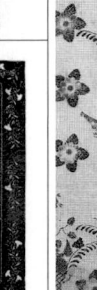

A late 18thC stenciled cotton bed cover, the bed cover with baskets of fruit and flowers, birds, and flowerheads stenciled on a natural woven cotton ground, the initials "AC" embroidered in cross-stitch at top center, some discoloration.

*78in (198cm) long*

**$12,000-15,000**     **SK**

A late 19thC pieced cotton 'striped star' quilt, with stars alternating with yellow dots on a printed green ground within a red border, diagonal line quilting, machine and hand-sewn.

*80in (203cm) square*

**$500-800** **FRE**

A late 19thC pieced cotton 'Star of Bethlehem' quilt, comprised of printed patches arranged with a central star enclosed by starbursts on a muslin ground, heightened with conforming and scroll device quilting, some fading.

*96in (244cm) long*

**$1,200-1,800** **FRE**

A late 1930s Amish quilt, double nine patch design on point, purple field and outer border, blocked corners, mixed fabrics including cotton, floral quilting.

*84in (210cm) long*

**$5,000-7,000** **BRU**

A mid-1930s Amish quilt, blue diamond with green, pink, and purple borders, undulating floral-quilted borders with floral wreath in center, cross stitched signature in corner on back "EB", minor insect damage and soiling.

*79in (197.5cm) long*

**$1,800-2,200** **BRU**

A 20thC floral appliqué quilt, eagle central medallion below tulip, with meandering vine and floral borders, slight stains and wear.

*95in (237.5cm) long*

**$2,200-2,800** **BRU**

An Amish quilt, sawtooth diamond design, quilting with wreath and scroll border and wreath and star center, mixed fabrics including cotton, some fading and stains.

*86in (215cm) long*

**$600-900** **BRU**

An Amish quilt, sawtooth diamond design, diamond inside square, block corners, feathered scroll quilting, tide line across one end, rod pocket for hanging.

*83in (207.5cm) long*

**$800-1,200** **BRU**

A pieced quilt, Bear Paw or Lily variant on white field, slight wear and losses.

*81in (202.5cm) long*

**$300-500** **BRU**

A pieced quilt, 30 blocks with brown sashing and red at intersections, pattern similar to Castle Wall, scattered light abrasions, browning.

*85in (212.5cm) long*

**$300-500** **BRU**

A pieced and appliquéd quilt, variant of Whig's Defeat with alternating green and red diamond border, detailed quilting with floral bouquets, some flowers stuffed, possibly an unfinished quilt.

*96in (240cm) long*

**$800-1,200** **BRU**

A pieced cotton hexagon medallion quilt, the quilt featuring hexagons containing a six-point star, made of printed cotton calico fabric, the white field quilted with fine stitching and trapunto work with flowering and feathered vines and circles, enclosed in a wide rust-red floral printed chintz cotton border.

*According to oral history which accompanied this quilt, Catherine Nead, born in 1793 to Daniel Nead and his wife Anna Mary (Polly) Hoefligh, probably made this quilt. In 1864 the family was said to have wrapped their valuable items in this and other family quilts to carry them to safety from fire during the Civil War. The town of Chambersburg was set on fire, as documented by a letter describing the event and given to the Kittochtinny Historical Society in Chambersburg.*

*100in (250cm) long*

**$10,000-12,000** **SK**

An early 19thC American yarn stitched wool bed rug, with central motif of five entwined flowers in an urn, enclosed on three sides with a wide flowering vine border, dated "1804" at top center above the intitials "L.L.", fringed on three sides, minor repair.

*1804*     *86.5in (219.5cm) wide*

**$50,000-60,000**     **SK**

An early 19thC American hooked rug, central leafy medallion enclosed by border of leafy fronds and flowers on stems, the corner blocks with glowers on stems, worked in polychrome wool and cotton fabrics on a burlap ground.

*80in (200cm) long*

**$3,000-5,000**     **FRE**

A 19thC American wool floral hooked rug, composed of woven wool and wool yarns hooked onto a burlap backing with floral leaf, striped border, restoration.

*73.5in (186.5cm) long*

**$4,000-6,000**     **SK**

A late 19thC New England hooked rug, with a central stylized flowering tree flanked by red deer within a geometric border with red and yellow horses in each corner.

*48in (122cm) long*

**$1,800-2,200**     **POOK**

An American pictorial hooked rug, of two birds flanking potted flowers within a green border.

*c1900*     *37in (94cm) high*

**$500-800**     **POOK**

An American pictorial hooked rug, depicting a brown and black dog.

*c1900*     *44in (112cm) high*

**$1,200-1,800**     **POOK**

A vibrant American folk art hooked rug, with two cats within a foliate border.

*c1900*     *46in (117cm) wide*

**$1,800-2,200**     **POOK**

An early 20thC American hooked rug, inscribed "Hail Columbia", with figure standing over a defeated lion.

*40in (100cm) long*

**$1,800-2,200**     **POOK**

An early 20thC American yarn-sewn pictorial rug, with a beaver on a log enclosed by a border of maple leaves worked in wool yarns, soiled.

**$220-280**     **FRE**

A 19thC New England sleigh, with bow runners and floral painted decoration.

*35.5in (90cm) long*

**$1,200-1,800**                                                    **BCAC**

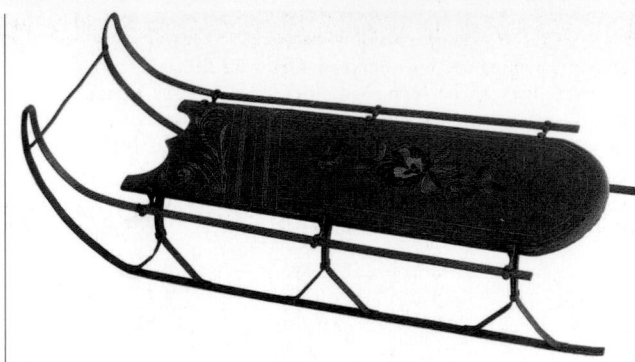

A 19thC American child's sleigh, with simplistic decoration.

*33.5in (85cm) long*

**$1,200-1,800**                                                    **BCAC**

A child's toy cart, with original painted decoration, probably by Joel Ellis, Springfield, Vermont.

*c1880*                                                  *35in (90cm) long*

**$220-280**                                                        **BCAC**

A folk art weather vane, painted steel cutout with stag and hunter with early 20thC-style cap and gun, metal reinforced backings, mounted on early steel rod with turned urn-form pedestal and oak cross-stretcher base with some hand-cut nails.

*57in (142.5cm) high*

**$800-1,200**          **BRU**

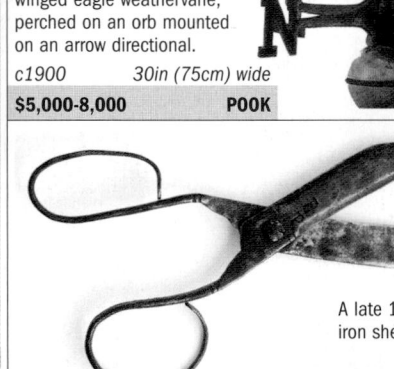

A full-bodied copper spread-winged eagle weathervane, perched on an orb mounted on an arrow directional.

*c1900*          *30in (75cm) wide*

**$5,000-8,000**          **POOK**

A late 18thC pair of Canadian wrought iron shears, with initials "PP".

*8in (20.5cm) long*

**$280-320**                          **BP**

A Canadian 19thC primitive wrought iron fork, found in the Brampton Ontario area.

*24.5in (62cm) long*

**$800-1,200**                    **BP**

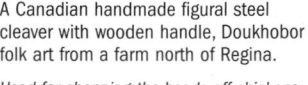

A Canadian handmade figural steel cleaver with wooden handle, Doukhobor folk art from a farm north of Regina.

*Used for chopping the heads off chickens.*

*c1920*          *11in (28cm) long*

**$600-900**          **BP**

## CHINESE REIGN PERIODS AND MARKS

Imperial reign marks were adopted during the Ming dynasty, and some of the most common are reproduced here. Most marked pieces were made in kilns at controlled Imperial workshops, which made ceramics for the Emperor's household and as tribute for foreign dignitaries. During periods when Imperial control was relatively lax, ceramics made outside the confines of these exalted workshops would sometimes be painted with reign marks. Many Chinese ceramics have reign marks that actually pre-date the object. This was designed not to deceive, but to show reverence for a golden age of production.

### Early periods and dates

| | | | |
|---|---|---|---|
| Xia Dynasty | c2000 - 1500BC | Northern and Southern Dynasties | 420 - 581 |
| Shang Dynasty | 1500 - 1028BC | Sui Dynasty | 581 - 618 |
| Zhou Dynasty | 1028 - 221BC | Tang Dynasty | 618 - 906 |
| Qin Dynasty | 221 - 206BC | The Five Dynasties | 907 - 960 |
| Han Dynasty | 206BC - AD220 | Song Dynasty | 960 - 1279 |
| Three Kingdoms | 221 - 280 | Jin Dynasty | 1115 - 1234 |
| Jin Dynasty | 265 - 420 | Yuan Dynasty | 1260 - 1368 |

### Ming Dynasties

| | | | |
|---|---|---|---|
| Hongwu | 1368 - 1398 | Jingtai | 1450 - 1457 |
| Jianwen | 1399 - 1402 | Tianshun | 1457 - 1464 |
| Yongle | 1403 - 1424 | Chenghua | 1465 - 1487 |
| Hongxi | 1425 - 1425 | Hongzhi | 1488 - 1505 |
| Xuande | 1426 - 1435 | Zhengde | 1506 - 1521 |
| Zhengtong | 1436 - 1449 | | |

### Ming Dynasty Marks

| 靖年製 大明嘉 | 慶年製 大明隆 | 曆年製 大明萬 | 啟年製 大明天 | 年製 崇禎 |
|---|---|---|---|---|
| Jiajing<br>*1522 – 1566* | Longqing<br>*1567 – 1572* | Wanli<br>*1573 – 1619* | Tianqi<br>*1621 – 1627* | Chongzhen<br>*1628 – 1644* |

### Qing Dynasty Marks

| 治年製 大清順 | 熙年製 大清康 | 正年製 大清雍 | 隆年製 大清乾 | 年製 嘉慶 | 光年製 大清道 |
|---|---|---|---|---|---|
| Shunzhi<br>*1644 – 1661* | Kangxi<br>*1662 – 1722* | Yongzheng<br>*1723 – 1735* | Qianlong<br>*1736 – 1795* | Jiaqing<br>*1796 – 1820* | Daoguang<br>*1821 – 1850* |

| 豐年製 大清咸 | 治年製 大清同 | 緒年製 大清光 | 統年製 大清宣 | **Republic Period**<br>年製 崇禎 |
|---|---|---|---|---|
| Xianfeng<br>*1851 – 1861* | Tongzhi<br>*1862 – 1874* | Guangxu<br>*1875 – 1908* | Xuantong<br>*1909 – 1911* | Hongxian (Yuan Shikai)<br>*1915 – 1916* |

**ORIENTAL CERAMICS**

## THE ORIENTAL CERAMICS MARKET

The market for Oriental ceramics is generally buoyant, although increasingly polarized. Buyers from mainland China are now beginning to dominate the world market and have forced up prices in many sectors. They are especially keen to acquire so-called 'mark and reign' pieces that bear the correct reign mark for their period. Kangxi and Transitional blue and white porcelain is proving extremely popular in China, where there has been a marked increase in the number of registered antique dealers in the last year. Figurative art has long been an important part of Chinese culture, and vases with figurative decoration are attracting particular interest at the moment.

A fundamental shift in the attitude of Chinese buyers is their newfound desire to acquire export ware, provided it does not deviate too far from the traditional Chinese aesthetic. The market for Famille Rose decoration and ceramics based on European silver shapes, has softened over the last year for only exceptional pieces and rare shapes have remained strong. The preference for minimalist decorative arts is a contributory factor in the stagnation of this sector of the market.

Damaged pottery and porcelain has probably shown the most dramatic increase in value over the last year. Whereas a minute rim chip would once have been enough to consign an otherwise beautiful vase to the back shelf, buyers are increasingly willing to overlook such minor imperfections. Items with more obvious cracks are now attracting up to half the value one would expect for a pristine example, rather than the 10% that was previously the norm. Once confined to the very best examples of a particular genre, this trend is now affecting more ordinary pieces.

*Robert McPherson, Oriental ceramics expert*

## EARLY CHINESE DYNASTIES

A Chinese Eastern Jin dynasty Yueyao ewer, the shoulders with a dragon head spout and faceted lugs, rim restored.

*The kilns of Yueyao are situated in the Ningbo region of China, one of the starting points for the Silk Road.*

cAD300     9in (22cm) high

**$500-800**     **DN**

A Chinese Eastern Jin dynasty Yueyao vase, with an olive green glaze, the shoulders with four taotie heads.

*The taotie is a fearsome horned beast that has been used in Chinese decorative arts for 3000 years.*

cAD300     6.5in (16.5cm) high

**$500-800**     **DN**

One of a pair of Chinese Tang dynasty mottled glaze teabowls, with green and ocher glazes over a white slip ground, the feet unglazed.

2.5in (6.5cm) diam

**$180-220 pair**     **CHEF**

A Chinese Liao dynasty pottery cockscomb vase, with short neck and tapering sides incised with lotus, covered with an olive green glaze, losses.

cAD1000     10.5in (26.5cm) high

**$500-700**     **DN**

A Chinese Tang dynasty ovoid vase and cover, covered with an amber brown glaze falling short of the foot, with a single blue splash, rim chipped.

AD618-907     9in (22cm) high

**$1,200-1,800**     **DN**

A Chinese Tang dynasty pottery straw-glazed model of a princess, her hair tied up in a chignon, with traces of original black pigment, her shoes upturned at the front, restored.

AD618-907

**$700-1,000**     **WW**

A Chinese Tang dynasty ewer, the design based on metal work, made of dense iron-splashed stoneware.

AD618-907     7.5in (19cm) high

**$800-1,200**     **R&GM**

A Chinese Tang dynasty horse and rider burial piece, with cold painted decoration, losses and restoration.

*This piece comes with thermoluminescence test results indicating its authenticity. There are many fakes on the market, often reassembled from mismatched fragments retrieved from the ground which are sometimes repainted.*

*AD618-907*                    *13.75in (35cm) high*

**$2,200-2,800**                              **R&GM**

An unusually large pair of Chinese Song dynasty Qingbai jars and covers, of slender baluster form, the necks molded with dragons, lingxhi fungus, deer, and bands of accolytes, the covers with bird finials.

*29in (74cm) high*

**$1,200-1,800**                              **DN**

A 12thC Chinese Song dynasty Qiangbai jar and cover.

*These vessels were made in large numbers for use as storage containers.*

*8.25in (21cm) high*

**$300-400**                              **R&GM**

A Chinese Song dynasty Qingbai vase, with cylindrical neck incised with fluting and ovoid body molded with bands of flowers beneath a pale ice blue glaze.

*11in (28cm) high*

**$400-600**                              **CHEF**

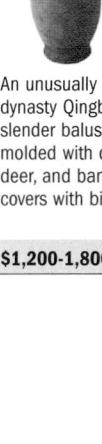

A large Chinese Southern Song dynasty Henan bottle vase, with ribbed body, short neck and flared rim, covered in a black glaze falling short of the foot, restored.

*12in (30.5cm) high*

**$600-900**                              **DN**

A 12th/13thC Chinese Southern Song dynasty molded Qingbai box.

*The Qingbai glaze was developed at the Xinping kilns. The blue tinge is from iron impurities in the glaze recipe.*

*2in (5cm) wide*

**$180-220**                              **R&GM**

An 11th/12thC Chinese Song dynasty fruit-form box and cover, restored.

*In better condition, this piece would be worth around $400.*

*2.5in (6cm) high*

**$120-180**                              **R&GM**

A Chinese 12thC Song dynasty Qingbai bowl, with incised fish, chipped.

*7in (18cm) diam*

**$800-1,200**                              **R&GM**

A Chinese late Ming dynasty celadon duck water dropper, with removable wing for filling the interior chamber, the bird's open beak forming the spout and its rocky perch the circular foot.

*6.75in (17cm) high*

**$4,000-6,000**                              **CHEF**

A Chinese late Ming dynasty celadon monkey, modeled sitting, with a hole in his back open to an interior chamber, holding a sacred peach, the octagonal base with flange foot.

*6.5in (16.5cm) high*

**$1,800-2,200**  **CHEF**

A Chinese Jin dynasty carved Yaozhou celadon bowl.

*'Yaozhou' refers to the kiln group where this piece was made. The decoration was achieved by incising the bowl before the clay dried. When the green celadon glaze was applied it pooled in these depressions, creating a design in varying tones of green.*

*AD1115-1234*    *5in (13cm) diam*

**$800-1,200**    **R&GM**

---

## A CLOSER LOOK AT A CHINESE CUP STAND

*Cup stands of this shape would have held small, straight-sided cups with slightly recessed bases and narrow feet.*

*The clarity of the glaze is excellent, with little of the typical graying or clouding associated with the aging process.*

*The copper underglaze used in this piece is relatively unsuccessful in the kiln, and few examples survive. An example with no firing faults is a real rarity.*

*A similar slightly smaller cup stand is owned by the British Museum in London, and another can be seen in the Avery Brundage Collection. Pieces of 'museum quality' are excellent illustrative examples of their type and invariably attract great interest.*

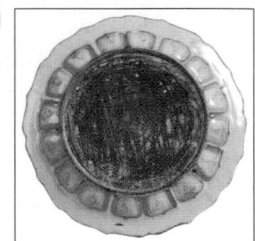

A Chinese Yuan period porcelain cup stand, decorated in underglaze copper red with peony blossom and ruyi heads, the scalloped border with fan-shaped panels decorated with lotus flower sprays, the unglazed base with a pale orange wash.

*The ruyi is a stylized lotus flower whose name translates as 'as you wish'. It is a symbol of favor and a traditional birthday gift.*

*8in (20cm) diam*

**$70,000-90,000**    **L&T**

A 15thC Chinese Ming dynasty celadon dish.

*10.5in (26.5cm) diam*

**$600-900**    **R&GM**

A Chinese late Ming dynasty earthenware table, from northern China, laid with food and drink offerings, lead glazed and cold painted, probably a burial piece, chipped.

*1550-1600    8.25in (21cm) wide*

**$500-800**    **R&GM**

---

## WANLI BLUE & WHITE

A mid-16thC Chinese blue and white dish, painted with a central floral rosette within a band of ruyi lappets and four mythical beasts on the rim, the reverse with five horse roundels and Buddhist objects, pseudo seal mark.

*12.25in (31cm) diam*

**$800-1,200**    **CHEF**

One of a pair of Chinese Wanli period blue and white Kraak dishes, painted with birds and insects within floral panelled borders.

*11.25in (29cm) diam*

**$800-1,200 pair**    **HAMG**

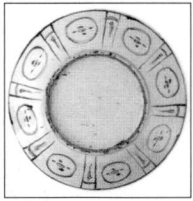

A Chinese Wanli period Kraak dish, decorated in underglaze blue with a panel of birds and flowers within a radiating panel of flowers and precious emblems.

*1573-1619*    *11in (28cm) diam*

**$800-1,200**    **DN**

A Chinese late Ming dynasty blue and white plate, with a central phoenix design.

1560-1620          7.75in (19.5cm) diam

**$220-280**                        **R&GM**

A Chinese late Ming dynasty Kraak dish.

*Kraak porcelain was made c1580-1640. It was named after the Portugese ships called 'carracks' in which it was carried.*

1600-1630          7.75in (19.5cm) diam

**$400-600**                        **R&GM**

A Chinese Ming dynasty dish, decorated with fowl on a white ground, for the Japanese export market.

1620-1640          6in (15cm) diam

**$500-700**                        **R&GM**

A late 16thC Chinese blue and white jar, the sides painted with a band of dragons and phoenix amongst clouds, between lappet bands.

7in (17.5cm) high

**$1,800-2,200**                    **CHEF**

An unusual Chinese Wanli period blue and white box and cover, painted with lotus flowers and scrollwork, restored.

*This piece would originally have been part of a set that would fit together.*

3in (7.5cm) high

**$8,000-10,000**                   **BEA**

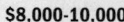

A Chinese Wanli period blue and white kendi.

*A kendi is a Persian drinking vessel without a handle.*

1575-1610          7.75in (19.5cm) high

**$4,000-6,000**                    **BEA**

A Chinese Transitional period blue and white vase.

*The price of this vase is relatively low as its cover has been lost and it has poor quality painting.*

7.25in (18.5cm) high

**$280-320**                        **CHEF**

A large mid-17thC Chinese Transitional period Wucai brush pot, the body incised with a band of five horizontal lines, damaged.

*In perfect condition, a pot like this would be worth $6,000-9,000.*

8.5in (21cm) diam

**$4,000-6,000**                    **WW**

A Chinese late Ming dynasty molded kraak dish, decorated with a cricket.

*Kraak porcelain is prone to chips at the edges, caused by blisters that form under the glaze during firing.*

1600-1630          5.25in (14cm) diam

**$280-320**                        **R&GM**

A Chinese blue and white cylindrical vase, with waisted neck and flared rim, the shoulder and foot decorated with anhua bands, the body with figures and a horse beside a waterfall, rim chips.

c1640             18.75in (47cm) high

**$20,000-25,000**                  **WW**

A Chinese Transitional period blue and white ewer, painted with a broad band enclosing a garden scene and a scholar with attendants, small chips.

*8.25in (21cm) high*

**$2,800-3,200** **BEA**

A pair of Chinese Kangxi period blue and white dishes, chipped.

*1662-1722* *8.5in (21.5cm) diam*

**$2,200-2,800** **R&GM**

## A CLOSER LOOK AT A KANGXI PERIOD BLUE AND WHITE DISH

*This dish was made in the Kangxi period (1662-1722) when blue and white ceramics dominated the export market.*

*The base of the dish contains reign marks from the Kangxi period, which are always written in conventional script. The presence of correct reign marks increases the value of the piece.*

*The decoration is beautifully executed, and the central image of two figures in parkland has been replicated several times in the border – an unusual design feature.*

*It is unusual to find a Kangxi ceramic dish in such good condition, with no chips to the outer edges. The fact that this example is pristine makes it especially valuable to collectors.*

A Chinese Kangxi period dish, with a central roundel depicting figures in a landscape, with Kangxi reign marks.

*c1690* *13.5in (34.5cm) diam*

**$5,000-8,000** **R&GM**

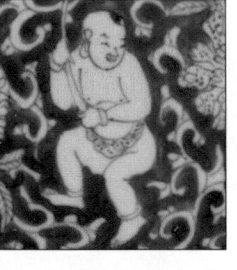

One of a pair of Chinese Kangxi period dishes, depicting a figure amid foliage.

*1690-1710* *11in (28cm) diam*

**$4,000-6,000 pair** **R&GM**

A Chinese Kangxi period dish, with a seascape scene, rim chips.

*c1700* *8.75in (22cm) diam*

**$700-1,000** **R&GM**

A Chinese Kangxi period Kraak dish.

*This is late revival of Kraak decoration, usually associated with the Wanli period.*

*1662-1722* *8.75in (22cm) diam*

**$800-1,200** **R&GM**

A pair of Chinese Kangxi period dishes, decorated with items representing cultural and artistic pursuits, including books and flowers arranged in vases.

*This is a Chinese pair – the dishes are not identical, as they were probably worked on by several artists. They are handpainted to a similar theme and have the same border design.*

*c1700* *11in (28cm) diam*

**$2,200-2,800** **R&GM**

A Chinese Kangxi period reticulated saucer, with foliate decoration.

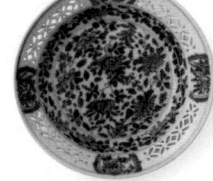

*This highly delicate technique involves the pattern being cut out while the clay is semi-hard, before glazing. European factories such as Worcester experimented with similar techniques in the late 19thC.*

*c1700* *4.25in (11cm) diam*

**$1,200-1,800** **R&GM**

A pair of Chinese Kangxi period blue and white plates, decorated with the eight horses of Mu Wang, with flower marks.

*1662-1722*　　*8.5in (21.5cm) diam*

**$3,000-5,000**　　**WW**

A pair of Chinese Kangxi period blue and white plates, each painted with the eight horses of Mu Wang.

*8.75in (22cm) diam*

**$2,800-3,200**　　**WW**

A 17thC Chinese blue and white bowl, decorated with peony flowers and foliage, with six-character mark for the Hall of Admiring Frugality.

*8.25in (20.5cm) diam*

**$800-1,200**　　**WW**

A Chinese Kangxi period bowl, with Chenghua reign marks.

*1662-1722*　　*5.5in (14cm) wide*

**$2,200-2,800**　　**R&GM**

A Chinese Kangxi period brush pot, decorated with figures, with chips to inner rim and footrim, unmarked.

*In perfect condition, a pot like this would be $15,000-18,000.*

*7.5in (18.5cm) wide*

**$6,000-9,000**　　**WW**

A pair of Chinese Kangxi period blue and white bowls, decorated with a continuous hibiscus scroll above a band of lappets, with six-character Kangxi marks, chipped.

*In perfect condition, a pair of bowls like this would be worth $5,000-7,000.*

*6.5in (16.5cm) high*

**$3,000-4,000**　　**WW**

A Chinese Kangxi period blue and white bowl, boldly painted with eight tribute bearers, the interior painted with a dragon in pursuit of a flaming pearl amongst clouds, seal mark.

*In Chinese mythology, the dragon represents the powers of air and water, while the flaming pearl symbolizes the quest for virtue and wisdom.*

*8.75in (22cm) diam*

**$700-1,000**　　**WW**

A Chinese Kangxi period salt, decorated with a typical Chinese landscape.

*This shape is based on European silverware. A complete pair in good condition would be worth around $2,500.*

*c1700*　　*3.5in (9cm) wide*

**$600-900**　　**R&GM**

A Chinese Kangxi period blue and white molded bowl, rim chips.

*c1700*　　*6in (15.5cm) high*

**$500-800**　　**R&GM**

One of a pair of Chinese European shape blue and white salts.

*1710-1735*　　*3in (7.5cm) long*

**$1,200-1,800 pair**　　**R&GM**

A small Chinese Batavia ware teabowl.

*Batavia, now called Jakarta, was the trading center of the Dutch East India Company. Batavia ware, recognizable by its iron red exterior, was particularly popular with the Dutch market. Teabowls were small because the tax on tea made it expensive.*

*1720-40*　　*3in (7.5cm) wide*

**$40-60**　　**R&GM**

A large Chinese Kangxi period blue and white molded baluster vase and cover, decorated with panels of peony, the knop a wooden replacement.

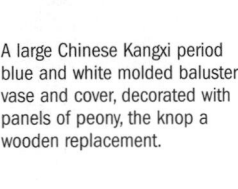

A Chinese Kangxi period blue and white bombe censer, decorated with the Eight Daoist Immortals, small rim chip.

A Chinese Kangxi period goblet, based on the shape of a European wine glass.

| | | |
|---|---|---|
| *1622-1722* | *7.75in (20cm) high* | |
| **$1,200-1,800** | **WW** | |

| | |
|---|---|
| *23.25in (59cm) high* | |
| **$6,000-9,000** | **WW** |

| | |
|---|---|
| *1690-1700* | *5.75in (14.5cm) high* |
| **$1,800-2,200** | **R&GM** |

A Chinese Kangxi period blue and white oviform vase, some damage.

*In perfect condition, this vase would be worth $3,000-5,000.*

A Chinese Kangxi period gu vase.

*The gu vase shape is based on the ritual bronze wine vessels of ancient China.*

A Chinese Kangxi period blue and white brushpot, decorated with the 'Hundred Antiques' pattern.

A 17thC Chinese Kraak teapot, extensively damaged, lacking cover.

*In perfect condition, a teapot like this would be worth $1,200-1,800 and more than double that with its cover.*

| | |
|---|---|
| *13.5in (34cm) high* | |
| **$1,800-2,200** | **ROS** |

| | |
|---|---|
| *7.5in (19cm) high* | |
| **$1,200-1,800** | **R&GM** |

| | |
|---|---|
| *1690-1720*    *4.75in (12cm) high* | |
| **$2,800-3,200** | **R&GM** |

| | |
|---|---|
| *7.75in (20cm) high* | |
| **$220-280** | **CHEF** |

A rare Chinese Kangxi period blue and white teapot and cover, with raised handle and spout modeled as a snake, the spherical body raised on a domed foot.

A Chinese Kangxi period blue and white ewer, decorated with two shaped panels containing figures.

A Chinese Kangxi period blue and white teapot and cover, the ribbed sides painted with flowers below molded key fret bands, the cover with a chrysanthemum knop.

| | |
|---|---|
| *7in (18cm) high* | |
| **$3,000-5,000** | **CHEF** |

| | |
|---|---|
| *10.5in (26.5cm) high* | |
| **$1,200-1,800** | **WW** |

| | |
|---|---|
| *5in (12.5cm) high* | |
| **$180-220** | **CHEF** |

A Chinese Kangxi period blue and white ewer, the ovoid body painted with a band of flowers and foliage, swastika mark.

*8in (20.5cm) high*

**$2,200-2,800**    **WW**

A 17thC Chinese blue and white kendi, decorated with figures in a landscape beneath a scroll band, chipped.

*7in (18cm) high*

**$500-800**    **WW**

A Chinese Kangxi period incised jar and cover, made for the European market, with Chenghua mark.

*The mark relates to the 15thC Emperor Chenghua. It denotes reverence for a bygone era.*

*1690-1720*    *9.5in (24cm) high*

**$3,000-5,000**    **R&GM**

A Chinese Kangxi period European shape mug, with firing crack, chipped.

*Although the form of this piece is European, the decoration is distinctly Chinese in style.*

*c1700*    *3.25in (8cm) high*

**$700-1,000**    **R&GM**

A Chinese Kangxi period cruet, with 19thC Dutch silver mounts.

*This shape is based on European glassware. It is in the form of two conjoined bottles, creating separate chambers for oil and vinegar.*

*1690-1710*    *8.25in (21cm) high*

**$5,000-8,000**    **R&GM**

A Chinese Kangxi period blue and white porcelain candlestick, after a European silver shape, the canted square base painted with exotic birds, with a band of leaves on the column.

*7in (18cm) high*

**$1,200-1,800**    **HAMG**

## YONGZHENG BLUE & WHITE

An Chinese Yongzheng period, with three feet, small chip to spout.

*This teapot is desirable as it has three feet and is of good color with varied tones of rich, strong blue.*

*1723-1735*    *3.25in (8.5cm) high*

**$2,200-2,800**    **JES**

A Chinese Yongzheng period blue and white sugar castor, chipped.

*Designs for these European shapes were sent to China for manufacturers to copy.*

*1723-1735*    *4.75in (12cm) high*

**$700-1,000**    **R&GM**

A Chinese Yongzheng period blue and white baluster vase, painted with a broad band enclosing a garden scene with go players, repaired neck.

*14.5in (37cm) high*

**$2,200-2,800**    **BEA**

**ORIENTAL CERAMICS**

A Chinese Yongzheng period blue and white rosewater sprinkler.

*The decoration here is made up of simple blue lines. Pieces decorated with different tones of blue are worth more.*

1723-35     7.75in (20cm) high

**$700-1,000**     **R&GM**

A pair of Chinese Yongzheng period blue and white double phoenix dishes, with Yongzheng reign mark.

*The phoenix, emblematic of the Empress, is one of the four supernatural creatures, along with the dragon, tortoise, and kylin, symbol of Imperial power.*

1723-35     7.75in (20cm) diam

**$8,000-12,000**     **R&GM**

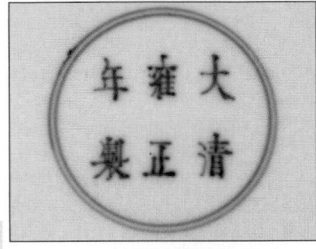

A Chinese Qianlong period Pompadour plate, with fish vignettes, rim chips.

*The fish refer to Pompadour's original surname, Poisson, and the crowned eagle to Louis XV, to whom she was mistress.*

c1750     9in (23cm) diam

**$500-800**     **R&GM**

A Chinese Qianlong period blue and white export ware dish, made in imitation of a Dutch Delft herring dish.

c1765     9.5in (24cm) wide

**$4,000-6,000**     **R&GM**

A Chinese Qianlong period blue and white Ming-style bowl, heavily potted and decorated with a continuous flower and leaf scroll, beneath a band of jui heads.

8.75in (22cm) diam

**$3,000-4,000**     **WW**

A large 18thC Chinese blue and white vase, of archaic form, with molded animal mask and ring handles, decorated with stylized bands of taotie masks, stiff leaves and key fret band.

18in (46cm) high

**$10,000-15,000**     **WW**

A Chinese Qianlong period blue and white baluster vase and cover, painted with prunus issuing from rockwork, the domed cover with bud finial, damaged.

14.25in (36cm) high

**$400-600**     **ROS**

## A CLOSER LOOK AT A CHINESE QIANLONG BLUE & WHITE VASE

*This vase has a six-character Qianlong period (1736-1795) reign mark, enclosed in a double circle. Having the correct reign mark can double the value of a piece.*

*This octagonal form is relatively unusual and marks this piece out from comparable Qianlong ceramics.*

A large Chinese Qianlong period blue and white vase, the octagonal section body painted with exotic pheasants, cranes, and ducks beneath a leafy tree flanked by peony and hydrangea, the reverse with sparrows and butterflies above chrysanthemums and rockwork.

*This vase has no manufacturing faults and is in excellent condition. The well-executed painting remains bright and clearly defined, further increasing the appeal of this vase.*

*Blue and white wares dominated the export market during this period and tended to imitate early Ming versions, with carefully spaced decoration. These formal and measured arrangements of scrolling foliage and animals are typical of the period.*

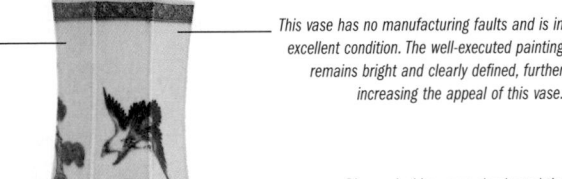

22in (56cm) high

**$28,000-35,000**     **WW**

A rare and early Chinese Blanc-de-Chine figure of Guanyin, from Dehua in Fujian province.

*1630-50*   9.5in (24cm) high

**$2,800-3,200**          **R&GM**

A 17thC Chinese Blanc-de-Chine figure of Guanyin.

*Guanyin, the goddess of mercy, is sometimes also represented with a child. In some pieces made for the European market the figure was modeled as the Virgin Mary.*

4.25in (11cm) high

**$1,200-1,800**          **R&GM**

A large Chinese Kangxi period Blanc-de-Chine figure of Guanyin, seated on rockwork, a child on her lap.

15.75in (40cm) high

**$1,200-1,800**          **WW**

A late 19thC Chinese Blanc-de-Chine figure of Guanyin, sitting cross legged on a double lotus throne and holding a pearl.

13in (33cm) high

**$120-180**          **CHEF**

A late 19thC Chinese Blanc-de-Chine figure of Guanyin, holding a child and seated on a lotus.

9in (22cm) high

**$180-220**          **DN**

A pair of Chinese Kangxi period Blanc-de-Chine figures from Dehua in Fujian province, known as 'Adam and Eve'.

*c1690*   9in (23cm) high

**$4,000-6,000**          **R&GM**

A Chinese Kangxi period Blanc-de-Chine group.

*The holes under the nose would have held a horsehair mustache.*

*1662-1722*   9in (23cm) high

**$1,200-1,800**          **R&GM**

A Chinese Kangxi period Blanc-de-Chine Buddhist lion, from Dehua in Fujian Province.

*This piece was made in a mold and handfinished. Some pieces feature more handcarved work.*

*c1700*   2in (5cm) high

**$400-600**          **R&GM**

A pair of late 19thC Chinese Blanc-de-Chine Buddhist lions, each with a raised paw, on pierced ball and plinth bases.

9in (23cm) high

**$300-400**          **ROS**

A 17thC Chinese Blanc-de-Chine vase, from Dehua in Fujian province.

5.5in (14cm) high

**$1,200-1,800**          **R&GM**

A 17thC Chinese Blanc-de-Chine stem cup, from Dehua in Fujian province.

5.25in (13.5cm) diam

**$2,200-2,800**          **R&GM**

An 18thC Chinese An hua decorated stem cup, complete with leather, cotton, and wicker carrying case.

*'An hua' means 'secret decoration'. The design is only visible when held to the light.*

5.5in (14cm) diam

**$2,200-2,800**          **R&GM**

**ORIENTAL CERAMICS**

## FAMILLE VERTE

- Famille verte, literally meaning the 'green family', was adopted during the Kangxi reign (1662-1722), having evolved from the five color Wucai style.
- The predominant famille verte colors are a bright apple green and iron red, combined with hues of blue, yellow, and eggplant. These enamels pigments are painted over the glaze, with the exception of cobalt blue and copper red.
- Patterns often incorporate flowers, such as chrysanthemums, lotus and prunus, combined with black speckled diapers. Larger designs include rocky oriental gardens and landscapes, figures, the Eight Precious Things and the Eight Buddhist Emblems.
- Wealthy northern European clients commissioned large famille verte dinner services decorated with their own coat of arms.
- The production of famille verte continued well into the 20thC. The most sought after pieces, however, are those dating from the Kangxi period, and these command a premium.

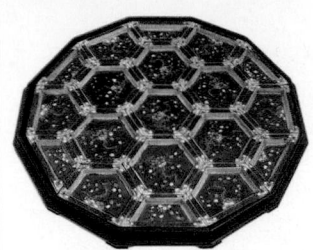

A Chinese Kangxi period famille verte supper set, decorated with prunus sprays on a green ground, comprising 19 shaped dishes in a fitted wood tray, some damage.

*16.25in (41.5cm) wide*

**$1,200-1,800**    **WW**

A Chinese Kangxi period famille verte fluted saucer dish, decorated with a small kylin issuing from the breath of a larger kylin, within alternate radiating panels of birds and Imari iron red mons, chipped.

*8in (20.5cm) diam*

**$800-1,200**    **DN**

A Chinese Kangxi period famille verte charger, with shaped rim, decorated with a basket of flowers within radiating panels of flowers and cell borders.

*14.5in (36cm) diam*

**$1,200-1,800**    **DN**

One of a pair of Chinese Kangxi period famille verte plates, decorated with the Hundred Antiques.

*c1700*    *8.5in (21.5cm) diam*

**$800-1,200 pair**    **R&GM**

A Chinese Kangxi period famille verte ovoid vase, decorated with cartouches containing fan-shaped panels of figures, flowers and buildings, with wooden cover, leaf mark.

*10.5in (26.5cm) high*

**$1,800-2,200**    **WW**

A 19thC Chinese famille verte vase, of baluster form painted with dignitaries and a rocky outcrop with a tree, painted marks.

*8.5in (22cm) high*

**$700-1,000**    **HAMG**

A pair of 19thC Chinese famille verte vases, converted as table lamps, each painted with eight figures conversing and holding fans and scrolls, with wooden stands, four-character Qianlong marks.

*14in (36cm) high*

**$1,200-1,800**    **WW**

A late 19thC Chinese famille verte ginger jar and cover, enameled with panels of flowers and insects, on a celadon foliate scroll ground, within stylized borders, blue four-character marks to base, with wooden stand.

*9.75in (25cm) high*

**$300-400**    **H&L**

A Chinese Kangxi period famille verte jug, painted with birds and flowers on a green-seeded ground, the sides with panels of insects amongst lotus, roses, chrysanthemums and prunus, cover missing.

*8.75in (22cm) high*

**$3,000-4,000**    **BEA**

An early 18thC Chinese famille verte wine pot, with yellow arch handle, gilt metal lid and mounted spout tip, the bell-shaped sides painted with two reserves of ladies seated at tables.

*7in (17.5cm) high*

**$1,200-1,800**    **CHEF**

A Chinese Qianlong period famille rose 'Hunting' punch bowl, the exterior decorated in the Mandarin palette with panels depicting huntsmen and hounds, the interior with a huntsman with two dogs and a pheasant, damaged.

*c1770*                                                     *11.75in (30cm) diam*

**$3,000-4,000**                                                               **H&L**

A pair of Chinese famille rose medallion bowls, decorated on the exterior with roundels of auspicious characters on a pink sgraffito ground, six-character Qianlong seal marks, one well repaired.

*5.75in (14.75cm) diam*

**$1,800-2,200**                         **WW**

A Chinese Qianlong period famille rose bowl and cover, painted in the Meissen style with panels of female figures in a garden, the final reglued.

*4.75in (12cm) diam*

**$300-500**                         **WW**

A 19thC Chinese Canton famille rose bowl, richly decorated with panels of figures, the borders with birds, butterflies and bats amid foliage.

*5in (13cm) diam*

**$1,200-1,800**                         **WW**

## FAMILLE ROSE

- Famille rose became popular in the Yongzheng period (1723-35), and virtually replaced famille verte. It is characterized by opaque rose-pink or purple overglaze, combined with greens and yellows.
- The palette was known to the Chinese as 'yang cai', meaning 'foreign colors', because the pink hue derived from the gold chloride first introduced to China by Jesuit missionaries.
- These new enamels were favored due to their superior brightness, quality, and opacity, which gave artists a greater range.
- Panels of figures, oriental landscapes or interior scenes were typical subjects for famille rose ceramics, often combined with rockwork, branches, flowers, and birds.
- The porcelain was very popular throughout the 18th and 19thC, and many armorial designs were exported to Europe.
- Famille rose from the Yongzheng period, with its brilliant colors and the delicate painterly quality of its decoration, is the most highly prized amongst collectors.

A large 19thC Chinese famille rose jardinière, painted with panels of dragons and phoenix on a pink ground decorated with bats, shou characters, flowers and foliage, the interior painted with fish, on a wooden stand.

*18.5in (47cm) high*

**$1,200-1,800**                         **WW**

A pair of Chinese Qianlong period export baluster vases, with panels of flowers in iron red and famille rose enamels, the ground with scrolling lotus, one neck damaged.

*1726-95*                         *11in (28cm) high*

**$1,200-1,800**                         **DN**

A pair of 19thC Chinese famille rose vases, decorated with birds, flowers, and rocks on a turquoise ground, minor faults.

*9.5in (24cm) high*

**$800-1,200**                         **WW**

### A CLOSER LOOK AT A PAIR OF FAMILLE ROSE VASES

*Famille rose was exported to Europe in vast quantities during the 18th and 19thC. This pair of vases date from the first half of the 19thC, before the quality of decoration began to deteriorate.*

*These vases bear iron red Jiaqing marks, which are correct for their period and therefore considerably increase their value.*

*The handles are in the form of animals, adding visual interest to this piece. The high overall quality of the decoration makes these vases highly collectible.*

*Although not from the Yongzheng period, which was the golden age of famille rose decoration, this pair of vases exhibits the intricate, painterly style associated with the very best famille rose work.*

A pair of Chinese famille rose yellow ground vases, each with four animal handles and decorated with stylized foliage, flowers, bats, and endless knots, the rims with jui bands, the feet with blue key fret designs, each with an iron red Jiaqing mark.

*c1810*                                                     *10in (25.5cm) high*

**$7,000-10,000**                                                               **WW**

**ORIENTAL CERAMICS**

One of a pair of Chinese late Kangxi period Imari plates.

*1700-1720*     *8.5in (21.5cm) diam*

**$500-700 pair**     **R&GM**

One of a pair of Chinese Qianlong period armorial plates, inscribed "RS".

*c1750*     *9in (23cm) diam*

**$1,200-1,800 pair**     **R&GM**

A Chinese Qianlong period Meissen-style dish, rim chips.

*c1750*     *14in (35.5cm) diam*

**$2,200-2,800**     **R&GM**

A Chinese Qianlong period export armorial dish, with flowers and floral garlands.

*15.25in (38.5cm) diam*

**$1,200-1,800**     **BEA**

A Chinese Qianlong period Meissen-style dish, painted with overglaze enamels and gilding, rim chips.

*c1750*     *14.25in (36cm) diam*

**$2,200-2,800**     **R&GM**

One of a pair of Chinese enameled dishes, decorated in green and eggplant with dragons on a yellow ground, six-character Kangxi marks.

*6.75in (17cm) diam*

**$2,800-3,200 pair**     **WW**

An early 20thC Chinese saucer, finely enameled with a water chestnut, gourd, cricket, and bamboo shoot beneath a poem, with gilt rim and four-character "Eternal China Hall" mark.

*5in (12cm) diam*

**$500-700**     **DN**

A Chinese Qianlong period oval dish, decorated with floral swags and sprays.

*16in (40.5cm) long*

**$1,200-1,800**     **BEA**

A Chinese Qianlong period canted rectangular meat dish, boldly painted with flowering branches and rockwork in Imari colors, within a flower paneled scroll border.

*17.25in (44cm) wide*

**$800-1,200**     **LFA**

A Chinese Qianlong period armorial plate, after a European shape, decorated with the arms of Seton.

*c1780*     *9.75in (25cm) long*

**$1,200-1,800**     **R&GM**

One of a pair of Chinese Qianlong period export meat dishes.

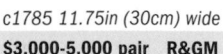

*c1785 11.75in (30cm) wide*

**$3,000-5,000 pair**     **R&GM**

A rare 18thC Chinese celadon bowl, fitted at the neck and base with later ormolu borders incorporating scrolling foliate motifs and acanthus, on scrolling feet.

*11.75In (30cm) diam*

**$30,000-40,000**     **BLA**

A Chinese cache pot, painted with peony and chrysanthemum sprays, with gilt ormolu mounts in Régence style, damaged.

c1750          8.75in (22cm) high

**$1,200-1,800**          **BEA**

## A CLOSER LOOK AT A CELADON GUAN

Celadon is a glaze derived from iron, with a distinctive blue-green color. It was first adopted by craftsman over 2000 years ago in an effort to imitate nephrite jade, and is often carved or molded.

This vase and cover dates from the Ming period (1368-1644), when exported celadon guans remained a vital source of revenue for the Chinese government. Ceramic forms were often dictated by the demands of the export market.

The ormolu mounts actually enhance the value of this piece as they have been executed to the highest standard and add to the original aesthetic of the guan vase.

During this period, decoration became increasingly ornate, which is evident here in the abundance of flowering lotus and chrysanthemum sprays carved into the body of the vase.

A large 18thC Chinese shallow bowl, decorated with a pagoda landscape, damaged.

15.25in (38.5cm) diam

**$180-220**          **WW**

A fine Chinese Ming dynasty gilt bronze mounted celadon guan, carved with flowering lotus, camellia, and chrysanthemum sprays and finely molded in relief with 'qing xiang mei jiu' decoration, with later ormolu mounts in the Louis XV style.

20.5in (52cm) high

**$35,000-45,000**          **BEA**

An unusual late 18thC Chinese tureen and cover, with cone knop and cross-over handles, painted with four circular panels with views of mansions within formal border patterns, probably for the American market.

12.5in (31.5cm) diam

**$1,800-2,200**          **WW**

A Chinese bowl, the interior painted with figures, an ox, birds, and cloud scrolls, the exterior with roundels of figures in landscapes, ground decorated with stylized flowers, six-character Daoguang mark.

c1835          6in (15cm) diam

**$500-700**          **WW**

A Chinese yellow ground jardinière, painted with flowering branches.

c1870          13.5in (34cm) high

**$800-1,200**          **SWO**

A late 19thC Chinese Canton porcelain bowl, decorated in colored enamels with figures, birds, insects, and flowers.

14.25in (36cm) diam

**$800-1,200**          **SWO**

A Chinese Guangxu period green glazed bowl, rising from a straight foot to rounded sides everted at the rim, Guangxu mark, small chip.

1875-1908          5.75in (14.5cm) diam

**$1,200-1,800**          **BEA**

A rare Chinese rice bowl, made during the Cultural Revolution, with a portrait of Dr Norman Bethune, with marks for Hunan Zijiang Porcelain Factory 1970, and inscribed "Never selfish, only to help others".

1970          6.25in (16cm) diam

**$800-1,200**          **BP**

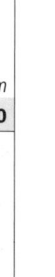

**ORIENTAL CERAMICS**

A Chinese porcelain coffee cup and saucer, with solid loop handle, painted in the style of James Giles, with landscape and ruins, unmarked.

1765-1768          4in (12cm) wide

**$3,000-4,000**                    **SHF**

A 19thC Cantonese mug, with interlaced handle, decorated with figures and trophies.

5.5in (14cm) high

**$700-1,000**                    **GORL**

A large Chinese Qianlong armorial tankard, decorated with famille rose sprays and a large crest with motto "Insperata Floruit".

7in (18cm) high

**$700-1,000**                    **JN**

A late Chinese Kangxi period tea canister, with later Dutch decoration.

*This canister would be worth around $1,200 if it was complete with its cover.*

c1720          3.75in (9.5cm) high

**$500-700**                    **R&GM**

A Chinese Yongzheng period teapot, with silver mounts, decorated in underglaze blue with iron oxide red and gilding, on a new stand, with later silver mounts.

*This teapot is decorated in a Chinese version of the Japanese Imari palette.*

1723-1755          4in (10cm) high

**$500-800**                    **R&GM**

A pair of Chinese Ming dynasty sancai glazed rooftile figures, of officials wearing long green and yellow glazed robes.

17.5in (44.5cm) high

**$3,000-4,000**                    **BEA**

A Chinese Qianlong period export group, fan restored.

*The group is not from a shipwreck, but similar pieces found on the Nanking cargo help to date this piece to the Qianlong period.*

c1750          6.75in (17cm) high

**$800-1,200**                    **R&GM**

A pair of Chinese Jiajing period incense stick holders, in the form of dragons, damaged.

c1810          9in (23cm) high

**$500-800**                    **R&GM**

A pair of late 19thC Chinese glazed models of roosters.

14.75in (37.5cm) high

**$800-1,200**                    **BEA**

A 19thC Chinese 'spinach and egg' glazed incense stick holder, modeled as a two-tier corral with cows under a tree, the mottled glazes in blue, brown, yellow, and green.

5in (13cm) wide

**$300-500**                    **CHEF**

A pair of Chinese porcelain bird feeders, with reticulated containers, painted in green, iron red, turquoise, and gilt, one restored.

c1800          4.25in (11cm) high

**$700-1,000**                    **WW**

Two large 17thC Japanese Arita Kraak-style blue and white porcelain chargers.

*17.75in (44.5cm) diam*

**$5,000-7,000**     **NAG**

A 17thC Japanese Kakiemon porcelain dish, decorated in blue and white, with flashes of red and green enamel.

*7.5in (19cm) diam*

**$700-1,000**     **NAG**

One of a pair of early 18thC Japanese Arita blue and white dishes, painted in the Kraak style.

*16.5in (42cm) diam*

**$4,000-6,000 pair**     **WW**

A small Japanese Nabeshima dish, painted with cloud scrolls, the reverse with stylized brocade balls tied with ribbons, on a comb foot, with applied silver handle, restored.

*6in (15cm) high*

**$700-1,000**     **WW**

A Japanese blue and white Nabeshima-type dish, painted in blue with flowers and leaves issuing from rockwork, raised on a high comb foot.

*8.25in (21cm) diam*

**$80-120**     **WW**

A large Japanese blue and white dish, decorated with peony and prunus.

*c1900*     *21.5in (54.5cm) diam*

**$300-500**     **WW**

A Japanese blue and white porcelain sake ewer.

*c1685*     *8.75in (22cm) high*

**$1,200-1,800**     **NAG**

A 19thC Japanese Hirado blue and white porcelain ewer, molded as a figure riding a carp through waves.

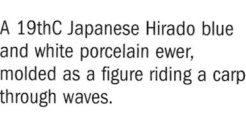

*9in (23cm) long*

**$700-1,000**     **WW**

A 19thC Japanese Hirado porcelain blue and white vase and cover, applied with three chrysanthemum sprays, the body painted with flowers floating on water, chipped.

*4.25in (10.5cm) high*

**$1,200-1,800**     **WW**

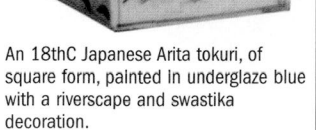

An 18thC Japanese Arita tokuri, of square form, painted in underglaze blue with a riverscape and swastika decoration.

*7.25in (18.5cm) high*

**$2,800-3,200**     **BEA**

An unusual Japanese porcelain condiment pot, after a German stoneware shape, with a loop handle, applied with prunts, cover missing.

*c1700*     *3.5in (9cm) high*

**$500-700**     **WW**

A Japanese Imari blue and white dish, with a crab design.

*1700-1730    16.25in (41.5cm) diam*

**$2,200-2,800**    **R&GM**

## JAPANESE IMARI

■ In the early 17thC ceramics were first made on Hyushu island, in the south of the Japanese archipelago. The largest city on Hyushu is Arita, which is served by the port town of Imari.

■ Clay in the vicinity of Arita and Imari has the requisite high kaolin content for making porcelain. Wares made for export became known as Imari after the port from which they sailed.

■ Imari potters first used enamels in the 1640s. Colored pigments were eventually supplemented with the use of silver and gold.

■ Production of Imari porcelain received a boost when instability in China disrupted the Dutch East India Company's supply of porcelain, and the Dutch turned to Japanese producers.

■ Genuine Japanese Imari porcelain was rarely signed until the 20thC. Exceptions include rare pieces that are marked by the artist who decorated them.

A Japanese Imari dish, the central vase of flowers painted within three blue scrolls dividing chrysanthemums and peonies to rim.

*c1800    10.75in (27cm) diam*

**$220-280**    **CHEF**

An 18thC Japanese Imari circular dish, decorated in red and gilt.

*12.75in (32.5cm) diam*

**$700-1,000**    **JN**

A large 19thC Japanese Imari charger, decorated with three panels of dragons.

*23.5in (59.5cm) diam*

**$800-1,200**    **WW**

A large 19thC Japanese Imari charger.

*22in (55cm) diam*

**$5,000-7,000**    **NAG**

One of a pair of Japanese Imari chargers, painted with a vase of peonies, the fluted border with panels of flowers and foliate designs.

*1880-1910    18.5in (46.5cm) diam*

**$1,200-1,800 pair**    **HAMG**

An early 20thC Japanese Imari deep dish, painted with a phoenix.

*12in (30.5cm) diam*

**$280-320**    **CHEF**

A pair of early 20thC Japanese Imari chargers, decorated with bowls of flowers within fluted rims, painted with shishi panels alternating with peonies.

*18.5in (47cm) diam*

**$800-1,200**    **CHEF**

A late 17thC Japanese Imari covered standing bowl, with ruyi lappet handles, standing on a trumpet foot, the domed cover surmounted by a shishi and flower finial, the sides painted with flowers.

*8.25in (21cm) high*

**$1,800-2,200** CHEF

A Japanese Arita Imari bowl and cover, decorated with flowers, foliage and fan-shaped panels, with later ormolu mounts comprising a foliate finial, scrolling side handles, reticulated rim and Rococo base.

*c1700* *9in (23cm) wide*

**$2,800-3,200** WW

A Japanese Imari porcelain bowl and cover, the later ormolu mounts probably French.

*c1700* *12in (30cm) high*

**$2,800-3,200** NAG

An 18thC Japanese Imari bowl and cover, decorated with vases of flowers, gilt highlights, chips to cover.

*c1700* *10.25in (26cm) diam*

**$2,800-3,200** BEA

A pair of late 19thC Japanese Imari pear-shaped vases, painted with panels of birds and a geisha practicing calligraphy, one with small drill hole.

*12.25in (31cm) high*

**$500-800** WW

A large Japanese Imari vase, decorated with panels of pine, prunus, and chrysanthemum.

*c1900* *23.5in (60cm) high*

**$300-500** WW

A Japanese Imari bush holder, painted in blue and gilt with chrysanthemums and prunus flowers.

*c1700* *3.5in (9cm) high*

**$1,200-1,800** BEA

A Japanese Imari teapot and cover, made for the European market.

*1700-1730* *6.25in (16cm) wide*

**$800-1,200** R&GM

A rare Japanese Imari tokkuri, modeled as Hotei seated on a gourd holding a fan, decorated in iron red and green enamels with flowers, body cracked.

*'Tokkuri' is a generic term for sake flasks, which come in many different shapes and sizes. Figural forms are relatively scarce.*

*c1680* *8.25in (21cm) high*

**$5,000-7,000** WW

A rare Japanese Genroku period Arita Imari porcelain wall vase, in the form of a standing bijin, restored.

*c1700* *13.5in (34cm) high*

**$3,000-4,000** NAG

A late 19thC Japanese Kakiemon style plate, painted with a phoenix, a pomegranate and prunus spray, the reverse with three cloud scrolls.

9.5in (24cm) diam

**$300-500**　　　　**WW**

A 19thC Japanese foliate molded bowl, decorated in the Kakiemon style, the interior a flowering prunus tree.

*If this was an original 18thC piece it would be worth $15,000-18,000.*

7.5in (19cm) wide

**$2,800-3,200**　　　　**WW**

A small Japanese Kakiemon dish.

*Kakiemon pieces from this period are rare. European porcelain factories copied this palette, particularly Chelsea and Chantilly.*

1690-1710　　5in (12.5cm) diam

**$1,200-1,800**　　　　**R&GM**

A Japanese Hododa Satsuma bowl, of square shape, with an applied figure in one corner, painted with immortals in gilt and enamel, signed.

c1890　　　4.5in (11.5cm) wide

**$220-280**　　　　**SWO**

A Japanese Meiji period Satsuma shallow bowl, on three feet, decorated with a water dragon rising from waves, overglaze blue Satsuma mon and two-character gilt mark, faint rim crack.

9in (23cm) high

**$500-700**　　　　**WW**

A Japanese Kozan Satsuma bowl and cover, the cover painted with seated ceremonial figures, the interior painted with women in a garden, signed to the base.

c1900　　　　5in (12.5cm) diam

**$1,200-1,800**　　　　**HAMG**

A late 19thC Satsuma vase, of square section with re-entrant corners, painted with panels of figures in a landscape, birds and foliage, the shoulder decorated with flowerheads.

6in (15cm) high

**$220-280**　　　　**ROS**

## A CLOSER LOOK AT A SATSUMA VASE

*Satsuma ware ranges from high quality to decidedly mediocre pieces. The faces of figures on high quality Satsuma are very expressive.*

*Unsigned pieces are often considered inferior and were sold in department stores in the West. This piece has the gilt signature of its maker and therefore commands a premium.*

*This vase is similar in style to pieces made by the Kinkozan family, who made ornate, cream-coloured pottery in the Satsuma style, usually heavily embellished with gilding, for the Western market In the 19thC and early 20thC.*

*The exquisite decoration here represents the best of Satsuma ornamentation, with traders and warriors interacting in a busy marketplace, scrolling flowers and gilding.*

A large Japanese Meiji period Satsuma vase, in Kinkozan style, one side decorated with a samurai beneath wisteria wrapped around a ginko tree, the reverse with figures in a market place, the blue ground with a gilt scroll design, gilt signature.

c1890　　　　12.5in (31cm) high

**$4,000-6,000**　　　　**WW**

A Japanese Meiji period Satsuma vase, decorated with panels of figures and buildings, two-character mark, minor faults.

*9.5in (24cm) high*

| $400-600 | WW |

A pair of Japanese Meiji period Satsuma vases, with elephant's head mask handles, painted with chrysanthemums and prunus trees, chipped.

*7.25in (18.5cm) high*

| $280-320 | HAMG |

A pair of Japanese Meiji period Satsuma vases, each painted with a landscape panel and wild flowers.

*9.5in (24cm) high*

| $400-600 | GORL |

A pair of Japanese Meiji period Satsuma vases, painted with bijin beneath maple trees before lakes and mountains, signed.

*7in (18cm) high*

| $700-1,000 | WW |

A Japanese Meiji period Satsuma vase, formed as two conjoined square sections, decorated with butterflies above wild flowers and a banded hedge, signed "Hododa" and "Satsuma Yaki" with four-character blue enamel mark.

*6.25in (16cm) high*

| $700-1,000 | WW |

A 19thC Japanese Satsuma vase, with a green decorated acorn top over a twin gourd style body, highly decorated with relief painted floral and crane patterns.

*8.5in (21.5cm) high*

| $1,800-2,200 | FRE |

A Japanese Meiji period Satsuma jar and cover, decorated with flowering branches, with chrysanthemum knop, signed "Tozan", with impressed seal mark.

*6.5in (16.5cm) high*

| $600-900 | BEA |

A late 19thC Japanese Satsuma pot and cover, of squat form, painted with landscape and figural panels against a maple tree ground, signed "Shizan".

*3in (7cm) high*

| $800-1,200 | HAMG |

A small Japanese Meiji period Satsuma koro and cover, with chrysanthemum knop and angled side handles, decorated with overlapping panels of figures in various pursuits, signed to the base.

*3.25in (8cm) high*

| $1,800-2,200 | WW |

A late 19thC Japanese Satsuma earthenware lidded koro, with reticulated domed lid, fish handles, enameled decoration, and pierced sides, on three feet, with painted signature.

*4in (10cm) high*

| $500-800 | ROW |

A Japanese Kiyozan period Satsuma koro and cover, with gilt elephant's trunk handles, painted with Japanese ladies seated on a terrace and landscape scenes, painted marks.

*c1900* *6in (15cm) high*

| $280-320 | HAMG |

A Japanese Yasuda Satsuma baluster vase, with pierced cover and chrysanthemum knop, decorated with panels of ladies in gardens with flowering prunus, the red ground with gilt brocade decoration, with Satsuma mon, Yasuda factory mark and signature.

*9in (23cm) high*

| **$2,800-3,200** | **DN** |

A late 19thC Japanese vase, of shouldered form, painted with figures walking in a garden setting, signed "Kinkozan Zo".

*4.75in (12cm) high*

| **$400-600** | **HAMG** |

A late 19thC Fukugawa-style vase, painted in white with herons against a shaded blue ground.

*7.25in (18.5cm) high*

| **$280-320** | **HAMG** |

An early 18thC Japanese Arita charger, painted with peony and lotus plants in underglaze blue, iron-red and gilt, the reserve with floral sprays.

*21in (62cm) diam*

| **$1,800-2,200** | **GORL** |

A pair of Kutani Showa period chargers, of eight-petaled form, painted in blue and green with birds on camellia branches, within an eggplant decorated yellow ground.

*11in (28cm) diam*

| **$400-600** | **ROS** |

A small 17thC Japanese Arita teabowl and saucer, printed in colored enamels and gilt with flowers and leaves, within red, blue, and gilt borders.

*4.5in (11.5cm) diam*

| **$400-600** | **LFA** |

A Japanese fluted pink luster bowl, painted with a mythological hoho bird, with reeded molding on the interior.

*c1720*   *4.25in (11cm) diam*

| **$300-400** | **R&GM** |

A Japanese earthenware lobed bowl, with a river landscape, wisteria floribunda, bridge and mountains, signed.

*6.75in (17cm) high*

| **$80-120** | **DN** |

A late 19thC Japanese ivory okimono, carved as an old farmer with a young child by his side, with a signed red tablet to the base.

*8.25in (21cm) high*

| $500-800 | ROS |

A late 19thC Chinese ivory figure, carved as a man holding a child and lion mask above his head, the base with red two-character mark.

*7.5in (19cm) high*

| $500-700 | ROS |

A Japanese Meiji period ivory okimono, carved as a mythical character with three Oni, red lacquer seal, signature, slight damage.

*7in (18cm) high*

| $800-1,200 | WW |

A Japanese Meiji period ivory okimono, carved as a Bijin carrying a flower and a tea kettle, damaged.

| $700-1,000 | WW |

A Japanese Meiji period ivory okimono, carved as an elderly man with his dog, red lacquer signature seal.

*7.25in (18.5cm) high*

| $1,200-1,800 | WW |

A Japanese Meiji period ivory group, carved as three men in a heated argument, their robes inset with lacquer and glass.

*2in (5cm) high*

| $800-1,200 | WW |

Two large Japanese Meiji period marine ivory carvings, each carved with figures and dragons, one with a shi shi, each with a two-character signature.

*14.5in (37cm) high*

| $1,800-2,200 | WW |

A large 19thC Japanese ivory carving of an Immortal, standing on a dragon, signed on a pad.

*11in (28cm) high*

| $6,000-9,000 | WW |

A Japanese Meiji period ivory okimono, carved as a hunter, standing holding a tethered bird of prey on his shoulder, holding a gun in his other hand, signed on an Inlaid tablet "Isshi".

*7.75in (20cm) high*

| $800-1,200 | ROS |

A Japanese Meiji period ivory okimono, carved as a group of rats, signed "Masatami".

*3.75in (9.5cm) wide*

| $7,000-10,000 | NAG |

An early 20thC Japanese ivory okimono, carved as a geisha, standing holding a songbird and cage, with engraved kimono, signed "Gyoku".

*10.75in (27cm) high*

| $1,200-1,800 | HAMG |

An early 20thC ivory figure by Shizuo, carved as a man kneeling with a basket of precious objects, signed on a red lacquer tablet.

*3.75in (9.5cm) high*

| $2,800-3,200 | CHEF |

A 19thC Chinese ivory figure, carved as an Immortal, carrying a basket of flowers, a writhing dragon at her feet.

*8.25in (21cm) high*

**$2,800-3,200**    **WW**

A Japanese Meiji period ivory okimono, carved as a fisherman, standing holding a basket of fish and a club, his coat with engraved, stained decoration, incised signature.

*14in (35cm) high*

**$3,000-4,000**    **HAMG**

A Japanese Meiji period ivory okimono, carved as an archer, standing holding a staff, a quiver of arrows on his back, his costume with engraved and stained detail.

*21in (53.5cm) high*

**$3,000-5,000**    **HAMG**

A Japanese Meiji period ivory okimono, carved as a musician with a basket of masks over his shoulder, his costume with engraved and stained detail, signed.

*21in (53.5cm) high*

**$3,000-4,000**    **HAMG**

A Japanese Meiji period ivory okimono, carved as a Samurai warrior standing beside a young boy fending off monkeys, signed.

*9in (23cm) high*

**$7,000-10,000**    **GORL**

A Japanese Meiji period ivory okimono, carved as a group of hunters trying to catch a giant crane, signed "Haruyoshi".

*6.25in (16cm) high*

**$3,000-4,000**    **BEA**

A Japanese Meiji period ivory okimono, carved as a woman playing flute, with three Oni, signed "Yoshi".

*10.75in (27cm) high*

**$800-1,200**    **BEA**

A Japanese Meiji period black wood and ivory okimono, carved as a farmer seated on a pile of wood, signed.

*5in (12.5cm) high*

**$3,000-4,000**    **BEA**

A Japanese Meiji period ivory okimono, carved as a fisherman carrying a cormorant in a basket, signed.

*9.5in (24cm) high*

**$3,000-4,000**    **BEA**

A Japanese Meiji period ivory okimono, carved as a salesman, with horn and mother-of-pearl inlaid details, signed "Gyokuzan".

*7.25in (18.5cm) high*

**$2,200-2,800**    **BEA**

## A CLOSER LOOK AT AN IVORY OKIMONO

*The very dense structure of ivory prevents splintering, making it an ideal material for finely detailed carving such as this bundle of branches.*

*Despite its size, this okimono was carved from a single piece of tusk, requiring great skill on the part of the craftsman.*

*Japanese carved figures often feature flowing lines, animated poses and vividly expressed emotions.*

*Export pieces tend to have smooth surfaces, without chisel marks. This was preferred in the West, where highly finished pieces characterized good craftsmanship.*

*Genuine ivory has a dark cross grain that can be seen in strong light.*

A Japanese Meiji period ivory okimono, carved as a woodsman seated on a pile of faggots, signed.

*7.25in (18.5cm) high*

**$5,000-7,000**    **BEA**

A Japanese ivory okimono, carved as a fisherman carrying a boy, on a naturalistic plinth, signed "Nobuyuki".

*7in (18cm) high*

**$1,200-1,800**    **BEA**

A Japanese ivory okimono, carved as the Seven Immortals, huddled together holding their attributes, red seal mark.

*2.25in (5.5cm) wide*

**$800-1,200**    **DN**

An early 20thC Japanese ivory figure, carved as a gold prospector, holding gold pieces in his hand and with a jar of gold on the ground, signed with red inset seal.

*8.25in (21cm) high*

**$1,200-1,800**    **WW**

A 20thC Japanese Meiji period carved ivory group, depicting an old fisherman and a young boy, with two-character mark to the base.

*10.25in (26cm) high*

**$300-500**    **ROS**

## NETSUKE

A late 18thC Japanese ivory netsuke, by Masanao, carved as a boar reclining on a bed of leaves, signed on red coral tablet.

*2.25in (5.5cm) wide*

**$2,800-3,200**    **CHEF**

A 19thC Japanese ivory netsuke, carved as Kinko reading as he rides a giant carp through the waves, the eyes of the fish inlaid.

*2.25in (5.5cm) high*

**$3,000-4,000**    **CHEF**

A 19thC Japanese ivory netsuke, by Masatami, carved as a monkey singing and dancing to a drum while supporting a youngster holding a peach stem on his back, the eyes and drum inlaid with cannel coal, signed on the leg.

*2.25in (5.5cm) high*

**$2,200-2,800**    **CHEF**

An early 19thC Japanese ivory netsuke, by Tomotada, carved as the dragon witch sitting on top of a temple bell, holding a lock of her hair in one hand and a crutch in the other, her tail coiled around the body of the bell, signed on the lip.

*2.25in (5.5cm) high*

**$2,200-2,800**    **CHEF**

A 19thC Japanese ivory netsuke, carved as a group of warriors battling around a warhorse, signed.

*1.75in (4.5cm) high*

**$4,000-6,000**    **CHEF**

An early 19thC Chinese cricket cage, the ivory-rimmed gourd incised with a dragon amongst clouds, the pierced cover carved with flowering cherry.

4.25in (11cm) high

$500-700　　　CHEF

An early 19thC Chinese cricket cage, the vegetable gourd with ivory rim and domed tortoiseshell top pierced and carved with two phoenix amongst flowers.

5.75in (14.5cm) high

$800-1,200　　　CHEF

A 19thC Cantonese ivory miniature table cabinet, carved with ptarmigan amongst undergrowth, the handles carved as insects, with a single-character signature tablet fitted to the stand, complete with wooden fitted carrying cabinet.

13in (33cm) high

$1,800-2,200　　　ROS

## A CLOSER LOOK AT A CHINESE IVORY PUZZLE BALL

Puzzle balls are made up of numerous concentric spheres, all carved from the same piece of ivory. The painstaking piercing and carving required to produce this example would have taken many weeks.

Years of handling produces a patina that can vary in tone from golden to dark brown and is difficult to fake.

The production of ivory pieces is now strictly monitored due to dwindling elephant populations. Despite bans on the trade in elephant ivory, illicit dealing continues and purchasers should check the origin of ivory articles that are offered as 'antique'.

Only the finest puzzle balls were made of ivory, as opposed to jade or other materials, making this example particularly desirable.

A 19thC Chinese Canton ivory tusk vase, intricately carved with peony flowers and leaves on a reticulated ground, with wooden stand.

9in (23cm) high

$500-700　　　WW

A Chinese ivory card case, carved and pierced with figures in a river landscape.

c1860　　　4.5in (11.5cm) high

$700-1,000　　　DN

A large Chinese ivory puzzle ball, carved with flowers, foliage, and birds, containing at least ten concentric balls, damaged.

4.75in (12cm) diam

$1,800-2,200　　　WW

A Japanese ivory Buddhist shrine, the roof bearing a swastika and dragons above opening doors with the goddess Kwannon flanked by acolytes on a stepped gallery, signed "Kuniaki".

c1880　　　18.5in (47cm) high

$1,200-1,800　　　SWO

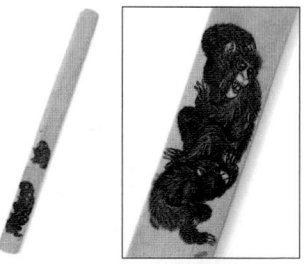

A 20thC Japanese ivory book page turner, intricately engraved with monkeys chasing a fly, red single-character mark.

18in (45.5cm) long

$180-220　　　ROS

A Chinese ivory cylindrical box and cover, carved in low relief with flowers on the domed lid and decorated with figures by pavilions amongst trees on the sides.

3.75in (9.5cm) diam

$300-500　　　CHEF

A small Japanese engraved and gilded ivory table cabinet, with brass edges and hinges, the front with a small pair of double doors concealing four drawers, with one long drawer below.

5in (12.5cm) wide

$1,200-1,800　　　JN

A Chinese Canton enamel snuff bottle, with a lapis lazuli stopper, the body painted with butterflies and flowers above rockwork, with four-character Qianlong mark, restored.

*2in (5cm) high*

**$180-220** WW

A 19thC Chinese rock crystal ovoid snuff bottle, carved with bands of lappets.

*2.25in (6cm) high*

**$400-600** WW

A 19thC Chinese glass snuff bottle, with four color overlay, carved with flowers and insects.

*2.5in (6.5cm) high*

**$1,200-1,800** WW

A 19thC Chinese glass snuff bottle, with four color overlay, carved with flowers and insects.

*2.5in (6.5cm) high*

**$700-1,000** WW

A 19thC Chinese jade snuff bottle, of mottled black and green color, the sides carved with lion mask handles.

*2.75in (7cm) high*

**$700-1,000** WW

A 19thC Chinese amber snuff bottle, of flattened oval shape, with gilded copper mounts and spoon.

*2.75in (7cm) high*

**$280-320** BMN

A 19thC Chinese cut glass snuff bottle, painted in between two layers of glass, partially red lacquered, damaged.

*2.75in (7cm) high*

**$280-320** BMN

A 19thC Chinese chalcedony snuff bottle, carved with ring handles and stylized mark, damaged.

*2.25in (6cm) high*

**$70-100** CHEF

A 19thC Chinese glass snuff bottle, black ground with five color overlay, carved with fish and lotus.

*3.25in (8cm) high*

**$700-1,000** WW

A Chinese amethyst snuff bottle and stopper, with flattened rectangular sides below a short neck, damaged.

*2.25in (6cm) high*

**$700-1,000** CHEF

A Chinese pale jade snuff bottle, of fluted ovular form, with coral stopper.

*2.25in (6cm) high*

**$2,800-3,200** GORL

A Chinese amber snuff bottle, carved with fish, lotus, and calligraphy.

*3.25in (8cm) high*

**$1,200-1,800** WW

A 19thC Chinese circular footed cloisonné bowl, the exterior decorated with scrolling leaves and lotus flowers, the interior with two writhing dragons and the well with fruit.

*8.25in (21cm) diam*

**$1,200-1,800**　　　　**L&T**

A late 19thC Japanese simulated cloisonné vase, of tapered square section, with short flared turquoise ground neck, bronze ground body decorated with lotus flowers and mon, and narrow yellow frieze to base.

*11in (28cm) high*

**$280-320**　　　　**L&T**

A pair of 19thC Chinese gu-shaped cloisonné beaker vases, with flared necks and feet, decorated with flowers, lotus scrolls and key fret borders.

*14.75in (37.5cm) high*

**$800-1,200**　　　　**WW**

A pair of 19thC Chinese cloisonné hanging wall vases, formed as lanterns with quatrefoil bodies, decorated with lotus flowers and leaves on a turquoise ground.

*12.25in (31cm) high*

**$2,200-2,800**　　　　**WW**

A late 19thC Chinese cloisonné jardinière, enameled with four alternating turquoise and red floral ovals on a lapis blue ground with scrolling flora.

*10.25in (26cm) high*

**$400-600**　　　　**CHEF**

A Japanese hexagonal cloisonné lobed tray, finely decorated with a mallard in snow-covered grasses, the back with a ground of scattered flowers, with monogram for Namikawa Sosuke.

*c1900*　　　　*10.75in (27cm) wide*

**$2,800-3,200**　　　　**DN**

A pair of Japanese Meiji period cloisonné vases, decorated with sparrows in flight above peony and chrysanthemums, all on a dark ground flecked with aventurine.

*9.75in (24.5cm) high*

**$1,200-1,800**　　　　**WW**

A pair of Japanese Meiji period cloisonné vases, decorated with panels of birds amidst wisteria, chrysanthemums and phoenix, impressed koro marks.

*7.25in (18.5cm) high*

**$1,200-1,800**　　　　**WW**

A small Japanese ovoid cloisonné vase, with white metal mounted foot and rim, finely decorated with a bird in a flowering tree on a dark blue ground, in original fitted wooden case, with paper label printed "J. Ando, Cloisonné Ware, Tokyo, Nagoya, Japan".

*3.25in (8cm) high*

**$800-1,200**　　　　**LFA**

A pair of Canton enamel plant pots and stands, of tapered square section, decorated with figural panels reserved on a foliate scroll ground.

*c1900*　　　　*3.5in (9cm) high*

**$180-220**　　　　**H&L**

A Chinese Kangxi period silver and parcel gilt ewer and cover, with a lobed hexafoil body engraved with panels containing Chinese figures and trees on a matted ground, the knop formed as a curled prunus twig with three flower heads, the handle as a knotted pine branch, the spout modeled as bamboo, with detail picked out in gold, marked "Rui Long" in Chinese characters to the base.

The "Rui Long" inscription may be a Chinese personal name or an early Chinese rendering of a European surname. Oriental silver was popular in the West at this time and export items were sometimes marked to order.

*6in (15.5cm) high*

**$12,000-18,000**　　　　**WW**

## A CLOSER LOOK AT A CHINESE SILVER EWER

The word 'ewer' derives from the 14thC French word 'evier', signifying a stone sink. This large jug was originally designed to carry water and would have been placed on a table in a conspicuous place within the room.

The detailed ornamentation is crisp despite its intricacy, demonstrating the skill of the craftsman and adding considerable value to this ewer.

The use of precious metals such as silver and gold in the Far East was generally confined to decorative inlay. From the 17th to the mid-20thC, however, silver hollowware was produced specifically for export to the West.

The condition of silver should be checked carefully, as any holes, splits or cracks around joined or pierced areas will have a negative effect on value.

A 19thC Chinese silver ewer and cover, the hexafoil body decorated with panels of figures and animals in landscapes, the gold knop formed as a lion dog.

*6.75in (17cm) high*

**$12,000-18,000**　　　　**WW**

A 19thC Chinese bronze vase, cast with a band of stylized birds above formal lappets.

*15.75in (40cm) high*

**$300-500**　　　　**WW**

A 19thC Chinese two-handled bronze censer, cast with archaic taotie masks on a keyfret ground, with a fitted wood cover and stand.

*12.75in (32.5cm) high*

**$700-1,000**　　　　**WW**

A Japanese early Edo period iron tsuba.

*2.75in (7cm) high*

**$800-1,200**     **NAG**

A Japanese mid-Edo period sentoku tsuba, signed "Mori Terukazu", with artist's seal.

*2.75in (7cm) high*

**$5,000-8,000**     **NAG**

A Japanese mid-Edo period iron tsuba, with chrysanthemum design, inscribed "shin marugata, katachi niku bori sukashi".

*3.5in (9cm) high*

**$1,200-1,800**     **NAG**

A Japanese mid-Edo period iron tsuba.

*3.5in (9cm) high*

**$500-700**     **NAG**

A Japanese Edo period iron tsuba, with dragon design.

*2.75in (7cm) high*

**$300-500**     **NAG**

A Japanese Edo period iron tsuba, with dragon design, inscribed "Kiyobo sanjin Jakushi Ryuunken Koretaka", with artist's seal.

*3.75in (9.5cm) high*

**$300-500**     **NAG**

A Japanese late Edo period iron tsuba, with cloisonné inlays, signed "Hirata Harunari".

*3in (7.5cm) high*

**$2,800-3,200**     **NAG**

A Japanese late Edo period shakudo tsuba, with dragon design.

*Shakudo is an alloy of copper and gold.*

*3.25in (8cm) high*

**$2,800-3,200**     **NAG**

A Japanese late Edo period elaborate sentoku tsuba, with a depiction of Rakan Handaka Sonja, signed "Furukawa Genchin".

*4in (10cm) high*

**$5,000-7,000**     **NAG**

One of a pair of Japanese late Edo period daisho shakudo tsuba, in a wooden box.

*3.25in (8cm) high*

**$6,000-9,000 pair**     **NAG**

A Japanese late Edo period shakudo tsuba, in a wooden box.

*2.75in (7cm) high*

**$1,800-2,200**     **NAG**

A Japanese late Edo period iron tsuba, decorated with fishermen.

*3.25in (8cm) high*

**$1,800-2,200**     **NAG**

A large Japanese Meiji period copper tsuba, signed "Hitotsuyanagi Tomohisa", with artist's seal.

*A tsuba is a hand guard placed above the handle of a Japanese sword.*

*3.5in (8.5cm) high*

**$7,000-10,000**     **NAG**

A Japanese late Edo period sentoku tsuba, with a depiction of Rakan Handaka Sonja.

*Tsuba give information about the owner's social standing and beliefs.*

*4in (10cm) high*

**$2,800-3,200**     **NAG**

A Japanese lacquer kobako, of square section, the black nashiji lacquer ground decorated in gold hiramakie with inlays of mother-of-pearl depicting prunus flowers, restored.

*c1600*      *2.5in (6.5cm) wide*

**$800-1,200**     **BEA**

A Chinese Qianlong period red lacquer charger, carved with flowering branches and grasses.

*12in (30.5cm) diam*

**$5,000-7,000**     **BEA**

A 19thC Chinese lacquer table cabinet, the metal bound sides with Chinoiserie decoration, with two doors opening to reveal an arrangement of seven drawers, on scroll feet.

*24.5in (62cm) wide*

**$3,000-5,000**     **FRE**

An early 19thC Chinese black and gilt lacquer tray, of wavy outline, painted in gilt with attendants in a garden, within a stylized floral border.

*26.5in (67cm) diam*

**$500-700**     **ROS**

A late 19thC Japanese tortoiseshell lacquered cigar case, decorated in tones of gold, black, and red with exotic birds in trees above rock pools.

*4.75in (12cm) high*

**$80-120**     **CHEF**

A 19thC Chinese gilt lacquered spice box and stand, the two-tier lobed container fitted with eleven black and floral gilt lacquered boxes, the exterior with a Buddhist lion and cubs, butterflies and flower heads.

*5.25in (13.5cm) high*

**$280-320**     **H&L**

A 19thC Japanese lacquer box and cover, decorated in hiramakie and takamakie techniques with flowers, on a nashiji ground.

*5.5in (14cm) wide*

**$300-500**     **DN**

A Japanese Meiji period gold lacquer five-case inro, decorated with tsuba on a complex diaper ground, one end decorated with mother of pearl, with three-character signature for Kajikawa, together with a pink hardstone ojime.

**$1,200-1,800**     **WW**

# ORIENTAL COSTUME

A Chinese Qing dynasty fifu dress, embroidered with polychrome silk and metal thread on blue silk taffeta.

**$1,800-2,200**                                    **RSS**

A Chinese Qing dynasty fifu dress, embroidered with polychrome silk and metal thread on taffeta, faded.

**$500-700**                                        **RSS**

A 19thC Chinese long pao woman's court robe, decorated with silk embroidery on twill weave silk.

**$1,200-1,800**                                    **RSS**

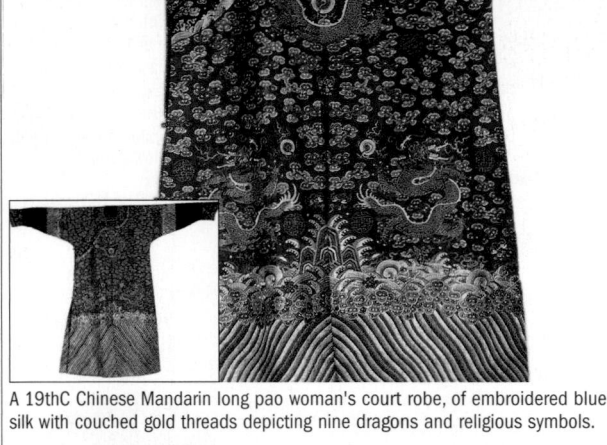
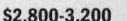

A 19thC Chinese Mandarin long pao woman's court robe, of embroidered blue silk with couched gold threads depicting nine dragons and religious symbols.

**$2,800-3,200**                                    **BEA**

A Chinese xia pei woman's ceremonial court vest, of indigo satin silk embroidered with phoenix amid clouds, flowers and auspicious emblems above waves and mountains, with tassel fringes.

**$300-500**                                        **RSS**

A Japanese Meiji period lime-green silk kimono, with floral and bamboo pattern.

*61.5in (154cm) high*

**$800-1,200**                                      **NAG**

## A CLOSER LOOK AT CHINESE CEREMONIAL ARMOR

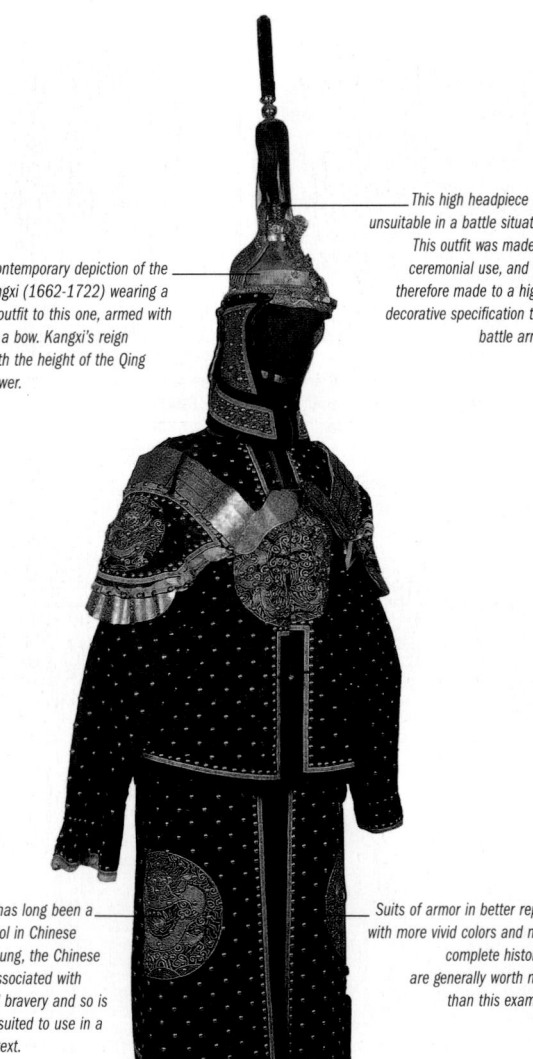

*There is a contemporary depiction of the Emperor Kangxi (1662-1722) wearing a very similar outfit to this one, armed with a saber and a bow. Kangxi's reign coincided with the height of the Qing dynasty's power.*

*This high headpiece was unsuitable in a battle situation. This outfit was made for ceremonial use, and was therefore made to a higher decorative specification than battle armor.*

*The dragon has long been a potent symbol in Chinese mythology. Lung, the Chinese dragon, is associated with heroism and bravery and so is particularly suited to use in a military context.*

*Suits of armor in better repair, with more vivid colors and more complete histories, are generally worth more than this example.*

A Chinese Qing dynasty ceremonial armor.

**$3,000-4,000**                                    **RSS**

A rare Chinese gouache on paper, depicting the interior of a Cantonese shop selling ceramics.

c1820                                          14in (35.5cm) wide

**$30,000-35,000**                                    NA

A rare and important Chinese gouache on paper, depicting a Cantonese shop making furniture in the Western style.

*This is the only known depiction of a Cantonese shop making Western-style furniture. Although caned recamiers, chests of drawers and Empire-style chairs made in China are well documented, few gate-leg tables and no candlestands have so far been identified with Chinese provenance.*

c1820                                          14in (35.5cm) wide

**$30,000-35,000**                                    NA

A rare Chinese gouache on paper, depicting the interior of a Cantonese shop making Chinese-style furniture for the West.

*The beds represented in this scene were not generally exported to the West. They were used by Westerners living at Macao and Canton. Trunks and desks, however, were common export items.*

c1820                          14in (35.5cm) wide

**$30,000-35,000**                          NA

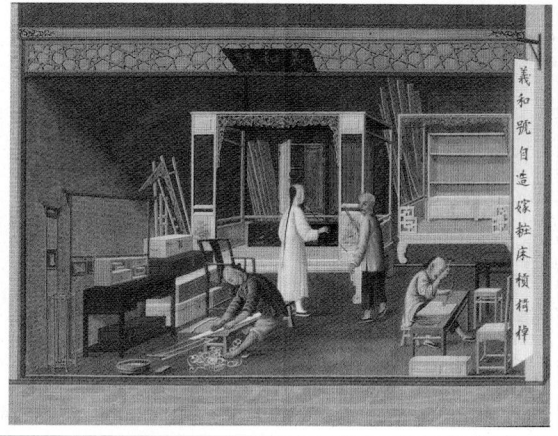

A rare and important Chinese gouache on paper, depicting the interior of a bamboo furniture shop.

c1820                                          14in (35.5cm) wide

**$60,000-70,000**                                    NA

A color woodcut, 'Fireworks at Ryogaku Bridge', by Ando Hiroshige, from the series 'Famous Places in the Eastern Capital', published by Sanoki, unframed.

15in (38cm) wide

**$500-700**                          FRE

A fan print, 'Hakone Tonosawa Yuba', by Ando Hiroshige, from the series 'Five Designs from an Untitled Series of Famous Places in Sagami Province', with aratame seal and date seal, published by Maruya Jinpachi, unframed.

1855                                          10in (25.5cm) wide

**$7,000-10,000**                                    FRE

A color woodcut, 'Kanasugi Bridge and Shibaura', by Ando Hiroshige, plate 80 from the series '100 Views of Places in Edo', unframed.

15in (38cm) high

**$700-1,000**                          FRE

A color woodcut, 'The City Florishing, Tanabata Festival', by Ando Hiroshige, plate 73 from the series '100 Views of Famous Places in Edo', unframed.

15in (38cm) high

**$700-1,000**                          FRE

A color woodcut, 'Yoshiwara', by Hiroshige, plate no 15 form the series 'Tokaido Goju-san Tsugi no Uchi' published by Hoeido.

| 1834 | 15in (38cm) wide |
|---|---|
| **$1,200-1,800** | **BEA** |

A woodcut, 'Shono', by Ando Hiroshige, plate number 46 from the series 'Fifty Three Stations of the Tokaido', published by Hoeido, signed "Hiroshige ga".

*This plate is considered the masterpiece of the series. In no other design does Hiroshige depict the raging elements more convincingly.*

| 1835 | 15in (38cm) wide |
|---|---|
| **$6,000-9,000** | **BEA** |

A woodblock print, 'The Hill at Kanagawa Station 4', by Hiroshige, from the series 'Fifty Three Stations of the Tokaido', published by Hoeido, the print depicts travelers climbing a hill lined with houses and restaurants facing Tokyo Bay.

| 1834 | 15in (38cm) wide |
|---|---|
| **$700-1,000** | **BEA** |

A woodcut by Hokusai, from the series 'Hyakunin isshu uba ga etoki', signed "Zen Hokusai", published by Éijudo.

| 1835 | 15in (38cm) wide |
|---|---|
| **$8,000-10,000** | **BEA** |

A color woodcut, 'Nichiren Walking Barefoot Up a Steep Mountainside', by Kuniyoshi, plate 10 from the series 'The Life of Nichiren', printed by Iseya Rihe, signed "Ichiyusaï Kuniyoshi".

| 1836 | 15in (38cm) wide |
|---|---|
| **$4,000-6,000** | **BEA** |

A 19thC Japanese color woodcut, 'Mount Fuji From Midzukubo', by Takahashi Hiroaki, signed and sealed.

| | 18.25in (46.5cm) wide |
|---|---|
| **$300-500** | **S&K** |

A Japanese color woodcut, 'Suzaku Gate Moon', by Taiso Yoshitoshi, plate 20 from the series '100 Views of the Moon', unframed.

| c1890 | 15in (38cm) high |
|---|---|
| **$500-700** | **FRE** |

One of a set of five Japanese color woodcuts, by Tsukioka Kogyo, from the series 'One Hundred Noh Pictures', unframed.

| c1900 | 13in (33cm) high |
|---|---|
| **$300-500 set** | **FRE** |

A Japanese mezzotint, 'Oiseau Et Poissons En Sympathie' by Kiyoshi Hasegawaon, signed and inscribed "ep. d'artiste" in the margin, pencil titled, dated, and inscribed "maniere noire" along bottom edge of sheet, and with artist's blindstamp in lower margin, framed.

| 1964 | 14in (35.5cm) high |
|---|---|
| **$5,000-7,000** | **FRE** |

A Japanese woodcut, 'Seated Deity', by Munakata Shiko, pencil signed, dated, and sealed in the margin, framed.

| 1961 | 11.75in (30cm) high |
|---|---|
| **$3,000-5,000** | **FRE** |

A pair of Japanese Edo period red lacquer folding chairs, with brass fittings.

*39.25in (98cm) high*

**$6,000-9,000**     **NAG**

A pair of 18thC Chinese hard wood armchairs, with rectangular seats, open-work backs and ornamental armrests.

*44.75in (112cm) high*

**$10,000-15,000**     **NAG**

A Chinese Qing dynasty hardwood low stand.

*c1780*     *12in (30.5cm) high*

**$400-600**     **DL**

A 19thC Chinese hardwood ceremonial open armchair, the paneled back decorated with open scrollwork above similarly carved open arms and caned seat, with shaped and carved apron.

**$1,200-1,800**     **L&T**

A large Chinese gilt and red lacquer cabinet, with two panel doors opening to an interior with one shelf, painted to depict precious objects.

*81in (202.5cm) high*

**$500-800**     **S&K**

A Chinese red lacquer and elmwood cabinet, from Shanxi province, with two doors opening to a single shelf.

*c1850*     *51in (127.5cm) high*

**$500-800**     **S&K**

An early 19thC Chinese red lacquer soft wood presentation case, divided into compartments of various shapes and sizes, on square legs terminating in hoof-shaped feet.

*58.5in (146cm) high*

**$1,800-2,200**     **NAG**

A Chinese black lacquer cabinet, the doors inlaid with mother-of-pearl foliage, with brass mounts.

*31.5in (80cm) high*

**$1,800-2,200**     **BEA**

A Korean rosewood display cabinet, the rectangular framed structure supported on a base with ornamental panels, comprising two shelves and a shelf cover, with metal fittings, lock, hinges, corner pieces, and handles.

*c1850*     *66.25in (168cm) high*

**$300-500**     **NAG**

A Japanese red lacquer cabinet, carved and painted with flowers and foliage, the panel doors decorated with bone and mother-of-pearl inlays of flowers and birds.

*1880*     *51.5in (131cm) high*

**$2,800-3,200**     **BEA**

A Chinese red lacquer whatnot, decorated with flowering trees, comprising five tiers, three with galleried open shelves and two enclosed by sliding panel doors, decorated with mountainous seascape scenes.

*64.25in (163cm) high*

**$700-1,000**     **L&T**

A Chinese Canton black lacquer paravent, decorated with young women and children in a pagoda garden, within a border of floral foilage.

*90.5in (230cm) high*

**$7,000-10,000**     **BEA**

A 19thC Korean travel cabinet, in two parts, with metal fittings, ornamental hinges, handles and corners, and fish-shaped locks.

*41in (102cm) high*

**$500-700**      **NAG**

A Chinese late Qing dynasty red and black lacquer soft wood cupboard, with a three-part brass lock plate and handles.

*37.5in (93.5cm) high*

**$2,200-2,800**      **NAG**

A Chinese hardwood medicine chest, overpainted in ocher, the rectangular top above six rows of seven drawers with three drawers below, each painted with Chinese symbols, the whole raised on square legs with decorative brackets.

*47.25in (120cm) wide*

**$1,200-1,800**      **L&T**

A late 19thC Japanese lacquer cabinet, decorated with combined lacquer and inlay techniques, in three parts, the four-legged stand a later addition.

*58.75in (147cm) high*

**$8,000-10,000**      **NAG**

A Japanese Meiji period two-panel black lacquer wood screen, with inlaid silk paintings and gilt mounts.

*82.75in (207cm) high*

**$5,000-8,000**      **NAG**

## THE FURNITURE MARKET

The market for fine and unusual furniture is extremely buoyant. Provenance is important and furniture from a respected source can attract a premium. A record price of $1.8 million was secured at Skinner in Boston, MA last year for a Boston Queen Anne japanned high chest of drawers in untouched condition. This piece caused particular excitement as it was previously unknown to the market. Items of this caliber are fought for at auction with ever-increasing ferocity, as collectors at the top end of the market remain undeterred by the anxiety that pervades elsewhere.

There is a general feeling that media coverage of extraordinary auction successes has left the buying public with the impression that prices overall are prohibitively high. This has exacerbated the general slump that is affecting all but the most faultless furniture that comes to auction in the current climate. American and British antique furniture at the lower end of the market remains difficult to sell. For some pieces, prices have fallen by as much as 50 percent over the last two to three years. This general downturn makes the present an ideal time to invest, and middle market pieces currently represent particularly good value.

*– Stephen L. Fletcher, Executive Vice President, Skinner, Inc.*
*Auctioneers and Appraisers of Antiques and Fine Art*

## BEDS

An early 19thC New Hampshire Federal mahogany canopy bed, the scalloped headboard with rosettes supported by turned posts with tobacco leaf decoration.

*61in (155cm) wide*

**$14,000-16,000**　　**POOK**

An early 19thC Federal mahogany carved and inlaid tall post bed, the vase and ring-turned swelled and reeded foot posts on square double tapering legs inlaid with stringing and crossbeading, maple square tapering head posts and arched pine headboard.

*49in (124.5cm) wide*

**$4,000-6,000**　　**SK**

A Federal mahogany carved reeded tall post bed, the ring-turned leaf-carved capitals on swelled reeded foot posts, on chamfered square tapering legs joined to the head posts with capitals and shaped headboard, old patina.

*c1810　　50in (127cm) wide*

**$13,000-15,000**　　**SK**

A Federal cherry canopy bed and chamber stand, attributed to Abner Toppan, the bed with vase and ring-turned, reeded, and swelled foot posts, chamfered tapering head posts, old red stained surface, the chamber stand with incised beaded drawer.

*c1810　　bed 49in (124.5cm) wide*

**$10,000-12,000**　　**SK**

An early 19thC Federal maple red stained canopy bed, the arched canopy above the vase and ring-turned, reeded, and swelled foot posts on vase and ring-turned legs joined to the ring-turned tapering head posts and acred headboard, old surface, minor imperfections.

*51in (129.5cm) wide*

**$5,000-8,000**　　**SK**

A Montgomery County, Pennsylvania, painted rope bed, retaining its original orange and red grain decoration.

*c1820　　75.25in (191cm) long*

**$700-1,000**　　**POOK**

A turned tiger maple tall post bed, the four ball-top vase and ring-turned posts continuing to vase and ring-turned legs joined by a turned foot rail and shaped headboard, refinished, alterations.

*c1825　　48in (122cm) wide*

**$3,000-5,000**　　**SK**

An important Pennsylvania William and Mary maple daybed, the serpentine crest over five vertical slats, flanked by ring- and baluster-turned stiles, the rush seat supported by boldly turned legs and stretchers.

*c1730　　72in (183cm) long*

**$17,000-20,000**　　**POOK**

A New England William and Mary maple daybed, with a craved arched crest over a vasiform splat flanked by square model stiles supported by turned and blocked legs joined by stretchers.

c1720

72in (183cm) long

$2,200-2,800                    POOK

An 18thC maple open cradle, possibly Pennsylvania or Maryland, with oval turned finials, double arched head and footboards with cut-out panels to sides of front.

41in (102.5cm) wide

$1,200-1,800                    FRE

## EIGHTEENTH CENTURY SECRETAIRE BOOKCASES

A George II kingwood and mahogany small secretaire bookcase, with simple parquetry veneering to sides and drawers, astragal glazed mirror doors enclosing adjustable shelves and fitted interior, on bracket feet.

74.75in (187cm) high

$12,000-18,000                    L&T

A George II mahogany bureau bookcase, with a later Grecian bust above mirrored panel doors, the lower section with a fall front enclosing pigeonholes, drawers, and a later leather writing surface, on ogee bracket feet.

96in (240cm) high

$12,000-18,000                    FRE

An 18thC mahogany bureau bookcase, with beveled mirror doors enclosing adjustable shelves above candle slides and a vitruvian scroll, the fall front with a fitted interior, on ogee bracket feet.

84in (210cm) high

$8,000-12,000                    L&T

A George III mahogany secretaire bookcase, with rosewood banding and boxwood stringing, the astragal glazed doors enclosing adjustable shelves, the base with secretaire drawer and fitted interior, on shaped bracket feet.

96.75in (242cm) high

$4,000-6,000                    L&T

A George III mahogany secretaire bookcase, with astragal glazed doors enclosing shelves, on a deeper base with an ebony-strung fall front and doors enclosing four drawers.

100.75in (252cm) high

$4,000-6,000                    L&T

A Scottish George III mahogany secretaire bookcase, with boxwood and ebony stringing, the astragal glazed doors enclosing shelves, on a bowfront base with drawers and turned bun feet.

93.5in (234cm) high

$4,000-6,000                    L&T

A George III mahogany secretaire bookcase, inlaid with a vase of flowers, the astragal glazed door enclosing shelves, the lower section with drawers and fitted interior.

102.5in (256cm) high

$8,000-12,000                    L&T

An 18thC George III and later mahogany bookcase, with astragal glazed doors enclosing a later interior, the base with drawers and fluted columns, on ogee bracket feet.

93in (232.5cm) high

$8,000-12,000                    FRE

A George III mahogany library bookcase, with a dentil cornice over two astragal glazed doors, on splayed bracket feet.

*c1810*     *90in (225cm) high*

**$5,000-8,000**     **FRE**

A George III mahogany secretaire bookcase, the Greek key cornice over two glazed panel doors enclosing two adjustable shelves, the lower section with a fitted secretaire drawer over three long drawers, on bracket feet.

*c1780*

**$10,000-15,000**     **FRE**

## A CLOSER LOOK AT A SECRETAIRE BOOKCASE

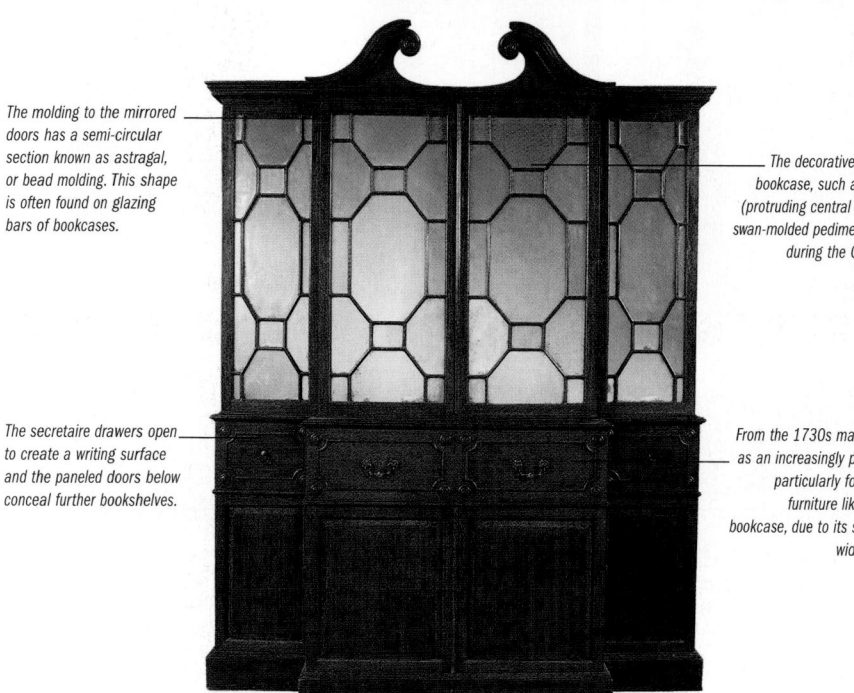

*The molding to the mirrored doors has a semi-circular section known as astragal, or bead molding. This shape is often found on glazing bars of bookcases.*

*The decorative features on this bookcase, such as the breakfront (protruding central section) and the swan-molded pediment, were popular during the George III period.*

*The secretaire drawers open to create a writing surface and the paneled doors below conceal further bookshelves.*

*From the 1730s mahogany emerged as an increasingly popular material, particularly for larger items of furniture like this secretaire bookcase, due to its strength and the width of its boards.*

A George III mahogany breakfront secretaire bookcase, the cornice with central swan neck molded pediment above four astragal mirrored doors enclosing adjustable shelves, the lower section with central paneled secretaire drawer enclosing interior, flanked by paneled doors enclosing three drawers, over four further paneled doors, each enclosing adjustable shelves, the whole raised on a plinth.

**Provenance**: *Gillingham Hall, Norfolk, England. Probably supplied for Francis Schutz of Gillingham who married in 1755; then by descent.*

*76.75in (192cm) wide*

**$45,000-55,000**     **L&T**

---

A Georgian mahogany secretaire bookcase, with dentil-molded cornice above two doors, the base with dovetailed and cockbeaded drawers, original brass hinges, ogee bracket feet.

*c1800*     *90in (225cm) high*

**$10,000-15,000**     **BRU**

An unusual George III mahogany and inlaid secretaire bookcase, probably from the Channel Islands, with beveled mirror doors, the inlaid fall front with a fitted interior, above two further doors and drawers, bracket feet.

*c1800*     *99in (247.5cm) high*

**$8,000-12,000**     **FRE**

A Victorian mahogany bureau bookcase, of early George III style, with astragal glazed doors enclosing adjustable shelves, hinged fall front and graduated drawers, on carved ogee bracket feet.

*98in (245cm) high*

**$5,000-7,000**     **L&T**

A Dutch 18thC-style walnut veneer and marquetry bombe bureau bookcase, with glazed panel doors, the lower section with a fall front and three long drawers, on carved paw feet.

*89in (222.5cm) high*

**$3,000-5,000**     **FRE**

A late 18thC American Chippendale mahogany carved reverse serpentine desk bookcase, scrolled doors flanked by pilasters, shelf over candle slides, lower case with a desk with fan-carved serpentine drawers, fan-carved prospect door, molded base with four carved ball and claw feet, old surface, replaced brasses, minor repairs.

*94.25in (239cm) high*

**$30,000-35,000** SK

An American Chippendale cherry carved desk bookcase, the top section with flat cove-molded cornice above two hinged doors opening to a valanced compartmented interior, fall-front desk, the lid opening to an interior of concave fan-carved prospect drawers, on ogee bracket feet, replaced wooden pulls, lacks finish, unrestored.

*c1770* *39in (99cm) wide*

**$8,000-12,000** SK

A late 18thC American Chippendale walnut inlaid desk bookcase, the top with urn finial above a crossbanded frieze, doors enclosing adjustable shelves with candle slides, on a base with fall front opening, string-inlaid document boxes, on ogee bracket feet, replaced brasses, refinished, restoration.

*40in (101.5cm) wide*

**$8,000-10,000** SK

A late 18thC American Chippendale cherry three-part secretary bookcase, the molded cornice resting on an upper section with two paneled cupboard doors, above a lower section with fall front enclosing a fitted interior, over four long drawers supported by straight bracket feet.

*85.75in (218cm) high*

**$5,000-8,000** POOK

A late 18thC American Chippendale cherry carved desk bookcase, the top section with two glazed doors opening to shelves set into a fall front desk, the lid opening to an interior of central pinwheel carved drawers, on ogee bracket feet, alterations.

*39.5in (100.5cm) wide*

**$7,000-10,000** SK

An inlaid mahogany Federal secretary, shaped cornice with three brass urn finials above two eight-pane doors with through muntins, base with fold-out writing surface with black string inlay, pit-sawn drawer bases with hand-wrought nails, old refinishing, wear and damage.

*41in (102.5cm) wide*

**$3,000-5,000** BRU

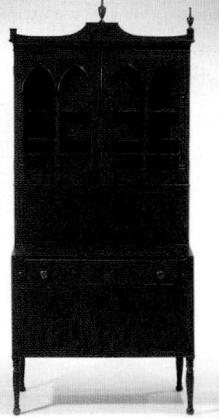

A Federal mahogany inlaid desk with bookcase top, two glazed Gothic arched doors with gilt tracery, two panel doors, the base with a sloping foldover writing surface, on short turned and round reeded legs, ball feet.

*c1800* *85.5in (214cm) high*

**$6,000-9,000** FRE

A Baltimore Federal mahogany secretary desk, broken arch cornice, upper case with two lattice-glazed doors with oval mirror panels, on a base with upper drawers with oval inlays on a satinwood reserve, on French bracket feet.

*c1795* *99in (251.5cm) high*

**$20,000-25,000** POOK

A Boston or Salem, Massachusetts, Hepplewhite mahogany secretary, the arched pediment above two glazed gothic arch doors, a central prospect door, flanked by tambour doors over a fall front writing surface, a scalloped skirt, on French feet.

*83in (211cm) high*

**$3,000-5,000** POOK

# The Complete Showcase

- From primitive pieces to elegant modernity, the definitive guide to 3,000 years of furniture design

- Packed with over 3,500 beautiful photographs illustrating every style and form

- Tips on how to recognize the key elements of style for each period

- Expert analysis of principal pieces, feature profiles and estimated values

An early 19thC Gothic mahogany breakfront library bookcase.

127.25in (318cm) wide

$10,000-15,000     LC

An early 19thC mahogany dwarf breakfront bookcase, with four astragal glazed doors enclosing adjustable shelves, the projecting base with a frieze drawer and cupboard door enclosing further shelves, plinth base.

87.25in (218cm) high

$7,000-10,000     L&T

A Regency simulated rosewood library bookcase, with two Gothic arched astragal glazed doors enclosing shelves, the lower section with two conforming cupboard doors, on a plinth base.

c1820     96in (240cm) high

$5,000-8,000     FRE

An early 19thC Anglo-Indian rosewood bookcase cabinet, with leaf-molded cresting above twin doors enclosing adjustable shelves, the lower section with two carved frieze drawers and two foliate and rosette panel doors, on carved bracket feet, bears maker's label "Deschamps & Co., Madras".

41in (104cm) wide

$15,000-20,000     L&T

A 19thC mahogany bureau bookcase, the molded cornice with blind fretwork frieze, the astragal glazed doors with fluted Corinthian pilasters, on an associated bureau, on ogee bracket feet.

89.5in (224cm) high

$3,000-5,000     L&T

A 19thC mahogany bookcase cabinet, with astragal glazed doors enclosing adjustable shelves, the base with paneled doors, plinth with flattened bun feet.

88.5in (221cm) high

$2,200-2,800     L&T

A 19thC English mahogany secretary, the two doors with through muntins, the base with a fold-down drawer, dovetailed drawers and cubbyholes, the two lower doors enclosing dovetailed drawers, on French feet.

89in (222.5cm) high

$5,000-7,000     BRU

A 19thC mahogany breakfront bookcase, the astragal glazed doors enclosing adjustable shelves, raised on a deeper base with paneled doors enclosing sliding trays, drawers, and shelves, on shaped apron with ogee bracket feet.

96.5in (241cm) high

$4,000-6,000     L&T

A 19thC mahogany breakfront bookcase, with four astragal glazed doors enclosing shelves, the lower section with four paneled cupboard doors enclosing shelves, bracket feet.

100in (250cm) high

$7,000-10,000     L&T

A 19thC George III-style mahogany library breakfront bookcase, with four astragal glazed panel doors enclosing adjustable shelves, the lower section with four panel doors enclosing shelves, raised on plinth base.

89in (222.5cm) high

$2,800-3,200     FRE

A 19thC Federal mahogany carved and veneer glazed bookcase, the top with a shaped gallery, doors with beaded Gothic arches, on a projecting base with drawers, corners carved with acanthus leaves and fluting with punchwork, ring-turned reeded tapering legs, old refinish.

*50in (127cm) wide*

**$10,000-12,000**    **SK**

An early 19thC walnut secretary-bookcase, found in Georgia, top with two doors, base with twelve drawers below eight cubbyholes flanking prospect door, four lipped and graduated dovetailed drawers, original dovetailed bracket feet, original rosehead nails, replaced brass pulls and hinges, repairs throughout.

*39in (97.5cm) wide*

**$5,000-8,000**    **BRU**

An early 19thC Classical mahogany veneer glazed desk and bookcase, molded cornice and frieze, glazed doors with Gothic revival shaping, a felt-lined writing surface above a convex drawer, boldly shaped frontal feet, some pulls orginal, imperfections.

*52.25in (133cm) wide*

**$4,000-6,000**    **SK**

A Philadelphia painted poplar three-part breakfront, the arched pediment over four glazed doors with arched recessed panels, base with four cupboard doors, retains its original ebonized surface with gold highlights.

*c1830*    *101.75in (254cm) high*

**$14,000-16,000**    **POOK**

A Philadelphia late Federal mahogany breakfront, the scalloped cornice over two glazed cupboard doors, over a lower section with two recessed panel doors resting on a flat base.

*c1830*    *115in (292cm) wide*

**$8,000-12,000**    **POOK**

An Empire mahogany breakfront bookcase, a step molded removable pediment with outset ends, center section with two glazed doors above slender center section, foldout writing surface, two recessed panel doors, two single glass door bookcase cabinets, cabinet doors below.

*c1835*    *89.25in (223cm) high*

**$7,000-10,000**    **FRE**

A Pennsylvania late Federal mahogany veneer breakfront, the carved and scalloped crest over four glazed doors over six drawers on a base with four recessed panel doors over a scalloped skirt, cutout bracket feet.

*c1840*    *136in (340cm) wide*

**$15,000-17,000**    **POOK**

**FURNITURE**

An early 19thC waterfall bookcase, with a solid back and sides and three open shelves, on bracket feet and castors.

*37.25in (93cm) wide*

**$2,200-2,800**     **L&T**

A matched pair of George III mahogany bookcases, each freestanding with three shelves and brass drop handles to the ends, plinth bases and castors.

*46in (115cm) wide*

**$5,000-8,000**     **L&T**

A pair of Regency rosewood waterfall bookcases, each with boxwood strung decoration, open shelves, brass carrying handles and a drawer below, the turned legs with brass caps and castors.

*40.5in (101cm) high*

**$15,000-20,000**     **L&T**

A fine late 19thC Louis XVI-style kingwood and gilt-bronze mounted dwarf bookcase attributed to Francois Linke, with a molded marble top, on turned legs and toupie feet.

*37in (92.5cm) high*

**$3,000-5,000**     **FRE**

A pair of Edwardian mahogany open bookcases, by Morison & Co., Edinburgh, each with adjustable shelves flanked by canted corners with carved terminals and scroll tops, stamped.

*50.5in (126cm) wide*

**$3,000-5,000**     **L&T**

## CABINETS

An early 18thC walnut cabinet chest, with a cushion frieze drawer and twin cupboard doors inlaid with feather banded panels, the base with further drawers, labeled "Gill & Reigate Ltd, Oxford Street, London".

*47.25in (118cm) wide*

**$3,000-5,000**     **L&T**

A Queen Anne-style red japanned cabinet, of two sections, in gilt and colors with Chinese figures and flowers, the domed pediment above two cupboard doors, over a lower section with two cupboard doors, on bun feet.

*37.75in (96cm) wide*

**$3,000-5,000**     **B**

A 19thC Swiss painted cabinet, the top and base each with a molded cornice above two paneled doors enclosing three drawers, on end supports.

*80.75in (205cm) high*

**$1,500-2,000**     **DN**

A 19thC mahogany estate cabinet, with sliding doors enclosing pigeonholes and three short drawers below, on acanthus carved legs and brass castors.

**$1,500-2,000**     **SWO**

## A CLOSER LOOK AT A GOTHIC CABINET

This cabinet is in the Gothic style, which was revived in the 18th and 19thC. The 19thC Revival was far less fanciful than the 18thC Gothic style and tended to be more archeologically exact. The influence of medieval design can clearly be seen in this cabinet.

The superb quality of this piece is evident from the use of marquetry and the exquisitely carved arched top, depicting a host of mythological beasts. It is also in an excellent condition.

A 19thC European marquetry Gothic cabinet, probably Portuguese or German, with a frieze arched door and drawer finely inlaid with figures, lions, and angels, flanked by Corinthian pilasters, the conforming lower section with a further cupboard door flanked by spiral turned pilasters, raised on block feet.

**$28,000-35,000**

This piece has a distinctly architectural feel to it, with arches raised on Corinthian and spiral turned columns. Gothic motifs were used primarily in church architecture, such as tracery and columns.

Block feet are vulnerable and prone to water damage and wear. Original feet will increase the value of the piece. Inspect the base for different woods and new additions.

*119in (297.5cm) high*

**FRE**

An early 20thC Louis XVI-style mahogany and gilt-bronze mounted side cabinet, in the manner of Francois Linke, the white molded marble top above a pair of paneled doors applied with draped cherubs, three long drawers, on turned legs with toupie feet.

*58.25in (145.5cm) high*

$2,800-3,200    **FRE**

A lacquered Buddha cabinet, with an open shelf enclosed by carved and pierced panels centered by roundels of fighting warriors, three drawers and pair of cupboard doors below flanked by carved panels, on stile feet.

*59.5in (149cm) high*

$700-1,000    **L&T**

**WRITING CABINETS**

A Queen Anne walnut escritoire, with a molded cornice, over a cushion frieze drawer, the crossbanded fall front opening to reveal a fitted interior with a cupboard flanked by drawers and pigeon holes.

*44in (110cm) wide*

$8,000-12,000    **SWO**

A Queen Anne-style walnut secretaire cabinet, the molded cornice with a cushion frieze drawer, above a boxwood inlaid fall front enclosing drawers and pigeon holes, the base with two short and two long drawers, on turned feet.

*65.25in (163cm) high*

$2,200-2,800    **L&T**

A George II walnut secretaire cabinet, attributed to William Old and John Ody, with a cavetto cornice over two mirrored doors enclosing an arrangement of eleven drawers with herringbone bands.

$15,000-20,000    **SWO**

A George III mahogany and brass-inlaid library secretaire, with twenty-four small drawers each inlaid with a letter, the lower section with a fal-front with leather writing surface and pigeonholes.

*74.5in (186cm) high*

$8,000-12,000    **FRE**

A 19thC mahogany Biedermeier secretaire cabinet, with a mirror door, cupboards and Carrara marble columns with gilt-brass composite capitals, the base with marquetry inlaid fall front.

*40.5in (103cm) wide*

$3,000-5,000    **L&T**

A 19thC French mahogany secretaire abbatant, with a gray marble top above a gilt-metal mounted frieze drawer, the fall flap enclosing a fitted interior, above three drawers on plinth base.

*58.25in (145.5cm) high*

$2,200-2,800    **L&T**

**DISPLAY CABINETS**

An 18thC Dutch walnut and marquetry inlaid cabinet chest, the serpentine molded cornice above twin astragal glazed doors enclosing shelves, the bombe base with two short above two long graduated drawers, raised on paw-carved front feet.

*76.75in (192cm) wide*

$5,000-7,000    **L&T**

A Louis XVI style D-shaped mahogany vitrine, with a marble top, brass gallery and three Vernis Martin rustic panels, glass shelves, on turned toupie feet.

*58.75in (147cm) high*

$2,200-2,800    **L&T**

A Regency rosewood and brass-inlaid display cabinet, with a pair of glazed doors raised on later plinth, the reverse breakfront base with a frieze drawer, glazed doors and brass-inlaid consoles.

*78.5in (196cm) high*

$8,000-12,000    **L&T**

A Louis Phillipe walnut and gilt-brass mounted vitrine, with mahogany banding and boxwood and ebony stringing, the single glazed door and glazed sides enclosing glass shelves, with cast rams head brackets to the angles, on flattened bun feet.

*54.5in (136cm) high*

**$8,000-12,000**  **L&T**

A late Victorian elm and marquetry display cabinet, in the manner of Gillows & Co., the cornice above a floral marquetry frieze and four glazed doors enclosing velvet-lined interior with glass shelves, raised on a breakfront base with marquetry panel doors.

*85in (216cm) wide*

**$4,000-6,000**  **L&T**

A Victorian mahogany display cabinet, with inlaid decoration and gilt-metal mounts.

*26.75in (67cm) wide*

**$1,800-2,200**  **SWO**

An early 20thC Louis XV-style rosewood bombe vitrine, with gilt-brass mounts, a glazed door and glazed serpentine sides, the lined interior with glass shelves, above Vernis Martin panels of lovers in a landscape, on splayed legs with sabots.

*73.5in (184cm) high*

**$5,000-7,000**  **L&T**

An Edwardian satinwood display cabinet, the crossbanded top above a pair of astragal glazed doors enclosing velvet-lined shelved interior, bears label of Druce & Co., Baker Street, London.

*42in (107cm) wide*

**$1,200-1,800**  **L&T**

A mahogany and inlaid display cabinet, with boxwood stringing, the astragal glazed door and bowed glass panels enclosing glass shelves, the whole raised on square tapered legs.

*72.5in (181cm) high*

**$2,200-2,800**  **L&T**

## CABINET-ON-STANDS

A 17thC-style walnut writing cabinet-on-stand, the fall front with geometric paneling enclosing a door and drawers, flanked by Mannerist pilasters, the stand with barley twist legs.

*64.75in (162cm) high*

**$2,200-2,800**  **L&T**

An 18thC black lacquered cabinet-on-stand, decorated with Chinoiserie panels to cupboard doors, enclosing eleven drawers, on square section legs.

*42.75in (107cm) wide*

**$1,800-2,200**  **L&T**

An 18thC or later William and Mary-style oyster veneer cabinet-on-stand, the two doors enclosing twenty drawers and a cupboard door, the stand with two drawers and bun feet.

*47in (117.5cm) wide*

**$5,000-7,000**  **FRE**

A George III mahogany writing cabinet-on-stand, with arched fielded paneled doors enclosing drawers and shelves, on a deeper base with writing slide and drawer, on molded chamfered legs.

*74in (185cm) high*

**$1,200-1,800**  **L&T**

A George III mahogany cabinet-on-stand, with twin doors enclosing a shelf, on an 18thC Venetian gilt and silvered wood stand, the top with lion rampant and silvered lozenge with "S. G. de C."

*25.5in (65cm) wide*

**$4,000-6,000**  **L&T**

An 18th/19thC Italian ebonized and ivory table cabinet-on-stand, with ten drawers and a cupboard door enclosing three further drawers, all inlaid with hunting scenes, on associated stand.

*58.5in (146cm) high*

**$5,000-7,000**  **FRE**

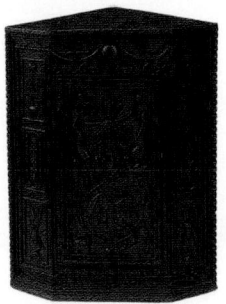

An early 19thC provincial carved and stained corner cabinet, unusual sliding bolt mechanism to the door, hidden drawer to the interior and false bottom to base.

*40.5in (102cm) high*

**$5,000-7,000**      **CATO**

A late 19thC Dutch satinwood corner cabinet, with Neo-classical faux marquetry decoration and leaf-cast gilt-brass mounts, the shaped triangular top centered by oval panel of oak leaves, with padouk banding, the single door centered by a putti mask in a panel, raised on pyramidal legs with brass bun feet.

*35.5in (89cm) wide*

**$8,000-12,000**      **L&T**

A 19thC light oak and mahogany standing corner cabinet, with one astragal glazed door over two paneled doors.

*44.75in (114cm) wide*

**$1,800-2,200**      **SWO**

## SIDE CABINETS

A 17thC and later Italian walnut side cabinet, molded rectangular top over a frieze drawer, one paneled door, raised on bracket feet.

*25in (62.5cm) wide*

**$800-1,200**      **FRE**

An Italian walnut side cabinet credenza, probably 18thC, molded top above three drawers with nailed construction, single door, on later bracket feet.

*34.25in (85.5cm) high*

**$3,000-5,000**      **BRU**

An 18thC Dutch mahogany cabinet, with checker stringing, the top with canted angles above a frieze drawer and pair of cupboard doors centered by shell paterae, on spade feet.

*37.5in (95cm) wide*

**$2,200-2,800**      **L&T**

A Louis XV-style mahogany and kingwood bombe cabinet, the serpentine marble top above a single door with floral marquetry and gilt-brass scrolling mounts enclosing shelves.

*35in (89cm) wide*

**$5,000-7,000**      **L&T**

An Italian Neo-classical-style painted and parcel-gilt side cabinet, the inverted breakfront top centered by a star motif, over two bead-molded frieze drawers and two fielded panel doors carved with laurel wreaths, opening to reveal a shelf, raised on a plinth base.

*57in (142.5cm) wide*

**$5,000-7,000**      **FRE**

An adapted Scottish George III mahogany side cabinet, with boxwood stringing, the stage back with hinged top and shell and leaf paterae, above a pair of dummy fronted doors, on square section tapered legs.

*36in (90cm) wide*

**$1,500-2,000**      **L&T**

A kingwood marquetry and parquetry side cabinet, the center panel with a scrolled cartouche, stamped "Gillows".

c1800      *48in (122cm) wide*

**$7,000-10,000**      **LC**

A Regency rosewood side cabinet, the crossbanded top with burr wood banding and foliate marquetry, the two doors with later pleated silk panels, on carved and gilded paw feet.

*43.75in (111cm) wide*

**$7,000-10,000**    **L&T**

An early 19thC Dutch mahogany and marquetry inlaid side cabinet, of demi-lune form, the inlaid top above a single frieze drawer and pair of tambour action doors, raised on block feet.

*36in (90cm) wide*

**$1,800-2,200**    **L&T**

A William IV rosewood and brass-inlaid side cabinet, with a green marble top above serpentine sides with applied castings of Ceres and Flora, two boulle-inlaid doors.

*46.75in (117cm) wide*

**$1,800-2,200**    **L&T**

A 19thC rosewood breakfront dwarf side cabinet, the green marble top above scroll brackets, the four doors with pleated silk panels, between a pair of shallow scroll pilasters.

*70.5in (176cm) wide*

**$3,000-4,000**    **SWO**

An 18thC-style painted Italian side cabinet, the canted top above a paneled frieze with two drawers and five further paneled doors, on bracket feet.

*84.5in (211cm) wide*

**$3,000-5,000**    **FRE**

A pair of Napoleon III ebonized gilt-bronze-mounted and 'pietra dura' side cabinets, each decorated in relief with exotic birds and foliage, the canted sides surmounted by female carytid and boulle panels, raised on a plinth base.

*49in (122.5cm) high*

**$20,000-30,000**    **FRE**

A Victorian ebonized parcel-gilt and gilt-metal side cabinet, with a white marble top, the paneled door between turned columns, on a plinth base.

*43.25in (108cm) wide*

**$700-1,000**    **SWO**

A Renaissance Revival walnut and part-ebonized side cabinet, attributed to Pottier and Stymus, with an inlaid central door, flanked by gilt-metal stylized acanthus capitals, with graffito-work and decorative burr veneers, on castors.

*c1880*    *61in (152.5cm) wide*

**$5,000-7,000**    **FRE**

### A CLOSER LOOK AT A GOTHIC REVIVAL CABINET

This walnut cabinet is attributed to the designer Frank Furness, who is noted for working with gothic themes. A piece by such a reputable designer is desirable and commands a premium.

The two oval copper panels have been replaced. This does not dramatically affect value, as the repair has been executed in a sympathetic manner.

A Victorian Gothic Revival walnut side cabinet, attributed to Frank Furness, with two frieze drawers and paneled doors, raised on a plinth base, the two copper panels replaced.

This piece comes with a copy of a letter from the Philadelphia Museum of Art discussing it.

This piece is typical of the 'Eastlake' style, pioneered by English architect Charles Eastlake, who published "Hints on Household Tastes" in 1868. In this publication Eastlake brought incoming Gothic Revival forms to simple household furniture. The Eastlake style was particularly popular in the US.

The extended curvilinear hinges on the paneled doors play an important part in the decoration.

*85.5in (214cm) high*

**$8,000-12,000**    **FRE**

A pair of 20thC George III-style satinwood and painted side cabinets, the cupboard door and paneled sides centered by oval panels depicting classical females, on carved square tapered legs with blocked feet.

*48in (120cm) wide*

**$8,000-12,000**    **FRE**

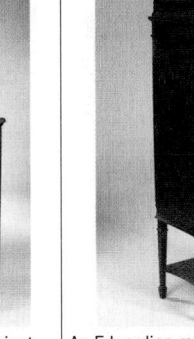

An Edwardian satinwood side cabinet, with open quadrant shelves and astragal glazed doors enclosing shelves, the base with grotesque marquetry.

*42.5in (108cm) wide*

**$3,000-5,000**    **L&T**

An Edwardian mahogany side cabinet, with boxwood and checker stringing, kingwood crossbanding and an astragal glazed door, on square tapered legs.

*19.25in (48cm) wide*

**$800-1,200**    **L&T**

## CREDENZAS

A pair of kingwood veneered serpentine side cabinets, each with a veined purple marble top and twin quarter-veneered and boxwood-strung serpentine doors, enclosing shelves, on square cabriole legs and cast sabots.

*40.5in (103cm) wide*

**$8,000-12,000**    **L&T**

A Victorian ebonized and gilt-metal mounted credenza, with an inlaid foliate frieze and four glazed doors, the turned and fluted columns with leaf-carved knops, the whole raised on a plinth base.

*78.75in (200cm) wide*

**$1,800-2,200**    **L&T**

A large Victorian ebonized credenza, with brass stringing and gilt-brass mounts, the frieze with metal panels decorated with applied floral sprays, carved from semi-precious stones, the central door with similar oval panel in ribbon-tied gilt-brass frame, flanked by glazed doors, framed by four fluted Corinthian columns and bases, on bun feet.

*74.75in (190cm) wide*

**$2,800-3,200**    **L&T**

A Victorian walnut inlaid and gilt-bronze mounted credenza, of serpentine form, the frieze inlaid with floral sprays, the door with a central inlaid oval flanked by shaped glazed doors, on a plinth base.

*76in (190cm) wide*

**$5,000-8,000**    **SWO**

**FURNITURE**

An 18thC pine hanging cabinet, a flat cove-molded top with a single raised panel door, carved sides below with shallow shelf.

*34in (85cm) high*

$1,800-2,200     FRE

A late 18thC inlaid cherrywood spice chest, Pennsylvania, rectangular molded top on case with single hinged door opening to four drawers, on molded base with ogee bracket feet, refinished, inlay loss.

*14in (35cm) high*

$3,000-5,000     FRE

An early 19thC Chester County, Pennsylvania, Federal walnut spice chest, the star and line inlaid door enclosing an interior with eight small drawers supported by French bracket feet.

*15in (37.5cm) high*

$12,000-14,000     POOK

A cherry cupboard, the rectangular top with breadboard ends on case with single chamfered drawer over paneled door opening the shelf, on ball feet, staining to top.

*45.75in (114cm) high*

$2,800-3,200     FRE

---

A painted two door cupboard, molded cornice above two paneled doors opening to shelves, molded base.

*39.25in (98cm) high*

$800-1,200     FRE

A Virginia walnut pie safe, probably mid-19thC, Scott County, Virginia, two drawers with nailed construction above two doors, each with two punched tin panels with eagles, secondary wood poplar, old refinishing.

*43in (17.5cm) wide*

$2,800-3,200     BRU

A walnut and poplar pie safe, Sullivan County, Tennessee, frame-and-panel ends, three dovetailed drawers above two doors, punched tin, chamfered horizontal backboards, on turned feet, refinished.

*55.25in (138cm) wide*

$10,000-12,000     BRU

A mid-19thC Pennsylvania poplar pie safe, the rectangular top over two cupboard doors with punched tin eagle panels flanked by sides with similar panels.

*53.75in (136.5cm) high*

$4,000-6,000     POOK

---

A Pennsylvania painted poplar jelly cupboard, the rectangular top above three short drawers over two panel cupboard doors, half turned stiles and paneled sides resting on turned feet, original ocher sponge and grain decoration.

*c1830*     *49in (122.5cm) high*

$3,000-5,000     POOK

A walnut cupboard, Buncombe County, North Carolina, dovetailed splash panel with scrolled cutouts above two dovetailed drawers and two frame-and-panel doors, cut nails, tongue-and-groove backboards, old green-painted surface, damage and replacement.

*44in (110cm) wide*

$1,200-1,800     BRU

A late 19thC pine counter or tabletop cupboard, frame door with two panels, added center decoration in front, interior with 16 cubbyholes, one with four drawers, single drawer below, cut nail construction, old refinishing.

*33in (82.5cm) high*

$500-800     BRU

A Canadian pine washstand, with two towel bars, square nails, with original yellow paint to the rear.

*c1870*     *33in (84cm) wide*

$700-1,000     PER

**FURNITURE**

A late 17thC ash and hickory carver armchair, from New Haven County, Connecticut.

*One of eight chairs known with these distinctive turnings.*

c1680                                    45in (114cm) high

**$50,000-$60,000**                                    **PH**

A Connecticut transitional Brewster/Carver armchair.

**Provenance:** *John Kenneth Byard, Silvermine, Connecticut.*

c1685       42.5in (108cm) high

**$45,000-55,000**       **PH**

A late 17thC Long Island, New York, transitional carver/great armchair.

48in (121cm) high

**$12,000-15,000**       **PH**

A mid-18thC maple and ash banister back, rush-seat armchair, molded arms, on baluster-and-block turned legs.

51in (127.5cm) high

**$300-500**       **FRE**

An 18thC black-painted New England banister-back armchair, turned finials, flaring arms, turned posts and legs, rush seat, restoration.

50.75in (127cm) high

**$700-1,000**       **FRE**

An 18thC Pennsylvania red painted comb-back Windsor armchair, serpentine crest rail with voluted ears, on rakish turned legs and stretchers.

40in (100cm) high

**$6,000-9,000**       **FRE**

A Philadelphia comb-back Windsor armchair, the crest with volute-carved ears, outscrolled arms, rakish turned legs.

c1770

**$6,000-9,000**       **FRE**

A set of four 18thC William and Mary black-painted turned and carved side chairs, New England, each with concave crest above molded back rest flanked by turned stiles, rush seat on turned legs and stretchers.

**$2,200-2,800**       **FRE**

A late 18thC black painted carved fan-back Windsor side chair, seven spindles, vase and ring-turned stiles, shaped saddle seat, splayed vase and ring-turned legs, old black/brown paint.

36in (91.5cm) high

**$8,000-12,000**       **SK**

A late 18thC Windsor comb-back armchair, carved ears on shaped crest above nine spindles and back rest with carved hand-holds, shaped seat and baluster-turned legs joined by swelled stretchers, refinished.

**$1,800-2,200**       **FRE**

Two Windsor chairs, serpentine crest with carved ears, the armchair with turned arm supports and back rest, peaked plank seats on rakish turned legs, refinished.

c1800

**$4,000-6,000**       **FRE**

A Connecticut sack-back Windsor armchair, the spindle back over boldly carved handholds, over an oval seat resting on baluster-turned legs joined by stretchers, signed "T.C. Howard".

*c1780*

**$3,000-5,000**   **POOK**

A late 18thC assembled set of four braced bow-back Windsor side chairs, the arched crest rails with eight spindles, saddle seats on vase and ring-turned splayed legs joined by turned swelled stretchers, old brown paint, imperfections.

*c1780*   *35in (89cm) high*

**$2,200-2,800**   **SK**

A set of six Philadelphia bowback Windsor chairs, the delicately pinched backs with nine spindles, above deep saddle seats supported by bamboo-turned legs, joined by stretchers.

*c1790*

**$8,000-12,000**   **POOK**

A set of six black painted bow-back Windsor side chairs, the crest rails above seven spindles on shaped seats and bamboo-turned swelled splayed legs joined by stretchers, later black paint.

*c1790*   *36in (91.5cm) high*

**$6,000-9,000**   **SK**

An assembled set of six sack-back Windsor armchairs, the bowed crest rails above seven spindles, shaped handholds on shaped saddle seats and splayed vase and ring-turned legs, refinished, minor imperfections.

*c1790*   *37.5in (95.5cm) high*

**$10,000-12,000**   **SK**

A Philadelphia bowback Windsor armchair, attributed to John Letchworth, the six-spindle back flanking an unusual vase form splat over a shield form seat, on bamboo legs joined by stretchers, retaining original Spanish brown finish.

*c1795*

**$7,000-10,000**   **POOK**

A pair of Pennsylvania loop-back Windsor chairs, having nine bamboo-turned spindles, walnut urn-turned posts, shaped seats on rakish turned legs with turned stretchers.

*c1800*

**$1,800-2,200**   **FRE**

**FURNITURE**

A 17thC rare low-back red oak and maple chair, square stiles, block and ring-turned legs, on turned feet, seat and back with 19thC leather, imperfections.

*Wood microanalysis is red oak, ash, and maple.*

c1680                    36in (91.5cm) high

**$38,000-40,000**                        **SK**

Four 18thC Queen Anne walnut side chairs, New England, shaped crest rail above rounded stiles and shaped splat above slip seat, cabriole legs ending in pad feet, repairs, sun bleached, age splits.

**$3,000-5,000**                        **FRE**

A Chester County, Pennsylvania Queen Anne walnut dining chair, shell-carved cupid's bow crest, trapezoidal slip seat with original upholstery, shell carved seat frame, cabriole legs with shell-carved knees terminating in trifid feet.

c1750

**$9,000-11,000**                        **POOK**

A Queen Anne maple carved side chair, the shape crest with C-scrolls, pierced spooned splat and stiles, molded compass seat on frontal cabriole legs outlined with C-scrolls over flat shaped reverse-curved stretchers, refinished, some imperfections.

c1750                    39in (99cm) high

**$2,800-3,200**                        **SK**

A pair of Queen Anne maple side chairs, with spooned crest rails on raking vasiform splats and chamfered stiles above upholstered trapeziodal seats on frontal cabriole legs, raking chamfered rear legs, block, vase, and ring-turned stretchers, refinished, imperfections.

c1750                    41.75in (106cm) high

**$5,000-7,000**                        **SK**

A Queen Anne mahogany carved side chair, the serpentine crest centers a fluted carved fan, a compass-shaped seat on frontal cabriole legs with shell carving, drop pendants above the frontal ball and claw feet, old refinish, imperfections.

c1760                    40in (102cm) high

**$8,000-12,000**                        **SK**

## A CLOSER LOOK AT A QUEEN ANNE DINING CHAIR

*This Newport chair has characteristic shell ornaments on the knee and cresting.*

*Newport was along with Philadelphia and Boston, one of the centers of furniture production before the Revolution of 1776.*

*Being an original and early piece of Newport furniture, this chair, in good condition, with only some signs of usage is very appealing to collectors.*

*In the first half of the 18thC American furniture underwent a basic change through the introduction of the cabriole leg. The curving line became a dominant feature of American furniture.*

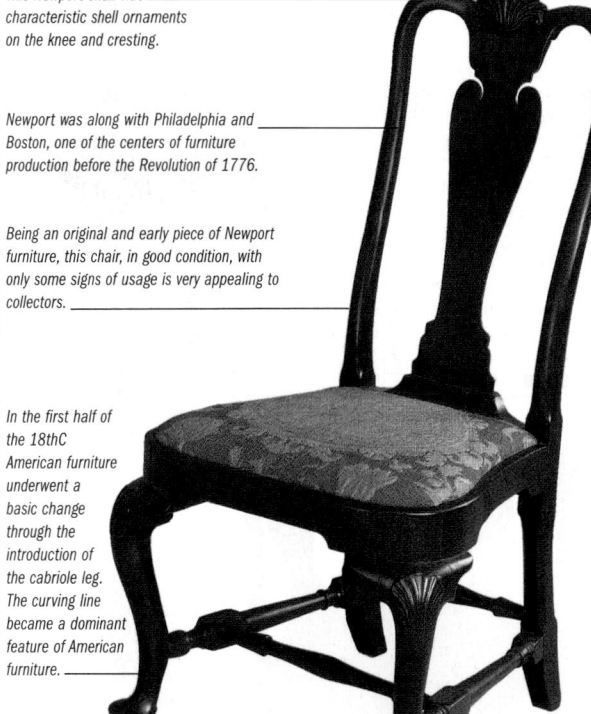

A late 18thC assembled set of five Queen Anne maple carved side chairs, vasiform splats and beaded raked stiles on rush seats, block, vase, and ring-turned frontal legs ending in carved Spanish feet, refinished.

41in (104cm) high

**$7,000-10,000**                        **SK**

A set of six late 19thC Massachusetts Queen Anne-style dining chairs, in the Boston tradition, each with an oxbow crest above a solid vasiform splat and compass seat, cabriole front legs, pad feet, joined by turned and blocked stretchers.

**$7,000-10,000**                        **POOK**

A Newport, Rhode Island Queen Anne walnut dining chair, the shell carved crest rail above a vasiform splat, a compass slip seat, cabriole legs with shell carved knees, pad feet, joined by turned and blocked stretchers.

c1750

**$23,000-25,000**                        **POOK**

## THE INFLUENCE OF CHIPPENDALE

- Published in April 1754, Thomas Chippendale's "The Gentleman and Cabinet-Maker's Director", was the most influential Rococo pattern book, containing 161 engraved plates of furniture designs.
- Subscribers included several aristocratic patrons of the arts.
- Designs that imitated desirable imports from the East, called Chinese Chippendale, were highly sought after, resulting in many prestigious commissions for the business.
- "The Director" became the 'bible' for furniture makers in Britain and also gave impetus to the American Chippendale style.

A late 18thC pair of Philadelphia Chippendale mahogany ribbon-back side chairs, shaped crest rail above four pierced and carved slates, trapezoidal seat on molded and squared legs.

**$5,000-7,000**     **FRE**

A pair of Philadelphia Chippendale walnut dining chairs, the arched crest rail above a C-scrolled gothic splat, over a trapezoidal slip seat resting on cabriole legs, terminating in stocking trifid feet.

*c1770*

**$17,000-20,000**     **POOK**

An 18thC Chippendale side chair, cherry, original glue blocks with 45-degree angles and hand-wrought nails, possibly Virginia or Connecticut, old, probably original surface, repairs, lacking drop-in seat.

*36.25in (90.5cm) high*

**$2,800-3,200**     **BRU**

A set of five Chippendale colonial period walnut carved side chairs, with serpentine crest rails that terminate in raked molded ears, leaf-carved arris cabriole legs, frontal ball and claw feet, with raking talons and squared legs ending in squared feet, old surface, with minor imperfections.

*c1770*     *38.5in (98cm) high*

**$60,000-65,000**     **SK**

A pair of Philadelphia Chippendale mahogany dining chairs, with foliate carved crest rail and pierced splat, above a slip seat, straight square legs with molded corners joined by stretchers.

*c1780*

**$5,000-8,000**     **POOK**

A pair of Delaware Valley Chippendale mahogany side chairs, each with a serpentine crest rail, pierced splat, slip seat, and cabriole front legs, ball and claw feet.

**Provenance:** *Direct descendants of Captain John Green of Philadelphia.*

*c1785*

**$9,000-11,000**     **POOK**

A late 18thC American Chippendale side chair, probably Virginia, mahogany with openwork splat, scrolled crest rail and ears, original glue blocks and hand-wrought nails, drop-in seat with later upholstery, damage and repair to top of crest rail.

*21.5in (54cm) wide*

**$1,800-2,200**     **BRU**

**FURNITURE**

One of a set of four mahogany chairs, in the George III Chippendale style, with a pierced and interlaced vase splat, each with a drop-in seat, on straight chamfered legs with H-stretcher.

*39.25in (98cm) high*

**$1,000-1,500 set** — DN

A set of six early 20thC Chippendale-style mahogany chairs, with two armchairs and four side chairs, each with an openwork splat with shaped crest rail and scrolled ears, scrolled arms, drop-in upholstered seats and cabriole legs with ball-and-claw feet.

*39in (97.5cm) high*

**$5,000-7,000** — BRU

Two of a set of six 19thC mahogany dining chairs, in the George III Chippendale style, each with a serpentine top rail with molded lugs above pierced vase-shaped splats and drop-in seat, on square chamfered legs with decorative brackets.

**$2,200-2,800 set** — L&T

Two of a set of eight 19thC mahogany dining chairs, in the Chippendale style, with two carvers, each with a serpentine top rail above pierced vase-shaped splats, above stuffover upholstered seat on square tapering and chamfered legs.

**$4,000-6,000 set** — L&T

Two of a set of four George III mahogany dining chairs, each with an arched back and anthemion pierced splat, above a drop-in needlework seat and chamfered square section legs joined by an H-stretcher.

**$1,200-1,800 set** — L&T

One of a set of ten walnut dining chairs, each with a molded frame and pierced and shaped splat, with an upholstered seat, the turned and fluted legs with an X-stretcher, two with arms.

**$3,000-5,000 set** — DN

## THE INFLUENCE OF HEPPLEWHITE

■ English cabinet-maker George Hepplewhite (d. 1786) became known through his pattern book, "The Cabinet-maker and Upholsterer's Guide", posthumously published in 1788.

■ Hepplewhite's designs, found in both his Guide and "The Cabinetmakers London Book of Prices" (1788), proved to be extremely influential in both Europe and America.

■ Hepplewhite furniture is distinguishable by its lightness, grace, and delicacy, especially when compared to Chippendale designs.

■ The elaborately carved cabriole and square legs, preferred by Chippendale and his contemporaries, contrast greatly by the slender, tapered legs seen on Hepplewhite pieces.

■ Characteristic features of the style include curvilinear forms, inlaid and painted decoration, shallow carving, and motifs such as sunbursts, husks, scrolls and paterae.

■ Chairs often have distinctive shield-shaped backs or square backs incorporating Prince of Wales feathers.

■ Due to the difficulty in identifying an actual piece or design by Hepplewhite himself, his name has come to represent a particular style rather than the handiwork of one man.

Three of a harlequin set of eight mahogany dining chairs, including two carvers, in the Hepplewhite style, the serpentine top rails above pierced and waisted splats and drop-in seats, raised on square legs linked by stretchers.

**$2,800-3,200 set** — L&T

Two of a set of eight Georgian-style mahogany shield back dining chairs, with drop-in seats.

**$1,200-1,800 set** — **SWO**

Two of a set of six 19thC Hepplewhite-style walnut dining chairs, including two carvers, each with a shaped top rail above carved uprights and three splats, one with pierced and carved Prince of Wales feathers, bowfront stuffover seat with plaid upholstery, on molded square section tapering legs joined by H-stretchers.

**$2,800-3,200 set** — **L&T**

Two of a set of six late 19thC Sheraton-style mahogany dining chairs, the square backs with three pierced splats with wheat ear capitals, above studded leather upholstered seats, on paneled square tapering legs.

**$3,000-5,000 set** — **L&T**

## FEDERAL CHAIRS

A set of six Federal mahogany inlaid shield-back dining chairs, the beaded backs with arched crests containing five shaped spindles converging at inlaid fans, overupholstered serpentine seats, square tapering molded legs joined by stretchers.

c1795

38.75in (98.5cm) high

**$28,000-30,000** — **SK**

A late 18th/early 19thC set of five Federal mahogany carved pedestal-back side chairs, molded serpentine crests, carved splats, with Neo-classical elements including kylixes, serpentine front rails on molded tapering front legs joined by square stretchers to the raking square rear legs, old refinish, imperfections.

c1800

39in (99cm) high

**$25,000-30,000** — **SK**

A set of six Philadelphia late Federal dining chairs, possibly by John W. Patterson, retain their original gilt decoration on a salmon ground.

c1835

**$2,800-3,200** — **POOK**

A set of 19thC Federal mahogany veneer side chairs, with curving ring-turned crests above veneered tablets and horizontal beaded splats enclosing spherules, slip seats with moulded edges on ring-turned front legs with raking rear legs, old refinish, minor imperfections.

c1815

32.75in (83cm) high

**$8,000-12,000** — **SK**

Two of a set of eight Regency mahogany dining chairs, with curved and paneled top rail above bound leafy mid-rail, the stuffover seat raised on square tapering legs linked by stretchers.

**$3,000-5,000 set**      **L&T**

Two of a set of seven Regency mahogany dining chairs, including one carver, each with curved top rail above anthemion carved mid-rail and drop-in seat, on turned and saber legs.

**$2,800-3,200 set**      **L&T**

Two of a set of six mahogany and satinwood crossbanded dining chairs, each with rectangular top rail above 'X' pierced mid-rail and stuffover seat, raised above square tapering legs.

**$2,200-2,800 set**      **L&T**

Two of a set of eight William IV mahogany dining chairs, including two carvers, each with leaf-carved and gadrooned top rails and drop-in seats, raised on saber legs.

**$1,200-1,800 set**      **L&T**

Two of a set of ten Edwardian mahogany dining chairs, including two carvers, in the Regency style, each with twin paneled yoke back, raised on reeded uprights with pierced lyre splat, stuffover seat with serpentine front, on turned and reeded tapering legs.

**$12,000-18,000 set**      **L&T**

One of a set of eight mahogany dining chairs, in late George III style, each with a satinwood crossbanded crest rail above a lattice back rail, upholstered seat and square tapering legs with spade feet, two with reeded arms.

**$2,800-3,200 set**      **DN**

Two of a set of four Regency mahogany dining chairs, with tablet backs, carved splats and stuffover seats on reeded tapering legs.

**$700-1,000 set**      **SWO**

Two of a set of twelve Regency mahogany dining chairs, ten original and two modern reproductions, each with a curved back with inset upholstered panel, above stuffover seat and paneled frieze, raised on paneled saber legs.

**$10,000-15,000 set**      **L&T**

Two of a set of eight Regency mahogany dining chairs, including two carvers, each with curved top rail above reeded uprights and paneled mid-rail, the drop-in seat raised on turned and tapering reeded legs.

Two of a set of twelve Regency mahogany dining chairs, each with paneled yoke back supported by saber uprights with Corinthian capitals, nailed stuffover leather seats, molded seat rail and turned and reeded front legs.

Two of a set of six early 19thC japanned parlor chairs, each with curved top rail above slatted back, painted in gilt with mother-of-pearl inlay, the plush stuffover seat on square cabriole legs linked by a stretcher.

| $3,000-5,000 set | L&T | $28,000-35,000 set | L&T | $3,000-5,000 set | L&T |

## VICTORIAN CHAIRS

One of a set of eight late Victorian mahogany dining chairs, each with reeded panels to the rail and supports, with blue leather buttoned upholstered seat, on fluted turned legs.

A Victorian Carolean-style oak side chair, with beadwork panel and seat, the turned and blocked frame with pierced foliate decoration, H-stretcher.

*34.75in (87cm) high*

| $1,800-2,200 set | DN | $280-320 | L&T |

Two of a composite set of fourteen Victorian mahogany balloon back chairs, the molded backs above stuffover seats with molded rails, on turned and tapering front legs with toupie feet.

Two of a set of six late Victorian mahogany parlor chairs, of George III style, each with vine carved and molded back with damask upholstered panel, above stuffover serpentine seat, on square tapering molded legs with rosette terminals and spade feet.

A set of four oak and antler horn dining chairs, each with a oval upholstered back supported by an antler frame, above a stuffover seat and on antler supports.

| $7,000-10,000 set | L&T | $12,000-18,000 set | L&T | $3,000-5,000 | L&T |

An early 19thC pair of mahogany inlaid shield-back chairs, with heart-back molded crests, the inlaid fans flanked by heart-carved splats and inlaid lunettes, the molded and curved back supports above over-upholstered seats with serpentine front rails, above string and bellflower-inlaid square tapering front legs ending in spade feet, with rounded rear legs.

*c1800*

*38in (96.5cm) high*

**$30,000-40,000**

**SK**

A set of six Victorian rosewood and tapestry-upholstered spoon-back side chairs, the shaped backs with shell and C-scroll carved crestings, over serpentine stuffover seats, raised on molded cabriole legs and castors.

*c1860*

**$7,000-10,000**  **FRE**

A pair of Empire-style parcel-gilt mahogany chairs, each with a tapering padded back with curved paneled crest rail carved with berried laurel, above a shaped padded seat on acanthus carved tensed animal legs, upholstered in gold floral silk.

**$12,000-18,000**  **FRE**

A set of four European carved walnut side chairs, the shaped backs modeled as elephants' heads with downswept rope-twist arms above drop-in seats, raised on outswept legs surmounted by elephant masks.

**$3,000-5,000**  **FRE**

A set of eight Classical mahogany dining chairs, attributed to Anthony Quervelle, slender rosette and leaf-carved horizontal splat, black Naugahyde-upholstered seats, on saber legs, two armchairs and six side chairs.

*c1820*

**$2,800-3,200**  **FRE**

A set of six 19thC Classical tiger maple carved and turned side chairs, with baluster turned cresting above an acanthus carved, pierced splat joining raked stiles above the rush seats on vase and ring-turned outward flaring frontal legs and turned stretchers, refinished, imperfections.

*34.5in (87.5cm) high*

**$1,800-2,200**  **SK**

A set of six mid-19thC Classical carved mahogany veneer side chairs and matching armchair, the curving crests flanked by molded curving stiles above splats with carved classical elements, rolled seat rails flanked by leaf carving, the klismos-style molded front legs.

*32.5in (82.5cm) high*

**$3,000-5,000**  **SK**

A set of five Pennsylvania Classical painted, stenciled, and paint-decorated side chairs, shaped seat on ring-turned tapering legs, decorated with baskets of fruit and flourishes, gilt highlights, with a chair of the same form without decoration.

*c1850*

**$600-900 set**  **FRE**

Two Belter rosewood chairs, one laminated armchair with carved crest rail with fruit and flowers, probably "Rosalie" pattern, scrolled arms, shield-shape back, cabriole legs, one laminated side chair, carved floral and fruit crest rail above double-scrolled supports, cabriole legs with carved roses, probably original surface, small chips and losses.

*larger 40in (100cm) high*

**$3,000-4,000**  **BRU**

A set of six Pennsylvania painted dining chairs, retaining their original stenciled fruit decoration on an ocher ground with green and yellow highlights.

*c1830*

**$2,200-2,800**  **POOK**

A set of six paint-decorated Windsor side chairs, original mustard yellow paint with gilt stencil designs and striping in black and orange, with putty painted seats, minor imperfections.

*c1830*  *32.5in (82.5cm) high*

**$6,000-9,000**  **SK**

One of a set of four New Jersey fancy chairs, with original paint and seats.

*c1840*  *33.5in (85cm) high*

**$1,200-1,800 set**  **BCAC**

155

A Delaware Valley Chippendale walnut armchair, the shell-carved cupid's bow crest with voluted ears, flanked by carved arms with voluted knuckled hand holds, above a slip seat resting in a scalloped frame, cabriole legs with shell carved knees, on ball-and-claw front feet.

c1770

**$7,000-10,000**　　　　　　**POOK**

A Delaware Valley Chippendale walnut armchair, the shell-carved cupid's bow crest, flanked by outward scrolling arms, above a scalloped seat frame with incised edge, cabriole legs, ball and claw feet.

c1770

**$7,000-10,000**　　　　　　**POOK**

## A CLOSER LOOK AT A DELAWARE VALLEY ARMCHAIR

*A naturalistic shell was a favorite ornament for the center of the seat frame during the second half of the 18thC.*

*Important and interesting provenance always adds value. This chair descended in the Howell family. They were well-known early settlers of Welsh origin.*

*The serpentine arms end in carved and voluted hand holds, which is typical of the bold Chippendale style.*

*The Chippendale style is marked by three general characteristics which can clearly be seen on this chair: the tendency to complex curved forms; the use of 'cross bow' type of cresting in chair backs; and the almost universal use of the claw and ball foot with the cabriole leg.*

A Delaware Valley Chippendale walnut armchair, shell carved crest rail, serpentine arms, slip seat resting in a shaped seat frame, cabriole legs, ball and claw feet.

**Provenance**: *Descended in the Howell family of Chester County.*

c1770

**$12,000-14,000**　　　　　　　　　　　　　　　　**POOK**

A George II mahogany armchair, with figural gros and petit point needlework upholstery, stuffover seat, and molded curved supports, on leaf-carved cabriole front legs with hairy paw feet.

**$15,000-20,000**　　　**L&T**

A George II mahogany armchair, with serpentine back, stuffover seat, shaped apron, and scrolling arms with squabs, on leaf-carved cabriole French front legs, the rear legs with scroll toes.

**$5,000-8,000**　　　**L&T**

A George II mahogany armchair, with gros and petit point needlework upholstery, the stuffover seat with padded arms and cabochon carved supports, on cabriole front and rear legs with pad feet.

**$10,000-15,000**　　　**L&T**

A George II mahogany open armchair, the serpentine arms with scroll terminals, on cabriole legs and pad feet united by a turned and blocked stretcher.

**$3,000-5,000**　　　**L&T**

A late George III mahogany elbow chair, with a slatted splat, shaped arms, a drop-in seat and chamfered straight legs with an H-stretcher.

*37.75in (94.5cm) high*

**$500-700** **DN**

A George III mahogany provincial Chinese Chippendale chair, the upholstered seat on square chamfered legs.

*25in (63.5cm) high*

**$1,200-1,800** **WW**

A George III mahogany open armchair, with carved tablet top rail, pierced lattice back and upholstered seat, on reeded tapering legs and toupie feet.

**$1,800-2,200** **L&T**

A George III mahogany tub armchair, with later drop-in 18thC needlework seat, on square section tapered legs.

**$1,800-2,200** **L&T**

A George III mahogany elbow chair, with an interlaced hoop back and swept arms, raised on molded square tapering legs.

**$1,200-1,800** **SWO**

A George III mahogany Gainsborough open armchair, with a serpentine back, swept arms and velvet upholstery, on square legs, united by an H-stretcher, castors lacking.

**$2,200-2,800** **SWO**

A George III mahogany Gainsborough armchair, with replaced silk upholstery, outswept arms with carved scrollwork, and a serpentine fronted seat, on molded square tapering legs.

**$3,000-5,000** **SWO**

A pair of Regency mahogany carvers, each with a paneled yoke back above a single mid-rail, downscrolled arms with turned supports and a nailed stuffover leather seat, on saber legs.

**$2,200-2,800** **L&T**

A Regency simulated rosewood tub-shaped showframe chair, with caned back and sides, on saber legs with brass terminals and castors, paintwork worn and lacking carving to seat.

*31.5in (79cm) high*

**$500-700** **DN**

A Regency mahogany elbow chair, the ebony strung crest rail above a roundel centered X-back, with downswept arms and upholstered seat, on square tapering legs.

*34in (85cm) high*

**$500-800** **DN**

A Regency mahogany open armchair, the brass line inlaid tablet toprail above a horizontal splat, channeled down scrolled arms and lemon upholstered seat, on channeled saber legs.

**$700-1,000** **L&T**

A pair of Regency ebonized and painted open armchairs, each with a pierced horizontal splat with a tablet painted with putti, the rattan seat with squab cushion, turned legs with toupie feet.

**$4,000-6,000** **L&T**

c1760

**$35,000-45,000**

The pierced vase splat beneath the carved top rail incorporates Gothic-style elements, which is typical of Georgian design.

This impressive needlepoint upholstery is in very good condition, and this will add to the desirability and consequently its value.

Spandrels flanking the knee of the legs are often carved separately and glued on. Originals will add considerable value.

Used by both Chippendale and Sheraton, downswept arms became very fashionable in the second half of the 18thC.

A George II carved walnut reading armchair, with needlepoint upholstery.

**CATO**

The classically inspired swags and ribbons that surround this coat of arms were popular motifs during the Renaissance Revival.

This inlaid shield back is a distinctive feature of the Hepplewhite style, which was clearly a source of inspiration for Wright and Mansfield.

These sunburst pieces are again typical of Hepplewhite's designs, which feature slender furniture with inlaid and carved decoration.

The crisply carved, mythological ram's heads are inspired by Etruscan art, which was introduced by the architect Robert Adam.

One of an important pair of mahogany armchairs, in the manner of Robert Adam, attributed to Wright and Mansfield, each with an inlaid satinwood back and carved front.

c1860

**$70,000-100,000 pair**

**CATO**

A rare early 19thC China trade armchair, Canton (Guangzhou), in Asian hardwood with a caned seat.

*The Neo-classical design motifs and Greek key carved crest suggest the design for this chair originated from London pattern books. The shaped carved rail suggests a family crest, possibly making the chair unique.*

*33in (84cm) high*

**$20,000-25,000**    **MJM**

Three of a set of four Louis XVI giltwood and upholstered fauteuils, the rope twist-carved backs with musical or gardening trophies, the padded scroll arms over serpentine stuffover seats, on fluted turned legs, one lacking seat upholstery.

*c1780*

**$3,000-5,000 set**    **FRE**

Two late 18th to early 19thC Spanish Colonial leather chairs, with scroll arms and headcrests, ornately carved with abstract floral designs, Hapsburg eagles, and heraldry crests.

*58in (147.5cm) high*

**$8,000-12,000**    **SK**

Two late 18thC mahogany open armchairs, with serpentine seat rails on square molded and slightly chamfered legs with H-stretchers.

*41in (102.5cm) high*

**$2,200-2,800 each**    **FRE**

A maple and ebony Federal armchair, New York, a curved flat crest rail, pierced back rest, scrolled arms above a cane seat covered with fixed cushion, on round ebonized ring-turned tapering and slightly outflaring legs.

*c1820*    *32.5in (81cm) high*

**$2,800-3,200**    **FRE**

A pair of Classical mahogany armchairs, each with shaped molded crest with Gothic arches above three molded slats and open scrolled arms, molded seat rail, tapering ring-turned front legs.

*c1830*

**$3,000-5,000**    **FRE**

A Rococo Revival carved rosewood armchair, attributed to George Henkels (1819-1883), with floral cresting to oval molded back, shaped seat rail carved with bellflowers and medallion, on cabriole legs carved with leafage, scrolled feet on castors.

*A similar chair attributed to Henkels is in the Philadelphia Museum of Art.*

**$3,000-5,000**    **FRE**

Part of a five-piece Rococo Revival carved rosewood suite, including sofa, two side chairs and an armchair, with molded, serpentine rail deeply carved with flowers and leafage, the crest of sofa carved with pot of grapes, cabriole legs carved with bellflowers on scrolled feet, and castors, old repairs.

*c1850*

**$5,000-8,000 suite**    **FRE**

A Louis XV-style walnut fauteuil, with needlework upholstery and carved outscrolled open arms and seat rail, on cabriole legs with scroll toes joined by wavy X-stretcher.

$800-1,200     L&T

A 19thC Louis XV-style beechwood fauteuil, with foliate tapestry centered by two panels of lovers and a dog, padded arms and serpentine stuffover seat, raised on cabriole legs.

$1,200-1,800     FRE

A 19thC Louis XV-style beechwood and walnut fauteuil, the shaped back, padded arms and seat covered in figural and foliate tapestry, raised on cabriole legs.

$800-1,200     FRE

Three of a set of four 19thC walnut framed open armchairs, in the French 17thC style, each covered in 17thC verdure wool tapestry, the scrolling open arms with acanthus-carved terminals, above leaf-carved and pierced front stretchers and turned and blocked legs, on stylized paw feet.

$7,000-10,000 set     L&T

A pair of 19thC carved pine open armchairs, in the Louis XVI manner, each with ribbon-carved molded frames with foliate crestings, the open arms and upholstered seats raised on turned and fluted front legs.

$1,200-1,800     L&T

A 19thC Spanish folding elbow chair, of folding savonarola form, the crest rail with a pierced motif, the slatted sides, seat and legs with rectangular bases.

*32in (80cm) high*

$1,800-2,200     DN

One of a set of three late 19thC French provincial open armchairs, each with a shaped crest rail and a pierced splat, with a drop-in seat, on cabriole legs.

*22.5in (56cm) high*

$500-800 set     DN

One of a pair of 19thC Swedish Empire-style painted open armchairs, with spool-turned X-form splats and an upholstered seat, on circular tapered legs with leaf banding.

*36.5in (91cm) high*

$5,000-7,000 pair     EVE

A pair of late 19thC Russian birch open armchairs, each with a stepped yoke backrest with a fan carving, scrolled armrests and an upholstered seat, raised on saber legs.

*36in (90cm) high*

$7,000-10,000     EVE

A pair late 19th to early 20thC Louis XVI-style armchairs, of pegged construction, the shield backs with scrolled arms, tapered and fluted legs, old pale yellow and olive paint.

*38in (95cm) high*

$3,000-4,000     BRU

An Italian ivory inlaid Mooresque open armchair, the shaped back rail centered by an urn issuing flowers, with a panel seat and X-frame supports, on sled bases.

$800-1,200     L&T

A Selanese ebony planter's armchair, with a carved back and seat and carved and turned arm supports, on reeded seat rail and turned front legs.

$1,200-1,800     L&T

An early George II upholstered wingback armchair, on shell and leaf-carved front cabriole legs, one back leg re-spliced, some restoration.

*c1730*

**$1,200-1,800**    **B**

A George III mahogany-framed bergère armchair, with an arched molded back, padded armrests and upholstered seat, on square tapering legs.

**$1,200-1,800**    **L&T**

A Regency upholstered and mahogany wing armchair, in foliate damask fabric, on ring and baluster turned legs with brass caps and ceramic castors.

**$3,000-5,000**    **L&T**

A pair of Regency simulated rosewood and upholstered library armchairs, the uprights and rail with gilded reeding, raised on turned tapering front legs with gilded embellishments.

**$6,000-9,000**    **L&T**

An American Chippendale mahogany carved easy chair, the serpentine crest above the shaped wings, outscrolled arms on the cabriole front legs, on carved ball and claw feet, rear maple square, chamfered, raking legs, modern wool damask red show cover.

*The chair's conservation report was prepared by the Society for the Preservation of New England Antiques in 1994 when the show cover was hand-loomed for the chair, appropriate for the period.*

*c1770*    *46in (117cm) high*

**$150,000-160,000**    **SK**

A pair of Federal mahogany upholstered easy chairs, with serpentine back and sides, outward scrolling arms and projecting serpentine seats on frontal vase and ring-turned legs and raked square rear legs, minor imperfections.

*c1810*    *46.5in (116cm) high*

**$17,000-20,000**    **SK**

A late Federal barrel-back upholstered armchair, the flaring ribbed back, scrolled arms and loose seat cushion raised on turned front legs, with squared back legs on castors, repair to back legs.

*c1820*

**$1,800-2,200**    **FRE**

A 19thC George III-style tapestry wing armchair, covered in 18thC fabric and raised on square tapered legs.

**$2,800-3,200**    **FRE**

An 18thC mahogany settee, with paneled back and solid seat, on cabriole legs.

*72.75in (182cm) wide*

**$3,000-4,000**     **SWO**

An early 18thC walnut double-chairback settee, the serpentine top rail above two crossbanded splats, with outscrolled arms and drop-in seat, on cabriole front legs with pad feet, later arms and restorations.

*58in (145cm) wide*

**$1,800-2,200**     **L&T**

An early 18thC William and Mary maple carved couch, the adjustable back with molded scroll-carved cresting, molded banisters flanked by bulbous turned finials on canted vase and ring-turned stiles, turned legs by bulbous turned stretchers, old surface, minor imperfections.

*66in (167.5cm) long*

**$8,000-12,000**     **SK**

An early Pennsylvanian Windsor maple and pine bench, with rodback and curved arms over a deep plank seat supported by bamboo turned legs joined by stretchers.

*78.5in (199.5cm) wide*

**$3,000-4,000**     **POOK**

An early 19thC painted and stenciled arrowback Windsor settee, a flat crest rail, scrolling arms, plank seat, on turned legs with turned and panel stretchers, painted Spanish brown with gilt flower panels at crest rail, pin striping on 'arrows', overall paint wear.

*77.5in (194cm) high*

**$800-1,200**     **FRE**

A yellow paint decorated Windsor bench, the triple-paneled rectangular crest above bamboo-turned spindles, plank seat flanked by arms all on eight legs joined by stretchers, old yellow paint with freehand painted tulip designs.

*82in (208.5cm) wide*

**$5,000-8,000**     **SK**

A New England rodback Windsor diminutive settee, the straight crest over 14 bamboo spindles, resting on splayed legs.

*c1815*     *41in (102.5cm) wide*

**$5,000-8,000**     **POOK**

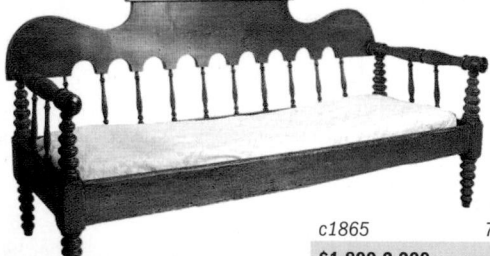

A Canadian pine country settle, from Quebec, with traces of original paint.

*c1865*     *70in (178cm) wide*

**$1,800-2,200**     **PER**

### A CLOSER LOOK AT A CHIPPENDALE SOFA

Replacement fabric should be in keeping with the piece.

The hump or curved back at the center of this sofa gave it its name.

Chippendale is more famous for making chairs and cabinets, making this sofa less common.

Straight legs with block feet were first designed for the Duke of Marlborough and are known as Marlborough legs today.

An American Chippendale upholstered mahogany camel-back sofa, the serpentine back on sloping scrolled arms on a serpentine seat, on three Marlborough frontal legs and three raked rear legs joined by stretchers, restoration.

*c1770*

*90in (228.5cm) wide*

**$12,000-14,000**　　　　　　　　　　　　　　　　　　**SK**

A late 18thC carved mahogany sofa, serpentine-shaped upholstered back enclosed by scrolling arms above molded and beaded legs joined by pierced stretchers.

**$6,000-9,000**　　　　**FRE**

An early 19thC Federal mahogany sofa, a slight curved back with reeded knuckles, vasiform and ringturned posts, vasiform-shaped reeded legs, turned feet, covered in yellow scalamandre.

*81in (202.5cm) long*

**$2,200-2,800**　　　　**FRE**

An early 19thC Sheraton mahogany upholstered settee, a flat crest rail, drapery, ribbon and tassel carved, reeded down-curved arms, scrolls, round reeded posts on round turned and reeded legs, tall turned feet, covered in yellow and ivory scalamandre, cushion seat, restoration.

*57in (142.5cm) wide*

**$3,000-5,000**　　　　**FRE**

An early 19thC Federal mahogany veneer sofa, paneled crest with reeding, the reeded arm supports, the bird's-eye maple inlaid dies on the front swelled and reeded legs, turned feet with square raked rear legs, old refinish, feet repairs.

*32.25in (82cm) high*

**$3,000-5,000**　　　　**SK**

A New York Federal mahogany sofa, possibly by Duncan Phyfe or a contemporary, the swag-and-bow carved crest above reeded arms, supported by turned and reeded legs with brass castors.

*c1815*　　　*77.5in (197cm) long*

**$2,200-2,800**　　　　**POOK**

A late Federal mahogany sofa, the plain scrolled backrail, upholstered back enclosed by molded and scrolled arms, the upholstered seat on molded seat rail and turned feet, old repairs.

*c1830*　　　*76.5 in (191cm) long*

**$1,200-1,800**　　　　**FRE**

A Regency mahogany sofa, the framed scrolling back and outscrolled arms with reeded fronts, squab and bolsters, reeded seat rail, on splayed reeded legs with leaf cast-brass caps and castors.

*90in (225cm) long*

**$2,800-3,200**                L&T

A Regency ebonized and painted settee.

*60.75in (152cm) wide*

**$4,000-6,000**                L&T

A Regency mahogany and brass-inlaid settee, with a shaped back and scroll ends, raised on reeded legs.

*77.25in (193cm) wide*

**$1,800-2,200**                SWO

A Regency mahogany chaise longue, with a scroll end and a reeded show frame.

**$1,000-1,500**                SWO

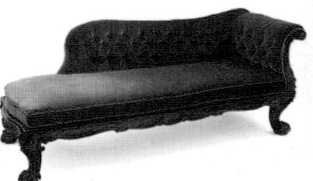

A William IV carved rosewood chaise longue, with a button upholstered back and end, on short cabriole legs, claw and ball feet and brass castors.

*78.25in (195.5cm) wide*

**$6,000-9,000**                WW

A 19thC George III-style mahogany and tapestry-upholstered settee, raised on gadrooned square legs with foliate-carved pierced angle brackets.

*82in (205cm) wide*

**$3,000-5,000**                FRE

A late 19thC George III-style mahogany triple back settee, with shell-carved scroll arms, raised on acanthus carved cabriole legs and paw feet.

*65in (162.5cm) wide*

**$3,000-5,000**                FRE

A Victorian chaise longue, with a buttoned back, upholstered in green damask with fringe and piping, on ebonized turned legs with horn castors.

*62.25in (158cm) wide*

**$1,200-1,800**                DN

A late Victorian ebonized settee, with buttoned stuffover upholstery, the balustraded sides with ring-turned uprights, molded front seat rail, on brass castors.

*62.5in (156cm) wide*

**$1,200-1,800**                L&T

A late Victorian painted satinwood settee, decorated with classical scenes and foliage.

*139.25in (348cm) wide*

**$1,800-2,200**                L&T

A Victorian rosewood and tapestry-upholstered salon suite, comprising a serpentine-back settee and two armchairs, all raised on molded cabriole legs, terminating in castors.

*74.5in (186cm) wide*

**$3,000-5,000**                FRE

An early 20thC Louis XV-style gilt-wood and painted salon suite, comprising a settee and two fauteuils, all raised on foliate-carved cabriole legs.

*73in (182.5cm) wide*

**$1,800-2,200**                FRE

A late Gustavian Swedish painted and upholstered settee, with turned uprights and central X-form supports, above a Neo-classical frieze, three loose cushions and upholstered cushion seat, on circular turned legs.

*c1805*     *75in (187.5cm) wide*

**$15,000-20,000**     **EVE**

A Danish Louis XVI elmwood daybed, the upholstered seat between outscrolled vertical slat armrests, raised on square tapered and fluted legs.

*c1800*     *78in (195cm) wide*

**$7,000-10,000**     **EVE**

A Classical carved mahogany sofa, Middle Atlantic states, shaped rail and upholstered back scrolled arms, the bolection seat rail on fruit-carved paw feet.

*85in (212.5cm) wide*

**$1,200-1,800**     **FRE**

A Classical carved mahogany sofa, the turned crest rail with acanthus carved scrolled ends above a shaped back above scrolled acanthus carved arms continuing to seat rail and leaf-carved brackets raised on hairy paw feet.

*c1825*

**$2,200-2,800**     **FRE**

A mid-19thC Classical mahogany sofa, the straight crest with voluted ends over foliate carved arms supported by animal paw feet.

*c1830*     *76.5in (194cm) wide*

**$1,800-2,200**     **POOK**

A 19thC Empire carved mahogany sofa, shaped crestrail with carved center of eagle heads and wings, bowl of flowers, flaring arms with acanthus leaf and rosette carving, claw feet, covered with yellow woven fabric, old repair.

*103.5in (163cm) long*

**$2,200-2,800**     **FRE**

A Belter rosewood sofa, laminated rosewood construction, carved crest rail and scrolls, probably Rosalie pattern, serpentine front, cabriole legs with original brass castors, red velvet upholstery, repairs.

*62in (155cm) wide*

**$3,000-5,000**     **BRU**

A Pilgrim Century oak chest with drawer, Essex County, Massachusetts, well with till, on paneled vase ornamented with applied ebonized split balusters, bosses and rectangles inscribed "The 19 of the 11 Mo. 1685 G.I. P", raised on straight feet with carved brackets, replaced lid.

*Provenance: The underside of lid bears plates inscribed with a partial descent of the chest, "Thomas Albert Newhall (1813-1892) to Lydia Jane Clark (1858-1936) to Frances Bernon Stoddard 1888," and "T. A. N. - L. J. N. - Walnut Cottage."*

1685                    51in (127.5cm) wide

**$45,000-50,000**                    **FRE**

A Pennsylvania Chippendale walnut blanket chest, the lift lid over a dovetailed case with inlaid initials "HL 1774", over two drawers supported by ogee bracket feet.

                        50in (127cm) wide

**$5,000-8,000**                    **POOK**

A Pennsylvania walnut blanket chest, the lift over a dovetail case with two short drawers resting on straight bracket feet.

c1790            47.25in (120cm) wide

**$3,000-5,000**                    **POOK**

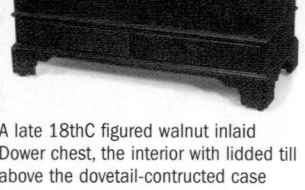

A late 18thC figured walnut inlaid Dower chest, the interior with lidded till above the dovetail-contructed case inlaid with "17 MM 85", applied molding and two thumb-molded half drawers, all on bracket feet, two original escutcheons, old surface, minor imperfections.

                    47in (119.5cm) wide

**$15,000-18,000**                    **SK**

A Berks County, Pennsylvania painted dower chest, the lift lid with three tombstone panels flanking two tulip stems, over a case with similar front panels with sawtooth and heart decoration, above a mid-molding and three short drawers with floral motifs, bracket foot base with central drop.

c1800                    50in (127cm) wide

**$40,000-50,000**                    **POOK**

A Pennsylvania painted dower chest, the top with applied molded edge, a dovetailed case, the front and sides with tombstone panels, decorated with flowers on ivory field, molded base and bracket feet.

c1790            49in (124.5cm) wide

**$5,000-8,000**                    **POOK**

A Pennsylvania painted pine dower chest, the front decorated with panels of potted tulips, framed by columns flanking the inscription "Pamlla HR 1803" on ocher ground, two short drawers, straight bracket feet.

1803            48in (122cm) wide

**$7,000-10,000**                    **POOK**

An early 19thC inlaid walnut Tennessee blanket chest, Greene County, top with applied molding, interior with lidded till and dovetailed drawer, top of front with tassel, vine, turnip, and teardrop inlay, sides with shaped skirt and barberpole inlay, shaped skirt with fan, barberpole and tassel inlay.

                    38in (95cm) wide

**$45,000-50,000**                    **BRU**

A Pennsylvania Queen Anne walnut sulphur inlaid blanket chest, the rectangular top over a dovetailed case, inscribed "MK 1800", resting on straight bracket feet.

1800            53in (134.5cm) wide

**$3,000-5,000**                    **POOK**

A rare Schwenkfelder decorated dower chest, with overall feather grained decoration, the front with a black edged cartouche, inscribed "Jacob Hubner 1815" above two drawers resting on ogee bracket feet.

*An identical chest is pictured in 'The Flowering of American Folk Art', by Lipman, plate 305. As suggested in the book, these chests were very likely decorated by Fraktur artists Daniel or David Kriebel.*

                    49in (124.5cm) wide

**$45,000-55,000**                    **POOK**

An early 19thC inlaid walnut blanket chest, the hinged lid with molded edge lifts to interior with till, the case inlaid with tulips, shaped reserve with "E.B. 1804," the sides inlaid with compass star, molded base, dated.

*1804*      *42.5in (108cm) wide*

**$6,000-9,000**     **FRE**

An early 19thC Pennsylvania painted poplar diminutive dower chest, the lift lid with two potted tulip panels with column sides over a case with similar decoration resting on straight bracket feet.

*39in (99cm) wide*

**$3,000-5,000**     **POOK**

An early 19thC Pennsylvania painted pine dower chest, panel with spread winged eagle, with shield and banner clutching tulip form battens, below two pinwheels all on a stippled salmon ground, straight bracket feet.

*48in (122cm) wide*

**$12,000-14,000**     **POOK**

An early 19thC Pennsylvania painted blanket chest, the lift lid with two painted circles within a sawtooth border, a case with recessed panel front and sides, turned feet, retaining its original ocher grain decorated surface.

*36in (91.5cm) wide*

**$3,000-5,000**     **POOK**

A Pennsylvania painted pine blanket chest, the lift lid over a dovetailed case resting on spurred straight bracket feet, retains its original red and black swirl decoration.

**Provenance:** *Dittmar Collection.*

*c1800*      *49in (122.5cm) wide*

**$800-1,200**     **POOK**

A Southern painted pine blanket chest, the rectangular lid over a dovetailed case and elaborate scalloped skirt resting on square legs, retaining its original green painted surface.

*c1820*      *49in (122.5cm) wide*

**$2,200-2,800**     **POOK**

A Pennsylvania painted pine and poplar blanket chest, the lift lid over a raised panel case above mid-molding over three short drawers with original glass pulls, on turned feet, original red painted surface.

*c1820*      *49.75in (124cm) wide*

**$5,000-8,000**     **POOK**

A mid-18thC paint-decorated pine chest over drawer, the molded lift top above a single thumb-molded drawer, base with turned ball feet, old red paint with hearts and leaves design, imperfections and restoration.

*36in (93cm) wide*

$1,200-1,800 — SK

A chest-over-drawer, the hinged top with reeded edge opens to a well, single drawer and case bordered by reeding, all on vase and ring-turned legs, some original brass, old surface, minor imperfections.

*c1810* — *42in (106.5cm) wide*

$1,800-2,200 — SK

A 19thC grain-painted, one drawer blanket chest, hinged rectangular top above a well, one long drawer, a shaped apron and bracket feet.

*41.5in (105.5cm) wide*

$1,800-2,200 — FRE

A 19thC Pennsylvania paint-decorated dome top box, retaining its original yellow demilune and wave decoration on a red ground.

*27.5in (69cm) wide*

$2,800-3,200 — POOK

A Soap Hollow, Pennsylvania painted poplar blanket chest, the lift lid over a case inscribed "JK 1901", flanked by three decoupage bouquets all on a red and black grained surface.

*1901* — *41.25in (103cm) wide*

$2,800-3,200 — POOK

A Pennsylvania painted pine dower chest, painted by David Y. Ellinger, (American, 1913-2003), with a dovetailed case, straight bracket feet, the lid and front decorated with panels depicting men on horseback, tulips, and birds, the sides with unicorns and tulips, the front dated, the inside of lid inscribed "painted by D.Y. Ellinger 1938".

*1938* — *46.5in (118cm) wide*

$4,000-6,000 — POOK

A Pennsylvania painted poplar dower chest, a dovetailed case, signed "Michael Scheiele", over a central cartouche with ocher sponge decoration, the sides with pinwheel motif, over short drawers, straight bracket feet.

*49.75in (126.5cm) wide*

$3,000-5,000 — POOK

A mahogany mule chest, of George III style, the hinged rectangular top above a plain front, on earlier hairy claw and ball feet.

*39.5in (99cm) wide*

**$1,200-1,800** | **L&T**

An Eastern European pine marriage chest, with iron side handles, painted overall with urns of flowers in red and green on a gold ground within yellow borders.

*25.5in (65cm) high*

**$500-800** | **DN**

A 19thC oak kist, of plank construction, the hinged lid with a molded edge above a front with crimped edges, the sides with cut-out feet.

*35.25in (88cm) wide*

**$500-700** | **L&T**

## CHEST OF DRAWERS

A late 17thC oak chest of drawers, with an ogee molded frieze, four long drawers with geometrical molded panel fronts and applied moldings, later cast brass handles and escutcheons.

*45in (114cm) wide*

**$2,200-2,800** | **WW**

A late 17th to early 18thC oak chest of drawers, with two short and three long graduated drawers with geometric paneling, on bun feet.

*41.5in (104cm) wide*

**$1,200-1,800** | **L&T**

An early 18thC oyster veneered walnut chest of drawers, with boxwood inlay and molded edge, above two short and three long graduated drawers, on shaped bracket feet.

*40.75in (102cm) wide*

**$4,000-6,000** | **L&T**

An 18thC Italian chest of drawers, with four graduated dovetailed drawers and frame-and-panel sides and back, formerly a lift-top chest with faux drawer fronts, the drawers and front rebuilt.

*41.5in (104cm) wide*

**$1,800-2,200** | **BRU**

An inlaid English chest of drawers, probably late 18thC, with burlwood top and dovetailed drawers with banded inlay, openwork brass pulls and escutcheons, the secondary woods pine and oak, partially replaced bracket feet.

*41in (102.5cm) wide*

**$1,200-1,800** | **BRU**

A late 18thC walnut serpentine chest of drawers, the shaped top above three graduated drawers and a shaped apron, raised on splayed bracket feet.

*42in (105cm) wide*

**$1,800-2,200** | **L&T**

A late 18thC Indo-Portugese rosewood serpentine chest of drawers, with two short and four long drawers, the brass handles stamped "W.I", the apron carved with scrolls and a flowerhead, on bracket feet.

*45.75in (116cm) wide*

**$4,000-6,000** | **DN**

A George III mahogany bowfront chest of drawers, with boxwood stringing, the crossbanded top above two short and three long graduated drawers, on shaped bracket feet.

*32in (80cm) wide*

**$3,000-5,000**　　　　　　**L&T**

A George III mahogany bowfront chest of drawers, with ebony and boxwood stringing, bird's eye maple panel and two short over three long graduated drawers, shaped apron and bracket feet.

*40.75in (102cm) wide*

**$1,800-2,200**　　　　　　**L&T**

A George III mahogany and crossbanded bowfronted chest of drawers, with two short and three long drawers and original handles, raised on splayed bracket feet.

*42.25in (107cm) high*

**$1,200-1,800**　　　　　　**B**

A George III mahogany chest of drawers, of small proportions, with two short and three long drawers, raised on bracket feet.

*31in (79cm) wide*

**$3,000-5,000**　　　　　　**B**

---

A George III mahogany bachelor's chest, the molded top above a baize-lined brushing slide and four long graduated drawers, on bracket feet.

*32in (80cm) wide*

**$4,000-6,000**　　　　　　**L&T**

A George III mahogany bowfront chest, the line-inlaid top above two short and three long drawers, with a shaped apron, on bracket feet.

*42in (105cm) wide*

**$3,000-4,000**　　　　　　**L&T**

A George III mahogany serpentine chest, the molded shaped top above four long graduated drawers, on bracket feet.

*42.75in (107cm) wide*

**$6,000-9,000**　　　　　　**L&T**

A George III mahogany serpentine chest, with four long graduated drawers and a shaped apron, on splayed bracket feet.

*46in (115cm) wide*

**$3,000-5,000**　　　　　　**L&T**

---

A George III mahogany serpentine chest of drawers, the molded shaped top above a brushing slide and four long graduated drawers, on ogee bracket feet.

*48.75in (122cm) wide*

**$8,000-12,000**　　　　　　**L&T**

A George III mahogany secretaire chest of drawers, the fall-front opening to reveal a fitted interior, on bracket feet.

*32in (80cm) wide*

**$1,200-1,800**　　　　　　**SWO**

A George III mahogany chest, with a molded top over two short and three long drawers, flanked with canted corners, on ogee bracket feet.

*36in (90cm) wide*

**$1,200-1,800**　　　　　　**SWO**

A Philadelphia Chippendale mahogany chest of drawers, drawers with cockbeaded edges, flanked by fluted quarter columns, on bold ogee bracket feet, retaining original brasses.

*c1770*          *37.75in (96cm) wide*

**$12,000-14,000**          **POOK**

An 18thC Philadelphia Chippendale mahogany chest of drawers, the top with molded edge above four beaded graduated drawers and molded base with ogee bracket padded feet.

*Provenance: Probably partial descent Elizabeth Buckley (1771-1797) and Luke Wistar Morris (1768-1830) to Samuel Buckley Morris (1791-1859) and Hannah Perot (1792-1831) to one of their three children.*

*40in (100cm) wide*

**$13,000-15,000**          **FRE**

A Massachusetts Chippendale mahogany-finished maple blockfront four-drawer chest, a lip-molded top conforming to the four blockfront drawers, the center of the apron carved with a scallop shell, on bracket feet, old large bat-wing brasses.

*c1770*          *35.5in (89cm) high*

**$45,000-50,000**          **FRE**

A Massachusetts Chippendale mahogany chest of drawers, the case with a serpentine front with four graduated drawers, on straight bracket feet, retaining original bail and rosette brasses.

*c1780*          *40.5in (103cm) wide*

**$11,000-13,000**          **POOK**

A Delaware Valley Chippendale diminutive mahogany low chest of drawers, with a molded edge top above four drawers, flanked by fluted quarter columns, on ogee bracket feet, retains original pierced brasses.

*c1780*          *36in (91.5cm) high*

**$11,000-13,000**          **POOK**

A late 18thC Chippendale cherry chest of drawers, the overhanging top with applied molded edge above a case of four thumb-molded graduated drawers flanked by reeded quarter-columns, ogee bracket feet on platforms, replaced brasses, refinished.

*36in (91.5cm) wide*

**$5,000-8,000**          **SK**

A late 18thC Chippendale walnut chest of drawers, the overhanging top with applied molded edge, a case of four thumb-molded graduated drawers, flanked by reeded quarter-columns all on ogee bracket feet, replaced brasses, refinished, some minor imperfections.

*36in (91.5cm) wide*

**$5,000-8,000**          **SK**

A Chester County Pennsylvania Chippendale walnut chest of drawers, with molded edge top over four drawers, flanked by fluted quarter columns, resting on bold ogee bracket feet.

*c1785*          *37.5in (95.5cm) wide*

**$4,000-6,000**          **POOK**

A late 18thC Chippendale tiger maple chest of drawers, the thumb-molded overhanging top above a case of four scratchbeaded graduated drawers, on ogee bracket feet, old bale brasses, refinished, restoration.

*39in (99cm) wide*

**$10,000-12,000**          **SK**

**FURNITURE**

An 18thC painted chest-over-drawers, the molded lift-top above a double-arch molded case of two graduated false drawers and two working drawers with turned wooden pulls, all on high bracket feet centering a cut-out pendant, original red painted surface.

*37.75in (96cm) wide*

**$9,000-11,000**                    **SK**

A late 18thC Virginia mahogany chest, two-over-four graduated and dovetailed drawers, Williamsburg, Virginia, vertical backboards, full dust panels, secondary wood yellow pine.

*39.25in (98cm) wide*

**$3,000-5,000**                    **BRU**

A late 18thC Chinese-style Virginia walnut chest of drawers, dovetailed drawers with scribed borders, bracket feet, original brass pulls, inlaid kite escutcheons, secondary wood yellow pine, damage and repairs.

*42in (105cm) wide*

**$4,000-6,000**                    **BRU**

A Southern inlaid walnut chest, top with light-wood corner inlay, two-over-three dovetailed drawers with triple dark and light string inlay, inlaid kite escutcheons, shaped skirt with French feet, original brass pulls, cut nails.

*42in (105cm) wide*

**$3,000-5,000**                    **BRU**

A Southern inlaid walnut chest, string inlay with canted corners, hand wrought nails and teardrop inlay, French feet, triple-line inlay on edge of top and at base, brass pulls original, hand wrought nails, small repairs, other separations.

*37in (92.5cm) wide*

**$3,000-5,000**                    **BRU**

A Kentucky swell-front chest, four graduated dovetailed and cockbeaded drawers, original brass pulls, inlaid diamond escutcheons, original yellow pine skirt with cherry veneer, horizontal backboards, feet facings with "V" joints, old refinishing.

*39.5in (99cm) wide*

**$15,000-18,000**                    **BRU**

An inlaid Tennessee cherry chest, originally found in Tate Springs, Tennessee, top with double-string inlay on edges with overhang at back, dovetailed drawers with string inlay, inlaid ivory kite escutcheons, on French feet, shaped skirt, cherry veneers with small band of walnut inlay, original feet.

*40in (100cm) wide*

**$5,000-8,000**                    **BRU**

A cherry sugar chest, dovetailed case, turned legs below dovetailed drawer, lift top with breadboard ends, original lock, secondary wood poplar, original wooden pulls.

*28in (70cm) wide*

**$9,000-11,000**                    **BRU**

A Federal carved mahogany four-drawer chest, attributed to Samuel McIntire (1757-1811) Salem, Massachusetts, a bow-shaped carved molded edge top, corners with stippled tops above floral cornucopia ring-turned, leaf-carved, reeded three-quarter round corners, bow-shaped cockbeaded drawers.

| | |
|---|---|
| c1800 | 44in (110cm) wide |
| **$10,000-12,000** | **FRE** |

Left: A Delaware Valley Federal walnut chest of drawers, the rectangular top over four graduated drawers above a scalloped skirt resting on French feet.

| | |
|---|---|
| c1800 | 39.5in (99cm) high |
| **$2,800-3,200** | **POOK** |

Right: A Mid-Atlantic States Federal cherry bowfront chest of drawers, the four graduated drawers over a scalloped skirt resting on French feet with overall line inlay.

| | |
|---|---|
| c1800 | 43.25in (108cm) wide |
| **$2,800-3,200** | **POOK** |

A Federal mahogany and mahogany veneer reverse serpentine chest of drawers, the shaped thumb-molded overhanging top on a base of four cockbeaded drawers with flanking canted corners, all on bracket feet, old replaced brasses.

| | |
|---|---|
| c1805 | 39in (99cm) wide |
| **$6,000-9,000** | **SK** |

A Western Pennsylvania Federal cherry chest of drawers, case with drawers, over a scalloped skirt, resting on flaring French feet with extensive line and light and dark inlays, retaining original brasses.

| | |
|---|---|
| c1820 | 37.25in (94.5cm) wide |
| **$6,000-9,000** | **POOK** |

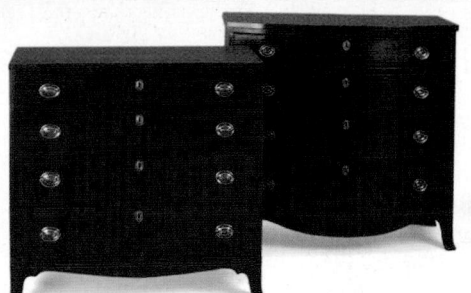

Left: A Pennsylvania Federal mahogany chest of drawers, the rectangular top with line inlay edge, over a case with four cockbeaded drawers, and a line inlay skirt, French feet.

| | |
|---|---|
| c1805 | 39in (99cm) wide |
| **$2,200-2,800** | **POOK** |

Right: A Pennsylvania Federal mahogany bowfront chest, with four long drawers over an inlaid skirt, on French feet.

| | |
|---|---|
| c1805 | 42.5in (108cm) wide |
| **$2,800-3,200** | **POOK** |

An early 19thC Federal mahogany veneer chest of drawers, the bowed top with crossbanded veneered edge overhangs a case of cockbeaded veneered drawers on a molded base with shaped feet, original brass, old refinish.

| | |
|---|---|
| | 41.25in (105cm) wide |
| **$4,000-6,000** | **SK** |

A Federal mahogany inlaid chest of drawers, molded top above four graduated drawers, shaped skirt and French bracket feet.

| | |
|---|---|
| c1800 | 39.25in (98cm) wide |
| **$2,200-2,800** | **FRE** |

An early 19thC Federal cherry inlaid chest of drawers, the bowfront top with string-inlaid edge overhangs a case of inlaid drawers with stringing in outline, quarter fans, and central paterae above a shaped skirt flanked by flaring French feet, replaced brasses, old refinish, repairs.

| | |
|---|---|
| | 42.75in (108.5cm) wide |
| **$3,000-5,000** | **SK** |

An early 19thC Federal cherry chest of drawers, the top with crossbanded edge overhangs a case of four graduated scratchbeaded drawers above a cut-out bracket base, replaced brass, refinished.

| | |
|---|---|
| | 40.25in (103cm) wide |
| **$3,000-5,000** | **SK** |

**FURNITURE**

An early 19thC Scottish mahogany chest of drawers, with boxwood and ebony stringing, the three short and three long cockbeaded drawers flanked by bead and reel angles, on bracket feet.

*49.5in (124cm) wide*

**$700-1,000**    **L&T**

An early 19thC English mahogany chest, the dovetailed and cockbeaded drawers with original brass pulls, full dust panels and horizontal backboards with hand-wrought nails, on original bracket feet with stacked glue blocks.

*44in (110cm) wide*

**$5,000-7,000**    **BRU**

An early 19thC English mahogany chest, the molded top over dovetailed drawers, on original bracket feet.

*38in (95cm) wide*

**$1,800-2,200**    **BRU**

An early 19thC overpainted pine Wellington secretaire chest, with six drawers and a secretaire drawer, opening to reveal an interior fitted with drawers and pigeonholes, enclosed by a hinged lockable faux pilaster, raised on a plinth.

*30.25in (77cm) wide*

**$4,000-6,000**    **L&T**

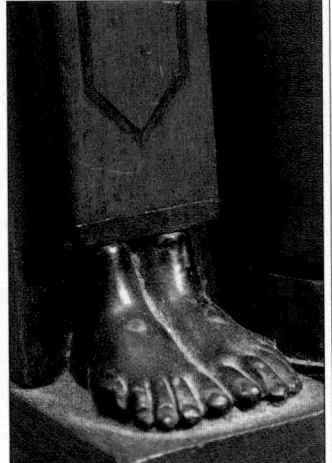

A fine Regency Egyptian Revival mahogany bowfront chest, possibly by Oakley.

*c1815*

**$3,000-5,000**    **BAM**

An early 19thC pitch pine chest of drawers, the rectangular top with a molded edge, above two short and three long graduated drawers, raised on a plinth base.

*48.75in (122cm) wide*

**$1,200-1,800**    **L&T**

A 19thC teak campaign chest, with brass binding and sunken handles, two short and three long drawers, on turned feet, divided into two sections.

*41.25in (103cm) high*

**$2,200-2,800**    **L&T**

A 19thC oak chest of drawers, the rectangular top with a molded edge, above four long graduated drawers with turned ebonized handles, on bracket feet.

*32in (81cm) wide*

**$1,200-1,800**    **L&T**

An unusual mid-19thC French Empire concave secretaire chest, the raised top with one drawer, compartment frieze drawer and two further ivory drawers, flanked by bobbin-turned pilasters, on conforming legs, formerly a dressing chest.

*42in (105cm) wide*

**$3,000-5,000**    **FRE**

A Chester County, Pennsylvania Queen Anne walnut semi-tall chest, the rectangular molded top over a case with raised panel sides and five long drawers, on straight bracket feet.

*c1750*          54.5in (136cm) high

**$12,000-14,000**          **POOK**

A rare Pennsylvania Queen Anne curly maple tall chest, the molded cornice above three over two short and three long drawers, flanked by raised panel sides, over a skirt with central drop supported by straight bracket feet.

*c1760*          59.25in (150.5cm) high

**$4,000-6,000**          **POOK**

A Pennsylvania Chippendale walnut tall chest, the ogee cornice above two rows of dentil molding with drawers flanked by fluted quarter columns, supported by bold ogee bracket feet, original brasses and old dry surface.

*c1770*          66.75in (169.5cm) high

**$17,000-20,000**          **POOK**

A Pennsylvania Chippendale walnut tall chest, the molded cornice above an applied scalloped frieze molding, drawers flanked by fluted quarter columns, supported by ogee bracket feet.

*c1780*          39in (99cm) wide

**$8,000-12,000**          **POOK**

## A CLOSER LOOK AT A QUEEN ANNE CHEST-ON-FRAME

*Tiger maple is also known as curly maple and is prized for its unusual grain.*

*The patina and condition of this piece have much appeal to collectors.*

*Details such as the short cabriole legs with pad feet and the batwing brasses add to the overall appeal of this handsome chest-on-frame.*

*The quality of the timber is one of the most important considerations when assessing the value of chests. This one is of particularly high quality.*

A rare 18thC Queen Anne tiger maple chest-on-frame, with a cove cornice above two short drawers over five long drawers, supported by a frame with short spurred cabriole legs with pad feet, retaining an old if not original dry surface and batwing brasses.

35.75in (91cm) wide

**$30,000-35,000**          **POOK**

A Pennsylvania Chippendale walnut tall chest, possibly from Lancaster County, the molded cornice above drawers, flanked by quarter columns, supported by ogee bracket feet.

*c1780*          64in (162.5cm) high

**$5,000-7,000**          **POOK**

An English George III mahogany chest-on-chest, with three short over three long graduated drawers enclosed by canted and fluted angles, the base with three long graduated drawers, raised on bracket feet.

70.5in (176cm) high

**$2,200-2,800**          **L&T**

An English George III mahogany chest-on-chest, with two short and three long graduated drawers flanked by fluted angles, the base with three long graduated drawers and shaped bracket feet.

73.5in (184cm) high

**$4,000-6,000**          **L&T**

An English George III mahogany chest-on-chest, with graduated drawers flanked by inlaid canted angles, the base with three long graduated drawers raised on bracket feet.

48in (120cm) wide

**$2,200-2,800**          **L&T**

A late 18thC Chippendale walnut tall chest, Pennsylvania, molded cornice above drawers, molded base, tall ogee bracket feet, replaced feet, changed brasses.

*68in (170cm) high*

**$7,000-10,000**  **FRE**

An 18thC Chester County, Pennsylvania Chippendale walnut tall chest, the molded cornice over a fan carved bonnet drawer flanked by drawers flanked by fluted quarter columns, on bold spurred ogee bracket feet.

*59.75in (149cm) high*

**$6,000-9,000**  **POOK**

An 18thC American Chippendale maple tall chest of drawers, the flat molded cornice above a case of drawers all on bracket feet, brasses appear to be original, old red stained surface, minor imperfections.

*36in (91.5cm) wide*

**$9,000-11,000**  **SK**

A late18thC Pennsylvania Chippendale walnut tall chest, the molded cornice above drawers flanked by fluted quarter columns, on ogee bracket feet.

*37.75in (96cm) wide*

**$8,000-12,000**  **POOK**

A late 18thC Chippendale maple tall chest of drawers, the molded cornice above a case of six thumb-molded graduated drawers on bracket feet, replaced brasses, refinished, minor imperfections.

*38in (96.5cm) wide*

**$6,000-9,000**  **SK**

A late 18thC Chippendale walnut tall chest, Pennsylvania, molded cornice above reeded frieze and drawers flanked by fluted three-quarter columns, on a molded base with tall ogee bracket feet, imperfections.

*89in (222.5cm) long*

**$8,000-12,000**  **FRE**

A Federal inlaid mahogany and mahogany veneer chest-on-chest, Mid-Atlantic States, in three parts, the molded cornice and inlaid frieze, horizontally reeded waist band on lower section, shaped skirt and tall bracket feet, repairs, changed brasses.

*c1800*  *78in (195cm) high*

**$4,000-6,000**  **FRE**

A Pennsylvania Federal cherry and mahogany tall chest of drawers, the molded cornice over a case with drawers, on flaring French feet.

*43in (109cm) wide*

**$6,000-9,000**  **POOK**

A Federal walnut inlaid tall chest of drawers, the flat-molded cornice above a case drawers, all with string inlay, escutcheons, vines and vases, on cut-out feet and a shaped skirt centering an inlaid fan, old brass bail pulls, old refinish, imperfections.

*c1800*  *40in (101.5cm) wide*

**$6,000-9,000**  **SK**

An 18thC Chippendale carved tiger maple chest-on-chest, the molded top with flame carved side finials above the raised paneled faux drawers and six thumb-molded working drawers on the lower case of four similar graduated drawers on a molded base with ogee feet, with some dark mahogany stain, some original brass, central finial is a later addition.

38.5in (98cm) wide

**$25,000-30,000** SK

A late 18thC Chippendale maple carved chest-on-chest, the top section with flat-molded cornice above a fan-carved central drawer flanked by two short drawers and four thumb-molded graduated drawers below, set into a lower section of three graduated drawers on tall bracket base, replaced brasses, old refinish, repairs.

73.5in (187cm) high

**$12,000-18,000** SK

A Pennsylvania Chippendale figured walnut chest on frame, the molded cornice drawers flanked by fluted quarter columns, on a base with a scalloped skirt supported by cabriole legs, on ball and claw feet.

*Provenance*: *Descended in the Schoener family of Pennsylvania.*

c1770          69.75in (174cm) high

**$7,000-10,000** POOK

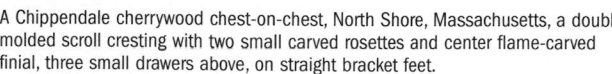

A Chippendale cherrywood chest-on-chest, North Shore, Massachusetts, a double molded scroll cresting with two small carved rosettes and center flame-carved finial, three small drawers above, on straight bracket feet.

*Provenance*: *Descended in the Sewall Family, shipbuilders, and early settlers of Newburyport and Bedford, Massachusetts.*

c1775          86in (215cm) high

**$35,000-40,000** FRE

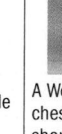

A late 18thC Pennsylvania Chippendale walnut chest-on-chest.

*Provenance*: *Descended in the Danenauer family of Montgomery County, Pennsylvania, to the present owner.*

84in (210cm) high

**$25,000-35,000** FRE

A Western Pennsylvania Federal walnut chest-on-chest, the cornice over three short drawers, the center with a tulip and fan inlays, above two short over two long drawers, base with two drawers and ending in flaring French feet.

c1800          69.75in (174cm) high

**$10,000-12,000** POOK

A Queen Anne maple carved high chest, with scrolled molded cornice, flame-carved finial, upper case with three small drawers, lower case with four long graduated drawers, flat-headed arches, cabriole legs, pad feet, imperfections.

*c1760*                    *84in (213.5cm) high*

**$30,000-35,000**                          **SK**

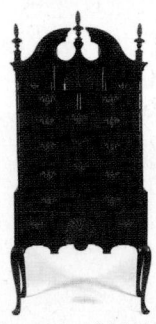

A Queen Anne walnut inlaid high chest, scrolled molded top, concave fan, inlaid small drawers with stringing in outline, lower case of similar drawers, central demi-lune drop flanked by flat headed arches, cabriole legs, pad feet, old refinish, restoration.

*c1735*                    *36in (91.5cm) wide*

**$45,000-50,000**                          **SK**

### A CLOSER LOOK AT A QUEEN ANNE HIGHBOY

*Walnut and mahogany were the woods of choice for Philadelphia Queen Anne and Chippendale carvers and joiners, although curly maple or tiger maple was a viable alternative. This rarity of wood use makes this piece an exceedingly rare example of Queen Anne Delaware Valley furniture.*

*Highboys were a development of the chest-of-drawers. It became a singularly American form after c1730.*

*The original 18thC paper label identifying the original owner, adds to the desirability of this piece.*

An important Delaware Valley Queen Anne tiger maple highboy, the molded cornice above three over two short drawers over three long drawers resting on a base with three over two short drawers above a scalloped skirt resting on squared cabriole legs terminating in Spanish feet, retains its original batwing brasses.

**Provenance**: *Descended in the Howell family and bears an 18thC paper label identifying the original owner as G. Howell.*

*c1760*

*73.5in (184cm) high*

*Spanish feet can also be called 'paintbrush feet' and are a type of feet in which the diagonal grooves suggest the bristles of a brush.*

**$150,000-160,000**                          **POOK**

A Queen Anne cherry high chest of drawers, the molded and scratchbeaded swan's neck crest above a cove-molded frieze drawer, single arch-molded case of drawers, lower section of drawers on valanced skirt, cabriole legs, pad feet on platforms, old brasses, refinished.

*c1770*                    *38in (96.5cm) wide*

**$13,000-15,000**                          **SK**

A rare Delaware Valley Queen Anne tiger maple flat-top highboy with Spanish feet, the upper with projecting stepped cornice over a case with drawers, the lower with mid-molding over drawers, shaped skirt on angular cabriole legs.

*41in (102.5cm) wide*

**$35,000-40,000**                          **NA**

An important Delaware Valley Queen Anne tiger maple high chest in two parts, molded cornice, resting on a lower section with two over two short drawers, above a scrolled apron, squared cabriole legs, crooked feet, retaining its original brass hardware.

*c1755*                    *68.5in (174cm) high*

**$65,000-70,000**                          **POOK**

A Queen Anne tiger maple high chest of drawers, the top section with flat-molded cornice, two thumb-molded short drawers and four long drawers, lower section of long drawer and three short drawers, cabriole legs, pad feet in platforms, old brasses, refinished.

*c1750*                    *38.25in (97cm) wide*

**$17,000-20,000**                          **SK**

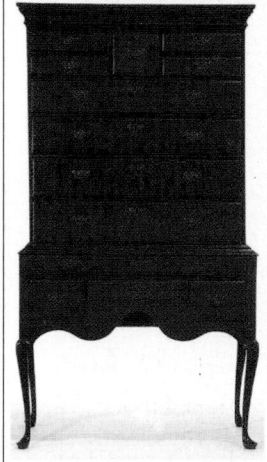

An early 18thC Connecticut Queen Anne maple and tulipwood highboy, the upper half with molded cornice, eight thumb-molded drawers, the lower with molded waist with four thumb-molded drawers, shaped skirt, cabriole legs, pad feet, old repairs.

*73.5in (184cm) high*

**$10,000-15,000**     **FRE**

A Queen Anne maple high chest of drawers, the top section with flat-molded cornice above thumb-molded drawers, set into a lower section of three short drawers joined by a cockbeaded valanced skirt on four cabriole legs ending in pad feet, engraved brasses, refinished.

*c1740*     *35.5in (90cm) wide*

**$13,000-15,000**     **SK**

A Queen Anne cherry carved high chest of drawers, the top section with deep cove-molded cornice and five thumb-molded drawers, lower section of long drawer and fan-carved central drawer, valanced skirt, cabriole legs, pad feet, replaced brasses, refinished, restoration.

*c1750*     *38in (96.5cm) wide*

**$15,000-18,000**     **SK**

A Queen Anne maple high chest of drawers, the top section with flat-molded cornice, upper case of three short thumb-molded drawers and four long drawers, lower section of drawers on cabriole legs, pad feet on platforms, valanced skirt, old replaced brasses, refinished, minor imperfections.

*c1750*     *38.75in (98.5cm) wide*

**$10,000-15,000**     **SK**

A Pennsylvania Queen Anne walnut high chest of drawers, in two parts, the molded cornice above three over two short drawers and three long drawers, lower section with two over two short drawers, a scalloped skirt, cabriole legs, on Spanish brush feet.

*c1760*     *38in (96.5cm) wide*

**$18,000-20,000**     **POOK**

An 18thC cherry highboy, swan's-neck pediment and urn finials, top with lipped and dovetailed drawers, base with frieze drawer above three drawers with shell-carved center drawer, shaped skirt, brass pulls, backboards with original hand-wrought nails, old refinishing, repairs.

*38.5in (96cm) wide*

**$9,000-11,000**     **BRU**

A Philadelphia Chippendale walnut high chest, the broken arch bonnet, drawers flanked by acanthus carved quarter columns, base with a long drawer over three short drawers, the center one with shell carving, acanthus carved cabriole legs, ball and claw feet.

*c1775*

*91in (227.5cm) high*

**$25,000-28,000 POOK**

An 18thC inlaid walnut highboy, Pennsylvania, upper section with molded cornice above three short drawers and four long drawers, the lower section with molded waist, three short drawers and one long drawer, inlaid cabriole legs, ball and claw feet.

*75in (187.5cm) high*

**$3,000-5,000**     **FRE**

A Lancaster County, Pennsylvania Chippendale walnut high chest of drawers, the molded cornice, drawers flanked by fluted quarter columns, a base with one long drawer over two short drawers, a scalloped skirt, cabriole legs with shell-carved knees, ball and claw feet.

*c1785*     *43in (109cm) wide*

**$14,000-16,000**     **POOK**

**FURNITURE**

A late 17thC oak chest on later stand, with paneled drawers, marquetry inlaid with mother-of-pearl and stained wood, the stand with barley twist and blocked legs, linked by stretchers.

*52in (130cm) high*

| $1,200-1,800 | L&T |
|---|---|

An 18thC oak tallboy, with graduated crossbanded drawers, on a base with a central drawer flanked by deeper small drawers, above shaped crossbanded apron and leaf-carved cabriole legs.

*63.25in (158cm) high*

| $3,000-5,000 | L&T |
|---|---|

An early 19thC mahogany campaign dressing chest, the fitted interior above a brushing slide, with a writing slope and an arrangement of drawers, brass carrying handles, on removable turned legs.

| $1,200-1,800 | SWO |
|---|---|

A French marble-top cabinet, with an openwork brass gallery, three drawers, a door opening onto two drawers, and a drop-front drawer concealing two further drawers, extensive geometric light and dark wood inlay.

*c1900*          *54.5in (136cm) high*

| $1,800-2,200 | BRU |
|---|---|

## A CLOSER LOOK AT AN INDO-PORTUGUESE CABINET-ON-STAND

The form and decoration of this cabinet is typical of a type of furniture made in India, probably Goa, under Portuguese patronage.

During the second half of the 17thC, large multiple drawers were very much in fashion in Europe.

High quality furniture of the period is also characterized by intarsia of various types, including seaweed marquetry named after the inlaid interlacing designs and dense arabesques.

The inlay pattern of stars and intersecting circles is recorded and is identical to a cabinet-on-stand in the collection of the Victoria and Albert Museum in London.

A rare late 17thC Indo-Portuguese cabinet-on-stand or contador, teak and rosewood inlaid with ebony and ivory.

*49in (125cm) high*

| $60,000-70,000 | MJM |
|---|---|

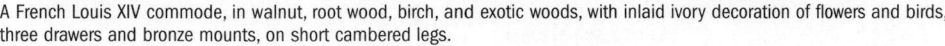

A French Louis XIV commode, in walnut, root wood, birch, and exotic woods, with inlaid ivory decoration of flowers and birds, three drawers and bronze mounts, on short cambered legs.

*c1710*                                                                   52in (130cm) wide

**$70,000-100,000**                                                                 **GK**

A French Louis XV commode, in veneered walnut, ash, and plum wood, of bombé shape with marble top, banding and marquetry and pierced bronze decoration, original locks and keys, on splayed feet.

*c1745*                         49.25in (123 cm) wide

**$5,000-7,000**                                 **KAU**

A mid-18thC Louis XV provincial walnut commode, with three long drawers, raised on squat cabriole legs.

50in (125cm) wide

**$6,000-9,000**                                 **FRE**

A mid-18thC Louis XV kingwood and crossbanded bombé commode, with gilt-bronze mounts, the marbled top over two short and two long drawers, raised on splated legs with sabots.

51in (127.5cm) wide

**$12,000-18,000**                 **FRE**

A kingwood and marquetry inlaid commode, in the French mid-18thC style, the serpentine veined rouge marble top above three drawers, marquetry inlaid with figural panels, on tapering legs and cast sabots.

46in (117cm) wide

**$3,000-5,000**                 **L&T**

A Transitional breakfront commode, in rosewood and satinwood with parquetry and marquetry and decorated with musical instruments, with two drawers and gilded ormolu mounts and sabots, profiled 'Campan rubané' top, signed "Jean Girardau".

*c1775*                 54in (135cm) wide

**$45,000-65,000**                 **GK**

A small Transitional marquetry commode, in rosewood and satinwood and decorated with musical instruments, with a 'Brèche d'Alep' top, two drawers and ormolu mounts and sabots, signed "Louis-Noel Malle".

*c1775*                         31.25in (78cm) wide

**$45,000-65,000**                                 **GK**

**FURNITURE**

A late 18thC Louis XV bombé kingwood and cross banded commode, with gilt-bronze mounts, the marble top over drawers, on square splayed legs and sabots.

*51in (127.5cm) wide*

**$12,000-18,000**  FRE

A good Louis XVI provincial mahogany commode, with drawers carved with drapery, ribbon-tied motifs and paterae, on square tapered legs.

*c1780*  *55in (137.5cm) wide*

**$5,000-7,000**  FRE

A Louis XVI kingwood and gilt-metal mounted commode, the later marble top above a frieze drawer with inlaid faux fluting and two quarter-veneered drawers, on turned tapering legs with cast gilt caps.

*36.5in (93cm) wide*

**$3,000-4,000**  L&T

A pair of French Transitional-style walnut and kingwood-banded commodes, with gilt-metal mounts, the marble tops over four long drawers, on bracket feet ending in sabots.

*28in (70cm) wide*

**$3,000-5,000**  FRE

A Louis XV kingwood marquetry bombé commode, with later gilt-metal mounts, the later marble top above two foliate-inlaid drawers, raised on square cabriole legs ending in sabots.

*57.5in (144cm) wide*

**$1,800-2,200**  FRE

A pair of mahogany Empire-style commodes, the drawers inlaid with sphinx, foliage and reclining females, on squat square tapering legs.

*28in (70cm) wide*

**$2,800-3,200**  FRE

An early 19thC French walnut commode, with a gray veined marble top above three drawers flanked by a cupboard door, applied and inlaid brass stringing, on short square tapering legs.

**$4,000-6,000**  SWO

A Louis XV-style kingwood and cherrywood marquetry commode, with gilt-brass casts mounts, the rouge marble top above drawers, on splayed legs with sabots.

*48.5in (121cm) wide*

**$5,000-8,000**  L&T

A late 19thC Louis XV or Louis XVI gilt-bronze mounted commode, by Gouverneur, in mahogany, tulipwood, and kingwood, the molded marble top over two long drawers veneered with lattice parquetry panels and applied with cast gilt-bronze floral garlands, the hipped legs ending in massive paw feet, the apron applied with foliate scrolls and centered by Bacchic and angel masks, the lock plate signed "Gouverneur Fabricant, 68 Rue Street, Paris".

*67in (167.5cm) wide*

**$90,000-110,000**  FRE

An 18thC Italian and walnut crossbanded commode, with two short and three long drawers raised on bracket feet.

*58in (145cm) wide*

**$8,000-12,000** FRE

A late 18thC Italian walnut commode, crossbanded and boxwood strung, the three drawers with floral marquetry and a marquetry architectural oval, gilt metal lion mask handles and escutcheons, on square tapering legs.

*46.25in (117.5cm) wide*

**$7,000-10,000** DN

An 18thC-style Italian green-painted and parcel gilt bombé commode, the serpentine molded marble top above two drawers, raised on cabriole legs united by a shaped apron.

*58in (145cm) wide*

**$5,000-7,000** FRE

An Italian Neo-classical walnut and marquetry commode, the later marble above three long drawers inlaid with flaring urns, foliate swags and a central circular panel inlaid with two draped maidens and a cupid, raised on square tapered legs.

*c1800* *53in (132.5cm) wide*

**$5,000-7,000** FRE

An early 19thC Italian olive wood and tulipwood crossbanded bedside commode, lift up lid above fall front and fitted interior, square tapering legs.

*31in (79cm) high*

**$4,000-6,000** CATO

A 19thC Italian bombé kingwood parquetry commode, the molded marble top above two checker veneered drawers centered by flower-head motifs, raised on square cabriole legs ending in sabots.

*47in (117.5cm) wide*

**$4,000-6,000** FRE

## LINEN PRESSES

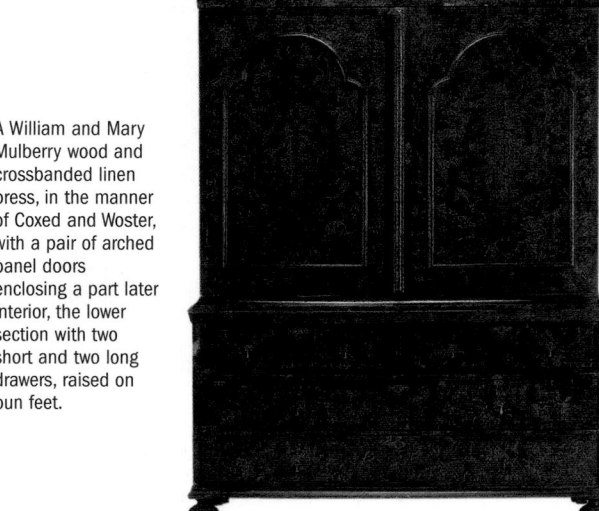

A William and Mary Mulberry wood and crossbanded linen press, in the manner of Coxed and Woster, with a pair of arched panel doors enclosing a part later interior, the lower section with two short and two long drawers, raised on bun feet.

*c1690*

**$25,000-35,000** FRE

A George II mahogany linen press, the dentiled cornice and cavetto frieze above a pair of doors with shaped fielded panels enclosing sliding trays, the base with two short and two long graduated drawers, on cut shaped bracket feet.

*The exposed timber hinges are characteristic of the work of Francis & William Brodie, Cabinet makers in Edinburgh, Scotland.*

*65.25in (163cm) high*

**$3,000-5,000** L&T

185

A Lancaster County, Pennsylvania William and Mary walnut kas, the molded cornice above two paneled doors, flanked by and centering on fluted pilasters, a base with two short drawers above a bold base molding, bun feet.

*c1750*                                      *61.5in (156cm) wide*

**$7,000-10,000**                                          **POOK**

A Philadelphia Queen Anne mahogany linen press, the top section with molded cornice over two recessed panel doors, five sliding shelves, over a lower section, on straight bracket feet, retaining original brasses.

*c1770*                                      *71in (180.5cm) high*

**$12,000-15,000**                                          **POOK**

A Hudson River Valley gumwood kas, the molded cornice resting on a case with two raised paneled doors flanked by and centering on column pilasters, a base with single long drawer resting on bun feet.

*c1780*                                      *77.5in (194cm) high*

**$18,000-20,000**                                          **POOK**

A late 18thC pine and poplar two-part kas, the stepped cornice over two raised panel cupboard doors, flanked by paneled pilasters resting on a base with one long drawer flanked by applied diamond panels, on ebonized bun feet, retaining a 19thC ocher grain decorated surface.

*59.75in (152cm) wide*

**$48,000-52,000**                                          **POOK**

A late 18thC Pennsylvania Federal inlaid cherrywood linen press, in two parts, the upper section with molded cornice above two recessed paneled doors, lower case with four graduated long drawers, on French bracket feet.

*79in (197.5cm) high*

**$7,000-10,000**                                          **FRE**

A late 18thC Pennsylvania walnut kas, the stepped cornice over two recessed panel line inlaid doors, with line and heart inlaid divider, above three over two short drawers, supported by ogee bracket feet.

*c1790*                                      *56in (142cm) wide*

**$15,000-18,000**                                          **POOK**

A Pennsylvania walnut schrank, the molded cornice above a case, with two recessed panel doors with rattail hinges, above three short drawers, supported by flaring French feet.

*c1800*                                      *65.5in (166.5cm) wide*

**$10,000-15,000**                                          **POOK**

A Pennsylvania cherrywood linen press, a flat cove-molded cresting with date, panel doors with inlaid corners and center panel, above four wide cockbeaded drawers, quarter-round fluted corners, on straight bracket feet.

***Provenance:*** *Hattie Klapp Brunner, Reinholds, Pennsylvania, 1940s.*

*1812*                                      *79.5in (199cm) high*

**$20,000-25,000**                                          **FRE**

An early 19thC Federal walnut schrank, the upper section with a dentil molded cornice above two paneled doors, recessed panels and chamfered corners, base with four drawers and flaring French feet.

*c1800*                                      *67.5in (171.5cm) wide*

**$4,000-6,000**                                          **POOK**

A mid-19thC Pennsylvania painted pine wardrobe, the molded cornice above two recessed panel doors, over a single drawer, above a scalloped skirt, bracket feet, retaining its original ocher swirl decoration.

*38.5in (98cm) wide*

**$3,000-5,000**                                          **POOK**

An early Victorian rosewood wardrobe, by John Kendell & Co, with seven long graduated drawers and bowed hanging cupboards with paneled side doors, paper label "J Kendell & Co, No. 96388", workman's signature.

**$4,000-6,000**     **SWO**

A Victorian mahogany breakfront linen press, with an architectural cornice, two paneled doors enclosing slides and two short and three long drawers, within full length double panel doors, on a plinth base.

*96in (240cm) wide*

**$3,000-4,000**     **SWO**

A 19thC mahogany and crossbanded breakfront wardrobe, the molded cornice with boxwood stringing, the central section with two paneled doors above two short and two long graduated drawers, the hanging sections to either side with twin panel doors, on shaped bracket feet.

*81.25in (203cm) wide*

**$3,000-4,000**     **L&T**

An Edwardian mahogany bowfront linen press, with checker and boxwood stringing, the paneled doors enclosing sliding trays, on a base with brushing slide and three long graduated drawers, on splayed bracket feet.

*80.75in (202cm) high*

**$3,000-5,000**     **L&T**

A mid-18thC Louis XV provincial oak armoire à deux corps, with a kingwood and checker banded frieze and shaped fielded paneled doors, the lower section with three central drawers, flanked by two further cupboard doors, on squat cabriole legs.

*92in (230cm) high*

**$8,000-12,000**     **FRE**

A fine Louis XV provincial oak and kingwood banded armoire, with two panel doors centered by star motifs, opening to reveal hanging space, two apron drawers, molded cabriole legs.

*c1780*     *88.5in (221cm) high*

**$5,000-7,000**     **FRE**

### A CLOSER LOOK AT A DUTCH BOMBÉ BURL WALNUT LINEN PRESS

*In the second half of the 17thC there was a demand for domestic furniture, like the linen press. Used to store linen and candles, they are traditionally in walnut or oak and were sometimes commissioned to celebrate a marriage.*

*The influence of the Rococo Movement is evident in the curvaceous and organic form. The Rococo linen press is distinguished by a waved cornice, above serpentine molded panel doors and deep shaped aprons.*

*The division of the form into two parts, with a high waist, was the most important evolution from the 17thC linen press. The doors of the upper section were reduced considerably in size to allow for the introduction of a series of long drawers in the base. This arrangement provided a far more effective means of storage.*

*Look out for alterations. Linen presses have often been converted to make room for a hanging space by removing shelves or by cutting through a top drawer. An unaltered example will command a higher price.*

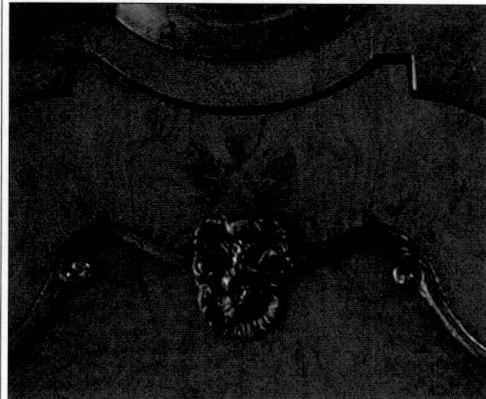

A Dutch bombé burl walnut linen press, the shaped top centered by a shell and scroll carved surmount, below are two shaped panel doors enclosing shelves and five drawers, the lower section with two short and two long drawers, raised on scroll feet.

*c1760*

*68in (136cm) wide*

**$12,000-18,000**      **FRE**

A German oak and marquetry armoire, the molded cornice above a parquetry frieze and sides, the paneled doors and sides inlaid with birds, cartouches and leaves.

*Once owned by Stopford Brooke, who was Chaplain to the Kaiser in the mid-19thC and a friend of William Morris.*

*116in (294cm) wide*

**$5,000-7,000**      **DN**

A French 19thC mahogany dwarf wardrobe, the pagoda top and molded cornice above a frieze drawer, false fronted door and drawers enclosing hanging space, on molded plinth and bun feet.

*71.25in (178cm) high*

**$700-1,000**      **L&T**

A Central European painted pine folk art marriage cupboard, initialed "A.F.R" and dated "Anno 1780".

*Dated 18thC Folk Art furniture of this quality and condition is extraordinarily rare. This example, with fine painted panels depicting the Ages of Man through the symbolic representation of the four seasons, was probably made to commission as a wedding gift for a prominent family.*

| 1780 | 75.75in (189cm) high |
|------|----------------------|
| **$35,000-55,000** | **RY** |

A European painted marriage cupboard, in molded pine, re-dated "1856".

*It was a tradition in rural alpine communities for families to commission cupboards of this type as wedding gifts. Examples such as this were sometimes re-dated to serve as wedding gifts for a subsequent generation.*

| c1830 | 77.5in (194cm) high |
|-------|---------------------|
| **$5,000-8,000** | **RY** |

An Italian 18thC bombé painted commode, with three long drawers, decorated with the 'Arte Povera' technique including relief collages.

| | 32.75in (82cm) high |
|-|---------------------|
| **$8,000-12,000** | **IF** |

A French Directoire semainier, in cherrywood with an oak carcass and a marble top, original painted decoration.

| c1810 | 59.5in (149cm) high |
|-------|---------------------|
| **$8,000-12,000** | **RY** |

A Charles II oak press cupboard or Duodarn, the molded cornice over a foliate-carved frieze dated "1673", the triple panel front carved with fleur-de-lys and scrolls, the two cupboard doors enclosing a void interior, three further cupboard doors, raised on style feet.

*74in (185cm) wide*

**$5,000-7,000**       **FRE**

A small mid-18thC French Provincial walnut armoire, the later cornice over a paneled frieze centered by a flowerhead motif, below are two grill and fielded panel doors, opening to reveal later shelves, on a later shaped plinth base.

*78in (195cm) high*

**$2,800-3,200**       **FRE**

A Swedish Gustavian painted step-back cabinet, with leaf-tip carved cornice molding, two fluted panel cupboard doors and a niche, the lower section with two conforming panel doors, on square fluted and tapered feet.

*c1800*       *101in (252.5cm) high*

**$12,000-18,000**       **EVE**

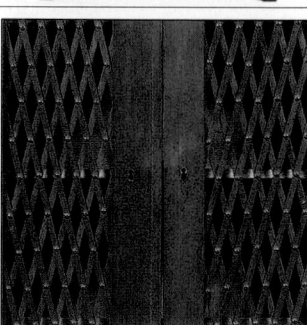

A George III oak press cupboard, the dentil molded cornice over a pair of paneled doors, with two short dummy drawers over two short and one long drawer, on bracket feet.

*52.75in (132cm) wide*

**$1,800-2,200**       **SWO**

A 19thC English three-piece mahogany corner cupboard, the molded cornice above two frame and panel doors, the interior with a faux marble grain-painted face and three dovetailed drawers, the base with two doors, inlaid teardrop escutcheons and vertical pine backboards with rosehead nails, on bracket feet.

*89in (222.5cm) high*

**$5,000-7,000**       **BRU**

An early 19thC Italian walnut bow-front cupboard, in two pieces, the figured walnut top with openwork lattice doors and four interior shelves, the base with a demilune top with conforming doors, on tapered and paneled legs.

*88.5in (221cm) high*

**$3,000-5,000**       **BRU**

## COUNTRY STYLE CUPBOARDS

A late 18thC pine glazed corner cupboard, molded keystone and beaded arch and two hinged arched doors flanked by molded pilasters, lower section of thumb-molded hinged doors flanked by pilasters on flat-molded base, exterior refinished, imperfections.

*58in (147.5cm) wide*

**$4,000-6,000**    **SK**

An early 19thC yellow pine corner cupboard, probably Georgia, double frame-and-panel doors, base with two frame-and-panel doors, original bracket feet, vertical yellow pine backboards with original cut nails, original iron latch, wear, refinishing and losses.

*51in (127.5cm) wide*

**$6,000-9,000**    **BRU**

A Pennsylvania Federal tiger maple corner cupboard, with a glazed upper section above a base with two drawers and two doors, supported by straight bracket feet.

*c1815*    *87in (221cm) high*

**$20,000-25,000**    **POOK**

A Southern pine one-piece corner cupboard, dentil-molded frieze with fan carving, two glazed doors, two recessed panel doors with fan carving, a scalloped skirt resting on bracket feet.

*c1815*    *49in (124.5cm) wide*

**$7,000-9,000**    **POOK**

An inlaid Tennessee corner cupboard, cove-molded inlaid cornice above two six-pane doors framed with rope and tassel inlay, medial molding, doors with through muntins, vertical backboards with original nails, old refinishing, panes reglazed.

*49in (122.5cm) wide*

**$10,000-15,000**    **BRU**

## FORMAL CUPBOARDS

A Pennsylvania Federal cherry two-piece corner cupboard, the dentil molded cornice above two glazed doors, base with matchstick molding over two raised panel doors, on ogee bracket feet.

*c1800*    *84.5in (211cm) high*

**$12,000-18,000**    **POOK**

A Federal cherrywood corner cupboard, flaring cornice above glazed door opening to a painted interior with three shelves on base with recessed paneled doors, shaped apron and bracket feet refinished.

*c1800*    *46in (117cm) wide*

**$5,000-8,000**    **FRE**

A Pennsylvania Federal cherry two-piece corner cupboard, the broken arch crest with inlaid rosettes flanking three urn-turned finials, arched glazed panel door, lower section with tiger maple drawers, over two recessed panel doors, flaring bracket feet.

*c1800*    *42.25in (107.5cm) wide*

**$7,000-10,000**    **POOK**

A Federal walnut inlaid glazed corner cupboard, inlaid plinth above the arched and molded doors, a lower section doors centering inlaid ovals bordered by stringing, inlaid panels on cutout feet and valanced skirt, imperfections, restoration.

*c1800*    *51in (129.5cm) wide*

**$9,000-11,000**    **SK**

A Pennsylvania Federal cherry two-part architectural corner cupboard, the molded cornice over two glazed arched doors flanked by reeded stiles, base with two drawers above two recessed panel cupboard doors, ogee bracket feet.

*c1810*    *101in (252.5cm) high*

**$9,000-11,000**    **POOK**

**FURNITURE**

A late 18thC Chippendale pine cupboard, Pennsylvania, molded cornice and frieze above arched recessed paneled door, recessed paneled door below, bracket base, refinished.

*Provenance*: Hattie Klapp Brunner, Reinholds, Pennsylvania.

*89in (222.5cm) high*

**$2,200-2,800**     **FRE**

An early 19thC walnut cupboard, possibly Piedmont, North Carolina, two frame-and-panel doors above two larger frame-and-panel doors, scalloped skirt with shaped feet, chamfered panels throughout, original brass hinges, old refinishing.

*42in (105cm) wide*

**$2,800-3,200**     **BRU**

---

**A CLOSER LOOK AT A SHAKER CUPBOARD**

The Shakers are a religious community and so named because of their tendency to shake during their lively prayer meetings.

The rich patination as well as the excellent provenance add considerably to the value of this piece.

Many copies of Shaker furniture can be found today. Later examples lack authentic patination.

They made simple, pared-down furniture, rejecting applied ornamentation in favor of clean line and color as can be seen on this example.

A Shaker pine one-piece wall cupboard, the molded cornice over seven drawers over two raised panel cupboard doors, resting on cutout bracket feet.

*Provenance*: Charles Heler Upton, Shaker Museum in Chatham, New York.

*c1820*

**$70,000-75,000**     **POOK**

---

A New England painted pine wall cupboard, the molded cornice over a case with two double recessed panel door and sides, over straight bracket feet, retains old blue painted surface.

*c1820*     *51.5in (131cm) wide*

**$8,000-12,000**     **POOK**

A walnut step cupboard, probably Georgia, probably mid-19thC, top with double-panel doors, sides with reverse-chamfered panels, base with single nailed drawer above two double-panel doors, tapered feet, old refinishing.

*41in (102.5cm) wide*

**$1,800-2,200**     **BRU**

A pie safe, Carter County, Tennessee, shaped back panel above two paneled doors with punched tins with heart and circle decoration, doors with pegged construction, old brown paint with losses, tins with scattered light rust.

*40in (100cm) wide*

**$1,800-2,200**     **BRU**

An eight-tin ash or chestnut pie safe, found in Blountville, Tennessee, molded cornice above two frame-and-panel doors with hand-punched tins, mortise-and-tenon construction, front and molding with later red paint, sides with old peeling brown paint, tins with scattered rust.

*52in (130cm) wide*

**$2,200-2,800**     **BRU**

A Queen Anne giltwood and gesso pier glass, with two beveled mirror plates in an arched shell and harebell molded frame.

*75.25in (188cm) high*

$6,000-9,000     **L&T**

An English Trumeau mirror, probably early 18thC, painting with village scene, losses to paint and silvering.

*50in (125cm) high*

$2,800-3,200     **BRU**

A Queen Anne mahogany looking glass, the scalloped crest with a gilt shell, over a rectangular mirror plate with a gilt liner.

*c1755*     *42.5in (106cm) high*

$2,800-3,200     **POOK**

A late 18thC Danish Louis XVI giltwood mirror frame, with a beaded inner edge and a leaf carved outer edge, surmounted by a carved ribbon crest.

*29in (72.5cm) high*

$5,000-7,000     **EVE**

A late 18thC Russian Neo-classical brass-inlaid mahogany mirror, the flat frame with a Greek key brass inlay, and a flat frieze with a brass arch inlay, the corners with gilt metal mounts.

*43.5in (109cm) high*

$8,000-12,000     **EVE**

A large Regency-style convex wall mirror, the circular plate within reeded ebonized slip and gilt, the ebonized frame with ball spacers.

*47.5in (119cm) diam*

$1,800-2,200     **L&T**

A Regency giltwood mirror, the molded cornice with ball spacers, the original plate flanked by latticework columns with shell cresting.

*43.5in (109cm) high*

$2,800-3,200     **L&T**

A pair of late 18th to early 19thC English mirrors, in the Chinese style, the top panels with raised and painted decoration of figures in a landscape, on red ground.

*56in (140cm) high*

$12,000-18,000     **BRU**

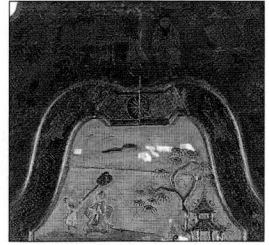

A 19thC European looking glass, the carved wood and gesso frame with an openwork wreath pediment and leaf and berry decoration, mahogany backboard.

*32in (80cm) high*

$500-700     **BRU**

A Regency giltwood and gesso convex mirror, with an eagle surmount and sea serpent flanks, the leaf-carved frame with ball spacers, issuing twin wire branch sconces with crystal nozzles.

*40in (100cm) wide*

$5,000-7,000     **L&T**

A Chippendale mahogany looking glass, the scrolled crest with gilt phoenix and foliate carved appliqués, above a rectangular plate with a gilt liner, flanked by gilded floral drops, over a scalloped base.

c1780      48.5in (123cm) high

**$3,000-5,000**      **POOK**

A New York Chippendale mahogany mirror, the urn and floral finial above a broken arch crest with floral rosettes, above an oval inlaid moth, over a line-inlaid frame flanked by floral and leaf appliqués, over a scrolled base.

c1780      58.5in (148.5cm) high

**$5,000-8,000**      **POOK**

An American Chippendale mahogany and giltwood constitution mirror, the broken arch crest with carved rosettes, centering a shell finial over a rectangular mirror plate, flanked by pierced oval stiles, above a base with shell appliqué.

c1780      55.25in (140.5cm) high

**$9,000-11,000**      **POOK**

A Federal giltwood mirror, the molded cornice over a foliate carved frieze, over an églomizé landscape panel, flanked by a fluted and turned half columns, beveled plate.

c1790      42.5in (108cm) high

**$2,800-3,200**      **POOK**

A late 19thC American carved and giltwood mirror, the crest with oval plaque with wheatsheaf, flanked by bellflower chain drops, mirror with floral carved frame, above a fruit and foliate carved base.

14.75in (37.5cm) high

**$1,200-1,800**      **POOK**

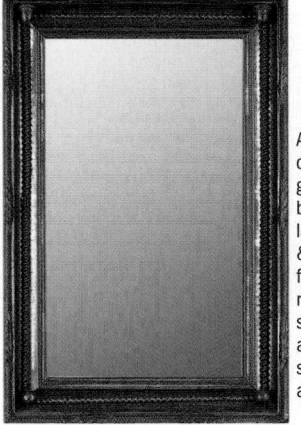

A Federal carved and giltwood mirror, bearing the label of "Earps & Co", with foliate and rope turned surround with acorn and spherule appliques.

c1825      17.75in (45cm) wide

**$1,200-1,800**      **POOK**

An early 19thC Classical carved giltwood and ebonized looking glass, the turned split-baluster frame encloses panel with basket of fruit.

18in (46cm) high

**$700-1,000**      **FRE**

A Federal gilt wood mirror, by Hosea Dugliss, New York, an eagle on a rocky perch, shaped acanthus leaf plinth, beaded frame with an églomisé tablet of musical instruments, imperfections.

*Backboard bears label of maker, "Hosea Dugliss Looking Glass, Manufacturer, 11 Chatham Row, between Ann Street and the Park Theatre, New York."*

c1815

**$15,000-18,000**      **SK**

An early 19thC circular gilt framed Federal mirror, a large spread-wing eagle on rocky crag with a chain and two acorns in his beak, the circular deep molded frame decorated with beads, acorns and composite leaf molding, beveled-edge glass.

40in (100cm) high

**$3,000-5,000**      **FRE**

An early 19thC Classical carved giltwood girandole mirror, with deer on rocky outcrop on foliate scrollwork and molded mirror surround enclosing reeded liner and mirror plate flanked by curving candle arms, foliate scrolled pendant, repairs, some losses and regilded.

37in (94cm) high

**$3,000-5,000**      **FRE**

A Regency giltwood and gesso convex wall mirror, the circular mirror plate in reeded ebonized slip and a ball molded frame, surmounted by an eagle and foliate scrolls, still leaf carving to the base.

*49.5in (124cm) high*

**$5,000-8,000**     **L&T**

A massive Philadelphia carved and gilded mirror, with a flower and ears of corn frame, ending in winged griffins.

*c1845*     *141in (352.5cm) high*

**$30,000-50,000**     **POOK**

A Regency carved giltwood convex wall mirror, the circular mirrored plate with a reeded ebonized slip and ball molded frame, surmounted by a dragon, flanked by two sea serpents, above a leaf carved apron.

*c1815*     *46in (115cm) high*

**$7,000-10,000**     **FRE**

A German Biedermeier wall mirror, in cherry wood veneer, the ebonized columns with gilded bases and capitals, supporting a cornice and pediment, the central brass mount depicting the goddess Diana.

*c1825*     *68in (170cm) high*

**$1,200-1,800**     **BMN**

A 19thC Italian giltwood wall mirror, in carved pine and white gesso, with a red paint undercoat and gilt surface.

*26.75in (67cm) high*

**$3,000-4,000**     **CATO**

A 19thC giltwood convex mirror, the circular plate within ebonized reeded slip and rope-twist frame, eagle surmount and floral pendent, two spiral wire sconces with cut glass drip trays.

*31.5cm (79cm) high*

**$2,200-2,800**     **L&T**

A 19thC giltwood and gesso convex mirror, of Adam style, with a molded frame surmounted by a gadrooned urn, the lower section with a green jasperware Wedgwood-style plaque.

*30in (75cm) high*

**$1,200-1,800**     **L&T**

A 19thC Italian Neo-classical-style giltwood and gesso pier mirror, decorated in relief with a classical scene, the beveled plate within a scale molded frame.

*74in (185cm) high*

**$3,000-5,000**     **FRE**

A Victorian carved giltwood and gesso overmantel mirror, the frame with curved canted angles, Neo-classical husk and guilloche and grotesque decoration, inset velvet border.

*54.5in (138cm) high*

**$2,800-3,200**     **L&T**

An early 20thC Empire-style buffet mirror, in three panels, with half columns and corner bosses, traces of original gilding, losses and chips, replaced mirrors.

*64in (160cm) wide*

**$500-700**                    **BRU**

One of a pair of Indian carved hardwood hall mirrors, each decorated with a bird crest, the frames with foliate scrolls and flowers, now painted white.

*60.25in (153cm) high*

**$700-1,000 pair**              **DN**

## A CLOSER LOOK AN ITALIAN MICRO MOSAIC MIRROR

The link between this piece and a prominent glassmaker like Salviati, who helped to revitalize the Venetian glass industry in the 19thC, adds considerable value to this mirror.

The exquisite quality and precision of decoration, seen in the micro mosaic, is extremely desirable to collectors.

The depiction of popular Venetian sites, such as one of the columns of San Marco and the first floor arcading of the Palazzo Ducale, would be attractive to any Venetian or Murano glass enthusiast.

Replacing glass should be avoided, as this will reduce value. If the glass is cloudy it may be possible to have it re-silvered. A mirror with original glass and little sign of repair commands a premium.

A late 19thC Italian walnut framed micro mosaic mirror, possibly by Salviati of Venice, with rectangular beveled plate, the lugged frame decorated with scenes of Venice and relief molded foliate sprays.

*70in (175cm) high*

**$20,000-25,000**                                    **L&T**

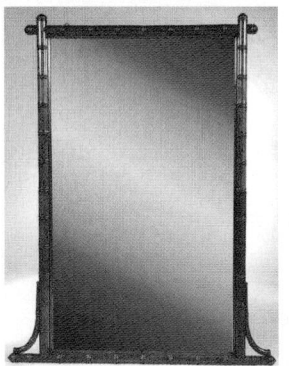

A faux bamboo overmantel mirror, of rectangular form with curved brackets to the base.

**$1,200-1,800**          **L&T**

A William and Mary-style oyster veneered mirror, the rectangular plate in bolection molded frame.

*31.25in (78cm) high*

**$700-1,000**            **L&T**

An American or English giltwood mirror, with a spread-winged eagle crest atop a molded cornice with spherules.

*c1810*      *52in (132cm) high*

**$7,000-10,000**        **POOK**

An American or English giltwood convex mirror, with a spread-winged eagle pediment and two girondole arms.

*c1800*      *40in (100cm) high*

**$12,000-18,000**       **POOK**

A pair of walnut and marquetry mirrors, the beveled plates with foliate and scroll inlaid frames.

*29.5in (74cm) wide*

$800-1,200     **FRE**

A pair of European gilt bronze wall mirrors, surmounted by an oval medallion with ribbon-tied drapery and flanked by two cherubs, the beveled plates within pierced frames.

*34in (85cm) high*

$2,200-2,800     **FRE**

An oval oak gilt-framed mirror, mounted with gilt composition figures, the pediment with an angel and oval coat of arms.

*58in (145cm) wide*

$4,000-6,000     **BRU**

A Regency mahogany cheval mirror, with a molded swing frame, ring turned supports and hipped reeded scroll legs with cast brass sabots and castors, later rectangular beveled plate.

*25.75in (65.5cm) wide*

$1,800-2,200     **WW**

A Regency mahogany cheval mirror, with reeded uprights and Greek key decorated top, the sides with brass candle holders, on reeded saber legs ending in brass caps and castors.

*32in (80cm) wide*

$5,000-7,000     **L&T**

A 19thC French rosewood cheval mirror, with a rectangular glass on turned columns and downswept legs united by a turned stretcher.

$5,000-8,000     **SWO**

A mahogany rectangular cheval mirror, the crossgrained frame flanked by molded supports with brass sphere finials, on downswept square section legs with brass terminals and castors.

*61.5in (154cm) high*

$1,200-1,800     **DN**

A Regency faux bamboo dressing mirror, painted in black and gray on a green ground, the rectangular plate supported by turned and blocked uprights, on corresponding trestle base with bun feet.

*24.5in (61cm) high*

$600-900     **L&T**

An early 19thC mahogany and boxwood strung mirror, the oval plate on stepped supports, the bowfronted base with three drawers, on ogee bracket feet.

*22.5in (56cm) high*

$500-700     **DN**

A Victorian walnut and gilt-metal mounted toilet mirror, with serpentine uprights, on a crossbanded serpentine base inlaid with strapwork marquetry, serpentine apron and cast scrolling feet.

*28in (71cm) wide*

$2,800-3,200     **L&T**

An Edwardian Chippendale-style giltwood dressing mirror, within a molded frame supported by fluted and turned leaf-carved uprights with acorn finials, on cabriole legs with scroll toes.

*36.75in (92cm) wide*

$300-500     **L&T**

A pair of Regency framed Chinoiserie canvas panels, each depicting an Oriental gentleman in garden setting on black ground, within gilt scrolled border.

*78.5in (196cm) high*

$5,000-8,000    L&T

A pair of late Regency rosewood pole screens, each with gilt brass pole supporting screen with gros point floral tapestry, on triform base and scrolling feet.

*14.5in (36cm) wide*

$4,000-6,000    CATO

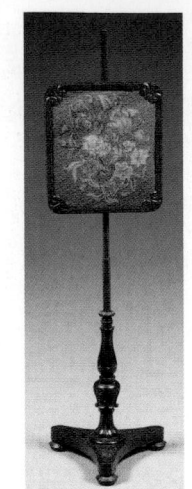

A Regency rosewood pole screen, with floral needlepoint, turned and shaped standard above a footed base, the veneer with chips.

*51.5in (129cm) high*

$300-500    BRU

A William IV rosewood pole screen, the banner inset with a woolwork panel, on a turned and lappet carved column, with a concave base on paw feet.

*59.5in (149cm) high*

$700-1,000    DN

A 19thC four-fold Chinoiserie screen, decorated with panels of domestic scenes and vases of flowers, a border of birds and scrolling vine, the reverse with monochrome decoration.

*72in (183cm) high*

$700-1,000    L&T

A 19thC Louis XVI-style painted and giltwood four-fold screen, depicting figures in a church.

*28in (70cm) wide*

$7,000-10,000    FRE

A 19thC Dutch marquetry walnut fire screen, the shaped top inlaid with figures, exotic birds, insects, and scrolling foliage, above a pleated fabric panel, raised on downswept legs.

*49.5in (124cm) high*

$2,800-3,200    FRE

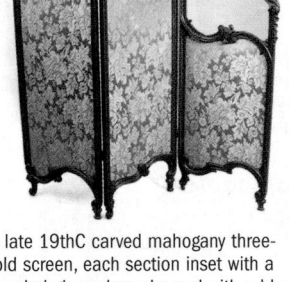

A late 19thC carved mahogany three-fold screen, each section inset with a beveled glass shaped panel with a blue silk lined panel below.

*61.25in (153cm) high*

$800-1,200    SWO

A pair of early 20thC Edwardian painted fire screens, the cartouche shaped panels painted with draped classical maidens and cherubs, raised on tripod bases.

*61.5in (154cm) high*

$2,800-3,200    FRE

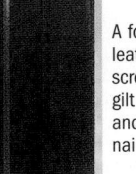

A four-fold leather screen, with gilt tooling and brass nailing.

*79.5in (199cm) high*

$1,000-1,500    L&T

A four-fold Spanish polychrome gilt leather screen, each fold with a serpentine top, gilt nailing.

*82.5in (206cm) high*

$3,000-5,000    L&T

A George III mahogany silver table, the rectangular top with a dished edge and cusped corners, raised on cabriole legs with ball and claw feet.

*37.35in (93cm) wide*

**$3,000-5,000** **L&T**

A Regency rosewood center table, the circular top with plain frieze raised on bulbous octagonal column and concave triform base with paw feet and brass castors.

*51.25in (128cm) diam*

**$3,000-4,000** **L&T**

**A CLOSER LOOK AT A REGENCY CENTER TABLE**

*This table has a tilt-top, an ingenious device that allowed circular tables to double up as a firescreen or to be stored neatly and compactly.*

*A true center table is one without a specific purpose; designed purely to furnish the space in the middle of a room and to be the center of attention. Therefore the center table's function is largely ornamental.*

*Round and oval tables tend to be more popular than rectangular tables – as a result many table tops have been reshaped. Look out for poor reshaping, a lack of signs of real wear to the outside edges, or a top that is too small for its base. An original and unaltered center table, like this piece, is worth considerably more.*

*The luxurious brass inlay and brass foliate banding typifies the rich ornamentation of the Regency style. This can also be seen on the reeded stem and the fine ram's head cappings and castors.*

A Regency rosewood and brass inlaid center table, the circular tilt-top with brass foliate banding, reeded stem and four bold S-scroll supports with fine rams head cappings and castors.

*48.5in (123cm) diam*

**$28,000-35,000** **CATO**

A Classical carved veneered rosewood center table, ten-facet pedestal terminating in rosewood petals on a platform with rosewood veneered rays ending in a molded edge above the three carved paw feet flanked by carved scrolled returns.

*c1830* *55in (140cm) diam*

**$4,000-6,000** **SK**

A Rococo Revival carved rosewood and marble 'turtle top' center table, the serpentine marble molded top on beaded apron carved with leafage and flowers, the cabriole legs with floral swags, scrolling stretchers centering a leaf-carved and beaded turned pendant.

*c1850* *48in (122cm) wide*

**$6,000-9,000** **FRE**

A late 19thC Victorian Aesthetic ebonized and marquetry center table, attributed to Herter Brothers, New York, inlaid with foliage and a musical trophy, on four turned legs.

**$3,000-5,000**   FRE

An early 20thC mahogany center table, in the manner of Robert Lorimer, the oval top raised on scrolling trestle supports joined by a central cross-frame.

*58in (145cm) wide*

**$2,200-2,800**   L&T

A Victorian Grecian Revival marquetry and ebonized center table, attributed to Herter Brothers, New York, inlaid with a marquetry musical trophy panel and decorated with gilt incised graffito work, raised on elaborate carved trestle supports joined by a turned stretcher, on bun feet with recessed castors.

*c1880*

**$8,000-12,000**   FRE

A Blackamoor and simulated marble table, the geometric top inlaid with flowerhead motifs within a Greek key border, raised on twin figural carved end supports.

*72in (180cm) wide*

**$5,000-7,000**   FRE

An early 19thC Austrian Neo-classical thuya wood and kingswood veneer center table, the circular top above a waisted support, raised on giltwood paw feet.

*51in (127.5cm) diam*

**$12,000-18,000**   FRE

A pair of Louis XV-style mahogany and gilt-bronze mounted center tables, the white marble inset tops above a shaped frieze with lions' mask motifs, raised on square cabriole legs ending in sabots.

*23in (57.5cm) wide*

**$1,800-2,200**   FRE

A Louis XV-style malachite and bronze center table, the circular top supported by a figural column modeled as the Three Graces, ending in three claw feet and a triform base.

*35in (87.5cm) high*

**$15,000-20,000**   FRE

A Louis XV-style marble and gilt-bronze Sèvres-style porcelain table, the top inset with transfer-printed porcelain panels depicting lovers, centered by a panel of Louis XV, the turned marble column and triform base applied with gilt-bronze mounts.

*45in (112.5cm) diam*

**$10,000-15,000**   FRE

A French Empire-style mahogany and specimen marble center table, raised on a bulbous turned column support ending in five outswept legs with flowerhead motifs.

*36in (90cm) diam*

**$5,000-7,000**  **FRE**

A Charles X mahogany and marble center table, the circular reeded top above a wavy frieze on three reeded turned supports ending in downswept legs with paw feet.

*41.5in (104cm) diam*

**$5,000-7,000**  **FRE**

A 19thC French carved giltwood and gesso center table, the top with a faux marble inset supported by three cherubs and a naturalistic hexagonal base.

*From an important Hollywood studio.*

*34in (85cm) wide*

**$7,000-10,000**  **FRE**

A 17th to 18thC Italian walnut table, the hexagonal top raised on a baluster turned column and three scale-carved scroll feet.

*30.5in (76cm) high*

**$10,000-15,000**  **FRE**

A Russian mahogany and parcel-gilt center table, the octagonal top above a conforming frieze, raised on curved supports with gilded eagle heads, on gilded ball and paw feet ending with a concave quatrepartite plinth base.

*c1825*  *41.75in (104cm) diam*

**$15,000-20,000**  **EVE**

A 19thC Russian birch center table, the marble top with a raised rim and reeded edge above a chamfered frieze and leaf-clasped column, with three anthropomorphic legs and paw feet with sunken castors.

*38.75in (97cm) diam*

**$2,200-2,800**  **L&T**

A Swedish Neo-classical birchwood pedestal table, the top with a conforming apron, on a waisted stem and concave tripartite base ending in scrolled feet.

*c1830*  *30.75in (77cm) high*

**$12,000-18,000**  **EVE**

A Swedish Biedermeier birch circular table, raised on a column support and four feet.

*c1835*  *33.5in (85cm) diam*

**$5,000-7,000**  **LANE**

A 19thC Swedish Gustavian-style painted center table, with a bead and leaf frieze and paneled rosette corners, the laurel leaf swags between tapered fluted legs headed with leaf banding and ending with acanthus leaves.

*34.75in (87cm) wide*

**$5,000-7,000**  **EVE**

One of a pair of Neo-classical-style marble and gilt-bronze center tables, each with two graduated tiers supported by scaly cast scroll legs headed by rams' masks and terminating in hairy hoof feet.

*30in (75cm) wide*

**$7,000-10,000 pair**  **FRE**

# The Bicentennial Pennsylvania Sale 11/19 & 20/05

Even as Freeman's extends our reach to the four corners of the globe, the fact remains that Pennsylvania items sell best in Pennsylvania. Just as our Paintings Department has established Freeman's as the country's premier auction house for Pennsylvania Impressionists with the annual Pennsylvania Academy of the Fine Arts sale, so will Americana, Books, and 20th Century Design with Pennsylvania origins find the country's best auction platform at Freeman's.

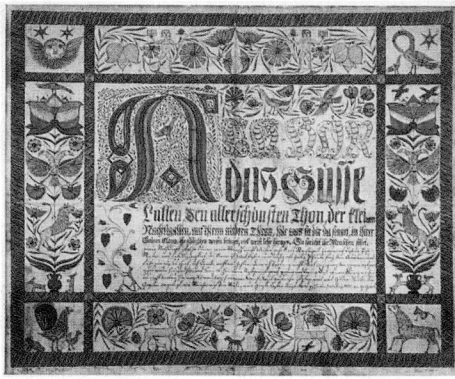

**George Nakashima
Burl oak coffee table**
Sold for $35,250

**Fraktur, A verse from A Hymn to the Nightingale, Rev. George Geistweite**
Sold for $366,750
**WORLD RECORD**

**Philadelphia Queen Anne Transitional Side Chair**
Sold for $336,000

From Pennsylvania German fraktur to early Philadelphia ceramics to the remarkable 20th century craftsmanship of Samuel Yellin and George Nakashima, many world records for Pennsylvania masterpieces already reside at Freeman's. With the establishment of this annual Pennsylvania Auction we have a singular aim - to elevate awareness of and prices achieved for work with Pennsylvania origins - and to replicate on a regular basis the boast very few auction houses have ever been able to make. . .

**More World Records than Unsold Lots**

. . .just as we were able to do after our December 2003 Fine Paintings auction, a sale in which new world auction records outpaced unsold lots by a ratio of three to one.

Our team of specialists in the above fields is ready to examine and appraise items on behalf of clients throughout North America and, through our partners at Lyon & Turnbull, throughout Europe.

To arrange for an appointment with one of our Pennsylvania specialists, please contact Stephanie Welch at 215.563.9275, ext. 3032 or pennsylvania@freemansauction.com

**Gothic writing table by Samuel Yellin**
Sold for $57,500
**WORLD RECORD**

**Glazed and slip-decorated redware jar, dated 1790**
Sold for $56,400

## A CLOSER LOOK AT A EUROPEAN WALNUT TABLE

This luxurious walnut table is richly decorated with seaweed marquetry, oyster veneering, and ivory and ebony starbursts. The quality in ornamentation in this example makes it a particularly desirable piece.

This table has been executed in a 17thC style. The bun feet, spiral turned legs, X-stretcher, and seaweed marquetry were all popular features. These characteristics were adopted in the 19thC, when all-things 'Jacobethan' enjoyed a revival.

It is common for rosewood or calamander crossbanding and decorative inlay to have been added at a later date, as this will boost the table's commercial appeal. Therefore examine the table carefully: a table with original crossbanding will command a higher price.

Oyster veneering is so-called because the grain resembles an oyster shell. This type of veneering was executed by slicing the veneer transversely across the end grain of smaller branches.

A European walnut table in the 17thC style, with panels of seaweed marquetry and oyster veneers, with an ivory and ebony starburst to each corner, rosewood crossbanding and checker bands, on spirally turned legs and bun feet.

*80in (200cm) long*

**$2,800-3,200**　　　　　　　　　　　　　　　　　　　　　　　　**DN**

A mid-19thC European giltwood center table, the serpentine veined carrara marble top above a scrolling frieze carved with alternate shell and floral cartouches, supported on cabriole legs with foliate carving and linked by molded stretchers centered by a leafy rosette.

*57.5in (146cm) wide*

**$15,000-20,000**　　　　　　　　　**L&T**

A 19thC European ebonized carved center table, the circular top raised on three crane form supports, terminating on a triform base with bun feet.

*23in (57.5cm) diam*

**$1,200-1,800**　　　　　　**FRE**

Pietre Dure, an Italian term meaning hardstones, was traditionally used in ancient Rome, and later in the Renaissance period. As a result of the 19thC Renaissance Revival, Italian furniture of the late 1860s and 1870s often features pietre dure such as the lapis lazuli and black marble seen here.

This scene shows the Temple of Vespasian in the Roman Forum, and the extraordinary precision and detail in its execution is evident. These exquisite micro mosaic tables were widely exported during the 19thC and today a piece of this quality, in such a good condition, is extremely valuable.

The Doves of Pliny motif was a popular design in Italy. It is named after an ancient mosaic by Sosos of doves on the rim of a drinking bowl, mentioned by Pliny the Elder as 'the finest ever found.'

A late 19thC Italian micromosaic table top, centered with the Doves of Pliny, encircled with eight scenes of ancient Roman structures including the Panthenon, the Arch of Titus, the Capitoline Hill, the Colosseum, St. Peter's Basilica and Square, the Temple of Vespasian in the Roman Forum, the Tomb of Cecilia Metella, and the Temple of Vesta, with three bands of lapis lazuli or African Blue, within an outer Greek key border, on a black marble ground, later black marble base.

*32.75in (83cm) diam*

**$50,000-70,000**

**DN**

A rare Regency rosewood, ebonized and parcel gilt console table in the manner of George Smith, the mottled red marble top above twin animal legs, the supports united by a foot board.

*49.5in (126cm) wide*

**$20,000-30,000** **CATO**

A Scottish Regency mahogany side table, in the manner of William Trotter, the veined white marble top with ledge back, above twin scrolling front consoles carved with acanthus leaves and with bead and reel panels, raised on a plinth with bead and reel moldings.

*46.5in (118cm) wide*

**$4,000-6,000** **L&T**

A William IV mahogany pier table, the top with a molded edge above a crossbanded frieze with gilt molding, raised on octagonal spreading columns and a mirrored back, on a platform base with pad feet.

*39.25in (98cm) wide*

**$4,000-6,000** **L&T**

An early Victorian rosewood and scagliola-topped console table, with two scrolled consoles, each carved with acanthus leaves, mirrored back, raised on a plinth base.

*44.5in (113cm) wide*

**$7,000-10,000** **L&T**

A pair of New York Classical mahogany and Atlantic white cedar pier tables, marble tops with cut corners, frame with acanthus corners, two dolphin supports and a mirror back, over a scalloped base resting on foliate carved feet.

*c1815* *52.5in (133.5cm) wide*

**$12,000-15,000** **POOK**

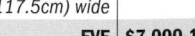

A late 18th to early 19thC Swedish Neo-classical worn giltwood and painted console, the rectangular faux marble top above a foliate and bird painted frieze, raised on fluted supports ending with a faux marble stepped plinth base.

*47in (117.5cm) wide*

**$12,000-18,000** **EVE**

A pair of Charles X mahogany console tables, each rounded rectangular marble top over an ogee molded frieze drawer, raised on scroll supports ending in a shaped platform base, with carved claw feet.

*42in (105cm) wide*

**$7,000-10,000** **FRE**

A Queen Anne maple drop-leaf table, the half-round hinged leaves flank serpentine skirts above cabriole legs ending in pad feet, old refinish, minor imperfections.

43in (109cm) wide

**$10,000-15,000**    **SK**

A mid-18thC Queen Anne figured walnut inlaid drop-leaf dining table, the top with thumb-molded edge is outlined in stringing, hinged leaves flanking serpentine shaped skirts, the cabriole legs, pad feet, old surface, imperfections.

c1750    42in (106.5cm) wide

**$12,000-14,000**    **SK**

### A CLOSER LOOK AT A DROP-LEAF TABLE

To provide sufficient strength for the solid drop-leaves, the central section is firmly secured to the table frame by numerous glueblocks and often by tenoned joints.

The large American sycamore supplies a hardwood popular for use in carpentry or furniture. Copies and fakes are about. Look for original wood and joints.

Gateleg tables are characterized by their hinged action, which enables flaps to be rotated through 90 degrees.

Gateleg tables are more robust in construction than cabriole-legged drop-leaf tables.

A William and Mary maple, sycamore, and pine gateleg table, the circular drop-leaf top on block, vase, and ring-turned legs, turned feet joined by a beaded apron with drawer and block, case and ring-turned stretchers, old refinish, imperfections.

c1715    42.5in (108cm) diam

**$20,000-25,000**    **SK**

A Queen Anne maple and tiger maple drop-leaf table, the square overhanging top on block turned tapering legs ending in pad feet on platforms joined by a straight skirt, refinished.

c1750    35.75in (91cm) wide

**$3,000-5,000**    **SK**

A Queen Anne birch tea table, the oval drop-leaf overhanging top on four cabriole legs, pad feet joined by a valanced skirt, refinished, minor imperfections.

c1750    35.75in (91cm) wide

**$6,000-9,000**    **SK**

An early 18thC William and Mary figured maple butterfly table, the circular drop-leaf overhanging top on splayed block, vase, and ring-turned legs, turned stretchers centering shaped supports for the leaves, refinished, minor height loss.

40in (101.5cm) diam

**$17,000-20,000**    **SK**

A Queen Anne walnut dining table, the molded edge top, with hinged demi-lune leaves, block and swelled turned straight legs ending in pad feet, old finish, imperfections.

*57.75in (146.5cm) extended width*

**$6,000-9,000**  **SK**

A mid-to-late 18thC Queen Anne mahogany drop-leaf table, the top with hinged square leaves which flank shaped skirts and block and turned legs ending in pad feet, old refinish, repaired.

*51.5in (131cm) wide*

**$4,000-6,000**  **SK**

A Salem, Massachusetts Chippendale mahogany dining table, with drop leaves over a scalloped skirt, on cabriole legs ending in ball and claw feet.

*c1780*  *52.25in (128cm) wide*

**$6,000-9,000**  **POOK**

A Pennsylvania Chippendale walnut drop-leaf table, the top over a scalloped skirt, supported by cabriole legs terminating in ball and claw feet.

*49in (124.5cm) wide*

**$3,000-5,000**  **POOK**

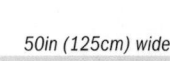

An Irish Chippendale mahogany hunt table, with a drop-leaf top, supported by eight square legs with beaded edges.

*c1780*  *78in (198cm) wide*

**$8,000-12,000**  **POOK**

A George III mahogany drop-leaf dining table, the central legs opening to support the extending leaves, on slight cabriole legs and pad feet.

*50in (125cm) wide*

**$800-1,200**  **SWO**

A George III-style mahogany drop-flap table, the top with reeded edge above a frieze and four club legs with reeded panel terminals and brass club feet.

*57.5in (144cm) wide*

**$1,200-1,800**  **L&T**

A George III mahogany drop-leaf table, the oval top raised on four club legs with pad feet.

*64.75in (162cm) wide*

**$6,000-9,000**  **L&T**

A large modern mahogany 'wake' table, with two leaves opening to an oval, on eight legs.

*90.75in (227cm) wide*

**$2,200-2,800**  **SWO**

A George II-style mahogany gateleg table, the oval top raised on four club legs, with pad feet.

*42.5in (106cm) diam*

**$500-800** | **L&T**

A Regency mahogany, dining table, on turned urn pedestals above three reeded saber legs with brass cuffs and castors, with two sets of poles for extension.

*46in (115cm) wide*

**$5,000-7,000** | **BRU**

A Regency-style mahogany triple pedestal dining table, the rosewood crossbanded top, on baluster turned pedestals with reeded saber legs and brass paw cast caps and castors, includes two further leaves.

*143in (363cm) wide*

**$5,000-7,000** | **L&T**

A Victorian mahogany three pedestal dining table, with re-entrant corners on a plain frieze, raised on octagonal tapering stems, quadripartite bases, and claw feet, each section with drop flaps.

**$4,000-6,000** | **SWO**

A George III D-end dining table, with boxwood stringing, the central gateleg section with drop leaves, above a panelled frieze with checker stringing, raised on tapered legs with spade feet, brass caps and castors.

*111.75in (284cm) wide*

**$4,000-6,000** | **L&T**

A late 18thC Federal three-part mahogany dining table, attributed to Silas Cheney, Litchfield, Connecticut, the D-shaped, beaded ends with deep leaf, squared tapering leaves, legs ended out, old mends.

*54in (135cm) wide*

**$8,000-12,000** | **FRE**

An early 19thC mahogany dining table, with a plain cockbeaded frieze, the central gateleg section with six legs and a pair of D-ends, the legs turned and reeded with brass caps and castors.

*124.75in (312cm) wide*

**$12,000-18,000** | **L&T**

An early 19thC dining table, with a central gateleg section, on ring turned and reeded tapering legs, toupie feet.

*118.5in (301cm) long*

**$2,200-2,800** | **L&T**

A Regency D-end mahogany dining table, the central gateleg section with one hinged leaf, one end with a further hinged leaf and one additional leaf, with reeded edge above ebony lined paneled frieze and coromandel crossbanded tablets, raised on ring turned and reeded tapering legs and toupie feet.

*142in (355cm) wide*

$6,000-9,000                                      L&T

A 19thC mahogany D-end dining table, with extensive boxwood stringing, two extra leaves, and a paneled frieze above paneled square section tapering legs.

*52in (130cm) high*

$3,000-5,000                                      L&T

An early Victorian mahogany telescopic dining table, with D-ends and reeded edge, on rosette headed lobed baluster legs, brass caps and castors, including five leaves.

*163.25in (408cm) wide*

$7,000-10,000                                     L&T

An early Victorian mahogany telescopic dining table, with four leaves, the top with D-ends and molded edge, raised above a plain frieze and five molded and bulbous baluster legs, brass caps and castors.

*156.25in (397cm) wide*

$18,000-22,000                                    L&T

A Victorian mahogany extending dining table, the top with molded edge and rounded angles, raised on four carved and fluted baluster legs with sunken brass castors, includes three leaves.

*121.2in (303cm) wide*

$7,000-10,000                                     L&T

A Victorian mahogany telescopic dining table, the top with demilune ends and molded edge, raised on paired baluster trestle supports with scroll feet and castors, includes three leaves.

*80.75in (202cm) wide*

$5,000-8,000                                      L&T

A Victorian mahogany dining table, the rectangular top with D-ends above a plain frieze, the telescopic pull out action with central leg, on turned and buckle carved tapering legs with brass caps and castors, six extra leaves with frieze to each leaf.

*17.25in (44cm) wide*

$10,000-15,000                                    L&T

## SIDEBOARDS

A Scottish George III mahogany sideboard, with boxwood and purplewood stringing and inlaid rosewood panels to the uprights, the stage back with tambour, above central frieze drawer, single drawers, dummy fronted cupboard and cellaret drawer, on carved square section tapering legs with collar feet.

*79.5in (202cm) wide*

$4,000-6,000                                      L&T

209

A Philadelphia Hepplewhite mahogany sideboard, the rounded corner top over three drawers above four cupboard doors supported by square tapering legs with overall line inlay.

*c1800*                                              72.25in (180.5cm) wide

**$4,000-6,000**                                                    **POOK**

A New York Federal mahogany sideboard, the top with ovolo cut corners, a case with a single long drawer above two inset doors, two cupboard doors, all with elaborate line inlays, square tapering legs with matchstick inlaid capitals, banded cuffs.

*c1790*                                                  69in (172.5cm) wide

**$18,000-22,000**                                                 **POOK**

A late 18thC Federal mahogany inlaid sideboard, the veneered top with ovolo corners and string inlay, case with a central drawer and cupboard doors with veneered ovals outlined in banding and interspersed with maple veneered rectangles, square tapering legs with stringing, the case with old surface, replaced brass.

*c1800*                                                  75in (190.5cm) wide

**$16,000-20,000**                                                   **SK**

A Federal mahogany inlaid sideboard, probably New York, the top with serpentine front, square ends and ovolo corners, the string inlaid case with convex panels flanked by hinged doors, square tapering inlaid legs, cuffs, replaced brasses, refinished, imperfections.

*c1795*                                                  71in (180.5cm) wide

**$30,000-35,000**                                                   **SK**

An early 19thC Federal mahogany sideboard, probably New York, shaped back panel with conforming front, bowed central section with drawers and cellaret drawer, sides with dovetailed drawer above large bay door with band inlay, all drawers dovetailed and cockbeaded, tapered legs, secondary wood white pine, wear and repairs.

*78.25in*

**$5,000-8,000**                                                     **BRU**

A diminutive Federal mahogany inlaid sideboard, top with ovolo corners and crossbanded edge, a case with a central drawer, wine drawers below, with crossbanded and string-inlaid borders, on ring-turned, reeded, tapering legs, imperfections.

*c1810*                               55in (140cm) wide

**$8,000-12,000**                                  **SK**

A cherry sideboard, possibly Catawba Valley, North Carolina, shaped top with four central dovetailed drawers, two frame-and-panel doors, double split-spindle columns on front, on turned feet, inlaid diamond escutcheons, back with frame-and-panel construction with cut nails, wear.

*48in (120cm) wide*

**$5,000-8,000**                                                     **BRU**

A George III mahogany bowfront sideboard with a central frieze drawer flanked by two drawers, on square tapering legs.

*67.25in (168cm) wide*

**$2,800-3,200**    **SWO**

A George III mahogany bowfront sideboard, with an inlaid and crossbanded central drawer, flanked by a drawers and cupboards, raised on turned tapering legs.

*54in (135cm) wide*

**$2,800-3,200**    **SWO**

A Regency mahogany serving table, the paneled ledge back above a rectangular top and deep frieze, with three cushion drawers, on turned and reeded legs with toupie feet.

*81.25in (203cm) wide*

**$4,000-6,000**    **L&T**

A Regency-style mahogany pedestal sideboard, with a pair of paneled drawers and scrolling paneled ledge back, flanked by taller pedestals with a drawer and cupboard containing sliding trays, on carved and turned feet.

*75.5in (189cm) wide*

**$2,800-3,200**    **L&T**

---

A Scottish Regency mahogany sideboard, with brass stringing, the breakfront stage with tambour doors and rosewood panels surmounted by a gallery, with drawers, cupboards and arched kneehole, on tapering legs with spade feet.

*79.5in (199cm) wide*

**$7,000-10,000**    **L&T**

A Regency mahogany bowfront sideboard.

*71.25in (178cm) wide*

**$2,800-3,200**    **GIL**

---

A Regency mahogany bowfront sideboard, with an ebony line-inlaid frieze drawer, curved deep drawers and two cupboard doors, line-inlaid spandrels, on ring turned tapering legs with toupie feet.

*61in (152.5cm) wide*

**$5,000-7,000**    **L&T**

A Regency mahogany pedestal sideboard, with three central molded frieze drawers, flanked by two tapered pedestals, raised on outswept paw feet.

*c1820*    *90in (225cm) wide*

**$5,000-7,000**    **FRE**

A Regency mahogany pedestal sideboard, with a raised shell and acanthus carved back over four frieze drawers, the breakfront pedestals carved with lions paw feet and opening to reveal shelves and a cellaret drawer, on plinth bases.

*c1820*    *88.5in (221cm) wide*

**$3,000-5,000**    **FRE**

A William IV mahogany serving table, of large proportions, possibly Scottish, with a raised gallery to the back, the top with gadrooned border, on reeded turned legs with beaded bands and carved with leaves.

*95.25in (242cm) wide*

**$10,000-15,000**    **DN**

---

A William IV mahogany serving table, the scrolling ledge back centered by a floral spray above a molded top with plate rack to rear, plain deep frieze and monopodial supports.

*76in (190cm) wide*

**$5,000-7,000**    **L&T**

A William IV mahogany twin pedestal sideboard, the semi-bowed top with a reeded edge above drawers and paneled doors, enclosed by spirally reeded columns, on a plinth.

**Provenance:** *Membury Court, Axminster, England.*

*67.25in (168cm) wide*

**$3,000-4,000**    **L&T**

**FURNITURE**

An early 18thC Pennsylvania William and Mary tavern table, the top over a frame with single drawer, supported by bold turned legs, joined by a box stretcher.

*61in (155cm) wide*

**$5,000-8,000**     **POOK**

An 18thC turned black walnut tavern table, probably Pennsylvania, the top with rounded edges, two small lip molded apron drawers with wood pulls, vasi-form turned legs with grooved stretchers on bun feet.

*top 52in (130cm) wide*

**$3,000-5,000**     **FRE**

An American hutch table on chair, with birch arms and a pine seat, painted with old red paint.

*c1800*     *table 50in (127cm) diam*

**$7,000-10,000**     **PST**

An early 19thC pine chair table, the tilting rectangular overhanging top on cutout ends joining a lift-top compartment, refinished.

*70in (178cm) wide*

**$6,000-9,000**     **SK**

A cherry sugar table, Sullivan or Washington County, Tennessee, lift top above interior compartments, one interior shelf, tapered and turned legs, old refinishing.

*29in (72.5cm) wide*

**$3,000-5,000**     **BRU**

A New England pine trestle table, rectangular top with baluster-shaped uprights joined by molded medial stretcher, old repairs.

*92in (230cm) wide*

**$6,000-9,000**     **FRE**

A Canadian pine harvest table.

*Harvest tables are large kitchen tables, so-called because of the old Canadian farmers' custom of helping each other gather their harvest, and sitting down together for a large meal at the end of a long day in the fields.*

*c1860*     *66in (167.5cm) long*

**$2,200-2,800**     **PER**

A Canadian painted single drawer work table, the rectangular top overhanging the plain frieze with single drawer, raised on tapering turned legs with toupie feet.

*30in (76cm) wide*

**$1,200-1,800**     **WAD**

A small Canadian pine dressing table from Ontario.

*c1860*     *38.5in (98cm) wide*

**$500-700**     **PER**

A George III mahogany, tulipwood, and satinwood crossbanded dressing table, the top with oval panels enclosing a bowl recess and a mirror, drawer with a fitted interior and two doors, on square tapering legs.

*34.25in (87cm) high*

| $700-1,000 | DN |

A George III mahogany dressing table, the double hinged top enclosing an adjustable mirror and fittings, above a false drawer front, on square tapering legs with an H-stretcher.

*33.5in (85cm) high*

| $700-1,000 | DN |

A George III mahogany gentleman's washstand, the hinged lid opening to reveal a mirror and lidded compartments, over three false and three deep drawers, on square tapering legs, with caps and castors.

| $1,200-1,800 | SWO |

A China Trade Huang Hua Li wood metamorphic combined dressing and writing table, the hinged lid enclosing a fitted interior, mirror and candle slides, a drawer to the reverse, fluted legs, brass castors.

*c1800*          *29in (72.5cm) high*

| $3,000-5,000 | FRE |

An early 19thC mahogany kneehole dressing table, the top with a banded edge above an arrangement of five drawers, raised on ring turned tapering legs with brass caps and castors.

*48.75in (122cm) wide*

| $1,200-1,800 | L&T |

An early 19thC mahogany kidney-shaped dressing table, the top with a reeded edge above a plain frieze and turned and reeded tapering legs, with brass caps and castors.

*48.75in (122cm) wide*

| $5,000-7,000 | L&T |

A 19thC mahogany dressing table, the top with apertures for bowl, cups and counterbalanced mirror, the kneehole flanked by drawers and pedestals containing paneled doors concealing a toilet bowl and bidet, sprung handles.

*48.75in (122cm) wide*

| $2,200-2,800 | L&T |

A Victorian bird's eye maple dressing table, with purplewood stringing, the mirror with pierced strapwork cresting, raised on a reverse breakfront kneehole desk with nine drawers and a recessed paneled cupboard, on plinth base.

*69.25in (173cm) high*

| $1,200-1,800 | L&T |

A late 19thC French mahogany and kingwood poudreuse, with banding and boxwood stringing, the top with a marquetry urn of flowers, the triple section hinged top enclosing a mirror and two recesses, on square tapering legs.

*29.75in (74.5cm) wide*

| $1,200-1,800 | DN |

A Queen Anne solid walnut lowboy, the rectangular molded top above three drawers and a shaped apron, raised on circular tapering legs and pad feet.

*29.25in (74cm) high*

**$4,000-6,000**                                                              **B**

A George II mahogany lowboy, with one long and three short drawers, original brass handles and a wavy frieze, on cabriole legs with pad feet.

*30in (76cm) wide*

**$12,000-18,000**                                                        **CATO**

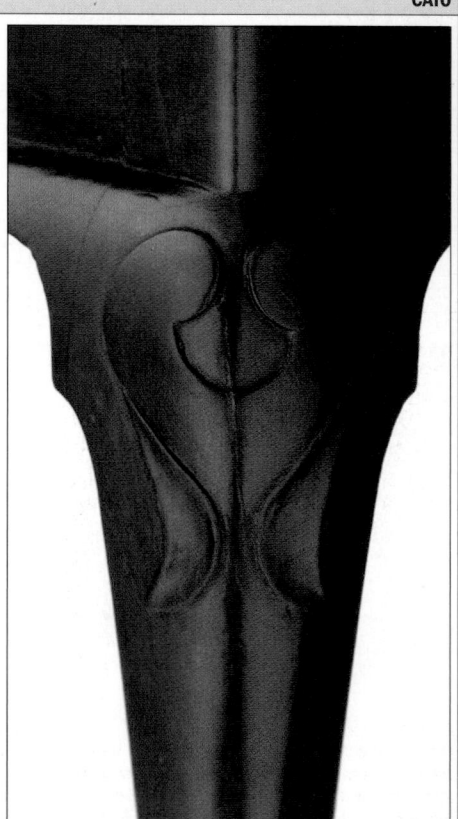

A late 18thC fruitwood country lowboy, the twin drawer frieze with oak lining above heart and scroll carved cabriole legs and pad feet.

*30.5in (77.5cm) wide*

**$5,000-8,000**                                                          **CATO**

A Queen Anne walnut inlaid dressing table, the thumb-molded top above drawers with string-inlaid borders, on four cabriole legs ending in pad feet and joined by a shaped valanced apron, replaced brasses, repairs, imperfections.

*c1740*      *27in (68.5cm) wide*

**$8,000-12,000**      **SK**

An American Queen Anne tiger maple dressing table, thumb-molded top, case with drawers bordered by double cockbeading on cockbeaded valanced apron with two turned drop pendants, cabriole legs ending in pad feet, engraved brasses, refinished, minor imperfections.

*c1750*      *29in (73.5cm) wide*

**$22,000-26,000**      **SK**

A Delaware Valley Queen Anne walnut dressing table, the top with notched corners, above one long and three short drawers, over an scalloped apron, cabriole legs, stocking trifid feet.

*c1750*      *30.75in (78cm) wide*

**$10,000-12,000**      **POOK**

A mid-18thC Massachusetts walnut and maple dressing table, molded top with breadboard ends and cusped corners, central drawer with carved circular concave recess, drawer bases with original rose-head nails, cabriole legs with pad feet, original brass pulls and escutcheons.

*35.5in (89cm) wide*

**$16,000-20,000**      **BRU**

An 18thC walnut lowboy or dressing table, Pennsylvania, lip-molded top with notched corner, one wide and three small lip-molded drawers, scalloped apron, on shell-carved cabriole legs on trifid feet, old brasses.

*34.5in (86cm) wide*

**$9,000-11,000**      **FRE**

A late 18thC tiger maple dressing table, top with molded edge and front notched corners above the case of three-thumb-molded drawers, a cut out front skirt, cabriole legs ending in carved, stockinged feet, original brasses and lock, refinished, some imperfections.

*34in (86cm) wide*

**$17,000-20,000**      **SK**

A late 18thC Pennsylvania Chippendale walnut dressing table, top with molded edge with notched corners, graduated lip-molded drawers, scalloped apron and shell-carved cabriole legs, on ball and claw feet.

*34.5in (87.5cm) wide*

**$18,000-22,000**      **FRE**

A Baltimore Federal mahogany card table, the demilune top over a conforming frame, square tapering legs with acorn and oak leaf capitals and overall line inlay.

*c1795*                    *38.5in (98cm) wide*

**$5,000-8,000**                    **POOK**

A late 18thC Federal mahogany inlaid card table, the folding top with ovolo corners and crossbanded and string-inlaid edges, skirt with central inlaid oval flanked by panels, with ovolo corners, with crossbanded string-inlaid lower edge, minor imperfections.

*c1790*                    *36in (91.5cm) wide*

**$6,000-9,000**                    **SK**

### A CLOSER LOOK AT A CARD TABLE

*This card table is of great interest to collectors for its decorative and functional appeal. It could also be used as a side table.*

*If the refinishing is done in a professional manner, like with this example, it will hardly affect the value.*

*Original features such as these brass handles make this table valuable.*

*The bulbous ball and claw feet add significant stability to this table.*

A Chippendale carved mahogany card table, Philadelphia, hinged top above frieze with molded edge drawer and gadrooned skirt on flower and leaf carved cabriole legs, on ball and claw feet, original brasses, refinished.

*c1770*                    *35in (89cm) wide*

**$22,000-26,000**                    **FRE**

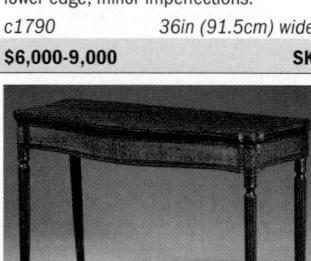

A Federal birch inlaid card table, the folding top with bowed front centering a projecting panel with inlaid edge, base with bird's-eye maple panel framed by stringing and crossbanding, old surface, imperfections.

*36in (91.5cm) wide*

**$6,000-9,000**                    **SK**

An inlaid Federal card table, probably North Shore, Massachusetts, shaped mahogany top, frieze with crotch-figure birch with turret corners and double-line inlay on edges, tapered and reeded legs, damage and repairs.

*c1805*                    *37.5in (94cm) wide*

**$5,000-8,000**                    **BRU**

A Federal carved mahogany folding-top card table, attributed to William Hook, Salem, Massachusetts, a serpentine top with outset corners, plain apron, on slender vasiform reeded legs, tall turned feet.

*c1810*     *35.75in (89cm) wide*

**$3,000-5,000**                    **FRE**

## TEA TABLES

A George II mahogany foldover tea table, the rectangular top raised on cabriole legs with pad feet.

*34in (85cm) wide*

**$2,200-2,800**                    **L&T**

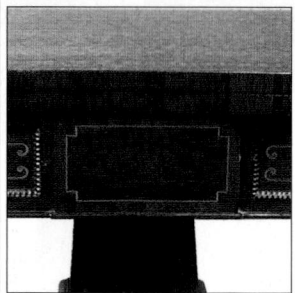

A Regency rosewood and crossbanded tea table, the rectangular top above a strung frieze with a central raised tablature, on a stepped column support with four downswept feet and lapette carved knees, on brass castors.

**$2,200-2,800**                    **SWO**

A Queen Anne maple tea table, the circular overhanging chamfered top on a shaped and valanced skirt joining four cabriole legs ending in pad feet, refinished.

*c1750*                                                    *32.25in (82cm) wide*

**$20,000-25,000**                                                        **SK**

An inlaid Southern stand, top with rounded corners and band of double string inlay, tapered legs with extensive string and elliptical inlay below bird's-eye maple panels, dovetailed drawer, MESDA label "S-11872", wear and repair.

*26.25in (65.5cm) wide*

**$45,000-50,000**                                                       **BRU**

A late 18thC Captain John Green Jr., Philadelphia, Chippendale mahogany pie crust tea table, with a carved top, birdcage support, baluster standard, and cabriole legs terminating in ball and claw feet, retains an early mellow finish.

**Provenance:** *Direct descendants of Captain John Green of Philadelphia.*

*33.25in (83cm) diam*

**$70,000-75,000**                                                     **POOK**

A Queen Anne cherry tea table, the oval overhanging top with chamfered edge on four block-turned tapering legs ending in pad feet, joined by valanced apron, old red stained surface, minor restoration.

*c1750*                                                      *33in (84cm) wide*

**$30,000-35,000**                                                        **SK**

A George III mahogany foldover card table, with boxwood and ebony stringing, the demilune top with satinwood crossbanding, above a paneled frieze, on stop-fluted and leaf carved turned tapering legs, toupie feet.

*33.5in (84cm) wide*

**$3,000-4,000**    **L&T**

A Regency mahogany and brass-strung card table, the rosewood crossbanded foldover top raised on a spreading pair of pierced trestle supports, on a plinth with four saber legs, paw cast brass caps and castors.

*36.5in (91cm) wide*

**$7,000-10,000**    **L&T**

A Regency mahogany and satinwood banded foldover card table, with boxwood stringing, hinged top and lion masks to the frieze, on bamboo form supports and a quadripartite base with saber legs, ending in brass paw caps and castors.

*36.75in (92cm) wide*

**$4,000-6,000**    **L&T**

A George IV rosewood card table, the hinged top on turned legs with acanthus leaf ornament.

*37.5in (94cm) wide*

**$3,000-4,000**    **SWO**

A 19thC Dutch walnut and floral marquetry card table, on square tapering legs with gilt-metal feet.

*32.75in (83cm) long*

**$1,800-2,200**    **DN**

A 19thC Gillows foldover amboyna card and writing table, the top with inset tooled leather skiver, opening to reveal a baize-lined interior, the paneled frieze with a gilded band raised above two twin columnar supports, on scrolling saber legs, stamped "Gillows & Co. 4362".

*37in (94cm) wide*

**$7,000-10,000**    **L&T**

A 19thC Colonial campaign card table, probably padouk wood, the foldover top with a brass inlaid central medallion, the interior with a circular baize within brass inlaid scrolling foliage and birds, detachable legs, brass fittings.

**$1,800-2,200**    **SWO**

An early Victorian rosewood foldover card table, with an anthemion decorated frieze, on an octagonal tapering column and quadruped platform base.

**$700-1,000**    **SWO**

One of a pair of Edwardian painted demilune foldover card tables, each decorated with gilt lattice work, flowers and figural panels of 18thC lovers, on club legs with pad feet.

*35.5in (89cm) wide*

**$5,000-7,000 pair**    **L&T**

An Edwardian rosewood and gilt-metal mounted foldover card table, the quarter-veneered and crossbanded top with a baize-lined interior, on cabriole legs with scrolled mounts, cast sabots.

*35.75in (91cm) wide*

**$4,000-6,000**    **L&T**

An Edwardian mahogany painted demilune foldover card table, the top with peacock feather border and a panel of a goddess and cherubs, above festoon frieze, tapering legs, spade feet.

*36.5in (91cm) wide*

**$6,000-9,000**    **L&T**

An Edwardian mahogany and inlaid card table, the hinged top inlaid with a satinwood and harewood patera within a foliate border, on square tapered legs, terminating in spade feet.

A Dutch floral marquetry folding card table, the serpentine top with outset corners, enclosing a baize-lined surface with marquetry playing card motifs, over a frieze drawer, on carved cabriole legs with claw and ball feet.

A walnut crossbanded card table, with a single frieze drawers, on cabriole legs.

*36.5in (91cm) wide*

*29.5in (75cm) high*

*33.5in (84cm) wide*

$1,800-2,200                    SWO

$3,000-5,000                    B

$1,200-1,800                    SWO

## A CLOSER LOOK AT A CHINA TRADE BACKGAMMON TABLE

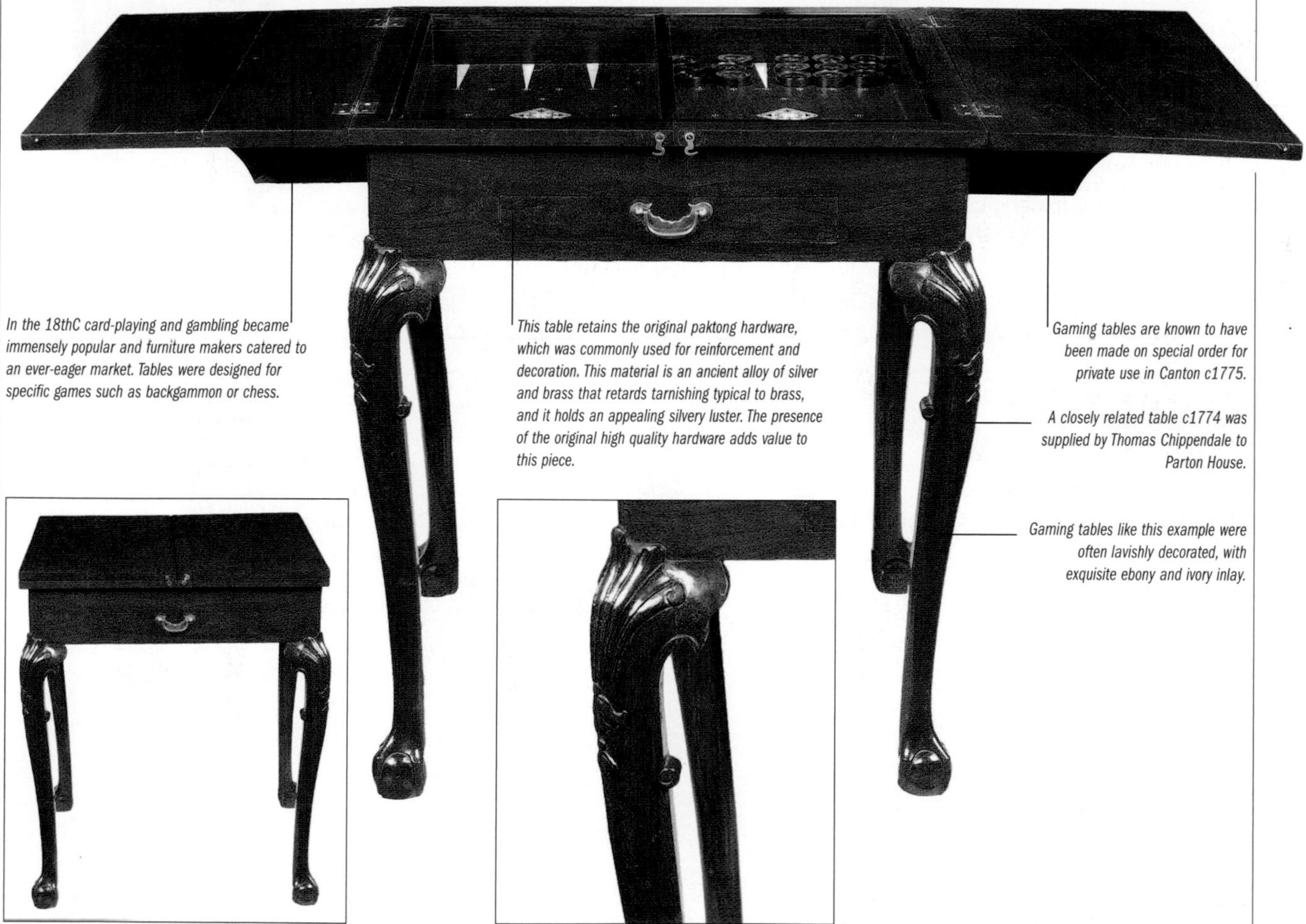

*In the 18thC card-playing and gambling became immensely popular and furniture makers catered to an ever-eager market. Tables were designed for specific games such as backgammon or chess.*

*This table retains the original paktong hardware, which was commonly used for reinforcement and decoration. This material is an ancient alloy of silver and brass that retards tarnishing typical to brass, and it holds an appealing silvery luster. The presence of the original high quality hardware adds value to this piece.*

*Gaming tables are known to have been made on special order for private use in Canton c1775.*

*A closely related table c1774 was supplied by Thomas Chippendale to Parton House.*

*Gaming tables like this example were often lavishly decorated, with exquisite ebony and ivory inlay.*

A late 18thC rare China trade backgammon table, from Canton (Guangzhou), in Asian hardwood with ebony and ivory inlays, original paktong hardware, the square top divided into two hinged flaps.

*c1775*

*54.75in (137cm) long*

$50,000-70,000                    MJM

A Regency square penwork chess table, the squares with alternating flowers and chinoiserie scenes of oriental buildings and figures in landscapes, within a wide foliate border, inscribed "Drawn by James W Beeson, Derby", on later column.

**$4,000-6,000** SWO

A Regency mahogany games table, the crossbanded foldover top enclosing a baize playing surface, on a stepped column, saber legs with hairy paw caps and castors.

*c1820* 35.5in (89cm) wide

**$2,800-3,200** FRE

A 19thC Damascus games table, with a mosaic inlay of exotic woods, mother of pearl and ivory, the top swiveling and opening to reveal a card surface, chessboard and backgammon board.

**$700-1,000** SWO

A George IV rosewood games table, with a molded edge and reversible checkerboard, the base with parcel gilt gesso husks and scrolls, on slender end supports with a turned stretcher, with gilt metal scroll and paw terminals with brass castors.

26.5in (66.5cm) wide

**$1,800-2,200** DN

A 19thC Louis XV-style kingwood and marquetry games table, the rectangular top with outset corners above two lateral frieze drawers, raised on square cabriole legs ending in sabots.

33in (82.5cm) wide

**$5,000-7,000** FRE

A Victorian burr walnut games and work table, the hinged top enclosing a backgammon and checker board, above a frieze drawer and sliding wool bag, on turned end supports with a double stretcher and carved outswept cabriole legs, ceramic castors.

29.25in (73cm) high

**$800-1,200** DN

A Federal mahogany and mahogany veneer astragal-end work table, the shaped hinged top with reeded edge, beaded case, ring-turned tapering legs on castors, old refinish, imperfections.

*c1810*      26in (66cm) wide

**$2,200-2,800**    **SK**

A Federal mahogany astragal-end work table, the top with two hinged lids above two cockbeaded drawers flanked by reeded pilasters, seven-sided compartments, vase and ring-turned support, scrolled shaped legs, minor imperfections.

*c1810*     25.75in (65.5cm) wide

**$3,000-5,000**    **SK**

A Shaker cherry and tiger maple stand, probably by Abner Allen, with inscription on the drawer side "April 12 1818", the top supported by parallel chamfered supports, overhangs the case of two small drawers, tapering legs, original red surface.

*Abner Allen (1776-1855) was a Shaker cabinetmaker who worked in both the Hancock, Massachusetts, and Enfield, Connecticut, communities. Some signed furniture with tapered drawer sides exist that have been identified with Abner Allen's work. Other Abner Allen construction techniques found in this stand include a heavily chamfered back edge of the drawer and the distinctive extended and chamfered top supports. Abner Allen died at the Enfield, Connecticut, community in 1855.*

*1818*      26.5in (67.5cm) high

**$50,000-75,000**    **SK**

A late Federal tiger maple work table, the shaped hinged top above a two-drawer façade, turned pedestal on four incurvate legs, on tiny ball feet, brasses replaced, refinished.

*c1820*      22.5in (57cm) wide

**$3,000-5,000**    **SK**

An early 19thC Federal bird's-eye maple and oak veneer work stand, the top with hinged leaves above two working and two faux string-inlaid drawers, the top one fitted, over ring-turned swelled legs, scrolled feet, old refinish, imperfections.

17.25in (44.5cm) wide

**$3,000-5,000**    **SK**

An early 19thC Massachusetts Federal mahogany work table, the top with ovolo corners, above two drawers with barber pole inlaid edges, turned and reeded tapering legs.

28.25in (72cm) high

**$3,000-5,000**    **POOK**

A rare Classical mahogany carved and mahogany veneer child's work table, the top with inset cast brass rosettes, ring-turned legs carved with fruit against a punchwork background, spiral carving and turned feet on castors, top with a fitted interior and the lower with bag compartment.

*c1825*     15.75in (40cm) wide

**$10,000-12,000**    **SK**

A mid-19thC Salem, Massachusetts Federal mahogany and birdseye maple sewing stand, the top with ovolo corners, above a single long drawer and sewing bag, turned legs.

30in (76cm) high

**$2,800-3,200**    **POOK**

A Regency figured work table, the top inlaid with ebony bellflowers over one frieze drawer and two opposing dummy drawers, raised on a lyre shaped support, terminating in saber legs with hairy paw cappings and castors.

*18in (45cm) wide*

**$2,800-3,200**                                                            **FRE**

A 19thC Louis XV-style kingwood inlaid work table, the quarter-veneered, kidney-shaped top over a brushing slide and three cloth-lined drawers, raised on shaped end supports ending in downswept legs.

*23in (57.5cm) wide*

**$2,800-3,200**                                                            **FRE**

A Federal academy painted tiger maple work table and portrait, the work table-top overhangs a case of two cockbeaded drawers, the top one fitted for writing, ring-turned tapering legs on castors, the shaded ink drawings of landscapes appear on the top and four facades, original turned pulls, old surface, together with a portrait in watercolor, pencil, and ink by Hannah Stone Brown, of a young brown-eyed woman, in a reverse-painted black and gilt mat lettered in gilt "Imagine" within an original gilt molded frame with ropetwist, imperfections.

*Private academies for teaching art to young women existed in Newbury, Boston. Mrs Brown of Newbury advertized her school for young ladies as offering instruction in "plain needlework, painting on wood, silk or paper, flowers, figures, landscapes, transparencies, and the new much admired art of drawing and shading in durable ink." It is likely that Hannah Stone attended the Newbury School of Mrs Brown.*

c1820
c1825

*work table 20in (51cm) wide*
*portrait 21in (53.5cm) high*

**$15,000-20,000**                                                          **SK**

An early 19thC mahogany work table, the dropleaf top above a frieze drawer, on three reeded saber legs.

*12.5in (32cm) wide*

**$1,200-1,800**                                    **L&T**

An early 19thC mahogany work table, with two drawers, raised on baluster turned pedestal, triform plinth, bun feet.

*20in (50cm) wide*

**$700-1,000**                                    **L&T**

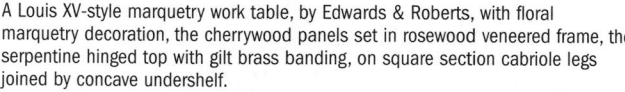

A Louis XV-style marquetry work table, by Edwards & Roberts, with floral marquetry decoration, the cherrywood panels set in rosewood veneered frame, the serpentine hinged top with gilt brass banding, on square section cabriole legs joined by concave undershelf.

*14.25in (36cm) wide*

**$1,200-1,800**                                    **L&T**

A William IV rosewood work table, the top with rounded corners, with a drawer and sliding wool bag, on fluted end supports and acanthus castors.

*28.75in (72cm) high*

**$1,200-1,800**                                    **DN**

A William IV rosewood work table, with two false drawers and a cotton wool bag, on an octagonal column and a concave platform base, with bun feet.

*28.5in (71cm) high*

**$700-1,000**                                    **DN**

A 19thC parquetry specimen wood ladies' work table, containing a single frieze drawer, with a sliding silk-covered bag below, on standard end supports united by a stretcher.

*22.5in (56cm) wide*

**$2,200-2,800**                                    **SWO**

A Victorian burr walnut games and work table, the hinged serpentine shaped top enclosing a backgammon and checker board, above a frieze drawer and sliding wool bag, on turned end supports with carved outswept cabriole legs and ceramic castors.

*29.25in (73cm) high*

**$800-1,200**                                    **DN**

A Victorian or Edwardian inlaid rosewood work table, with a carrying handle and beveled glass opening to reveal a buttoned silk interior, on square tapering legs, united with an undertier.

**$1,200-1,800**                                    **SWO**

**A CLOSER LOOK AT A GEORGE III DWARF SIDE TABLE**

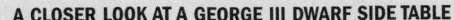

*From the 15thC side tables, which were intended to stand against the wall, were used as an additional surface at meal times or for holding ornaments. They became fashionable in the mid-18thC, when they were included in grand sets of furniture and were also used as writing and dressing tables.*

*During the George III period, furniture designers were inspired by the Classical world and used delicate decorative motifs. There was a move to a further refinement of form, which can be seen in this example, where newly imported timbers from all over the world, like satinwood and purpleheart, were used for sophisticated veneers.*

*Purpleheart is a dense hardwood (of the genus Peltogyne) from the Caribbean and is so-called due to the purplish color it becomes when freshly cut.*

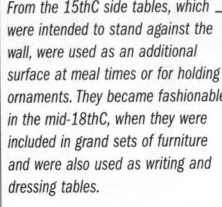

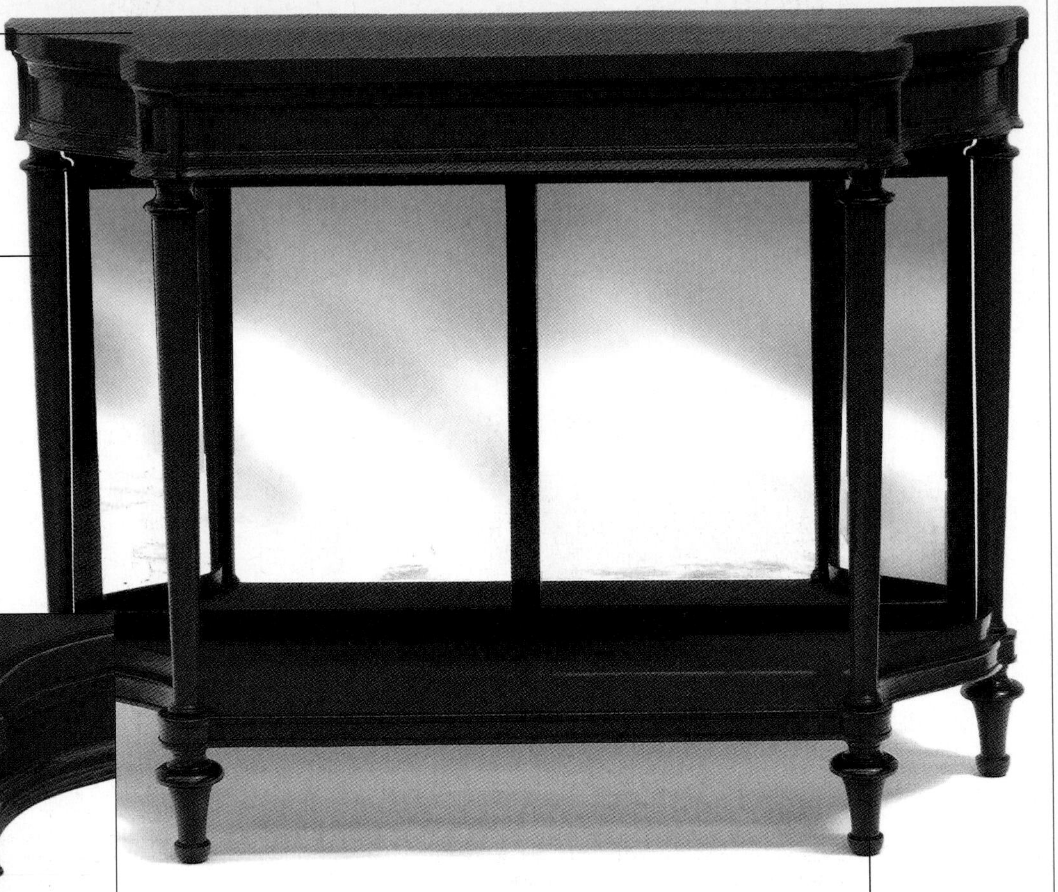

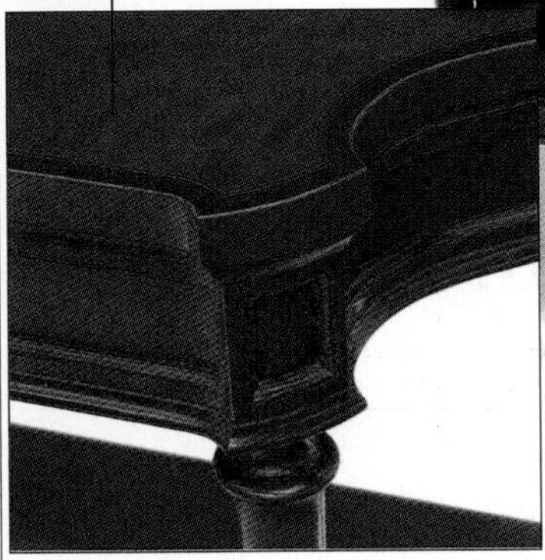

*The spade feet seen here are typical of the period. Check that none of the feet have been replaced – a side table that has its original feet is extremely desirable.*

An George III English satinwood veneer dwarf side table, crossbanded in purpleheart.
*c1790*

**$15,000-20,000** **CATO**

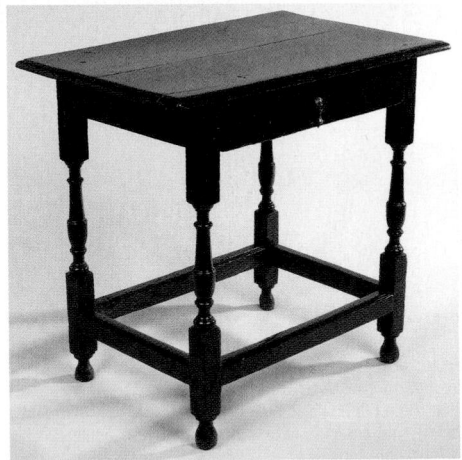

A Queen Anne oak side table, with turned legs linked by stretchers.

*28in (71cm) wide*

**$5,000-7,000** **EP**

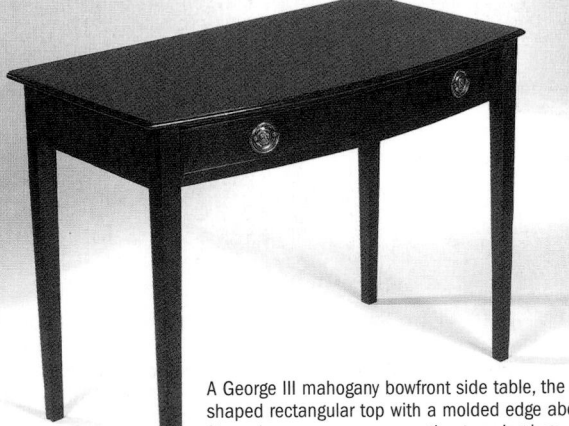

A George III mahogany bowfront side table, the shaped rectangular top with a molded edge above frieze drawers, on square section tapering legs.

*36in (90cm) wide*

**$1,800-2,200** **L&T**

A pair of Victorian overpainted tables, each with faux marble tops above friezes carved with Vitruvian scrolls and rosettes, the whole raised on square tapering legs with deep fluting, terminating in left carved feet.

*52.75in (134cm) wide*

**$7,000-10,000**          **L&T**

A pair of early Victorian burr oak side tables, the modern marble tops above a paneled frieze, on square tapering baluster front and pilaster rear legs.

***Provenance***: *Haggerston Castle, Northumberland.*

*66in (165cm) wide*

**$8,000-12,000**          **L&T**

An Edwardian oak side table, the breakfront top with rounded angles and verde antico marble, inset above a plain frieze, on turned and fluted supports joined by a shaped undershelf, on corresponding feet.

*47.25in (118cm) wide*

**$700-1,000**          **L&T**

A late 17thC Iberian walnut side table, the rounded rectangular plank top above two frieze drawers, raised on bobbin turned legs united by a peripheral stretcher.

*62in (155cm) wide*

**$3,000-5,000**          **FRE**

A late 18thC French mahogany table, with a frieze drawer and paneled sides, on square tapering legs with brass terminals and castors, stamped "MBF".

*28.25in (71.5cm) high*

**$4,000-6,000**          **DN**

A 19thC Scandinavian pine rectangular table, with a leather inset top and molded border, above a dentil and fluted frieze of shaped form, on fluted square tapering legs, some repairs.

*33.75in (86cm) wide*

**$300-500**          **DN**

A pair of Louis XVI-style walnut and brass inlaid side tables, with gilt-metal mounts, each rectangular top above a frieze drawer, raised on square tapered legs ending in toupie feet.

*29in (72.5cm) wide*

**$2,800-3,200**          **FRE**

A 19thC Dutch marquetry and parquetry mahogany and satinwood side table, the cubic-veneered top centered by a coat of arms, above conforming veneered sides, with one drawer, raised on faceted tapered legs joined by a wavy triform stretcher terminating in bun feet.

*44.5in (111cm) wide*

**$5,000-8,000**          **FRE**

A Scottish George III mahogany Pembroke table, with boxwood stringing, the satinwood crossbanded top above a frieze drawer, on square section tapering legs with 'round dot' terminals, brass caps and castors.

*44in (110cm) wide*

| $4,000-6,000 | L&T |

A George III mahogany and satinwood-banded Pembroke table, attributed to Young and Trotter, Edinburgh, with a single drawer and opposing dummy drawer, on square tapering legs, terminating in brass caps and castors.

*38.5in (98cm) wide*

| $2,200-2,800 | L&T |

A New York Hepplewhite mahogany Pembroke table, oval line inlaid top, demilune drop leaves, over a case with single drawer, square tapering legs with paterae and bookend inlaid capitals, overlaying bellflower chain and banded cuffs.

*c1800*                                      *30in (76cm) wide*

| $11,000-14,000 | POOK |

A George III mahogany Pembroke table, the hinged oval top on turned and tapered legs terminating in claw and ball feet.

*65.6in (164cm) wide*

| $1,000-1,500 | SWO |

A George III mahogany oval Pembroke table, with a single frieze drawer on square tapering legs.

*33.5in (83.5cm) wide*

| $1,200-1,800 | SWO |

A George III satinwood and crossbanded Pembroke table with a hinged oval top, containing one true and an opposing dummy drawer, on square tapering legs terminating in brass cappings and castors.

*40.75in (102cm) wide*

| $2,200-2,800 | SWO |

A late 18th to early 19thC English Pembroke table, with a single board top and a bowfront dovetailed drawer with inlaid borders, on tapered legs with oval, floral and string inlay, original glue blocks and iron hinges, pit-sawn surface under top.

*30.5in (76cm) wide*

| $2,800-3,200 | BRU |

A Regency mahogany pedestal Pembroke table, the figured twin flap top above an end frieze drawer and false verso, on a turned column, four reeded and fluted splay legs and brass castors.

*48.75in (122cm) wide*

| $2,200-2,800 | WW |

A late Regency mahogany Pembroke supper table, the top with a pair of drop flaps above a shallow frieze fitted with two opposing drawers, on a ring-turned column, four fluted legs, brass lion paw caps and castors.

*42.5in (107cm) wide*

| $1,200-1,800 | B |

A Regency rosewood sofa table, with a drop-leaf top above two frieze drawers opposed by false drawers, on dual standard ends, brass cappings and castors.

*This is a good example of the effect of sunlight on rosewood. The back of the table has been hidden from sunlight and has a richer coloring.*

*59in (150cm) wide*

**$20,000-30,000**                                                                    **CATO**

A Regency mahogany sofa table, possibly Scottish, with boxwood stringing and satinwood banding, two frieze drawers and dummies, raised on trestle supports with scroll toes and inlaid decoration.

*62.5in (156cm) wide*

**$8,000-12,000**          **L&T**

A Regency mahogany sofa table, with satinwood crossbanding and boxwood and ebony stringing, two frieze drawers with opposing dummy drawers, on trestle supports with downswept legs, brass caps and castors.

*52.75in (132cm) wide*

**$2,200-2,800**          **L&T**

A Regency mahogany sofa table, with ebony inlay and opposing frieze and dummy drawers, on balustraded trestle supports joined by an arched stretcher, with splayed feet with cast paw caps and castors.

*65.5in (164cm) wide*

**$1,800-2,200**          **L&T**

A late Regency rosewood sofa table, with a pair of frieze drawers and opposing dummies, on leaf-clasped trestle supports and sled bases, with carved scroll toes and castors.

*59.25in (148cm) wide*

**$3,000-5,000**          **L&T**

A Regency mahogany sofa table, the hinged top above two freeze drawers, on twin turned column ends and reeded dual splayed legs, united by a turned stretcher, terminating in brass cappings and castors.

*68in (173cm) wide*

$7,000-10,000 **H&L**

A Regency coromandel wood sofa table, with satinwood crossbanding and two frieze drawers opposing dummy drawers, raised on rectangular section supports on inlaid saber legs terminating in anthemion cast brass caps and castors.

*57.5in (146cm) wide*

$3,000-5,000 **L&T**

A Regency mahogany pedestal sofa table, the top with rounded angles above two frieze drawers opposing alternate dummy drawers, on an anthemion carved column, raised on base with gadrooned apron and boldly carved lions' paw feet.

*59.75in (152cm) wide*

$1,800-2,200 **L&T**

A Regency mahogany sofa table, the crossbanded top above a pair of frieze drawers with opposing dummies, raised on pierced lyre trestles joined by pot stand, on saber legs with coromandel panels, cast brass paw feet and castors.

*61.5in (154cm) wide*

$3,000-5,000 **L&T**

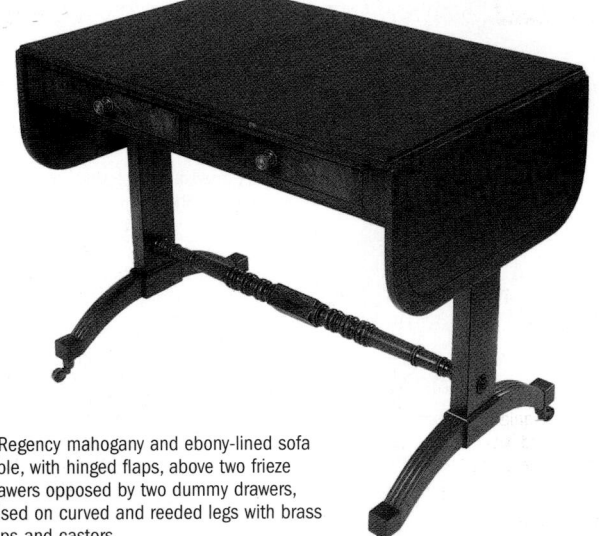

A Regency mahogany and ebony-lined sofa table, with hinged flaps, above two frieze drawers opposed by two dummy drawers, raised on curved and reeded legs with brass caps and castors.

*46in (115cm) wide*

$1,800-2,200 **L&T**

A Danish Empire mahogany ebonized sofa table, with fruitwood inlay and parcel-gilt the D-shaped drop-leaves above a rectangular frieze with a rootwood drawer, the end supports flanked by curved giltwood and ebonized bird head supports with paw feet.

*c1815*

*59.5in (149cm) wide*

$18,000-25,000 **EVE**

A 19thC rosewood sofa table, the frieze drawer with applied beading, raised on baluster turned supports and downscrolled sled bases with a turned and blocked stretcher with urn finial.

*53.5in (136cm) wide*

$1,200-1,800 **L&T**

A 19thC European mahogany sofa table, the oval drop-leaf top with ripple molded edge above two frieze drawers, raised on spiral supports joined by a conforming stretcher, terminating in downswept legs.

*62in (155cm) wide*

$1,800-2,200 **FRE**

A Chippendale mahogany kettle stand, the top with shaped gallery and candle slide on a vase and ring-turned post and tripod cabriole leg, arris pad feet on platforms, old refinish, imperfections.

c1770                    12in (30.5cm) wide

**$12,000-16,000**                    **SK**

A New England Federal figured maple one-drawer stand, the rectangular top raised on ring and tapering reeded legs ending in peg feet with castors.

c1800                    30in (75cm) high

**$3,000-5,000**                    **FRE**

A Federal mahogany and cherry inlaid stand, the square top with ovolo corners and inlaid edge above a bird's-eye maple veneered drawer and inlaid sides, quarter-engaged vase and ring-turned tapering legs, minor imperfections.

c1815                    17.25in (44cm) wide

**$9,000-11,000**                    **SK**

## CANDLESTANDS

A Pennsylvania Queen Anne candlestand, walnut and maple, with original blue paint.

c1750                    28.5in (72cm) high

**$3,000-5,000**                    **PH**

A late 18thC Federal mahogany tilt-top candlestand, the oval tilt-top on a vase and ring-turned post on a tripod base with cabriole legs ending in arris pointed pad feet on platforms, old surface, very minor imperfections.

28in (71cm) high

**$10,000-12,000**                    **SK**

An 18thC Pennsylvania walnut tilting-top candlestand, with a tilting dish-molded top, columnar turned pedestal with suppressed ball, on cabriole legs, snakehead feet.

27.75in (69cm) high

**$1,800-2,200**                    **FRE**

A late 18thC Chippendale mahogany tilt-top candlestand, the serpentine molded top tilts on a vase and ring-turned post on tripod cabriole leg base, arris pad feet on platforms, old finish, very minor imperfections.

28.75in (73cm) high

**$4,000-6,000**                    **SK**

A Boston Federal mahogany and satinwood candlestand, attributed to the cabinet shop of John and Thomas Seymour, the top with a central satinwood panel and edge, tilting over a baluster turned standard, tapering and downward curving legs.

c1800                    29.75in (75.5cm) high

**$4,000-6,000**                    **POOK**

A George I walnut bureau, the fall-front revealing a pigeonhole interior and well, above two short and two long drawers, on bracket feet, some alterations.

*37in (94cm) high*

**$5,000-8,000**                    **B**

A George II burr elm veneered and mahogany banded bureau, the sloping fall enclosing an interior fitted with five pigeonholes above ten short drawers, with a green baize lined writing surface, above four cock-beaded drawers, on shaped bracket feet, restorations.

*43.5in (110.5cm) high*

**$1,200-1,800**                    **B**

An early George III mahogany bureau, the fall front enclosing a fitted interior above four long graduated drawers and lopers, on paneled bracket feet.

*37.75in (96cm) wide*

**$1,200-1,800**                    **L&T**

A small George III mahogany bureau, with a fitted interior over four long drawers, original brass handles and oak lined drawers, on bracket feet.

*30.5in (76cm) wide*

**$2,800-3,200**                    **SWO**

A George III painted and satinwood bureau, with ribbon-tied foliate swags and scrolling foliage, the fall front centered by an oval panel depicting a classical female with two cherubs, opening to reveal a fitted interior with pigeonholes, drawers, a central cupboard door and inset leather writing surface, over two short and three long graduated drawers, raised on bracket feet.

*c1800*                    *42.5in (106cm) high*

**$8,000-12,000**                    **FRE**

A George III oak bureau, the slope front opening to reveal a pigeonholed interior, over four graduated long drawers, on shaped bracket feet.

*33.5in (83.5cm) wide*

**$700-1,000**                    **SWO**

An 18thC North Italian walnut and sycamore marquetry bureau, of small size, the banded and quarter-veneered sloping fall enclosing fitted interior with three small central drawers, two long drawers below, on cabriole legs.

*32.25in (82cm) wide*

**$2,200-2,800**                    **H&L**

A mid-18thC French Provincial Louis XV walnut bureau, the paneled fall centered by a marquetry medallion, with a stepped interior and covered well, below is one central frieze drawer flanked by two cupboard doors, on square cabriole legs.

*35in (87.5cm) wide*

**$7,000-10,000**                    **FRE**

A mid-18thC American Queen Anne tiger maple and pine slant-lid desk, opens to a stepped interior of valanced compartments and drawers, the case with thumb-molded drawers on bracket feet, replaced brasses, refinished, minor imperfections.

*35in (89cm) wide*

| $7,000-10,000 | SK |
|---|---|

A mid-18thC Queen Anne tiger maple and maple desk on frame, interior of central fan-carved drawer, compartments and drawers, thumb-molded drawer below, valanced frame, cabriole legs ending in pad feet, old replaced brasses, refinished, minor imperfections.

*34in (86.5cm) wide*

| $20,000-25,000 | SK |
|---|---|

An 18thC Connecticut cherrywood slope front desk on frame, the lip-molded-edge lid concealing cubbyholes and six small drawers, four wide lip-molded drawers, on frame with shell-carved apron and cabriole legs with pad feet.

*43in (107.5cm) high*

| $5,000-8,000 | FRE |
|---|---|

A Newport, Rhode Island Chippendale mahogany slant front desk, attributed to Townsend-Goddard School, the fall front, a shell carved interior, a case with drawers, on ogee bracket feet, original plate brasses.

*c1765*          *42.5in (108cm) high*

| $10,000-15,000 | POOK |
|---|---|

A Connecticut tiger maple secretary desk, with two upper raised panel doors, over a fall front, enclosing a fitted interior, above three drawers, resting on straight bracket feet.

*c1780*          *38in (96.5cm) wide*

| $10,000-15,000 | POOK |
|---|---|

A Chippendale cherry fall-front desk, interior of a central prospect door flanked by drawers, on case of thumb-molded graduated drawers, ogee bracket feet, original brasses, old surface, imperfections.

*c1780*          *39.75in (101cm) wide*

| $4,000-6,000 | SK |
|---|---|

A late 18thC Chippendale maple slant-lid desk, interior of drawers and valanced compartments, the central valance concealing a drawer, a case of thumb-molded graduated drawers on bracket feet, minor imperfections.

*Attached label reads "Came in original condition from Leonard A. Tuner...Athol. Mass".*

*38.75in (98.5cm) wide*

| $4,000-6,000 | SK |
|---|---|

A late 18thC Chippendale mahogany carved oxbow serpentine slant-lid desk, interior of prospect door with valanced compartments and drawers, cockbeaded case of drawers on carved cabriole legs, claw and ball feet, refinished, imperfections.

*41in (104cm) wide*

| $6,000-9,000 | SK |
|---|---|

A late 18thC Chippendale mahogany slant ox bow desk, Massachusetts, slant top with molded edge, fitted interior above four drawers, molded base with ball and claw feet, replaced brasses, old repairs.

*42in (106.5cm) wide*

| $4,000-6,000 | FRE |
|---|---|

A Pennsylvania painted pine accountant's desk, the slant lid over a case with four double recessed panel doors supported by turned feet, retaining overall vibrant ocher sponge decoration, dated.

*1841*          *51in (127.5cm) high*

| $20,000-25,000 | POOK |
|---|---|

## A CLOSER LOOK AT A NAPOLEON II BUREAU MAZARIN

*The bureau mazarin was made from the late 17thC through to the early 18thC and experienced a revival in the 19thC. Bureau mazarins are usually supported on legs joined by double X-shaped stretchers to allow for leg room.*

*The quality of this bureau is evident from the exquisite boulle work, with brass and pewter inlay, and popular classical motifs such as carytids, exotic birds, and foliate scrolls, which were typical of the era.*

*This piece is a 19thC copy, but unlike most of these revival pieces it has a boulle work top (a type of marquetry) rather than the more common leather inset top. The best copies show a good understanding of the originals and command a premium.*

*Examine the boulle work as the brass should be engraved – if it is not it may have been rubbed off through wear. Beware of damage because this will be extremely expensive to repair and has a negative impact on its value.*

A 19thC Napoleon II bureau mazarin, inlaid in brass and pewter with figures, carytids, exotic birds and foliate scrolls, with one central frieze drawer and recessed fall front cupboard with six further drawers, flanked and divided by outset scroll corners, raised on four square tapered legs joined by wavy stretchers and ending in toupie feet.

*54in (135cm) wide*

**$28,000-35,000** **FRE**

A Federal mahogany and mahogany veneer swell-front bureau, the top with swell-front and thumb-molded edge above a case of cockbeaded drawers, valanced skirt, on French feet, the brasses appear original, refinished, imperfections.

*c1800* *40in (101.5cm) wide*

**$2,800-3,200** **SK**

A Federal mahogany and mahogany veneer inlaid bowfront bureau, the overhanging top with string inlaid edge on base of cockbeaded drawers with inlaid escutcheons and string inlaid borders, flaring French feet joined by a cutout skirt, replaced brasses, repairs.

*c1800* *39in (99cm) wide*

**$4,000-6,000** **SK**

A New York late Federal cherry and birds-eye maple bureau, scalloped backsplash, top with notched front edge above drawers flanked by architectural columns, a bobbin-turned base molding resting on turned feet.

*c1825* *57.5in (144cm) high*

**$5,000-8,000** **POOK**

A 19thC Louis XV-style rosewood bonheur de jour, with a brass gallery, inlaid decoration and a fitted interior with well.

*56in (140cm) high*

**$2,200-2,800**      **SWO**

A late 19thC French kingwood bonheur de jour with gilt-metal mounts, the top with two glazed doors and two drawers, the serpentine base with a velvet-lined writing surface, on cabriole legs.

*48.5in (123cm) high*

**$2,200-2,800**      **DN**

A late 19thC quarter-veneered kingwood and tulipwood bonheur de jour, with gilt-brass mounts, the pagoda top with a gallery above doors centered by Sèvres-style panels, raised on serpentine base with frieze drawer enclosing a writing slide, on square section tapered cabriole legs with scrolled sabots, stamped "Tahana, Paris".

*31.5in (80cm) wide*

**$5,000-8,000**      **L&T**

## CYLINDER DESKS

A George III mahogany roll-top desk, with a tambour front enclosing a fitted interior with sliding writing surface, above two short drawers, on square tapering legs joined by stretchers, with brass caps and castors.

*40.5in (101cm) wide*

**$5,000-7,000**      **L&T**

A George III mahogany roll-top desk, the tambour top opening to reveal a fitted interior with candle slides, drawers, pigeonholes and a leather writing surface, two frieze drawers, raised on square tapered legs terminating in brass cappings and castors.

*c1790*      *37in (92.5cm) wide*

**$5,000-8,000**      **FRE**

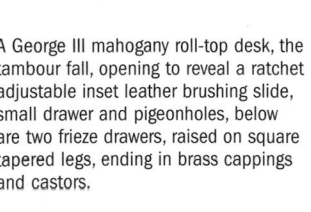

A George III mahogany roll-top desk, the tambour fall, opening to reveal a ratchet adjustable inset leather brushing slide, small drawer and pigeonholes, below are two frieze drawers, raised on square tapered legs, ending in brass cappings and castors.

*c1790*      *36.5in (91cm) wide*

**$5,000-7,000**      **FRE**

A George IV mahogany twin pedestal roll-top desk, the three-quarter galleried reeded top above solid ebony-strung roll front enclosing a fitted interior with sliding writing surface, above a frieze drawer and kneehole flanked by two columns of four graduated drawers, on bracket feet, stamped "T Willson 68 Great Queen Street London".

*Thomas Willson is entered in directories as a furniture broker and appraiser at 68 Great Queen Street between 1821 and 1829. He was also a cabinet maker from 1818. The business was continued by his widow Mary from 1830 and his son Matthew from 1838, when the stamp 'M Willson' was used.*

*54in (135cm) wide*

**$10,000-15,000**      **L&T**

**FURNITURE**

A Victorian mahogany cylinder desk, the three-quartered gallery top above a fall-front, enclosing a fitted interior and brushing slide with pigeonholes, drawers, inkwells, and a leather inset writing surface, each pedestal with four graduated drawers and molded plinth bases, stamped "maple and co."

*c1860*                                         *60in (150cm) wide*

**$7,000-10,000**                                                FRE

A late Victorian satinwood pedestal cylinder desk, with a gilt-metal pierced gallery above a paneled cylinder front, enclosing interior drawers and a pull-out adjustable leather writing slope, the three drawers to each pedestal above plinth bases, the lockplate stamped "J.T. Needs, 100 New Bond Street, late Bramah 124 Picadilly".

*45in (114.5cm) high*

**$2,800-3,200**                DN

A late Victorian rosewood and satinwood-inlaid ladies' writing desk, fitted with an arrangement of drawers and pigeonholes and a pull-out ratcheted writing surface enclosed by a roll-top, on square tapered legs.

**$800-1,200**                SWO

An Edwardian rosewood cylinder bureau, with boxwood stringing and floral marquetry, the ledge back with an hexagonal panel, above an interior with a sliding writing surface and drawers, on square section tapering legs.

*43.5in (109cm) high*

**$1,200-1,800**        L&T

A mahogany and brass-inlaid Directoire cylinder bureau, with gilt-bronze mounts, the marble top over three frieze drawers and a cylinder fall, the fitted interior with drawers and a central shelf and a pigeonhole, the lower section with three long drawers, and fluted pilasters, on a shaped plinth base.

*c1800*        *51in (127.5cm) wide*

**$12,000-18,000**                FRE

A Dutch mahogany marquetry bombé cylinder bureau, inlaid with scrolling foliage, urns and exotic birds, the brushing slide and rising fall opening to reveal a serpentine fitted interior with pigeonholes, drawers and a secret compartment, over three further long drawers, on outswept feet.

*c1800*        *47.5in (119cm) wide*

**$7,000-10,000**        FRE

A Louis XV gilt-bronze-mounted cylinder bureau, in kingwood, tulipwood, and rosewood, with a three-quarter pierced galleried top above a cylinder fall enclosing a fitted interior with an inset leather brushing slide, over three shaped frieze drawers, on square cabriole legs ending in sabots, some later mounts.

*c1760*                                        *32in (80cm) wide*

**$18,000-25,000**                                        FRE

A 19thC English mahogany folding writing desk, constructed as a games table, a swing-leg supporting one leaf, the other leaf with a rising leather writing surface and three dovetailed drawers with brass clips and hinges, on tapered legs with molded feet and brass castors.

*38in (95cm) wide*

**$3,000-5,000** **BRU**

A late Victorian mahogany writing desk, with a brass pierced three-quarter gallery and seven short drawers with blind fret-carved decoration, on carved cluster legs, stamped "Edwards and Roberts".

**$1,800-2,200** **SWO**

A New York late Federal mahogany 'Aaron Burr Desk', patent April 1854, by Stephen Hedges, the oblong top opening to a single drawer and upholstered seat, cabriole legs and scrolled feet with brass castors, bearing patent label underside, "by Stephen Hedges".

*33.25in (84.5cm) wide*

**$7,000-10,000** **POOK**

A massive Edwardian oak partner's desk, with a green gilt tooled leather top and rounded angles, above frieze drawers and kneeholes to each side, flanked by drawers and cupboards, on plinth base.

*106.5in (266cm) wide*

**$5,000-7,000** **L&T**

## WRITING TABLES

A Regency rosewood library table, with a tooled inset skiver, the three frieze drawers opposed by dummy drawers, on belt-waisted supports with gilt-decorated milled panels in the manner of John Maclean, later brass feet and pot castors.

*c1825* *60in (152.5cm) wide*

**$28,000-35,000** **CATO**

A Milanese mid-19thC ebony penwork and ivory-inlaid library table, the top with intricate floral inlay, over four frieze drawers, on fluted turned tapering legs.

*35in (89cm) wide*

**$35,000-45,000** **CATO**

A Regency mahogany and rosewood crossbanded library table, in the manner of Gillows of Lancaster, with two drawers opposed by dummy drawers, above dual spindle-filled ends, brass cappings and castors.

*42in (105cm) wide*

**$45,000-55,000**     **CATO**

A Regency rosewood library table, with an inset writing surface above two frieze drawers opposing dummy drawers, raised on spindle-filled supports with saber legs, united by a stretcher, terminating in brass caps and castors.

*49in (124cm) wide*

**$5,000-7,000**     **L&T**

A late Regency rosewood and brass-inlaid library table, the top inlaid with a band of foliage, above two frieze drawers on tapering supports, raised on saber legs with applied cast rosettes and terminating in leaf cast caps and castors.

*39.5in (99cm) wide*

**$4,000-6,000**     **L&T**

A Victorian mahogany library table, with a leather inset top and two frieze drawers, on turned tapering legs and brass caps and castors.

*48in (120cm) wide*

**$800-1,200**     **SWO**

A Victorian Aesthetic walnut and burl walnut library table, possibly Philadelphia, with an inset writing surface over one frieze drawer, raised on twin open-end supports united by a turned stretcher and ending in scroll feet.

*c1880*     *47in (117.5cm) wide*

**$3,000-5,000**     **FRE**

A mahogany library table, with a gilt tooled leather skiver, above a paneled frieze with two drawers to each side, on tapering molded legs with scrolled and carved brackets, block feet with brass caps and castors, lacking one drawer.

*59.75 (152cm) wide*

**$1,800-2,200**     **L&T**

A mahogany Chippendale-style writing table, with a blind fret frieze and drawers to each end, on square section tapered chamfered legs with tassel feet.

*48in (122cm) wide*

**$1,200-1,800**     **L&T**

An 18thC European writing table, with marquetry decoration of a banded panel, trees, and baskets of fruit, secret drawer, on cabriole legs and hoof feet.

*33.75in (86cm) wide*

**$1,200-1,800**     **L&T**

A Directoire-style brass-inlaid mahogany writing table, the top with an urn of flowers in a cartouche, above a single frieze drawer and turned and fluted legs, joined by a stretcher with a central tablet, on toupie feet.

*44in (110cm) wide*

**$2,200-2,800**     **L&T**

An Italian writing table, probably late 18thC and from the Duchy of Parma, with an ornate burlwood inlay, four side drawers with hand-wrought nails and original brass pulls, pencil inscription in one drawer "Carolina Lorenzetti", old paper label to base "Camera Della Franducclessa(?)".

*42.5in (17cm) wide*

**$4,000-6,000**     **BRU**

A Regency mahogany writing table, inset with a tooled leather writing surface, above three opposing drawers, one with fitted interior, the whole raised on turned and reeded tapering legs.

*54in (137cm) wide*

$4,000-6,000    **L&T**

A George IV mahogany writing table, the leather-inset top above two frieze drawers, on bold reeded legs and original brass cappings and castors.

*48in (122cm) wide*

$6,000-9,000    **CATO**

A William IV mahogany writing table, with a molded top over two frieze drawers, raised on turned and gadrooned legs, brass caps and castors.

*52.5in (131cm) wide*

$2,800-3,200    **SWO**

A 19thC mahogany writing table, the three frieze drawers with paneled brackets, on ring turned tapering legs.

*36.5in (91cm) wide*

$700-1,000    **L&T**

A Gothic Revival mahogany and ebonized writing desk, the inlaid top with inset rounded angles above a twin panel frieze drawer, on four turned and blocked legs joined by pierced H-stretcher, brass castors, stamped "Johnston and Jennings".

*54.75in (137cm) wide*

$2,800-3,200    **L&T**

A mid-19thC satin birch writing table, in the manner of Gillows of Lancaster, with an inset writing surface, ebony stringing and a frieze drawer, on cabriole legs.

*44.5in (113cm) wide*

$2,800-3,200    **L&T**

A 19thC Louis XVI-style mahogany and gilt-bronze-mounted writing table, with an inset leather writing surface, three frieze drawers, on turned fluted tapered legs.

*17.25in (43in) wide*

$3,000-5,000    **FRE**

A mid-Victorian walnut and marquetry inlaid kidney-shaped writing table, the top with molded and crossbanded edge inlaid with sprays of flowers and enclosing a tooled leather writing surface, on cabriole legs with gilt-metal Rococo mounts.

*49in (114cm) wide*

$2,800-3,200    **L&T**

A Regency-style tortoiseshell and boulle work bureau plat, the top with cast brass mounts and gilt tooled leather lining above a frieze drawer and opposing dummy, on square section cabriole legs with cabochon mounts and sabots.

*52.5in (131cm) wide*

$1,800-2,200    **L&T**

A Louis XVI-style kingwood walnut and gilt-brass-mounted bureau plat, the top with leather inset writing surface, above five drawers and a kneehole, on turned fluted tapering legs with gilt-brass sabots.

*68in (170cm) wide*

$4,000-6,000    **L&T**

A 19thC kingwood crossbanded and gilt-bronze-mounted bureau plat, by Paul Sormani, the serpentine quarter-veneered top with a rockwork and shell-cast edge.

*69.5in (174cm) wide*

$28,000-35,000    **FRE**

A late 19thC Louis XV-style parquetry bureau plat, in kingwood and rosewood, the top with flowers and a marquetry courting couple panel, one drawer, on square cabriole legs and sabots, "Forest, Paris" label.

*39in (97.5cm) wide*

$7,000-10,000    **FRE**

An early Victorian rosewood dwarf folio stand, the two fixed splayed folio supports with scrolling brackets, above a base with two pierced sides and open ends, on a plinth with scroll feet and sunken castors.

*28in (70cm) high*

**$4,000-6,000**                    **L&T**

A late 18thC Federal mahogany three-tier stand, the molded trays revolve on a turned urn-shaped shaft above a cabriole leg tripod base with arris pad feet, old refinish, minor imperfections.

*43.25in (110cm) high*

**$8,000-12,000**                    **SK**

A near pair of 19thC Dutch mahogany ice buckets or jardinières, with slatted, tapered sides raised on triform bases and bun feet.

*16in (40cm) high*

**$2,800-3,200**                    **FRE**

A pair of French Empire-style burl walnut, veneered and gilt-metal jardinières, raised on Egyptian Revival gilt-metal-mounted legs.

*22.5in (56cm) high*

**$2,200-2,800**                    **FRE**

A George III mahogany basin stand, the divided hinged caddy top enclosing apertures for basin and cups, over an undershelf with single drawer, on square section tapering legs joined by shaped X-stretcher.

*32.75in (82cm) high*

$500-800     **L&T**

A late 18thC English mahogany washstand fitted with a slate top, molded top fitted with well, shaped skirt over medial shelf with two drawers and lower shaped shelf, raised on molded legs.

***Provenance****: Teina Baumstone, New York, 1980. Ex. Garbisch Collection.*

$2,200-2,800     **FRE**

A George III mahogany kettle stand, the serpentine gadrooned top above frieze with slide to the front, on channeled and molded chamfered square legs with acanthus carved spandrels.

*13.25in (33cm) wide*

$5,000-7,000     **L&T**

A Regency mahogany teapoy, with ebony and boxwood stringing and satinwood banding, the hinged lid with canted angles enclosing interior, raised on turned and spirally reeded pedestal with gadrooned foot, the base with gilt-brass ball and claw feet.

*12in (30cm) wide*

$1,800-2,200     **L&T**

A mid-19thC English adjustable walnut candle stand, with a six-sided pedestal above three heavily carved tapered square legs with lions' head, iron adjusting mechanism.

*31in (77.5cm) high*

$600-900     **BRU**

A 19thC octagonal burlwood candle stand, probably Italian, the top with inlaid frieze, on four tapered legs with pad feet and shaped returns, lacking original slide-out tray for candle.

*25.5in (64cm) high*

$2,200-2,800     **BRU**

A Victorian walnut folio stand, the hinged open sides locked by brass fittings with leaf castings, the whole raised on a baluster 'jeweled' column, on four scroll supports terminating in scroll feet.

*40in (100cm) wide*

$5,000-7,000     **L&T**

A late Victorian Sheraton Revival satinwood and checker-strung pedestal, of square tapering form with a stepped plinth and shaped apron, painted with floral and garrya motifs.

*44.75in (112cm) high*

$800-1,200     **DN**

An early 19thC overpainted wood grotto stand, carved with a clam shell held by three caryatids, their tails wreathed with foliage, extending to three outswept legs linked by a lower tier.

*29in (74cm) wide*

$5,000-7,000     **L&T**

A Dutch 19thC mahogany jardinière, with floral marquetry decoration, pierced leaf supports, lift-out liner and hinged handle, on a turned foot and circular base with ball feet.

*13.75in (35cm) diam*

$1,200-1,800     **L&T**

**FURNITURE**

A George II mahogany two-tier dumb waiter, with molded octagonal tiers, on cannon turned columns and octagonal base with cabriole legs, adapted.

*29.25in (73cm) high*

| $1,200-1,800 | L&T |

A George III mahogany three-tier dumb waiter, the graduated shelves of dished form, with baluster columns, cabriole legs and pad feet with castors.

*40.5in (101cm) high*

| $700-1,000 | DN |

An early 19thC gilt-brass and mahogany dwarf whatnot, with turned supports and brass edging, acorn finials and castors.

*28.5in (71cm) deep*

| $5,000-7,000 | L&T |

A 19thC brass and mahogany two-tier whatnot, the kidney-shaped shelves with pierced three-quarter galleries and tubular supports, bell finials and castors.

*30in (75cm) high*

| $1,200-1,800 | L&T |

A Victorian rosewood whatnot, with a fret cut gallery, on turned supports and a base drawer.

| $1,200-1,800 | SWO |

An early Victorian mahogany three-tier whatnot, on roundel and lotus carved supports, brass cappings and castors.

*30in (75cm) high*

| $8,000-12,000 | CATO |

A Victorian rosewood whatnot, with a pierced fretwork gallery and raised on turned circular supports above a single drawer, on brass castors.

*37in (94cm) high*

| $2,800-3,200 | B |

A Victorian mahogany whatnot, the four serpentine-fronted shelves on turned supports, the lower shelf with a drawer.

*27.5in (69cm) wide*

| $800-1,200 | SWO |

A Victorian walnut four-tier whatnot, with pierced fret-cut gallery and spiral twist supports.

*46.75in (117cm) high*

| $500-800 | SWO |

## ÉTAGÈRES

A late 19thC rosewood and marquetry inlaid étagère, in the French mid-18thC manner, the kidney-shaped top with pierced gilt-metal gallery, the crossbanded top with floral marquetry inlay above a single inlaid drawer, on cabriole legs with gilt-metal cast mounts.

*27.25in (69cm) wide*

| $2,800-3,200 | L&T |

A pair of mahogany and gilt-metal mounted étagères, each with three tiers with bamboo-cast moldings, supported by cast faux bamboo uprights, terminating in outswept feet.

*24.75in (93cm) wide*

| $3,000-5,000 | L&T |

A Regency mahogany cellaret, the hinged top enclosing divided interior, on rope turned plinth and ring turned legs with brass caps and castors.

*27.25in (68cm) high*

**$2,800-3,200**     **L&T**

A Regency mahogany and bronze-mounted cellaret, of sarcophagus form, with a fitted interior, the sloping sides with cast foliate beading and anthemion motifs to the angles, on turned and gadrooned feet with brass caps and castors.

*29in (74cm) wide*

**$8,000-12,000**     **L&T**

A William IV mahogany sarcophagus cellaret, with a raised top above a cavetto molded border, scroll molded corner brackets with palmette incised carving, on four lion paw feet.

*29in (74cm) wide*

**$6,000-9,000**     **WW**

A George IV mahogany wine cooler, with an everted rim and lead lining, the plinth base with a nulled border, gilt-metal side handles and recessed castors.

*29.25in (73cm) wide*

**$5,000-7,000**     **DN**

An early 19thC inlaid cherry cellaret on stand, probably Piedmont North Carolina, dovetailed top, lid and front with string and star or floral inlay, base with dovetailed drawer, tapered legs with bellflower inlay and string inlay, original brass hinges, secondary woods yellow pine and poplar, old refinishing.

*13in (32.5cm) wide*

**$15,000-20,000**     **BRU**

An Edwardian mahogany cellaret on stand, with checker stringing and fan medallions, the hinged top inlaid with musical trophy, enclosing divided interior later lined for sewing, the legs inlaid with ribbon tied husk drops.

*26.5in (66cm) high*

**$1,800-2,200**     **L&T**

An octagonal mahogany cellaret, the satinwood crossbanded hinged lid with an inlaid rosette, over a lead-lined interior and brass bound sides with carry handles, on splayed square section tapering legs with brass caps and castors.

*28in (70cm) high*

**$4,000-6,000**     **L&T**

An English mahogany spirits cabinet, the panel lift top above an interior compartment, above a dovetailed drawer with wood pulls, on compressed turned bun feet, secondary woods pine and ash.

*31in (77.5cm) wide*

**$700-1,000**     **BRU**

A mahogany and brass-bound oval jardinière, with lion mask handles and a metal liner, on a stand with cabriole legs and pad feet.

*27.25in (68cm) wide*

**$2,200-2,800**     **DN**

A Flemish oak book press, with ebony-veneered frieze and finial surmounts and a molded rectangular press, raised on leaf-carved cup-and-cover supports linked by stretchers, the drawer inscribed "Anno 1630".

*1630*                    *31in (79cm) wide*

**$5,000-7,000**                    **L&T**

A late 19thC American glass and grain-painted cane display case, domed hinged lid opens to a fitted interior on a cylindrical base raised on four arched rectangular feet.

*52in (132cm) high*

**$10,000-15,000**                    **FRE**

An early 20thC mahogany and glass cane display case, marked Simons Bro. & Company, Philadelphia, glazed upper section with a molded lid, fitted interior, molded waist and base, shaped handles at sides and four arched feet.

*Simons Bro. & Co. was founded in 1840 by George W. Simons and his three sons. They began making silver thimbles and pencils and gradually expanded production to tea services, flatware, and umbrella heads.*

*53.75in (136.5cm) high*

**$3,000-5,000**                    **FRE**

A late 19thC oak easel of Albert Pinkham Ryder, of traditional form, on wheels.

**Provenance:** *Originally belonging to artist Albert Pinkham Ryder (1847-1917), the easel was given to artist Philip Evergood by his mother, Flora.*

*67in (167.5cm) high*

**$1,800-2,200**                    **FRE**

A Philadelphia Chippendale mahogany carved cartouche and pediment to chest-on-frame, attributed to John Pollard (1740-1787), cornice of double-molded scrolls with leafage-carved rosettes, pierced latticework with blind fret band, and centering a phoenix finial.

*c1775*                    *84in (210cm) high*

**$40,000-45,000**                    **FRE**

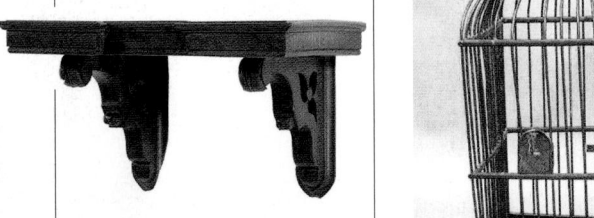

A 19thC English walnut burlwood bracket, the top with rectangular well and brass hangers, with tag "From the Estate of Jim Jefferson".

*15in (37.5cm) wide*

**$300-500**                    **BRU**

A Victorian double dome top birdcage, with a single opening, lacking lock and two base trays.

*35.5in (88.5cm) wide*

**$400-600**                    **SWO**

A mahogany terrarium, with turned wood and brass rod supports, a pagoda top with urn finial, the base with tapered and fluted legs and copper liner, damage and wear.

*72in (180cm) high*

**$2,200-2,800**                    **BRU**

An 18thC Italian miniature walnut and crossbanded commode, with three drawers, on squat bun feet.

*14.5in (36cm) wide*

**$3,000-5,000** **FRE**

A mid-19thC child's painted and grained high top dry sink, molded top above two recess paneled doors opening to shelves, above sink with single drawer and pair of recess panel doors below, bracket base.

*20.5in (52cm) wide*

**$800-1,200** **FRE**

A vibrantly decorated miniature pine blanket chest, by Jacob Weber, the lift lid with white flower within a green border, the front with a white farmhouse within a landscape, the ends with tulips, the chest with a tin hasp and straight bracket feet.

*c1840* *7.5in (19cm) wide*

**$80,000-100,000** **POOK**

A miniature Empire chest, top with drawers with fancy crotch-figure veneer, tapered columns with scrolled feet, secondary wood white pine, pencil inscription under full top drawer "Wife Ellen P.T(?)uttle by her father when a baby. Made at Bath, Maine, 1842 by Robert Tuttle. Took first premium at Bath fair", old refinishing.

*19in (47.5cm) wide*

**$1,800-2,200** **BRU**

A 19thC German Baroque-style miniature inlaid commode, in walnut and fruitwood, with three molded drawers, on four splayed feet.

*14.75in (37cm) wide*

**$700-1,000** **KAU**

A 19thC Dutch miniature walnut china cabinet, with a pair of astragal glazed doors enclosing shaped shelves, on a bombé base with three long drawers, on carved claw feet.

*40in (100cm) high*

**$1,200-1,800** **WW**

A Scottish miniature stained pine chest of drawers, with an ogee molded frieze drawer and four further drawers flanked by carved brackets, on a plinth and turned legs, labeled "These drawers were bought at the Franchise Demonstration which took place at Falkirk on 27th September 1884", inscribed.

*15.5in (39.5cm) wide*

**$3,000-4,000** **L&T**

A late Victorian miniature oak linen press, with a pair of paneled cupboard doors enclosing three slide-out trays, the base fitted with two short and two long drawers with brass drop handles, on a stepped plinth and shaped bracket feet.

*26.5in (67cm) high*

**$1,200-1,800** **B**

A Victorian miniature mahogany chest, with two short and three long graduated drawers and turned bone handles, on a plinth base.

*6in (15cm) high*

**$600-900** **B**

**FURNITURE**

An 18th or 19thC carved wooden figure of woman, wearing flowing gown and holding musical pipes, one finger missing, damage.

*42.5in (106cm) high*

$5,000-7,000      **BRU**

A pair of early 19thC carved oak allegorical figures, in the manner of Richard Bridgens, depicting Justice and Plenty, raised on plinths carved with blind strapwork and figural panels.

*largest 66in (168cm) high*

$7,000-10,000      **L&T**

A pair of 19thC European carved limewood figures, depicting a portly couple on shaped bases.

*largest 14.5in (37cm) high*

$280-320      **ROW**

A pair of European Blackamoor figures, each modeled as a man in 18thC costume holding a flaming torch and standing on a pillow, raised on a square base terminating in carved paw feet.

*71.75in (179cm) high*

$12,000-18,000      **FRE**

---

A European carved walnut figurehead, modeled as an admiral.

*30in (75cm) high*

$3,000-5,000      **FRE**

An 18th or 19thC gilt-wood sconce, with eagle and lion's head boss.

*27in (67.5cm) high*

$3,000-5,000      **BRU**

A 19thC Black Forest oak figure of a bear, with a rocky naturalistic base.

*26in (66cm) high*

$1,800-2,200      **L&T**

A 19thC Black Forest oak stick stand, carved as a bear with a 'branch' hoop.

*36in (91cm) high*

$5,000-7,000      **L&T**

---

A late 19thC German carved boxwood inkwell, modeled as a hound's head with a hinged lid and glass eyes.

*8.5in (21.5cm) wide*

$300-500      **GORL**

A Black Forest carved bear liqueur set, modeled holding a staff and carrying a young bear, the basket with glass decanter and six glasses.

*10in (25.5cm) high*

$2,800-3,200      **GORL**

A carved wooden tobacco jar, in the form of a skull, with an entwined carved snake and a lid.

*7.5in (19cm) high*

$280-320      **GORL**

An 18thC carved and painted wood relief, with a bishop and angels, signed "Joseph Go..." and dated "Ano de 1745", later frame.

*11in (27.5cm) high*

$1,800-2,200      **CHEF**

A pair of late 19thC bronze figural twin branch candelabrum, modeled as two jovial putti holding cornucopia.

*16.5in (41.5cm) high*

**$1,200-1,800**     **SWO**

A pair of Italian 18thC style Blackamoor torchères, modeled as full-length figures dressed in blue and red waistcoats, holding cornucopia, with vine branch candelabra, on scrolled triangular bases.

**$2,800-3,200**     **SWO**

A pair of Regency gilt and patinated bronze candelabra, each with winged angel, holding a candelabra with flaming sconces, on square pedestal with applied maiden to front holding a dove and a bee, on vine cast plinth.

*28.25in (73cm) high*

**$10,000-15,000**     **L&T**

One of a pair of bronze Barbadienne five-branch candelabra.

*36in (91.5cm) high*

**$1,200-1,800 pair**     **JN**

A set of four 19thC European Popeian-style iron and brass candlesticks, the knop molded stems raised on triform openwork bases.

*69.5in (174cm) high*

**$2,200-2,800**     **FRE**

## LAMPS

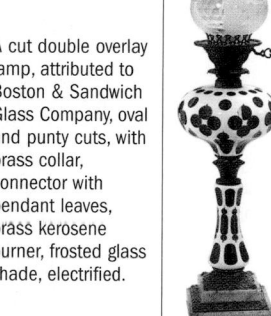

A cut double overlay lamp, attributed to Boston & Sandwich Glass Company, oval and punty cuts, with brass collar, connector with pendant leaves, brass kerosene burner, frosted glass shade, electrified.

*c1870*     *25.5in (65cm) high*

**$1,200-1,800**     **SK**

A cut double overlay lamp, attributed to Boston & Sandwich Glass Company, oval, punty and vesica cuts, with brass collar and connector, brass kerosene burner, a frosted glass shade, wear, electrified.

*c1870*     *25.5in (65cm) high*

**$1,800-2,200**     **SK**

A cut double overlay lamp, attributed to Boston & Sandwich Glass Company, oval and punty cuts, brass kerosene burner, a frosted glass shade with cut flowering vines, damage, electrified.

*c1870*     *26.75in (68cm) high*

**$1,200-1,800**     **SK**

A 20thC mushroom shade raised over base, cut in a variety of patterns, shade ring suspends cut glass prisms.

*25in (63.5cm) high*

**$600-900**     **SK**

A Mt. Washington Crown Milano lamp, the base decorated with seven snow geese flying against a sunburst, shade has matching decoration, base is signed with purple "CM" crown mark, excellent condition.

*19in (48cm) high*

**$4,000-6,000**     **JDJ**

A cobalt blue pear-shaped table lamp, font mounted on a crystal-stemmed foot, no. 1 burner.

*9.75in (24cm) high*

**$180-220**     **JDJ**

An amethyst pear-shaped table lamp, font-mounted on a brass and marble foot, zero size Coronet burner and old flange chimney.

*9.25in (23cm) high*

**$280-320**     **JDJ**

A pair of brass table lamps in Victorian ecclesiastical style, with glass cabochons and round bases, each with three feet.

*31.5in (79cm) high*

**$700-1,000**     **DN**

**FURNITURE**

A 19thC pair of Federal giltwood sconces, each with a ribbon crest above a shaft with arrows and garlands supporting a profile bust portrait on a blue reserve and two candlearms, some losses.

*28in (71cm) high*

**$2,800-3,200**    **POOK**

An 18thC style silvered electrolier and four sconces en suite, the electrolier with eight branches supported on turned column cast with foliate bands and surmounted by three opposed caryatid figures, with chain and ceiling rose, together with four matching two branch sconces.

*31in (79cm) diam*

**$5,000-8,000 set**    **L&T**

## A CLOSER LOOK AT A PAIR OF SCONCES

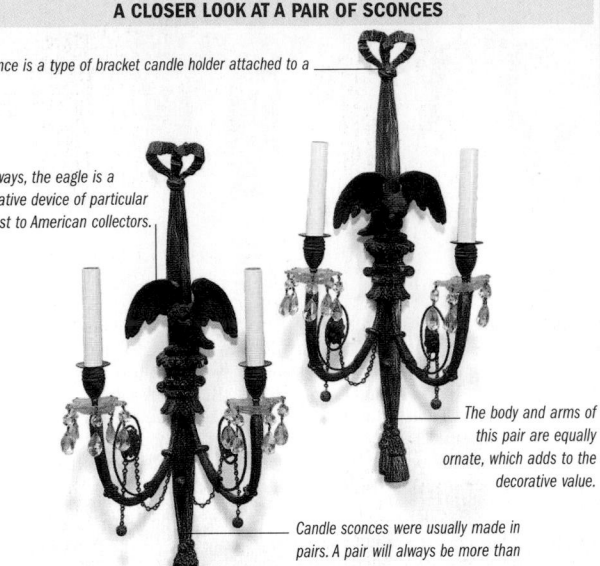

A sconce is a type of bracket candle holder attached to a wall.

As always, the eagle is a decorative device of particular interest to American collectors.

The body and arms of this pair are equally ornate, which adds to the decorative value.

Candle sconces were usually made in pairs. A pair will always be more than double the value than that of a single example.

A late 18thC pair of Classical giltwood, brass, and glass two-light candle sconces, each with carved eagle figures on a giltwood pilaster of acanthus leaves, scrolled giltwood and wirework scrolled arms with brass candlecups suspending glass prisms and giltwood balls, the whole mounted on a giltwood bowknot with tassel terminals, minor imperfections.

*26in (65cm) high*

**$22,000-25,000**    **SK**

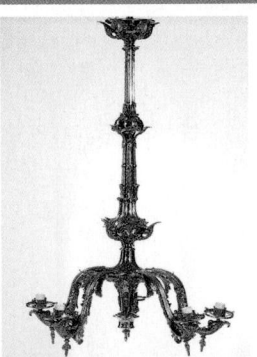

A pair of gilt bronze wall sconces, the ornate openwork back plates surmounted by shells, and cast with a horned grotesque mask issuing three acanthus cast S-scroll branches terminating in candle nozzles and with leafy drip trays, below are drapery aprons, signed "Henry Dasson" and dated.

*1887*    *23.5in (59cm) high*

**$10,000-15,000**    **FRE**

Two 19thC English brass-mounted candle sconces, glass globes with brass acorn drop finials, chevron-shaped wall mounts.

*14.25in (35.5cm) high*

**$2,800-3,200**    **BRU**

## CEILING LIGHTS

A late 19thC five-light cast-brass chandelier, attributed to Cornelius & Baker, Philadelphia, the shaped shaft and arms with cast leafage and decorative bosses, restored and electrified.

*46in (117cm) high*

**$4,000-6,000**    **FRE**

A late 19thC European Gothic Revival hall lantern, wrought iron, with fleur-de-lys finials enclosing a scrolling pendant and linked by pierced frieze below, converted to electricity.

*52in (132cm) high*

**$2,200-2,800**    **L&T**

A late 19thC Swedish alabaster chandelier, white with hand-carved flower design.

*25in (63.5cm) diam*

**$6,000-9,000**    **LANE**

A late 19thC Swedish alabaster amber chandelier, carved with leaf design.

*24in (61cm) diam*

**$5,000-7,000**    **LANE**

An 18thC mahogany tea caddy, of Chippendale design, with an ornate brass handle and escutcheon.

**$500-700** SWO

A George III mahogany tea caddy, the rectangular top with concave sides and a brass handle, enclosing divisions, and a secret drawer to one side, on ogee bracket feet, restored.

*9.5in (24cm) wide*

**$500-800** DN

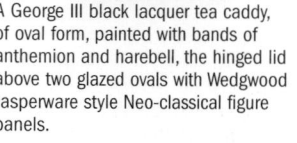

A George III black lacquer tea caddy, of oval form, painted with bands of anthemion and harebell, the hinged lid above two glazed ovals with Wedgwood Jasperware style Neo-classical figure panels.

*4.25in (11cm) high*

**$1,200-1,800** L&T

A George III burr fruitwood tea caddy, of octagonal form, the lid with chevron and rope-twist inlay.

*4.25in (11cm) high*

**$800-1,200** SWO

A George III mahogany tea caddy, the hinged lid concealing a compartmented interior, on bracket feet.

*9in (23cm) wide*

**$300-500** SWO

A George III mahogany tea caddy, the six sides and lid with inlaid ovals and narrow crossbanding.

**$1,200-1,800** SWO

A George III inlaid satinwood octagonal tea caddy, with rope-twist inlay to the corners, the body with alternate inlay of fluted columns and ovals with floral sprays.

**$1,200-1,800** SWO

A George III inlaid mahogany elliptical tea caddy with crossbanded and rope-twist inlay to the edges and urn and husk inlay to the front, opening to reveal two lidded compartments.

*7.25in (18.5cm) wide*

**$3,000-4,000** SWO

A George III inlaid mahogany tea caddy.

*c1800* *10.25in (26cm) wide*

**$500-800** MB

A Regency tortoiseshell and mother-of-pearl tea caddy, of square shape with canted corners and geometric lozenge design, with silver escutcheon and initialed mount.

*6in (15cm) wide*

**$10,000-15,000** GORL

A Regency mahogany and line-inlaid tea caddy, of sarcophagus form, the hinged cover enclosing three lidded canisters, the sides mounted with pressed brass handles, on four compressed bun feet.

*12.25in (31cm) wide*

**$300-500**     **B**

A Regency oak and marquetry sarcophagus-shaped three division tea caddy, inlaid with satinwood and rosewood geometric motifs, on bracket feet.

*11.25in (28.5cm) wide*

**$180-220**     **GORL**

A Regency rosewood and tulipwood crossbanded sarcophagus-shaped tea caddy, with checker banding and foliate brass loop handles, on bun feet.

*12in (30.5cm) wide*

**$280-320**     **GORL**

An early 19thC rectangular mahogany tea caddy, with a hinged lid enclosing two lidded compartments and a cut glass mixing bowl.

*12in (30.5cm) wide*

**$180-220**     **GORL**

A Regency tortoiseshell tea caddy of rounded sarcophagus shape, with white metal stringing and ball feet, the interior with two lidded compartments with white metal stringing and ivory knobs.

*6.75in (17cm) high*

**$4,000-6,000**     **SWO**

An early 19thC mahogany, boxwood, and ebony-strung tea caddy, of plain rectangular shape, with an elliptical handle and ivory escutcheon, fitted with two lidded compartments and a later glass bowl.

**$120-180**     **SWO**

A Georgian boxwood and ebony-inlaid tea caddy.

*c1810*     *7.75in (19.5cm) wide*

**$500-700**     **MB**

A Regency giltwood and papier mâché tea caddy, of oval section, the top with dragons in the Chinoiserie style on a black lacquer ground, opening to reveal the interior fitted with a hidden caddy, the gadrooned body raised on a leaf-carved pedestal.

**$2,800-3,200**     **L&T**

A late 18thC mahogany-framed paper scroll tea caddy, of six-sided section, inset with panels of scrolled paper under glass.

*8in (20.5cm) wide*

**$1,200-1,800**     **L&T**

A late Georgian blonde tortoiseshell and pewter-strung tea caddy, of rounded rectangular form, the dome hinged cover enclosing a pair of lidded zinc-lined compartments standing on four metal bun feet, restored.

*6.25in (16cm) wide*

**$1,200-1,800**     **B**

A William IV blonde tortoiseshell bombe sarcophagus-shaped two division tea caddy, the hinged lid opening to reveal two zinc-lined compartments, the covers with turned ivory knops, on brass ball feet.

*6.5in (16.5cm) wide*

**$3,000-5,000**     **B**

A small 19thC tortoiseshell tea caddy, raised on ivory bun feet.

*5in (13cm) wide*

**$500-700**  **CHEF**

A 19thC tortoiseshell tea caddy, the interior with two lidded compartments.

*7.75in (20cm) wide*

**$1,200-1,800**  **CHEF**

A 19thC tortoiseshell and mother-of-pearl tea caddy, of serpentine outline.

*5.5in (14cm) wide*

**$700-1,000**  **CHEF**

A 19thC black japanned papier mâché tea caddy, with painted floral decoration.

*14.25in (36cm) wide*

**$180-220**  **B**

A mid-19thC Cantonese lacquered tea caddy, of canted rectangular form, the exterior decorated in gilt with panels and borders of birds amongst trees and flowers, the domed cover enclosing a pair of engraved pewter canisters and covers, above a bombe-shaped body, on four carved and stylized bat feet.

*8.5in (21.5cm) wide*

**$3,000-5,000**  **B**

A Victorian mahogany tea caddy, with two lidded compartments and a glass mixing bowl.

*12.75in (32.5cm) wide*

**$180-220**  **GORL**

## WRITING BOXES

A large Georgian mahogany gentleman's writing box, inlaid with a compass star.

*c1800  14in (35.5cm) wide*

**$700-1,000**  **MB**

An early 19thC coromandel traveling writing box, profusely carved with flowering and scrolling foliage, the interior inlaid in bone with dotted lines and enclosing a folding writing surface.

*16.5in (41cm) wide*

**$300-500**  **L&T**

A Regency rosewood and mother-of-pearl inlaid stationery cabinet, the hinged lid and twin doors enclosing a tray and three drawers, on gadrooned plinth and bun feet.

*12.5in (32cm) wide*

**$500-700**  **GORL**

A William IV rosewood ladies' compendium, inlaid with mother-of-pearl and pewter, with jewelry and writing compartments.

*c1830*  *12.25in (31cm) wide*

**$1,800-2,200**  **MB**

A late 19thC boullework inkstand, fitted with two glass inkwells, box and pen tray, on button feet.

*16in (40.5cm) wide*

**$280-320**      **GORL**

A 19thC Jennings & Bettridge papier mâché stationery box, black lacquered finish with sloped lid and swept sides enclosing fitted interior, impressed mark and crown cipher to base.

*6.5in (16.5cm) wide*

**$180-220**      **GORL**

A Victorian walnut writing slope, the hinged lid concealing a removable fitted tray, with a secret sprung writing slope below.

*15.25in (39cm) wide*

**$500-700**      **SWO**

An early Victorian writing slope with brass bindings and inlay, hinged to enclose a leather writing inset, recesses and a pen tray.

*20in (50.5cm) wide*

**$280-320**      **DN**

An early Victorian rosewood writing box, of rectangular form, with a pair of hinged covers flanking a turned carrying handle, enclosing an interior fitted with a single lidded compartment.

*37.5in (95cm) wide*

**$280-320**      **B**

A Victorian mother-of-pearl writing and ink box.

*3in (7.5cm) wide*

**$220-280**      **MB**

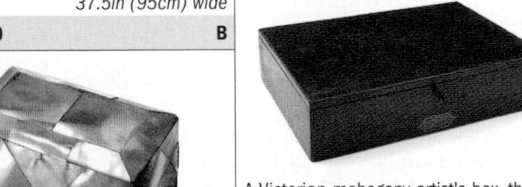

A Victorian mahogany artist's box, the compartmentalized interior with watercolor blocks in a labeled tray together with other artist's materials and equipment, stamped "Reeves and Sons", inscribed with owner's name and dated "March 24th 1860".

*11.5in (29cm) wide*

**$280-320**      **GORL**

A Victorian Isle of Man stationery box, in bird's-eye maple and inset rosewood, the hinged top and fall-front enclosing a well stand and bone pen rack, with two spring-loaded drawers and carved bone Manxman device initialed "EL".

*15in (38cm) wide*

**$280-320**      **GORL**

A rosewood drawing box.

*c1870*      *8in (20.5cm) wide*

**$220-280**      **MB**

A Victorian brass-bound coromandel desk inkstand.

*c1870*      *11.5in (29cm) wide*

**$500-800**      **MB**

A Victorian inlaid rosewood stationery cabinet.

*c1890*      *12in (30.5cm) wide*

**$1,200-1,800**      **MB**

An ivory and shagreen writing box and cover, with turquoise-coloured exterior, the handle gilt-embossed "London Made".

*13in (33cm) wide*

**$2,800-3,200**      **ROS**

An early 19thC penwork work basket, the lid decorated with a view of Brighton Pavilion within a foliate border, with turned ivory handle and feet.

*10in (25.5cm) wide*

$1,200-1,800                                   GORL

A Regency penwork work box, with foliage decoration and later lined interior, the sides with brass petal plate ring handles, on foliate paw feet.

*13in (33cm) wide*

$500-700                                          WW

A Regency tooled Morocco leather work box, with gadrooned hinged lid revealing a compartmented interior with seven mother-of-pearl and treen spools, on gilt metal scroll feet, damaged.

*11in (28cm) wide*

$120-180                                         GORL

An early 19thC octagonal penwork box, the lid decorated with a harbor scene within a scrolling acanthus leaf border.

*11in (28cm) wide*

$280-320                                         GORL

A Regency painted boxwood work box, decorated with a rustic landscape with flowers and leaves.

*10in (25.5cm) wide*

$800-1,200                                       GORL

An early 19thC penwork work box, the lid decorated with Oriental figures in a garden within a foliate border, the sides with scrolling acanthus leaves, on gilt metal scroll feet.

*9.5in (24cm) wide*

$300-500                                         GORL

An early 19thC penwork work box, the molded lid decorated with a lion and four music-making cherubs, with a compartmented interior housing various sewing accessories, on gilt ball feet.

*9in (23cm) wide*

$300-500                                         GORL

A William IV satinwood and ebony banded sarcophagus-shaped work box, the interior with a compartmented tray, on gilt metal paw feet.

*12.5in (32cm) wide*

$120-180                                         GORL

A 19thC mother-of-pearl inlaid and gilt-painted papier mâché toilet or work box, the cover inset and painted with a scene of Windsor Castle from the river below, the inside with six matched jars, with fitted stationery drawer to the base.

*11in (28cm) wide*

$280-320                                          ROS

A late 19thC Anglo-Indian work box, of sarcophagus shape, veneered in ivory and sadeli work, the hinged cover enclosing a detachable mirror and various dedicated compartments, above a pull-out slide containing a plush-lined writing surface.

*Sadeli work is a mosaic of ivory, pewter, and wood inlaid in geometric patterns.*

*16.5in (43cm) wide*

$1,200-1,800                                      WW

A 19thC burr elm and steel pique work box, with fitted interior tray housing various bone and glass accessories.

*Pique work makes use of gold and silver pins to create an inlaid design.*

*9.75in (25cm) wide*

$700-1,000                                       GORL

**BOXES & TREEN**

A 19thC stained pine workbox, in the form of a cottage, with a hinged lid, damaged.

*10in (25.5cm) wide*

**$800-1,200**    **SWO**

A Victorian rosewood sarcophagus-shaped work box, the lid inset with a mother-of-pearl presentation plaque, inscribed "Presented to Miss Bower by her pupils 1838".

*11.5in (29cm) wide*

**$300-500**    **GORL**

A walnut oyster-veneered lace box, the top with an inlaid circle and crossbanding.

An early 19thC Federal inlaid mahogany veneer table box, hinged lid on rectangular box with crossbanded and string-inlaid edges, the lid and front with ovals, carved shield-shaped ivory escutcheon, on base with cut-out skirts and flared French feet, minor imperfections.

**$5,000-8,000**    **SK**    **$700-1,000**    **SWO**

## JEWELRY BOXES

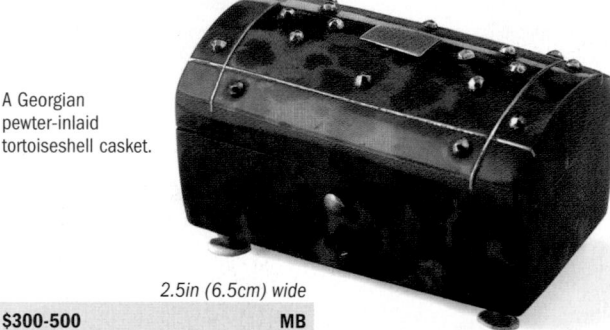

A Georgian pewter-inlaid tortoiseshell casket.

*2.5in (6.5cm) wide*

**$300-500**    **MB**

A William IV mother-of-pearl inlaid rosewood box.

*c1830*    *11in (28cm) wide*

**$500-700**    **MB**

A William IV mother-of-pearl inlaid coromandel cigar case.

*5.25in (13.5cm) wide*

**$280-320**    **MB**

An Austrian burr cedar, ebony, and specimen agates box.

*c1870*    *2.75in (7cm) wide*

**$180-220**    **MB**

A Victorian walnut jewelry box.

*12in (30.5cm) wide*

**$300-500**    **MB**

An Edwardian walnut jewelry box, with inscription.

*c1905*    *9.75in (25cm) wide*

**$500-700**    **MB**

A Tunbridgeware work box, by Thomas Barton, the domed lid decorated with a central floral spray within a foliate border, with similar decoration to side panels, with paper label.

*11in (28cm) wide*

**$600-900**       **GORL**

A large Tunbridgeware parquetry box, by Edmund Nye, the dark ground with geometric inlay with tesserae banding, with maker's paper label on base.

*11in (28cm) wide*

**$1,200-1,800**       **B**

An early 19thC Tunbridgeware rosewood work box, the hinged lid with perspective cube panel between a pair of green velvet pin cushions.

*12in (30.5cm) wide*

**$300-400**       **B**

A Victorian Tunbridgeware inlaid walnut writing slope.

*c1880*     *10.25in (26cm) wide*

**$220-280**       **MB**

A Victorian Tunbridgeware mosaic snuff box.

*c1820*     *3.25in (8.5cm) diam*

**$120-180**       **MB**

A 19thC Tunbridgeware rosewood box, with eight-point star design.

*1.5in (4cm) diam*

**$120-180**       **MB**

A William IV Tunbridgeware stickware box, with geometric design.

*4.25in (11cm) wide*

**$120-180**       **MB**

A Victorian Tunbridgeware rosewood box, with perspective cube design.

*c1870 3.75in (9.5cm) wide*

**$120-180**       **MB**

A 19thC Tunbridgeware rosewood jewelry box, the top inlaid with a stag, with a silk-lined interior.

*6in (15cm) wide*

**$220-280**       **SWO**

A Victorian Tunbridgeware inlaid brush, with floral design.

*c1860*     *6.25in (16cm) wide*

**$50-70**       **MB**

A Victorian Tunbridgeware inlaid rosewood box, with floral design.

*4.5in (11.5cm) wide*

**$120-180**       **MB**

**BOXES & TREEN**

A Tunbridgeware rosewood sewing companion, the turned central stem with a circular pin cushion with 'Van Dyke' inlay, the middle tier with a smaller pincushion, thread waxer, tape measure and thimble stand, between four cotton reel pegs.

*'Van Dyke' inlay is a pattern of elongated triangles in contrasting colors.*

*6.75in (17cm) high*

**$1,200-1,800**     **B**

A novelty Tunbridgeware pin wheel, by Thomas Barton, modeled as a table, the ebony top inlaid with a Barton star on a stickware baluster-turned stem and tesserae mosaic decorated circular base, losses.

*3.25in (8cm) diam*

**$800-1,200**     **B**

A Victorian Tunbridgeware inlaid frame.

*c1880*     *6.25in (16cm) high*

**$120-180**     **MB**

A Tunbridgeware oblong rosewood box, with sloping sides and pin cushion top. the sides with a tesserae mosaic band of daffodils.

*9.75in (24.5cm) wide*

**$280-320**     **B**

A Tunbridgeware rosewood box, the oblong-shaped lid with tesserae mosaic rose banding within checker stringing, the cedar-lined interior with single boat-shaped division.

*5.75in (14.5cm) wide*

**$220-280**     **B**

A Tunbridgeware inlaid rosewood box.

*2in (5cm) wide*

**$120-180**     **MB**

A Victorian Tunbridgeware stamp box.

*1.75in (4.5cm) wide*

**$120-180**     **MB**

A Tunbridgeware 'saucepan' caddy spoon, with turned handle.

*3.5in (9cm) long*

**$300-500**     **WW**

A Tunbridgeware 'saucepan' caddy spoon, with geometric eight-point star motif inside the pan and turned handle.

*3.5in (9cm) long*

**$300-500**     **WW**

A Tunbridgeware 'saucepan' caddy spoon, with turned handle.

*4in (10cm) long*

**$300-500**     **WW**

A Tunbridgeware 'saucepan' caddy spoon, with turned handle.

A Tunbridgeware 'saucepan' caddy spoon, with turned handle.

*3.5in (9cm) long*

**$300-500**     **WW**

A Tunbridgeware 'saucepan' caddy spoon, with turned handle.

*3in (7.5cm) long*

**$300-500**     **WW**

A Victorian Mauchlineware watch case.

*c1850*          *2.75in (7cm) high*

**$80-120**          **MB**

An early Victorian Mauchlineware sycamore snuff box, painted with green grapes growing with foliage on brown vines against a black background.

*2.75in (7cm) wide*

**$280-320**          **CHEF**

A Mauchlineware miniature saucepan, with a print of the Parade at Skegness.

*c1860*

**$70-100**          **MB**

A Victorian Mauchlineware larch and sycamore box, with a print of Porthcawl.

*2.75in (7cm) wide*

**$80-120**          **MB**

A Victorian Mauchlineware sycamore box.

*4in (10cm) wide*

**$50-80**          **MB**

A Victorian Mauchlineware hat pin box, with a print of York Minster.

*4in (10cm) wide*

**$70-100**          **MB**

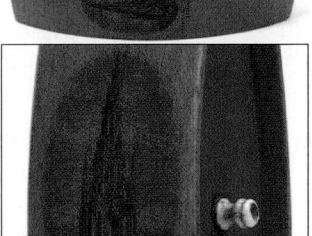

A Victorian Mauchlineware boat-shaped desk sealer.

*4.75in (12cm) wide*

**$120-180**          **MB**

A Mauchlineware larch and sycamore watch barrel.

*c1880*          *3.25in (8.5cm) high*

**$80-120**          **MB**

A Mauchlineware cylindrical box and cover, the lid with a print of Hawkhurst in Kent, the side with a print of the Queens Hotel in Hawkhurst.

*3.25in (8cm) diam*

**$80-120**          **B**

A Mauchlineware hexagonal hinged box, containing a glass inkwell.

*2in (5cm) high*

**$120-180**          **GORL**

**BOXES & TREEN**

A Mauchlineware string box, with a print of Campbeltown harbor.

*3.5in (9cm) diam*

$120-180     **GORL**

A Mauchlineware napkin ring.

*2.25in (5.5cm) wide*

$30-50     **MB**

A Mauchlineware ruler, with a print of Wimborne Minster in Dorset, England.

*12in (30.5cm) wide*

$50-70     **MB**

A Mauchlineware sycamore watch box.

$80-120     **MB**

An early Mauchlineware cigar case, with a portrait print.

*5in (13cm) wide*

$220-280     **MB**

## TARTANWARE

A tartanware specimen wood snuff box, with a hinged lid and presentation inscription, dated.

*1849*

$700-1,000     **CHEF**

A mid-19thC tartanware snuff box, possibly from Mauchline.

*Tartanware boxes were made by the Smith works at Mauchline from 1825.*

$120-180     **CHEF**

A tartanware stamp box, printed with the 'McBeth' tartan.

*1.5in (4cm) diam*

$70-100     **WW**

A tartanware go-to-bed, printed with the 'MacDuff' tartan.

*2.75in (7cm) high*

$70-100     **WW**

A tartanware string box, printed with the 'Caledonia' tartan.

*3in (7.5cm) diam*

$80-120     **WW**

## A CLOSER LOOK AT A PEG TANKARD

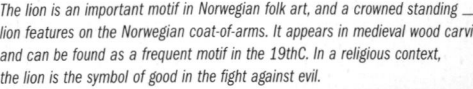

A rare 17thC carved beech Friesland mangle board, carved with traditional decoration and with date "Anno 1670".

*30.75in (78cm) long*

**$700-1,000** | **L&T**

The lion is an important motif in Norwegian folk art, and a crowned standing lion features on the Norwegian coat-of-arms. It appears in medieval wood carving and can be found as a frequent motif in the 19thC. In a religious context, the lion is the symbol of good in the fight against evil.

The lid is beautifully carved with traditional Norwegian motifs and chip-carved, or 'karverskurd', ornament.

Apart from a patch to the side and repairs to the base, this tankard appears to be in good condition. Both the scroll handle and the crowned lion are still intact.

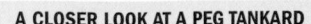

A mid-19thC Norwegian birch peg tankard, the domed hinged lid carved with a crowned lion, with a scrolled handle and stylized lion feet, restored.

Peg tankards were used for communal drinking. Each drinker had to drain the tankard down to the next peg.

The lion motif is repeated on the base in the form of four stylized pressed lions supporting the vessel.

*9.5in (24cm) wide*

**DN**

An early 18thC wrought iron rush light, on a bell-shaped wood base.

*8.25in (21cm) high*

**$500-700** | **DN**

**$1,200-1,800** | **DN**

---

A rare 18thC carved beech Friesland mangle board, carved with traditional decoration, initialed "HM BV" and dated 1728.

*34.75in (88cm) long*

**$1,200-1,800** | **L&T**

An early 18thC wrought iron rush light, on a round oak base, traces of paint.

*10.75in (27cm) high*

**$500-700** | **DN**

A lignum vitae goblet and cover, with later silver mounts inscribed "To friendship, Mirth & good Humour, ever Sacred", hallmarks undated, maker's marks for Thomas Phipps and Edward Robinson II.

*c1785*     *10in (25cm) high*

**$12,000-18,000** | **L&T**

An early 19thC mahogany and laburnum egg epergne, the central baluster column supporting two graduated tiers with removable egg cups and with lidded finial above, the whole raised on a spreading turned base.

*19.25in (49cm) high*

**$1,800-2,200** | **L&T**

---

A 19thC turned lignum vitae string barrel, with brass tap and cutter.

*3.5in (9cm) high*

**$280-320** | **WW**

A 19thC knitting sheath, inlaid with heart, star, and diamond shapes and inset with a paper label inscribed "Miss M Brown, White House, March 16th 1838".

*8.25in (21cm) long*

**$120-180** | **WW**

A 19thC European yew wood nut cracker, modeled as a squirrel, with a screw handle.

*7in (18cm) high*

**$120-180** | **WW**

A 19thC fruitwood pen box, the carved sliding top with a button release.

*9in (23cm) long*

**$80-120** CA

A 19thC turned fruitwood glove powder box.

*4.25in (11cm) high*

**$80-120** CA

A late 19thC Swiss carved pine gnome coat hook, with glass eyes and two ibex horns, dated.

*1887* *14.25in (36cm) long*

**$800-1,200** DN

A Victorian fruitwood chemist's jar and cover with stoppered glass bottle, by S. Mawson & Sons.

*5.5in (14cm) high*

**$80-120** CA

A Victorian turned fruitwood box and cover, containing a small measuring glass and a phial measure, by S. Mawson & Sons.

*3.25in (8.5cm) high*

**$120-180** CA

An Edwardian turned mahogany urn, on a concave-sided square base, with brass paw feet.

*20.5in (52cm) high*

**$500-700** WW

A 19thC turned olive-wood wool winder, the baluster stem with clamp, adjustable arms with pegs, and a wool bowl.

*10in (25.5cm) high*

**$120-180** WW

An antique treen cup and cover.

*4.75in (12cm) high*

**$180-220** CA

A treen money box, in the form of a round castle.

*3.5in (9cm) high*

**$180-220** CA

A fruitwood boot in the 18thC style, with a spur.

*3in (7.5cm) high*

**$70-100** CA

A treen campana-form pin cushion stand.

*4in (10cm) high*

**$120-180** CA

A treen glove powder box.

*4.75in (12cm) high*

**$80-120** CA

A treen barrel-form box and cover.

*3.25in (8.5cm) high*

**$80-120** CA

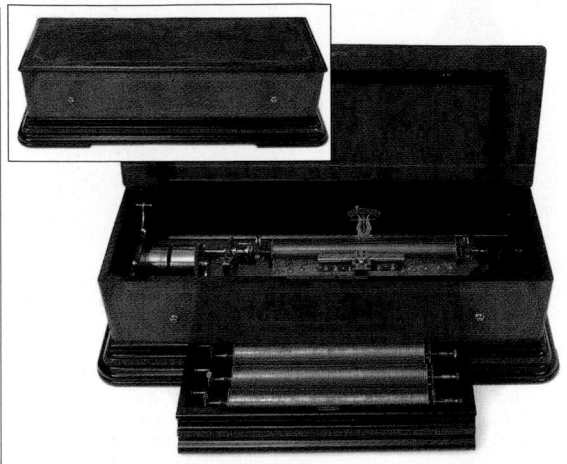

A large Harpe-Harmonique interchangeable music box, by Bremond, with four cylinders playing eight airs each, double-spring motor, tune indicator, speed regulator and zither attachment, in a walnut veneered case with a cylinder drawer.

*50in (127cm) wide*

**$5,000-8,000**     **EG**

An automaton music box, by Karrer, with one cylinder playing six airs, further bells struck by a monkey, three-piece comb and silvered zither attachment signed "S. Karrer, Manufacturer of Musical Boxes, Teufenthal, Switzerland", in an ebonized case, the lid painted with a three-masted schooner, signed and dated "Capt. Elisha Jonas 1876", on an associated ebonized writing table by Hernedon.

*40in (101cm) wide*

**$4,000-6,000**     **EG**

A Nicole Frères music box, the rosewood case inlayed with a classical bust, stamped "Nicole Frères a Geneve" on the brass bed, with serial number.

*18in (46cm) wide*

**$4,000-6,000**     **H&L**

A Regina music box, in a serpentine mahogany case, with 71 steel discs.

*18in (46cm) wide*

**$5,000-8,000**     **BRU**

## A CLOSER LOOK AT A REGINA UPRIGHT MUSIC BOX

The Regina Music Box Co. was founded in 1892 by Gustav Brachhaussen and based in New Jersey. Originally the company sold imported music boxes from Polyphon of Leipzig, but later they began producing their own. Between 1894 and 1921 Regina was the most prominent maker of music boxes in America.

This piece is one of Regina's earlier music boxes, made in 1899, and retains original features such as the automatic changer and an original paper plate printed with the patent date. A music box in this condition is extremely desirable.

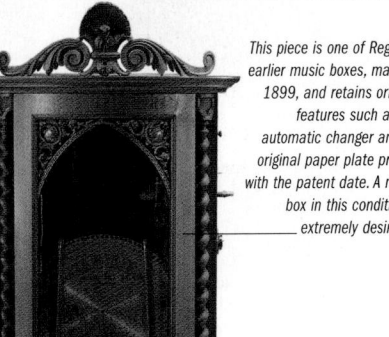

The mechanism is in good, unrestored condition, which is essential if a music box is to realize the best possible price.

The upright case has been skillfully constructed from fine mahogany and the legs remain undamaged despite frequent movement, which further enhances its value.

A Regina mahogany upright case music box, with automatic changer, original paper plate with patent date "Nov. 21, '99" and partial paper label "Regina Music Box Co.", complete with 50 discs.

*27in (68.5cm) wide*

**$15,000-18,000**     **FRE**

A Sublime Harmony music box, by Mermod, with one cylinder playing 12 airs, nickeled movement, tune indicator, speed regulator, Jacot safety check and coin mechanism, in an oak case with carved front, paneled lid and bead and reed molding.

*38in (96.5cm) wide*

**$2,800-3,200**     **EG**

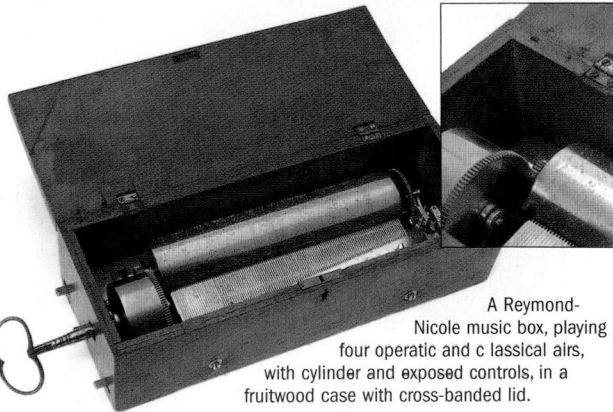
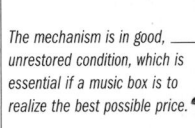

A Reymond-Nicole music box, playing four operatic and classical airs, with cylinder and exposed controls, in a fruitwood case with cross-banded lid.

*12in (30.5cm) wide*

**$5,000-8,000**     **EG**

**MUSICAL**

A Reymond-Nicole music box, playing six airs, with cylinder and exposed controls, in a fruitwood case with cross-banded lid, winding key and manuscript tune list.

*11.75in (30cm) wide*

**$1,800-2,200**    **EG**

A German upright walnut polyphon, inlaid in brass with the name "Polyphon", with a plaque to the side of the case stamped with retailer's label "H. Peters & Co. London. Made in Leipzig", complete with 12 discs.

*c1870*    *42.25in (107cm) high*

**$6,000-9,000**    **H&L**

A German upright walnut polyphon, with a crank-wound movement and coin slots, a bone plaque to the door stamped with retailer's label "T. Rhodes and Sons Ltd 18 Silver Street Halifax", complete with 20 discs.

*c1870*    *50.5in (128cm) high*

**$7,000-10,000**    **H&L**

A 19thC Swiss musical box, with lever-operated mechanism, one silvered metal cylinder playing 30 airs and colored lithographic card to the lid, contained in a rosewood inlaid case transfer-decorated with floral sprays.

*26.5in (67.5cm) long*

**$2,800-3,200**    **H&L**

A late 19thC Visible Bells Swiss music box, with one cylinder playing eight airs on a comb and three bells, the rosewood lid with marquetry inlay, the sides painted to simulate rosewood.

*16.5in (42cm) wide*

**$400-600**    **CHEF**

A Swiss carved wood musical log cabin, with pitched roof and embellishments, in original pine box.

*7.5in (19cm) high*

**$180-220**    **GORL**

A Sublime Harmonie musical box, with one cylinder playing eight airs, double comb and winding lever, stamped with the serial number "12411", with decorated tune sheet, in a burr walnut case with brass and ebonized inlay.

*28.75in (73cm) wide*

**$3,000-5,000**    **H&L**

A musical sewing box, with a two air movement under a glazed cover, contained in a walnut case with inlaid central cartouche and cross banding, the base with tune card.

*9.5in (24cm) wide*

**$120-180**    **EG**

A singing bird cage, containing a pair of birds with moving heads, beaks and tails, on a gilt gesso square base with floral and foliate decoration.

*18.5in (47cm) high*

**$2,200-2,800**    **EG**

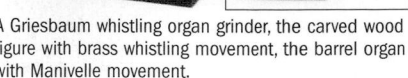

A Griesbaum whistling organ grinder, the carved wood figure with brass whistling movement, the barrel organ with Manivelle movement.

*13in (33cm) high*

**$1,200-1,800**    **EG**

An Edison Model B Fireside phonograph, with four-minute gearing, Diamond B reproducer, oak case and No.10 Cygnet horn.

**$1,200-1,800**     **EG**

An Edison Opera phonograph, with Diamond A reproducer, traversing mandrel, brown enameled top plate and upper works, oxidized fittings, mahogany case, and self-supporting Music Master horn.

**$5,000-8,000**     **EG**

An Edison Model G Triumph phonograph, with Diamond B reproducer, double-spring motor, oak case with corner columns, and oak Music Master horn.

**$10,000-15,000**     **EG**

A Victor Type C phonograph, with Concert sound box, oak traveling arm, nickeled extension arm, wood dust ring, brass-belled horn, chromed turntable and oak case.

**$2,800-3,200**     **EG**

A Victor MS phonograph, with Exhibition sound box, goose-neck tone arm, oak case with fluted corner columns, and fluted oak 'spear tip' horn.

*21.5in (54.5cm) diam*

**$2,800-3,200**     **EG**

A Victor Type P phonograph, with Exhibition soundbox, metal top plate, oxidized extension arm, oak case and traveling arm and brass-belled horn.

*11in (28cm) diam*

**$800-1,200**     **EG**

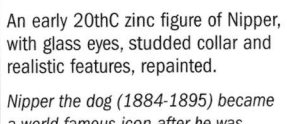

An early 20thC zinc figure of Nipper, with glass eyes, studded collar and realistic features, repainted.

*Nipper the dog (1884-1895) became a world famous icon after he was immortalized in Francis Barraud's painting 'Dog looking at and listening to a phonograph', later renamed 'His Master's Voice'.*

*18in (45.5cm) high*

**$4,000-6,000**     **EG**

A Zonophone Concert phonograph, with Universal soundbox on tapering tone arm, double-spring motor, oak case and blue Morning Glory horn, retailer's label "So. Cal. music Co., Los Angeles, Cal."

*23in (58.5cm) diam*

**$1,200-1,800**     **EG**

Four items of phonograph paraphernalia, comprising a record case by Hawthorne & Sheble, a framed advertizement for Columbia Art Models, a modern ceramic Nipper money bank, and a plastic Nipper.

**$120-180**     **EG**

## THE GLASS MARKET

A quiet and uneventful year in the antique glass market has been a mixed blessing for collectors. Values have remained relatively stable and predictable, but the lack of quality glass reaching the market is beginning to stifle certain areas of this sector.

Color continues to spell popularity. Antique wine glasses with color-twist stems and the enameled and brightly painted armorial glasses of William Beilby have been market leaders for some time now. However, even in these popular areas of the market, price rises have not been particularly dramatic. This may well be because so few pieces are offered for sale that collectors abandon hope of acquiring them and move on to other fields.

Glimmers of hope were afforded by the publication of an authoritative book 'The Decanter' by Andy McConnell, published by The Antiques Collectors Club. An influx of new knowledge and good quality glass will recruit new collectors and re-enthuse those already familiar with antique glass.

Buyers should concentrate their resources on acquiring one or two pieces of top quality glass rather than a greater number of inferior items. Collectors of Brilliant Period glass are keen on buying pieces by Dorflinger, Libbey, Hawkes, Hoare, and Clark. These firms produced some of the finest cut and engraved glass in history and are highly collectible today.

## AIR-TWIST WINE GLASSES

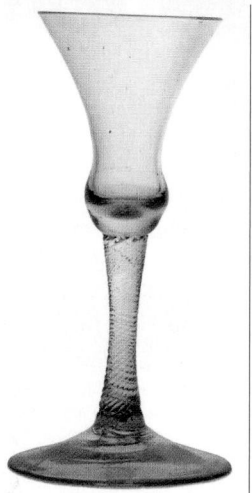

A mid-18thC European wine glass, with a bell bowl and incised twist stem, made from soda glass.

*6.5in (16.5cm) high*

**$180-220**    **JH**

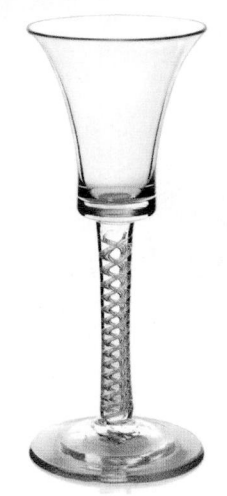

An air-twist wine glass, the flared bucket bowl supported on a stem with a pair of multi-ply tapes, on a conical foot.

*c1750    6.5in (16.5cm) high*

**$800-1,200**    **DN**

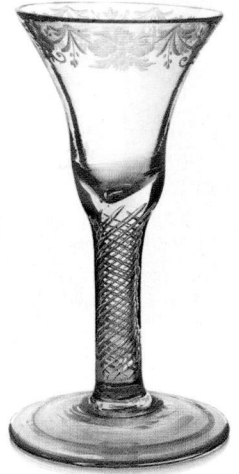

A mid-18thC engraved air-twist wine glass, the bell bowl decorated with a stylized foliate band, on a folded conical foot.

*6in (15cm) high*

**$1,200-1,800**    **DN**

A mid-18thC wine glass, the bell bowl supported on an air-twist stem filled with spiral threads.

*7in (18cm) high*

**$180-220**    **DN**

A mid-18thC engraved air-twist wine glass, the bell bowl on an annular knop and decorated with a rose, bud, and a thistle.

*7in (17.5cm) high*

**$500-700**    **DN**

An air-twist wine glass, the bell bowl supported on a shoulder-knopped stem filled with spiral threads, on a conical foot.

*c1750    7in (18cm) high*

**$700-1,000**    **DN**

A mid-18thC Jacobite air-twist wine glass, of drawn trumpet form, engraved with a rose and thistle, the stem with a pair of entwined cables, on a conical foot, inscribed "Fiat".

*7.5in (19cm) high*

**$2,800-3,200**    **DN**

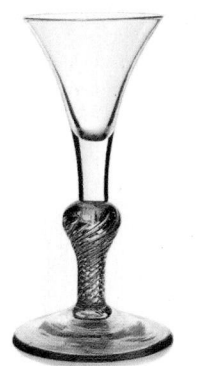

A wine glass of drawn trumpet form, with a solid plain section supported on an air-twist inverted baluster stem and conical foot, foot-rim chip.

*c1750*          7in (18cm) high

**$700-1,000**          DN

A mercury-twist wine glass, of drawn trumpet form, the stem with a pair of spiral tapes, on a conical foot.

*c1750*          6.5in (16.5cm) high

**$1,200-1,800**          DN

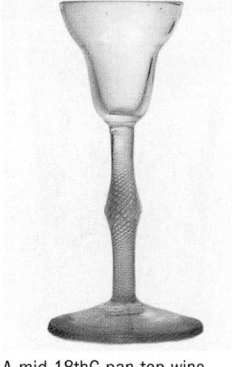

A mid-18thC air-twist wine glass, the round funnel bowl supported on an annular cushion knop, on a conical foot.

6.5in (16.5cm) high

**$1,200-1,800**          DN

A mid-18thC pan-top wine glass, with multi-spiral air-twist stem.

6in (15cm) high

**$220-280**          JH

A small mid-18thC air-twist wine glass, the round bowl with a gilt dentil rim, supported on a stem with central swelling knop, on a conical foot.

4.5in (11.5cm) high

**$800-1,200**          DN

An air-twist wine glass, the round funnel bowl supported on a shoulder-knopped stem, with a basal-knopped lower section on a conical foot.

*c1750*          6in (15cm) high

**$500-700**          DN

A pair of engraved air-twist wine glasses, the round funnel bowls with a band of fruiting vine, the centrally knopped stems filled with spiral threads.

*c1750*          6in (15cm) high

**$1,200-1,800**          DN

An engraved air-twist wine glass, the round bowl with everted rim and engraved with a floral band, the stem filled with spiral threads.

*c1750*          6in (15cm) high

**$800-1,200**          DN

A mid-18thC engraved air-twist wine glass, the round funnel bowl decorated with a floral band, on a domed foot.

6.25in (16cm) high

**$1,200-1,800**          DN

An air-twist goblet, the ogee bowl with honeycomb-molded lower section, on a conical foot.

*c1760*          8in (20cm) high

**$700-1,000**          DN

An opaque-twist toasting glass or ale flute, of drawn trumpet form, with double-series stem and conical foot.

*c1770*          7.5in (19cm) high

**$700-1,000**          DN

A color-twist wine glass, the round funnel bowl supported on a stem with a red corkscrew core entwined by a broad opaque spiral, on a conical foot.

*c1765*

**$3,000-4,000**          DN

**GLASS**

A Riesengebirge allegorical armorial tumbler, chipped.

c1700    3.75in (9.5cm) high

**$3,000-5,000**    **FIS**

An 18thC enameled tankard with the arms of Saxony and Poland.

c1720    9in (23cm) high

**$1,800-2,200**    **FIS**

A late 18thC 'Lynn' tumbler, typically worked with horizontal ribs on tapering cylindrical sides.

4.5in (11.5cm) high

**$700-1,000**    **CHEF**

An early 19thC commemorative shipping tumbler, with fluted lower section, engraved with a single-masted fishing boat, inscribed "Adelaide", and "JH".

4in (10.5cm) high

**$700-1,000**    **DN**

## A CLOSER LOOK AT AN ENGRAVED TUMBLER

Johann Wolfgang Schmidt was a glasscutter who worked in Nuremberg during the late 17thC.

Glass made from potash lime was developed in Germany at around this time. It was far more suitable for this kind of engraved decoration than soda glass.

The fleeing doe and captured buck is a romantic take on the hunting motif, which was typical of the German decorative arts throughout the medieval period and into the Renaissance.

Nuremberg was a center of the European glass industry during this period, and was especially famed for detailed Baroque engraving such as this.

An engraved tumbler by Johann Wolfgang Schmidt of Nuremberg, depicting a hunting scene.

c1680    3in (7.5cm) high

**$7,000-10,000**    **FIS**

An engraved tumbler, decorated with a hunting scene in a continuous band.

c1820    4in (10cm) high

**$400-600**    **DN**

## GOBLETS & RUMMERS

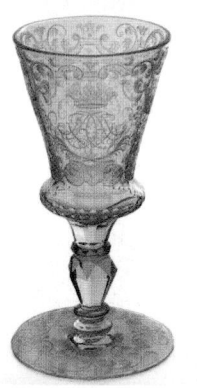

A Riesengebirge goblet with a mirror monogram.

c1730    6.75in (17cm) high

**$2,800-3,200**    **FIS**

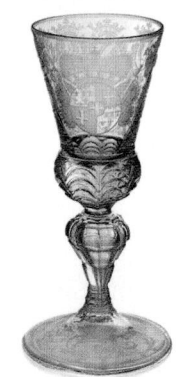

A goblet by the Glasburger Hütte, with the arms of the Prince of Fulda.

9.75in (24.5cm) high

**$7,000-10,000**    **FIS**

A mid-18thC Dutch light baluster marriage goblet, the round funnel bowl engraved with a rocaille cartouche with love-hearts on an altar and a cornucopia of fruit and flowers, the reverse inscribed, on a stem with cushion knop above an inverted baluster section with bead inclusions, on a conical foot.

8in (20.5cm) high

**$4,000-6,000**    **DN**

A late 18thC trumpet-shaped goblet, with a band of engraved decoration.

*8.5in (21.5cm) high*

**$1,200-1,800** FIS

A pair of engraved rummers, the barrel-shaped bowls with foliate sprigs above fluted lower sections, on centrally knopped stems and circular feet, initialed "RAK".

*c1820*     *5in (13cm) high*

**$280-320** DN

A large early 19thC Admiral Lord Nelson commemorative rummer, the round funnel bowl engraved with the HMS Victory under sail, the reverse with the Admiral's funeral barge, on a knopped stem and conical foot, inscribed "Nile", "Trafalgar", and "Victory", cracked.

*8.5in (21.5cm) high*

**$1,800-2,200** DN

A large coin rummer, the bucket bowl with a fluted lower section, the hollow stem with a George III coin insert, on a conical foot, engraved "WAL".

*c1820*     *6.75in (17cm) high*

**$500-700** DN

A commemorative rummer, the tapered bucket bowl engraved with the London to York mail coach with figures and horses, on a facet-knopped stem and square foot, initialed "GC".

*c1825*     *6in (15cm) high*

**$1,200-1,800** DN

An engraved rummer, the tapered bucket bowl with a two-masted ship sailing beneath Sunderland Bridge, on a capstan stem and circular foot, inscribed "Sunderland Bridge River Wear" and initialed "EB".

*c1825*     *6in (15cm) high*

**$500-800** DN

A mid-19thC German rummer, with octagonal tapered bowl, faceted knop and strawberry-cut octagonal foot, engraved with a Munich landscape, inscribed "Baberte" and "Zur Erinnerung" amidst vine motifs.

*6.25in (16cm) high*

**$280-320** L&T

Two of a set of six Edwardian rummers, with tall bell bowls on stepped plinth bases.

**$600-900 set** L&T

An engraved crested rummer, the generous bucket bowl with a crest of an anchor entwined with a serpent, on a plain stem and conical foot.

*6.25in (16cm) high*

**$400-600** DN

## OTHER GLASSES

A mid-18thC ribbed sweetmeat glass, with molded pedestal stem and folded foot.

*6in (15cm) high*

**$700-1,000** JH

A mid-18thC baluster sweetmeat glass, the round bowl with everted and notched rim and fluted lower section, supported on a centrally knopped stem and domed foot.

*7in (18cm) high*

**$500-800** DN

**GLASS**

## A CLOSER LOOK AT A FAÇON DE VENICE GLASS

'Façon de Venice' means 'in the manner of Venice'. Factories all over Europe emulated the lampwork designs of the Venetian master glassblowers.

Belgium and southern Holland, from where this piece originates, were the great centers of Façon de Venice production during the 17thC. Most examples are made from clear glass combined with these characteristic blue colors.

The delicacy, age, and technical accomplishment of this piece combine to make it a valuable and desirable item.

Most of the Façon de Venice glass on the market today dates from the 19thC revival. This piece is a far more valuable 17thC original.

A very rare 17thC 'Façon de Venice' stemmed glass, from the southern Netherlands.

12.25in (31cm) high

| $3,000-5,000 | FIS |

A 19thC ruby-flashed German rummer.

7in (17.5cm) high

| $500-700 | FIS |

Two of a set of eighteen quatrefoil-shaped glasses, by Lobmeyr of Vienna.

c1890 largest 6in (15cm) high

| $2,800-3,200 set | AL |

A set of three green wine glasses, with clear stems.

4.75in (12cm) high

| $80-120 | H&L |

One of a set of eight cranberry champagne glasses.

| $120-180 set | H&L |

## DECANTERS

A Victorian oak and silver-plated tantalus, by Walker & Hall, with three square cut-glass decanters for gin, whisky, and brandy.

c1890          13.75in (35cm) wide

| $400-600 | CSA |

A Sheffield silver decanter carrier, by James Deakin & Sons, with three cut-glass decanters and later silver labels.

1904          12in (30cm) wide

| $1,200-1,800 | CSA |

Three mid-19thC slender colored decanters, with silver-plated stoppers and a plated tripartite stand, in amethyst, blue, and green glass.

13.75in (35cm) high

| $500-800 | DN |

## A CLOSER LOOK AT A TANTALUS

*Invented in the mid-18thC, the tantalus is a wooden frame used to display decanters whilst keeping them locked away from the servants. The name is taken from Greek mythology. Tantalus abused the hospitality of the gods and was punished by being surrounded by inaccessible food and drink for eternity.*

*In order to attract a good price, it is essential that a tantalus is complete with original, matching decanters and stoppers in good condition, without chips or losses.*

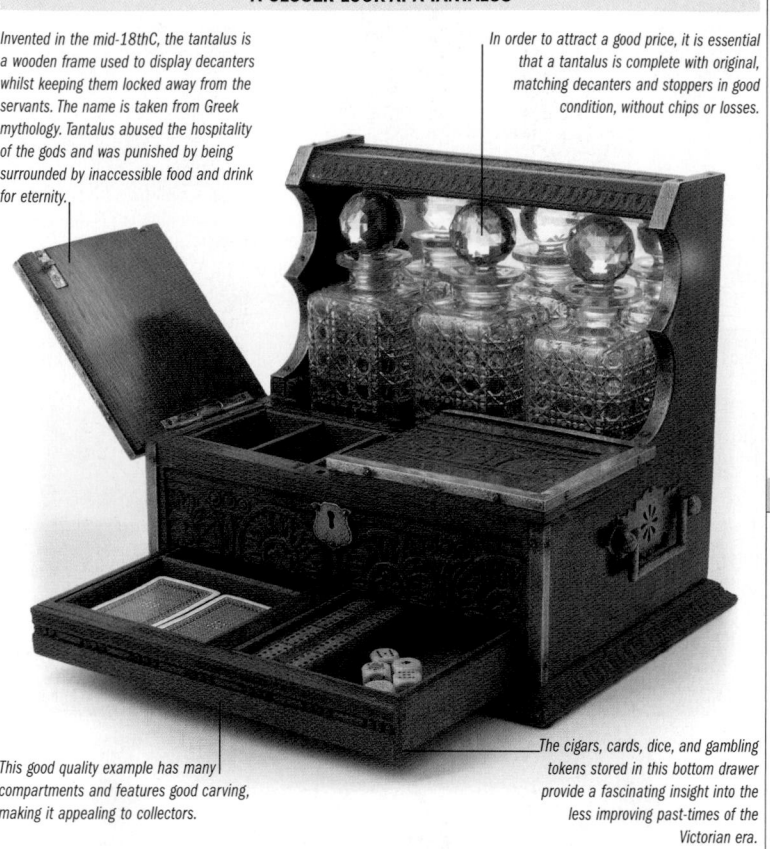

*This good quality example has many compartments and features good carving, making it appealing to collectors.*

*The cigars, cards, dice, and gambling tokens stored in this bottom drawer provide a fascinating insight into the less improving past-times of the Victorian era.*

A carved oak tantalus, with nickel mounts, panels for cigarettes and cigars, four lidded compartments, and bottom drawer with catch containing two packs of cards, dice, gambling tokens, cribbage, and dice.

*c1900*                                                          14.5in (37cm) wide

**$800-1,200**                                                              **CSA**

A pair of blue club-shaped decanters and stoppers, each inscribed in gilt with faux bottle labels and chains "Hollands" and "Brandy", with later papier-mâché stand.

*c1800*          9in (23cm) high

**$500-700**                **DN**

An early 19thC mallet-shaped toddy lifter, of decanter form, with fluted neck and inscribed "Bitters" within a foliate cartouche.

7.75in (20cm) high

**$280-320**                **DN**

An Irish engraved club-shaped decanter and stopper, with a pair of notched neck rings, decorated with fruiting vine above a flute-molded lower section.

*c1800*       9.75in (25cm) high

**$700-1,000**              **DN**

An Irish mallet-shaped decanter and stopper, with three notched annular neck rings, the body with a band of engraved and polished stars.

*c1810*      10.25in (26cm) high

**$800-1,200**              **DN**

### BOWLS

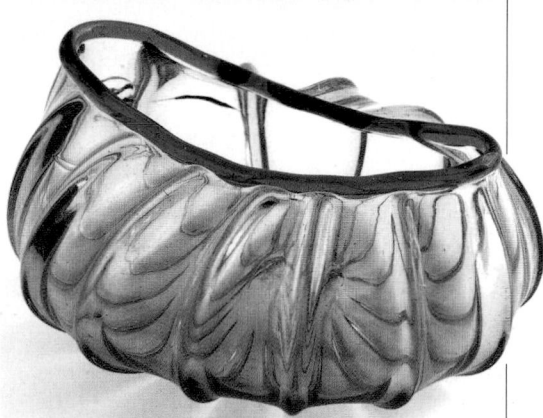

A rare 17thC German Maigelein cup.

4.5in (11.5cm) high

**$2,200-2,800**            **FIS**

A turquoise club-shaped decanter, stopper and bottle coaster, the neck applied with three plain rings, the stopper with radiating flutes.

*c1820*   10.75in (27.5cm) high

**$500-800**               **DN**

A pair of club-shaped decanters and stoppers, with triple rings over fluted necks, the shoulders cut with fan-shaped bands above diamond fields, chipped.

*c1840*          9.75in (25cm) high

**$300-500**               **DN**

A pair of plain mallet-shaped decanters and flattened disc stoppers, stoppers replaced.

12.25in (31cm) high

**$800-1,200**             **DN**

**GLASS**

A cut glass pedestal bowl, of ogee form, cut with a fan-shaped rim above a field of large strawberry and hobnail diamonds, on a knopped stem and circular foot, chipped.

c1820          8.75in (22cm) diam

**$500-700**          DN

A bowl from a Whitefriars 'straw opal' sixteen-piece port service.

c1850          5.75in (14.5cm) high

**$500-700 set**          AL

A Salviate & Co. Venetian revival bowl and underdish.

c1890          3in (8cm) high

**$300-500**          AL

Two of a set of ten early 20thC dimpled and ribbed bowls and stands, possibly Venetian, gilded with rural scenes.

stands 6in (15cm) diam

**$300-500**          AG

A Victorian cut glass and gilt bronze mounted comport, by F. & C. Osler, the circular lattice-cut bowl with rim mounts supporting twin handles cast as exotic birds, the base with cast curved paw feet.

c1890          14in (35cm) diam

**$1,200-1,800**          L&T

A circular cranberry bowl and cover, the bowl with a flared rim, the domed cover with a clear glass finial.

6in (15cm) diam

**$70-100**          H&L

## BOTTLES & JUGS

An unusual pair of early 18thC green wine bottles, the flattened oval bodies with slim conical necks and string rims, with kick-in bases.

7in (18cm) high

**$700-1,000**          H&L

An 18thC purple Alpine bottle, with flattened fluted body and narrow neck.

6.25in (15.5cm) high

**$400-600**          FIS

A rare 18thC flat bottle, by Lauenstein, with a hunting scene relief.

5.75in (14.5cm) high

**$400-600**          FIS

A 19thC blue Alpine bottle, with flat body, narrow neck and wide rim.

7.5in (19cm) high

**$120-180**          FIS

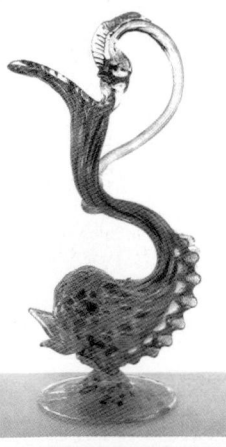

A 19thC miniature sample pressed glass jug, with applied handle.

3.25in (8.5cm) high

**$12-18**          AG

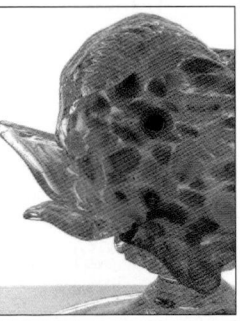

A Salviati & Co. Venetian revival dolphin pitcher.

c1890          9.5in (24cm) high

**$800-1,200**          AL

A cranberry glass ewer with a reeded clear glass handle and tear-shaped stopper.

7in (18cm) high

**$50-70**          H&L

An early 19thC Nailsea-type olive green shouldered jug, with white inclusions, cracked.

7in (18cm) high

**$500-700**          DN

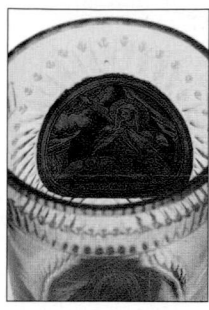

A beaker by Johann Joseph Mildner, with the arms of Joseph Edlen von Fürnberg in gilt within a red lacquered medallion.

c1790                    4.5in (11.5cm) high

**$5,000-7,000**                    FIS

A late 19thC gilded beaker, by J. Pohl, depicting riding and hunting scenes.

3.75in (9.5cm) high

**$1,200-1,800**                    FIS

A beaker by Anton Kothgasser of Vienna, with gilded edges and a depiction of Cupid, inscribed "Blühe immer".

c1825        4.25in (11cm) high

**$8,000-12,000**                    FIS

A dark red lithyalin cup, by Friedrich Egermann, with gilded decoration.

*Lithyalin glass resembles semi-precious stones.*

c1830        4.25in (11cm) high

**$2,800-3,200**                    FIS

An enameled beaker, by Friedrich Egermann, with checkered decoration and faceted stepped mouth.

c1835    4.25in (10.5cm) high

**$1,200-1,800**                    FIS

A rare clear glass Artel beaker, decorated in colors with a church, animal grotesques and symmetrical arabesques.

c1925    4.25in (10.5cm) high

**$1,200-1,800**                    FIS

A tall goblet and cover by August Böhm, clear and red engraved glass with deep-cut engravings depicting stags in a woodland setting.

c1850        20.75in (53cm) high

**$5,000-7,000**                    FIS

A tall green glass rummer, by Harrach, with gilded rim and enameled coat of arms, on a trumpet-shaped foot.

c1880        12.5in (31.5cm) high

**$800-1,200**                    FIS

A red overlay goblet, by F.P. Zach of Munich, engraved with a hunting scene.

c1850        8.75in (22cm) high

**$7,000-10,000**        FIS

A light green 'Emanuel' goblet and cover, by the Rhineland Glassworks, on a footed base, stamped.

1893        17.75in (45cm) high

**$2,200-2,800**                    FIS

A 'Jodphur' wine glass, by Fritz Heckert, engraved with silver, gold and polychrome enamel.

c1900        7.5in (19cm) high

**$280-320**                    FIS

An enameled wine glass, by Meyr's Neffe, with green stem and clear bowl with polychrome enameling and gilding.

c1900        9in (22.5cm) high

**$800-1,200**                    FIS

271

**GLASS**

A faceted Baccarat paperweight, with two interlocking garlands of blue and red millefiori canes between small flowers, large white flower to center.

*c1845*                    *3in (7.5cm) diam*

**$1,800-2,200**                    **WKA**

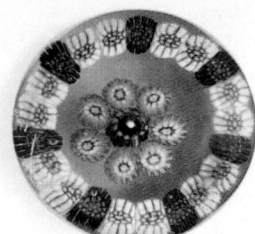

A mid-19thC French concentric paperweight, possibly Baccarat, the central green and red millefiori cane within two rings of colored canes, scratched.

                    *2.5in (6cm) diam*

**$500-700**                    **DN**

A Clichy scattered millefiori paperweight, with colored flowers on a clear ground.

*c1845*                    *2.5in (6.5cm) diam*

**$1,200-1,800**                    **WKA**

A large Clichy paperweight, set with various colored canes on a lace ground.

*c1845*                    *3.25in (8cm) wide*

**$2,800-3,200**                    **WW**

A Clichy paperweight, set with concentric canes and a border of white stars and rose canes.

*c1845*                    *2.5in (6.5cm) wide*

**$1,200-1,800**                    **WW**

A mid-19thC Clichy checker paperweight, set with colored millefiori canes on a ground of latticinio tubing, some surface scratches.

                    *2.5in (6.5cm) diam*

**$800-1,200**                    **DN**

## A CLOSER LOOK AT A BACCARAT PAPERWEIGHT

These 'Gridel' silhouettes are named for Emile Gridel, the nephew of a Baccarat manager, whose paper animals inspired the deceptively simple designs.

Densely packed millefiori canes are a signature feature of Baccarat paperweights, which are considered among the very best on the market.

Date canes like this one were first used by Baccarat in 1846. Genuine date canes will not be placed centrally.

A 20thC Baccarat paperweight, decorated with a central deer 'Gridel' silhouette and alternate green and yellow concentric rows of canes within a twist of blue canes.

                    *3in (7.5cm) diam*

**$500-800**                    **GORL**

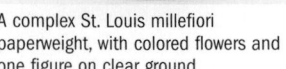

A complex St. Louis millefiori paperweight, with colored flowers and one figure on clear ground.

*1845*                    *2.75in (7cm) diam*

**$1,200-1,800**                    **WKA**

A 19thC St Louis glass paperweight, with central red and white cogwheel design surrounded by rows of blue, red, and white wavy cut canes.

                    *3in (7.5cm) diam*

**$1,200-1,800**                    **GORL**

A mid-20thC Paul Ysart paperweight, with thirteen polychrome canes on a green ground, complete with original presentation box.

                    *3in (7.5cm) diam*

**$500-800**                    **GORL**

A 20thC Perthshire paperweight, dark blue glass base with yellow and pink millefiori canes, centered with a flower and a butterfly, with signature "P" cane to the base.

                    *2.75in (7cm) diam*

**$500-700**                    **WKA**

A very rare center flower holder, possibly Libbey, Brilliant Period, cut and polished.

*Later pieces were acid dipped, which made the corners less 'sharp'.*

**$1,200-1,800**     **AJK**

A J. Hoare two piece egg nog bowl, Brilliant Period, Hobstar pattern.

*10in (25cm) high*

**$1,800-2,200**     **AJK**

A flower holder, Hobstar and Cane pattern, Brilliant Period, unknown maker.

*Reputedly two of these were used as centerpieces at the Russian Embassy in Washington, DC.*

*12in (30cm) high*

**$1,800-2,200**     **AJK**

A butter ball server or bonbon dish, Brilliant Period, Pinwheel pattern, dated from before 1917.

*7in (17.5cm) high*

**$300-500**     **AJK**

A rare late 19thC cut, etched, and blown glass presentation trumpet, the bell decorated with crossed ladders, hooks and crossed axes enclosing the inscription "From C.R.B to W.W.W: Sept. 12th, 1885 Harrisburg".

*1885 was the Centennial of the founding of Harrisburg.*

*c1885*               *23in (58.5cm) long*

**$11,000-14,000**     **FRE**

A Wheeling peachblow cruet, with applied handle and stopper, chip to stopper.

*7in (18cm) high*

**$800-1,200**     **JDJ**

A Wheeling peachblow vase, of classic bulbous form.

*6.25in (16cm) high*

**$800-1,200**     **JDJ**

A Wave Crest 'Iris' pattern vase, with ormolu handles and dolphin feet.

*12in (30.5cm) high*

**$2,800-3,200**     **JDJ**

**SILVER & METALWARE**

## THE SILVER & METALWARE MARKET

Over the last few years, buyers have become increasingly knowledgeable and are more selective about what they buy. Silver and metalware at the lower ends of the market is being rejected in favor of high quality and unusual pieces without restoration.

As well as 20thC pieces by designers such as Jensen and Ramsden, smaller 19thC items, including boxes and vinaigrettes, have remained popular, particularly examples with unusual decoration. Highly regarded English 19thC makers, such as Hennell, Hunt Roskell and Storr, have also held their appeal.

With earlier pieces, buyers look for good, simple silver with original engraving. Bright-cut tea sets are popular.

Traditionally, silver with engraved coat-of-arms and inscriptions have attracted little interest but buyers, increasingly fascinated by provenance, now intentionally seek out original examples.

Scottish and Irish silver is also in demand, especially provincial hollowware. To command high prices, the pieces should bear distinct hallmarks.

Early American silver is rare and desirable. Collectors also favor pieces by S. Kirk & Sons and Tiffany & Co.

The market is poor for pieces of low quality, including mass-produced 20thC silver.

## SILVER BOWLS & BASKETS

A pair of George II 'Duty Dodgers' pomanders, by Abraham Buteux, each with a hinged body, reticulated design and engraved crest of Bernard of Dunsinnan and Buttergask of Perthshire, on spreading circular foot, marks for London.

*'Duty dodgers' inserted hallmarks from lighter pieces into new silver to avoid paying the tax levied from 1719 to 1758.*

| 1727 | 3.75in (9cm) high |
|---|---|
| **$12,000-18,000** | **FRE** |

A matched group of four 19thC French small silver comports, each of circular form, inscribed with various mottos, applied Napoleonic bee motifs and engraved Heroic inscriptions, dated 1811 and 1808.

| | 7in (17.5cm) wide |
|---|---|
| **$1,200-1,800** | **L&T** |

A pair of George III silver oval dishes, by Paul Storr, the wavy rim with engraved frieze of floral and C-scrolls forming four cartouches, on a bold cast base of four scrolling leaf-form feet, with marks for London, formerly with armorial bearings.

| 1817 | 12.5in (31.5cm) wide |
|---|---|
| **$2,800-3,200** | **L&T** |

A 19thC European silver gilt and enamel urn, of campana form, the ornate foliate chased sides with twin ram's mask handles and applied bloodstone lobes, set with rubies, on a spreading oval base.

| | 5.5in (14cm) high |
|---|---|
| **$8,000-12,000** | **FRE** |

A Victorian Irish silver melon-fluted sugar bowl, by J. Mahoney, with a shell and leaf chased border, embossed with foliate sprays and cartouches, marks for Dublin.

| 1868 | 6in (15cm) diam |
|---|---|
| **$600-900** | **DN** |

A Victorian silver monteith, by Elkington and Co., of traditional form, demi-fluted with a cartouche and engraved monogram, a spreading foot and gilt interior, marks for Birmingham.

| 1898 | 10.5in (26.5cm) diam |
|---|---|
| **$1,200-1,800** | **L&T** |

A set of four Victorian silver baskets, each with cast interwoven handles, reticulated sides and a floral swag, pierced oval back, by "JC" and marks for London.

| 1893 | 7in (17.5cm) wide |
|---|---|
| **$2,200-2,800** | **L&T** |

A George III silver vinaigrette, by Samuel Pemberton, the hinged cover engraved with "J.C." within a repeating leaf border, gilt interior with filigree and scrollwork grille, marks for Birmingham.

*1802*          *1.25in (3cm) wide*

**$300-400**          **B**

A George III agate inset silver snuff box, by "WH" of London, the hinged lid with a raised panel of pink and brown banded stone, on an overall vermicular, stippled, and engraved ground.

*1806*          *3in (7.5cm) wide*

**$280-320**          **CHEF**

A George III silver gilt snuff box, made by Matthew Linwood of Birmingham, of rectangular form with basket weave decoration.

*1810*          *3in (7.5cm) wide*

**$600-900**          **HAMG**

A silver snuff box, made by Nathaniel Mills of Birmingham, the cover cast and chased with a foliate border, the base and sides with engine-turned decoration.

*1839*          *3.5in (9cm) wide*

**$800-1,200**          **HAMG**

A silver table snuff box, by Nathaniel Mills of Birmingham, the cover engraved with an inscription to "William Hardman" dated "May 1849", with red velvet lining, marks for Birmingham.

*1846*          *3.25in (8.5cm) wide*

**$2,800-3,200**          **B**

A Russian Niello silver cigarette case, the cover engraved with figures in a wagon pulled by three horses, against a scrolling foliate ground, with a letter of provenance.

*c1870*          *5.5in (14cm) wide*

**$800-1,200**          **HAMG**

A silver and parcel-gilt cornucopia vinaigrette, by Sampson Mordan and Co., applied with die-stamped and pierced borders, the cover enclosing a foliate pierced grille, London.

*1873*          *8cm (3.25in) long*

**$700-1,000**          **B**

A Victorian oval tobacco box, by John and Frank Pairpoint, embossed with scrolls and a later inscribed cartouche, the cover with a figure in a rural landscape, marks for London.

*1883*          *6in (15cm) wide*

**$300-500**          **DN**

A late Victorian silver and enamel cigarette case, with an oval panel depicting a Boer War soldier at a carriage-mounted machine gun, engraved verso "T.B.S", marks for Birmingham.

*1899*          *3.5in (9cm) high*

**$600-900**          **DN**

An Edwardian silver snuff box by The Goldsmith's and Silversmith's Company of London, with central "FM" initials and a wavy edged hinged lid, gilt interior.

*3.5in (9cm) high*

**$220-280**          **CHEF**

## A CLOSER LOOK AT A VICTORIAN SILVER SNUFF BOX

The inscription adds to the desirability, as silverware collectors are increasingly interested in historical context. Pieces that have a strong link with a historical figure can command a premium.

The crisp high relief decoration, depicting specific military campaigns, adds to the unique nature of the piece, which appeals to both collectors of snuff boxes and of militaria.

This piece is accompanied by documents of provenance, indicating a specific regiment, which adds to its appeal.

This was made by Yapp and Woodward of Birmingham for the silversmiths Magnus and Son of Chatham. This demonstrable link with a respected silversmiths will attract a premium.

An early Victorian silver military table snuff box, a unique commission by Yapp & Woodward of Birmingham for silversmiths Magnus & Son of Chatham, with inscription to Sergeant Major Henry Whearing on retirement in 1849, cast in high relief depicting his campaigns and regimental details, with documents of provenance.

*4.25in (10.5cm) wide*

**$6,000-9,000**          **B**

**SILVER & METALWARE**

One of an early 20thC pair of sterling silver five-light candelabra, in the Louis XV style, with scroll arms with floral hand-chased bobeches, on cast scroll feet, base marked "Goldis Blum".

*19in (47.5cm) high*

**$8,000-12,000 pair** | **FRE**

A pair of George III silver candlesticks, by John Carter of London, with hexagonal scroll edged foot embossed with shells below a knopped stem, spool socket with detachable shell decorated nozzle.

*1775* | *10.5in (26.5cm) high*

**$3,000-5,000** | **CHEF**

A pair of George II cast silver candlesticks, by Ebenezer Coker, of traditional knopped form with removable sconce, the base engraved with crest and motto, marks for London.

*1748* | *8.25in (21cm) high*

**$4,000-6,000** | **L&T**

A pair of George II candlesticks, by William Gould, with vase shaped capitals, leaf chased knopped stems and shaped square bases with anthemion corners, engraved armorials, marks for London.

*1749* | *8.75in (22cm) high*

**$3,000-4,000** | **DN**

A set of four early George III silver cast candlesticks, by Ebenezer Coker, with spiral fluted knopped columns and nozzles and stepped square bases, numbered 1 to 4, with scratch weights beneath "21: 7", "21: 14", "21: 10" and "21: 2", marks for London.

*1766* | *10.5in (26.5cm) high*

**$12,000-18,000** | **DN**

## A CLOSER LOOK AT A PAIR OF SILVER CANDLESTICKS

These detachable nozzles are discreet, conforming with the outline to the base of the candlestick, and with the decoration to the stem.

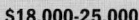

Nozzles have been added at a later date; they are detachable and prevent the wax from pouring down the stem of the candlestick. By the 1740s these were a regular feature on candlesticks.

These candlesticks are in very good condition. Cast silver candlesticks are stronger and less prone to damage than those stamped from sheet and are therefore especially attractive to the buyer.

The production of cast candlesticks became rare after the 1770s. Therefore, cast candlesticks are much more desirable and command a premium.

A pair of George II cast silver candlesticks, by Edward Feline, the round leaf chased capitals with later nozzles, knopped stems headed with oval medallion busts, sunk centers with armorials, the bases with concave corners, engraved scale-work panels and applied cherubs, scratch weights beneath 28 and 28-15, London.

***Provenance***: *Rushbrooke Hall, Suffolk, England.*

*1743* | *9in (23cm) high*

**$18,000-25,000** | **DN**

A pair of George III silver table candlesticks, by John Green & Co., of circular tapered form, with removable sconces and spreading feet, marks for Sheffield.

*1800* | *11.75in (30cm) high*

**$1,200-1,800** | **L&T**

A pair of George II cast silver candlesticks, by John Pollock, of traditional knopped form with removable sconce, the base with engraved crest, marks for London.

*1750* | *8.25in (21cm) high*

**$4,000-6,000** | **L&T**

A George I hexagonal taperstick, by Gabriel Sleath, with a knopped stem and molded base, with a later monogram, marks for London.

*1718* | *4.25in (11cm) high*

**$2,800-3,200** | **DN**

A pair of silver mounted tortoiseshell candlesticks, on turned spreading bases, marks for Birmingham.

*1921* | *4.75in (12cm) high*

**$1,200-1,800** | **L&T**

A pair of George III pierced oval pedestal salt cellars, by Robert Hennell, with scroll handles, beaded rims, and engraved with bright cut floral swags, blue glass liners, marks for London.

*1783*     *4.75in (12cm) wide*

**$800-1,200**     **DN**

One of a pair of George IV round salt cellars, by Emes and Barnard, each on a triform paw stem and round base, marks for London.

*1822*     *3.5in (9cm) diam*

**$280-320 pair**     **DN**

A pair of salt cellars modeled as ducks, by E. & J. Barnard, with silver gilt interiors, one marked beneath "Thomas's, Bond St, London", marks for London.

*1862*     *4.75in (12cm) wide*

**$2,200-2,800**     **DN**

A pair of Danish silver salt and pepper pots, each in the form of a squirrel with a bushy tail crouching on a circular removable base, "NM" maker's marks and "925S".

    *2.5in (6.5cm) high*

**$180-220**     **DN**

A set of four Victorian silver gilt salt cellars, by John S. Hunt, of lobed-oval trencher form on eagle supports, engraved with scrolls, cartouches and arms, marked to base with "Hunt and Roskell Late Storr and Mortimer", blue glass liners, London.

*The arms are an early and unauthorized shield and motto used by Wells City Council in Somerset, England.*

*1856*     *4in (10cm) long*

**$5,000-8,000**     **DN**

## SILVER MARKS

- During the 14thC laws were passed to fix the purity of English silver at 925 parts in every thousand. A London Assay Office was set up to test and mark silver. This type of silver was known as 'sterling' – a term thought to derive from Easterling, a part of Germany known for the quality of its silver.
- A maker's mark was introduced in 1363 and in 1478, the date letter, which changed every year, was added.
- Assay offices opened all over the country to test the quality of silver. Each had its own mark. Important English assay marks include: leopard's head: London (est. 1544); sword and three wheatsheaves: Chester (1686-1962); castle: Exeter (1701-1883); three castles: Newcastle (est.1702); anchor: Birmingham (est.1773); crown: Sheffield (est. 1773).
- Assay offices were established in Russia from 1700 and a standard system was introduced in the USA in 1869, although in both these countries other marks had been used prior to these dates.
- Beware of fake marks that are badly punched or incorrectly positioned, or marks that have been lifted from other pieces.

## CASTORS

A Queen Anne silver castor, with a pierced and engraved domed top and ball finial, the baluster body engraved with initials "VSH", with marks for London.

*Provenance: Purchased at Spink & Son of 5 King St, St James's, London, October 1929.*

*1705*     *8.25in (21cm) high*

**$3,000-4,000**     **L&T**

A George I castor, probably by Glover Johnson, engraved with an armorial, on a stepped foot, the foliate pierced cover with a finial, London, maker's mark rubbed.

*The arms are those of Townshend of Raynham, Norfolk, England with a crescent for a second son.*

*1718*     *7in (18cm) high*

**$3,000-4,000**     **DN**

A George II vase-shaped castor, by John White, with a molded girdle and borders, later chased with leaf scrolls and rocaille, a crest within a cartouche, pierced cover with vase shaped finial, cover unmarked, London.

*1731*     *6.75in (17cm) high*

**$1,200-1,800**     **DN**

A matched pair of silver castors, by Samuel Wood, of plain vase form, with pierced cover and turned finial, together with a facsimile, with marks for London.

*1742*     *6.25in (16cm) high*

**$800-1,200**     **L&T**

A George II vase-shaped castor, by Samuel Wood, later embossed with foliate scrolls, the pierced cover with a turned finial, the cover with lion passant only, London, the body repaired.

*1744*     *5.5in (14cm) high*

**$120-180**     **DN**

**SILVER & METALWARE**

A George III pear-shaped castor, by Robert Pearcy, with beaded borders and bright-cut engraved cover with a flame finial, London.

*1777*     *6in (15cm) high*

**$300-400**     **DN**

A George III vase-shaped sugar castor, by Hester Bateman, with beaded border, diaper engraved cover and acorn finials, on a round foot, London.

*1788*     *6in (15cm) high*

**$400-600**     **DN**

A George III vase-shaped castor, possibly by William Abdy, with spiral fluted and foliate embossed body, the shaped cover with acorn finial on a reeded foot, London.

*1798*     *6.75in (17cm) high*

**$220-280**     **DN**

A pair of George III castors, with urn-shaped fluted bodies and crests, gadrooned borders on spreading reeded feet, the domed top pierced covers with ball-turned finials, London, maker's marks indistinct.

*1819*     *3in (8cm) high*

**$300-400**     **DN**

An urn-shaped silver castor, by George Fox, with a bead and reel border, part spiral fluted and chased with shells and scrolls, the pierced cover with a finial, London.

*1901*     *8.25in (21cm) high*

**$500-800**     **DN**

A vase-shaped castor, embossed with spiral flutes and leaves, the cover with spiral turned finial, on a molded foot, Birmingham.

*1904*     *5.5in (14cm) high*

**$120-180**     **DN**

A Scottish vase-shaped sugar castor on a molded foot, Edinburgh.

*1914*     *7.5in (19cm) high*

**$300-400**     **DN**

A William IV silver oval cylindrical nutmeg grater, by Rawlings and Sumner, with two hinged covers, engraved with script initials, London.

*1835*     *2.75 in (7cm) long*

**$800-1,200**     **DN**

A Victorian silver egg epergne, probably by Rawlings and Sumner or Reily and Storer, with acanthus-clasped base, hands and rims to the six gilt egg cups, each engraved with a crest, the whole on C-scroll feet, London.

*1840*     *11in (28cm) high*

**$800-1,200**     **L&T**

## SILVER CUPS & GOBLETS

A Charles II silver porringer and cover, embossed with lions and gazelles amidst leaves, makers mark "WW" and a fleur-de-lys below, London.

*1668*

**$7,000-10,000**     **DN**

A William III silver porringer, possibly by Alexander Roode of London, the lower body fluted below a rope twist girdle, initialed "EL SS".

*1696*     *3.25in (8.5cm) high*

**$1,800-2,200**     **CHEF**

A Queen Anne silver porringer and cover, initialed by William Keat, part swirl fluted with a ropework band around the cover, the body engraved on one side with a later lozenge-shaped cartouche, London.

*1711*     *5.75in (14.5cm) high*

**$2,800-3,200**     **WW**

A Queen Anne porringer, by William Gamble, the part spiral lobed and fluted bowl with an embossed ropework band and an acanthus cartouche with pricked initials "B" over "W S", London.

*1713*     *3.5in (9cm) high*

**$800-1,200**     **DN**

A George II silver cup, by Richard Bayley, with two reeded scroll handles and a foot, with later initials "A.M.P.", London.

*1747*                      *4in (10cm) high*

**$700-1,000**                      **DN**

A George III silver goblet, of plain vase form, with engraved inscription and crest, pedestal base and spreading foot, London.

*1802*            *8.75in (22cm) high*

**$800-1,200**                      **L&T**

A George II 'The Pytchley Cup', in silver gilt, by George Methuen, embossed with flowers, scrolls and shells, with scroll handles, the body engraved with a baron's armorial and "Aequo Animo", acanthus decorated finial, inscribed "Presented to Ronald Lambert Tree Esq by members of the Pytchley Hunt on relinquishing his Mastership 1927-1933", London.

*Ronald Lambert Tree (1901-1976) served in the Ministry of Information in WWII and became a friend of the Prime Minister, Winston Churchill, who used to stay at the Tree's house, at Ditchley, in Oxfordshire, for safety from German bombers 'when the moon was high' and Chequers was thought too dangerous.*

*1750*                      *13.75in (35cm) high*

**$8,000-12,000**                      **CHEF**

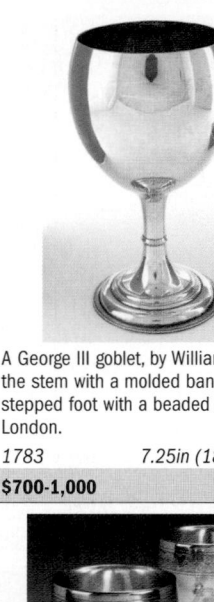

A George III goblet, by William Smith II, the stem with a molded band on a stepped foot with a beaded border, London.

*1783*            *7.25in (18.5cm) high*

**$700-1,000**                      **DN**

A pair of George III Irish silver goblets, by Augustavus Burn and retailed by Law, with an engraved border and cartouche, plain stem and spreading circular foot, threaded rim, with marks for Dublin.

*1808*            *6.5in (16.5cm) high*

**$2,800-3,200**                      **L&T**

A George III silver goblet, by Joseph William Story, the circular foot with tongue and dart border, the lower body of the bowl with an applied fruiting vine border, London.

*1808*            *6.35in (15.75cm) high*

**$800-1,200**                      **CHEF**

A large early 20thC Dutch parcel gilt silver wager cup, formed as a female in late 16thC attire, the swivel cup with import mark for Chester 1898, the body with later import marks for Chester.

*1906*            *13.5in (34.5cm) high*

**$1,800-2,200**                      **CHEF**

**CADDY SPOONS**

A 16thC silver mounted natural shell caddy spoon, by Matthew Linwood of Birmingham, with a bifurcated thread pattern stem, crested.

**$1,200-1,800**                      **WW**

An Onslow pattern silver caddy spoon, with a fluted circular bowl, engraved on the back of the stem with a cipher within a strap and buckle, below a crest, unmarked.

*c1770*            *3.5in (9cm) long*

**$700-1,000**                      **WW**

An early 18thC Scottish silver circular stand, by Robert Luke, with a domed center and on a circular foot, initials "MR" in script, marks for Glasgow.

1725     7.75in (19.5cm) diam

**$4,000-6,000**     **L&T**

A George II Scottish small silver waiter, by Robert Luke, with shell and acanthus-carved inner border on four hoof feet, marks for Glasgow.

c1725     6.5in (16.5cm) wide

**$2,200-2,800**     **L&T**

A George II silver salver, by Edward Pocock, with chased decoration and a C-scroll and floral border, on four scroll feet, with marks for London.

1732     12.5in (32cm) diam

**$800-1,200**     **L&T**

A George III Scottish small silver waiter, maker James Hewitt, with gadrooned edge and engraved inner leaf border, on short cabriole legs with hoof feet, marks for Edinburgh.

1770     7in (18cm) diam

**$600-900**     **L&T**

A William IV silver tray, by J.E. Terry, with a heavy cast deep border of C-scrolls and flowers and vine-clasped handles, blank central cartouche surrounded by a deep chased border on a diaper ground and two C-scroll cartouches, one with armorial bearings and a shield, on heavy-cast shell feet, with marks for London.

1833     32.75in (83cm) wide

**$12,000-18,000**     **L&T**

## INTEGRAL DECORATIVE TECHNIQUES

- The term 'integral decoration' refers to decoration that is formed from the body of the piece.
- Engraved decoration is cut into the surface with a 'graver' or 'burin'. Bright-cut engraving is angled to reflect the light.
- Embossing or 'repoussé' creates raised (relief) or hollow (incuse) designs. Hammers are used to bulge the material to one side. The technique also adds strength to the object.
- Chasing is often used to add definition to embossing and involves drawing a design on silver and then hammering it with a blunt ball-point chisel to distort the surface.
- In the 19thC, the technique of die stamping, where sheets of silver were sandwiched between shaped metal molds, was developed, making it easier to mass-produce decorative silver.
- When buying, check that the style of the decoration matches the date of the hallmark. Engraved and chased designs may be later than the date of a piece, as decoration was sometimes added during the Victorian period to suit the tastes of the time. Earlier coats of arms and initials were also occasionally removed.
- Be aware of decoration that conceals repairs to silver, particularly where a worn area has been patched or replaced.

A George III silver gilt sideboard dish, by William Pitts, the base later engraved with "Presented to William Rome Corporation of the City of London Chairmanship 1892", London.

1789

**$2,800-3,200**     **L&T**

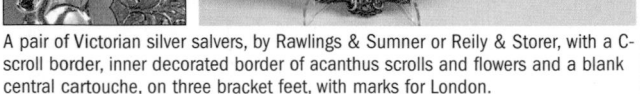

A pair of Victorian silver salvers, by Rawlings & Sumner or Reily & Storer, with a C-scroll border, inner decorated border of acanthus scrolls and flowers and a blank central cartouche, on three bracket feet, with marks for London.

1843     13.5in (34cm) wide

**$2,200-2,800**     **L&T**

A Scottish George II circular stand, by Archibald Ure, assaymaster Edward Penman, with marks for Edinburgh.

1728     8in (20.5cm) diam

**$4,000-6,000**     **L&T**

A George III Irish helmet-shaped silver cream jug, by John Shields, embossed with rocaille cartouches, with a molded girdle, double scroll handle and chased lion's mask, on paw feet, Dublin.

c1765          4in (10cm) high

**$700-1,000**          **DN**

A George III vase-shaped cream jug, by Hester Bateman, embossed with panels of fruit and vines and a scroll cartouche, punched rim, loop handle and square base, London.

1789          5.75in (14.5cm) high

**$500-800**          **DN**

A George III silver wine jug, of large helmet shape, with an engraved full armorial and demi-fluted oval foot, hardwood handle, marks for London.

1801          11in (28cm) high

**$1,200-1,800**          **L&T**

An early 19thC silver ewer, with a later engraved crest, central band of applied foliate grotesques and chased acanthus base and stem, with a pedestal base on ball feet, inscription, probably contemporary, to crest "This formerly belonged to the... 1st EMPEROR NAPOLEON, AT FONTAINBLEUE".

*Provenance: Purportedly once the property of Napoleon Bonaparte.*

7.5in (19cm) high

**$2,800-3,200**          **ROS**

A Regency Scottish silver ewer, by Robert Gray & Son of Glasgow, of baluster form, the body embossed with flowers above a gadrooned circular foot, the flared spout chased with acanthus and anthemion, over a hinged cover.

1819

**$2,200-2,800**          **CHEF**

A Victorian silver claret jug, probably by Rawlings & Sumner or Reily & Storer, of classical ewer shape, horn scroll handle, the body engraved with classical figures, on a pedestal foot, with marks for London.

1840          12.5in (32cm) high

**$1,800-2,200**          **L&T**

## APPLIED DECORATIVE TECHNIQUES

- The term 'applied decoration' indicates designs which are not part of the basic form of a piece.
- Cut-card decoration, most common on Huguenot silver, refers to designs cut from plates of silver and then soldered to an object.
- Gilding is used to give silver the appearance of gold. The term 'parcel gilt' refers to gilding in a limited area rather than an all-over coating. The process of mercury gilding is highly toxic and was replaced with electrogilding in the mid-19thC.
- Electrogilding involves coating silver objects with a film of gold using an electric current. The gold can be brassy in color.
- Other types of applied decoration was also used, such as beaded rim wires or cast foliate, figural and shell decoration.

A Victorian Irish silver presentation claret jug, by "P.L.", inscription, Dublin.

1844          12.25in (31cm) high

**$1,800-2,200**          **L&T**

A Victorian silver hot water jug, with a scroll capped handle, London.

1892          6.5in (17cm) high

**$280-320**          **SWO**

A late Victorian helmet-shaped cream jug, by J. Millward Banks, embossed with flowers, birds and animals and with a shaped rim, molded girdle and lion mask and paw feet, Birmingham.

1895

**$300-400**          **DN**

**SILVER & METALWARE**

A late 17thC Scandinavian silver peg tankard, with a beaded scroll handle and shield terminal, the hinged lid with lion and ball thumbpiece, engraved with "Olle Peders * Anne Nielsd 1680" and shields with scrolling flowers, on floral capped melon feet.

*6.5in (16.5) high*

**$4,000-6,000**    **DN**

A Queen Anne silver tankard, by Gabriel Sleath, London, with molded foot, edge and girdle, S-scroll handle and peaked cover with scrolled thumbpiece, later embossed presentation inscription, dated "24 June 1842".

*1710*    *7.5in (19cm) high*

**$1,200-1,800**    **CHEF**

## A CLOSER LOOK AT A SILVER TANKARD

*Thumbpieces with little sign of wear, like this one, contribute to the value of a piece. Although the thumbpieces were for use, the silversmith combined practicality with beauty when crafting them.*

*The tapered cylindrical sides and shallow domed lid is emblematic of pre-1765 tankard design. Chased and embossed foliate and fruit decoration, along with the chased décor on the S-scroll handle is typical of tankards from the William and Mary period, which tend to have plain shapes and simple decorative borders.*

*The floral ornamentation was typical of the William and Mary style of decoration. The style was heavily influenced by the French Louis XIV style, whose classical motifs and formality were brought to England by the Huguenot refugees.*

*Between the two mullets are the initials "H.I." Tankards were expensive purchases and were recognized as a symbol of the owner's wealth, therefore most were marked with the owner's initials.*

A William and Mary silver tankard, the lid and tapered cylindrical sides with chased and embossed foliate and fruit decoration, the S-scroll handle with chased decoration, "H.I." between two mullets, London.

*1693*    *8in (20cm) high*

**$10,000-15,000**    **FRE**

A George III English provincial silver quart tankard, by John Langlands I, with a molded border and band, the scroll handle with a heart-shaped terminal, inscribed "H" over "I.M", Newcastle.

*1770*

**$3,000-5,000**    **DN**

A William and Mary silver mug, by John Sutton, with molded borders and a scroll handle with two armorials, the sides engraved with a shield and crest, inscribed, London.

*The shield and crest of George Donnington, Armiger, and an inscription marking this gift to the Town of Wells in Somerset, England.*

*1693*

**$4,000-6,000**    **DN**

A George II silver baluster-shaped mug, by Thomas Whipham II and Charles Wright with a leaf-capped double scroll handle and broad spreading foot, London.

*1757*    *5in (13cm) high*

**$400-600**    **DN**

A late George II baluster mug, by John Wilks, with leaf capped scroll handle on a molded spreading foot, London.

*1758*    *6in (14.5cm) high*

**$800-1,200**    **DN**

A Victorian drum-shaped silver mustard pot, by Henry Wilkinson & Co., with a shaped foot-rim, engraved with a bird and vines on a diaper ground, the cover with a cartouche and presentation inscription, green glass liner, Sheffield.

*1843*    *2.75in (7cm) diam*

**$400-600**    **DN**

A George III silver three piece tea service, by J.E. Terry, the teapot lid with a fluted ivory finial, the body with an engraved crest in a C-scroll and floral ground, reserve panels of an oriental person fishing and eagle surmount, with marks for London.

1819

$2,200-2,800                                      CHEF

A Scottish Victorian three piece silver tea service, comprising teapot, sugar bowl and cream jug, engraved with birds and C-scrolls, floral finial to teapot, "JM" maker's marks, marks for Glasgow.

1857

$1,200-1,800                                      CHEF

A four-piece silver tea service, by Barraclough and Barraclough, with fluted covers, shell-chased and formal engraved bands and borders, the teapot and hot water jug with ivory handle and finial, London.

1939                    teapot 6.25in (16cm) diam

$1,200-1,800                                        DN

A George I small bullet-shaped teapot, by Abraham Buteux, with a molded spout and foot, a fruitwood scroll handle and a turned finial, the rim with and engraved band and with a later crest, London.

*The Irish crest and coronet are those of Earl Winterton of Gort in the county of Galway, Ireland. Buteux married Eliza Godfrey, one of the most prolific silversmiths of the time.*

1721

$12,000-18,000                                      DN

A Scottish George II silver bullet teapot, by Charles Dickson, assaymaster Edward Lothian, chased foliate and C-scroll banding, scrolling spout, with marks for Edinburgh.

1743                              6in (15cm) high

$3,000-5,000                                      L&T

A George III silver teapot and matching stand, with bright-cut decoration and blank cartouche, the base similarly engraved and with a mahogany base. "G.B." marks for maker, London.

1800                            11.75in (30cm) wide

$1,200-1,800                                      L&T

A George III Irish silver teapot, with bold Rococo chased decoration, the lid with later butterfly finial, the scroll spout with eagle and mask support, with marks for Dublin.

1816                              6in (15cm) long

$2,200-2,800                                      L&T

An early Victorian silver melon-shaped teapot, with marks for London.

1844

$300-500                                          SWO

A Victorian oval silver teapot, by Thomas Smily, with an angular handle, engraved cartouches with an elephant crest and presentation inscription dated 1871, hinged cover with knop finial, London.

1869                            12in (31cm) wide

$400-600                                            DN

A George III silver coffee pot, by John Swift of London, with embossed decoration and engraved coat of arms.

1776          11.5in (29cm) high

$2,200-2,800                      WW

A fine Maltese silver coffee pot, by Gio Andrea Azzopardi, hinged dome cover, ebonized handle, raised on caprine legs.

c1800          10.5in (27cm) high

$4,000-6,000                    HAMG

A silver coffee pot, wooden handle and Duncan crest, Goldsmiths & Silversmiths Company marks, Sheffield.

1918          11in (28cm) high

$1,800-2,200                      L&T

A George III silver tea urn on stand, with a hinged wicker handle, the spout with an ivory handle, marks for "IS", London.

1795          18in (46cm) high

$5,000-7,000                      L&T

A George III large lidded silver ewer, by Robert William, with a cartouche and crest, marks for Dublin.

1796          11.5in (29cm) high

$5,000-7,000                      L&T

**METALWARE**

## AMERICAN SILVER

- Silver has been a sign of wealth in America since the 1600s.
- New England, the state of New York, Pennsylvania, and later Delaware and South Carolina were the centers for the silversmithing trade. Each state and city developed its own designs and characteristics, which were influenced by the heritage of the colonists.
- American silver usually only has a single mark. This alone does not guarantee an American piece, it could also indicate an Irish or Scottish one.
- Most pre-1850 American silversmiths used their last name, or initials, or first initial and last name.
- The word "Sterling" indicated a piece made in America after c1860. Sterling means that 925 out of 1,000 parts are silver. This is still the standard for silver today.
- Pieces of tea or coffee services did not necessarily match. A set often had pieces made by several makers which does not affect the overall value much.

A late 19thC silver coffee service, by Samuel Kirk, including tea pot, creamer, covered sugar, and hot water urn, and an associated water jug, ornamented with exotic buildings, palm trees and marine views, the covers with turbaned head knops, the water urn with knight head knop.

*218 oz.*

**$15,000-20,000**     **FRE**

A rare and ornate S. Kirk & Son silver tea service in a floral repoussé pattern with dragonfly, heron, and fish embellishments and Chinese figural finials inscribed on base "S. Kirk & Son 1102. Elizabeth J. Smith Dec. 25, 1892".

*tallest 14in (35.5cm) high*

**$20,000-25,000**     **POOK**

An S. Kirk & Son sterling silver five-piece tea service, in a floral repoussé pattern, including coffee pot, teapot, sugar bowl and cover, creamer, and a waste bowl, coffee pot.

*11in (28cm) high*

**$6,000-9,000**     **POOK**

An early 20thC American sterling silver tea and coffee service, by S. Kirk & Sons, each piece with allover architectural, floral and shell repoussé decoration, the pots and sugar bowl with a demi-rampant English lion finial to lids, cross-hatch center.

*c456oz.*

**$30,000-35,000**     **FRE**

An early 20thC sterling silver tea and coffee service, urn form with chased urn finials to lids, floral and leaf repousse lids and bodies, rosette and ribbon chased circular feet, ornate chased leaf and bellflower handles, sold by Bailey Banks & Biddle.

*Total weight 210 oz.*

**$20,000-25,000**     **FRE**

A five-piece silver tea service, marked Tiffany and Co., New York, including coffee pot, tea pot, creamer, covered sugar, and waste bowl, each decorated with ivy pattern within panels, and ivy-form medallions at foot.

**$8,000-12,000**     **FRE**

A silver butter plate, by Samuel Edwards (1705-1762), Boston, rim engraved with the Jackson arms in a sheaf and scroll cartouche and crest, in script "E. Jackson," and has the touchmark of Samuel Edwards.

*c1730*     *6in (15cm) diam*

**$40,000-50,000**     **SK**

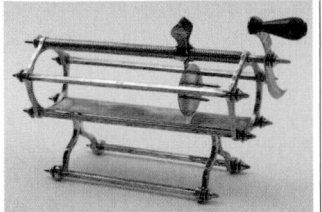

A silver cucumber slicer, the open framework supporting a screw with moving back plate opposing a rotating blade, set on an ogee form base, London.

$400-600 — **ROS**

A Britannia silver photograph frame, of rectangular form, enriched with repoussé putti playing among flowering vines, London.

11in (28cm) high

$400-600 — **ROS**

A late Victorian Irish dish ring, by Charles Lamb, pierced and embossed with figures and animals, the rocaille cartouche with a presentation inscription, blue glass liner, Dublin.

1897

$2,200-2,800 — **DN**

A silver and mother-of-pearl child's teether, by Crisford & Norris, in the form of spaniel's head, Birmingham.

1902          4.75in (12cm) long

$180-220 — **DN**

A Dutch silver miniature longcase clock, the hood cast with a figure and scrolls, the white enamel dial painted with a harbor scene, 18thC London pocket watch movement, on a Bombay shaped base, the case 833 standard with date letter.

1904          9.75in (24.5cm) high

$600-900 — **B**

A silver mounted pin cushion, by Adie and Lovekin Ltd., in the form of a Venetian gondola decorated with scrolls, Birmingham.

1906          3.75in (9.5cm) long

$400-600 — **DN**

A silver fluted and engraved rattle, by Crisford and Norris, hung with six bells and with a coral teether, Birmingham.

1910

$300-500 — **DN**

A pair of silver mounted glass vesta holders, of ribbed globular form, with marks for "JG&S", London, 1912, and another larger, Birmingham, 1911.

largest 4.75in (12cm) high

$1,800-2,200 — **L&T**

A silver desk ruler, with loop handle, engraved with initials "J A L D" with marks for Asprey & Co., London.

1917          10in (25.5cm) long

$1,200-1,800 — **L&T**

A European articulated model of a salmon, with scale detail, textured fins, hinged head with glass eyes, the hinged mouth with realistic teeth, English import marks for London.

1927          26in (66cm) long

$12,000-18,000 — **WW**

An Eastern silver scent bottle, modeled as an articulated fish, the head hinged to reveal a bottle, jeweled eyes, chain with finger ring, unmarked.

4.5in (11.5cm) wide

$220-280 — **CHEF**

An Edwardian silver pastry dish, by C Westwood & Sons, Birmingham.

1903          11in (28cm) wide

$120-180 — **CHEF**

An 18ct gold goblet, engraved to commemorate the Royal Silver Wedding, by A. T. Cannon, numbered "12", Birmingham.

1972

$2,800-3,200 — **DN**

## SILVER PLATE

An early 19thC Old Sheffield plate tea urn, the chamber with a cast iron frog.

15.75in (40cm) high

$800-1,200 — **CHEF**

An early Victorian silver-plated tea kettle on a stand, with a lamp, embossed with scrolls and cartouches and with a bird of prey finial.

$500-700 — **DN**

A Victorian silver-plated on copper double tea caddy, of bombé form and serpentine body, decorated with C-scrolls and scroll feet, divided interior, the lid with floral finial and lock.

8.25in (21cm) wide

$500-700 — **L&T**

**SILVER & METALWARE**

A large Victorian silver-plated soup tureen and cover, of oval shape, with all-over bright-cut decoration and cast mounts.

*19.25in (49cm) wide*

**$1,200-1,800**     **L&T**

An early 20thC tortoiseshell mounted vesta/match case, in the form of a tortoise with a plated base and a press-molded tortoiseshell hinged cover.

*3.25in (8.5cm) wide*

**$700-1,000**     **DN**

An electroplate reproduction of an Old Sheffield plate ewer by Walker & Hall, the body of scrolled and fluted form, with foliate handle, hinged cover with acanthus thumbpiece.

*13.5in (34cm) high*

**$280-320**     **CHEF**

Two of a set of four Old Sheffield plate extending candlesticks, with gadrooned borders, round columns and oblong bases and nozzles.

**$180-220 set**     **DN**

A pair of Old Sheffield plate candelabra, each with a central gadrooned urn finial, the scrolled candle branches with trumpet sconces, the swag embossed tapering column on a spreading circular foot.

*14.5in (37cm) high*

**$1,800-2,200**     **L&T**

## WINE ANTIQUES

A George III beaded silver wine label, probably provincial or Scottish, in the shape of a narrow kidney, incised "Port", maker's mark "WS" struck twice, unascribed.

*c1785*

**$280-320**     **WW**

A George III English silver oval-shaped port label, by John Whittingham of London.

*1791*     *2in (5cm) wide*

**$80-120**     **CSA**

A rare George III Irish silver wine label, of canted oblong form with a molded border, incised "Tenerif", maker's mark "JT" possibly for J. Teare of Dublin.

*1800*

**$800-1,200**     **WW**

A George III English silver oblong brandy label, by John Angel of London, with cut corners.

*1806*     *1.75in (4.5cm) wide*

**$70-100**     **CSA**

## WINE ANTIQUES

- Wine antique collectors often specialize in a particular area of collection. Corkscrews, labels, funnels, champagne taps, tastevins, and ladles are especially popular.
- Wine labels, made from ivory, wood or silver, were produced to hang around the neck of bottles and decanters to identify the contents. When legislation was introduced in 1860 forcing retailers to label their own bottles prior to sale, the use of hanging wine labels declined.
- Wine funnels, used for pouring liquid into decanters for serving, were made from the mid-17thC. The curve to the base of the spout allowed wine to pour gently against the side of the decanter. Early funnels are rare and often valuable.
- Tastevins were a professional tool designed for wine tasting to assess color and clarity.
- The corkscrew became popular from the 18thC when wine producers began to seal bottles by driving the cork well into the neck. Major manufacturers include Thomason, James Heeley, Dowler, and Robert Jones. Types include peg and worm, concertina and waiter's friends.

A cast silver madeira wine label, by Charles Rowlings and William Summers, with grapevine border.

*1809*     *2.75in (7cm) wide*

**$120-180**     **CSA**

A George III silver wine label, probably Scottish, of plain oblong form, incised "Soterne", maker's mark "PG" in an oval, unascribed.

*c1815*

**$1,200-1,800**     **WW**

A George III provincial silver wine label, by John Walton of Newcastle, canted oblong with a reeded border, incised and filled "Rum".

*1815*

$220-280                                    WW

A George III English silver sherry label, by George Knight of London.

*1819*                    *1.75in (4.5cm) long*

$50-80                                       CSA

A 19thC Colonial mounted tiger claw wine label, probably Indian, with engraved decoration, incised "Port", unmarked.

*c1850*

$180-220                                    WW

A pair of Birmingham silver decanter labels, by Yapp & Woodward, with pierced lettering "port" and "sherry", in the form of vine leaves, hallmarked "Birmingham".

*1852*                      *3.5in (9cm) wide*

$280-320                                    CSA

A Birmingham silver "SCOTCH WHISKEY" label, by C.H. Cheshire, escutcheon-shaped with scrolled border.

*c1865*                    *2in (5cm) wide*

$180-220                                    CSA

A Victorian stamped-out silver wine label, by Edward Charles Brown of London, with a decorative border of husks and scrolls and pendant thistles, pierced "GIN".

*1868*

$120-180                                    WW

A pair of English Victorian silver spirit decanter labels, marked "Rum" and "Gin", with "Free (trade)" on the ribboned edge frame, among cornucopia, wheatsheaves and farming tools.

*2.25in (6.5cm) wide*

$300-500                                    CSA

A Dutch cast-silver corkscrew, with cavorting ladies and cherubs, the base with piped hamper.

*c1760*                    *3in (8cm) long*

$500-700                                    CSA

An English silver pocket corkscrew, by Samuel Pemberton, stamped "SP".

*c1780*                    *3.5in (9cm) long*

$400-600                                    CSA

### A CLOSER LOOK AT A CORKSCREW

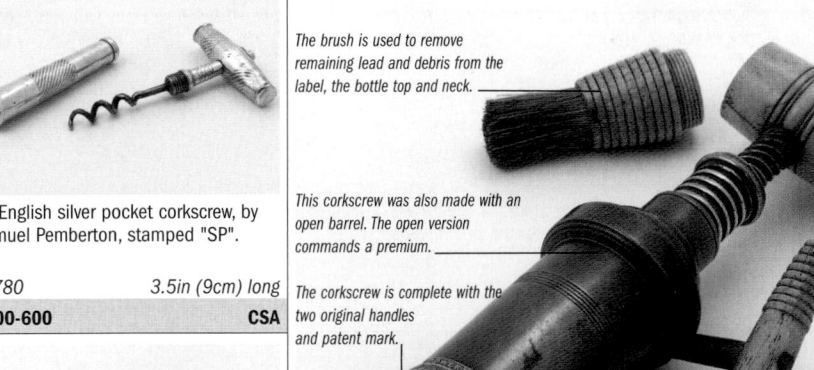

*The brush is used to remove remaining lead and debris from the label, the bottle top and neck.*

*This corkscrew was also made with an open barrel. The open version commands a premium.*

*The corkscrew is complete with the two original handles and patent mark.*

*The top handle is used to insert the worm into the cork whilst the side handle operates a rack and pinion mechanism to remove the cork from the bottle.*

A Birmingham silver-sheathed corkscrew, by Wardell and Kempson, with a two-finger ivory grip.

*c1790*                    *3.25in (8.5cm) long*

$800-1,200                                  CSA

An English bronze-barreled wide-rack king's screw, with a turned bone handle and a lion and unicorn tablet inscription "Dowler Patent".

*c1820*                    *extended 11in (28cm) wide*

$800-1,200                                  CSA

**SILVER & METALWARE**

An English straight-pull corkscrew, with carved turned bone handle and dusting brush, mobed stem, helical worm.

c1840      4.25in (11cm) long

**$80-120**      **CSA**

An English six-tool steel folding bow, with horse hoof pick, button hook, corkscrew, screwdriver, gimlet and spike.

*The more tools and the larger the piece, the more this type of tool is worth.*

c1850      2.75in (7cm) long

**$220-280**      **CSA**

c1860

**$280-320**      **CSA**

A rare English silver roundlet corkscrew, with folding baluster stem, fluted steel worm, hallmarked "TJ" by Thomas Johnson of Birmingham.

3in (8cm) long

**CSA**

A steel concertina-type corkscrew, with copper finish, marked "Weir's Patent 12804, 25 Septr 1884".

extended 12.5in (32cm) long

**$80-120**      **CSA**

An English two-part cast steel level corkscrew, with hinge plate bearing the inscription "Lund Patentee, 24 Fleet Street and 57 Cornhill, London 1884".

*Lund was a retailer in Cornhill who was known to sell stationery and gentlemen's accessories and accoutrements. There are some pieces marked "Lund".*

8.25in (21cm) long

**$120-180**      **CSA**

An English steel concertina-type corkscrew, inscribed "H.D. Armstrong Patent", with bladed worm.

c1885      extended 10.5in (27cm) long

**$80-120**      **CSA**

A French steel bladed corkscrew, with rivetted cow horn handle and corkscrew helix.

c1890      3in (8cm) long

**$22-28**      **CSA**

A double-lever steel corkscrew, with copper finish, stamped "'A1' Heeley's Double Lever".

c1900      6.75in (17cm) long

**$80-120**      **CSA**

An Italian four-pillar, open-frame bladed worm corkscrew, fixed brass 'T-shaped driving handle on a threaded shaft.

c1920      5.5in (14cm) long

**$80-120**      **CSA**

A French nickel-plated concertina-type corkscrew, marked "Perfect Revete S.G.D.G.".

c1920      extended 7.75in (20cm) long

**$30-40**      **CSA**

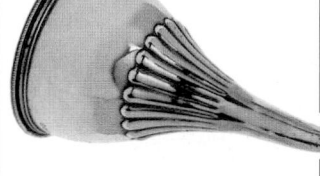

A George III part-fluted wine funnel, by Thomas Johnson, with gadrooned and molded borders, London.

1810      6in (15cm) long

**$500-700**      **DN**

A Scottish silver wine funnel and drip stand, by J. McKay, Edinburgh, with pierced pattern, one-shell tab, family crest and motto.

1826      5in (12.5cm) long

**$700-1,000**      **CSA**

A George III silver wine funnel, by Thomas James of London, with a deep circular bowl, reeded borders and a shaped tang.

1805      6in (15.5cm) high

**$800-1,200**      **WW**

An English George III silver-gilt toddy ladle, with a turned bone handle.

c1820      12in (30.5cm) long

**$220-280**      **CSA**

A Scottish silver toddy ladle, with turned rosewood handle, hallmarked "F.F." for Finlay and Field.

1828     18.5in (47cm) long

**$280-320**     **CSA**

A French silver tastevin on a chain with a French 50 cents coin, rim engraved with stars and "Dieu protege la France".

1872     2.5in (6.5cm) diam

**$500-700**     **CSA**

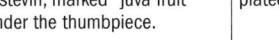

A French miniature silver-plated tastevin, marked "juva fruit" under the thumbpiece.

c1905     2.75in (7cm) diam

**$22-28**     **CSA**

A 1960s French chromium-plated tastevin.

4.25in (10.5cm) wide

**$8-12**     **CSA**

A George III silver tumbler cup, by Benjamin Brewood of London, initialed "RGL" below a crest.

1764     3.25in (8.5cm) diam

**$800-1,200**     **WW**

A George I silver tumbler cup, by Richard Bailey of London, with slightly tapered sides and a gilt interior.

1719     2.75in (7cm) diam

**$3,000-5,000**     **WW**

An English silver-plated leather-cased champagne tap, with two detachable spikes and a silk case lining printed with directions for use.

c1890     4in (10cm) long

**$80-120**     **CSA**

A pair of electroplate on copper wine coolers, each on a circular reed edged fluted foot supporting a half-fluted vase-shaped body with two foliate and shell scroll handles, reed-edged removable liner.

10.5in (26.5cm) high

**$400-600**     **CHEF**

An Old Sheffield silver-plate wine cooler or planter, of plain serpentine form raised on four bun feet and fitted with two ram's mask and ring handles, crested.

8.75in (22cm) diam

**$400-600**     **CHEF**

A pair of George III large silver wine coasters, by Edward Farrell of London, with cast husk and scroll rims and turned wooden bases, engraved with a coat of arms within an embossed scene, one depicting men and riders apprehending a man in the woods and conveying another back on a horse, the other with putti on a boar hunt in the woods.

1818     6.75in (17cm) diam

**$2,800-3,200**     **WW**

## BRASS

An 18thC Dutch brass hexagonal wedding presentation foot warmer, the pierced and embossed body with decoration of hearts, flowers, and busts of man and woman.

7in (18cm) high

**$3,000-6,000**     **POOK**

A penny foot brass trivet, with pierced decoration.

c1800

**$800-1,200**     **BP**

A pair of George II silver waiters, with pie crust borders and the coat of arms of a lady or widow in the center, by William Tuite of London.

1733     6.25in (16cm) diam

**$1,200-1,800**     **WW**

A 19thC Boulle inkstand, with covered inkwells and raised on scroll feet cast with female masks.

14.5in (37cm) wide

**$800-1,200**     **CHEF**

A late 19thC gilt brass urn, with two handles cast with double head finials, above boar's heads, the body with bands of oak, shell and Greek key decoration, on a fluted foot and square base.

*22.75in (57cm) high*

**$2,200-2,800**     **L&T**

A massive brass and copper wine cooler, in the form of a Renaissance goblet, with mask handles and circular armorial and figural panels.

*42.75in (107cm) high*

**$4,000-6,000**     **L&T**

A copper and brass log bin, of cylindrical form with a rolled edge and two lion mask handles, on three paw feet.

*18.75in (47cm) diam*

**$280-320**     **L&T**

## BRONZE

An American 'The Pioneer Woman' bronze group, by Bryant Baker, with a brown patina, on a marble base, inscribed and dated "Bryant Baker c 1927" and stamped "R. B. W. INC.".

*1927*     *11in (27.5cm) high*

**$5,000-8,000**     **FRE**

A Franz Bergman cold-painted bronze figure of a cock pheasant, in a standing posture, stamped monogram.

*10.5in (26cm) high*

**$2,200-2,800**     **L&T**

A Franz Bergman cold-painted bronze model of a golden pheasant, marked "B" within a vase stamp, and "Gesch 5724".

*17.5in (44.5cm) wide*

**$1,200-1,800**     **WW**

### BRONZE FIGURES

- Bronze figures were either sand-cast or cast using the 'lost wax' (cire perdue) technique which involves molding an object in wax, covering it with a clay or plaster mold and then heating it to allow the wax to run out and leave a shaped mold.
- The fluidity of bronze makes it particularly well suited to casting sculpture and decorative objects.
- In 1830, the pantograph was invented. This tracing instrument allowed artists to accurately scale down large antique sculptures and produce copies to meet the increased demand for decorative objects of a domestic size.
- During the 19thC Paris was considered the center of sculpture and attracted sculptors from all over the world. Many based work on Classical statues until the advent of the Art Nouveau movement.
- Austria was also a center for the production of high quality miniature bronzes. Several makers had studios in Vienna, including Franz Bergman.
- Known for its bronze groups, birds and animals, the Bergman factory was founded in Austria by Franz Bergman. Many pieces were exported and were extremely popular.
- Bergman signed some of his work with a "B" inside a two handled vase. The word "Namgreb" (Bergman spelled backward) is also found.

A Franz Bergman Austrian cold-painted bronze model of a woodcock, vase stamp.

*8in (20.5cm) high*

**$1,800-2,200**     **WW**

A French 'Racehorse with Jockey Up' bronze group, by Isidore Bonheur, with a brown patina, on marble base, inscribed "I. Bonheur" and stamped "28/100".

*23.5in (59cm) high*

**$8,000-12,000**     **FRE**

A Maurice Bouval figure, of a bronze hunter, with birds strapped to his waist, shielding his eyes and holding a sling, with a greenish brown patination.

*12in (31cm) high*

**$800-1,200**     **CHEF**

A French Jean Baptiste Auguste Clesinger 'Tauredo Romain' bronze standing bull, signed "J. Clessinger Rome, F. Barbedienne".

*10in (25.5cm) wide*

**$1,800-2,200**  JN

A French Paul Edouard Delabrierre bronze group of two fighting bulls, one standing over the other, on a rocky ground with branches, signed.

*10.5in (26.5cm) wide*

**$2,200-2,800**  JN

A 19thC French calling stag bronze, by Christophe, lying on a naturalistic base, signed.

*12.5in (32cm) wide*

**$1,800-2,200**  JN

A rare French Emmanuel Fremiet group of goats, the large goat feeding two kids, on a shaped naturalistic base, stamped "Fremiet".

*7.75in (19.5cm) long*

**$2,200-2,800**  JN

A Ferdinand Frick 'Male Cryer' bronze figure, with a rich dark brown patina, inscribed "Frick fec.".

*24.5in (61cm) high*

**$3,000-4,000**  FRE

An Austrian cold-painted bronze model of a bulldog, stamped "Gesch".

*4.5in (11.5cm) wide*

**$500-700**  WW

A Russian Ievgueni Alexandrovitch Lanceray 'Cossack on Horseback' bronze group, inscribed "Lanceray" in Cyrillic.

*11.25in (28cm) high*

**$7,000-10,000**  FRE

A German Hugo Lederer 'Man With Sword' bronze figure, with a brown patina, on a marble base, inscribed "H. Lederer fec".

*37.5in (94cm) high*

**$5,000-7,000**  FRE

A 19thC American 'Shepherd Boy' bronze group, by Kate Lizard, with a brown patina, inscribed "K. Lizard", stamped "Bronze Garantiau Titre C & L Déposée" and "12 6649".

*20.25in (50.5cm) wide*

**$3,000-5,000**  FRE

A 19thC French Jules Moigniez 'Merinos Nes A Wildeville' cast group, of a family of sheep, signed.

*15.5in (39.5cm) wide*

**$6,000-9,000**  JN

## A CLOSER LOOK AT A BRONZE GROUP

The 19thC French sculptor Pierre Lenordez specialized in the medium of bronze. He was very popular among the socially elite in the French Riviera, especially those within horseracing circles.

Lenordez' equestrian bronzes were often portraits of specific thoroughbreds or the favorite horses of prominent horse owners. This bronze is signed, in script, and is accompanied by an inscription.

This particular bronze, 'Graux Marley', demonstrates the artist's skill in the medium, and his firm knowledge of the anatomy of horses.

The quality of the casting is flawless, with no sign of foundry marks, as is typical of Lenordez.

A 19thC French Pierre Lenordez 'Graux Marley' large bronze group, with three horses and riders at fence, the first horse fallen, the second leaping clear of the fence and the third startled, the bronze signed and inscribed.

*30in (76cm) wide*

**$18,000-25,000**  JN

A 19thC Jules Moigniez large bronze stallion, standing before a rustic fence, signed.

*20.5in (52cm) high*

**$12,000-18,000**  JN

A 19thC bronze figure of Cupid, his hands tied by a ribbon, on a tree trunk, his bow and arrows on the oval base at his feet, dark brown patination.

*8.25in (21cm) high*

**$120-180**  CHEF

An early 19thC 'The Dancing Faun' bronze figure, after the Antique, in a naked contraposto pose, standing on a square plinth, dark green patination.

*12.75in (32cm) high*

**$700-1,000**    **L&T**

A bronze figure of a naked male after the Antique, on a rectangular base, with a brown patina.

*20.5in (51cm) high*

**$2,800-3,200**    **FRE**

A bronze statue of William the Conqueror, holding a boot and sword, on a circular base.

*19in (58cm) high*

**$700-1,000**    **JN**

A bronze figure of Cupid, with a staff and tambourine, on a circular base.

*22.5in (57cm) high*

**$2,800-3,200**    **JN**

A small Vienna bronze of a native American on horseback, wearing full length head feathers and carrying a club, signed.

*10.5in (26.5cm) wide*

**$3,000-5,000**    **JN**

A pair of Marly rearing horses, with attendants, each on an ovoid naturalistic base.

*15.75in (40cm) high*

**$1,200-1,800**    **DN**

A large bronze group of a Chinese pheasant and lizard, on a rectangular base, signed.

*29in (73.5cm) wide*

**$1,200-1,800**    **JN**

A 19thC gilt-bronze table lamp, the stem and circular foot heavily cast in relief with leaves, fitted for electricity.

*19.75in (50cm) high*

**$1,200-1,800**    **CHEF**

## CAST IRON

A massive Philadelphia painted cast iron, double-wheel coffee grinder, by Enterprise Mfg. Co., Patent July 12.98, retains original black pinstripes and floral decals on a red ground.

*60in (150cm) high*

**$4,000-6,000**    **POOK**

## COPPER

A copper strong box, weighing nine pounds, with a key.

*c1820*    *9.5in (24cm) wide*

**$500-700**    **BP**

A late 19thC copper wash basin of circular form, with flattened rolled rim.

*12.5in (32cm) diam*

**$80-120**    **BP**

A set of twelve graduated 'Crosby' copper measures, each of tapering cylindrical form with brass banding and applied handles, ranging from 5 gallons to 0.8 fluid oz.

*largest 18.5 in (47cm) high*

**$5,000-7,000**    **L&T**

## PEWTER

- American pewter was made as early as as 1639. The first colonists made pewter identical to the English wares. Any American pewter before 1875 is rare.
- Pewter is made from a mixture of tin, lead, copper, and other metals. Some pieces appear dull, while others are almost silver in appearance.
- Marks on pewter are called 'touchmarks'. Pewter from America is marked with a crowned rose. American makers almost always used names and letters to mark their pieces. However, some of the finest examples of American pewter were never marked.
- Use reference books and Internet sites that picture the marks in detail to decipher pewter marks.
- Beware of some 20thC English-made pewter that appears old and has a mark on the front of the plate. American pewter is almost always marked on the bottom, not the face of the piece.

An 18thC pewter quart mug, by Jacob Whitmore, flared cylindrical form with fillet, S-scroll handle with bud terminal, molded base, rare rose mark to interior base, round rose touchmark.

*6in (15cm) high*

**$10,000-12,000**     **SK**

An early 19thC pewter quart flagon, disk finial on domed, molded cover with 'chairback' thumbpiece, scroll handle with bud terminal, molded base, marked "TD & SB" and "X".

*9in (23cm) high*

**$5,000-8,000**     **SK**

An early 19thC three-quart pewter flagon, domed cover with 'chairback' thumbpiece, with molded fillet and base, double-scrolled handle with bud terminal, "BOARDMAN & HART", "N-YORK", and two round eagle touchmarks.

*13in (33cm) high*

**$4,000-6,000**     **SK**

A late 18thC pewter deep dish, with rare eagle mark.

*6in (15.5cm) diam*

**$1,800-2,200**     **SK**

An early 19thC three-quart pewter flagon, domed cover with 'chairback' thumbpiece, with molded fillet and base, double-scrolled handle with bud terminal, "BOARDMAN & HART", "N-YORK", and two round eagle touchmarks.

*Although items made by Boardman and Hart are marked New York, where they had a sales office, they were actually made in Hartford, Connecticut.*

An 18thC set of three pewter plates, the plates each with hammered booge, bear left facing lion touchmarks, owner's marks, minor wear.

*8.5in (21.5cm) diam*

**$2,200-2,800**     **SK**

A matched set of four pewter deep dishes, with single-reed brim, touchmarks include two oval eagles, "BOARDMAN & CO. NEW-York", and "X" quality mark.

*13in (33cm) high*    c1825          *9.5in (24cm) diam*

**$3,000-5,000**     **SK**    **$1,200-1,800**     **SK**

## THE CLOCKS MARKET

Luxury products are the first to feel the pinch during periods of economic uncertainty, and mid-range antique clocks are bearing the brunt of the current slowdown. Whereas buyers were previously clamouring for pressed oak gingerbread clocks, late 19thC black mantel clocks and other such typical American timepieces, these markets seem to have stalled in recent months. Auction prices have fallen by as much as half across vast swathes of the middle market as buyers tighten their belts and reject frivolity in favour of necessity.

Hardcore clock enthusiasts, however, remain undeterred by the gloomy economic climate. Caseless movements, bought in the main by hobbyists and restoration experts, have been selling well. Rare timepieces and clocks by the most admired makers continue to attract healthy interest and accrue value. It is still the case that a good American weight-driven wall regulator is among the best investments one can make in the antiques market.

Fine clocks such as Pennsylvania pillar-and-scroll tall cases currently fetch up to $10,000. Historic examples from the Connecticut River valley, cradle of the American clock industry, can be expected to find enthusiastic bidders for the foreseeable future despite the bearish sentiments felt elsewhere in the sector.

*Bob Schmitt, R.O. Schmitt Fine Arts*

## TALL CASE CLOCKS

A walnut and floral marquetry tall case clock, by John Lowe of London, with month duration six-pillar movement.

*c1690*  81in (205cm) high

**$45,000-55,000**  **DR**

A walnut and Arabesque marquetry tall case clock, by Joseph Bates of Holborn, England, with fretwork to the sides and front of the hood, walnut spiral-twist columns and giltwood capitals, the trunk door with three panels of Arabesque marquetry and a lenticle in the center, five-pillar movement with internal count.

*c1700*  84in (213.5cm) high

**$32,000-40,000**  **DR**

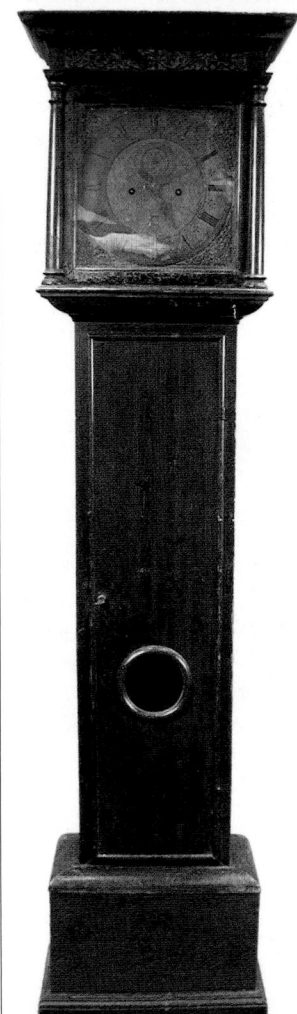

An early 18thC tall case clock, the square brass dial with seconds and date apertures, inscribed "Richard Fennell, London", with an eight day striking five-pillar movement.

**$2,200-2,800**  **SWO**

An early 18thC walnut tall case clock, the square brass dial with cherub and crown spandrels, subsidiary seconds dial, winding holes and date wheel, inscribed "Sam. Townson, London".

**$5,000-7,000**  **SWO**

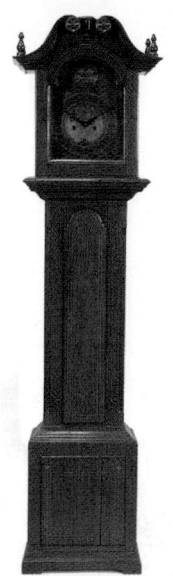

A mid-18thC walnut carved and inlaid tall case clock, by John Miller, the engraved brass dial inscribed "John Miller, Germantown, 1705" in the arch, brass weight-driven movement, the case with stringing, refinished, imperfections.

*86in (218.5cm) high*

**$6,000-9,000**     **SK**

A Philadelphia Queen Anne walnut tall case clock, the sarcophagus top over a tombstone door enclosing eight-day works, inscribed "Joseph Wills Philadelphia", rectangular base resting on ball feet.

*c1740*     *93in (236cm) high*

**$22,000-28,000**     **POOK**

A Georgian-style diminutive mahogany tall case clock, probably late 18thC, face marked "Rd James, Worcester", brass works, case with shell and bellflower inlay, probably late 19th or early 20thC, with keys, pendulum and weights.

*69in (172.5cm) high*

**$3,000-5,000**     **BRU**

A late 18thC Chippendale walnut tall case clock, by Duncan Beard, Appoquinimink, Delaware, the face with a curved steel hemispheric ring inscribed "Duncan Beard / Appoquinimink", original lead weights.

*99in (247.5cm) high*

**$50,000-55,000**     **FRE**

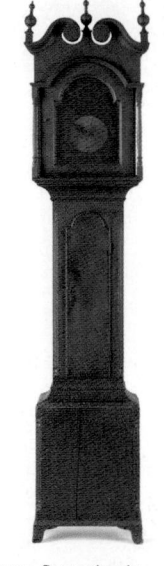

A Hilltown, Pennsylvania, painted poplar tall case clock, with a tombstone door enclosing a 30-hour brass works, inscribed "Benjn Morris Hill Tn No 23", case retaining a vibrant red and black grain decoration.

*c1780*     *95in (241.5cm) high*

**$60,000-65,000**     **POOK**

---

## A CLOSER LOOK AT A TALL CASE CLOCK

*Few clocks of this quality, with engraved brass-work, and an important provenance, appear on the market.*

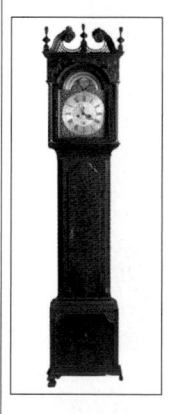

*The swan-neck pediment, which derives from Classical architecture, is highly elaborate with dentil moldings and carved rosettes.*

*This clock has a strong provenance, and is the heirloom from an important family. The family in question are direct descendants of Captain John Green, who sailed the Empress of China, the ship that opened the American China Trade.*

An important Philadelphia Chippendale mahogany tall case clock, the bonnet with a swan's neck pediment enclosing the original engraved brass works inscribed "David Paterson, Sunderland", above a waist with a scalloped door flanked by fluted quarter columns, resting on a base with applied moldings and foliate carvings, all supported by bracket feet.

**Provenance:** *Direct descendants of Captain John Green of Philadelphia.*

*c1775*

**$160,000-170,000**     *101in (252.5cm) high*     **POOK**

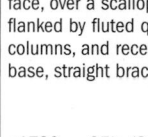

A Chippendale walnut tall case clock, by Solomon Parke, Newtown, Bucks County, Pennsylvania, the face etched with corner leaves and "Solomon Parke / Newtown Bucks County", double arched raised panel base.

*c1780*     *93.5in (234cm) high*

**$45,000-50,000**     **FRE**

A Pennsylvania Chippendale walnut tall case clock, with 30-hour works and white painted face, over a scalloped door flanked by fluted quarter columns, and recessed panel base, straight bracket feet.

*c1780*     *95in (241.5cm) high*

**$3,000-5,000**     **POOK**

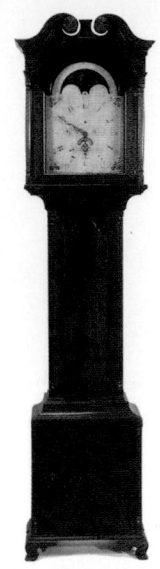

A late 18thC Chippendale walnut carved tall case clock, by George Faber, the gilt and painted iron dial inscribed "George Faber, Sumneytown, PA", with brass weight-driven pull-up movement, refinished, restoration.

*89in (226cm) high*

**$6,000-9,000**  SK

An important East Hampton, Long Island, New York stained gumwood tall case clock, by Nathaniel Dominy IV, the white dial inscribed "N.D. 1793", on straight bracket feet.

*The template for this clock's design survives in Nathaniel's tool collection, now at Winterthur Museum where the Dominy clock shop has been reconstructed. This piece is rare as, according to Charles F. Hummel, only about 90 clocks were produced by the Dominy shops from 1768 to 1828.*

*1793*  *81.5in (207cm) high*

**$40,000-45,000**  POOK

A Philadelphia Chippendale mahogany tall case clock, the flat top bonnet with step-fluted columns, enclosing an eight-day works with painted oval of a gentleman fishing, above the signature "R. Shearman Philadelphia".

*c1795*  *91.25in (232cm) high*

**$6,000-9,000**  POOK

A Federal mahogany inlaid tall case clock, the gilt iron dial with moon phase indicator, inscribed "Isaac Brokaw, Bridgetown", and eight-day brass weight-driven movement, the cove-molded base centering an inlaid sailing ship.

*c1800*  *91in (231cm) high*

**$12,000-14,000**  SK

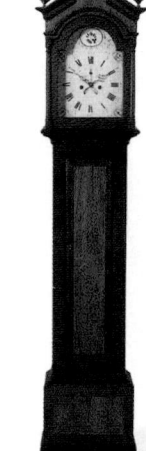

A Pennsylvania cherrywood tall case clock, with an arched painted face with painted moon-phase dial, white field signed "Emanuel Meily / Lebanon", slender columnnettes, lip-molded arched waist door, on French bracket feet.

*c1800*  *98.5in (246cm) high*

**$5,000-8,000**  FRE

A Lancaster County, Pennsylvania Federal cherry tall case clock, with eight-day works, signed "George Fisher Lancaster" above an arched herringbone inlaid door, above a scalloped skirt with fan inlay, on French feet.

*c1805*  *101.25in (257cm) high*

**$18,000-20,000**  POOK

A Federal cherry inlaid tall case clock, by Joseph Mulliken, the iron dial with floral and fruit spandrels inscribed "J. Mulliken, CONCORD", and eight-day brass weight-driven movement, inlaid base centering a patera, on ogee bracket feet.

*c1805*  *87.5in (217.5cm) high*

**$35,000-40,000**  SK

A Massachusetts Federal mahogany tall case clock, the arched bonnet enclosing brass works with white painted face, above a waist with an oblong door flanked by fluted quarter columns with brass capitals, on French feet.

*c1805*  *91in (231cm) high*

**$11,000-13,000**  POOK

An early 19thC grain painted pine, satinwood, and mahogany veneer tall case clock, brass eight-day weight-driven movement, dial signed in script on reverse "John Minot 207", old surface, movement possibly of different origin.

*88.5in (225cm) high*

**$4,000-6,000**  SK

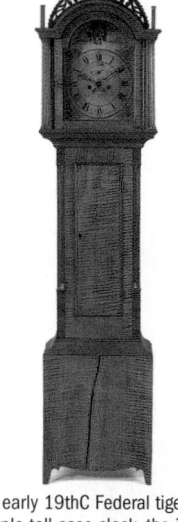

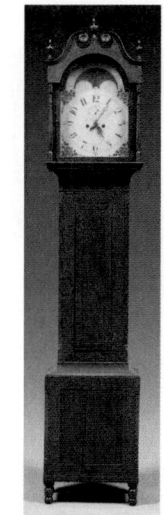

An early 19thC Federal cherry tall case clock, the painted iron dial with floral design, the tombstone door flanked by quarter-engaged columns with spiral inlaid stringing, over the similarly inlaid base with flaring French feet, refinished.

*c1805* 97.25in (247cm) high

**$8,000-12,000** **SK**

A Federal mahogany and mahogany veneer tall case clock, by Edward Hudson, a gilt polychrome painted dial inscribed "Edwd Hudson Mount Holly", eight-day brass weight-driven movement, refinished, repairs, and imperfections.

*c1810* 92.5in (235cm) high

**$10,000-12,000** **SK**

An early 19thC Federal tiger maple tall case clock, the iron polychrome and gilt dial showing a flower in the arch with American shield spandrels, eight-day brass weight-driven movement, refinished, restoration, and imperfections.

*c1810* 84in (213cm) high

**$12,000-14,000** **SK**

An early 19thC cherry tall case clock, probably Kentucky, with mahogany veneers, central cabinet and base with lambs' tongue chamfers, iron face with original painted floral spandrels, original brass works with bell mechanism, some losses.

98in (245cm) high

**$6,000-9,000** **BRU**

A 19thC Federal cherry tall case clock, by John Osgood, the polychrome gilt iron dial with American shield spandrels, seconds hand, and calendar aperture inscribed by "John Osgood", refinished, imperfections.

*c1810* 93.5in (237.5cm) high

**$12,000-14,000** **SK**

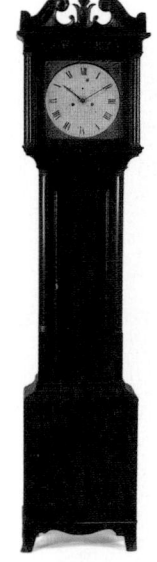

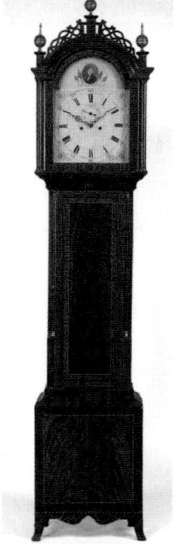

An early 19thC tiger maple tall case clock, polychrome and gilt iron dial, eight-day brass weight-driven movement, the thumb-molded waist door on cove molding and base resting on bracket feet, refinished, restoration.

88in (223.5cm) high

**$7,000-10,000** **SK**

An early 19thC Federal mahogany veneer inlaid tall case clock, by Aaron Willard, Boston, the iron dial inscribed with maker's name, and eight-day brass weight-driven movement, interior of door has engraved label of Aaron Willard, restored.

*c1815* 92in (233.5cm) high

**$16,000-18,000** **SK**

A walnut grandmother's tall case clock, with painted face with pink rose above red and floral corners, arched lip-molded waist door with reeded sides, recessed panel base on turned feet.

*c1815* 67in (167.5cm) high

**$5,000-8,000** **FRE**

An early 19thC American Federal mahogany tall case clock, a portrait of G. Washington and flags in the arch, with a two-train movement and subsidiary seconds dial, the mid-case with brass stop-fluted quarter columns.

*c1815* 95in (241.5cm) high

**$10,000-12,000** **SK**

An early 19thC cherrywood tall case clock, by Silas Hoadley, Plymouth, Connecticut, with an arched painted face with oval reserve of a landscape with farm buildings above, on straight bracket feet, 30-hour wooden movement.

98in (245cm) high

**$3,000-5,000** **FRE**

*John Benson won admiration in his day for the tidal, lunar, musical, and astronomical mechanisms he fitted to his clocks.*

*The fine mahogany case is well proportioned with good quality carving, and has acquired an attractive dark patina.*

*This chapter ring giving the relative altitude of the sun is an unusual feature of great interest to collectors.*

*Fewer than two dozen clocks by this maker are known to exist today, making them very rare and valuable commodities.*

An extremely rare tall case automaton clock, by Samual Toumlin of London, the trunk door decorated with mahogany veneers.

*c1770*      *95in (241cm) high*

**$45,000-55,000**      **DR**

A mahogany tall case clock, by Lawson of Newton, England, with conventional striking movement, rotating moon disc, and lunar calendar.

*c1770*      *87in (221cm) high*

**$25,000-30,000**      **DR**

A very rare mid-18thC astronomical tall case clock by John Benson of Whitehaven, England, the dial with Rococo engraving and stylized dolphins, two further chapters show the rising and setting sun, signed.

*89in (226cm) high*

**$60,000-70,000**      **DR**

A George III mahogany tall case clock, the twin-train eight day movement with anchor escapement striking on a bell, the false plate inscribed "Walker & Finemore, Birmingham".

*84.5in (211cm) high*

**$2,800-3,200**      **L&T**

A George III oak tall case clock, the twin-train eight day movement with anchor escapement striking on a bell, false plate inscribed "Dallaway & Son, Edinburgh".

*88in (220cm) high*

**$1,800-2,200**      **L&T**

A George III mahogany tall case clock, the twin-train eight day movement with anchor escapement striking on a bell.

*81.5in (204cm) high*

**$1,800-2,200**      **L&T**

An early 19thC painted satinwood tall case clock, with Adams-style decoration, the face marked "Ogeden, Darlington", losses.

*83in (211cm) high*

**$5,000-7,000**      **BRU**

A George III mahogany tall case clock, by John Hamilton of Glasgow, the twin-train eight day movement with anchor escapement striking on a bell.

*78.75in (200cm) high*

**$1,800-2,200**      **L&T**

A Regency mahogany and brass inlaid bracket clock, by Wieland of Watworth, with enamel dial, stepped gadrooned rectangular top and gilt brass pineapple finial.

*19in (48cm) high*

**$5,000-8,000**     **L&T**

An English Regency mahogany bracket clock, the painted dial signed "Sutherland, Davies and Co. Liverpool", with twin-train striking anchor escapement mechanism.

*c1830*     *18.5in (47cm) high*

**$1,800-2,200**     **ROS**

An Edwardian bracket clock, by Marshall & Sons of Edinburgh, the triple-train movement with circular silvered dial, and subsidiary dials.

*24.5in (62cm) high*

**$3,000-5,000**     **L&T**

A George I-style ebonized bracket clock, the triple-train movement striking on eight bells and Westminster chimes on bells and a gong, the brass dial with silvered Roman chapter ring and subsidiary tune dials.

*29.25in (73cm) high*

**$3,000-5,000**     **L&T**

## A CLOSER LOOK AT A BRACKET CLOCK

*The original sarcophagus top, or stepped pediment, make this bracket clock very special. It has all four of the original finials. On many clocks finials have been replaced – this is less desirable.*

*The term 'bracket' clock came in use when lantern clocks were given wooden cases and mounted on a wooden bracket. Bracket clocks are distinguished by having a handle on the top and they are taller and narrower than a mantel clock.*

*By the beginning of the 18thC arched dials became more common.*

A late 18thC Philadelphia Chippendale mahogany bracket clock, the case with a sarcophagus top with brass carrying handle, pineapple finials, and ogee bracket feet, the painted face signed by the retailer "John Hall Philad.", the backplate engraved "Thos. Parker Philadelphia".

*18.5in (47cm) high*

**$8,000-12,000**     **POOK**

## MANTEL CLOCKS

A 19thC French gilt metal and porcelain-mounted mantel clock, with floral painted dial and panels.

*15in (38cm) high*

**$500-800**     **CHEF**

A 19thC French ormolu timepiece, within a sunburst-topped lyre frame on a variegated marble base.

*15.75in (40cm) high*

**$1,200-1,800**     **CHEF**

A 19thC French mantel clock, the eight-day movement striking on a bell inscribed "Leroy à Paris".

*19in (48cm) high*

**$500-800**     **WW**

A 19thC ebonized amboyna and gilt-metal-mounted mantel clock, of Louis XV-style, with circular silvered dial.

*13.75in (35cm) high*

**$1,000-1,500**     **L&T**

A large 19thC rosewood mantel clock, with brass dial, silvered chapter ring and triple-train musical movement.

**$2,800-3,200**     **SWO**

An early 19thC marble and ormolu mounted mantel clock, the eight day striking movement with an external count wheel, the enamel dial inscribed "Jeannin à Paris", the case with a flaming urn finial, flanked by reeded pilasters with urns, on turned feet.

13in (33cm) high

$700-1,000          WW

A 19thC gilt brass and champlevé decorated mantel clock, the circular dial surmounted by a cherub holding a torch and flanked by urns, on two caryatid supports.

18.5in (47cm) high

$1,200-1,800          L&T

An early 19thC French bronze and ormolu-mounted pillar clock, the dial marked "Angevin à Paris", with silk suspension countwheel movement, case entwined with fruiting vine, upon a canted base with leaf and beaded bands.

14.5in (37cm) high

$1,200-1,800          CHEF

A late 18thC Swiss Carrara marble mantel clock, with a musical mechanism incorporating eleven bells and twenty hammers, the white enamel numeral ring with Arabic numbers and decorated hands.

18.5in (46cm) high

$8,000-12,000          NAG

An early 19thC mahogany stepped case shelf clock, by W. Cummings, the shaped cresting with an eagle, the face painted in ivory enamel, inscribed.

*34in (85cm) high*

**$3,000-5,000**     **FRE**

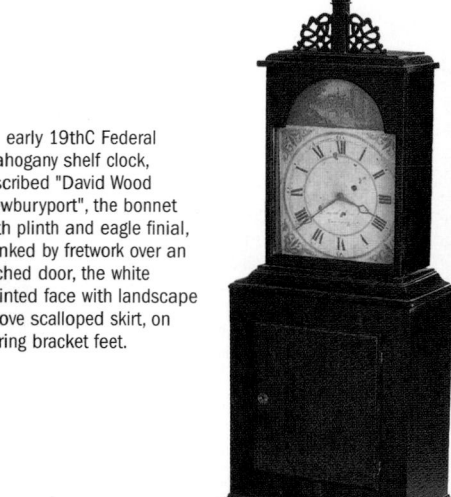

An early 19thC Federal mahogany shelf clock, inscribed "David Wood Newburyport", the bonnet with plinth and eagle finial, flanked by fretwork over an arched door, the white painted face with landscape above scalloped skirt, on flaring bracket feet.

*41.75in (106cm) high*

**$12,000-14,000**     **POOK**

An early 19thC New England maple shelf clock, with a center finial support and brass eagle, brass face, on straight bracket feet, shaped apron.

*28.25in (70.5cm) high*

**$5,000-8,000**     **FRE**

A Federal mahogany shelf clock, the upper églomisé panel inscribed "Aaron Willard/Boston", white painted face, turned brass feet.

*c1815     35.25in (82cm) high*

**$5,000-8,000**     **POOK**

A Federal mahogany and mahogany veneer pillar and scroll shelf clock, by Eli Terry, with 30-hour weight-driven movement with outside escapement, old refinish, restoration.

*c1815     29.5in (74cm) high*

**$3,000-5,000**     **SK**

A mahogany pillar and scroll shelf clock, by Eli Terry, Plymouth, Connecticut, face painted with two baskets of flowers, spandrel corners.

*c1815     31in (77.5cm) high*

**$2,800-3,200**     **FRE**

## ELI & SAMUEL TERRY

- Eli (1772-1852) and Samuel Terry (1774-1853) were born to Samuel and Hildah Terry in Connecticut. Eli completed his apprenticeship in brass movements and became a talented businessman, issued with nine patents from 1797 to 1845.
- Eli invented and perfected the wood movement shelf clock and was a master of difficult horological principles. He was determined to make a new kind of clock that is small, affordable, and quick to manufacture.
- Eli joined forces with brother Samuel Terry from 1824 to 1827. Together they created the pillar and scroll mantel clock, with elegant pillars and a scrolling pediment with finials. Most of these clocks were embellished with verre églomisé panels on the front.
- The Terry family were soon operating three factories that produced about 9,000 clocks annually.
- By the 1840s wooden movements were in decline and brass movements became more popular.
- The Eli and Samuel label is highly prized among collectors and pieces attributed to the Terry brothers are in high demand.

A mahogany pillar and scroll shelf clock, by Eli and Samuel Terry, Plymouth, Connecticut, white-painted face with basket of flowers and corner enamels.

*c1825     31.75in (79cm) high*

**$2,800-3,200**     **FRE**

A Federal mahogany and mahogany veneer pillar and scroll shelf clock, by Eli Terry & Sons, with 30-hour wooden weight-driven movement, refinished, minor restoration.

*c1825     31in (77.5cm) high*

**$2,200-2,800**     **SK**

A Federal mahogany and mahogany veneer pillar and scroll shelf clock, by Eli and Samuel Terry, with 30-hour wooden weight-driven movement, refinished.

*c1825     32in (81cm) high*

**$1,800-2,200**     **SK**

A Classical mahogany carved triple-decker shelf clock, by Eli Bartholomew and Co., white painted and gilt dial, weight-driven wooden movement, with mirror glass, on claw feet.

*c1825     35in (89cm) high*

**$500-800**     **SK**

A Classical mahogany carved triple decker shelf clock, by John Birge, the eight-day weight-driven brass movement with mirror glass, on carved hairy paw feet.

*c1825     38in (96.5cm) high*

**$1,200-1,800**     **SK**

**CLOCKS**

A Federal mahogany and mahogany veneer pillar and scroll shelf clock, by Ephraim Downes, with 30-hour wooden weight-driven movement, refinished, minor imperfections.

*c1825*          *31in (77.5cm) high*

**$2,800-3,200**                    **SK**

A mahogany pillar and scroll shelf clock, by Ethel North, Torrington, Connecticut, with three brass urn finials, painted face, gilt and red enamel corners, on tall bracket feet.

*c1835*          *29.5in (74cm) high*

**$3,000-5,000**                    **FRE**

A mid-19thC Gothic mahogany 'candlestick' double steeple wagon spring shelf clock, the case with original painted tablets, painted zinc dial, and eight-day time and strike "J. Ives Patent Accelerating Lever Spring" movement.

*c1845*          *13.75in (35cm) wide*

**$8,000-12,000**                    **SK**

A mid-19thC Gothic rosewood acorn shelf clock, the shape laminated case with original reverse-painted tablet, painted zinc dial, and eight-day fusee movement, dial probably repainted.

*10in (25.5cm) wide*

**$7,000-10,000**                    **SK**

A mid-19thC 30-day rosewood shelf clock, with an iron and brass "patent equalizing lever spring" movement.

*This 30-day wagon spring movement was invented by Joseph Ives.*

*13.5in (34.5cm) wide*

**$2,800-3,200**                    **SK**

A mid-19thC Gothic rosewood acorn shelf clock, the laminated case with painted zinc dial, reverse-painted glass tablet, eight-day time and strike wood barrel fusee spring movement.

*15in (38cm) wide*

**$6,000-9,000**                    **SK**

A mid-19thC Gothic mahogany double steeple wagon spring shelf clock, the case with original painted tablets, painted zinc dial, and 30-hour "J. Ives Patent Accelerating Lever Spring Movement."

*11.5in (29cm) wide*

**$3,000-5,000**                    **SK**

A mid-19thC 30-day rosewood shelf clock, painted zinc dial, with a brass "patent equalizing lever spring" movement, maker's label.

*13.5in (34.5cm) wide*

**$4,000-6,000**                    **SK**

A painted iron figural 'Topsy' blinking-eye shelf clock, attributed to Bradley & Hubbard, figure of a black lady, Roman numeral chapter ring, on oval plinth, crack at neck.

*c1880*          *17in (42.5cm) high*

**$1,800-2,200**                    **FRE**

An enamel painted iron figural blinking-eye 'Organ Grinder and Monkey' shelf clock, attributed to Bradley & Hubbard, with Roman numeral chapter ring, standing on an oval plinth.

*c1880*          *17.5in (44cm) high*

**$3,000-5,000**                    **FRE**

A 19thC French malachite and gilt bronze clock garniture, the clock with white enamel dial and eight day movement, with a pair of later figural five-light candelabra.

*candelabra 31in (77.5cm) high*

**$12,000-18,000**     **FRE**

A 19thC French gilt metal clock garniture, the urn-topped case molded with scrolls, masks, and flowers, with numbered Marti movement, restored.

*clock 13in (33cm) high*

**$500-800**     **CHEF**

A 19thC ormolu and bronze clock garniture, the eight day striking timepiece set within an ornate case with strapwork and artistic trophies.

*20.25in (51.5cm) high*

**$1,800-2,200**     **ROW**

## POCKET WATCHES

An early 20thC French 18ct gold, diamond and enamel round pendant watch by Le Roy & Sohn of Paris, signed "Grand Prix Paris 1900".

**$1,000-1,500**     **DN**

An 18ct gold cuckoo clock coat pin, set with diamonds in platinum mounts, with movable weights and pendulum winding mechanism, marked on face "Walser Wald".

*3in (7.5cm) long*

**$1,800-2,200**     **BRU**

A rare early silver pair cased pocket watch, by Isaac Austin, with verge escapement, chain, and fusee movement with pierced scrolled foliate designs and engraved "Isaac Austin Philadela No. 12", with ten American late 18thC round paper watch maker's labels, chip to dial edge.

*c1785*     *2.25in (6cm) diam*

**$1,200-1,800**     **SK**

### A CLOSER LOOK AT A FOB WATCH

*These appendages are similar to those found on charm bracelets, which are currently in vogue. Popular fashions can have a substantial effect on the market value of any antique.*

*Natural pearls have a thicker nacre — the shiny outer surface — than the cultured variety. Intensive harvesting has devastated natural pearl beds, with the result that they are extremely valuable today.*

*The hands are encrusted with diamonds - a luxurious touch that adds to the general opulence of this fine piece of jewelry.*

A gold, enamel, and half-pearl fob watch and chatelaine, the cover enameled, with white enamel face, diamond hands, and half-pearl bezel, the fob suspension mounted with natural pearls, with four appendages, comprising a pair of tassels, a watch key, and a monogrammed seal.

*c1800*

**$5,000-7,000**     **WW**

A gold open-faced fob watch, the silvered dial with black Roman numerals, engraved with foliate scroll decoration, the reverse decorated with enamel painted flowers, the gold dust cover signed "Mare Dupan", with watch key.

*1in (2.5cm) diam*

**$500-700**     **WW**

An open-faced pocket watch, signed "Patron", the scroll hands and bezel set with small diamonds, the back cover painted with an enamel scene within a guilloche and scroll enamel border, signed and numbered "2263".

*1.5in (4cm) diam*

**$2,200-2,800**     **WW**

**CLOCKS**

A late 18thC mahogany and mahogany veneer shelf timepiece, by Aaron Willard, a brass engraved dial, marked "A. Willard, Grafton", brass weight-driven 30-hour movement.

*9.25in (23.5cm) wide*

**$5,000-8,000**    **SK**

A 19thC gilt gesso and wood mirror timepiece, the door with stencil and painted tablet and mirror, the dial inscribed "A. Chandler", eight-day weight-driven movement, maker's label.

*13.75in (35cm) wide*

**$8,000-12,000**    **SK**

A 19thC gilt gesso and wood mirror clock, the door with a glass tablet and mirror, a dished painted iron dial and eight-day weight-driven rack and snail striking movement, alterations.

*c1825*    *13.75in (35cm) wide*

**$800-1,200**    **SK**

A 19thC gilt gesso and wood mirror timepiece, with reverse-painted frame, stenciled tablet and mirror, a painted iron dial and brass eight-day weight-driven movement, minor imperfections.

*c1825*    *12.75in (32.5cm) wide*

**$3,000-5,000**    **SK**

## A CLOSER LOOK AT A WALL CLOCK

*The detailed carved eagle finial with its spread wings is especially appealing for American collectors.*

*Few American wall clocks are signed on the dial, preferring a maker's label at the back of the inside case. This clock is rare as it has been signed by Dunning on the painted iron dial.*

*This clock is weight-driven, meaning the movement is powered by a constant pull of weights that are attached to a line wound around a barrel. A functioning clock, with original mechanical features like this one is very desirable.*

*Attributed to the renowned clockmaker J.L. Dunning of Burlington, Vermont, this wall clock commands a premium.*

An early 19thC Classical mahogany carved girandole wall timepiece, attributed to J. L. Dunning, the molded wooden bezel opens to a painted iron dial inscribed "...Dunning" and brass weight-driven movement, imperfections.

*39in (99cm) long*

**$65,000-70,000**    **SK**

An early 19thC mahogany and parcel gilt banjo case wall clock, with a carved and gilded phoenix finial, pierced brass spandrels.

*34.5in (86cm) high*

**$600-900**    **FRE**

A mid-19thC rosewood lyre wall acorn timepiece, painted zinc dial and eight-day 'ladder' spring movement, labeled "... J. C. Brown & CO., Bristol ...".

*13in (33cm) wide*

**$16,000-18,000**    **SK**

A late 19thC gilt gesso and wood mirror clock, reverse-painted glass, iron concave dial inscribed "E. P. Moulton Saco", eight-day striking movement.

*14in (35.5)cm) wide*

**$3,000-5,000**    **SK**

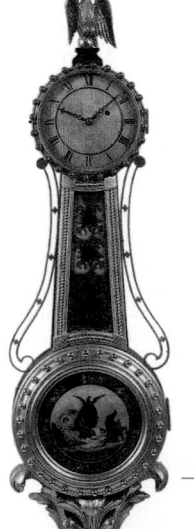

An early 20thC Federal style gilt gesso and mahogany girandole timepiece, carved gilt eagle finial, eight-day weight-driven movement, the throat with églomisé tablet lettered "L. Curtis, Concord" above an eagle and shield, a tablet depicting "Commerce".

*44.5in (113cm) high*

**$13,000-15,000**    **SK**

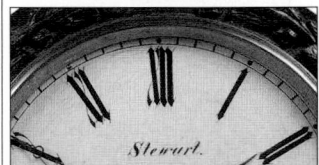

A Victorian oak wall regulator by Stewart of Glasgow, the single-train eight day fusee movement with dead beat escapement.

*15.5in (39cm) diam*

**$500-800**     **L&T**

A Victorian mahogany trunk dial wall clock, the dial marked "Honeybone Nottingham", the trunk with glass panel and pierced side mounts, the four-pillar brass fusee movement with tapered plates.

*23.25in (59cm) high*

**$1,000-1,500**     **CHEF**

A George III mahogany banjo barometer, by Lione & Somalvico of London, with silvered circular dial and brass frame, spirit level at base in corresponding dial, engraved "Lione & Somalvico, 125 Holborn Hill, London".

*42.75in (107cm) high*

**$1,200-1,800**     **L&T**

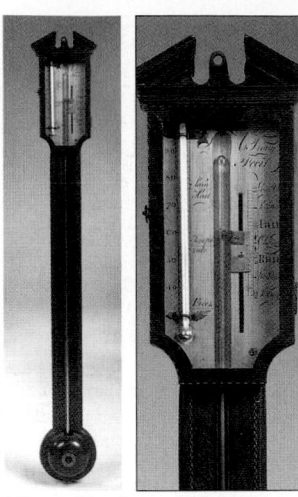

A George III mahogany stick barometer, by A. Trony, with checker stringing, broken pediment, vernier slider, and narrow shaft with circular reservoir panel and domed cover.

*38in (97cm) high*

**$1,800-2,200**     **L&T**

A George III mahogany barometer, by A. Lione of London, with a silvered circular dial, subsidiary humidity dial, thermometer and spirit level.

*41.25in (105cm) high*

**$2,800-3,200**     **L&T**

A George III mahogany stick barometer, with boxwood stringing and silvered scale, the body with exposed mercury tube and square reservoir cover inlaid with oval shell patera.

*38.25in (97cm) high*

**$1,800-2,200**     **L&T**

A George III cased stick barometer, by F. Bird of London, the rubbed silvered dial above a rectangular body with exposed mercury tube.

*36.25in (92cm) high*

**$2,200-2,800**     **L&T**

A Regency mahogany stick barometer, by Adie & Son of Edinburgh, with silvered vernier slider and thermometer.

*42.5in (106cm) high*

**$15,000-20,000**     **L&T**

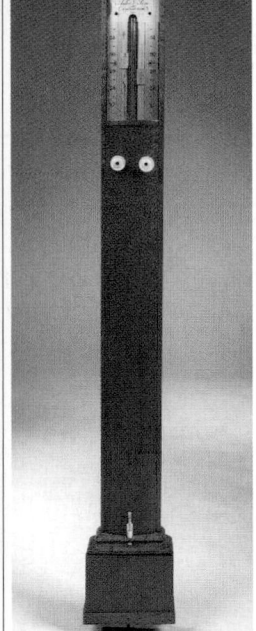

A mid-19thC bird's-eye maple stick barometer, by Adie & Son, the square silvered scale with glass mercury tube, the bowed case with dual apertures and two ivorine adjusters.

*41.75in (106cm) high*

**$8,000-12,000**     **L&T**

## THE PRECIOUS JEWELRY MARKET

The very top end of the jewelry market is extremely buoyant and prices for the most attractive, finely crafted pieces made from the best materials remain high. Unusual items and signed jewelry by well-known designers, such as Cartier and Van Cleef & Arpels, continue to attract a great deal of attention.

Jewelry buyers currently tend to favor wearable pieces that sit happily with contemporary dress and can be worn for both day and evening. This has lead to an increase in demand for jewelry from the 1940s and 1950s, particularly that made in America by companies such as Rubel and Trabert & Hoeffer Mauboussin. Bold jewels, such as rubies, and semi-precious stones that create a striking visual effect, including amethyst and aquamarine, are very desirable, although diamonds remain enduringly popular.

Interest in pieces from the 1960s and 1970s, that were largely ignored until recently, has also grown and prices have risen accordingly. Grima and Charles de Temple pieces from this period have recently fetched startling prices. In comparison, 19thC jewelry has somewhat fallen out of fashion and can struggle to attract interest.

In terms of types of jewelry, earrings are the most sought after and prices tend to be high because they are also the most difficult to come by. Bracelets and pendants are also popular, whilst brooches move in and out of fashion.

The market for middle and lower end pieces is faring less well. Buyers are rejecting poor quality, unsigned and semi-mass-produced jewelry.

*– Ian Harris, N. Bloom & Son*

An antique Egyptian winged scarab pin, with carved blue glazed ceramic from the Middle Empire (2000BC) and French set in the 1880s.

5.75in (14.5cm) wide

**$8,000-12,000**     **NBLM**

An early 19thC gold en-tremblant pin, in the form of a filigree bird with a ruby eye and drop, mounted on a spring within a flowerhead and turquoise surround, with a small hair-glazed back panel, in a fitted case.

**$800-1,200**     **DN**

An early 19thC gold pendant pin, the heart-shaped locket with wirework floral motifs and a repoussé scroll border, suspended by snake chain inter-links, set with rubies and emeralds, one stone a later green paste.

**$500-800**     **DN**

An early 19thC serpent pin, set with graduated half-pearls and a ruby eye, the glazed center with needlework, hinged glazed locket section to reverse.

1.5in (3.5cm) wide

**$1,200-1,800**     **WW**

An early Victorian gold and gem cruciform pin, with a round hessonite garnet, four oval mixed-cut Imperial topaz and chrysolite spacers and terminals.

**$2,800-3,200**     **DN**

An early Victorian coiled serpent pin, partly set with graduated turquoise cabochons and garnet eyes, set in gold, missing pin.

1.75in (4.5cm) wide

**$700-1,000**     **WW**

A mid-19thC architectural micromosaic pin, depicting the Vatican and St. Peter's Church in Rome, in a rectangular gold mount.

*2in (5cm) wide*

**$1,200-1,800**    **CHEF**

A 19thC oval cameo pin, carved with an image of a Roman soldier, surrounded by a bead-decorated silver frame.

*2in (5cm) high*

**$50-80**    **FRE**

A Victorian gold and garnet pin, in the form of entwined hoops, with an oval drop and a hair-glazed back panel, later pin.

**$400-600**    **DN**

A Victorian diamond-set star pin, with graduated cushion-shaped diamonds and larger diamonds set in gold, in a fitted case.

*In the Victorian era, there was a revival of interest in 18thC court jewelry which typically used star or sunburst motifs.*

*1.25in (3cm) wide*

**$2,800-3,200**    **WW**

A gem-set butterfly pin, with a diamond and emerald body, sapphire and diamond wings and cabochon ruby eyes, set in silver on gold.

*Insect jewelry, using forms such as bees, wasps, butterflies, and dragonflies, first became popular in the 1860s. Butterfly pins are very popular with collectors.*

*2in (5cm) wide*

**$4,000-6,000**    **WW**

A Victorian owl and moon pin, set with graduated circular-cut diamonds, the owl with cabochon ruby eyes, set in silver on gold.

*2.25in (5.5cm) wide*

**$5,000-7,000**    **WW**

A late Victorian gold pin, with a fox walking into a bush, set with diamonds.

*1.75in (4.5cm) wide*

**$2,800-3,200**    **NBLM**

A late Victorian rose diamond and enamel pin, in the form of a cockerel and two hens, on a knife-edge bar with pearl terminals, set throughout in silver and gold, in a Hancock's case.

**$2,800-3,200**    **DN**

A late Victorian moonstone and diamond pin or pendant, with a heart-shaped moonstone carved with a classical cameo of Apollo, set within an old-cut diamond border with a ribbon tied bow surmount, set in silver and gold, removable pin fitting.

*This pin has all the classic ingredients of late Victorian sentimentality, the 'lovers knot' surmount, the use of moonstone with its reference to night and dreams and carved to depict Apollo, a god legendary for his love affairs, in a pin of heart-shaped outline set with diamonds, the eternal gemstone.*

**$5,000-8,000**    **DN**

A late Victorian frog pin, set with rose-cut diamonds, a line of demantoid garnets and cabochon ruby eyes, set in silver on gold, French control mark to the pin.

*1in (2.5cm) wide*

**$1,800-2,200**    **WW**

A late Victorian jewelry model, with two gold rabbits, running over a hill of pearls.

*1in (2.5cm) wide*

**$1,800-2,200**    **NBLM**

A late Victorian diamond horseshoe pin, pavé-set throughout in silver and gold with graduated old-cut diamonds in three rows, in a case.

**$2,200-2,800**    **DN**

A late Victorian closed crescent diamond pin, the graduated old-cut stones set in silver and gold.

$1,800-2,200      DN

An Art Nouveau scroll and diamond platinum pin, adaptable as a pendant, with openwork.

*The design is Art Nouveau, but the use of materials is typical of the Edwardian era.*

2in (5cm) wide

$8,000-12,000      NBLM

A Belle Epoque pierced pin, set with graduated circular and rose-cut diamonds in platinum, with a border of untested pearls, detachable pin and pendant loop.

1.75in (4.5cm) wide

$6,000-9,000      WW

A French gold pin, with a winged chimera holding a diamond in her mouth.

c1900      1.75in (4.5cm) wide

$1,800-2,200      NBLM

A Tiffany diamond pin, with a central emerald-cut diamond mounted in free-form branches set with old European-cut diamonds, stamped "Tiffany Schlumberger".

*French master jewelry designer Jean Schlumberger opened his salon at Tiffany & Co. in 1956.*

$20,000-30,000      BRU

An Edwardian gold and pearl shield-shaped openwork pin, the central flowerhead with a small old-cut diamond, scroll work surmount and a half-pearl collet swag and drop, removable pin fitting, unmarked.

$1,200-1,800      DN

An Edwardian Caduceus pin, with red enameled wings, old-cut diamond entwined snakes and pearl terminals, set throughout in silver and gold.

*The Caduceus was the magic staff of Greek god Hermes, or Roman god Mercury. The messenger gods were also associated with incantations and conducting the dead.*

$1,200-1,800      DN

An Edwardian gold pin, with three cushion-shaped rubies, probably of Burmese origin, spaced by pairs of old-cut diamonds.

$15,000-20,000      DN

An Edwardian diamond openwork pin, with a lobed lozenge-shaped outline, millegrain set throughout with old-cut diamonds.

$4,000-6,000      DN

An Edwardian opal and diamond pin, centered with a round white opal, millegrain set within an open-lobed border with old-cut diamonds.

**$800-1,200** DN

An Edwardian gold crescent pin, set with two rows of graduated seed pearls.

*1in (2.5cm) wide*

**$280-320** WW

An Edwardian bicycle lapel pin, with articulated wheels and set with small diamonds.

*1.5in (4cm) wide*

**$2,800-3,200** NBLM

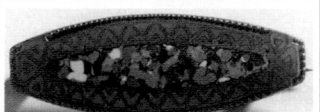

An enameled pin.

*c1910* *1.5in (4cm) wide*

**$50-70** GKA

A French tree in a bucket pin, with carved emerald leaves and ruby and diamond fruit.

*The carved emerald detail suggests an Indian influence.*

*c1930* *2.25in (6cm) high*

**$8,000-12,000** NBLM

A French fintail fish pin, set with sapphires and diamonds.

*c1940* *3in (7.5cm) high*

**$7,000-10,000** NBLM

An hourglass watch drop pin, set with rubies.

*c1940* *3in (7.5cm) high*

**$2,800-3,200** NBLM

A fine plique-a-jour enamel bird of paradise pin, with a blue feathered body and perched on a diamond branch, signed 'Mellerio Dits Mellers Paris'.

*c1945* *2.75in (7cm) high*

**$8,000-12,000** NBLM

A 'sunshine and clouds' gem-set pin, in the style of Simon Schepps, American-set with blue and yellow sapphires and diamonds.

*c1940* *3in (7.5cm) high*

**$8,000-12,000** NBLM

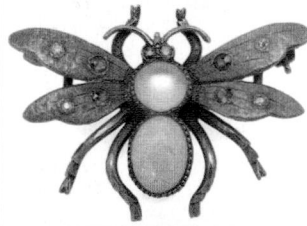

A 20thC opal and moonstone 'bumble bee' pin, with brushed gold wings inset with small diamonds, the head with garnet eyes, stamped "BBB".

*1.5in (4cm) wide*

**$500-800** FRE

**JEWELRY**

A 20thC 14ct gold and enamel duck pin, with a green enameled hat, jade dangle, yellow enameled body, green and blue enameled wings.

*1.75in (4.5cm) long*

**$280-320**    **FRE**

A 20thC yellow gold and diamond 'Rooster' pin, with inset diamond eye.

*1.75in (4.5cm) long*

**$220-280**    **FRE**

## A CLOSER LOOK AT AN OSCAR HEYMAN DIAMOND PIN

*Oscar Heyman & Brothers, founded in New York in 1912, hand-produced precious stone jewelry in the European style to the very highest standard. Pieces are produced with great skill using the best materials and are thus extremely desirable.*

*The firm produced jewelry for Cartier, Van Cleef & Arpels and other prestigious brands. Elizabeth Taylor and the Sultan of Brunei have featured on its list of clients. Pieces by such an important company attract a premium.*

*Until relatively recently, the firm's work was generally not signed. However, many pieces have registration numbers that can help with identification.*

*The unique design makes this pin extremely versatile and thus very appealing to collectors. The pin can be worn alone or with one of the two detachable bars.*

An Oscar Heyman diamond set spray pin, with two adaptable bars, one in sapphire and diamonds, the other in emerald and diamonds.

*c1950*                    *2.25in (6cm) wide*

**$35,000-45,000**    **NBLM**

A gem-set flower spray pin, with 4ct of rubies and 7ct of diamonds.

*c1950*        *2.25in (6cm) high*

**$8,000-12,000**    **NBLM**

A Tiffany double-heart pin set, with two diamonds.

*c1950*        *1.5in (4cm) wide*

**$2,200-2,800**    **NBLM**

A Tiffany pin pendant set with diamonds, 4.5ct.

*c1950*        *3in (8cm) high*

**$15,000-20,000**    **NBLM**

A Meister secretary bird pin, with spectacles and emerald eyes.

*1965*                    *1.75in (4.5cm) high*

**$5,000-7,000**                    **NBLM**

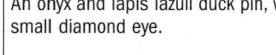

An onyx and lapis lazuli duck pin, with a small diamond eye.

*c1980*                    *0.75in (2cm) wide*

**$700-1,000**                    **NBLM**

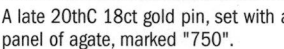

A jade and diamond leaping fish pin, with maker's mark "WAD" for Wendy Anne Dan, Birmingham.

*c1986*                    *2.25in (6cm) high*

**$5,000-7,000**                    **NBLM**

A late 20thC 18ct gold pin, set with a panel of agate, marked "750".

**$500-700**                    **GS**

A late 20thC seated hound pin, with an enameled head.

*1.5in (4cm) high*

**$1,800-2,200**                    **NBLM**

A late 20thC carved labradorite 18ct moonface pin, by Stephen Webster, with cabochon sapphires, emeralds, and cultured pearls.

*2.5in (5cm) wide*

**$5,000-7,000**                    **NBLM**

A jade pin, mounted with pierced jade in the form of a dragon, the shaped gold frame decorated with enamel.

*2.75in (7cm) wide*

**$3,000-4,000**                    **WW**

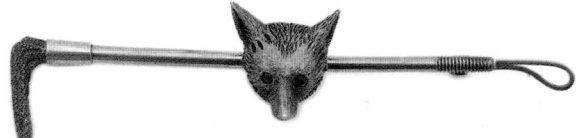

A fox mask stick pin, designed as a riding crop and applied with a realistically formed fox mask with ruby eyes, fitted case.

*3.25in (8.5cm) wide*

**$280-320**                    **WW**

A goshawk stick pin, with a realistically formed bird, pavé-set with graduated turquoise cabochons, with ruby eyes and two small rose-cut diamonds to the beak, set in gold, the fitted case by Mappin and Webb.

*3.75in (9.5cm) high*

**$800-1,200**                    **WW**

A Cartier 18ct gold turtle pin, set with turquoise cabochons and sapphire eyes, signed "Cartier Paris no 7383".

*1.5in (3.5cm) high*

**$1,800-2,200**                    **WW**

A French gold pheasant pin, with a ruby eye, rose-cut diamond feathers and a polychrome enameled body, indistinct lozenge-shaped maker's mark.

**$1,200-1,800**                    **DN**

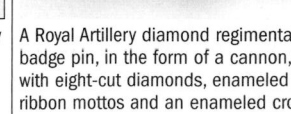

A Royal Artillery diamond regimental badge pin, in the form of a cannon, set with eight-cut diamonds, enameled ribbon mottos and an enameled crown.

**$700-1,000**                    **DN**

**JEWELRY**

**A CLOSER LOOK AT A RARE KASHMIR SAPPHIRE AND DIAMOND NECKLACE**

*The sapphire mines of Kashmir are situated in the Padar region of the Himalayas. When sapphires were first discovered there after a landslide in 1881, they were so plentiful that locals used the hard blue rocks as flints for their rifles, starting fires and as cutting tools.*

*The quality of these Kashmir stones is such that they reveal their rich yet 'velvety' quality under a range of light sources.*

*The necklace can be converted in to five pins, and this adaptable quality, together with provenance, adds to its desirability.*

*Kashmir sapphires of this size and color rarely come onto the open market. They have been cataloged by the London Precious Stone Laboratory.*

A rare Kashmir sapphire and diamond necklace, formed of eight graduated oval 'target' clusters, with sapphire and diamond five stone saltire-shaped inter-links, each oval cluster centered with a sapphire within two old-cut diamond graduated borders, each silver and gold mounted cluster with two suspension loops and screw apertures, with five removable screw-in pin fittings, the diamonds weigh 37ct, in a fitted case.

*With the necklace is a contemporary hand-written note from the vendor's grandmother; "Marjorie's sapphire and diamond necklace, given to me to give to her by Mama on March 30th 1888".*

*c1885*

**$450,000-550,000**

DN

A George III flat garnet cruciform pendant, set with five garnets, half-pearls and turquoise cabochons to the gold canetille mount, later gold chain.

*1.5in (4cm) wide*

**$400-600** WW

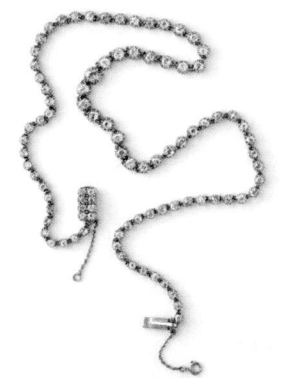

A Victorian diamond riviere necklace, set with graduated circular-cut diamonds in cut down silver and gold collets, the clasp with eight similar diamonds, 7ct.

*16.25in (41.5cm) long*

**$8,000-12,000** WW

A Victorian black pearl and diamond pendant, the half-pearl in a surround of circular diamonds suspending a pear-shaped diamond, set in silver and gold.

*1.25in (3cm) high*

**$3,000-4,000** WW

An unusual Victorian gem-set gold horseshoe pendant, with a carved amethyst and assorted stone beads, set with a small diamond to the pendant hoop.

*2.5in (6.5cm) high*

**$600-900** WW

A late 19thC gilt-metal ship pendant, in the Renaissance style, mounted with pearl and decorated with emeralds, rubies and smaller pearls.

*1.75in (4.5cm) wide*

**$600-900** WW

An American necklace pendant, with moonstones and moonstone drops.

*c1900* *drop 1.5in (4cm) high*

**$1,200-1,800** NBLM

An Edwardian diamond trefoil pendant necklace, designed as leaf scrolls with old-cut diamonds, set in silver and gold, with a small pearl drop, later chain.

**$1,200-1,800** DN

An Edwardian diamond pendant necklace, millegrain set with old-cut and rose diamonds, with three graduated diamond drops, on a fine trace-link back chain.

**$3,000-4,000** DN

An Edwardian pendant watch, in blue enamel and platinum set with small rose-cut diamonds, the dial signed "Agassiz".

*Agassiz supplied movements to Tiffany.*

*1.75in (4.5cm) high*

**$15,000-20,000** NBLM

An Edwardian winged cherub pendant, set with rubies, diamonds, and pearls, adapts as a pin.

*1.75in (4.5cm) wide*

**$4,000-6,000** NBLM

A pink satin glass drop necklace.

*c1930* *drop 2.75in (7cm) high*

**$50-70** GKA

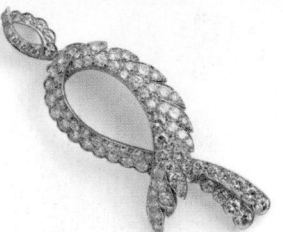

A mid-20thC 6.5ct diamond swirl pendant.

*2.5in (6.5cm) high*

**$8,000-12,000**     **NBLM**

A suite of seed pearl and peridot jewelry, with a necklace, earrings, and a pin, each with gold framing, the pin and earrings with tear-drop shaped stones.

**$800-1,200**     **ROW**

A rope design necklace, by Mellerio Dits Mellers of Paris, with a watch pendant set with diamonds, adaptable as a bracelet.

*c1950*     *1in (2.5cm) wide*

**$15,000-20,000**     **NBLM**

A unique Van Cleef & Arpels triple rope-twist necklace, with an articulated gem set center, diamonds, emeralds, and rubies.

*c1950*     *panel 2.5in (6.5cm) wide*

**$18,000-25,000**     **NBLM**

## BRACELETS

An early 19thC hardstone itaglio yellow metal bracelet, formed from seven hardstone itaglio links, each carved with a classical maiden.

**$400-600**     **ROW**

A Victorian cased demi-parure, in the Etruscan style, comprising a hinged bangle, pin, and drop earrings, each with a pink foiled back cabochon stone and white coral beads to the gold filigree mounts.

*bangle 2.25in (5.5cm) wide*

**$1,200-1,800**     **WW**

### A CLOSER LOOK AT AN EDWARDIAN PEARL & DIAMOND BRACELET

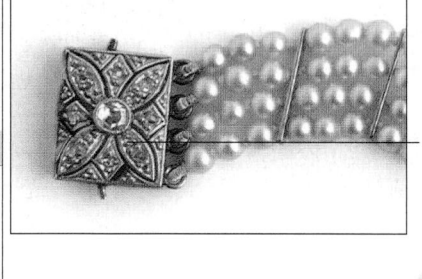

*The quality of this piece is evident in the standard of the materials and the smoothness, delicacy and strength of the connections and settings.*

*Millegrain, popular in the Edwardian period, is a setting in which stones are subtly held in place by small beads or grains of metal. It also refers to a surface that is decorated with tiny beads of metal.*

*Edwardian jewelry tended to be delicate and feminine with dainty and intricate decoration that would compliment the fashions of the period. Diamonds were a favored stone.*

*Higher quality pearls, like these, have less imperfections. Examples with blemishes should be avoided.*

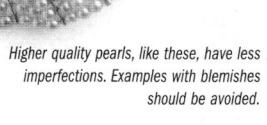

An Edwardian pearl and diamond bracelet, adaptable as a choker, with openwork and millegrain.

*7.75in (20cm) long*

**$15,000-20,000**     **NBLM**

A Victorian garnet and gold hinged bangle, mounted with three garnet cabochons, each centered with a diamond to the star mount.

*2.5in (6.5cm) wide*

**$700-1,000**    **WW**

An Edwardian ruby caliber sapphire and diamond bracelet.

*2.75in (7cm) wide*

**$7,000-10,000**    **NBLM**

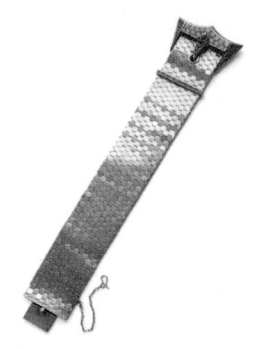

A honeycomb-patterned belt bracelet, in pink gold, with a sapphire and diamond set buckle.

*c1940*

**$8,000-12,000**    **NBLM**

A modern 18ct gold erotic hinged bangle, by Carrera y Carrera, chased with a group of nudes, with a gold ring with associated subject, in original fitted cases.

*bangle 2.5in (6.5cm) wide*

**$2,800-3,200**    **WW**

## RINGS

A Russian Imperial presentation ring, with a black opal and eleven cushion-shaped diamonds, inscription, cyrillic maker's mark "AR", St Petersburg marks for 1856.

*The inscription probably refers to the botanist Henry Bradbury (1831-1860).*

*1in (2.5cm) wide*

**$3,000-5,000**    **WW**

### A CLOSER LOOK AT A GEORGE WASHINGTON MEMORIAL RING

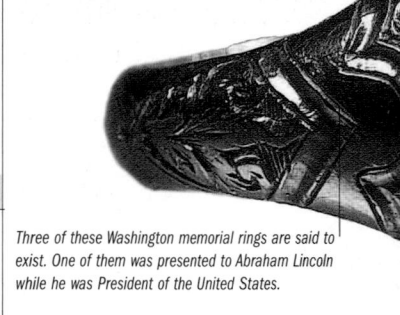

*A stone-cutter named John Struthers donated two marble tombs to reinter the remains of George and Martha Washington after the originals were found to be in bad repair. Mr. Struther was present at the time of the re-entombing and obtained a piece of the original wooden casket which was shaped into the form of a coffin and set into this ring.*

*The inside of the hinged lid is engraved with floral motifs.*

*Three of these Washington memorial rings are said to exist. One of them was presented to Abraham Lincoln while he was President of the United States.*

*This ring was made in Birmingham, England, and has a date mark for 1858-59.*

A 22ct gold and intaglio-carved onyx George Washington memorial ring, with an oval hinged bezel, set with a white onyx stone intaglio-carved with a bust profile of George Washington with a laurel wreath, opens to reveal a fragment of George Washington's coffin, shaped in the form of a coffin and studded with 13 gold disks set under crystal, the ring exterior with engraved scrolled foliate designs, impressed hallmarks including "C.G." a crown, anchor, date mark, and "22."

**$14,000-18,000**    **SK**

An Art Deco carved emerald and diamond platinum ring, the Indian emerald probably 19thC.

*c1930*    *0.5in (1.5cm) wide*

**$22,000-28,000**    **NBLM**

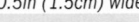

An American gold ring, shaped as a pelican forming a square.

*c1965*    *1.5in (4cm) wide*

**$1,800-2,200**    **NBLM**

A diamond cluster ring, by Boucheron, with a central 2ct brilliant-cut diamond and baguette and brilliant-cut diamonds to the shoulders, 18ct yellow gold, signed and numbered "885795".

*1in (2.5cm) wide*

**$10,000-18,000**    **WW**

A 9ct Tanzanite set cluster ring, with a 5ct diamond pave border.

*Only discovered in 1967 in Tanzania, Tanzanite was championed by Tiffany's as the gemstone of the 20thC.*

*c1980*    *1in (2.5cm) wide*

**$18,000-22,000**    **NBLM**

**COSTUME JEWELRY**

## THE COSTUME JEWELRY MARKET

The costume jewelry market has altered significantly over the last few years as fashions changed. Bright bold colors are now very much in demand as buyers favor turquoise and coral over classic designs in pale colors with pearls and crystals. Miriam Haskell has remained extremely popular, although high prices have led to an increase in popularity of Stanley Hagler, which is often more keenly priced. European and Japanese buyers in particular, are increasingly interested in his work. The exuberant work of Kramer, Regency, and Lea Stein is also in demand.

The trend for color has affected the market for some Trifari – buyers look for colorful pieces, such as fruit salad pins, and are more likely to reject the company's classic pearl jewelry.

As in previous years, jewelry by top name designers, such as Dior, Schiaparelli, and Chanel, continues to be highly sought after. The trend for all things 1980s has lead to an increase in interest in pieces epitomizing the era, such as Larry Vrba.

Long drop earrings are selling extremely well, particularly Hagler's 'Jewels of India range'. Buyers favor longer examples, especially in the summer season. Brooches, wide diamanté bracelets and striking tasseled necklaces are also very much in demand.

*– Yai Thammachote, Cristobal*

## CORO

A Coro Duette, in the form of horses' heads, in vermeil sterling silver with ruby and aquamarine crystal navettes.

*c1940*  2.25in (6cm) high

**$280-320**  CRIS

A Coro Duette, in the form of owls, in vermeil sterling silver with topaz and clear crystal rhinestones.

*c1940*  1.5in (4cm) high

**$220-280**  JJ

A bow pin, possibly by Coro, of rhodium-plated casting with round, baguette and pavé-set clear crystal rhinestones, unsigned.

*c1935*  3.25in (8cm) high

**$120-180**  CRIS

A Corocraft 'bunch of grapes' pin, with prong-set faux moonstone, chalcedony glass stones and sterling silver leaves.

*c1940*  3in (7.5cm) high

**$300-400**  CRIS

### A CLOSER LOOK AT A CORO DUETTE

*The double clip design was patented by the French jeweler, Louis Cartier in 1927. Coro developed its own version, the Duette, in 1931.*

*Clips became very popular during the 1920s. They were worn on lapels, furs, or necklines.*

*Sometimes sold with matching earrings, Coro Duettes are now avidly collected.*

*The two identical clips are mounted on a detachable back which allows the pair to be worn as a single pin.*

A Coro Duette, in the form of a bouquet of flowers, in enameled silver with red glass beads and clear crystal rhinestones.

*c1935*  2.75in (7cm) high

**$300-400**  ROX

A gold Coro necklace with bow detail.

**$50-80**  MILLB

A late 1940s Coro chatelaine pin, with a pair of ballerinas in gold-tone metal, linked by a a twin-strand gilt metal chain.

*chains 6in (15.5cm) long*

**$120-180**  JJ

A pair of Coro Native American chief earrings, in pewter-tone white metal castings.

*c1960*  1in (2.5cm) high

**$50-70**  MILLB

A Cristobal butterfly pin, from the 'Butterfly' collection, ruthenium-plated, with navette-cut, round and square-cut clear rhinestones.

*c1995*        *3.75in (9.5cm) wide*

**$120-180**                    **CRIS**

A Cristobal butterfly pin, from the 'Butterfly' collection, ruthenium-plated with round and navette-cut sapphire and lime green and aurora borealis rhinestones.

*c1995*           *3in (7.5cm) wide*

**$80-120**                     **CRIS**

A Cristobal apple pin, from the 'Secret Garden' collection, with prong-set ruby, fuchsia, aquamarine, amethyst, and emerald rhinestones of various cuts, mostly dating to the 1950s.

*c1995*      *3in (9cm) high*

**$120-180**            **CRIS**

A Cristobal sunflower pin from the 'Secret Garden' collection, ruthenium-plated, with Swarovski jet, emerald, peridot, and rainbow rhinestones.

*c1995*         *4.75in (12cm) high*

**$120-180**                    **CRIS**

A Cristobal necklace, with 1950s amber and topaz rhinestones, in a ruthenium-plated casting.

*c1995*           *15.25in (39cm) long*

**$180-220**                    **CRIS**

A Cristobal necklace with bow pendants and earrings, ruthenium-plated with prong-set amethyst and jet crystal rhinestones.

*c1995*      *17.25in (44cm) long*

**$180-220**            **CRIS**

A Dior pendant necklace with earrings, of gilt metal with rectangular-cut jonquil pastes, black enamel cabochons, faux pearls and clear rhinestones.

*c1965*                                    *14.5in (37cm) long*

**$1,800-2,200**                                         **FM**

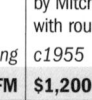

A Dior necklace with bracelet and earrings, of interlinked hoops of gilt metal with topaz rhinestones.

*c1955*           *14.5in (37cm) long*

**$800-1,200**                    **FM**

A pendant tassel necklace and earrings, by Mitchell Maer for Dior, of faux gold with round-cut haemetite stones.

*c1955*      *pendant 4in (10cm) long*

**$1,200-1,800**            **WAIN**

A Dior necklace with earrings, of rhodium-plated metal with prong-set faux moonstones, pale ruby pastes and clear rhinestones.

*c1960*           *14in (35.5cm) long*

**$1,200-1,800**                    **FM**

A Dior stylized floral necklace, with textured gilt squares, triangles and black and fluorescent blue pastes.

*c1965*      *16.75in (43cm) long*

**$1,200-1,800**            **FM**

## A CLOSER LOOK AT A MAISON GRIPOIX ORNAMENT

*Maison Gripoix was founded in Paris in the 1870s. Originally focusing on glass buttons and beads, it soon branched out in jewelry. By the mid-1920s, the firm made pieces for Chanel.*

*Jeweled ornaments were made to be displayed in retailers' windows. Flower versions were made by Maison Gripoix from the 1950s.*

*The leaves have been made from poured glass or pate-de-verre, a technique favored by the company. The effect is achieved by grinding, molding, and gently melting colored glass.*

*Most ornaments, like this example, were 5-8in (12-20cm) high. Large trees measuring 3ft (90cm) were also produced and are extremely scarce today.*

A Maison Gripoix basket of flowers ornament, in antiqued gold-tone metal with emerald poured glass and faux baroque pearl drops.

*c1955*

*6.25in (16cm) high*

**$800-1,200**

**CRIS**

A Maison Gripoix flower pin, with poured glass leaves and turquoise, emerald, and black glass cabochons in an antiqued gilt-metal frame.

*c1945*     *3.25in (8cm) high*

**$800-1,200**     **SUM**

A Maison Gripoix berries and leaves necklace, with green poured glass leaves and cherry poured glass beads.

*c1985*     *17.5in (45cm) long*

**$700-1,000**     **RITZ**

A late 1930s Maison Gripoix glass bracelet, the clasp marked "MADE IN FRANCE".

*3.25in (8cm) wide*

**$180-220**     **ROX**

## MIRIAM HASKELL (1899-1981)

- Miriam Haskell made glamorous and fashionable costume jewelry from the mid-1920s.
- She helped to establish costume jewelry as a valued art form in its own right. Her pieces were worn by high profile individuals, such as Joan Crawford.
- Although not a designer herself, she possessed a talent for spotting good designs and skilled designers.
- Frank Hess was appointed Chief Designer of the company from 1926. He introduced innovative designs well into the 1960s.
- Talented designers included Robert Clark and Peter Raines in the 1960s, Larry Vbra in the 1970s, and Millie Petronzio in the 1980s.
- Haskell's pieces broke with traditional jewelry design.
- Materials included Japanese faux pearls, Murano glass beads, and Austrian facetted crystals.
- Pieces were finished to high standards, often by hand. The appeal today rests with the high quality and the innovation of designs.
- The company is still in production today.

A Miriam Haskell pin, with large French jet cabochons set in antiqued gilt metal with rings and clusters of clear rose montées.

*c1945*   3.25in (8.5cm) high

**$700-1,000**   SUM

A Miriam Haskell two-tier pendant pin, of antiqued gilt metal with clusters of clear rose montées and three faux baroque pearl drops.

*c1950*   3.75in (9.5cm) high

**$700-1,000**   SUM

---

A Miriam Haskell floral motif pin, of antiqued gilt metal with lavender, amethyst and moonstone glass cabochons and clear rose montées.

*c1950*   4in (10cm) high

**$700-1,000**   SUM

A Miriam Haskell floral motif pin and bracelet, with clear and aurora borealis rose montées and antiqued gilt metal leaves.

*c1950*   bracelet 7.5in (19cm) long

**$1,200-1,800**   SUM

A Miriam Haskell festoon necklace, of filigree gilt metal, clusters of faux seed pearls and round-cut clear rhinestones.

3.5in (9cm) long

**$2,200-2,800**   SUM

A Miriam Haskell necklace, with five strands of faux pearls of various size, terminating in gilt metal plates with small, faux pearl floral motifs.

*c1950*   10.5in (26.5cm) long

**$700-1,000**   SUM

---

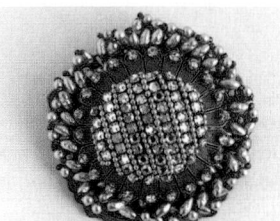

A Miriam Haskell floral pin, of antiqued gilt metal with rings and rows of faux seed and baroque pearls and clear rose montées.

*c1950*   2.25in (6cm) diam

**$600-800**   SUM

A Miriam Haskell pin, with bands of antiqued gilt metal and faux baroque pearls, topped with antiqued gilt-metal leaves covered with clear rose montées.

*c1960*   3in (7.5cm) high

**$700-1,000**   SUM

---

A Miriam Haskell parure, with a pendant necklace, two pins and earrings, all with black resin beads and cabochons and square-cut clear rhinestones.

*c1960*   necklace 14.75in (38cm) long

**$4,000-6,000**   SUM

A pair of Miriam Haskell large floral motif earrings, with seed pod and foliate pendants, of filigree and textured silvered metal.

*c1975*   4.25in (10.5cm) high

**$120-180**   ABIJ

A pair of Miriam Haskell earrings, of antiqued gilt metal with clusters of small faux baroque pearl beads and prong-set clear rhinestones.

*c1950*   2in (5cm) high

**$400-600**   SUM

An Alcozer 'vase of flowers' pin, with semi-precious stones, cultured pearls and clear and ruby rhinestones, on a rosegold-plated casting.

*c1995*      *4.5in (11cm) high*

**$280-320**     **CRIS**

A Fred A. Block cat pin, of vermeil sterling silver, with turquoise glass beads to the whiskers and tail and clear crystal rhinestone eyes.

*c1945*      *4cm (10cm) high*

**$300-400**     **BY**

A Chanel flower and bow pin, with poured glass stones, glass beads, clear crystal rhinestones and faux pearls, in gilt-metal settings.

*c1935*      *2.5in (6.5cm) high*

**$500-700**     **BY**

A Chanel pendant pin, with green and blue glass stones and faux pearls, in gold-plated settings.

*c1955*      *3.25in (8cm) high*

**$400-600**     **RITZ**

A pair of Chanel pendant earrings, of antiqued, stamped gilt metal with faux pearls, green glass cabochons and glass drops.

*c1975*      *3.75in (9.5cm) high*

**$400-600**     **SUM**

A De Rosa bowl of flowers pin, in vermeil sterling silver with red enameled roses.

*c1945*      *2in (5cm) high*

**$300-400**     **ROX**

A Deposé necklace, with strands of faux pearls, faux pearl drops, clear crystal rhinestones and a silver clasp.

*c1920*      *15in (39cm) long*

**$300-400**     **CRIS**

A German black and silver pin, possibly by Fahrner.

     *2in (5.5cm) wide*

**$1,800-2,200**     **TR**

An Art Deco Fahrner pin, in silver and marcasite with amazonite bars, blue glass cabochons and a pink quartz stone.

*c1925*      *1.75in (4.5cm) wide*

**$1,200-1,800**     **TR**

A Fahrner stylized leaf pin, in silver and marcasite with a single pearl highlight.

*c1925*      *1.75in (4.5cm) wide*

**$500-700**     **RBRG**

A 1930s Fischel and Nessler necklace, in sterling silver and carved glass.

     *2.5in (6.5cm) wide*

**$280-320**     **RG**

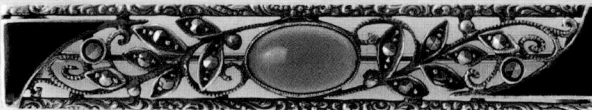

A Fahrner floral motif bar pin, in silver with matte black enamel and an aventurine quartz cabochon.

*c1925*      *2.75in (7cm) wide*

**$700-1,000**     **RBRG**

A Har pendant bracelet, the oriental Lucite head with jade glass cabochons and small aurora borealis crystal rhinestones, on a silver-plated chain.

*c1955*      *pendant 1.5in (3cm) high*

**$120-180**     **CRIS**

A pair of Har cobra heads earrings, with aurora borealis lava stones, green enamel and topaz crystal rhinestones, on gold-plated castings.

*c1955*          *1.5in (3.5cm) high*

**$220-280**          **CRIS**

A Har serpent bangle, gold-plated with green enamel and green and aurora borealis glass stones.

*c1955*          *2.5in (7cm) wide*

**$500-800**          **CRIS**

A 1950s Hattie Carnegie plastic and diamanté 'Aztec Man' pin, the plastic imitating jade and coral.

*2.25in (6cm) high*

**$300-400**          **ROX**

A Hattie Carnegie leaf pendant necklace and earrings, of gold-washed metal with faux pearl highlights.

*c1965*          *necklace 17in (43cm) long*

**$220-280**          **JJ**

A 1940s Schreiner pink glass and faux pearl pin and earrings, unsigned.

*pin 3in (7.5cm) wide*

**$300-500**          **ROX**

A Schreiner necklace and earrings, in gilt metal with rhinestone, moonstone, citrine, and aurora borealis.

*c1955*          *necklace 2in (5cm) wide*

**$1,200-1,800**          **SUM**

An Ian St. Gielar tasseled scarf of mauve, cranberry, red, and pale green glass beads.

*c1995*          *44in (112cm) long*

**$500-700**          **CRIS**

A Larry Vrba vase of flowers pin, in glass, mother-of-pearl, jade, and coral.

*c1995*          *4.75in (12cm) high*

**$280-320**          **CRIS**

A Larry Vrba vase of flowers pin, in mother-of-pearl, glass, and rhinestones.

*c1995*          *4.5in (11.5cm) high*

**$280-320**          **CRIS**

## A CLOSER LOOK AT A SCHREINER BUSH PIN

*Schreiner jewelry, like this striking red and green pin, is characterized by unconventional combinations of colors and paste stones.*

*Output was limited as pieces were made by hand. This increases their desirability today.*

*Glamorous and exuberant, Schreiner pieces were worn by stars such as Marilyn Monroe during the 1940s and 1950s.*

*This piece was made shortly after Henry Schreiner's death in 1951, when the firm was taken over by his daughter, Terry Schreiner.*

A Schreiner bush pin, in gilt wire backing with prong-set ruby, emerald and clear crystal rhinestones, square-cut aquamarine pastes and carved, pear-cut emerald glass drops.

*c1955*          *4.25in (11cm) wide*

**$1,800-2,200**          **SUM**

A Marcel Boucher pin, in scrolling sterling silver with clear crystal rhinestone highlights, around a faux ruby paste.

c1935     2.25in (5.75cm) wide

**$220-280**     **ABIJ**

A 1930s Mazer ruby glass and diamanté inset necklace and earrings.

centerpiece 2in (5cm) diam

**$700-1,000**     **ROX**

A 1940s figural Nettie Rosenstein brooch, in faux ivory inset with diamanté inset.

1.75in (4.5cm) high

**$280-320**     **ROX**

A Pennino Bros. bow with pendant tassels necklace and earrings, rhodium-plated with clear crystal rhinestones.

c1940     necklace 14.5in (37cm) long

**$700-1,000**     **CRIS**

A Pennino Bros. bouquet of flowers pin and earrings, of rose-gold vermeil sterling silver with rose-pink and clear crystal rhinestones.

c1945     pin 2.75in (7cm) high

**$700-1,000**     **CRIS**

A Pennino Bros. stylized flower pin, with trailing tendrils, of vermeil sterling silver with aquamarine and clear crystal rhinestones.

c1945     2.75in (7cm) wide

**$300-400**     **CRIS**

A Regency butterfly pin, gold-plated with prong-set round and navette aurora borealis and aquamarine and jade rhinestones.

c1955     1.75in (4.5cm) wide

**$120-180**     **CRIS**

A Canadian floral pin, in the style of the Regency company, with green navettes, aquamarine, emerald, clear, and aurora borealis rhinestones, unsigned.

c1960     3in (7.5cm) wide

**$70-100**     **CRIS**

A Regency flower and leaf motif necklace and earrings, silver-plated with navette and round-cut aurora borealis and clear rhinestones.

c1955     necklace 15.3in (39cm) long

**$220-280**     **CRIS**

A Robert horse pin, in silver gilt-metal, the head set with polychrome crystal beads and rhinestones.

c1955     5in (12.5cm) wide

**$280-320**     **ROX**

A Robert de Mario floral motif pin, of gilt-metal with large, faceted emerald green crystal stones and small clear crystal rhinestone highlights.

c1955     2.25in (95.5cm) wide

**$120-180**     **ROX**

A 1940s Sandor plastic pin, in the form of a bunch of green berries or grapes.

2.5in (6.5cm) high

**$280-320**     **ROX**

A Secrett brooch, in the form of a butterfly, custom made from black opal for the Lieutenant Governor of Ontario.

c1980     2in (5cm) wide

**$4,000-6,000**     **TCF**

A 1950s Selro glass bracelet and earrings.

bracelet 7in (18cm) long

**$180-220**     **ROX**

A Stanley Hagler diamanté brooch and earrings, with faux pearls.

c1955     brooch 2.5in (6.5cm) wide

**$180-220**     **PC**

A Stanley Hagler necklace, with strands of filigree gilt-metal capped faux pearls and rose montées.

c1975     15.75in (40cm) long

**$300-500**     **CRIS**

A gilt-metal snake necklace, the head with an inset facetted faux amethyst and faux sapphire eyes, unsigned.

*c1925*                                    *11.5in (29cm) long*

**$300-400**                                    **BY**

An unsigned necklace, with faceted crystal spheres, silver filigree work in the form of flowers.

*c1925*        *19.25in (49cm) long*

**$220-280**                **BY**

A necklace, with faceted clear crystal stones and three emerald green poured glass stones, unsigned.

*c1935*        *15.25in (39cm) long*

**$180-220**                **BY**

A pendant necklace, attributed to Rousselet, with cranberry colored glass beads and clusters of faux pearls, unsigned.

*c1935*                    *necklace 20in (51cm) long*

**$500-700**                                    **BY**

A Murano glass fruits and leaves necklace and bracelet, with aquamarine cabochons, orange and red fruits and unusual opaque green leaves, unsigned.

*c1955*                    *necklace 16.25in (42cm) long*

**$300-400**                                    **BY**

A necklace, bracelet, and earrings, of gilt metal with faux amethysts, faux coral glass beads and green crystal rhinestones, unsigned.

*c1965*                    *necklace 17in (43cm) long*

**$220-280**                                    **BY**

A Blackinton bangle, of gold-washed sterling silver with graduated bead molding and turquoise glass cabochons.

*c1890*  3in (7.5cm) diam

**$220-280**  CGPC

A Blackinton bangle, of gold-washed sterling silver with scrolling leaf motifs and amethyst glass cabochons.

*c1895*  3in (7.5cm) diam

**$300-400**  CGPC

A Gorham & Co. twin fish pin, of gold-washed sterling silver with green enameling and a central amethyst glass cabochon.

*c1900*  2.25in (5.75cm) wide

**$700-1,000**  CGPC

A rare Gorham & Co. 14ct gold pin, with a miniature, enameled romantic bacchanalian portrait.

*1906*  1in (2.5cm) wide

**$1,200-1,800**  CGPC

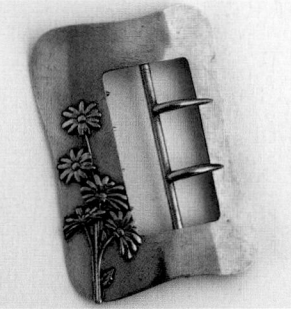

A Howard & Co. belt buckle, of sterling silver with applied sterling silver flowers.

*c1885*  3.25in (8.25cm) high

**$120-180**  CGPC

A Howard & Co. circular buckle, of goldwashed and textured sterling silver, with ruby and amethyst glass stones and a blister pearl center.

*c1900*  1.5in (3.75cm) diam

**$300-400**  CGPC

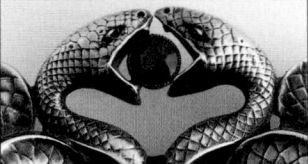

A Kerr & Co. belt buckle, with coiled cobras in silver plated metal and a central ruby red crystal rhinestone.

*c1900*  5in (12.75cm) wide

**$500-700**  CGPC

A rare Kerr & Co. gold-wash over sterling silver necklace, comprising floral swags intertwined with cherubs.

*c1900*  15in (38cm) long

**$700-1,000**  CGPC

A Kerr & Co. two-part cherub belt clasp, in silver-plated metal, the male and female cherubs dancing when fastened.

*c1900*  2.75in (7cm) wide

**$500-800**  CGPC

A Kerr & Co. belt buckle, adapted to a pin, of engraved silver bordered with enamel.

*c1905*  3in (7.5cm) wide

**$300-400**  CGPC

An S. & B. Lederer & Co. medal pin, of hand-beaten and textured sterling silver with copper and gold-plated dragon and antiqued gold soldier's face.

*c1900*  1.5in (3.75cm) wide

**$1,200-1,800**  CGPC

A La Pierre belt buckle, the sterling silver frame with scrolling leaves and two romantic celluloid miniatures.

*c1905*  4in (10cm) wide

**$700-1,000**  CGPC

A Pryor Novelty Co. sterling silver belt pin, in the form of a bust with stylized flowing hair and floral motifs.

*1903*  2.5in (6.25cm) wide

**$500-700**  CGPC

A pair of Reddall & Co. Inc. winged suspender or garter clips, in gold-washed sterling silver.

*c1900*     *1in (2.5cm) wide*

**$220-280**                    **CGPC**

A Reddall & Co. Inc. buckle, with scrolling leaf forms in gold-washed sterling silver with a faceted, dark amethyst-colored center stone.

*c1900*     *2.25in (5.75cm) diam*

**$300-400**                    **CGPC**

## A CLOSER LOOK AT A SHIEBLER SILVER BELT PIN

The frog and snake decoration on this belt pin exemplify Shiebler's use of naturalistic motifs, which he realized with great attention to detail. He also favored Classical motifs, like this bust.

Known for their creativity and fine workmanship, pieces by silversmith George W. Shiebler of Brooklyn, New York, are hotly collected today.

A Shiebler twin leaf pin, of engraved sterling silver with applied insects, one in sterling silver, the other in matt-finish copper alloy.

*c1900*     *2.75in (7cm) high*

**$500-800**                    **CGPC**

A Shiebler cross pin, of asymmetrical shape, with sterling silver casting and a large, faceted, sapphire blue crystal cabochon.

*c1900*     *2.25in (5.75cm) wide*

**$700-1,000**                  **CGPC**

Pieces are marked with an "S" within a circle and flanked by wings.

The influence of the Aesthetic Movement can be seen in Shiebler's pieces, while the overall shape and scrolling forms are Art Nouveau in style.

A Shiebler sterling silver belt pin, with a frog, snakes and wings encircling a gilded neo-classical-style bust of a female.

*c1900*     *5in (12.75cm) wide*

**$1,800-2,200**                **CGPC**

A Shiebler open cuff bangle, of sterling silver with applied, highly naturalistic floral and foliate imagery.

*c1900*     *2.5in (6.25cm) diam*

**$1,800-2,200**                **CGPC**

A Thomas F. Brogan buckle, with looped wire border, gold-washed sterling silver scrolls and a dark amethyst-colored center stone.

*c1900*     *2.25in (5.75cm) high*

**$180-220**                    **CGPC**

An Unger Bros. gold-wash over sterling silver bracelet, with filigree scrolling leaf and flower cartouches.

*c1900*     *7.5in (19cm) long*

**$400-600**                    **CGPC**

A very rare Unger Bros. bonneted lady head belt pin, in sterling silver, with naturalistic detail.

*c1905*

**$800-1,200**                  **CGPC**

An Unger Bros. belt pin, with a duck or goose head bursting out of an egg, in textured sterling silver with a ruby red glass cabochon eye.

*c1905*     *1.75in (4.5cm) wide*

**$500-800**                    **CGC**

A rare pair of Unger Bros. eagle head cufflinks, in gold-wash over sterling silver castings, with ruby red glass cabochon eyes.

*c1905*     *0.75in (2cm) high*

**$700-1,000**                  **CGC**

A rare pair of Unger Bros. owl head cufflinks, of sterling silver with amber and dark brown glass cabochon eyes.

*c1905*     *0.5in (1.5cm) diam*

**$500-800**                    **CGPC**

An English enamel snuff box, the cover painted with a piper, the sides with flowers.

*c1750*                    *2.75 (7cm) wide*

**$280-320**                    **ROS**

A late 18thC enamel box, with a hinged mirrored lid, painted with two birds in a garden and inscribed, "Keep this for my sake", within a jeweled border.

*1.75in (4.5cm) high*

**$500-700**                    **WW**

An 18thC enamel box, in the form of a goldfinch, the hinged lid painted with a dog chasing birds.

*3.5in (8.5cm) wide*

**$1,200-1,800**                    **WW**

A late 18thC enamel box, with a hinged mirrored lid, printed in puce with a view of a harbor, inscribed "Sold at Thompson & Co. on the Corn Hill, Bridgewater".

*2in (5cm) high*

**$500-700**                    **WW**

An 18thC erotic enamel box, the hinged lid painted with two figures and concealing two erotic panels, the sides with figures and landscape vignettes.

*3.5in (9cm) wide*

**$1,200-1,800**                    **WW**

A South Staffordshire enamel box, the cover depicting a house in a landscape within pink borders, the base and sides with flowers and diaper panels.

*c1800*                    *2in (5cm) wide*

**$180-220**                    **DN**

A 19thC enameled copper patch box, with a pink ground and a scene of a cottage and tree.

**$280-320**                    **WW**

A 19thC enameled copper patch box, with a trophy of arms and the inscription "May British Valour Conquests Gain and Make our Foes our Friends Again".

**$300-500**                    **WW**

A 19thC enameled copper patch box, with a pink ground and the inscription "Who Opens this Will have a Kiss".

**$180-220**                    **WW**

A 19thC enameled copper patch box, with a floral design and inscribed "Present from Dover".

**$300-500**                    **WW**

A 19thC to 20thC enamel pill box, the lid decorated with an English sailing ship in battle.

*1.5in (4cm) wide*

**$280-320**                    **FRE**

A South Staffordshire enameled patch box, with "Constant to thee I'll ever be" and two ladies in a landscape, the base in pink, restored.

**$180-220**                    **DN**

A 19thC Limoges enamel on brass beaker, made for the Persian market, of flared form with enamel decoration of vignettes depicting mother and child, within floral borders.

*3.25in (8.5cm) diam*

**$300-500**     **ROS**

A Limoges silver and enamel jewelry box, decorated with three young women in Rococo dress, signed "A. Juan", marked for Paris and Limoges.

*c1900*     *6in (15.5cm) wide*

**$500-700**     **VZ**

An early 20thC French enameled mirror pendant, with a portrait, set in a paste frame.

*1.5in (4cm) diam*

**$280-320**     **WW**

A Viennese enameled ladies' cigarette case, with mauve, black, and white stripes, heightened with gilding, English import marks for London.

*1923*     *3.5in (9cm) wide*

**$700-1,000**     **WW**

## CLOISONNÉ

A silver cloisonné-enameled milk jug, sugar pot, and tong, made in Moscow, silver mark "GK", maker's mark "A.A", dated.

*1896*     *3.25in (8.5cm) high*

**$2,800-3,200**     **HMN**

A Russian silver and gilded cloisonné-enameled spoon, 84 zolotnik mark.

*1850*     *5.5in (14cm) long*

**$180-220**     **KAU**

A Russian cloisonné-enameled caddy scoop, decorated in shaded polychrome within a white pelleted border and a toffee-colored ground, with state marks for 1896 to 1908.

*4in (10cm) long*

**$1,200-1,800**     **WW**

Six silver and gilded cloisonné-enameled spoons, silver mark.

*1850*     *5.5in (14cm) long*

**$300-500**     **KAU**

A Russian cloisonné-enameled and amethyst silver-gilt beaker, of trumpet form, decorated with polychrome fruiting and flowering vines bordering floral panels, below four cabochon amethysts, on a cream ground.

*c1885*     *5.25in (13.5cm) high*

**$800-1,200**     **ROS**

An early 20th Russian cloisonné-enameled kovsch, decorated in blues, mauve, white, and red, with state marks for 1908-1917.

*4.25in (10.5cm) wide*

**$700-1,000**     **WW**

## STOBWASSER

- Johann Heinrich Stobwasser was born in 1740 in Lobenstein, Germany.
- After an apprenticeship at a lacquer factory, he began to experiment with new techniques with the help of his pharmacist brother.
- He soon became famous for his delicate miniature paintings on lacquered papier-mâché snuff boxes. These were produced at his father's Brunswick factory.
- His boxes became the height of fashion among the German bourgeoisie in the late 18thC.

- His erotic snuff boxes were also very popular and were sold all over the world.
- The company soon branched out into other areas, producing furniture and royal carriages.
- In 1772, Johann Heinrich founded a subsidiary in Berlin with J. Guérin, a French carpenter who had married into the Stobwasser family.
- In 1818, Johann Heinrich's son moved the entire Stobwasser business to Berlin. It was taken over in 1829 and closed after WWI.
- The snuff boxes are often signed.

An early 19thC Stobwasser snuff box, painted with 'Mile Lundens la...de Rubens', numbered "906", with a note giving the history of Stobwasser, taken from "The Connaisseur", by PAS Phillips.

**$4,000-6,000**    **CHEF**

An early 19thC Stobwasser snuff box, painted with 'Le Credo D'apres Raphael', a lady holds up a chalice and witnesses transubstantiation, numbered "13904", signed in red inside.

*4in (10cm) diam*

**$2,800-3,200**    **CHEF**

An early 19thC papier-mâché snuff box, attributed to Stobwasser, the lid painted with a Dr Syntax-like figure about to carve into 'The Tythe Pig' on a table backed by decanters on shelves, the interior with later gilding possibly obscuring inscription.

*4.25in (10.5cm) diam*

**$500-800**    **CHEF**

A Stobwasser snuff box, with 'Stowe Buckinghamshire in England', "5430".

*The firm probably made this snuff box after an 1806 visit by the Prince of Wales to Sir John Soane's new library at Stowe.*

*3.75in (9.5cm) diam*

**$4,000-6,000**    **CHEF**

A John Obrisset pressed tortoiseshell and silver snuff box.

*c1690*      *3.75in (9.5cm) wide*

**$800-1,200**      **MB**

A Neopolionic horn snuff box, modeled as a cocked hat, with an ivory rosette to one side and molded on the other with Napoleon and plans by a camp fire, titled "La Veillee D'Austerlitz".

*3in (8cm) wide*

**$500-800**      **CHEF**

An 18thC French Vernis Martin snuff box, the circular lift-off lid inset with a brass framed watercolor miniature of a lady, the interior and exterior lacquered to simulate tortoiseshell.

*3in (8cm) diam*

**$280-320**      **CHEF**

A late 18thC French mother-of-pearl mounted snuff box, of paneled form with reeded cagework borders, inlaid with mother-of-pearl flowers and a butterfly, maker's mark "AD" probably for Antoine Daroux of Paris.

*3in (7.5cm) wide*

**$3,000-5,000**      **WW**

A Queen Anne tortoiseshell snuff box, with ridged decoration.

*c1705*      *3.75in (9.5cm) wide*

**$700-1,000**      **MB**

A Napoleonic snuff box, the lid inset with glazed-over yellow metal, embossed by Morel with Napoleon urging his troops on up a pass, titled "Napoleon au Mont St Bernard".

*3.25in (8.5cm) diam*

**$400-600**      **CHEF**

An early 19thC japanned tole snuff or tobacco box, possibly Pontypool, the lid with a magnifying glass, inscribed "Bright Sol Through This Your Pipe will Light and Help Old Age to Read and Write".

**$500-700**      **CHEF**

An early 19thC penwork snuff box, the cover depicting a steeplechase, titled "A Slap at a Stone Enclosure".

*3.25in (8.5cm) wide*

**$400-600**      **DN**

An oval tortoiseshell snuff box, with gold standaway hinges and gold pique-work decoration, the cover depicting cranes, peacocks and exotic foliage, the base with a small bird, unmarked.

*c1715*      *3in (7.5cm) long*

**$2,800-3,200**      **WW**

An 18thC painted mahogany table snuff box.

*3.5in (9cm) wide*

**$300-500**      **MB**

An early 19thC snuff box, the hinged lid slightly arched and printed with an overall stipple of yellow crosses on a green ground.

*2.5in (6cm) wide*

**$280-320**      **CHEF**

An oval horn snuff box, possibly American.

*c1830*      *3.5in (9cm) wide*

**$500-700**      **MB**

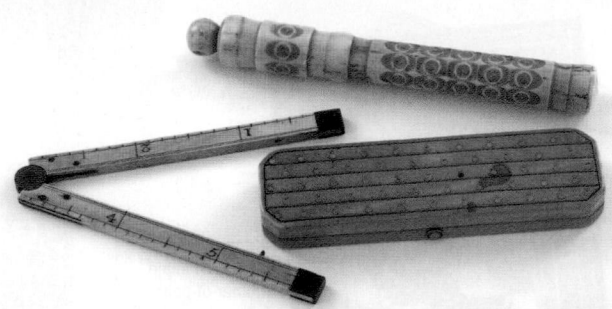

A late 18th to early 19thC ivory pique canted box, with an ivory folding ruler and a carved bone cylindrical bodkin case.

*box 3.25in (8cm) long*

**$280-320** | DN

An early 18thC French mounted ivory patch box, with a pique-work cover and base and a stand-away hinge, the cover opening to reveal a symbolic miniature portrait of a lady with a bow and arrow, above a further portrait of a young lady at her toilette and a portrait of a young gentleman in a powdered wig, struck with charge and discharge marks.

*c1710*

**$1,800-2,200** | WW

A 19thC Dieppe ivory triptych figure of the Empress Josephine, with glass jewels, her dress revealing a scene of her coronation by Napoleon, with another figure, probably Joan of Arc.

*9.5in (24cm) high*

**$2,200-2,800** | L&T

A 19thC sailor-made ivory and bone yarn swift, the ring-turned ivory axis topped with a yarn cup and with an engraved eagle and turned thumbscrew, highlighted with red and black wax, expanding carved whale bone cage joined by metal rivets and red and blue silk ribbons, dovetail constructed mahogany case with hinged lid.

*25.5in (65cm) high*

**$18,000-25,000** | SK

An ivory silver-mounted ladies' aide memoire, with six sheets.

*c1870* | *3in (7.5cm) wide*

**$80-120** | CSA

An ivory circular box and cover, carved in relief with roses and briars and stylized bands of foliage.

*3.5in (9cm) diam*

**$180-220** | GORL

A Victorian carved bone sewing Jenny, formed as a classical urn with a pin cushion and a table screw mechanism to base.

*8in (20.5cm) long*

**$180-220** | GORL

An 18thC English School portrait of a gentleman, wearing a rust-colored jacket, watercolor on ivory, mounted in a gold brooch setting.

**Provenance:** *By descent from Frank Arthur Cecil Richardson (1874-1940) and Winifred Eva Richardson (1878-1945).*

1.5in (4cm) high

$500-700    DN

An American oil on ivory miniature sepia landscape, in a locket, of Germantown near the Schuylkill river, mother and children in the foreground, the reverse with a later Victorian photograph of a lady.

c1800    2in (5cm) high

$8,000-12,000    POOK

An American miniature portrait on ivory of a baby, in a long dress, in a gold leaf mount with a pin and necklace loop.

c1840    2.25in (5.5cm) high

$1,800-2,200    PST

A 19thC oils on ivorine portrait miniature, painted with a young lady in a white dress, with molded gilt frame.

c1840    8.75in (22cm) high

$1,800-2,200    L&T

A 19thC American School miniature portrait of Margaretta Rentz Benfer, watercolor on ivory, indistinct initials.

2.75in (7cm) wide

$700-1,000    FRE

A 19thC Anglo-American School miniature portrait of Mrs. Holbrook, watercolor on paper, framed, unsigned.

5in (12.5cm) high

$180-220    FRE

A late 18thC English School portrait of a gentleman, wearing a wig and a brown coat, watercolor on ivory, in a rose gold clasp mount with later brooch pin and loop.

1.5in (4cm) high

$300-500    DN

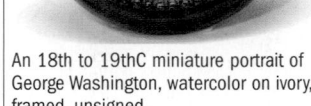

An 18th to 19thC miniature portrait of George Washington, watercolor on ivory, framed, unsigned.

2.75in (7cm) diam

$3,000-5,000    FRE

## A CLOSER LOOK AT A MINIATURE PORTRAIT

Miniature portraits became fashionable in the second half of the 18thC. They were a popular way of recording the faces of family members and were worn as jewelry, given as gifts or displayed around the home.

Mary Jane Simes was a member of the Peale family of successful American artists. She was taught to paint by her nieces, the artists Anna and Sarah Peale. Her mother was a daughter of James Peale.

The work of Mary Jane Simes is thought to be the rarest of the Peale family, and this is a very good example.

Ivory was used in many miniature portraits as they were produced as treasured and decorative objects, in the same way as precious jewelry.

A miniature portrait by Mary Jane Simes, watercolor on ivory, gold locket setting, the back with an oval of woven hair, signed and dated "Mary Jane Simes 1834", Baltimore, Maryland, in a fitted red leather case.

1.5in (4cm) high

$12,000-18,000    FRE

A 19thC English School portrait of a lady, half length, probably Lady de Grey, watercolor on ivory, in an ebonized and gilt metal mounted frame.

*2.5in (6.5cm) high*

**$500-700** **DN**

A 19thC portrait miniature, of a gentleman wearing a black coat.

*5in (12.5cm) high*

**$120-180** **ROW**

A portrait of the Duchess of Kent and Princess Victoria, by G. Cruickshank after Sir William Beachey, watercolor on ivory, in an ebonized frame.

*4.5in (11.5cm) high*

**$500-800** **DN**

A portrait of a young lady, wearing a low-cut dress and a turquoise hair-ribbon, after Cosway, bust length, watercolor on ivory, inscribed verso "Lady Selina, Sir J. Laurence".

*3in (7.5cm) high*

**$180-220** **DN**

A miniature portrait on ivory, depicting a woman wearing a dress with a high lace collar, in an ivory frame.

*3.5in (9cm) high*

**$180-220** **AAC**

A watercolor on ivory miniature portrait of a gentleman, enclosed with a lock of his hair and enameled initials "F.C." within a seed pearl border, all within a fitted leather case.

*2in (5cm) high*

**$2,800-3,200** **POOK**

A late 19thC silhouette of Mrs. Overton, (nee Betty Stoddart), painted on the reverse of the oval glass, within a wood frame with embossed brass coverlet.

*5in (13cm) high*

**$280-320** **CHEF**

A pair of silhouettes, by Auguste Edouart, signed and "1842 Hartford".

*5.5in (14cm) high*

**$3,000-5,000** **POOK**

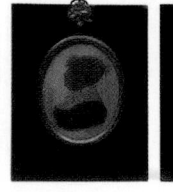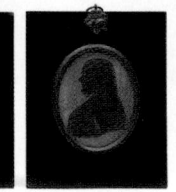

A pair of Regency miniature painted silhouettes, of "Mr. and Mrs. Whitty", each mounted in an ebonized frame and inscribed on the reverse.

*5.25in (13.5cm) high*

**$300-500** **ROW**

A 19thC wax commemorative portrait medallion, of Mrs Steward, Greco-Roman dress, by F. Tathe, encased in a mahogany box frame against a velvet background.

*7in (17.5cm) high*

**$280-320** **AGO**

A 19thC wax commemorative portrait medallion, encased in a mahogany diamond frame against a velvet background, inscription reads "Courijuer".

*6.25in (16cm) high*

**$280-320** **AGO**

A 19thC wax commemorative portrait medallion, encased in a mahogany hexagonal frame against a velvet background, inscribed "F/Uni Aequus Virtute 1799", possibly James Tassie.

*6.5in (16.5cm) high*

**$300-500** **AGO**

A pair of 19thC waxwork figures of maids in a garden, under white muslin linen blossom, in glass domes.

*8.5in (21.5cm) high*

**$180-220**                    **AG**

A 19thC octagonal sailor's 'valentine', the mahogany box with reeded framed hinged lid enclosing concentric geometric arrangement of shells.

*10.75in (27cm) wide*

**$3,000-5,000**                **L&T**

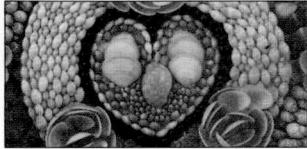

A shell sailor's 'valentine', contained in a hinged wooden octagonal case.

*8.5in (21.5cm) wide*

**$1,200-1,800**                **WW**

A late 19thC tortoiseshell parasol handle, in the form of a bust of a winking bald headed man.

**$800-1,200**                  **DN**

A pair of Belle Epoque diamond set platinum lorgnettes, the handle set overall with graduated circular cut diamonds, the spring loaded eyepieces release with a button to the upper section.

*3.75in (9.5cm) high*

**$2,800-3,200**                **WW**

A Pietra Dura framed plaque, depicting two chickens in mottled white and orange stone, frame with wear and two missing beads.

*7in (12.5cm) wide*

**$1,200-1,800**                **JDJ**

An American gutta percha photograph case, the front molded in relief with the Washington Memorial, with angels above and eagles below, the reverse of similar design but with plain oval panel, enclosing a tinted ambrotype photograph of a lady.

*Gutta percha is an oil-based material from the resin of a Malaysian tree called Isonandra Gutta. Its potential was discovered in 1842 by Dr William Montgomerie, a British doctor in India.*

*It was initially used to make splints and various medical implements. In the mid-19thC it was used to make a variety of items, from 'gutties' or golf balls, to dolls.*

*It became universally known for making golf balls from 1848-1900. It was so successful that the 'featherie' ball disappeared almost immediately after its introduction. From c1860-1900 it became a fashionable material for making photo frames.*

*6.5in (16cm) long*

**$400-600**                    **CHEF**

A Victorian double-ended cranberry glass scent bottle, with a faceted tubular body, embossed caps, unmarked.

*c1870*     4in (10cm) long

**$120-180**     **WW**

A Victorian English cranberry glass perfume bottle, with white enameling.

*c1890*     4in (10cm) high

**$400-600**     **TRIO**

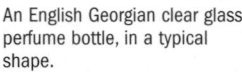

An English Georgian clear glass perfume bottle, in a typical shape.

*c1830*     5.5in (14cm) high

**$220-280**     **TRIO**

An English Georgian clear glass perfume bottle, probably for a man, in a typical shape with a simple stopper and silver top.

*c1830*     3in (7.5cm) high

**$280-320**     **TRIO**

A Georgian gold and cornelian flat scent bottle, with original chain.

1.25in (3cm) wide

**$300-500**     **SSP**

A 19thC clear glass perfume bottle, with blue overlay, silver top, probably English.

5.5in (14cm) high

**$400-600**     **TRIO**

A Victorian scent bottle, in black enamel on gilt silver, with cupid and floral detail, hinged cover, glass liner and stopper, interior flaw.

2.5in (6.5cm) high

**$1,800-2,200**     **RDL**

A mid- to late 19thC English latticino blue and white perfume bottle, with a pinchbeck stopper.

2.5in (6.5cm) high

**$280-320**     **TRIO**

An Victorian English green smelling salts bottle.

*Smelling salts were often worn on a chain around the neck.*

*c1870*     4in (10cm) high

**$280-320**     **TRIO**

A 19thC shell perfume bottle, with pinchbeck stopper, chain and ring.

*c1875*     3.5in (9cm) high

**$180-220**     **TRIO**

An English Victorian smelling salts bottle, with a silver top.

*c1870*     5in (13cm) high

**$280-320**     **TRIO**

An English Victorian clear cut-glass perfume bottle, with blue enameling and silver top.

*c1870*     3.75in (9.5cm) high

**$400-600**     **TRIO**

A Lalique 'L'Effleurt' perfume bottle for Coty, in clear and frosted glass with gray patina, molded "LALIQUE", stopper edges slightly ground.

c1910

4.5in (11.5cm) high

**$5,000-7,000**      RDL

A Lalique 'Panier de Roses' perfume bottle, in clear and frosted glass with blue patina, engraved "R. Lalique".

c1910     4in (10cm) high

**$3,000-5,000**    RDL

A Lalique 'Flausa' perfume bottle for Roger et Gallet, in clear and frosted glass with sepia patina, molded "LALIQUE" to stopper.

c1915     4.75in (12cm) high

**$4,000-6,000**    RDL

A Lalique 'L'Elegance' perfume bottle for D'Orsay, in clear and frosted glass with sepia patina, molded "R. LALIQUE".

c1915     3.25in (9cm) high

**$2,800-3,200**    RDL

A Lalique 'Salamandres' perfume bottle, in clear and frosted glass with blue patina, engraved "R. Lalique France".

c1915     3.5in (9.5cm) high

**$1,800-2,200**    RDL

341

A Lalique 'Styx' perfume bottle for Coty, in clear and frosted glass with sepia patina, a variation with a central stopper, molded "LALIQUE".

*c1910*  5in (12.5cm) high

**$1,800-2,200**  RDL

A Lalique 'Ambre' perfume bottle for D'Orsay, in black glass with a whitish patina, molded "LALIQUE".

*c1910*  5.25in (13.5cm) high

**$1,200-1,800**  RDL

A Lalique 'Au Coeur des Calices' perfume bottle for Coty, in blue glass with gray patina, molded and impressed "LALIQUE".

*c1915*  2.25in (6cm) high

**$7,000-10,000**  RDL

A Lalique 'Mystère' perfume bottle for D'Orsay, in black glass, engraved "R. Lalique", label, chip to one corner and stopper.

*c1910*  3.75in (9.5cm) high

**$500-800**  RDL

A Lalique 'Pan' perfume bottle, in clear and frosted glass with sepia patina, molded "R. LALIQUE".

*c1920*  5in (12.5cm) high

**$1,800-2,200**  RDL

A Lalique 'Lepage' perfume bottle, in clear and frosted glass with green patina, molded "R. LALIQUE", engraved "France".

*c1920*  4.5in (11.5cm) high

**$4,000-6,000**  RDL

A Lalique 'Le Parisien' atomizer for Molinard, in clear and frosted glass with sepia patina and gilt metal, with molded "R. LALIQUE MADE in FRANCE".

*c1925*  5in (13cm) high

**$1,200-1,800**  RDL

A Lalique 'Figurines No. 1' atomizer for Marcas et Bardel, in clear and frosted glass with blue patina and gilt metal, molded "R. LALIQUE MADE in FRANCE".

*c1925*  5in (12.5cm) high

**$800-1,200**  RDL

A Lalique 'Le Jade' perfume bottle for Roger et Gallet, in green glass, with silk display box, paper label on box, bottle molded with "RL FRANCE" mark.

3in (7.5cm) high

**$8,000-12,000**  RDL

A Lalique 'Toutes les Fleurs' perfume bottle for Gabilla, in clear and frosted glass with red patina, molded "LALIQUE MADE in FRANCE", stopper frozen and hairline to neck.

*c1925*  3.75in (9.5cm) high

**$800-1,200**  RDL

A Lalique 'Bouquet de Faunes' perfume bottle for Guerlain, in clear and frosted glass with gray patina, molded "MADE in FRANCE".

c1925          4.25in (11cm) high

**$1,200-1,800**          RDL

A Lalique 'La Belle Saison' perfume bottle for Houbigant, in clear and frosted glass with sepia patina, in a large size, molded "R. LALIQUE MADE in FRANCE".

c1925          5.75in (14cm) high

**$1,800-2,200**          RDL

A Lalique 'Pavots d'Argent' perfume bottle for Roger et Gallet, in clear glass, sealed, with card box, numbered, box printed with "RL" mark.

c1925          3.75in (9cm) high

**$1,200-1,800**          RDL

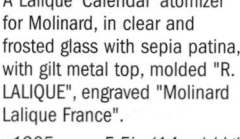

A Lalique 'Calendal' atomizer for Molinard, in clear and frosted glass with sepia patina, with gilt metal top, molded "R. LALIQUE", engraved "Molinard Lalique France".

c1925          5.5in (14cm) high

**$1,200-1,800**          RDL

A Lalique 'Le Parfum des Anges' perfume bottle for Oviatt of Los Angeles, in clear and frosted glass with sepia patina, molded "R. LALIQUE FRANCE".

c1930          3.25in (8cm) high

**$1,800-2,200**          RDL

A Lalique 'Myosotis Flacon No. 3' perfume bottle, in clear and frosted glass with green patina, engraved "R. Lalique France".

c1930          9in (23cm) high

**$5,000-7,000**          RDL

A Lalique 'Sans Adieu' perfume bottle for Worth, in green glass, on chrome and wood stand, molded "R. LALIQUE".

c1930          5.5in (13.5cm) high

**$800-1,200**          RDL

**$1,800-2,200**          RDL

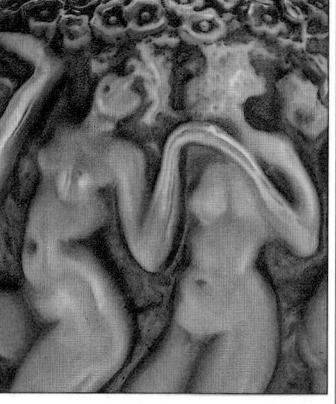

A Lalique 'Habanito' perfume bottle for Molinard, in clear and frosted glass with sepia patina, with original box, with stenciled "R. LALIQUE MADE in FRANCE, MOLINARD PARIS FRANCE" mark.

4.5in (11.5cm) high

RDL

A Lalique 'Je Reviens' perfume bottle for Worth, in blue glass with chromed metal case, with stenciled "R. LALIQUE WORTH MADE in FRANCE" mark.

c1930          5.5in (14cm) high

**$800-1,200**          RDL

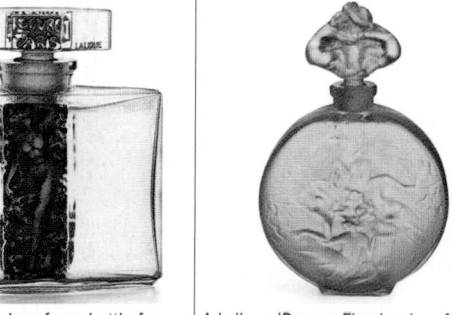

A Lalique 'Danae' perfume bottle for Magasin du Louvre, Paris, in clear and frosted glass with sepia patina, with molded "LALIQUE" mark.

c1930          3.25in (8.5cm) high

**$1,800-2,200**          RDL

A Lalique 'Rosace Figurines' perfume bottle, originally designed 1912, in clear and frosted glass, with stenciled "LALIQUE" mark.

c1940          5in (12.5cm) high

**$2,800-3,200**          RDL

A Lalique 'Fille d'Eve' miniature perfume bottle for Nina Ricci, in frosted glass with screw cap and hang tag, in wicker basket, with molded "LALIQUE" mark.

c1950          2.5in (6cm) high

**$1,200-1,800**          RDL

A Baccarat 'Parfum des Champs-Elysees' perfume bottle for Guerlain, in clear and frosted crystal with gray stain, label and display box, slight stain.

c1900      4.5in (11.5cm) high

**$2,800-3,200**      RDL

A Baccarat 'Le Parfum D'Antan' perfume bottle for D'Orsay, in clear and frosted crystal, with gray stain, with label and box.

c1915      3in (7.5cm) high

**$1,800-2,200**      RDL

A Baccarat 'Moda' perfume bottle for Gabilla, in clear crystal with recessed and enameled detail, stenciled "Baccarat".

c1920      3.75in (8.5cm) high

**$3,000-5,000**      RDL

A Baccarat 'Toquade' perfume bottle for Silka, in clear and frosted crystal with recessed name labels, stenciled "BACCARAT".

c1925      4in (10cm) high

**$1,200-1,800**      RDL

A Baccarat 'Le Secret de Dieux' perfume bottle for Yardley, in clear and frosted crystal, with recessed gilt detail.

c1915      4.5in (11.5cm) high

**$5,000-7,000**      RDL

A Baccarat 'Mitsouko' perfume for Guerlain, with a label and box.

*This perfume was used by many celebrities of the time including De Agalef, the ballerina. Guerlain used a variety of glassmakers to make their bottles.*

c1920      4.75in (12cm) high

**$220-280**      LB

A Baccarat 'Le Dandy' perfume bottle, designed by Louis Sue for D'Orsay, in black crystal with label and seal in box.

c1920      3.5in (9cm) high

**$500-700**      RDL

A Baccarat 'L'Heure Bleu', perfume bottle for Guerlain, in clear crystal with a label, seal and display box, stenciled "BACCARAT" mark.

c1920      4.75in (12cm) high

**$700-1,000**      RDL

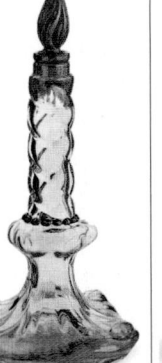

A Baccarat 'Sleeping' perfume bottle for Schiaparelli, in clear and red crystal with gilded details and a stenciled "Baccarat".

c1940      8in (20cm) high

**$700-1,000**      RDL

A Baccarat 'It's You' perfume bottle for Elizabeth Arden, in clear and frosted crystal with an enameled ring, on a display stand, with stenciled "BACCARAT" mark.

c1940      6.5in (16.5cm) high

**$800-1,200**      RDL

A Baccarat 'Cyclamen' perfume bottle for Elizabeth Arden, in white and clear crystal with gold detail, with stenciled "Baccarat".

c1940      5.5in (13.5cm) high

**$2,200-2,800**      RDL

A Hoffman perfume bottle, in clear and frosted green crystal, with stenciled oval "MADE in CZECHOSLOVAKIA" mark.

*c1920*    *5.75in (14.5cm) high*

**$800-1,200**                    RDL

A Hoffman perfume bottle, in pink crystal, mounted with jewels and an ivory miniature, with "HOFFMAN" intaglio mark, the metal marked "AUSTRIA".

*c1920*    *5.5in (13.5cm) high*

**$1,800-2,200**                RDL

A Hoffman perfume bottle, in black crystal with applied green crystal plaque and unusual stopper of St. George slaying a dragon, stopper edge flaked.

*c1920*    *6.5in (16.5cm) high*

**$2,800-3,200**                RDL

The perfume industry blossomed in the 1920s as cosmetics became increasingly fashionable. Glassmakers competed for a share of the market by making ever more exquisite and original bottles, like this bust and column bottle.

Joseff Hoffman was one of the foremost European glass designers. He attempted to improve standards of workmanship and design in the face of cheap mass-produced products. His pieces are of high quality and are therefore highly desirable.

Hoffman favored geometric design and this is evident in this bottle. Even his earlier Art Nouveau pieces were often unusually angular in form.

The Classical design of a bust on a column has been updated, with simplified lines and striking colors, and has a distinctive 1920s look.

A Hoffman perfume bottle, in black and opaque green crystal, with stenciled divided circle marked with "FBS" and "FRANCE".

*c1920*                    *9.5in (23.5cm) high*

**$5,000-8,000**                                RDL

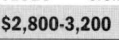

An Ingrid perfume bottle, in clear and frosted amber crystal, with stenciled oval "MADE in CZECHOSLOVAKIA" mark.

*c1920*    *5.75in (14.5cm) high*

**$2,800-3,200**                RDL

An Ingrid perfume bottle, in opaque black crystal, with frosted stopper and dauber.

*c1920*    *5.25in (13cm) high*

**$1,800-2,200**                RDL

An Ingrid perfume bottle, in opaque green crystal with clear and frosted stopper.

*c1920*    *6.5in (16.5cm) high*

**$1,800-2,200**                RDL

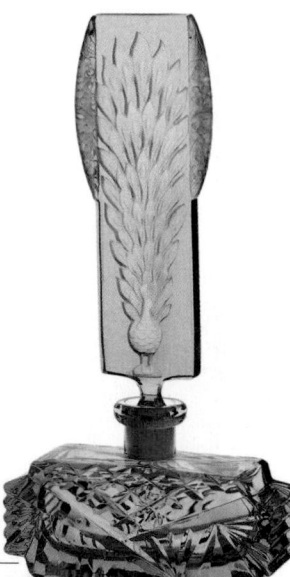

A Czechoslovakian perfume bottle, in blue crystal, with stenciled oval "MADE in CZECHOSLOVAKIA" mark, and silver paper label.

*c1930*    *7.75in (19.5cm) high*

**$800-1,200**                RDL

A Czechoslovakian perfume bottle, in amber crystal, with blue and pearl jeweled metalwork, stenciled circle "CZECHOSLOVAKIA" mark, missing jewels.

*c1920*    *4.5in (11.5cm) high*

**$800-1,200**                RDL

A Czechoslovakian perfume bottle for Shimy, in green crystal with enameled details and metal filagree cap, with metal plaque, marked "CZECHOSLOVAKIA".

*c1930*    *6in (15cm) high*

**$1,200-1,800**                RDL

An 'Apres L'Ondee' perfume bottle for Guerlain, in clear glass with enameled detail, paper label and display box, box lid loose.

*c1900*                                    3in (7.5cm) high

$800-1,200                                    RDL

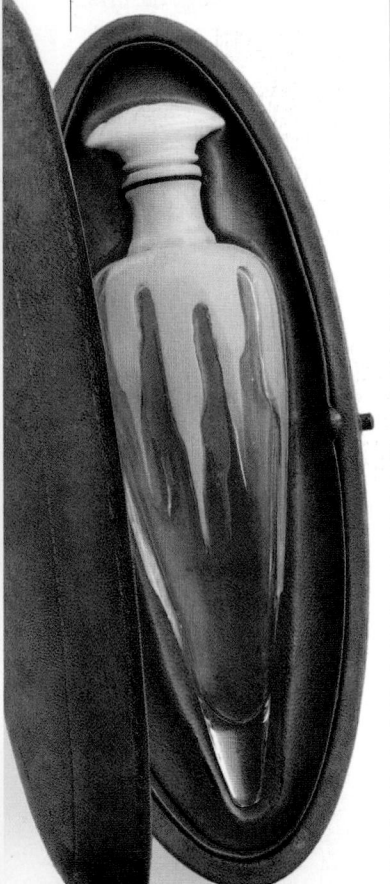

A Cristallerie De Pantin 'Parfum Precieuse' perfume bottle, a J. Viard design for Caron, in opal and white crystal with deluxe leather box.

*c1915*          6in (15cm) high

$3,000-5,000          RDL

A 'Giardini' perfume bottle for Babani, in green glass with gilded and enameled detail.

*c1920*          4.5in (11cm) high

$1,800-2,200          RDL

A Devilbiss Imperial perfume bottle, with dauber, in yellow glass shading to opal, with glass jewels in metal filagree.

*c1920*                                    7.75in (19.5cm) high

$8,000-12,000                                    RDL

A European silver-gilt and mauve enameled scent bottle, the translucent enamel on an engine turned ground, the interior fitted with a stoppered glass bottle, with English import marks for London.

c1910     1.5in (4cm) high

**$800-1,200**    **WW**

A Devilbiss atomizer, in decorated glass with amber glass foot and finial, removable insert and paper label.

c1920     6.75in (16cm) high

**$700-1,000**    **RDL**

A 'Miss Kate' Saint-Louis perfume bottle for Bourjois, in clear and black crystal, with label and box.

c1920     4.75in (12cm) high

**$1,200-1,800**    **RDL**

A rare 'Heure Exquise' perfume bottle for Breyenne, in blue glass with gilt detail and label to base, in velvet cushion box, chip, missing stopper.

c1925     3.5in (9cm) high

**$3,000-5,000**    **RDL**

A Depinoix perfume bottle, a J. Viard design for Dubarry, in clear and frosted glass with stained and painted details, stenciled "MADE in FRANCE" mark.

c1920     3.5in (9cm) high

**$3,000-5,000**    **RDL**

A 'Chypre' perfume bottle for Sauze, of cube form, in clear glass, with screw cap, bakelite cover, label and display box.

c1920     3in (7.5cm) high

**$3,000-5,000**    **RDL**

A J. Viard 'Ambre de Carthage' perfume bottle for Isabey, in clear and frosted glass with gray stain and faux Spanish leather box, molded "J. VIARD".

c1925     5in (12cm) high

**$2,800-3,200**    **RDL**

A J. Viard 'Vers la Joie' perfume bottle for Rigaud, gilt details and black pearl finished cover, Art Deco box, stenciled "J. Viard" mark, lacking stopper.

c1925     2.5in (6cm) high

**$3,000-5,000**    **RDL**

A Depinoix 'Lune de Miel' perfume bottle for Sari, in opaque black glass with silver-gilt detail and label.

c1925     4.5in (11cm) high

**$1,800-2,200**    **RDL**

A 'Bibelot' perfume bottle for Lydes, in black glass, with bakelite stopper, cover and stand.

c1925     4.5in (11.5cm) high

**$1,800-2,200**    **RDL**

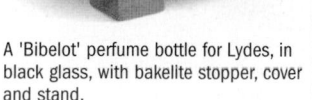

A 'Jicky' perfume bottle for Guerlain, in French opaline crystal with bronze neck, gilt stopper, and enameled decoration signed by R. Noirot, slight gold wear.

c1950     6.5in (16.5cm) high

**$1,800-2,200**    **RDL**

A relative dearth of important textiles auctions in the last year has dampened the market in rugs, curtains, and tapestries. Dealers, and consequently collectors, have been struggling to source top quality items and these are snapped up quickly when they do surface. Run-of-the-mill fabrics, on the other hand, can be found in abundance and as such are failing to realize anything but rudimentary prices. The weak dollar is contributing to this general malaise, as the U.S. has traditionally been one of the main markets for antique European textiles. American collectors of Colonial and Federal needlework samplers, on the other hand, remain unaffected by international financial markets and are very active right now. Prices over $35,000 are not unheard of for the finest early American textiles.

Buyers should be especially aware of condition when purchasing textiles. A degree of sun damage is acceptable, although examples with bright colors that have been protected from ultra-violet radiation invariably attract a substantial premium. Many fabrics, such as silk, will begin to rot after too much exposure to sunlight, and this can be a particular problem with curtains. Many collectors are now showing interest in ethnographic pieces in preference to traditional French, Flemish, and American textiles. This new trend looks set to continue as the tribal art market attracts more devotees who find that tribal forms and motifs gel well with modern interiors.

*Joanna Booth, antique textiles dealer, London*

A late 19thC Heriz carpet, from northwest Persia.

167in (417.5cm) long

**$5,000-8,000**          **FRE**

A Heriz carpet, from northwest Persia.

c1940          129in (322.5cm) long

**$4,000-6,000**          **FRE**

A late 20thC Heriz carpet, from northwest Persia.

74in (185cm) long

**$5,000-8,000**          **FRE**

A Heriz rug, with a large central medallion on a salmon and blue field, with corner work in blue and olive, with rebound selvedge.

129in (327.5cm) long

**$5,000-8,000**          **BRU**

A large Heriz carpet, the brick red field with indigo and sky blue medallions and ivory spandrels, within an indigo turtle palmette border.

236.25in (600cm) long

**$30,000-35,000**          **L&T**

A Heriz carpet, the brick red field with a small central medallion, flanked by large palmettes and surrounded by angular yellow vines, within an indigo scrolling vine border.

141.75in (360cm) long

**$3,000-5,000**          **L&T**

A late 19thC Mohtashem Kashan rug, from central Persia.

*79in (197.5cm) long*

**$1,200-1,800**     **FRE**

An Indo-Kashan prayer rug, from central Persia.

*c1900*     *60in (152.5cm) long*

**$3,000-5,000**     **FRE**

---

## A CLOSER LOOK AT A MOHTASHEM KASHAN CARPET

Kashan, in northern Iran, has been a center of carpet production for many years. Before the 1930s, Kashani weavers actually used wool spun in Manchester.

This medallion repeats the 'Tree of Life' pattern in miniature, attesting to the cyclical nature of creation.

Unlike most Persian rugs, which are symmetrical, this 'Tree of Life' pattern has a top and a bottom. It is decorated with many varieties of flowers and foliage.

There are records relating to a prolific carpet factory known as Mohtashem, but the name has now become a by-word for any high quality rug of the Kashan region.

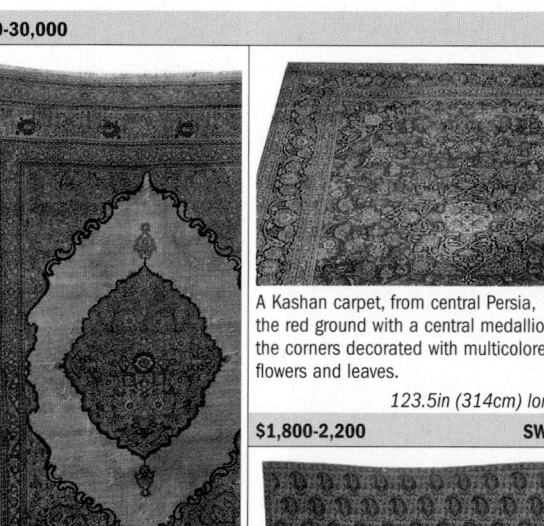

A late 19thC Mohtashem Kashan carpet, from central Persia.

*116in (290cm) long*

**$25,000-30,000**     **FRE**

---

A Mohtashem Kashan carpet, the indigo field with a central medallion suspending pendants and rose and ivory spandrels, within an indigo hunting border between bands decorated with birds.

*118.5in (301cm) long*

**$10,000-15,000**     **L&T**

A Kashan rug, the cream field with a central medallion suspending pendants and similar spandrels, within a cream palmette and angular vine border between bands.

*66.25in (168cm) long*

**$2,200-2,800**     **L&T**

A Kashan carpet, from central Persia, the red ground with a central medallion, the corners decorated with multicolored flowers and leaves.

*123.5in (314cm) long*

**$1,800-2,200**     **SWO**

A Kashan carpet, from central Persia, the red ground with a central medallion, the corners decorated with multi-colored flowers, leaves, and motifs.

*123.5in (314cm) long*

**$2,200-2,800**     **SWO**

An early 20thC Kerman rug, from southeast Persia.

*83in (207.5cm) long*

**$10,000-15,000**     **FRE**

A Lauer Kerman rug, from Persia.

*c1920*     *81in (202.5cm) long*

**$2,200-2,800**     **FRE**

**TEXTILES**

A late 19thC Ziegler Mahal wagireh rug, from west Persia.

*146in (371cm) long*

**$3,000-4,000** **FRE**

A Mahal carpet, from west Persia.

*c1920* *149in (372.5cm) long*

**$3,000-4,000** **FRE**

A late 19thC Sarouk Fereghan carpet, from west Persia.

*119in (297.5cm) long*

**$15,000-20,000** **FRE**

A Sarouk Fereghan rug, from west Persia.

*c1910* *80in (203cm) long*

**$1,800-2,200** **FRE**

A Sarouk Malayer rug, with an ivory medallion on a rust field, with overall floral design.

*c1920* *81in (205.5cm) long*

**$2,800-3,200** **POOK**

A Sarouk carpet, from west Persia.

*c1930* *257in (642.5cm) long*

**$4,000-6,000** **FRE**

A Sarouk Fereghan rug, from west Persia.

*c1940* *50in (125cm) long*

**$3,000-5,000** **FRE**

A Sarouk Fereghan rug, with rows of boteh designs on an ivory field, worn.

*59in (150cm) long*

**$800-1,200** **BRU**

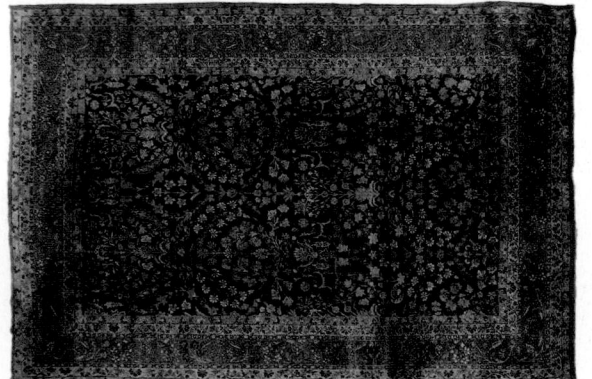

A finely woven Sarouk or Kashan rug, with repeating floral designs on a blue field, within ivory and red borders, worn.

*188in (477.5cm) long*

**$3,000-4,000** **BRU**

A Sarouk Fereghan rug, with a central medallion on an ivory field, with repeating floral and geometric motifs.

*77in (195.5cm) long*

**$1,800-2,200** **BRU**

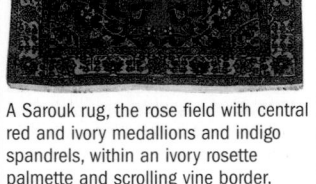

A Sarouk rug, the rose field with central red and ivory medallions and indigo spandrels, within an ivory rosette palmette and scrolling vine border, between similar bands.

*80in (203cm) long*

**$1,200-1,800** **L&T**

A Mosul rug, with a multiple diamond ivory central medallion on a red field with blue corner work, damaged.

*74in (188cm) long*

**$500-800** **BRU**

A Mushkabad rug, with repeating geometric and blossom designs on an ivory field, damaged.

*139in (353cm) long*

**$1,800-2,200** **BRU**

A Shahsavan runner, from northwest Persia.

*c1900* *173in (439.5cm) long*

**$1,200-1,800** **FRE**

A Shiraz rug, with three stepped central medallions on a brown field, with ivory, blue and salmon borders and a flat-woven fringe with alternating stripes.

*88in (223.5cm) long*

**$800-1,200** **BRU**

A Tabriz carpet, from northwest Persia, the claret ground with a central blue medallion, the inner field with quarter medallion corners, decorated with multicolored flowers and motifs.

*156in (396cm) long*

**$4,000-6,000** **SWO**

A late 19thC corridor carpet, from northwest Persia.

*Corridor carpets, also known as 'runners', are designed for use in entranceways and hallways.*

*201in (510.5cm) long*

**$1,200-1,800** **FRE**

## CAUCASIAN RUGS & CARPETS

A Kazak throw rug, with three central medallions on a blue field, with multiple borders.

*c1900* *96in (240cm) long*

**$5,000-7,000** **POOK**

A Kazak Karatchopf rug, the red field with a central ivory and indigo square panel, flanked by two similar blue and cream panels, within ivory rosette borders between bands.

*85in (216cm) long*

**$4,000-6,000** **L&T**

A Kazak rug, the lemon field with three hooked medallions, within ivory hooked lozenge borders between skittle bands.

*80in (203cm) long*

**$6,000-9,000** **L&T**

A 19thC Shirvan rug, from east Caucasus.

*56in (140cm) long*

**$5,000-8,000** **FRE**

A late 19thC Shirvan throw rug, with four central medallions on a navy field, with a kufic and running dog border.

82in (205cm) long

**$7,000-10,000**     **POOK**

A Daghestan prayer rug.

c1910     70in (175cm) long

**$1,200-1,800**     **POOK**

An Erivan rug, the rust field with an olive lozenge medallion suspending pendants and similar spandrels, within a red and blue script style, border between scrolling bands.

78in (198cm) long

**$400-600**     **L&T**

A late 19thC Karabagh runner, from south Caucasus.

242in (605cm) long

**$3,000-4,000**     **FRE**

A late Karagashli rug, from northeast Caucasus.

60in (152.5cm) long

**$4,000-6,000**     **FRE**

A late 19thC Leshgi rug, from south Caucasus.

76in (190cm) long

**$3,000-4,000**     **FRE**

An Oushak carpet, from west Anatolia.

187in (467.5cm) long

**$2,800-3,200**     **FRE**

A Perpedil rug, the dark indigo field with a ram's horn pattern, within an indigo kufic border between various bands, signature cartouche.

73.25in (186cm) long

**$1,200-1,800**     **L&T**

A Sechour throw rug, with two central lime and ivory medallions, on a blue field within an elaborate running border.

c1900     81in (202.5cm) long

**$3,000-4,000**     **POOK**

An early 20thC Sivas carpet, from Anatolia.

150in (375cm) long

**$2,800-3,200**     **FRE**

A Caucasian rug, the rust red field with large flowerheads, within multiple borders.

114.25in (290cm) long

**$1,800-2,200**     **L&T**

A 20thC French Aubusson carpet.

*189in (472.5cm) long*

**$18,000-22,000**  FRE

A French Aubusson carpet, with a floral design.

*c1900*  *117in (292.5cm) long*

**$3,000-5,000**  FRE

An Aubusson-style needlepoint rug, with a central medallion with floral bouquet, and panels with stitched seams.

*162in (411.5cm) long*

**$1,200-1,800**  BRU

An early 20thC Turkish rug.

*73in (182.5cm) long*

**$1,200-1,800**  FRE

An Agra rug, with repeating floral designs on an ivory field, within green, ivory and red minor borders, damaged.

*129in (327.5cm) long*

**$7,000-10,000**  BRU

An Agra rug, the claret field with a palmette and scrolling vine pattern, within a claret palmette border.

*80in (203cm) long*

**$800-1,200**  L&T

A mid-20thC Indian runner.

*237in (592.5cm) long*

**$2,200-2,800**  FRE

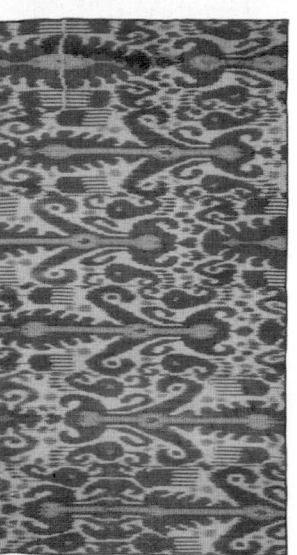

An 19thC Ikat panel, from central Asia.

*61in (155cm) long*

**$1,800-2,200**  FRE

A 19thC Tibetan saddle rug, mounted on linen, affixed to a wood stretcher.

*51in (127.5cm) wide*

**$2,200-2,800**  FRE

A Chinese carpet.

*c1900*  *116in (290cm) long*

**$7,000-10,000**  FRE

A Chinese carpet.

*c1930*  *140in (350cm) long*

**$2,200-2,800**  FRE

A 17thC French Royal Aubusson verdure tapestry, in silk and wool on a linen foundation, depicting a woodland scene, within a ribbon-bound floral border.

*136.25in (346cm) wide*

$15,000-18,000     RSS

A 17thC French Aubusson historical verdure tapestry, within a later foliate border, restored.

*80.75in (205cm) high*

$5,000-8,000     RSS

A 17thC French Aubusson mythological tapestry, woven in silk and wool.

*95in (241cm) high*

$1,800-2,200     RSS

A Louis XIV Aubusson mythological tapestry, woven in silk and wool, depicting warriors, within a scrolling foliate and flower head border, restored.

*114.25in (290cm) high*

$4,000-6,000     BEA

An early 18th French Royal Aubusson verdure tapestry, in silk and wool on a linen foundation, depicting woodland scenes, within a ribbon-bound floral border.

*112.25in (285cm) wide*

$2,800-3,200     BEA

A French Aubusson verdure tapestry, woven in silk and wool, depicting a wooded landscape within a ribbon-bound floral border.

*109.5in (278cm) high*

$3,000-5,000     BEA

An 18thC French Aubusson verdure tapestry, woven in silk and wool, depicting a wooded landscape within a ribbon-bound floral border.

*114.25in (290cm) wide*

$2,000-2,500     BEA

An18thC French Royal Aubusson verdure tapestry, woven in silk and wool on a linen foundation, depicting woodland scenes, within a ribbon-bound floral border, in the manner of Pillement.

*91.25in (232cm) high*

$5,000-8,000     RSS

An 18thC French Royal Aubusson verdure tapestry, woven in silk and wool on a linen foundation, within a ribbon-bound floral border.

*100.5in (255cm) high*

$3,000-5,000     RSS

An 18thC French Aubusson pastoral tapestry, woven in silk and wool, depicting a group hunting game birds, restored.

*80.75in (205cm) high*

**$7,000-10,000** **RSS**

An 18thC French Royal Aubusson verdure tapestry, woven in silk and wool on a linen foundation, depicting a woodland scene with birds, within a ribbon-bound floral border, restored.

*98.75in (251cm) wide*

**$5,000-8,000** **RSS**

A French Royal Aubusson verdure tapestry, woven in silk and wool on a linen foundation, depicting an exotic woodland scene, within a ribbon-bound floral border, restored.

*75.5in (192cm) wide*

**$4,000-6,000** **RSS**

An 18thC French Royal Aubusson verdure tapestry, woven in silk and wool on a linen foundation, depicting an autumnal woodland scene, within a ribbon-bound floral border, restored.

*88.5in (225cm) high*

**$5,000-8,000** **RSS**

An 18thC French Royal Aubusson verdure tapestry, woven in silk and wool on a linen foundation, depicting a woodland scene, within a blue border.

*108.25in (275cm) wide*

**$8,000-12,000** **RSS**

An 18thC French Royal Aubusson verdure tapestry, by Finet, woven in silk and wool on a linen foundation, depicting a woodland glade, within a ribbon-bound floral border, restored.

*151.5in (385cm) wide*

**$8,000-12,000** **RSS**

An 18thC French Royal Aubusson verdure tapestry, woven in silk and wool on a linen foundation, depicting a woodland scene with birds and buildings, within a ribbon-bound floral border, restored.

*106.75in (271cm) high*

**$5,000-8,000** **RSS**

An 18thC French Royal Aubusson verdure tapestry, woven in silk and wool on a linen foundation, depicting a woodland scene, within a ribbon-bound floral border, in the Pillement style, restored.

*81in (206cm) wide*

**$3,000-5,000** **RSS**

An 18thC French Royal Aubusson verdure tapestry, woven in silk and wool on a linen foundation, depicting a woodland scene in the distance, within a ribbon-bound floral border, restored.

*99.25in (252cm) high*

**$5,000-7,000** **RSS**

**TEXTILES**

A French Aubusson tapestry, woven in silk and wool, depicting urns, trophies, flowers, and scrolling foliage, with a central cartouche depicting a romantic scene.

*102in (259cm) high*

**$15,000-20,000 BEA**

A late 18thC French Royal Aubusson verdure tapestry, woven in silk and wool on a linen foundation, depicting a woodland scene, within a ribbon-bound floral border, restored.

*114.25in (290cm) high*

**$5,000-7,000 BEA**

A late 18thC French Royal Aubusson verdure tapestry, woven in silk and wool on a linen foundation, depicting a woodland scene.

*198.75in (505cm) high*

**$5,000-8,000 BLA**

A late 18thC French Royal Aubusson verdure tapestry, woven in silk and wool on a linen foundation, depicting a woodland scene.

*169.25in (430cm) wide*

**$7,000-10,000 BLA**

A late 18thC French Royal Aubusson verdure tapestry, woven in silk and wool on a linen foundation, depicting a woodland scene, within a ribbon-bound floral border.

*193in (490cm) wide*

**$7,000-10,000 BEA**

An 18thC French Royal Aubusson verdure tapestry, woven in silk and wool, depicting a woodland scene.

*95.25in (242cm) wide*

**$3,000-4,000 BEA**

An 18thC French Aubusson mythological tapestry, woven in silk and wool, restored.

*72in (140cm) wide*

**$3,000-5,000 BEA**

A 19thC French Aubusson pastoral tapestry fragment, in the 18thC manner, woven in silk and wool.

*47.25in (120cm) wide*

**$1,200-1,800 RSS**

A pair of 19thC Aubusson pastoral tapestries, depicting hunting scenes.

*112.25in (285cm) high*

**$15,000-18,000 PIL**

A 19thC French Aubusson pastoral tapestry, in the 18thC manner after Téniers, woven in silk and wool, depicting a gypsy fortune teller with peasants in a wooded landscape, within a simulated picture frame border, signed "Aubusson Manufacture Royale 1847".

*106in (269cm) high*

**$5,000-8,000 RSS**

A late 17thC French silk and wool needlepoint chair cover, with a central image surrounded by scrolling foliage and large flowerheads.

*27.5in (70cm) wide*

**$500-700**     **RSS**

An early 18thC French verdure tapestry, manufactured by De la Marche, woven in silk and wool on a linen foundation, depicting woodland scenes.

*96in (244cm) wide*

**$3,000-4,000**     **RSS**

An 18thC Beauvais mythological tapestry panel, woven in silver thread, silk and wool, in a gilt frame.

*85.75in (218cm) high*

**$15,000-18,000**     **BEA**

An early 18thC verdure tapestry, by Felletin, woven in silk and wool on a linen foundation, depicting woodland scenes, within a ribbon-bound floral border.

*193in (490cm) wide*

**$7,000-10,000**     **BEA**

An 18thC pastoral tapestry, by Felletin, woven in silk and wool, within a large ribbon-bound floral border, restored.

*93in (236cm) high*

**$5,000-7,000**     **RSS**

A pair of 18thC French wool needlepoint seat covers.

*32.25in (82cm) wide*

**$2,200-2,800**     **RSS**

A 19thC French tapestry, woven in silk and wool in the 18thC manner, depicting a woman picking flowers.

*The floral swags and garlands that frame this scene are typical motifs of 18thC Neoclassicism. A rural French twist is provided by the use of native wild flowers and sheaves of wheat.*

An 18thC French silk and wool needlepoint panel, restored.

*57.5in (146cm) wide*

**$1,200-1,800**     **RSS**

A French 18thC silk and wool needlepoint chair cover, depicting a mythological scene.

*29.25in (74cm) high*

**$1,200-1,800**     **RSS**

*99in (252cm) high*

**$7,000-10,000**   **RSS**

## FLEMISH TAPESTRIES

A 16thC Flemish tapestry, woven in silk and wool on a linen foundation, depicting a hunting scene.

*64.5in (164cm) wide*

**$3,000-5,000**     **RSS**

A 16thC Flemish mythological tapestry, woven in silk and wool, depicting a hunting scene with archers, cavalry and spear bearers bringing down a large boar within a later blue outer slip, restored.

*Hunting was a favorite pastime of the European aristocracy in the 16thC. In Belgium, one of the greatest prizes was a wild boar.*

*74.75in (190cm) wide*

**$5,000-8,000**     **RSS**

A 16thC Flemish mythological tapestry, woven in wools and silks, within a scrolling foliate and flower head border, restored.

*147.75in (375cm) wide*

**$30,000-35,000**

RSS

A Flemish Audenarde mythological tapestry, woven in wools and silks, with a war-scene, within a scrolling foliate and flowerhead border, restored.

*c1590* *167.25in (425cm) wide*

**$7,000-10,000**

RSS

A late 16thC Flemish Audenarde mythological tapestry fragment, restored.

*80.75in (205cm) high*

**$5,000-8,000**

RSS

A Flemish mythological tapestry fragment, within a later simulated picture frame border, restored.

*74.75in (190cm) high*

**$5,000-8,000**

RSS

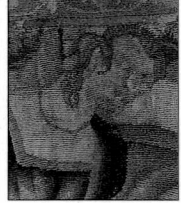

A late 16thC Flemish mythological tapestry fragment, woven in silk and wool, within a later beige and gray outer slip, restored.

*74.75in (190cm) high*

**$2,800-3,200**

RSS

A 17thC Flemish mythological tapestry, woven in silk and wool, depicting Diane, goddess of the hunt, within a scrolling foliate and flower head border, restored.

*214.25in (544cm) wide*

**$25,000-30,000**

RSS

A 17thC Flemish mythological tapestry, woven in silk and wool, within a rich decorated border, restored.

*107in (272cm) high*

**$5,000-8,000**

RSS

A 17thC Flemish mythological tapestry, woven in silk and wool, within a rich decorated border, restored.

*107in (272cm) high*

**$5,000-8,000**

RSS

4 lot page

An early 18thC Brussels allegorical tapestry, 'The Feast of the Continents', by Jasper van der Borght, woven in wool, depicting men and women of four continents seated at a banquet, with a puppet show, musicians and dancers to one side, the border woven to resemble a carved frame, bearing the Brussels town mark "BB" and signed "I V D BORGHT".

*Jasper van der Borght was born into one of the leading families of Brussels weavers, and two further generations continued the family business after him. This tapestry represents one of a set of five known as 'The Four Continents', the others in the series each focusing on a single continent. Nine sets of tapestries on this theme are believed to exist — the only extant full set is at the Kunsthistorisches Museum in Vienna. In Britain there are examples in the Royal Collection at Holyrood House in Edinburgh, which has two panels, and Mereworth Castle in Kent, which has four.*

157.5in (400cm) wide

$100,000-150,000                                                                   L&T

A pair of 19thC curtains, made from 16thC Italian red velvet, silvered threads.

*123.25in (313cm) high*

**$3,000-5,000** | **RSS**

A red silk and velvet valance, Spanish or Italian, with applied motifs in silk, embroidered with metal thread.

*95.75in (243cm) wide*

**$3,000-5,000** | **RSS**

One of a set of four French Aubusson tapestry curtains, silk and wool.

*118in (300cm) high*

**$7,000-10,000 set** | **RSS**

A late 16thC Flemish tapestry portière, woven in silk and wool.

*126.75in (322cm) high*

**$2,800-3,200** | **RSS**

One of a pair of late 19thC French Aubusson cantonnières.

*92.5in (235cm) high*

**$3,000-5,000 pair** | **RSS**

A late 19thC damask valance, in the Regence style, with applied ivory and satin border.

*166.25in (422cm) long*

**$800-1,200** | **RSS**

## FABRIC

A length of 17thC Italian velvet.

*47.25in (120cm) long*

**$500-700** | **RSS**

A length of late 17thC French green and gold damask, with a scrolling pattern of stylized flowers.

*213.5in (542cm) long*

**$300-500** | **RSS**

A French Abbeville damask furnishing panel, with a floral pattern.

*c1710*   *27.25in (69cm) long*

**$1,800-2,200** | **RSS**

A French Regence silk panel, with a cream and green floral pattern.

*551.25in (1400cm) long*

**$2,800-3,200** | **RSS**

A length of French Lyon naturalist brocaded lampas silk.

*c1740*   *204in (518cm) long*

**$300-500** | **RSS**

A piece of 18thC French furnishing fabric, from the Rhône valley, with flower and urn motifs on a blue ground.

*140.25in (356cm) long*

**$500-700** | **RSS**

A French linen and silk bed cover.

*111.5in (283cm) long*

**$800-1,200** | **RSS**

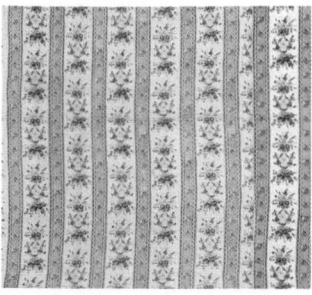

A length of 18thC French cotton, by Haussmann, with a woodblock print.

*82.25in (209cm) long*

**$300-500**    RSS

A piece of 18thC furnishing fabric panel, in blue woven silk damask.

*245.25in (623cm) long*

**$800-1,200**    RSS

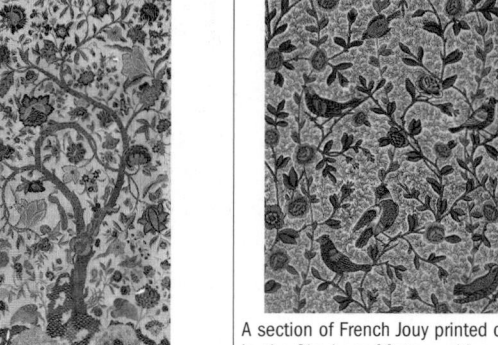

An section of 18thC Indian quilting, painted and printed with a tree of life.

*96in (244cm) long*

**$8,000-12,000**    RSS

A section of French Jouy printed cotton, by the Oberkampf factory, with a repeating pattern of flowers and birds.

*This design was created for Christophe-Philippe Oberkampf's bedroom.*

*c1775        106.25in (270cm) long*

**$3,000-4,000**    RSS

## TOILE DE JOUY

- 'Toiles peintes', literally translated as 'painted fabrics', first arrived in France along the Silk Road in the 17thC. They were also known as 'Indiennes' because of their Eastern origin.
- French workshops soon began to make their own versions to meet demand but small textile producers, fearful for their livelihoods, successfully lobbied for a ban on this enterprise.
- Christophe-Philippe Oberkampf established the Manufacture Royale at Jouy-en-Josas in 1760, a year after the ban was lifted.
- The Jouy factory used French cotton as well as fabric imported from India, the Middle East, and Britain.
- Chief designer Jean-Baptiste Huet produced floral and allegorical patterns, primarily in monochrome red, blue, green, or yellow on white, although combinations of these colors were also used.
- Jouy became especially well known for printed fabrics designed for use as furniture coverings and wall hangings. The generic term 'toile de Jouy' came into use to describe these wares.
- Oberkampf's factory was closed in 1843 after the hardships of the Napoleonic Wars irreparably eroded his business.

A piece of French Jouy Indienne cotton, printed from a wooden matrix, depicting stylized flowers, by the Oberkampf factory.

*c1780        67in (170cm) long*

**$1,200-1,800**    RSS

A piece of French Jouy furnishing cotton, printed from copper plates, by the Oberkampf factory, entitled 'Pagode sur un pont de rochers'.

*c1780        41in (104cm) long*

**$500-700**    RSS

A piece of furnishing cotton, by the Oberkampf factory, printed from copper plates.

*c1785        22.75in (58cm) long*

**$500-700**    RSS

A length of French Lyon woven silk lampas.

*This pattern was created in 1784 for the games salon at Versailles.*

*55in (140cm) long*

**$800-1,200**    RSS

A French furnishing cotton, printed from copper plates, by Petitpierre Frères of Nantes, entitled 'Panurge dans l'île des lanternes'.

*c1785        85.75in (218cm) long*

**$800-1,200**    RSS

A French furnishing cotton, printed from copper plates, by the Gorgerat factory in Nantes, entitled 'A la gloire de Louis XVI'.

*c1790        35.5in (90cm) long*

**$180-220**    RSS

A French Indienne quilt, manufactured by Hartmann of Alsace, printed from woodblocks with an Indian tree of life design and flowers.

*c1800        112.25in (285cm) long*

**$1,200-1,800**    RSS

A French boutis cotton quilt, manufactured in Jouy or Beautiran, printed from wood blocks with flowers on a patterned red ground.

*c1800*                    *109.5in (278cm) long*

**$800-1,200**                                    **RSS**

A 19thC French Lyon brocade sample, in the Grand Frères manner, the cream ground brocaded in blue with flowers.

*50.75in (129cm) long*

**$400-600**                    **RSS**

A French 19thC lampas sample, woven in silk with grotesques, in the 18thC manner, marked "TC".

*58.75in (149cm) long*

**$400-600**                    **RSS**

A 19thC French Lyon woven silk lampas sample, based on a late 18thC design.

*87in (221cm) long*

**$500-700**          **RSS**

A 19thC French Lyon woven silk lampas brocade, in the 18thC manner.

*230in (584cm) long*

**$400-600**          **RSS**

A 19thC French Empire-style Gros de Tours panel and runners, with gold embroidery.

**$15,000-20,000**                                    **RSS**

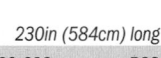

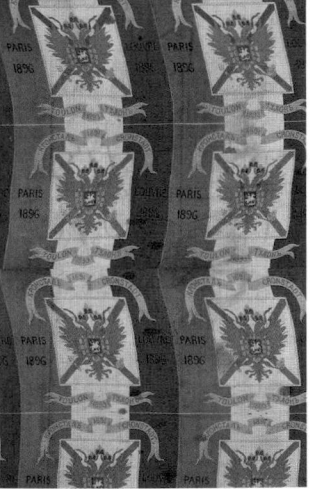

A length of 19thC French Lyon woven silk and satin furnishing brocade, in the Byzantine style.

*25.25in (64cm) long*

**$300-500**          **RSS**

A 19thC French silk lampas seat cover, manufactured by La Maison Grand Frères for the Vice King of Egypt, after an 18thC design by Gaudin.

*1862*          *100in (254cm) long*

**$1,200-1,800**          **RSS**

A late 19thC French table runner, embroidered in silk with bullion cruciform appliqué, stamped dedication to Tsar Nicholas II and Tsarina Alexandra Fedorovna, restored.

*94in (228cm) long*

**$15,000-18,000**          **RSS**

A section of 19thC French Rouen roller-printed cotton, with the arms of the Russian Imperial family, designed by Laveissiere and Chamont-Deville, labelled "Toulon 1893", "Cronstadt 1891" and "Paris Louvre 1896".

*63.75in (162cm) long*

**$500-700**          **RSS**

A section of 18thC French Régence wallpaper, manufactured by Les Associé of Paris.

*33.75in (86cm) long*

**$800-1,200** RSS

A French wallpaper, designed by Jean-Baptiste Réveillon, with flowers and love birds on a cream ground.

*c1785* *23.25in (59cm) wide*

**$2,800-3,200** RSS

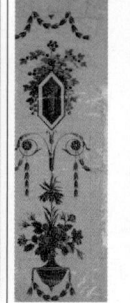

One of a set of 11 late 18thC French wallpaper strips and borders.

**$800-1,200 set** RSS

A French wallpaper, by Jacquemart and Bénard, printed from wood blocks in gouache with flowers, on a blue ground.

*c1795* *20.75in (53cm) long*

**$300-500** RSS

A French wallpaper, by Jacquemart et Bénard, printed from wood blocks in gouache with laurels and a landscape, on a blue ground with 'Directoire' motifs.

*1796* *20.75in (53cm) long*

**$300-500** RSS

A French wallpaper, printed in color from wood blocks with flocks, with 'Directoire' motifs and a bust of Barras in gray, on a blue ground, dated.

*1798* *139.75in (355cm) long*

**$500-700** RSS

A pair of French wallpaper panels, designed to imitate drapery.

*c1800* *100.5in (255cm) long*

**$3,000-5,000** RSS

An early 19thC Belgium scenic wallpaper, block-printed with a landscape scene with trees.

*145in (368cm) long*

**$280-320** RSS

A 19thC French block printed wallpaper.

*87.75in (223cm) wide*

**$2,800-3,200** RSS

An early 19thC French block printed wallpaper border, depicting flowers and antic scenes in reserves, in the style of Dugourc.

*78.75in (200cm) wide*

**$300-500** RSS

A block-printed wallpaper, with drapery.

*c1820*

**$7,000-10,000** RSS

One of a pair of 19thC French scenic wallpaper rolls.

*39.25in (100cm) long*

**$280-320 pair** RSS

A 19thC wallpaper strip, probably designed by Défossé and Karth.

*91.25in (232cm) long*

**$280-320** RSS

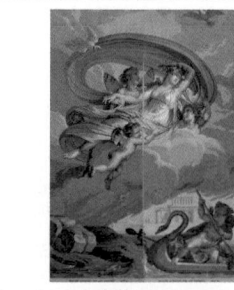

One of a set of 22 scenic wallpaper panels, after designs by Merry-Joseph Blondel and Louis Laffitte.

*c1870*

**$4,000-6,000 set** RSS

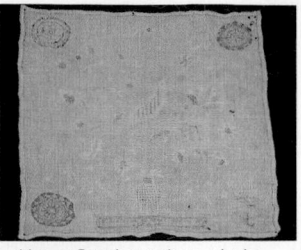

A white- or Dresden-work sampler by Elizabeth M. Buckley, Philadelphia, four cut and drawn-work circles and hollie-point panel with "Eliza M. Buckley/ 1784," linen and cotton on linen, unframed.

*1784*                    *10.5in (26cm) high*

**$12,000-18,000**                    **FRE**

A linen needlework sampler, embroidered in silk with the alphabet, decorative bands and the inscription "Abigail Bond Her Sampler Age 15 in Year 1753 MB MH RB", framed.

*21.25in (53cm) high*

**$2,800-3,200**                    **FRE**

*This shepherdess is part of an idyllic pastoral scene, typical of 18thC needlework samplers with their emphasis on industry and piety.*

A woollen needlework sampler by Mary Susannah Lambeth, embroidered in silk with rows of stylized flowers, the alphabet and numerals, above a pictorial band with shepherdess and flock, angels, pious verse and the inscription "Mary Susannah Lambeth works this in the 10th year of her age, 1789", framed.

*Girls in the 18thC were encouraged to stitch samplers as a sign of their virtue. Needlework was an important part of a wealthy young woman's education.*

*This extensive verse includes meditations on the nature of God's love and how to live a righteous life.*

*The standard of needlework on this sampler is particularly high. It has been thoughtfully composed and has many and varied attractive features. It is an interesting document of social history.*

*1789*          *27.5in (69cm) high*

**$40,000-45,000**                    **FRE**

A late 18thC needlework sampler by Amy Cougill "Done at L. Peck School," in silk threads on a linen ground, framed.

*11.5in (29cm) high*

**$700-1,000**                    **FRE**

A New York linen sampler, embroidered in silk with a tree of life, Adam and Eve, a Federal house and the inscription "Elizabeth Vermillya, aged 13 years, New York June in the year 1796", within a strawberry border.

*17.5in (44.5cm) high*

**$4,000-6,000**                    **POOK**

A woolen sampler, embroidered in silk with four verses, rows of alphabet, numerals, weeping willow and decorations, with the inscription "Mary Burbery's Work Finished October 27th in the year 1796", in a simple painted wooden frame.

*16.5in (42cm) high*

**$800-1,200**                    **BRU**

A Maine linen sampler, embroidered in silk with multiple alphabets above central potted trailing floral vines, within a vine border, with the inscription "Sophronia Robinson's sampler, wrought in the twelfth year of her age".

*18in (45.5cm) wide*

**$7,000-10,000**                    **POOK**

A Connecticut linen sampler, embroidered in silk with a floral and ribbon swag garland above the Wells family record, over a landscape of the village of Wethersfield, wrought by Hannah Wells, losses.

*20in (51cm) wide*

**$4,000-6,000**                    **POOK**

A 19thC American linen sampler, embroidered in silk with the Gallison family genealogy, wrought by Julia A. Gallison, the central record with a floral and vine border.

*20.5in (52cm) wide*

**$2,200-2,800**                    **POOK**

A George III sampler, embroidered in silk and chenille with moral sentiments and decorative devices, within a floral border.

*c1800*      21in (53.5cm) high

**$800-1,200**      **GORL**

A Pennsylvania silk on linen sampler by Sarah L. Taylor of West-Town school, with two doves surrounded by birds, flowers, and half medallions.

*1802*      12in (30.5cm) high

**$5,000-8,000**      **POOK**

An early 19thC needlework sampler, signed "Christiana Golder Ackworth School" and dated, one panel inscribed "Token of Love", dated.

*1805*      16in (41cm) high

**$1,800-2,200**      **ROW**

An English Adam and Eve linen sampler, embroidered in silk and wool, with two lines of alphabet and initials.

*1808*      15.75in (40cm) high

**$400-600**      **BRU**

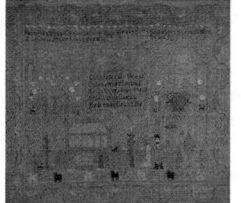

A 19thC needlework sampler, by Elizabeth Marshall, silk threads on a linen ground, with a vine border, original frame, some wear.

*Some design elements are similar to those in the Federal period in Philadelphia, such as spindly legged sheep.*

*c1815*      20in (51cm) wide

**$10,000-12,000**      **SK**

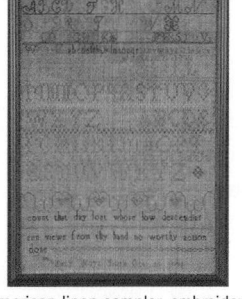

An American linen sampler, embroidered with rows of alphabet and a stylized floral vine above pious verse, framed.

*c1810*

**$2,800-3,200**      **FRE**

A 19thC silk linen needlework sampler, silk threads on a linen ground, with inscription "Lucy Parham born October 27, 1811, she wrought this in the 11th year of her age," above a verse, with house, trees and deer, toning, stains.

     18in (45cm) wide

**$30,000-35,000**      **SK**

A linen sampler, embroidered in silk with rows of alphabet, numerals and stylized flowers, dated.

*1822*      18in (45cm) high

**$700-1,000**      **FRE**

A Philadelphia silk on linen sampler, by Elizabeth Jolley, possibly of the E. Brunnell School, landscape with brick house, trees and husband and wife, floral and vine border.

*1824*      25.5in (65cm) wide

**$15,000-20,000**      **POOK**

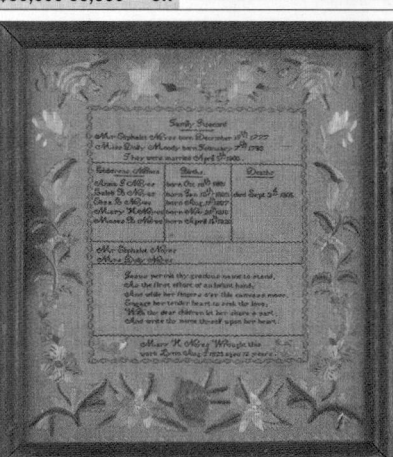

A Massachusetts linen family record, embroidered in silk with a central record and verse within a scrolling border, surrounded by large flowers and a sawtooth border, with the inscription "Mary H. Noyes Lynn Aug. 3 1823 aged 12 years".

     19.25in (49cm) high

**$2,800-3,200**      **POOK**

A Philadelphia silk-on-linen needlework sampler, possibly Hamilton School, by Ann T. Mack, with verse, trees and flowers above a lawn with animals, dated.

*1830*      21.25in (54cm) high

**$4,000-6,000**      **POOK**

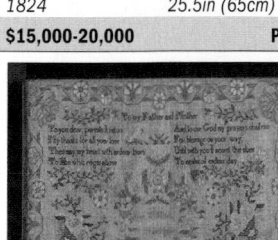

A North Carolina linen sampler, embroidered in silk with the alphabet and numerals above the inscription "M H Bell Tarboro Academy NC", damaged.

*1833*      16.75in (42.5cm) wide

**$1,200-1,800**      **BRU**

A pair of linen samplers, one embroidered in silk with verse over twin homes and the inscription "Ellen Wood May 29, 1835", the other with verse above a building flanked by flowers, trees and other designs, within a vine border and the inscription "Hannah Wood 1835".

*1835*     *14.5in (37cm) wide*

**$3,000-4,000**    **POOK**

A Connecticut silk-on-linen needlework sampler, by Abigail C. Phipps, with alphabet above family history and house with lawn, trees, and sheep, all within a vine border, dated.

*1836*     *17.75in (45cm) high*

**$2,200-2,800**    **POOK**

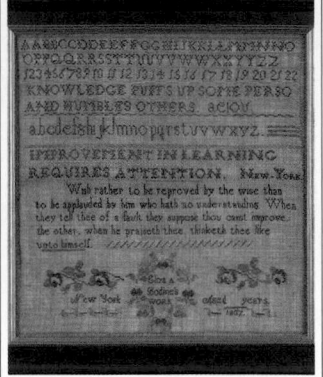

A silk on linen needlework sampler, inscribed "Eliza A. Bodine's Work, New York, Aged_ Years 1837" with alphabet, verse, floral wreath, and roses.

*Family history accompanies this item. Eliza's mother, Polly Bodine (the witch of Staten Island), was involved in a sensational murder case in the 19thC.*

*17.5in (44.5cm) high*

**$4,000-6,000**    **POOK**

---

A mid-19thC Virginia silk on linen needlework sampler, by Lucinda Parker, with alphabet and family record, with a house, trees and a fence.

*c1840*     *23.25in (59cm) high*

**$30,000-35,000**    **POOK**

A linen sampler, embroidered with a petit-point floral border, religious poem and maker's name, framed.

*1843*

**$280-320**    **TA**

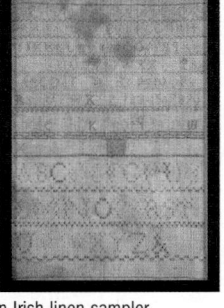

An Irish linen sampler, embroidered in silk with the inscription "Sarah Gowan, Belfast January 1844", in a wooden frame, faded.

*1844*     *11.75in (30cm) high*

**$300-400**    **BRU**

A Pennsylvania linen sampler, embroidered in wool with a basket of flowers, a church, birds, a heart, trees, and a strawberry vine border enclosing verse, with the inscription "Sarah Knight's Work Aged 10 1848", framed.

*1848*     *21in (52.5cm) wide*

**$800-1,200**    **FRE**

A mid-19thC needlework sampler, embroidered in colors with the alphabet, spring flowers, potted fruit trees, biblical subjects, a peacock, and vases of flowers, in a giltwood frame.

*16in (40.5cm) wide*

**$400-600**    **S&K**

---

A needlework sampler by Hannah J. Craft, polychrome silk threads on a linen ground, framed, unfinished.

*c1860*     *19in (48cm) high*

**$1,200-1,800**    **FRE**

A 19thC linen marking sampler, embroidered with alphabets in four lettering styles.

*17in (43cm) high*

**$220-280**    **BRU**

A linen needlework sampler, embroidered in silk with an alphabet, potted flowers and birds, in a decorated frame.

*12in (30.5cm) high*

**$500-800**    **POOK**

An Adam and Eve linen sampler, embroidered in silk with a verse entitled "The Fall of Adam", with Adam and Eve, cupids, flowers, birds, butterflies, and dogs.

*16in (40.5cm) high*

**$700-1,000**    **BRU**

A 17thC stumpwork panel, with raised sculptural forms on an ivory silk ground, alluding to a period of political calm and prosperity, depicting a lady with a musical instrument, encased in an oak box with sloping mirrored sides.

*16in (40.5cm) wide*

**$4,000-6,000**     **GORL**

A 17thC stumpwork panel, with a central oval cartouche depicting a young woman gathering a posy in a castle and country landscape, flanked by leopard, deer, insects, flowers, and foliage.

*11.5in (29cm) wide*

**$3,000-5,000**     **GORL**

A 17thC woolwork panel, worked in colored wools, depicting the angel Gabriel and Mary at the scene of the Annunciation.

*9.75in (25cm) wide*

**$700-1,000**     **L&T**

A late 18thC needlework map of Ireland, by A. Wolfe, the county borders worked in silks and their names in black thread, within numbered degrees of latitude and longitude, in a verre églomisé slip, framed.

*16.5in (42cm) high*

**$1,200-1,800**     **CHEF**

An early 19thC silk pictorial needlework, 'Rebecca at the well with Eliezer', probably American, in silk chenille satin stitch on a silk ground, the facial features and sky painted in watercolors, in a painted wood and composition frame with oval églomisé mat, damaged.

*14in (35.5cm) high*

**$800-1,200**     **BRU**

An early 19thC silk on silk oval pictorial needlework, possibly Folwell School, depicting a young girl wearing a white dress, petting a lamb in a pastoral landscape.

*7in (17.5cm) wide*

**$800-1,200**     **POOK**

A pair of 19thC English silkwork pictures, one depicting a harvest scene, the other a mother with her two children in a wooded landscape, framed.

*28in (70cm) wide*

**$2,200-2,800**     **FRE**

A late 19thC sailor's woolwork picture, depicting a ship in full sail, inset with a Victorian photograph of a sailor and his wife.

*23.5in (60cm) wide*

**$4,000-6,000**     **SWO**

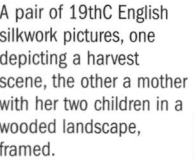

A Charleston woolen needlework, embroidered in silk chenille and wool crewelwork with a basket of flowers and the inscription "Worked by Mary E. Ward at the Academy of the Sisters of Our Lady of Mercy, Charleston SC", worn.

*15.25in (38.5cm) wide*

**$2,800-3,200**     **BRU**

A Chester County Pennsylvania wool on linen pictorial needlework, with the initials "SW" and "HW" over the name "R.Webb 1787".

*9.5in (24cm) high*

**$6,000-9,000**  **POOK**

A late 18thC New England silk-on-linen needlework picture, the reverse inscribed "Bath, Maine".

*13in (33cm) high*

**$6,000-9,000**  **POOK**

A late 18thC New England silk-on-silk needlework picture, of a woman and her dog within a landscape.

*14in (35.5cm) high*

**$800-1,200**  **POOK**

A late 18thC family register needlework, probably worked by Margaret Padelford, first wife of Dr. Philip Padelford, on linen with a landscape, minor imperfections.

*16.75in (42.5cm) high*

**$7,000-10,000**  **SK**

A late 18thC crewel work panel, worked in wool yarn and silk thread, some discolorations and wool losses.

*25in (63.5cm) wide*

**$1,200-1,800**  **FRE**

A silk on linen needlework, wrought by Hannah Hollyman, with potted thistle surrounded by four landscape vignettes with figures, dated.

*1794*  *11.75in (30cm) wide*

**$3,000-5,000**  **POOK**

A needlework picture of a Native American, worked with silk threads, watercolor and gilt metallic threads, églomisé mat, framed.

*c1800*  *10.5in (27cm) high*

**$1,200-1,800**  **FRE**

A Pennsylvania silk on gauze needlework, by Sarah L. Taylor of Westtown School, with "Emblem of Innocence" within half-medallion border, dated.

*1804*  *19.25in (49cm) high*

**$1,200-1,800**  **POOK**

An early 19thC silk needlework memorial, by Eliza B. Padelford in memory of her family, with cascading willow trees over four memorial sarcophagi, background restored and reframed.

*27in (68.5cm) wide*

**$8,000-12,000**  **SK**

An early 19thC family record, for the McEndree family, possibly Pennsylvania or Ohio, with woven hair from each of the 28 family members with various symbols.

*16in (40cm) long*

**$1,800-2,200**     **POOK**

An early 19thC pictorial needlework, attributed to the school of Samuel Folwell, worked with chenille, silk threads, paint, and ink on a silk ground, framed, imperfections.

*20.5in (52cm) wide*

**$1,800-2,200**     **FRE**

A needlework picture by Mary Heister Muhlenberg, worked in silk, chenille, and watercolor on a silk ground, framed, breaks to silk.

*c1820*     *17in (43cm) high*

**$4,000-6,000**     **FRE**

A needlework picture by Emma Matilda Seal, Chester County, Pennsylvania, silk on gauze, inscription "Matilda M. Seal 1828", with weeping willows, and mourning figures at tombs.

*1828*

**$35,000-40,000**     **FRE**

A mid-19thC Pennsylvania silk on silk needlework, with the State Seal of Pennsylvania, inscribed "Virtue Liberty and Independence".

**Provenance**: *Dittmar Collection.*

*28.75in (72cm) wide*

**$2,800-3,200**     **POOK**

An 18thC needlework pocketbook, with crewel embroidery and the initials "Z S", various flowers, the interior lining of glazed wool with two compartments, imperfections.

*c1760*     *7.5in (19cm) wide*

**$12,000-15,000**     **SK**

A rare Chester County, Pennsylvania Florentine stitch pin cushion, dated and initials "SP".

*1763*     *7in (17.5cm) long*

**$18,000-22,000**     **POOK**

A Florentine stick pocket, probably Chester County, Pennsylvania, dated, initials "SI", repaired.

*1761*     *13in (32.5cm) long*

**$4,000-6,000**     **POOK**

**TEXTILES**

A late 18thC crewelwork pocket, from Chester County, Pennsylvania, embroidered in overall trailing vine, initialed "SB".

*15.5in (39cm) long*

$2,800-3,200     **POOK**

An early 19thC painted and embroidered silk globe, Westtown School, Chester County, Pennsylvania, some losses.

$1,800-2,200     **POOK**

A boxed kashmir paisley shawl with advertising pillow, for Sharpless & Sons, Philadelphia, the twill-tapestry woven, pieced and embroidered shawl in wool yarns, box lid with inscriptions "India Camel's Hair Shawl" and "Sharpless & Sons, Philadelphia".

*Townsend Sharpless, a member of the Society of Friends, began a dry good business in Philadelphia in 1814.*

*c1880*

$1,800-2,200     **FRE**

A Grand Army of the Republic Commemorative thirty-eight star flag, "PRESENTED JAN 8 1886 BY MRS. EUNICE B. NORRIS BORN APR 15, 1816," pieced cotton with appliqued and embroidered decoration, symbolic Civil War Corps patches, lettering "GAR/FRATERNITY CHARITY/LOYALTY ALBERT M. PERKINS POST 80".

*56in (142cm) high*

$5,000-8,000     **SK**

## OTHER AMERICAN NEEDLECRAFT

A Boston silk and paint on silk embroidery, attributed to Mrs Rowson's Academy, titled "Landing of Columbus", reverse-painted mat with title and name "Jane Seely".

*This embroidery belongs to a small group of needleworks done after the print "The Landing of Christopher Columbus", engraved by David Edwin (1776-1841), after a painting by Edward Savage published in 1800.*

*c1805*     *24.5in (62cm) high*

$4,000-6,000     **POOK**

An early 19thC oil on velvet memorial theorem, with two women in front of a church flanking a grave, inscribed "Giles Blodget and Bethiah Quick".

*22in (56cm) wide*

$1,200-1,800     **POOK**

A New England silkwork watercolor memorial, inscribed "Sacred to the Memory of Charles McConn who died July 9th 1815 Aged 18 years".

*18in (46cm) wide*

$3,000-5,000     **POOK**

A mid-19thC American watercolor on silk New England townscape, inscribed lower left.

*11in (28cm) wide*

$800-1,200     **POOK**

A mid-19thC silkwork and watercolor mourning picture, "Wrought by Mary Mirick, AE14.", silk threads on a silk ground with watercolor background, imperfections, in a gilt gesso frame.

*19.5in (49.5cm) wide*

$5,000-8,000     **SK**

An 18thC European cut velvet panel, the plum ground decorated with raised embroldered sllk work and silver threads, depicting a stylized tree of life, with exotic flowers, peacocks, and smaller birds.

*101.25in (253cm) long*

**$2,800-3,200** **L&T**

A Pennsylvania cut-work picture, with eagles, horses, and doves within foliate and geometrically patterned borders, backed with painted pale blue, green, and yellow paper, framed.

*This picture is backed with newspaper dated 1859.*

*c1860* *21in (52.5cm) wide*

**$35,000-40,000** **FRE**

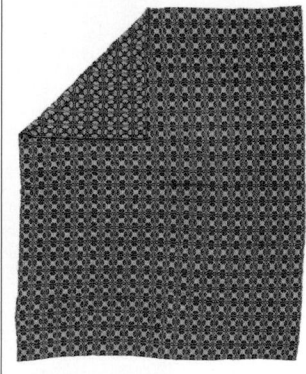

A late 19thC American green overshot coverlet, comprising two hand-sewn panels, with three shades of green wool on cotton.

*The term 'overshot' refers to a method of weaving popular from the late 17thC.*

*98in (249cm) long*

**$280-320** **BRU**

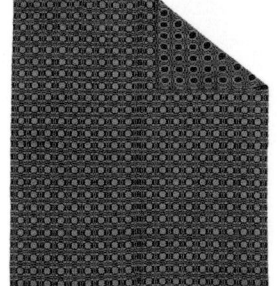

An American four-color overshot coverlet, comprising two panels, with multicolored wool on cotton.

*87in (221cm) long*

**$400-600** **BRU**

An orange paisley coverlet, with tassels.

**$300-400** **DRA**

A multicolored paisley shawl.

**$500-700** **DRA**

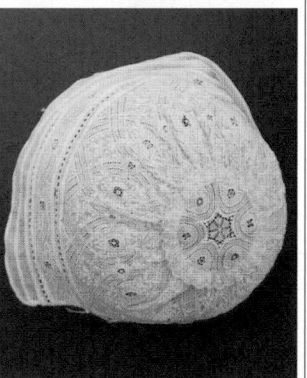

A 19thC baby's white work bonnet, with fine needle lace insert.

**$500-800** **BONM**

A set of three jet and black bead decorative panels.

*longest 14in (35.5cm) long*

**$70-100 each** **PSA**

A Victorian jet and black bead collar.

*18in (45.5cm) high*

**$120-180** **PSA**

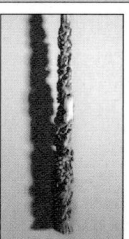

A mid-19thC black lace parasol, with cream silk lining and elaborate ivory handle.

*26in (66cm) high*

**$500-700** **GMC**

A 15thC English dalmatic garment, in red velvet with embroidery in silk and silver gilt thread.

*41in (104cm) long*

**$5,000-7,000** RSS

A formal French ensemble, in embroidered satin with Beauvais needlepoint in silver thread.

*c1780*

**$1,800-2,200** CSB

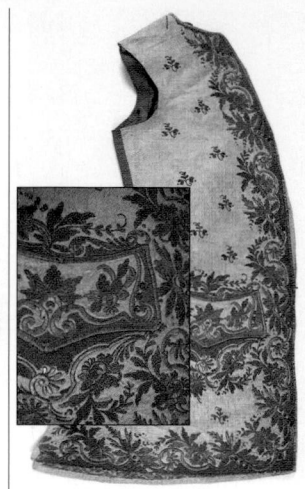

A late 18thC French waistcoat, in embroidered silk.

**$1,200-1,800** CSB

A late 18thC French formal breeches and coat ensemble, in aubergine silk velvet, embroidered with polychrome silk and metal thread, backed with ivory linen.

A late 18thC French green taffeta coat.

**$800-1,200** CSB   **$3,000-4,000** RSS

A late 18thC French waistcoat, in iridescent silk, the collar with large lapels.

*c1790*

**$1,200-1,800** RSS

A French Empire Court suit, comprising breeches and coat, in silk and velvet embroidered with silk and metallic thread, backed with ivory linen.

**$500-700** RSS

## WOMEN'S CLOTHING

An early 18thC French silk and linen jacket and billowing skirt, embroidered with flowers, insects, and birds.

**$3,000-4,000** RSS

An 18thC dress, in iridescent green and pink silk taffeta.

*c1745*

**$6,000-9,000** CSB

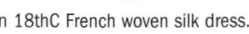

An 18thC French woven silk dress.

**$3,000-4,000** RSS

A French silk taffeta waistcoat and skirt.

c1795

$1,200-1,800    RSS

An early 19thC French silk taffeta dress, with very high waist and long sleeves.

$1,200-1,800    RSS

An 18thC French Regence coat, worn with a dress, in silk woven with taffeta.

$3,000-4,000    RSS

A 19thC French dress, in Gros de Tours heavy tartan silk with a matt finish, on a blue ground.

c1860

$800-1,200    RSS

## OTHER CLOTHING

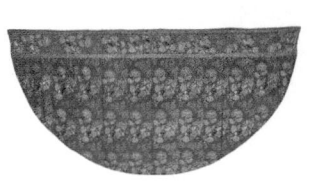

An Italian or French silk cape, with a multicolored pattern on a green ground.

c1735

$8,000-12,000    RSS

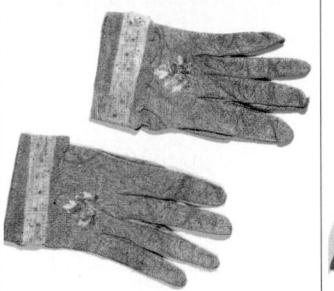

A pair of French Louis XV gloves, of hand stitched leather with silk thread.

c1750

$3,000-4,000    RSS

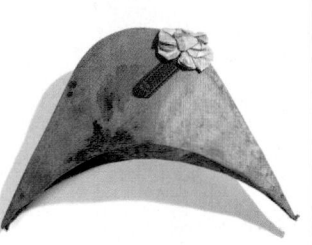

A late 18thC French bicorne hat, with applied satin rose detail.

$700-1,000    RSS

An early 19thC Russian hat, of red velvet embroidered with gold.

$500-700    RSS

An Italian hat, with a wooden hat box.

c1835

$1,800-2,200    CSB

A pair of 19thC gloves, of hand stitched leather with silver thread.

*These gloves were made for Napoleon III, Emperor of France.*

$4,000-6,000    BEA

A late 19thC pair of early tooled leather cowgirl boots, the tall high heeled forms with red leather insets at the ankles and fancy stitching, cracks in leather.

*22in (56cm) high*

**$1,800-2,200**　　　**SK**

An early 20thC pair of leather cowboy cuffs, with stamped and overall brass stud decoration, oval "H.B. Brand" cartouche.

*6.75in (17cm) high*

**$500-800**　　　**SK**

A Western saddle, with slick fork, rounded skirt, and stamped decoration, marked "Texas Tanning Mfg. Co. Yoakum, Texas", silver engraved plate reads "2 Tophand C. M. Rancho Chuck".

*This saddle belonged to Carl Moon, who was famous for photographing Native Americans in their environment.*

*c1935*

**$4,000-6,000**　　　**SK**

A pair of South American gaucho spurs, with multi-spiked rowels, the rowel arms pierced and overlaid with silver, the heel pieces decorated with inlaid silver chevrons and overlay, the rowel washers formed from South American silver coins.

*6in (15cm) diam*

**$220-280**　　　**W&W**

A 17thC French fan, painted in gouache on vellum, with later carved and pierced mother-of-pearl sticks and guards, inlaid with silver and gold, restored.

*9.5in (24cm) long*

**$2,200-2,800**  **RSS**

An 18thC French fan, 'Le commerce du Levant', painted in gouache on cabretille, with painted, varnished, engraved, and carved sticks and guards, restored.

*10.75in (27.5cm) long*

**$5,000-7,000**  **RSS**

An 18thC French fan, painted in gouache with a mythological scene, with carved and pierced mother-of-pearl sticks and guards, inlaid with silver and gold.

*10in (25.5cm) long*

**$3,000-4,000**  **RSS**

An 18thC French fan, painted in gouache on cabretille leaf, with carved and pierced sticks and guards.

*c1765*  *9.5in (24cm) long*

**$3,000-5,000**  **RSS**

An 18thC French fan, painted in gouache on cabretille leaf, with carved and pierced ivory sticks and guards.

*Cabretille a is very fine vellum made from kid leather.*

*10in (25.5cm) long*

**$8,000-12,000**  **RSS**

An 18thC French fan, 'Les mariages dans l'île de Cayenne', painted in gouache on paper, with wooden sticks and guards inlaid with bone.

*10in (25.5cm) long*

**$1,200-1,800**  **RSS**

A French fan, 'Le banquet champêtre', painted in gouache on paper with a pastoral scene, with carved and gilt painted ivory sticks and guards.

*c1780*  *10in (25.5cm) long*

**$1,200-1,800**  **RSS**

A late 18thC French fan, painted in gouache on silk leaf, with ivory and tortoiseshell sticks and guards.

*10.5in (26.5cm) long*

**$1,200-1,800**  **RSS**

A late 18thC French fan, painted in gouache on vellum with three medallions of romantic and pastoral scenes, with carved, pierced, and varnished ivory sticks and guards, inlaid with gilt.

*9.5in (24cm) long*

**$800-1,200**  **RSS**

A French fan, painted in gouache on silk, with pierced ivory sticks and guards inlaid with silver, dated.

*1783*  *10in (25.5cm) long*

**$3,000-4,000**  **RSS**

A late 18thC French fan, the paper leaf decorated with a printed and gouache military scene depicting Lafayette, with wooden sticks and guards.

*10in (25.5cm) long*

**$1,200-1,800**  **RSS**

**TEXTILES**

A French fan, 'La quiétude de la campagne', painted in gouache on vellum, with pierced mother-of-pearl sticks and guards with metal pique.

*c1820*      7in (18cm) long

**$2,800-3,200**      **RSS**

A 19thC French fan, painted in gouache on vellum, with carved, pierced and engraved mother-of-pearl sticks and guards, with a cut crystal scent bottle.

9.75in (25cm) long

**$1,200-1,800**      **RSS**

A 19thC French lace fan, decorated with golden sequins and spangles, with gilt and pierced ivory sticks and guards.

11.75in (30cm) long

**$500-800**      **BO**

A French fan, 'Souvenir of The Paris Exhibition 1867', lithograph on paper by Guilletat, printed by Truillot, with wooden sticks and guards.

*1867*      10in (25.5cm) long

**$400-600**      **RSS**

A 19thC French fan, designed by Alexandre, painted in gouache on silk leaf with a pastoral scene, with ivory sticks and guards, signed "Marius b.d."

10.5in (26.5cm) long

**$500-700**      **RSS**

A late 19thC French fan, painted in gouache on cabretille, with carved and pierced mother-of-pearl sticks and guards, signed "Mok Revers" and "MM".

10.5in (26.5cm) long

**$1,200-1,800**      **RSS**

A French vellum fan, 'Nonchalance', with carved and pierced wooden sticks and guards, signed "Jacques Blanche" and "MM", dated.

*1878*      10in (25.5cm) long

**$3,000-4,000**      **RSS**

A French fan, lithograph on paper after John Lewis Brown, with carved wooden sticks and guards, signed "Buissot" and dated "May 1889", restored.

*1889*      12in (30.5cm) long

**$1,200-1,800**      **RSS**

A late 19thC French fan, painted in gouache on cabretille leaf, with ivory sticks and guards, signed "b.d. Cécile Chennevière" and "A. Rodien Paris", restored.

13in (33cm) long

**$4,000-6,000**      **RSS**

A 19thC French fan, of lace leaf and gouache on paper, with carved and gilt painted ivory sticks and guards.

13in (33cm) long

**$500-700**      **RSS**

A French vellum fan, painted with an Italian palazzo, with carved and pierced bone sticks and guards, dated.

*1898*      6in (15cm) long

**$1,800-2,200**      **RSS**

A French Art Nouveau fan, of silk leaf with gouache and gilt scroll decoration, with pierced and carved mother-of-pearl sticks and guards.

*c1900*      9in (23cm) long

**$300-500**      **RSS**

A microbeaded purse, with a floral design.

*c1910*                           *8in (20.5cm) high*

**$500-700**                                    **AHL**

A 1920s beaded purse, with a multicolored organic design, triangular beaded fringing and circular base, fauxtortoise Lucite clasp and Lucite chain strap.

*7.5in (19cm) wide*

**$500-700**                                    **AHL**

An Art Deco beaded evening purse, in cream.

*c1920*                           *6in (15cm) wide*

**$50-80**                                      **TDG**

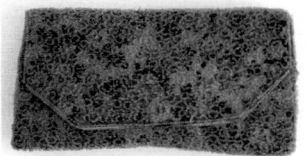

A 1930s French hand-beaded evening purse, with clear beadwork over floral satin, lined with ivory satin, marked "Made in France, Hand made".

*7.35in (18.5cm) wide*

**$80-120**                                      **RG**

An Art Deco beaded purse, in cream and white.

*c1925*                          *6.25in (16cm) wide*

**$50-80**                                      **TDG**

A 1930s Belgian woven beadwork purse, with cream silk lining and label reading "HANDMADE IN BELGIUM", metal frame, sprung cover and beadwork handle.

*8.5in (21.5cm) high*

**$180-220**                                     **PC**

A 1930s beadwork purse, in gold, cream, and white, with a sprung top lip and white beadwork handle.

*8in (20.5cm) wide*

**$120-180**                                     **PC**

A 1930s beadwork purse, with curling thread motif, circular catch and cream fabric lining, woven label reading "Bags by Josef HAND BEADED IN FRANCE".

*9.25in (23.5cm) wide*

**$180-220**                                     **BY**

A 1930s black beadwork purse, with a woven basketwork pattern, on a gilt metal frame with inlaid bands of tiny rhinestones, beadwork handle, the interior lined with black silk.

*6.75in (22cm) wide*

**$280-320**                                     **BY**

A 1940s black satin and hand-embroidered evening purse, with a beaded and enamel frame, yellow satin lining and a satin handle, unmarked, probably French.

*11.75in (30cm) wide*

**$300-400**                                     **RG**

A 1940s Fre-Mor hexagonal beaded box purse, with relief metal surround and five internal compartments.

*7in (18cm) high*

**$280-320**                                     **FAN**

A 1950s beaded evening purse, the flamingo with gem detail to its tail, satin interior and chain handle.

*12in (30cm) wide*

**$280-320**      **AHL**

A 1950s beadwork purse, with gilt metal frame, cream silk lining and swinging circular catch.

*9in (23cm) wide*

**$180-220**      **ROX**

A 1940s copper-colored beaded clutch purse, with an etched clasp and frame.

*7in (18cm) wide*

**$280-320**      **AHL**

A 1950s French beaded purse, made for the US market, with a beaded frame and clasp, lined with ivory satin, marked "Davids Fifth Avenue".

*8.25in (21cm) wide*

**$120-180**      **RG**

A 1950s French beaded evening purse, with beaded frame and clasp, gilt chain handle, lined with ivory satin, marked "Made in France".

*7.5in (19cm) wide*

**$120-180**      **RG**

## A CLOSER LOOK AT A BEADED TAPESTRY PURSE

Beaded purses were hugely popular in the 1920s, and were revived in the 1950s. The shape of the purse has been updated to suit 1950s fashions.

Following the end of WWII, clothing and accessories once again became more heavily ornamented and colorful. The design on the purse is finely realized and appeals today.

Based in New York, Austrian-born Nettie Rosenstein was an influential designer between the 1930s and 1960s. The value of this purse is increased by the known maker, as well as the high quality.

The purse is made from thick tapestry fabric. Glass beads have been carefully embroidered onto the cloth to highlight the woven design.

A 1950s tapestry purse, by Nettie Rosenstein, New York, with applied glass beads and satin lining, made in Florence, Italy, minor bead loss.

*9.5in (24cm) wide*

**$1,200-1,800**      **MGL**

A Jolles Original purse, applied with beading, leaves, and a bunch of large plastic cherries, pink felt interior.

*12.5in (32cm) high*

**$180-220**      **FAN**

A hand-beaded purse, by Veldore of Texas, with a country scene.

*11in (28cm) wide*

**$80-120**      **FAN**

A Belgian beaded purse, in white silk, overlaid with faceted iridescent glass and rope beads, gilt metal frame, acorn shaped clasps and cream silk lining, fabric label "MADE IN BELGIUM".

*7.75in (19.5cm) wide*

**$80-120**      **BY**

A beaded purse, with black and cut steel beads.

*6in (15cm) wide*

**$300-500**      **AHL**

An Art Deco embroidered purse, in the style of Sonia Delaunay.

*c1925*                              *15.75in (40cm) high*

**$500-700**                                        **MOD**

A black silk evening purse, with a bakelite clasp.

*c1930*              *8in (20.5cm) high*

**$180-220**                        **TDG**

A French satin purse, custom made, with double self handles.

*c1950*              *9.5in (24cm) wide*

**$500-700**                        **GOL**

A 1960s carpet purse, in the style of Pucci.

*12in (30.5cm) wide*

**$80-120**                        **CHA**

A mid-1970s Jeanesse white ostrich purse, with shoulder strap of cut steel, lined in gold leather.

*7.5in (19cm) wide*

**$500-700**                        **GOL**

A 1980s Diane Love 'Envelope' purse.

*12in (30.5cm) wide*

**$300-500**                        **GOL**

A 1930s Argentine brown crocodile purse, marked "Industria Argentina".

*11.75in (30cm) wide*

**$180-220**                        **RG**

A 1930s alligator purse with brass hardware.

*12in (30.5cm) wide*

**$280-320**                        **AHL**

A 1930s French lizard purse, with enameled and cut steel silver frame.

*8.5in (21cm) wide*

**$1,200-1,800**                        **GOL**

An Art Deco-style small suedette purse, with integral geometric pattern, brass clasp and fabric handle.

*c1940*              *6.75in (17cm) wide*

**$280-320**                        **AHL**

A British Art Deco leather purse, with a stitched geometric design, silver frame, with integral leather purse fixed to frame.

*c1930*              *7in (18cm) wide*

**$500-700**                        **AHL**

**TEXTILES**

A 1940s Brazilian Aveda ponyskin purse, with lanyard hand-stitched detail, and a clear Lucite and brass clasp.

*12.5in (31.5cm) wide*

**$300-500**  AHL

A 1940s Gucci black lizard clutch purse.

*7.5in (19cm) wide*

**$500-700**  GOL

A 1950s lizard purse.

*11.5in (29cm) wide*

**$280-320**  AHL

A rare 1950s calfskin purse, by Holzman, US, Lucite clasp and Lucite circle handles.

*c1950*  *11.25in (28.5cm) wide*

**$300-500**  MGL

An early 1960s Gucci leather purse, with woven effect.

*9.5in (24cm) wide*

**$120-180**  CHA

A 1960s ponyskin purse.

*11in (28cm) wide*

**$180-220**  AHL

A 1960s calfskin purse, by De Leon, US, of elongated circular design with satin lining.

*20in (51cm) wide*

**$300-500**  MGL

A 1960s Hermes 'Kelly' calfskin box purse, with lock, keys, and clochette.

*11.25in (28.5cm) wide*

**$1,800-2,200**  MGL

A 1970s red calfskin clutch purse, with a Gucci shoulder strap.

*10.5in (26.5cm) wide*

**$180-220**  MGL

A 1960s Hermes leather purse, known as the 'piano purse'.

*10in (25.5cm) wide*

**$1,800-2,200**  MGL

A 1950s Llewellyn gray shell Lucite purse, in a a rare shape, with gray handles.

*9in (23cm) wide*

**$700-1,000**     **DJI**

A 1950s Wilardy black Lucite travel purse, with handpainted decoration.

*11in (28cm) wide*

**$500-800**     **DJI**

A 1950s Wilardy pearl gray Lucite purse, of 'beanpot' design, with rhinestones.

*5in (13cm) wide*

**$600-900**     **DJI**

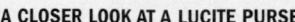

## A CLOSER LOOK AT A LUCITE PURSE

*Plastic box purses were very popular in the 1950s and come in a wide range of shapes and styles. Additional decorative features, such as the clear top, add value.*

*This wedding purse has a clear plastic top that can be filled with brightly colored flowers to compliment an outfit. Other popular 1950s purses had clear sides that could be lined with colored fabrics of the owner's choice.*

*Check that plastic box purses have not started to decay. Look out for warping and damage as they will affect value.*

A 1950s Rialto Lucite purse, with a clear top and hand-carved decoration.

*6.5in (16.5cm) wide*

**$300-500**     **DJI**

An early 1950s Myles Original Lucite purse, in caramel and striated butterscotch, with clear plastic hand-carved rose and leaf decoration.

*8.25in (21cm) wide*

**$700-1,000**     **DJI**

A 1950s Lucite purse, with a caramel waffle-carved body and apple juice colored top.

*4.5in (11.5cm) wide*

**$300-500**     **DJI**

A 1950s Lucite wedding purse, unsigned, with a clear lid for removable flowers or other decoration.

*7.5in (19cm) wide*

**$500-700**     **DJI**

A 1950s Llewellyn Lucite purse, the gray circular panel with a tapestry of pearls and rhinestones.

*9in (23cm) wide*

**$500-800**     **DJI**

A 1950s Tyrolean Lucite purse, basket-shaped, with gold decoration.

*8in (20.5cm) wide*

**$300-500**     **DJI**

A 1950s Rialto bone-color pearl Lucite purse, with an amber and aurora rhinestone disc.

*7in (18cm) wide*

**$1,200-1,800**     **DJI**

A late 1950s Wilardy black Lucite purse, with aurora rhinestones to the base of handle and clasp.

*10in (25.5cm) wide*

**$600-900**     **DJI**

A French cut-steel beaded purse, with rose decoration.

*c1910*                    *8in (20.5cm) high*

**$300-500**                           **AHL**

A 1930s evening compact purse, with a fitted interior and strap.

*The fitted interior adds to the value of this stylish compact purse.*

*5in (13cm) wide*

**$180-220**                           **TDG**

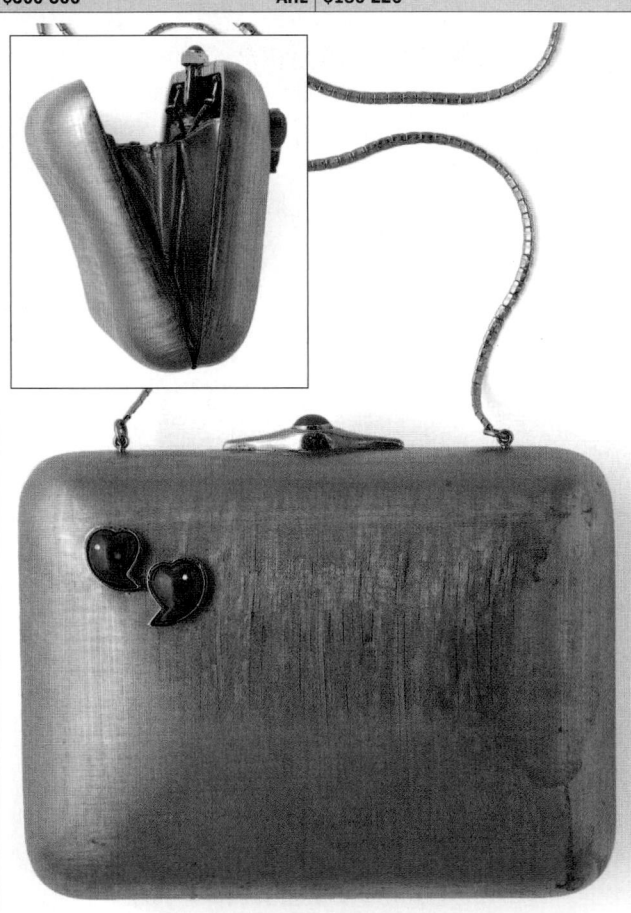

A 1970s Judith Leiber purse, in brushed gold over metal, with coral accents and diamonds, the clasp with coral top, strap inside, the back with a concave shape to follow the line of the hand.

*7.5in (19cm) wide*

**$1,200-1,800**                       **GOL**

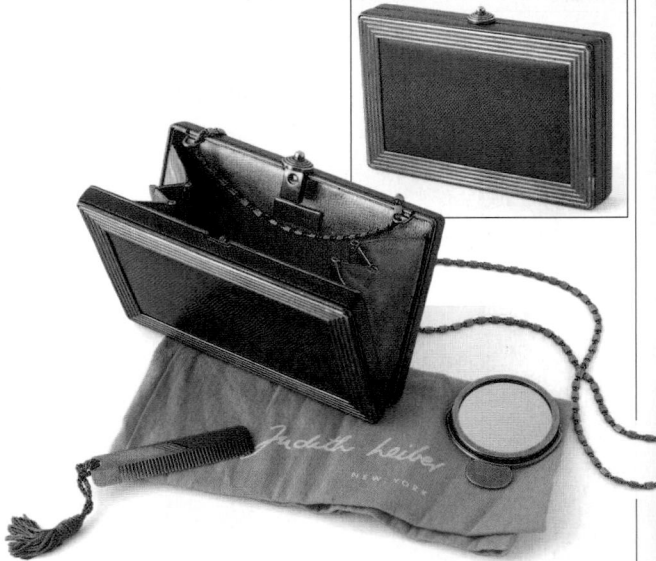

A 1970s Karung box purse by Judith Leiber, with sleeper bag, mirror and tassel comb.

*6.75in (17cm) wide*

**$300-500**                           **MGL**

A purse, by Holzman, US, design probably in silkscreen on leather, the wrapped frame with piped edges and silk lining, with signature "Holzman", ball clasp.

c1960          8in (20.5cm) wide

**$300-500**                    **MGL**

A 1960s US telephone purse, in black patent leather.

10in (25cm) wide

**$600-900**                    **AHL**

**A CLOSER LOOK AT A NOVELTY PURSE**

Novelty purses are popular with collectors, especially animal examples like this poodle.

It is rare to find a purse like this in such good condition as the beadwork is vulnerable to breakage and loss.

Poodles were a fashionable 1950s motif as they symbolized glamor and sophistication. Today they appear rather kitsch, but continue to have great appeal.

A 1950s black poodle beaded purse, by Walborg, Belgium.

8in (20.5cm) wide

**$1,800-2,200**          **DJI**

A 1970s red plastic telephone purse, by Dallas Handbags, with a working telephone.

9.75in (25cm) wide

**$300-500**                    **DJI**

A 1960s unusual wooden box purse, in a satchel style, with brass handles and fittings, probably French.

5.5in (14cm) wide

**$300-500**                    **GOL**

A Paco Rabanne purple metal purse, branding applied to metal.

c1990          9in (23cm) wide

**$1,200-1,800**          **MGL**

**TOYS, DOLLS & MODELS**

## THE TOYS, DOLLS & MODELS MARKET

Whilst the market for some antiques has been fairly subdued in the last year, the toy market has been extremely buoyant. The reasons for this are diverse: as well as being a fun collecting area and having great nostalgic appeal to a wide range of buyers, toys have the potential to rise in value in the future, making them an alternative investment to stocks and shares. Toys are also particularly appealing to collectors who are focused on completing sets, as many were produced in numbered series.

Television and film related toys of all kinds are currently very desirable, and this trend seems likely to continue as cult figures, such as James Bond and Batman, are continually re-invented and introduced to new audiences. Diecast toys in mint condition are also performing well, especially examples by the well-known makers Dinky and Hotwheels. Condition is increasingly essential.

Tinplate continues to be desirable and early and clockwork pieces can command huge prices. The market for later Japanese tinplate remains strong, particularly for space related toys. Collectors are also increasingly expressing interest in Chinese tinplate toys, although prices are generally yet to reach the levels of Japanese toys.

Teddy bears and dolls, especially examples by well-known English and German makers, such as Steiff, Merrythought, and Simon and Halbig, are continuing to fetch high prices.

Model railways are almost always popular, although interest tends to tail-off to some extent during the summer months.

Cast iron money banks are becoming more and more desirable. Unusual shapes and pieces in mint condition are particularly sought after by collectors.

An early 18thC wax carved creche doll, with painted features, wearing a full-length dress and underwear, inscribed in French, hands and legs missing.

*11in (28cm) high*

**$120-180** | **GORL**

A mid-Victorian poured wax shoulder doll, possibly Montanari, with inset blue glass paperweight eyes, inserted hair, cloth body with wax lower limbs, clothed.

*c1860* | *20.5in (52cm) high*

**$300-500** | **GORL**

A Victorian wax doll, dressed as a Christmas fairy in a silk layered dress, displayed under a glass dome.

*17in (43cm) high*

**$280-320** | **ROS**

A poured wax Lucy Peck-type fashion doll, with rare sleep eyes.

*c1880* | *17in (43cm) high*

**$1,200-1,800** | **BEJ**

## COMPOSITION DOLLS

A Biedermeier shoulder head doll, with a waxed papier-mâché shoulder head and fixed blue glass eyes, fabric body, blonde mohair wig and painted yellow boots, damage.

*20.75in (52cm) high*

**$280-320** | **WDL**

A very rare Biedermeier doll, with waxed papier-mâché shoulder head on a horn shaft, painted blue eyes and black hair, the dress with cardboard stars, remains of a hat.

*10.75in (27cm) high*

**$600-900** | **WDL**

A pair of 19thC wax over composition shoulder dolls, with inserted real hair, inset glass eyes and cloth bodies with leather forearms.

*largest 25.5in (65cm) high*

**$500-700** | **GORL**

A large wax over composition shoulder doll, with fixed glass paperweight eyes, cloth body and painted composition limbs, in a velvet dress.

*c1880* | *38in (96cm) high*

**$280-320** | **GORL**

A tall Dressel wax doll, with fixed brown eyes, an old blonde mohair wig, papier-mâché limbs and a fabric body, in a faded train dress with an old brooch, stamped mark.

*26in (65cm) high*

**$800-1,200** | **WDL**

A wax composition old crone doll, with a mask-like face and stick legs, carrying a child by the hand.

*16.5in (42cm) high*

**$700-1,000** | **GORL**

A Jumeau bisque character doll, dressed as a nun with a pendant rosary, fixed glass eyes, open mouth, and pierced ears, on a jointed wood and composition body, wearing original leather shoes.

*19in (48cm) high*

**$1,800-2,200**                                    **GORL**

A Jumeau bisque doll, with fixed glass eyes, open mouth and a jointed composition body with voice box, label attached to lower back "Bebe Jumeau, Diplome d'Honneur".

*26in (66cm) high*

**$1,200-1,800**                                    **GORL**

A Jumeau bisque 'closed mouth' character doll, with fixed blue glass paperweight eyes, pierced ears and a jointed wood and composition body, printed mark in red "Tete Jumeau 8".

*c1885*                                    *22in (56cm) high*

**$1,800-2,200**                                    **GORL**

A French Jumeau bébé, in original woolen dress.

*c1880*                                    *16in (40.5cm) high*

**$6,000-9,000**                                    **BEJ**

385

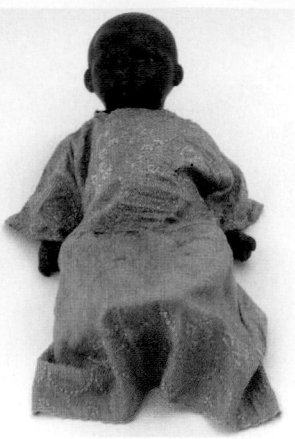

An Armand Marseille 'My Dream Baby' baby doll, mold 341, with closed mouth, sleep eyes, and a jointed composition body.

*16in (41cm) high*

**$220-280**      **GORL**

An Armand Marseille bisque 'My Dream Baby' doll, mold 351, with sleep eyes, an open mouth with two teeth and a jointed composition bent-limb body, chipping.

*16in (40.5cm) high*

**$220-280**      **W&W**

An Armand Marseille bisque 'My Dream Baby' doll, mold 351, with sleep eyes, open mouth showing two teeth and a composition body, wearing a long white dress.

*14in (35.5cm) high*

**$220-280**      **W&W**

An Armand Marseille bisque 'My Dream Baby' doll, with weighted blue eyes, open mouth and a five piece curved limb composition body, impressed "A M 351 /3 1 /2 K", dated, firing speck.

*1926*      *14in (36cm) high*

**$220-280**      **VEC**

An Armand Marseille bisque 'My Dream Baby' doll, mold 353, with sleep eyes, closed mouth and a bent-limb composition body, wearing a hand-woven outfit.

*15in (38cm) high*

**$1,200-1,800**      **GORL**

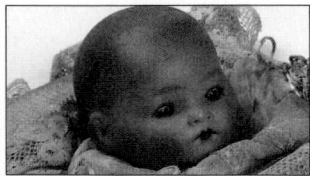

An Armand Marseille 'Puppet Dream Baby', in original bedding.

*c1920*      *doll 10in (25.5cm) high*

**$1,200-1,800**      **BEJ**

A bisque doll, by Armand Marseille, mold 390n, with sleep eyes, open mouth and a jointed wood and composition body, seated within an early 20thC steel push chair.

*26in (66cm) high*

**$700-1,000**      **GORL**

A large Armand Marseille porcelain bisque doll, mold 390, with sleep eyes, open mouth and a jointed composition body, impressed "A 15 M", on an Edwardian mahogany chair.

*31in (79cm) high*

**$500-700**      **GORL**

An Armand Marseille child doll, mold '390', dressed as a goose girl in an apron and plaits.

*c1920*      *19in (48.5cm) high*

**$600-900**      **BEJ**

A late 19thC French bisque fashion doll, with fixed glass eyes, pierced ears, a closed mouth and a kid leather body, in a lace-trimmed dress, some damage.

*13in (33cm) high*

**$700-1,000**     **GORL**

A 19thC French bisque fashion doll, the swivel head with fixed blue glass eyes, closed mouth and pierced ears, on a kid leather body, in a satin and lace dress.

*15in (38cm) high*

**$1,200-1,800**     **GORL**

A French fashion doll, attributed to Madame Huret, with a bisque shoulder head, glass eyes, closed mouth and a kid leather body, dressed as a bride, chemise with "S & S Hibernia" label.

*c1860*     *19in (48cm) high*

**$1,200-1,800**     **GORL**

A French Simonne young lady fashion doll, with rare neck articulation, wearing original clothes with red trim.

*c1870*     *20in (50cm) high*

**$5,000-7,000**     **BEJ**

An early Bru fashion doll, wearing an original outfit with ribbons and bonnet, in display case, the head marked "C".

*c1870*     *14in (35.5cm) high*

**$5,000-7,000**     **BEJ**

A very rare French mignonette with rare peach boots, in original red outfit and bonnet, with box.

*c1880*     *6in (15cm) high*

**$5,000-7,000**     **BEJ**

A late 19thC French bisque fashion doll, with fixed glass eyes, pierced ears, closed mouth and a kid leather body, in a lace-trimmed dress, cracks to neck.

*13in (33cm) high*

**$700-1,000**     **GORL**

## SIMON & HALBIG

A Simon & Halbig character toddler girl doll, with a white dress and shoes.

*c1900*     *20in (51cm) high*

**$1,200-1,800**     **BEJ**

A German bisque shoulder doll, attributed to Simon & Halbig, with fixed glass paperweight eyes and closed mouth, on kid leather body, clothed in blue silk, unmarked.

*18in (46cm) high*

**$500-700**     **GORL**

### A CLOSER LOOK AT A SIMON & HALBIG DOLL

*Most Simon & Halbig dolls are marked. The mark was changed slightly in 1905 – dolls with marks without an ampersand were generally produced prior to 1905.*

*Simon & Halbig, established in Thuringia in Germany in 1839, began producing dolls in the early 1870s. This makes this c1880 doll a fairly early example.*

*Dolls made by Simon & Halbig before the 20thC tend to have open mouths, while the mouths on later examples are usually closed.*

*Collectors look for all original dolls, especially attractive examples in outstanding condition.*

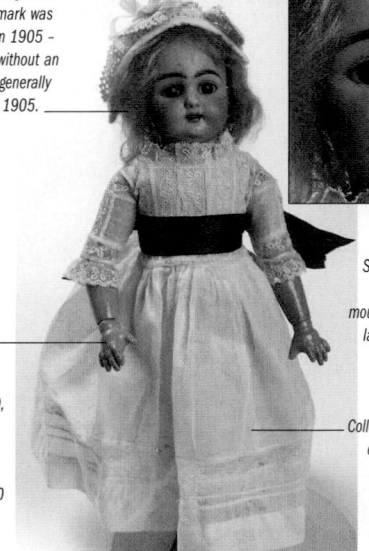

A Simon & Halbig all original child doll, in a white dress.

*c1880*     *17in (43cm) high*

**$1,200-1,800**     **BEJ**

A Simon & Halbig bisque-headed doll, model number 126.

**$300-500**     **JN**

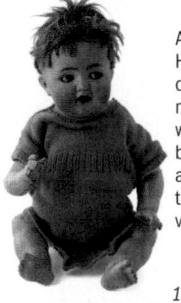

A Simon & Halbig character doll, model number 126, with composition body, flirty eyes and tremble tongue, inactive voice box.

*18in (46cm) high*

**$300-500**     **ROS**

**TOYS, DOLLS & MODELS**

A 19thC bisque shoulder doll, with molded hair, blue eyes, fabric body and bisque limbs, in original outfit.

13.5in (34cm) high

$500-700          ROS

A Parian sailor boy shoulder doll, with molded hair and painted features, cloth body and bisque arms and legs.

c1870          12in (31cm) high

$220-280          GORL

A Parian shoulder doll, with molded hair and painted features, above a cloth body and bisque arms and legs.

c1870          12in (31cm) high

$700-1,000          GORL

A Parian shoulder doll, with molded hair and painted features, cloth body and bisque arms and legs, in a green satin dress and carrying a violin.

c1870          12in (31cm) high

$700-1,000          GORL

A Parian 'Annie' shoulder doll, with molded hair and painted features, wearing a white dress and a pink hat, unmarked.

c1895          12in (31cm) high

$700-1,000          GORL

## OTHER DOLLS

An Altbeck & Gottschalk 'Sweet Nell' character doll.

c1890          25in (63.5cm) high

$1,200-1,800          BEJ

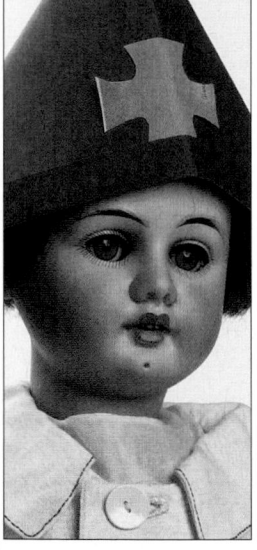

An A. M. of Austria character boy, with a hat and sword.

c1890          25in (63.5cm) high

$1,800-2,200          BEJ

A rare French Belton child, with a box and extra clothes.

c1880          13in (33cm) high

$3,000-4,000          BEJ

A German double-ended doll, possibly by Karl Bergner, with one smiling and one serious face, fixed glass eyes and closed mouths, on kid leather body with bisque forearms, in a velvet suit.

12in (31cm) high

$500-700          GORL

A Chad Valley 'Princess Margaret Rose' doll, with original clothing.

c1930                     17in (43cm) high

**$500-700**                          **BEJ**

An Eden Baby bisque character doll, impressed "no.8, Paris Depose", with fixed glass eyes, open mouth and pierced ears, on a jointed composition body, in a black velvet suit.

c1900                     22in (56cm) high

**$800-1,200**                        **GORL**

## A CLOSER LOOK AT A FRENCH EDEN BÉBÉ

*French Bébés, popular between 1860 and 1900, are among the most sought-after bisque dolls. This is a medium-sized example – Eden Bébés were produced up to 34in (86cm) high and larger examples tend to command more.*

*Eden Bébé is a trade name for the Fleischmann and Bloedel Doll Factory, of Bavaria and France. This doll predates the firm becoming part of the Société Francaise de la Fabrication de Bébés et Jouets (S.F.B.J.) in 1899.*

*Heads are made from bisque and bodies are composition. Eyes are usually paperweight and mouths are slightly open.*

*Minor repairs will not have a great effect on price. Damage to the porcelain however, could reduce value by up to fifty percent.*

A French Eden bébé, wearing a cream suit with velvet trim.

c1885                     16in (40.5cm) high

**$3,000-4,000**                      **BEJ**

An Eden Bébé porcelain bisque doll, with fixed paperweight eyes, open mouth and pierced ears, on a five-piece composition body, in hand-embroidered clothes, impressed size "11".

25in (64cm) high

**$800-1,200**                        **GORL**

An Farnell Alpha Toys Princess Elizabeth cloth doll, with side glancing painted blue eyes, blonde mohair wig and a velveteen jointed body, in an original cotton dress, blue label to foot.

1930                     14in (36cm) high

**$300-500**                          **VEC**

A Max Handwerck bisque headed No. 3 doll, with wood and composition jointed body.

21.75in (55cm) high

**$300-500**                          **ROS**

A Heubach Koppelsdorf child doll, dressed as Alice in Wonderland, wearing a white apron and plaits.

17in (43cm) high

**$800-1,200**                        **BEJ**

A Gebrüder Heubach bisque Piano baby girl, wearing a blue bonnet and pinnafore.

c1910                     8.5in (21.5cm) high

**$300-500**                          **BEJ**

A Kämmer & Reinhardt/Halbig bisque doll, with sleeping eyes, pierced ears, on a jointed composition body, in blue velvet with underwear.

18.5in (37cm) high

**$700-1,000**                        **GORL**

A Kämmer & Reinhardt German girl doll, with a dark wig and wearing a blue dress.

7in (18cm) high

**$300-400**                          **BEJ**

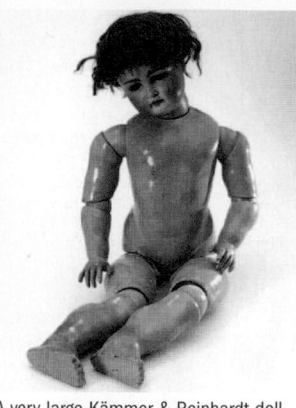

A very large Kämmer & Reinhardt doll, with a bisque head, sleeping eyes, open mouth with teeth, pierced ears and a mohair wig, on a wooden and papier-mâché 15-part body, red mark "192".

c1905          28.75in (72cm) high

**$1,800-2,200**          WDL

A rare Käthe Kruse number 1 doll, the painted head with one seam.

c1910          18in (45cm) high

**$3,000-5,000**          WDL

An early Käthe Kruse type VII boy, 'Kleines Du mein' (My little darling), with a wood wool-stuffed body, stamped "Käthe Kruse 34...4".

c1930          14in (35cm) high

**$3,000-5,000**          WDL

A 1950s Käthe Kruse 'German Child' doll, the plastic head with painted eyes and a real hair wig, on a fabric body.

20.5in (51cm) high

**$1,200-1,800**          WDL

A 1950s Käthe Kruse 'Friedebald' doll, with a plastic head, painted eyes and blonde hair, on a fabric body, later cardigan, stamped "...a.d. Saale".

20.5in (51cm) high

**$1,200-1,800**          WDL

A German Max Oscar Arnold child doll.

c1900          18in (45.5cm) high

**$600-900**          BEJ

A Pintel & Godchaux French bébé.

c1880          17in (43cm) high

**$2,800-3,200**          BEJ

A German Recknagel child, with painted shoes and socks.

13in (33cm) high

**$500-700**          BEJ

A doll with a Schildkröt celluloid head, with an open mouth with teeth, white leather body with wooden arms and original worn silk dress, socks and black wax shoes, marked "Germany SiR Schutz-Marke 12", damaged eyes.

16in (40cm) high

**$80-120**          WDL

A Schoenau and Hoffmeister bisque headed doll, with jointed composition body, marked "1909, 6".

21.75in (55cm) high

**$300-500**          ROS

A S.F.B.J. bisque doll, with brown sleep eyes, open mouth with teeth and a brown mohair wig, on a composition body with national costume, paper tag to wrist, marked "Unis 60", some mottling.

19in (48.5cm) high

**$300-500**          W&W

An S.F.B.J. bisque boy doll, mold 227, with painted hair to the domed head, fixed glass eyes and an open mouth, on clothed composition body.

c1900          21in (53cm) high

**$2,200-2,800**          GORL

A French Steiner 'A' series bébé.

*c1880*        *17in (43cm) high*

**$5,000-7,000**        **BEJ**

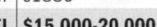

*c1880*

**$15,000-20,000**        **BEJ**

A large French Steiner 'C' series bébé, dressed in layered white clothing and a bonnet.

*30in (76cm) high*

A Jules Steiner bisque doll, with fixed blue glass eyes, closed mouth and a jointed composition body, in a cotton dress with elaborate lacework and bonnet.

*9.5in (24cm) high*

**$3,000-5,000**        **GORL**

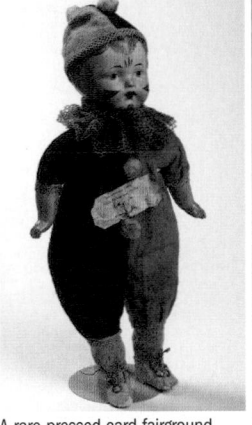

A rare pressed card fairground prize doll, in original clothing.

*c1920*        *18in (45.5cm) high*

**$700-1,000**        **BEJ**

A Japanese brocade and bisque play doll.

*c1920*        *12in (30.5cm) high*

**$280-320**        **BEJ**

A composition baby doll, in a knitted outfit and hat.

*c1930*        *22in (55.75cm) high*

**$400-600**        **BEJ**

## DOLL'S HOUSES & FURNITURE

A large mid-19thC three-story doll's house, with furniture.

*This house was originally built in a closet in the Morris Longstreth Hallowell House in Philadelphia in 1840. In 1917, the house was razed and the interior walls were saved and stored until 1929 when they were placed in the present cabinet and donated to Stenton House museum. The contents, original to the doll's house, include period furniture, cutlery, portraits, and porcelain accessories.*

*79in (197.5cm) high*

**$28,000-35,000**        **POOK**

A British Georgian-style wooden doll's house, the lift-off front revealing four rooms, a wooden staircase, a fitted range and open cast-iron fireplaces, with glazed windows, damaged.

*c1900*        *38in (97cm) high*

**$1,200-1,800**        **VEC**

A Triang Tudor-style doll's house, with half-timbered gables, five rooms, staircase, opening metal-framed windows with imitation shutters, electric wall lights with switches, repainted.

*1938*        *47in (120cm) wide*

**$400-600**        **VEC**

An unusual American Gothic wooden doll's house, with a papered brick finish, a tinplate spiral staircase and extensive fittings, with spare panes of glass and Pollock's wallpaper, damage.

*c1920*        *42in (107cm) high*

**$1,800-2,200**        **VEC**

A Noah's Ark with elaborate decoration and hinged roof with two birds, 74 animals, four insects, and five people.

*21.75in (54cm) wide*

**$2,200-2,800**    **POOK**

A Noah's Ark with polychrome decoration and 39 animals.

*20in (50cm) wide*

**$1,800-2,200**    **POOK**

A French musical 'L'Ecole' schoolroom automaton, with a clockwork mechanism, possibly Jumeau.

*c1900*    *17in (43cm) wide*

**$2,200-2,800**    **GORL**

A miniature Landau carriage.

*c1880*    *24in (61cm) wide*

**$2,800-3,200**    **BEJ**

A Lines Bros. child's cart with original paintwork.

*c1890*    *36in (91.5cm) wide*

**$700-1,000**    **BEJ**

## TEDDY BEARS

- The first teddy bears are attributed to German seamstress Margarete Steiff (b1847), who started producing toys in 1884.
- The first Steiff bear appeared at the 1903 Leipzig fair. An American visitor ordered three thousand, knowing that, after President Roosevelt well-publicized refusal to shoot a bearcub, American children would love the new 'Teddy bear'.
- Steiff bears are the most sought after teddy bears. Pre-1930s bears have humped backs and long arms. Glass eyes replaced boot buttons after WWI, and following WWII, artificial and wool plush was used. White and cinnamon coloring are rare.
- American teddy bear companies faced stiff competition from all the teddy bears imported from Germany, and many of the U.S. companies did not last long.
- Bears by Dean's, Farnell and Schuco are also collectible, as are Pre-WWII bears by other makers.
- An attractive faces tends to command a premium.
- Condition is crucial to value, especially on more recent bears.

A Chad Valley golden mohair teddy bear, with vertically stitched black nose and shaven muzzle, fully jointed, with black claw stitching and cloth pads, replacement eyes, inoperative growler, damage and wear.

*c1920*    *17in (43cm) high*

**$280-320**    **VEC**

A pre-WWII English teddy bear, probably Chad Valley, with gold mohair plush and wood-wool filling, glass eyes, stitched snout and jointed limbs some wear.

*Wood-wool stuffing indicates an early teddy bear.*

*43.5in (110cm) high*

**$300-500**    **GORL**

An early post-WWII Chad Valley teddy bear, with gold plush, glass eyes and a stitched snout, the jointed body with brown velour pads, maker's label to foot.

*27in (69cm) high*

**$500-700**    **GORL**

A 1920s to 1930s Chiltern golden mohair teddy bear, with clear glass eyes and vertically stitched nose, fully jointed, with black claw stitching and cloth pads, growler inoperative, wear.

*16in (41cm) high*

**$280-320**    **VEC**

A Chiltern pink mohair and wool teddy bear, with vertically stitched nose, fully jointed, remains of black claw stitching and velveteen pads, replacement glass eyes, inoperative squeaker, some wear.

*c1930*    *14in (35cm) high*

**$220-280**    **VEC**

A pink mohair Chiltern 'Hugmee' teddy bear, with a vertically restitched nose with longer upward stitches, fully jointed, replacement glass eyes, repairs, damage.

*c1930*            20in (51cm) high

**$300-400**                        **VEC**

An English cinnamon plush mohair teddy bear, with plastic eyes, a stitched snout, growler and jointed limbs, labelled "Le Fray".

*c1950*            31in (78cm) high

**$220-280**                        **GORL**

A Merrythought blonde mohair teddy bear, with amber and black glass eyes and vertically stitched black nose with long downward stitches, fully jointed, squeaker, missing label, some wear.

*c1930*            19in (48cm) high

**$120-180**                        **VEC**

A large blonde mohair Steiff teddy bear, with extensive restoration and replacements, with notes and photographs relating to the restoration process, stains.

*c1910*            22in (56cm) high

**$800-1,200**                        **VEC**

A Steiff limited edition Alfonzo red mohair teddy bear, number 440 from an edition of 5000, white tag "406195", for Teddy Bears of Whitney, box and certificate.

14in (35cm) high

**$800-1,200**                        **VEC**

An English golden mohair teddy bear, with glass eyes and jointed limbs, wear.

28in (71cm) high

**$400-600**                        **GORL**

## A CLOSER LOOK AT A MERRYTHOUGHT TEDDY BEAR

*Colored bears, made by a variety of manufacturers, were popular throughout the 1930s. Look for examples that have retained their bright colors.*

*Merrythought bears were made with metal ear buttons as well as white labels until WWII.*

*This bear has retained the white label, which is often missing.*

*The claw stitching is webbed. This feature was brought to Merrythought c1930 by Director A.C. Janisch, who had previously worked for J.K. Farnell.*

A Merrythought red artificial silk plush teddy bear, with a shaven muzzle, fully jointed, with a metal button and white embroidered label to foot, replacement plastic eyes, wear.

*Although Merrythought was known for making colored bears, red is hard to come by.*

*c1935*            17in (43cm) high

**$500-700**                        **VEC**

A golden mohair American teddy bear, with black boot button eyes and horizontally stitched black nose, fully jointed, black claw stitching and felt pads, inoperative growler, wear.

*c1920*            11.5in (29cm) high

**$280-320**                        **VEC**

An American blonde mohair teddy bear, with boot button eyes and horizontally stitched black nose, fully jointed, remains of black claw stitching, in a tailor-made tweed suit, wear and repairs.

*c1920*            14in (36cm) high

**$300-500**                        **VEC**

A British curly blonde mohair teddy bear, with pronounced hump and remains of horizontally stitched black nose, fully jointed, replacement eyes and repairs.

*c1920*            16in (40cm) high

**$300-500**                        **VEC**

A British golden mohair teddy bear, with black boot button eyes, fully jointed, restoration and losses to mohair.

*c1910*            13in (33cm) high

**$300-500**                        **VEC**

A large golden blonde teddy bear, stuffed with wood wool, with long arms, brown glass eyes and a black stitched nose.

*c1920*            24in (60cm) high

**$400-600**                        **WDL**

A rare French curly plush teddy bear, with a red ribbon, probably Jopi or Helvetica.

*c1920*                        **BEJ**

**$1,200-1,800**

A British Farnell golden mohair teddy bear, with glass eyes and a small hump, growler inoperative, repairs, with photographs of owner and a tinplate box.

*1930*            19in (48cm) high

**$700-1,000**                        **VEC**

A Merrythought mohair plush monkey, with a cloth face, paws and feet, jointed.

*22in (56cm) high*

$280-320     **GORL**

A good Roullet et Descamps 'Springing' lion, with glass eyes, a fur mane and beard, whiskers and a skin covered body and tail, the mechanism partly inoperative.

*This lion is classed as an automaton, it winds up and 'jumps' forward. The body and legs are rigid.*

*17in (43cm) wide*

$1,200-1,800     **ROS**

A Schuco 'Biego Bello' plush crow, with original label, slightly dirty.

*10in (25cm) high*

$80-120     **LAN**

A Steiff soft toy terrier, with glass eyes, a squeak and spotted white mohair plush.

*16in (40.5cm) wide*

$220-280     **GORL**

A Steiff curly plush lamb.

*c1950*     *16in (40.5cm) high*

$700-1,000     **BEJ**

A British black mohair Felix the Cat, with boot button eyes, black painted metal nose, embroidered mouth simulating teeth and an internal wire frame, inoperative squeaker, wear, restitched.

*c1920*     *9in (23cm) high*

$80-120     **VEC**

## DINKY TOYS

A Dinky No.504 second cab Foden 'Mobilgas' tanker, with a red body, filler caps and supertoy hubs, in a dark blue box with an orange and white label.

$700-1,000     **VEC**

A Dinky No.982 Bedford Pullmore car transporter, with large baseplate print and model number to base, in a blue striped box, card packing and No.994 ramp.

$400-600     **VEC**

### A CLOSER LOOK AT A DINKY TRUCK

This No.935 Leyland flatbed truck with chains was produced by Dinky between 1964 and 1966.

The blue version of this truck is rare and can be worth up to twice as much the green.

Scratches, bruises, and damage can reduce value significantly, particularly on post-WWII models.

Correct boxes in excellent condition increase the value of Dinky vehicles.

A Dinky No.935 Leyland Octopus flat truck, with chains, in a rare colorway, dark blue cab and chassis, primrose yellow cab band and bumper, silver radiator grille, in a yellow box with a detailed picture panel.

$7,000-10,000     **VEC**

A Dinky No.31c trade box of six 'Chivers Jellies' Trojan vans, all dark green with mid-green ridged wheels, in a repaired trade box with repro dividers.

*Before c1953 most Dinky toys were sold from retailers packs like this, and were not individually boxed.*

$1,200-1,800     **VEC**

A Dinky No.23f trade box of six Alfa Romeo racing cars, five with No.23f baseplate, and one with No.232 baseplate, trade box with repro dividers.

$700-1,000     **VEC**

A rare Dinky No.141 Vauxhall Victor estate car, a promotional issue with "Lightning Fastners Ltd Technical Service", in maroon, with a blue interior, paper labels, sun-faded.

*The colorway and transfers are rare and appeared as part of a US promotion.*

A Dinky No.140a Trade Box of six Austin Atlantic convertibles, two pink and four light blue, in a yellow trade box complete with original dividers.

$700-1,000 VEC

A rare Dinky Set No.3 Private Automobiles, with No.30d Vauxhall Saloon, No.36b Bentley Coupe, No.36d Rover Streamlined Saloon, No.38a Fraser Nash, No.38c Lagonda, boxed.

$4,000-6,000     **VEC**

$1,200-1,800     **VEC**

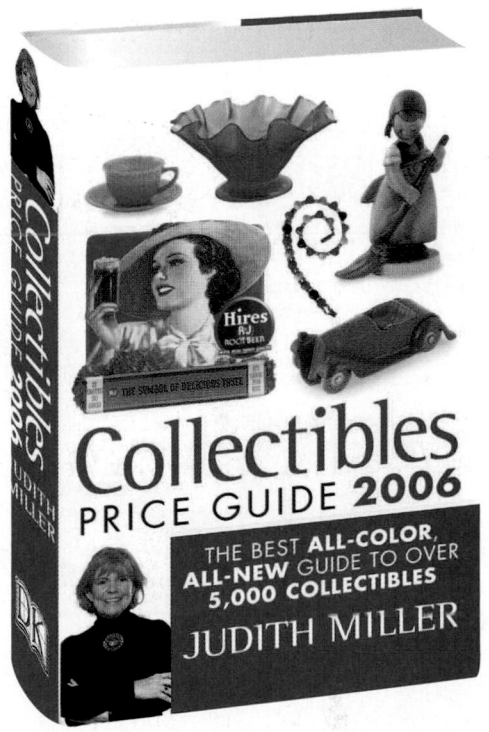

A Corgi 'Mister Softee' Smiths Karrier van, with spun hubs, in a blue and yellow card box.

**$700–1,000** VEC

A Corgi No.471 'Joe's Diner' Smiths Karrier mobile canteen, with spun hubs, in a blue and yellow carded box.

**$400–600** VEC

A Corgi No.413 'Family Butchers' Smiths Karrier Bantam Mobile Shop, with flat spun hubs, in a blue box with a folded leaflet.

**$700–1,000** VEC

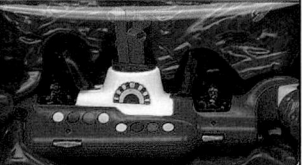

A Corgi No.803 'The Beatles' Yellow Submarine, in yellow with a red front and rear hatches, in an inner plastic stand and picture window box.

**$700–1,000** VEC

A Corgi No.207m Standard Vanguard, in yellow with flat spun hubs, in a blue box with a color folded leaflet.

**$500–700** VEC

## A CLOSER LOOK AT A CORGI MONKEEMOBILE CAR

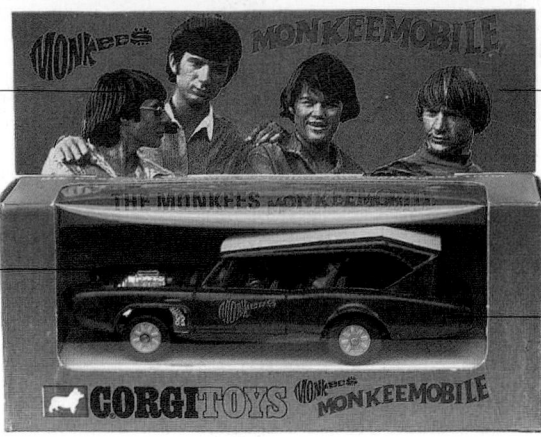

Corgi made the 'Monkeemobile' between 1968 and 1972, at the height of the TV pop group's popularity.

This car was also sold in a box without a header card. The version with the card tends to command a premium.

The theme of the car appeals to fans of cult TV and retro collectors as well as Dinky enthusiasts. This increases its desirability and value.

The car featured figures of Mike, Mickey, Davey, and Pete. During the 1960s Corgi were known for producing especially detailed models.

A Corgi No.277 The Monkees 'Monkeemobile' car, with a red body, white roof and blue and yellow windows, cast hubs, the box with a colorful detachable header card.

**$1,800–2,200** VEC

A Corgi No.422 'Corgi Toys' Bedford van, with flat spun hubs, in a blue and yellow box with a folded leaflet.

**$1,200–1,800** VEC

A Corgi No.803 'The Beatles' Yellow Submarine, in yellow with a red front and rear hatches, in an inner plastic stand and picture window box.

A Corgi No.GS31 'Riviera' gift set, with a Buick in pale blue, with a red interior and wire wheels, a boat on a trailer, and a figure and Skier on skis, pictorial stand, packing, box and instruction sheet.

**$700–1,000** VEC

A Corgi No.1109 Bristol Bloodhound guided missile, on a loading trolley, with an inner carded tray and blue and yellow lift-off lid box, complete with correct 'Rocket Age' folded leaflet.

**$500–700** VEC

A Corgi No.303s Mercedes Benz 300SL Open Roadster, in blue with a yellow interior, figure, spun hubs and racing number "7", in inner packing ring and blue and yellow box.

**$400–600** VEC

A Corgi No.300 Austin Healey sports car, in cream with red seats and flat spun hubs, in blue box with color folded leaflet.

**$800–1,200** VEC

## SCHUCO

- German factories led the toy market for much of the 19thC and early 20thC, and Schuco was one of the country's most influential firms.
- The company was established as Schreyer & Co. in 1912 by Heinrich Schreyer and Heinrich Müller, who had worked at Bing.
- Despite mass-producing toys for a wide range of markets, Schuco is known for the relative high quality of its products.
- Vehicles, such as cars, fire engines, and lorries, tended to be highly detailed and were sold with accessories. Boxes were well-made with fitted compartments.
- Look out for the prewar gear-operated open Mercedes, the rare 'Turn-About Motor Car' of 1935, the 'Radio-Auto' and Sir Malcolm Campbell's 'Bluebird'.
- Vehicles were marked on the base plate. Examples produced between 1945 and 1952 read "Made in the US zone Germany", while later models are marked "Made in Germany".
- The company is still in production today.

A Schuco tinplate No.5306 Elektro-Fernlenk truck, based on the MAN Diesel open lorry, with a red cab, dropdown rear tailgate and electric operation, in an illustrated box, wear.

*13.75in (35cm) wide*

**$500-700**     **VEC**

A Schuco tinplate No.6084 Elektro Lastomat truck, based on the MAN Diesel open lorry, in various shades of red, with a black chassis and electrically operated loading ramp, wear, missing parts.

*14.25in (36cm) wide*

**$280-320**     **VEC**

A Schuco tinplate No.6080 fire engine presentation set, with a turntable ladder and a long bonnet, two firemen figures in cab, steering control, battery compartment, in box with a card base, parts missing.

*11.75in (30cm) wide*

**$1,200-1,800**     **VEC**

A Schuco tinplate fire engine, with a turntable ladder and a long bonnet, back rest, silver platform and four-sectional ladder, plated parts, missing elements, wear.

*11.75in (30cm) wide*

**$700-1,000**     **VEC**

A Schuco tinplate No.5720 Mercedes Hydro-car sports car, with an open top, battery operation and plated parts, lacks control wire and accessories, box for No.5311.

*10.25in (26cm) wide*

**$800-1,200**     **VEC**

A Schuco tinplate No.2095 Mercedes 190 SL sports car, with a printed dashboard, clockwork operation and plated parts, missing cable, illustrated card box.

*9in (23cm) wide*

**$280-320**     **VEC**

A Schuco tinplate No.5509 Mercedes Elektro Razzia police car, with plated parts, clockwork and battery operation and two interior policeman figures, in an illustrated box with key and instructions.

*8.75in (22cm) wide*

**$300-500**     **VEC**

A Schuco tinplate No.5720 Electro Hydro-car sports car, with a printed dashboard, steering wheel, opening boot with battery compartment and remote control wire, with two wooden bollards, in correct box.

*10.25in (26cm) wide*

**$1,200-1,800**     **VEC**

A Schuco tinplate No.5307 Mercedes 230SL electric sports car, with ignition key, printed dashboard and plated parts, battery compartment, in a card box, lacks control cable.

*11in (28cm) wide*

**$800-1,200**     **VEC**

A Schuco tinplate No.4003 combination car, in beige with a red interior and clockwork operation, key, some wear.

*8in (20cm) wide*

**$700-1,000**     **VEC**

A Schuco tinplate No.5509 Elektro Razzia car, with clockwork and battery operation, red revolving roof beacon and plated parts, with two plastic uniformed figures, illustrated card box.

*9in (23cm) wide*

**$700-1,000**     **VEC**

TOYS, DOLLS & MODELS

An Arnold tinplate No.2500 military jeep, with clockwork operation and key, dashboard mounted semaphore, jerry can and three figures, card box.

6.75in (17cm) wide

**$1,200-1,800**     VEC

An Arnold tinplate No.11500 lorry-mounted crane, with an orange cab and body, detailed tin printed interior, on an illustrated card box with instructions slip, wear.

10.25in (26cm) wide

**$700-1,000**     VEC

An Arnold tinplate MAN diesel breakdown lorry, with a long bonnet, pale yellow plastic cab and detailed tin printed interior, plated parts and friction drive, light wear and retouching.

12.5in (32cm) wide

**$800-1,200**     VEC

An Arnold tinplate container lorry, with control cab and friction drive, the wheeled plastic tank with "Esso" to sides, light wear, hard to find variation.

11in (28cm) wide

**$800-1,200**     VEC

An Arnold tinplate DAF high-sided open-backed truck, with a long wheel base, drop down tailgate and red hubs, a rare friction drive model, in a plain card box.

17.25in (44cm) wide

**$800-1,200**     VEC

An Arnold tinplate Dutch Post Office delivery van, in yellow and light gray with opening rear door, friction drive and plated parts, printed interior, light wear.

11.75in (30cm) wide

**$800-1,200**     VEC

## EARLY TINPLATE TOYS

### TINPLATE

- Tinplate was the most widely used toy material from c1850.
- German factories, such as Lütz, Rock & Gräner, Tipp & Co., Bing, and Märklin, led the tinplate market during the late 19thC and early 20thC. Early handpainted German toys were made to high standards and are among the most sought-after today.
- 'Penny toys', produced inexpensively in the early 20thC and sold by street vendors throughout Europe, are also collectible. Look for early complex examples in good condition and by a recognized maker, such as Meier, Distler, or Fischer.
- By the end of WWI, tinplate designs had generally become less complex and lithography had replaced painted decoration.
- After the 1930s, the American Marx company became the world's largest toy manufacturer and produced popular tinplate models.
- Japan established its own toy industry after WWII and successfully reached European markets with its exciting array of new and cheap products.
- By the late 1960s plastic had largely replaced tinplate.

An early Bing tinplate Kiddy Phone Junior Gramophone, with clockwork operation, turntable, stylus and key, selection of early records and a tin of HMV stylus needles, the horn detached.

*Gebrüder Bing, one of best known tinplate makers, made several of these children's gramophones.*

**$220-280**     VEC

A rare Branko tinplate clockwork acrobat, with a celluloid doll and original box.
c1920

16in (40.5cm) high

**$800-1,200**     BEJ

A Bub tinplate limousine, with driver and battery-operated motor, in green with chromolithography decoration and two faux lamps.

*Limousines are particularly popular with collectors.*

*10.75in (27cm) wide*

**$1,200-1,800** | **LAN**

### A CLOSER LOOK AT A MÄRKLIN ZEPPELIN

*This airship is made by Märklin, one of best known tinplate toy manufacturers.*

*The D-LZ-127 Graf Zeppelin was launched in 1928 and set a number of flying records. The historical interest of this and other airships makes items depicting them desirable.*

*The handpainted rather than lithographed finish suggests an early date and increases the value.*

*The airship is complete with its box and has a working movement. It therefore commands a premium.*

A Märklin 'Zeppelin D-LZ 127' handpainted airship, with working movement, propeller and original hangings, in original box.

*16in (40cm) wide*

**$5,000-8,000** | **LAN**

---

A DRG tinplate wind-up musical model of Cologne Cathedral, with lithographed detail, plays church-organ-style music when handle is rotated, the box with colorful illustration to lid.

*6.75in (17cm) high*

**$300-500** | **VEC**

A DRG tinplate 'Buckingham Palace' clockwork diorama, with Coldstream Guards marching at Palace gates on operation, in an illustrated box.

*8.75in (22cm) wide*

**$800-1,200** | **VEC**

An unusual DRG tinplate 'Hitler's Palace' clockwork diorama, modeled as Buckingham Palace, with German sentries holding rifles and marching on operation, includes key.

**$1,200-1,800** | **VEC**

---

An S. Guntherman tinplate clockwork double decker bus, with printed decoration, some rubbing and wear.

*13.75in (35cm) wide*

**$800-1,200** | **SWO**

A Lehmann No.445 'Tame Seal' model, hand-painted, the movement in working order, with original key.

*7.5in (19cm) wide*

**$500-700** | **LAN**

A Lehmann No.770 'Express Boy' with cart, chromolithographed decoration.

*6.5in (16cm) wide*

**$400-600** | **LAN**

A Märklin No.1151 constructor low-wing monoplane, with lithographed decoration and "D-ALBA", tail fatigue, in original box with instruction manual.

*21in (53cm) wide*

**$800-1,200** | **GORL**

**TOYS, DOLLS & MODELS**

A large 1950s Marx tinplate clockwork racing car, with single seat and driver.

*13.5in (34.5cm) wide*

| $500-700 | W&W |

A Modern Toys tinplate 'Moon Explorer' vehicle, with clear perspex cockpit and tinplate astronaut, battery operated with mystery action, light wear, Japan.

*14.25in (36cm) wide*

| $300-400 | VEC |

A rare Rock & Graner tinplate castle landscape, with rope bridge and lake with fountain, handpainted, partly restored.

*11.5in (29 cm) wide*

| $1,200-1,800 | LAN |

A TN Toys tinplate and plastic Pinocchio with xylophone, battery operated and lithographed, in an illustrated card box, Japan, dated, damage.

*1962*     *9in (23cm) high*

| $300-500 | VEC |

A TN Toys tinplate 'Bartender' toy, the figure makes a cocktail on battery operation, with smoke and sound effects, in illustrated box with card inserts, Japan.

*11.75in (30cm) high*

| $80-120 | VEC |

A tinplate clockwork figure at a snooker table, lacks ball and accessories, man's arm detached but present.

| $220-280 | VEC |

## ROBOTS

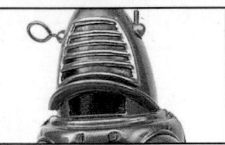

A rare Yoshiya 1950s tinplate 'Planet Robot', with battery-operated remote control box and cable, light corrosion, Japan.

*8.75in (22cm) high*

| $700-1,000 | VEC |

An early American Ideal plastic 'Robert the Robot', with manual remote control operating movement and voice, card box, lacks antenna.

*13.75in (35cm) high*

| $220-280 | VEC |

A Horikawa tinplate 'Swivel-o-matic Astronaut', battery operated, with firing guns, in an illustrated card box, Japan.

*11.5in (29cm) high*

| $300-400 | VEC |

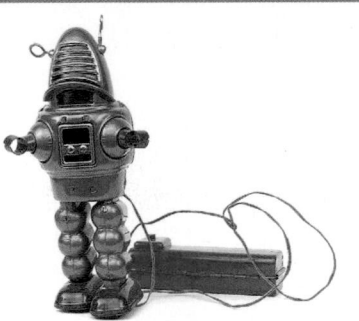

An early Marx tinplate and plastic 'Mr Mercury' robot, with battery operated remote control and sponge pads to hands, light wear.

*c1960*     *13in (33cm) high*

| $700-1,000 | VEC |

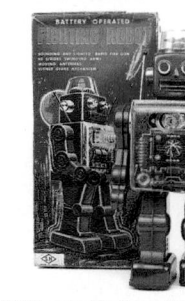

An SH Toys for Horikawa tinplate 'Fighting Robot', battery operated, in a colorful illustrated box, small crack, Japan.

*11.5in (29cm) high*

| $300-500 | VEC |

An SH Toys tinplate 'Attacking Martian' robot, battery operated, with plastic lights to front, in a colorfully illustrated box, Japan.

*11.5in (29cm) high*

| $220-280 | VEC |

A Bing for Bassett-Lowke 1-gauge L&NWR No.44 'Precursor' tank locomotive, clockwork, complete with winding handle, wear.

**$800-1,200**     **VEC**

## A CLOSER LOOK AT A BASSETT-LOWKE LOCOMOTIVE

Bing made a wide range of trains for Bassett-Lowke, to be retailed in Great Britain, from c1900. Quality varied – this train is an example of the company's better-quality work.

The decoration was lithographed on flat sheets of tinplate, which were then shaped. Handpainted details were added later.

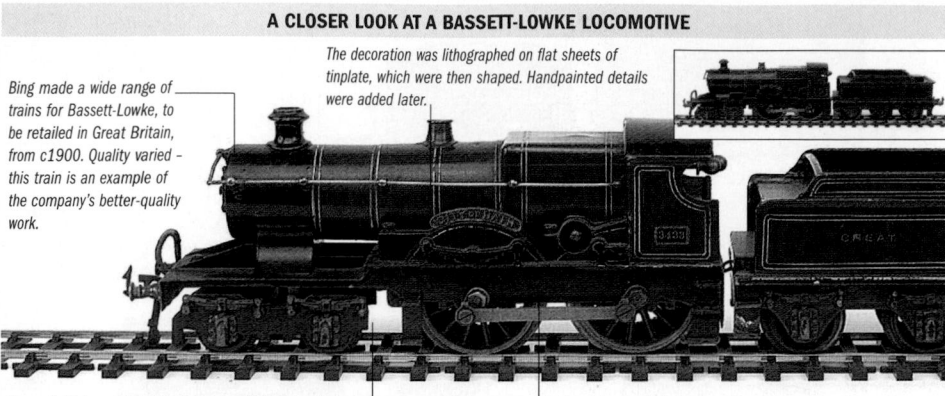

As a relatively early Bing train, the bearings and springs are visible outside, rather than within, the wheels.

Look out for repainting and replacement parts as these will reduce value.

A Bing for Bassett-Lowke 4-4-0 No.3433 'City of Bath' locomotive and tender, in Great Western green, clockwork, with nameplate and running number "3433", wear and crazing.

**$10,000-15,000**     **VEC**

A Bassett-Lowke O-gauge 4-6-2 LMS No.6232 'Duchess of Montrose' locomotive and tender, 12v electric, with LMS lettering, some restoration and repainting.

**$1,800-2,200**     **VEC**

A Bassett-Lowke 2-6-0 LNER No.33 'Mogul' locomotive and tender, 12v DC electric, with running number "33".

**$800-1,200**     **VEC**

A Bing cast iron 1-gauge 2-B steam locomotive and '1012' tender, handpainted, with cow catcher and bell, working movement, restored.

**$500-700**     **LAN**

A Craigard Railway Collection 4-6-2 LMS No.6200 'The Princess Royal' locomotive and tender, three-rail Electric, skate pick-up, some repainting.

**$1,800-2,200**     **VEC**

## HORNBY

- Established in 1907 by Frank Hornby, the Hornby company initially concentrated on producing Meccano construction toys.
- A range of 0-gauge trains were introduced in 1920. Trains made before 1923 had a simple nut and bolt construction, while Hornby Series trains made after this time were tinplate.
- From 1925 trains were made with clockwork and electric motors. Clockwork motors were phased out after WWII.
- In 1938, the smaller Hornby Dublo 00-gauge range was launched. Locomotives had diecast bodies and were well-made and more affordable. They became the most popular toy train.
- Prewar Hornby Dublo is hard to come by and can be identified by its blue boxes with date codes and distinctive coupling.
- Southern Railway trains are the most popular with collectors and tend to fetch higher prices.
- Sets that have not been played with command a premium.
- Hornby still produces trains, largely for the collector's market.

A Hornby O-Gauge 0-4-0 No.1 Southern B343 Special locomotive and tender, clockwork, retouching and coupling replaced.

**$1,200-1,800**     **VEC**

A Hornby O-Gauge E320 Riviera train set, consisting of a 20v electric 4-4-2 No.3 locomotive and tender, two coaches, 12 pieces of electric three-rail track, three boxes of connecting plates and one corridor connector, in box.

**$2,800-3,200**     **VEC**

A Hornby 0-gauge 4-4-0 No.2 Special 'Yorkshire' locomotive and No.234 LNER tender, clockwork, some restoration and re-wheeled.

**$2,200-2,800** VEC

A Hornby Dublo 'EDP2' passenger train set, with a 4-6-2 Canadian Pacific locomotive, tender and coaches, instructions dated "7/52".

*This train, a British 'Duchess of Atholl' in Canadian colors for the Canadian market, was a financial disaster.*

**$1,800-2,200** VEC

A Hornby Dublo EDG16 tank goods train set, with a 2-6-4 BR black standard class tank No.80054 locomotive, brick wagon and bolster wagon, BR brake Van and track, boxed.

**$800-1,200** VEC

A Pre-WWII Hornby Dublo LNER Gresley teak 1st/3rd Coach, with minor rusting around windows and some bare metal parts.

*The Gresley was one of the first Hornby Dublo issues.*

**$220-280** VEC

A Hornby 0-Gauge No.2 Special Pullman set, with a 4-4-0 locomotive and tender, clockwork, an early version with "Hornby Made in England limited Liverpool" transfer to front, with two Pullman coaches, box, guarantee and instructions, dated "11/29".

**$3,000-5,000** VEC

A Hornby 0-Gauge 4-4-0 No.2 locomotive and 'L1' "Southern 1759" tender, 20v electric, overpainting.

**$1,800-2,200** VEC

A Hornby 0-Gauge 0-4-0 No.1 Special tank locomotive, in green with "Southern 516", clockwork.

**$800-1,200** VEC

A Hornby 0-Gauge 0-4-0 No.1 Special tank locomotive, with "Southern A129", clockwork.

*This version was only issued in 1929 and 1930.*

**$4,000-6,000** VEC

## MÄRKLIN TRAINS

- The German Märklin company produced high quality and expensive toys from 1859. It introduced regular gauge trains at the 1891 Leipzig toy fair.
- After 1900, Märklin trains became more realistic and sophisticated.
- Electric motors were introduced in 1898.
- Live steam trains are fairly rare. Produced for only a short time around 1900, they were dangerous and messy.
- Trains can often be dated by the coupling. A tin loop was used 1904-1909, a hook was used 1909-1913 and, between 1913 and 1954, a sliding drop was used.
- A wide range of buildings and other accessories were produced. Post-WWI examples tend to be less detailed.
- After WWI, Märklin produced trains for all levels of the market. Collectors look for high quality realistic examples.
- Early paintwork had a tendency to craze. By the 1930s, paint was finely applied.
- The gauge was changed from '00' to a smaller 'H0' in 1948.
- Märklin is still in production today.

A Märklin 1-gauge 2-B steam 'Queen of Scots' locomotive 1443 and a 3-A LNER tender, electric, painted in green, wear.

**$700-1,000** LAN

A Märklin 1-gauge 2-B steam locomotive EE1021 and a 4-A tender, electric, with two electrified headlights, one tender cover missing.

**$700-1,000** LAN

A Märklin direction indicator, with eight direction signs, handpainted, wear.

*8.75in (22cm) high*

**$300-400** LAN

A Märklin 1-gauge mail carriage 1802, handpainted in green, with gothic windows, replaced footboards.

*4.75in (12cm) wide*

**$300-500** LAN

A Märklin 1-gauge canvas-covered carriage, hand-painted in green, with three wax cows.

*8.75in (22cm) wide*

**$300-500** LAN

A rare Märklin 1-gauge handcar 1100, handpainted, with three original figures, the movement in working order, flags replaced, one hat restored.

**$12,000-18,000** LAN

A Märklin 2-C-1 PLM steam locomotive H 64/13021 and a 4-A tender, electrified, handpainted in green, two electrical headlights, cover of tender missing.

**$5,000-7,000** LAN

A Märklin 1-gauge platform carriage 1766, carrying two cars, tinplate wheels, handpainted.

*9.75in (24.5cm) wide*

**$1,800-2,200** LAN

A Märklin 0-gauge carriage 1886, with 4-A tinplate wheels, no interior decoration.

*8.5in (21.5cm) wide*

**$120-180** LAN

A Märklin 0-gauge luggage carriage 1846, handpainted, with interior decoration and 4-A tinplate wheels, one axis and wheels missing, old finish, buffer replaced.

*6.5in (16cm) wide*

**$1,200-1,800** LAN

A Märklin 0-gauge 2-B-1 tender locomotive TCE 66/12920, electric, partly restored.

**$1,800-2,200** LAN

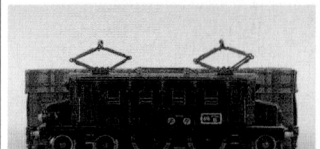

A Märklin 0-gauge 2-B-1 electro-locomotive CS 66/12920, chromolithographed, with two moving panthographes and two electric lanterns, some wear.

**$2,800-3,200** LAN

A Märklin 0-gauge carriage 1983, with a Sarrasani animal cage and a lion, 2-A tinplate wheels, lion's tail missing.

*6.5in (16.5cm) wide*

**$500-700** LAN

A Rocket and three wagon set, consisting of 0-2-2 locomotive and tender, three-rail electric, four-wheeled Liverpool to Manchester coach, four-wheeled two container open wagon and a flat wagon with Landau.

**$2,800-3,200** VEC

A Triang D31 station set, part assembled, with a T32 island platform set labeled "Plymouth" and a T28 Engine Shed.

**$80-120** VEC

A Trix No.1540 4-6-2 BR 'Scotsman' blue A3 class locomotive and tender No.60103, three-rail AC, with box and some internal packaging.

**$500-700** VEC

A Trix No.244 diesel shunter three-rail Set, comprising 0-6-0 green shunter and shunter's match truck, box.

**$280-320** VEC

A Wrenn W2296 (ins) 4-6-2 BR 'Dartmoor' West Country class locomotive and tender No.34021, box.

**$700-1,000** VEC

A Wrenn W2278 (ins) 4-6-2 SR 'Blue Funnel' Wartime black Streamlined Merchant Navy class locomotive and tender No.21C13, box.

**$700-1,000** VEC

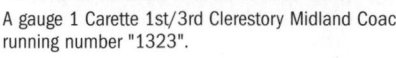

A gauge 1 Carette 1st/3rd Clerestory Midland Coach, running number "1323".

**$700-1,000** VEC

## MONEY BANKS

- Mechanical banks first appeared during the 1800s. They are often considered the epitomy of late 19thC American toys because they were developed during a period when industrialization changed many facets of life. This included a shift in the materials used to create toys – from wood and tin to cast iron. Cast iron was durable and affordable.
- When penny banks arrived in America a common phrase of the day was "A penny saved is a penny earned."
- Animals, birds, fish, political personalities, and many types of architecture, served to beguile several generations of youngsters into saving their money.
- Faded, colorless or worn banks should never be repainted as their worn appearance enhances their value.
- Look for original features and signs of usage. Reproductions of older banks are common.
- Collectors should look through the internet, flea markets, antique shops, and auctions to expand their collection.

A 19thC American cast iron Piccaninny money bank, no. 3000.

5.25in (13.5cm) high

$180-220        B&H

A late 19thC cast iron eagle and eaglets mechanical bank, by J. & E. Stevens Co., raised patent mark on base "PAT JAN 23 1883", plug mark "PAT FEB 1875", paint wear.

5in (13cm) high

$600-900        SK

A polychrome cast iron William Tell mechanical bank, by J. & E. Stevens Co., William Tell aiming his rifle at a boy with apple in front of a castle, raised patent mark on base "PAT JAN 23 1883", plug marked "PAT FEB 1875", paint wear.

6.5in (16.5cm) high

$800-1,200        SK

### A CLOSER LOOK AT A MECHANICAL BANK

The building opens to reveal a teller. When a coin is placed on his tray and the door is closed, the coin is deposited in a slot in the teller's cage.

The J. & E. Stevens Company was famous for making cast iron toys and was in business until the 1930s.

Iron was the most popular material for toy banks as it could be cast inexpensively and was virtually indestructible.

This bank is very appealing to collectors despite its worn paint and the spring not working. The damage is consistent with honest usage.

A cast iron novelty mechanical bank, by J. & E. Stevens Co., patent marks impressed on side "PATd JUNE 25 1872 OCT 23 1873", paint wear.

c1875        6.75in (17.5cm) high

$1,200-1,800        SK

A cast iron lighthouse mechanical bank, the signal tower on a hexagonal rockery base, old repaint.

c1890        10.5in (26.5cm) high

$800-1,200        SK

A cast iron 'Dinah' mechanical bank, by John Harper & Company, bust-length figure with yellow dress, raised lettering "DINAH" on the back, some old repaint.

c1920        6.5in (16.5cm) high

$500-800        SK

A Staunton-pattern weighted boxwood and ebony chess set, together with a 19thC leather covered chessboard.

*king 4in (10cm) high*

**$800-1,200** CO

A 19thc Jaques Staunton ivory chess set, the white king stamped "Jaques London", the pieces with Victorian registration lozenges, with a Jaques Cartonpierre box with separate lid.

*king 3.5in (9cm) high*

**$2,800-3,200** CO

A Jaques Staunton boxwood and ebony chess set, both kings stamped "Jaques London", boxed, some damage.

*king 3.5in (9cm) high*

**$1,800-2,200** CO

An ivory Macao-type 'bust' chess set, probably Cantonese.

*c1830* *king 3.5in (9cm) high*

**$1,800-2,200** CO

An ivory Burmese-type chess set, probably Cantonese, boxed, the pieces varnished.

*c1840* *king 3.5in (9cm) high*

**$1,200-1,800** CO

An ivory Burmese-type chess set, probably Cantonese.

*c1840* *king 3.25in (8.5cm) high*

**$700-1,000** CO

An ivory Burmese-type set, Cantonese.

*c1840* *king 4.25in (10.5cm) high*

**$700-1,000** CO

A 20thC German large Volksteder porcelain 'Crusader' chess set, marked on underside of base.

*king 7in (18cm) high*

**$5,000-7,000** CO

A Schoenhut Manufacturing Co. indoor golf game, with Tommy Green and Cissy Lofter figures, three clubs and balls, papier-mâché and wood hazards, sand traps, mounds and felt fairways, Philadelphia.

*c1920*

**$1,800-2,200** FRE

A Victorian table croquet game, in original wooden box with pictorial chromolithographic label to inside of lid, with mallets, balls, and other equipment.

**$220-280** FRE

A Victorian mahogany traveling chess set, by Pearce and Maker, with inlaid checkering, and boxwood and ebony pieces.

*8in (20.5cm) wide*

**$220-280** GORL

A Victorian boxwood and ebony chess set and board.

*13in (33cm) wide*

**$180-220** MB

A boxed set of building bricks.

*c1890* *box 18in (45.5cm) wide*

**$180-220** BEJ

A boxed set of wooden ninepins with jack.

*c1895* *pins 8in (20.5cm) high*

**$220-280** BEJ

## THE TRIBAL ART MARKET

The tribal art market has remained fairly buoyant. This is particularly true of items at the higher end of the market. Early, rare, and fine pieces in good condition tend to perform extremely well at auction and can far exceed even optimistic sales estimates. Provenance is crucial. The most desirable pieces can be traced back, through prominent owners or museums, to the original point of collection by missionaries or military men.

Many serious European and American collectors tend to favor sculptural forms from the classic West and Central African cultures, fine beaded or quilled buckskin clothing from the Great Plains tribes, or figurative antiquities from Pre-Columbian cultures of Meso-America.

Native American, Inuit, and African masks can all easily obtain five-figure prices at auction. The distinctive Southwest blankets

of the Navajo and others are particularly popular, for example.

Despite some heady auction prices, pieces can still be purchased at for reasonable amounts, particularly basketry work, polychrome pottery or weaponry. However, some tribal pieces have been produced in recent times specifically for sale in the western art market, rather than used in ceremonial situations. These pieces are not considered to have sufficient authenticity to be seriously collected. Nevertheless, because they can be purchased for modest sums, and are often well crafted and aesthetically pleasing, they may be acquired and enjoyed in their own right, and should act as an introduction to wider study for the novice collector.

*– Philip Keith*

## PLAINS CLOTHING

A Central Plains beaded hide and cloth man's vest, the European-style form with cloth liner and back, multicolored beads on a white ground, worn.

c1875  22.5in (57cm) long

**$2,800-3,200**  SK

A late 19thC Central Plains beaded hide man's vest, Lakota tribe, the calico-lined vest beaded on both sides, minor bead loss.

*The Lakota were the most western of the Sioux tribes. From spring to fall they were a nomadic tribe, following the herds of bison.*

20in (50cm) long

**$4,000-6,000**  SK

A late 19thC Central Plains beaded hide boy's vest, Lakota tribe, with print cloth liner, beaded with multicolored and metallic geometric devices on a white ground.

18.5in (47cm) long

**$2,200-2,800**  SK

A late 19thC Northern Plains hide man's vest and pants, possibly Métis tribe, vest with blue cloth back, embroidered with flowers and butterflies, the Spanish-style hide pants with floral embroidery and red cloth trim, metal buckles to back, brass buttons, minor damage.

*The Métis were people of French-Canadian and Indian extraction.*

pants 43in (109cm) long

**$1,800-2,200**  SK

A Northern Plains beaded cloth and hide man's vest, the back from a commercial vest, the hide front with unusual blue human forms, light green border, bead loss.

c1900  22in (55cm) long

**$1,200-1,800**  SK

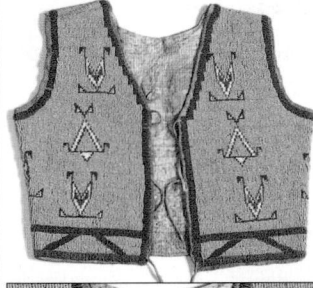
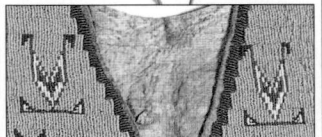

An early 20thC Central Plains beaded hide man's vest, beaded on both sides on a light blue ground, made from an old recycled painted buffalo robe.

**$1,200-1,800**  SK

An early 20thC Plains commercial leather man's vest, the European form beaded with two mounted warriors and two sun and moon images, the back with two mounted warriors and an eagle.

22in (56cm) long

**$2,500-3,000**  SK

## A CLOSER LOOK AT A PLAINS HIDE COAT

The Great Plains of America cover a wide area and the natural conditions in this region were ideal for nomadic hunting, with its treeless grasslands. The Plains tribes mainly hunted buffalo and used the hide for robes and coats.

Clothing was often decorated with strips of elaborate beadwork in a variety of color combinations, to create geometric patterns.

A late 19thC Southern Plains beaded hide child's coat, stained yellow with red details, fringed at the hem, elbows, and collar, with multicolored beaded trim, including large black faceted and mescal beads, patina of use.

The bones of hunted animals were transformed into awls for sewing. The tendons of larger animals, or plant fibers, were used to stitch together material.

The free edges on items of clothing were generally fringed for decorative effect.

38.5in (96.5cm) long

**$22,000-28,000**     SK

---

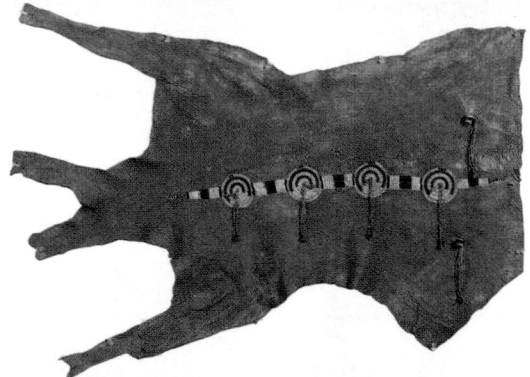

A rare Northern Plains beaded hide child's robe, the animal-shaped form with yellow pigment, the strip beaded on to the hide, bold geometric devices on a white ground, the roundels with quill-wrapped hide suspensions and tin cone danglers.

c1865     39in (99cm) long

**$25,000-30,000**     SK

A late 19thC Plains beaded and painted hide doll's dress, fringed along the sides and hem, painted with blue outlined red triangles, the yoke with two rows of beadwork, stains.

11in (28cm) high

**$3,000-5,000**     SK

An early 20thC Southern Plains man's beaded hide leggings, red and white border beading, tabs with fringed tassel tips, thin fringe below tabs and along cuffs.

32in (81.5cm) long

**$2,200-2,800**     SK

---

An early 20thC Southern Plains beaded hide woman's dress, buckskin fringed at the arms and hem, split up the back, beaded with multicolored glass and metallic beads, and cowrie shells, minor bead loss.

48in (122cm) long

**$2,200-2,800**     SK

An early 20thC Central Plains beaded cloth and hide girl's dress, Lakota tribe, the beaded yoke reinforced with red and white striped canvas, possibly part of an American flag, beaded bands and short fringe along the lower dress, bead loss, minor hide damage.

40in (100cm) long

**$4,000-6,000**     SK

A Northern Plains beaded hide girl's dress, the beaded yoke on a blue background, beaded fringe, and with four red trade cloth circles with beaded borders, bead loss.

c1925     38in (95cm) long

**$1,200-1,800**     SK

A Northern Plains hide man's beaded shirt and leggings, Blackfoot tribe, the shirt open to sides with long fringed arms, the beaded strips and heart-shaped ornaments with geometric devices, the leggings with identical strips.

c1935     shirt 44in (112cm) long

**$1,500-2,000**     SK

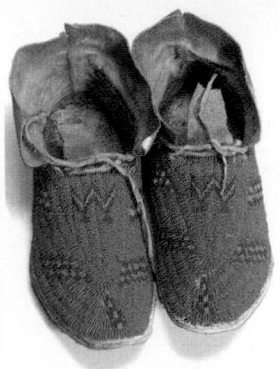

A pair of late 19thC Central Plains beaded hide moccasins, fully beaded uppers and soles with multicolored geometric, some damage to hide.

*10in (25.5cm) long*

**$2,200-2,800** SK

A pair of late 19thC Central Plains beaded hide man's moccasins, hard sole forms with fully beaded uppers, minor bead loss and wear.

*10.5in (26.5cm) long*

**$800-1,200** SK

A pair of late 19thC Central Plains beaded hide man's moccasins, with rawhide soles, the uppers beaded with flags and a six-point star, traces of red pigment.

*10.5in (26.5cm) long*

**$2,500-3,000** SK

A late 19thC Southern Plains beaded hide woman's high-top moccasins, Arapaho tribe, stained yellow and green, fringe top, fully beaded moccasins and partially beaded tops, bead loss.

*These moccasins probably had German silver buttons at one time.*

*23in (58.5cm) high*

**$12,000-18,000** SK

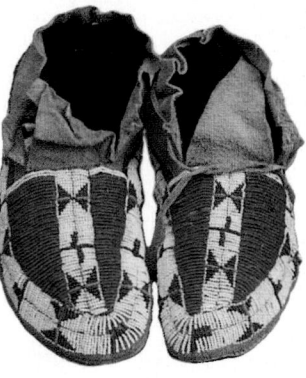

Two pairs of early 20thC Central Plains beaded hide man's moccasins, Lakota tribe, hard sole forms with multicolored geometric uppers, minor bead loss.

*10in (25.5cm) long*

**$1,500-2,000** SK

A pair of late 19thC Northern Plains beaded hide leggings, Crow tribe, fringed down one side, multicolored floral devices to front, a single horseshoe device on the back of each legging.

*22.5in (57cm) long*

**$2,200-2,800** SK

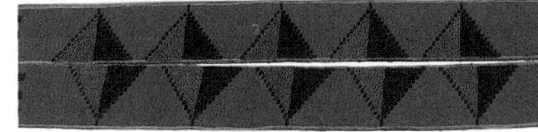

A pair of Northern Plains beaded cloth legging strips, Blackfoot tribe, muslin strips with stepped triangles on a blue ground.

*29in (74cm) long*

**$800-1,200** SK

A19thC Central Plains beaded and quilled hide pipe bag, Lakota tribe, the soft bag with roll-beaded opening, panel with bar design, quill-wrapped rawhide slats and fringe to base, quill loss, minor damage.

*c1865*     *39in (99cm) long*

**$10,000-12,000** SK

A late 19thC Northern Plains beaded and quilled hide pipe bag, the soft hide bag roll-beaded at the top, lower panel beaded with box and border pattern, polychrome quilled rawhide slats and fringe to base, traces of red pigment on the hide, old tag, quill loss.

*c1875*     *37in (94cm) long*

**$5,000-7,000** SK

A Northern Plains beaded and quilled hide pipe bag, Lakota tribe, roll-beaded at the top, sides quilled rawhide slats and fringe to base, traces of yellow stain, damage.

*Possibly owned by 'Rain in the Face'.*

*c1875*     *37in (94cm) long*

**$14,000-16,000** SK

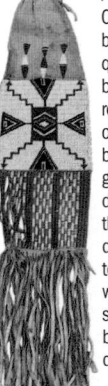

A late 19thC Central Plains beaded and quilled hide pipe bag, Lakota tribe, roll-beaded at the opening, panel beaded with geometric devices, with three feather devices at the top, quill-wrapped rawhide slats and fringe to base, some damage.

*38in (96.5cm) long*

**$2,200-2,800** SK

A late 19thC Central Plains beaded hide pictorial pipe bag, Lakota tribe, with horse and tipi devices in metallic and multicolored beads, remnant quill-wrapped rawhide slats and fringe to base, damage.

*29in (74cm) long*

**$2,800-3,200** SK

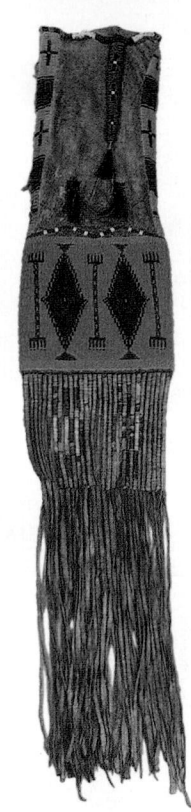

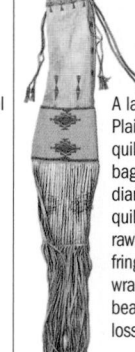

A late 19thC Central Plains beaded and quilled hide pipe bag, Lakota tribe, roll-beaded at the opening, beaded with geometric patterns, quill-wrapped rawhide slats, quill loss.

*33in (84cm) long*

**$2,800-3,200** SK

A late 19thC Central Plains beaded and quilled soft hide pipe bag, blue panel with diamond devices, quill-wrapped rawhide slats and fringe to base, quill-wrapped and roll-beaded drops, quill loss.

*39in (99cm) long*

**$800-1,200** SK

A late 19thC Central Plains beaded and quilled hide pipe bag, one side with box and border design, the other with crossed flags, quill-wrapped rawhide slats and fringe to base, damage.

*32in (81.5cm) long*

**$3,000-5,000** SK

A late 19thC Central Plains beaded and quilled hide pipe bag, Lakota tribe, with roll-beaded opening, panel with geometric devices, tin cone and horsehair danglers, quill-wrapped rawhide slats with fringe to base, traces of yellow pigment.

*36in (91.5cm) long*

**$22,000-25,000** SK

An early 20thC Central Plains beaded and quilled hide pipe bag, beaded with spiderweb, pipes, and crosses, a sunburst, polychrome quilled rawhide slats.

*27in (68.5cm) long*

**$1,800-2,200** SK

A Central Plains beaded hide pictorial pipe bag, the panel beaded on both sides with a horse and geometric devices in metallic and colored beads, quill-wrapped rawhide slats and fringe to base, damage, loss.

*29in (74cm) long*

**$3,000-5,000** SK

A late 19thC Central Plains beaded hide bag, Cheyenne tribe, beaded with bold multicolored geometric bar patterns, red dyed horsehair and tin cone danglers, tears in hide, bead loss.

*c1880*     *22in (56cm) wide*

**$6,000-9,000** SK

A late 19thC Central Plains beaded buffalo hide bag, Cheyenne tribe, beaded with geometric devices, red dyed horsehair and tin cone danglers from the side and flap, minor damage.

*19.5in (49.5cm) wide*

**$4,000-6,000** SK

A late 19thC Eastern Plains beaded hide bag, Dakota tribe, three-sided soft form with cloth and remnant ribbon top, abstract floral beadwork, and quill-wrapped drops with tin cones from base, damage.

*bag 8.5in (21.5cm) long*

**$800-1,200** SK

A late 19thC Central Plains beaded hide bladder bag, Lakota tribe, with hide cuff and rondel at the base, geometric beading, with fringe and tin cone danglers, quill-wrapped drops from the base and top.

*bag 10in (25cm) long*

**$800-1,200** SK

A late 19thC Central Plains beaded hide bag, the trapezoidal form beaded to front with a forked diamond pattern, short fringe from the base, stitch separation.

*11in (28cm) long*

**$400-600** SK

A late 19thC Central Plains beaded animal hide bag, Lakota tribe, with remnant red trade cloth at the edge, beadwork at the top, and beaded applications where the features would have been, remnant tin cone and red horsehair danglers.

*15.5in (39.5cm) long*

**$1,200-1,800** SK

A late 19thC Plains hairpipe breastplate, four strips of commercial leather, hide-strung bone hairpipes and glass trade beads, and a glass bead and shell disc pendant, minor loss.

*19in (48cm) long*

$1,200-1,800                                    SK

A late 19thC feather headdress, Lakota Sioux tribe, South Dakota, eagle feathers, buckskin.

*30.75in (77cm) long*

$4,000-6,000                                    BLA

A late 19thC Native American feather headdress.

*18in (45cm) long*

$2,200-2,800                                    BLA

A late 19thC Plains beaded hide knife sheath, stiff rawhide liner covered with buckskin and beaded on one side, decorated with tin cones and an unusual row of German silver discs, twisted hide strap, tin cone loss.

*8.75in (22cm) long*

$6,000-9,000                                    SK

A late 19thC Plains hair pipe breast plate, four strips of commercial leather strung with bone hair pipes, globular hollow brass beads, shell discs, glass bead attachments, partially unstrung.

*18in (45.5cm) long*

$2,800-3,200                                    SK

A late 19thC Plains bone hairpipe breastplate, three sections of hairpipes, strung on red-stained hide with commercial leather spacers.

*21.5in (54.5cm) long*

$1,800-2,200                                    SK

A pair of Central Plains beaded hide legging strips, Lakota tribe, beaded on one side with geometric devices.
*c1900*

*27in (68.5cm) long*

$800-1,200                                    SK

An early 20thC Northern Plains beaded cloth blanket strip, Blackfoot tribe, the muslin strip with geometric devices alternating with four-point rondels, faded blue cloth binding.

*61in (155cm) long*

$2,200-2,800                                    SK

A Northern Plains beaded cloth and hide martingale, Crow tribe, decorated with classic Crow geometric patterns, trade cloth inserts, the straps with tab bottoms and roll-beaded cloth danglers, the central panel with hide fringe and hawk bells.

*c1900*          *42in (107cm) long*

$8,000-12,000                                    SK

A late 19thC Central Plains beaded hide, cloth, and wood miniature cradle, Cheyenne tribe, hide form with cotton print liner, beaded on the outside with stepped devices, damage to boards.

*8in (20cm) high*

**$2,200-2,800** SK

A late 19thC Central Plains fully beaded hide cradle, Lakota tribe, with rawhide tab, with multicolored and metallic geometric devices, with bugle beads, with cowrie shell and brass hawk bell danglers, fringed hide to base.

*22in (55cm) long*

**$7,000-10,000** SK

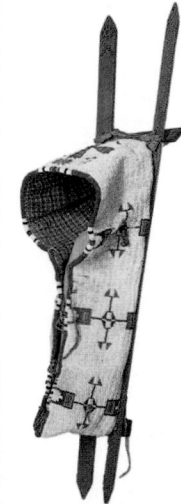

A late 19thC Central Plains beaded hide and cloth cradle, Cheyenne tribe, with long printed cotton and muslin extension, the hide with rawhide tab and beaded geometric devices, large 'morning star' over the head area, minor bead loss, tears in cloth.

*34in (85cm) long* c1900

**$4,000-6,000** SK

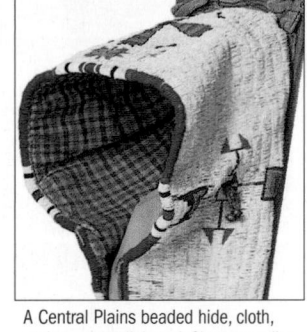

A Central Plains beaded hide, cloth, and wood cradleboard, Cheyenne tribe, the canvas form with cloth liner and rawhide insets, with striped cloth backing, the outside fully beaded with classic Cheyenne geometric designs, the pointed wood slats with tacks on one tip.

*46.5in (116cm) long*

**$10,000-15,000** SK

An early 20thC Southern Plains beaded miniature cradle, Comanche tribe, the muslin form net-beaded with linear and diamond devices, mounted stained boards, inside a small cloth doll with beaded eyes.

*8.25in (21cm) long*

**$4,000-6,000** SK

A late 19thC Plains quilled hide and cloth cradle cover, Lakota tribe, with blue cloth base and cotton lining, the hide hood with geometric devices on top, feather remnants, minor quill loss, fading.

*27in (68.5cm) high*

**$2,800-3,200** SK

A Plains Indian doll, with hide dress and beaded shoes, belt, face, and trim.

*14in (35.5cm) high*

**$4,000-6,000** POOK

A late 19thC Northern Plains polychrome parfleche envelope, the rectangular rawhide form with geometric devices, remnant buffalo hide ties.

*25in (63.5cm) long*

**$2,800-3,200** SK

A late 19thC Northern Plains beaded hide possible small bag, Crow tribe, with edge-beaded flap and two triangular tabs from the base, the front partially beaded with barred devices, remnant red trade cloth edge.

*8.25in (21cm) long*

**$600-900** SK

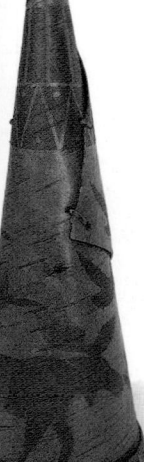

A 20thC Chippewa incised birchbark moose-calling horn, depicting moose, beaver, and flying geese.

*16in (40.5cm) high*

**$400-600** ALL

A late 19thC Plains painted hide dance shield, painted with two warriors on horseback, the lower third painted with a buffalo, trade cloth attachments, original tag on back of frame, part of the original wood hoop, restoration.

*18in (45.5cm) diam*

**$10,000-12,000** SK

Two late 19thC framed portrait paintings of Plains Native American men wearing native attire, includes pieces of original cardboard backing and attribution to "Ada K. Farnsworth" (1857-1921), some damage.

*images 5.5in (14cm) high*

**$1,800-2,200** SK

411

Two photographs by Carl Moon, depicting Plains male figures, one painting a stretched hide, both in original cardboard studio frames, with the artist's stamp, warping to both.

*Carl Moon (1879-1948) is well-known for photographing Native Americans in their natural surroundings and dress.*

*9.25in (23.5cm) high*

**$700-1,000**      **SK**

## A CLOSER LOOK AT A HIDE DRUM

*Music was an important cultural practice for the American Indian tribes. Through music and dance the tribesmen were preserving traditional values and honoring the Great Spirits.*

*The hide strap handle was necessary for ceremonies, as tribesmen would often dance, sing, and play the drum simultaneously.*

*Instruments like this hide drum had sacred symbolism and were considered to be works of art themselves. The rawhide cover has been painted with a dark pigment and depicts a bear, which was a highly respected animal in Native American culture.*

*The hide has become worn, which can be seen from the dark patina around the edges. This adds to the value, as signs of ceremonial use and genuine age are appealing to collectors of tribal artefacts.*

A 19thC Plains painted wood and hide drum, with bell on the inside, the rawhide cover painted with dark blue-green pigment, a ground line and walking bear on one side, a circle and dot on the other, dark patina from use, hide strap.

*19in (48.5cm) diam*

**$60,000-65,000**      **SK**

A large Apache coiled pictorial storage jar of classical form, with central band of six horses and six male figures, all within geometric and checkerboard designs.

*17.5in (44cm) high*

**$8,000-12,000**      **POOK**

A late 19thC Plains red pipestone pipe bowl, Dakota tribe, in the form of a European man's head, with long beard, incised mustache, and wearing a cap.

*4in (10cm) high*

**$1,200-1,800**      **SK**

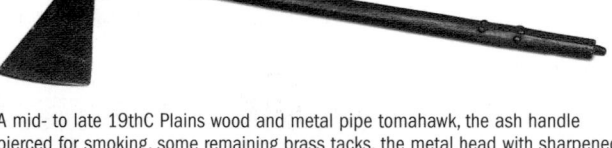

A mid- to late 19thC Plains wood and metal pipe tomahawk, the ash handle pierced for smoking, some remaining brass tacks, the metal head with sharpened blade and slightly swelled bowl, dark patina of use.

*handle 24.5in (68.5cm) long*

**$14,000-16,000**      **SK**

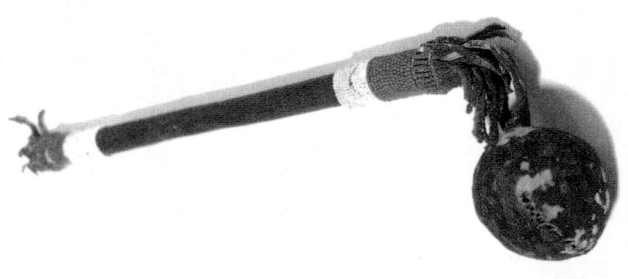

A Plains 'flop knob' war club, with partially beaded handle and yellow ochered head.

*c1890*      *17in (43cm) long*

**$700-1,000**      **ALL**

A late 19thC Plateau tribes parfleche envelope, bold geometric pattern, hide ties.

*27in (68.5cm) long*

**$2,200-2,800** SK

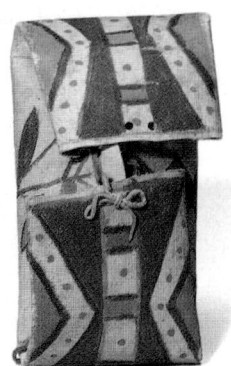

An early 20thC small Plateau tribes painted parfleche envelope, the rawhide form with both floral and geometric devices in pigments.

*9.5in (24cm) long*

**$1,800-2,200** SK

An early 20thC Plateau tribes parfleche envelope, painted on the flaps with multicolored geometric devices, hide ties.

*26.5in (67.5cm) long*

**$1,200-1,800** SK

A late 19thC Plateau tribes cornhusk bag, with stepped cross devices on both sides, red yarn used on one side.

*15in (38cm) long*

**$500-800** SK

---

A Plateau tribes cornhusk bag, decorated on both sides with geometric devices using commercial yarn, in a double-glass frame, wool loss.

*c1900*          *15in (38cm) wide*

**$1,200-1,800** SK

An early 20thC large Plateau tribes wood and hide beaded cradle, the round-top covered with native tanned hide, cut seed beads forming geometric devices, swags of trade beads on cloth hood, hide fringe and strap at back, minor bead loss.

*38in (96.5cm) high*

**$5,000-7,000** SK

An early 20thC Plateau tribes wood and hide beaded cradle, the top covered in hide, the cloth covered hood with remnant ribbon borders, beaded with metallic and colored abstract floral devices, fringe from the upper back, bead loss.

*39in (99cm) high*

**$5,000-7,000** SK

An early 20thC Plateau tribes beaded cloth vest, the canvas front with geometric devices in glass and metallic seed beads, the velveteen back with cloth trim and four beaded fringed panels with hawk bell attachments, bead loss.

*24in (61cm) long*

**$1,200-1,800** SK

---

## PRAIRIE TRIBES

A pair of mid-19thC Prairie beaded cloth and hide moccasins, Delaware tribe, beaded on the vamps and heels with abstract floral devices using small seed beads, edge-beaded two-color silk cuffs.

*8.25in (21cm) long*

**$23,000-25,000** SK

A pair of late 19thC Prairie beaded cloth and hide moccasins, Delaware tribe, beaded on the vamps with abstract floral devices on a 'pony trader' blue ground, brown cloth cuffs edged in silk and partially beaded with celestial motifs, wear.

*9.75in (25cm) long*

**$1,800-2,200** SK

Two early 20thC Prairie breechcloth panels, blue cloth panels decorated along the sides, and with three bands of abstract silk appliques and white edge beading.

*9.5in (24cm) wide*

**$1,200-1,800** SK

A pair of Prairie silk appliqué blue cloth man's leggings, each with one strip of multicolored geometric silk appliqué down one side, white edge beading.

*31in (79cm) long*

**$500-800** SK

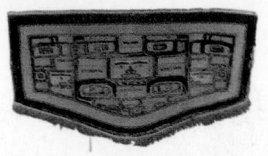

A 19thC classic Northwest Coast dance blanket, finger-woven with mountain goat wool and cedar bark strands, black-form line designs, remnant fringe, loss, fading.

*61in (155cm) wide*

**$5,000-8,000**     **SK**

A late 19thC Northwest Coast dance blanket, woven with mountain goat wool and cedar bark, with bilateral form line animal imagery, some fading, minor damage.

*44in (112cm) wide*

**$18,000-22,000**     **SK**

A 19thC Northwest coast twined spruce root basketry hat, with traces of black and red form-line painting, stiff, patina of use.

*15in (38cm) diam*

**$12,000-15,000**     **SK**

## A CLOSER LOOK AT A DANCE BLANKET

The highly structured and linear arrangement in this blanket is typical of Northwest Coast Native American art.

Decorative fringing was commonly used on the lower edge of ceremonial blankets.

A male artist would paint a pattern for a dance blanket onto a wooden board and highly skilled women would weave the design from goat wool and cedar bark.

The two dimensional design on this blanket is known as 'Northern formline,' a complex art style used by the Northwest coast Native Americans. The basic outline was defined by curvilinear 'formlines', which have a variety of widths.

A 19thC classic Northwest Coast dance blanket, finger woven in mountain goat wool and cedar bark warp strands, in an abstract line pattern, a strip of otter hide sewn across the top.

*63in (160cm) long*

**$40,000-45,000**     **SK**

Two rare late19thC Northwest Coast copper bracelets, both etched, one with an abstract human or animal face, the other with abstract avian imagery.

*2.5in (6.5cm) long*

**$3,000-5,000**     **SK**

An early 20thC Northwest polychrome carved wood totem pole, the hollow-back form with stylized animal, human, and bird forms, the separately carved beak is missing from bird.

*60in (152.5cm) high*

**$2,800-3,200**     **SK**

An early 20thC Northwest Coast polychrome carved wood totem pole, the flat-backed form on a carved and painted base, with eagle and animal forms.

*20in (50cm) high*

**$600-900**     **SK**

An early to mid-20thC Northwest Coast carved wood forehead mask, representing a bird, with commercial paint, domed copper overlaid eyes, articulated lower beak, cedar bark and painted cloth head covering attached at back.

*18in (45.5cm) long*

**$5,000-8,000**     **SK**

A mid 20thC Northwest Coast painted wood forehead mask, representing a wolf, articulated lower jaw, cedar bark and cloth strip attachments at the back.

*13.5in (34.5cm) long*

**$600-900**     **SK**

Two Northwest Skookum dolls, both female forms with painted pressed fiber faces, wearing cloth head scarves and commercial blankets, the larger with glass pinhead pupils.

*15in (38cm) high*

**$1,200-1,800**     **SK**

A Western pictorial coiled basketry bowl, tightly woven vertical black panels with zigzag and track devices alternating with natural panels decorated with quadrupeds, whirling logs, roosters, and one human figure.

*5.5in (14cm) high*

**$23,000-25,000**     **SK**

A 19thC large California basketry bowl, the rounded form with dark brown stacked diagonal geometric pattern, patina of use, breaks, stitch loss.

*13in (33cm) high*

**$6,000-9,000**  SK

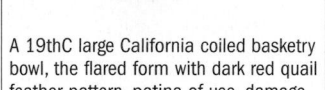

A 19thC large California coiled basketry bowl, the flared form with dark red quail feather pattern, patina of use, damage.

*15.5in (39.5cm) high*

**$2,200-2,800**  SK

A 19thC large California coiled basketry bowl, the flared form decorated with a dark red and brown diagonal track-like pattern with diamond spacers, severe rim damage.

*15.5in (39.5cm) high*

**$3,000-5,000**  SK

A late 19thC Northern California twined harvest basket, decorated with bands of dark brown geometric devices on a medium brown ground.

*4.5in (11.5cm) high*

**$800-1,200**  SK

A late 19thC California coiled basketry bowl, with three bands of zigzag decoration, stitch loss, rim damage.

*19.5in (49.5cm) diam*

**$2,200-2,800**  SK

A late 19thC California coiled basketry jar, Yokuts tribe, tightly woven bottleneck form with rattlesnake pattern and zigzag devices from the rim, topknot feathers at the shoulder, feather loss.

*9.25in (23.5cm) diam*

**$6,000-9,000**  SK

A Californian coiled basketry bowl, Yokuts tribe, with rattlesnake and abstract decoration, stitch loss, wear.

*8.5in (20.5cm) diam*

**$700-1,000**  SK

A California coiled basketry jar, Kern tribe, tightly woven with bands of two-color meandering devices, remnants of red wool at shoulder, wear.

*c1900*   *8.25in (21cm) diam*

**$8,000-12,000**  SK

A Northern California twined basketry bowl, the flared form decorated with three sets of stepped chevron devices on a natural ground.

*c1900*   *8.5in (21.5cm) diam*

**$1,800-2,200**  SK

A Southern California pictorial coiled basketry bowl, Miwok tribe, decorated with two large spread winged birds, two scorpions and two upside-down human figures.

*c1900*   *6.5in (16cm) diam*

**$7,000-10,000**  SK

An early 20thC California pictorial basketry bowl, tightly woven, decorated with eight human forms, all but one with an unusual geometric framing device.

*c1900*   *3.25in (8.5cm) high*

**$4,000-6,000**  SK

An early 20thC California pictorial coiled basketry jar, decorated with diamond and twelve human figure devices, remnant top knot feathers and wool at shoulder.

*c1900*   *5.25in (13.5cm) high*

**$10,000-15,000**  SK

An early 20thC California coiled basketry bowl, with flat base and flared sides, the base decorated with feathers in a five-point star pattern, clamshell and abalone pendants, row of quail top knot feathers, some loss and damage.

*c1900*      *2.5in (6.5cm) high*

**$3,000-5,000**      SK

An early 20thC California coiled basketry bowl, Pomo tribe, the bottom decorated with remnant feathers in a pinwheel variant, with glass bead and abalone shell pendants, feather loss, rim damage.

*9.5in (24cm) diam*

**$3,000-5,000**      SK

---

## A CLOSER LOOK AT A CALIFORNIA DANCE SKIRT

Originally, beads were made from coral, shells, animal bones, and various other natural materials. However, glass beads that were brought to the continent by colonists some 500 years ago became the primary material for beadwork in most tribes.

The peoples of warm climates often did not bother with much clothing except at festivals.

The thimbles, acquired through trading, were pierced and attached to traditional clothing as decorative features, particularly on dance costumes.

During ceremonial dances the jostling glass beads and brass thimbles were controlled by the dancers movements so that the sound produced was in perfect harmony with the drums.

A late19thC Northern California dance skirt, the heavily fringed buckskin wrap folded laterally, decorated with vegetal wrapped strips and strands of cut glass beads terminating in brass thimbles, interspersed with spaced seeds.

*34in (86.5cm) wide*

**$21,000-23,000**      SK

---

A California coiled basketry bowl, Pomo tribe, the compressed round form with dark red diagonal stepped fret design, with white clamshell additions, minor stitch loss.

*c1900*      *11in (28cm) diam*

**$1,200-1,800**      SK

A Northern California polychrome twined basketry bowl, possibly the work of Elizabeth Hickok, tightly woven, decorated with half-twist overlay of triangle and linear devices, minor stitch loss.

*3in (7.5cm) high*

**$7,000-10,000**      SK

A Northern California twined lidded basket, the globular form decorated with geometric devices on a natural ground, the lid with small central handle.

*8.5in (21.5cm) diam*

**$3,000-4,000**      SK

---

A late 19thC Northern California Dentalia necklace, multiple strands of geometric engraved shells with large white center red glass bead spacers.

*19in (48.5cm) long*

**$7,000-10,000**      SK

A Northern California beaded choker, possibly Pitt River, with dark blue and bottle green geometric devices on a white ground, beaded fringe and abalone pendants, minor loss.

*c1900*      *15in (38cm) long*

**$300-500**      SK

A California beaded wood bow, with cloth covering and multicolored beaded stacked diamond devices, banded background, minor bead loss.

*18.5in (47cm) long*

**$1,200-1,800**      SK

A late 19thC Great Lakes loom beaded bandolier bag, Winnebago tribe, cloth bag with strap and front beaded in geometric and heart devices, the tabs with remnant silk ribbons, framed.

*33in (84cm) long*

**$3,000-5,000**    **SK**

A late 19thC Great Lakes loom beaded bandolier bag, velvet front with cloth backing and silk edging, beaded with abstract floral devices, beaded tabs with wool tassels from the bottom, bead loss, damage.

*36in (90cm) long*

**$3,000-5,000**    **SK**

A late 19thC Great Lakes loom beaded bandolier bag, with strap, beaded with geometric devices, loom beaded tabs with red wool tassels, minor loss.

*32in (81.5cm) long*

**$4,000-6,000**

A late 19thC Great Lakes loom beaded bandolier bag, Ojibwa tribe, backed with commercial cloth, with geometric and floral devices, the beaded tabs with red wool tassels.

*35in (89cm) long*

**$2,200-2,800**    **SK**

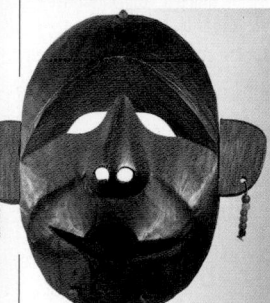

A Great Lakes beaded cloth bandolier bag, Ojibwa tribe, backed with commercial cloth, the shoulder strap and pouch with floral devices, remnant bugle bead swags from the bottom, damage.

*c1900*    *35.5in (34cm) long*

**$1,800-2,200**    **SK**

A late 19thC Western Great Lakes man's beaded cloth vest, the commercial cloth with narrow lapels and velvet trim, partially beaded on the front with abstract floral devices.

*22in (55cm) long*

**$800-1,200**    **SK**

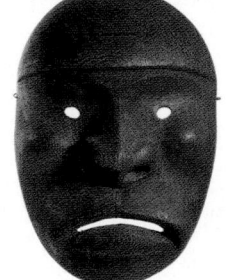

A late 19thC Great Lakes beaded cloth man's shirt, Winnebago tribe, calico pullover with wool tape ribbons, loom beaded panels with stylized leaf pattern, the tabs decorated with trade beads and wool tassels, damage.

*29in (74cm) long*

**$2,200-2,800**    **SK**

Two pairs of late 19thC Great Lake loom beaded garters, both with geometric devices and braided wool ends, one pair with tabs and trade beads hanging from one end, bead loss.

*14in (35.5cm) long*

**$1,200-1,800**    **SK**

An early 19thC Great Lakes turtle effigy bowl, with stylized head and tail, the holes in the burl surface had been filled with wood putty, was removed, and recently filled with lead.

*13.5in (34.5cm) long*

**$1,200-1,800**    **SK**

## INUIT TRIBES – MASKS

A mid-19thC Alaskan Athabascan Eskimo wooden face mask, from Ingalik.

*12in (30cm) high*

**$30,000-35,000**    **M&D**

A mid-19thC Alaskan Eskimo wooden face mask, with labrets, from Andreafsky.

*9.5in (24cm) high*

**$10,000-12,000**    **M&D**

A mid-19thC Alaskan Eskimo wooden face mask, from Diomede Island.

*10.5in (26.5cm) high*

**$7,000-10,000**    **M&D**

A mid-19thC Alaskan Eskimo wooden face mask, from King Island.

*8.5in (21.5cm) high*

**$7,000-10,000**    **M&D**

A mid-19thC Alaskan Eskimo wooden face mask, from King Island.

*9in (23cm) high*

**$7,000-10,000**    **M&D**

**TRIBAL ART**

A portion of a complex mid-19thC Alaskan Eskimo mask, from the Nushugak area.

*10in (25cm) wide*

**$25,000-30,000**     **M&D**

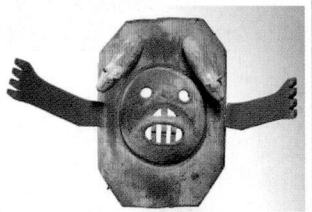

A portion of a complex mid-19thC Alaskan Yupik mask, from Goodnews Bay.

*9.5in (24cm) high*

**$30,000-35,000**     **M&D**

## A CLOSER LOOK AT AN ALASKAN DUAL-IMAGE MASK

*Masks were carved from driftwood and whalebone and used to evoke powerful spirits during ceremonial dance.*

*This mask was probably worn by a Shaman who acted as an intermediary between the spiritual and visible world.*

*The Eskimos of Western Alaska called themselves Yupik, literally meaning 'real person.' Most Yupik masks were destroyed after use, making them extremely rare and very valuable.*

*Design elements like this toothy mouth were common, and Yupik craftsmen would re-use these features in subsequent creations.*

An Alaskan dual-image shamanic Yupik mask, from the Kuskokwim area.

*c1880*     *12in (30cm) high*

**$110,000-120,000**     **TB**

An Eskimo red cedar male dance mask, from the lower McKenzie river.

*c1855*     *13in (33cm) long*

**$30,000-35,000**     **D&G**

An Alaskan Eskimo human effigy salmon fishing net float, from Point Hope.

*c1870*     *2.5in (6.5cm) wide*

**$2,000-3,000**     **M&D**

A late 19thC Alaskan Eskimo wooden face mask, from Point Hope.

*9in (23cm) high*

**$10,000-12,000**     **M&D**

## CEREMONIAL PIECES

An Old Bering Sea III culture Eskimo woman's ceremonial knife, or 'ulu', of walrus ivory and slate, decorated with stylized animal effigies, excavated at Kukulik, St. Lawrence Island, Alaska.

*c300-500AD*     *5in (12.5cm) wide*

**$4,000-6,000**     **M&D**

## INUIT ART

- The Inuit region spans a distance of 3,500 miles. It covers the coastal Arctic regions of Northern America, Greenland, and parts of Eastern Siberia.
- Three main periods of Inuit Art exist. The first spans from c2000BC to c1700 before the Inuit tribes were in contact with Europeans. The second is the contact period, which dates from c1700 to 1948, and the last period refers to contemporary Inuit art.
- Inuit tribesman were extremely talented artists, particularly gifted at sculpting forms from stone, whale bone, walrus ivory, and wood.
- Inuit craftsmen decorated everyday objects, like tools, amulets, clothing, or weapons, with stylized, anthropomorphic designs.
- The Inuit people believed in animism. These spiritual preferences are reflected in Inuit artwork, particularly in the carved masks and amulets used in Shamanistic rituals.

An Old Bering Sea II culture Eskimo shaman's birthing wand, of walrus ivory relief-carved with mother, father, and child's faces, excavated at Kukulik, St. Lawrence Island, Alaska.

*c100-300AD*     *7in (18cm) high*

**$10,000-12,000**     **M&D**

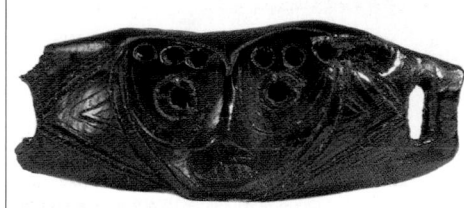

An Old Bering Sea III culture Eskimo child's ceremonial wrist band, of walrus ivory, to signify elevated social status, excavated at Kitneapaluk, St. Lawrence Island, Alaska.

c300-500AD · 1.5in (4cm) wide

**$3,000-4,000** · **M&D**

An 18thC Thule culture Eskimo shaman's drum handle, with bone rim attachment, excavated at Port Clarence, Alaska.

4.75in (12cm) long

**$10,000-12,000** · **M&D**

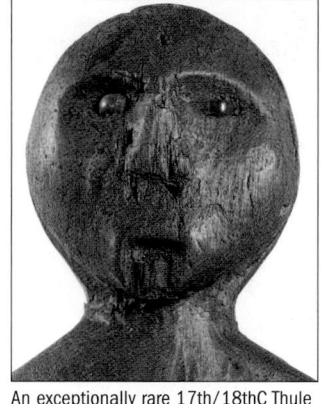

An exceptionally rare 17th/18thC Thule culture Eskimo wooden handheld shaman's effigy, with trade bead eyes and ray motif on chest, excavated at Igloo, Alaska.

12in (30.5cm) high

**$15,000-20,000** · **M&D**

An early 19thC Alaskan Eskimo multiple effigy walrus ivory ceremonial box handle, from Diomede Island.

6.25in (16cm) long

**$10,000-12,000** · **M&D**

An early 19thC Alaskan Eskimo walrus ivory ceremonial wound plug, from Diomede Island.

7.25in (18.5cm) long

**$15,000-20,000** · **M&D**

A mid-19thC Alaskan Eskimo shaman's drum, carved wood and ivory frame covered with walrus intestine fastened with sinew, from Point Hope.

19in (48.5cm) diam

**$10,000-15,000** · **M&D**

An Inuit engraved walrus skull, the tusks profusely decorated with images of birds, fish, a hunter and bear, an elephant, insects, and a spider crab, one tusk reglued.

c1900 · 27in (68.5cm) long

**$4,000-6,000** · **SK**

An Alaskan Eskimo shaman's walrus ivory box handle, from Cape Nome.

c1880 · 2.75in (7cm) long

**$4,000-6,000** · **M&D**

## WEAPONS & TOOLS

Three prehistoric ivory Inuit items, two pierced objects with incised decoration, and a long object with an animal head finial, all with custom-made stands.

6.5in (16.5cm) high

**$300-500** · **SK**

An Old Bering Sea II culture Eskimo sealing harpoon head, bone with a slate blade, excavated at Ivetok, St. Lawrence Island.

c100-300AD · 3.5in (9cm) long

**$600-900** · **M&D**

An Old Bering Sea II culture Eskimo walrus ivory harpoon socket piece, excavated at St. Lawrence Island, Alaska, damaged.

*The pointed end of this piece fixes to the wooden shaft of the harpoon, and the other end has a socket which fixes to an ivory foreshaft.*

c100-300AD · 8in (20cm) long

**$4,000-6,000** · **M&D**

A late 19thC Northeastern splint basketry fishing creel, with commercial leather straps.

*11in (28cm) long*

$300-500    SK

An early 19thC Northeastern painted wood splint basket, the lidded rectangular form with red and black abstract medallions and a band of connected diamonds, wood loss.

*12in (30cm) long*

$5,000-8,000    SK

A Northeastern splint basketry fishing creel, the oblong form with wood lid and rawhide lashings at the rim.

*11in (28cm) long*

$300-400    SK

An early 20thC Northeastern splint hamper, the lidded form with bulging sides, painted cream and blue, damage.

*28in (71cm) high*

$400-600    SK

A 19thC Northeastern moosehair embroidered birch bark tray, decorated on the interior with polychrome moosehair depicting various human and animal scenes with an eagle in the center, wear and damage, stand included.

*10in (25cm) diam*

$1,800-2,200    SK

A pair of mid-19thC Northeastern beaded cloth and leather moccasins, Seneca, commercial leather forms with hard soles, the black cloth cuffs and vamps with multicolored stylized floral devices, silk edging.

*9.5in (24cm) long*

$3,000-5,000    SK

An early 20thC Northeastern beaded cloth skirt, Iroquois tribe, black wool trimmed along the bottom with ribbon and white and blue beaded geometric devices, commercial buttons at the waist.

*29in (74cm) long*

$400-600    SK

A rare 16thC Northeastern carved stone pipe, the gray-green elbow form with tapered stem, U-shaped, angled bowl, stylized male head projecting from the front of the bowl, crack at elbow.

*5.5in (14cm) high*

$10,000-12,000    SK

A mid-19thC Northeastern carved stone pipe bowl, the bowl with three attached carved animals, an otter, beaver, and bear, further decorated with bands of incised concentric circles, lower flange pierced for an attachment, includes stand, damage.

*2.75in (7cm) high*

$4,000-6,000    SK

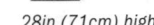

A 19thC Northeastern wood and metal cane, the gracefully curved form depicting a snake, with lead inlay detail and pyrographic decoration, dark patina, stand included.

*28in (71cm) high*

$1,200-1,800    SK

A 19thC Navajo late classic 'Moki' blanket, natural and commercially dyed homespun wool woven in a banded pattern, with a dark brown and indigo background.

*72x48in (183x122cm)*

**$10,000-12,000**  SK

A Southwestern Navajo 'Moki'-style Germantown weaving, tightly woven with multicolored stepped diamond pattern over a variegated striped ground.

*75x51in (190.5x129.5cm)*

**$10,000-12,000**  SK

### A CLOSER LOOK AT A NAVAJO SLAVE BLANKET

After the Navajo were forced from their land in 1864 by the US government, many were sold into slavery.

The style and technical characteristics of this blanket date it to the early 1860s.

The overall design concept of large radiating concentric diamonds is very different from the usual Navajo aesthetic which was always based on horizontal bands.

The narrower, longer format and exaggerated terracing, implies a different type of weaving environment and lead to the belief it is a Navajo slave blanket.

An early 1860s classic period man's serape Navajo slave blanket, wool loss.

*78x48in (198x122cm)*

**$60,000-80,000**  SK

A Southwestern Navajo Germantown weaving, tightly woven in a variant Chief's blanket pattern.

*67x45.5in (170x115.5cm)*

**$21,000-23,000**  SK

A late 19thC Southwestern Germantown weaving, tightly woven with concentric crosses, whirling logs, and arrows on a red ground, damage, wood loss.

*56x79in (142x200.5cm)*

**$4,000-6,000**  SK

A late 19thC Southwestern Germantown weaving, with rows of multicolored serrated diamonds on a red ground, two-color fret border and rare fringed edge.

*73x45in (185.5x114.5cm)*

**$8,000-12,000**  SK

A Southwestern Germantown weaving, Navajo, saddle blanket with fringe on one end, multicolored 'eye-dazzler' pattern on a red ground.

*31.5x26.5in (80x67.5cm)*

**$2,200-2,800**  SK

A large Southwestern weaving, Navajo, natural and commercially dyed homespun wool, with bold geometric and whirling log devices on a variegated ground, edge binding on two sides, wool loss, repairs, stains.

*c1880*

*107x91in (272x231cm)*

**$1,800-2,200**  SK

A Southwestern Germantown weaving, Navajo, multicolored diagonal serrated bands, fringed at the ends, wool loss.

*45.5x29in (115.5x74cm)*

**$2,200-2,800**  SK

A late 19thC Southwestern weaving, Navajo, woven with natural and commercially dyed homespun wool in a 'Third Phase' Chief's pattern, wool loss, repairs, fading.

*73x59in (185.5x150cm)*

**$2,200-2,800** SK

A late 19thC Southwestern weaving, Navajo, natural and commercially dyed homespun wool, in a variant Chief's pattern, with 'eye-dazzler' devices on a 'Moki'-style background, fading.

*72x59in (183x150cm)*

**$1,800-2,200** SK

An early 20thC Southwestern weaving, Navajo, natural and commercially dyed homespun wool, with stepped cross center and five red crosses on a variegated ground, wool loss, some dye run.

*94x74in (239x188cm)*

**$3,000-5,000** SK

An early 20thC Southwestern regional weaving, Navajo, natural and commercially dyed homespun wool, interlocking cross devices on a variegated ground, fret border, red warp, stains.

*106x61in (269x155cm)*

**$2,800-3,200** SK

An early 20thC Southwestern weaving, Navajo, large regional rug of natural and commercially dyed homespun wool, fret pattern on a variegated gray ground, with fret border, wool loss, stains.

*116x79.5in (295x202cm)*

**$3,000-5,000** SK

An early 19thC Southwestern regional weaving, Navajo, possibly J. B. More style or early ganado, natural and commercially dyed homespun wool, with crosses and whirling log devices, minor wool loss.

*63x45in (160x114cm)*

**$1,200-1,800** SK

An early 20thC Southwestern 'eye-dazzler' weaving, Navajo, natural and commercially dyed homespun wool woven in an overall concentric serrated diamond pattern, insect damage.

*84x51in (213.5x129.5cm)*

**$2,800-3,200** SK

A Southwestern pictorial weaving, Navajo, natural and commercially dyed homespun yarns, depicting seven Yei dancers, the lead dancer with feathered headdress, on a variegated ground.

*c1925*    *58x28in (147.5x71cm)*

**$1,500-2,000** SK

A Southwestern pictorial weaving, Navajo, natural and commercially dyed homespun wool, the central panel with central cornstalk and cows, lizards, and horses on a variegated ground, with a large geometric border.

*c1930*    *81x47in (206x119.5cm)*

**$8,000-12,000** SK

A Southwestern pictorial weaving, handspun wool, the central panel with three horses on a variegated ground, multiple stepped border.

*c1930*    *49.5x37.5in (126x95cm)*

**$1,200-1,800** SK

A Southwestern weaving, Navajo, woven in natural and commercially dyed homespun wool, concentric serrated diamonds on a variegated ground, sawtooth border.

*c1935*    *105x60.5in (267x154cm)*

**$2,800-3,200** SK

A Southwestern pictorial weaving, Navajo, five Yei figures, with central female figure, the border with two-color bird and feather devices, minor stains.

*70.5x42in (179x107cm)*

**$5,000-7,000** SK

A 20thC Southwestern weaving, Navajo, natural and commercially dyed homespun wool, concentric stepped crosses and feather devices on a variegated gray ground, wool loss.

*66x44in (167.5x112cm)*

**$600-900** SK

A Southwestern 'Moki'-style weaving, Germantown wool woven in a variant 'third phase' Chief's pattern, minor discoloration on one side.

*'Third Phase' Chief's pattern indicates the usage of new diamond-shaped elements.*

*72.5x64.5in (184x164cm)*

**$15,000-20,000** SK

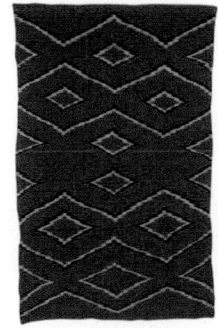

A 19thC Southwestern weaving, woven with natural and commercially dyed homespun wool in a late classic serape pattern, with a serrated diamond pattern, minor damage.

*71x44in (183x122cm)*

**$3,000-5,000** SK

A 19thC Southwestern weaving, natural and commercially dyed homespun wool woven in a variant-style Chief's pattern, with bands of concentric crosses on a variegated ground, alternating with stripes, old repair.

*70x58in (178x147.5cm)*

**$4,000-6,000** SK

A late 19thC Southwestern weaving, woven with natural and commercially dyed homespun wool, concentric diamond and linear devices on a red ground, damage.

*57x38in (145x96.5cm)*

**$1,800-2,200** SK

An Arts & Crafts Southwestern Indian rug, geometric patterns on charcoal field with black and tan band border.

*83x53.5in (211x134.5cm)*

**$2,200-2,800** FRE

An early 20thC Southwestern pictorial weaving, woven in natural and commercially dyed homespun wool depicting Yei figures, lizards, fish, feathers, lightning corner devices, and a central avian figure, all on a variegated background, minor damage.

*89x63in (226x160cm)*

**$8,000-12,000** SK

An early 20thC Southwestern weaving, woven with natural and commercially dyed homespun wool, central X-pattern with feather and lightning offshoots on a variegated ground, minor damage.

*66x39in (167.5x99cm)*

**$1,800-2,200** SK

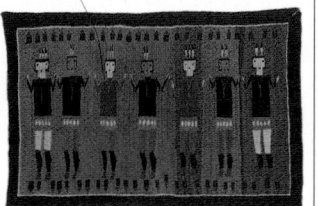

A 20thC Southwestern pictorial weaving, seven Yei figures on a variegated brown background.

*59x38in (150x96.5cm)*

**$1,500-2,000** SK

A Southwestern regional rug, natural and commercially dyed homespun wool tightly woven in a polychrome 'eye-dazzler' pattern, with fret pattern border.

*c1930    79x46.5in (200.5x118cm)*

**$1,200-1,800** SK

A 20thC Southwestern weaving, natural and commercially dyed homespun wool, the central panel with two bold Vallero stars, feather devices, and an unusual woman's dress pattern in the center.

*105x58in (266.5x147.5cm)*

**$1,800-2,200** SK

A 20thC Southwestern regional weaving, with natural and commercially dyed homespun wool, geometric elements on a variegated ground, with a bold border, minor damage.

*96x48in (244x122cm)*

**$2,800-3,200** SK

A 20thC Southwestern weaving, woven with natural and commercially dyed homespun wool, abstract bird devices on a variegated ground, serrated border, stains, minor loss.

*72x44in (183x112cm)*

**$800-1,200** SK

A Southwestern pottery bowl, the round globular form with short neck, decorated with red and black geometric and scroll devices on a buff ground.

c1200-1500AD

$600-900       SK

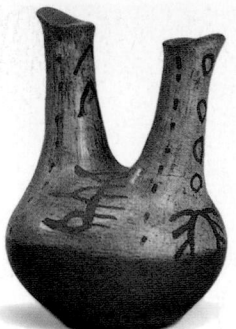

A 19thC Southwestern painted pottery wedding jar, San Ildefonso, double-spout form painted with dark red symbolic devices, broken, old metal pipe repair.

11in (28cm) high

$300-500       SK

A 19thC Southwestern pottery Olla, Zuni, the body with black and red-brown geometric, abstract foliate, and animal devices including heart-line deer and neck-crested birds, chips at rim, small hole.

*An Olla is a storage pot, used for water, grain and other foodstuff.*

12.5in (32cm) diam

$14,000-16,000       SK

A late 19thC Southwestern pottery Olla, Acoma, with bold geometric foliate and large stylized parrots, reglued crack, repainting on one bird and one leaf.

11.5in (29cm) diam

$14,000-16,000       SK

A late 19thC Southwestern pottery seed jar, Hopi, possibly Nampeyo, painted with dark brown and red-brown abstract bird and moth devices, crack and wear.

13.5in (34cm) diam

$27,000-30,000       SK

A late 19thC Southwestern pottery seed jar, Hopi, Nampeyo, with stylized bird and feather devices, restored by Andrew Goldsmidt, break lines visible.

*Includes typed provenance on part of an old playing card "Bowl bought in 1893? at mesa by potter named Nampeyo C.E.M.-Keams."*

11in (28cm) diam

$7,000-10,000       SK

A late 19thC Southwestern pottery Olla, Zia, decorated with black and orange geometric, foliate, and quadruped devices, fire clouds, surface wear.

12.5in (32cm) diam

$6,000-9,000       SK

A late 19thC Southwestern pottery jar, Zuni, dark brown and red-brown volutes, cross-hatching, and other classic abstract curvilinear devices on a cream-colored ground, wear at rim, stabilized hairline crack from rim.

12.25in (30.5cm) diam

$7,000-10,000       SK

A late 19thC Southwestern pottery Olla, Zuni, painted with classic black and red-brown 'rainbird' pattern, restored.

12in (30cm) diam

$4,000-6,000       SK

A late 19thC Southwestern Pottery Olla, Zuni, the body decorated with geometric and animal devices, two sunflower rosettes, heart-line deer, neck-crested birds, and other classic abstract decoration, minor chips to rim.

12in (30cm) diam

$8,000-12,000       SK

A late 19thC Southwestern pottery jar, painted with red and black sections of foliate devices, long body crack and repair.

*8in (20.5cm) diam*

**$500-700** SK

An early 20thC large Southwestern pottery vessel, signed "Maire san Ildefonso, N.M.," black-on-black form with 'Avanyu' pattern, minor scratches.

*c1920* *8.5in (21.5cm) high*

**$15,000-17,000** SK

An early Southwestern painted Olla, with abstract geometric and foliate devices and three stylized parrots, restoration.

*c1900* *12.5in (32cm) high*

**$23,000-25,000** SK

A Southwestern pottery jar, Acoma, painted with geometric devices on a cream-white ground, surface wear, chips.

*c1925* *10.25 (26cm) high*

**$700-1,000** SK

A Southwestern painted pottery dough bowl, Santo Domingo, with panels of black abstract devices on a buff ground, fire clouds, fading.

*15.25in (39cm) diam*

**$1,200-1,800** SK

A Southwestern pottery jar, Zia, with bands of geometric and foliate devices connecting three medallions with birds.

*c1930* *10.5in (27cm) diam*

**$2,800-3,200** SK

A Southwestern pottery jar, Acoma, with geometric and stylized feather devices on a cream-white ground, reglued at the rim.

*c1935* *11in (28cm) diam*

**$1,200-1,800** SK

A Southwestern carved and painted pottery vase, by Margaret Tafoya, with deeply carved 'Avanya' pattern, the white paint background possibly a later addition, damage, broken in half and reglued.

*10.5in (26.5cm) high*

**$1,800-2,200** SK

A late 19thC Southwestern painted pottery figure, Tesuque, made of mica-containing clay, the large head painted with yellow and dark green devices, broken and reglued in three spots.

*13.25in (34cm) high*

**$5,000-7,000** SK

A late 19thC Southwestern shell necklace, one strand of white shell heishi and turquoise, the silver tubular beads and turquoise and shell jaclas possibly a later addition.

*21in (53.5cm) long*

**$300-400** **SK**

A late 19thC Southwestern silver squash blossom necklace, with eighteen serrated edge blossoms, the Naja set with one large oval turquoise stone, strung on buckskin.

*15in (38cm) long*

**$5,000-7,000** **SK**

A Southwestern silver cross necklace, with a double-barred Naja, globular silver beads, and ten silver crosses, strung on original hide strand.

*c1900* *14in (35.5cm) long*

**$3,000-5,000** **SK**

A Southwestern silver squash blossom necklace, Navajo, with twelve squash blossoms, the double-barred Naja with turquoise set in serrated bezel, slight damage.

*c1900* *13.5in (34cm) long*

**$2,200-2,800** **SK**

A Southwestern silver cross necklace, globular silver beads, seven differing small crosses, and one large cross pendant.

*c1900* *14.5in (37cm) long*

**$2,800-3,200** **SK**

A Southwestern silver and turquoise necklace, the squash blossom form with 'needlepoint' turquoise settings.

*15in (38cm) long*

**$300-500** **SK**

A Southwestern silver and turquoise squash blossom necklace, Navajo, with heavy compressed globular beads, twelve squash blossoms, the double-barred Naja with three irregular-cut turquoise settings.

*c1950* *16.5in (41cm) long*

**$800-1,200** **SK**

A 20thC Southwestern copper squash blossom necklace, the Naja with a turquoise setting.

*The Naja is the crescent-shaped centerpiece. It has Moorish derivation.*

**$300-400** **SK**

A mid-20thC Southwestern silver squash blossom necklace, Navajo, two strands of compressed globular beads, with squash blossoms with a turquoise setting, the Naja with similar ends and a turquoise pendant.

*15in (38cm) long*

**$300-500** **SK**

A mid-20thC Southwestern squash blossom necklace, Navajo, two strands of silver beads, with sand-cast squash blossoms, turquoise settings, sand-cast double-barred Naja with two turquoise settings.

*14.5in (37cm) long*

**$800-1,200** **SK**

A mid-20thC Southwestern silver squash blossom necklace, Navajo, stamped silver beads, twelve stamp-decorated blossoms, double-barred Naja with twisted wire center and single oval turquoise setting.

*13.5in (34cm) long*

**$300-500** **SK**

A mid-20thC Southwestern turquoise and shell nugget necklace, large irregular-cut, heavily matrixed turquoise stones with small white heishi spacers.

*13.5in (34cm) long*

**$800-1,200** **SK**

A 20thC Southwestern silver and coral necklace, multiple strands of tubular-shaped pink-red coral and silver beads.

*12in (30cm) long*

**$400-600** SK

A Southwestern inlaid 'battery' necklace, with ten tabs and a large bird pendant set with crushed turquoise and other materials, losses.

*14in (35.5cm) long*

**$300-400** SK

A late 19thC Southwestern First Phase concha belt, Navajo, six oval diamond-slot silver conchas with early stampwork, later sand-cast silver buckle and leather backing.

*belt 39in (99cm) long*

**$3,000-5,000** SK

A late19thC Southwestern First Phase concha belt, seven oval diamond-slot silver conchas with classic stampwork, on original leather backing, commercial buckle.

*Concha is the Spanish term for shell. It is now mainly used as a Navajo design for a belt.*

**$10,000-12,000** SK

A late 19thC Southwestern silver and stone First Phase concha belt, with seven stamped and chiseled scallop-edged conchas, stamped sand-cast buckle with six greenish turquoise settings, patina of use.

*35in (89cm) long*

**$14,000-16,000** SK

A late 19thC Southwestern First Phase concha belt, seven diamond slot oval conchas with scalloped, stamped, and perforated edgework, original round buckle, on original commercial leather backing.

*conchas 4in (10cm) wide*

**$18,000-20,000** SK

A late 19thC Southwestern First Phase concha belt, Navajo, six oval diamond-slot silver conchas with classic stampwork, the silver buckle with elaborate stamp and repoussé work, mounted on original leather belt.

*38in (95cm) long*

**$7,000-10,000** SK

A Southwestern child's silver concha belt, Navajo, twelve stamped oval conchas, the rectangular scallop-edge buckle with stamped and repoussé decoration, commercial leather belt.

*c1940* *25in (63.5cm) long*

**$500-800** SK

A mid-20thC Southwestern man's silver and turquoise concha belt, eight scalloped oval conchas with Jell-O mold domes and set with a single stone, the oval buckle with repoussé work, on commercial leather, old pawn tag.

*40in (100cm) long*

**$1,800-2,200** SK

A mid-20thC Southwestern silver and turquoise concha belt, Navajo, oval conchas and butterfly forms, each with stamped and repoussé work and central turquoise settings, the buckle with stamped and repoussé work and four turquoise settings.

*belt 50in (127cm) long*

**$600-900** SK

A 20thC Southwestern silver concha belt, Navajo, attributed to Roger Skeet, six large oval conchas with stamped and repoussé work, winged buckle.

*concha 4.5in (11.5cm) long*

**$800-1,200** SK

A Southwestern silver-mounted leather pouch, Navajo, decorated with stamped, fluted, and domed buttons, the pouch flap with large sunburst-shaped concha with serrated bezel turquoise setting.

*c1900* *35in (89cm) long*

**$6,000-9,000** SK

A late 19thC large Southwestern coiled basketry bowl, the flared form with a radiating whirling log design, dark patina, minor stitch loss.

*8in (20cm) high*

**$4,000-6,000** **SK**

An early 20thC Southwestern twined burden basket, the conical form with two-color geometric design bands and strips of buckskin and buckskin fringe.

*12in (30.5cm) high*

**$2,800-3,200** **SK**

An early 20thC large Southwestern coiled basketry Olla, decorated in a diagonal grid pattern, a band of human forms, quadrupeds, and chickens at the shoulder, some restoration to rim, stitch loss.

*24in (61cm) high*

**$8,000-12,000** **SK**

An early 20thC Southwestern coiled basketry bowl, flared sides decorated with stepped pinwheel design, damage.

*15.5in (39.5cm) diam*

**$700-1,000** **SK**

A large 20thC Southwestern Native American basketry bowl.

*28in (70cm) diam*

**$3,000-5,000** **FRE**

## THE HOPI PUEBLO

A Southwestern carving, possibly Hopi, the flat cutout form depicting a woman wearing traditional clothing and jewelry, with a water Olla balanced on her head, patina, paint loss.

*c1900* *15in (38cm) high*

**$1,800-2,200** **SK**

An early 20thC Southwestern carved wooden Katsina, Hopi, twisted cottonwood form with large tablita, with European doily used as a manta.

*10.5in (27cm) high*

**$800-1,200** **SK**

### A CLOSER LOOK AT A HOPI CANTEEN

The Hopi Pueblo, from Northwestern Arizona, lived in hot desert like conditions, with no steady supply of water. The women of the tribe were assigned to collecting and storing water in these large pottery canteens.

The Kachina image represents one of a number of Hopi ancestral spirits, who occupied the Pueblo region for part of the year.

Hopi potters use the traditional coil and scrape technique. Their designs are hand-painted using the yucca leaf brush and vegetal and mineral paints.

This canteen is attributed to the Nampeyo family who were the most recognized of all Hopi potters, making this piece particularly valuable.

A late 19thC Hopi canteen, attributed to Hano Nampeyo, decorated with a Kachina image in brown shades on a cream slip ground.

*10.5in (26cm) high*

**$35,000-40,000** **POOK**

A Hopi wooden pigment figure, from New Mexico, Kachina Karosta area.

*c1940* *7.5in (19cm) high*

**$1,800-2,200** **BLA**

An early 20thC Hopi jar, possibly Nampeyo, with black decoration on an orange ground.

*10.5in (26.5cm) wide*

**$3,000-5,000** **POOK**

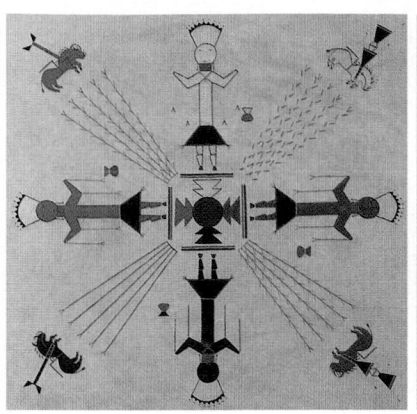
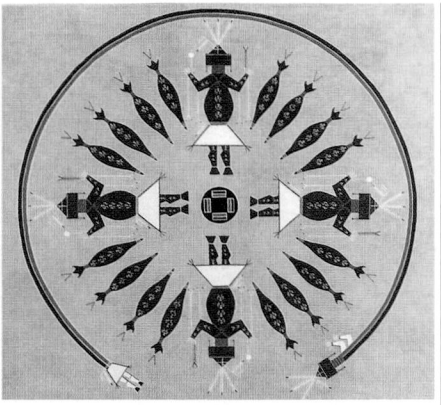

Two 20thC Southwestern paintings on cloth, with four human figures and other symbolic forms in a circular pattern.

*32x35in (81.5x89cm)*

**$400-600**     **SK**

A 20thC Southwestern watercolor painting on paper, depicting a Katsina dancer.

*11x7.25in (28x18.5cm)*

**$300-500**     **SK**

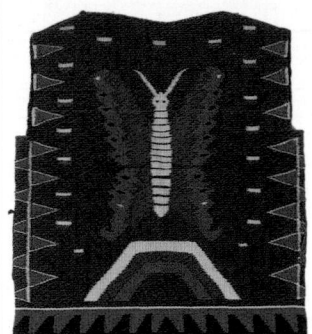

A Southwestern Navajo pictorial Germantown yarn vest, with down-turned lapels, two pockets, three Navajo silver buttons, the front with geometric devices, the back with a large central butterfly.

*c1900*     *22in (55cm) long*

**$800-1,200**     **SK**

A Southwestern girl's outfit, Navajo, includes traditional moccasins with silver buttons, cotton skirt, and a velvet blouse decorated with fluted buttons and conchas, repoussé worked brooches with turquoise settings, and silver and turquoise collar tabs.

*38in (96.5cm) long*

**$2,800-3,200**     **SK**

An early 20thC Southwestern net beaded collar, with bold blue and white geometric pattern, remnant large white beads from the beaded fringe, old illegible tag.

*24in (61cm) long*

**$400-600**     **SK**

A Southwestern inlaid silver and stone pin, Zuni, large 'knifewing' man with stamped decoration and inlaid with shell, turquoise, and jet.

*3.5in (9cm) high*

**$1,200-1,800**     **SK**

A late 19thC Southwestern silver and leather bridle, Navajo, mounted on its original leather, the two large conchas and brow band pieces with elaborate stamped, punched, and repoussé work, uncleaned condition.

*19in (47.5cm) long*

**$5,000-7,000**     **SK**

An early 20thC Southwestern silver and bridle, Navajo, with Navajo iron bit, the silver with stamped decoration and eighteen round and oval domed turquoise settings.

*24in (61cm) long*

**$4,000-6,000**     **SK**

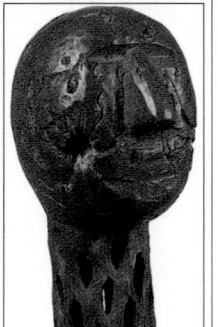

A Southwestern carved mesquite wood walking stick, possibly from a Northern Mexico Indian group, the finial carved as a head with peyote symbols on the cheeks and head, patina of use.

*30.5in (77.5cm) long*

**$300-400**     **SK**

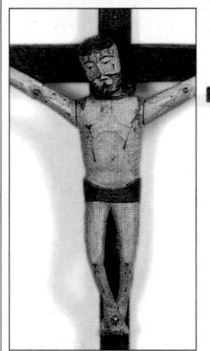
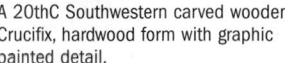

A 20thC Southwestern carved wooden Crucifix, hardwood form with graphic painted detail.

*53in (135cm) high*

**$800-1,200**     **SK**

A late 19thC photograph mounted on card stock, by photographer D.F. Barry (American, 1854-1934), the famous image of Lakota dancers standing in front of a log structure, damage.

*9x7.5in (23x19cm)*

**$800-1,200**　　　　　　　　　　SK

A late 19thC large photograph mounted on card stock, by D.F. Barry, depicting a Lakota war dance, pinholes in mount.

*9x6.25in (23x16cm)*

**$1,800-2,200**　　　　　　　　SK

A late 19thC large photograph on card stock, by D.F. Barry, depicting Lakota men before the dance.

*8.25x6.25in (21x16cm)*

**$1,200-1,800**　　　　　　　SK

A 19thC cabinet card, by E. A. Bonine (American, 1843-1916), depicting three Yuma men, marked "Yuma Indians, E. A. Bonine, Photo, Lamanda park, Los Angeles Co., Cal."

*7x4.5in (18x11.5cm)*

**$600-900**　　　　　　　　SK

A cabinet card photograph, by George W. Scott (American, 1854-1910), depicting 'Low Dog,' seated and holding a rare three-bladed knife club, Fort Yates, Dakota, stains, some fading.

*6.5x4.25in (16.5x11cm)*

**$500-800**　　　　　　　　SK

A cabinet card photograph, by George W. Scott, depicting 'Chief Gall,' Lakota, wearing war shirt and feathered bonnet, Fort Yates, Dakota, slightly faded.

*6.5x4.25in (16.5x11cm)*

**$600-900**　　　　　　　　SK

A cabinet card photograph, by George W. Scott, depicting 'Rain in the Face,' Fort Yates, Dakota, faded.

*6.5x4.25in (16.5x11cm)*

**$2,200-2,800**　　　　　　SK

A cabinet card photograph, by George W. Scott, depicting 'Sitting Bull', the mount marked "Fort Yates, Dakota," faded, stains.

*6.5x4.25in (16.5x11cm)*

**$800-1,200**　　　　　　SK

A 19thC cabinet card photograph, by Will Soule (American 1836-1908), depicting a Kiowa boy reclining on a buffalo robe, written on the front "Tar-lo, Kiowa Boy," stamped on the back "W. S. Soule, Fort Sill, I. T."

*6.5x4in (16.5x10cm)*

**$600-900**　　　　　　SK

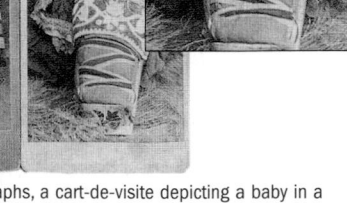

R. ANTELOPE and FAMILY.

Two late 19thC Woodlands photographs, a cart-de-visite depicting a baby in a traditional cradle, and a cabinet card depicting "R. Antelope and Family" in traditional dress, trimmed down at top.

*larger 5.25x38in (13.5x96.5cm)*

**$220-280**　　　　　　SK

432

## MAYAN ART

- The Mayan civilization originates from Central America, in the region of modern day southeast Mexico, Western Honduras, Guatemala, and Belize.
- The Mayans were highly skilled in pottery and carving jade. Jade was particularly important to Mayan society. Its green hues, reminiscent of young crops and the life-giving waters of nearby rivers, represented ideas of fertility and renewal, giving jade spiritual significance and added value in Mayan culture.
- Their terracotta and jade sculptures were not only reserved for deities and priests, but also for wealthy, powerful men and women who wished to memorialize themselves in stone.
- Sculptured figurines often depict females, animals, birds, and mythical creatures. Mayan artists were highly skilled at relief carving and many of these designs protrude from the surface.
- Pottery vessels were large and covered with ornate designs painted with slip-paint, a combination of watered-down clay and colored minerals.

### A CLOSER LOOK AT A MAYAN JADE VESSEL

The ancient Maya considered jade to be divine and therefore far more important than gold. The stone brimmed with religious meaning and was used to make both artistic and sacred objects.

The depicted dignitary is wearing a bead necklace with a large face pendant, ear ornaments, and avian headdress.

This urn was a ceremonial and ritual container, carved from a green jade and polished to a high shine.

The carvings are in high relief with a dignitary seated cross-legged in a relaxed and animated posture.

A Pre-Columbian Mayan green jade vessel, from Mexico.

cAD650                                    4in (10cm) high

**$15,000-20,000**                              **BLA**

A Pre-Columbian molded Mayan Ocarina pottery piece, from Mexico or Guatemala.

c400BC        4.5in (11.5cm) long

**$1,500-2,000**              **BLA**

---

A Pre-Columbian Mayan pottery seated figure, from Honduras, Itzapa area.

c450BC        5in (12.5cm) high

**$1,800-2,200**              **BLA**

A Pre-Columbian ceremonial Maya hacha from Guatemala, carved and drilled stone, in the form of human face in profile.

cAD650        11.5in (29cm) high

**$10,000-15,000**            **BLA**

A Pre-Columbian Mayan jade mask, from Mexico.

cAD750        4.5in (11.5cm) high

**$7,000-10,000**             **BLA**

A Pre-Columbian Mayan pottery figure, from Mexico.

cAD750        11.5in (29cm) high

**$7,000-10,000**             **BLA**

A Pre-Columbian Mayan jade pectoral or ceremonial dagger, from Mexico or Guatemala.

c650BC        10.5in (26cm) high

**$7,000-10,000**             **BLA**

---

A Pre-Columbian Mayan ceremonial flint, from Mexico or Guatemala.

cAD750        5.75in (14.5cm) high

**$4,000-6,000**              **BLA**

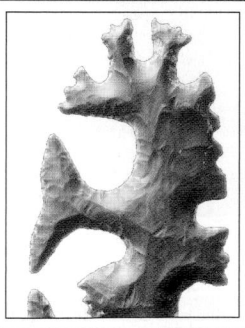

A Pre-Columbian Mayan excentric ceremonial flint, from Mexico or Guatemala.

cAD750        7.25in (18cm) high

**$10,000-15,000**            **BLA**

A Huari tapestry, from Peru.

*The Huari, or Wari tribe, were the dominant tribe in the Andes region from around AD700-1100, before the rise of the Incas.*

c AD800

**$4,000-6,000**　　　**BLA**

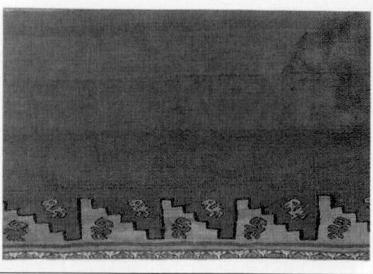

A Pre-Columbian Chimu cloth panel, from Peru, made predominantly of red, white, ocher, and black, with typical iconography including geometric and tortoises motifs.

*c1200*　　　*18.75in (47cm) wide*

**$600-900**　　　**BLA**

A Pre-Columbian Chancay cloth panel, from Peru.

*c1200*　　　*16.75in (42cm) wide*

**$600-900**　　　**BLA**

A Pre-Columbian ceremonial Chancay painted cloth, from Peru, painted with a shaman.

*The Chancay were from the Chancay Valley north of Lima.*

*c1200*　　　*48in (120cm) wide*

**$3,000-4,000**　　　**BLA**

A Chimu tapestry, from Peru.

*c1200*　　　*39.25in (98cm) high*

**$1,200-1,800**　　　**BLA**

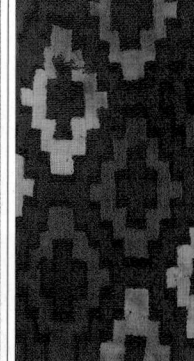

An Inca cloth tunic, mostly in red, olive green, black, and yellow, from Peru.

*c1200*　　　*32in (80cm) wide*

**$800-1,200**　　　**BLA**

A Pre-Columbian Chimu cloth tunic, decorated with colorful and stylized motifs, from Peru.

*c1250*　　　*88.75in (222cm) long*

**$3,000-4,000**　　　**BLA**

A Mochica stone conopa, animal shape, black to greenish-black and highly polished, from Peru.

c AD100

**$1,200-1,800**　　　**BLA**

A Mochica stone scepter, from Peru.

c AD200　　　*19.25in (48cm) high*

**$10,000-15,000**　　　**BLA**

A Mochica terracotta human jar, from Peru.

c AD500　　　*10.25in (25.5cm) high*

**$700-1,000**　　　**BLA**

A Mochica III stirrup-spot animal effigy vessel, from Peru.

*cAD500*      *12.25in (30.5cm) high*

**$1,800-2,200**      **BLA**

A Mochica III terracotta animal effigy vessel, from Northern Peru.

*cAD500*      *9.75in (24.5cm) high*

**$800-1,200**      **BLA**

A Nazca double spout and bridge terracotta vessel, from Southern Peru.

*cAD500*      *7.75in (19.5cm) high*

**$1,200-1,800**      **BLA**

A Tihuanaco Huari stone conopa, animal shape, black to greenish-black and highly polished, from Peru or Bolivia.

*cAD800*

**$1,200-1,800**      **BLA**

A Chancay terracotta vessel, from Peru.

*c1200*      *20in (50cm) high*

**$5,000-7,000**      **BLA**

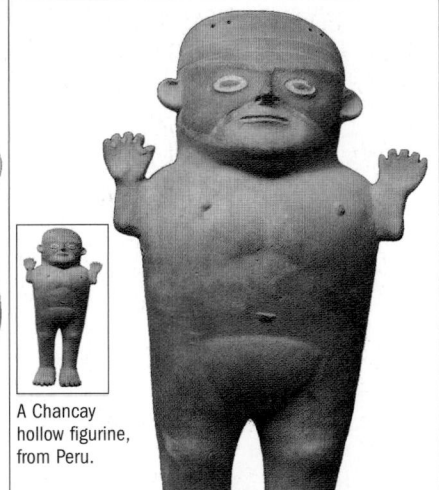

A Chancay hollow figurine, from Peru.

*c1200*      *23.25in (58cm) high*

**$1,500-2,500**      **BLA**

A Chimu terracotta erotic vase, from Peru.

*c1200*      *9.5in (23cm) high*

**$1,200-1,800**      **BLA**

A Chimu stirrup spout vessel, from Peru.

*c1200*      *8.25in (20.5cm) high*

**$300-400**      **BLA**

A Chimu terracotta vessel, from Peru.

*The Chimu culture flourished from the 13th to the 15th centuries.*

*c1300*      *6.5in (16cm) high*

**$400-700**      **BLA**

A Pre-Columbian jade pectoral pendant, from Costa Rica.

c100BC          3.5in (9cm) high

**$1,500-2,000**                    **BLA**

A volacanic stone ceremonial table, from Costa Rica.

c500AD          12.5in (31cm) high

**$5,000-8,000**                    **BLA**

A jade ring from Costa Rica.

c500AD          1.25in (3cm) high

**$700-1,000**                    **BLA**

A Pre-Columbian Guanacaste jade pectoral pendant, from the Nicoya area, Costa Rica.

c650AD          3.75in (9.5cm) high

**$4,000-6,000**                    **BLA**

A Nicoya greenstone mace head, from Costa Rica.

c700AD          3.5in (8.5cm) high

**$1,800-2,200**                    **BLA**

A seated polychrome human figure, from Costa Rica, Nicoya area.

c1000          7in (17.5cm) high

**$500-800**                    **BLA**

A terracotta vessel, from Costa Rica, Nicoya area.

c1000          10.5in (26cm) high

**$800-1,200**                    **BLA**

A terracotta vessel, from Costa Rica, Nicoya area.

c1200          9.25in (23cm) high

**$3,000-5,000**                    **BLA**

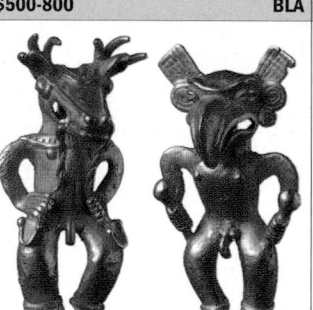

A gold Diquis shaman pendant, Veragas, Panama, Costa Rica, 1.8oz.

c1200          3.75in (9.5cm) high

**$5,000-8,000**                    **BLA**

Two gold Shaman pendants, Diquis, Veragas, Panama, Costa Rica, 1.4oz and 1.5oz.

c1200          larger 2.5in (6.5cm) high

**$30,000-40,000**                    **BLA**

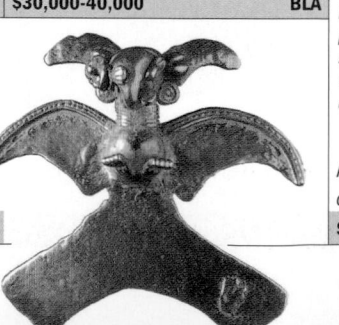

A gold avian pendant, Diquis region, Veragas, Panama, Costa Rica, 2oz.

c1200          3.25in (8cm) high

**$5,000-8,000**                    **BLA**

## A CLOSER LOOK AT A ZOOMORPHIC PENDANT

Gold was highly prized in this region and signified political power and wealth to the competitive chiefs of Costa Rican tribes.

Amphibian subjects were a favorite among Diquis goldsmiths.

The stylized legs of the frogs demonstrate the Disquis' imaginative portrayal of their surrounding environment. This artistry is extremely desirable to collectors.

The anthropomorphic figures have the bodies of frogs, and a long double-headed snake slithers behind them. It is thought that the combination of the amphibious creatures and the dual-headed snake denote ideas of rebirth and fertility.

A zoomorphic pendant, Diquis, Veragas, Panama, Costa Rica, 3.8oz.

c1200          3.25in (8cm) high

**$35,000-45,000**                    **BLA**

A Veraguas terracotta stemmed dish, with painted stylized creatures all in rust, black, and mauve on an orange ground, Panama.

*cAD600*       *12in (30cm) diam*

**$3,000-4,000**       **BLA**

A Pre-Columbian Calima gold mask, from Colombia.

*cAD300*       *3.25in (8cm) wide*

**$6,000-9,000**       **BLA**

A Chorrera terracotta idol figure, from Ecuador.

*c1200*       *12in (30cm) high*

**$3,000-5,000**       **BLA**

A Jama Coaque sculpture of a shaman, from Ecuador.

*cAD100*       *20in (50cm) high*

**$7,000-10,000**       **BLA**

A Valdivian greenstone hatchet, from Ecuador.

*c2000BC*　　　*6.5in (16cm) high*

**$800-1,200**　　　**BLA**

Five Chorrera terracotta heads, from Ecuador Tumaco-La Tolita area.

*c600BC*　　　*tallest 2.5in (6cm) high*

**$700-1,000**　　　**BLA**

Five terracotta heads, from Ecuador, Tumaco area.

*c200BC*　　　*tallest 3.25in (8cm) high*

**$700-1,000**　　　**BLA**

A Jama Coaque sculpture, depicting a shaman, from Ecuador.

*cAD100*　　　*10.5in (26cm) high*

**$3,000-5,000**　　　**BLA**

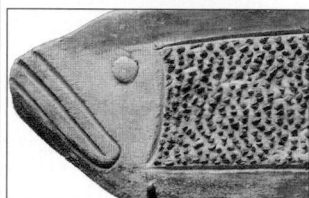

A terracotta fish-shaped vessel, from Ecuador, Tumaco area.

*cAD100*　　　*11.5in (28.5cm) wide*

**$800-1,200**　　　**BLA**

A Pre-Columbian Tumaco terracotta female figure, from Columbia, La Tolita/Monte alto area.

*c100BC*　　　*6.75in (17cm) high*

**$800-1,200**　　　**BLA**

A Veraguas terracotta stemmed dish, painted with stylized animals, flared foot with superimposed triangles all in rust, black mauve on orange ground, Panama.

*cAD650*　　　*10.25in (25.5cm) diam*

**$1,800-2,200**　　　**BLA**

A 19thC terracotta Venus figure with polychrome pigments, from the Amazonian region.

*6.75in (17cm) high*

**$600-900**　　　**BLA**

A Pre-Columbian carved jade, one side with the image of an important male figure with elaborate headdress, earplugs, and necklace, part of the headdress broken off.

*cAD750*　　　*2in (5cm) high*

**$1,200-1,800**　　　**SK**

A Pre-Columbian carved wood figure, probably worn as a pendant, with large head, short legs, the hands to the abdomen, pierced at the upper arms and top of head.

*2.25in (5.5cm) high*

**$700-1,000**　　　**SK**

An early 20thC South American woven poncho, indigo with concentric stepped cross devices, with two inset bands of red and white geometric devices, fringe to bottom.

*50in (125cm) long*

**$8,000-12,000**　　　**SK**

## CHOKWE TRIBE

- The Chokwe tribe has its roots in the 15thC, when an alliance between a Lunda queen and a Luba prince prompted a section of the Lunda aristocracy to resettle in what is now Angola.
- Chokwe society is administered by the Mwanangana, a ruler who apportions hunting and farming plots, supported by societies for male and female subjects called Mugonge and Ukule respectively.
- Art in Chokwe society is divided into two distinct schools. Folk art, for use in everyday family life, is made by craftsmen called Songi. Higher status artists, known as Fuli, craft artifacts for the royal court.
- The Western form of the Chokwe chief's chairs comes from contact with Portuguese colonialists. They are elaborately carved with caryatid supports.
- A great deal of Chokwe figurative art depicts venerated ancestors. Typical subjects include the prince Tshibinda Ilunga and deceased Mwanangana.
- Most sculptural depictions of women are based on an unknown female ancestor who inspired the Pwo mask. The characteristic feature of these masks is the elaborate coiffure.

### A CLOSER LOOK AT A CHOKWE MASK

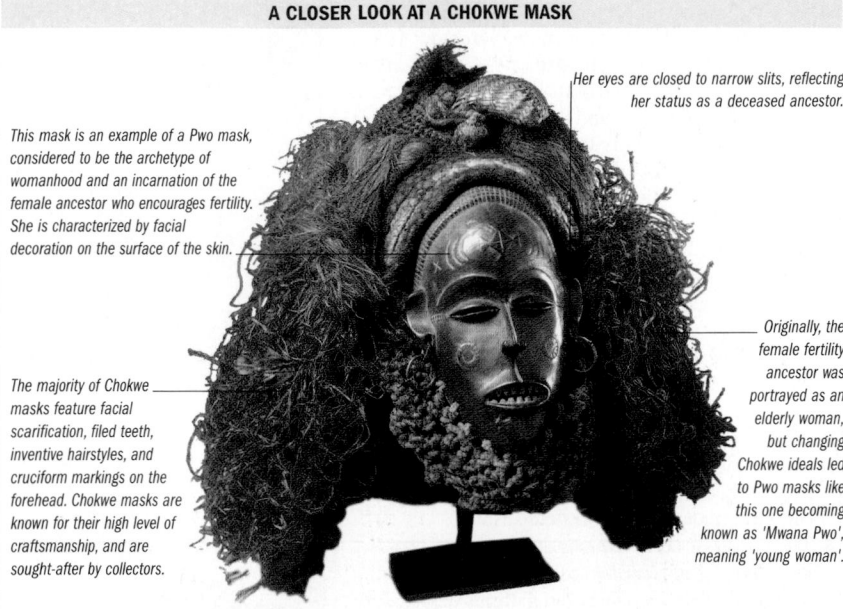

*This mask is an example of a Pwo mask, considered to be the archetype of womanhood and an incarnation of the female ancestor who encourages fertility. She is characterized by facial decoration on the surface of the skin.*

*Her eyes are closed to narrow slits, reflecting her status as a deceased ancestor.*

*The majority of Chokwe masks feature facial scarification, filed teeth, inventive hairstyles, and cruciform markings on the forehead. Chokwe masks are known for their high level of craftsmanship, and are sought-after by collectors.*

*Originally, the female fertility ancestor was portrayed as an elderly woman, but changing Chokwe ideals led to Pwo masks like this one becoming known as 'Mwana Pwo', meaning 'young woman'.*

An early 20thC Chokwe mask, with a headdress made of loofah and an overlay of raffia hair.

*12in (30cm) high*

$7,000-10,000  BLA

A late 19thC Chokwe Pwo dance mask, from Angola or the Democratic Republic of Congo.

*9in (22.5cm) high*

$2,800-3,200  BLA

An early 20thC Chokwe dance mask, with elaborate hairstyle, keloid facial scarification patterns, remnants of kaolin pigment around the eyes and cruciform on forehead, from the Democratic Republic of Congo.

*7.5in (19cm) high*

$3,000-4,000  BLA

A late 19thC Chokwe carved wooden cane, from Angola.

*33in (84cm) high*

$800-1,200  BLA

An early 20thC Chokwe figure, from Angola.

*9.25in (23.5cm) high*

$700-1,000  BLA

An early 20thC wooden Chokwe chief's chair, from Angola.

$1,200-1,800  BLA

An early 20thC small carved Chokwe chief's chair, with enthronement scenes.

*24.5in (61cm) high*

$1,800-2,200  BLA

A mid-19thC wooden Kuba figure, from the Democratic Republic of Congo.

*10.5in (26cm) high*

$1,200-1,800  BLA

A late 19thC Kuba wooden medicine cup, from the Republic Democratic of Congo.

*8.5in (21cm) high*

$2,800-3,200  BLA

## LUBA

- Luba artists and craftsmen carry a ceremonial axe as a symbol of their high status in society. Members of the clan with birth defects are thought to have a propensity for magic, and are often inducted into the artistic community for this reason.

- The Luba have a special reverence for women and believe that the clan was established by Vilie, a female spirit who assures fertility.

- Luba chieftains would offer women from their family lines as wives to neighboring rulers, forging alliances cemented by female influence.

- When a Luba ruler died, his spirit traditionally transferred to a woman who would move into the deceased chief's residence and continue his reign by proxy.

- Luba stools, supported by a kneeling or standing female caryatid figure, are very distinctive. They are invariably carved from a single tree trunk and display a high degree of craftsmanship.

- The power of Luba rulers is demonstrated by flaunting art objects, including stools and canes. The coiffure and scarification patterns depicted on a chief's artifacts relate to his own prestige.

A 19thC Luba stool, supported by a female caryatid, from the Democratic Republic of Congo.

*18in (45cm) high*

**$3,000-4,000**    **BLA**

A late 19thC Luba Suku wooden fetish figure, from the Democratic Republic of Congo.

*12.75in (32cm) high*

**$2,800-3,200**    **BLA**

A late 19thC Luba male ancestral Hemba figure, from the Democratic Republic of Congo.

*8in (20cm) high*

**$1,200-1,800**    **BLA**

A late 19thC Luba ancestral wooden medicine cup, in the form of a woman, from the Democratic Republic of Congo.

*6.25in (15.5cm) high*

**$300-500**    **BLA**

An early 20thC Luba figure of a crouching woman, holding her breasts, from the Democratic Republic of Congo.

*6.75in (17cm) high*

**$300-500**    **BLA**

An early 20thC Luba stool, supported by female caryatids, from the Democratic Republic of Congo.

*17.25in (43cm) high*

**$7,000-10,000**    **BLA**

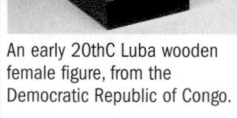

An early 20thC Luba stool, supported by a female caryatid, from the Democratic Republic of Congo.

*6in (15cm) high*

**$2,200-2,800**    **BLA**

An early 20thC wooden Luba chief's cane, with a bust in the form of a female figure, from the Democratic Republic of Congo.

*59.5in (149cm) high*

**$800-1,200**    **BLA**

An early 20thC Luba ceremonial wooden Kasai figure, in the form of a female, from the Democratic Republic of Congo.

*12.5in (31cm) high*

**$800-1,200**    **BLA**

An early 20thC Luba Hemba ancestral male figure, in wood, from the Democratic Republic of Congo.

*12.75in (32cm) high*

**$7,000-10,000**    **BLA**

An early 20thC Luba wooden female figure, from the Democratic Republic of Congo.

*10in (25cm) high*

**$500-800**    **BLA**

An early 20thC Luba Hemba stool, supported by a female caryatid, from the Democratic Republic of Congo.

*12in (30cm) high*

**$1,200-1,800**    **BLA**

A late 19thC dance mask, from the Democratic Republic of Congo.

*12.5in (31cm) high*

**$5,000-7,000**　　　　　　**BLA**

A rare early 20thC Ngbawka wooden dance mask, of Cubist form, from the Democratic Republic of Congo.

*10.5in (26cm) high*

**$12,000-15,000**　　　　　**BLA**

## A CLOSER LOOK AT A NBAWKA DANCE MASK

*Many African tribes believe masks to be the faces of gods and spirits. This mask conforms to an ideal of an aesthetically pleasing narrow, well-proportioned face with a high forehead, arching eyebrows and a narrow nose.*

*These scarification marks are a reference to bodily scarification, a process that holds important societal value in some tribes. A scarificator is used to pierce the skin and aid blood-letting, possibly as an initiation ritual or a way of preparing girls for the ordeal of childbirth.*

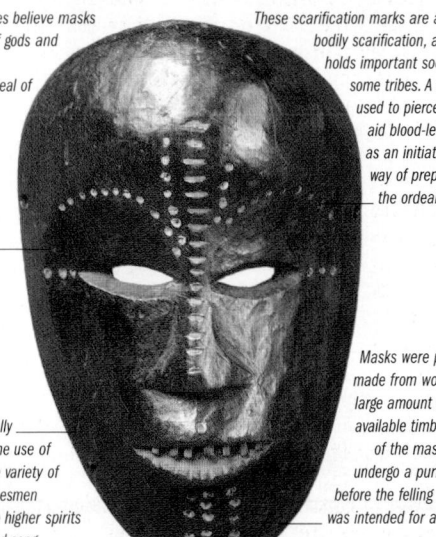

*Masks are generally associated with the use of dance and a wide variety of rituals involve tribesmen communicating to higher spirits through dance and song.*

*Masks were predominantly made from wood due to the large amount and variety of available timber. The carver of the mask would often undergo a purification ritual before the felling of a tree that was intended for a dance mask.*

An early 20thC wooden Nbawka dance mask, with facial scarification patterns, from the Democratic Republic of Congo.

*10.5in (26cm) high*

**$12,000-15,000**　　　　　**BLA**

An early 20thC oblong Lélé helmet mask, from the Democratic Republic of Congo.

*18in (45cm) high*

**$1,800-2,200**　　　　　**BLA**

An early 20thC Lega wooden chief's mask, decorated with white pigment, from the Democratic Republic of Congo.

*7.25in (18cm) high*

**$500-700**　　　　　　　**BLA**

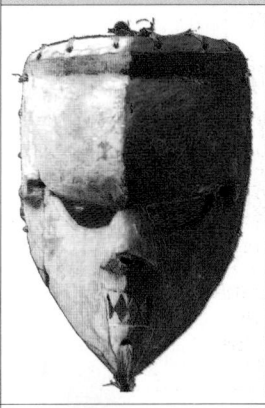
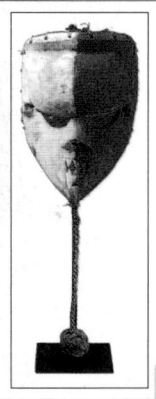

An early 20thC Salampasu wooden dance mask, decorated with polychrome pigments, from the Democratic Republic of Congo.

*10.75in (27cm) high*

**$2,800-3,200**　　　　　**BLA**

A rare mid-19thC patinated Mbole ivory figure, from the Democratic Republic of Congo.

*4.25in (10.5cm) high*

**$1,200-1,800**　　　　　**BLA**

An early 20thC wooden Kongo fetish figure, from the Democratic Republic of Congo.

*9in (22.5cm) high*

**$1,800-2,200**　　　　　**BLA**

An early 20thC Bas Yaka maternity figure with a child, from the Democratic Republic of Congo.

**$1,200-1,800**　　　　　**BLA**

An early 20thC Salampasu wooden male figure, from the Democratic Republic of Congo.

*11.5in (28.5cm) high*

**$1,200-1,800**　　　　　**BLA**

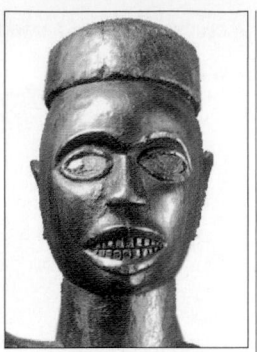

An early 20thC wooden Vilie fetish, encrusted with mirror and metal splinters, form the Democratic Republic of Congo.

*25.5in (63.5cm) high*

**$12,000-15,000**    BLA

An early 20thC statue of a Kusu ancestral male figure, from the Democratic Republic of Congo.

*18.75in (47cm) high*

**$5,000-7,000**    BLA

An early 20thC Bassikassingo fetish figure, with an elongated oblong face terminating in a stylized beard, marked with sacrifice symbols, from the Democratic Republic of Congo.

*14.5in (36cm) high*

**$1,200-1,800**    BLA

An early 19thC ivory pounder, with carved geometric design, from the Democratic Republic of Congo.

*11in (27.5cm) high*

**$280-320**    BLA

A wooden Yaka hand drum, the carved head with pierced ears, above an open cylinder, from the Democratic Republic of Congo.

*17in (42.5cm) high*

**$800-1,200**    FRE

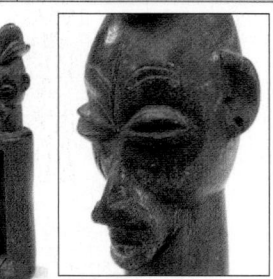

## GABON

An early 20thC wooden Punu dance mask, decorated with kaolin pigments, from Gabon.

*11.5in (29cm) high*

**$1,800-2,200**    BLA

A 19thC iron and carved ivory Mangbetu battle knife, from the Central African Republic.

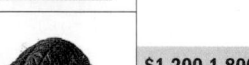

*16in (40cm) high*

**$1,200-1,800**    BLA

A late 19thC Kota reliquary figure, with oval face, crescent crest and lobed lateral flanges, all covered with brass, from Gabon.

*22.5in (56.5cm) high*

**$8,000-12,000**    BLA

An early 20thC miniature Punu wooden mask, from Gabon.

*8in (20cm) high*

**$1,800-2,200**    BLA

An early 20thC wooden Fang Byeri reliquary figure, from Gabon.

*19.5in (48.5cm) high*

**$18,000-25,000**    BLA

## BAOULÉ

- Originally from Ghana, the Baoulé people migrated westward with their queen Aba Pokou when the Asante tribe rose to influence in their traditional territory during the 18thC.
- Now settled in the Ivory Coast, the Baoulé are one of the most prolific and culturally dominant tribes in Western Africa.
- Craftsmen used carved wood with gold and brass castings to produce an abundance of artwork including masks, statues and everyday decorative objects such as carved doors and boxes.
- The Baoulé use a variety of mask forms. One of them, known as Bonu Amwin, represents a buffalo head. Its heavy, stylized features inspired Picasso and the Cubist movement. Other mask types include the Goli festival mask, used to celebrate the harvest.
- Spirit statues have great importance in Baoulé culture. Asie Usu statues help ensure fruitful harvests and hunting, whereas Blolo Bian and Blolo Bla statues symbolize male and female spouses from the spirit world. These statues are characterized by detailed coiffures and keloid scarification marks.

### A CLOSER LOOK AT A BAOULÉ MASK

This mask was made by the Baoulé people, who account for around a quarter of the population of the Ivory Coast. The Baoulé tribe was greatly influenced by the neighboring Senufo and Guro tribes, particularly in the design of masks and figure carving.

This example is typical of a Baoulé mask, with its realistic rounded face, pointed chin, T-shaped nose, raised scarification marks, semi-circular eyes, and distinctive coiffure.

Masks were designed for specific people and it was believed that when a person's face came into contact with the inside of a mask, the individual would become the entity that the mask represented. It was therefore dangerous for others to wear ceremonial masks because each one had received an individual's soul.

This mask does not appear to have had a specific sacred function and was probably worn during festivals held for important dignitaries. The ownership of masks was usually restricted to powerful and specially trained individuals and families.

A 19thC wooden Baoulé mask, representing a dignitary, with scarification marks, from the Ivory Coast.

9.75in (24.5cm) high

$5,000-7,000    BLA

An early 20thC hardwood Baoulé or Guro mask, with traces of vegetable and mineral pigments, from the Ivory Coast.

16.5in (41cm) high

$1,200-1,800    BLA

A late 19thC male Baoulé Blolo Bian figure, from the Ivory Coast.

21.5in (54cm) high

$5,000-7,000    BLA

A late 19thC Baoulé figure of a dignitary or important ancestor, from the Ivory Coast.

17.5in (44cm) high

$1,800-2,200    BLA

An early 20thC abstract Baoulé figure, from the Ivory Coast.

8.25in (20.5cm) high

$300-500    BLA

An early 20thC Baoulé anthropomorphic Blolo Bla figure, from the Ivory Coast.

16.75in (42cm) high

$1,800-2,200    BLA

An early 20thC Baoulé wooden masculine figure, from the Ivory Coast.

18.75in (47cm) high

$800-1,200    BLA

An early 20thC Baoulé wooden figure, from the Ivory Coast.

13.25in (33cm) high

$800-1,200    BLA

A pair of early 20thC ancestral Baoulé figures, from the Ivory Coast.

20in (50cm) high

$8,000-12,000    BLA

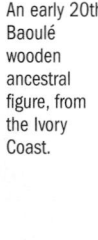 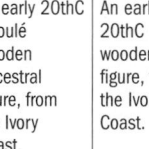

An early 20thC Baoulé wooden ancestral figure, from the Ivory Coast.

18.5in (46.5cm) high

$3,000-5,000    BLA

An early 20thC Baoulé wooden figure, from the Ivory Coast.

13.25in (33cm) high

$800-1,200    BLA

**TRIBAL ART**

## DAN MASKS

- The characteristic features of Dan masks include a concave face, protruding mouth and high-domed forehead.
- The rich brown patina on these masks is achieved by applying vegetable extracts. Once dry, these extracts act like a varnish or lacquer, imparting a dark hue to the wood.
- Most Dan masks are produced and kept by powerful societies such as Poro, a men's society, and Sande, a secret women's society.
- As well as ritual and ceremonial use, Dan masks are used for education and entertainment. They also provide an important social function by helping to arbitrate in disagreements.
- Dan masks are vessels for an essence known as 'du', bestowed by the creator god Zlan on all living things. Bodiless du appear in dreams to initiates of Dan societies to reveal how they want to be represented.
- The business of bridging the gap between the village and the dark forest, where the formless du reside, is considered very dangerous in Dan society, and is therefore a serious undertaking.

### A CLOSER LOOK AT A DAN MASK

This very smooth brown patina may have been produced by immersing the mask in mud, as opposed to the application of vegetable dyes which tends to produce a more uneven finish.

This mask would originally have had an elaborate coiffure attached to holes around the edge. Its absence detracts from the value of this piece.

In order to appeal to collectors, it is important that any tribal mask was originally crafted for use by the clan, and not for the tourist trade. Indicators include signs of wear on the interior, particularly around the lip and nose areas.

This protruding mouth is typical of Dan masks used to entertain, especially those related to mischief-making characters.

An early 20thC anthropozoomorphic wooden Dan mask, from the Ivory Coast.

9.75in (24.5cm) high

**$1,800-2,200**     **BLA**

A Dan mask, from the Ivory Coast.

c1870     9.5in (24cm) high

**$5,000-8,000**     **JBB**

A late 19thC Dan mask, from the Ivory Coast or Nigeria.

16in (40cm) high

**$2,800-3,200**     **BLA**

A late 19thC Dan mask, from Liberia.

10in (25cm) high   **BLA**

**$1,200-1,800**   **BLA**

An early 20thC Dan mask, from the Ivory Coast.

9.5in (24cm) high

**$500-800**     **BLA**

An early 20thC Dan dance mask, from the Ivory Coast.

8.5in (21cm) high

**$500-700**     **BLA**

An early 20thC wooden Dan mask, from the Ivory Coast.

8in (20cm) high

**$800-1,200**     **BLA**

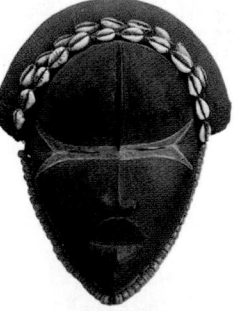

A carved wood Dan mask, of hollowed oval form, pierced around the rim for attachments, with pointed chin, broad mouth, pierced slit eyes, traces of kaolin, cowrie shell, and yellow trade bead attachments.

10.5in (27cm) high

**$300-500**     **SK**

A carved wood Dan mask, of hollowed oval form, pierced around the rim for attachments, with pierced protruding mouth, triangular nose, narrow pierced eyes, incised frame lines and a dark patina.

9.25in (23.5cm) high

**$300-500**     **SK**

A late 19thC male wooden Dan figure of an ancestor, from the Ivory Coast.

21.25in (53cm) high

**$2,800-3,200**     **BLA**

A late 19thC Dogon door lock, from Mali.

*20in (50cm) high*

**$1,200-1,800**     **BLA**

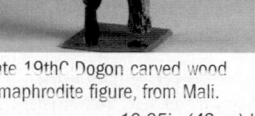

A late 19thC Dogon carved wood hermaphrodite figure, from Mali.

*19.25in (48cm) high*

**$3,000-5,000**     **BLA**

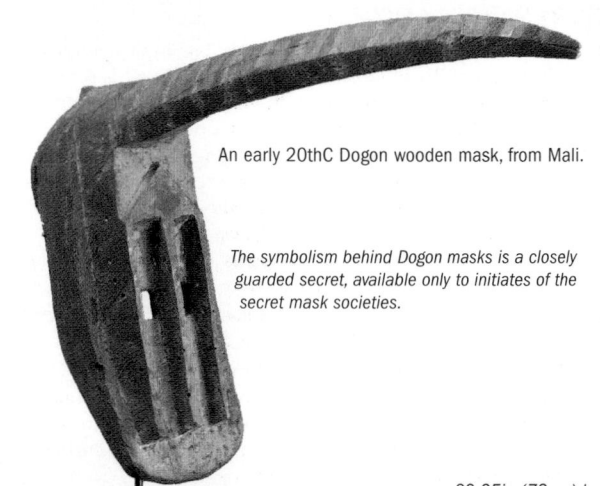

An early 20thC Dogon wooden mask, from Mali.

*The symbolism behind Dogon masks is a closely guarded secret, available only to initiates of the secret mask societies.*

*29.25in (73cm) long*

**$3,000-4,000**     **BLA**

## NIGERIA

An early 20thC Eket hardwood dance mask, from Nigeria.

*6.5in (16.5cm) high*

**$300-500**     **BLA**

An early 20thC Eket wooden solar mask, from Nigeria.

*6.5in (16.5cm) high*

**$1,200-1,800**     **BLA**

A monolithic Ekoi stone sculpture, from Cameroon.

*42.75in (107cm) high*

**$15,000-20,000**     **BLA**

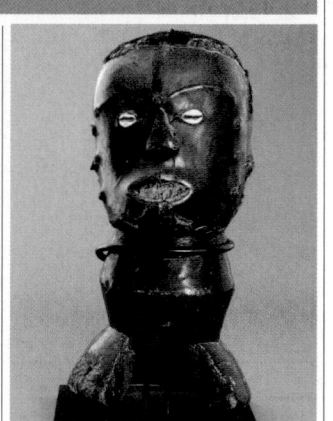

A late 19thC wooden Ekoi ritual dance head, decorated with paint and bronze, from Nigeria.

*14.5in (36cm) high*

**$800-1,200**     **BLA**

A late 19thC Ekoi Janus helmet mask, the wooden base covered with leather, from Nigeria.

*23.5in (59cm) high*

**$5,000-8,000**     **BLA**

A pair of Ibeji carved wood figures, one with beaded belt, the other with beaded necklace.

*10.5in (26cm) high*

**$280-320**     **FRE**

A set of three Ibeji carved wood figures, all with beaded necklaces, two with beaded belts.

*11in (27.5cm) high*

**$500-800**     **FRE**

## YORUBA MATERNITY FIGURES

- The Yoruba people inhabit the southwest region of Nigeria and the Republic of Benin, in Africa. Yoruba civilization is centered around the sacred city of Ife, which is considered the birthplace of all humanity and has a prestigious artistic heritage.

- Among the most celebrated Yoruba carvings are Ibjebu figures, representing deceased twins. The Yoruba region has the highest dizygotic twinning rate in the world, although premature births and living conditions mean high infant mortality. Yoruba maternity figures, signifying fertility and lineage, are therefore of great importance.

- The maternity figure represents the ideal of feminine beauty, fertility, and character. The archetypal mother is often depicted seated, suckling an infant and surrounded by other children.

- The worship of these statues, by way of sacrificial ceremonies and offerings, appeases the maternal spirit and brings the Yoruba people many children and good fortune, particularly during pregnancy and labor.

An early 20thC Yoruba maternity fetish figure, with traces of blue indigo pigments on the hair, from Nigeria.

*14.25in (35.5cm) high*

**$2,800-3,200**    **BLA**

An early 20thC Yoruba Gelede dance mask, from Nigeria.

*11.5in (29cm) high*

**$800-1,200**    **BLA**

A Yoruba Shango carved wood staff, with a figure holding a drum with a traditional double axe form, from Nigeria.

*19.5in (49cm) high*

**$1,800-2,200**    **FRE**

A pair of Yoruba carved wood figures, each supported by a staff with leather straps and cowrie shells, with traces of white pigment, from Nigeria.

*14.5in (36cm) high*

**$1,200-1,800**    **FRE**

A late 19thC Ogoni bronze ritual Edan scepter, from Nigeria.

*9.25in (23cm) high*

**$1,200-1,800**    **BLA**

A large early 20thC Wurkum Anyang hardwood dance mask, from the border of Nigeria and Cameroon.

*42.75in (107cm) high*

**$2,800-3,200**    **BLA**

An early 20thC wooden Igbo Alusi figure, from Nigeria.

*42.75in (107cm) high*

**$2,800-3,200**    **BLA**

An early 20thC Igbo wooden dance mask, from Nigeria.

*9in (22.5cm) high*

**$800-1,200**    **BLA**

An early 20thC Zulu ceremonial war shield, of wood covered with buffalo hide and monkey skin, painted with pigments, from South Africa.

*24in (61cm) high*

**$800-1,200**      **BLA**

An early 20thC Zulu ceremonial shield, of wood covered with monkey skin and buffalo hide, from South Africa.

*25.25in (64cm) high*

**$800-1,200**      **BLA**

A carved Zulu female figure, with linear carving to the head and neck, from South Africa.

*16in (40cm) high*

**$1,200-1,800**      **FRE**

A late 19thC Mbunda wooden divinity figure, from Angola.

*28in (71cm) high*

**$5,000-7,000**      **BLA**

A Bapende carved wood mask, highlighted with pigments, from the Democratic Republic of Congo.

*10in (25.5cm) wide*

**$60-90**      **GORL**

A late 19thC Kwere wooden ancestor buti figure, from Tanzania.

*15.5in (39.5cm) high*

**$5,000-8,000**      **BLA**

An early 20thC wooden Makondé figure, from Tanzania or Mozambique.

*33in (84cm) high*

**$3,000-4,000**      **BLA**

A large carved wood drum, of hollow cylindrical form, with pegged animal hide skin, depicting a kneeling mother nursing an infant, with encrusted patina, damaged.

*46in (117cm) high*

**$500-700**      **SK**

An African carved monkey, with bent knees, long cylindrical torso, heart-shaped face and carved teeth, standing on a base, damaged.

*31in (79cm) high*

**$500-700**      **SK**

## MODERN AFRICA

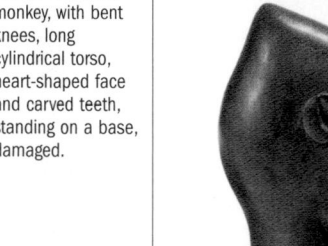

A Bernard Matemera stone bust, unsigned.

*15in (37.5cm) high*

**$800-1,200**      **FRE**

A Fanizani Akuda stone bust, with carved signature "Fanizani".

*13in (32.5cm) high*

**$500-700**      **FRE**

A 20thC Luizi Purumero stone bust, with carved signature "Luizi".

*16in (40cm) high*

**$500-700**      **FRE**

An early 19thC Totokia carved wooden chief's war club, from Fiji.

*The sharp beak was designed to deliver a fatal blow while preserving the enemy's skull as a trophy. The mass of the club head meant that even a weak swing was enough to kill a foe.*

35.5in (90cm) high

**$5,000-7,000** BLA

A Polynesian carved wood throwing club, with chip-carved hand grip, two teeth inlaid in the head and a dark patina, from Fiji.

14in (35.5cm) long

**$400-600** SK

A Polynesian carved wood headrest, the long cylindrical form with flared ends, two sets of arched legs lashed on with braided fibers and dark patina, from Fiji.

28.5in (72.5cm) long

**$500-700** SK

A Polynesian carved wood throwing club, with bulbous head, chip-carved handle and dark patina, from Fiji.

16in (40.5cm) long

**$280-320** SK

A Fijian gunstock club and a Samoan club with serrated edge, elaborate chip-carving and dark patina, "Fana Fana" incised on the handle.

38in (96.5cm) long

**$280-320** SK

A Polynesian carved wood throwing club, with a heavy bulbous head, chip-carved grip and dark patina, from Fiji.

15.5in (39.5cm) long

**$300-500** SK

An early 20thC Asmat wooden pole, from Irian Jaya.

59.5in (151cm) high

**$18,000-22,000** BLA

An early 20thC Asmat pole, from Irian Jaya.

43.25in (110cm) high

**$800-1,200** BLA

An early 20thC carved wood gobi, from the Santini Lake area of Irian Jaya.

22.75in (57.5cm) high

**$1,200-1,800** BLA

A 20thC tapa, from the Lake Sentani area of Irian Jaya.

27.5in (70cm) high

**$1,800-2,200** BLA

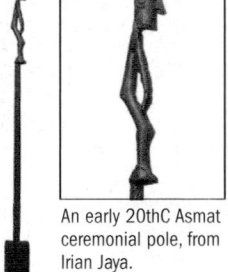

An early 20thC Asmat ceremonial pole, from Irian Jaya.

47.5in (120.5cm) high

**$1,200-1,800** BLA

An early 19thC carved wooden canoa stirrup, engraved with stylized and geometric motifs, from the Marquesas Islands.

*These symbolic wooden stirrups were used by children and young adults for a sport that was practiced on stilts.*

15in (38cm) high

**$5,000-7,000** BLA

An early 19thC carved wooden canoa stirrup, shaped as a tiki figure, engraved with stylized and geometric motifs, from the Marquesas Islands.

11.5in (29.5cm) high

**$3,000-5,000** BLA

An early 19thC carved wooden canoa stirrup, shaped as a tiki figure, engraved with stylized and geometric motifs, from the Marquesas Islands.

13in (33cm) high

**$2,800-3,200** BLA

## MAORI

- The Maori people probably arrived in New Zealand from eastern Polynesia over a thousand years ago.
- Favored materials for Maori art are the native woods toa, whale bone, and nephrite, a jade mineral known in New Zealand as 'greenstone'.
- Rival Maori sects were engaged in intermittent warfare for many years, and this is reflected in their art. Weapons reserved for the best warriors were decorated with representations of Tu Matuenga, the war deity.
- Hei-Tiki, or greenstone pendants, were among the first Maori artifacts given to Westerners. They generally represent stylized human figures, and have become symbolic of Maori culture.
- The art of Moari carving is known as Te Toi Whakairo, and is subject to Tapu, the series of laws that govern many aspects of traditional Maori culture.
- The lizard is the only animal to feature in Maori sculpture, and represents the fearsome god Whiro, representative of evil.

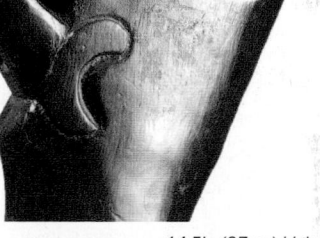

A late 19thC Maori Wahaika club, of toa wood, carved in relief with stylized motifs and incised ornament, with a dark glossy patina.

*'Wahaika' is a Maori word that means 'mouth of the fish'. The first enemy killed in battle was often referred to as 'the first fish'.*

A mid-19thC Maori greenstone Hei Tiki pendant, with pierced, bowed legs and arms and circular eyes filled with red wax.

*6.25in (16cm) high*

**$5,000-7,000**    **BLA**

**$5,000-7,000**    **BLA**

*14.5in (37cm) high*

**BLA**

A late 19thC Maori club, of toa wood, each side carved in relief with a Janus head and further incised ornament, with a dark glossy patina.

*This end of the club would be used in a dummy attack against an enemy. The club would then be spun around to deliver a blow to the opponent's skull with the heavier end.*

*61.5in (156.5cm) high*

**$1,200-1,800**    **BLA**

A Maori jade Hei Tiki pendant, the head tilted to the left, with recessed round eyes, pierced at the top for suspension.

*3in (7.5cm) high*

**$3,000-5,000**    **SK**

An early 20thC carved wood pigmented gobi, from the Papuan Gulf of Papua New Guinea.

*36.25in (92cm) high*

**$8,000-12,000**　　　　**BLA**

An early 20thC male Ramu river figure, from Papua New Guinea.

*5.5in (14cm) high*

**$5,000-7,000**　　　　**BLA**

An early 20thC Biwat wooden ancestral figure, in the Mundugumor style, from South Sepik in Papua New Guinea.

*28.75in (73cm) high*

**$1,800-2,200**　　　　**BLA**

A mid-20thC carved wood ancestor board, with traces of red and white pigment, from the Wapo Creek area of Papua New Guinea.

*44in (110cm) high*

**$400-600**　　　　**FRE**

A carved wood ancestor board, painted with red and white pigment, from the Papuan Gulf of Papua New Guinea.

*62in (155cm) high*

**$300-500**　　　　**FRE**

A carved wood skull rack, with brown and white pigment, from the Papuan Gulf of Papua New Guinea.

*39in (97.5cm) high*

**$500-700**　　　　**FRE**

A carved and painted wood Bioma figure, with traces of white and red pigment and plaited fiber, from the Papuan Gulf of Papua New Guinea.

*46in (115cm) high*

**$700-1,000**　　　　**FRE**

An early 20thC Abelam wooden mask, decorated in polychrome pigments, from Maprik village in Papua New Guinea.

*22in (56cm) high*

**$1,200-1,800**　　　　**BLA**

An early 20thC Baba helmet mask, with polychrome pigments, from the Maprik area of Papua New Guinea.

*16.5in (42cm) high*

**$1,200-1,800**　　　　**BLA**

An early 20thC Tambuan mask, with pigments, from the Ramu River in Papua New Guinea.

*16.5in (42cm) high*

**$1,200-1,800**　　　　**BLA**

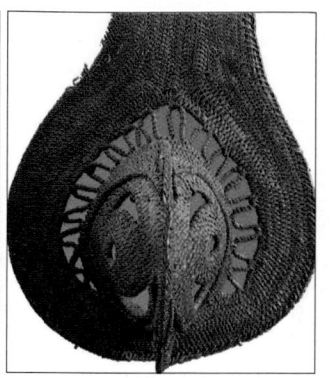

An early 20thC Abelan ceremonial yam mask, from Papua New Guinea.

*22.5in (57cm) high*

**$300-500**    **BLA**

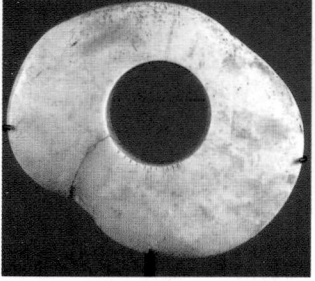

An early 19thC Boiken giant kina shell currency, from Papua New Guinea.

*8.25in (21cm) diam*

**$1,800-2,200**    **BLA**

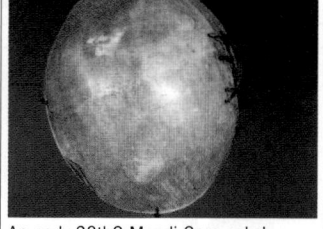

An early 20thC Mendi Gam pakol pectoral shell ornament, worn by elders in the Mendi Valley area of Papua New Guinea.

*9.75in (25cm) diam*

**$500-700**    **BLA**

## A CLOSER LOOK AT A MALANGGAN HEADDRESS

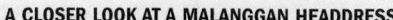

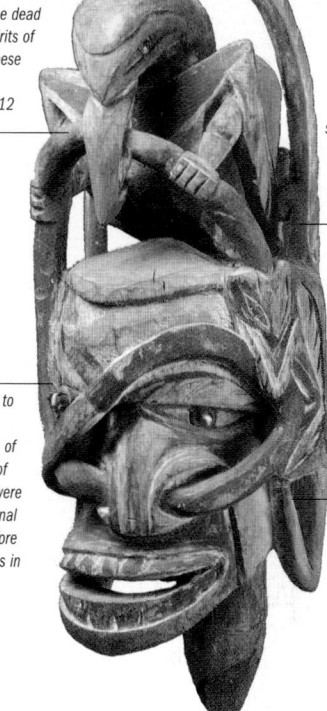

*'Malanggan' is a generic term for ceremonies honoring the dead on New Ireland. The spirits of the ancestors attend these ceremonies, arriving in visible form, often in a 12 foot long boat.*

*Malanggan headdresses exhibit some of the most sophisticated carving to be found in the South Pacific Islands. They are indigenous to northwest New Ireland.*

*This intricately carved sculpture was designed to decay over time as a symbolic representation of the dead. The majority of Malanggan sculptures were left to rot in the traditional fashion. They are therefore rare, and early examples in particular command a premium.*

*The pigments used on this headdress are unique to Oceanic tribal art. Although faded in places, much of the polychrome coloring remains, increasing the value of this piece.*

An early 19thC Malanggan wooden headdress, with polychrome pigments, used in ceremonies to honor the dead, from New Ireland.

*23.75in (60.5cm) high*

**$15,000-18,000**    **BLA**

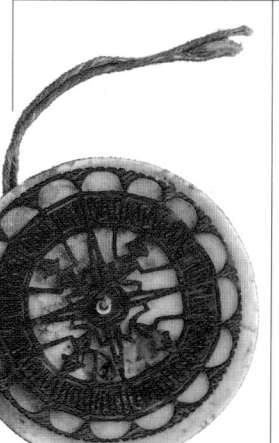

An early 20thC shell disk ornament, with filigree turtleshell.

*Commonly known as 'kapkaps', these ornaments were made in the Solomon Islands. They are worn as far west as the Papuan Gulf in Papua New Guinea.*

*4.5in (11.5cm) diam*

**$1,200-1,800**    **BLA**

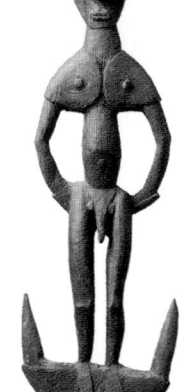

An early 20thC Sepik figural food hook, from Papua New Guinea.

*30in (76cm) high*

**$2,800-3,200**    **BLA**

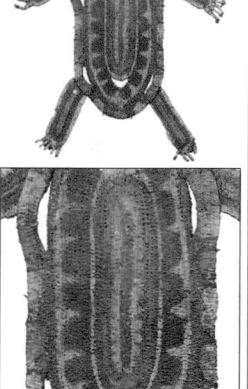

An early 20thC cult banner, of stylized animal form, woven from multicolored fibers, from New Guinea.

*32.75in (83cm) high*

**$2,800-3,200**    **BLA**

A 20thC Sepik spirit hook, of carved wood colored with pigments, from the Sepik River area of Papua New Guinea.

*13.75in (35cm) high*

**$300-500**    **BLA**

A carved wood drum, of hourglass form, with stylized animals at the waist, geometric carving on the reptile skin drum head and a dark patina, damaged, from New Guinea.

*31.5in (80cm) high*

**$1,200-1,800**    **SK**

**ARCHITECTURAL ANTIQUES**

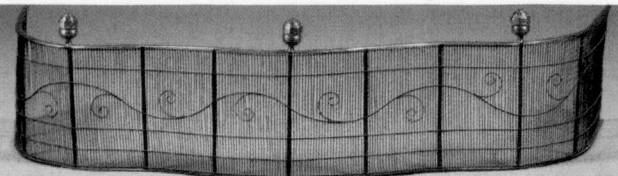

An early 19thC wirework fender, the serpentine front with scrolled wire decoration, brass rims and finials, scattered light rust.

*59in (150cm) wide*

**$1,200-1,800** | **BRU**

A steel fire fender, in cast and laminated iron with copper mounts, the central section with tool rests and handle rests to sides.

*53in (135cm) wide*

**$220-280** | **BRU**

## FIREMARKS & OTHER ACCESSORIES

A wrought iron fender stool, by Thomas Hadden of Edinburgh, of rectilinear three-quarter form, the green leather padded seats with studded decoration above a slatted frieze enhanced with panels of entwined foliage.

*71in (180cm) wide*

**$2,800-3,200** | **L&T**

A 'Sun Fire Office 1710' firemark, embossed in relief and gilded with the wording above a sun on a black ground, mounted on a mahogany plaque.

*7.25in (18.5cm) diam*

**$180-220** | **CHEF**

Two 19thC American firemarks, the first, from Baltimore, of cast iron in oval form enclosing a figure of a fireman blowing a horn and holding a burning torch, the second, from Philadelphia, with a cast-lead tree mounted on a painted pine shield.

*Provenance: The first mark was originally issued in 1848 by the Associated Fireman's Insurance Company of Baltimore. The second mark, the 'Green Tree', was originally issued by the Mutual Insurance Company for Insuring Houses, Philadelphia, from 'Loss by Fire' in 1784.*

*larger 15.75in (39cm) high*

**$1,200-1,800** | **FRE**

A painted and gilt firemark, worked in relief with a gold lion resting a paw on a union shield, on a red ground with "British", mounted on mahogany plaque.

*8.5in (21.5cm) diam*

**$300-500** | **CHEF**

A 17thC cast iron Coat-of-Arms fire back, dated.

*Provenance: Sorber Collection.*

*1635*      *26in (65cm) wide*

**$2,800-3,200** | **POOK**

A cast iron stove plate, the two arched panels with the inscription "God's well has water in plenty", dated.

*Provenance: Sorber Collection.*

*1748*      *27.5in (69cm) wide*

**$5,000-7,000** | **POOK**

An 18thC Pennsylvania cast iron stove plate, depicting Samson and Delilah inscribed "When at last Delilah...".

*Provenance: Sorber Collection.*

*24.75in (62cm) wide*

**$4,000-6,000** | **POOK**

A cast iron stove plate, with a rampant horse above a foliate cartouche, dated.

*Provenance: Sorber Collection.*

*1758*      *26in (65cm) high*

**$300-500** | **POOK**

A Pennsylvania cast iron stove plate, with tulips and hearts, inscribed "George Ross Ann Mary Ann Furnace".

*Provenance: Sorber Collection.*

*1763*      *26in (65cm) wide*

**$2,200-2,800** | **POOK**

A Pennsylvania cast iron 'Depart from Evil' stove plate, inscribed "John Potts Warwick Furnace", dated.

*Provenance: Sorber Collection.*

*1764*      *26.75in (67cm) wide*

**$4,000-6,000** | **POOK**

An ornate cast iron parlor stove, with open central bay flanked by lyre-shaped supports, one central burner, removable cabriole legs and pad feet, damage.

*86.5cm (34in) wide*

**$500-800** | **BRU**

An Alexander the Great bronze and marble bust, in military dress, the breastplate with silhouette medallion, bronze doré fringed chlamys, head and helmet in figured red marble, chest and base of gray and dark red mottled marble, losses, chips, and corrosion.

*48in (122cm) high*

**$40,000-45,000**  **BRU**

An early 19thC lead garden figure, cast in lead as a young girl in a smock dress, raised on a turned socle base.

*26.75in (67cm) high*

**$1,200-1,800**  **L&T**

A green patinated bronze figure of a Bacchic faun, after the Antique, with arms aloft and tail to rear, on stepped base.

*32in (81cm) high*

**$3,000-5,000**  **L&T**

A Gothic-style cast iron bird bath, the basin mounted with openwork twig decoration, the pedestal base formed as a tree trunk with roots, marked "Miller Iron/Prov./RI", rust, central rod replaced.

*46in (117cm) high*

**$8,000-12,000**  **BRU**

An American School life-size portrait of a gentleman wearing a frock coat, in bronze with a dark brown patina, on a circular wooden base supported by castors.

*66in (165cm) high*

**$18,000-25,000**  **FRE**

An early Victorian tole urn and cover, with a pineapple knop, the flattened ovoid body and footed socle painted with flowers, the lion mask and ring handles in gilt.

*11.5in (29cm) high*

**$500-700**  **CHEF**

A 19thC English church bell, inscribed "Thomas Mears of London, Founder 1836".

*24in (60cm) diam*

**$1,200-1,800**  **L&T**

An 18thC Dutch church bell, foliate cast bands, inscribed "Mr GR Van Kingschoten, Amstelodam", dated.

*1739*  *26.75in (67cm) diam*

**$2,200-2,800**  **L&T**

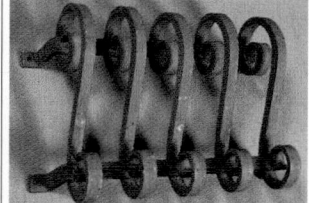

A cast iron window grille, of scrolled construction, overall rust and pitting.

*24in (61cm) wide*

**$120-180**  **BRU**

A Regency tole peint plate warmer, painted with gilt borders on a black ground, with a dome top above a door enclosing shelves and an open back, flanked by gilt metal handles, on cabriole legs with pad feet.

*27.5in (70cm) high*

**$300-500**  **DN**

A painted metal horse head, probably French, with an open mouth, covered with traces of old yellow and red paint, once used as a sign, wear and damage.

*17in (43cm) high*

**$2,200-2,800**  **BRU**

## THE BOOKS MARKET

The increased public and press attention given to literary awards has had repercussions for the market in modern first editions over the last year. Crime and mystery fiction, traditionally the strongest genres in this sector, have lost ground to 21stC literary fiction.

Many collectors now specialize almost exclusively in first novels by contemporary authors. Inclusion on the Booker, Orange, or Whitbread prize shortlist tends to fuel an increase in value, a situation exacerbated by the lower print runs now favored by risk-wary publishers. Other areas to watch include foreign language writers, such as Turkey's Orhan Pamuk, and books aimed at young adults, such as 'Mortal Engines' by Phillip Reeve.

Up to 80 percent of the value of a first edition book is in its dust wrapper, so it is vital that buyers choose examples with intact dust wrappers in the best possible condition.

It is also worth bearing in mind that, despite the booming market in books still warm from the press, one of the most successful titles at auction in the last year was J.R.R. Tolkien's "Lord of the Rings" trilogy. Allen & Unwin's 1954-5 editions have enjoyed steady growth for more than a decade, and are now outperforming J.K. Rowling's early Harry Potter titles.

*Chris Fruin, biblion.com*

## CLASSIC BOOKS

Aretz, Gertrude, "Napoleon and his Women Friends", first English translation, cover set with five watercolor on ivorine portraits by C.B. Currie, Cosway binding, inner gilt doublures, t.e.g., by Riviere, in original fleece-lined slipcase, Allen & Unwin, London.

*1927*

**$28,000-35,000**   L&T

Couch, Jonathan, "A History of the Fishes", first edition, in four volumes, 252 colored plates, 8vo., Groombridge, London.

*1862-65*

**$2,800-3,200**   L&T

Austen, Jane, "The Novels", Winchester edition in 12 volumes, red cloth boards, spines with gilt decoration, Grant, Edinburgh.

*1911-12*

**$5,000-8,000**   L&T

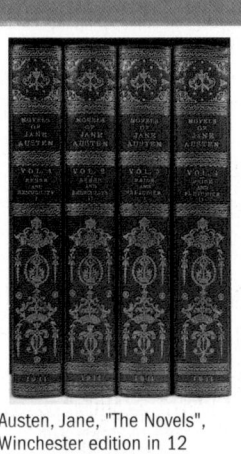

Bacon, Francis, Viscount St. Alban, "Essays, Moral, Economical, and Political", cover with watercolor on ivorine portrait of Bacon by C.B. Currie, Cosway, Sharpe, London.

*1828*

**$12,000-18,000**   L&T

Beardsley, Aubrey, "The Savoy: An Illustrated Monthly", with original bands and wrappers, volumes 1-8, cover decorations and other illustrations by Beardsley, London.

*1896*

**$1,800-2,200**   FRE

Beebe, William, "A monograph of the pheasants", first edition, in four volumes, with 90 chromolithographed plates, 88 photogravure plates by Thorburn and others, and 20 maps, Witherby, London.

*No. 35 of 600 copies, this was one of the last books printed using chromolithography.*

*c1920*

**$5,000-8,000**   L&T

Burns, Robert, "Poems chiefly in the Scottish dialect", with a watercolor on ivorine portrait miniature of Burns by C.B. Currie, inner gilt doublures, by Riviere, Cosway binding, in fleece-lined slipcase, John Smith, Glasgow.

*1927*

**$12,000-18,000**   L&T

Colley, Cibber, "She wou'd and she wou'd not; or, the kind imposter", with a watercolor portrait on ivorine by C.B. Currie of Mrs Jordan as Hypolita, engraved frontispiece and titlepage, Cosway binding, inner gilt doublures, t.e.g., by Riviere, in its original slip case, published by Bell, London.

*1792*

**$12,000-18,000**   L&T

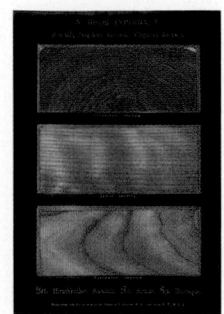

Hough, Romeyn Beck, "American Woods", green cloth portfolios with cloth sleeves, gilt lettered portfolio spines and metal clasps, with six text volumes in original wrappers and 468 wood samples window-mounted in 156 card mounts, New York.

*c1890*

**$3,000-5,000** FRE

Humphreys, H.N. & Westwood, J.O. "British moths and their transformations", 2 volumes, 124 hand-colored plates, Smith, London.

*1848*

**$2,800-3,200** L&T

Ireland, W.H., editor, "Life of Napoleon Bonaparte...", engravings by G. Cruikshank, first edition, four volumes, engraved titlepages, hand-colored plates, 8vo., Fairburn, London.

*1823-28*

**$1,800-2,200** L&T

Takeji Iwamiya, "Forms, Textures, Images: Traditional Japanese Craftsmanship in Everyday Life", first English-language edition, original red cloth, gilt, color and black and white photo plates.

*1979*

**$120-180** FRE

Lawrence, TE, "Seven pillars of wisdom: a triumph", Cosway morocco binding no. 691, cover with watercolor portrait of Lawrence on ivorine by C.B. Currie, t.e.g., by Riviere, in original fleece-lined slipcase, 4to., Cape, London.

*1935*

**$12,000-18,000** L&T

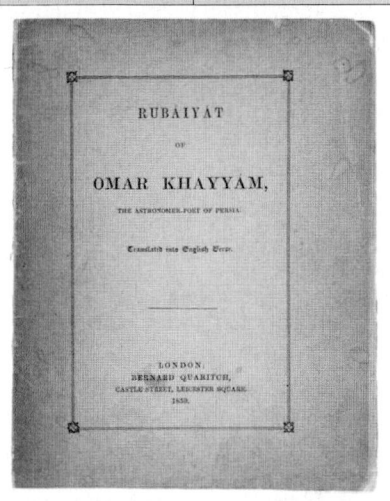

Fitzgerald, Edward, editor and translator, "Rubáiyát of Omar Khayyám", first edition, one of 250 copies, original printed wrappers, preserved in a brown morocco solander case, gilt, 4to., published by Bernard Quaritch, London, wear.

*Many copies of this edition were unsold and remaindered, making this book rare.*

*1859*

**$15,000-20,000** BLO

Lilford, Thomas L. Powys, Baron, "Coloured figures of the birds of the British Islands", first edition, seven volumes, litho plates by Thorburn et al, Porter, London.

*1885-87*

**$2,800-3,200** L&T

Lipscomb, George, "The history and antiquities of Buckingham", first edition, four volumes, 38 engraved plates, nine maps, 940 hand-colored coats of arms, Nichols, London.

*1831-47*

**$2,800-3,200** L&T

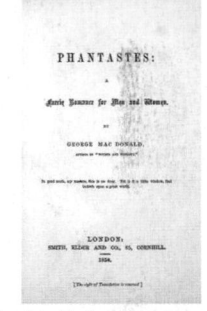

Macdonald, George, "Phantastes: A Faerie Romance for Men and Women", first edition, original embossed cloth, 8vo., wear.

*1858*

**$500-800** BLO

Nicholson, William, "The History of the Wars Occasioned by the French Revolution", folio, 21 color plates, London, back cover detached.

*1820*

**$500-800** FRE

Drummond, Comte de Melfort, "Trait sur la Cavalerie", folio, gilt-paneled spine, raised bands, red morocco spine label, red-stained edges, Paris.

*1776*

**$220-280** FRE

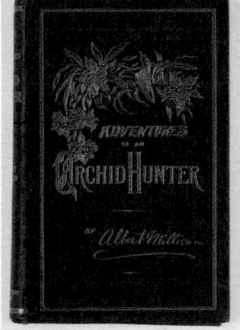

Millican, Albert, "Orchid Hunting: The Adventures of an Orchid Hunter", gilt-lettered and pictorial blue cloth, black and white plates, London.

*1891*

**$600-900** FRE

Pilkington, Matthew, "A general dictionary of painters", new edition, two volumes, with 450 engravings, morocco binding, McLean, London.

*1824*

**$5,000-8,000** L&T

Dana, Mrs. William Starr, "How to Know the Wild Flowers: A Guide", silver and green stamped brown cloth, illustrations by Marion Satterlee, with 30 watercolor drawings of American wild flowers, unsigned, dated, New York.

*1895*

**$400-600** FRE

Stock, St. George H., "The Romance of Chastisement: Select Tales form the Original Manuscript", London, cloth-backed bands, paper spine label, text with ornamental red borders, edge wear.

*1869*

**$120-180** FRE

Strutt, Joseph, "A biographical dictionary containing an historical account of all the engravers", first edition, two volumes extended to four, with 19 original plates, two hand-colored, 450 additional engravings, 4to., Robert Faulder, London.

*1785*

**$8,000-12,000** L&T

Tennyson, Alfred, Lord, "A selection from the works... (Moxon's miniature poets)", Cosway binding no. 911, with a watercolor portrait on ivorine of Tennyson by C.B. Currie, in original fleece-lined slipcase, 8vo., Moxon, London.

*1865*

**$10,000-15,000** L&T

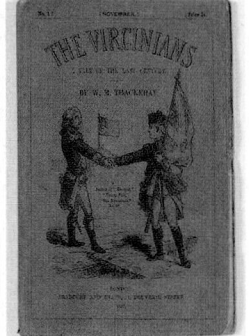

Thackeray, William Makepeace, "The Virginians", first edition, original printed pictorial yellow wrappers, 48 plates, adverts, custom cloth box, Bradbury and Evans, London.

*1858*

**$300-500** FRE

Thackery, William Makepeace, "The History of Henry Esmond", first edition, three volumes, half calf cover patterned boards, 8vo., wear.

*1852*

**$500-800** BLO

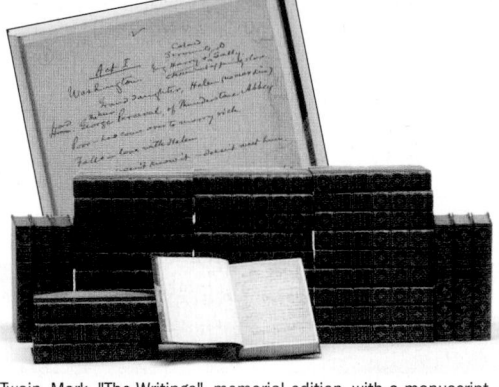

Twain, Mark, "The Writings", memorial edition, with a manuscript leaf in Mark Twain's hand tipped-in, levant morocco binding, marbled bands, gilt, gilt-paneled spines, maroon morocco spine labels, plates, Harpers & Brothers, New York.

*1929*

**$15,000-20,000** FRE

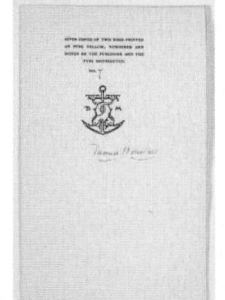

Whitman, Walt, "Memories of President Lincoln and Other Lyrics of the War", on vellum, signed by Thomas Mosher, unbound and unopened, Thomas B. Mosher, Portland, Maine.

*1906*

**$1,200-1,800** FRE

Williamson, George C., Cosway, Richard, R. A. et al., "Miniaturists of the 18th century", first edition, one of 350, Cosway binding no. 889, with watercolor portrait miniatures on ivorine by C.B. Currie, inner gilt doublures, in fleece-lined slipcase, 4to., Bell, London.

*1897*

**$30,000-35,000** L&T

The "Holy Bible containing the Old Testament and the New ", John Baskett, Oxford.

*This edition is known as the "Vinegar Bible", infamous as "A Baskett-ful of Errors", including the misprint "vinegar" for "vineyard".*

*1717*

**$7,000-10,000** L&T

"The New Cries of London", printed stiff wrappers, 22 engraved vignettes and vignettes on each title and front wrapper, London.

*1813*

**$800-1,200** FRE

Adams, Herbert "Roger Bennions Double", first edition, published for the Crime Club, original cloth, dust jacket, discolored, worn and repaired, 8vo.

*1941*

**$280-320**    **BLO**

Baker, Josephine, "La Revue des Folies Bergere, 1926-1927", blue wrappers, gilt and color illustrations, Paris.

*1926*

**$400-600**    **FRE**

---

### A CLOSER LOOK AT A MODERN FIRST EDITION

This world famous and much-loved tale, published in 1900, was an immediate bestseller. The story was further popularized by the 1939 movie starring Judy Garland as Dorothy.

The Wizard of Oz is a hugely popular collecting area making competition for items fierce and prices relatively high.

As a first edition of a popular title in excellent condition, this book is very desirable.

This first edition book is in its second state. An older, first state, first edition could command $35,000 or more.

Baum, Frank L., "The Wonderful Wizard of Oz", first edition, second state, published by George M. Hill, Chicago.

*1900*

**$22,000-32,000**    **BRB**

---

Bellow, Saul, "Dangling Man", first English edition, original cloth, dust jacket, 8vo.

*This was the first book by the author of "Herzog".*

*1946*

**$180-220**    **BLO**

Blake, Nicholas, "The Beast Must Die", first edition, original cloth, dust jacket, repaired on verso, 8vo, extremities worn, spine ends chipped, together with two other titles by Blake.

*1938*

**$600-900**    **BLO**

---

Blixen, Karen, (Isak Dinesen), "Out of Africa", first edition, original burgundy cloth, dust jacket, 8vo., soiled, rubbed at extremities, small tears to spine ends.

*1937*

**$400-600**    **BLO**

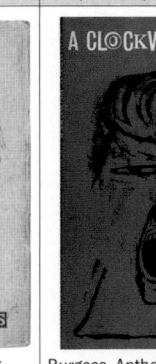

Buchan, John, "The Dancing Floor", first edition, with original cloth, 8vo., tanned, faded and rubbed at extremities.

*1926*

**$220-280**    **BLO**

Burgess, Anthony, "A Clockwork Orange", first edition, first issue dustwrapper, original cloth, 8vo., published by Heinemann, London, spotting.

*1962*

**$2,200-2,800**    **L&T**

Burroughs, William S., "The Naked Lunch", No. 76, The Traveller's Companion Series, first edition, original printed wrappers, 8vo., published by Olympia Press, Paris.

*1959*

**$700-1,000**    **BLO**

Burton, Miles, "The Three Corpse Trick", first edition, published for the Crime Club, original cloth, dust jacket, 8vo., slightly rubbed and soiled.

*1944*

**$220-280**    **BLO**

Carroll, Lewis, "Alice's Adventures in Wonderland and Through the Looking Glass", photo-play edition, stamped pictorial gray cloth, light edge wear.

*1918*

**$180-220**      **FRE**

Chesterton, G.K., "The Secret of Father Brown", first edition, ink signatures on front endpaper, slight peripheral and end foxing, original cloth, dust jacket, 8vo., creased and chipped.

**$800-1,200**      **BLO**

Chesterton, G.K., "Tales of the Long Bow", first edition, half-title, original cloth, dust jacket, 8vo., edge and end foxing, worn and internally strengthened.

*1925*

**$500-700**      **BLO**

Christie, Agatha, "A Pocket Full of Rye", early edition, Collins.

*This early edition, printed one year after the first edition, is rare.*

**$180-220**      **BIB**

Agatha Christie, "The Moving Finger", first edition, published by Collins/The Crime Club.

*1943*

**$500-800**      **BIB**

Christie, Agatha, "Why Didn't They Ask Evans?", first edition, published by Collins/The Crime Club.

*This is a rare dust jacket.*

*1950*

**$500-800**      **BIB**

Churchill, Sir Winston, "The Eve of Action: A Verbatim Report of Mr. Churchill's Speech", first edition, original red printed wrappers, 4to., published by W. & G. Baird Ltd., Belfast.

*1944*

**$1,200-1,800**      **BLO**

Conrad, Joseph, "The Arrow of Gold", first English edition, published by T. Fisher Unwin.

*1919*

**$300-500**      **BIB**

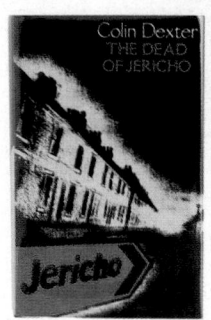

Dexter, Colin, "The Dead of Jericho", first edition, published by MacMillan.

*1981*

**$500-700**      **BIB**

Dinesen, Isak, "Seven Gothic Tales", first English edition, color frontispiece, original cloth, dust jacket, printer's band still present, 8vo., tanned at edges and spine.

*The frontispiece and dust jacket were designed by Rex Whistler.*

*1934*

**$400-600**      **BLO**

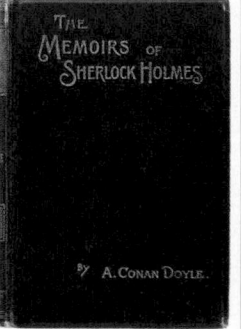

Conan Doyle, Arthur, "The Memoirs of Sherlock Holmes", first edition, published by George Newnes.

*1892*

**$1,200-1,800**      **BIB**

Conan Doyle, Arthur, "The Return of Sherlock Holmes", first edition in book form, 16 plates by Sidney Paget, advertizements at end, published by George Newnes.

*1905*

**$1,800-2,200**      **BLO**

Conan Doyle, Arthur, "The History of Spiritualism", first edition, two volumes, original cloth, dust jackets, with "Pheneas Speaks", original publisher's wrappers, foxed.

*1926*

**$500-800**      **BLO**

Conan Doyle, Arthur, "The Hound of the Baskervilles", first edition, frontispiece and 15 plates by Sidney Paget, half-title, original gilt pictorial cloth, 8vo., bubbling of cloth, slight scuffing to extremities.

*1902*

**$2,200-2,800** BLO

Fleming, Ian, "From Russia With Love", first edition, published by Jonathan Cape.

*1957*

**$2,800-3,200** BIB

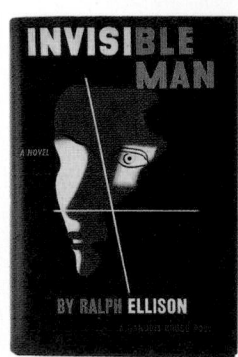

Ellison, Ralph, "Invisible Man", first edition, published by Random House, New York.

*1952*

**$2,800-3,200** BRB

Faulkner, William, "The Wild Palms", first English edition, original cloth, 8vo., dust jacket a little tanned, rubbed at extremities.

*1939*

**$180-220** BLO

Faulkner, William, "Intruder in the Dust", first edition, first printing, original gilt and blue lettered and decorated black cloth, Random House, New York.

*1948*

**$500-700** FRE

Fleming, Ian, "Moonraker", first edition, later printing, published by Jonathan Cape.

*1955*

**$300-500** BIB

Fleming, Ian, "Diamonds are Forever", first edition, published by Jonathan Cape.

*1956*

**$1,800-2,200** BIB

Fleming, Ian, "Goldfinger", first edition, original embossed boards, gilt, 8vo., dust jacket slightly soiled.

*1959*

**$500-800** BLO

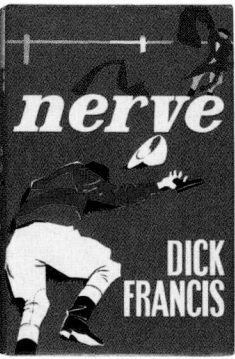

Francis, Dick, "Nerve", first edition, 8vo., remains of small labels on front endpaper, original boards, dust jacket worn.

*1963*

**$800-1,200** BLO

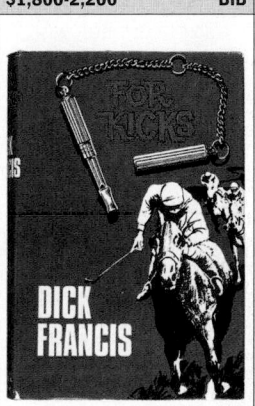

Francis, Dick, "For Kicks", first edition, original boards, dust jacket, 8vo., worn at extremities.

*1965*

**$800-1,200** BLO

Francis, Dick, "Flying Finish", first edition, original boards, dust jacket, 8vo., ink inscription on front endpaper.

*1966*

**$300-500** BLO

463

Robert Frost, "A Witness Tree", first trade edition, published by Henry Holt & Co., New York, Pulitzer Prize winner, inscribed by the author.

*1942*

**$8,000-12,000** BRB

Golding, William, "Lord of the Flies", first edition, published by Faber & Faber, London.

*1954*

**$7,000-10,000** BRB

Gray, Alasdair, "Lanark, A Life in Four Books", first edition, original cloth, gilt spine, dust jacket, 8vo., slightly creased at spine ends, Edinburgh.

*1981*

**$300-500** BLO

Greene, Graham, "Stamboul Train", first edition, published by Heinemann, with rare dust jacket, distressed.

*1932*

**$2,800-3,200** BIB

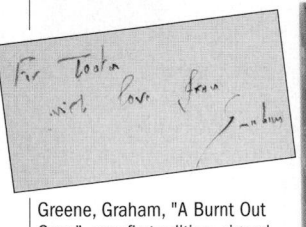

Greene, Graham, "A Burnt Out Case", rare first edition, signed by the author, published by Heinemann.

*1960*

**$1,200-1,800** BIB

Greene, Graham, "It's A Battlefield", and eight other English first editions including "Stamboul Train", "The Quiet American", "Our Man in Havana" and "A Burnt Out Case", published by Heinemann, London.

*1932-1961*

**$1,200-1,800 set** L&T

Greene, Graham, "The Third Man and The Fallen Idol", first edition, original cloth, dust jacket, 8vo., edges slightly creased, tape repairs to jacket.

*1950*

**$400-600** BLO

Greene, Graham, "The Lost Childhood", first edition, original cloth, dust jacket, 8vo.

*1951*

**$500-700** BLO

Grogan, E.S. and Sharp, A.H., "From Cape to Cairo: The First Traverse of Africa from South to North", first edition, illustrated by A.D. McCormick, published by Hurst and Blackett, wear.

*1990*

**$400-600** L&T

Hammett, Dashiell, "The Maltese Falcon", first edition, published by Alfred A. Knopf, New York and London.

*1930*

**$2,200-2,800** BRB

Heinlein, Robert A., "Stranger in a Strange Land", first edition, original cloth, Putnam's, New York.

*1961*

**$1,800-2,200** FRE

Hemingway, Ernest, "The Old Man and the Sea", first edition, publisher's seal and "A" to copyright page, original cloth, dust jacket, 8vo., rubbed, New York.

**$1,200-1,800** BLO

Herrick, Robert, "One Hundred and Eleven Poems", from an edition of 500, with eight extra plates, signed by the author, illustrated by Sir W. R. Flint, Golden Cockerel Press.

*1955*

**$500-800** BLO

## A CLOSER LOOK AT A MODERN FIRST EDITION

*This is one of the first two novels to be written by Haggard, who is best known for "King Solomon's Mines" and "She".*

*First editions by emerging authors were often produced in small print runs to minimize the risk to the publisher's finances. Only 500 first edition copies of this novel were printed, making it scarce and increasing its desirability.*

*Age does not necessarily influence the value of books. Books dating from after the mid-19thC are fairly common. Value is determined by edition, author, rarity, and condition.*

*This novel is typical of Haggard's adventure fantasies and explores the evil magic surrounding a witchdoctor's severed head. This subject matter would have appealed to mid-Victorian Colonial and Gothic sensibilities.*

Haggard, H. Ryder, "The Witch's Head", first edition, three volumes, half-titles, eight pages of advertizments at end of volume three, original gray/green cloth, 8vo., endpapers splitting, knocked, fraying to spine-ends and fore-corners.

*1885*

**$12,000-18,000** BLO

---

Huxley, Aldous, "Brave New World", first edition, original cloth, gilt spine, 8vo., some foxing, rubbed at extremities, worn, creasing.

*1932*

**$1,200-1,800** BLO

---

Ishiguro, Kazuo, "A Pale View of Hills", first ed., Faber & Faber.

*The first novel by the author of "The Remains of the Day".*

*1982*

**$800-1,200** BIB

---

James, P.D., "The Black Tower", first edition, published by Faber & Faber.

*1975*

**$400-600** BIB

---

Knowles, John, "A Separate Peace", with "Morning in Antibes" and "Double Vision", first editions, dust jacket.

*1959*

**$300-500** BLO

---

Kennedy, John F., "Why England Slept", first edition, second printing, in first printing dust jacket, signed "Jack Kennedy", published by Wilfred Funk, Inc., New York.

*1940*

**$12,000-18,000** BRB

---

Lee, Harper, "To Kill a Mockingbird", first English edition, original boards, dust jacket, 8vo., stained.

*1960*

**$220-280** BLO

---

Mailer, Norman, "The Naked and the Dead", first edition, original cloth, dust jacket, New York, with "Barbary Shore", first English edition, ownership inscription on front endpaper, original cloth, worn.

*1957*

**$300-500** BLO

---

Masterman, Walter, "The Green Toad", first edition, original cloth, dust jacket by E. McKnight Kauffer, slight foxing, rubbed and worn, 8vo.

*1928*

**$800-1,200** BLO

Maugham, W. Somerset, "The Razor's Edge", first English edition, inscribed by the author, published by Heinemann, London.

*1944*

**$5,000-7,000**    **BRB**

Miller, Arthur, "Death of a Salesman", first edition, winner of the Pulitzer Prize, inscribed by the author, published by The Viking Press, New York.

*1949*

**$7,000-10,000**    **BRB**

Miller, Henry, "Black Spring", first edition, first issue, from an edition of 1,000, original wrappers, 8vo., browned, worn, uncut.

*1936*

**$800-1,200**    **BLO**

Miller, Henry, "Max and the White Phagocytes", first edition, first issue, from an edition of 1,000, 8vo., original wrappers, neat ink ownership signature on half-title, slight edge creasing.

*1938*

**$800-1,200**    **BLO**

---

Miller, Henry, "The Rosy Crucifixion Book Two Plexus", first edition, two volumes, from an edition of 2,000 for private circulation, original wrappers, Olympia Press, Paris.

*1953*

**$500-700**    **BLO**

Morrison, Toni, "The Bluest Eye", first edition, the cover with a text design, published by Holt, Rinehart & Winston, New York.

*1970*

**$5,000-7,000**    **BRB**

Murdoch, Iris, "The Flight from the Enchanter", first edition, original cloth, 8vo., dust jacket in protective wrapper, creasing to head of spine.

*1956*

**$800-1,200**    **BLO**

Murdoch, Iris, "The Bell", first edition, original boards, 8vo., dust jacket, price clipped, slight top edge creasing.

*1958*

**$80-120**    **BLO**

Murdoch, Iris, "The Sea, The Sea", first edition, original boards, 8vo., dust jacket, slight creasing to head of spine.

*1978*

**$120-180**    **BLO**

---

Orwell, George, "Nineteen Eighty-Four", first edition, original cloth, green dust jacket, 8vo., ink ownership signature on front free endpaper, wear and restoration.

*1949*

**$1,200-1,800**    **BLO**

Pasternak, Boris, "Doctor Zhivago", first English edition, original cloth, dust jacket, 8vo., very slightly rubbed, spine slightly darkened and chipped at head.

*1958*

**$220-280**    **BLO**

Plath, Sylvia, "The Bell Jar", original boards, dust jacket, small ink signature on front free endpaper, Faber & Faber.

*This is the first edition published under the author's true name.*

*1966*

**$400-600**    **BLO**

Pynchon, Thomas, "V.", first English edition, original boards, dust jacket, a little rubbed, tanned, head of spine a little creased.

*This was Pynchon's first book.*

*1963*

**$300-500**    **BLO**

Rossetti, Christina, "Speaking Likenesses", first edition, wood-engraved frontispiece, title vignette, plates and illustrations by Arthur Hughes, original blue cloth, gilt, wear.

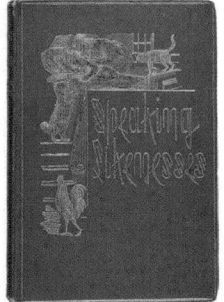

*1874*

**$300-500**    **BLO**

Rhys, Jean, "Voyage in the Dark", first edition, slightly darkened, original cloth, 8vo., a little faded at spine, worn at extremities and head of spine.

*1934*

**$700-1,000**  **BLO**

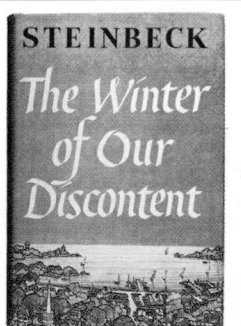

Steinbeck, John, "The Red Pony", first edition, from an edition of 699 copies, numbered and signed by the author, in original numbered cardboard slipcase, published by Covici-Friede, New York.

*1937*

**$5,000-8,000**  **BRB**

Saint-Exupery, Antoine de, "Le Petit Prince", first French-language edition, from a limited edition of 260, signed by the author, published by Reynal & Hitchcock, New York.

*Issued simultaneously with the English limited edition, which was a larger run, the French edition is rarer and more desirable.*

*1943*

**$18,000-25,000**  **BRB**

Steinbeck, John, "Of Mice and Men", first English edition, frontispiece and pictorial headpieces by Michael Rothenstein, original cloth, 8vo., dust jacket, wear and tear, spine trimmed.

*1937*

**$500-800**  **BLO**

Sayers, Dorothy L., "The Unpleasantness at the Bellona Club", first edition, original purple cloth, name in pencil on front endpaper, wear, tape repaired at folds, price clipped, New York.

*1928*

**$280-320**  **BLO**

Steinbeck, John, "The Grapes of Wrath", first English edition, original cloth, 8vo., worn at peripheries, slightly tanned, small chips to spine ends, New York.

*1939*

**$180-220**  **BLO**

Tom Sharpe, "Riotous Assembly", first edition, original boards, dust jacket, 8vo.

*1971*

**$220-280**  **BLO**

Steinbeck, John, "Cannery Row", first edition, first issue, original mustard cloth, 8vo., wear and restoration, New York.

*This is the true first state first edition with the mustard colored cloth as opposed to the brighter yellow cloth of the second state first edition.*

*1945*

**$500-700**  **BLO**

Steinbeck, John, "The Winter of Our Discontent", first edition, original publisher's boards, 8vo., dust jacket, spine tanned, price clipped, uncut, New York.

*1961*

**$220-280**  **BLO**

Thomas, Dylan, "Under Milk Wood", first edition, original cloth, dust jacket, 8vo.

*1954*

**$400-600**  **BLO**

Trevor, William, "A Standard of Behaviour", first edition, wear.

*This was the Whitbread award winner's first book.*

*1958*

**$280-320**  **BLO**

Verne, Jules, "The Purchase of the North Pole", first English edition, engraved frontispiece and illustrations throughout, tissue-guard, quires loose, several plates detached.

*1891*

**$2,800-3,200**  **BLO**

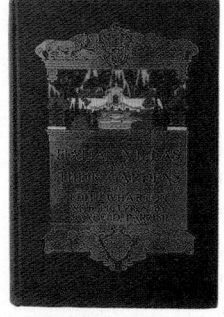

Wharton, Edith, "Italian Villas and Their Gardens", first American edition, published by The Century Co., New York.

*1904*

**$2,200-2,800**  **BRB**

# LITHOGRAPHS

Gould, J. and E., "Sparrow Hawk", a hand-colored lithograph, folio sheet, matted.

*c1835*        *19in (47.5cm) high*

**$280-320**                    **FRE**

Roberts, David, "Oblique View, Hall of Columns, Karnak", a hand-colored lithograph, framed.

*c1845*        *19in (47.5cm) high*

**$800-1,200**                  **FRE**

Currier, N., a hand-colored lithograph of "Young America'", after James Butterworth, by Frances Flora Palmer, New York.

*Palmer was a prominent 19thC graphic artist and one of the few women in her field.*

*27.75in (69cm) wide*

**$7,000-10,000**               **FRE**

Cogniaux, Alfred, "Dictionnaire Iconographique des Orchides", six volumes of text and 768 chromolithographic plates, wrappers preserved, the plates and accompanying text arranged by genus.

*c1900*

**$4,000-6,000**                **FRE**

## A CLOSER LOOK AT A LITHOGRAPH

*Royal Academy of Arts alumini, Thomas Rowlandson, portrayed political subjects and London characters. He also illustrated a number of contemporary books by the likes of Henry Fielding and Oliver Goldsmith.*

*These high quality works were produced for Samuel Fores, one of the top dealers at the higher end of the market, although Rowlandson also produced some cheaper, less well-executed work.*

*This series of plates satirizes the activities of the affluent in the fashionable town of Bath. This one, 'The Portrait', shows a gentleman sitting for his portrait, while the viewer can see the couple behind the door.*

*Satirical prints became popular during the period as a result of political volatility, social excesses and a lack of censorship. The print captures the feeling of an age and is desirable.*

Rowlandson, Thomas, "The Comforts of Bath" 12 hand-colored plates loosely inserted into a full red crushed morocco over-beveled boards album, with white watered silk endpapers, 4to., Fores, London.

*1798*

**$7,000-10,000**                               **L&T**

Pennell, Joseph and Robins, Elizabeth, "Lithography and Lithographers", with three original lithographs by Joseph Pennel, original gilt-lettered white vellum and gilt-lettered white vellum portfolio, in worn and soiled original box.

*1916*

**$300-500**                    **FRE**

Wawra von Fernsee, Heinrich, "Botanische Ergebnisse der Reise Seiner Majestät des Kaisers von Mexico Maximillian I nach Brasilien", folio, original printed bands, 104 lithographic plates, 32 of which are partially colored, Vienna.

*1866*

**$4,000-6,000 set**            **FRE**

Cappiello, Leonetto, "Cognac Pellisson", color lithographic poster by, linen-backed, Vercasson, Paris.

*1907*        *46in (115cm) high*

**$400-600**                    **FRE**

Sabartes, Jaime, "Picasso Toreros", with four original lithographs by Picasso, one in color, other plates, original pictorial black stamped red cloth, New York.

*1961*

**$1,200-1,800 set**                            **FRE**

Munting, Abraham, 'Ananas', a hand-colored engraving, folio sheet, framed.

1696     12.25in (30.5cm) high

**$280-320**     FRE

Catesby, Mark, "Pseudoo & C. Flos. Passionins", a hand-colored engraving, matted, depicting a Catesby snake.

c1745     14in (35cm) high

**$500-800**     FRE

An 18thC Persian "Anthology of Poems" manuscript, with contemporary flexible red morocco, double-page richly gilt and color illuminated title and 176 pages with gold borders, Khate Shikest script, scuffed.

**$700-1,000**     FRE

Piranesi, Giovanni Battista, "A Sua Eccellenza...", an etching of a perspective view of candelabrum.

1778     27in (67.5cm) high

**$220-280**     FRE

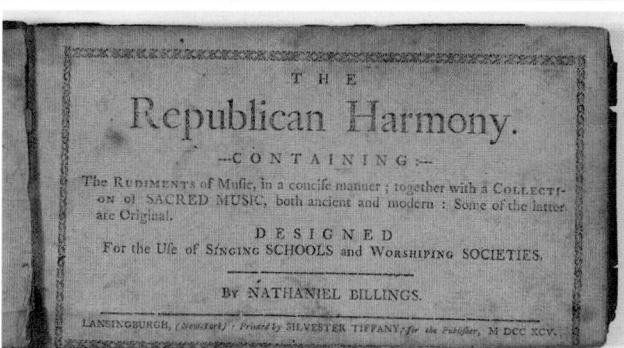

Michaux, Francois Andre and Nuttall, Thomas, "The North American Sylva", gilt-pictorial green cloth, 278 hand-colored engraved plates, Philadelphia.

1855

**$4,000-6,000**     FRE

Billings, Nathaniel, "The Republican Harmony", unrecorded 18thC American song writer, with ink inscription on front paste-down, Lansingburgh.

1795

**$1,800-2,200**     FRE

Beaton, Cecil, an original watercolor costume design drawing on paper.

c1950     14.5in (36cm) high

**$800-1,200**     FRE

Arp, Hans and Ernst, Max, "Geh durch den Spiegel", small folio, original pictorial red and white cloth, light wear, Cologne.

1960

**$300-500**     FRE

Thornton, Dr. Robert John, "The Night Blowing Cereus", a mezzotint engraving printed in color and finished by hand, original color, London.

1800     19in (47.5cm) high

**$5,000-8,000**     FRE

A US ten dollar gold piece, NST graded at MS 62.

*1801*

**$10,000-13,000** FRE

A US two-and-a-half dollar gold piece, ANA graded at MS 64.

*1907*

**$1,200-1,800** FRE

A US one dollar gold piece, ANA graded at MS 64.

*1851*

**$700-1,000** FRE

A US one dollar gold piece.

*1854*

**$1,000-1,500** FRE

A US five dollar gold piece, ANA graded at MS 64.

*1909*

**$2,200-2,800** FRE

An US three dollar gold piece, ANA graded at MS 63.

*1854*

**$2,800-3,200** FRE

A US one dollar gold piece, ANA graded at MS 64.

*1874*

**$400-600** FRE

A US two-and-a-half dollar gold piece, ANA graded at MS 64.

*1929*

**$400-600** FRE

A US ten dollar gold piece, PCGS graded at MS 64.

*1932*

**$1,200-1,800** FRE

A US silver dollar, ANA graded at MS 68.

*1880*

**$1,800-2,200** FRE

A US commemorative half-dollar, PCGS graded at MS 66.

*1920*

**$120-180** FRE

A Massachusetts State Colonial currency note, codfish, signed "D. Chever".

**$400-600** FRE

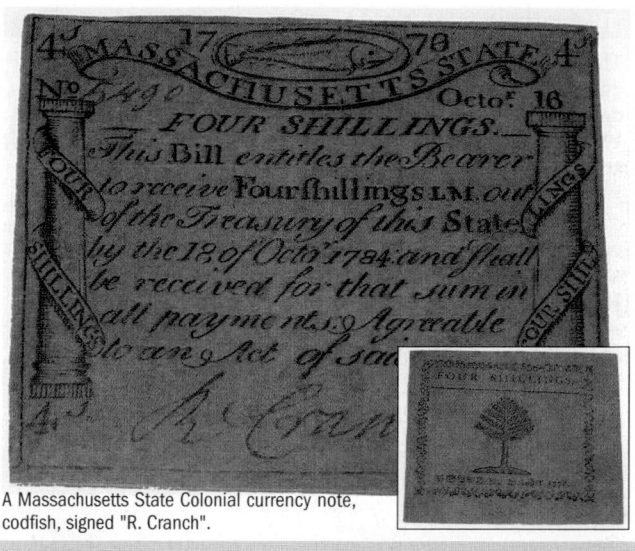

A Massachusetts State Colonial currency note, codfish, signed "R. Cranch".

**$400-600** FRE

A European five dollar currency note, signed "S. Lewis".

**$400-600** FRE

A Massachusetts State Colonial currency note, Rising Sun, signed by "J. Moore".

**$400-600** FRE

A European thirty dollar Colonial currency note, use of 'nature' prints designed and engraved by order of Paul Revere, emitted by 'The United States', signed by "Jacob Masoner" and "Jno. Graff".

**$400-600** FRE

A Colony of Massachusetts Bay two shillings Colonial currency note, dated. *1775*

**$120-180** FRE

## THE GOLF MARKET

The market for golfing antiques is less buoyant than during its heyday a decade ago. Despite this, pieces at the high end of the market are commanding greater prices than ever before. Buyers are currently attracted to golfing ceramics, particularly examples dating from c1900 and made by well-known English factories such as Royal Doulton, Doulton Lambeth, and Spode. Pieces need to be in good condition without restoration. Ceramics produced in Germany for the American market by makers such as Gerz, are also popular. Books and pictures continue to perform well.

In terms of equipment, golf clubs have perhaps suffered the most from a declining market. Prices have come down for many examples, although this has enabled collectors on smaller budgets to buy quality clubs that have the potential to rise in value. Clubs at the very top of the market however, are attracting high prices. Examples by Hugh Phillips of St. Andrews can sell for $18,000 or more, while clubs and balls by Tom Morris are also desirable. At the lower end of the market, collectors are becoming increasingly keen on other types of memorabilia, such as scorecards and Open programs – even recent ones – and favor examples signed by players.

*– Manfred Schotten, Manfred Schotten Antiques*

## CLUBS

A long nose putter, by John Allan of Westward Ho, scared fruitwood head, horn insert and lead counterweight, hickory shaft, replacement grip.

*Allen was the golf professional at Prestwick, UK. This piece is rare as he only made a few clubs.*

c1870

**$2,800-3,200**    **L&T**

A B.W. Day long nose play club, with horn insert to sole, lead backweight and hickory shaft, the scared head stamped with maker's name, replacement wrapped leather grip.

**$1,200-1,800**    **L&T**

An R. Dickson long nose putter, with horn insert to sole, lead backweight and hickory shaft, the scared head stamped with maker's name, replacement wrapped leather grip.

**$700-1,000**    **L&T**

A one-piece straight-faced brassie, in hickory, a John Dunn patent for B.G.I. Co., the sole with ebony insert and brass plate, the face with a leather insert, lead counterweight, wrapped smooth leather grip.

**$1,200-1,800**    **L&T**

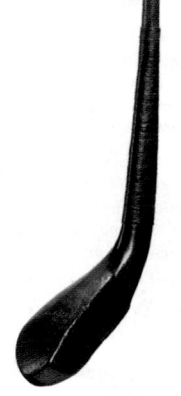

A long nose wood, by Tom Dunn of Musselburgh, with a horn insert to sole, leather insert to face, hickory shaft, lead counterweight, the head stamped "T Dunn".

c1880

**$1,800-2,200**    **L&T**

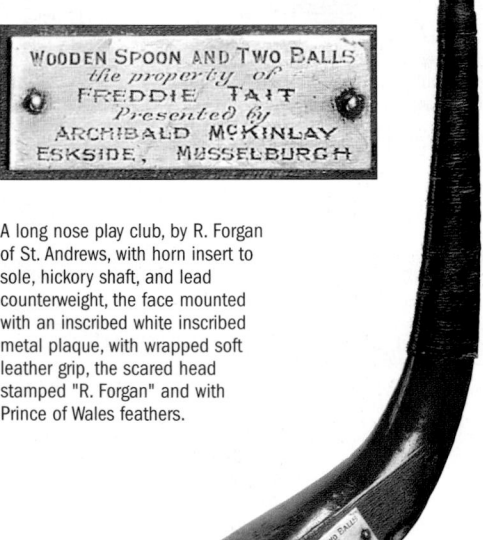

A long nose play club, by R. Forgan of St. Andrews, with horn insert to sole, hickory shaft, and lead counterweight, the face mounted with an inscribed white inscribed metal plaque, with wrapped soft leather grip, the scared head stamped "R. Forgan" and with Prince of Wales feathers.

**$18,000-28,000**    **L&T**

A long nose play club, by W. Frier of Edinburgh, the scared head with horn insert to sole, lead counterweight, hickory shaft and wrapped leather grip.

**$2,200-2,800**    **L&T**

A William Gibson anti-shank Putter, with a wry neck, hickory shaft and wrapped leather square section grip, the head stamped "Lillywhite's London Woodfaced Putter, Special" and with star mark.

**$2,800-3,200**    **L&T**

An early Karsten Co. 'Ping' putter, No. 1A, the brass head with a central shaft.

**$1,800-2,200**    **L&T**

A rare Pro-swing practice club, with leaded brass ball head, hickory shaft and wrapped smooth leather grip.

**$1,200-1,800** L&T

A hand-forged iron, by George Nichol of Leven, with gutta percha crimped hosel, hickory shaft and wrapped leather grip, stamped with patent number.

*c1900*

**$4,000-6,000** L&T

A patent iron, by R.L. Urquhart, of conventional form, with an adjustable head and marked face, hickory shaft and wrapped leather grip, loose.

**$1,200-1,800** L&T

An early unfinished blacksmith iron head.

**$8,000-12,000** L&T

## BALLS

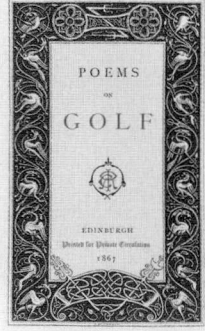

A 'The Lunar' bramble rubber core ball, by the Scottish Golf Ball Manufacturing Co., with dot and crescent markings.

*1912*

**$2,800-3,200** L&T

A Faroid 75 rubber core ball, with raised concentric circles, stamped at each pole in red.

**$4,000-6,000** L&T

A hand-hammered gutta ball, by Andrew Patrick of Leven, stamped "A. Patrick, 27 1/2".

**$18,000-28,000** L&T

A rare feather ball, of unusual proportions, inscribed in ink "Presented to Rev. H.M. Lamont by J.W.. Inglis C.B (?), an old student in St. Andrews, 18**" and "This ball was made by Wil. Robertson, 1790, Father (?) of Allan, the famous golfer", with protected lacquer to ball.

**$45,000-55,000** L&T

## BOOKS

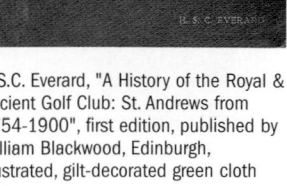

Robert Clark, "Poems on Golf", first edition, privately printed in Edinburgh for subscribers and one of a limited edition of 58, illustrated with printer's vignettes, gilt stamped and lettered ribbed green cloth, inscription.

*This work includes poems such as Mathison's "The Goff" and Carnegie's "Golfiana".*

*1867*

**$2,200-2,800** L&T

Bernard Darwin, "The Golf Courses of the British Isles", first edition, published by Duckworth, London, illustrated with sixty-four color plates from paintings by Harry Rowntree, original gilt-decorated green cloth and gray cloth dust jacket.

*This famous book covers the courses of Scotland, England, and Ireland.*

*1910*

**$8,000-12,000** L&T

H.S.C. Everard, "A History of the Royal & Ancient Golf Club: St. Andrews from 1754-1900", first edition, published by William Blackwood, Edinburgh, illustrated, gilt-decorated green cloth cover.

*1907*

**$1,200-1,800** L&T

Harold H. Hilton & Garden G. Smith, "The Royal & Ancient Game of Golf", first edition, published by London & Counties Press, London, No. 40 of 900 copies, the Subscriber's edition, illustrations from paintings and photographs, the red vellum cover with gilt-tooled lion, gilt lettering to cover and spine.

*1912*

$2,800-3,200     L&T

E.C. Potter, "Midlothian Melodies, Mnemonic Maunderings of the Merry Muse", first edition, by appointment by the Midlothian Country Club, red cloth cover, gilt lettering, Chicago.

*1900*

$1,800-2,200     L&T

W.W. Tulloch, "The Life of Tom Morris, with Glimpses of St. Andrews and its Golfing Celebrities", first edition published by T. Werner Laurie, London, illustrations from 27 photographs, original pictorial green cloth cover, the spine lettered in gilt.

*1908*

$1,200-1,800     L&T

An Amateur Championship at St. Andrews "Official Programme", for 28th May 1930, with brown paper wrappers.

$5,000-8,000     L&T

## OTHER GOLFING MEMORABILIA

A lithographed "Life Association of Scotland" advertising calendar, printed by Banks & Co., Edinburgh, with a golfing view of North Berwick and further golfing vignettes to the border.

*1893*     22in (54cm) wide

$3,000-5,000     L&T

John Blair, "North Berwick From The West", watercolor, with the links in the right middle distance, signed and inscribed lower right.

10.25in (26cm) wide

$2,800-3,200     L&T

Thomas Hodge, "The Slogger, Robert Clark", a pencil drawing of a profile portrait laid down on card, inscribed on the mount.

4.25in (11cm) high

$2,800-3,200     L&T

Life Magazine, "Fore! Life's Book for Golfers", first edition, published by Life Publishing, New York, illustrated with green cloth-backed pictorial boards and a cover design of a female golfer in the style of Charles Dana Gibson.

*1900*

$1,200-1,800     L&T

A Gerz salt-glazed stoneware jug and stopper, relief-molded with golfers and caddies.

9in (23cm) high

$2,800-3,200     L&T

A pair of Bohemian iridescent glass vases, with enamel and gilt decoration of lady golfers.

(12.5in) 32cm high

$15,000-18,000     L&T

A pair of Copeland pottery golfing tygs, the body with relief molding, decorated in white in the round with a scene of golfers and caddies, printed and impressed marks.

5.5in (14cm) high

$3,000-5,000     L&T

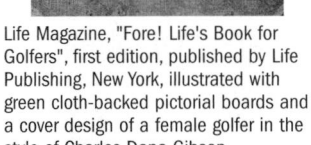

A Lenox pottery tobacco humidor, with a golfing scene in shades of green, the sterling silver cover by Shreve & Co., printed mark.

6in (15.5cm) high

$7,000-10,000     L&T

## THE DECORATIVE ARTS MARKET

A landmark exhibition in Indianapolis and San Francisco will attract media attention to the Arts & Crafts style this year. Endorsements by celebrity collectors should help to raise the profile of this exciting area of the decorative arts market. Furniture by the Stickleys is a perennial favorite among collectors, with pieces by Gustav Stickley the most sought-after. Unusual examples of Gustav Stickley's art – particularly metalwork and textiles – could well see substantial increases in value over the coming months, as could furniture by other virtuosos such as Charles Rohlfs.

Similarly, ceramics by smaller, more esoteric producers such as Grueby, whose international appeal is currently keeping prices high, are gaining popularity. Larger potteries such as Roseville are collected more avidly now than ever, although only the most remarkable pieces are appreciating significantly. Whereas an experimental or otherwise rare example of Roseville pottery might now fetch upwards of $15,000, the mass-produced 'Futura' range has actually lost value in the last year. This is due at least in part to the easy availability of items like this through online auction sites.

Not all mass-produced products are feeling the detrimental effects of the online auction revolution. Inter-war Lalique glass has been the subject of healthy interest in recent months. This trend looks set to continue as a new generation starts to build specialist collections of perfume bottles and car mascots. The quantity of Lalique glass on the secondary market is actually dwindling while demand increases, and this potent combination of factors can only lead to higher prices at auction.

*Nicholas M. Dawes*

## AMPHORA

An Amphora cylindrical vase, of tapering form with inverted rim, painted with cattle in a landscape, the base with stylized flowerhead frieze in relief, the rim with gilt decoration, printed and impressed marks "3731".

*15.25in (38cm) high*

**$500-800** **L&T**

A large Amphora shouldered vase, of ovoid form, with everted rim, painted with cattle in a landscape, stylized flowerhead frieze to base, the rim with gilt decoration, printed and impressed marks "3760".

*17in (42.5cm) high*

**$800-1,200** **L&T**

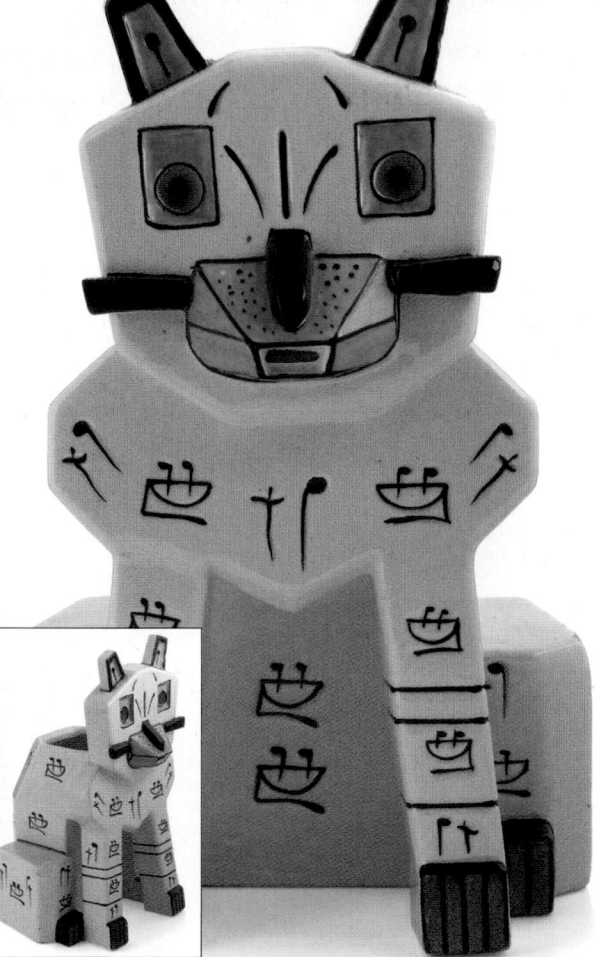

A tall Amphora water jug, with crossed handles, enamel-decorated with Egyptian motifs in polychrome, stamped numbers.

*14.5in (37cm) high*

**$500-700** **DRA**

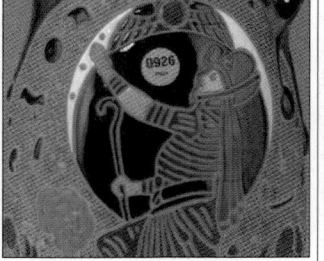

A large Amphora pottery spill vase, designed by Louis Wain, modeled as a white cat, with printed mark and impressed facsimile signature.

*10.25in (26cm) high*

**$7,000-10,000** **WW**

A Boch Frères 'Gres Keramis' blue vase, with a cockerel design.

*c1925*      *11.5in (29cm) high*

**$1,800-2,200**      **MOD**

A Boch Frères 'Gres Keramis' green vase, with a cockerel design.

*c1925*      *6.75in (17cm) high*

**$1,200-1,800**      **MOD**

## BOCH FRÈRES

- Boch Frères was founded by Pierre-Joseph Boch in Luxembourg in 1767 and was passed down through subsequent generations.
- It became Villeroy and Boch in 1836.
- In 1841, the Belgium branch of the Boch family set up a factory at La Louvière and traded as Boch Frères.
- The Boch Frères company became well known for its Art Deco ceramics. Pieces were of high quality and simple in form.
- Charles Catteau (1880-1966) was one of the factory's leading designers. He had worked as a potter at Sèvres and Nymphenburg before joining Boch Frères as Design Director in 1907. He was influenced by Japanese and African design as well as the Avant Garde and Bauhaus movements.
- Catteau joined the 'Circle of Friends of the Fine Arts' in 1908. His Art Deco work won him a grand prix at The International Exhibition of Decorative Arts in 1925.
- The company is still in production today.

A rare and early Boch Frères 'Gres Keramis' stoneware vase, by Charles Catteau, in brown and beige.

*c1925*      *7.75in (20cm) high*

**$1,200-1,800**      **MOD**

An early Boch Frères bulbous vase, by Charles Catteau, stamped "Boch Frères Keramis/Ch. Catteau", numbered.

*8.75in (22cm) high*

**$3,000-4,000**      **DRA**

A Boch Frères bulbous stoneware vase, by Charles Catteau, green ink stamps, "Boch Frères/Keramis/Made in Belgium/CH. Catteau" with numbers, and incised "Gres Keramis".

*10.25in (26cm) high*

**$2,200-2,800**      **DRA**

An early Boch Frères 'Keramis' vase, designed by Charles Catteau, in green and white with a stylized deer design.

*c1925*      *12.5in (32cm) high*

**$3,000-4,000**      **MOD**

A Boch Frères Keramis pottery vase, with geometric flowers on a craquelure ground, printed "Keramis" mark.

*10.75in (27.5cm) high*

**$700-1,000**      **WW**

## A CLOSER LOOK AT A BOCH FRÈRES VASE

Boch Frères Keramis produced some of the finest ceramics in Belgium during the Art Deco period. With its geometric detailing, this is a classic Art Deco design.

Pieces identified as being by the renowned designers Arthur Finch or Charles Catteau will usually attract a premium. The maker of this vase is unknown.

Boch Frères Keramis often used enamels to decorate its ceramics. As well as the colored metal mounts seen on this vase, the company also produced cloisonné work.

The colors on this vase have lost none of their vibrancy, so it has held its value particularly well.

A very rare Art Deco Boch Frères facetted vase, covered in Persian blue crackled glaze, with French enameled metal mounts, black ink stamp to body, metal stamped "France", some wear to enamel.

*10in (25.5cm) high*

**$4,000-6,000**      **SDR**

A Carlton ware 'Chevron' Handcraft vase, pattern number 3657, with printed and painted marks.

*4.25in (10.5cm) high*

**$500-700** WW

A Carlton ware 'Heron and Magical Tree' vase, with printed factory mark.

*5in (13cm) high*

**$500-800** WW

A Carlton ware 'Fantasia' vase, pattern number 3406, with printed and painted marks.

*7in (17.5cm) high*

**$800-1,200** WW

A Carlton ware oviform luster jug, painted with highly stylized flowers and foliage against a mottled orange luster ground, with a gilded handle, factory marks to base.

*7.75in (19.5cm) high*

**$700-1,000** DN

An Art Deco Carlton ware 'Fantasia' wall plaque, pattern number 3388, printed and painted marks, paper label, repair to foot rim.

*15.75in (40cm) diam*

**$1,200-1,800** WW

## CLARICE CLIFF

A Clarice Cliff Bizarre 'Applique Avignon' octagonal plate, with printed mark, restored.

*8.75in (22cm) diam*

**$1,200-1,800** WW

A Clarice Cliff Bizarre 'Applique Palermo' octagonal plate, with printed mark.

*8.5in (21.5cm) diam*

**$1,800-2,200** WW

A Clarice Cliff Fantasque Bizarre two-handled grapefruit bowl, painted in colored enamels with a version of the 'Autumn' pattern, printed marks in black.

*6.75in (17cm) wide*

**$300-500** NEA

A Clarice Cliff Bizarre 'Autumn' cachepot, painted with a pattern of trees with sinuous trunks and a small cottage, black printed marks.

*c1930* *6.25in (16cm) high*

**$700-1,000** HAMG

## DOULTON LAMBETH

A Doulton Lambeth stoneware vase by Hannah Barlow, of shouldered cylindrical form with applied foot, decorated with a frieze of children, goats, and donkeys, impressed and incised marks, restored base.

*10.75in (27cm) high*

**$1,200-1,800**          **L&T**

A Doulton Lambeth stoneware biscuit barrel and cover by Florence Barlow, with electroplated mounts and hinged cover, decorated with a frieze of horses, impressed and incised marks, cracks under mounts.

*8in (20cm) high*

**$700-1,000**          **L&T**

A Doulton and Watts Lambeth stoneware spirit barrel, the sides decorated in relief with bands of fruiting vine and the Royal Coat of Arms.

*c1840          15in (38cm) high*

**$280-320**          **H&L**

A large Doulton Lambeth stoneware vase, by Hannah Barlow, incised with a band of grazing horses between foliate borders, on a buff ground, impressed mark, incised monogram.

*17in (43cm) high*

**$1,800-2,200**          **WW**

A Doulton Lambeth stoneware jardinière, by Mark V. Marshall, incised with mythical beasts below a band of scrolling foliage, impressed marks, incised monogram.

*6.5in (16.5cm) high*

**$1,200-1,800**          **WW**

A Doulton Lambeth candlestick designed by Edith Lupton, incised and impressed marks with date "1876".

*8.75in (22cm) high*

**$300-500**          **CHEF**

## ROYAL DOULTON

A pair of Royal Doulton stoneware vases, of shouldered baluster form, tubeline decoration with white roses and foliage, on a mottled blue ground, impressed mark and "MB" monogram.

*14in (36cm) high*

**$500-700**          **HAMG**

A pair of Royal Doulton vases, by Hannah Barlow, incised with grazing donkeys in a landscape between applied foliate borders, incised marks, one with restored chip to base rim.

*11in (28cm) high*

**$2,200-2,800**          **WW**

A Royal Doulton 'Seaweed' stoneware baluster vase, by George Tinworth, with applied and incised foliage decoration, and white tubelining, factory marks and signed with "GT" monogram.

*10.5in (27cm) high*

**$500-700**          **DN**

A Royal Doulton 'Calumet' figure, number HN2068, by C.J. Noke.

*6.5in (16cm) high*

**$300-400**          **DN**

A Royal Doulton figure, 'The Wizard', designed by A. Maslankowski, HN 2877.

*9.75in (25cm) high*

**$220-280**     **CHEF**

A Royal Doulton 'Mamselle' figure by L. Harradine, with printed and painted marks, HN786, chip to hat.

*7in (17.5cm) high*

**$4,000-6,000**     **WW**

A Royal Doulton figure, 'The Welsh Girl', designed by E.W. Light, in bronze finish, repaired neck and plinth.

*13.5in (34cm) high*

**$500-700**     **GORL**

A Royal Doulton plate, painted by R. Carnock, with colored enamel flowers within raised paste gilded trellis and vase bands, signed, printed green mark and retailer's mark for "Davis Collamore & Co Ltd, New York".

*8.75in (22cm) diam*

**$180-220**     **LFA**

An unusual Royal Doulton tea trio, modeled in low relief with fish amongst waterweed, the cover modeled with a seated frog, comprising teapot and cover, milk and sugar, impressed marks.

*5in (13cm) high*

**$2,800-3,200**     **WW**

## GOLDSCHEIDER

- Goldscheider was established in Vienna in 1885. It produced Art Nouveau figures in a variety of materials including terracotta.
- During the 1920s and 1930s, the factory became one of the few Austrian ceramic firms to concentrate on Art Deco pieces.
- The company produced a wide range of models, many depicting female figures in elaborate modern costumes decorated in rich bright colors. Pieces, many of which are marked "Goldscheider", included ballerinas, Pierrettes, and cast plaster copies of bronze sculptures.

- The boldly colored wall masks made by the company during the Art Deco period are highly collectible. They are handpainted with stylized and simplified features and typically have curled hair. They were made from terracotta and are prone to chipping and damage.
- The Staffordshire firm Myott, Son & Co. produced Goldscheider from the late 1930s. These pieces, marked "Goldscheider made in England", are less sought-after than Austrian examples.
- The Goldscheider factory closed in 1954.

A large Goldscheider ceramic sculpture of Diana the Huntress, by Latour, with polychrome glaze, mounted on a bow-front base, black ink stamp "Goldscheider Wien/Made in Austria", with numbers and artist's signature, restoration, missing bow and arrow.

*23.25in (33.5cm) high*

**$1,200-1,800**     **DRA**

A Goldscheider pottery figure of a dancer, by Josef Lorenzl, signed to the skirt, base with black stamp and model number "5715/49/8".

*c1930*

**$2,800-3,200**     **DOR**

A Goldscheider pottery figure of a girl standing on a drum, from a model by Josef Lorenzl, printed and impressed marks, restored.

*14.5in (37cm) high*

**$1,800-2,200**     **WW**

A Goldscheider figure, by Dakon, depicting a lady holding aloft the trail of her red floral skirt.

*15in (38cm) high*

**$3,000-4,000**     **BEV**

A Goldscheider figure, by Joseph Lorenzl, of an elegant lady in white hat and red dress.

*13in (33cm) high*

**$2,200-2,800**     **BEV**

A Goldscheider pottery figure of a dandy, designed by Lorenzl, with printed and impressed marks.

*11.5in (29cm) high*

**$700-1,000**     **WW**

A Goldscheider figure, 'Mephistopheles', by Josef Lorenzl, printed marks.

*14.25in (36cm) high*

**$2,200-2,800**     **WW**

A Goldscheider Art Deco figure of 'The Captured Bird', modeled as a dancing girl wearing batwing sleeves outstretched, painted and impressed marks, restored leg.

*12.75in (32cm) high*

**$1,200-1,800**     **L&T**

A large Goldscheider terracotta group, modeled as a woman and lion on an architectural base with lion masks, impressed factory marks and a metal retail label from Bordeaux.

*20in (51cm) high*

**$1,200-1,800**     **DN**

A Goldscheider ceramic bust of a woman with wavy hair, holding a flower in her hand, stamped "Goldscheider / Wien / Made in Austria", with incised numbers and remnant of foil label, restoration.

*8.75in (22cm) high*

**$700-1,000**     **DRA**

A Goldscheider earthenware head of a woman in dark brown clay, her features in turquoise and orange glaze, mounted on an ebonized wood block, marked with metal tag, minor damage.

*10.75in (27.5cm) high*

**$700-1,000**     **SDR**

A Goldscheider figure modeled as a draped maiden holding a conch to her ear, impressed marks, artist's signature, glaze flakes and chip to base rim.

*26in (66cm) high*

**$700-1,000**     **WW**

### A CLOSER LOOK AT A GOLDSCHEIDER CLOCK

Goldscheider sculptural models are very popular. Rare examples will attract a premium, especially if they bear the mark of Ludwig Goldscheider.

Cabochons are precious stones that have been polished but remain uncut, and so have no facets. Opal cabochons of various colors have been applied to this piece.

This clock was made as a unique exhibition piece, which increases its market value substantially.

The large scale and dramatic subject matter of this clock makes it an impressive and unusual commodity.

A monumental Art Nouveau sculptural clock, by Ludwig Goldscheider, with a semi-nude maiden and an eagle, with gray glaze, glass and genuine opal cabochons, marked "Ludwig Goldscheider/Wien", with stamped numbers, chip to one corner and replaced works.

*c1870*     *25in (64cm) high*

**$4,000-6,000**     **DRA**

A miniature William Moorcroft 'Orchid' pattern flambé vase, decorated in shades of red, yellow, green, and blue.

*3in (8cm) high*

**$220-280** **GORL**

A Moorcroft 'Orchid' pattern ovoid jug, with loop handle, tube-line decorated in colored enamels on a mottled blue ground, impressed and painted initial marks, paper label.

*8.25in (21cm) high*

**$700-1,000** **NEA**

A Moorcroft circular bowl, decorated in the 'Plum Wisteria' pattern, impressed marks, signed in blue.

*10.5in (26cm) wide*

**$3,000-4,000** **L&T**

A William Moorcroft 'Pansy' pattern vase.

*c1914* *5in (12.5cm) high*

**$2,200-2,400** **RUM**

A William Moorcroft 'Pomegranate' pattern vase.

*c1930* *6in (15cm) high*

**$700-1,000** **RUM**

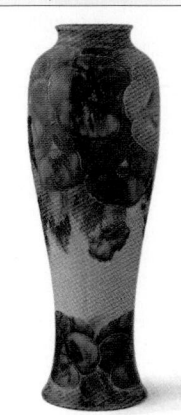

A William Moorcroft 'Pansy' pattern vase, dated.

*1913* *(29.5cm) high*

**$6,000-9,000** **RUM**

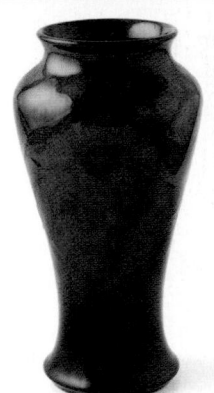

A Moorcroft 'Pomegranate' flambé vase, with a painted blue signature.

*10in (25.5cm) high*

**$2,200-2,800** **WW**

A Moorcroft candlestick, decorated in the 'Pomegranate' pattern, cylindrical form with spreading base, impressed marks, initialed in green.

*8.25in (21cm) high*

**$300-500** **L&T**

A William Moorcroft 'Pomegranate' pattern dish, with hammered pewter rim.

*11in (29cm) high*

**$500-800** **GORL**

A William Moorcroft 'Pomegranate' pattern inkwell, with plated mount.

*4.5in (11cm) wide*

**$800-1,200** **GORL**

A William Moorcroft 'Poppy' pattern tobacco jar.

*c1900* *3.5in (8.5cm) high*

**$1,200-1,800** **RUM**

A William Moorcroft 'Spanish' design vase.

*c1910* *8.75in (22cm) high*

**$6,000-9,000** **RUM**

A William Moorcroft 'Willow' pattern vase.

*c1930* *9in (23cm) high*

**$3,000-4,000** **RUM**

## PILKINGTON

- The Pilkington factory was founded in Manchester, England in 1891 to produce architectural ceramics.
- From 1912, it was also known as Royal Lancastrian.
- At the advice of William Burton, a chemist for Josiah Wedgwood & Sons, it began to produce tiles which had become increasingly fashionable. Burton later took over as manager of the company.
- Pilkington soon expanded its range to include decorative vases. Distinctive glazes included Sunstone, Eggshell, Luster, and Lapis.
- The respected illustrator Walter Crane (b. 1845) produced a number of designs for the company in the early 20thC.
- Talented artists, including Lewis F. Day, C.F.A. Voysey, Gordon Forsyth and W.S. Mycock, also contributed to the firm.
- An impressed 'P' and bees mark and date marks were used between c1904 and 1914. A 'P' within a rose was used after c1914.
- The company is still in operation today.

A Pilkington's Lancastrian vase, by Annie Burton, decorated with scrolling foliage, impressed mark, painted "B".

*4in (10cm) high*

**$500-800**    **WW**

A Pilkington's Lancastrian vase, by Charles Cundall, painted with a hunting scene, impressed mark, painted monogram, date mark.

*1910*    *8.25in (21cm) high*

**$3,000-5,000**    **WW**

A Pilkington's Lancastrian vase, by Walter Crane, painted by William S. Mycock, decorated with a band of heraldic lions, impressed mark, painted Crane monogram, artist monogram.

*5in (13cm) high*

**$2,800-3,200**    **WW**

### A CLOSER LOOK AT A PILKINGTON'S VASE

Pilkington's Lancastrian ware is named for the county where its clay seam was discovered.

Pilkington is best known for its glazes, which came in a dazzling variety of colors and textures.

Walter Crane was an illustrator, political activist and academic who had links with William Morris. This vase is more valuable because it was designed by Crane.

Richard Joyce was one of Pilkington's most successful artists. His signature on this piece is another indication of its superior quality and value.

A Pilkington's Lancastrian vase, designed by Walter Crane and painted with maidens by Richard Joyce, impressed mark "RJ", monogram date mark, probably "1912".

*9in (23cm) high*

**$3,000-5,000**    **WW**

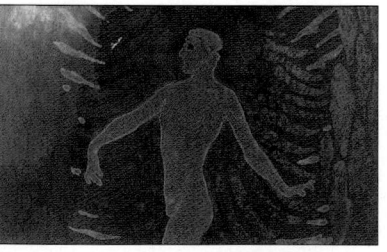

A Pilkington's Lancastrian vase, by Charles Cundall, decorated with grapevines in shades of copper and ruby luster, painted monogram and date mark.

*1909*    *5.75in (14.5cm) high*

**$2,800-3,200**    **WW**

A Pilkington's Lancastrian vase, by Gordon Forsyth, painted with winged classical figure and horses between cypress trees, impressed mark.

*9in (23cm) high*

**$3,000-4,000**    **WW**

A Pilkington's Royal Lancastrian vase, by William S. Mycock, with cranes flying through foliage, impressed mark, incised monogram, dated "Dec 28 1911".

*8.25in (21cm) high*

**$800-1,200**     **WW**

A Pilkington's Royal Lancastrian book end, modeled as a gazelle, impressed marks.

*6.5in (16.5cm) high*

**$180-220**     **WW**

A Pilkington's Royal Lancastrian limited edition figure, by David Evans, modeled as a cherub with a galleon, impressed marks "19/36", restored shell.

*9in (22.5cm) high*

**$400-600**     **WW**

A Pilkington's Royal Lancastrian leopard, probably designed by Richard Joyce, impressed marks, small chip to inside rim.

*5in (12.5cm) high*

**$400-600**     **WW**

A pair of Pilkington's Royal Lancastrian book ends, probably by David Evans, modeled as Classical dolphins, impressed marks.

*6in (15.5cm) high*

**$500-700**     **WW**

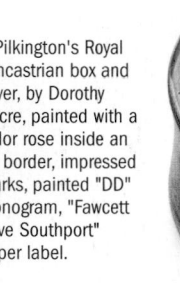

An early 20thC Pilkington's Royal Lancastrian scarab paperweight, with turquoise glaze, on an oval base, impressed mark.

*4in (10cm) long*

**$280-320**     **HAMG**

A Pilkington's Royal Lancastrian box and cover, by Dorothy Dacre, painted with a tudor rose inside an ivy border, impressed marks, painted "DD" monogram, "Fawcett Cave Southport" paper label.

*4in (10cm) diam*

**$800-1,200**     **WW**

## POOLE

- In 1921, the Poole-based manufacturer of architectural ceramics, Carter & Co., established the subsidiary Carter, Stabler and Adams to produce decorative domestic pottery. The company became known as Poole Pottery.
- Truda Adams (later Truda Carter), wife of the Managing Director John Adams, became a leading designer for the company. She produced ceramics painted with stylized flowers and animals in the 1920s and 1930s. Pieces by Ruth Pavely, who became head of the painting department after WWII, are also widely collected.
- Pieces from the 1920s and 1930s tend to command the highest prices, especially those decorated with stylised geometric patterns in bright colours that exemplify the style of the period. 'Ship Plates', based on a series of drawings by Arthur Bradbury and made from the 1930s are also desirable.
- During the 1950s, Poole introduced an innovative 'Freeform' range of contemporary pieces, designed by Alfred Read and Guy Sydenham. Large examples in popular patterns such as 'PRP' are particularly sought after and valuable.
- The words "Poole England" appear on early pieces, occasionally with "Carter, Stabler & Adams Ltd". A dolphin was added to the mark in the 1950s and from c1956 the words and dolphin image appear within a box. Special wares produced after c1963 are marked "Poole Studio".
- The company is still in operation today.

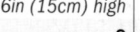

A Poole Pottery hand-thrown vase, painted in the 'WL' design by Gwen Haskins.

*6in (15cm) high*

**$220-280**     **C**

A 1930s Poole pottery vase, painted by Iris Skinner, with blue bell flowers on a downswept neck and an hemispherical body, incised "267", impressed and painted marks.

*5.75in (14.5cm) high*

**$180-220**     **CHEF**

A 1930s Poole pottery vase, painted by Hilda Hampton, with jazzy blooms on each side, the downswept shoulders above a hemispherical body, incised "443", impressed and painted marks,

*7in (17.5cm) high*

**$180-220**    **CHEF**

An Art Deco Poole pottery hand-thrown vase, decorated in the 'DU' pattern by Ruth Paveley.

**$300-500**    **C**

A Carter, Stabler & Adams Poole Pottery 'The Bull' group, by Harold and Phoebe Stabler, depicting two children with garlands sitting on a bull above a shaped canted base, impressed factory marks.

*13in (33cm) high*

**$2,200-2,800**    **DN**

A Carter, Stabler & Adams Poole Pottery 'The Buster Boy' and 'The Buster Girl' pair of figures, designed by Phoebe Stabler, both with impressed factory marks.

*largest 7in (17.5cm) high*

**$1,200-1,800**    **DN**

A pair of 1930s Poole pottery pair of Springbok bookends, No. 831, with brown glaze.

**$300-500**    **C**

A Poole pottery 'Atlantis Helmet' lamp, by Guy Sydenham, with internal grotesque face and outward chainmail carving.

*12in (30.5cm) high*

**$2,800-3,200**    **C**

A Poole Studio vase, No. 20, finished in turquoise-blue glaze on a white ground, impressed Poole Studio mark.

*9.5in (24cm) high*

**$2,800-3,200**    **C**

A 1930s Poole pottery ship bookend, designed by Harold Stabler and modeled by Harry Brown, minor chip.

**$400-600**    **C**

## ROYAL DUX

A Royal Dux table centerpiece, modeled as a maiden sitting on a large shell, triangular pad mark and printed mark.

*11in (28cm) high*

**$400-600**    **HAMG**

A Royal Dux pottery centerpiece, modeled as a classical girl catching fish and wearing pale green and gilt robes, between a pair of large shell-shaped bowls, raised on a rockwork and seaweed base, pink triangle mark.

*14in (35.5cm) high*

**$800-1,200**    **DN**

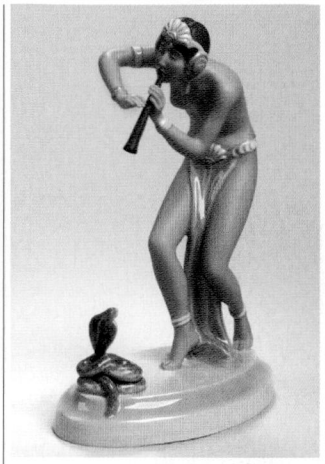

A Royal Dux Art Deco figure of a snake charmer.

*9.5in (24cm) high*

**$500-800**          **GCL**

A Royal Dux figure group, modeled as an eastern dancers, applied pink triangle mark.

*14.25in (36om) high*

**$800-1,200**          **WW**

An unusual Royal Dux figure of a Chinese man with a cart.

*c1915          10in (25.5cm) wide*

**$700-1,000**          **GCL**

A pair of Royal Dux figures of musicians, on mound and scroll bases.

*22in (56cm) high*

**$1,200-1,800**          **GORL**

## ROYAL WORCESTER

A large late 19thC Royal Dux figural vase, in the form of a woman holding a amphora beside a palm tree, raised on a naturalistic base, triangular seal and impressed "12800, 111/59", repairs to rim.

*37in (92.5cm) high*

**$1,200-1,800**          **FRE**

A Royal Dux Art Nouveau pottery vase, with basket weave texturing, embellished in shallow relief with blossom, olive green strapwork, gilded angular handles and female masks near the base, pink triangle mark on base.

*10.5in (27cm) high*

**$500-700**          **DN**

A Victorian Royal Worcester pedestal ewer, relief-molded with birds and flowers against an unusual petrol-iridescent ground of crimson blue, shoulder and handle modeled with masks, date code.

*1897          9in (23cm) high*

**$1,200-1,800**          **GORL**

A Royal Worcester two-handled globular potpourri vase and cover, with painting of Durham Cathedral by Harry Davis, inscribed "Durham Cathedral", puce printed marks, date code, shape number 1515.

*1912          8.5in (21cm) high*

**$5,000-7,000**          **DN**

## HARRY DAVIS

- Harry Davis (1885-1970) is considered to be one of greatest 20thC Royal Worcester artists.
- Davis joined the company as an apprentice in 1898 at the age of 14 and continued to work until 1970.
- He is known for meticulously handpainted landscapes, highland scenes, and architectural views, which are usually found on richly gilded vases and decorative services.
- A number of Harry Davis' designs are still in production today, including 'Lavinia', which was originally designed in 1946.
- Because his pieces date from the 20thC and were made for display rather than use, many have survived in good condition. This means that any damage greatly affects value.
- Pieces are marked "Royal Worcester". A dot was added to this mark for every year between 1892 and 1916. After this time, an asterix was added to the dots.
- Royal Worcester continues to operate today.

### A CLOSER LOOK AT A ROYAL WORCESTER EWER

*The shape is complex and thus suitable for display.*

*Harry Davis worked for Worcester for over 70 years and was awarded the MBE (Member in The Most Excellent Order of the British Empire) for his work.*

*Although the date code is for 1902, when Davis was just 18, this ewer may have been painted later, after a period of storage.*

*Davis's landscape scenes are particularly admired by collectors for their restraint and attention to detail.*

A Royal Worcester ewer, painted by Harry Davis, with sheep in a Highland landscape, puce printed marks, shape no.1209, date code, restored handle.

| | |
|---|---|
| 1902 | 17in (42.5cm) high |
| **$8,000-12,000** | **DN** |

A Royal Worcester two-handled oviform vase and cover, painted by Harry Davis, with sheep in a Highland landscape, shape no. 2158, puce printed marks, date code, restored cover.

| | |
|---|---|
| 1912 | 11in (28cm) high |
| **$6,000-9,000** | **DN** |

A Royal Worcester two-handled globular potpourri vase and cover, with Durham Cathedral painted by Harry Davis, puce printed marks, date code, shape no.1515, the underside inscribed "Durham Cathedral".

| | |
|---|---|
| 1912 | 8.5in (21.5cm) high |
| **$5,000-8,000** | **DN** |

A Royal Worcester slender ovoid vase, painted by Harry Davis with hill sheep in a Highland landscape, shape no.2217, puce printed marks, date code.

| | |
|---|---|
| 1914 | 9in (22cm) high |
| **$6,000-9,000** | **DN** |

A Royal Worcester oviform vase, painted by Harry Davis, with sheep in a Highland landscape, puce printed marks, shape no.287/H, date code.

| | |
|---|---|
| 1922 | 8in (20.5cm) high |
| **$4,000-6,000** | **DN** |

A Royal Worcester two-handled vase and cover, painted by Harry Davis, with Highland cattle, puce printed mark, shape no.2701, date code, finial gilt restored.

| | |
|---|---|
| 1922 | 5in (12.5cm) high |
| **$1,200-1,800** | **DN** |

A Royal Worcester cylindrical spill vase, painted by Harry Davis, with sheep in a landscape, with a pierced gilt japanesque lower section, puce printed mark, shape no.6/161, date code.

| | |
|---|---|
| 1922 | 6.5in (16cm) high |
| **$3,000-4,000** | **DN** |

A Royal Worcester ovoid vase with flared neck, painted by Harry Davis, with sheep in a landscape of bluebells, puce printed mark, shape no.202/H, date code.

| | |
|---|---|
| 1926 | 6.5in (16cm) high |
| **$8,000-12,000** | **DN** |

A Ruskin Pottery high-fired stoneware vase and cover, with a mottled and running sang-de-boeuf, lavender and silver glaze, impressed marks, dated, repaired finial.

*1909*     *10.5in (26cm) high*

**$3,000-5,000**     **WW**

A Ruskin stoneware vase covered in a speckled silver and gray luster glaze, impressed mark, dated.

*1923*     *6in (15.5cm) high*

**$1,200-1,800**     **WW**

A Ruskin high-fired stoneware vase mottled sang-de-boeuf and purple glaze, impressed mark, painted scissor mark, dated.

*1905*     *8.5in (21cm) high*

**$2,200-2,800**     **WW**

A Ruskin high-fired stoneware tyg, in mottled sang-de-boeuf and lavender on white, impressed marks, dated.

*1933*     *8in (20cm) high*

**$2,200-2,800**     **WW**

A Ruskin high-fired stoneware candlestick, of hexagonal section, mottled sang-de-boeuf and lavender on a white ground, impressed mark.

*4in (10cm) high*

**$1,200-1,800**     **WW**

A Ruskin high-fired stoneware stand, with streaked lavender and sang-de-boeuf on silver, impressed mark.

*4.75in (12cm) high*

**$1,200-1,800**     **WW**

A Ruskin high-fired stoneware vase, applied with silver mount to base rim, mottled pink, purple and turquoise on a white ground, impressed marks, silver marked "S*B Birmingham 1906".

*9.5in (24cm) high*

**$2,800-3,200**     **WW**

A Ruskin lamp base, of hexagonal section raised on bracket feet, covered in streaked and crystalline blue, yellow, orange and buff glazes, impressed marks.

*10.5in (26cm) high*

**$500-700**     **L&T**

## WEDGWOOD

A Wedgwood Fairyland luster 'Amherst Pheasant' bowl, designed by Daisy Makeig-Jones, printed mark, minor wear.

*8.75in (22cm) diam*

**$2,800-3,200**     **WW**

A Wedgwood luster 'Flying Humming Birds' bowl, painted in gilt with birds against a mottled blue ground, the mottled red interior with orange border, gilt Portland vase mark.

*c1925*     *11.5in (29cm) diam*

**$400-600**     **HAMG**

A Wedgwood Fairyland luster 'Willow' vase, designed by Daisy Makeig-Jones, pattern number Z5760, on flame luster ground, with printed and painted marks, missing cover, wear to ground.

*7.75in (20cm) high*

**$2,200-2,800**                    **WW**

## A CLOSER LOOK AT A WEDGWOOD FAIRYLAND BOWL

*Daisy Makeig-Jones designed Wedgwood's Fairyland luster range during the 1920s. Along with Keith Murray, she was one of the many innovative designers employed by the company during the early 20thC.*

*Fairyland luster pieces portray magical landscapes inspired by fairytales. They are highlighted in gold. The distinctive style of the pieces inspired other manufacturers to produce similar ranges.*

*Lusterware has been produced since the 8thC. The iridescent effect is made using a mixture of metallic oxides in oil that forms a thin film of metal on the surface of the pot when fired at a temperature of 1,380°F (750°C).*

A Wedgwood Fairyland luster 'Moorish' octagonal bowl, designed by Daisy Makeig-Jones, pattern number Z5125, the interior decorated in the 'Smoke Ribbons' pattern, printed and painted marks, minor ware to gilt interior.

*7.75in (20cm) diam*

**$5,000-7,000**                    **WW**

---

A Wedgwood Fairyland luster 'Willow' coral and bronze vase, designed by Daisy Makeig-Jones, with printed mark, missing cover, wear to bronze.

*8.75in (22cm) high*

**$2,200-2,800**                    **WW**

A Wedgwood moon flask, by Norman Wilson, covered in a pale blue glaze, impressed and printed mark "NW".

*8.75in (22cm) high*

**$500-700**                    **WW**

A Wedgwood earthenware 'Matt Blue' vase, designed by Keith Murray, of flaring shoulder form, with printed mark and "KM" monogram, slight damage.

*11.75in (30cm) high*

**$700-1,000**                    **WW**

A Wedgwood sculpture, 'Duiker', by John Skeaping, covered in an ocher glaze, impressed "Wedgwood J Skeaping", minor overpainting to one ear.

*7in (18cm) high*

**$120-180**                    **WW**

---

A Wedgwood earthenware Moonstone coffee set for four, designed by Keith Murray, various marks.

*pot 8.25in (21cm) high*

**$800-1,200**                    **WW**

Two of a set of six Wedgwood coffee cans and saucers, with Houses of Parliament design in gold and green band below rim.

*saucer 4.75in (12cm) diam*

**$50-70 set**                    **B&H**

## WEMYSS

- Wemyss ceramics were made at Robert Heron's pottery in Sinclairtown, Fife, from 1882.
- The firm was named after local patrons, the Wemyss family.
- It produced everyday tableware, affordable household items and the famous decorative cats and pigs.
- Chief decorator from the mid-1880s, Karel Nekola, is well known for his cabbage rose designs.
- Heron closed his factory in 1929 and Bovey Pottery bought the right to produce Wemyss.
- Large quantities were made to order by Bovey for the London wholesaler Jan Plichta, many pieces from this period are marked with his name.
- In the 1950s, Wemyss ware returned to Fife, where it is still produced today.
- Early Wemyss has been immensely collectible since the 1960s.
- Pieces signed by Nekola attract a premium today.

A large Wemyss circular bowl, of tapered cylindrical form, decorated with 'Cabbage Roses', printed retailer's mark.

*14.5in (36.5cm) diam*

**$800-1,200**     **L&T**

A large Wemyss 'Roses' circular bowl, painted with branches of cabbage roses, restored chip to rim, impressed mark "Wemyss".

*11.25in (28cm) diam*

**$500-800**     **L&T**

A Wemyss 'Roses' jardinère, painted with a frieze of cabbage roses, yellow painted mark "Wemyss".

*6.75in (17cm) high*

**$500-800**     **L&T**

A Wemyss 'Roses' small ewer and basin, painted with branches bearing cabbage roses, green painted marks "Wemyss".

*11.5in (29cm) diam*

**$700-1,000**     **L&T**

A Wemyss medium-sized pig, decorated with roses and leaves on a white ground, with pale pink decoration to ears, snout and trotters.

*11in (28cm) diam*

**$1,200-1,800**     **RDER**

A Wemyss cat, the body painted with large roses and leaves against a white ground, with black glass eyes and painted whiskers.

*12in (30cm) high*

**$4,000-6,000**     **RDER**

A large early 20thC Wemyss pig, modeled seated on its haunches, painted with pink cabbage roses, painted green mark "Wemyss Ware no 5 Made in England", damage to tail.

*16in (41cm) wide*

**$3,000-5,000**     **HAMG**

A Wemyss 'Dog Roses' circular cake plate, painted with branches of dog roses, green painted mark "Wemyss", also a Wemyss 'Dog Roses' tea cup, saucer and side plate, each painted with dog roses, green painted marks "Wemyss".

*large plate 9.25in (23cm) diam*

**$700-1,000**     **L&T**

A Wemyss 'Dog Roses' Lady Eva vase, impressed mark "Wemyss", yellow painted mark "Wemyss".

*8in (20cm) high*

**$500-700**      **L&T**

A pair of Wemyss candlesticks, each decorated in the 'Dog Roses' pattern, impressed marks.

*7.5in (18.5cm) high*

**$1,800-2,200**      **L&T**

A Wemyss Gordon plate, decorated with a yellow iris.

*8.25in (21cm) diam*

**$700-1,000**      **RDER**

A Wemyss quaich, decorated with a yellow iris.

*c1900*      *10.75in (27.5cm) wide*

**$700-1,000**      **RDER**

A small Wemyss Plichta pig money bank, painted with clover, signed "NEKOLA PINET".

*c1930*      *6.25in (16cm) wide*

**$800-1,200**      **RDER**

A Wemyss pottery pig, for Goode & Sons, painted with clover leaves, impressed "Wemyss Ware", printed retail mark, damages.

*6.25in (16cm) wide*

**$700-1,000**      **WW**

A small Wemyss pig, painted with green shamrocks, impressed "RH & S" mark.

*6.75in (17cm) wide*

**$800-1,200**      **L&T**

## A CLOSER LOOK AT A WEMYSS PIG

*Jan Plichta was a wholesaler who bought up large quantities of Wemyss ware in the early 20thC. Pieces predating this period tend to sell for a much higher price.*

*Wemyss pigs are iconic and much loved ceramics, with very strong collectible appeal.*

*Repeated designs inspired by flora and fauna, like these shamrocks, are typical Wemyss motifs.*

*Wemyss animals were made in various sizes. This large pig is more valuable than smaller examples, except the small rare sleeping pig.*

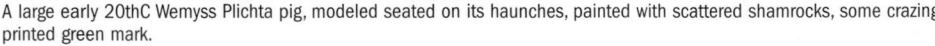

A large early 20thC Wemyss Plichta pig, modeled seated on its haunches, painted with scattered shamrocks, some crazing, printed green mark.

*16in (41cm) wide*

**$1,800-2,200**      **HAMG**

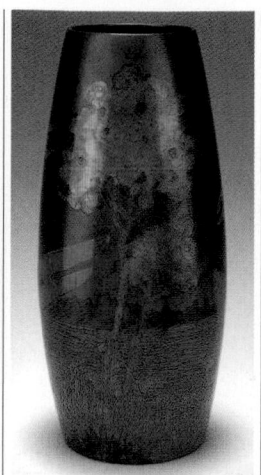

A Zsolnay faience vase, with landscape decoration depicting a coastal scene with boat and a gliding swan, glazed in red, purple, and green, marked on base "Zsolnay Pécs", model no. 5282 S 49 56.

*c1900*                  *13in (33.5cm) high*
**$12,000-18,000**                **QU**

A rare Art Nouveau Zsolnay trumpet vase with ruffled rim in lustered red glaze, surrounded with gold leaves, stamped "ZSOLNAY PECS" with "Castle/53/83/M".

*9.5in (24cm) high*
**$10,000-15,000**                **DRA**

A Zsolnay vase and cover, painted with butterflies and foliage in shades of blue, red, and gold luster, printed Zsolnay circular mark, painted "3252", small glaze frit to base.

*7in (17cm) high*
**$2,800-3,200**                **WW**

A large Zsolnay moonflask vase, with a molded, glazed and gilt peacock on a flowering branch, above a Chinese style base, impressed marks.

*16.75in (42cm) high*
**$1,800-2,200**                **L&T**

A Zsolnay pottery dish, modeled as three grotesque birds watching a frog, painted mark.

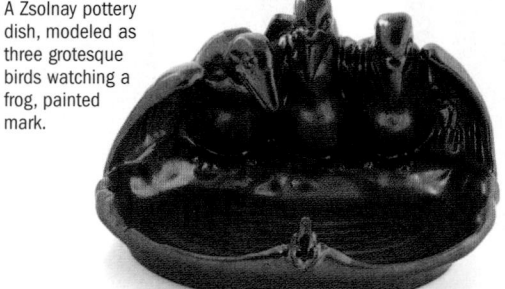

*6.25in (16cm) wide*
**$500-700**                **WW**

A tall Art Nouveau Zsolnay reticulated vase, with blood-red blossoms alternating with lustered green-gold leaves, over an incised matte green base, small chips and drilled hole to base, stamped "ZSOLNAY/6531/M".

*14.5in (36cm) high*
**$30,000-40,000**                **DRA**

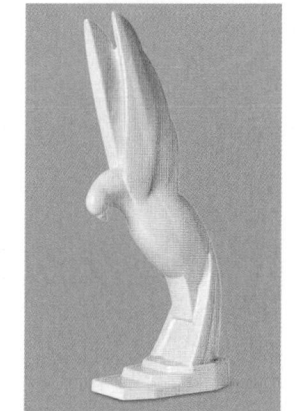

An Art Deco Adnet dove, signed.

*c1925*                  *19in (48cm) high*
**$700-1,000**                **TDG**

A rare Adnet bowl, in cream, with a floral design.

*Adnet is better known as a furniture maker.*

*c1925*                  *10.25in (26cm) diam*
**$800-1,200**                **MOD**

A circular vase, with green, olive and gray decoration, marked "EF Alsace".

*c1925*                  *14.5in (37cm) diam*
**$2,800-3,200**                **MOD**

An Art Nouveau pair of Denbac porcelain vases, each with a circular neck surrounded by three openings and embossed with stylized sprigs of flowers, covered in flowing microcrystalline glaze, stamped "Denbac/89".

*8in (20cm) high*

**$500-700**     DRA

An Ault vase, designed by Christopher Dresser, with one tall neck surrounded by four smaller necks, each molded with owls, the body molded with stars and clouds, glazed, applied and impressed marks, "Ault England 365."

*15.25in (38cm) high*

**$4,000-6,000**     L&T

Between 1892 and 1895, the influential designer Christopher Dresser produced designs for Ault pottery, based in Derbyshire, England. Pieces were made in earthenware, sometimes with a shimmering glaze like this vase.

Inspiration for Dresser's organic pieces came partially from his training as a botanist.

The swirling shape of this vase pre-empts the Art Nouveau movement, whilst its simplicity looks forward to more minimalist Modernist design.

Ault continued to produce Dresser pieces after the designer died in 1904, but these later pieces usually lack the facsimile signature.

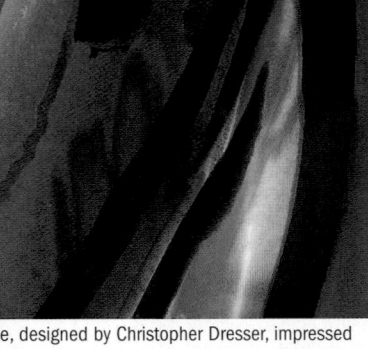

An earthenware plate by J. Selwyn Dunn, painted with a galleon at full sail, painted marks, Johnson Bros plate mark.

*12.25in (31cm) diam*

**$120-180**     WW

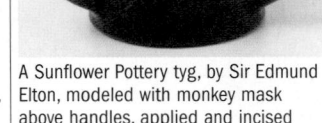

A Sunflower Pottery tyg, by Sir Edmund Elton, modeled with monkey mask above handles, applied and incised with foliate panels, unmarked.

*8.5in (21cm) high*

**$300-400**     WW

A large Ault pottery 'propeller' vase, designed by Christopher Dresser, impressed facsimile signature, minor nicks to glaze.

*14in (33.5cm) high*

**$3,000-5,000**     WW

An Editions Etling of Paris porcelain box and cover, the cover modeled with a female figure, printed marks and original paper label, cover restored.

*9in (23cm) wide*

**$700-1,000**     WW

A Sunflower Pottery ewer, by Sir Edmund Elton, incised and applied with flowers, in a blue glaze, painted "Elton" mark.

*19.75in (50cm) high*

**$500-700**     WW

A Sunflower Pottery vase and cover, by Sir Edmund Elton, covered in a gold craquelure glaze, painted signature.

*10.5in (26.5cm) high*

**$700-1,000**     WW

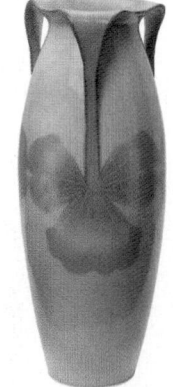

An Art Nouveau Rorstrand porcelain vase, designed by Algot Erikson, factory marks, numbered "6031" and with "AE" initials, some restoration.

*12.25in (31.5cm) high*

**$280-320**     DN

A pair of Linthorpe molded 'Iris' baluster vases, in green, brown, and blue glaze, pattern no. 168, "SL" monogram for William Sheldon Longbottom, design attributed to Christopher Dresser, chip on base.

*c1880*                                        *19in (48.5cm) high*

**$3,000-5,000**                                                **TCS**

An Art Deco plate by J. Lurçat of Sant-Vicens, with brown and white design.

*c1925*           *9.75in (25cm) diam*

**$800-1,200**                    **MOD**

A Clement Massier vase, of tapered form with four loop handles, covered in luster glaze, impressed and painted marks, chips.

*4in (10cm) high*

**$120-180**                    **WW**

A group of mallards, by Leo Mol (Leonid Moludizhanyn), signed and dated "Canada 58" in the glaze to base.

*This important painter and sculptor began modeling clay in his father's pottery workshop in Ukraine at the age of six. After moving to Canada in 1948, Leo began producing ceramic dancers, skiers and wildlife figurines which were exhibited in Winnipeg from 1949.*

*8.5in (21.5cm) high*

**$500-700**                    **WAD**

A German china jug and bowl, designed by Raymond Loewy for Rosenthal.

*jug 4.25in (11cm) high*

**$400-600**                    **MOD**

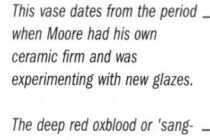

A blue, black, and white plate by J. Lurçat.

*c1925*           *9.75in (25cm) diam*

**$800-1,200**                    **MOD**

## A CLOSER LOOK AT A BERNARD MOORE VASE

This vase dates from the period when Moore had his own ceramic firm and was experimenting with new glazes.

The deep red oxblood or 'sang-de-beouf' glaze was a Ming Dynasty glaze that Moore revived in his own work.

A signature invariably adds value to any item, particularly if the maker is known to have employed other potters or decorators.

The large size of this piece and its fine proportions add to its value.

A tall Bernard Moore bottle-shaped vase with cylindrical body and ringed neck, covered in a fine lustered oxblood glaze, signed "Bernard Moore".

*18.5in (47cm) high*

**$1,800-2,200**                    **DRA**

A Fulper 'Bell Pepper' vase, with an unusual ocher crystalline matte glaze over a flowing blue-to-brown flambé, mark obscured by glaze.

*4.5in (11cm) high*

**$500-800** DRA

A Fulper faceted vase of Chinese shape covered in a fine leopard skin crystalline glaze, vertical mark.

*7.5in (19cm) high*

**$800-1,200** DRA

A large Fulper vase, with a thick gunmetal over Chinese Blue crystalline flame glaze, vertical mark, minor glaze nicks to rim.

*12in (30cm) high*

**$2,200-2,800** DRA

A Fulper vase, with cream colored top and blue and black flowing glaze to the base, marked with an incised vertical Fulper mark, some typical factory grinding flakes at the base.

*9.5in (24cm) high*

**$400-600** BEL

A Fulper Arts & Crafts vase, in shades of green, marked with vertical Fulper ink stamp.

*6.75in (17cm) high*

**$280-320** BEL

A Fulper bottle-shaped vase covered in a fine mahogany, green, and matte blue-gray glaze, scratches to base, vertical mark.

*8in (20cm) high*

**$280-320** DRA

A rare and exceptional early Fulper bulldog doorstep, in mustard matte and 'Elephant's breath' flambé glazes, unmarked, two small nicks to face.

*11in (27.5cm) wide*

**$1,200-1,800** DRA

A rare Fulper candlestick bowl with a dynamic green crystalline overglaze on a mottled blue and green ground, race track mark.

*11.25in (28cm) diam*

**$1,800-2,200** DRA

## FULPER

- The Fulper Pottery Company was born in 1899, when Abraham Fulper's sons reincorporated their father's pottery in Flemington.
- William H. Fulper II, grandson of Abraham, developed Fulper's 'Vasekraft' range of art pottery in 1909.
- Unlike many Arts and Crafts ceramicists, the Fulper Pottery used moulds to manufacture its wares. This kept costs down and made Fulper pottery affordable for ordinary American families.
- The 'Vasekraft' range is distinguished by the vast range of fine glazes developed by Martin Stangl, Fulper's ceramic engineer.
- Valuable Fulper pieces today include table lamps with shades made from inset glass panels and artist-signed lusterware.
- Fulper withdrew from the art pottery market in 1935, when Martin Stangl concentrated the firm's efforts on dinnerware.

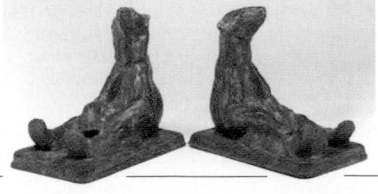

A pair of rare Fulper polar bear bookends covered in amber and ivory mottled matte glaze, restoration to several areas, vertical ink mark.

*8.25in (20.5cm) wide*

**$3,000-4,000** DRA

A tall Grueby vase, by Willhemina Post, with five-sided neck, the body with full height tooled and applied leaves alternating with ivory buds, covered in a leathery matte brown glaze, with Grueby Pottery stamp.

*11.25in (28.5cm) high*

**$8,000-12,000**　　　**DRA**

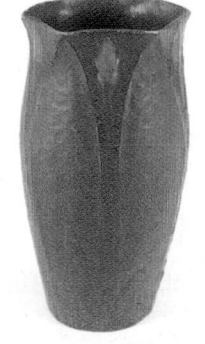

A Grueby vase, by Willhemina Post, with tooled and applied full height leaves alternating with yellow buds, the vase covered in a leathery matte green glaze, some chipping, circular pottery stamp, "WP" mark and paper labels.

*8in (20cm) high*

**$5,000-7,000**　　　**DRA**

An early Grueby tall ovoid vase, by Marie Seaman, decorated with green buds alternating with spade-shaped leaves, under a rich cucumber matte glaze, die-stamped faience mark "28 MS."

*11.5in (29cm) high*

**$3,000-5,000**　　　**DRA**

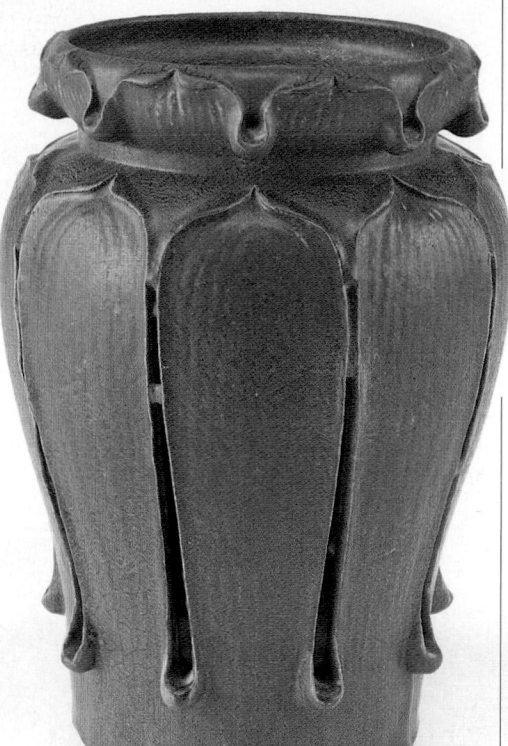

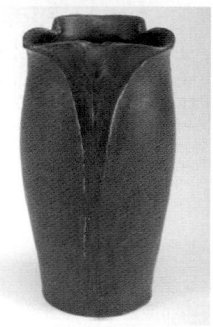

A Grueby bulbous vase with three-lobed opening, tooled and applied full-height leaves alternating with buds, and covered in a fine, smooth matte green glaze, restoration to one lobe, stamped "GRUEBY FAIENCE/W.F."

*7.5in (19cm) high*

**$1,800-2,200**　　　**DRA**

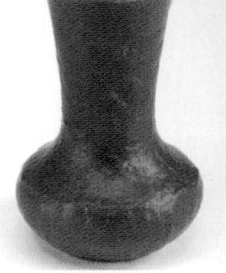

A Grueby bulbous vase with squat base covered in curled, rounded leaves under a flaring neck, in a thick matte green glaze, stamped "GRUEBY POTTERY/?.M.?/1-9."

*6.5in (16cm) high*

**$1,800-2,200**　　　**DRA**

A rare and exceptional tapering Grueby vase, crisply molded with broad, flat leaves under a flowing ocher matte glaze, circular die-stamp mark.

*7.25in (18.5cm) high*

**$5,000-7,000**　　　**DRA**

An exceptional Grueby Kendrick vase, by Wilhemina Post, its full height tooled and applied leaves reticulated below a row of shorter, flat leaves, covered in a feathered matte green glaze, minor restoration.

*12in (30cm) high*

**$30,000-35,000**　　　**DRA**

## GRUEBY

- William Henry Grueby established the Grueby Faience Co. in 1894 in Boston, Massachusetts.
- He had become fascinated with French matt glazes and the strong organic shapes used by Auguste Delaherche after visiting the World's Columbian Exposition in 1893.
- Grueby Faience Co. became known for quality opaque matt glazes in rich shades of brown, ocher, aqua, and pink. Then as now, it was Grueby's moss green glaze that was most celebrated.
- Grueby collaborated with Tiffany Studios to produce a collection of lamps which are highly prized today.
- Despite bouncing back from bankruptcy in 1909, Grueby Faience Co. was closed in 1920.

A rare and monumental Grueby Faience Co. pottery jardinière, green glaze with a band of broad leaves, two impressed marks on base, stress cracks at rim and nicks to leaf edges.

*c1900　　12.25in (31cm) high*

**$17,000-20,000**　　　**SK**

A late 19thC Art Nouveau pottery vase, five handles joined to the organic form with repeating design of modeled broad ribbed leaves in light green semi-gloss crackle glaze.

*This vase shares form and design elements with Grueby pottery. Grueby was inspired by the work of the French ceramicists such as Lachenal.*

*12in (30cm) high*

**$3,000-5,000**　　　**SK**

A Grueby/Pardee rare tile decorated in cuerda seca with a hilly landscape in blues, greens and amber, mounted in a fine Arts & Crafts frame, small chip to one corner, stamped "The C. Pardee Works."

*4.25in (10.5cm) square*

**$2,200-2,800**　　　**DRA**

A Newcomb College bulbous vase, with modeled and painted fern leaves in green on a cobalt and light blue ground, no artist's mark.

*c1902*                8.25in (20.5cm) high

**$10,000-12,000**                DRA

An early Newcomb College large vase, painted by Marie Delavigne with stylized pods in green on cobalt and light blue ground, two restored hairlines.

*c1902*                10.75in (27.5cm) high

**$5,000-7,000**                DRA

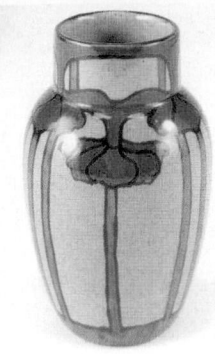

An early Newcomb College bulbous vase, painted by Sara Levy, with bright yellow blossoms on green stems against a pale ground.

*1903*                5.5in (14cm) high

**$7,000-10,000**                DRA

An early tall Newcomb College vase, incised and painted by Henrietta Bailey in indigo and dark green on a white and medium blue ground.

*1904*                9.5in (24cm) high

**$11,000-13,000**                DRA

A rare and early Newcomb College corseted vase, carved by Leona Nicholson, with a band of green scarabs on a blue, green, and yellow ground, complete with original stand covered in gunmetal glaze.

*c1905*                6.25in (16cm) high

**$10,000-12,000**                DRA

A rare and early Newcomb College bulbous vase, decorated by Leona Nicholson with incised, modeled and surface-painted freesia blossoms and stems, with green spiked leaves on a dark blue ground.

*c1910*                8.5in (21.5cm) high

**$30,000-32,000**                DRA

An unusual early Newcomb College squat vessel, painted by M. L. Dunn, with stylized leaves and blossoms in dark blue, white, and medium blue.

*1908*                4in (10cm) high

**$5,000-8,000**                DRA

A tall Newcomb College vase, carved by A.E. Simpson, with a moonlit scene of live oaks and Spanish moss.

*c1930*                11in (28cm) high

**$16,000-18,000**                DRA

An early Newcomb College tall milk pitcher, painted by Marie de Hoa LeBlanc, with a broad band of cows under stylized trees in blues and greens, small glaze flakes.

*1902*                8in (20cm) high

**$7,000-10,000**                DRA

An early 20thC Newcomb College art pottery lamp base, with three handles with line and broad leaf decoration, impressed potter's mark "JM" for Joseph Meyer, NC cipher, painted number "BS100", numbered paper label, inscribed circular mark with "New Orleans", possibly the initials "KW" and "April, 1907."

*1907*                4.25in (11.5cm) high

**$4,000-6,000**                SK

## NEWCOMB COLLEGE

■ Newcomb Pottery was established in 1895 at the H. Sophie Newcomb Memorial College, in New Orleans.

■ Its founder, the skilled designer Ellsworth Woodward (1861-1939), saw the department as a vehicle for training a new generation of women potters. The distinguished potter Mary G. Sheerer was hired to teach pottery making and decorating.

■ The college thrived under the direction of Woodward and Sheerer, attracting talented designers and instructors like Sadie Irvine, Harriet Joor, Anna Frances Simpson, and Henrietta Bailey.

■ Although influenced by the Arts & Crafts movement, their designs exhibited a unique aesthetic with distinctive imagery of flora and fauna native to the southern states.

■ Newcomb vessels were given soft curvaceous shapes inspired by peasant pottery and Oriental wares. They are best known for their unique soft blue and green glazes.

■ The company won international acclaim at the Paris Exposition of 1900. However, the quality of Newcomb's pottery declined after Woodward retired in 1931 and the company closed in 1940.

A bulbous George Ohr vase with folded rim covered in bottle green gunmetal glaze, stamped "GEO. E. OHR, BILOXI, MISS."

*4in (10cm) wide*

**$3,000-5,000** DRA

A large George Ohr vase, with deep in-body twist and folded rim, covered in brown gunmetal and green speckled glaze, stamped "G.E. OHR, Bilox, Miss.", restoration to rim chips.

*6.25in (15.5cm) high*

**$7,000-10,000** DRA

A tall George Ohr vase, with a deep folded rim, covered in brown and black speckled glaze, stamped "G. E. OHR, Biloxi, Miss."

*7.75in (19cm) high*

**$8,000-12,000** DRA

A George Ohr bulbous vase, with a pinched and collapsed neck, covered in a rare green, gun-metal, indigo, and raspberry sponged-on glaze, mark obscured by glaze.

*5.5in (14cm) high*

**$8,000-12,000** DRA

## GEORGE OHR

- Before setting up his own studio in 1883, George Ohr (1857-1918) had begun an apprenticeship with the potter Joseph Meyer in New Orleans. On leaving this formal training, Ohr worked alone until 1907.

- Ohr established a small studio in Biloxi, Mississippi, in 1883. He sold his ceramics in his shop, called 'Pot-Ohr-E', having dug his own clay locally and crafted the vessels by hand.

- Ohr was an eccentric with a rebellious spirit, which is reflected in his unique and flamboyant designs. He was fond of discovering different ways of manipulating clay by pinching, twisting, crushing, folding, and pressing earthenware into distinctive sculptural forms.

- He used rich and lustrous glazes of brown, blue, bronze, black, salmon, and orange, which were often combined to create mottled, speckled, and metallic effects.

- His later works were left unglazed, in accordance with his maxim "God put no color in souls so I'll put no color in my pots."

- Ohr closed his studio in 1907. His work was forgotten until the 1960s, when Jim Carpenter stumbled across it in a Biloxi garage.

A tall lobed vase, by George Ohr, with pinched rim and burgundy, gunmetal green and light green volcanic sponged stripes on ivory ground, stamped "G.E. Ohr Biloxi Miss," rim nicks.

*6.75in (17cm) high*

**$19,000-21,000** DRA

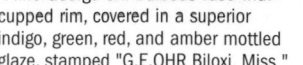

A fine George Ohr bulbous vase with cupped rim, covered in a superior indigo, green, red, and amber mottled glaze, stamped "G.E.OHR Biloxi, Miss."

*4.75in (12cm) high*

**$8,000-12,000** DRA

A George Ohr small baluster vase covered in a cobalt and green sponged pattern on amber ground, small stilt-pull chips, stamped "G.E. OHR, Biloxi, Miss."

*3.75in (9cm) high*

**$1,200-1,800** DRA

A George Ohr spherical vase covered in lustered brown-green glaze with melt fissures, minor nick to rim, stamped "G.E. OHR, Biloxi, Miss."

*3.75in (9cm) diam*

**$1,800-2,200**              **DRA**

A large and early George Ohr corseted vase, with two curled handles, the body glazed in four panels, over a marbleized clay body, stamped.

*8.25in (20.5cm) high*

**$12,000-14,000**           **DRA**

A George Ohr vessel with flaring base and tapering top, covered in an unusual gunmetal crystalline glaze over dark brown ground, script signature.

*3.5in (9cm) high*

**$2,800-3,200**             **DRA**

A cylindrical George Ohr vessel with neat piecrust rum, covered in gunmetal brown glaze over bubbled texture, several small nicks to rim folds, script signature.

*5in (12.5cm) diam*

**$3,000-5,000**             **DRA**

A George Ohr vessel with horizontally-dimpled shoulder and closed-in rim, the interior in an amber and black tortoise-shell glaze, the exterior in gunmetal black, stamped "G.E. OHR, Biloxi, Miss."

*5.5in (14cm) diam*

**$2,200-2,800**             **DRA**

A George Ohr whimsical face vessel, of richly colored marbleized clay, with a folded rim, pinched nose and applied eyes, script signature, two small chips to rim folds.

*5.5in (14cm) diam*

**$4,000-6,000**             **DRA**

A fine George Ohr ruffled open bowl of collapsed form with a green flambé hanging unevenly over a rich, ripe pink, script signature.

*4.5in (11.5cm) wide*

**$6,000-9,000**             **DRA**

A George Ohr vessel of red bisque clay with folded middle, one side with oxidized pattern, script signature.

*4.75in (12cm) wide*

**$2,200-2,800**             **DRA**

A George Ohr bisque potato-shaped bank, stamped mark.

*3.25in (8cm) high*

**$1,200-1,800**             **DRA**

A George Ohr chamberpot complete with contents covered in green, brown, and gunmetal-sponged amber glaze, restored chip at rim, stamped "G.E. OHR, BILOXI, MISS."

*4.5in (11cm) diam*

**$1,200-1,800**             **DRA**

A George Ohr tall hat-shaped trinket covered in dark brown speckled glaze, stamped "G.E. OHR, Biloxi, Miss."

*3.5in (9cm) diam*

**$2,200-2,800**             **DRA**

A fine George Ohr bungalow inkwell in butter yellow on a brown floral ground, small glaze nicks to body only, stamped "GEO. E. OHR, BILOXI, MISS."

*5.25in (13cm) wide*

**$2,800-3,200**             **DRA**

An exceptional and large George Ohr teapot, with a squat body, a curving handle and a serpentine spout, covered in a dynamic blood red to emerald green flambé glaze, with original lid, die-stamp marked twice.

*9in (22.5cm) wide*

**$25,000-30,000** **DRA**

A George Ohr bottle-shaped vase, with a folded rim, covered in rare white, turquoise, and amber glaze sponged on a raspberry ground, stamped "G. E. OHR, Biloxi, Miss."

*4.75in (12cm) high*

**$8,000-12,000** **DRA**

A large George Ohr vase with squat folded base, stovepipe body and ruffled rim, covered in gunmetal brown speckled glaze, marked "Geo E. Ohr Biloxi Miss."

*9in (23cm) high*

**$22,000-28,000** **DRA**

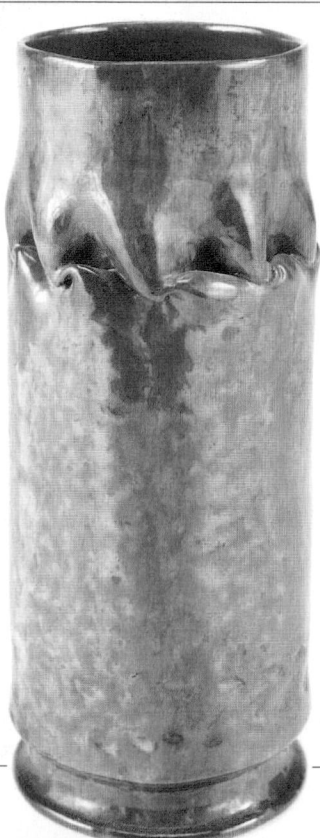

A tall cylindrical George Ohr vase with deep in-body twist and footed base, covered in a superior raspberry, white, and amber frothy striped glaze, marked "G.E. OHR Biloxi Miss."

*8.75in (22cm) high*

**$20,000-25,000** **DRA**

A Rookwood unusual silver-overlaid Standard glaze vase, painted by Caroline Steinle, with clover blossoms and leaves, and covered in woven sterling bands, dated and stamped with flame mark "381C/W/CS/STERLING."

1893                 6.75in (17cm) high

**$1,800-2,200**                 **DRA**

A Rookwood Standard glaze pillow vase, painted by Charles Dibowski, with a portrait of a man wearing a wig, flame mark, artist cipher, dated.

1894          5.75in (14cm) high

**$1,200-1,800**                 **DRA**

A large Rookwood Standard glaze baluster vase, painted by Kataro Shirayamadani, with molded and slip painted lotus blossoms and leaves, dated, flame mark and "S1411C/Artist cipher".

1898          13in (32.5cm) high

**$3,000-5,000**                 **DRA**

A large Rookwood Standard glaze Indian vase, painted by Matthew A. Daly, with a portrait of a Native American in profile, cracked and drilled.

c1900          12in (30.5cm) high

**$2,800-3,200**                 **DRA**

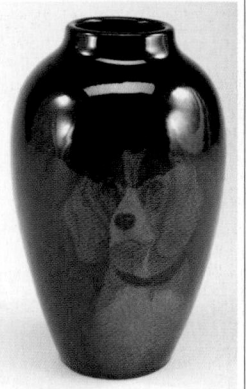

A Rookwood Standard glaze bulbous vase, painted by E.T. Hurley, with a portrait of a beagle, dated, flame mark and "II/900B/E.T.H."

1902          9in (22.5cm) high

**$2,200-2,800**                 **DRA**

A Rookwood Standard glaze vase painted by Grace Young, with a portrait of the artist Van Dyck, scratches to body.

c1902          10in (25cm) high

**$1,800-2,200**                 **DRA**

A late 19thC Rookwood pottery ewer, by Albert Robert Valentien, the spirally fluted body slip decorated with poppies, marked.

17in (42.5cm) high

**$300-500**                 **CHEF**

## ROOKWOOD

- Rookwood Pottery, established in 1880 by Maria Longworth Nichols (1849-1932) in Cincinnati, Ohio, was one of the most influential pottery firms in the US.
- Early inspiration came from Japanese ceramics and one of their most important designers was Japanese artist Kataro Shirayamadani.
- Equally distinctive are the portraits of Native Americans that adorn plaques and vessels.
- Rookwood was renowned for its innovative glazing techniques, employing talented artists like Artus Van Briggle to experiment with high quality glazes. Glazes of particular note include the Standard, Sea Green, Matte, and Vellum Glazes.
- Rookwood also introduced new effects like silver appliqué in 1892. In 1900 it won a Grand Prix award at the Paris Exhibition for its designs.
- After filing for bankruptcy in 1941 Rookwood had a number of owners. Production ceased in 1960.

A large silver-overlaid Rookwood Standard glaze ewer, painted by Kataro Shirayamadani, with roses and leaves, covered in Gorham silver with latticed floral and arabesque patterns, crazing, loss to overlay.

c1890          12.75in (32.5cm) high

**$2,200-2,800**                 **DRA**

A Rookwood silver-overlaid Standard glaze pitcher, painted by Kate C. Matchette, with leaves and blossoms under Gorham silver with birds nesting, minor lifting to overlay.

c1890          9in (23cm) high

**$3,000-4,000**                 **DRA**

An exceptional Rookwood Standard glaze pitcher, with pinched rim painted by Albert R. Valentien, with praying Japanese elder, uncrazed.

c1890          9in (23cm) high

**$3,000-4,000**                 **DRA**

A fine Rookwood Standard glaze three-sided pitcher, painted by Harriet Wilcox, with a peasant holding a bowl and a pitcher of wine, dated and stamped with flame mark "259C/W/H.E.W."

*1892*                    *7.5in (19cm) wide*

**$1,200-1,800**                    **DRA**

An unusual Rookwood silver-overlaid Standard glaze tri-corner pitcher by Edith Felten, with a Brownie sitting on a crescent moon, covered with Gorham silver in floral pattern, restored cracks.

*c1895*                    *8.75in (22cm) high*

**$1,200-1,800**                    **DRA**

A fine Rookwood standard glaze 'Negro' portrait mug painted by Sturgis Laurence, depicting a smiling boy, firing crack to body.

*c1896*                    *5in (12.5cm) high*

**$1,800-2,200**                    **DRA**

A Rookwood Standard glaze tankard, painted by Grace Young, with a Native American portrait 'White Man Bear, Sioux', with handle and rim overlaid in silver, dated and stamped.

*1900*                    *7.5in (19cm) high*

**$1,800-2,200**                    **DRA**

An unusual, early silver overlay Rookwood Standard glaze basket, painted by Harriet E. Wilcox, with flowers, buds, and leaves under Gorham silver with chased flowers and arabesques, losses to silver.

*c1895*                    *10.5in (26.5cm) wide*

**$2,200-2,800**                    **DRA**

A Rookwood Standard glaze 'Indian' humidor, painted by Harriet E. Wilcox, depicting two Native Americans dancing with lit torches.

*c1895*                    *6.5in (16.5cm) high*

**$1,200-1,800**                    **DRA**

A Rookwood Standard glaze humidor, painted by A.D. Sehon, with 'Chief Whiteman -Kiowa-,' dated and stamped "Flame mark/I/813/A.D.S./Chief Whiteman -Kiowa-," damage and restoration.

*1901*                    *5.75in (14cm) high*

**$3,000-4,000**                    **DRA**

An unusual Rookwood silver-overlaid Standard glaze inkwell on a pen tray, painted by C.A. Baker, with clover and a feather, inkwell covered in sterling arabesques, dated and stamped with flame mark "586C/C.A.B."

*1900*                    *10in (25cm) wide*

**$2,200-2,800**                    **DRA**

## A CLOSER LOOK AT A ROOKWOOD PLAQUE

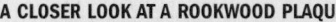

*Rookwood is not only known for its ceramic vases, but also for its exquisite painted and framed ceramic plaques.*

*The Native American subjects are the rarest and most distinctive. These Native American designs reflected the growing appreciation for indigenous cultures in the United States.*

*William P. McDonald was one of Rookwood's most distinguished artists, executing highly detailed and realistic portraits.*

*The detail in this portrait, especially in the clothing and the quiet dignity of the subject's face, make this a particularly attractive example of one of Rookwood's most sought-after lines.*

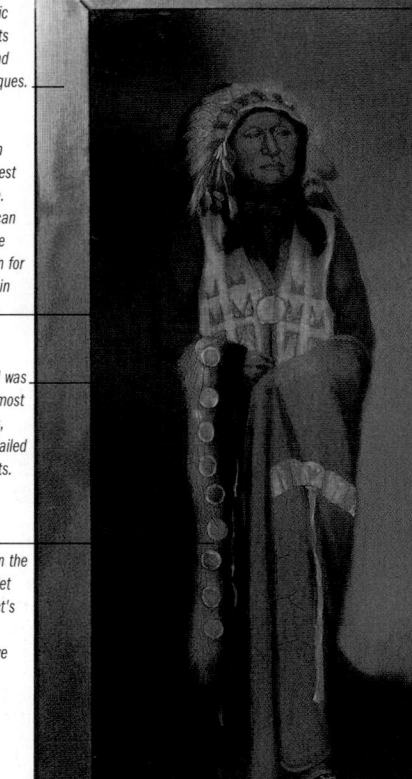

A fine and important Rookwood Standard glaze 'Indian' portrait plaque, painted by William P. McDonald, depicting a standing Native American chief in headdress, first fire crazing, framed.

*c1885*                    *23.25in (58cm) high*

**$50,000-55,000**                    **DRA**

A Rookwood iris glaze vase, painted by Constance A. Baker with apple blossoms on shaded green ground, dated, flame mark and "I/30E/C.A.B."

*1901*          *7.5in (19cm) high*

**$1,200-1,800**                    **DRA**

A Rookwood iris glaze baluster vase painted by Rose Fechheimer with gray mistletoe, dated, flame mark and "II/842C/A/R.F."

*1902*          *7in (17.5cm) high*

**$1,800-2,200**                    **DRA**

A fine Rookwood iris glaze ovoid vase, painted by Sara Sax, with gray roses in a shaded pink-to-green ground, crazing, dated, flame mark "VII/932C/W."

*1907*          *9.75in (24cm) high*

**$4,000-6,000**                    **DRA**

A Rookwood iris glaze vase by Elizabeth Lincoln, with white roses on a pink-to-green ground, crazing, dated.

*1911*          *6in (15cm) high*

**$800-1,200**                    **DRA**

A rare and important Rookwood iris glaze plaque, painted by Sturgis Laurence with 'Summer Afternoon: Long Island Sound,' depicting a rocky coast with distant boats, framed.

*c1905*          *14in (35cm) wide*

**$35,000-38,000**                    **DRA**

A Rookwood painted matte vase by Albert Valentien, with branches of red cherry blossoms on a dark teal green ground, with flame mark and signature.

*c1900*          *12in (30.5cm) high*

**$15,000-17,000**                    **DRA**

A Rookwood carved matte vase by William Hentschel with green leaves on green and indigo ground, flame mark, dated and "X679V/WEH".

*1910*          *7.25in (18cm) high*

**$1,200-1,800**                    **DRA**

A matte Rookwood vase painted by C.S. Todd with roosters in polychrome on an indigo-to-red ground, with flame mark, number and painter's initials.

*c1910*          *5.75in (14.5cm) high*

**$8,000-12,000**                    **DRA**

A Rookwood carved matte vase with bronze overlay, by Kataro Shirayamadani, with yellow and ivory waterlilies on a light green ground, with flame mark and artist's cipher, dated.

*1901 11in (28cm) high*

**$20,000-25,000   DRA**

A Rookwood carved matte baluster vase, painted by C.S. Todd with peacock feathers in celadon and brown on matte brown ground, bruise to base, dated.

*1914*          *9in (22.5cm) high*

**$1,200-1,800**                    **DRA**

A Rookwood carved matte vase with flat shoulder, decorated by C.S. Todd, with stylized floral panels in red and green on cobalt ground, flame mark, dated and "C.S.T.," restoration.

*1915*          *9.5in (24cm) high*

**$800-1,200**                    **DRA**

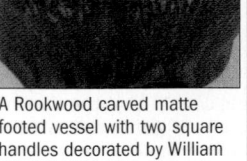

A Rookwood carved matte footed vessel with two square handles decorated by William Hentschel with a stylized pattern, flame mark, dated and "WEH," restoration to hairline.

*1914*          *6.75in (17cm) wide*

**$800-1,200**                    **DRA**

A rare Rookwood vellum plaque, painted by Sara Sax with a heron standing in water, scratched frame.

c1910  10.5in (26cm) high

**$16,000-18,000**    **DRA**

A large Rookwood scenic vellum plaque, painted by Edward Diers with grand purple cliffs and valleys of tall trees, framed.

c1915  14in (35cm) high

**$10,000-12,000**    **DRA**

A Rookwood scenic vellum plaque, painted by Ed Diers with tall trees by a creek, mounted in original ebonized frame, with flame mark, illegible paper label and artist's initials.

c1915  10.75in (27.5cm) high

**$11,000-13,000**    **DRA**

A Rookwood scenic vellum plaque, painted by Lorinda Epply with 'Over the Hills,' depicting a bucolic scene with trees and a river, minor pitting, original frame, flame mark, dated.

1914  7.5in (19cm) wide

**$2,800-3,200**    **DRA**

A Rookwood marine scenic vellum plaque, painted by Carl Schmidt with 'The Close of Day, Venice,' depicting ships at sunset, framed.

c1915  14.5in (36cm) wide

**$11,000-13,000**    **DRA**

A fine Rookwood scenic vellum landscape plaque, painted by Lenore Asbury with a scene of trees at dusk against snow-capped mountains, uncrazed, framed.

c1930  8.5in (21cm) wide

**$7,000-10,000**    **DRA**

A Rookwood scenic vellum plaque, painted by E. Timothy Hurley, depicting a tree-lined lake in a mountainous landscape, uncrazed, framed.

c1945  12in (30cm) wide

**$17,000-20,000**    **DRA**

A fine Rookwood scenic vellum plaque, painted by E. Timothy Hurley with 'The Crags,' with tall pines against mountains, uncrazed, framed.

c1940  11in (27.5cm) high

**$20,000-22,000**    **DRA**

A Rookwood scenic vellum plaque, painted by E. Timothy Hurley, with a group of figures at shore and sailboats, uncrazed, framed.

c1945  11.5in (29cm) high

**$20,000-22,000**    **DRA**

A Rookwood scenic vellum plaque, painted by E. Timothy Hurley with 'Birches and the Lake,' mounted in original frame, uncrazed, "E.T.H." on front, title label on back.

11.75in (29cm) high

**$8,000-12,000**    **DRA**

510

A Rookwood scenic vellum plaque, painted by Lorinda Epply with 'A Quiet Scene,' with birch and elm trees in a verdant landscape, mounted in original frame, some wear to edges, flame mark, tile and artist label.

*7.75in (19cm) wide*

**$3,000-5,000**     **DRA**

A Rookwood unusual scenic vellum flaring vase, painted by E. Timothy Hurley with a forest scene in fall colors, dated and stamped with flame mark "1369D."

*1908*    *9in (22.5cm) high*

**$4,000-6,000**     **DRA**

A large Rookwood vellum vase, painted by Carl Schmidt with purple irises on a shaded ground, with flame mark, number and artist's cipher.

*c1910*    *15.5in (39.5cm) high*

**$4,000-6,000**     **DRA**

A Rookwood vellum flaring vase, painted by M.H. McDonald with poppies on a shaded ground, seconded mark, two sort parallel lines to rim, dated, flame mark and "XIV/1369E/MHM/X".

*1914*    *7.25in (18cm) high*

**$1,800-2,200**     **DRA**

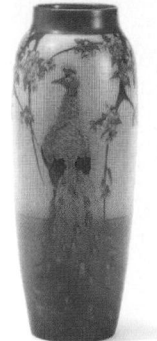

A 20thC Rookwood vellum 'Peacocks' vase by Sara Sax, painted and glazed ceramic, incised artist's cipher, flame mark for 1918.

*1918*    *17.75in (45cm) high*

**$50,000-70,000**     **FRE**

A Rookwood jewel porcelain vase, painted by Kataro Shirayamadani, with cornflowers, dated and stamped with flame mark "XXV/2719" and artist cipher.

*1925*    *6.5in (16cm) high*

**$2,800-3,200**     **DRA**

A Rookwood jewel porcelain trumpet vase, painted by Sara Sax with stylized blossoms, dated, stamped with flame mark "XXVI/2735" and artist cipher.

*1926*    *8.5in (21cm) high*

**$3,000-4,000**     **DRA**

A Rookwood jewel vase, painted by Jens Jensen with Art Deco flowers, butterfat glaze on ivory ground, dated, stamped with flame mark "XXXII/S."

*1932*    *7.75in (19cm) high*

**$3,000-5,000**     **DRA**

A large Rookwood Production urn impressed with a geometric pattern under butterfat glaze, restoration to base chips, handle, flame mark, dated.

*1912*    *18in (45cm) high*

**$1,800-2,200**     **DRA**

A tall Rookwood Production vase covered in black glossy glaze, restoration to drill hole at base and to rim, flame mark, dated.

*1922*    *17.5in (42.5cm) high*

**$500-700**     **DRA**

A Rookwood Production baluster vase covered in a matte black butterfat glaze with crackled turquoise interior, flame mark, dated.

*1923*    *11in (27.5cm) high*

**$800-1,200**     **DRA**

A rare Rookwood Production eagle paperweight by Louise Abel, with gunmetal brown glaze, flame mark, dated.

*1934*    *8in (20cm) wide*

**$1,200-1,800**     **DRA**

A Rookwood pottery dish, modeled as a bird, covered in a pale ocher glaze, impressed Rookwood mark.

*6.75in (17cm) wide*

**$500-700**     **WW**

A Rookwood bronze-overlaid sea-green vase by Anne Marie Valentien, covered in verdigris patina, dated, stamped "28Z/A.M.V."

*1900*    *5.25in (13cm) high*

**$18,000-20,000**     **DRA**

A Rookwood Japanese hand-thrown flaring vase, carved with abstract square pattern, medallion and script, and an Oriental peasant in high relief.

*c1880*    *11.5in (29cm) high*

**$2,800-3,200**     **DRA**

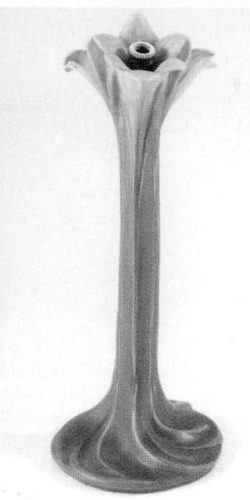

A rare Rookwood lamp base designed by Anne Marie Valentien with three white lilies, with flame mark, number and designer's initials, some damage and restoration.

c1905     17.5in (44.5cm) high

**$6,000-9,000**     **DRA**

A tall Rookwood aventurine vase, by Lorinda Epply, the base painted with large abstracted blossoms under a green and blue ground with light green neck, uncrazed.

c1920     15.5in (39.5cm) high

**$5,000-8,000**     **DRA**

A Rookwood Art Nouveau glazed pottery baluster-formed vase by Kataro Shirayamadani, with flowering branches, crimson-red interior, bears firm's logo incorporating date, artist's signature and "2720" underfoot.

c1925     6.5in (16.5cm) high

**$2,200-2,800**     **ISA**

A Rookwood black opal vase, carved and decorated by Kataro Shirayamadani, with large modeled fish on a cobalt, celadon, brown, and purple ground, uncrazed.

c1925     9.75in (25cm) high

**$8,000-12,000**     **DRA**

A Rookwood vase, painted in squeezebag by William Hentschel, with an Art Deco pattern and brown sprigs on rich brown ground, dated.

1929     5.25in (13cm) high

**$1,200-1,800**     **DRA**

A large and unusual Rookwood vase, slip-painted by Elizabeth Barrett, with a group of dancing women silhouetted in black against a brilliant sky blue ground.

c1935     11.75in (30cm) high

**$3,000-5,000**     **DRA**

A late Rookwood porcelain vase, painted by Loretta Holtkamp with magnolia blossoms on a gray ground, some crazing, flame mark, dated, and "LI/2984A".

1951     15.5in (37.5cm) high

**$1,800-2,200**     **DRA**

A fine and rare Rookwood splashback, in the Arts & Crafts Gothic style with diagonal tiles, and a green tree at the top, slight damage, grout on back hides signature.

43in (107.5cm) high

**$3,000-4,000**     **DRA**

A fine and large Rookwood ginger jar and cover by E. Timothy Hurley, the lobed body painted with flowers, topped by a cover with pierced geometric decoration.

*c1920*          *15.5in (39.5cm) high*

**$5,000-8,000**          **DRA**

A Rookwood two-handled garden urn, with crackled blue glaze over unglazed ground, with factory-drilled base, small chips, stamped "RP/410/331AY."

*26.5in (66cm) high*

**$1,800-2,200**          **DRA**

A Rookwood Pottery tea tile, carved pattern of grapes, vines, and leaves, impressed flame, dated, numbered "1683".

*1920*          *5.5in (14cm) wide*

**$300-500**          **SK**

A Rookwood trivet tile with an indigo rook against an Oriental trellis, flame mark, dated.

*1927*          *5.75in (14cm) square*

**$800-1,200**          **DRA**

A fine and unusual Rookwood diamond-shaped tile with two tall ships, a few small chips to edges, stamped "RP, 417, G352."

*8in (20cm) square*

**$1,200-1,800**          **DRA**

A fine and large Rookwood tile decorated in cuenca with a tall ship, small nick to cuenca wall, mounted in a fine Arts & Crafts frame.

*12in (20cm) square*

**$2,200-2,800**          **DRA**

A rare Rookwood Barbotine plaque, painted by Mary Keenan, with waves crashing against a rocky shore under hovering seagulls, framed.

*c1885*          *11in (27.5cm) wide*

**$33,000-35,000**          **DRA**

A rare and important red clay 'Indian' Rookwood portrait charger by H.F. Farny, with a Native American chief in headdress, painted in black.

*Farny designed the first trademark for Rookwood and was the first to suggest Indian designs for its pottery. This charger is recorded in the shape record book as "189. Red clay plaque. Pressed. Decorated by H. Farny. Could not be fired hard enough to set colors in manner desired by artist without destroying effect", 'The Book of Rookwood Pottery' by Herbert Peck, p.15.*

**Provenance:** *From the Rookwood Pottery Museum Collection, deaccessioned in 1937.*

*c1880*          *11in (28cm) diam*

**$15,000-17,000**          **DRA**

## ROSEVILLE

- Established in 1890 near Zanesville in Ohio, the Roseville Pottery Co. concentrated on producing utilitarian stoneware.
- From 1900, Roseville produced a range of art ware called 'Rozane' ware. Characterized by molded, incised and painted foliage, these wares were encased in luminous glazes.
- Designs for other art pottery ranges were produced under art director John Herold by the potters Frederick H. Rhead and Frank Ferrell.
- After 1914 Roseville turned away from hand-decorated wares in favour of more economical machine production.
- The 'Futura' and 'Fuchsia' ranges, produced in the late 1920s and 1930s respectively, were among Roseville's most successful.
- Having weathered two wars and the Depression, Roseville ceased trading in 1954.

A Roseville 'Blackberry' hanging basket, unmarked.

*7in (18cm) high*

**$800-1,200**    **DRA**

A Roseville 'Blackberry' vase, no. 571-6, unmarked.

*6.25in (15.5cm) high*

**$400-600**    **BEL**

A large Roseville 'Blackberry' vase, very crisp mold and color, unmarked.

*12in (30.5cm) high*

**$1,800-2,200**    **DRA**

A Roseville 'Blackberry' corseted two-handled vase, minute bruise to rim, touch-up to one handle, unmarked.

*10.25in (26cm) high*

**$800-1,200**    **DRA**

A scarce Roseville brown 'Fuchsia' ice lip pitcher, marked "1322", tight line to spout.

*8.25in (20.5cm) high*

**$300-500**    **BEL**

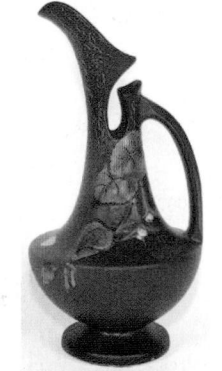

A Roseville brown 'Fuchsia' ewer, marked "902-10", with the original foil label.

*10.25in (25.5cm) high*

**$280-320**    **BEL**

A Roseville brown 'Fuchsia' basket, faintly marked "350-8".

*8.25in (20.5cm) high*

**$280-320**    **BEL**

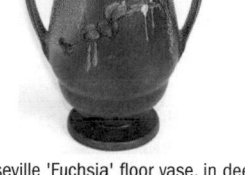

A Roseville 'Fuchsia' floor vase, in deep blue, marked "905-18".

*18.25in (45.5cm) high*

**$3,000-4,000**    **BEL**

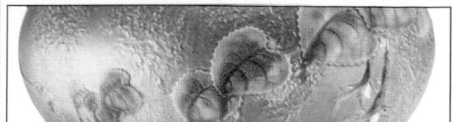

A Roseville blue 'Fuchsia' jardinière and pedestal set, raised mark "645-10".

*10in (25cm) high*

**$3,000-4,000**    **DRA**

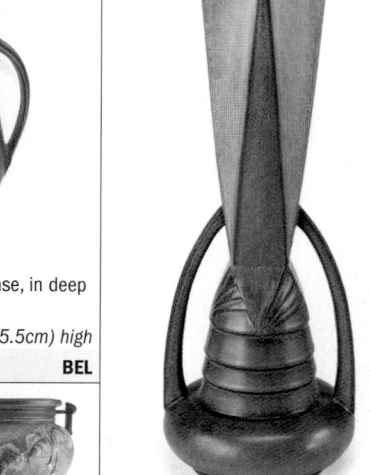

A rare Roseville 'Futura' 'Arches' vase, one handle cracked and reglued, black paper label.

*14.25in (36cm) high*

**$2,200-2,800**    **DRA**

A Roseville 'Futura' 'Shooting Star' vase, marked with black paper label on base "392-10", some restoration.

*10.25in (26cm) high*

**$400-600**    **BEL**

A Roseville 'Futura' telescopic urn vase, no. 382-7, unmarked.

*7.25in (18cm) high*

**$300-500**       **BEL**

A Roseville 'Futura' tombstone vase, in shades of tan and brown with blue flowers, unmarked.

*6.25in (15.5cm) high*

**$300-400**       **BEL**

A Roseville blue 'Futura' hibachi, no. 198-5, unmarked, repairs to two areas of the rim and two darkened lines at the rim among the crazing.

*5.25in (13cm) wide*

**$400-600**       **BEL**

A Roseville 'Imperial II' bulbous vase, with ribbed bands around body, covered in a turquoise and blue mottled glaze, unmarked.

*7.75in (19.5cm) high*

**$1,800-2,200**       **DRA**

---

A Roseville 'Imperial II' ovoid vase, covered in mottled glaze, small drill hole to underside of base, paper label.

*11.5in (29cm) high*

**$1,800-2,200**       **DRA**

A Roseville 'Imperial II' vase, with ribbed band around the body, covered in a blue and yellow mottled glaze, glazed over factory chip at rim, unmarked.

*11.5in (29cm) high*

**$2,200-2,800**       **DRA**

A Roseville 'Imperial II' flaring vase, with embossed branch-like design near rim, covered in a mottled glaze, restoration to minor nick at rim, unmarked.

*6.5in (16.5cm) diam*

**$2,200-2,800**       **DRA**

A Roseville 'Imperial II' flaring vase, covered in a mottled green and orange glaze, unmarked.

*8.5in (21.5cm) high*

**$3,000-4,000**       **DRA**

---

A Roseville blue 'Montacello' tall vase, marked faintly "565" in red crayon, old restoration.

*10.75in (27cm) high*

**$500-800**       **BEL**

A Roseville blue 'Montacello' vase, no. 564-9, with two handles, unmarked, old repairs to rim, crazing heavy and darkened.

*9.25in (23cm) high*

**$400-600**       **BEL**

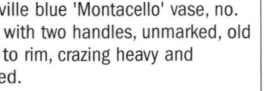

A Roseville blue 'Montacello' vase, no. 562-7, unmarked.

*7.25in (18cm) high*

**$500-800**       **BEL**

A Roseville brown 'Montacello' broad vase, marked "562" in red crayon.

*7.25in (18cm) high*

**$800-1,200**       **BEL**

A Roseville brown 'Montacello' vase, marked "564" in red crayon, repaired hairlines, factory grinding roughness at the base.

*9.25in (23cm) high*

**$400-600**     **BEL**

A Roseville brown 'Montacello' vase, no. 559-5, with two small handles, marked with black A Roseville Pottery paper label.

*5.25in (13cm) high*

**$500-800**     **BEL**

A Roseville 'Sunflower' ovoid vase, crisp mold, good color, unmarked.

*10.25in (26cm) high*

**$2,800-3,200**     **DRA**

A large Roseville 'Sunflower' vase, no. 492-10, unmarked.

*10in (25cm) high*

**$3,000-5,000**     **DRA**

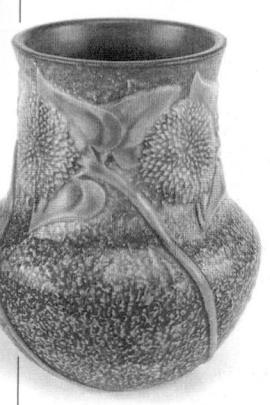

A Roseville 'Sunflower' bulbous vase, very crisp mold, unmarked.

*8.5in (21.5cm) high*

**$2,800-3,200**     **DRA**

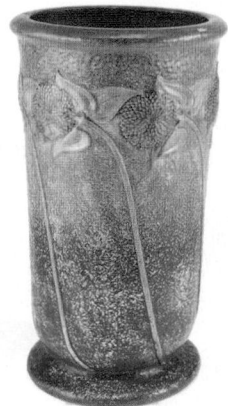

A rare Roseville 'Sunflower' umbrella stand, crisp mold, excellent color, very minor X-shaped spiderlines to underside, unmarked.

*20in (50cm) high*

**$6,000-9,000**     **DRA**

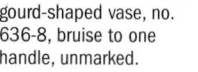

A Roseville 'Sunflower' window box, with three tight lines to base, unmarked.

*11.5in (29cm) wide*

**$800-1,200**     **DRA**

A Roseville blue 'Wisteria' gourd-shaped vase, no. 636-8, bruise to one handle, unmarked.

*8in (20cm) high*

**$1,200-1,800**     **DRA**

A Roseville brown 'Wisteria' vase, foil label.

*8.5in (21.5cm) high*

**$1,200-1,800**     **DRA**

A Roseville brown 'Wisteria' double-handled vase, no. 680-8, unmarked.

*8.25in (20.5cm) high*

**$500-800**     **BEL**

A Roseville blue 'Wisteria' vase, no. 634-7, unmarked.

*7in (17.5cm) high*

**$800-1,200**     **BEL**

A Roseville brown 'Wisteria' vase, no. 633-8, unmarked, shallow glaze nick on the rim.

*8in (20cm) high*

**$400-600**     **BEL**

A Roseville blue 'Wisteria' gourd-shaped vase, no. 635-8, with foil label.

*8in (20cm) high*

**$800-1,200**     **DRA**

A Roseville blue 'Wisteria' vase, lightly marked "242" in red crayon.

*4in (10cm) high*

**$500-800**     **BEL**

A Roseville brown 'Wisteria' low bowl, marked with Roseville Pottery foil label on base.

*8in (20cm) diam*

**$600-900**     **BEL**

A Roseville brown 'Wisteria' jardinière and pedestal set, unmarked.

*24.5in (62cm) high*

**$3,000-5,000**     **DRA**

A Roseville pink 'Apple Blossom' floor vase, marked "USA 393-18."

*18.75in (47cm) high*

**$800-1,200**     **BEL**

A Roseville pink 'Bleeding Heart' floor vase, marked "USA 977-18," top rim restored.

*18.5in ((46cm) high*

**$300-400**     **BEL**

A Roseville 'Artcraft' jardinière, no. 629-4, unmarked.

*4in (10cm) high*

**$300-500**     **BEL**

A Roseville pink 'Baneda' bulbous vase, no. 929-9, crisp mold and good color, unmarked.

*9.25in (23.5cm) high*

**$1,200-1,800**     **DRA**

A Roseville 'Jonquil' jardinière, faintly marked "621-6" in red crayon.

*6in (15cm) high*

**$400-600**     **BEL**

A Roseville red 'Laurel' vase, no. 250-6 1/4, marked with Roseville Pottery foil label.

*7.25in (28cm) wide*

**$280-320**     **BEL**

A tall Roseville brown 'Pine Cone' vase, no. 850-14, impressed mark.

*14in (35.5cm) high*

**$800-1,200**     **DRA**

A rare Roseville Experimental brown 'Silhouette' vase, touched-up chip to base, marked in crayon "765/G-233."

*9.5in (24cm) high*

**$3,000-5,000**     **DRA**

A Roseville matte blue 'Topeo' vase, no. 245-6, with green and pink highlights, unmarked.

*7in (17.5cm) wide*

**$300-500**     **BEL**

An early Roseville 'Velmoss' jardinière, with broad leaves and buds, unmarked.

*9.5in (24cm) diam*

**$1,200-1,800**     **DRA**

A tall Roseville Rozane 'Woodland' bulbous vase, incised with chrysanthemums, professional restoration to base and rim, Rozane seal.

*15in (38cm) high*

**$1,800-2,200**      **DRA**

A Roseville green 'Baneda' jardinière and pedestal set, restoration to rim and base of jardinière, unmarked.

*29in (73.6cm) high*

**$4,000-6,000**      **DRA**

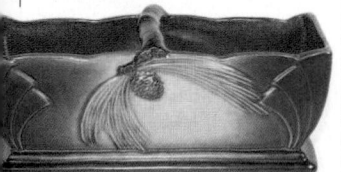

A Roseville blue 'Pine Cone' window box, marked "USA 468-8".

*8.75in (22cm) wide*

**$500-800**      **BEL**

---

**A CLOSER LOOK AT A ROSEVILLE VASE**

*'Experimental' vases are the stuff of legend among Roseville collectors. There are many fakes on the market so it is important to be very wary.*

*'Experimental' vases were made as trials for factory use only. Most of them never went into production and accordingly only a handful of each type exist. Many are unique, hence the special interest among collectors.*

*This raised decoration is typical of a genuine 'Experimental' Roseville piece. These patterns were hand-sculpted rather than cast in a mold as Roseville's production pottery was. The decoration here is far crisper than it would be on a mold-made vase.*

*A genuine 'Experimental' Roseville piece will often have pattern numbers or notes etched or otherwise marked on a blank area towards the rear of the vase.*

A rare Roseville Experimental two-handled vase, embossed with fish, minute flecks to base, tight hairline to rim, marked in crayon "49/660/61/921."

*9.5in (24cm) high*

**$7,000-10,000**      **DRA**

A Roseville blue 'Cosmos' basket in blue, marked "357-10".

*10.5in (25.5cm) high*

**$280-320**      **BEL**

A Roseville large blue 'Magnolia' ewer, marked "USA 15-15".

*15.5in (39cm) high*

**$400-600**      **BEL**

A rare Roseville 'Vista' wall pocket, unmarked.

*9.5in (24cm) high*

**$1,200-1,800**      **DRA**

A small rare Saturday Evening Girls bowl, decorated in cuerda seca with pairs of roosters around the motto "Early to Bed & Early to Rise Makes a Child Healthy Wealthy and Wise."

*5in (12.5cm) diam*

**$8,000-12,000**    **DRA**

A Saturday Evening Girls closed-in bowl decorated in cuerda seca with stylized blue blossoms and brown leaves on a green ground, short line to rim.

*8in (20cm) diam*

**$2,800-3,200**    **DRA**

A Saturday Evening Girls bullet-shaped wall pocket, decorated in cuerda seca with yellow poppies on a white and lime green ground, minor abrasions to hanging hole.

*6in (15cm) high*

**$4,000-6,000**    **DRA**

## A CLOSER LOOK AT A SATURDAY EVENING GIRLS BOWL

*The Saturday Evening Girls, also known as Paul Revere Pottery of Boston, embodied the Arts and Crafts ideal of marrying craftsmanship with social goals. Immigrant girls would gather on a weekly basis and learn to make and decorate pottery.*

*Pieces were often decorated using the 'cuerda seca' technique, whereby certain areas of the bowl are protected from the glaze with the application of wax.*

*Incised decoration like this is typical of Saturday Evening Girls ceramics. The geese motif, however, is relatively scarce. The animation and whimsy of this design is particularly appealing.*

*This piece is exceptional for its large size and bold colours. It is both a highly decorative object and a great example of the Saturday Evening Girls' work.*

An exceptional and large Saturday Evening Girls bowl, decorated by Fannie Levine in cuerda seca with white geese on a bright yellow ground.

*Provenance: Previously from the estate of Fanny Goldstein, editor of the S.E.G. Newsletter, 1912-1917. Ms. Goldstein, the first Jewish librarian in the state of Massachusetts, was instrumental in the early ecumenical movement in Boston.*

*11.5in (29cm) diam*

**$38,000-40,000**    **DRA**

## AMERICAN TERRA COTTA AND CERAMIC COMPANY

A Teco bulbous vase with two buttressed angular handles, under a matte glaze with charcoaling around the edges, stamped "Teco."

*3.5in (9cm) high*

**$2,200-2,800**    **DRA**

A Teco vase, with two whiplash handles, covered in matte glaze, invisible restoration, short line under rim, stamped "Teco."

*8.5in (22cm) high*

**$1,800-2,200**    **DRA**

A Teco pitcher with organic handle and faceted body, covered in matte glaze, no visible mark.

*12.75in (32cm) high*

**$2,200-2,800**    **DRA**

A tall Teco vase, embossed with tulip blossoms alternating with leaves above a squat round base, covered in smooth matte glaze, stamped "Teco."

*13.75in (34cm) high*

**$22,000-24,000**    **DRA**

A large Teco vase with four webbed handles, covered in smooth matte green glaze, stamped "Teco," restored chip.

*14in (35.5cm) high*

**$15,000-17,000**    **DRA**

An early Van Briggle tapered vase, covered in a superior burgundy and green mottled glaze, slight imperfections, "AA Van Briggle 1903."

*1903*          *8in (20cm) high*

**$1,800-2,200**                    **DRA**

An early Van Briggle two-handled vase, covered in deep red over lime green matte glaze.

*c1905*          *7.75in (19cm) high*

**$1,800-2,200**                    **DRA**

An early Van Briggle large two-handled vase, embossed with cornflowers under a burgundy and blue-green frothy glaze, the beige clay showing through.

*c1905*          *10in (25cm) high*

**$4,000-6,000**                    **DRA**

An early Van Briggle squat vase, embossed with leaves and stylized blossoms under mustard and olive green dead-matte glaze, dated, marked.

*1904*          *5.25in (13cm) high*

**$2,200-2,800**                    **DRA**

An early Van Briggle vase, covered in a purple and dark blue elephant's skin glaze.

*c1905*          *11.5in (29cm) high*

**$1,800-2,200**                    **DRA**

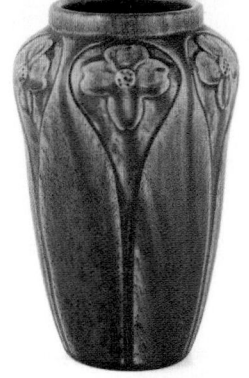

A Van Briggle vase, embossed with dogwood blossoms and leaves under a superior frothy cucumber green glaze, kiln kiss to heart of one flower.

*c1905*          *8in (20cm) high*

**$1,200-1,800**                    **DRA**

A tall rare Van Briggle flaring vase, embossed with peacock feather motif and covered in a blue-green, purple, gold, and mauve lustered glaze.

*c1910*          *10in (25cm) high*

**$4,000-6,000**                    **DRA**

A Van Briggle corseted vase, crisply embossed with full-height tulips under frothy glaze, the beige clay showing through.

*c1910*          *5.75in (14cm) high*

**$800-1,200**                    **DRA**

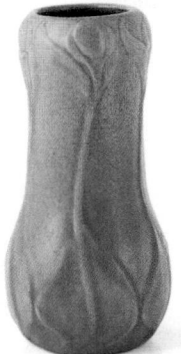

A Van Briggle bulbous vase, embossed with blossoms and leaves under feathered matte turquoise glaze, the beige clay showing through.

*c1910*          *7.5in (19cm) high*

**$1,200-1,800**                    **DRA**

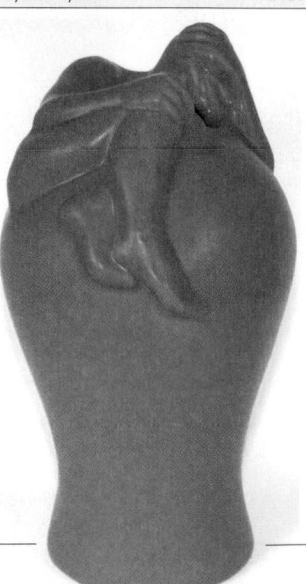

A Van Briggle despondency floor vase, in Ming turquoise glaze, marked "Van Briggle" with logo, "Colo Spgs Co", finisher's initials "DR" and esoteric markings.

*This vase is a reproduction of an original that is currently on display at the Louvre.*

*16in (40cm) high*

**$500-800**                    **BEL**

A Van Briggle bowl, Ming turquoise glaze with high relief decoration, with logo and limited edition number.

*Van Briggle continue to produce pots today, many of them from designs originally produced in the early 1900s.*

*9.75in (24cm) wide*

**$300-500**                    **BEL**

A Weller 'Coppertone' flaring vase, with two frogs perched on the side, short, tight firing line to rim, unmarked.

*10.25in (26cm) diam*

**$1,200-1,800**     **DRA**

A Weller 'Coppertone' pitcher, with fish handle, stamped mark.

*8in (20cm) high*

**$1,800-2,200**     **DRA**

A Weller 'Glendale' bulbous vase, embossed with birds and their nest, stamped mark.

*9.25in (23.5cm) high*

**$1,800-2,200**     **DRA**

A Weller 'Glendale' vase, with birds and butterflies among thistles and daisies, unmarked with the exception of "D" in green slip.

*12in (30cm) high*

**$800-1,200**     **BEL**

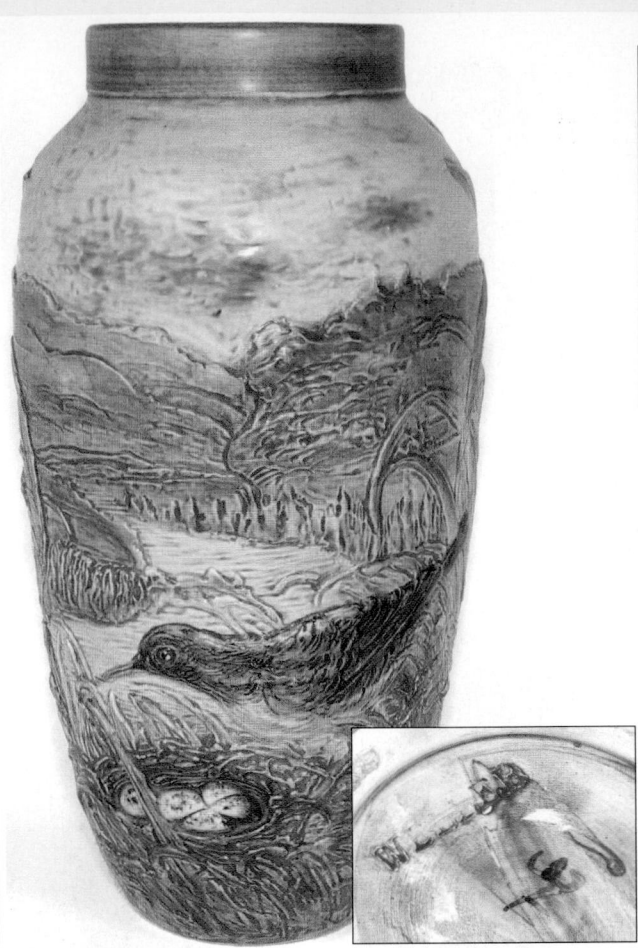

A Weller 'Glendale' vase, decorated with a bird watching over her nest in a marsh, marked "WELLER."

*13in (32.5cm) high*

**$2,200-2,800**     **BEL**

A Weller 'Hudson' vase by Ruth Axline, with double square handles decorated with very heavy slip, marked with Weller Pottery full kiln stamp and signed "Axline" at the base, slight imperfections.

*9.75in (24cm) high*

**$300-500**     **BEL**

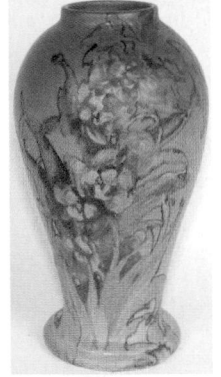

A Weller 'Hudson' vase by Claude Leffler with blue florals on a pastel background, signed "Leffler" at the base, marked with Weller Ware ink stamp and a Weller Hudson Ware paper label.

*11.75in (29cm) high*

**$1,800-2,200**     **BEL**

A Weller 'Hudson' bulbous vase, painted by McLaughlin, with blue columbine on a shaded blue to pink ground, impressed mark/artist's signature.

*12in (30cm) high*

**$1,800-2,200**     **DRA**

A large Weller 'Hudson' vase, painted by Hester Pillsbury, with yellow and blue irises on both sides, small blue glaze run, stamped mark/artist's signature.

*15.5in (39.5cm) high*

**$1,800-2,200**     **DRA**

A Weller 'Hudson' vase by Hester Pillsbury, with lilies of the valley, marked "WELLER" and with a Weller Ware stamp, signed "Pillsbury" at the base.

*8.75in (22cm) high*

**$700-1,000**     **BEL**

A Weller 'Hudson' vase, by Hester Pillsbury, showing three large blossoms on a gray to pink background, marked "A Weller" in script and signed "HP" at the base.

*10.5in (25.5cm) high*

**$800-1,200** **BEL**

A large Weller 'Louwelsa' bulbous vase, painted by L. Burgess, with a portrait of a pirate, small line from rim, minor lifting of glaze, stamped mark/artist's signature.

**$1,200-1,800** **DRA**

## WELLER

- Weller Pottery was established in Ohio in 1871, by Samuel A. Weller, and produced a range of utilitarian, handmade red earthenware ceramics.
- These early wares included hanging baskets, vases, jardinières, and umbrella stands.
- By the late 1880s, the company had moved to larger premises in Zanesville and acquired Lonhuda Pottery, admired for its slip-painted wares. The Lonhuda slip-decorated designs were developed and remarketed as Louwelsa.
- Weller exploited the fashion for hand-thrown wares and was greatly influenced by the international Arts & Crafts style. From the 1890s and for the next 50 years, ceramics became a fashionable medium for artistic expression.
- In a bid to trump its main competitors, Rookwood and Roseville, the company employed distinguished artists and designers for its new lines.
- These included the iridescent glazes of Jacques Sicard's 'Sicardo' range and Charles Babcock Upjohn's 'Dickensware' line. Albert Haubrich, Frederick H. Rhead and Frank Ferrell also contributed.
- Weller Pottery eventually closed in 1948, having suffered a dramatic slump in sales during the Depression of the 1930s.

A rare Weller 'Louwelsa' cabinet jug, painted with small yellow blossoms, overlaid with silver, impressed mark.

*3.75in (9.5cm) high*

**$1,200-1,800** **DRA**

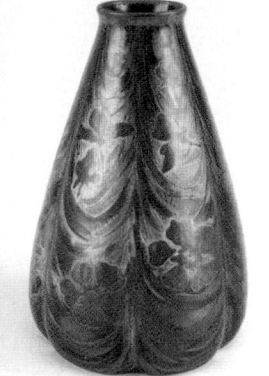

A Weller 'Sicard' lobed vase, with flowers and leaves in gold on a nacreous red and purple ground, impressed "27".

*8in (20cm) high*

**$1,800-2,200** **DRA**

A Weller 'Sicard' gourd-shaped vase, minor glaze nick near rim, marked "Sicard", impressed "41."

*8in (20cm) diam*

**$1,200-1,800** **DRA**

A large and unusual Weller 'Sicard' jardinière, decorated with sunflowers, well fired around the entire piece, marked in script.

*12in (30cm) diam*

**$3,000-5,000** **DRA**

A tall Weller 'Woodcraft' tree-shaped vase, with a squirrel and an owl in the tree, very minor damage, unmarked.

*18in (45cm) high*

**$1,800-2,200** **DRA**

A rare Weller 'Woodcraft' tree-shaped vase, with an owl perched on a branch, small chip to base ring, impressed mark.

*15.5in (39.5cm) high*

**$1,800-2,200** **DRA**

A rare Chelsea Keramic Art Works cabinet pillow vase on scrolled feet, carved with blue violets and leaves, stamped "CKAW," and artist signed "TT" or "TM."

*4.25in (11cm) wide*

**$800-1,200** DRA

A rare Denver Denaura vase with squat top and small opening, molded with poppies under a matte vellum glaze, stamped "Denaura Denver 169."

*5.5in (14cm) high*

**$3,000-5,000** DRA

A Kelmscott Studio china-painted vase by R.M. Dowie with tall pines by a mountain lake, nick and wear to gilt at rim, artist-signed and "Kelmscott Studio."

*6in (15cm) high*

**$1,200-1,800** DRA

A McCoy Arts & Crafts vase, four buttresses encircle the body, with a crystalline blue semi-high glaze, unmarked.

*14in (35cm) high*

**$500-800** BEL

A large North Dakota School of Mines vase 'Tulips,' in a chocolate brown matte glaze, circular ink stamp, title.

*8in (20.5cm) high*

**$2,800-3,200** DRA

A rare Redlands covered jar carved with swimming sharks under a terracotta and green burnished glaze, Redlands Pottery mark.

*5.5in (14cm) diam*

**$14,000-16,000** DRA

A Paul Revere dinner plate with a landscape medallion on a blue-gray ground and "FG", circular stamp.

*12in (30cm) diam*

**$1,200-1,800** DRA

A Union Porcelain Works urn, painted in Chinese style, with poppy finial and pair of dragon handles, stamp "UNION PORCELAIN WORKS/GREEN POINT, NY".

*20.5in (51cm) high*

**$4,000-6,000** DRA

An early 20thC Marblehead pottery vase, decorated by Hanna Tutt, with stylized grape leaf motifs, berries with ocher banding on a light blue-gray ground, impressed ship cipher and artist's initials "HT".

*Hanna's work is exhibited at the Newark museum and other nationally recognized museums. The subtle use of color and decoration is a characteristic of her work.*

c1908 *4.75in (12cm) high*

**$6,000-9,000** SK

A tall Walrath vase, matte-painted with full-height stylized pink blossoms and green foliage on a green mottled matte ground, incised "Walrath Pottery."

*8.75in (22cm) high*

**$7,000-10,000** DRA

A tall Rick Wisecarver vase, with a portrait of a Native American, signed "Rick Wisecarver", marked "Wihoa's Hand Painted Art Pottery 1995."

*21in (52.5cm) high*

**$1,200-1,800** BEL

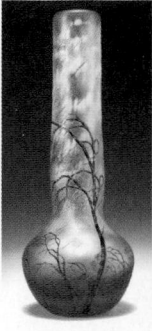

A rare Daum Frères vase, in clear and green glass overlaid in blue with etched and cut branches, signed "Daum Nancy" with Cross of Lorraine.

c1900          12.5in (31cm) high

**$10,000-15,000**          DOR

A Daum Frères 'Une Pluie' or 'Arbres sous l'Averse' etched vase, designed by Henri Bergé for the Paris World's Fair, with overlaid glass and colored powder inclusions, signed "DAUM NANCY", Cross of Lorraine and "5".

c1900          12.5in (31cm) high

**$10,000-12,000**          QU

A Daum Frères 'Arbres Roux' vase, designed by Henri Bergé, the bell-shaped body in overlaid clear glass, with blue and purple powder inclusions, enameled in brown and green, etched decoration, signed "Daum Nancy", Cross of Lorraine.

c1905          5.5in (13.5cm) high

**$20,000-25,000**          QU

A Daum Frères glass vase, with apple blossoms and yellow, orange, and dark-brown inclusions, overlaid in brown and white, etched cut blossom and leaves, signed "Daum Nancy" with Cross of Lorraine.

c1910          12.25in (30.5cm) high

**$8,000-12,000**          DOR

A Daum Frères cameo vase, decorated with brown stems and padded white cameo flowers, all against a mottled blue background, incised signature to side "Daum Nancy".

7.5in (19cm) high

**$10,000-15,000**          JDJ

## A CLOSER LOOK AT A DAUM FRÈRES VASE

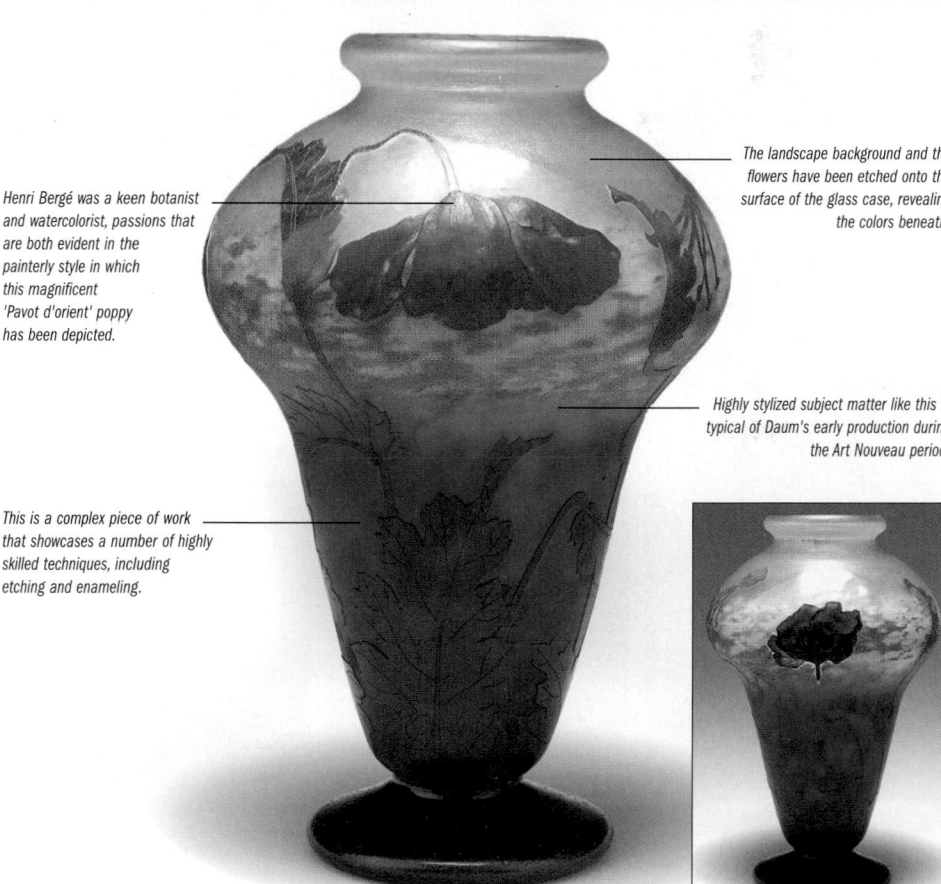

Henri Bergé was a keen botanist and watercolorist, passions that are both evident in the painterly style in which this magnificent 'Pavot d'orient' poppy has been depicted.

The landscape background and the flowers have been etched onto the surface of the glass case, revealing the colors beneath.

Highly stylized subject matter like this is typical of Daum's early production during the Art Nouveau period.

This is a complex piece of work that showcases a number of highly skilled techniques, including etching and enameling.

A Daum Frères cameo vase, decorated with a butterfly, flower blossoms, and leaves in gold enamel on a green and amber background, signed "Daum Nancy" on base.

3.75in (9.5cm) high

**$1,800-2,200**          JDJ

A Daum Frères 'Pavot d'orient' baluster vase, designed by Henri Bergé, in clear overlaid glass with blue, white, and yellow powder inclusions, enameled in dark-blue with etched decoration of poppies, signed "DAUM NANCY", Cross of Lorraine.

**$35,000-40,000**          QU

An Emile Gallé cylindrical glass vase, in two sections, with red overlay, etched decoration of a grasshopper and fern, signed to lower wall "Gallé", etched Cross of Lorraine, etched "Modèle et Décor Déposés".

*c1895*     8in (20.5cm) high

**$5,000-8,000**     **FIS**

A tall Gallé 'Pavonina' floor vase, in clear glass overlaid in auburn, with etched blossoms, flower buds and leaves, etched "Gallé" to inside and outside.

*c1895*     17.5in (43.5cm) high

**$2,800-3,200**     **FIS**

A Gallé enameled and acid-etched amber glass vase, the ovoid, textured surface decorated with thistles and gilt highlights, engraved to base "Gallé/depose" within a stylized star.

*c1895*     7in (18cm) high

**$3,000-5,000**     **S&K**

An Emile Gallé 'Pâques Fleuries' glass vase, with overlay in three colors and silver inclusions, painted "Pâques Fleuries", etched and painted "Gallé Nancy déposé G.G.", silver mounting with head of Minerva, "M" and "V".

*c1895*     4in (10cm) high

**$5,000-8,000**     **FIS**

 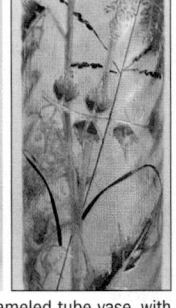

A Gallé floral cameo vase, in opalescent on clear glass decorated with spider chrysanthemum and pink, blue, yellow, and brown enamel, signed within the decoration "Galle".

5in (12.5cm) high

**$5,000-7,000**     **JDJ**

An early Gallé enameled tube vase, with enameled acid-cut and gilded floral decoration on amber swirled glass, engraved signature "E. GALLE NANCY".

8in (20.5cm) high

**$1,800-2,200**     **JDJ**

A rare Emile Gallé large vase, in clear glass with a four layers of semi-opaque overlay, etched decoration of lilies, rim formed as a blossom with five leaves, signed on the lower wall, etched "Gallé", cracked.

*c1895*     41.5in (105.5cm) high

**$18,000-22,000**     **FIS**

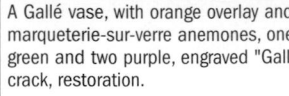 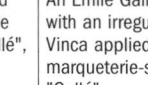 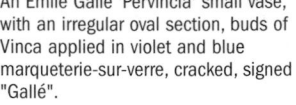

A Gallé vase, with orange overlay and marqueterie-sur-verre anemones, one green and two purple, engraved "Gallé", crack, restoration.

*c1895*     7.25in (18cm) high

**$2,800-3,200**     **FIS**

An Emile Gallé 'Pervincia' small vase, with an irregular oval section, buds of Vinca applied in violet and blue marqueterie-sur-verre, cracked, signed "Gallé".

*c1900*     4.25in (11cm) high

**$10,000-15,000**     **FIS**

A rare Gallé marqueterie-sur-verre cameo glass vase, on a cushion foot, with a freeform three-pronged connector decorated with a wheel-carved martelé finish, the background glass internally streaked with russet, sienna, and green shading and decorated in marqueterie-sur-verre with crocus blossoms and foliage, with engraved signature "Gallé" to side.

14in (35.5cm) high

**$100,000-120,000**     **JDJ**

A signed Gallé cameo vase, with red anemone flowers on an amber background, signed in cameo "GALLE" to side.

*5in (13cm) high*

**$2,800-3,200**      **JDJ**

A Gallé cameo vase, decorated with amethyst leaves and blossoms over clear frosted glass, signed to side "Gallé".

*5.25in (13.5cm) high*

**$1,800-2,200**      **JDJ**

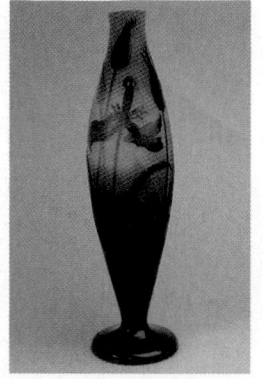

A Gallé cameo vase, decorated with green and amethyst flower blossoms and leaves, signed on side "Gallé", ground top.

*18in (45.5cm) high*

**$2,800-3,200**      **JDJ**

A Gallé fluid lamp, decorated with flowers and pond lilies in amethyst over blue, signed within the design "Gallé", later metal hardware.

*10in (25cm) high*

**$2,200-2,800**      **JDJ**

A Gallé cameo vase, decorated with amethyst and blue fuchsia blossoms, leaves and stems on a frosted amber background, signed "Gallé" on the side.

*18.25in (46.5cm) high*

**$5,000-8,000**      **JDJ**

A Gallé cameo bowl, with amethyst over pink over clear glass, decorated with flower blossoms, leaves, and stems, matt finish, signed "Gallé" on the side.

*6in (15cm) diam*

**$2,200-2,800**      **JDJ**

A Gallé cameo bowl, with overlaid brown over pink over yellow and white, decorated with blossoms and leaves, signed within the design, the side collapsed during manufacture, four open bubbles to base.

*6in (15cm) diam*

**$1,500-2,000**      **JDJ**

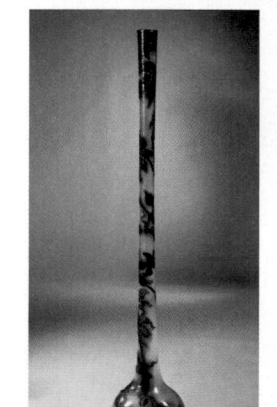

A large Gallé wheel-carved, fired, and polished cameo solifleur vase, the gray glass overlaid in shades of purple and acid-etched with clematis, lacks signature, base hollowed.

*53in (135cm) high*

**$5,000-7,000**      **L&T**

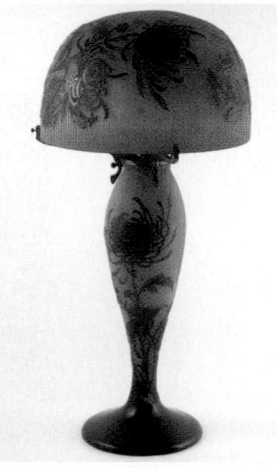

A Gallé cameo table lamp, decorated with chrysanthemum sprays, cameo signature, small chip to top rim of base.

*20in (51cm) high*

**$12,000-18,000**      **WW**

A pair of Gallé cups, with redcurrants, in the shape of a stylized calyx, on a trumpet-shaped foot, overlaid in orange and red, etched decoration, signed "Gallé".

**$2,800-3,200**      **QU**

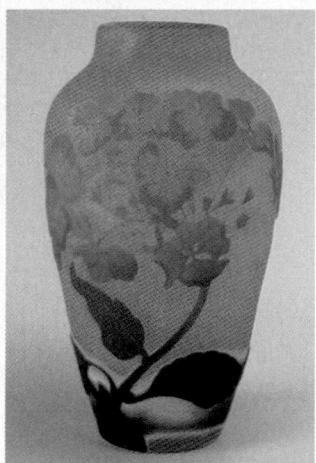

A Gallé cameo vase, overlaid with green amethyst and white on a frosted background, floral decoration with signature to base, signed "Gallé" with a star, two chips to cameo signature.

*10in (25.5cm) high*

**$1,800-2,200**      **JDJ**

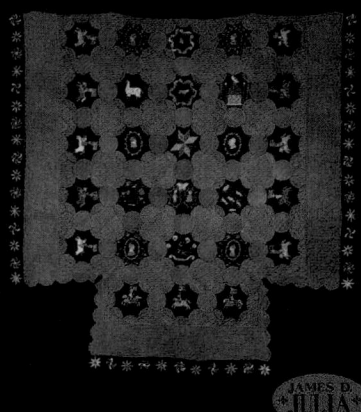

A 1920s Gallé 'Gentiane' disc-shaped vase, overlaid with amber and blue glass, etched decoration of a gentian, signed "Gallé".

**$2,800-3,200**    QU

A Gallé cameo vase, decorated with amber pine cones on a mottled green background, signed "Gallé" with a star.

*6in (15cm) high*

**$2,200-2,800**    JDJ

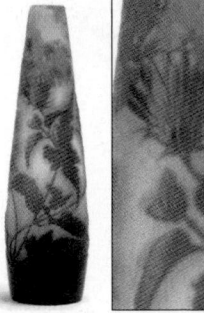

A Gallé cameo vase, overlaid decoration of green leaves and purple lilac blossoms, signed on side of vase "Gallé" with a star.

*11in (28cm) high*

**$1,500-2,000**    JDJ

## LALIQUE

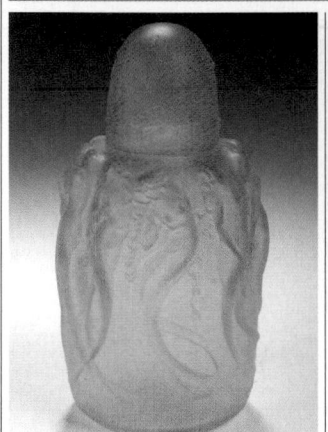

A Lalique 'Sirenes' frosted glass perfume burner and cover, molded with a frieze of naked female forms, the domed lid molded with their flowing hair, includes original wick, etched mark "R. Lalique, France".

**$2,200-2,800**    L&T

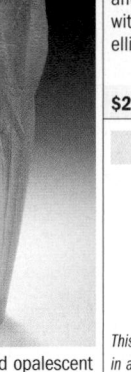

A Lalique 'Ceylan' frosted and opalescent glass vase, of tapering cylindrical form, molded with a frieze of budgerigars, wheel-etched marks, traces of blue staining, "R.Lalique, France", "No.905".

*9.5in (24cm) high*

**$4,000-6,000**    L&T

A Lalique frosted glass centerpiece, with two disc-like handles molded with an openwork design of antelopes leaping through foliage, with leaves extending on to the plain elliptical vessel, marked "R. Lalique".

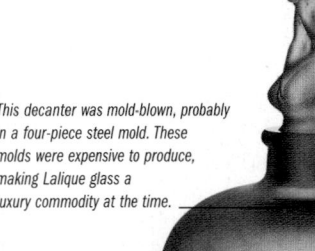

*19in (48cm) long*

**$2,800-3,200**    DN

### A CLOSER LOOK AT A LALIQUE VASE

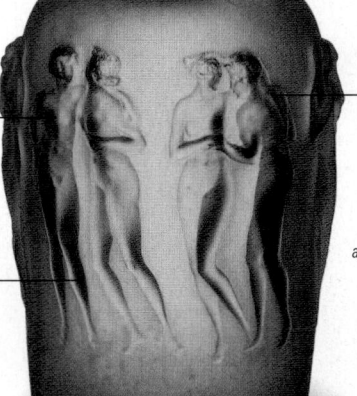

*This decanter was mold-blown, probably in a four-piece steel mold. These molds were expensive to produce, making Lalique glass a luxury commodity at the time.*

*The stopper, depicting a kneeling female figure, is particularly vulnerable to chipping or loss. The fact that this one remains in excellent condition enhances the value of this decanter.*

*Look for crispness in the molded figures.*

*These diaphanous figures almost seem to melt into the body of the decanter. This kind of sophisticated design marks Lalique out as a master of his art.*

*This is a very complex design depicting an amorous couple in six different poses.*

A Lalique 'Moissac' opalescent, clean and frosted glass vase, number 992, with remains of blue staining, molded mark "R Lalique France".

*5in (13cm) high*

**$1,800-2,200**    WW

A Lalique 'Domremy' amber glass vase, number 979, with etched signature.

*8.75in (22cm) high*

**$3,000-5,000**    WW

A Lalique 'Douze Figurines avec Bouchon' vase, with stopper, in clear and frosted glass, engraved "R. Lalique" mark.

*c1920*    *11.5in (29.5cm) high*

**$8,000-12,000**    RDL

A reissued Lalique 'Danseuse Bras Baisse' statuette, after an earlier figure, with engraved "No. 11910" mark.

*c1975*      9.5in (19cm) high

**$700-1,000**      **RDL**

A Lalique 'Longchamps' frosted glass car mascot, modeled as a horse's head with highly stylized mane, the glass with a pale amethyst tint, with a chromed collar mounted on a rectangular marble base, marked "R.Lalique", some trimming and nicks.

7in (17.5cm) high

**$4,000-6,000**      **DN**

A Lalique 'Ato Pendule électrique Moineau' frosted glass timepiece, with a curved top, the front molded with sparrows resting on prunus, 'Ato' glass dial, molded 'R. Lalique' near the base.

*This model was created for and sold exclusively by 'Ato' and never appeared in the commercial catalogs of Maison Lalique.*

6in (15.5cm) high

**$2,200-2,800**      **DN**

A Lalique clear and frosted opalescent box, with a later enameled silver top depicting cherry blossom, inscribed "R. Lalique France", English silver marks Birmingham 1933.

5.5in (14cm) wide

**$700-1,000**      **ROS**

## LOETZ

A Loetz-style enameled iridescent glass vase, the spirally ribbed and dimpled ovoid body in pale green glass, painted with flowering clover and a gilt border, inscribed "Loetz/Austria".

10in (25.5cm) high

**$280-320**      **S&K**

A Loetz iridescent Art Nouveau vase, designed by Friedrich Adler, with a gilt pewter mount, signed "Orion", model number 315.

*c1905*      6in (15cm) high

**$5,000-7,000**      **BMN**

An overlaid vase, attributed to Loetz, of lustered glass with silver blossoms, etched number "21309".

8in (20cm) high

**$1,500-2,000**      **DRA**

A Loetz glass vase, of dimple ovoid form with everted rim, the green body covered in a tracery of peacock iridescence.

7.75in (19.5cm) high

**$500-700**      **L&T**

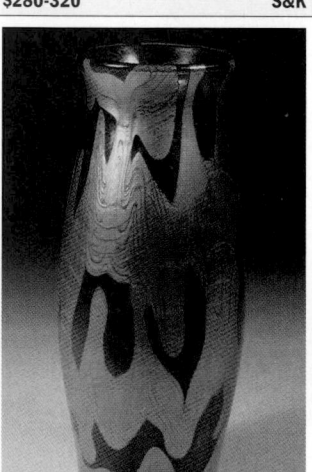

A Loetz-Witwe 'Gre 29' vase, in light olive-green glass with wide bands of silvery yellow, engraved "Loetz Austria".

*c1900*      10in (25cm) high

**$4,000-6,000**      **FIS**

A Loetz iridescent glass, vase with incised leaf veining.

*c1905*      8.75in (22cm) high

**$15,000-18,000**      **LN**

A Loetz iridescent small vase, with sterling silver overlay.

*c1905*      5in (13cm) high

**$4,000-6,000**      **LN**

A Monart tapering glass vase, in mottled orange and amethyst.

*8.5in (21cm) high*

**$220-280**    **L&T**

A Monart glass vase, of bulbous tapering form with cylindrical neck, the mottled orange body with amethyst inclusions to the rim.

*8.5in (22cm) high*

**$400-600**    **L&T**

A Monart posy vase, with broad flaring rim, the mottled pea green body with amethyst and aventurine inclusions to the rim.

*5.5in (14cm) diam*

**$50-80**    **L&T**

A rare Monart cameo glass lamp, the domed shade above a baluster shaped body, the mottled orange glass overlaid with green and brown glass, acid-etched with a frieze of trees, possibly unique, bears paper label "etched lamp".

*18.75in (47cm) high*

**$7,000-10,000**    **L&T**

A Vasart pink glass basket, with handles.

**$30-50**    **L&T**

A Monart circular tapering bowl, the red, orange and mottled body with amethyst inclusions to the rim, bears paper label "No.MC.VII".

*5.25in (13cm) high*

**$70-100**    **L&T**

## ORREFORS

### ORREFORS

- Glass was first manufactured at Orrefors, Småland, Sweden in 1898.
- Simon Gate (1883-1945) was taken on as artistic director in 1916 and was joined by Edward Hald (1883-1980) a year later. The company then gained an international reputation for high quality glass.
- Graal, a type of cased engraved glass, was introduced by Gate in 1916.
- At the 1925 Paris International Exposition Orrefors was awarded the Grands Prix and gold medals.
- Ariel glass, sandblasted with intaglio decoration and cased, was introduced by Edvin Öhrström (b.1906) in 1937, and developed by Vicke Lindstrand (1904-83).
- Two other notable designers were Sven Palmqvist (1906-84), who produced abstract designs, and Ingeborg Lundin (b.1921) who used a variety of techniques including engraving and latticino.
- Orrefors continues to produce quality glass today and became part of Royal Scandinavian in 1997.

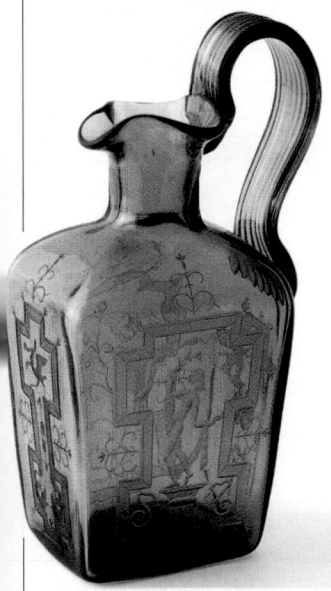

An Orrefors jug, by Simon Gate, engraved with a female dancer.

*c1925*    *8.75in (22cm) high*

**$2,800-3,200**    **LN**

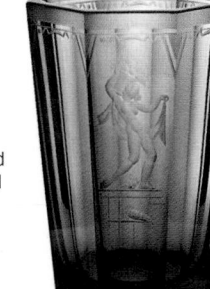

An engraved glass vase, probably Orrefors, designed by Vicke Lindstrand, engraved with a classical nude, etched "L. 1935".

*6.5in (16.5cm) high*

**$280-320**    **WW**

A 1930s Orrefors 'Ariel' bright blue glass vase, by Öhrström.

*6.75in (17cm) high*

**$5,000-8,000**    **LN**

A 1930s Orrefors 'Mermaid' vase.

8.5in (22cm) high

$1,800-2,200          LN

An engraved Orrefors decanter, by Nils Landberg, with an image of a sailor.

c1940          9.5in (24cm) high

$300-500          JH

An Orrefors 'Graal' glass vase, by Edward Hald, in clear glass with green and brown overlay, acid-etched decoration of fishes and water plants, signed.

1944          7.5in (19cm) high

$800-1,200          FIS

## A CLOSER LOOK AT AN ORREFORS VASE

The designer of this vase, sculptor Edvin Öhrström, was hired in 1936 to develop new designs before the world exhibition in Paris in 1937.

Öhrström, together with Vicke Lindstrand, developed a technique known as Ariel, which was named after the spirit of the air in Shakespeare's 'The Tempest'.

A design is cut into multi-layered glass, revealing the colors beneath. The whole piece is then cased in clear glass, trapping air in the cavities.

Due to the way light is reflected in the cased cavities, the design has a silvery finish.

An Orrefors 'Ariel' pink glass vase, by Edvin Öhrström.

c1940          6.25in (16cm) high

$20,000-25,000          LN

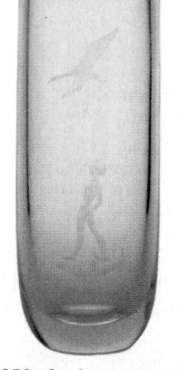

A 1950s Orrefors engraved vase, by Palmqvist, with a scene of a boy and a bird.

9in (22.5cm) high

$120-180          JH

A 1950s Orrefors 'Utopia' vase, by Boran Varsh.

10.5in (27cm) high

$800-1,200          JH

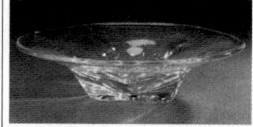

An Orrefors window cut vase.

c1935          5in (13cm) high

$180-220          JH

An Orrefors glass bowl, on a trefoil foot, incised "Orrefors/ No 3516/211".

13in (33cm) diam

$180-220          S&K

## STEVENS & WILLIAMS

- Established in 1847 in Stourbridge, England, Stevens & Williams started developing new types of art glass in the late 19thC.
- The high relief decorative technique of 'Mat-Su-Noke' ('The Spirit of the Pine Tree') was registered in 1884. This expensive process was widely copied.
- Innovations included the Silveria range, developed by John Northwood c1900. The technique involved carefully encasing thin sheets of silver foil between layers of glass. The range was only produced for a short period and is highly sought after today.
- As well as attractive decoration, collectors look for the work of particular craftsmen such as Joshua Hodgetts and Frederick Carder, who went on to found Steuben Glass Works in New York.
- The firm later employed Keith Murray who produced over 150 designs, including the Cactus vase, before he joined Wedgwood.
- Still in production today as Royal Brierley.

A Stevens & Williams double case hock glass.

c1900          8in (20cm) high

$500-700          AL

A Stevens & Williams two color 'Hock' glass, in yellow and orange.

c1905          8in (20cm) high

$500-800          AL

A Stevens & Williams two color 'Hock' glass, predominantly purple.

c1905          8in (20cm) high

$500-800          AL

## THE STEUBEN GLASS WORKS

- The Steuben Glass Works was established in 1903 in Corning, Steuben County, New York.
- Under Frederick Carder (1864-1963), an English chemist and glassmaker, Steuben produced a wide range of art glass, including the popular 'Aurene' range, which has a bright gold iridescence.
- In 1918 the company was acquired by the Corning Glass Works but continued under Carder's directorship until Arthur Houghton took over in 1933.
- Technological advances led to the development of a pure form of clear glass, '10M', in 1932, which did not need decolorizing agents. This became known as Steuben crystal.
- Some of Carder's original glass designs were made in the new clear glass but new ranges, influenced by the sculptor Sidney Waugh (1904-63) and architect John Monteith Gates (b. 1905), were also introduced and the company became famous for its distinctive Art Deco style glass.
- The company is still running successfully today, combining technological advances with the work of skilled craftsmen.

A Steuben art glass shade, iridescent gold with blue and purple highlights, signed with Steuben Fleur-de-Lis mark.

*4.5in (11.5cm) high*

**$400-600**    JDJ

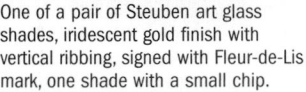

One of a pair of Steuben art glass shades, iridescent gold finish with vertical ribbing, signed with Fleur-de-Lis mark, one shade with a small chip.

*4.75in (12cm) high*

**$400-600 pair**    JDJ

One of a pair of Steuben Ivrene shades, vertical ribs with a slight scalloped edge, iridescent white coloring, unsigned, one fitter with a chip.

*4in (10cm) high*

**$300-500 pair**    JDJ

A Steuben Aurene on calcite shade, iridescent gold interior with a calcite exterior, vertical ribbing, unsigned.

*5.5in (14cm) high*

**$300-400**    JDJ

An extremely rare Steuben art glass shade, with platinum haphazard design on brown Aurene ground, unsigned.

*5.75in (14.5cm) high*

**$3,000-5,000**    JDJ

A Steuben green glass shade, with applied border, the green Aurene body with gold or platinum applied border and a zigzag design.

*5.25in (13.5cm) high*

**$4,000-6,000**    JDJ

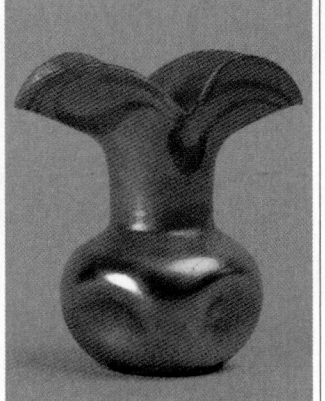

A Steuben gold Aurene millefiori vase, with blue and purple highlights with leaf and vine decoration interspersed with millefiori flowers, signed on base.

*6.25in (16cm) high*

**$7,000-10,000**    JDJ

A Steuben decorated vase, iridescent gold with green swirls and four pinched in sides, flaring four-sided top, signed on base "Aurene 131B."

*4.5in (11.5cm) high*

**$2,200-2,800**    JDJ

A Steuben gold Aurene three-stump vase, with bright gold stumps, strong blue overtones on foot, signed on base "Aurene 1744."

*6in (15cm) high*

**$800-1,200**    JDJ

A gold Aurene glass dome, attributed to Steuben, iridescent gold finish with blue highlights and silver-plated metal rim.

*8.5in (21.5cm) high*

**$1,800-2,200**    JDJ

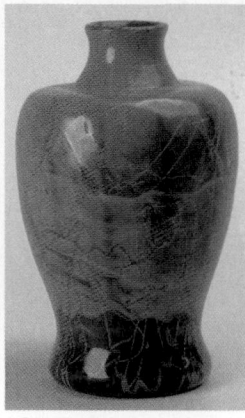

A Steuben Tyrian vase, heart and vine decoration on purple and blue glass, signed on base "Tyrian."

*7.25in (18.5cm) high*

**$10,000-12,000**    JDJ

A yellow Steuben Cintra lamp base, with acid cut back design against a yellow cintra base, unsigned.

*14in (35.5cm) high*

**$1,200-1,800**    JDJ

A Steuben green jade perfume bottle, green shouldered with clear crystal twisted stopper.

*11.75in 29cm) high*

**$400-600**    JDJ

Three Steuben Celeste blue glass candlesticks, with vertical ribbing, signed with Fleur-de-Lis acid-etched mark.

*12in (30cm) high*

**$1,200-1,800**    JDJ

A Steuben Art Deco hanging shade, with starburst cut into center and a pebble pattern all over, scalloped border, signed "Steuben" with the Fleur-de-Lis mark.

*13.5in (35.5cm) diam*

**$300-500**    JDJ

A rare 1920s Steuben Rouge flambé plate, in rich red color.

*8.5in (21cm) diam*

**$7,000-10,000**    JDJ

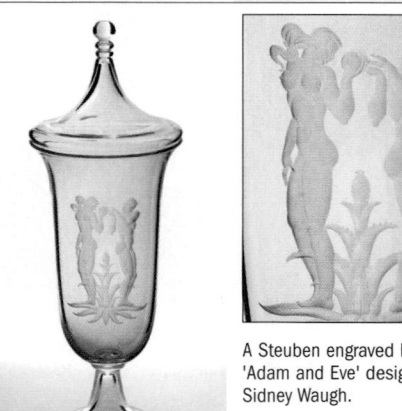

A Steuben crystal castle, molded and polished crystal, engraved "Steuben," in original box.

*9.75in (24cm) wide*

**$3,000-4,000**    FRE

A Steuben engraved bottle with 'Adam and Eve' design by Sidney Waugh.

*c1940*    *16in (40cm) high*

**$11,000-13,000**    LN

## A CLOSER LOOK AT A STEUBEN BOWL

*This famous 'Gazelle' design reflects the typical geometrical design of Art Deco and the influences of Swedish simplicity. This design owes a specific debt to the work of Vicke Lindstrand, designer of Orrefors in the 1930s.*

*Steuben's chief designer Waugh engraved this bowl with twelve graceful gazelles, leaping in cinematic motion.*

*All of Steuben's renowned glassmaking techniques are combined in this bowl: blowing, cutting, polishing, and copper-wheel engraving.*

*This piece juxtaposes the heavy angular Art Deco base with a hemispherical glass bowl.*

A Steuben engraved 'Gazelle' bowl with stand, designed by Sidney Waugh.

*c1935*    *7.25in (18cm) high*

**$23,000-25,000**    LN

One of a pair of Quezel shades, in iridescent green with white pulled feather decoration, signed on fitter "QUEZEL," one fitter with a small chip.

*24.25in (60.5cm) high*

**$1,200-1,800 pair**    **JDJ**

Three Quezal shades, iridescent gold finish with vertical ribbing and flaring edge, all signed on fitter "Quezal," one with a small chip to fitter.

*5.25in (13.5cm) high*

**$400-600**    **JDJ**

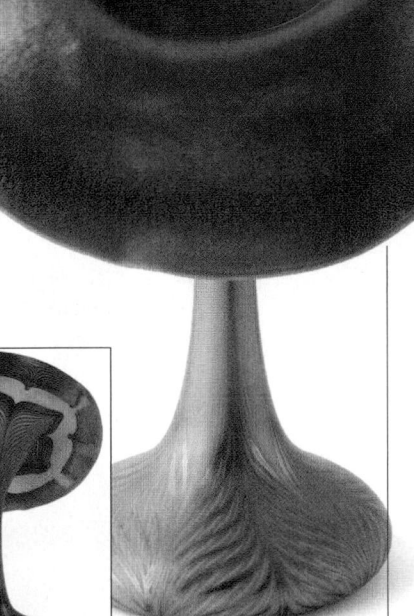

A Quezal green flower shade, model no. R#55, green flower decoration and gold lily pads and vines on an opal ground with gold interior, signed "Quezal."

*4.75in (12cm) high*

**$3,000-5,000**    **JDJ**

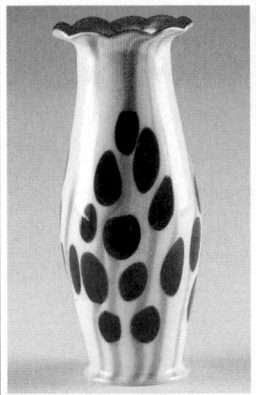

A very rare Quezal grape shade, with purple grapes and green vertical lines, ruffled lip with internal gold iridescence, signed "Quezal."

*7in (18cm) high*

**$5,000-7,000**    **JDJ**

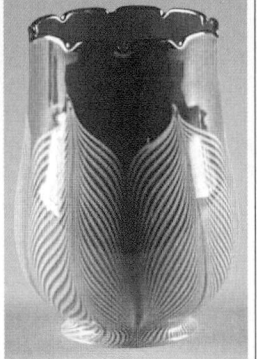

A rare Quezal paperweight shade, lemon yellow background with white feather decoration, crimped border, signed "Quezal".

*5in (12.5cm) high*

**$1,800-2,200**    **JDJ**

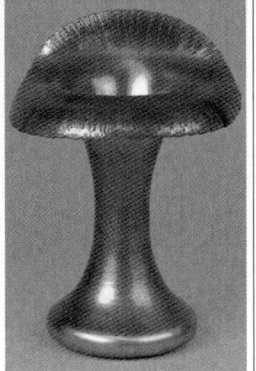

A Quezal 'Jack in the pulpit' vase, iridescent gold finish with purple highlights, signed in polished pontil "Quezal."

*8.5in (21.5cm) high*

**$3,000-4,000**    **JDJ**

A Quezal art glass cabinet vase, blown glass, etched "Quezal F 639."

*6.25in (15.5cm) high*

**$6,000-9,000**    **FRE**

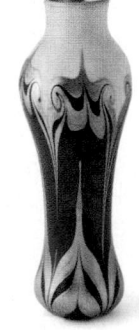

A Quezal vase, of shouldered and waisted form, with pulled-feather decoration in iridescent blue, green, and gold, on an opaque white ground.

*13in (32.5cm) high*

**$4,000-6,000**    **LN**

A Quezal compote, with green iridescent rim shading to blue shading to iridescent gold in the bowl section, on gold foot, unsigned.

*9.5in (24cm) diam*

**$800-1,200**    **JDJ**

A Quezal 'Jack in the Pulpit' vase, with a gold iridescent interior, on a green and gold stem.

*13in (32.5cm) high*

**$10,000-12,000**    **LN**

535

An unusual Tiffany bulbous vase, decorated with applied pods and tendrils, the pods of very rare blue glass on a gold and platinum ground and decorated with an Art Nouveau hooked pattern design, signed "LCT R3291."

*6in (15cm) high*

**$20,000-22,000**     **JDJ**

An extremely rare Tiffany reactive glass shade, model no. R#123, mauve and pink wavy marvering decoration on white, opal interior, signed "L C Tiffany Favrile."

*5in (12.5cm) high*

**$4,000-6,000**     **JDJ**

A Tiffany flower form vase, decorated with an Art Nouveau feather design in highly unusual browns, golds, and mauves, the scalloped bowl tapering into a rich rum and green hued stem supported by a ribbed platform base, signed "LCT M1940," with minor open and trapped bubbles.

*9in (23cm) high*

**$10,000-12,000**     **JDJ**

A rare L.C. Tiffany Favrile cypriote paperweight vase, model no. V196, etched signature and numbered underfoot.

*4.5in (11.5cm) high*

**$12,000-15,000**     **ISA**

A Tiffany wheel-carved Favrile glass vase, with a shaped lip, in iridescent amber glass with trailing vines and carved leaves, inscribed "L.C. Tiffany. Favrile/2352K", numbered "14178".

*c1915*                    6in (15cm) high

**$5,000-8,000**                    **S&K**

A Tiffany glass vase, of iridescent gold with vertical ribbing and five folded petals, button pontil, signed "L.T.C. Y2390".

4.25in (11cm) high

**$1,200-1,800**                    **JDJ**

A Tiffany blue iridescent vase, with silver decoration of leaves and vines with iridescent flashes of green, gold, and blue, signed on base "Louis C. Tiffany LCT D1420".

4.5in (11.5cm) high

**$7,000-10,000**                    **JDJ**

A Tiffany bulbous vase, in opaque yellow Favrile glass with threaded blue leaves and opaline dogwood blossoms, etched "L.C.T./T5284".

6in (15cm) high

**$14,000-18,000**                    **DRA**

A small Tiffany paperweight vase, with a pink floral decoration.

*c1910*            6.25in (16cm) high

**$18,000-22,000**                    **LN**

A Tiffany floriform vase with broad flat rim and pulled feather decoration, two manufacturing bubbles to rim, etched "L.C.T./T3241".

11.25in (28cm) high

**$12,000-18,000**                    **DRA**

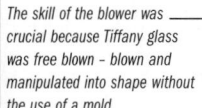

A large Tiffany iridescent wine glass, with carved vines.

*c1910*            6in (15cm) high

**$800-1,200**                    **LN**

## A CLOSER LOOK AT A TIFFANY CAMEO VASE

Paperweight vases were produced by Tiffany c1905-1915.

Patches of glass were laid into the body in layers, the whole was reheated and then cased with a layer of clear glass known as paperweight glass.

The glass used was of high quality and the decorative techniques required a great deal of skill. Speciality Tiffany glassware is rare and expensive.

The skill of the blower was crucial because Tiffany glass was free blown – blown and manipulated into shape without the use of a mold.

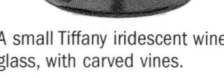

A small Tiffany iridescent wine glass, with carved vines.

*c1910*            5in (13cm) high

**$500-700**                    **LN**

A Tiffany pastel wine glass.

*c1910*            6.25in (16cm) high

**$1,800-2,200**                    **LN**

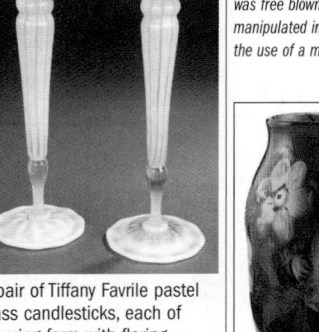

A pair of Tiffany Favrile pastel glass candlesticks, each of tapering form with flaring scalloped rim, in opalescent shading to teal green glass, inscribed "L.C. Tiffany. Favrile/1901", one numbered "993T".

*c1925*            9.5in (24cm) high

**$2,800-3,200**                    **S&K**

A rare Tiffany cameo carved paperweight vase, inlaid with different colors and then engraved.

*c1910*                    7in (18cm) high

**$50,000-60,000**                    **LN**

A Thomas Webb three color cameo vase, with cameo floral decoration of roses and leaves, signed "Tiffany & Co. Paris Exposition 1889 Thomas Webb & Sons Gem Cameo".

7.5in (19cm) high

**$4,000-6,000** **JDJ**

A cameo glass vase, in the style of Thomas Webb, of bulbous form in ruby glass overlaid with branching flowers and butterflies.

13in (33cm) high

**$5,000-7,000** **S&K**

A Thomas Webb cameo scent bottle, with original silver cover, decorated in white over red with lily of the valley, base signed "Thomas Webb & Sons".

5.25in (13.25cm) high

**$5,000-7,000** **JDJ**

A Webb cameo perfume bottle, with white cameo vines and leaves, silver top marked "Gorham Sterling".

10.5in (26.5cm) long

**$2,800-3,200** **JDJ**

A Webb cameo glass bowl, in Moorish style.

c1890 4.5in (11.5cm) diam

**$1,800-2,200** **MW**

A pair of Webb cameo glass salad servers.

c1890 11.5in (29cm) long

**$1,800-2,200** **MW**

A Webb Burmese vase, with a bulbous body and rolled rim, enameled with red flowers and green leaves, marked on underside "Thomas Webb & Sons Queen's Burmeseware Patented Rd 67648".

4.75in (12cm) high

**$500-800** **JDJ**

A Webb vaseline glass fruit dish.

c1905 5.5in (14cm) high

**$500-800** **MW**

A 1930s Thomas Webb vase, designed by Anna Fogelberg, decorated with cacti.

*Anna Fogelberg was married to the Managing Director of Thomas Webb.*

11.5in (29cm) long

**$1,800-2,200** **JH**

A 1930s Webb cut and acid-etched vase.

*This vase is similar to Webb's 'Cameo Fleur' but has a single casing.*

8in (20.5cm) high

**$300-500** **JH**

A Webb Corbett decanter, original label.

*The ban on the production of luxury goods for the British market following WWII suggests that this was made for export.*

c1945 13in (34cm) high

**$500-700** **JH**

A pair of Arts & Crafts leaded glass windows, in polychrome glass with different textures, one depicting a medieval maiden with hand-painted face and hands, the other with "Gather ye rosebuds while ye may, Old Time is still a-flying", in original sashes.

*frames 33x23in (84x58.5cm)*

**$3,000-5,000 pair**      DRA

A late 19thC stained, painted, and leaded glass panel, inscribed "Literature", the central panel painted with an allegorical female figure within an archway, surrounded by panels of foliage, within foliate borders, unframed.

*112in (280cm) wide*

**$6,000-9,000**      L&T

A leaded glass panel, depicting a medieval maiden in flowing robes and collecting flowers, with a poem.

*10.5in (26.5cm) high*

**$1,200-1,800**      WW

A pair of leaded glass landscape windows, in the manner of Louis Comfort Tiffany, blown, mottled, striated, drapery, and confetti glass with lead, iron, oak, each in oak frames with protective clear glass to one side.

*66in (165cm) high*

**$4,000-6,000**      FRE

An Arts & Crafts stained glass panel, with a scene from Lewis Carroll's 'Alice in Wonderland', showing the rabbit looking at his watch.

*c1930*      *36in (91.5cm) high*

**$35,000-45,000**      PUR

An Arts & Crafts stained glass panel, with a scene from Lewis Carroll's 'Alice in Wonderland', showing the rabbit at the court of the Queen of Hearts.

*c1930*      *36in (91.5cm) high*

**$25,000-35,000**      PUR

An Arts & Crafts stained glass panel, with a scene from Lewis Carroll's 'Alice in Wonderland', showing Alice's first encounter with the Cheshire cat.

*c1930*      *36in (91.5cm) high*

**$70,000-100,000**      PUR

An Arts & Crafts stained glass panel, with a woodland scene of a dark-haired nymph sitting by a stream.

*c1930*        *36in (91.5cm) high*

**$35,000-50,000**        **PUR**

An Arts & Crafts stained glass panel, with a woodland and setting sun scene.

*c1930*        *36in (91.5cm) high*

**$8,000-12,000**        **PUR**

An Arts & Crafts stained glass panel, depicting a scene from Lewis Carroll's 'Alice in Wonderland'.

*c1930*        *36in (91.5cm) high*

**$18,000-22,000**        **PUR**

## OTHER GLASS FACTORIES

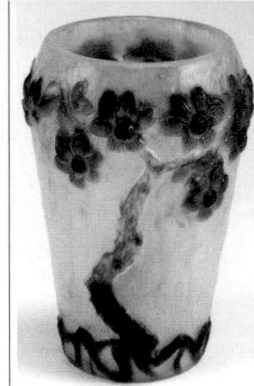

An Argy Rousseau pâte-de-verre nightlight, with cast iron mounts, signed "G Argy Rousseau".

*8.25in (21cm) high*

**$3,000-5,000**        **WW**

An Argy-Rousseau pâte-de-verre vase, embossed with prunus, minor nicks, stamped "G. Argy-Rousseau, 8874".

*6in (15cm) high*

**$6,000-9,000**        **DRA**

An Argy-Rousseau pâte-de-verre vase, embossed with thistles in purple and red on a mottled ground, stamped "G. Argy-Rousseau, France".

*4in (10cm) wide*

**$3,000-5,000**        **DRA**

An Argy-Rousseau table lamp 'La Coupe Fleurie', pâte-de-verre and relief decoration, wrought-iron mounting, signed "G.Argy-Rousseau France".

*c1925*        *6.25in (16cm) high*

**$4,000-6,000**        **FIS**

A Baccarat vase decorated with a grasshopper with colored wings.

*c1885*

**$1,800-2,200**        **MW**

An Art Deco Baccarat glass box and cover, the pressed lid molded with a naked couple, the body decorated with a white metal filigree band set with carved jadeite panels on reeded jadeite feet, molded butterfly monogram.

*5in (12cm) high*

**$600-900**        **L&T**

A 1920s or 1930s Bimini Workshop blue and white vase, with decorative birds.

*9in (23cm) high*

**$1,000-1,500**        **LN**

Two Bimini glasses, of blown glass lampwork, with glass roosters inside.

*taller 8in (20cm) high*

**$300-400 each**        **LN**

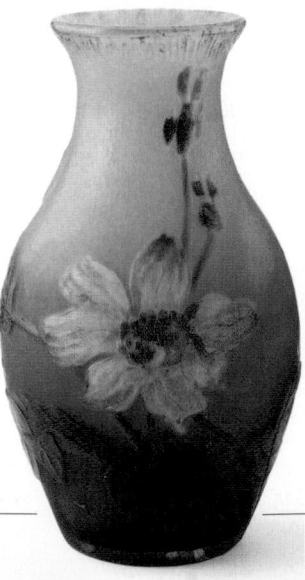

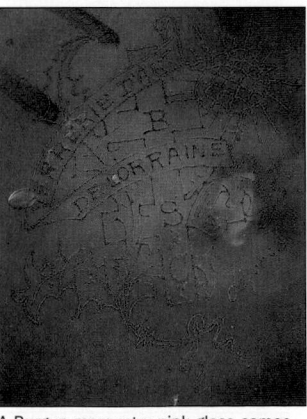

A Burgun marquetry pink glass cameo carved vase, with gilt details.

*c1900*        *8in (20cm) high*

**$12,000-18,000**        **LN**

A Burgun marquetry purple glass, cameo carved vase, with gilt details.

*c1900*          *8.75in (22cm) high*

**$15,000-20,000**                          **LN**

A Leerdam 'Serica' series glass vase, designed by A.D. Copier, the clear glass internally decorated with tiny blue bubbles arranged in horizontal rows, etched triangular mark with "Serica Copier" and scratch numbered "108".

*4.5in (11.5cm) high*

**$300-400**                                **DN**

A rare Crown Milano ewer, the background decorated to represent water and coral with applied decoration of fish, shells, and coral, with rare applied glass rope handle.

*10in (25.5cm) high*

**$10,000-12,000**                          **JDJ**

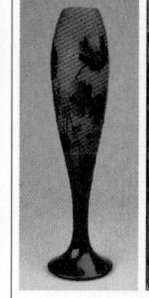

A d'Argental cameo vase, decorated with rust-colored floral blossoms and leaves on an amber background, signed on body "d'Argental".

*14in (35.5cm) high*

**$2,800-3,200**                            **JDJ**

A D'Argyl amethyst vase, with frosted and silver paint decorated with tulips, the applied metal top with handles, metal foot and band, signed on the side in silver paint "D'Argyl", minor scratches.

*14in (35.5cm) high*

**$700-1,000**                              **JDJ**

An Emil Dugay Art Deco table lamp, with flaring pink glass shade on a bright chrome hemispheric base, from the Chateau de Grenany in Lyons, France, unmarked.

*13.5in (34.5cm) high*

**$1,200-1,800**                            **DRA**

An Art Deco opaque milk glass vase with aquatic design, by Pierre D'Avesn.

*c1925*          *9.5in (24cm) high*

**$2,800-3,200**                            **MOD**

An Art Deco opalescent glass vase, by H. Dieupart.

*c1925*          *13.5in (34cm) high*

**$1,500-2,000**                            **MOD**

A rare Durand platinum vase, of tapering form with 'King Tut' decoration on green, with gold circular pedestal foot, signed "Durand 2028-19".

*14in (35.5cm) high*

**$3,000-5,000**                            **JDJ**

A 1920s or 1930s Marcel Goupy enameled vase, the design of blue and green trees with gilt details.

*7in (18cm) high*

**$5,000-7,000**                            **LN**

A Marcel Goupy clear glass decanter and stopper, of teardrop form, painted in green and red enamels with stylized leaves, signed on the base.

*11in (28cm) high*

**$400-600**                                **L&T**

A Handel teroma covered jar, painted with birds flying in a bamboo thicket, in polychrome on dark green, unmarked, chip and flakes.

*7.5in (19cm) high*

**$3,000-5,000**                            **DRA**

A Wiener Werkstätte purple glass bowl, by Josef Hoffmann.

c1915        9.75in (25cm) diam

**$5,000-7,000**                                    **LN**

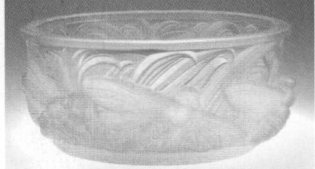

An opalescent glass bowl, with dragonfly decoration, frosted patina, pressed mark on base "Verlys France".

c1930        9.75in (24.5cm) diam

**$2,200-2,800**                                    **QU**

A French vase, by Auguste Jean, with enamel work in Japanesque style.

c1880        6.75in (17cm) high

**$2,800-3,200**                                    **MW**

A 1930s clear glass Mermaid vase, by Kjellander.

*Kjellander was the workshop manager at Kosta but later set up his own factory. This vase was made in heavy and lightweight versions. This is a heavy example.*

6.5in (16.5cm) high

**$400-600**                                    **JH**

An important floor vase, by Auguste Jean, Paris, in brown smoke glass, the rim with bright blue molding, with gilded and auburn decoration, painted on base with gold "T. Ducy, 53 Rue de Chateaudun" and painted in red "A Jean", restored.

c1880        22.4in (55.9cm) high

**$8,000-12,000**                                    **FIS**

A 1920s enameled vase, by Josephinen glassworks, Silesia, in blue glass with opaque enameling depicting a bird perched on stylized golden branches surrounded by butterflies.

4.25in (10.5cm) high

**$500-800**                                    **VS**

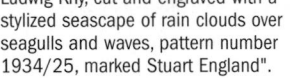

A Stuart flared vase, designed by Ludwig Kny, cut and engraved with a stylized seascape of rain clouds over seagulls and waves, pattern number 1934/25, marked Stuart England".

c1935        7in (18cm) high

**$1,000-1,500**                                    **JH**

A mid-1930s cut glass bowl, designed by Ludwig Kny for Stuart.

11.75in (30cm) diam

**$700-1,000**                                    **JH**

A Legras tall cameo glass vase, decorated with swags of ribbons and flowers in dark pink on a light pink mottled ground, signed "Le Gras".

13.5in (34.5cm) high

**$700-1,000**                                    **DRA**

A Legras tall-necked cameo bottle, with purple wisteria and brown branches on a pearl gray ground, signed "Legras".

13in (32.5cm) high

**$1,500-2,000**                                    **DRA**

One of a pair of 1950s intaglio and engraved decanters, designed by Jack Lloyd for Crystal.

13.75in (35cm) high

**$500-700 pair**                                    **JH**

An extremely rare Maurice Marinot bottle with stopper, with enameling around the rim.

c1915        6.25in (16cm) high

**$22,000-28,000**                                    **LN**

A Val Saint Lambert double-cased footed vase.

c1915          8.75in (22cm) high

**$1,500-2,000**          **AL**

A Val Saint Lambert vase, in clear glass with cobalt blue overlay, etched decoration of tendrils of wild vine with blue grapes.

c1910          12in (30.5cm) high

**$1,800-2,200**          **FIS**

An important Vallerysthal vase, the clear glass with copper overlay and stylized etched tendrils of wild vine, a butterfly and stars, the rim decorated with a geometric design, etched signature to base "Vallerysthal".

c1905          14in (35.5cm) high

**$7,000-10,000**          **FIS**

A Walsh Walsh vaseline glass vase, with a ruffled rim.

c1905          4.25in (10cm) high

**$500-800**          **MW**

A pair of enameled vases, designed by Wally Weisenthiel for Wiener Werkstätte.

c1915          8.25in (21cm) high

**$15,000-20,000**          **LN**

A rare WMF 'Myra-Kristall' footed bowl, by Karl Wiedmann, in opaque red glass with yellow flashes and etched decoration of stylized pine leaves.

c1930          10in (25.5cm) diam

**$700-1,000**          **FIS**

A WMF green crystal cut glass bowl, number '3172', with silver-plated lid and glass knop.

c1935          8.5in (21cm) high

**$280-320**          **QU**

A pair of Arts & Crafts Aesthetic Movement red glass vases, with birds and a spider painted in gold.

c1885

**$800-1,200**          **PUR**

An Arts & Crafts hanging lantern, in caramel and green slag glass with a wrought copper frame, original reddish brown patina, line to one panel.

15in (37.5cm) high

**$3,000-5,000**          **DRA**

An English vaseline glass shade.

c1900          7.25in (18.5in) high

**$1,800-2,200**          **MW**

A bell-shaped vaseline glass shade.

c1900          6.75in (17cm) high

**$180-220**          **MW**

One of a set of six naturalistically enameled drinking glasses.

c1890 set          6.75in (17cm) high

**$1,000-1,500**          **AL**

A vaseline opalescent and enameled shade.

c1900      5.75in (14.5cm) high

**$180-220**      **MW**

One of a pair of English glass water jugs, the silver mounts by John Grinsell & Sons, stamped marks for London.

1901      7in (18cm) high

**$1,500-2,000 pair**      **WW**

A 1920s mushroom top millefiore table lamp.

15.5in (39.5cm) high

**$600-900**      **GCC**

An Art Deco glass vase, with green and gold swirls.

c1925      8.25in (21cm) high

**$700-1,000**      **MOD**

An Art Deco Décorchement glass bowl, in brown and smoky glass, with an angular design.

c1925      4.75in (12cm) wide

**$12,000-18,000**      **MACK**

## A CLOSER LOOK AT AN ART DECO DÉCORCHEMENT GLASS BOWL

The French glassmaker François-Emile Décorchemont (1880-1971) set up a workshop in Coches in 1902. Here he produced thick-walled pâte-de-verre vases and bowls.

Décorchemont's pieces tended to have smooth interiors and textured exteriors.

Décorchemont pieces were colored with metallic oxides and decorated with pâte-de-crystal. In this technique, a paste of adhesive substance and powdered glass was applied to a mold in layers and then fired. The technique is fairly rare as it was prone to failure.

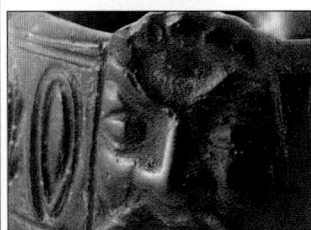

An Art Deco Décorchement glass bowl, in greens, brown, and black, decorated with a male face.

c1925      4.75in (12cm) high

**$5,000-8,000**      **MACK**

An Art Deco Décorchemont glass bowl, in blue, black, and turquoise, with a stylized flower design.

c1925      11in (28cm) wide

**$2,800-3,200**      **MACK**

An Arts & Crafts brass-washed hammered metal chandelier, with five cylindrical fixtures lined in caramel slag glass hanging from a ring frame, minor wear, unmarked.

*30in (75cm) high*

**$2,200-2,800** **DRA**

An Arts & Crafts hammered copper hanging fixture, with four pendant lanterns of yellow slag glass, suspended by hanging chains from a square ceiling plate, original patina, unmarked.

*30in (76cm) high*

**$1,800-2,200** **DRA**

An Arts & Crafts table lamp, with a four-sided oak base and flaring shade inset with four panels of newer caramel slag glass, one loose, refinished, unmarked.

*22in (55cm) high*

**$700-1,000** **DRA**

An Arts & Crafts brass and copper extending standard lamp, in the manner of W.A.S. Benson, with a turned column and applied tendril decoration, three scrolling and twisted brackets on a tripod base.

*57.5in (144cm) high*

**$500-700** **L&T**

Three Arts & Crafts wicker shades, each lined in new silk, two conical, one with a flat top.

*largest 18in (45.5cm) diam*

**$600-900** **DRA**

Two Arts & Crafts wicker shades, each lined in silk with a flat top, one with original silk.

*16in (40.5cm) diam*

**$400-600** **DRA**

## HANDEL

■ The Handel factory (1885-1936), Meriden, Connecticut, is famed for its extensive range of decorative glass lamps.

■ The factory is known for its reverse-painting – a painstaking technique that involved sandblasting the shade, coating it with glue and firing it, before painting the interior with a design.

■ It also produced leaded shades and a range with a 'pebbled' texture achieved by melting glass beads on the surface of a lamp.

■ Lamps are typically hemispherical and are usually signed. Early versions have holes to the top to allow for oil or kerosene.

■ From 1902, the company began to design and produce its own bases – usually in white metal, but sometimes in bronze.

■ Shades by named and well-known designers are particularly valuable. Look for examples painted by John Bailey.

■ It also made glassware and china, which are rare and valuable.

An Arts & Crafts Handel oak leaf lamp, with overlay style leading.

*c1910* *14in (35cm) high*

**$5,000-8,000** **GAL**

An Arts & Crafts Handel lamp, bronze leading on a mixed metal base, simulated rivet detail to the shade.

*c1910* *21.75in (55cm) high*

**$5,000-8,000** **GAL**

An Arts & Crafts Handel boudoir lamp.

*c1910* *13.75in (35cm) high*

**$3,000-4,000** **GAL**

An Arts & Crafts Handel desk lamp, with a band of roses design.

*14.25in (36cm) high*

**$3,000-4,000** **GAL**

An Arts & Crafts Handel lamp, with a painted floral band.

*c1910* *20.5in (52cm) high*

**$4,000-6,000** **GAL**

An Arts & Crafts Handel reverse-painted scenic lamp.

c1910     23.5in (60cm) high

**$12,000-18,000**     **GAL**

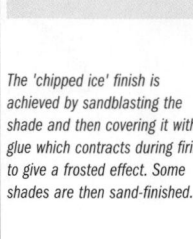

An Arts & Crafts Handel hanging lamp, in frosted and handpainted etched glass with a hammered copper mount.

c1910     26in (66cm) high

**$7,000-10,000**     **GAL**

A Handel table lamp, with bronzed base and reverse-painted chipped glass shade, cloth label and "Handel 7039".

23.5in (60cm) high

**$7,000-10,000**     **DRA**

A Handel reverse-painted table lamp, with a Winter dusk landscape, marked "Handel".

24.5in (62.5cm) high

**$1,800-2,200**     **DN**

## A CLOSER LOOK AT A HANDEL LAMP

The 'chipped ice' finish is achieved by sandblasting the shade and then covering it with glue which contracts during firing to give a frosted effect. Some shades are then sand-finished.

The design was painted, with great skill, on the interior and exterior of the shade. This technique creates a dramatic effect.

Most Handel lamps are signed on the shade border and metalwork.

Handel opened a foundry in 1902 and began to produce bases as well as shades. Bases were designed to complement the shade. Most were made of patinated white metal.

Rare Handel lamps can rival Tiffany lamps in value.

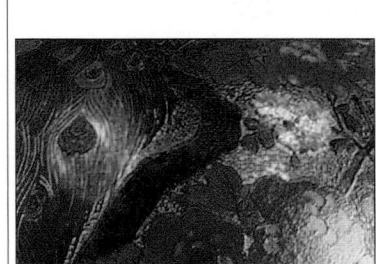

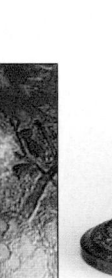

A rare Handel 'Peacock' lamp, the reverse and obverse painted shade with a cameo peacock with gold iridescent finish, flowers and leaves, against an amber chipped ice background, the Handel base with marble disk foot, three legs and a three-socket cluster, the base and shade ring heavily enameled with gold, some chipping to enamel on base and minor corrosion.

24.5in (62cm) high

**$40,000-50,000**     **JDJ**

A rare Handel 'Bird of paradise' table lamp, reverse-painted against a black background with chipped ice exterior, enameled gold base, with original amber glass prisms and matching glass finial, shade signed "Handel 7026" and artist signed "Broggi".

24in (61cm) high

**$20,000-30,000**     **JDJ**

An early 20thC Handel glass and patinated metal desk lamp, cloth label on felt base, shade inscribed "No 6577".

13.25in (33.5cm) high

**$800-1,200**     **S&K**

An early 20thC Handel leaded glass chandelier, composed of tiles with stylized cornucopia and flowers, impressed "HANDEL".

20.5in (51cm) diam

**$1,800-2,200**     **S&K**

A Handel hanging chandelier, the chipped ice shade, the mounting fixture in bronze, marked "5-66827".

2in (30.5cm) diam

**$4,000-6,000**     **JDJ**

A Handel table lamp, with apple blossom leaded slag glass shade, new base patina, new cap, stamped "HANDEL".

22in (55cm) high

**$1,800-2,200**     **DRA**

A Handel piano lamp with cylindrical caramel leaded glass shade, overlaid with brick pattern and lyre, bronze-patinated adjustable base, unmarked.

*12in (30cm) high*

**$1,200-1,800**  DRA

A Handel floor lamp stand, with a new art glass shade by Lundberg Studios, the adjustable harp-shaped shade holder with original mottled, bronzed patina, base unmarked.

*57in (142.5cm) high*

**$2,200-2,800**  DRA

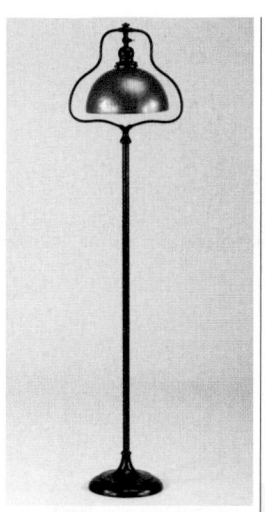

A Handel double student lamp, the base with bronze finish and two high sweeping arms supporting contemporary damascene replacement shades, base signed with cloth tag "Handel Lamps", minor blistering.

*20in (51cm) high*

**$1,800-2,200**  JDJ

## TIFFANY

A Tiffany 'Crocus' table lamp, with a leaded glass shade, the patinated bronze foot decorated with 'Celtic knobs', signed "TIFFANY STUDIOS NEW YORK 25904".

*c1910    23.5in (58.5cm) high*

**$40,000-45,000**  QU

An unusual Tiffany table lamp, with a feather-pull twin-socket glass base, copper foot and a painted and quilted mesh Chinese shade, stamped "Tiffany Furnaces", damage.

*22in (55cm) high*

**$5,000-8,000**  DRA

### A CLOSER LOOK AT A TIFFANY LAMP

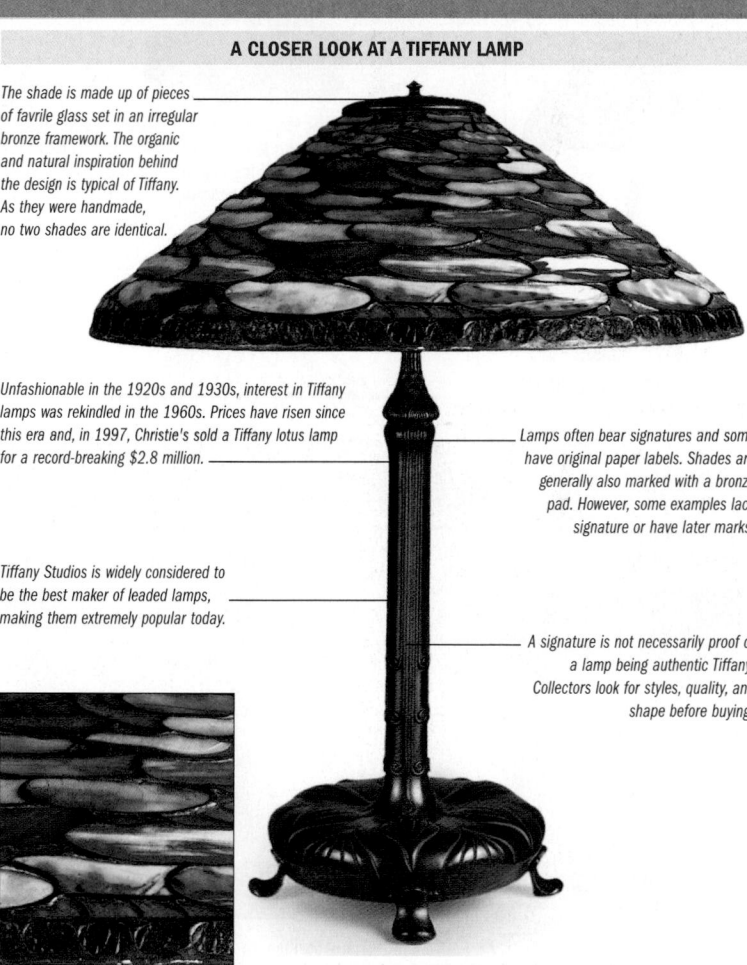

The shade is made up of pieces of favrile glass set in an irregular bronze framework. The organic and natural inspiration behind the design is typical of Tiffany. As they were handmade, no two shades are identical.

Unfashionable in the 1920s and 1930s, interest in Tiffany lamps was rekindled in the 1960s. Prices have risen since this era and, in 1997, Christie's sold a Tiffany lotus lamp for a record-breaking $2.8 million.

Lamps often bear signatures and some have original paper labels. Shades are generally also marked with a bronze pad. However, some examples lack signature or have later marks.

Tiffany Studios is widely considered to be the best maker of leaded lamps, making them extremely popular today.

A signature is not necessarily proof of a lamp being authentic Tiffany. Collectors look for styles, quality, and shape before buying.

A Tiffany 'Lily Pad' mushroom-shaped table lamp, with a shallow, conical, leaded glass shade, the slender reeded stem with bud ornaments above a bronze foot with four leaf-like feet, stamped on underside "TIFFANY STUDIOS NEW YORK 357".

*c1910    25.25in (64cm) high*

**$80,000-100,000**  QU

## TIFFANY

- Louis Comfort Tiffany founded an interior design firm in 1879. Designs included stained-glass windows. In the 1890s he established Tiffany Studios to produce his own glass.
- Tiffany had been fascinated by stained glass since visiting Byzantine churches in his youth, in particular, the effects of daylight on colored glass.
- By making lamps, he was able to experiment with decorative glass and artificial light while bringing his work to a wider domestic audience.
- The first leaded shades included Nautilus, Dragonfly, and Wisteria. By 1906, over 125 types were on sale.
- Shades tended to be hemispherical in shape and designs ranged from simple geometrical patterns to complex depictions of flowers, foliage, and insects.
- The lamps were handmade by laying stained glass onto wooden molds.

DECORATIVE ARTS

A Tiffany table lamp, decorated with green acorns, the base with floral design, the shade marked "Tiffany Studios New York", the base marked "Tiffany Studios New York 357" and "S171".

*22in (56cm) high*

**$20,000-25,000**          **JDJ**

A Tiffany 'Arrowroot' table lamp, the green paneled shade with mottled arrowroot leaves, shade marked "Tiffany Studios New York 1496-8", base on five ball feet, lightly ribbed stem with a three light cluster, marked "Tiffany Studios New York 394".

*25in (63.5cm) high*

**$65,000-70,000**          **JDJ**

A 20thC Tiffany 'Crocus' table lamp, four inverted clusters of spring flowers, knob with seven cabochon jewels, baseplate stamped "S216 437 Tiffany Studios New York".

*24in (61cm) high*

**$20,000-25,000**          **SK**

A Tiffany 'Daffodil' table lamp, the base with teardrop design and teardrop cluster, the shade marked "Tiffany Studios New York", the base marked "Tiffany Studios New York 6842".

*22.5in (57cm) high*

**$40,000-45,000**          **JDJ**

An early 20thC Tiffany 'Daffodil' table lamp, cylindrical standard with wirework, leaf decoration on base, shade signed "Tiffany Studios New York", base signed "Tiffany Studios, 6840".

*22.25in (56.5cm) high*

**$30,000-35,000**          **SK**

An early 20thC Tiffany Studios 'Dragonfly' table lamp, a conical shade depicting seven dragonflies with twenty-one oval gold jewels and dore metalwork, shade stamped "Tiffany Studios New York 1495", on standard base in turtle back design with verdigris dore finish, baseplate stamped "Tiffany Studios New York 587".

*24in (61cm) high*

**$45,000-50,000**          **SK**

An early 20thC Tiffany Studios 'Poinsettia' table lamp, leaded mottled glass, shade stamped "TIFFANY STUDIOS NEW YORK 548", replaced pulls.

*22in (56cm) high*

**$47,000-50,000**          **SK**

An early 20thC Tiffany Studios 'Pomegranate' table lamp, green Favrile segments, openwork base, shade signed "Tiffany Studios New York", base signed.

*19.5in (49.5cm) high*

**$22,000-24,000**          **SK**

A Tiffany 'Pomegranate' table lamp, the base with a red-brown patina, the shade marked "Tiffany Studios New York", the base marked "Tiffany Studios New York 533".

*21.75in (55cm) high*

**$18,000-20,000**          **JDJ**

A Tiffany Studios leaded glass and bronze library lamp, the bronze standard with green patina, signed and numbered, the shade with leaf-motif horizontal band, signed.

*16in (40.5cm) diam*

**$7,000-10,000**          **ISA**

An early 20thC Tiffany Studios geometric table lamp, with lower border accented by triangular line decoration, stamped "1900 Tiffany Studios New York", baseplate stamped.

*21in (53.5cm) high*

**$20,000-25,000**          **SK**

An early 20thC Tiffany table lamp, dore shade of caramel and green slag glass, on a gold dore base, signed on shade and base "Tiffany Studios New York".

*20in (51cm) high*

**$7,000-10,000** SK

A Tiffany Colonial lamp, the mottled dichroic glass panels golden-yellow, the shade signed "Tiffany Studios New York 1684", the base marked "Tiffany ...".

*21.5in (54.5cm) high*

**$17,000-20,000** JDJ

A large Tiffany table lamp, with a green leaded glass geometric shade on a bronze base, with verdigris patina, marked "Tiffany Studios New York".

*30.5in (77.5cm) high*

**$24,000-26,000** DRA

A Tiffany leaded glass and bronze 'Nautilus' desk lamp, the shell-form shade paneled in opalescent green glass, "Tiffany Studios New York 400".

*15.5in (39.5cm) high*

**$10,000-12,000** DRA

A Tiffany bronze and leaded glass floor lamp, re-patinated stand, the green tile and leaded domed shade signed "TIFFANY STUDIOS NEW YORK 1507".

*66in (168cm) high*

**$24,000-26,000** ISA

An early 20thC Tiffany Studios counterbalance floor lamp, gold dore finish, base stamp "Tiffany Studios New York 681", and shade with four rows of fourteen panels, unsigned.

*52.5in (133.5cm) high*

**$3,000-5,000** SK

An early 20thC Tiffany 'Pomegranate' hanging lamp, inverted geometric dome, signed "Tiffany Studios, New York".

*27in (68.5cm) high*

**$11,000-13,000** SK

An early 20thC Moorish Tiffany gold Favrile glass chandelier, the main ring scroll wirework suspending six Favrile shades and 18 chains, centered by a Favrile glass shade, signed.

*34in (86.5cm) high*

**$23,000-25,000** SK

One of a pair of 20thC Tiffany-style bronze large wall lanterns, square form with arched bracket, leaded green glass-paneled sides.

*22in (56cm) high*

**$6,000-9,000 pair** FRE

A pair of Tiffany turtleback glass and bronze wall sconces, each with four iridescent turtlebacks within a verdigris bronze framework with hinged slag glass base panel.

*21.5in (54.5cm) long*

**$65,000-70,000** SK

## OTHER LEADED LIGHTING

A Bigelow & Kennard water lily leaded table lamp, the base with three light cluster, marked "Bigelow. Kennard & Co. Boston" and "Bigelow Studios".

*22.5in (57cm) high*

**$8,000-12,000** JDJ

A signed Bradley & Hubbard table lamp, the ten-panel shade with metal overlay, backed by carmel slag glass, on a cast base.

*29in (73.5cm) high*

**$1,800-2,200** JDJ

A Chicago mosaic water lily table lamp, on a classically shaped base with three-light cluster, slight damage.

*25in (63.5cm) high*

**$2,200-2,800** JDJ

An American Art Nouveau slag glass table lamp, the stand patinated metal molded as a leafy column, marked "Hubbell".

*c1900*     *29in (72.5cm) high*

**$2,800-3,200**    **S&K**

A Wilkinson table lamp with a pink and green leaded glass shade on a bronzed three-socket classical base with rams' heads, stamped "250".

*24in (60cm) high*

**$3,000-4,000**    **DRA**

An Arts & Crafts table lamp with a four-sided metal base with two sockets in verdigris patina topped by a flaring double-layered leaded glass shade with stylized pattern, crack to one pane, unmarked.

*24in (60cm) high*

**$1,800-2,200**    **DRA**

A Roycroft hammered copper table lamp, designed by Dard Hunter, the shade of leaded slag glass on a classical base with riveted bands and ring pulls, topped by three sockets, orb and cross mark, replaced cord.

*23in (58.5cm) high*

**$38,000-40,000**    **DRA**

An early 20thC bronze and slag glass table lamp, on a single socket with acorn pull, base relief decorated with leaves and berries, unsigned.

*14.5in (37cm) high*

**$1,200-1,800**    **SK**

A slag glass and bronze table lamp, green and white geometric glass paneled shade on baluster-form bronze base, unsigned.

*c1920*     *26.25in (67cm) high*

**$5,000-8,000**    **SK**

An early 20thC Pansy table lamp, stained and leaded glass, three-socket standard, verdigris weighted metal base.

*17.25in (44cm) diam*

**$12,000-14,000**    **SK**

A mid-20thC slag glass and metal overlay table lamp, of hexagonal form, green slag glass overlaid in blackened sheet metal, hand-signed.

*c1940*     *24.75in (63cm) high*

**$800-1,200**    **SK**

A 20thC metal overlay and slag glass table lamp, shade with gridwork and border of cherries, riveted strapwork standard, moss-green patina, unsigned.

*25in (63.5cm) high*

**$2,200-2,800**     **SK**

A 20thC table lamp, six curved slag glass panels with stylized Art Nouveau metal overlay, on ribbed standard with relief decoration at base.

*15.75in (40cm) diam*

**$220-280**     **SK**

A bent panel table lamp, the shade with eight metal filigreed panels backed by carmel slag glass, on an embossed metal base with single socket.

*22in (56cm) high*

**$500-800**     **JDJ**

A Rayo kerosene floor lamp, the heavy cast base decorated with garland and leaves, the bent slag glass panel shade with overlay metal design, signed.

*69in (175.5cm) high*

**$2,200-2,800**     **JDJ**

## A CLOSER LOOK AT A GUSTAV STICKLEY LANTERN

*Artisans who worked in the Arts & Crafts style, like Gustav Stickely, often used handcrafted techniques such as planishing. The copper here has been shaped using this method which leaves a pleasing hammer-textured surface.*

*The inclusion of original features such as the chain and square ceiling cap gives this piece added desirability.*

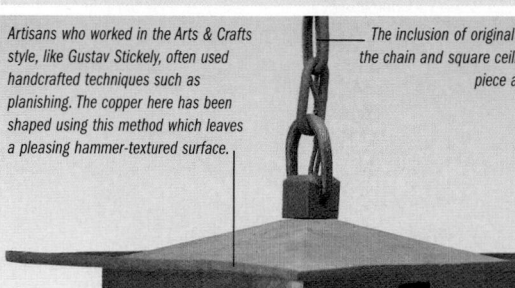

*This rare example, marked by one of the leading figures in the Arts & Crafts movement, is highly sought after.*

*The stylized motifs in the leaded glass are typical of the Arts & Crafts style, looking to nature for inspiration and incorporating organic shapes into designs.*

A rare four-sided lantern, by Gustav Stickley, with an overhanging hammered copper top on panels of hammered amber leaded glass depicting stylized flowers, complete with original chain and square ceiling cap, circular Craftsman stamp.

*13in (33cm) high*

**$350,000-380,000**     **DRA**

A 20thC leaded glass chandelier shade, parasol form of mottled spring green slag glass with drop border of leaves, undulating rim, cracks.

*14in (35.5cm) drop*

**$800-1,200**     **SK**

A geometric leaded glass piano lamp, attributed to Suess, on a bronze tone base with impressed design of lyre and reeds, marked "5-66637".

*9.5in (24cm) wide*

**$1,200-1,800**     **JDJ**

An early 20thC Bradley & Hubbard table lamp, reverse-painted shade depicting eight lilies, shade decorated on the exterior with textured brown blades, on a patinated metal strapwork base, maker's stamp on standard.

*22in (56cm) high*

**$3,000-5,000**     **SK**

A reverse-painted table lamp, by Moe Bridges, shade with scenic view of trees and hills, signed to edge "Moe Bridges-Co-18-2" and inside with artist's initials "H.H.", the copper colored base with green enamel highlights to the impressed designs.

*22.5in (57cm) high*

**$3,000-4,000**     **JDJ**

An early 20thC reverse-painted table lamp, by Moe Bridges, textured exterior, base with incised linear decoration, patinated black body, shade signed, initialed and with raised maker's mark on base.

*c1925*     *20.25in (51.5cm) high*

**$1,800-2,200**     **SK**

A pair of Jefferson mantel lamps, shades reverse-painted with a sunset scene, each shade is marked "1001-R", base with rope-turn stem.

*15.5in (39.5cm) high*

**$1,200-1,800**     **JDJ**

An early 20thC Jefferson reverse-painted table lamp, shade decorated with hollyhocks, raised on patinated bronze color base, shade no. 1884, base with maker's stamp.

*21in (53.5cm) high*

**$3,000-5,000**     **SK**

A Phoenix reverse-painted table lamp, the shade with a night scene, the base with embossed leaf and flower design, some corrosion to base.

*22in (55cm) high*

**$300-500**     **JDJ**

A reverse-painted parrot table lamp, the milk glass shade with parrots sitting on a branch, base painted in bright gold, numbered "5-66853".

*23.5in (59.5cm) high*

**$2,200-2,800**     **JDJ**

An early 20thC reverse-painted table lamp, dome shade depicting a winter landscape at sunset with a mill house and flowing water, double socket, scroll, and leaf relief decorated standard base.

*24.5in (62.5cm) high*

**$1,800-2,200**     **SK**

A 20thC Tiffany Studios bronze dore lily lamp, three gold Favrile shades on arched stems, faint "L.C.T." signature on shade, base with impressed mark, fracture repairs to shades.

*13in (33cm) high*

**$2,200-2,800** SK

A Tiffany Studios bronze dore lily lamp, with slender gold iridescent glass lily-form shades, shades unsigned, lamp signed on base "Tiffany Studios 320".

*8.75in (22cm) high*

**$2,200-2,800** SK

A Tiffany 'Arabian' lamp, decorated with a gold and platinum snakeskin design on a butterscotch ground, shade signed "LCT", base signed "L.C. Tiffany Favrile", harp on base reattached.

*13in (33cm) high*

**$5,000-7,000** JDJ

A Tiffany six-light lily lamp, with a rare base and six gold Favrile glass lily shades, signed "Tiffany Studios New York S1554", shades signed "LCT".

*20in (51cm) high*

**$20,000-25,000** JDJ

A Tiffany Studios ten-light lamp, with a gold dore ten stem lily base, supporting ten Favrile glass lily shades with butterscotch colored vertical ribbing, shades signed "LCT", base signed "Tiffany Studios New York" and numbered.

*20in (51cm) high*

**$45,000-50,000** JDJ

A Tiffany counter-balance desk lamp, with platinum damascene decoration, on a bronze counter balance base, shade signed "LCT Favrile", base signed "Tiffany Studios New York 415".

*16in (40.5cm) high*

**$17,000-19,000** JDJ

A Tiffany damascene desk lamp, the green Favrile shade decorated in a damascene pattern, on a bronze base, shade signed "LCT", base signed "Tiffany Studios New York 331".

*12in (30.5cm) high*

**$11,000-13,000** JDJ

A Tiffany table lamp with a glass shade in green and gold damascene on a fluted bronze base in verdigris patina, base stamped "Tiffany Studios New York 617", shade signed "L.C.T. Favrile".

*19in (48.5cm) high*

**$12,000-14,000** DRA

A Tiffany desk lamp, with decorated and ribbed Favrile glass shade, on a Tiffany Studios base with brown patina finish and Art Nouveau leaf pattern, the shade signed "LCT", the base signed.

*14in (35.5cm) high*

**$10,000-12,000** JDJ

A Tiffany lamp, with a tapering Arabian Favrile glass shade, the base with original Bakelite switch, shade marked "L.C.T.", base stamped "Tiffany Studios New York, 606", slight damage.

*16in (40cm) high*

**$5,000-8,000** DRA

A Tiffany Studios bronze and glass lamp, the shade etched "L.C.T." and base stamped "TIFFANY STUDIOS NEW YORK 424," original finial and one foot missing.

*18in (45cm) high*

**$7,000-10,000** FRE

A Tiffany bronze lamp, with fluted base and single-socket adjustable harp top around a grapevine shade with green glass lining, stamped "Tiffany Studios New York, 419".

*13.5in (34cm) high*

**$5,000-8,000** DRA

A Tiffany table lamp, with bronze and a Corona art glass feather-pulled shade, base stamped "Tiffany Studios New York, 424", shade unmarked, damage, restoration.

*17.25in (43cm) high*

**$2,800-3,200** DRA

A Tiffany bronze fluted table lamp base with adjustable harp top with a single socket, brass acid-etched finish, stamped "Tiffany Studios, New York".

*13.5in (34cm) high*

**$2,200-2,800** DRA

A rare Tiffany student oil lamp, with an adjustable bronze base with an Oriental-style rope pattern, two hemispherical gold Damascene glass shades, original patina, shades etched "L.C.T.", base unmarked, electrified.

*37in (92.5cm) wide*

**$18,000-22,000** DRA

A Tiffany Studios bronze and leaded glass double student lamp, with blown glass shades, old fittings, each shade with a tag stamped "TIFFANY STUDIOS NEW YORK".

*29in (72.5cm) high*

**$18,000-22,000** FRE

A Tiffany counter-balance floor lamp, with a five-legged bronze base topped by an adjustable arm with a ball and a Favrile glass shade, original patina, shade marked "L.C.T.", base stamped "Tiffany Studios, New York, 468".

*52in (130cm) high*

**$12,000-18,000** DRA

A Tiffany Studios bronze light fixture, with six lights and bronze balls on chains, some flaking to original verdigris patina, unmarked.

*18in (45cm) diam*

**$28,000-35,000** DRA

## ART GLASS

A pair of Quezel shades, in iridescent green with white pulled feather decoration, signed on fitter "QUEZEL", one fitter has small chip.

*9.5in (24.25cm) high*

**$1,200-1,800** JDJ

One of a pair of art glass shades, attributed to Luster Art, with iridescent gold and green pulled feather decoration with iridescent gold interior, minor wear.

*6in (15cm) high*

**$1,200-1,800 pair** JDJ

One of a pair of Quezel sconces, each with a shaped arm supporting a signed gold iridescent Quezel shade, possible repairs.

*Shade 5in (13cm) high*

**$400-600 pair** JDJ

An iridescent gold art glass shade, with vertical ribbing and a scalloped edge, unsigned.

*5.25in (13.5cm) high*

**$120-180** JDJ

An early 20thC Pairpoint puffy 'Papillon' table lamp, blown-out domed shade with butterflies, mounted on a silvered metal base, signed "Pairpoint".

*base 21in (53.5cm) high*

**$5,000-7,000** SK

An American Arts & Crafts hammered copper lamp, by Roycroft.

*c1910* *20.5in (52cm) high*

**$3,000-4,000** GAL

A Roycroft hammered copper and mica single socket table lamp with riveted heraldic shade lined with a band of mica, original dark patina and mica, orb and cross mark.

*15in (38cm) high*

**$3,000-5,000** DRA

A fine Samuel Yellin wrought iron table lamp, isinglass, stamped.

*c1925* *24.5in (61cm) high*

**$8,000-12,000** FRE

A 20thC Samuel Yellin large wrought iron table lamp with mica shade, pricket-form finial, spiral-turned standard, ribbed dish base on tripod ribbed pad feet.

*30in (76cm) high*

**$8,000-12,000** FRE

An American Arts & Crafts copper and glass lamp.

*19.75in (50cm) high*

**$1,200-1,800** GAL

An early 20thC Quezal hanging lamp, pulled feather decoration in green and gold, white interior, held by three chains, signed "Quezal" on fitter.

*23in (58.5cm) high*

**$4,000-6,000** SK

A Steuben blue moss agate crackle glass lamp base, mounted on an ornate acanthus leaf base, with a two light cluster and blue glass finial.

*29in (73.5cm) high*

**$6,000-9,000** JDJ

A rare Steuben Pegasus lamp base, style #8496, the yellow background with acid-cut back and enameled Pegasus winged horse, with gold Aurene, black Aurene and black enamel, mounted on a brass or bronze ornate openwork foot, with a four light cluster.

*35in (89cm) high*

**$13,000-15,000** JDJ

A rare Gustav Stickley hammered copper chandelier, with pierced hearts hanging from a central ring, with frosted glass liners, with chain and ceiling cap, original patina.

*12in (30cm) diam*

**$12,000-18,000** DRA

An early 20thC Carder Steuben brown Aurene glass shade on a brass bridge lamp base, shade of iridescent light brown glass with iridescent 'Intarsia' rim border, supported on a brass harp.

*c1910* *57in (145cm) high*

**$3,000-5,000** SK

## ART DECO

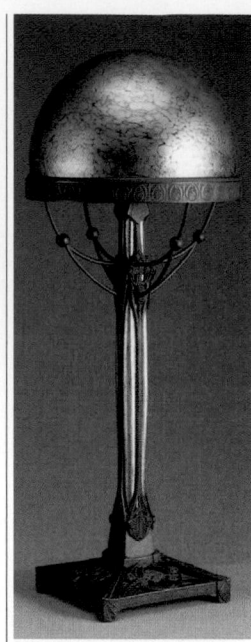

A rare Austrian Secessionist table lamp, with two sockets, its embossed and pierced bronze base with Glasgow roses on a mahogany frame and blown art glass stem, topped by an art glass shade with oilspot pattern, re-wired, unmarked.

*27in (68.5cm) high*

**$8,000-12,000**     **DRA**

An Art Deco decorated lamp, by Oscar Bach.

*26in (66cm) high*

**$5,000-8,000**     **MOD**

One of a pair of Art Deco candlestick-style lamps, by Edgar Brandt, with dove, berries, and foliage decoration.

*Frenchman Edgar Brandt (1880-1960) began creating metalwork from an early age. He became famous for his 'Oasis' screen which took a prize at 1925 Paris Exhibition. Brandt opened a studio, Ferrobrandt, in New York, to complete commissions for skyscrapers and domestic ware. His work captured the essence of the machine age.*

*c1925*    *16.25in (41cm) high*

**$12,000-18,000 pair**    **MOD**

An Art Deco silver and glass lamp by Desny.

*c1925*     *5in (13cm) high*

**$3,000-5,000**    **MOD**

An Art Deco lamp, in glass and metal by Marc Erol.

*c1925*    *15.75in (40cm) high*

**$2,800-3,200**    **MOD**

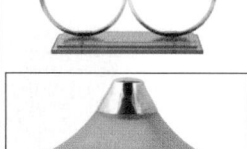

An Art Deco three-lamp set, by Marc Erol.

*c1925*    *20.75in (53cm) wide*

**$3,000-5,000**    **MOD**

An Art Deco wrought iron lamp base by Serva, with leaf and berry decoration, the orange glass shade by Muller Frères.

*c1925*    *17.75in (45cm) high*

**$3,000-4,000**    **MOD**

An Art Deco dinanderie lamp, with original shade, with floral decoration.

*c1925*    *12.25in (31cm) diam*

**$2,800-3,200**    **MOD**

A French Art Deco wrought-iron and bronze lamp, unsigned.

*c1925*     *17in (43cm) high*

**$3,000-4,000**    **MOD**

A large Art Deco lamp, in wood and metal, with a bird design.

*c1940*    *23.25in (59cm) high*

**$1,200-1,800**    **MOD**

A large Art Deco glass ceiling light, of canted square form, the frosted glass sides with deeply molded and ribbed glass blocks, a frosted glass base, with a patinated brass frame and original hanging chain.

*23.25in (58cm) wide*

**$1,800-2,200**    **L&T**

A Samuel Yellin wrought iron lantern and bracket, Philadelphia, with brass fittings.

***Provenance:*** *This lantern flanked an entrance to the Central Savings Bank in New York City, one of Yellin's largest bank commissions.*

*c1925*    *85in (212.5cm) high*

**$7,000-10,000**    **FRE**

A Swedish Art Deco alabaster chandelier, with angular design.

*c1925*    *16in (40.5cm) diam*

**$3,000-4,000**    **LANE**

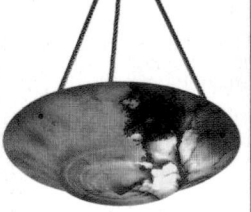

A Swedish Art Deco alabaster chandelier, with angular design.

*c1925*     *17in (43cm) diam*

**$3,000-4,000**    **LANE**

An Art Deco chromium and black lacquered electrolier, with four stepped branches, each with square section nozzles and cube pendants, a square column with cube pendant and box ceiling fixture.

*77in (192.5cm) high*

**$300-500**    **L&T**

An Arts & Crafts ebonized mantel clock, in the Anglo-Japanese style, inset with satsuma tiles.

*c1885*      16in (40.5cm) high

**$3,000-5,000**      **PUR**

An Arts & Crafts ebonized clock with red pillars, in the style of Bruce Talbert.

*c1880*      20in (51cm) high

**$800-1,200**      **PUR**

An Arts & Crafts oak bracket clock of architectural form, attributed to George Walton, with Queen Anne top, tapering sides and the stylized intertwined initials "GWB" carved above clock face, with Camerer Cuss movement.

*c1900*      23in (59cm) high

**$3,000-5,000**      **PUR**

An English Arts & Crafts hammered copper mantel clock, with Ruskin cabochons and dial, riveted faceted top and sides, inscribed "Dum Spectas Fugit" in repoussé, some damage, unmarked.

17.5in (44cm) high

**$3,000-5,000**      **DRA**

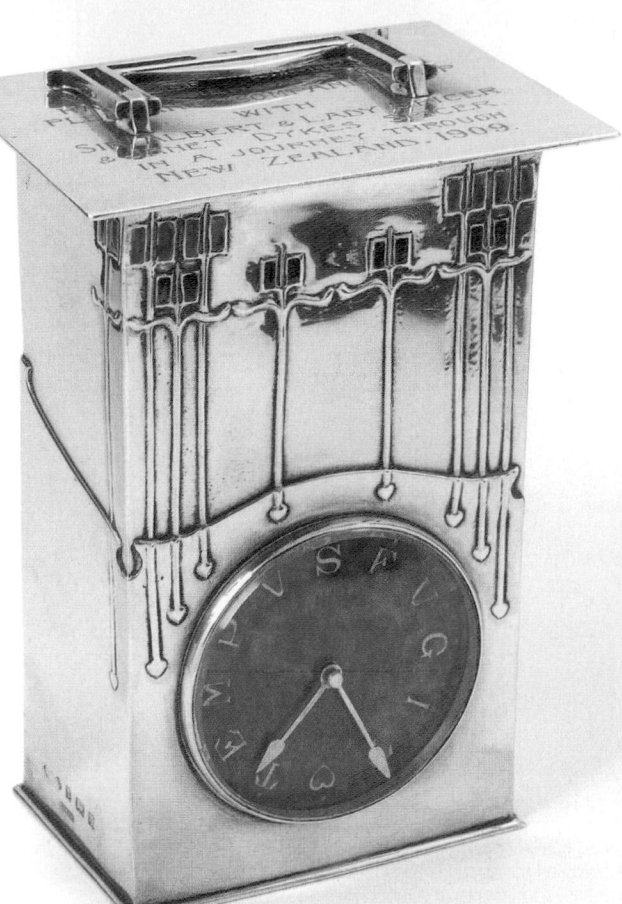

A Liberty & Co. silver Magnus clock of architectural form, with overhanging top, enameled face with "Tempus Fugit" about the dial in silver letters, with inscription to the top.

*1903*      5in (13cm) high

**$30,000-35,000**      **VDB**

An Arts & Crafts silver-plated mantel clock with a copper face, brass plaque inscription reads "Presented to Mr. H.V.H. Everard by the members of the Ramblers Club of the Southwestern Polytechnic, Chelsea, S.W., on the occasion of his marriage, 1909".

14in (36cm) high

**$1,800-2,200**      **PUR**

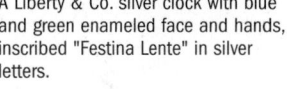

A Liberty & Co. silver clock with blue and green enameled face and hands, inscribed "Festina Lente" in silver letters.

*c1905*      3.5in (9cm) high

**$8,000-12,000**      **VDB**

A Liberty & Co. silver repoussé mantel clock, of swept rectangular form with blue and green enameled dial.

4in (10cm) high

**$3,000-5,000**      **GORL**

An Arts & Crafts longcase grandfather clock, by Robert 'Mouseman' Thompson.

*c1930*      77in (195.5cm) high

**$18,000-25,000**      **PUR**

An Art Deco 'ATO' black and silver clock.

c1925      7.5in (19cm) wide

**$2,200-2,800**      **MOD**

A Garrad-Le Cautre clock with green face, British made with French movement.

1925      4in (10cm) high

**$800-1,200**      **TDG**

A Jaeger Le Coultre mantel timepiece, the double-sided green glass dial with pierced filigree border and pierced hands, raised on shaped base with stepped and pierced trefoil terminals.

9.25in (23cm) high

**$700-1,000**      **L&T**

An Art Deco clock by Kienzle, with a bronze case with glazed front and back, resting on a ribbed rectangular base, eight-day ruby movement.

7.5in (19.5cm) high

**$400-600**      **DN**

## A CLOSER LOOK AT AN ART DECO CLOCK

The relief decoration around the top and sides of this clock is known as 'monnaie de pape' after the plant it portrays. Lalique also used it frequently.

The pierced gilt bronze case over the face of this clock carries exceptional sculptural detailing.

Simonet Frères was an important French bronze manufacturer specializing in light fittings. Henri Dieupart was an occasional collaborator who contributed some of their best designs.

A French Art Deco bronze and enamel clock by Simonet Frères, designed by Henri Dieupart, with impressed signature.

c1925      11.5in (29cm) high

**$10,000-15,000**      **MOD**

An Art Deco wooden clock by Paul Follot, carved with a leaf pattern and stained with red, brown, and silver.

c1925      18.5in (47cm) wide

**$3,000-4,000**      **MOD**

An Art Deco frosted blue glass mantel timepiece, the machine-turned silvered dial enclosed by frame molded with scantily clad maidens kneeling on a reeded bed.

43in (17cm) high

**$700-1,000**      **L&T**

An Art Deco electric clock by Herman Miller, attributed stylistically to Gilbert Rohde, burr-wood veneered case applied with three chromed bands, dial with abstract numerals in black, maker's mark to dial and stamped underneath with number "4082B".

*The stamped number corresponds closely to design numbers known to be by Rohde.*

12.5in (33cm) wide

**$220-280**      **DN**

An Art Deco marble-faced clock, the stepped base with a geometric dial and numerals, surmounted with two spelter models of German shepherd dogs.

26in (68cm) wide

**$300-400**      **DN**

A Scottish School Arts & Crafts brass wall mirror, in the manner of Talwin Morris, the beveled plate enclosed by repoussé decorated frame with opposing peacocks enclosing five triangular turquoise Ruskin panels, inset to repoussé bosses.

*34.75in (87cm) wide*

**$4,000-6,000**     **L&T**

A Scottish School Arts & Crafts brass wall mirror, of octagonal outline, the circular beveled plate enclosed within a repoussé decorated frame with winged angels and meandering flowering tendrils.

*23.5in (59cm) wide*

**$500-800**     **L&T**

A Scottish Arts & Crafts brass wall mirror, of rectangular outline with lobed angles, the beveled plate enclosed by a repoussé decorated frame with flowering branches.

*24in (60cm) wide*

**$280-320**     **L&T**

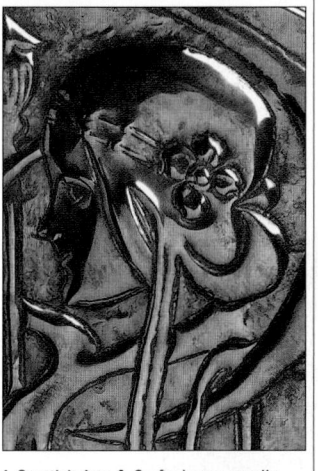

A Scottish Arts & Crafts brass candle sconce, in the manner of Margaret Gilmour, repoussé decorated with a dragonfly on a beaten ground with candle nozzle and drip tray below.

*14in (35cm) high*

**$400-600**     **L&T**

A Scottish Arts & Crafts brass candle sconce by Agnes Bankier Harvey, the shaped backplate repoussé decorated with the profile of a girl amidst poppies, above twin candle nozzles and drip tray.

*15in (37.5cm) high*

**$1,200-1,800**     **L&T**

A pair of copper and brass candlesticks, decorated with flowerheads and tendrils, unmarked.

*10.5in (26cm) high*

**$700-1,000**     **WW**

An Arts & Crafts brass ceiling light, with three tulip-shaped lamp sockets on curved stems and five brass petal-like extensions radiating from the ceiling rose.

*14.5in (37cm) diam*

**$280-320**     **DN**

A Scottish Arts & Crafts brass jardinière, of hexagonal form, repoussé decorated with panels of poppy flowers, raised on square feet.

*9.5in (24cm) diam*

**$400-600**     **L&T**

A Scottish Arts & Crafts brass jardinière, of square tapering form with projecting rim and ring handles, repoussé decorated to two sides with Celtic galleons in full sail.

*12in (30cm) wide*

**$400-600**     **L&T**

A fluted brass bowl, attributed to the Artificers' Guild and a design by Edward Spencer, internally decorated with radiating flutes with a relief medallion of a sickle and branches of mistletoe.

*6.25in (16cm) diam*

**$400-600**     **DN**

A Jan Eisenloeffel tea service, by J.K.C. Sneltjes of Haarlem, Holland, made in brass, wicker, and glass, comprising a kettle on warming stand, creamer, sugar bowl, and associated tray, kettle and creamer both marked.

*Jan Eisenloeffel's metalwork was considered avant-garde for its purity of form and functionalist aesthetic. He drew influences from Eastern and Western traditions, all of which contributed to his native Dutch 'Neue stile'.*

c1905                                                                                  tray 12in (30cm) diam

**$1,200-1,800**                                                                                          **FRE**

An Alexander Ritchie circular brass tray on stand, the pierced gallery with a broad repoussé band decorated with Celtic knotwork and centered with a roundel bearing the inscription "Iona", on a mahogany barley-twist column, the base inset with a brass panel.

38.5in (96cm) high

**$1,200-1,800**                                                                                          **L&T**

A Scottish Arts & Crafts brass wall clock, the square dial repoussé decorated with a chapter ring enclosed by four roundels depicting fairy nymphs, includes pendulum and weights.

13.5in (33.5cm) wide

**$1,200-1,800**                                                                                          **L&T**

A brass box and cover, design attributed to Edward Spencer, with fine wirework banding, centered with a circular silvered medallion showing a pelican in piety, engraved on base "From three not ungrateful young pelicans", dated "Christmas 1925".

3in (8cm) high

**$700-1,000**                                                                        **DN**

A large Lucien Bazar brass paper knife, decorated with a female figure.

c1930                       10in (25.5cm) long

**$500-800**                                      **TDG**

A Cotswold School Arts & Crafts brass fender, pierced and repoussé decorated with a frieze of opposed red squirrels eating nuts, held at the angles by brackets with decorative screws.

*The squirrel motif resembles a wrought iron radiator grille by C.A. Llewellyn-Roberts for The Birmingham Guild. Ernest Gimson also produced metalwork with squirrel and oak leaf designs, in particular a pair of brass andirons now in Cheltenham Museum.*

49.25in (123cm) wide

**$4,000-6,000**                                                                                          **L&T**

## BRONZE

A French bronze group, 'Souviens', by Henri Allouard, brown patina with golden brown highlights, inscribed "H. Allouard".

29in (72.5cm) high

**$2,800-3,200**                                                                        **FRE**

A bronze sculpture of an athlete, with dark brown patina, on a marble base, with "R. Bellair & Co. Friedrichstr 182 Berlin" foundry seal.

12.75in (32cm) high

**$1,200-1,800**                                      **FRE**

An early 20thC cold-painted Austrian bronze group by Franz Bergman, of two Arabs seated playing chess at a table on a rug base, a lamp hung from a bamboo pole above them, stamped "Bergman" under the base.

16in (40cm) high

**$800-1,200**                                      **GORL**

A cold-painted bronze figure in the style of Bergman, modeled as an Egyptian seated flanked by panthers, on red marble desk tidy base, unmarked.

*15.75in (40cm) wide*

**$2,800-3,200**          **WW**

A silvered bronze group, 'First Prize Bull', by Isidore Jules Bonheur, on silver mounted marble base, stamped "Christofle & Cie. 1274706".

*18.75in (47cm) high*

**$4,000-6,000**          **FRE**

A French Art Nouveau bronze and dore bronze plate, with fully molded dore chestnut leaves and nuts on a patinated ground, signed "A. Bouny".

*c1910          10.5in (26cm) diam*

**$400-600**          **S&K**

A bronze figure of 'Moses', after Michelangelo Buonarroti, medium brown patina, with "Reduction Meccanique a Collas" foundry seal.

*This piece is after the original, executed in 1515 in San Pietro, Rome.*

*16.5in (41cm) high*

**$2,800-3,200**          **FRE**

## A CLOSER LOOK AT A FRENCH GILT-BRONZE VASE

*This woman's features have an Asian aspect. Chalon was very influenced by Japanese style, so it is not surprising that he looked East for his idealized depiction of feminine beauty.*

*The iris is often used as a representation of night and sleep. The irises around this woman's face seem to suggest that she is waking from a dream.*

*This figure is decorated with multiple patinas, ranging from the rose-colored background to the golds on the body.*

*This woman's dress and stance are evocative of a pre-Raphaelite painting. The erotic undertones of this vase make it an enticing piece.*

*L. Chalon*

A French silvered and gilt-bronze vase, by Louis Chalon, of flaring stylized heart form with relief decoration of a smiling maiden, on a shaped square base, signed "L. Chalon".

*16in (40cm) high*

**$18,000-22,000**          **MACK**

A bronze group, 'Classical woman', by Henri Michel Antoine Chapu, brown patina, set on a marble base, inscribed "H. Chapu" and "F. Barbedienne Fondeur" and stamped "HH Made in France MM".

*27.75in (69cm) high*

**$3,000-5,000**          **FRE**

A bronze figure, 'La Zingara', by Jean Baptiste Auguste Clesinger, golden brown patina, inscribed "J. Clesinger Rome 1858" with foundry seal.

*1858*        *41in (102.5cm) high*

**$7,000-10,000**                    **FRE**

A bronze figure, 'The Shipwreck', by Georges Colin, signed on the base and inscribed on the reverse "To Frank Bailey 1885-1914".

*34in (85cm) high*

**$5,000-8,000**        **L&T**

A bronze figure, 'Gladiator', from the Continental School, with rich dark brown patina, on marble base.

*26in (65cm) high*

**$800-1,200**        **FRE**

Two 19thC Continental School bronzes, Diomedes and a classical Greek head, with dark brown patina.

*14.75in (37cm) high*

**$2,800-3,200**                    **FRE**

A bronze bust of a young woman, the drapery signed "G. Coudray", the plinth inscribed "Bakie" in relief.

*c1900*        *24.75in (63cm) high*

**$5,000-8,000**                    **RGA**

A 20thC bronze figure, by Le Couflet, of a female nude reclining in a rocking chair.

**$800-1,200**        **ROS**

A bronze group, 'The Last Drop', cast by T. Curts, with a standing cavalry officer giving his horse a drink from his hat, on naturalistic base, with signed and impressed foundry marks and stamped mark "Made in Austria".

*11.5in (29cm) high*

**$1,800-2,200**        **L&T**

A bronze group by Antoine Coysevox, depicting a classical maiden with a cherub on a bronze base with inlaid champlevé panels, brown and gilt patinas, signed by the artist and stamped "F. Barbedienne Fondeur".

*1710*        *27.5in (69cm) high*

**$3,000-5,000**        **FRE**

A bronze, 'Porteur d'eau Tunisien', by Jean Didier Debut, brown and reddish brown patinas, inscribed "Debut".

*24.75in (62cm) high*

**$2,800-3,200**        **FRE**

A bronze figure, 'Maiden with Pitcher', by Anatole J. Guillot, golden brown patina, inscribed "A. Guillot".

*29.75in (74cm) high*

**$1,800-2,200**        **FRE**

A gilt-bronze figure, 'Pan', cast from a model by Emmanuel Fremiet, on a marble base, signed in the bronze "F Barbedienne, Fondeur Paris".

*13.5in (34cm) wide*

**$1,200-1,800** **WW**

A bronze, 'Nymph with Two Dogs', by Amadeo Gennarelli, greenish-gold patina, signed "A. Gennarelli" on the base.

*31in (77.5cm) wide*

**$3,000-5,000** **S&K**

A bronze with silver patina, 'Stella', by Maurice Guiraud-Riviere, on a marble base, inscribed "Guiraud-Riviere" and "Etling, Paris".

*23in (57.5cm) high*

**$4,000-6,000** **FRE**

A bronze with silver patina, 'Danseuse à La Boule', Maurice Guiraud-Riviere, inscribed "Guiraud-Riviere" and "Etling Paris".

*24.5in (61cm) high*

**$4,000-6,000** **FRE**

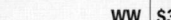

A pair of Hafenrichter Art Deco bronze figures of nude dancers, on green onyx bases, each signed "Hafenrichter".

*7.5in (19.5cm) high*

**$700-1,000** **HAMG**

A pair of Hagenauer bronze figures, cast as warriors with raffia skirts and polished brass spears, stamped marks.

*5.5in (14cm) high*

**$300-500** **L&T**

A Heintz sterling-on-bronze ashtray and matchbox holder with overlay of golfer and golf course on green patinated ground, some damage, stamped "HAMS".

*7in (17.5cm) wide*

**$180-220** **DRA**

A bronze crocodile, by Barry Jackson, brown and green patinas, on wood base, inscribed and numbered "Barry Jackson 5/10".

*35in (87.5cm) long*

**$3,000-5,000** **FRE**

A bronze figure, 'La Rosee', by E. Herbert, signed in the bronze.

*25.5in (64cm) high*

**$2,800-3,200** **L&T**

A bronze group, 'Retour de Peche', by Henryk Kossowski II, brown patina with golden brown highlights, inscribed "Kossowski Eleve de Math. Moreau".

*43.75in (109.5cm) high*

**$3,000-5,000** **FRE**

A bronze fish sculpture, by Georges Lavroff.

*c1925* *15.5in (39.5cm) high*

**$1,800-2,200** **TDG**

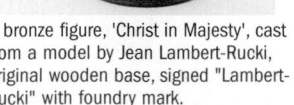

A bronze figure, 'Christ in Majesty', cast from a model by Jean Lambert-Rucki, original wooden base, signed "Lambert-Rucki" with foundry mark.

*17.75in (45cm) high*

**$5,000-7,000** **WW**

A 20thC female bronze nude, by F. de Luca, verdigris patina, signed by the artist.

*64in (160cm) high*

**$10,000-15,000**      **FRE**

A bronze group, 'Man with Child', by Gaston Veurenot Leroux, with brown patina, inscribed "G. Leroux" and "Boyer Fres Fondeur à Paris".

*37in (92.5cm) high*

**$3,000-5,000**      **FRE**

A bronze eagle by Jules Moigniez, brown patina, inscribed "J. Moigniez".

*30in (75cm) high*

**$1,800-2,200**      **FRE**

A bronze group, 'Retour de Moisson' by Mathurin Moreau, with brown patina, on a marble base, inscribed "Moreau Math".

*33.5in (84cm) high*

**$5,000-7,000**      **FRE**

A French Art Nouveau bronze and dore bronze ink stand, by Marionnet, with patinated beach nuts and leaves surrounding the single ink well, signed "A. Marionnet".

*c1910*    *7.5in (19cm) diam*

**$500-800**      **S&K**

A French Art Nouveau bronze and dore bronze ink stand and letter opener, the stand with oak leaves and acorns, the two inkwells with acorn finials, signed "A. Marionnet".

*c1910*    *13in (32.5cm) wide*

**$1,200-1,800**      **S&K**

## A CLOSER LOOK AT A BRONZE GROUP

*Mathurin Moreau flourished during the French Second Empire, a period marked by the Classical revival which can be seen at work in this piece.*

*Moreau is particularly famous for his depictions of women, including a massive statue of Marguerite, 13thC Countess of Anjou. This figure demonstrates the confidence with which he approached the female form.*

*The multiple patinas on this piece are a sign of technical expertise and an eye for subtle yet effective decoration.*

*Moreau's work often has a strong symbolic and allegorical content. This group is no exception, and has been modeled to depict 'Harmony'.*

A bronze group, 'Les Harmonies', by Mathurin Moreau, inscribed "Math. Moreau", medium and dark brown patinas.

*41.5in (104cm) high*

**$12,000-18,000**      **FRE**

A Tiffany Studios gilt bronze desk set, with stylized grapevine decoration, the vines cast as lines and scrolls, the grapes inlaid with mother-of-pearl, comprising a letter rack, inkwell, letter opener, and four blotter corners, marked "Tiffany Studios, New York".

*c1920*

**$1,800-2,200**     **S&K**

Two Tiffany pine needle desk accessories, one pine needle rocker blotter and pen brush holder, with bronze patina and carmel slag glass backing, impressed "Tiffany Studios New York" and numbered, missing brush.

**$400-600**     **JDJ**

### A CLOSER LOOK AT A TIFFANY BOX & COVER

*Louis C. Tiffany began his career as a painter. The stylized enamel strokes on this box have been executed almost as if they were oils applied with a brush.*

*Tiffany made only a small number of these enameled metal boxes. Scarcity, when combined with desirability, invariably leads to high prices at auction.*

*The colors on this box have darkened with years of handling. A similar box with better color could be expected to sell for around $10,000 more.*

*Tiffany is an iconic figure in the history of American decorative arts. His signature tends to increase the value of any given item dramatically.*

A rare Tiffany circular box and cover, enameled with a stylized spray of flowers in iridescent gold, blue, and green, in the Favrile style on a bronze ground, signed "Louis C. Tiffany".

*5in (12.5cm) diam*

**$25,000-30,000**     **DRA**

A rare Tiffany bronze pen tray with inkwell, embossed in a leaf pattern with lappets, with remnant of Favrile glass liner, original patina, stamped "TIFFANY STUDIOS NEW YORK, 10034".

*11.5in (29cm) high*

**$1,800-2,200**     **DRA**

A Tiffany Studios, New York, pen tray in cast bronze, decorated with enamel tendrils, with textured gilt finish, signed on base.

*c1920*     *10.5in (26.5cm) wide*

**$500-700**     **TDG**

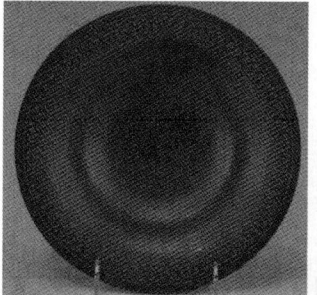

A Tiffany Studios bronze flaring bowl in gold dore finish, the rim embossed with a band of arabesques, original patina, signed "Tiffany Studios" along edge.

*8.75in (22cm) diam*

**$80-120**     **DRA**

A Tiffany Studios cast bronze paper knife, with textured gilt finish.

*c1925*     *10.5in (26.5cm) long*

**$300-400**     **TDG**

A dore finished bronze Venetian box, by Tiffany Studios, New York.

*c1915*

**$1,200-1,800**     **TDG**

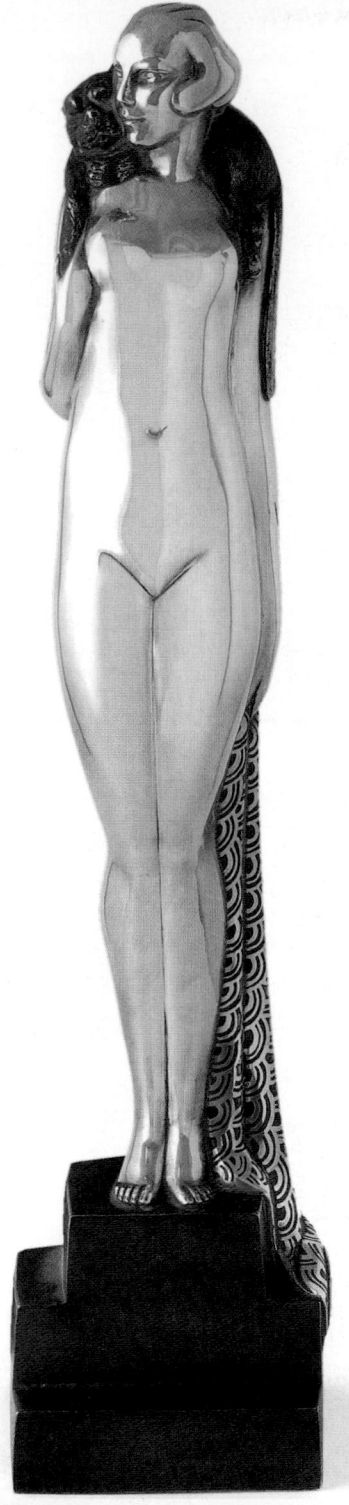

An Art Deco bronze figure, by Fayral, modeled as an exotic dancer holding a pose, on a lozenge-shaped black figured marble base, signed.

*15in (38cm) high*

**$700-1,000** ROS

An Art Deco bronze and ivory figure, inscribed "Elegante au Levrier", by Solange Bertrand.

*c1935* *11.75in (30cm) high*

**$15,000-20,000** JES

A 1930s Art Deco sculpture 'Standing Nude', by Marie-Louise Simard, of silvered, patinated, and damascened bronze, on a marble base.

*6.75in (17cm) high*

**$10,000-15,000** JES

A bronze and ivory figure of a Spanish dancer, on a rectangular marble base.

*11.75in (30cm) high*

**$2,200-2,800** WW

## A CLOSER LOOK AT A DEMÊTRE H. CHIPARUS FIGURE

Chryselephantine is the Classical technique of combining ivory with metals in sculpture. It was revived in the Art Deco period, and Chiparus was a particularly skillful exponent.

A figure with bronze hands, face, and naval would not be worth as much as this example. The ivory is carved to an extremely high standard.

Kapurthala is a district in the Punjab. Artists working within the Art Deco idiom frequently looked East for inspiration.

This dual-tone onyx base is very attractive and adds interest to this piece.

An Art Deco bronze and ivory figure, by Dakon, on marble base with alabaster dish, signed in the bronze "Dakon".

*7.5in (19cm) high*

**$2,200-2,800**　　**WW**

A cold-painted bronze and ivory figure, 'Dancer on Points', cast and carved from a model by Joe Descomps, engraved to the base "Joe Descomps".

**$18,000-22,000**　　**WW**

An Art Deco bronze and carved ivory figure, 'Dancer of Kapurthala', by Demêtre H. Chiparus, the figure raised on a stepped brown and green onyx base, signed to the base "Chiparus".

*c1925*　　　　　　　　　*22in (55cm) high*

**$35,000-45,000**　　**L&T**

A bronze figure, 'Archer', by Pierre Le Faguays, brown and silver patinas with ivory, on marble base, inscribed "Le Faguays".

*23.75in (59cm) high*

**$32,000-38,000**　　**FRE**

A cold-painted bronze and ivory figure, cast from a model by Hafenrichter, on alabaster base, signed in the bronze.

*9.75in (25cm) high*

**$1,200-1,800**　　**WW**

A cold-painted bronze and ivory figural lamp, 'Woman with Two Urns', from a model by S. Lipchytz, signed in the bronze.

*22.5in (57cm) high*

**$10,000-15,000**　　**WW**

A Lorenzl bronze and ivory figure, modeled as a dancing girl, signed in the bronze.

*11in (28cm) high*

**$2,200-2,800**　　**WW**

A bronze figure, cast from a model by Josef Lorenzl, on alabaster base, signed in the bronze "Lorenzl".

*15in (38cm) high*

**$3,000-5,000**    **WW**

A bronze figure, cast from a model by Josef Lorenzl, modeled as a female holding flowers, signed "Lorenzl".

*9in (23cm) high*

**$2,200-2,800**    **WW**

An Art Deco bronze and carved ivory figure, 'Grecian With Torch', by Ferdinand Preiss, signed in the bronze "F. Preiss".

*11.25in (28cm) high*

**$4,000-6,000**    **L&T**

A cold-painted bronze and ivory figure, 'Mandolin Player', cast and carved from a model by Ferdinand Preiss, signed.

*23.25in (59cm) high*

**$20,000-30,000**    **WW**

An Art Deco spelter lamp base, modeled as a figure with arched back, with frosted glass shade, unsigned.

*25.5in (65cm) high*

**$1,200-1,800**    **WW**

## COPPER

An Arts & Crafts copper goblet, the circular hammered bowl with three curved supports with stylized leaf terminals joined by a pierced band, bearing the legend "Then Came Spring" and with stamped mark "Geo. Spencer Baker".

*6.5in (16cm) high*

**$300-500**    **L&T**

A Benham & Froud galleried copper tray, the design attributed to Christopher Dresser, of rectangular form, the frilled rim enclosing central brass panel, engraved with a stork flying above rocks in a silver finish, apparently unmarked.

*12.25in (30.5cm) wide*

**$400-600**    **L&T**

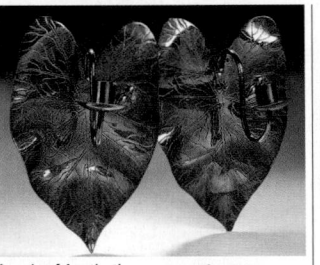

A pair of Aesthetic movement copper candle sconces, in the manner of W.A.S. Benson, each formed as a leaf stamped with veining and embossed with a frog chasing a fly, with detachable curved branches with candleholders, stamped registration mark, number 17801.

*11.25in (28cm) high*

**$700-1,000**    **L&T**

A brass, copper, and steel kettle stand, by W.A.S. Benson, the circular top pierced and cast with flowering branches raised above baluster columns resting on a floret-embossed circular base.

*7.5in (19cm) wide*

**$280-320**    **L&T**

## W.A.S. BENSON

- William Arthur Smith Benson was born in 1854 and died in 1924. Between 1880 and the outbreak of World War I, he produced art metalware of an extremely high standard from his studios in Kensington, London.
- His 1883 pamphlet, 'Notes on Some of the Minor Arts', explained his personal aesthetic, illustrated with a number of his designs.
- Unlike many of his Arts & Crafts contemporaries, Benson succeeded in making his work accessible to the mass market. He did this by embracing industrialization and mass-production techniques such as machine tooling.
- Benson's signature materials were copper and brass, the reflective properties of which he used to great effect in his light fittings.
- Pieces by Benson are often marked, sometimes with a monogram featuring his initials separated by metalworking tools.

A copper and brass twin-branch candlestick by W.A.S. Benson, the curved branches resting on a foliate support with circular copper drip-pans, counterbalanced by a fluted brass bud-shaped weight, stamped "W.A.S. Benson" in a shaped panel.

*12.5in (32cm) long*

**$3,000-4,000**    **DN**

A copper and brass plate warmer by W.A.S. Benson, with riveted decoration, the domed hinged lid with insulated handle enclosing divided interior for plates, the whole raised on shaped supports with pointed pad feet, raised on a rectangular platform base.

*17.5in (43.5cm) wide*

**$500-800**      **L&T**

A dished copper tray by W.A.S. Benson, of circular form, embossed with divided panels, the lobed edge enclosing a repoussé decorated band of flowering rose branches, stamped mark.

*19.25in (48cm) wide*

**$800-1,200**      **L&T**

A Birmingham Guild copper plate, with mark.

*c1920*      *8.25in (21cm) diam*

**$120-180**      **HBK**

A Duchess of Sutherland's Cripples' Guild copper box, of rectangular shape, the hinged domed cover with an embossed geometric border, applied with silver florets, shells and an oval plaque, stamped "D.S.C.G." with coronet.

*8.75in (22.5cm) wide*

**$500-800**      **DN**

A Duchess of Sutherland's Cripples' Guild copper goblet, based on a vessel from antiquity, with deep bowl, twin handles and spreading circular foot, with applied silvered winged cherubs, swags and other Classical motifs, stamped "D.S.C.G." below a coronet.

*7.5in (19cm) high*

**$500-800**      **DN**

A Newlyn copper tea caddy, of oval section, finely embossed with a seascape, lighthouse and sailing ship, the drop-in cover embossed "Tea" and stamped "H. Dyer".

*4.25in (10.5cm) high*

**$400-600**      **DN**

An Art Nouveau brass and copper box, with enamel decoration, stamped "Fisher 188 Strand".

*c1905*      *8.5in (21.5cm) wide*

**$800-1,200**      **TDG**

A Fivemiletown copper tray, of rectangular form with raised edges, decorated with two peacocks flanking a fruiting tree, unmarked.

*16in (40cm) wide*

**$280-320**      **WW**

A Birmingham Guild of Handicraft silvered copper mug, with scrolling frieze, inscribed "R.W.R. Nov.24 1912", stamped "BGH 41".

*1912*      *5in (12.5cm) high*

**$300-500**      **WW**

A Hagenauer copper ice bucket with applied brass trim and riveted handle, stamped "Handmade Hagenauer Wien WHW Made in Austria".

*14in (35.5cm) high*

**$2,200-2,800**      **DRA**

A rare Keswick School of Industrial Arts charger, the rim hammered in relief with a stag hunt frieze, the well with a Tudor rose, stamped "KSIA".

*18.75in (47cm) diam*

**$4,000-6,000**      **WW**

**DECORATIVE ARTS**

A Joseph Heinrichs hammered copper samovar, with sterling bands and wooden handles, stamped "Jos. Heinrichs, Paris, New York", replaced finials.

*13.5in (34cm) high*

**$180-220**　　　　　　　**DRA**

A Keswick lidded copper flagon, by W. H. Mawson, with applied strap handle, the hammer tapering body repoussé worked with the inscription "More Friends And Less Need of Them", stamped mark "W. H. Mawson".

*8.5in (21cm) high*

**$500-800**　　　　　　　**L&T**

A large Newlyn copper bowl, hammered in relief with a frieze of fish, stamped Newlyn mark.

*Newlyn metalware is the product of fishermen from the Cornish coast who took to metalwork when bad weather prevented sailing.*

*11.5in (29cm) diam*

**$800-1,200**　　　　　　　**WW**

A Newlyn twin-handled copper vase, of tapering cylindrical form with applied beaten handles, the body repoussé decorated with fish, unmarked.

**$280-320**　　　　　　　**L&T**

A John Pearson copper jardinière, with repoussé scrolling floral motifs on a hammered ground, numbered 2326 and incised "J Pearson 1897".

*8in (20cm) high*

**$400-600**　　　　　　　**HAMG**

## A CLOSER LOOK AT A COPPER CHARGER

*John Pearson's stylized bird designs are typical of pieces produced at the Newlyn Copper Class, where Pearson taught in the 1890s.*

*The slightly irregular line around the rim of this charger's shows that it was cut and beaten by hand. This kind of detail appeals to enthusiasts of the Arts & Crafts look.*

*The oak leaves and and foliage depicted on this plate are typical of the Arts & Crafts style as it was practiced in England.*

*Pearson pioneered the use of lead as a bed on which to beat copper — a closely guarded secret that allowed the development of ever-more intricate designs.*

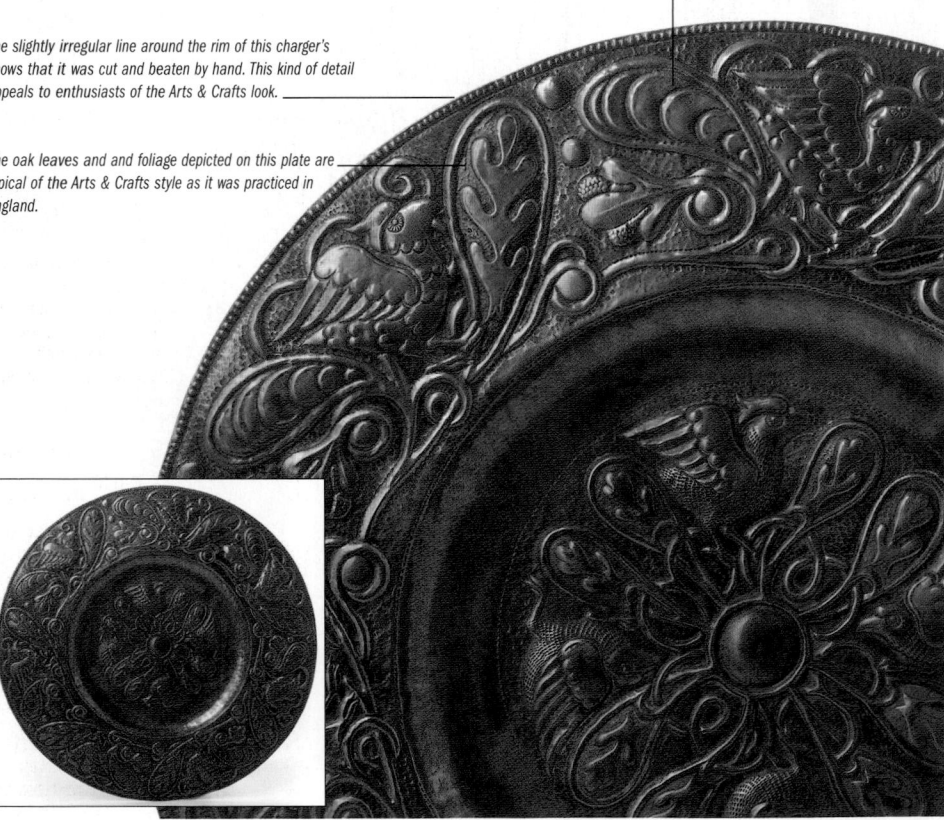

A large John Pearson copper charger, repoussé hammered with birds amongst foliage and incised "Jpearson", dated.

*1896*　　　　　　　*25.25in (63cm) diam*

**$3,000-5,000**　　　　　　　**WW**

An embossed copper jardinière, by John Pearson, the bulbous body with collar rim, initials "JP" and "1909" inscribed to underside.

*1909*      *7.75in (20cm) high*

**$700-1,000**      **ROS**

An Artificers' Guild silver and copper box and cover, designed by Edward Spencer, the finial formed as a bat with outspread wings, with mark for London.

*1831*      *4.75in (12cm) high*

**$800-1,200**      **DN**

An Artificers' Guild rectangular copper tray, the design attributed to Edward Spencer, the raised edge with silvered border and applied with silvered handles embelished with interwoven vines and foliage.

*21.5in (55cm) wide*

**$400-600**      **DN**

A copper picture frame, inset with a ceramic heart, on easel-support leather back, stamped "JS Vickery, Regent Street".

*13.25in (33cm) high*

**$700-1,000**      **WW**

An Artificers' Guild copper wall sconce, the design attributed to Edward Spencer, the back plate embossed and pierced with stylized branches of foliage, florets, and buds, the drip-pan with two wavy-edged cylindrical sconces.

*10.5in (27cm) high*

**$2,200-2,800**      **DN**

A Scottish Arts & Crafts copper mantel timepiece, by Marion Henderson Wilson, with repoussé decorated dial and case, the dial with Roman chapters, the case decorated with a flock of birds, a galleon and an angel, signed "MHW".

*16.5in (41cm) high*

**$6,000-9,000**      **L&T**

An Arts & Crafts copper timepiece, in the form of a miniature longcase clock with an overall stippled surface, the central panel embossed with Glasgow-style roses and tendrils.

*14.5in (36.5cm) high*

**$400-600**      **DN**

An Arts & Crafts silvered copper vase, the copper body overlaid with silver ivy leaves and tendrils.

*c1910*      *8in (20.5cm) high*

**$80-120**      **S&K**

An Arts & Crafts hammered copper jardinière with stylized flowers in repoussé on a rutile patinated ground, some damage, unmarked.

*10in (25cm) wide*

**$500-800**      **DRA**

An Arts & Crafts large hammered humidor with riveted hinges and corners, on ball feet, original zinc lining and excellent dark patina, unmarked.

*10in (25cm) wide*

**$800-1,200**      **DRA**

An Arts & Crafts hammered copper hinged miniature chest with pewter rivets, latch and handles, new felt lining, original patina, unmarked.

*7in (17.5cm) wide*

**$700-1,000**      **DRA**

A copper and enamel letter rack, by The Arts Shop.

*The Arts Shop was founded by ex-Roycrofters.*

8.25in (21cm) wide

**$800-1,200**      **GAL**

An Arts & Crafts copper and enamel roller blotter, by The Arts Shop.

c1910      5in (13cm) wide

**$300-500**      **GAL**

A round copper box, by Rebecca Cauman, with removable silver lid, orange enameled interior and carved agate rooster finial inside small ring on lid, signed with the Cauman mark.

c1935      6in (15cm) wide

**$2,200-2,800**      **CHI**

A large Kalo copper tray, with stones and applied strap handles in geometric pierced shape, base with raised border, five bezel-set carnelian cabochons on each handle, signed "Kalo".

*Stone-set hollowware pieces are unusual and especially rare on copper items.*

14.75in (37.5cm) wide

**$4,000-6,000**      **CHI**

A Kalo copper letter holder, of truncated pyramid shape, with large repoussé stylized tulip, leaf and stem design on front, small engraved "HHF" monogram at the base, original dark patina, signed "Hand beaten at Kalo Shops Park Ridge Ills."

c1910      5.5in (14cm) wide

**$3,000-4,000**      **CHI**

An American Arts & Crafts hammered copper plant holder, by Karl Kipp.

*Karl Kipp was a Roycrofter who set up on his own.*

12.5in (32cm) high

**$300-500**      **GAL**

A heavy gauge copper vase by Falick Novick, with tin interior, bulging form with tapering neck, cylindrical collar, angular strap handles with flat tops, applied wire around mouth.

c1915      9in (23cm) high

**$4,000-6,000**      **CHI**

An Arts & Crafts hammered copper plate, by Roycroft, with logo.

c1910      8in (20.5cm) diam

**$180-220**      **GAL**

An Arts & Crafts hammered copper bowl, by Roycroft, with a desirable chocolate patina.

c1910      4.25in (11cm) diam

**$400-600**      **GAL**

A rare American Arts & Crafts hammered copper vase, by the Stickley Brothers, with an unusual design, crudely hammered by Russian metalworkers.

*c1910*                     *14.25in (36cm) high*

**$600-900**                                    **GAL**

A Tiffany Studios Favrile glass and copper desk set, comprising of a letter rack, two blotting paper boards and a pen tray, stamped factory mark to the base.

*letter rack 12.5in (31.5cm) wide*

**$1,200-1,800**                               **ROS**

A rare Tiffany double inkwell, with an accessories tray on top and riveted front panel, curved doors to sides, swing-out cauldron-shaped inkwell with gold Favrile insert, the inkwell with red-brown patina and green highlights, marked on base "Tiffany Studios New York D1070 5", one Favrile glass inkwell cup missing.

*6.5in (16.5cm) wide*

**$19,000-21,000**                             **JDJ**

An American Arts & Crafts copper cigarette box, with enamel sailing ships, by Gertrude Twichell, Boston.

*Twichell was known for her skilled use of enamels.*

*c1920*                     *5in (12.5cm) wide*

**$2,200-2,800**                               **ARK**

A Dirk van Erp hammered copper bowl with medium patina, stamped mark.

*9.5in (24cm) diam*

**$800-1,200**                                 **DRA**

A Dirk van Erp hammered copper cabinet vase with closed-in rim, original dark patina, Windmill mark with open box.

*3in (7.5cm) wide*

**$1,200-1,800**                               **DRA**

A Dirk van Erp early hammered copper vessel with closed-in rim, restored patina, Windmill mark with remnant of "D'Arcy Gaw".

*4.25in (10.5cm) wide*

**$800-1,200**                                 **DRA**

A pair of Arts & Crafts hammered copper three-prong candlesticks.

*c1910*                     *7.75in (20cm) wide*

**$300-400**                                   **GAL**

An American Arts & Crafts hammered copper pipe rack.

*c1910*                     *8.25in (21cm) diam*

**$500-700**                                   **GAL**

An Arts & Crafts copper kettle on stand, the kettle of ovoid form repoussé decorated with a band of flowering foliage, raised on a scrolling wrought iron stand.

*23.5in (59cm) high*

**$300-400**     **L&T**

An Arts & Crafts wrought iron and copper firescreen, repoussé decorated with a domed central panel surrounded by scrolled foliage and centered with an enamel roundel, the frame with beaten finish and scrolling handle.

*28in (70cm) high*

**$800-1,200**     **L&T**

An Arts & Crafts copper and wrought iron plant holder, the copper vessel of tulip shape embossed with heart shapes and lily-of-the-valley, supported on an iron stem decorated with naturalistic leaves, spreading to form feet.

*16.25in (41cm) high*

**$500-800**     **DN**

A Gothic style copper candlestick, the lobed drip tray above a knopped column on a domed base.

*6.5in (16cm) high*

**$280-320**     **L&T**

A European Art Nouveau copper and brass mounted kettle and stand, embossed with stylized foliate motifs, with wicker covered carrying handle on tripod stand with burner, stamped marks.

*13.25in (33.5cm) high*

**$180-220**     **L&T**

A Swedish Art Deco copper and wicker coffee set.

*c1925*     *tray 11.5in (29cm) diam*

**$800-1,200**     **MOD**

A pair of Art Deco copper picture frames with a geometric design, unsigned.

*c1925*     *13.75in (35cm) high*

**$800-1,200**     **MOD**

A Scottish Arts & Crafts copper charger, of circular form, the central panel decorated with the profiled head of a girl enclosed within a rim decorated with knotted tendrils and iridescent rounded inlay.

*16.25in (40.5cm) wide*

**$1,200-1,800**     **L&T**

## PEWTER

A Liberty & Co. pewter bowl with green glass liner, cast with foliate motif, model number 0320, stamped marks.

*8.75in (22cm) diam*

**$700-1,000**     **WW**

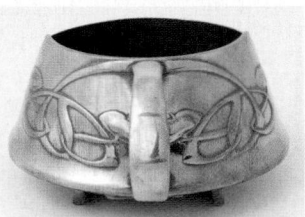

A Liberty & Co. Tudric pewter slop bowl, designed by Archibald Knox, model number 0231, stamped marks.

*6.5in (16cm) wide*

**$600-900**     **WW**

A hammered copper tray, rounded rectangular form, hammered with Tudor rose motif.

*21.75in (54.5cm) wide*

**$120-180**     **WW**

A Liberty & Co. Tudric pewter footed bowl, probably designed by Oliver Baker, model number 067, stamped marks.

*11.25in (28cm) diam*

**$700-1,000**     **WW**

A Liberty & Co. pewter and enamel rose bowl, designed by Archibald Knox, with green glass liner, model number 0320, stamped "English Pewter" mark.

*9in (23cm) diam*

**$1,800-2,200**     **WW**

## ARCHIBALD KNOX

- Archibald Knox (1864-1933) was inspired by the history and landscape of the Isle of Man, where he grew up.
- Knox worked primarily with pewter and silver, but also with other metals, textiles, ceramics, and graphics.
- Plain metalware by Knox is often more valuable than hammered, and pieces that incorporate glass by famous makers such as Whitefriars or Clutha are very sought-after.
- Knox's rarer designs include some of his clocks and belt buckles, particularly those with enamel or semi-precious stone inclusions.
- Although popular in his lifetime, Knox has only recently been recognized for the instrumental role he played in the development of the British Art Nouveau scene.
- Knox was a driving force behind the Celtic Revival at the turn of the 20thC.

A Liberty & Co. Tudric pewter bowl, designed by Archibald Knox, of ovoid form with single applied handle, cast with Celtic whiplash budding foliage, model 0231, stamped marks.

*6.25in (16cm) diam*

**$300-500**     **L&T**

A Liberty & Co. pewter biscuit barrel and cover, designed by Archibald Knox, of square form, the cover with twin fin handles, the sides cast with stylized plant forms, model 0237, stamped mark.

*4.75in (12cm) high*

**$2,200-2,800**     **L&T**

A Liberty & Co. Tudric enameled pewter vase, designed by Archibald Knox, cast with foliate decoration at the neck, with blue and green enamel bosses, model 0927, impressed marks.

*c1905*     *11.25in (28.5cm) high*

**$800-1,200**     **S&K**

A Liberty & Co. Tudric enameled pewter vase, designed by Archibald Knox, cast with foliate decoration at neck with blue and green enamel bosses, model 0927, impressed marks.

*c1905*     *11.25in (28.5cm) high*

**$800-1,200**     **S&K**

A Liberty & Co. Tudric bullet-shaped pewter vase, designed by Archibald Knox, cast with entwined and stylized foliage and with applied bracket supports, model 0927, stamped marks.

*11.5in (29cm) high*

**$800-1,200**     **L&T**

A Liberty & Co. Tudric bullet-shaped pewter vase, designed by Archibald Knox, cast with entwined and stylized foliage and with three applied bracket supports, unmarked.

*7.5in (19cm) high*

**$280-320**     **L&T**

A Liberty & Co. Tudric single-handled tankard, designed by Archibald Knox, of tapering ovoid form cast with entwined foliage and seed heads, model 0228, stamped marks.

*6in (15cm) high*

**$300-500**     **L&T**

An unusual pair of Liberty & Co. pewter solifleur vases, designed by Archibald Knox, model number 0819, stamped marks.

*6in (15cm) high*

**$800-1,200**     **WW**

A W.M.F. Jugendstil pewter plate, the rim cast with panels of flowering whiplash foliage and centering the head of an Art Nouveau maiden in profile, stamped marks.

*12.75in (32cm) wide*

**$700-1,000**                    **L&T**

A W.M.F. pewter tray, stamped in low relief with an Art Nouveau couple kissing, model number 196, stamped marks, minor scratches and wear.

*11in (28cm) wide*

**$280-320**                    **WW**

A W.M.F. pewter card tray, decorated with stylized motifs.

*c1905*          *10in (25.5cm) high*

**$1,200-1,800**                    **TO**

A W.M.F. Art Nouveau pewter claret jug, the green glass tapering body within mounts cast with maidens and flowering whiplash foliage, stamped marks.

*16.5in (41.5cm) high*

**$700-1,000**                    **L&T**

A W.M.F. pewter vase, decorated with dragons amongst scrolling foliage, stamped marks.

*12.75in (32cm) high*

**$300-400**                    **WW**

**A CLOSER LOOK AT A PEWTER CLARET JUG**

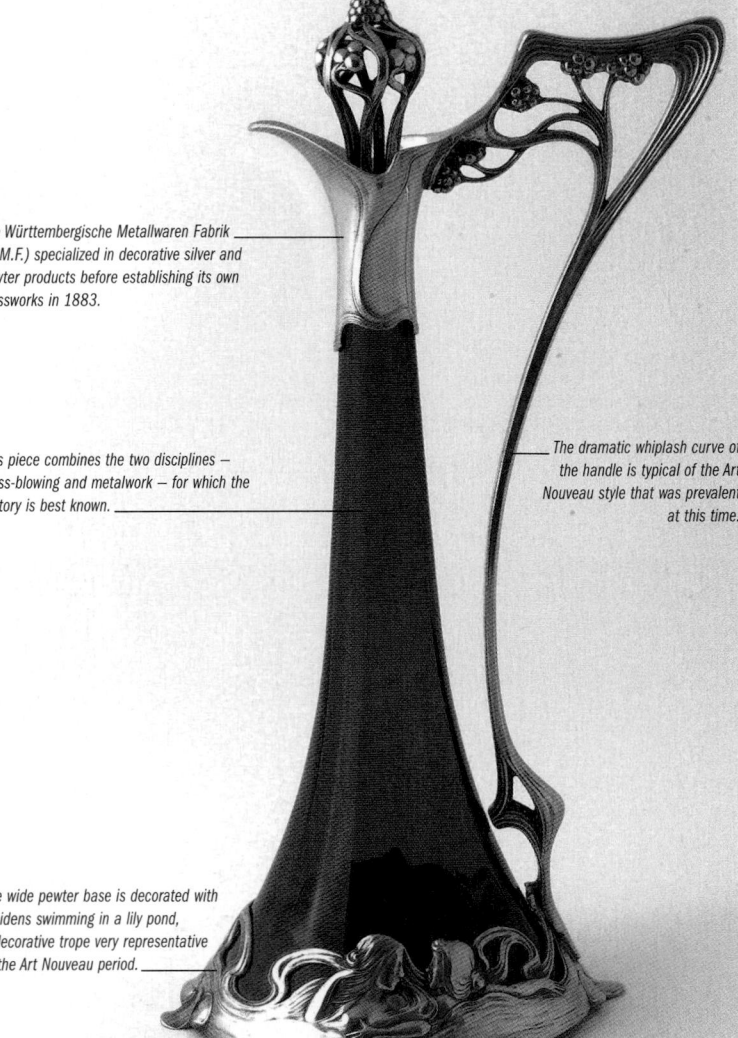

*The Württembergische Metallwaren Fabrik (W.M.F.) specialized in decorative silver and pewter products before establishing its own glassworks in 1883.*

*This piece combines the two disciplines — glass-blowing and metalwork — for which the factory is best known.*

*The dramatic whiplash curve of the handle is typical of the Art Nouveau style that was prevalent at this time.*

*The wide pewter base is decorated with maidens swimming in a lily pond, a decorative trope very representative of the Art Nouveau period.*

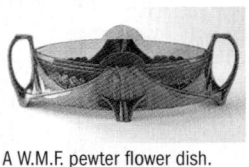

A W.M.F. pewter flower dish.

*c1905*          *14in (35.5cm) wide*

**$500-700**                    **TO**

A W.M.F. pewter siphon stand.

*c1905*          *8.5in (21.5cm) high*

**$400-600**                    **TO**

A W.M.F. pewter and green glass vase, of classical urn form, cast with griffin amongst foliate swags, stamped marks.

*15.5in (39cm) high*

**$500-700**                    **WW**

A W.M.F. polished pewter claret jug, with green glass.

*c1900*          *13.75in (35cm) high*

**$2,200-2,800**                    **STY**

A W.M.F. pewter flower dish.

c1905          10in (25.5cm) wide
**$500-700**                    **TO**

A pair of W.M.F. pewter and glass napkin holders.

c1905          5.25in (13.5cm) high
**$400-600**                    **TO**

A W.M.F. pewter picture frame.

c1905          9.5in (24cm) high
**$500-800**                    **TO**

A German Jugendstil pewter liquor set, comprising seven pieces, including tray, flagon, and cups.

c1900          tray 13.5in (34cm) wide
**$800-1,200**                    **FRE**

A Kayzerzinn pewter novelty ewer, modeled as a kangaroo, with glass eyes, unmarked.

10.5in (26cm) high
**$800-1,200**                    **WW**

A Danish pewter covered vase, designed by Edvin Ollers, of broad cup shape on a spreading circular foot, with scroll handles and drop-in cover domed in the center with a fluted ribbon and ball finial, maker's marks and signed "Ollers" in oval.

5in (13cm) high
**$180-220**                    **DN**

A set of six Sheffield pewter flaring cordials in the style of Desny, on buttressed bases with cones, one has small separation on stem, stamped "Manor Period" with trademark.

4.5in (11cm) high
**$700-1,000**                    **DRA**

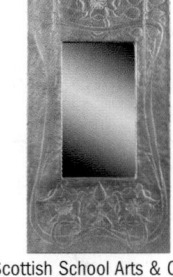

A Scottish School Arts & Crafts pewter wall mirror, of rectangular form, the mirrored plate enclosed by a frame repoussé decorated with sinuous tendrils and flowering rose plants.

22.75in (57cm) wide
**$2,200-2,800**                    **L&T**

## SILVER

### C.R. ASHBEE AND THE GUILD OF HANDICRAFT

- Charles Robert Ashbee (1863-1942) founded the Guild of Handicraft in 1888. It was conceived as a co-operative based on the medieval guild system, and trained many apprentices.
- Originally concerned with carpentry, the Guild was soon successful enough to expand its interests and build a forge for metalwork on its east London premises.
- The Guild moved to Chipping Camden in 1902. Craftsmen from east London relocated and settled permanently in the Cotswolds, taking apprentices from the local community.
- The hand-hammered finishes and simple designs of the Guild's silverware were very popular and much imitated.
- The Guild was wound up in 1908 after a period of decline. Many of its members remained in Chipping Camden working in the decorative arts.
- Ashbee held large retailers, such as Liberty & Co. who sold mass-produced goods, responsible for the failure of his experiment.

A Guild of Handicraft silver porringer and spoon, designed by Charles Robert Ashbee, the twin-handled form set with green chrysoprase stones, with later glass liner, stamped marks "GofHLtd, London 1902".

1902          10.75in (27cm) wide
**$15,000-20,000**                    **WW**

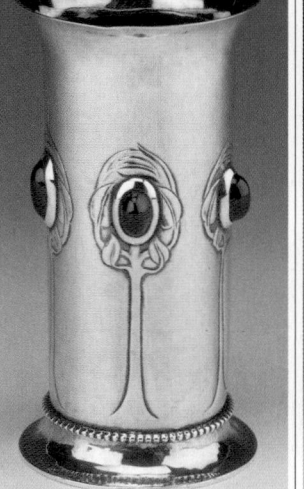

A silver vase, set with garnets, by C.R. Ashbee.

c1900          7in (18cm) high
**$5,000-8,000**                    **VDB**

A silver vase, by C.R. Ashbee.

c1900          7in (18cm) high
**$4,000-6,000**                    **VDB**

An Arts & Crafts symbolist silver and enamel panel, by Alexander Fisher, depicting William Morris' lyric poem 'Sigurd the Volsung', mounted in a silver pediment frame flanked by columns, unsigned.

*The inscription is based on Morris' and Eirikr Magnusson's translation of the Icelandic 'Volsunga Saga'.*

c1900                    13in (33cm) high

**$18,000-25,000**                    VDB

An Art Nouveau silver bonbon dish, by W.H. Haseler, of shaped oval form with pierced sides and floral border set with blue enameling and chased foliage, marks for Birmingham.

1905                    5.5in (14cm) diam

**$500-700**                    L&T

A Liberty & Co. silver bowl set with turquoise, by W.H. Haseler, design attributed to Archibald Knox, marks for Birmingham.

1905                    7in (18cm) diam

**$5,000-8,000**                    VDB

An Art Deco silver coffee pot, by the International Silver Company.

c1925                    8.75in (22cm) high

**$300-500**                    MOD

A Georg Jensen cigar ashtray, designed by Georg Jensen, design number 22.

c1910                    6.25in (16cm) long

**$1,800-2,200**                    SF

A Georg Jensen sterling grape tazza, marked "263A Georg Jensen Denmark".

5in (12.5cm) high

**$1,200-1,800**                    POOK

## GEORG JENSEN

■ Georg Jensen (1866-1934) established his business in April 1904 on Bredgade, a fashionable street in central Copenhagen.

■ He became well-known for his elegant and simple designs which were influenced by the Arts & Crafts movement.

■ Johan Rohde first worked with Jensen in 1906 when he engaged the firm to manufacture silver from his own drawn designs.

■ Rohde is particularly celebrated for his forward-looking holloware. His '432A' pitcher was held back from production for a number of years as it was considered 'too modern'.

■ Harald Nielsen started work for Jensen as a chaser in 1909. After leading the apprentice school for a period, he was appointed a director and also served as artistic director from 1958-62.

■ After Jensen's death, Nielsen trained a new generation, including Henning Kopel, to uphold the traditions of the Jensen brand.

■ Sigvard Bernadotte, second son of King Gustav VI of Sweden, joined Jensen in 1930 after studying at Uppsala University.

■ His 1939 'Bernadotte' cutlery is considered a classic, featuring his trademark motif of parallel lines.

■ The Jensen factory continues to produce silverware from classic Jensen patterns and contemporary designs.

A Georg Jensen grape-style wine coaster, designed by Georg Jensen, design number 229.

1927                    5.5in (14cm) diam

**$5,000-7,000**                    SF

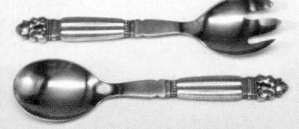

A Georg Jensen sterling silver salad fork and spoon, with fluted handles and pineapple tips, stamped "Georg Jensen Stainless" and "Sterling Denmark".

7.75in (19cm) long

**$400-600**                    DRA

A Georg Jensen cigarette case, designed by Sigvard Bernadotte, design number 712.

1935                    5.25in (13.5cm) wide

**$1,800-2,200**                    SF

A set of 12 Georg Jensen 'Acorn' pattern gilded coffee spoons, each with an oval bowl, reeded handle and scroll-and-acorn finial, marked "Sterling Denmark" and "Georg Jensen & Wendel A/S", in the original fitted case.

3.75in (9.5cm) long

**$500-700**                    DN

A Georg Jensen preserve jar, designed by Harald Nielsen, design number 891.

c1925                    5in (12.5cm) high

**$1,800-2,200**                    SF

A Georg Jensen vase, designed by Harald Nielsen, design number 676.

*c1925*     *7in (17.5cm) high*

**$2,200-2,800**     **SF**

A tall Georg Jensen vase, designed by Harald Nielsen, design number 757.

*c1935*     *8.75in (22cm) high*

**$1,800-2,200**     **SF**

A Georg Jensen bowl, decorated with leaves and berries, designed by Johan Rohde, design number 17.

*c1925*     *4in (10cm) high*

**$500-800**     **SF**

An Arts & Crafts silver candlestick by A.E. Jones, with cylindrical sconce and broad drip-pan on a strapwork stem above a slightly domed circular base punctuated with four tiny turquoise-glazed Ruskin pottery studs, fixed to a turned wooden base, maker's mark and mark for Birmingham.

*1904*     *5in (12.5cm) high*

**$800-1,200**     **DN**

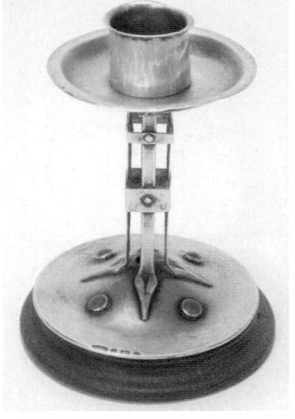

A silver muffin dish, by A. E Jones of Birmingham.

*1935*     *5.5in (14cm) high*

**$1,200-1,800**     **VDB**

A Liberty & Co. Cymric silver flower vase, the design attributed to Archibald Knox, broad rim, tapering cylindrical body, cast with stylized leaf forms and supported by three curved brackets raised on a dished circular base, stamped marks "L & Co.", "Cymric" and hallmarked for Birmingham.

*1903*     *5.5in (14cm) high*

**$4,000-6,000**     **L&T**

A Liberty & Co. Cymric silver cigarette case, designed by Archibald Knox, of rectangular outline with applied Celtic knotwork design with enamelled panels, applied to the reverse with a gold lizard, marks for Birmingham.

*3.5in (9cm) long*

**$700-1,000**     **L&T**

## LIBERTY & CO.

- Arthur Lasenby Liberty (1843-1917) started out in business in 1875 with a $3,000 loan and a lease on half a shop in Regent Street.
- Liberty & Co. soon became the most fashionable department store in London, catering to the wealthy elite and aspiring middle classes alike.
- Arthur Liberty sourced much of his merchandise from the near and far East, particularly Japan. The basement of the store was called the 'Eastern Bazaar'.
- By the 1890s, Liberty had forged links with many of the most prominent English designers, including Archibald Knox and Dr Christopher Dresser.
- Arthur Liberty strived to make good design affordable for the masses, and to this end he championed manufactured and even mass-produced goods.
- The distinctive Tudor-style building that Liberty & Co. now occupies was built in 1924 from timber salvaged from HMS Impregnable and HMS Hindustan.

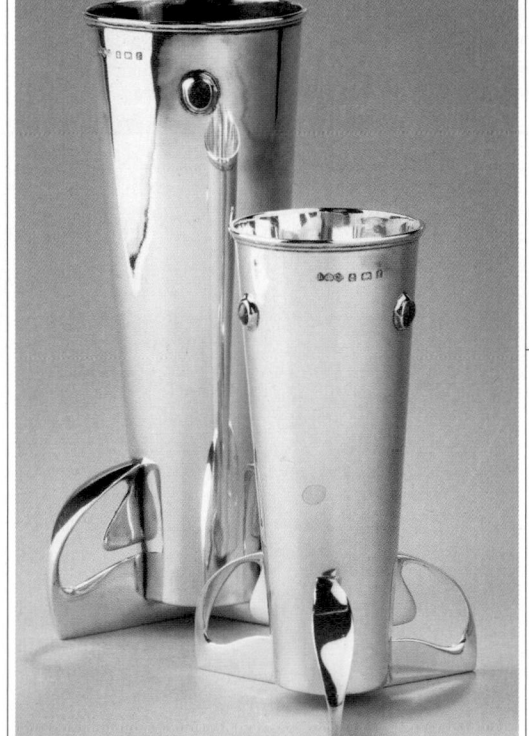

Two silver vases, designed by Archibald Knox for Liberty & Co.

*c1905*     *largest 8.75in (22cm) high*

**LEFT: $35,000-45,000 RIGHT: $25,000-35,000**     **VDB**

A pair of Liberty & Co. Cymric silver candlesticks, design attributed to Archibald Knox, the drip trays and sockets above nozzles cast with stylized buds and applied with tapering tendrils, Birmingham hallmarks.

*1905*     *8.5in (21cm) high*

**$10,000-15,000**     **L&T**

A Liberty & Co. Cymric silver coffee service, designed by Archibald Knox, comprising a lidded coffee pot with ivory handle, a cream jug, a sugar bowl and a twin-handled tray, set with turquoise cabochons, bearing hallmarks for Birmingham.

*1906*     *coffee pot 8.5in (21.5cm) high*

**$45,000-50,000**     **L&T**

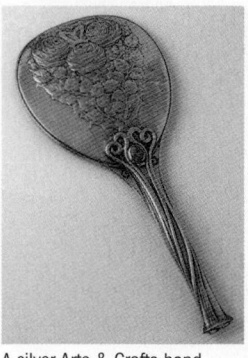

A silver Arts & Crafts hand mirror by Omar Ramsden and Alwyn Carr, marks for London.

*1907*     *11.75in (30cm) long*

**$3,000-5,000**     **VDB**

A silver and enamel box by Omar Ramsden, with blue enamel.

*5.5in (14cm) wide*

**$4,000-6,000**     **VDB**

An Arts & Crafts silver tea urn by Omar Ramsden and Alwyn Carr, with an ivory handle and bands of foliate motifs, raised on six lion's paw feet.

*1908*     *12.5in (32cm) high*

**$4,000-6,000**     **VDB**

A silver and electroplated presentation goblet by Omar Ramsden, surmounted by a naked boy and set with moonstone cabochons, with marks for London.

*1931*     *21.25 (53cm) high*

**$5,000-7,000**     **L&T**

An Artificers' Guild silver tureen spoon, by Edward Spencer, the tapering long handle with applied ropework decoration, with catch to reverse, stamped marks for London.

*1922*     *9in (23cm) long*

**$700-1,000**     **WW**

An Artificers' Guild circular silver box and cover, designed by Edward Spencer, with a wirework rim and a domed drop-in cover centered with a lion finial, maker's mark for London and designer's mark.

*1928*     *4in (10cm) diam*

**$1,200-1,800**     **DN**

A set of four silver goblets, by the Artificers' Guild of London, design attributed to Edward Spencer.

*1923*     *3.5in (9cm) diam*

**$5,000-8,000**     **VDB**

An Artificers' Guild silver 'Scorpio' napkin ring, the design attributed to Edward Spencer, with a relief medallion of a scorpion flanked by beading and two pink coral studs, maker's marks and marks for London.

*1915*     *1.75in (4.5cm) diam*

**$220-280**     **DN**

A Tattorini & Sons Ltd solid silver tray, with ivory handles.

*c1925*     *15in (38cm) wide*

**$1,800-2,200**     **TDG**

An Arts & Crafts silver cigar box with handpainted enamel panel of a wooded glade, by Fleetwood Vardley for the Guild of Handicraft.

*c1905*     *8in (20cm) long*

**$7,000-10,000**     **VDB**

A London silver and glass perfume bottle, by Walter Thornhill.

*1894*     *7.5in (19cm) high*

**$5,000-7,000**     **JBS**

A pair of silver candlesticks, by Williams of Birmingham.

*1906*     *11in (28cm) high*

**$10,000-15,000**     **VDB**

A silver W.M.F. sugar basket.

*c1900*     *5in (12.5cm) wide*

**$280-320**     **TDG**

An Arts & Crafts silver mounted oak and leather writer's traveling aid, the front mounted with a silver panel depicting an owl amongst flowers and foliage, stamped "JA & S", marks for Birmingham.

*1905*     *13.5in (34cm) high*

**$500-700**     **WW**

A Kalo silver pitcher, with applied wire to the rim and engraved tree in circle, inscribed "BMH 23 March 1899 / 23 March 1911", signed "Sterling Hand beaten at Kalo Shops Park Ridge Ills. 7978".

*1911*                   *8.75in (22cm) wide*

**$3,000-5,000**            **CHI**

A silver Kalo water pitcher, of paneled form, hammered surfaces, applied wire to rim, applied "GRH" monogram, signed "Sterling Hand wrought at the Kalo Shops Chicago 9318 18 X".

*The marks on this pot indicate that it may have been made in 1912-13, when plans were underway to open the second Kalo shop in New York but it was not yet in business.*

*1912*                   *7.25in (18.5cm) high*

**$5,000-7,000**            **CHI**

A Kalo silver pitcher, part of a matching six piece tea and coffee set, with outward-pointing flutes, applied wire to rim, with applied "ML" monogram, signed "Sterling Hand wrought at the Kalo Shop 10S".

*c1915*                   *8.75in (22cm) high*

**$3,000-4,000**            **CHI**

A large Kalo water pitcher, in wrought silver, with stylized leaves and angular handle, monogrammed "B", marked "Sterling Handwrought at the Kalo Shop 14".

                          *10in (25cm) high*

**$2,200-2,800**            **DRA**

An early Kalo silver bowl, with four concave hourglass-shaped outward lobes, and two hollow angled flat-top handles, applied "GH" monogram on side, hammered surfaces, signed "Hand beaten at Kalo Shops Park Ridge Ills 10".

*c1910   10in (25.5cm) wide*

**$5,000-7,000**      **CHI**

A Kalo silver bowl, unusually large version of the company's trademark '5811' form, with large low self-foot, five scalloped lobes, heavy applied wire to rim, engraved "CA" or "CX" on the side and "September 4 1918" on base, marked "Hand wrought at the Kalo Shop 5811L".

*This design was made between 1915 and 1970, and produced in at least three different sizes.*

*10.5in (26.5cm) wide*

**$1,800-2,200**            **CHI**

A pair of monumental Kalo silver candlesticks, with stepped circular feet, in tulip form, signed.

*c1925*              *14in (35.5cm) high*

**$15,000-20,000**            **CHI**

A pair of silver candlesticks, by Kalo, hammered surfaces with pedestal base, tulip form with fluted sides and spade shaped designs to the base, signed "Sterling Hand wrought at the Kalo Shop S402".

              *12in (30.5cm) high*

**$8,000-12,000**            **CHI**

A Kalo silver bud vase, of inverted trumpet form, with tapering neck, slightly flared top with wire applied to rim, hammered surface, signed "Sterling Handwrought at the Kalo Shop M627".

*c1925*       *6.75in (17cm) high*

**$2,800-3,200**            **CHI**

An early two-piece silver salad set, by Kalo, with spade-shaped bowls, notched handles with rounded ends, cut-outs on fork, unusual mark, signed "Sterling hand beaten at Kalo Shops Park Rdge Ills".

*8.75in (22cm) long*

**$800-1,200**            **CHI**

An early Kalo silver spoon, with round bowl and bezel-cut green onyx cabochon at end of handle, signed "Kalo sterling".

*7in (18cm) long*

**$1,800-2,200**            **CHI**

A silver Kalo tray, with pierced design and bezel-set dark green stone, hammered surface, raised border with a bezel-set oval cabochon agate at one end, rim with applied wire, engraved on the reverse "Louise Van Dyke", signed "Sterling Hand beaten at the Kalo Shop Park Ridge Ills. 0865".

*8in (20.5cm) long*

**$6,000-9,000**            **CHI**

**DECORATIVE ARTS**

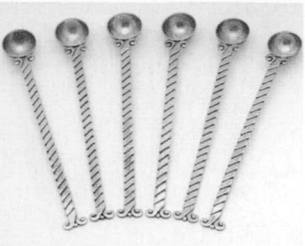

Six Hector Aguilar silver spoons, each stamped "TAXCO HA 990".

*7.75in (19cm) long*

**$1,200-1,800**                    **FRE**

A silver ribbed bowl, by Heinrich Eicher, two notched curving strap handles, foot with the repeated square ribbed form, applied wire to rim and foot, and applied "S" monogram, signed "Sterling hand wrought 158".

*c1920*              *7.5in (19cm) wide*

**$800-1,200**                    **CHI**

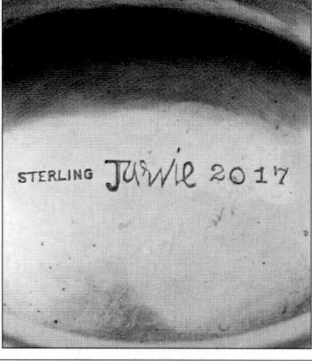

A silver sauce bowl with attached underplate, by Robert Jarvie, oval attached underplate, applied rim on top edge of bowl and around underplate with three chased lines, applied "L" monogram on underplate, signed "Sterling" with Jarvie logo.

*c1925*              *8.5in (21.5cm) long*

**$2,200-2,800**                    **CHI**

## A CLOSER LOOK AT A JARVIE PITCHER

Robert Jarvie set up The Jarvie Shop in 1904 in Chicago and specialized in candlesticks cast in bronze, copper, brass, and occasionally silver.

*This water pitcher has a lightly hammered bowl, which was a distinctive feature of metalwork pieces from the Arts & Crafts period.*

*The stylized organic decoration is typical of Jarvie's work, with a few simple decorative details on an elegant and simply shaped chalice.*

Interest in Jarvie's work has steadily increased among collectors. Silver objects by Jarvie are less common, and therefore particularly sought after.

An Arts & Crafts silver water pitcher by Robert Jarvie.

*c1925*              *7.75in (19.5cm) high*

**$8,000-10,000**                    **ARK**

A sauce or mayonnaise set, by Mary C. Knight, consisting of a bowl, underplate and spoon, all with blue champlevé enamel pattern of grapes and chased vines, the bowl and underplate with "F" monogram, the spoon with "Frp" monogram.

*Leather-working craft tools were used to produce the design on this plate.*

*1906*              *bowl 4.5in (11.5cm) wide*

**$4,000-6,000**                    **CHI**

A silver chocolate pot, from a five piece set by Lebolt and Co., melon-ribbed with high looping hollow handles, on broad round self-feet, with ivory insulators and applied "BDG" monogram, signed "Lebolt Hand beaten sterling 957 1 3/4 pints".

*c1925*              *12in (30.5cm)*

**$2,200-2,800**                    **CHI**

An American Arts & Crafts silver water pitcher, by Marshall Field Craft Shop, Chicago with a chased design.

*c1925*              *7.75in (19.5cm) high*

**$1,800-2,200**                    **ARK**

A John Pontus Petterson wrought sterling flaring bowl, its base tooled with a Native American motif, stamped "J.P.P. STERLING 901".

*Work by this artist is rare.*

*6in (15cm) diam*

**$700-1,000**                    **DRA**

Part of a five-piece silver tea and coffee set, by Julius O. Randahl, with hollow harp-shaped handles and domed lids with ivory insulators and finials, engraved "C" monograms, signed "JOR sterling hand wrought 695 Betteridge Company Inc. Fifth Ave New York".

*c1925*

**$3,000-5,000 set**              **CHI**

*coffee pot 9.75in (25cm) high*

An enameled silver dish, by Margaret Rogers, with flat broad rim with a repeating saw-pierced stylized floral design, enameled in green, signed "Sterling MR".

*c1910*              *4.5in (11.5cm) wide*

**$1,800-2,200**                    **CHI**

An enameled silver dish, by Margaret Rogers, with flat broad rim with a repeating saw-pierced stylized floral design, enameled in green, signed "Sterling MR".

c1910      4.5in (11.5cm) wide

**$1,800-2,200**      **CHI**

A Spratling silver box and candlesticks, hardwood handle, box stamped "SPRATLING WS MADE IN MEXICO STERLING", sticks stamped "WILLIAM SPRATLING 925 WS TAXCO MEXICO" and eagle 63 mark.

sticks 3.5in (9cm) high

**$1,800-2,200**      **FRE**

A William Spratling coffee service, sterling silver, wood, comprising of a creamer, sugar and coffeepot, and tray, each with stamped marks "WILLIAM SPRATLING TAXCO MEXICO" encircling "925" and stylized "WS", some pieces with shield hallmark.

coffeepot 9.5in (24cm) high

**$3,000-5,000**      **FRE**

A Spratling sterling silver box, stamped "STERLING WS MADE IN MEXICO STERLING".

4.5in (11cm) high

**$1,200-1,800**      **FRE**

A very rare Arts & Crafts pill box, by Arthur Stone, in sterling silver and 14ct gold.

c1920      2.25in (5.5cm) wide

**$3,000-5,000**      **ARK**

An American Arts & Crafts Arthur Stone silver bowl, hand-decorated with a chased stylized design.

9.5in (24cm) wide

**$3,000-4,000**      **ARK**

A Tiffany silver bowl.

c1925      5.5in (14cm) diam

**$700-1,000**      **MOD**

An Arts & Crafts silver and ebony spider tray.

c1880      16in (40.5cm) high

**$1,200-1,800**      **PUR**

An American Arts & Crafts bonbon spoon, with a pierced and chased cornflower design.

c1925      4.5in (11.5cm) long

**$220-280**      **ARK**

An Arts & Crafts bonbon spoon, with a pierced and chased berry design.

c1925      7in (18cm) long

**$220-280**      **ARK**

A pair Tiffany silver-plated lidded wine coolers, with scrolled shell-and-foliate borders, applied die-rolled scroll, floral and acanthus decoration, footed base with gadroon borders, interior liners, marks for Tiffany & Co., made by Adams & Shaw, lids matched and numbered, wear to plate, scratches.

12in (30cm) wide

**$3,000-5,000**      **BRU**

A fine silver-plated Art Deco teapot and creamer, by Paul Follot, of sweeping fluted design, marked "Pfollot", teapot inscribed "3050 XII" and creamer inscribed "3050 VI", slight damage.

*11.5in (29cm) high*

**$5,000-8,000**                                    **SDR**

## A CLOSER LOOK AT A SILVER-PATINATED BRONZE

*Maurice Guiraud-Rivière is considered one of the finest sculptors of the Art Deco period, and this is among his best-known works.*

*The streamlined form and strong sense of motion imparted by this sculpture make it instantly recognizable as a classic Art Deco image. A strong visceral association with a popular look will often enhance the value of a piece.*

*Different versions of this sculpture can be found — some are cold-painted, whereas this example is of unadorned, silver-patinated bronze.*

*The simple geometry of the lozenge-shaped base and the stylized clouds linking the figure to the base add to the Deco feel of this piece.*

A silver-patinated bronze, 'The Comet', by Maurice Guiraud-Rivière.

c1925                                              *24in (61cm) wide*

**$35,000-45,000**                                    **TDG**

A silver-plated chocolate set and tray, by Hukin & Heath.

*The stylized geometric form of this set is typical of Hukin & Heath. Pieces were usually electroplated or pure silver.*

c1920                      *tray 10.75in (27.5cm) wide*

**$400-600**                                    **TDG**

A Hukin & Heath electroplated lamp base, converted from a candle stick, the circular drip-tray above a rusticated turned column with frilled knop, on spreading domed base with frilled rim and stamped marks.

*12in (31cm) high*

**$180-220**                                    **L&T**

A silver-plated cocktail shaker, formed as the Boston lighthouse, marks for "Meridien Silver Plate", light scratches, both lids with small dents on edge.

c1920          *13.5in (4.5cm) high*

**$7,000-10,000**                                    **BRU**

A Keswick School of Industrial Arts electroplated bowl, of circular form with braided edge, centered by repoussé worked rose motif, stamped marks.

*11.25in (28cm) wide*

**$300-500**                                    **L&T**

One of two silver-gilt pedestal bowls, by Nathan & Hayes, designed in the Gothic style and part lobed, inscribed "in Dona Suis Srme Bene Dictus", marks for Chester.

c1910          *4.25in (11cm) high*

**$800-1,200 pair**                                    **ROS**

A tazza-shaped sweet dish by Saunders & Shepherd Ltd of London, with a round bowl and a stem in the form of 'The Spirit of Ecstasy', on a stepped round foot, with initials "GB".

1930          *5.5in (14cm) diam*

**$1,800-2,200**                                    **DN**

An early 20thC Mappin & Webb silver-plated desk inkwell stand and pen tray, on lion paw feet.

*7.25in (18.5cm) wide*

**$80-120**                                    **EPO**

A hexagonal part engine-turned table lighter, by Saunders & Shepherd Ltd of London, in the form of a petrol pump surmounted with a model of 'The Spirit of Ecstasy', with initials "GB".

*1934*

**$5,000-8,000**　　　　**DN**

An Arts & Crafts silver-plated brass vase, designed by Edward Spencer, of broad trumpet shape with horizontal ribs in relief edged with ropework banding, decorated with simple florets and foliage near the base, number 216.

*6.75in (17.5cm) high*

**$700-1,000**　　　　**DN**

A W.M.F. Jugendstil electroplated 'Echo' strut mirror, the rectangular shaped frame cast with sinuous flowering tendrils and an Art Nouveau maiden with a hand cupped to her ear, enclosing a mirrored plate, stamped marks.

*14.75in (37cm) high*

**$2,200-2,800**　　　　**L&T**

A W.M.F. Art Nouveau electroplated ewer, of tapering form with hinged lid set with leafy tendrils, the applied handle cast as a mermaid, her tail flowing into the foliage of the body, case with entwined iris, stamped marks.

*15in (37.5cm) high*

**$2,200-2,800**　　　　**L&T**

A W.M.F. table lamp, with original plating.

*c1900*　　　*16in (41cm) high*

**$5,000-8,000**　　　　**STY**

A pair of W.M.F. silver-plated figural candelabra, in the form of maidens holding stylized sconces.

*c1900*　　　*19.25in (49cm) high*

**$18,000-25,000**　　　　**STY**

A W.M.F. liquor service, with original glass.

*c1900*　　*14in (36cm) high*

**$2,800-3,200**　　　　**STY**

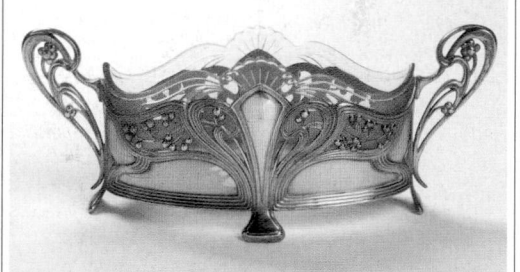

A W.M.F. electroplated jardinière and liner, the etched clear glass liner enclosed within an oval frame cast and pierced with fruiting whiplash foliage and with similarly cast twin handles, number 352, stamped and cast marks.

*12.5in (31cm) wide*

**$400-600**　　　　**L&T**

A W.M.F. silver-plated celery vase.

*c1905*　　*7.5in (19cm) high*

**$300-400**　　　　**TO**

A W.M.F. cookie jar.

*c1905*　　*10in (25.5cm) high*

**$300-400**　　　　**TO**

A W.M.F. silver-plated tea and coffee set on a tray.

*c1905*

*tray 28.25in (72cm) wide*

**$5,000-7,000**　　　　**TO**

585

A W.M.F. Art Nouveau silver-plated wall plaque, with W.M.F. mark.

*c1910    17.25in (44cm) diam*

**$700-1,000**                    **TDG**

A W.M.F. silver-plated cookie jar and glass liner, with sinuous stems and berries.

*9in (23cm) high*

**$700-1,000**                    **DN**

A W.M.F. electroplated desk set, in the Secessionist style, comprising an inkstand, a paper clip, a pen tray, and a blotter, each with stamped mark.

**$300-400**                    **L&T**

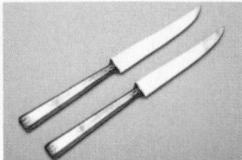

Two knives from a W.M.F. plated metal 12-piece dessert service, comprising six knives and six forks with steel blades and prongs, the handles embelished with geometric foliate motifs, in a fitted case for Zurich retailer A. Wiskemann-Knecks.

*knife 6.75in (17cm) long*

**$300-500 set**                    **DN**

A silver-plated Arts & Crafts wine cooler, with maker's marks.

*c1900    7.5in (19cm) high*

**$400-600**                    **TDG**

An Arts & Crafts white metal bowl, with deep rounded sides embossed with a band of foliage and berries, with applied green enamel roundels centered with a plaque of mother-of-pearl, on ball feet.

*9in (23cm) high*

**$800-1,200**                    **DN**

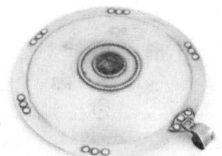

An Arts & Crafts plated circular hand-mirror, with central green and blue enameled plaque flanked by a wirework band, the mirror secured by florets and rivets.

*5.25in (13.5cm) diam*

**$500-700**                    **DN**

A silver-plated Art Deco plate, with a mermaid design and bakelite handles.

*c1930    15in (38cm) diam*

**$400-600**                    **TDG**

A European metal and enamel inkwell and desk tidy, the central inkwell with cloisonné enamel maiden, stamped "AE 9307".

*10.25in (25.5cm) wide*

**$500-700**                    **WW**

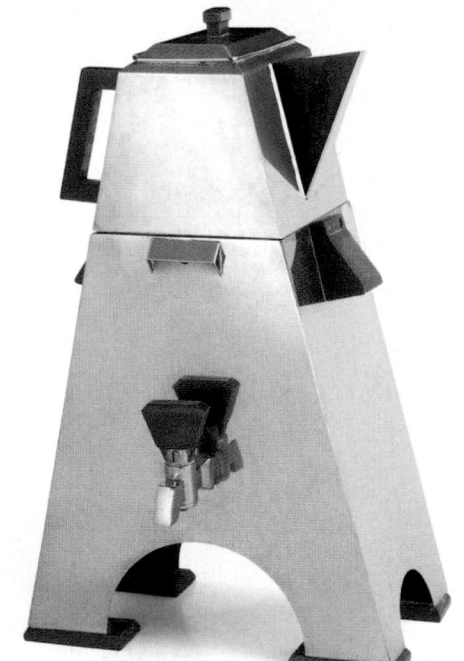

An English chrome and bakelite kettle and urn, stamped "Regd 849217" for 1946.

*16.5in (42cm) high*

**$700-1,000**                    **WW**

An Artificers' Guild wrought iron trivet, the openwork design of a stylized plant with sinuous scrolling stems, with plain tapering handle, raised on three loop feet.

*14.75in (37.5cm) long*

**$500-800**                    **DN**

An Artificers' Guild wrought iron toasting frame, of almost rectangular outline with scrolling stems extending from a flattened handle with brass hanging loop.

*18.25in (46.5cm) long*

**$400-600**                    **DN**

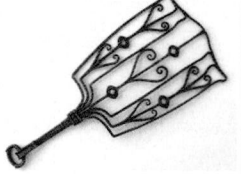

An unusual pair of Art Deco hand-wrought iron snake paperweights, by Edgar Brandt.

*c1925    4.75in (12cm) high*

**$5,000-8,000**                    **MOD**

A pair of Art Deco wrought iron gates in the style of Wilhelm Hunt Diederich, with leaping hounds and stags in a stylized landscape, within radially planished border, unmarked.

*62.75in (159.5cm) high*

**$22,000-28,000**                    **SDR**

## SAMUEL YELLIN

- Born in Poland in 1885, Samuel Yellin started his business 'Samuel Yellin Metalworkers' in Philadelphia in c1905. Often called a genius, Yellim refered to himself as a blacksmith, even though his most successful works are in the field of architecture. Hundreds of designs for gates, lighting fixtures, screens, railings, and doors were produced. Residences, cathedrals, banks, academic buildings – all could be enhanced with Yellin's unique approach to the use of metalwork. His clients included both Yale and Harvard Universities, as well as Washington Cathedral (DC), Grace Cathedral (San Francisco), and the Cathedral of St. John the Divine (New York, NY).

- He received several medals acknowledging his contributions, including awards from the Chicago Art Institute (1919), American Institute of Architects (1920), and Architectural League of New York (1922). Yellin died in 1940.

- The factory's high standards in design and craftsmanship can still be seen in their products today under the direction of Clare Yellin, Samuel's granddaughter.

A 20thC Samuel Yellin wrought iron candlestick, circular beaded dish base, tripod ribbed pad feet, stamped "YELLIN" on underside.

*10.5in (27cm) high*

**$3,000-5,000**       **FRE**

A Samuel Yellin wrought iron sconce, stamped "SAMUEL YELLIN" to arm.

*16in (40cm) high*

**$2,200-2,800**       **FRE**

A large Arts & Crafts wrought iron lantern, in the manner of Samuel Yellin, mica, with three hanging rods, electrified.

*62in (155cm) high*

**$1,200-1,800**       **FRE**

A pair of Jarvie 'Alpha' candlesticks, in spun brass with original bobeches, incised mark.

*Robert Jarvie created a range of designs named after Greek characters. The simplicity and elegance of these candlesticks is a signature of Jarvie's work.*

*11.5in (29cm) high*

**$800-1,200**       **DRA**

An early Bruno Paul brass thirteen-light candelabra, in the form of a stylized tree, impressed monogram.

*Bruno Paul, (1874-1968), a noted designer and architect, used similar ribbed ornamentation on the legs of his furniture. This design, introduced in 1901, was sold by the Vereinigte Werkstätte. Very few examples are known.*

*16in (40.5cm) high*

**$2,200-2,800**       **SK**

A Tiffany fine and large desk tray inkwell in the Venetian pattern in dore finish, complete with original liner, stamped "Tiffany Studios, New York, 1669".

*9.75in (24cm) wide*

**$2,800-3,200**       **DRA**

A Heinz art metalwork presentation trophy cup, decorated with sterling silver overlay, engraved for "George W. Currier Trophy, Nashua Police Department, Highest Revolver Score, 1920," awarded to patrolman Edward McCarthy, impressed maker's mark on base.

*12in (30.5cm) high*

**$400-600**       **SK**

**DECORATIVE ARTS**

A wrought iron fender stool, by Thomas Hadden of Edinburgh, of rectilinear three quarter form, the green leather padded seats with studded decoration above a slatted frieze enhanced with panels of entwined foliage.

*72in (180cm) wide*

**$3,000-5,000**     **L&T**

An Art Deco wrought iron hook, by Paul Kiss.

*c1925*     *9.5in (24cm) high*

**$2,800-3,200**     **MOD**

A pair of Art Deco hand-wrought iron candlesticks by Maury.

*c1925*     *11in (28cm) wide*

**$1,200-1,800**     **MOD**

A German Art & Crafts wrought iron casket, stamped with "FW" cipher and "GERMANY", retains original hand-wrought key.

*11in (27.5cm) wide*

**$1,800-2,200**     **FRE**

## A CLOSER LOOK AT A PAIR OF BRANDT WROUGHT IRON GATES

*Edgar Brandt is widely regarded as one of the 20thC's most accomplished manipulators of iron.*

*Brandt's oeuvre includes lighting, tableware, furniture, and decorative items. Large architectural pieces like this are particularly sought after as they make a bold statement.*

*The stylized symmetry of the fountain at the center of the gates provides a counterpoint to the leaves and tendrils swirling around it.*

*'L'Oasis', a brass and iron five-panel screen by Brandt, sold for $1.5million in June 2000. These gates date from the same period of Brandt's work.*

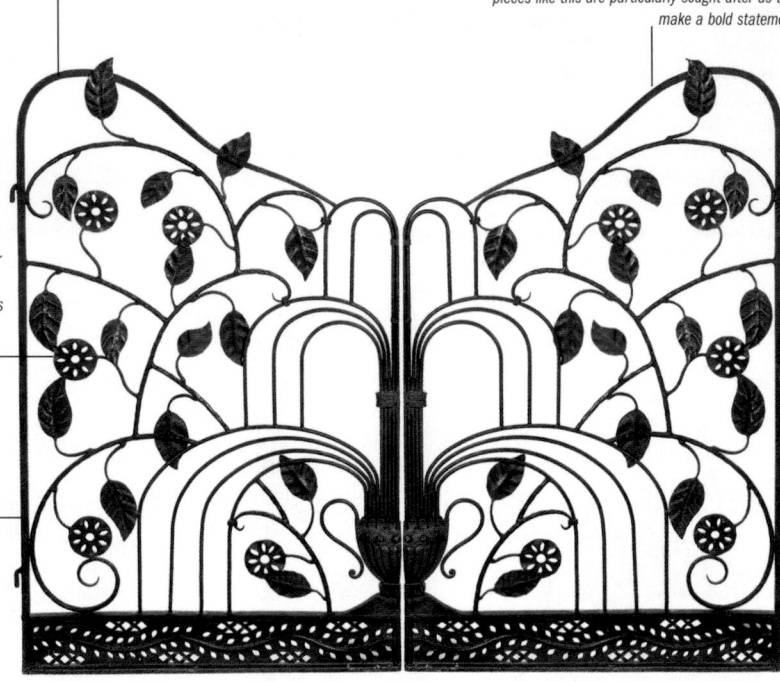

A pair of Art Deco wrought iron interior gates by Edgar Brandt, with stylized water fountain and swirling stems of leaves and pierced flowers, above vines along the base, stamped "E. Brandt France".

*c1925*     *51in (129.5cm) high*

**$10,000-15,000**     **SDR**

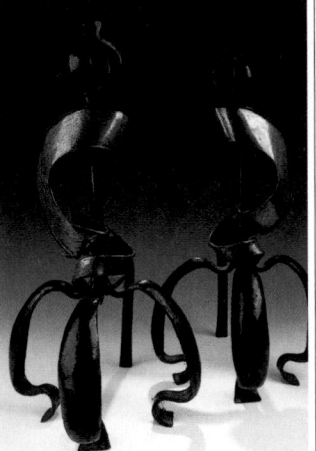

A pair of Arts & Crafts wrought iron fireirons, each with applied copper entwined banner on tripod base.

*20.75in (53cm) high*

**$400-600**     **L&T**

An Arts & Crafts cast-iron fireplace, in the manner of the Glasgow School and Margaret McDonald Mackintosh, with a high relief maiden's head with long, flowing hair, and stylized floral details either side and below the face.

*c1905*     *49.5in (126cm) high*

**$15,000-18,000**     **PUR**

A French Art Deco magazine rack, unsigned.

*1925*

**$800-1,200**     **MOD**

A unique Art Deco wrought iron and bronze aquarium, unsigned.

*c1925*                    *15.25in (39cm) wide*
**$1,200-1,800**                    **MOD**

A French Art Deco fish sculpture, unsigned.

*c1925*                    *15.75in (40cm) wide*
**$2,200-2,800**                    **MOD**

A gilt metal erotic figure of a dancer, after a model by Bergman, with hinged skirt, cast marks.

*7in (18cm) high*
**$1,200-1,800**                    **WW**

An Art Deco spelter figure of a female in a flowing dress holding hoops.

*c1925*                    *10in (25.5cm) high*
**$700-1,000**                    **TDG**

A spelter figural lamp base, on a marble base, unsigned.

*31.5in (80cm) high*
**$1,200-1,800**                    **WW**

A pair of French Art Deco metal vases with embossed decoration, signed "C. Terrers Lyon".

*c1925*                    *6.25in (16cm) high*
**$1,200-1,800**                    **MOD**

A Scottish Arts & Crafts tin jardinière, of circular form, repoussé decorated, with ring handles.

*10in (25cm) diam*
**$400-600**                    **L&T**

A polished steel candlestick, designed by Ernest Gimson, probably made by Alfred or Norman Bucknell, stamped with bands of geometric decoration, on three shaped feet, unmarked.

*9.5in (24.5cm) high*
**$2,800-3,200**                    **WW**

A Scottish Arts & Crafts polished tin hairbrush, by Margaret Gilmour, repoussé decorated with a panel of stylized flowers, stamped monogram.

*9.25in (23cm) long*
**$700-1,000**                    **L&T**

An Arts & Crafts multistone silver necklace, for the Artificer's Guild, with wirework, leaves, beads, and set cabochons.

*c1910*          *8.5in (21.5cm) long*

**$6,000-9,000**          **VDB**

An Arts & Crafts heart-shaped necklace, by Child & Child, with silver and gold citrine and pale aquamarine, the semi-precious stones encased in rubover settings.

*c1890*          *12in (30.5cm) long*

**$2,800-3,200**          **VDB**

An Arts & Crafts silver necklace, by Katie Eadie, of intricate intertwining foliate and floral design, with moonstone and a mother-of-pearl drop.

*c1905*          *19in (48cm) long*

**$7,000-10,000**          **VDB**

An English Arts & Crafts necklace, by Arthur and Georgina Gaskin, a central amethyst cabochon within a foliate mount, flanked by mother-of-pearl and with similar drops, signed "G".

*c1900*          *pendant 2in (4.5cm) long*

**$1,200-1,800**          **PC**

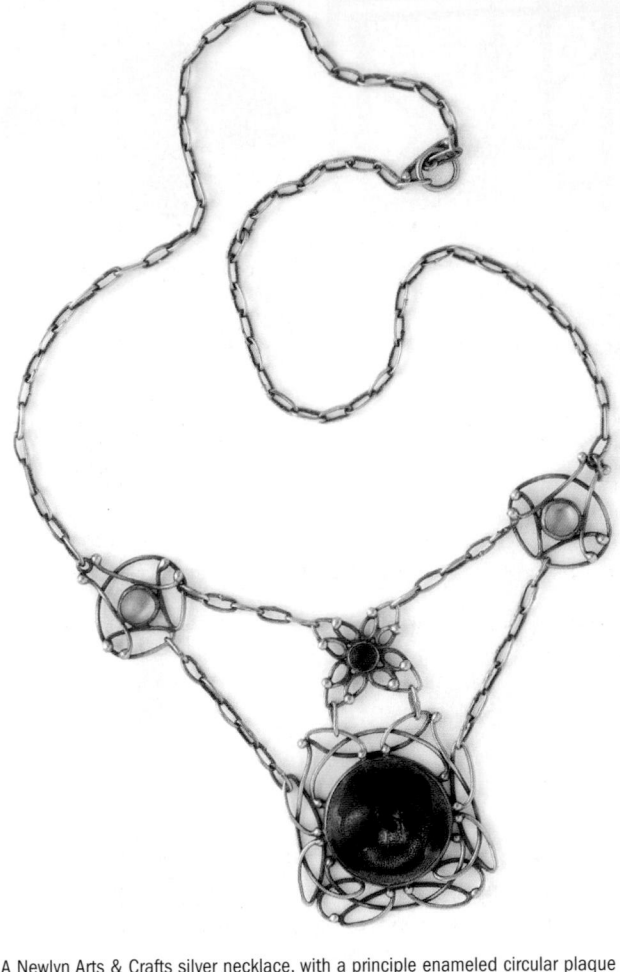

A Newlyn Arts & Crafts silver necklace, with a principle enameled circular plaque depicting a pansy below an enameled wirework flower, moonstone connections to an oval link chain, signed "Newlyn".

*plaque 2in (5cm) high*

**$3,000-4,000**          **WW**

An enameled necklace, by Charles Horner, with a pendant of elliptical shape with blue-green enameling and a plain openwork winged top, enameled drop and spacer to chains above, marked "C.H" and Birmingham marks for 1908.

*1908*          *2.75in (7cm) long*

**$700-1,000**          **DN**

An Arts & Crafts silver necklace, with sealed butterfly wing pendant, by Henry William King.

*c1905*          *12in (31cm) long*

**$220-280**          **AVW**

A Liberty & Co. silver and enamel necklace, with set mother-of-pearl, in an organic design.

*9in (23cm) long*

**$3,000-5,000**          **VDB**

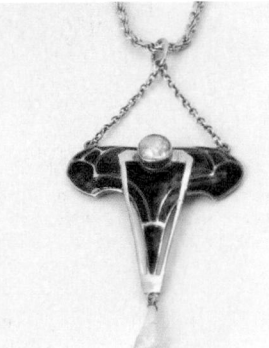

A silver pendant necklace, in the style of Liberty & Co., blue and green enamel, set with a blister pearl and a Mississippi pearl, unmarked, new chain.

*c1900*          *12in (31cm) long*

**$300-500**          **AVW**

An Arts & Crafts silver repoussé pendant necklace, with blue and green enamel, a blister pearl, seed pearls and Mississippi pearl drop, unmarked.

c1900   12in (31cm) long

**$500-800**   AVW

An Arts & Crafts heart-shaped silver and enamel pendant necklace, with blister pearl drop.

c1900   12.5in (32cm) long

**$500-700**   AVW

An Arts & Crafts silver blue and green enamel pendant necklace, with a blister pearl and a Mississippi pearl, enamel work verso, foliate motifs, unmarked.

c1900   10.5in (27cm) long

**$500-700**   AVW

An Arts & Crafts silver pendant necklace, with three enamel squares and a drop pearl, enamel work verso, unmarked.

c1900   12in (30.5cm) long

**$280-320**   AVW

An Arts & Crafts silver and turquoise pendant necklace, with three set turquoise stones.

c1900   9.5in (24cm) long

**$180-220**   AVW

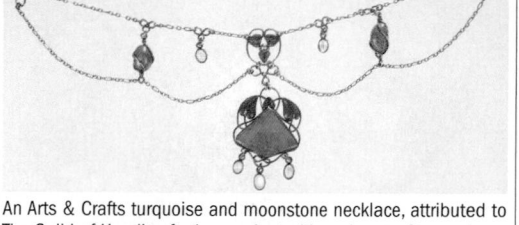

An Arts & Crafts turquoise and moonstone necklace, attributed to The Guild of Handicraft, the pendant with a plaque of turquoise within a foliate mount with three moonstone cabochon drops, suspended on chains with turquoise matrix pebbles and moonstones.

pendant 2in (5cm) long

**$1,200-1,800**   DN

An Arts & Crafts necklace, with a central malachite cabochon and drop below within fine wirework mounts, on a chain with two oval jade cabochon spacers.

**$280-320**   DN

A Swedish Arts & Crafts silver pendant necklace, with iridescent central blue enamel panel surrounded by enameled decoration, hallmarked "NM".

c1920   11.5in (29cm) long

**$280-320**   AVW

## A CLOSER LOOK AT AN ARTS & CRAFTS NECKLACE

*The use of moonstones and silver is characteristic of the Arts & Crafts movement.*

*The painted image depicts a Medieval figure. The Arts & Crafts movement was influenced by the designs of the Middle Ages.*

*Provenance tends to increase the desirability of a piece. This necklace belonged to the Hove-based artist Averil Burleigh (1883-1949), whose paintings can be seen in the Hove Art Gallery, Brighton, England.*

*The value of jewelry from this period rests on the quality of the design, rather than the use of expensive, precious materials.*

An Arts & Crafts silver and ivory necklace, with foiled moonstones and painted ivory panel.

**Provenance:** This piece belonged the British 20thC artist Averil Burleigh.

c1900   15in (38cm) long

**$7,000-10,000**   VDB

591

**DECORATIVE ARTS**

A Child & Child aquamarine and citrine pendant, of open-work double-scroll form, collet set with cushion, round and oval mixed-cut pale blue aquamarines and similarly cut citrines, with an hexagonal citrine drop, maker's mark only, adapted as a brooch.

**$800-1,200**　　　　　　　　　　　　　　**DN**

An Arts & Crafts pendant, with a plaque of blister pearl, the mount embellished with foliate stems and with a Swiss lapis cabochon drop, suspended from chain.

*pendant 2in (5cm) long*
**$300-500**　　　**DN**

An Arts & Crafts enameled pendant, formed as a stylized flowerhead with radiating petals and three simulated pearls in the center.

*1.75in (4.5cm) long*
**$280-320**　　　**DN**

An Arts & Crafts citrine pendant, with four facetted stones and wire ropework borders, linked by a foliate mount, the suspension loop engraved with foliage.

*2in (5cm) long*
**$300-500**　　　**DN**

A W.H. Haseler enameled pendant, with a spray resembling a fleur-de-lys extending from a blue and turquoise enameled band, stamped "W.H.H" and "Silver", suspended on chain.

*1.5in (3.5cm) long*
**$700-1,000**　　　**DN**

A Murrle Bennett white metal, enamel, and abalone shell pendant, with a garland of flowers and leaves, stamped "MB" mark.

**$500-700**　　　**WW**

An Arts & Crafts pendant in silver and aquamarine, attributed to Rhoda Wager.

*c1900*　　*1in (2.5cm) long*
**$220-280**　　　**TDG**

An Arts & Crafts silver pendant, with chalcedony chrysoprase, garnets, blister pearls, and a crystal heart.

*c1890*　　*3in (7.5cm) long*
**$500-800**　　　**TDG**

A heart-shaped 9ct gold and amethyst pendant, marked "HM" with Birmingham marks for 1908.

*1.5in (3.5cm) long*
**$220-280**　　　**DN**

An Arts & Crafts pendant, with abalone shell and a scrolling wirework mount, four mother-of-pearl studs, chain.

*1.5in (3.5cm) long*
**$220-280**　　　**DN**

An Arts & Crafts silver brooch, by C.R. Ashbee, of hexagonal shape with a large set agate cabochon.

*c1900*　　*1.75in (4.5cm) wide*
**$5,000-7,000**　　　**VDB**

An Arts & Crafts silver and turquoise brooch, by C.R. Ashbee for the Guild of Handicraft Ltd., shaped as a butterfly.

*c1900*　　*3in (7cm) long*
**$5,000-8,000**　　　**VDB**

An Arts & Crafts silver repoussé brooch, in the style of James Fenton, in the shape of an insect's wings, with blue and green enamel work, a blister pearl and a drop pearl, unmarked.

*c1900*                    *1.5in (3.5cm) wide*

**$300-500**                              **AVW**

An Arts & Crafts silver pin, by Arthur and Georgina Gaskin, with leaves, florets, four set green pastes, and a central blister pearl.

*c1910*          *3in (7.5cm) long*

**$1,200-1,800**              **VDB**

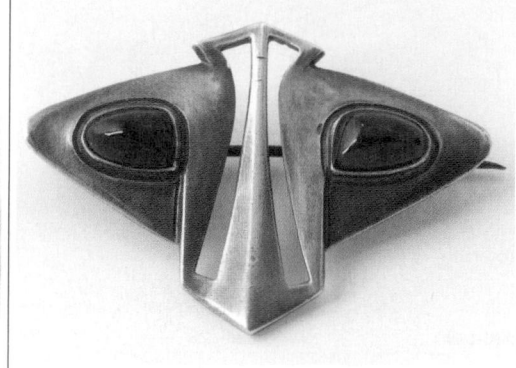

An Arts & Crafts silver brooch, designed by Max Gradl and made by Theodor Fahrner, with two stained oval agate cabochons, unsigned.

*c1900*

**$3,000-5,000**                          **VDB**

A Guild of Handicraft silver enamel brooch, with a painted pansy, of hexagonal form.

*c1900*        *1.75in (4.5cm) wide*

**$3,000-5,000**              **VDB**

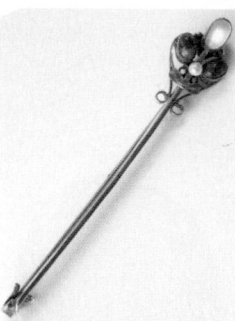

An Arts & Crafts Skonvirke brooch, by Bernhard Hertz, embossed with leaves and set with a green cabochon stone, a similar pendant below, stamped marks.

**$220-280**                **L&T**

A George Hunt white metal, enamel and moonstone pin, stamped "GH".

*4in (10cm) long*

**$400-600**            **WW**

An English Arts & Crafts oval brooch, by Bernard Instone, set with a central facetted citrine and flanked by slender leaves and pale smoky quartz.

*c1920*        *1.5in (4cm) wide*

**$400-600**              **PC**

A citrine and peridot brooch, by Bernard Instone, the oval facetted citrine within a mount of leaves, tendrils and berries punctuated with three peridots.

*c1920*        *1in (2.5cm) wide*

**$300-500**              **DN**

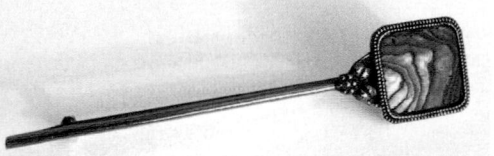

An English Arts & Crafts bar brooch, by Bernard Instone, with a plaque of abalone shell within a ropework border and flanked by a floret and leaves.

*c1920*        *2.5in (6cm) long*

**$180-220**              **PC**

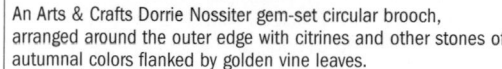

An Arts & Crafts silver brooch, by Bernard Instone, with a set cornelian and foliate decoration, unmarked.

*c1920*        *1.5in (3cm) wide*

**$180-220**              **AVW**

An Arts & Crafts silver brooch, designed by Georg Kleeman, with three oval chrysoprases, unsigned.

*c1900*    *1.75in (4.5cm) wide*

**$2,800-3,200**              **VDB**

A Dorrie Nossiter gem-set clip, with golden wirework scrolls flanked by garnets, turquoise cabochons and half-pearls.

*1.25in (3.5cm) high*

**$400-600**              **DN**

An Arts & Crafts Dorrie Nossiter gem-set circular brooch, arranged around the outer edge with citrines and other stones of autumnal colors flanked by golden vine leaves.

*c1905*                    *1.5in (4cm) wide*

**$700-1,000**                          **PC**

An Arts & Crafts silver brooch, with blister pearls and foliate decoration, unmarked.

c1900    1.25in (3cm) wide

**$80-120**    AVW

An Arts & Crafts silver repoussé lady's brooch, with an orange Ruskin pottery roundel, unmarked.

c1900    1.75in (4cm) wide

**$80-120**    AVW

An Arts & Crafts silver repoussé diamond-shaped lady's brooch, with blue Ruskin pottery roundel, unmarked.

c1900    2.5in (6.5cm) wide

**$70-100**    AVW

An Arts & Crafts silver brooch, with a large cabochon labradorite, flowers and serpents, hallmarked.

c1905    3.5in (9cm) wide

**$1,200-1,800**    VDB

An Arts & Crafts citrine brooch, centered with a facetted citrine flanked by foliage, stems, and berries.

1.5in (4cm) wide

**$280-320**    DN

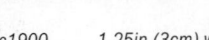

An Arts & Crafts silver and turquoise repoussé bar brooch.

c1900    3in (7.5cm) wide

**$80-120**    AVW

An Arts & Crafts silver brooch, with a blister pearl and stylized wheatsheaves, unmarked.

c1910    2.75in (7cm) wide

**$120-180**    AVW

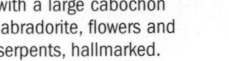

An Arts & Crafts silver, gold and amethyst brooch, with four thistles around the central cabochon, unmarked.

c1900    1.75in (4.5cm) wide

**$180-220**    AVW

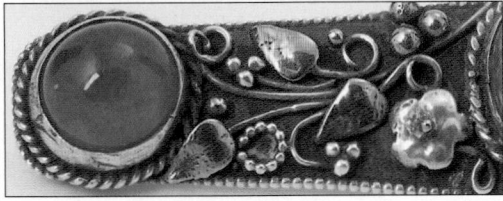

An Arts & Crafts silver, gold, and chalcedony brooch, with stylized foliate scrollwork and three cabochons, unmarked.

c1900    3in (7.5cm) wide

**$500-700**    AVW

An Arts & Crafts carnelian and fire opal brooch, with a central pale carnelian plaque within an openwork foliate mount punctuated with four facetted fire-opals.

1.75in (4.5cm) wide

**$300-400**    DN

An Arts & Crafts silver lady's ring, by Bernard Instone, with a square central amethyst and detailed wheatsheaf motifs, unmarked.

c1920    1in (2.5cm) wide

**$800-1,200**    AVW

An Arts & Crafts silver lady's ring, by Bernard Instone, with a Swiss lapis lazuli and grapevine motifs, unmarked.

c1920    1in (2.5cm) wide

**$800-1,200**    AVW

## BERNARD INSTONE

- Bernard Instone (1891-1987) won a scholarship to the Birmingham Central School of Art in England when he was only 12 years old.
- He continued his training in Birmingham's jewelry district, before working as a journeyman. He spent time with Emile Lettré in Berlin, Germany and John Paul Cooper in Kent, England.
- Instone established Langstone Silver Works in the West Midlands in 1920. Here, he specialized in jewelry and made custom pieces for clients.
- Despite the quality, he aimed to keep his work affordable. Semi-precious stones reduced costs.
- The English countryside inspired designs and wheatsheaves and berries are common motifs.
- In 1937, he became president of the 'Birmingham Jewelers' Association'.

An Arts & Crafts silver ring, with chrysoprase, chalcedony, and opal stones, attributed to Bernard Instone.

1.5in (4cm) wide

**$800-1,200**    TDG

An 18kt yellow gold ring by Edward Oakes, with pearls and blue-faceted zircons, with scrolls and beads, signed.

c1925    5in (12.5cm) high

**$6,000-9,000**    CHI

An oval Kalo brooch, with tapering pointed ends, cut-out and geometric work on both sides, centering a large green stone with brown streaks, raised rim around the outside and the stone, signed "Sterling Kalo".

c1915     2.25in (5.5cm) wide

**$800-1,200**     **CHI**

A Kalo bar pin with cut-out geometric pattern on the sides, centering a large square bezel-set yellow citrine stone, signed "Sterling Kalo".

c1915     1.75in (4.5cm) wide

**$800-1,200**     **CHI**

A Kalo bar pin, with a thin rectangular body, straight edged top, with an incised line running the length of the pin with small cutouts at each end, centered with a deep green oval bezel-set cabochon bloodstone with red inner highlights, flanked by small applied trillium flowers, signed "Sterling Kalo".

c1920     2.75in (7cm) wide

**$800-1,200**     **CHI**

## KALO SHOP

- Clara Barck Welles, a graduate of the Art Institute of Chicago, founded the Kalo Shop in 1900. Welles sought to train young women in the art of design, initially concentrating on weaving and leatherwork. After marrying the metalworker George Welles in 1905 her attention turned to silver and metal, and Welles went on to set up the Kalo School and Studio.

- The name Kalo originates from the Greek word 'kalos', which literally means 'beautiful' and the studio's motto or design brief of sorts was "Beautiful, Useful, and Enduring."

- Designs by the so-called 'Kalo girls' are usually crafted from silver, but occasionally gold was employed. The surface is often hammered, chased, and pierced.

- The most popular designs were embellished with semi-precious stones such as pearls or moonstones. These stones were typically set within stylized foliage, vine leaves, blossoms, and geometric motifs.

- After many successful years, the Kalo Shop closed in 1970.

A large oval Kalo brooch, in the form of a single flower blossom set in a saw-pierced and chased oval frame, centering a cluster of berries and a bezel-set oval cabochon moonstone, signed "Sterling Kalo Hand wrought 170".

c1935     2.25in (5.5cm) wide

**$800-1,200**     **CHI**

An American Arts & Crafts Kalo silver brooch, with an acorn and oak leaf design.

c1935     2.25in (5.5cm) wide

**$300-400**     **ARK**

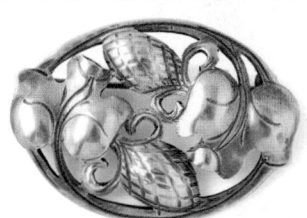

An American Arts & Crafts Kalo silver brooch, with a grape and grape leaf design.

c1935     1.75in (4.5cm) wide

**$280-320**     **ARK**

A Kalo necklace, with oval bezel-set lapis stones, and three teardrop-shaped lapis drops with silver tops, signed.

c1910     17in (43cm) long

**$6,000-9,000**     **CHI**

A rare gold Kalo pendant on a chain, with applied flowers and vines, blister pearl, pearl drop, signed "Kalo 14K".

c1910     pendant 2.25in (5.5cm) high

**$6,000-9,000**     **CHI**

A Kalo pendant necklace with pearl, with a blister pearl, applied trillium flowers, two silver bead drops, signed.

c1915     pendant 1.25in (3cm) high

**$3,000-5,000**     **CHI**

A Kalo link bracelet, with oval box clasp, safety chain, five round flower-shaped links, each containing a round carnelian bezel-set stone at its center, signed "Hand wrought sterling Kalo".

c1935     7.5in (19cm) wide

**$2,200-2,800**     **CHI**

A long and unusual Kalo belt, in the cherry motif, 28 links, signed.

*Cherry links are more usually used on Kalo bracelets and chokers.*

c1935     35in (89cm) long

**$2,800-3,200**     **CHI**

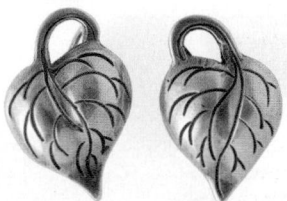

A pair of American Arts & Crafts Kalo silver leaf-design earrings, with screw backs.

c1935     1in (2.5cm) high

**$180-220**     **ARK**

A rare Kalo 14kt gold ring, with a jade cabochon, stamped "KALO 14KA".

**$800-1,200**     **DRA**

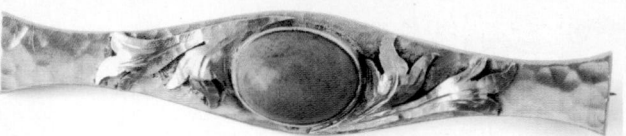

A silver bar pin, by the Art Silver Shop, with large bezel-set oval light blue-gray cabochon stone at center flanked with chased and applied leaves, hammered surfaces, signed with "SAS" mark, inscribed "Sterling, Hand made".

*c1920*      *2.25in (5.5cm) long*

**$500-700**      **CHI**

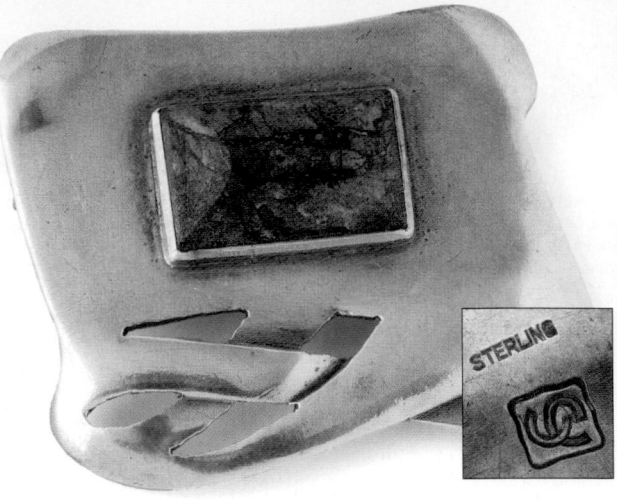

An American Arts & Crafts brooch, by George C. Frost, leaf-design in acid-etched brass.

*c1915*      *2.5in (6.5cm) wide*

**$180-220**      **ARK**

An American Arts & Crafts pin or belt buckle, by Frank Gardner Hale.

*c1915*      *1.5in (4cm) wide*

**$1,200-1,800**      **ARK**

An American Arts & Crafts brooch, in sterling and agate with Celtic interlacing detail, by Carence Crafters, Chicago.

*c1905*      *1.5in (4cm) wide*

**$700-1,000**      **ARK**

An American Arts & Crafts brooch, by Viven Lyke.

*Lyke was a student of Edward Oakes.*

*c1945*      *2in (5cm) wide*

**$180-220**      **ARK**

A gold brooch, by the Potter Studio, with maple leaves and winged seeds on an oval frame made to look like a curving twig, with hammered and carved details, signed "Potter Studio".

*c1915*      *1.5in (4cm) wide*

**$3,000-5,000**      **CHI**

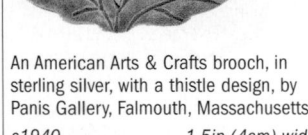

An American Arts & Crafts brooch, in sterling silver, with a thistle design, by Panis Gallery, Falmouth, Massachusetts.

*c1940*      *1.5in (4cm) wide*

**$120-180**      **ARK**

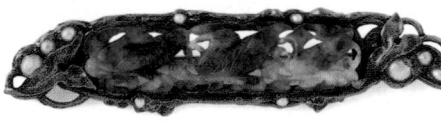

An American Arts & Crafts brooch, in 14ct gold with jade and pearls, by Potter Mellen Inc., Cleveland, Ohio.

*c1940*      *2.5in (6.5cm) wide*

**$1,800-2,200**      **ARK**

A silver bar pin, by Madeline Turner, with central oval turquoise cabochon with fine, saw-pierced scroll designs on either side of the stone, signed "M Turner handmade sterling".

*2in (5cm) wide*

**$500-700**      **CHI**

A silver brooch, by Peer Smed, designed as a lily with detailed beaded stamen and chased leaves, signed "Hand wrought Sterling Peer Smed".

*Dutch born silversmith, Peer Smed (1878-1943), established his shop in Brooklyn, New York in 1909. His 'Jack-in -the-pulpit' design for domestic silver wares, usually executed in heavy guage silver, was one of his most popular. Smed managed to attract a wealthy clientele, even during the years of he Great Depression of the 1930s. His daughter, Lona P. Schaffer, continued to make hollow and flatware in the 'Jack-in-the-pulpit' design throughout the 1940s, after her father's death.*

c1930                                              2.5in (6.5cm) long

**$600-900**                                                          CHI

A brooch and earrings set, by Clemens Friedell, with repoussé brooch in the shape of California poppies on intertwined stems and fern-like leaves, signed "Clemens Friedell Pasadena".

c1920                                    brooch 4in (10cm) long

**$3,000-4,000**                                              CHI

An American Arts & Crafts brooch, in nickel, or 'German silver', with an acid-etched design.

c1905                              2.5in (6.5cm) wide

**$220-280**                                        ARK

An American Arts & Crafts sterling silver pin, with a blister pearl, unsigned.

c1910                              2.5in (5.5cm) wide

**$220-280**                                          RK

An American Arts & Crafts bar pin, in 14ct gold and opal, unsigned.

c1915                            1.75in (4.5cm) wide

**$400-600**                                        ARK

An American Arts & Crafts pin, in green gold and green tournaline, unsigned.

c1920                            2.25in (5.5cm) wide

**$1,800-2,200**                                    ARK

An American Arts & Crafts pin, in 18ct gold and amythest, unsigned, Boston.

c1920                                2in (5cm) wide

**$700-1,000**                                      ARK

## AMERICAN NECKLACES

An American Arts & Crafts silver necklace, with dyed agate decoration, by the Art Silver Shop, Chicago.

c1920          pendant 1.5in (4cm) high

**$300-500**                            ARK

A pendant on chain, by Frank Gardner Hale, a garnet cabochon with four blister pearls, signed "F.G. Hale".

c1915          pendant 2in (5cm) high

**$5,000-8,000**                        CHI

A rare Robert Jarvie pendant on a paper clip chain, with pierced and tooled surfaces, three bezel-set chyroprase stone, with bezel-set chyroprase stone drop at the bottom, signed "Jarvie Sterling".

*Jarvie is best known as a maker of spun brass, cast bronze, and copper candlesticks, but he also worked with silver from c1905.*

c1915                          pendant 2in (5cm) high

**$6,000-9,000**                                    CHI

An enameled pendant by the Rokesley shop, with enamel in the form of an orchid or iris, pearl drop, signed.

                      1.75in (4.5cm) high

**$2,800-3,200**              CHI

An American Arts & Crafts silver and amethyst necklace, by James Scott of The Elverhoj Craft Colony.

c1925

**$500-800**                            ARK

An American Arts & Crafts necklace, in sterling silver and malachite, unknown maker.

c1905          neckpiece 4in (10cm) wide

**$500-700**                            ARK

**DECORATIVE ARTS**

An American Arts & Crafts sterling silver ring, with gold highlights and turquoise, by Frank Gardner Hale.

*c1920  0.75in (2cm) diam*

**$2,200-2,800**  **ARK**

An American Arts & Crafts sterling silver ring, with a turquoise matrix design, by Gilbert Oakes, Boston.

*c1945  0.75in (2cm) diam*

**$800-1,200**  **ARK**

An American Arts & Crafts ring, in green onyx and silver, by Bjarne.

*Bjarne was born in Denmark and emigrated to the US.*

*c1935  0.75in (2cm) diam*

**$300-400**  **ARK**

A pair of American Arts & Crafts screw back earrings, in sterling silver, by Gilbert Oakes.

*Gilbert Oakes was the son of Edward E. Oakes, the Arts & Crafts jeweler.*

*c1950  0.5in (1.5cm) wide*

**$500-800**  **ARK**

A handwrought 18kt gold bracelet, by the Rokesley Shop, with four plates joined by small oval links, each plaque with an applied water chestnut design with swirling branches in an Art Nouveau style, signed "Rokesley".

*c1910  7.5in (19cm) long*

**$6,000-9,000**  **CHI**

A 14kt gold bracelet, by Edward Oakes, alternating links, bezel-set and faceted rectangular golden topaz with all gold links in stylized leaf form.

*c1925  6.75in (17cm) long*

**$6,000-9,000**  **CHI**

A handwrought 18kt gold bracelet, by Margaret Rogers, with alternating links, bezel-set oval black onyx with smaller links comprised of gold fleur-de-lys with bezel-set pearls connected by tiny gold chain links, signed "MR".

*c1925  7.25in (18.5cm) long*

**$6,000-9,000**  **CHI**

## ART NOUVEAU JEWELRY

A Georg Jensen pendant, designed by Georg Jensen, design no. 15.

*c1910  2in (5cm) long*

**$3,000-5,000**  **SF**

A Liberty and Co. silver repoussé pendant and necklace, with stylized swirling motifs and blister pearls.

*c1900  9.5in (24cm) long*

**$500-800**  **AVW**

A set of six Liberty & Co. silver and enamel buttons, designed by Archibald Knox, each with enameled whiplash motif, in original fitted case, stamped marks "Birmingham 1903".

*1in (2.5cm) diam*

**$2,800-3,200**  **WW**

A bead belt with an Art Nouveau buckle.

*c1900  28.5in (72cm) long*

**$100-150**  **TDG**

### A CLOSER LOOK AT AN ART NOUVEAU PENDANT

*The difficult technique of plique-à-jour involves filling gaps in a metal framework with enamel, which is held in place by surface tension. The piece is then fired so that the enamel hardens.*

*There is usually no backing to the enamel so light is allowed to stream through and create a stained glass effect.*

*Innovative design in jewelry became more important during the Art Nouveau period as pieces became art forms in their own right, rather than a display of wealth.*

*Freshwater pearls are formed by shellfish found in fresh water and rivers. They are duller and less iridescent than saltwater pearls.*

A Heinrich Levinger plique-à-jour enamel and pearl pendant, of foliate form with three freshwater pearls flanked by pale blue translucent enameled panels and with a freshwater pearl drop, marked "HL 900 depose".

*1.25in (3cm) wide*

**$1,800-2,200**  **DN**

A Lalique 'Cabochon Pommier du Japon' glass brooch, of domed form molded with prunus blossom heightened with dark staining and held in a gilt metal mount, with internal green-tinted foil which reflects light, mount stamped "Lalique" and "RL".

*1.5in (4cm) diam*

**$800-1,200**     **DN**

## A CLOSER LOOK AT AN ART DECO BROOCH

*This brooch is platinum – more rare and expensive than gold and silver and generally used only in the finest jewelry. It was the most popular setting for diamonds.*

*Many of the best Art Deco pieces are signed or numbered by the maker.*

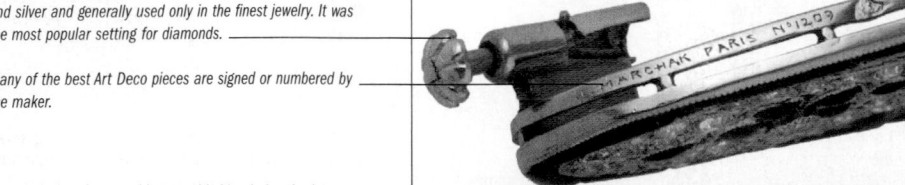

*Brooch designs became bigger and bolder during the Art Deco period to accommodate large, striking designs.*

*Good quality emeralds have fewer flaws and are deep in color. It is rare to find an example with very few or no inclusions. They are prone to chipping, so jewelry should be checked for damage.*

An Art Deco platinum, diamond, and sapphire bow pin.

*c1925*     *1.75in (4.5cm) wide*

**$12,000-18,000**     **MACK**

A rare Art Deco platinum brooch, by Marchale of Paris, set with a 5kt sugarloaf-cut emerald and 2kt diamonds, with onyx flower design, signed.

*c1925*     *2.25in (6cm) wide*

**$28,000-32,000**     **MACK**

An Art Deco platinum and diamond bow pin.

*c1925*     *2.5in (6.5cm) wide*

**$18,000-22,000**     **MACK**

A European Art Deco platinum brooch set with diamonds and rubies.

*c1925*     *1.75in (4.5cm) wide*

**$8,000-12,000**     **MACK**

A French-cut sapphire and diamond clip brooch, of openwork tapering shape, the banded mounts engraved with fine foliate decoration.

*1.25in (3cm) long*

**$800-1,200**     **DN**

A pair of dress clips, of geometrical form, with diamanté decoration.

*c1925*     *1in (2.5cm) long*

**$120-180**     **TDG**

A French silver brooch with marcasite decoration.

*c1935*     *2in (5cm) wide*

**$120-180**     **TDG**

A pair of Art Deco dress clips with paste decoration.

*c1930*   *1in (2.5cm) long*

**$50-80**   **TDG**

An Art Deco platinum semi-curve clip, set with a 12kt diamond.

*c1930*   *1.75in (4.5cm) wide*

**$18,000-22,000**   **MACK**

A pair of Art Deco sapphire and diamond double clips.

*c1930*   *1.5in (4cm) long*

**$22,000-28,000**   **MACK**

An Art Deco platinum clip, with a French mark.

*c1935*   *2.25in (5.5cm) wide*

**$8,000-12,000**   **MACK**

An Art Deco platinum ring, with filigree decoration, set with calibré rubies and diamonds.

*c1925*   *1in (2.5cm) high*

**$8,000-12,000**   **MACK**

An Art Deco platinum ring, with filigree work, set with old European-cut diamonds and sapphires.

*c1925*   *0.5in (1.5cm) high*

**$18,000-22,000**   **MACK**

An Art Deco platinum ring, of buckle design, set with one carat diamonds and rubies, with cabochon-cut sapphires to the side.

*This style of ring was often worn on the pinkie finger.*

*c1935*   *1in (2.5cm) high*

**$5,000-7,000**   **MACK**

An Art Deco Burmese platinum ring, set with rubies and diamonds.

*c1935*   *1in (2.5cm) high*

**$12,000-18,000**   **MACK**

An Art Deco platinum Van Cleef and Arpels calibré ruby ring.

*c1940*   *1in (2.5cm) high*

**$7,000-10,000**   **MACK**

An Art Deco platinum and ruby ring, signed by F. Folgert.

*c1940*   *0.75in (2cm) high*

**$4,000-6,000**   **MACK**

An Art Deco diamond, ruby and platinum ring, by Oscar Heyman, diamonds 50kt.

*c1950*   *1in (2.5cm) high*

**$8,000-12,000**   **MACK**

An Edgar Brandt necklace, with a mistletoe design, signed.

*This is an extremely rare piece as Brandt, who specialized in ironwork, made jewelry only in his early years. Only two pieces of jewelry by Brandt are known to have come to market. The Brandt family also have some examples and other pieces that were photographed during the period.*

*c1905*   *3.25in (8.5cm) high*

**$22,000-28,000**   **MOD**

An Art Deco pendant, by Edgar Brandt.

*c1925*   *2in (5cm) high*

**$12,000-18,000**   **MOD**

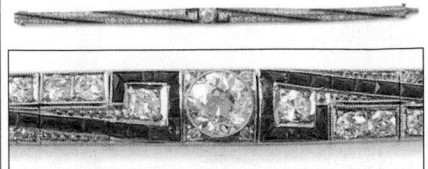

An Art Deco platinum bracelet, set with old European-cut diamonds and French-cut sapphires.

c1925     7in (18cm) long

**$22,000-28,000**     **MACK**

An Art Deco platinum bracelet, set with 32kt diamonds and emeralds.

c1925     7in (18cm) long

**$32,000-38,000**     **MACK**

An Art Deco articulated platinum bracelet, set with mixed-cut diamonds and hand-cut rubies.

c1935     7in (18cm) long

**$70,000-80,000**     **MACK**

An Art Deco celluloid bangle in shape of a serpent, with diamanté details.

c1930     3in (7.5cm) diam

**$120-180**     **TDG**

A gilt metal headdress, in Egyptian style, with a serpent.

c1920     7in (18cm) diam

**$500-700**     **TDG**

A pair of Art Deco earrings, with large central diamonds.

c1920     2.25in (6cm) long

**$35,000-40,000**     **MACK**

A pair of Art Deco diamond and sapphire pendant earrings.

c1925     2.5in (6.5cm) long

**$22,000-28,000**     **MACK**

A Cartier black onyx and diamond round dress set, in Art Deco style, comprising a pair of twin-panel cufflinks, four buttons, and two collar studs, the buttons and two of the cufflink panels engraved "Cartier", the studs stamped "18c", in a case.

**$7,000-10,000**     **DN**

A Mexican silver bracelet, with green gem.

c1940     9in (23cm) long

**$300-400**     **TDG**

A 20thC amber bead necklace, with beads of varying size.

40in (100cm) long

**$800-1,200**     **TDG**

A 1950s brooch, silver metal formed as a stylized figure.

**$220-280**     **MOD**

An Arts & Crafts mahogany bookcase, by Shapland and Petter of Barnstaple, the cavetto frieze with applied and embossed copper foliage, with leaded glazed doors and linen fold paneled doors, on square supports, inscribed "Reading Maketh a Full Man".

*84.5in (211cm) high*

**$5,000-7,000**          **L&T**

An Arts & Crafts oak bookcase, in the manner of the Scottish school, by Wylie and Lochhead of Glasgow, with stained glass floral panels flanked by angular stylized copper repoussé panels, above drawers and a bottom cabinet.

*c1900          72in (183cm) high*

**$10,000–15,000**          **PUR**

A Cotswolds Arts & Crafts oak compendium, retailed by Heal and Son, with a chest of drawers, bookcase and wardrobe.

*79in (197.5cm) high*

**$700-1,000**          **FRE**

An Arts & Crafts standing oak bookcase, retailed by Liberty & Co., of three tiers, with stylized floral repoussé panels and cut-outs to the sides.

*c1905          35in (89cm) high*

**$800–1,200**          **PUR**

An Arts & Crafts oak bookcase, by Harris Lebus, the flaring cornice with shaped supports, open bookcase and drop-down writing surface, above a single drawer with stylized heart fretwork to the sides and two open bookshelves below.

*c1900          65in (165cm) high*

**$3,000–5,000**          **PUR**

An Arts & Crafts oak bookcase, retailed by Liberty & Co., with adjustable shelves, stylized heart fretwork at the top, three long top shelves and a single central bottom cabinet flanked by two small short shelves.

*c1900          70in (175cm) high*

**$32,000-38,000**          **PUR**

## CABINETS

An Arts & Crafts oak music cabinet, attributed to Bruce Talbert for Gillows of Lancaster.

*c1885          43in (109cm) high*

**$2,800-3,200**          **PUR**

An Arts & Crafts mahogany music cabinet in the Anglo-Japanese style, with string ebony and boxwood inlay.

*c1895          49in (125cm) wide*

**$5,000-7,000**          **PUR**

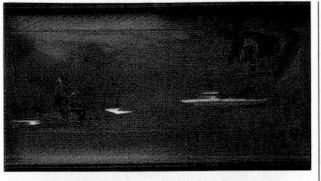

An Arts & Crafts sideboard, designed by E.A. Taylor for Wylie and Lochhead of Glasgow, with a marquetry panel depicting a knight before a medieval castle in flames.

*c1900*   *70in (170cm) wide*

**$15,000–18,000**   **PUR**

## A CLOSER LOOK AT AN ARTS & CRAFTS SIDEBOARD

Godwin worked on commissions from many of the great and good in his lifetime, including studios for Princess Louise and James Whistler, a house and costumes for actress Lily Langtry, and interiors for Oscar Wilde.

Godwin's celebrated Anglo-Japanese styling can clearly be seen in this sideboard, especially in the pagoda-style detailing and the use of lacquer panels.

The lacquer panels are decorated with trees and birds, in imitation of the Japanese style.

Godwin was keen to make his furniture as light as possible. Combined with the delicate fretwork, that makes this a fragile piece that has survived in remarkably good condition.

An Arts & Crafts Anglo-Japanese mahogany sideboard, designed by E.W. Godwin and made by William Watts, with Japanese lacquer panels set in embossed leather, lattice top with pagoda-style detailing, two drawers flanked by lacquer panels, engraved handles, hinges and escutcheons, on splayed feet.

*1878*   *50in (127cm) wide*

**$150,000-180,000**   **PUR**

## WYLIE & LOCHHEAD

- In 1829 brothers-in-law Robert Wylie and James Lochhead founded a company in Glasgow to retail furniture and upholstery. In the 1860s the firm became increasingly involved in designing and producing their own products, establishing workshops at Kent Road and Mitchell Street.
- Wylie and Lochhead produced stylish but commercial and affordable Arts & Crafts furnishings for the middle classes. Typical Wylie and Lochhead furniture is in solid oak, with stylized inlaid detail and cut-out or carved decoration.
- Many talented craftsmen and designers produced pieces for the firm, including George Logan and Ernest Archibald Taylor, husband of illustrator and jewelry designer Jessie M. King. Shapland and Petter also supplied them with stock.
- The company survived until 1957, when it became part of The House of Fraser.

An Arts & Crafts ebonized sideboard by Collcut, with bone inlay.

*54in (137cm) high*

**$5,000-8,000**   **PUR**

## DRESSING TABLES

A William Watt ash dressing table, designed by E.W. Godwin, the top with hinged extensions and fold-out supports, drawers with brass handles, and an enameled metal 'Heirloom' label, together with an en-suite washstand table, some damage.

*39.5in (100cm) wide*

**$18,000-25,000 set**   **WW**

An Arts & Crafts walnut lady's desk, by Shapland and Petter, with a leather writing surface and a stained glass back panel with stylized floral motifs, above two drawers and a shaped slatted bottom gallery.

*1903*   *42in (107cm) wide*

**$3,000-4,000**   **PUR**

A Gordon Russell 'Ilmington' cherrywood dressing table, designed by W.H. Russell, with hinged triptych mirror, semi-bowed twin pedestals and oak-lined drawers with inset handles, bears maker's label.

*This dressing table design differs from the standard stock and was probably made as a special commission for a client.*

*c1935*   *54.75in (137cm) wide*

**$1,200-1,800**   **L&T**

An Arts & Crafts iron stick stand, in the Anglo-Japanese style.

*30in (76cm) high*

**$5,000-7,000** **PUR**

An Arts & Crafts oak umbrella stand, by Shapland and Petter, with copper thistle repoussé panel, single drawer, three shaped spindles and central heart cut-out to the slatted bottom gallery, raised on square capped supports.

*c1905* *43in (109cm) high*

**$1,200-1,800** **PUR**

An Arts & Crafts oak stick stand, by Shapland and Petter, with stylized upper and lower copper floral repoussé panels, three umbrella compartments and lower slatted front and sides, raised on square supports.

*c1905* *41in (106cm) high*

**$2,200-2,800** **PUR**

An Arts & Crafts oak stick stand, retailed by Liberty & Co., with three compartments each decorated with a pierced heart, on capped feet.

*c1905* *32.5in (83cm) high*

**$500-700** **PUR**

An Arts & Crafts Gothic Revival oak hallstand, with angular pediment and stylized floral cut-outs above a mirror, butterfly fretwork detail at top corners, a row of tiles by Christopher Dresser above the serving area and a central drawer flanked by two Star of David roundels, raised on ring-turned front legs with ebony dot detailing.

*c1880* *97in (246cm) high*

**$3,000-5,000** **PUR**

An Arts & Crafts hallstand, by Harris Lebus, with dentil cornice above stylized floral carvings, with central mirror above a panel of tiles, stylized tubular floral motifs, seven stylized coat hooks, and central drawer flanked by side stick compartments, on stile feet.

*c1905* *82.5in (210cm) high*

**$3,000-4,000** **PUR**

An Arts & Crafts Gothic Revival oak hall seat with central mirror, ebonized floral details at the top and sides and chevron inlays to the front edges, with six ring-turned coat hooks and a lift-up store seat, raised on stile feet.

*c1880* *85in (216cm) high*

**$3,000-5,000** **PUR**

An Arts & Crafts oak hallrobe by Shapland and Petter, with classical carved panels at the top, stylized copper hinges and handles, and fitted interior.

*c1905* *82in (209cm) high*

**$4,000-6,000** **PUR**

## WARDROBES

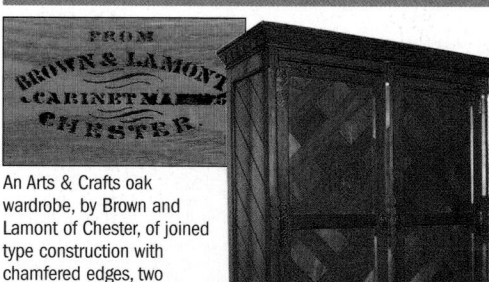

An Arts & Crafts oak wardrobe, by Brown and Lamont of Chester, of joined type construction with chamfered edges, two parquetry doors with pierced brass hinges, sliding trays and hanging space above two short drawers.

*83.5in (212cm) high*

**$2,200-2,800** **DN**

An Arts & Crafts oak wardrobe by Maple and Co., in the form of a house, the roof-shaped cornice with stylized eaves.

*86in (220cm) high*

**$700-1,000** **DN**

An Arts & Crafts mahogany wardrobe, designed by Barry Parker and Sir Raymond Unwin for Goodall, Lamb and Heighway Ltd. of Manchester, the doors with tongue-and-groove paneling and plant-form cut-outs, the canted sides with leaded glass doors, the doors containing shelves and drawers, with beaten copper fittings, raised on a plinth.

*This wardrobe once belonged to the English designer and ceramicist Clarice Cliff and stood in the bedroom of 'Chetwynd', her house in Northwood, Staffordshire, England. Designed by Parker and Unwin between 1899 and 1902 for C.F. Goodfellow, the house was bought and renamed in 1926 by Colley Shorter who lived there with his first wife before his marriage to Clarice Cliff in 1940. Clarice Cliff remained at 'Chetwynd' until her death in 1972.*

*8.75in (220cm) wide*

**$3,000-5,000**     **L&T**

A three-fold Arts & Crafts oak screen with brass disc detailing and gilded leather panels embossed with grapes, lemons, apples, and passion fruit.

*69in (175cm) high*

**$15,000–20,000**     **PUR**

## A CLOSER LOOK AT A MORRIS & CO. SCREEN

*The combination of well-worked wood and attractive silk embroidery make this an important and appealing document of the work done by Morris & Co.*

*Each of these three silk panels is decorated with a different pattern, significantly enhancing the interest of this piece. J.H. Dearle's textile designs for Morris & Co. were among the best they produced.*

*This piece could be put to practical use in a contemporary setting, perhaps to divide a large loft-style interior. Utility will invariably increase the value of an antique.*

*The pierced detail on these panels is typical of Arts & Crafts furniture, with decoration primarily used to display the skill of the maker and highlight the inherent charm of the wood.*

A Morris & Co. three-fold mahogany draught screen, each fold with a silkwork embroidered glazed panel, possibly designed by J. H. Dearle, with foliage worked in coloured silks, enclosed by a frame with shaped top and finials, the frieze below decorated with waved piercings, on turned feet.

*74.75in (187cm) high*

**$22,000-28,000**     **L&T**

An embroidered oak framed firescreen, the embroidered panel depicting two peacocks.

*33.5in (84cm) high*

**$400-600**     **WW**

A two-fold firescreen, in the style of Morris & Co., embroidered with panels of flowers and foliage.

*40in (100cm) high*

**$500-700**     **WW**

## CHAIRS

A leather-upholstered armchair by Ogden Farago.

*c1900*     *41.5in (105.5cm) high*

**$5,000-8,000**     **LM**

### E.W. GODWIN

- Edward William Godwin was an architect who designed furniture in the mid-19thC. His work is characterized by careful choice of materials and meticulous construction – the central tenets of the Arts & Crafts movement.
- Godwin embraced Japanese principles of design, as is evident in the balance of vertical and horizontal members in his furniture.
- His distinctive furniture is elegant, with a light touch and refined proportions.
- Ebonized woods were left unadorned, or else simply decorated with inset panels of embossed Japanese paper. A few pieces bear painted or stenciled stylized geometric patterns.
- Godwin submitted his designs for production by various cabinet-makers, including William Watt, John Gregory Crace, and the firm of Collinson and Lock.
- Furniture by Godwin is unmarked, making attribution problematic. Surviving sketches have helped identify a number of his designs.

An Arts & Crafts Anglo-Japanese armchair, by E.W. Godwin, with lattice details to the back support centred with an embossed leather back.

*c1875*          *40in (101.5cm) high*

**$7,000-10,000**          **PUR**

An Arts & Crafts oak armchair, attributed to E.W. Godwin, with slatted back and sides, and embossed leather back support.

*c1875*          *44in (112cm) high*

**$5,000-7,000**          **PUR**

An Arts & Crafts Jacobean ebonized all-round stretcher armchair, by E.W. Godwin.

*c1875*          *34in (86.5cm) high*

**$3,000-5,000**          **PUR**

An Arts & Crafts office chair, by E.W. Godwin.

*40in (101.5cm) high*

**$7,000-10,000**          **PUR**

An Arts & Crafts oak open armchair, possibly for Heal & Son, with a pierced splat and a padded seat.

**$400-600**          **DN**

A Swedish birch armchair, designed by Carl Malmsten.

*c1900*          *23.5in (60cm) wide*

**$3,000-5,000**          **LANE**

A Morris & Co. 'Sussex' ash armchair with rush seat, damaged.

*33.5in (85cm) high*

**$500-700**          **WW**

One of two similar late 19thC ebonized elbow chairs, by Morris and Co., each with a spindle back and caned seat.

*34in (86cm) high*

**$220-280 pair**          **DN**

A Morris & Co. 'Rossetti' chair, the design attributed to Dante Gabriel Rossetti, damaged.

*35.5in (89cm) high*

**$280-320**          **WW**

A mahogany armchair in the style of E.W. Godwin, possibly manufactured by James Peddle, with retailer's mark.

*35.25in (88cm) high*

**$500-700**          **WW**

An Arts & Crafts mahogany revolving chair, by James Peddle, attributed to E.W. Godwin, with curved slatted back and shaped seat on tripulitic legs.

*c1880*     *34in (86.5cm) high*

**$1,800–2,200**     **PUR**

An Arts & Crafts walnut armchair, by E. Punnet for William Birch of High Wycombe, the shaped back with stylized heart cut-out, slatted sides, solid bow-fronted seat, and elongated square tapering legs, on sledge feet.

*c1905*     *32in (82cm) high*

**$3,000–5,000**     **PUR**

A 'Gnomeman' oak armchair, with leather seat and carved gnome, signed.

*36in (90cm) high*

**$400-600**     **WW**

A pair of Arts & Crafts ladder-back dining room chairs with rush seats, associated with Charles Rennie Mackintosh.

*c1895*     *46in (117cm) high*

**$5,000–8,000**     **PUR**

## A CLOSER LOOK AT A MORRIS & CO. CHAIR

*Ebonizing was one of the few treatments that Morris & Co. used, as it enhanced rather than disguised the grain and texture of the woods the company worked with.*

*The original upholstery adds a great deal of value to this chair, as it is the most perishable part. This 'Bird' pattern is typical of Morris & Co. textile designs, and was very popular in its day.*

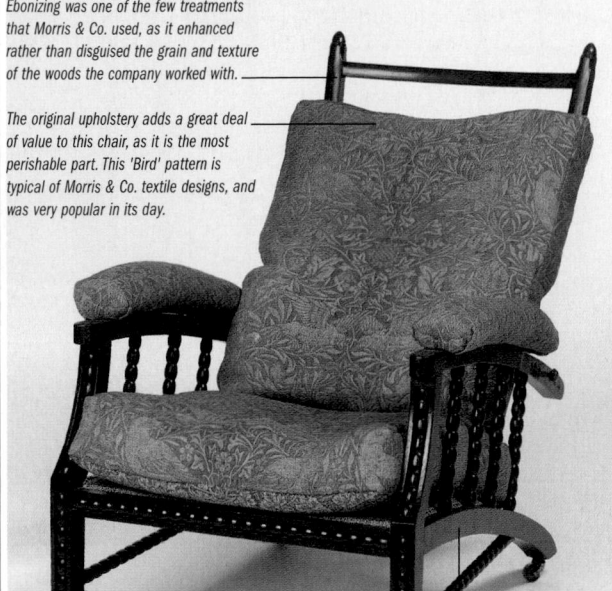

*The slatted sides and long, curving back legs that meet the front seat rail are classic components of the William Morris chair.*

An Arts & Crafts walnut armchair, designed by Philip Webb for Morris & Co., with original fabric upholstery depicting birds, of ebonized wood, with slatted sides.

*c1865*     *36.5in (92cm) high*

**$12,000-18,000**     **PUR**

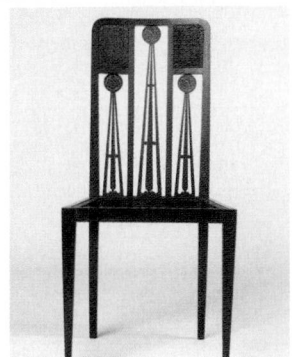

One of a set of six Arts & Crafts mahogany dining room chairs, designed by George Walton.

*c1900*     *38in (96cm) high*

**$2,800-3,200 set**     **PUR**

One of six oak and leather dining chairs by Robert 'Mouseman' Thompson, each carved with a mouse signature.

*34in (85cm) high*

**$5,000-7,000 set**     **FRE**

A Heal & Son rush-seated oak child's chair, of slat back form.

*36in (90cm) high*

**$120-180**     **WW**

A mahogany chair, retailed by Liberty & Co., the back carved with a Celtic panel, with original paper label.

*40.5in (101cm) high*

**$800-1,200**     **WW**

A Swedish birch side chair, designed by Carl Malmsten.

c1900    17.75in (45cm) wide

**$1,200-1,800**    LANE

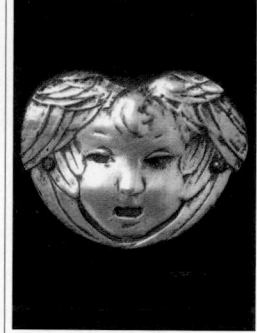

A Morris & Co. 'Sussex' chair, in ebonized beech, the spindle-filled back above a rush seat on turned legs.

**$300-500**    L&T

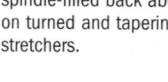

An Arts & Crafts mahogany high-backed side chair, by Shapland and Petter, in the Glasgow style, with a cherub head in pewter on the central slat, the upholstered seat not original.

c1905    42in (107cm) high

**$1,800-2,200**    PUR

A late 19thC Arts & Crafts walnut side chair, in the manner of George Walton or Arthur Simpson, with curved top rail, heart-pierced splat, and rush seat.

**$600-900**    DN

## SHAPLAND & PETTER

- Cabinet-maker Henry Shapland initially founded his furniture company c1855 at Barnstable in Devon, England. Accountant Henry Petter joined Shapland, and the firm rapidly expanded.
- Shapland had been impressed by an innovative wave-molding machine on a trip to America. He recreated this technology on his return, and his company continued to combine sophisticated machine production with skilled hand craftsmanship.
- Shapland and Petter's Arts & Crafts pieces are typically in mahogany or oak with inlaid decoration and carving. Designs often feature piercing, arches, stained panels, and cabochons.
- Shapland and Petter employees trained for many years to become fully qualified. Their mastery is evident in the work they produced for the company. The quality of their designs brought commissions from highly regarded retailers such as Morris & Co.
- When the market for hand-finished furniture declined after WWII, the firm began to focus on producing functional items.

A pair of 19thC ebonized side chairs, designed by Bruce Talbert, the curved spindle-filled back above a caned seat on turned and tapering legs linked by stretchers.

**$300-400**    L&T

A Morris & Co. 'Sussex' sofa, in ebonized beech, with spindle back, horizontally spindled open arms above later cord seat, on turned legs linked by stretchers.

54.75in (137cm) wide

**$800-1,200**    L&T

An Arts & Crafts Moorish settee, retailed by Liberty & Co.

c1890    34in (86.5cm) high

**$3,000-5,000**    PUR

An Arts & Crafts settee, designed by George Jack for Morris & Co.

c1900    37in (94cm) high

**$10,000-15,000**    PUR

An Arts & Crafts cast-iron garden bench, by Christopher Dresser for the Coalbrooke Dale, with an intricate and stylized floral cut-out panel.

A Scottish Arts & Crafts stained pine and pokerwork decorated hall settle, with molded top rail, tongue-and-groove back decorated with coloured pokerwork roses, and electroplated seat on square supports, with rose and checker decoration and decorative brackets.

74.75in (187cm) wide

**$2,800-3,200**    L&T

c1875    76in (193cm) wide

**$12,000-18,000**    PUR

A Swedish birch bench, designed by Carl Malmsten.

*Malmsten (1888-1972) was an important Swedish designer who promoted a more craft-orientated and functional approach to furniture design.*

*c1900      14.25in (36cm) wide*

**$800-1,200**                    **LANE**

An oak stool with embroidered seat, the uprights with overhanging arm rails, linked by a single stretcher.

*24.5in (61cm) wide*

**$120-180**                    **WW**

A Scott Morton oak stool, designed by Sir Robert Lorimer, with chamfered shaped trestle ends joined by a waved stretcher with exposed peg joints, bears maker's label.

*17.5in (44cm) wide*

**$800-1,200**                    **L&T**

A pair of Arts & Crafts oak Thebes stools, retailed by Liberty & Co., with carved Egyptian and astrological motifs.

*c1890                    13.5in (34cm) high*

**$3,000–5,000**                    **PUR**

## TABLES

A French 1930s limed oak dining table.

*59in (150cm) wide*

**$4,000-6,000**                    **LM**

A mahogany side table, in the style of M.H. Baillie Scott, the circular top inlaid to the edge.

*29.25in (73cm) high*

**$300-500**                    **WW**

### A CLOSER LOOK AT AN ARTS & CRAFTS TABLE

*The simple, robust form of the table is typical of Webb's Gothic sensibility.*

*The symmetrical form of the table and its stretchers mean that it retains its aesthetic interest from every angle.*

*This table was commissioned by Sir William Beale for use at Drumlamford House in Ayrshire, Scotland. The link to this illustrious family provides this piece with solid provenance.*

*Philip Webb designed this table while working for Morris & Co. An architect by trade, Webb also produced important designs for interiors, including metalware, furniture, and textiles.*

A large Morris & Co. mahogany dining table, designed in the 1860s by Philip Webb, the oval top with incised edge above a central turned support surrounded by six ring-turned legs linked by ring-turned stretchers.

**Provenance**: *Sir William Beale was the Liberal M.P. for Galloway. His younger brother James Beale commissioned Philip Webb to build 'Standen' at East Grinstead in 1891 and he in turn engaged Morris & Co. to furnish the interior with textiles, wallpapers and furnishings. William Morris became a personal friend of the Beale family and consequently his influence can be felt at all of their residences, including 32 Holland Park in London, 'Bryntirion' near Dongelan in Wales, and 'Drumlamford' in South Ayrshire, Scotland.*

*70.5in (176cm) long*

**$60,000-80,000**                    **L&T**

A pair of Arts & Crafts side tables by E.W. Godwin for Heal & Son, with open fretwork and staggered shelves, in the Anglo-Japanese style.

*c1890          tallest 27in (68.5cm) high*

**$4,000-6,000**                    **PUR**

An Arts & Crafts mahogany occasional table, probably Heal & Son, with checker banding, the rectangular top above an arched frieze and single drawer raised on six square supports linked by stretchers and raised on a trestle base.

*39.5in (99cm) long*

**$800-1,200**                    **L&T**

An Arts & Crafts rosewood side table, by Collinson and Lock.

*27in (68.5cm) wide*

**$8,000-12,000**  PUR

An Arts & Crafts ash bobbin side table, by E.W. Godwin.

*22in (56cm) high*

**$2,800-3,200**  PUR

An Arts & Crafts walnut three-leg bobbin side table, by E.W. Godwin.

*22in (56cm) high*

**$3,000-4,000**  PUR

An Arts & Crafts rosewood side table, in the style of William Morris.

*26in (66cm) high*

**$7,000-10,000**  PUR

## STANDS

A white painted Arts & Crafts occasional table, the rectangular top with molded edge above square tapering legs linked by a lower stretcher and with pierced heart supports to the sides.

*21.5in (55cm) high*

**$220-280**  L&T

An Arts & Crafts whatnot, attributed to Philip Webb for Morris & Co.

*c1855*   *60in (152.5cm) high*

**$10,000-15,000**  PUR

A Liberty and Co. oak étagere designed by Leonard Wyburd, the top above two lower galleried tiers linked by turned and blocked supports, the sides with latticed grilles, on bobbin-turned legs linked by stretchers.

*31.25in (78cm) high*

**$700-1,000**  L&T

An Arts & Crafts walnut plant stand, retailed by Liberty & Co., in the Anglo-Moorish style, with ebonized Moorish brackets and mushrabia bobbin turnings, on an angled kickout.

*c1890*   *33in (84cm) high*

**$1,800-2,200**  PUR

## MIRRORS

An Arts & Crafts copper mirror, retailed by Liberty & Co., with six turquoise Ruskin pottery roundels and stylized floral embossing to the frame.

*c1900*   *19in (48cm) long*

**$1,200–1,800**  PUR

An Arts & Crafts Glasgow School repoussé brass mirror, with interlaced Celtic details.

*c1905*   *22.5in (57cm) long*

**$2,200–2,800**  PUR

An Arts & Crafts oak swing mirror, in a plain rectangular frame, held between two tapering uprights, on splayed feet united by a stretcher.

*23.25in (59cm) high*

**$220-280**  DN

An Arts & Crafts ebonized burr and walnut mirror, with painted top.

*c1885*   *32in (81.5cm) high*

**$3,000-5,000**  PUR

A Gustav Stickley V-back armchair with vertical backslats and saddle seat, overcoated finish, replaced seat, unsigned.

*36in (90cm) high*

**$400-600** DRA

A Gustav Stickley V-back armchair with rush seat, refinished, replaced paper rush seat, unsigned.

*34in (85cm) high*

**$300-400** DRA

A Gustav Stickley V-back rocker with rush seat, refinished, replaced paper rush seat, repairs to underside of one rocker, unsigned.

*Paper rush is a man-made fiber of chemically treated twisted paper that was used in the early 20thC.*

*34in (85cm) high*

**$300-400** DRA

## A CLOSER LOOK AT STICKLEY ROCKER

*Stickley's heavy solid forms were simple and he used geometric lines, steering clear of the fussy ornamentation that was so typical of Victorian design.*

*Features like mortise-and-tenon joints and chamfered boards were given a decorative purpose in Stickley designs. This emphasized the solid craftsman approach.*

*This rocker features a Gustav Stickley branded shopmark, which includes a joiner's compass and the name "Stickley" or "Gustav Stickley", and beneath are the Flemish words "Als Ik Kan" (As I can).*

*Stickley furniture has a rich and dark patina.*

An American Arts & Crafts rocker, by Gustav Stickley, no. 323, with vertical slats and short corbels beneath flat arms, original finish, color added to tops of arms, replaced leather upholstery and branded on back stretcher.

*c1900* *32in (80cm) wide*

**$3,000-5,000** DRA

An American Arts & Crafts fixed-back armchair, by Gustav Stickley, with vertical slats under each arm, original finish, lighter on the arms, minor edge chipping, replaced leather, unsigned.

*c1900* *30.5in (76cm) wide*

**$3,000-5,000** DRA

A drop-arm Morris chair, by Gustav Stickley, with five slats under each arm, original finish and maker's decal, damaged.

*32.75in (83cm) wide*

**$7,000-10,000** DRA

A Gustav Stickley reverse-taper bow-arm chair, with adjustable pegs for three tilt settings.

*40in (100cm) high*

**$12,000-14,000** GAL

A Morris chair, by Gustav Stickley, adjustable back, vertical side slats, replaced rope seat support, signed under arm with red joiner's compass and "Stickley" marks, original fumed finish.

*36.5in (93cm) wide*

**$13,000-15,000** SK

A rare and early American Arts & Crafts armchair, by Gustav Stickley, with V-top rail, narrow arms, and flaring legs flanking a rush seat, refinished, replaced paper rush, unmarked.

*c1900* *24in (60cm) wide*

**$4,000-6,000** DRA

611

A rare and early 20thC American Arts & Crafts side chair, by Gustav Stickley, no. 2600, with V-rail and rush seat, original finish, some restoration, replaced rush, unsigned.

*c1900*    *33.5in (84cm) wide*

**$4,000-6,000**    DRA

Six Gustav Stickley ladderback side chairs, no. 306 1/2, original light red-brown finish, with tacked on leather seats, red decal on back slats and paper label under seats, some damage.

*36in (90cm) high*

**$4,000-6,000**    DRA

Six Gustav Stickley ladderback side chairs, no. 306 1/2, original dark brown finish, with replaced leather and original tacks, four chairs branded, one with paper label, one unsigned.

*36in (90cm) high*

**$4,000-6,000**    DRA

An American Arts & Crafts footstool, no. 300, by Gustav Stickley, with arched side stretchers, original finish, leather and tacks, decal inside side stretcher, paper label under seat.

*c1900*   *15.5in (39cm) wide*

**$2,200-2,800**    DRA

An American Arts & Crafts piano bench, by Gustav Stickley, with cut-out handles and feet, original finish, good condition and red decal inside side.

*c1900*   *36in (90cm) wide*

**$5,000-7,000**    DRA

## BOOKCASES

A Gustav Stickley two-door bookcase, with gallery top, iron pulls, thin original finish, missing piece from back right foot, paper label.

*45in (112.5cm) high*

**$5,000-7,000**    DRA

A Gustav Stickley oak bookcase, gallery top with through tenons, each of the mullioned doors with eight panes of glass, V-shaped pulls, paper label, veneer damage.

*c1905*    *47.75in (121.5cm) wide*

**$4,000-6,000**    SK

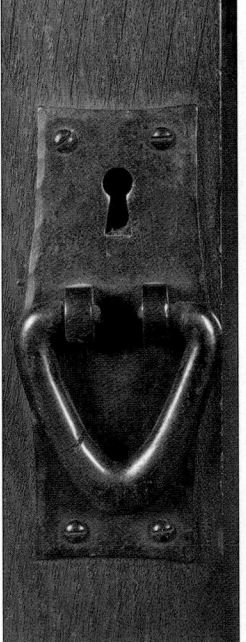

A Gustav Stickley single-door bookcase.

*55in (139.5cm) high*

**$6,000-9,000**    GAL

An early Gustav Stickley bookcase, with four mitered-mullion doors over four cabinet doors, copper ring pulls and strap hardware, broad backsplash, large red decal.

*59.75in (152cm) wide*

**$140,000-145,000     DRA**

A Gustav Stickley sideboard, with four centered drawers and two side doors.

*70in (178cm) wide*

**$22,000-26,000     GAL**

## STANDS

A Gustav Stickley 'Tree of Life' magazine stand, refinished, small burns and water spots on top, unmarked.

*43in (107.5cm) high*

**$1,000-1,500     DRA**

An early American Arts & Crafts magazine stand, by Gustav Stickley, with beveled top and paneled sides, some damage and restoration, decal under top.

*c1900     15.5in (39cm) wide*

**$5,000-8,000     DRA**

An American Arts & Crafts magazine stand, by Gustav Stickley, with semi-circle cut-outs and arched toe-board, original finish, red decal above handle cut out, paper label under top.

*c1900     13.5in (34cm) wide*

**$3,000-5,000     DRA**

## OTHER GUSTAV STICKLEY PIECES

A rare and early American Arts & Crafts clip-corner taboret, by Gustav Stickley, no. 52, with flush through-tenons and corseted cross-stretchers, fine new finish, red decal under top.

*c1900     22in (55cm) high*

**$3,000-5,000     DRA**

### A CLOSER LOOK AT A GUSTAV STICKLEY WRITING DESK

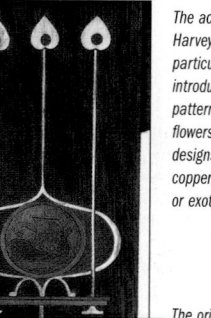

*The accomplished architect Harvey Ellis is particularly known for introducing subtle patterns, with decorative flowers or Jugendstil designs. He used inlays of copper, pewter and nickel, or exotic woods.*

*The original finish and fixtures add to the desirability and value of the piece.*

A rare Gustav Stickley writing desk, designed by Harvey Ellis, with pewter pulls, shoe feet and four flat legs inlaid with sailing ships surrounded by an Art Nouveau motif in various woods, copper, and pewter, original finish, unsigned, partial restoration to pewter.

*An extremely rare desk from a private residence in Maine, this is one of only three known.*

*Despite Ellis's lighter, subtle approach this table maintains the sturdy and solid form of earlier Stickley pieces, which can be seen from the shoe-feet with conjoining stretcher.*

*29.5in (74cm) wide*

**$55,000-60,000     DRA**

A Gustav Stickley oak-framed mirror with arched crest rail and wrought iron hanging hooks, remains of paper label.

*29in (72.5cm) wide*

**$1,200-1,800** **DRA**

A Gustav Stickley oak-framed mirror with arched crest rail, refinished, "Als Ik Kan" paper label and decal.

*29in (72.5cm) wide*

**$400-600** **DRA**

A Gustav Stickley blanket box.

*31.75in (80.5cm) wide*

**$6,000-9,000** **GAL**

A rare pair of hammered copper and wrought-iron single-socket electrified post lamps, by Gustav Stickley, composed of four curled straps holding a copper oil font, topped with a period wicker shade, original patina, some wear, stamped.

*33in (82.5cm) high*

**$18,000-20,000** **DRA**

A rare and early Gustav Stickley hammered copper floriform lamp base, two sockets, original dark patina, unmarked.

*23.5in (59cm) high*

**$3,000-4,000** **DRA**

A rare wrought-iron three-piece fireplace set, attributed to Gustav Stickley, with a pair of tongs and a poker on a stand with oval base and curled feet, tong handle resoldered, unmarked.

*30in (75cm) high*

**$2,800-3,200** **DRA**

## L. & J.G. STICKLEY

A set of six early 20thC oak chairs, by L. & J.G. Stickley, three horizontal slats, slip cushion seat, double side stretcher, straight seat rail, later upholstery, branded "The Work of L. & J.G. Stickley."

*36.5in (93cm) high*

**$5,000-8,000** **SK**

A set of five rush-seat side chairs, by L. & J.G. Stickley, with three vertical backslats, refinished, replaced rush, branded.

*36in (90cm) high*

**$2,200-2,800** **DRA**

Three of a set of six Arts & Crafts oak side chairs, by L. & J.G. Stickley, three vertical slats below crest rail, slip seat, double side-stretcher, branded marks.

*c1915* *35.75in (91cm) high*

**$2,800-3,200 set** **SK**

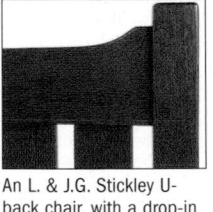

An L. & J.G. Stickley U-back chair, with a drop-in sprung cushion.

*36in (90cm) high*

**$800-1,200** **GAL**

An Arts & Crafts oak rocker, by L. & J.G. Stickley, the back with five center splats under a shaped rail, over paddled arm with mortise and tendon into the front square leg supports, joined by stretchers, paper label.

*32in (81cm) high*

**$800-1,200** **ISA**

An L. & J.G. Stickley octagonal taboret with legs mortised through the top, original finish with color added, wear, stains and repair, decal.

*17in (42.5cm) high*

**$800-1,200**      **DRA**

An L. & J.G. Stickley octagonal taboret with legs mortised through the top, original finish, wear, unmarked.

*17in (42.5cm) high*

**$1,200-1,800**      **DRA**

An L. & J.G. Stickley tea table, the legs mortised through the circular top and circular lower shelf, refinished, wear, unmarked.

*24.5in (61cm) diam*

**$500-800**      **DRA**

A 20thC oak dining table, by L. & J.G. Stickley, rectangular top on trestle base with extension arms and two leaves, branded oval "Stickley" mark.

*62in (157.5cm) wide*

**$2,200-2,800**      **SK**

A rare L. & J.G. Stickley book table with verticle slats all around, under a square overhanging top, unmarked, some restoration.

*27in (68.5cm) wide*

**$5,000-7,000**      **DRA**

An L. & J.G. Stickley plant stand with two straight cross stretchers, refinished, seam separations to plant shelf, wood loss around feet, unmarked.

*22in (55cm) high*

**$400-600**      **DRA**

An L. & J.G. Stickley drop front desk.

**$3,000-5,000**      **GAL**

An L. & J.G. Stickley tall clock, with square overhanging top, paneled sides, arched apron and copper clockface, original finish and maker's decal.

*45in (114.5cm) wide*

*80in (200cm) high*

**$22,000-28,000**      **DRA**

## STICKLEY BROTHERS

■ The five ambitious and talented Stickley brothers entered the furniture industry around the turn of the century, each with their own area of expertise. However, instead of working together the brothers formed their own separate and joint companies.

■ The eldest and most successful brother, Gustav, was greatly influenced by the philosophy of the Arts & Crafts movement. His designs were simple, geometric, and solid, with heavy quartered oak covered with fumed finishes. Charles, Albert, and Leopold Stickley all worked for Gustav at one stage.

■ John George Stickley and Albert established Stickley Bros in 1891. Albert's more decorative designs were marked with the 'Quaint' logo, which defined his style.

■ John George left Stickley Bros to set up L. & J.G. Stickley with Leopold in 1904. They took inspiration from Gustav, but rejected handcrafted techniques for mechanical production. As fashions changed the Stickley-endorsed firms changed hands or closed.

Six early 20thC Arts & Crafts oak side chairs, attributed to the Stickley Brothers, double side stretcher and front and back seat rail with through tenon, caramel-colored slip upholstery, unsigned.

37in (94cm) high

$1,800-2,200 — SK

Two of a set of six Stickley Brothers chairs with Mackmurdo feet.

*Arthur Heygate Mackmurdo (1851-1942) headed the Century Guild, established in 1882.*

39.5in (100.5cm) high

$5,000-8,000 set — GAL

A set of six Stickley Brothers armchairs, no. 375 1/2, refinished, seats recovered in brown vinyl, four with 'Quaint' tags.

38in (95cm) high

$3,000-5,000 — DRA

A Stickley Brothers Arts & Crafts mahogany rocker, flat arms over three vertical slats, front posts with through tenons, re-upholstered seat cushions in Morris designed fabric, restored finish, with paper label.

c1910 — 32in (81.5cm) high

$2,800-3,200 — SK

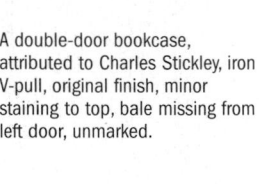

A three-piece library set, attributed to the Stickley Brothers, with pressed cane panels, restored original finish, replaced cane panels, stenciled model numbers.

table 48in (120cm) wide

$2,200-2,800 — DRA

A Stickley Brothers infant's high chair.

41in (104cm) high

$1,200-1,800 — GAL

A Stickley Brothers pedestal.

34in (86.5cm) high

$1,200-1,800 — GAL

A double-door bookcase, attributed to Charles Stickley, iron V-pull, original finish, minor staining to top, bale missing from left door, unmarked.

56in (140cm) high

$3,000-5,000 — DRA

A Stickley Brothers shaving mirror.

31in (78.5cm) wide

$1,800-2,200 — GAL

An Arts & Crafts taboret, the circular top on four legs combined by two X-stretchers.

*24in (61cm) diam*

**$500-800**     **GAL**

An early 20thC Tiffany & Co. bronze stand, top centered by a medallion relief decorated with classical figures, base accented with scroll and leaf decoration, impressed maker's mark and "0297 M."

*31.5in (80cm) high*

**$2,200-2,800**     **SK**

A Limbert café chair with cut-out back and sides and canted arms, new ebonized finish, replaced leather, branded under stretcher.

*25.5in (65cm) wide*

**$3,000-5,000**     **DRA**

A Morris chair, with padded back and armrests, seat cusion.

*40in (100cm) high*

**$1,200-1,800**     **GAL**

A Roycroft Morris chair with shaped arms and posts, laced leather covered foam cushions and four slats under each arm, carved orb and cross mark, restored.

*29.5in (75cm) wide*

**$3,000-5,000**     **DRA**

An Arts & Crafts child's chair.

*26in (66cm) high*

**$500-700**     **GAL**

An Arts & Crafts mirror hall bench.

*65in (165cm) high*

**$1,200-1,800**     **GAL**

A Batchelder tile-top table of rectangular unglazed tiles and three floral tiles with blue engobe, mounted on a black-enameled iron base, unmarked.

*19in (47.5cm) high*

**$1,200-1,800** DRA

A Flint tile-top table with geometric tiles arranged in a Persian carpet pattern, matte glazes, mounted in a white-enameled iron base, wear, unmarked.

*20in (50cm) high*

**$220-280** DRA

A Californian tile-top table with two tiles painted with a scene after Cecil Aulden, with a horsedrawn carriage in front of an inn, mounted in green enameled wrought-iron base, damage and wear.

*19.25in (48cm) high*

**$280-320** DRA

A Californian tile-top table and drink stand, with one floral tile in the hispano-moresque style surrounded by black and turquoise border tiles, mounted in a black-enameled iron stand with two ring drink holders, unmarked.

*24in (60cm) high*

**$700-1,000** DRA

A Midwestern small tile-top table with two horizontal tiles decorated in cuenca with gold, blue and green peacocks in a medallion, on a four-legged wrought-iron base.

*22in (55cm) high*

**$120-180** DRA

A Californian cut-corner tile-top table with a floral tile surrounded by smaller yellow and blue field tiles, mounted in a Mission wooden base with turned legs, slight wear, unmarked.

*19.25in (48cm) high*

**$300-500** DRA

A Catalina fine and rare tile-top sewing table with six-tile panel depicting birds of paradise on black ground, mounted in a flip-top Mission table with turned legs, unmarked.

*27.25in (68cm) wide*

**$4,000-6,000** DRA

An art glass inlaid marble and bronze table, inlaid in a geometric mosaic pattern of Tiffany glass in shades of green with gilt highlights, over bronze verdigris figural base, cross-stretcher missing.

*c1910*　　　　*42in (106.5cm) wide*

**$45,000-55,000** SK

**A CLOSER LOOK AT A ROSE VALLEY BOOKCASE**

*Rose Valley pieces are usually unmarked. If this bookcase had been marked it would add considerably to the value of the piece.*

*John Bisseger was a distinguished Philadelphia area architect and was head draftsman for Price and McLanahan, an important Philadelphia architect firm. By 1905 he was an active member of the Rose Valley community, designing and building his own chalet and furniture.*

*The Rose Valley community was fairly small and therefore examples of the style rarely come onto the market.*

*These symbols are typical of the Arts & Crafts style, which appropriated motifs and ornamental details from medieval times.*

*Handles and hinges are an important feature of Arts & Crafts furniture.*

A rare Rose Valley mahogany triple-door bookcase by John Bisseger, with a beveled top, leaded glass doors with medieval symbols, adjustable shelves, original finish, unmarked, some damage.

*c1907*

**$10,000-15,000**

*62.25in (158cm) wide*

**DRA**

An early 20thC Limbert Arts & Crafts oak sideboard, with drawers and cupboards, the top surmounted by an arched and mirrored backsplash with outwardly bowed shelf, signed with the firm's Grand Rapids and Holland burn mark.

*65in (165cm) wide*

**$6,000-9,000**　　　**ISA**

An American Arts & Crafts oak tall dresser with mirror, the rectangular swivel mirror above drawers and cupboard doors, all flanked by four square pencil columns.

*44in (112cm) wide*

**$1,200-1,800**　　　**ISA**

A Roycroft vanity unit with single drawer and swivel mirror, on Mackmurdo feet, with original finish and maker's mark.

*56in (142cm) wide*

**$4,000-6,000**　　　**DRA**

A McHugh slant-front desk with applied X-slats to top and sides, full gallery interior, original finish to outside, restoration to inside, unsigned.

*44.5in (111cm) high*

**$1,200-1,800**　**DRA**

A Roycroft magazine stand with arched tapering sides and three shelves, carved orb and cross mark, original finish.

*17.75in (45cm) wide*

**$5,000-8,000**　　　**DRA**

A Jamestown vice cabinet with cut-out front and legs, original finish, partial paper store label on back.

*56in (140cm) high*

**$700-1,000**　　　**DRA**

An octagonal occasional table in the manner of Bugatti.

*58cm (23in) wide*

**$3,000-4,000**  LC

A corner chair in the manner of Bugatti.

**$3,000-4,000**  LC

A Carlo Bugatti side chair, in wood, copper, parchment, rope, pewter and bone, label of "C.LONATI - FIRENZE" under seat, restored.

*36in (90cm) high*

**$4,000-6,000**  FRE

A Carlo Bugatti stool, in wood, pewter, bone, and wool, upholstered with a Soumac rug, some losses.

*18in (45cm) high*

**$2,200-2,800**  FRE

## CARLO BUGATTI

- Carlo Bugatti was an Italian designer trained at Brera Academy of Fine Arts who worked c1880-1910. He was to become the head of a very creative household, with a sculptor and a legendary automobile designer as sons.
- Bugatti's prodigious output included metalware, textiles, and ceramics, but it is for his furniture that he is most remembered today.
- Celebrated in his day, Bugatti was the recipient of a silver medal at the Exposition Universelle in Paris in 1900. His work is currently enjoying a revival in popularity after a period of relative neglect.
- Bugatti's work is indebted to the writing of Eugène Viollet-le-Duc, in particular his ideas on the use of decorative elements to draw attention to rather than disguise the structure of a piece.
- Some of the materials used by Bugatti were unorthodox – he incorporated brass, bone, silk, and parchment into his furniture design.

## MOORISH STYLE

- Notable for his rejection of the predominant European tradition of design, Bugatti instead looked to the East, especially to Islamic and Oriental cultures, for his inspiration.
- The use of ropework and tassels of silk and wool highlights the strong Moroccan influence running through Bugatti's design. Moorish forms, such as small side tables with multi-sided tops, also feature strongly in his work.
- Dark woods offset by bold colors and strong, geometric designs are also features of Moroccan furniture design that Bugatti appropriated in the search for his own unique aesthetic.

A Carlo Bugatti low table, in wood, copper, pewter, bone, and parchment.

*38.5in (96cm) wide*

**$6,000-9,000**  FRE

A Carlo Bugatti settee, in wood, parchment, copper and pewter.

*47in (117.5cm) long*

**$6,000-9,000**  FRE

## CABINETS

A Scottish School Art Nouveau mahogany sideboard, the central concave drawer with arched moldings, enclosed by four drawers above paneled doors flanking a void and raised on bracket feet.

*43in (109cm) high*

**$300-500**  L&T

A Louis Majorelle oak pantry, with a two-door lower part divided by carved columns and a glazed two-door display case on curved consoles, part of an eight-piece dining room suite also including an extendable table and six upholstered chairs.

*c1900*      *100in (250cm) high*

**$1,800-2,200 set**  QU

An Art Nouveau mahogany and inlaid display cabinet, by Shapland and Petter, the D-shaped top with spindled gallery centred by a shelf and floral marquetry plaque, with glazed doors, on square legs and feet.

*70in (175cm) high*

**$4,000-6,000**  L&T

An Art Nouveau dressing chest, with a rectangular mirror above three short and one long drawer on square supports linked by a platform stretcher, part of a suite along with a three-drawer wardrobe.

*45in (114cm) wide*

**$700-1,000 set** **L&T**

An Art Nouveau mahogany writing desk, the rectangular top above an asymmetrical glazed door and open shelf with heart piercings and a sloping fall, the sides pierced with tulips, on a stile base with bracket supports.

*56.75in (144cm) high*

**$700-1,000** **L&T**

## A CLOSER LOOK AT AN ART NOUVEAU ARMCHAIR

*This slender chair frame with its sweeping curves is an excellent example of high Art Nouveau furniture.*

*Many dealers and collectors would prefer to buy a chair like this in unrestored condition, rather than one that has mismatched replaced upholstery.*

A pair of Art Nouveau armchairs, by J.S. Henry, each with a mahogany frame, the tall backs with leaf finials above curving open arms, on turned and tapering legs linked by stretchers, one bearing a maker's label.

**$3,000-4,000** **L&T**

An early J. & J. Kohn side chair, with bentwood back and tapering legs, by Josef Hoffmann, with four spheres under the seat rail, and tacked-on brown leather upholstery, the stamp mark obscured.

*38.75in (98.5cm) high*

**$1,200-1,800** **SDR**

*Jallot's monogram signature is visible here, as the upholstery is missing. The mark of such a revered designer cannot fail to enhance value.*

*The exquisite sculpting on these front rails has acquired a fine patina and is free of chips and other losses.*

A French Art Nouveau sculpted armchair, by Leon Jallot.

*c1910* *32in (81.5cm) high*

**$15,000-20,000** **LM**

## TABLES

A French Art Nouveau Ecole de Nancy tea table, in walnut, brass, and glass, with a tray top and four fold-down sides.

*c1900* *31.5in (79cm) wide*

**$1,200-1,800** **FRE**

An Art Nouveau mahogany tray-topped tea table, with brass carrying handles and a pewter and copper inlaid panel depicting a teacup and saucer.

*29in (74cm) high*

**$500-700** **L&T**

An Art Nouveau mahogany foldover card table, probably by J.S. Henry, inlaid with stylized bands in specimen woods, brass, copper, and mother-of-pearl.

*27.25in (68cm) high*

**$2,200-2,800** **L&T**

A giltwood 'Aubepin' occasional table by Louis Majorelle, the circular marble top above molded frieze and tapering molded legs with foliate carving.

*32in (81cm) high*

**$2,200-2,800** **L&T**

An Austrian or German Jugendstil glazed ceramic tile-top table, unknown cabinet maker's stamp, original finish.

*c1900*　　　29.5in (74cm) high

**$1,800-2,200**　　　**FRE**

An Art Nouveau oak writing desk, with pierced brass grilles and ledge back, the bowed top inset with leather writing surface above a drawer, on square tapered legs linked by an undertier.

42.75in (107cm) high

**$1,800-2,200**　　　**L&T**

A Gallé wooden marquetry tray, depicting elephants and banana trees, signed "Gallé" in marquetry.

22.75in (58cm) wide

**$3,000-4,000**　　　**JDJ**

An Art Nouveau gilt and gesso picture frame, molded with a fringe of waterlilies and whiplash foliage on a ribbed ground.

37.5in (95cm) wide

**$400-600**　　　**L&T**

An Art Nouveau steel and applied brass duet stand, the music stops with sunburst decoration, applied candle sconces with cast and embossed leaf and floral decorations, on a tripod base with whiplash foliate embellishments.

49.5in (126cm) high

**$2,200-2,800**　　　**L&T**

An Art Nouveau mahogany jardinière stand, the canted square tapering supports linked by two further tiers and with decorative bracket supports.

47.25in (120cm) high

**$220-280**　　　**L&T**

## ART DECO FURNITURE – CABINETS

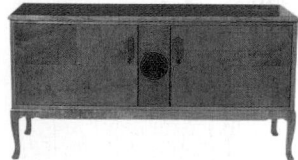

A Swedish Art Deco sideboard in birch, with typical Swedish sunburst motif and detailing in ebony and dark and light mahogany.

*c1930*　　　59in (150cm) wide

**$4,000-6,000**　　　**LANE**

A Swedish Art Deco bookcase in birch with fleur-de-lys detail to top.

*c1920*　　　39.25in (100cm) wide

**$1,800-2,200**　　　**LANE**

A Swedish Art Deco sideboard in birch, with ebony and burled ash detailing, the geometric dark wood motif influenced by Asian style.

*c1930*　　　59in (150cm) wide

**$2,800-3,200**　　　**LANE**

A red lacquer cabinet, by Maurice Jallot.

42in (106.5cm) wide

**$7,000-10,000**　　　**LM**

A cabinet by Guglielmo Ulrich of Milan, comprising a goat vellum-bound box on a rosewood veneered plinth, the doors with circular ivory fittings, the interior with a tuja-root veneer and fourteen drawers with ivory knobs.

*c1930*　　　60in (150cm) high

**$5,000-7,000**　　　**QU**

A wooden desk with a leather writing surface, by Maurice Jallot.

*47in (119.5cm) wide*

**$8,000-12,000**     **LM**

A desk by John Pascand, the surface and drawer fronts in blonde wood.

*c1930*     *44.25in (112.5cm) wide*

**$8,000-12,000**     **LM**

A Swedish Art Deco desk in birch, marked with maker's name "A.B. Axel Beckmans Möbelfabrik, Norrköping".

*c1930*     *58.25in (148cm) wide*

**$6,000-9,000**     **LANE**

A Swedish Art Deco desk cabinet in rosewood and birch.

*c1920*     *35.5in (90cm) wide*

**$3,000-4,000**     **LANE**

A 1930s Belgian black lacquer desk and chair, by De Coene Frères.

*68in (172.5cm) wide*

**$15,000-20,000 set**     **LM**

A Swedish Art Deco vanity unit, in birch with a mirror on top.

*c1925*     *47.75in (121cm) wide*

**$3,000-4,000**     **LANE**

An Art Deco skyscraper vanity unit.

*c1930*     *61in (155cm) high*

**$2,200-2,800**     **LOS**

A Swedish Art Deco birch vanity desk, of unusual design incorporating a lift-up desk, missing leg.

*c1925*     *35.75in (91cm) wide*

**$2,200-2,800**     **LANE**

One of a pair of Art Deco open armchairs with prominent reversed C-shape armrests on squat saber legs.

*c1930*

**$3,000-4,000 pair**      **BL**

A Swedish Art Deco birch club chair, with curved arms and black leather upholstery.

*c1930*      *25.25in (64cm) wide*

**$2,200-2,800**      **LANE**

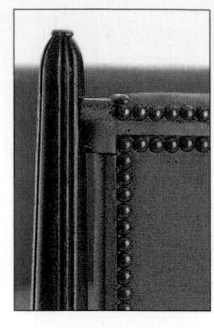

One of a pair of mid-1920s French Art Deco mahogany armchairs.

*31.5in (80cm) high*

**$5,000-7,000 pair**      **LM**

One of a pair of red checkered upholstered bridge chairs, by De Coene Frères.

*c1930*      *32.25in (82cm) high*

**$3,000-4,000 pair**      **LM**

A French wood and ropework chair by Wibo.

*c1935*

**$800-1,200**      **LM**

An Art Deco walnut framed three-piece suite, comprising a sofa and two armchairs, upholstered in red and buff uncut moquette, the backs and arms in walnut veneer, the arm uprights with fishscale carving, on stepped block feet.

*sofa 71.25in (178cm) wide*

**$4,000-6,000**      **L&T**

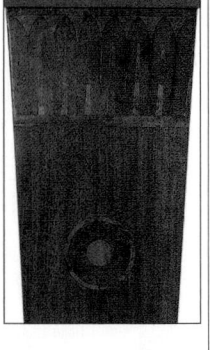

A Swedish Art Deco chair, with brown leather upholstery and burled elm and satinwood detailing to back.

*c1925*      *24in (61cm) wide*

**$2,200-2,800**      **LANE**

One of a set of six Art Deco chairs with red plush upholstery fastened to the frame with studs, with scroll back and slightly outswept legs.

*c1935*      *35in (89cm) high*

**$8,000-12,000 set**      **LM**

One of a set of eight French chairs, with red leather upholstery.

*c1935*            *34.5in (87.5cm) high*

**$12,000-18,000 set**            **LM**

**$700-1,000**

A Swedish Art Deco chair, with abstract design to roundel in central slat.

*19in (48cm) wide*

**LANE**

One of a set of four American Art Deco patinated steel stools, with upholstered padded seats above pierced aprons cast with scrolling foliage, with maker's label "Edge-Lite, Chicago, Illinois".

**$800-1,200 set**            **L&T**

A Swedish Art Deco stool, with a leopard skin seat.

*22.5in (57cm) wide*

**$700-1,000**            **LANE**

A Belgian wood and cowhide vanity stool.

*c1935*            *6.25in (16cm) long*

**$800-1,200**            **LM**

An Art Deco three-seat sofa, its frame and loose seat cushions re-upholstered in blue patterned fabric with black trim, on black enameled wood base, unmarked.

*c1930*            *80in (203cm) high*

**$500-800**            **SDR**

## TABLES

A French mahogany dining table, by Michel Roux Spitz.

*c1935*            *39.5in (100.5cm) wide*

**$8,000-12,000**            **LM**

An Art Deco extendable dining table of exotic wood veneers inlaid with an oval band to top, on a double-pedestal base, unmarked.

*80in (200cm) wide*

**$700-1,000**            **SDR**

Part of an eleven-piece Art Deco dining suite in ebonized oak, consisting of a large double-pedestal dining table with rectangular top and ten dining chairs, each upholstered in lavender leather, unmarked.

*98.5in (250cm) long*

**$5,000-7,000 set**            **SDR**

### A CLOSER LOOK AT AN ART DECO TABLE

Eugene Printz was an important French furniture designer who won numerous public commissions, including an office suite for the 1931 Exposition Coloniale Internationale.

This table has a strong but not overpowering design, making it ideal for use in any number of situations. This versatility makes it a desirable piece.

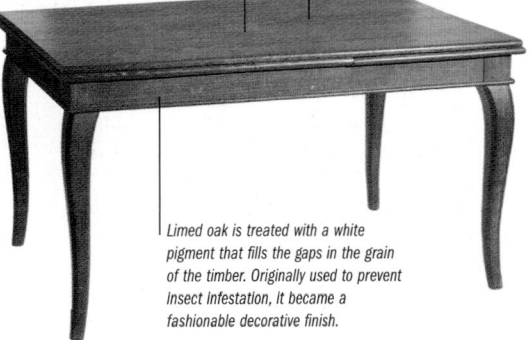

Limed oak is treated with a white pigment that fills the gaps in the grain of the timber. Originally used to prevent insect infestation, it became a fashionable decorative finish.

A Eugène Printz limed oak dining table, signed to the underside.

*c1935*            *50.5in (128.5cm) wide*

**$40,000-50,000**            **LM**

A late 1940s French oak coffee table, with a black glass top.

*32in (81.5cm) diam*

**$5,000-7,000** LM

A sculpted walnut and leather gueridon.

*c1925* *28.5in (72.5cm) diam*

**$4,000-6,000** LM

A Swedish Art Deco birch occasional table, with sunburst design to the top and chunky turned legs.

*c1920* *35.5in (90cm) wide*

**$1,800-2,200** LANE

A French round oak and leather table.

*c1945* *29.5in (75cm) diam*

**$5,000-7,000** LM

A 1940s French coffee table, with curved legs supported by pointed feet.

*23.5in (59.5cm) diam*

**$5,000-7,000** LM

A Belgian end table with a mahogany colored finish, inspired by Joseph Hoffmann's 'Fledermaus' model.

*c1925* *31in (78.5cm) high*

**$1,800-2,200** LM

A French Art Deco walnut marquetry gueridon.

*c1935* *24.25in (61.5cm) diam*

**$5,000-7,000** LM

A Swedish Art Deco birch table.

*c1925* *23.5in (60cm) wide*

**$1,200-1,800** LANE

## A CLOSER LOOK AT AN ART DECO TABLE

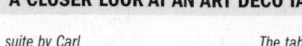

*This table was part of a suite by Carl Malmsten. If it had a factory mark or signature its value would be doubled.*

*The table top is made of bookmatched birch, the four quadrants set at 45 degree angles so as to reflect light differently.*

*This stylized fleur-de-lys is inlaid in mahogany. It is indicative of earlier Art Deco with its freeform style.*

*This kind of symmetrical, geometric pattern, especially in monochrome, is a hallmark of a more mature Art Deco style.*

A Swedish Art Deco birch occasional table, attributed to Carl Malmsten.

*c1925* *37.75in (96cm) wide*

**$3,000-4,000** LANE

A Swedish Art Deco birch table, with palisander veneer strips.

*c1925* *11.5in (29cm) wide*

**$2,200-2,800** LANE

A rectangular wooden coffee table in blonde wood.

*c1940* *31.5in (80cm) wide*

**$4,000-6,000** LM

A French padouk wood table.

c1925     31in (78.5cm) wide

**$3,000-4,000**     **LM**

An Belgian Art Deco lyre console, by De Coene Frères.

c1935     29.5in (75cm) high

**$3,000-4,000**     **LM**

## DE COENE FRÈRES

- De Coene Frères was a Belgian furniture manufacturer working during the inter-war period from Les Ateliers d'Art de Courtrai De Coene Frères in Brussels.
- The brothers specialized in producing elegantly designed furniture to extremely high standards, in contrast to the mass-produced Art Deco style that began to fill department stores as the movement gained momentum.
- High gloss finishes such as lacquer and polished veneers feature on a lot of De Coene furniture. They also used bright metals such as nickel and chrome to amplify this high sheen effect.
- Simple symmetry, and the contrast between straight lines and tight curves, are quintessential Art Deco motifs that the brothers made their own.
- The influence of tribal art and of Oriental aesthetics – both of which had an impact on the Art Deco scene – can be seen at work in some pieces by De Coene Frères.

An early 1930s rosewood coffee table, by De Coene Frères, with walnut veneer and chrome tubing.

24.5in (62cm) high

**$2,200-2,800**     **LM**

An English Art Deco two-tier occasional table, of chrome and laminate with a walnut base.

c1925     14.5in (36cm) wide

**$1,200-1,800**     **JK**

A Swedish Art Deco sewing table in ash.

24in (61cm) wide

**$1,200-1,800**     **LANE**

A Swedish Art Deco rectangular birch side table, with a black glass top.

c1930     26in (66cm) wide

**$1,800-2,200**     **LANE**

A rare Samuel Yellin wrought-iron side table, with a tripod base curled around a screw shaft and topped by a single four-sided tile covered in green crystalline glaze, fine original patina, stamped "Samuel Yellin 1933".

24in (60cm) high

**$28,000-35,000**     **DRA**

A Swedish Art Deco side table, in ash and dark wood, with curved edges.

13.5in (34cm) wide

**$1,800-2,200**     **LANE**

A pair of Art Deco style two-tier bedside tables, in blonde wood with ebonized supports and plinth bases.

*24in (60cm) high*

**$500-700** **S&K**

A pair of Swedish Art Deco birch bedside tables, with inlaid detailing and white marble tops.

*15.75in (40cm) wide*

**$1,800-2,200** **LANE**

An Art Deco wood veneer and black lacquered mantelpiece of asymmetric design, with rectangular and round-edged pedestals, unmarked.

*59.5in (151cm) wide*

**$1,000-1,500** **SDR**

A lacquer screen comprising four hinged panels, by Paul-Etienne Sain of France, of lacquered wood with brass fittings, signed in red "Paul Sain 32", some chipping.

*63in (157.5cm) high*

**$5,000-8,000** **FRE**

One of a pair of wooden lyre bedroom chests, with a single drawer.

*c1920* *23in (58.5cm) high*

**$3,000-4,000 pair** **LM**

## A CLOSER LOOK AT A PRINTZ BOOKSHELF

These shelves are part of a suite with which Printz won a design competition in 1932. Other entrants included Emile Ruhlmann and Maurice Jallot.

The brief was to design a study and bedroom suite for halls of residence at La Cité Internationale Universitaire de Paris, an institution founded in the 1920s to provide international students in Paris with suitable lodgings.

The symmetrical design is very simple, allowing for relatively cheap construction. Printz made a virtue of the necessity to create something simple, and produced a very elegant, understated piece of work.

The elongated sides allowed for the storage of books above the cupboard.

A well-designed piece of furniture like this, in unrestored condition with an attractive patina, can be put to good use in a modern interior. This versatility increases desirability and, as a consequence, value.

Antique shelves or cabinets that have been modified to accommodate modern equipment, such as televisions, will invariably be worth less, particularly if these amendments are visible from the front.

One of a pair of bookshelves, designed by Eugène Printz for students' quarters at La Cité Internationale Universitaire de Paris.

*1931* *71in (180.5cm) wide*

**$18,000-22,000 pair** **LM**

Two of three Arts & Crafts crewelwork panels, each rectangular panel worked in colored wools by Lady Phipson Beale, unbleached linen ground.

*c1880*                    largest 63.6in (159cm) wide

**$1,800-2,200 set**                    **L&T**

One of a set of eight Arts & Crafts crewelwork seat covers, worked in colored wools by Lady Phipson Beale with sprays of flowering foliage on an unbleached linen ground.

***Provenance:*** *Sir William Phipson Beale, Drumlamford House, Ayrshire, Scotland.*

*The Beale family became close friends with Morris after he was commissioned to design and furnish their East Grinstead home, Standen. Lady Phipson Beale was inspired by Morris' work and embroidered many pieces after his designs. One of a pair of Lady Phipson Beale's hangings in Morris' 'Artichoke' design now hangs in the Victoria and Albert Museum, London.*

17.5in (44cm) high

**$2,800-3,200 set**                    **L&T**

An Arts & Crafts embroidered panel, the design attributed to Walter Crane, possibly executed at the Royal School of Needlework, in ivory-colored silks, with panels of winged putti, one holding a scrolling foliate branch, another resting beside a dolphin and a third feeding a plumed bird from a bowl, flanked by ribbons and foliage, framed and glazed.

51.25in (130cm) wide

**$700-1,000**                    **DN**

## A CLOSER LOOK AT A MORRIS TAPESTRY

A Glasgow school net panel, by Irene Cherry, depicting a stylized flower, framed, with a pencil inscription to the reverse.

*Irene Cherry studied at the Glasgow School of Art.*

16.5in (41cm) high

**$280-320**                    **WW**

A pair of Aesthetic Movement curtains, designed in the manner of Christopher Dresser.

94in (235cm) high

**$700-1,000**                    **L&T**

*The trees and animals are species native to and commonly associated with the English countryside in keeping with the rural idyll that inspired the Arts & Crafts movement.*

*The banners are inscribed with 'Verses for Pictures', a poem by William Morris that featured in his 1891 collection entitled 'Poems by the Way'.*

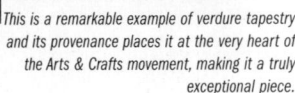

*This tapestry was originally commissioned by Percy Wyndham, a member of the intellectual 'Souls' society, formed in the 1880s to counteract perceived philistinism in the aristocracy.*

*This is a remarkable example of verdure tapestry and its provenance places it at the very heart of the Arts & Crafts movement, making it a truly exceptional piece.*

A Morris & Co. 'Greenery' tapestry, designed by John Henry Dearle, woven in colored wools and mohair by John Martin and William Sleath, with a woodland glade, millefleurs and animals in the foreground, the trees woven with banners bearing inscriptions.

***Provenance:*** *The Hon. Percy Scawen Wyndham, Clouds, East Knoyle, Wiltshire, England.*

*1892*                    184.5in (461cm) wide

**$350,000-400,000**                    **L&T**

**DECORATIVE ARTS**

A pair of Morris & Co. 'Strawberry Thief' chintz curtains, each with buff linen borders, lined and interlined.

*100in (250cm) high*

**$1,200-1,800 pair**          **L&T**

A pair of lined cotton curtains, designed by William Morris, wear and losses.

*84.75in (212cm) high*

**$300-500 pair**          **WW**

Five pairs of Morris & Co. 'Compton' printed cotton curtains, each pair lined.

*92.5in (235cm) high*

**$7,000-10,000 set**          **L&T**

Two pairs of Morris & Co. 'Acanthus' woven silk damask curtains, in Celadon green, lined, pelmets and bedspread.

*96in (240cm) high*

**$5,000-7,000 set**          **L&T**

A pair of Morris & Co. 'Vine and Pomegranate' wool curtains, each lined and lengthened with red woolen cloth, braided edges and tie backs.

**Provenance:** *Sir William Phipson Beale, Drumlamford House, Ayrshire, Scotland.*

*92in (230cm) high*

**$1,800-2,200 pair**          **L&T**

One of three Morris & Co. 'Peacock and Dragon' upholstered footstools, each of rectangular form, covered in woven wool fabric with braided edges, rexine bases.

*13.25in (33cm) wide*

**$500-800 set**          **L&T**

An Arts & Crafts woven cotton rug, printed in colors with a Persian-style design of entwined foliage, in the manner of Morris & Co.

*73.5in (184cm) long*

**$500-800**          **L&T**

An Arts & Crafts Wilton carpet, in the style of Morris & Co., machine woven, the field with allover scrolling and flowering foliage in shades of green, a meandering foliate border with guard bands.

*191.25in (478cm) long*

**$1,200-1,800**          **L&T**

A pair of Alexander Morton 'Isphurhan' velveteen and cotton curtains, with opposed bird motifs, each with buff linen borders, lined and interlined.

**$1,800-2,200 pair**          **L&T**

An Arts & Crafts Wilton carpet, designed by C.F.A. Voysey, woven by Tomkinson and Adam for Liberty & Co., with allover luxuriant flowering foliate design within a scrolling foliate band.

*108.5in (271cm) long*

**$7,000-10,000**          **L&T**

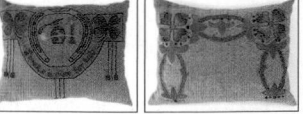

Three Arts & Crafts pillows, stenciled and embroidered, one with shamrocks, one with dog roses and the other with the motto "Smoke a Pipe for Luck".

*19.5in (49.5cm) wide*

**$300-400 set**          **DRA**

A woven cotton blanket, decorated in reds and greens with paisley design.

**$220-280** **WW**

An embroidered linen tablecloth, embroidered with bird panels in gold and black.

*84in (210cm) wide*

**$120-180** **WW**

An embroidered velvet bookcover.

*9.25in (23cm) wide*

**$120-180** **WW**

A Scottish silk embroidery, decorated with a medieval maiden picking roses in a garden setting, framed, unsigned.

*11.25in (28cm) high*

**$800-1,200** **WW**

An Art Deco belt, with red and white beads.

*c1935* *36in (91.5cm) long*

**$120-180** **TDG**

## WALLPAPER

A roll of Morris & Co. 'Acorn' wallpaper, printed "Morris & Co."

*22in (56cm) wide*

**$500-700 per repeat** **PC**

### WILLIAM MORRIS WALLPAPER

- William Morris established his company in 1861 under the name Morris, Marshall, Faulkner & Co., later renamed Morris & Co.
- The firm produced wallpapers, stained glass, textiles, furniture, tapestries, and illustrations.
- The first two wallpapers were 'Trellis' and 'Daisy'. In 1887 Morris designed a wallpaper for Queen Victoria's Balmoral residence.
- Apart from Morris, John Henry Dearle (1860-1932) was one of the firm's leading designers. He joined Morris & Co. in 1878 and designed wallpaper, textiles, and tapestry, taking over as artistic director of the firm after Morris's death in 1896.
- Wallpapers were printed by hand using wooden blocks. This technique made them comparatively expensive. The number of different blocks used tended to correlate to the price of the paper.
- Morris & Co. closed in 1940. Arthur Sanderson & Sons Ltd, who had been producing Morris & Co. wallpapers since the 1920s, continued to make Morris wallpaper designs.

A panel of Morris & Co. 'Celadine' wallpaper, printed "Morris & Co."

*Wallpaper produced by block printing was often retouched by hand. On this piece, handpainting marks and inconsistencies in the pattern can clearly be seen.*

*22in (56cm) wide*

**$500-700 per repeat** **PC**

A roll of Morris & Co. 'Golden Lily' wallpaper, designed by John Dearle, printed "Morris & Co."

*This pattern was designed after Morris' death.*

*22in (56cm) wide*

**$700-1,000 per repeat** **PC**

A roll of Morris & Co. 'Foliage' wallpaper, unmarked.

*This is a later example of a Morris & Co. design – there is no mark and the design has Art Deco elements in 1940s colors.*

*22in (56cm) wide*

**$180-220 per repeat** **PC**

**DECORATIVE ARTS**

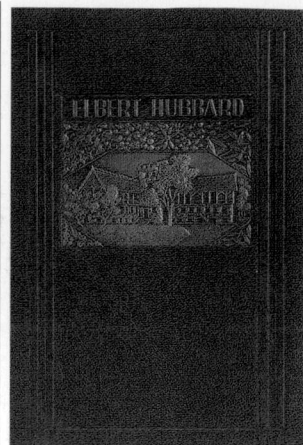

Elbert Hubbard, one of a set of 16 'Little Journeys' books.

*8.5in (21.5cm) high*

**$300-500 set**     **GAL**

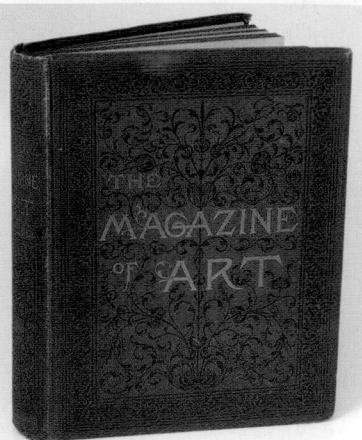

One of a selection of volumes of 'The Magazine of Art' 1881-1884, 1886, 1891, and 1895-1897, with various bindings.

**$280-320 set**     **WW**

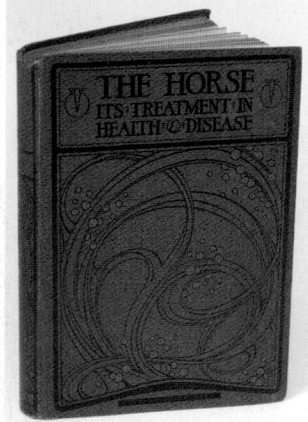

One of nine volumes of 'The Horse', with cover designs by Talwin Morris, published by The Gresham Publishing Company.

*11in (27.5cm) high*

**$120-180 set**     **WW**

One of six volumes of 'The Architectural Review', this one for 1897-1899.

**$500-700 set**     **WW**

**PRINTS & PAINTINGS**

Gustave Baumann, 'Eagle Ceremony at Tesque Pueblo', color woodblock print, matted and mounted in a new Arts & Crafts frame, initialed in print only.

*1932*    *image 6.5in (16.5cm) high*

**$280-320**     **DRA**

Ethel Isadore Brown, brown pen and ink with watercolor of a cityscape in winter, matted and mounted in a new Arts & Crafts frame.

*1904*    *6.75in (17cm) high*

**$280-320**     **DRA**

Sir Edward Coley Burne-Jones, 'Pan and Psyche', signed print.

*17.5in (44cm) wide*

**$800-1,200**     **L&T**

Waldo Chase, 'Tall Timbers', oil painting on board, mounted in a new Arts & Crafts-style frame, signed "Waldo S. Chase".

*18in (45.5cm) high*

**$300-500**     **DRA**

William S. Coleman, etching on paper, depicting a maiden playing a pipe, framed, signed in the print "WSC", pencil signature and blindstamp.

*11.5in (29cm) high*

**$500-800**     **WW**

Arthur Wesley Dow, 'Modern Art' lithograph, matted and framed, image signed.

*image 10in (25.5cm) high*

**$800-1,200**     **DRA**

J. Foord, chromolithograph print of chestnut blossoms, from 'Decorative Flower Studies', stamped "J. Foord" and dated, new mat and frame, tears and losses.

*1899*　　　　*10in (25.5cm) high*

**$220-280**　　　　**DRA**

J. Foord, chromolithograph print of peace rose, from 'Decorative Flower Studies', stamped "J. Foord" and dated, new mat and frame, tears and losses.

*1899*　　　　*9.5in (24cm) high*

**$220-280**　　　　**DRA**

May Gaerhart, 'St. Laurence Islanders', color etching depicting an Inuit family, matted and mounted in a new Arts & Crafts frame, pencil signed.

*c1925*　　　　*3in (7.5cm) high*

**$280-320**　　　　**DRA**

Clarence Hotvedt, 'Two Pines', color woodblock print, mounted and matted in new Arts & Crafts frame, pencil titled, signed and monogrammed in print.

*1929*　　　　*9.75 (25cm) high*

**$280-320**　　　　**DRA**

Dard Hunter, 'Entrance to Roycroft Inn', published as a cover of a Roycroft menu, menu intact within frame.

*c1920*　　　　*5.25in (13.5cm) wide*

**$300-500**　　　　**DRA**

Leonard Hutchinson, 'Road to Niagra', color woodblock print, 20/50, matted and mounted in new Arts & Crafts frame, pencil titled and signed.

*c1935*　　　　*8.5in (21.5cm) high*

**$400-600**　　　　**DRA**

Jessie M. King, 'Green Gate', design for a bookplate, ink on vellum.

**Provenance:** *The Estate of Merle Taylor.*

*4.75in (12cm) high*

**$500-700**　　　　**L&T**

Jessie M. King, 'Rose Trellis', ink on vellum.

*8.5in (21cm) high*

**$280-320**　　　　**L&T**

Blanche Lazzell, woodblock print depicting a Providence dock scene in black on white paper, framed.

*This piece featured as cover art for Ms. Lazzell's exhibition.*

*1928*　　　　*8in (13cm) high*

**$500-700**　　　　**DRA**

Sidney Lee (British 1866-1949), color woodblock print of fishermen and nets by a lighthouse, matted and mounted in new Arts & Crafts frame, signed.

*c1925*　　　　*15in (38cm) high*

**$500-700**　　　　**DRA**

Berta Lum, 'Snowballs', color woodblock print, matted and mounted in new Arts & Crafts frame, pencil signed, chop mark and No. "133", water stains to bottom left corner.

*10in (25.5cm) high*

**$500-800**　　　　**DRA**

W. Palmer, 'Seven Ages of Man', two of a set of seven prints of various sizes, in ebonized wood frames, signed in the print.

**$1,800-2,200 set**                                                                  **WW**

Henry van de Velde, 'Tropon', French version, a lithograph on cream-colored paper, artist's signature lower right and "l'Aliment le plus concentre", framed.

*1898*                    *11.25in (28cm) high*

**$500-800**                          **QU**

German School, 'Flowers with Tree and House' woodblock print, mounted and matted in new Arts & Crafts frame, pencil titled and signed.

*11.25in (28.5cm) high*

**$280-320**                          **DRA**

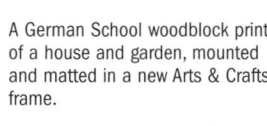

Eva Watson, 'Gull Rock', color linocut, matted and mounted in new Arts & Crafts frame, pencil titled and signed.

*8.5in (21.5cm) high*

**$800-1,200**                          **DRA**

A German School woodblock print of a house and garden, mounted and matted in a new Arts & Crafts frame.

*4.25in (11cm) wide*

**$280-320**                          **DRA**

Two framed stained glass window sketches, one depicting an angel, the other as the Virgin, pencil, ink, and ink wash.

**$1,200-1,800 pair**                          **L&T**

A Russian Arts & Crafts woodblock print of an industrial scene by mountains, matted and mounted in period Arts & Crafts frame, illegible pencil signature, some foxing and folds.

*16.75in (42.5cm) wide*

**$300-500**                          **DRA**

## THE MODERN DESIGN MARKET

Modern design, encompassing movements from the mid-20thC onward such as the Bauhaus, Pop Art, and Post-modernism, has consistently been one of the fastest growing sectors of the art market. While sales of some antique furniture and glass have struggled in recent years, many modern pieces such as 'Wassily' armchairs and contemporary studio glass have performed extremely well.

In our increasingly self-referential culture, iconic postwar design, whether from the 1950s or 80s, is perpetually stylish. The current taste for all things 1970s has led to price increases for original versions of designs first produced in that era, such as Verner Panton's 'Relaxer' rockers. Japanese design is another popular area, and contemporary reproductions of classic Japanese design from the late 20thC have made them accessible to a wider audience. Sculpture by Clive Barker was a runaway success at a sale in February 2005 and may be a sign that further recognition is on the way for the 1960s Pop Art sculptor.

Faded plastic and air bubbles underneath veneers will have a detrimental effect on value and can be difficult to restore. Despite this, it is important to be aware that furniture and accessories made in the first years of production are invariably worth far more than later pieces. A Bertoia barstool made by Knoll in 1952 will carry a very different price tag from one made in 2004, despite being made by the same company and to the same design. Most sought-after of all are unique commissions and prototypes by revered designers such as George Nakashima and Ercole Barovier.

*Lilian Fawcett, Themes & Variations*

## MARCEL BREUER

### MARCEL BREUER

- Marcel Breuer (1902-1981) moved from Hungary to Weimar, Germany in 1920 to study at the Bauhaus.
- A central tenet of Bauhaus teaching was the combination of good engineering with craftsmanship. This ideal, along with the commercial awareness instilled by the school, proved to be a great influence on Breuer throughout his career.
- In 1925, Breuer accepted a teaching post in the furniture workshop of the Bauhaus, which by then had relocated to Dessau. There he experimented with new materials such as plastics, laminated woods, aluminum, and tubular steel.
- Breuer won critical acclaim with the Wassily chair, a functional, low cost and sleek design that lent itself to mass production.
- Breuer taught alongside his former mentor Walter Gropius at Harvard's architecture faculty from 1937.
- He is remembered today primarily as an architect and for pioneering the use of tubular steel in furniture.

A pair of 'B-34' armchairs, by Marcel Breuer, one in chromium plated steel, the other in tubular aluminum, both with canvas Eisengarn upholstery.

*Eisengarn is a strong yarn developed by the Bauhaus to ensure that seat coverings maintained their shape.*

c1930                                    32in (81cm) high

**$1,800-2,200**                                    SK

A pair of 'Wassily' armchairs, by Marcel Breuer, with tubular chromium frames and tan leather strapwork.

*This iconic chair, designed at the Bauhaus in 1925, was named after the Russian artist Wassily Kandinski.*

30.5in (77.5cm) wide

**$700-1,000**                                    ISA

A Marcel Breuer 'B-35' lounge chair, in chromium-plated tubular steel, with black painted armrests, leather seat and paper label.

c1960                                    32in (81cm) high

**$1,200-1,800**                                    SK

A 'B-10' table, by Marcel Breuer, in chromium-plated tubular steel, with blue painted wood table top.

c1925                                    26.25in (67cm) high

**$1,800-2,200**                                    SK

LEFT: A single pedestal desk, by Marcel Breuer, with four drawers with recessed pulls, marked "Rhoads".

RIGHT: A wall-hanging shelf unit, by Marcel Breuer.

*These items were designed for the Rhoads Dormitory at Bryn Mawr College in Pennsylvania.*

shelf unit 72in (183cm) high

**$1,200-1,800**                                    SDR

## WENDELL CASTLE

- Born in Kansas in 1932, Wendell Castle obtained a BFA in industrial design and an MFA in sculpture from the University of Kansas. He went on to teach at the School of American Craftsmen in New York and set up his own studio.

- Castle describes himself as a furniture artist, and his playful designs explore the aesthetic qualities and technical possibilities of wood and metal, as well as contemporary materials such as fiberglass and plastics.

- Castle's designs are simultaneously sculptural and functional, for public and residential space. He has exhibited his work in galleries and also taken commissions from private clients.

- As a leading light of the Pop Art movement, Castle's work is infused with irreverence and a sense of the absurd, and takes inspiration from everyday objects and the human form.

- His 'Molar' line of furniture from the late 1960s, coated with fiberglass plastic, was inspired by human teeth. This is typical of Castle's playful style, also evident in later works such as the 'Star' series.

- Castle's innovative and imaginative designs have won him international awards such as the 1994 Visionaries of the American Craft Movement prize, which was sponsored by the American Craft Museum, and a gold medal from the American Craft Council.

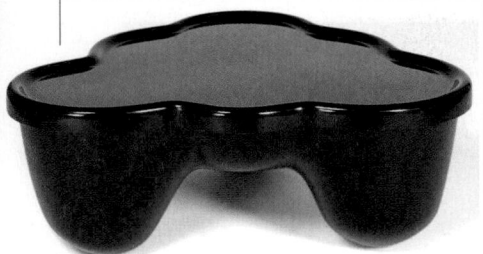

A 'Molar' coffee table, by Wendell Castle, with scalloped top, in black fiberglass, marked "WC".

*40in (101.5cm) wide*

**$4,000-6,000**      **SDR**

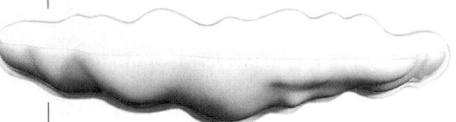

A 'Cloud' wall-hanging shelf, by Wendell Castle, in white fiberglass, marked "W.C. 69 03".

*65.75in (167cm) wide*

**$4,000-6,000**      **SDR**

An unusual bentwood music stand, by Wendell Castle, with brass inlay and ebonized finish, the rack mounted on an organic three legged base, marked "W. Castle 81".

*1981*      *52.5in (133.5cm) high*

**$18,000-25,000**      **SDR**

A lounge chair, by Charles and Ray Eames, constructed from molded mahogany plywood.

*This is the famous 'LCW' chair, named as the best design of the 20thC by Time magazine.*

*c1950*     26in (66cm) high

**$1,800-2,200**     **SK**

## EAMES

- Charles and Ray Eames helped to define postwar American design through their work with important companies and institutions such as IBM and the Smithsonian.
- The couple met in 1940 when they collaborated with Eero Saarinen on a competition design for the Museum of Modern Art. Their personal and professional partnership continued until Charles' death in 1978.
- Their goal to design a chair without joints or individual component parts was eventually realized after the emergence of fiberglass as a consumer material in the postwar years.
- Many Eames designs were distributed through Herman Miller, a company that continues to manufacture furniture to their original specifications today.
- Many of their pieces, such as the '670' lounge chair and '671' ottoman, have become world famous and entered the canon of modern design.
- True to Charles' maxim that "recognizing the need is the primary condition for design", utility is key to the Eames' work.

A 'DKW' wire chair, by Charles and Ray Eames, on dowel legs with a bikini pad.

*c1950*     33in (84cm) high

**$300-500**     **SK**

A 'DKW' wire chair, by Charles and Ray Eames, on dowel legs.

*c1960*     32.5in (82.5cm) high

**$800-1,200**     **LOS**

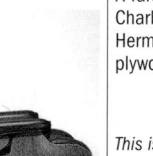

A rocker, by Charles and Ray Eames, with a plastic tub seat.

26.5in (67.5cm) high

**$700-1,000**     **LOS**

A set of six 'Aluminum Group' swivel chairs, by Charles Eames for Herman Miller, with black hessian upholstery.

**$2,800-3,200**     **L&T**

A pair of reproduction lounge chairs, by Charles and Ray Eames, with black leather seats on molded plywood shells with walnut finish, with paper labels.

*This design was first produced in 1956 for the film producer Billy Wilder.*

33in (84cm) high

**$3,000-4,000**     **SK**

A rare child's stool, by Charles Eames for Herman Miller, in bent plywood, unmarked.

*This is an early design and was never a commercial success.*

12in (30.5cm) wide

**$1,200-1,800**     **SDR**

A folding table, by Charles Eames for Herman Miller.

*c1955*     33.75in (85.5cm) wide

**$1,200-1,800**     **LOS**

A rare dowel leg table, by Charles Eames for Herman Miller, with a square wood veneer top, unmarked.

21.5in (54.5cm) wide

**$2,800-3,200**     **SDR**

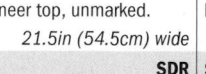

An 'ESU' desk, by Charles Eames for Herman Miller, with three drawers in black and white laminate with birch fronts and early Herman Miller label.

60in (152.5cm) wide

**$3,000-4,000**     **SDR**

One of a set of eight dining chairs, by Molly Gregory, with low back, single vertical slat, flared arms and hard brown leather sling upholstery, unmarked.

*24in (61cm) high*

**$2,800-3,200 set**     SDR

A Molly Gregory highchair, with low back, single vertical slat, flared arms and hard brown leather sling upholstery, unmarked.

*18.25in (46.5cm) wide*

**$280-320**     SDR

A pair of 20thC blonde wood occasional tables, by Molly Gregory, with triangular tops and graduated stretchers, unmarked.

*28in (71cm) wide*

**$600-900**     SDR

A small A-frame stepstool, by Molly Gregory, of pinned construction, with arched handle and two graduated steps, unmarked.

*11in (28cm) wide*

**$500-700**     SDR

## VLADIMIR KAGAN

One of a pair of library chairs, by Vladimir Kagan for Dreyfus, upholstered in dark green leather on a sculptural walnut frame, unmarked.

*1953*     *24in (61cm) wide*

**$5,000-7,000 pair**     SDR

A mid-20thC chaise-longue, by Vladimir Kagan, with low rounded armrests, upholstered in brown and beige fabric on a sculptural walnut base, unmarked.

*54in (137cm) wide*

**$6,000-9,000**     SDR

A rare '175SS' rocker and ottoman, by Vladimir Kagan, on highly polished stainless steel frames, upholstered in high grade elephant gray leather.

*25.5in (65cm) wide*

**$18,000-25,000**     SDR

An unusual drop-leaf dining table, by Vladimir Kagan, with an oblong top on a seven-legged wood base, unmarked.

*66.5in (169cm) wide*

**$4,000-6,000**     SDR

## JOHN MAKEPEACE

- John Makepeace trained under Keith Cooper in Dorset in England during the late 1950s before establishing his own workshop in the Midlands.
- Makepeace eventually returned to Dorset and founded Parnham College, a school for furniture designers housed in a country manor.
- Taking a lead from Arts & Crafts teachings, Parnham espouses a holistic approach and teaches design, craft, and entrepreneurial skills. An on-site arboretum supplies native British woods for research and timber.
- Makepeace favors English hardwoods such as oak, yew, holly, and sycamore. Some of these timbers are rarely seen in contemporary furniture design.
- The majority of Makepeace designs are bespoke, one-off commissions.

A 'Bird' personal desk, by John Makepeace, of burr elm and wych elm with Lebanon cedar drawer linings, with adjustable writing slope, two paper drawers and five revolving trays, on a bronze tripod base.

*45.75in (116cm) wide*

**$40,000-60,000**                                      **JM**

A 'Mollusc' desk, by John Makepeace, of washed oak, with a suede-lined pull-out writing surface, on laminated curving legs.

*The oak used for this desk was planted at Longleat in Wiltshire, England in the 1760s and harvested in 1980 to coincide with the late Lord Bath's 80th birthday.*

*c1980*                        *74.75in (190cm) wide*

**$70,000-90,000**                                      **JM**

A rosewood coffee display table, by John Makepeace, the rectangular framed glass top enclosing a green baize-lined well interior.

*30.5in (76cm) wide*

**$5,000-7,000**                                      **L&T**

A 'Desert Sand' chest of drawers, by John Makepeace, with solid ripple ash carcass, three shallow stationery drawers, suede-lined writing slide and six deep drawers.

*The undulating pattern was computer-generated so that the peaks conclude at the corners of the drawers and the hollows coincide with the maximum extent of the handles.*

*42.5in (108cm) wide*

**$120,000-150,000**                                      **JM**

A chest of 18 drawers, by John Makepeace, of English cherry, hornbeam, and burr elm, with cast bronze handles.

*32.25in (82cm) wide*

**$120,000-150,000**                                      **JM**

A plateau coffee table, by Paul McCobb, with a single drawer and vitriol top.

*32in (81.5cm) wide*

**$1,200-1,800**                                      **SK**

### PAUL McCOBB

A 'Planner' group desk and spindle-back chair, by Paul McCobb.

*29.5in (75cm) high*

**$500-700**                                      **SK**

A 'Planner' group chest of four drawers, by Paul McCobb, with a walnut finish.

*36in (91.5cm) wide*

**$220-280**                                      **SK**

A credenza, by Paul McCobb, with sliding cloth doors and two adjustable shelves.

*c1950*                        *60in (152.5cm) wide*

**$1,200-1,800**                                      **LOS**

A contemporary reproduction of a Paul McCobb 'Zither' chair.

*34in (86.5cm) high*

**$300-400**                                      **LOS**

**MODERN FURNITURE**

A lounge chair, by Modernage, upholstered in light gray ultra-suede, with loose seat cushion on ebonized block feet, unmarked.

*28in (71cm) wide*

**$300-400** SDR

A library table with black lacquered top, by Madame Majeska for Modernage, on a blonde wood base with four quarter-round shelves.

*36in (91.5cm) wide*

**$800-1,200** SDR

A large desk, by Modernage, with open shelves over three drawers with horizontal pulls, the center one a fall-front with fitted interior, with metal "Modernage" tag.

One of a pair of Art Deco square club chairs, by Madame Majeska for Modernage, upholstered in bias-cut maroon twill, with new cream linen seat covers.

*28in (71cm) wide*

*72in (183cm) wide*

**$500-700 pair** SDR

**$800-1,200** SDR

## GEORGE NAKASHIMA

A coffee table, by George Nakashima, of English burl oak and walnut, signed "George Nakashima Nov 1969".

A walnut 'Minguren II' coffee table, by George Nakashima, with one V-shaped end and one expressively figured free-edge end, with a rosewood butterfly key concealed underneath.

*58in (145cm) wide*

*55in (137.5cm) wide*

**$35,000-40,000** FRE

**$8,000-12,000** SDR

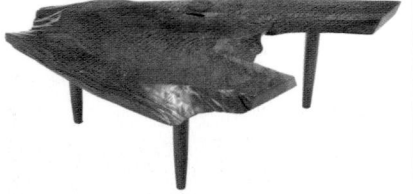

An English walnut coffee table, by George Nakashima, marked with client's name.

A 'Minguren II' Persian walnut coffee table, by George Nakashima, the sculptural top with a single rosewood butterfly joint, on a black walnut minguren base.

A black walnut 'Minguren I' coffee table, by George Nakashima, with a free-edge top with natural occlusions and two rosewood butterfly keys, signed "George Nakashima Oct 1979", also marked "Hand & Spirit".

*46.5in (116cm) wide*

*16.5in (42cm) wide*

*1979*

*70.5in (176cm) wide*

**$7,000-10,000** FRE

**$8,000-12,000** FRE

**$12,000-18,000** SDR

A 'Minguren I' side table, by George Nakashima, with a free-form Buckeye burl top on a rosewood base, marked with original owner's name.

32.5in (82.5cm) wide

**$25,000-35,000**  **SDR**

An English black walnut dining table, by George Nakashima, of hickory and rosewood, marked with client's name.

81in (202cm) wide

**$25,000-35,000**  **FRE**

A 1960s English walnut, black walnut, and oak dining table, by George Nakashima, marked with client's name.

68in (173cm) wide

**$15,000-20,000**  **FRE**

Two of a set of six 'New' hickory and walnut dining chairs, by George Nakashima, comprising two armchairs and four side chairs, marked with client's name.

armchair 39in (97.5cm) high

**$7,000-10,000 set**  **FRE**

A walnut 'Conoid' lounge chair and ottoman, by George Nakashima.

c1975  chair 30.5in (77.5cm) high

**$4,000-6,000**  **SK**

A walnut 'Conoid' bench, by George Nakashima, with hickory spindles and free-edge seat with natural occlusion, on tapering dowel legs, unmarked.

1977  71.5in (179cm) wide

**$18,000-25,000**  **SDR**

An early prototype walnut four-drawer chest, by George Nakashima, with louvered front, of pinned and dovetailed case construction, on a plinth base.

*This is a historically important piece that George Nakashima presented to Knoll in the 1940s.*

36in (91.5cm) wide

**$8,000-12,000**  **SDR**

A rare walnut cabinet, by George Nakashima, with dovetailed case, free-edge top, three grilled sliding doors and three interior compartments fitted with dividers and shelves.

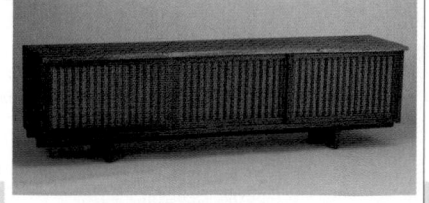

84in (210cm) wide

**$18,000-25,000**  **SDR**

A walnut wall-hanging shelf, by George Nakashima, with free-edge top, dovetails and two lower drawers, unmarked, some wear.

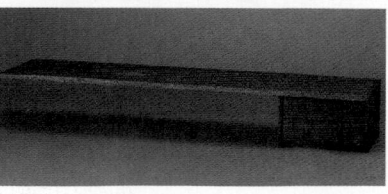

78in (195cm) wide

**$10,000-15,000**  **SDR**

A conference table in rosewood and steel, by George Nelson for Herman Miller, with circular metal tag.

*103.5in (236cm) wide*

**$1,200-1,800** | **FRE**

A home office desk, by George Nelson, with two leather-covered sliding doors over a rectangular top with hinged cabinet revealing a fitted interior, flanked by a leather writing surface with perforated metal basket.

*c1950* *54in (137cm) wide*

**$5,000-7,000** | **SK**

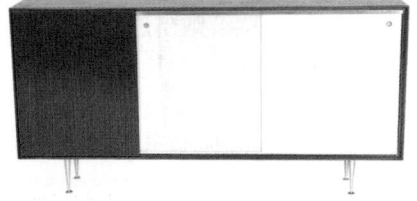

A 'Thin Edge' walnut veneer credenza, by George Nelson for Herman Miller, with a cabinet flanking two cream-colored sliding doors concealing three shelves, on tapering aluminum legs, unmarked.

*67.25in (171cm) wide*

**$3,000-4,000** | **SDR**

A 'Marshmallow' sofa, by George Nelson for Herman Miller, with 18 forest green naugahyde cushions mounted on a tubular steel frame, with circular Herman Miller tag and factory paper label.

*Naugahyde is a type of vinyl often used in mid-20thC upholstery.*

*51in (129.5cm) wide*

**$15,000-18,000** | **SDR**

## MIES VAN DER ROHE

A pair of 'Tugendhat' chairs, by Mies van der Rohe, each with two curved arms on a cantilevered flat bar metal frame, with S-shaped legs and tufted black leather cushions.

*c1930* *34in (86.5cm) high*

**$5,000-8,000** | **SK**

One of a pair of 20thC 'Barcelona' chairs, by Mies van der Rohe, with black leather cushions on a flat bar base.

*29.5in (75cm) high*

**$5,000-8,000 pair** | **SK**

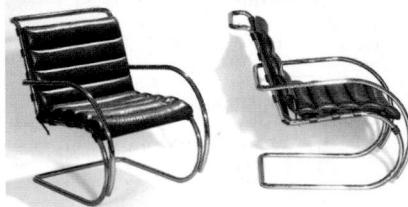

A pair of 20thC 'MR' chairs, by Mies van der Rohe, each with a cantilevered tubular steel frame and green leather padded and upholstered seat.

*33.5in (85cm) high*

**$6,000-9,000** | **SK**

A set of four 'BRNO MR50' chairs, by Mies van der Rohe, with green leather upholstery on a steel base.

*31.25in (79cm) high*

**$1,200-1,800** | **SK**

A pair of 'Barcelona' chairs, by Mies van der Rohe, with red leather upholstery on chromed flat metal bar frames.

*29.5in (75cm) high*

**$5,000-7,000** | **SK**

A 20thC 'Tugendhat'-style day bed, after a design by Mies van der Rohe, with rectangular black leather cushion and head rest, on a webbed wooden frame, raised on four cylindrical legs.

*38in (96.5cm) wide*

**$2,200-2,800** | **SK**

A valet chair, by Hans Wegner for Johannes Hansen, made from teak, oak, brass, and leather, with branded "JH" logo, marked "Johannes Hansen Copenhagen Denmark".

*37in (92.5cm) high*

**$6,000-9,000    FRE**

A peacock chair, by Hans Wegner, in ash and teak, with cord seat and maker's mark.

*43in (109cm) high*

**$2,200-2,800    SK**

A teak day bed, by Hans Wegner, with natural woven backrest, converts to create an upholstered day bed, with retail label to base.

*c1960*                    *78in (198cm) wide*

**$2,800-3,200                            SK**

A teak lounge chair and ottoman, by Hans Wegner, with a reclining upholstered cushion seat.

*c1960    34.5in (87.5cm) high*

**$4,000-6,000              SK**

A teak dining table, by Hans Wegner, with a circular top on a cross-stretcher frame, with metal mounts set into four tapered circular legs.

*c1960                    61in (155cm) diam*

**$1,800-2,200                            SK**

## EDWARD WORMLEY

A coffee table, by Edward Wormley for Dunbar.

*c1955                    60in (152.5cm) wide*

**$1,800-2,200                            LOS**

A mahogany coffee table, by Edward Wormley for Dunbar, with partial plank top and brass rods to one end over a low shelf, with yellow "Dunbar" tag.

*66in (168cm) wide*

**$1,200-1,800                            SDR**

A pair of mid-20thC side tables, by Edward Wormley for Dunbar, with round stone tops on mahogany tri-foot pedestal bases, with metal maker's tag.

*c1950    21.5in (54.5cm) high*

**$2,800-3,200              SK**

An easy armchair and ottoman, by Edward Wormley for Dunbar, upholstered in brown ultra-suede, raised on teak supports.

*31in (79cm) wide*

**$1,200-1,800                            ISA**

A floating back sofa, by Edward Wormley for Dunbar, fully upholstered in woven black and gray fabric on an ebonized wooden base with cross stretcher, with yellow "Dunbar" tag.

*90.5in (230cm) wide*

**$3,000-4,000                            SDR**

## FRANK LLOYD WRIGHT

- American architect Frank Lloyd Wright (1867-1959) studied engineering at the University of Wisconsin before joining an architecture firm in Chicago.
- Wright mainly worked in the Prairie style of architecture, a mid-western interpretation of the Arts & Crafts movement, infused with his own reaction against the historical revivalism that was popular in America at the time.
- Wright designed the interiors to most of his architectural projects, believing in a thematically consistent relationship between interior design and the architectural exterior.
- Rectilinear lines, intersecting planes and simple structures show a strong architectural influence on Wright's furniture. His high-back spindle chair is typical of his take on the Prairie style.
- Wright developed a more Modernist style in the later part of his career, using novel and innovative materials. His work reflected his interest in Japanese art and culture, combined with shapes and motifs that were often Cubist in origin.

A long mahogany bench, by Frank Lloyd Wright for Heritage Henredon, of rectangular form, raised on a pair of board supports with Taliesin motif edges, signed with red monogram.

*60in (152.5cm) wide*

**$2,200-2,800** ISA

A hexagonal mahogany coffee table, by Frank Lloyd Wright for Heritage Henredon, raised on triangular board supports with Taliesin motif edges, signed with red monogram and impressed marks.

*42in (107cm) wide*

**$3,000-4,000** ISA

An eight-drawer dresser, by Frank Lloyd Wright, with overhanging brass pulls, on a plinth base, unmarked.

*c1955*  *48in (122cm) wide*

**$2,800-3,200** SDR

A mahogany buffet, by Frank Lloyd Wright for Heritage Henredon, complete with removable open shelf unit, with Taliesin motif edges, raised on rail legs.

*86.5in (220cm) wide*

**$2,200-2,800** ISA

## OTHER NAMED FURNITURE

An highback 'Model 31' armchair, by Alvar Aalto for Artek, with padded seat, on laminated beech cantilever supports.

*c1935*

**$500-700** L&T

A pair of birch and plywood tables, by Alvar Aalto for Finmar Ltd., with celluloid "Finmar" tag.

*largest 39in (97.5cm) wide*

**$500-700** FRE

A 'Pony' chair, by Eero Aarnio for Asko, fully upholstered in black jersey, marked with tag "Eero Aarnio Adelta Made in Finland".

*35in (89cm) high*

**$2,800-3,200** SDR

A rosewood wardrobe, by Jacques Adnet, with single drawer and three cabinet doors, glass and brass pulls, four original shelves and original keys, marked "J. Adnet".

*49in (124.5cm) wide*

**$2,800-3,200** SDR

A 'Rover' chair, by Rod Arad for One Off Ltd, comprising a salvaged Rover car seat with headrest covered in black leather, mounted on a tubular steel scaffolding frame, unmarked.

*26.5in (67.5cm) wide*

**$3,000-4,000** SDR

A pair of foam lounge chairs, by Ron Arad for Moroso, fully upholstered in green wool, one with "Moroso" metal tag.

*32in (81.5cm) wide*

**$4,000-6,000** SDR

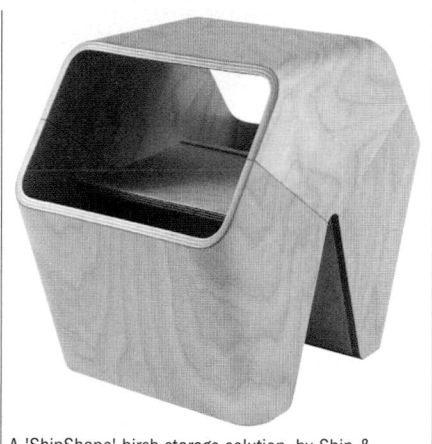

A 'ShipShape' birch storage solution, by Shin & Tomoko Azumi, inspired by the Isokon archives, dated.

*2003*                    *17.75in (45cm) wide*

**$500-700**                    **ISO**

Two Bär & Knell armchairs 'Deko' and 'Müll-Direkt', made from black recycled plastic with collage-like applications of plastic household waste, both stamped "BK 95".

*1995*          *21.5in (54.5cm) wide*

**$2,200-2,800**                    **QU**

A bench, by Milo Baughman for Thayer Coggin, with buttoned upholstery and four tapering legs.

*c1960*          *60in (152.5cm) wide*

**$1,200-1,800**                    **LOS**

A single-pedestal desk, by Studio BBPR for Olivetti, with clip-corner top and three drawers, on an enameled metal trestle base, unmarked.

*62.5in (159cm) wide*

**$2,800-3,200**                    **SDR**

A 'Landscape Chaise', by Jeffrey Bernett for B&B Italia, upholstered in orange felt sewn into segments, with magnetically attached leather pillow.

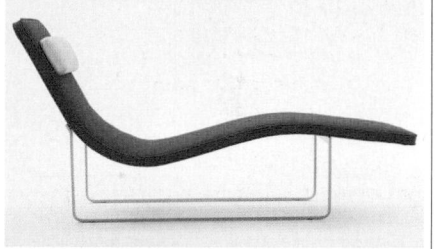

*24in (61cm) wide*

**$2,800-3,200**     **BBI**

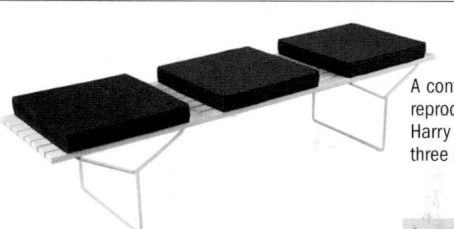

A contemporary reproduction of a 1950s Harry Bertoia for Knoll three seater sofa.

*72in (183cm) wide*

**$1,200-1,800**                    **LOS**

A 'Dinette' table, by Osvaldo Borsani for Tecno, with beveled circular top covered in mottled taupe leather, with embossed design, on four polished curved steel legs, unmarked.

*25in (63.5cm) high*

**$800-1,200**                    **SDR**

A lounge chair, by Osvaldo Borsani for Tecno, upholstered in peach, umber, purple, and blue striped fabric, on a steel base with low-slung hard rubber side grips, with "Tecno" metal tag.

*26.5in (67.5cm) wide*

**$1,200-1,800**                    **SDR**

An inflatable armchair, by Mario Botta.

*38.5in (98cm) wide*

**$1,200-1,800**     **SDR**

A 'Strap Chair', by Boym Partners, with a polypropylene strapping tape seating surface.

*'Strap Chair' was featured at the National Design Triennial in 2000.*

**$3,000-5,000**                    **BOY**

A 'Strap Chair', by Boym Partners, with a polypropylene strapping tape seating surface.

$3,000-5,000    BOY

A rolling cart, by Calvin, with a drop-leaf top and castors.

*c1965*                    *34in (86.5cm) wide*

$800-1,200    LOS

A bentwood chair, by Norman Cherner for Plycraft, with orange upholstered seat and partial paper label.

*c1955*                    *31in (79cm) high*

$600-900    SK

A 'Torso' armchair, by Paola Daganello for Cassina, with asymmetric fabric upholstered back and leather upholstered seat frame in dark teal, on enameled steel legs, unmarked.

*43in (17cm) wide*

$800-1,200    SDR

A satinwood buffet, by Desny, with beveled black glass insert to top and illuminated interior, flanked by cabinets with chrome hardware, marked "Desny France".

*83in (211cm) wide*

$7,000-10,000    SDR

A wicker chair, by Nanna Ditzel and Ludwig Pontoppidan, with a woven barrel seat, mahogany frame, and paper label.

*c1950*    *23in (58.5cm) wide*

$1,200-1,800    SDR

A Danish coatrack, attributed to Nanna Ditzel.

*c1960*    *65in (165cm) high*

$800-1,200    LOS

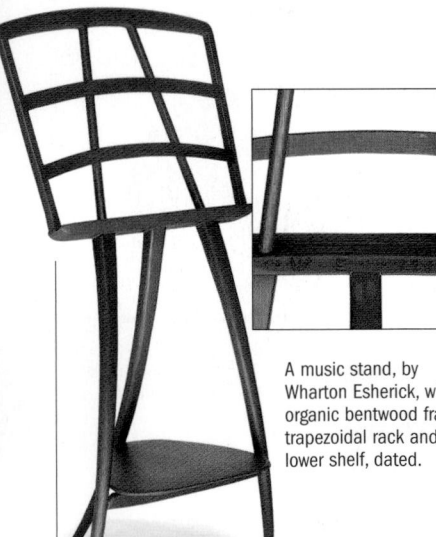

A music stand, by Wharton Esherick, with organic bentwood frame, trapezoidal rack and lower shelf, dated.

*1962  46in (117cm) high*

$80,000-120,000 SDR

A mid-20thC teak credenza, by Dryland, with rectangular top over four blind drawers and two sliding doors, fitted with sliding shelves and compartments, raised on tapering legs.

*82.5in (209.5cm) wide*

$800-1,200    SK

A walnut console table, by Wharton Esherick, with freeform beveled top over a sculptural tripod base, with carved cipher.

*c1950*                    *35in (89cm) wide*

$20,000-30,000    SDR

A unique dining table, by Paul Evans, executed in the Queen Anne style, with a rectangular rosewood top on a sculpted bronze base with cabriole legs, unmarked.

*This table was from the personal collection of Paul Evans and was used in the artist's home.*

*103in (262cm) wide*

$6,000-9,000    SDR

A card table, by Paul Frankl, with undulating laminated cork top, on four tapering legs with ebonized finish, stenciled mark "5002-180".

35.75in (91cm) wide

**$700-1,000** SDR

One of a set of four dining chairs, by Paul Frankl, with windowpane backs and black vinyl covered seat pads on ebonized frames, the bases numbered in crayon.

19in (48.5cm) wide

**$400-600 set** SDR

An 'Easy Edges' stool, by Frank Gehry, of masonite and corrugated cardboard, overpainted, unmarked.

12in (30.5cm) wide

**$700-1,000** SDR

## A CLOSER LOOK AT A LITTLE BEAVER ARMCHAIR

*The 'Little Beaver' armchair and ottoman were conceived as part of a project called 'Experimental Edges', in which Gehry used corrugated cardboard to challenge common perceptions of suitable furnishing materials.*

*This laminated, corrugated cardboard was originally designed for use in the packing industry.*

*Designs for Gehry's 'Experimental Edges' series were intended for gallery exhibition, and have never been developed commercially. This exclusivity adds to the value of this set.*

A 'Little Beaver' armchair and ottoman, by Frank Gehry for Vitra, of laminated cardboard construction, marked with brass tag and numbered "54/100".

1987    33.5in (85cm) wide

**$4,000-6,000** SDR

A rare 'Skyscraper' chest, by Paul Frankl, asymmetrically configured with drawers, cabinets and shelves, with pyramidal and horizontal brass pulls and metal "Skyscraper Furniture" tag.

36in (91.5cm) wide

**$8,000-12,000** SDR

A zaisu chair, produced to an original Kenji Fujimori design by Tendo Mokko, made from a single piece of molded beech with a zelkova veneer.

*The zaisu chair is a legless Japanese interpretation of the Western chair. The hole prevents warping and slipping.*

2004    13in (33cm) wide

**$80-120** TDO

A rare dining table, by Frank Gehry, with a circular plate glass top on a six-cylinder corrugated cardboard base, unmarked.

48in (122cm) diam

**$4,000-6,000** SDR

A 1950s birch sideboard, by T.H. Robsjohn Gibbings for Widdicomb, with rectangular top, fitted with three cabinet doors, the interior fitted with four drawers and shelves.

72in (183cm) wide

**$1,800-2,200** FRE

A mirrored glass, brass, and wood step table, by Billy Haines, the upper glass shelf raised on waisted supports rising from a shaped mirrored shelf, all raised on tapering ebonized legs.

1958    18in (46cm) wide

**$220-280** ISA

An early 'Butterfly' chair, by Bonet, Kurchan and Hardoy, with a leather sling seat on a rod iron frame.

c1950    34.25in (87cm) high

**$800-1,200** LOS

A wall unit, by Heywood-Wakefield, comprising a top case fitted with shelving over drawers and tambour door compartments, with a walnut color finish and branded mark.

*c1960*                                   *65in (165cm) wide*

**$1,200-1,800**                          **SK**

A unique handcrafted solid black walnut writing table, by Laurence Hendricks.

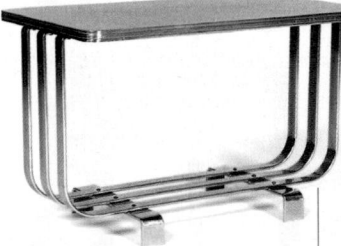

A side table, by Wolfgang Hoffmann for Howell, with a rectangular laminate top and chrome trim, on a polished chrome base, unmarked.

*1972*                    *30in (76cm) wide*

**$2,200-2,800**               **LOS**

*27in (68.5cm) wide*

**$800-1,200**               **SDR**

A harp chair, by Jorgen Hovelskov, made from wood and strung rope.

A mid-20thC birch veneer composition desk, retailed by the Interform Collection, with a rectangular top and sides enclosing a suspended bank of three drawers.

A bent plywood chair, produced to an original Saburoh Inuiby design by Tendo Mokko, in beech with a maple veneer.

*c1970*        *52in (132cm) high*

**$2,200-2,800**          **SK**

*64.5in (164cm) wide*

**$220-280**          **SK**

*2004*        *28.25in (72cm) wide*

**$500-700**          **TDO**

A low table, produced to an original Saburoh Inuiby design by Tendo Mokko, in beech with a zelkova veneer.

A birch 'Monroe' chair, produced to an original Arata Isozaki design by Tendo Mokko.

*48in (122cm) wide*

**$500-700     TDO**

*2004*        *21.25in (54cm) wide*

**$3,000-4,000**          **TDO**

A 'Swan' chair, by Arne Jacobsen, designed in 1957.

*30in (76cm) high*

**$1,200-1,800** LOS

An 'Egg' chair, by Arne Jacobsen, with blue upholstery, on a metal swivel base.

*c1960* *42in (106.5cm) high*

**$1,200-1,800** SK

A rosewood coffee table, by Georg Jensen, with a rectangular top inset on one side with abstract patterned studio tiles in olive green and teal blue, unmarked.

*23.25in (59cm) wide*

**$400-600** SDR

One of a pair of 'No.53' easy Chairs, by Finn Juhl for Niels Vodder, in teak with green fabric upholstery, horn-shaped arms brass hardware and branded mark.

*28in (71cm) wide*

**$1,800-2,200 pair** SDR

A teak 'No. 45' settee, by Finn Juhl for Niels Vodder, with brown vinyl upholstery, sculpted frame and branded mark.

*46in (117cm) wide*

**$7,000-10,000** SDR

An early teak 'Chieftan' chair, by Finn Juhl for Niels Vodder, re-upholstered in black leather, with branded mark.

*40.5in (103cm) wide*

**$12,000-18,000** SDR

A chair, produced by Tendo Mokko from an original design by Isamu Kenmochi, in beech with a maple veneer.

*2004* *20.25in (51.5cm) wide*

**$400-600** TDO

A 'Kashiwado' chair, produced by Tendo Mokko from an original design by Isamu Kenmochi, formed from blocks of cedar trunk sanded to reveal the grain.

*This wide chair is named after a famous Japanese sumo wrestler.*

*2004* *33.5in (85cm) wide*

**$4,000-6,000** TDO

A low table, produced by Tendo Mokko from an original design by Isamu Kenmochi, in beech with rosewood veneer.

*The indentation around the edge of the table top is called a 'mizukaeshi', which means 'water embankment'.*

*2004* *55in (140cm) wide*

**$2,800-3,200** TDO

649

**MODERN FURNITURE**

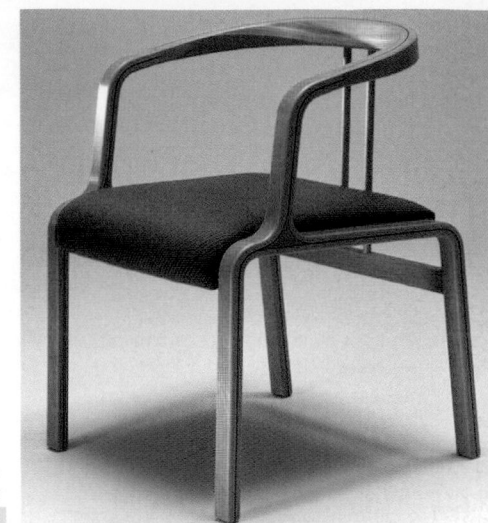

A beech armchair, produced by Tendo Mokko from an original design by Toshiyuki Kita.

*2004     21.25in 8(54cm) wide*

**$300-400     TDO**

A steel, oak, and marble dining table, by Poul Kjaerholm, with a green marble on top of the original oak surface.

*80in (200cm) wide*

**$2,200-2,800     FRE**

A conference table, by Florence Knoll, with an oval rosewood top, on a polished chrome pedestal base, with "Knoll International" label.

*78in (198cm) wide*

**$2,200-2,800     SDR**

A 'Terrazza' modular lounge sofa, by Ubald Klug for De Sede, consisting of two corner seats, upholstered in chocolate brown leather, with "Stendig" paper label.

*27.5in (70cm) high*

**$3,000-5,000     SDR**

A marble coffee table, by Florence Knoll, with a rust-colored variegated rectilinear marble top on a stainless steel base.

*c1975 45in (114.5cm) wide*

**$500-700     SK**

A beech and teak easy chair, by Ib Kofod-Larsen for Christensen & Larsen, with a fabric seat in red and cream on a tapering dowel leg frame, with "Selig Mfg. Co." paper labels.

*21.5in (54.5cm) wide*

**$280-320     SDR**

A wood and leather chair, by Kold of Denmark.

*c1960 29in (73.5cm) high*

**$2,200-2,800     LOS**

A high-back lounge chair, by Axel Larsson, with sculpted wood frame and reddish-brown leather webbing, missing pillow headrest, branded "SMF" monogram and 1939 World's Fair customs tag.

*1937     40in (101.5cm) high*

**$6,000-9,000     SDR**

A pair of chairs, by Kofod Larsen, with black metal frames, geometric patterned green imitation leather seats and shaped laminated beechwood backrests.

*c1950     29in (73.5cm) high*

**$500-800     SK**

A 'Fiberglass Group' armchair, by Erwine & Estelle Laverne, with a free-form cutout seat in ivory on a steel pedestal base, unmarked.

*24in (61cm) wide*

**$800-1,200** **SDR**

A rosewood and amboyna sideboard, attributed to Jules Leleu, with three cabinet doors enclosing interior shelves, with horizontal brass scroll pulls, unmarked.

*78.5in (199.5cm) wide*

**$2,200-2,800** **SDR**

A pair of box chairs, by Enzo Mari, with tubular frames and perforated plastic yellow and white seats.

*c1975* *32.5in (82.5cm) high*

**$320-380** **SK**

An 'Old Point Comfort' club chair, by Warren McArthur, on a tubular aluminum frame with taupe fabric upholstery, remnant of decal.

*23.5in (59.5cm) wide*

**$5,000-7,000** **SDR**

An 'S534' chromium-plated tubular metal armchair, by Eric Mendelsohn, upholstered with red vinyl cloth, with "Desta" label.

*c1930* *78in (198cm) high*

**$1,800-2,200** **SK**

A rare 'Rudder' stool, by Isamu Noguchi for Herman Miller, model number IN-22, in birch with two tubular steel legs, unmarked.

*17in (43cm) high*

**$20,000-30,000** **SDR**

A pair of high-back armchairs, by Herman Miller, with curvilinear seats in tangerine upholstery, on chrome frames with black armrests and chair supports, with paper labels.

*41in (104cm) high*

**$500-700** **SK**

A Danish settee, by Borg Mogenson.

*64in (162.5cm) wide*

**$2,200-2,800** **LOS**

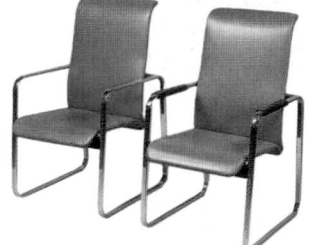
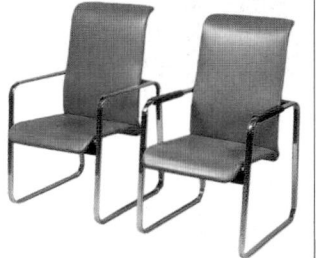

Two of a set of six teak chairs, similar to a design by Neils O. Moller, comprising two armchairs and four side chairs, newly upholstered.

*c1960* *31in (79cm) high*

**$1,200-1,800 set** **SK**

A daybed, by James Mont, with a slatted frame and cushions upholstered in finely woven brushed tan fabric, on bracket feet, unmarked.

*76in (193cm) wide*

**$1,800-2,200** **SDR**

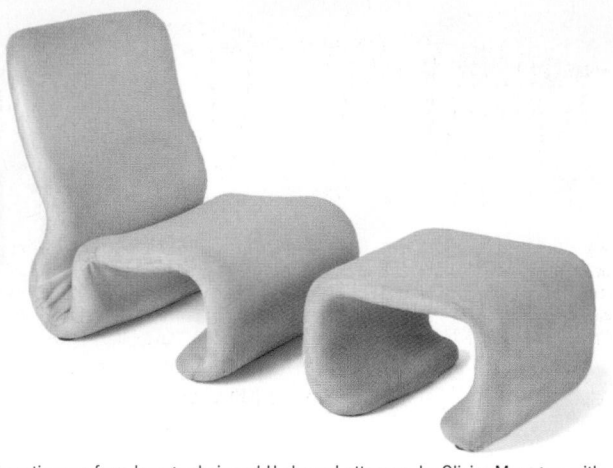

A continuous-form lounge chair and U-shaped ottoman, by Olivier Mourgue, with light gray fabric covering, unmarked.

*25in (65.5cm) wide*

**$800-1,200** SDR

A three panel screen, by Peter Niczewski, with trompe l'oeil marquetry, depicting newspaper, photographic images and geometric designs.

*48in (122cm) wide*

**$1,800-2,200** FRE

A 'Laminex' beech wood chair, by Jens Nielsen for Westnofa of Norway, in two parts.

*1966*          *30in (75cm) wide*

**$700-1,000** FRE

## OLIVIER MOURGUE

■ Born in 1939, Brittany-based Olivier Mourgue produces work firmly rooted in the Pop Art tradition. He owes a debt to the playful Modernism of designers such as Pierre Paulin, whose furniture designs combined comfort with an artistic statement.

■ Mourgue's iconic 'Djinn' series, including a two-seat stool, a chaise, and a chair and ottoman set, has become a classic. The name is taken from a malevolent spirit in Islamic mythology.

■ A magenta Djinn suite was used on the Space Station V set in Stanley Kubrick's film "2001: A Space Odyssey". Its continued cult status has led to its electronic replication for use in the popular computer game "The Sims".

■ Another design classic of Mourgue's is the Bouloum Chaise, made in the form of a reclining human figure, complete with head and legs. It is supposedly named after one of Mourgue's childhood friends.

■ Ever the eccentric, Mourgue always traveled with a Bouloum Chaise, taking photographs of it in places he visited.

A 'Cone' chair, by Verner Panton for Fritz Hansen.

*c1960*          *33.5in (85cm) high*

**$1,800-2,200** LOS

A 'Bachelor' chair, by Verner Panton, with teal blue canvas on a tubular polished chrome frame, unmarked.

*29in (73.5cm) high*

**$280-320** SDR

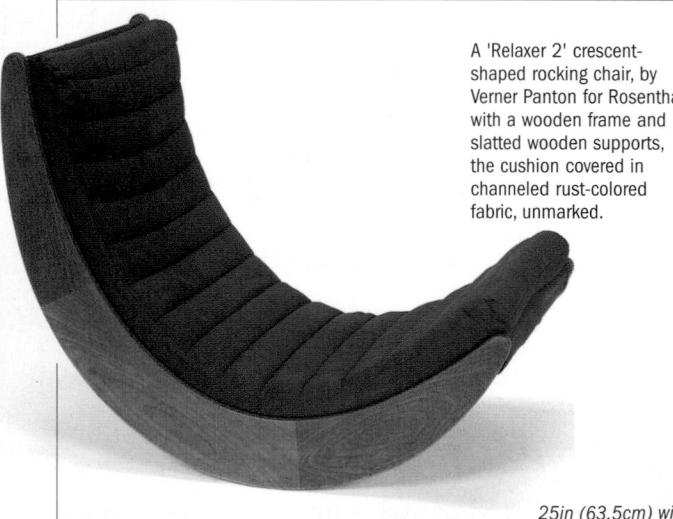

A 'Relaxer 2' crescent-shaped rocking chair, by Verner Panton for Rosenthal, with a wooden frame and slatted wooden supports, the cushion covered in channeled rust-colored fabric, unmarked.

*25in (63.5cm) wide*

**$2,200-2,800** SDR

A pair of high-back lounge chairs, by Ico Parisi, with burgundy damask upholstery and brocade trim, on flaring wooden legs, unmarked.

*28in (71cm) wide*

**$2,200-2,800** SDR

A brass and enameled metal coffee table, attributed to Ico Parisi, with a rectangular plate glass top, chipped, unmarked.

*36.5in (92.5cm) wide*

**$1,200-1,800** SDR

A rare day-bed, by Tommi Parzinger, with eight loose cushions upholstered in butter yellow embossed silk fabric, on a dark stained wooden frame with etched brass details, unmarked.

*65in (165cm) wide*

**$4,000-6,000** SDR

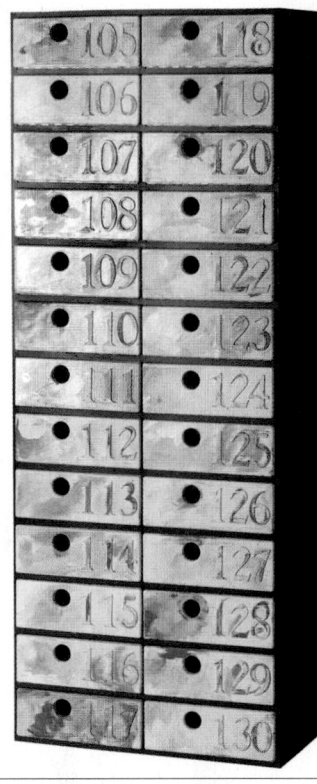

A post-modern storage unit, by Gaetano Pesce, comprising two racks of 13 numbered compartments with hinged fronts in polychrome wood, on an ebonized frame with open back, unmarked.

*1991*     *24.25in (61.5cm) wide.*

**$2,200-2,800**          **SDR**

A green marble and metal dining table, designed by Pasanella & Klein, the rectangular green marble top with white veining, on four tubular steel legs, with flat bar cross and side stretchers.

*104in (264cm) wide*

**$2,200-2,800**          **SK**

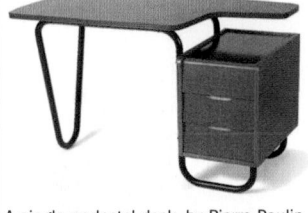

A single-pedestal desk, by Pierre Paulin for Mobilor, with raised free-form top over two drawers with black laminate surface, on a tubular black metal frame, with "Mobilor" paper label.

*47in (119.5cm) wide*

**$1,200-1,800**          **SDR**

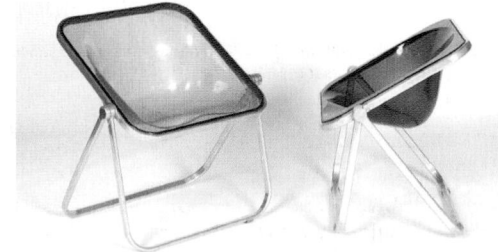

A pair of folding chairs, by Giancarlo Piretti, each with a smoky quartz molded plastic tub seat, on an aluminum frame, unmarked.

*30in (76cm) high*

**$400-600**          **SDR**

A lounge suite, by Warren Platner, comprising three chairs and a table formed of electronically welded steel rods, the chairs upholstered in oatmeal fabric, the table with a circular beveled glass top, chipped.

*1966*     *table 54in (137cm) diam*

**$1,800-2,200**          **SK**

A dining table, by Gio Ponti for Singer & Sons, in walnut and brass.

*1954*     *64in (162.5cm) wide*

**$5,000-7,000**          **LOS**

A single dining chair image

One of a set of four 'Superleggera' dining chairs, by Gio Ponti, each with two horizontal backslats and woven seat, unmarked.

*17in (43cm) wide*

**$1,800-2,200 set**          **SDR**

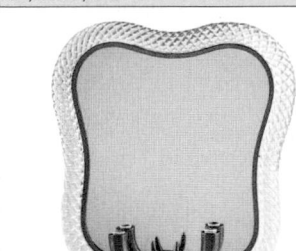

A large and rare illuminated wall mirror, by Gio Ponti for Venini, of scalloped form with braided glass border and two brass crossed horn fixtures, unmarked.

*c1940*     *19.5in (49.5cm) wide*

**$6,000-9,000**          **SDR**

A custom designed walnut dining table, by Phillip Lloyd Powell, unmarked.

*c1960*     *47.25in (120cm) wide*

**$1,800-2,200**          **SDR**

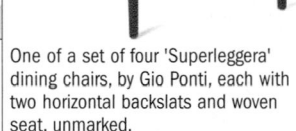

A wood and brass coffee table, by Harvey Probber.

*c1960*     *70.5in (179cm) wide*

**$2,200-2,800**          **LOS**

**MODERN FURNITURE**

One of a set of four side chairs, by Ernest Race, covered in black vinyl, on black metal legs with chrome capped feet.

*19in (48.5cm) wide*

**$600-900 set** SDR

A 'Polar Bear' chair, by Jean Royere, fully re-upholstered in hand-stitched alpaca fabric, on low wooden legs, unmarked.

*31.5in (78.5cm) wide*

**$18,000-25,000** SDR

A fine Brazilian rosewood pedestal dining table, in the style of Emile-Jacques Ruhlmann, with a radiating grain pattern to the ivory inlaid top, on four curved supports and a stepped base, unmarked.

*72in (183cm) diam*

**$6,000-9,000** SDR

A walnut free-edge dining table, by Gino Russo, with four butterfly joints and terminal supports conjoined by a stretcher, signed "Gino 87".

*Gino Russo worked for George Nakashima from the mid 1950s until 1968.*

*36in (91.5cm) wide*

**$1,200-1,800** FRE

A postmodern single-pedestal desk, by Peter Shire, with a trapezoidal black lacquered top on an enameled steel base in yellow, pink, and blue, unmarked.

*1979* *81.5in (207cm) wide*

**$1,200-1,800** SDR

A 'Crazy Horse' table, by Ettore Sottsass for Memphis, with a square laminated top in red and black trim, on a white enameled steel base, unmarked.

*40in (101.5cm) wide*

**$800-1,200** SDR

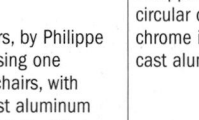

One of a set of five chairs, by Philippe Starck for Aleph, comprising one armchair and four side chairs, with bentwood backs and cast aluminum rear legs, stamped "Starck Aleph".

*18in (45.5cm) wide*

**$1,800-2,200 set** SDR

An 'M Serie Lang' dining table, by Philippe Starck for Aleph Driade, the circular dyed mahogany veneer top with chrome inlay, on three sharply tapered cast aluminum legs, unmarked.

*51in (129.5cm) wide*

**$1,200-1,800** SDR

Two of a set of four high-back chairs, by Philippe Starck, three in light green and one in dark green vinyl upholstery, all with laced trim on tapering white enameled wooden legs, unmarked.

*15in (38cm) wide*

**$2,200-2,800 set** SDR

A 'Murai' stool, produced to an original Reiko Tanabe design by Tendo Mokko, in beech with a teak veneer.

*2004* *17.75in (45cm) wide*

**$400-600** TDO

A 'Spoke' oak chair, produced by Tendo Mokko from an original design by Katsuhei Toyoguchi.

*This is an interesting example of a Western form adapted to the Japanese environment, where furniture is traditionally very low.*

*2004* *32in (81cm) wide*

**$700-1,000** TDO

A rare and early asymmetric server, by Russel Wright for Heywood-Wakefield, in a burlwood veneer and black lacquer finish, comprising a single drawer and two-door cabinet with horizontal pulls, unmarked.

*45in (114.5cm) wide*

**$3,000-4,000**      **SDR**

Two of a set of four rare and early 'Nikke 9019' side chairs, by Tapio Wrikkala for Stendig, each with vinyl upholstery on a tubular metal base, with "Stendig" labels.

*17.5in (44.5cm) wide*

**$1,200-1,800 set**      **SDR**

A butterfly stool, produced to an original Soir Yanagi design by Tendo Mokko, in beech with a rosewood veneer.

*2004*      *16.5in (42cm) wide*

**$280-320**      **TDO**

A drop leaf dining table, by Stanley Young for Glenn of California.

*c1955*      *60in (152.5cm) wide*

**$3,000-5,000**      **LOS**

## UNNAMED FURNITURE

Two of a set of five Danish rosewood and leather club chairs, with cotton webbing.

*26in (65cm) wide*

**$1,200-1,800 set**      **FRE**

An Italian cabinet, with an inlaid sliding door over a mirrored interior, on tapering columns, with a glass shelf and marble base, unmarked.

*37in (94cm) wide*

**$1,200-1,800**      **SDR**

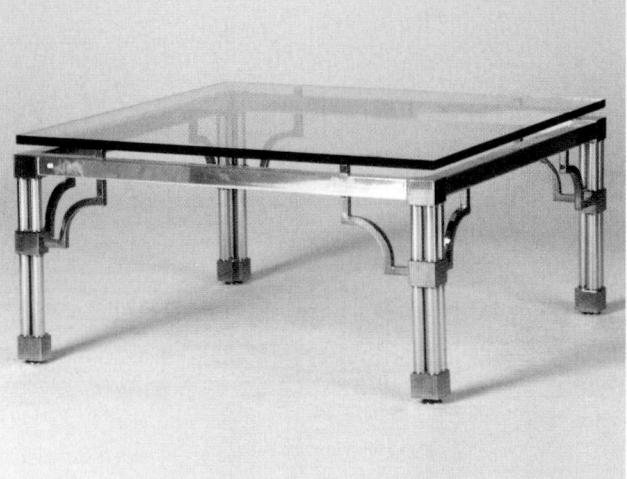

An American polished chrome and brass coffee table, with a raised square plate glass top on a base with bracket supports, unmarked.

*36in (91.5cm) wide*

**$220-280**      **SDR**

A solid glass cow, by Alfredo Barbini for Vetreria Alfredo Barbini, with protruding horns and ears and gray powder inclusions, signed "A. Barbini".

*c1955*  13.2in (33 cm) long

**$5,000-7,000**  VZ

An amorphous clear glass vase, by Alfredo Barbini for Vetreria Alfredo Barbini, with a drawn-in mouth, the inside drop-shaped hollow underlaid in strawberry red.

*c1960*  4in (10cm) high

**$800-1,200**  VZ

A flat oval 'Vetro Pesante' vase, designed by Alfredo Barbini, of thick transparent smoked and cased cherry red glass, signed on the base "A. Barbini".

*c1960*  8.75in (22cm) wide

**$2,800-3,200**  QU

A cylindrical black glass vase, by Alfredo Barbini for Vetreria Alfredo Barbini, with matt oil spot decoration, etched "Barbini Murano".

*c1965*  14.25in (36.5cm) high

**$500-700**  VZ

A glass vase, by Alfredo Barbini for Vetreria Alfredo Barbini, with a narrow inverted rim and double horizontal band inclusions in ocher, dated, etched "A. Barbini".

*1968*  10in (25cm) high

**$4,000-6,000**  VZ

A turquoise cased glass vase, by Vetreria Alfredo Barbini, with a narrow inverted rim and ocher inclusions in the center, etched "A. Barbini".

*c1970*  14in (35.5cm) high

**$3,000-4,000**  VZ

## BAROVIER & TOSO

### ERCOLE BAROVIER

- Born into a family of glassmakers, Ercole Barovier (1889-1974) abandoned a career in medicine to join his father's firm in 1919.
- In 1929 Barovier created his 'Primavera' series. The distinctive crackled white surface of these vessels was the result of an accidental chemical combination, and could not be reproduced.
- Barovier's experiments with new ways of introducing color and texture to glass resulted in a technique called 'colorazione a caldo senza fusione'. This literally means 'coloring glass while hot without fusing', and it was widely imitated by other glassworkers on the island of Murano.
- During the 1960s, Barovier produced the 'Intarsio' series, one of his most inventive. The design consisted of a mosaic effect composed of colorful diamond or triangular tesserae and was produced in several different color combinations from 1963.

A flat ovoid black glass vase, by Ercole Barovier for Vetreria Artistica Barovier & Co., with a thick rim and bands of amber aventurine.

*c1925*  7in (18cm) high

**$800-1,200**  VZ

An 'Aventurina' cased glass amphora vase, by Ercole Barovier for Vetreria Artistica Barovier, with double-scroll handles, and aventurine inclusions.

*c1930*  11.75in (29.5cm) high

**$1,800-2,200**  QU

A 'Primavera' vase, by Ercole Barovier for Vetreria Artistica Barovier, of teardrop form with opaque white craquelure effect and decorative branches in dark green.

*c1930*  12.5in (32cm) high

**$5,000-7,000**  VZ

A 'Vetro Mosaico' bell-shaped vase, by Ercole Barovier for Ferro Toso Barovier, with squared opaque yellow and brown murrines.

*c1930*  8.5in (21.5cm) high

**$7,000-10,000**  VZ

A 'Lenti' colorless iridescent glass vase, by Ercole Barovier for Barovier & Toso, with horizontal semi-spherical bosses.

*c1940*  8.5in (21.5cm) high

**$3,000-5,000**  QU

A 'Lenti' cylindrical amber glass vase, by Ercole Barovier for Barovier & Toso, with hobnail relief, unmarked.

c1940          8.25in (21cm) high

**$1,200-1,800**          VZ

An 'A Spirale' clear glass vase, by Ercole Barovier for Barovier & Toso, with thick ribbing, purple powder inclusions and a black diagonal spiral band.

c1940     10.25in (26cm) high

**$15,000-18,000**          VZ

A pale green glass bowl, by Ercole Barovier for Barovier & Toso, with applied emerald green flower decorations, painted iridescent gold and petrol blue.

c1940          5in (12.5cm) high

**$800-1,200**          VZ

A 'Cordonato Oro' clear glass oval bowl, by Ercole Barovier, ribbed throughout with scroll handles and spiral goldfoil inclusions.

c1950          3.75in (9.5cm) high

**$280-320**          VZ

An oval glass bowl, by Ercole Barovier for Barovier & Toso, with ocher and opaque orange powder inclusions and irregular bubbles.

c1955          10.25in (26cm) wide

**$280-320**          VZ

A 'Moreschi' cylindrical glass vase, by Ercole Barovier for Barovier & Toso, with alternating rectangular aventurine and amber glass plate inclusions in the 'Pezzato' pattern.

c1955          7.5in (19cm) high

**$5,000-8,000**          QU

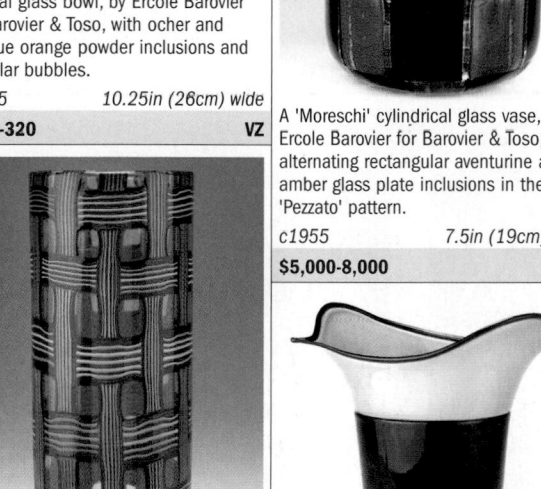

An 'A Canne Multiple' clear glass vase, by Ercole Barovier for Barovier & Toso, with spiraling bands in gold, copper, green, and black, marked to the base, with remains of paper label.

c1960          17.5in (44cm) high

**$1,800-2,200**          QU

A 'Efeso' bulbous glass vase, by Ercole Barovier for Barovier & Toso, with light blue and dark gray oxide and bubble inclusions.

c1965          16.25in (40.5cm) high

**$1,800-2,200**          QU

A cylindrical transparent glass vase, by Ercole Barovier for Barovier & Toso, with a pattern of woven horizontal and vertical violet, green, and white stripes.

c1980          13.5in (33.5cm) high

**$2,200-2,800**          QU

A 'Morbido' black glass vase, by Toni Zuccheri for Barovier & Toso, the applied light gray opaque glass neck with a broad waved rim outlined in black, turquoise interior, marked.

1984          11.75in (30cm) high

**$3,000-5,000**          VZ

A 'Tessere' cylindrical glass vase, by Ercole Barovier, with a continuous pattern of pale yellow and opaque white stripes with purplish brown rings, etched "Barovier & Toso Murano" to the base.

c1985          13in (33cm) high

**$3,000-5,000**          VZ

A 'Tiffany' murrine and amethyst-threaded pietini vase, by Vittorio Ferro for Fratelli Toso.

*The wavy rim of this vase is created by the murrines themselves which contract as they cool, pulling the rim downward.*

| | |
|---|---|
| c1960 | 11.75in (30cm) high |
| **$1,800-2,200** | **VET** |

A nerox glass bowl, by Vittorio Ferro, with blue and clear rectangular murrines.

*This very rare bowl was made for the 'Santi d'Oro' exhibition. By arranging the lined murrines alternately vertically and horizontally, Ferro has created an interesting optical effect.*

| | |
|---|---|
| c1970 | 9.75in (25cm) diam |
| **$4,000-6,000** | **FER** |

A 'Pezzato' vase, by Vittorio Ferro for De Majo, with a matte finish.

| | |
|---|---|
| c1990 | 9.5in (24cm) high |
| **$1,200-1,800** | **PC** |

A rare murrine vase, by Vittorio Ferro, signed "V&A Vittori Ferro Murano".

*These murrines came from a rival factory.*

| | |
|---|---|
| 1999 | 3.5in (9cm) high |
| **$1,200-1,800** | **VET** |

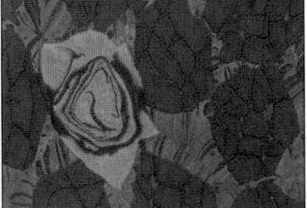

A red and yellow murrine vase, by Vittorio Ferro for Fratelli Pagnin, with iridescent areas between the murrines.

| | |
|---|---|
| 1998 | 11in (28cm) high |
| **$2,200-2,800** | **PC** |

A complex red murrine vase, by Vittorio Ferro for Fratelli Pagnin, signed to the base "2000 Vittorio Ferro".

| | |
|---|---|
| 2000 | 7.25in (18.5cm) high |
| **$2,200-2,800** | **VET** |

A gold aventurine and pietina vase, by Vittorio Ferro for Fratelli Pagnin, with blue and gold aventurine murrines, signed to the base "F'lli Pagnin Vittorio Ferro".

*This shape is sometimes called 'Dead Man's Bone'.*

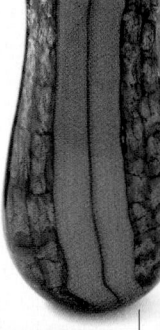

| | |
|---|---|
| | 13in (33cm) high |
| **$5,000-7,000** | **VET** |

## FRATELLI TOSO

A 'Stellata' oval clear glass vase, by Pollio Perelda for Fratelli Toso, with encased star-shaped polychrome murrines.

| | |
|---|---|
| 1953 | 10.5in (26.5cm) high |
| **$5,000-7,000** | **VZ** |

A 'Farfalle' ovoid transparent glass vase, by Pollio Perelda for Fratelli Toso, with dense multi-colored melted rectangular 'Pezzato'-style pattern.

| | |
|---|---|
| c1960 | 14.5in (36.5cm) high |
| **$10,000-15,000** | **QU** |

A 'Murrine' ovoid clear glass vase, by Ermanno Toso for Fratelli Toso, decorated with polychrome murrines, with maker's paper label.

| | |
|---|---|
| c1960 | 8.5in (21.5cm) high |
| **$3,000-4,000** | **QU** |

A 'Kiku' ovoid clear glass vase, by Ermanno Toso for Fratelli Toso, with dense polychrome murrine inclusions in flower shapes.

| | |
|---|---|
| c1960 | 8.75in (22cm) high |
| **$5,000-8,000** | **VZ** |

An oval clear glass vase, by Ermanno Toso for Fratelli Toso, with inverted neck and a dense pattern of aubergine and opaque white murrines.

| | |
|---|---|
| c1960 | 7.25in (18.5cm) high |
| **$5,000-7,000** | **VZ** |

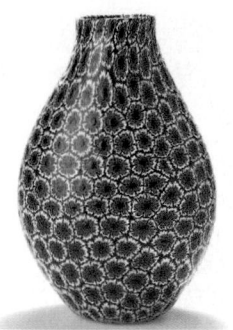

A baluster-shaped glass vase, by Ermanno Toso for Fratellli Toso, with narrow cylindrical neck and a dense pattern of flower murrines, outlined in cobalt blue and opaque white.

c1960          9.25in (23.5cm) high

**$3,000-5,000**          VZ

A 'Nerox a Petoni' irregular purple glass vase, by Ermanno Toso for Fratellli Toso, with star-shaped murrines of various colors, copper aventurine and matt graphite oxide inclusions.

c1960          16in (40cm) high

**$15,000-18,000**          VZ

A 'Nerox a Petoni' slender bottle vase, designed by Ermanno Toso for Fratelli Toso, the cylindrical neck with a slight bulge, with random colored spot decoration.

*The term 'Nerox' is used to describe the opaque black glass used to make this vase.*

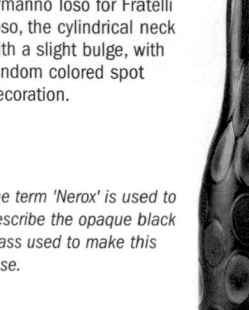

c1960          16in (40cm) high

**$7,000-10,000**          VZ

A 'Nerox a Petoni' slender clear glass bottle vase, by Ermanno Toso for Fratelli Toso, long slender neck, with oval opaque white, tomato-red, and opaque yellow spots and matt oxide powder inclusions in graphite.

c1960          16in (40cm) high

**$4,000-6,000**          VZ

## SEGUSO VETRI D'ARTE

A 'Vetro Pulegoso' light green cased glass vase, by Archimede Seguso, with a clear glass overlay and red spiral pattern.

c1950          12.75in (32cm) high

**$18,000-25,000**          QU

A wide oval clear glass vase, by Seguso Vetri d'Arte, with a wavy rim, etched to give a frosted appearance.

c1950          4.25in (10.5cm) high

**$500-700**          VZ

A light green flashed glass bowl, by Flavio Poli for Seguso Vetri d'Arte, of irregular shape with an oval base.

c1950          12.75in (32.5cm) long

**$300-400**          VZ

## SEGUSO VETRI D'ARTE

- Seguso Vetri d'Arte began in the early 1930s as a small workshop operated by brothers Archimede and Ernesto Seguso and their father, Antonio.
- After working for various glass manufacturers, Flavio Poli (1900-1984) began a collaboration with Archimede Seguso in 1934. This relationship proved successful for both Poli and Seguso's Vetri d'Arte factory.
- Poli served as artistic director to the Seguso factory for almost 30 years between 1934 and 1963.
- Poli launched the 'Bullicante' range in 1936, which combined clear colored glass with colored underlays infused with air bubbles.
- 'Sommerso' glass, designed by Poli in the 1940s and made from the 1950s, brought Seguso Vetri d'Arte international recognition.
- Poli's shell-shaped 'Conchiglie' vases and the 'Siderale' and 'Astrale' ranges, with their concentric rings, won him many accolades and secured his reputation as a glass master.

A 'Valva' sommerso glass vase, designed by Flavio Poli for Seguso Vetri d'Arte, of multi-layered ruby and purple cased glass.

c1950          9.5in (24cm) high

**$5,000-8,000**          VZ

A 'Valva a Forato' sommerso glass vessel, designed by Flavio Poli for Seguso Vetri d'Arte, of cherry red and honey colored cased glass.

c1950          8.5in (21.5cm) high

**$2,800-3,200**          VZ

A 'Siderale' glass bowl, by Flavio Poli, for Seguso Vetri d'Arte, of emerald-green and ocher cased glass arranged in concentric circles, with original factory label.

c1950      7.25in (18.5cm) diam

**$5,000-8,000**      VZ

A 'Siderale' flat oval glass bowl, by Flavio Poli for Seguso Vetri d'Arte, of beige and olive green cased glass arranged in concentric circles.

c1950      6.5in (16.5cm) diam

**$1,800-2,200**      VZ

A 'Siderale' flat round glass bowl, by Flavio Poli for Seguso Vetri d'Arte, of clear and emerald green cased glass arranged in concentric circles.

c1950      5.25in (13.5cm) diam

**$1,800-2,200**      VZ

A 'Siderale' round glass bowl, by Flavio Poli for Seguso Vetri d'Arte, of clear and emerald green cased glass arranged in concentric circles.

c1950      5.25in (13.5cm) diam

**$2,800-3,200**      VZ

A thick oval clear glass vase, by Archimede Seguso, with two elongated loop handles and dark purple and amber inclusions.

c1950      12.5in (31.5cm) high

**$1,200-1,800**      VZ

A 'Murrine' ovoid clear glass vase, by Archimede Seguso, with a short neck and murrines in shades of green and white.

c1950      8.25in (21cm) high

**$4,000-6,000**      VZ

A bulbous glass vase, by Archimede Seguso, with a long cylindrical neck, opaque white netting and pink and dark purple inclusions.

c1955      7.5in (19cm) high

**$8,000-12,000**      VZ

An opalescent sommerso glass vase, designed by Archimede Seguso, with spiralling ribbing and gold aventurine inclusions.

*Aventurine has a glimmering finish thanks to the introduction of copper or gold particles to the glass batch. It takes its name from the Italian 'avventura', meaning 'chance'.*

c1955      10.75in (27cm) high

**$3,000-4,000**      QU

A sommerso glass vase, by Flavio Poli for Seguso Vetri d'Arte, of beige and smoky brown cased glass, with a short narrow neck.

c1955      8.75in (22cm) high

**$1,800-2,200**      VZ

A honey yellow sommerso oval glass vase, by Seguso Vetri d'Arte, underlaid in red and blue, with an arched mouth.

c1955      13.5in (33.5cm) high

**$1,800-2,200**      VZ

A bottle green glass vase, by Flavio Poli for Seguso Vetri d'Arte, of teardrop shape on an oval base, encased with clear glass and an orange inclusion.

c1955    17.5in (44.5cm) high

**$800-1,200**    VZ

A fan-shaped sommerso glass vase, by Flavio Poli for Seguso Vetri d'Arte, of cased yellow and cherry red glass, with an arched rim.

c1955    10.25in (26cm) high

**$2,800-3,200**    VZ

A sommerso glass bowl, by Flavio Poli for Seguso Vetri d'Arte, of light green encased with sky blue glass.

c1955    10in (25.5cm) high

**$3,000-4,000**    VZ

A narrow oval glass bowl, by Flavio Poli for Seguso Vetri d'Arte, triple cased in purple, red, and clear glass.

c1955    21.5in (54.5cm) diam

**$8,000-12,000**    VZ

A deep oval glass bowl, by Flavio Poli for Seguso Vetri d'Arte, of cased pale turquoise and green colored glass.

c1955    12.5in (31.5cm) wide

**$1,200-1,800**    VZ

An ovoid emerald green glass vase, by Archimede Seguso, with fine goldfoil inclusions in a spiral pattern.

c1955    3.5in (9cm) high

**$1,800-2,200**    VZ

A sommerso glass vase, by Flavio Poli for Seguso Vetri d'Arte, of cased bottle green and turquoise glass, with deep amber glass at the base.

c1955    14.25in (36cm) high

**$700-1,000**    VZ

A sommerso glass vase, by Flavio Poli for Seguso Vetri d'Arte, of teardrop form, in blue and green cased glass.

c1960    2.25in (30.5cm) high

**$2,200-2,800**    QU

A sommerso funnel-shaped clear glass vase, by Flavio Poli for Seguso Vetri d'Arte, with blue and green inclusions.

c1960    9.5in (24cm) high

**$500-700**    QU

A tall clear glass vase, by Flavio Poli for Seguso Vetri d'Arte, with a concave hollow body, in layered cherry red and orange cased glass.

c1960    10in (25.5cm) high

**$2,200-2,800**    VZ

A flat glass vase, by Seguso Vetri d'Arte, of amethyst glass cased with turquoise.

c1960    7.75in (20cm) wide

**$500-800**    VZ

A sommerso glass vase, by Flavio Poli for Seguso Vetri d'Arte, of cased yellow and turquoise glass, with a squared opening.

c1960    10in (25.5cm) high

**$2,800-3,200**    VZ

A sommerso glass vase, designed by Flavio Poli for Seguso Vetri d'Arte, of deep yellow glass encased with cherry red.

*c1960*     *6in (15cm) high*

**$300-500**    VZ

A sommerso glass vase, by Flavio Poli for Seguso Vetri d'Arte, with funnel neck, of encased honey and chestnut glass.

*c1960*     *7.5in (19cm) high*

**$300-500**    VZ

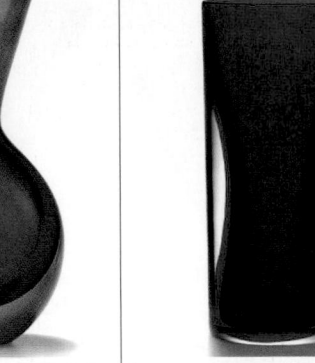

A sommerso glass vase, by Flavio Poli for Seguso Vetri d'Arte, of pale yellow glass cased with light red and orange.

*c1960*     *13in (33cm) high*

**$3,000-4,000**    VZ

A sommerso vessel, by Flavio Poli for Seguso Vetri d'Arte, with an asymmetrical opening, of brown and honey cased glass.

*c1960*     *7in (17.5cm) high*

**$1,200-1,800**    VZ

A sommerso vase, by Flavio Poli for Seguso Vetri d'Arte, with flared rim, of cased violet and olive green glass.

*c1960*     *7.5in (19cm) high*

**$180-220**    VZ

A sommerso glass bowl by Seguso Vetri d'Arte, with diamond-shaped rim, of turquoise glass, encased with amethyst.

*c1960*     *7.75in (19.5cm) wide*

**$500-800**    VZ

A sommerso glass bowl, by Flavio Poli for Seguso Vetri d'Arte, with convex walls, of turquoise glass double-cased in amber and green.

*c1960*     *3in (7.5cm) high*

**$700-1,000**    VZ

A sommerso ashtray, by Seguso Vetri d'Arte, of amber and turquoise glass.

*c1960*     *4.75in (12cm) diam*

**$120-180**    VZ

A sommerso glass bowl, by Flavio Poli for Seguso Vetri d'Arte, of ruby cased glass with pale green exterior, with inverted oval base, original label.

*c1960*     *12.25in (31cm) wide*

**$2,200-2,800**    VZ

A spiral ribbed glass vase, by Archimede Seguso, of cased clear and black glass with shimmering gold inclusions, and original factory label.

*c1960*     *6in (15cm) high*

**$300-400**    VZ

A glass vase, by Archimede Seguso, with diagonal lattice decoration of opaque pink squares with opaque white and gray stripes, with label bearing inscription in gold, and pencil mark "5222".

*c1960*     *8.5in (21.5cm) high*

**$12,000-18,000**    VZ

A sommerso glass vase, by Flavio Poli for Seguso Vetri d'Arte, with flat rim, of green and purple encased glass.

*c1960*     *21in (53.5cm) high*

**$6,000-9,000**    VZ

A turquoise cased glass fish, by Archimede Seguso, with dense gold foil inclusions, air bubbles, applied fins and clear glass eyes.

*c1960*     *8in (24cm) long*

**$2,200-2,800**    VZ

A glass vase, by Archimede Seguso, of stained petrol blue and flashed clear glass, with gold and air bubble inclusions.

*c1960*     6.25in (16cm) high

**$1,200-1,800**     **VZ**

A tapering oval glass vase, by Mario Pinzoni for Seguso Vetri d'Arte, with cylindrical neck, of orange glass encased with amber, with factory label.

*c1965*     13in (33cm) high

**$1,200-1,800**     **VZ**

A long oval rose glass vase, by Seguso Vetri d'Arte, with diagonal ribbing.

*c1970*     7in (17.5cm) high

**$300-400**     **VZ**

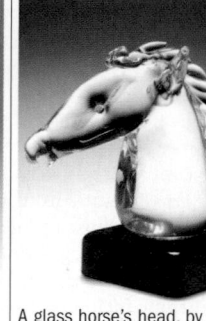

A glass horse's head, by Archimede Seguso, with wavy mane and applied black glass base.

*c1970*     6in (15.5cm) high

**$800-1,200**     **VZ**

## VENINI & CO.

A molded red glass bowl, by Napoleone Martinuzzi for Venini & Co., with a central rosette and wide flaring rim, the stand marked "Venini Murano".

*c1925*     14in (35cm) diam

**$220-280**     **VZ**

A round oval glass vase, by Napoleone Martinuzzi for Venini & Co., with five ribbed scroll handles on each side, of emerald green pulegoso glass.

*The pulegoso technique uses a chemical process to place large numbers of tiny air bubbles in the body of the glass.*

*c1930*     14.25in (36cm) high

**$15,000-20,000**     **VZ**

A cylindrical glass bowl, by Venini & Co., the wide rim with a trumpet-shaped stand, with spiral ribbing and applied bands.

17.5in (44.5cm) diam

**$500-800**     **VZ**

A glass apple, by Napoleone Martinuzzi for Venini & Co., of opaque green and clear cased craquelure glass, with burst gold foil inclusions and with applied stalk and leaf with relief decoration.

*c1930*     4in (10cm) high

**$1,200-1,800**     **VZ**

A cylindrical glass bowl, by Carlo Scarpa for Venini & Co., with a protruding glass handle on either side and encased air bubbles.

*c1935*     9.5in (24cm) wide

**$1,200-1,800**     **VZ**

A 'Foglia' leaf-shaped clear glass bowl, designed by Tyra Lundgren for Venini & Co., with iridescent blue band inclusions, signed to the base.

*Tyra Lundgren, a Scandinavian designer, was the first freelance artist to work at Venini.*

*c1940*     8.75in (22cm) long

**$1,800-2,200**     **VZ**

A tumbler-shaped glass vase, by Carlo Scarpa for Venini & Co., of ruby red and honey cased glass.

*c1940*     4.75in (12cm) high

**$1,800-2,200**     **VZ**

A 'Clessidra' hour glass, by Venini & Co., of petrol blue and gray flashed glass, marked to the stand "Venini Murano Italia".

*c1950*     6in (15cm) high

**$800-1,200**     **VZ**

## FULVIO BIANCONI

- After graduating from the art academy in Venice, Fulvio Bianconi (1915-1996) began a career in graphic design, working for large publishing companies.
- His greatest passion was glass, and he designed for great Murano factories such as Seguso Verti d'Arte and Vistosi.
- Bianconi's designs were often witty and playful. He exhibited a flair for caricature from an early age, and this talent found an outlet in his chosen profession within the glass industry.
- Bianconi's meeting with Paolo Venini lead to a magnificent partnership. From 1946, Bianconi produced numerous designs for Venini, including a series of small figures in regional costumes, the multicolored 'Pezzato' patterned vases and his 'Fasce Orrizontale' and 'Fasce Verticali' series.
- Bianconi's whimsical designs attracted international acclaim at the Venice Biennale Design fair in 1948 and, along with the numerous pieces that he designed for Venini, helped cement his reputation as one of the most inventive designers of Italian glass.

A tall clear glass vase, by Flavio Bianconi for Venini & Co., with cylindrical neck, decorated with six opaque red band inclusions, with original label to base.

*c1950*

**$1,800-2,200**　　VZ

A 'Fazzoletto' clear glass handkerchief vase, by Fulvio Bianconi for Venini & Co., with encased bands of opaque pink and turquoise glass, marked to the base.

*c1950*　　5.75in (14.5cm) high

**$2,200-2,800**　　VZ

A tumbler-shaped glass vase, by Fulvio Bianconi for Venini & Co., of encased gray, honey yellow and opaque green glass arranged in horizontal layers, marked to the base.

*c1950*　　5in (13cm) high

**$8,000-12,000**　　VZ

A 'Pezzato' flared glass vase, by Fulvio Bianconi for Venini & Co., with irregular rim, decorated with multicolored rectangular plates, marked "Venini Murano Italia" to the base.

*c1950*　　9in (23cm) high

**$12,000-18,000**　　VZ

A cylindrical glass vase, by Fulvio Bianconi for Venini & Co., of cased emerald and clear glass with matt gold iridescence and prunts.

*c1950*　　3.75in (9.5cm) high

**$800-1,200**　　VZ

A cylindrical glass vase, by Fulvio Bianconi for Venini & Co., of cased turquoise and clear glass with an oval opening in the center, marked "Venini Murano Italia" to the base.

*c1950*　　10.75in (27cm) high

**$2,200-2,800**　　VZ

A tapering club-shaped clear glass 'Obelisco', by Paolo Venini for Venini & Co., with internal multi-colored spiral bands, marked to the base "Venini Italia".

An 'A Murrina Romana' elongated flat glass dish, by Fulvio Bianconi for Venini & Co., with crimped rim and a dense mosaic pattern of fused murrines in various colors.

*c1955*　　11.5in (29cm) long

**$6,000-9,000**　　VZ

A tumbler-shaped emerald green flashed glass vase, by Venini & Co., with regular air bubble inclusions, marked "Venini Murano Italia" to the base.

*c1955*　　14in (35.5cm) high

**$1,200-1,800**　　VZ

*c1955*　　12in (30.5cm) high

**$3,000-4,000**　　VZ

An 'Al fasce ritorte e orizzontale' clear glass lantern, by Flavio Bianconi for Venini & Co., with three internal glass bands in red, blue, and green, signed to the base "Venini Murano Italia".

*c1955*　　12.5in (32cm) high

**$3,000-4,000**　　VZ

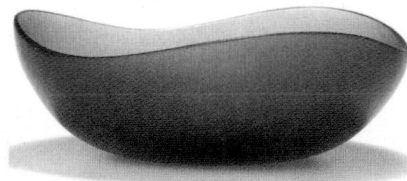

A 'Battuto' round glass bowl, by Tobia Scarpa for Venini & Co., of cased honey and clear glass, with wavy rim and mark to base.

c1955    3in (7.5cm) wide

**$1,800-2,200**    **VZ**

An 'Occhi' squared glass vase, by Tobia Scarpa for Venini & Co., with dense decoration of blue and green murrines outlined in red and remnants of etched stamp to the base.

*'Occhi' is Italian for 'eyes'.*

c1960    8.25in (21cm) high

**$5,000-7,000**    **VZ**

An 'Occhi' conical glass vase, by Tobia Scarpa for Venini & Co., with a dense pattern of yellow and gray murrines, marked "Venini 89" to the base.

c1960    13in (33cm) high

**$2,800-3,200**    **VZ**

A small amber flashed glass vase, by Venini & Co., with regular air bubble inclusions, marked to the base "Venini Murano Italia".

c1960    2.5in (6.5cm) high

**$180-220**    **VZ**

A conical tapering petrol green flashed glass vase, by Venini & Co., with horizontal veined band inclusions in various colors and remnants of original label to base.

c1960    12.25in (31cm) high

**$800-1,200**    **VZ**

An 'Occhi' club-shaped glass vase, designed by Tobia Scarpa for Venini & Co., shaped and pressed on four sides, with a grid pattern of lobster red murrines.

*Designed in 1960, this pattern is still made by Venini & Co. today.*

c1960    12.5in (32cm) high

**$7,000-10,000**    **VZ**

A 'Battuto' elongated oval gray flashed glass bowl, by Ludovico Diaz de Santillana for Venini & Co., with wavy rim and mark to the base.

c1960    8.25in (21cm) wide

**$700-1,000**    **VZ**

An 'Ad Incalmo' cylindrical opaque green glass vase, by Thomas Stearns for Venini & Co., with applied upper section of clear glass with band inclusions in reddish-black and blue, marked to the base.

c1960    10.75in (27.5cm) high

**$1,200-1,800**    **VZ**

A decorative solid glass egg, by Ludovico Diaz de Santillana for Venini & Co., with square opaque red murrines speckled in black and dark red, on a bobbin shaft, with engraved mark "Venini Italia".

c1965    11.25in (28.5cm) high

**$5,000-8,000**    **VZ**

A 'Chiacchera' oval glass vase, designed by Toots Zynsky for Venini & Co., signed and dated.

*Toots Zynsky is a renowned American studio glass artist who studied with Dale Chihuly.*

1984    10.25in (26cm) high

**$1,200-1,800**    **VZ**

## OTHER MODERN & CONTEMPORARY GLASS

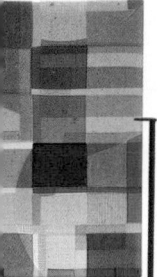

A fused glass panel, by Dorothy Hafner, entitled "On Call", on a metal stand.

25in (63.5cm) high

**$5,000-7,000**    **HOL**

A laminated glass sculpture, by Sidney Hutter, entitled "Twisted Solid Vase Form", joined with dyed glue.

2003    16in (40.5cm) high

**$12,000-18,000**    **HOL**

A glass sculpture, by Kreg Kallenberger, entitled "View at Kelly's Peak".

2003    23in (58.5cm) wide

**$10,000-15,000**    **HOL**

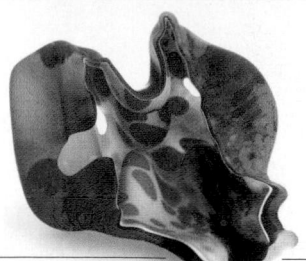

A cut and sandblasted mold-blown glass sculpture, by Marvin Lipofsky, entitled "IGS VII 2000-03 #9".

2003    16in (40.5cm) wide

**$15,000-20,000**    **HOL**

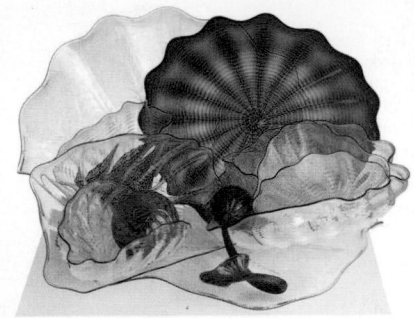

A glass sculpture series, by Dale Chihuly, entitled "Carnival Persian Set", comprising 12 pieces.

2000        22in (56cm) wide

**$28,000-35,000**      **HOL**

A glass sculpture series, by Dale Chihuly, entitled "Carnival Pheasant Macchia", comprising four pieces.

2002        21in (53.5cm) wide

**$20,000-30,000**      **HOL**

A glass sculpture series, by Dale Chihuly, entitled "Harrison Red Basket Set", comprising five pieces.

11in (28cm) high

**$20,000-25,000**      **HOL**

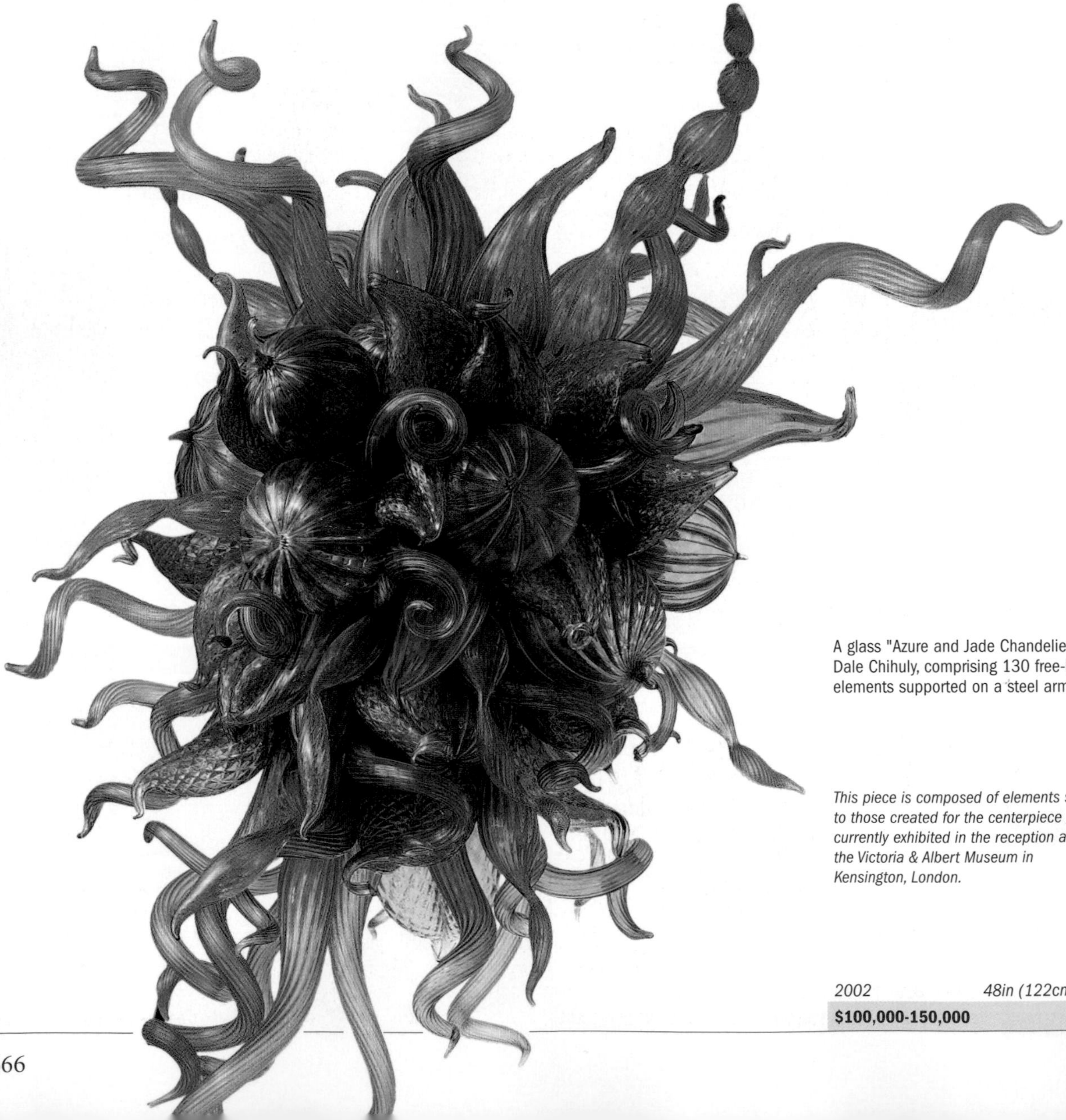

A glass "Azure and Jade Chandelier", by Dale Chihuly, comprising 130 free-blown elements supported on a steel armature.

*This piece is composed of elements similar to those created for the centerpiece currently exhibited in the reception area of the Victoria & Albert Museum in Kensington, London.*

2002        48in (122cm) high

**$100,000-150,000**      **HOL**

A cut and sandblasted mold-blown glass sculpture, by Marvin Lipofsky, entitled "IGS VI #3", made in three parts, signed.

*This piece was made at the International Glass Symposium at Novy Bor in the Czech Republic.*

1997          24in (61cm) wide

$28,000-35,000          HOL

A cast glass pâte-de-verre vase, by Charles Miner, entitled "Cleo".

2003          17in (43cm) high

$4,000-6,000          HOL

An 'Ariel' glass bowl, by Edvin Ohrstrom for Orrefors, the claret colored design cased in clear glass, engraved marks.

7.5in (19cm) diam

$300-400          ROS

An orange art glass chick, by Alessandro Pianon for Vistosi, with red encrustation accented by eye disks, unsigned.

c1960          9.5in (24cm) high

$1,800-2,200          SK

A glass vessel, by Stephen Powell, entitled "Ignited Lunar Lunacy", made using colured murrines.

2003          40in (101.5cm) high

$18,000-25,000          HOL

An optical crystal glass form, by Christopher Ries, entitled "Wild Orchid", with cut, ground, polished and engraved decoration.

2001          20.5in (52cm) high

$28,000-35,000          HOL

A cut and laminated glass sculpture, by Martin Rosol, entitled "Radius VI".

2003          11in (28cm) high

$7,000-10,000          HOL

A cylindrical gray flashed glass vase, by Dr. A. Salviati & Co, with opalescent finish.

c1950          14in (35.5cm) high

$1,200-1,800          VZ

A cut and sandblasted blown glass sphere by David Schwarz, entitled "ZAOF 12-19-00", on a metal stand.

2000          13in (33cm) high

$6,000-9,000          HOL

A cut and polished cast glass sculpture, by Steven Weinberg, entitled "Blue Cube", signed.

1996          8.25in (20cm) wide

$40,000-50,000          HOL

A cut and polished cast glass sculpture, by Steven Weinberg, entitled "Cutty Wow Rock Boat", signed.

2003          14in (35.5cm) wide

$8,000-12,000          HOL

A 'Banjo' kingfisher blue glass vase, designed by Geoffrey Baxter for Whitefriars, molded with concentric abstract shapes.

12.5in (32cm) high

$1,800-2,200          HAMG

A 'Banjo' vase, designed by Geoffrey Baxter for Whitefriars, in willow, labeled.

*The rarest color for a 'Banjo' vase is ruby red – only one is currently known to exist.*

12.5in (32cm) high

$1,800-2,200          TCM

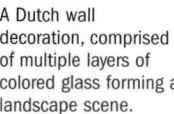

A Dutch wall decoration, comprised of multiple layers of colored glass forming a landscape scene.

19.75in (50cm) wide

$120-180          FD

A blue and brown vase, by Arroyave-Portella.

*2003*          *15.75in (40cm) high*

**$2,200-2,800**                    **MOD**

A pair of unicorn bookends, by Waylande Gregory for Cowan, covered in a mottled ocher and mahogany glaze, with stamped flower mark.

*7.25in (18.5cm) high*

**$500-700**                    **SDR**

A set of four 'Russian Peasant' figurines, by Alexander Blazys for Cowan, with a beige crackled glaze, comprising a Balalaika player, accordion player, tambourine player, and female dancer, stamped "Cowan" with numbers.

*largest 11.5in (29cm) high*

**$4,000-6,000**                    **SDR**

An Italian majolica jug, by Giovanni DeSimone, decorated with a sun face.

*DeSimone is an artist and ceramicist from Palermo who studied under Pablo Picasso.*

*10in (25.5cm) high*

**$120-180**                    **FD**

Five of a set of 12 porcelain plates, by Fornasetti, decorated in gilt with Roman scenes on a white ground, signed in gilt "Fornasetti-Milano".

*10in (25.5cm) diam*

**$600-700 set**                    **SK**

A rare 'L'Architetto' flared urn, by Gio Ponti and Richard Ginori, printed and filled with a Classical rendering of an architect and a draped urn, marked.

*13.5in (34.5cm) high*

**$10,000-15,000**                    **SDR**

A white porcelain couple, by Schwarzburger Werkstätten für Porzellankunst, Erbach, marked.

*14in (35.5cm) wide*

**$1,200-1,800**                    **SDR**

An early architectural tile frieze, by Henry Varnum Poor, painted with fig branches flanking a bas-relief panel of pears and a fruit bowl in yellow, green, and mauve glazes, mounted in an ebonized wood frame, signed "HVP".

*This is one of Poor's most influential commissions, from the Helen Haas house in Nyack, New York.*

*c1925*          *34.5in (87.5cm) wide*

**$5,000-7,000**                    **SDR**

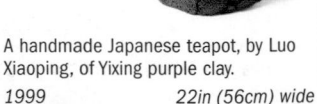

A handmade Japanese teapot, by Luo Xiaoping, of Yixing purple clay.

*1999*          *22in (56cm) wide*

**$1,800-2,200**                    **MOD**

A handmade Japanese teapot, by Luo Xiaoping, of Yixing purple clay.

*1999*          *22in (56cm) wide*

**$1,800-2,200**                    **MOD**

A handmade Japanese teapot, by Luo Xiaoping, of Yixing purple clay.

*1999*          *22in (56cm) wide*

**$1,800-2,200**                    **MOD**

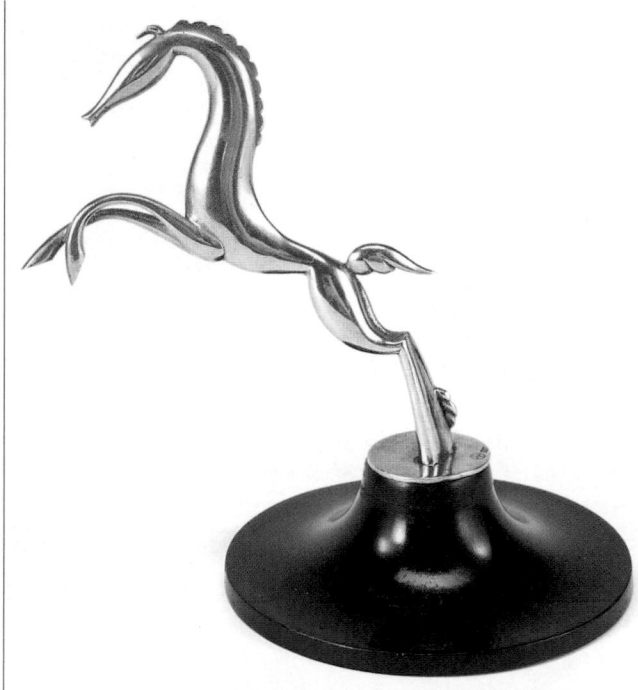

A chrome-plated figurine of a leaping horse, by Hagenauer, mounted on an ebonized circular base, stamped "Made in Vienna Austria WHW".

*8.75in (22cm) high*

**$2,800-3,200** SDR

A large polished chrome sculpture of a woman's head, by Hagenauer, in profile with stylized features and locks of hair, wearing a beaded choker and mounted on a flat rectangular base, stamped "WHW Hagenauer Wien Made in Austria".

*21in (53.5cm) high*

**$8,000-12,000** SDR

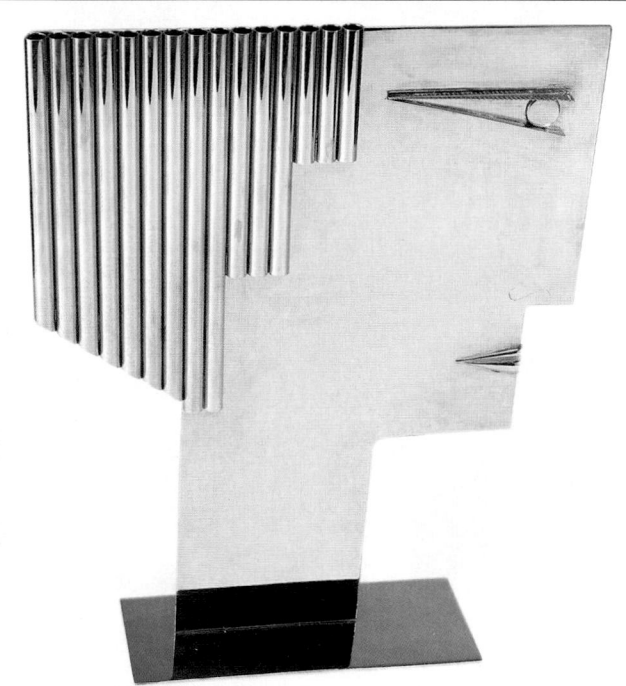

A large polished chrome sculpture of a man's head, by Hagenauer, in profile with stylized features and locks of hair, mounted on a flat rectangular base, with stamped marks.

*21in (53.5cm) high*

**$4,000-6,000** SDR

A bronze figure, by Hagenauer, depicting a tribal warrior, with stamped mark.

*9.75in (25cm) high*

**$700-1,000** WW

**MODERN SCULPTURE**

An aluminum sculpture, by Clive Barker, entitled "Head of Darth Vader", from an edition of six.

*1998*              *10.75in (27.5cm) high*

**$5,000-7,000**                    **TCM**

An aluminum sculpture, by Clive Barker, entitled "Superman", from an edition of ten.

*1999*              *17.5in (44.5cm) high*

**$4,000-6,000**                    **TCM**

A aluminum sculpture, by Clive Barker, entitled "Spiderman".

*1999*              *19.5in (49.5cm) high*

**$4,000-6,000**                    **TCM**

A bronze sculpture, by Clive Barker, entitled "The Emperor", depicting a Dalek, from an edition of nine.

*1999*              *6.5in (16.5cm) high*

**$2,800-3,200**                    **TCM**

## OTHER SCULPTURES

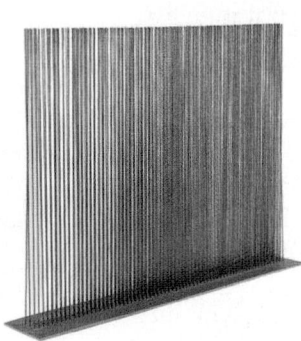

A large sonambient sculpture, by Harry Bertoia, with five rows of alternating rods in beryllium copper mounted on a long rectangular brass base, unmarked.

              *36in (91.5cm) wide*

**$35,000-55,000**                    **SDR**

A monumental turned burr walnut vase, by David Ellsworth.

*c1980*              *29in (73.5cm) high*

**$10,000-15,000**                    **MOD**

An art glass sculpture, by Jon Juhn, entitled "Rainbow's End", mounted on a base, signed and dated.

*1990*              *8.75in (22cm) high*

**$4,000-6,000**                    **SK**

An optical glass sculpture, by Kreg Kallenberger, cast over ceramic fiber, dated.

*1986*

**$10,000-15,000**                    **JH**

Three pieces of foam sculpture, by Verner Panton, from an exhibition commissioned by Littmann Kulturprojekte of Basel, shown at Gallery Softart in Zurich.

              *39in (99cm) wide*

**$1,800-2,200**                    **TCM**

A rare and early 'Hokus' elephant doorstop, by Russel Wright, from a limited edition of home accessories fashioned after circus animals, unmarked.

*c1935*              *12in (30.5cm) high*

**$15,000-18,000**                    **SDR**

A bronze sculpture of a camera, by Arman.

*This is a limited edition artist's proof.*

*c1980*              *23in (58.5cm) long*

**$3,000-4,000**                    **TCM**

An amethyst, malachite, and gold sculpture of an owl, by Andrew Grima.

*Grima is primarily known as a jeweler.*

*c1975*              *4.5in (11.5cm) wide*

**$1,800-2,200**                    **TCM**

A desk lamp, by Marianne Brandt and Hin Bredendieck, by black enameled metal and Bakelite.

c1930                    17in (43cm) high

**$800-1,200**                          **SK**

A 'Mini Topo' desk lamp, by Joe Colombo for Stilnovo.

14in (35.5cm) high

**$400-600**                           **TCM**

A 'KD27' lamp, by Joe Colombo for Kartel.

1967              13in (33cm) high

**$120-180**                            **FD**

A Swedish rise and fall lamp, by Fagerluchts.

26in (66cm) high

**$120-180**                            **FD**

A double-headed desk lamp, by Christian Dell, made from nickel plate, black enameled metal and Bakelite.

c1940               21.25in (54cm) high

**$1,800-2,200**                         **SK**

A metal and plastic desk lamp, by Fase.

c1965              23in (58.5cm) long

**$120-180**                            **FD**

## A CLOSER LOOK AT A DESNY TABLE LAMP

The French firm La Maison Desny produced high quality Modernist pieces, taking inspiration from progressive design movements of the period such as the Bauhaus.

This series of stacked discs has the characteristic symmetry and uniformity of the Desny style. These geometric constructions appear avant-garde even by today's standards, and appeal to fans of the Modernist style.

Little is known about the history of La Maison Desny, but it is thought that the company was founded by the designers Desnet and René Nauny.

Apart from a crack to the bottom disk, this lamp is in good condition. The crack does not seriously affect the value of this piece due to its overall quality and, more importantly, rarity.

An 'Umbrella' floor lamp, by Fortuny, with pivoting tan shade, the interior with polished chrome reflector, on an adjustable black enameled metal tripod base, unmarked.

70in (178cm) high

**$1,800-2,200**                         **SDR**

A rare spherical lamp, by Hanau, of green painted metal, with original quartz bulb, stamped "Original Hanau, Klein-Höhensonne S100".

c1935              12in (30.5cm) high

**$3,000-4,000**                         **SK**

A rare table lamp, by Desny, with seven plate glass discs mounted on a nickel-plated brass housing, bottom disk cracked, stamped "Desny Paris Made in France Depose".

6.75in (17cm) high

**$7,000-10,000**                        **SDR**

An artichoke lamp, by Poul Hennigsen for Louis Poulsen, made from copper and steel.

*18in (46cm) high*

**$3,000-5,000** FRE

A frosted glass and chrome floor lamp, by Laurel, with mushroom-shaped shade and blue "Laurel" label, worn.

*56in (142cm) high*

**$1,800-2,200** SDR

An 'Eclipse' table lamp, by Vico Magistretti, with a cream colored plastic body and adjustable dome shade.

*c1970   15.5in (39.5cm) high*

**$400-600** SK

A contemporary Murano glass hanging chandelier.

**$300-400** FRE

A floor lamp, by Nagel, with inter-changeable component parts.

*c1975   35.5in (90cm) high*

**$500-800** TCM

A 'Mingurea' burled walnut table lamp, by George Nakashima.

*30in (76cm) high*

**$3,000-5,000** SDR

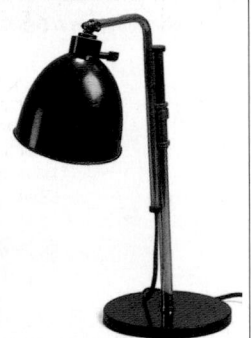

A 'Rondella' table lamp, made from nickel plate, black enameled metal and Bakelite.

*c1930   20in (51cm) high*

**$3,000-5,000** SK

A 'Triennale' three-arm floor lamp, by Gino Sarfatti for Arteluce, with enameled metal shades and handles in red, chartreuse, and dark green.

*62in (157.5cm) high*

**$4,000-6,000** SDR

An adjustable ceiling lamp, by Wolfgang Tumpel, comprising a white glass globe suspended from a chromed metal mount.

*c1930   19in (48.5cm) high*

**$700-1,000** SK

An adjustable table lamp, by Karl Trabert, made from nickel-plated black enameled metal and Bakelite.

*c1935   17.5in (44.5cm) high*

**$700-1,000** SK

An Italian chrome and marble desk lamp, with three adjustable bulbs.

*23.5in (59.5cm) high*

**$120-180** FD

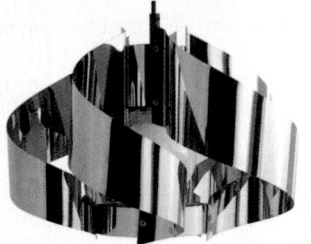

An aluminum hanging lamp.

*13.5in (34.5cm) wide*

**$80-120** FD

A chrome and glass chandelier.

*1960   18in (45.5cm) wide*

**$300-400** FD

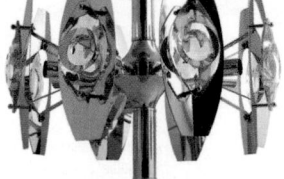

A 1960s chrome and glass 'Globe' light.

*18in (45.5cm) wide*

**$220-280** FD

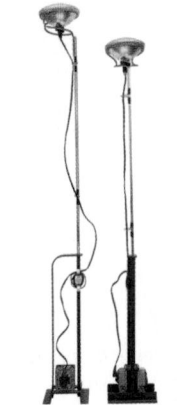

Two 'Toio' floor lamps, by Achille and Pier Giacomo Castiglione.

*c1960   62in (157.5cm) high*

**$600-900 each** TCM

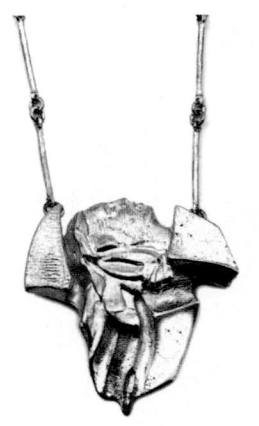

A Finnish silver pendant, in the form of a woman's profile, possibly by Majja Haavland.

c1965                    1.75in (4.5cm) long

$280-320                              TDG

A Canadian silver and enamel pendant.

c1970                    2in (5cm) long

$120-180                              TCF

A Scandinavian silver pendant, set with an agate stone.

c1965                    2in (5cm) long

$50-80                               TDG

A Scandinavian white metal pendant, set with rock crystal.

c1965                    2in (5cm) long

$80-120                              TDG

A Scandinavian silver ring, set with a semi-precious stone.

c1965                    1in (2.5cm) wide

$120-180                              TDG

A pair of Scandinavian silver earrings, set with agates.

c1965                    0.75in (2cm) long

$70-100                              TDG

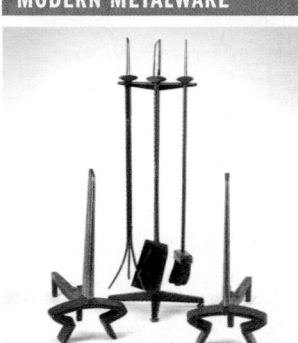

## MODERN METALWARE

A wrought-iron and brass set of andirons, by Donald Deskey for Bennett, with matching fireplace tool set on a stand with a black enameled metal finish, marked "Bennett" with flame motif.

tool set 33.5in (85cm) high

$700-1,000                           SDR

A silver-plated coffee set, by Lurelle Guild for International Silver, with die-stamped marks.

coffee pot 6.75in (17cm) high

$500-700                             SDR

A silver water jug, by Stuart Devlin, of flared form with hammered effect and abstract gilt handle, with impressed "SD" seal and hallmarks for London.

1973                    11.25in (28.5cm) high

$2,800-3,200                         ROS

A five-piece fireplace tool set, by Albert Paley, comprising a stand with brush, shovel, poker, and log tongs, unmarked.

67in (167.5cm) high

$7,000-10,000                        SDR

## VERNER PANTON

- Born on the island of Funen in Denmark, Verner Panton (1926-1998) studied architecture at the Academy of Art in Copenhagen before embarking on a remarkable career in design.
- Panton was interested in holistic design, and would create pieces that complemented each other in an interior setting.
- Despite being trained in the classic Scandinavian tradition, Panton consistently strove to create innovative and amuzing products.
- The Pantonaef range of modular toys was a collaboration with Kurt Naef. Kits were sold with instructions for making a variety of animals, but the pieces could be assembled into any shape. They have acquired cult status among aficionados of Panton's work.

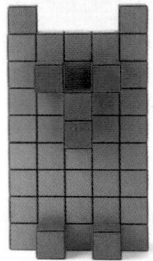

A Pantonaef modular toy owl, designed by Verner Panton and manufactured by Kurt Naef.

*c1975*          *21.5in (54.5cm) high*

**$1,200-1,800**          TCM

A mounted Mira-Spectrum 'Squares' velvet fabric, designed by Verner Panton.

*c1975*          *47.25in (120cm) wide*

**$1,200-1,800**          TCM

A Pantonaef modular toy fish, designed by Verner Panton and manufactured by Kurt Naef.

*c1975*          *30in (76cm) wide*

**$1,200-1,800**          TCM

## OTHER MODERN DESIGN

A length of synthetic fabric, possibly by Pierre Cardin for Dekoplus, printed in shades of blue.

*c1970*          *285in (724cm) long*

**$220-280**          FD

A length of printed 'Larch' fabric, by Lucien Day for Heal & Son.

*1961*          *144in (366cm) long*

**$300-400**          FD

A boxed 'Shocking' perfume bottle, by Allen Jones for Les Beaux Arts, the stopper in the form of a boot in shades of red, numbered and signed.

*1993*          *box 8in (20.5cm) high*

**$180-220**          TCM

A boxed 'Shining' perfume bottle, by Allen Jones for Les Beaux Arts, the stopper in the form of a boot in green and orange, numbered and signed.

*1993*          *box 8in (20.5cm) high*

**$180-220**          TCM

An inflatable plastic cushion, by Peter Max, depicting a running man with butterfly wings, surrounded by flowers and stars.

*c1975*          *12in (30.5cm) wide*

**$180-220**          TCM

An inflatable plastic cushion, by Peter Max, depicting a smiling mouth with tulip borders and the motto "Hello".

*c1975*          *12in (30.5cm) wide*

**$180-220**          TCM

An inflatable 'Nana' plastic doll, by Nikki Saint-Phalle.

*17in (43cm) high*

**$120-180**          TCM

A transparent plastic television set, by Zarach UK, dated.

*1978*          *15in (38cm) diam*

**$1,800-2,200**          TCM

'La Comedie', by Jules Cheret, with a dancing girl.

*Cheret only designed two decorative series, comprising six images in total.*

33in (84cm) wide

**$5,000-7,000** SWA

'L'Eldorado', by Jules Cheret, advertising the important Parisian music hall, restored losses in top margin, folds, creases, matted and framed.

c1895                32in (81.5cm) wide

**$7,000-10,000** SWA

'Bal Tabarin' in Montmartre, by Jules Alexandre Grun, restored, framed.

*This is the original version of the poster.*

34in (86.5cm) wide

**$5,000-7,000** SWA

'A La Scala', by the caricaturist and painter Albert Guillaume, advertising the opera house, rare.

c1910                35in (94cm) wide

**$7,000-10,000** SWA

'Reforme/Le Masque Anarchiste', by Privat Livemont, advertising a novel, restoration along folds and to image, two sheets.

*Unlike most Art Nouveau work, this image uses the decorative style to depict a gory scene from the story. Even the floral decorative border contains images of death.*

c1895                63.75in (162cm) wide

**$3,000-5,000** SWA

'Eugenie Buffet/Ambassadeurs', by Lucien Metivet, with an actress in a snowy scene, rare, trimmed left margin.

c1885                31in (79cm) wide

**$7,000-10,000** SWA

'Zodiac', by Alphonse Mucha, restoration and overpainting to top of the image, corners rounded, mounted on paper.

*This design for the Zodiac was one of Mucha's most popular, with nine variants. It exists as a calendar, a decorative panel, and as advertising for various companies.*

c1895                19in (48.5cm) wide

**$7,000-10,000** SWA

'Job', by Alphonse Mucha, advertising Job Rolling paper, with a girl in a circle, faded, matted and framed.

c1900        38in (96.5cm) wide

**$10,000-12,000** SWA

'Les Etoiles/Claire de Lune', by Alphonse Mucha, with pale moonlight and clouds in a night sky.

c1900                30in (75cm) high

**$18,000-25,000** SWA

The Times of the Day, by Alphonse Mucha, the four panels representing 'Nightly Rest', 'Morning Awakening', 'Evening Reverie', and 'Daytime Dash', matted and framed.

c1900                                                          14in (36cm) wide

**$40,000-50,000**                                                      **SWA**

'Exposition Decennale De L'Automobile', by Georges Rochegrosse, restoration and losses.

*This was Rochegrosse's third poster for the organization, for the 10th anniversary exposition.*

c1905   45.5in (115.5cm) wide

**$5,000-7,000**               **SWA**

'La Ligue Vinicole' (the French Wine Guild), by Manuel Orazi, representing the positive attributes of wine drinking, restoration, damage.

c1900                                    55in (140cm) wide

**$10,000-15,000**                              **SWA**

'Cie Francaise', by Theophile-Alexandre Steinlen, rare, folds, restoration and damage.

c1895            23in (58.5cm) wide

**$5,000-7,000**               **SWA**

'Chat Noir', by Theophile-Alexandre Steinlen, for the cabaret club, minor tears, paper discoloration.

c1895            16in (40.5cm) wide

**$15,000-20,000**               **SWA**

'La Revue Blanche', by Henri de Toulouse-Lautrec, advertising the avant-garde magazine, restored losses, tears, framed.

*Lautrec's image is uncharacteristically soft and endearing, representing 'Misia', the living incarnation of the magazine.*

c1895            36in (91.5cm) wide

**$28,000-35,000**               **SWA**

'La Chanson du Matelot', by Henri de Toulouse-Lautrec, rare lithograph poster of a British singer performing in Paris, paper skinning, minor creases, slight darkening.

*Only five copies of this poster are known to exist. They were possibly intended for insertion into a magazine. The presence of the registration marks implies that the prints were never trimmed for use.*

c1900            11.5in (29cm) wide

**$50,000-70,000**               **SWA**

'Transatlantique', by Jan Auvigne, with the 'Normandie' at sea, early version without text, probably designed for the 1937 Universal Exposition in Paris, rare.

c1935          40in (102cm) wide

**$5,000-7,000**                    **SWA**

'TWA/Trans World Airline', by Paul Colin, with a plane circling the globe.

*Travel is a rare subject for the artist. He typically depicted Paris's cultural scene.*

39in (99cm) wide

**$8,000-12,000**                    **SWA**

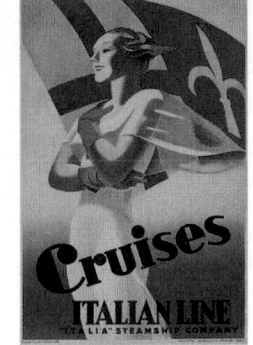

'Cruises Italian Line', by Marcello Dudovich, with a stylish passenger.

*Dudovich was awarded the gold medal at the 1900 Universal Exhibition in Paris.*

25in (63.5cm) wide

**$4,000-6,000**                    **SWA**

'Holland America Line', by Willem Frederik Ten Broek, with a view of a ship with an Art Deco curve to its profile, English version.

c1935          25in (63.5cm) wide

**$7,000-10,000**                    **SWA**

'To New York/Hamburg America Line', by Albert Fuss, with ships sailing side-by-side.

c1930          25.5in (65cm) wide

**$1,200-2,200**                    **SWA**

'Forth Bridge/L.N.E.R. to Scotland', by H. G. Gawthorn.

25.5in (65cm) wide

**$2,800-3,200**                    **SWA**

'Normandie/The world's most perfect ship', attributed to the British painter Herkomer, with the ship at night.

*Launched in 1935, the Normandie captured the Blue Ribband on her maiden voyage, making the fastest Atlantic crossing to date. Her interiors exemplified the finest French craftsmanship of the era, reflecting the prevailing Art Deco style.*

c1940          24.75in (63cm) wide

**$15,000-20,000**                    **SWA**

'Westminster from the Thames', by E. McKnight Kauffer, one in a series of three posters for London Transport.

c1935          25in (63.5cm) wide

**$3,000-4,000**                    **SWA**

'Calcutta', by Philip Kumar Das Gupta, with a fashionable street scene and the Art Deco Metro Cinema.

25in (63.5cm) wide

**$2,800-3,200**                    **SWA**

'Travel by Imperial Airways', by Tom Purvis, with a plane and elegant disembarking passengers.

c1935          20in (51cm) wide

**$2,800-3,200**                    **SWA**

'Travel at reduced rates to your favorite winter resorts/Pullman', by Welsh.

*This is one in a rare series of Art Deco posters for the Pullman railway company.*

c1935          21in (53.5cm) wide

**$4,000-6,000**                    **SWA**

'Europe/United States Lines', by Lester Beall, with an arrow and a boat.

*30in (75cm) high*

**$3,000-4,000**      **SWA**

'The Chap Book', by Claude Fayette Bragdon, with a stylized allegory of a Juggler and the sun.

*c1895*      *21in (52.5cm) high*

**$4,000-6,000**      **SWA**

'Josephine Baker', by Paul Colin, with Josephine's bust in a slanted frame and free-hand drawings of the dancer in the background.

*c1935*      *30.25in (75.5cm) high*

**$8,000-12,000**      **SWA**

'Now and until next May/Winter Shell', by Maurice Beck and Peter Morgan, with hot water bottles and bed warmers.

*c1935*      *44.5in (111cm) wide*

**$800-1,200**      **SWA**

'Persil', designed by Donald Brun, with a little girl against an orange background.

*c1950*      *50in (125cm) high*

**$300-500**      **SWA**

'British European Airways', by Lee Elliot, with a key made out of the logo and a beam of light.

*c1945*      *39.5in (99cm) high*

**$500-700**      **SWA**

'A Trip To Chinatown', by The Beggarstaff Brothers, James Pryde and William Nicholson, the orange balanced by a green square, in the Ukiyo-e tradition.

*The original design was sold to advertise a musical comedy, "A Trip to Chinatown" by Charles Hoyt, which opened at Toole's Theater on September 29, 1894. However, the design was altered by the printer, Dangerfield.*

*c1895*      *117in (292.5cm) high*

**$40,000-50,000**      **SWA**

'Cinzano', by Jean Carlu, lithography.

*This poster re-works the unofficial emblem created by Leonetto Cappiello in 1910.*

*c1950*      *63in (157.5cm) high*

**$7,000-10,000**      **SWA**

'Das letzte Stück Brot', by John Heartfield, with anti-fascist propaganda imagery, in an unusual size.

*c1930*      *55in (137.5cm) high*

**$15,000-18,000**      **SWA**

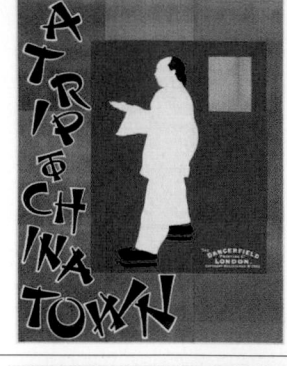

'Maison Prunier', by Adolphe Mouron Cassandre, announcing the opening of Prunier's London branch restaurant.

*c1935*      *117in (292.5cm) high*

**$30,000-40,000**      **SWA**

'Kaffee Hag', by Ludwig Hohlwein, with a character drinking coffee.

*c1915*      *34in (85cm) high*

**$15,000-20,000**      **SWA**

'Sirenella', by Max Huber, advertising a ballroom in Zürich, depicting a drummer surrounded by colorful circles representing the emanating tempo of Swing.

*c1945*     53in (132.5cm) high

**$2,800-3,200**     **SWA**

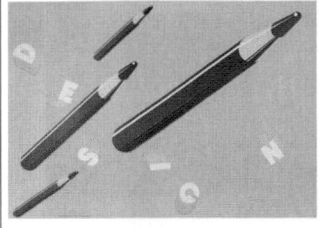

'Design', by Takenobu Igarashi, with flat tones and bold geometric letters.

*c1975*     40.5in (101cm) high

**$1,200-1,800**     **SWA**

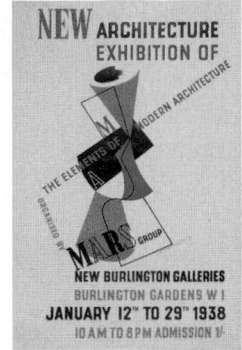

'Elements of Modern Architecture', by Edward McKnight Kauffer, with asymmetrical typography and post-cubist shapes.

*c1940*     30in (75cm) high

**$1,800-2,200**     **SWA**

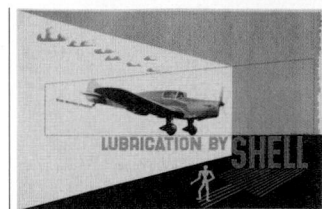

'Lubrication by Shell', by Edward McKnight Kauffer, with a Miles M-11 Whitney Straight airplane in photomontage.

*c1935*     44.75in (112cm) wide

**$5,000-8,000**     **SWA**

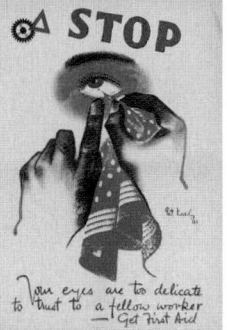

'Stop', by Pat Cokayne Keely, with a modernist design.

*c1940*     30in (75cm) high

**$280-320**     **SWA**

'Wireless War', by Patrick Cokayne Keely, with airplanes, battleships, and an engineer connected by concentric radio waves.

*This poster acknowledges the role of Post Office engineers in the field of radio technology. The visual effect has been achieved with an airbrush.*

*c1945*     36in (90cm) wide

**$3,000-4,000**     **SWA**

'Museum Rietberg', by Ernst Keller, for the Rietberg Museum, with a stylized eagle and snake engaged in combat.

*c1955*     50.5in (126cm) high

**$2,800-3,200**     **SWA**

'The Truth That Makes Men Free/American Bible Society' designed by Rockwell Kent.

*c1940*     32in (80cm) high

**$1,200-1,800**     **SWA**

'Zoologischer Garten', depicting a flamingo, with precise architectural rendering of the zoo buildings.

*c1910*     26.5in (66cm) high

**$1,200-1,800**     **SWA**

'Lincoln Center', by Roy Lichtenstein, advertising a film festival.

*1966*     45in (112.5cm) high

**$2,200-2,800**     **SWA**

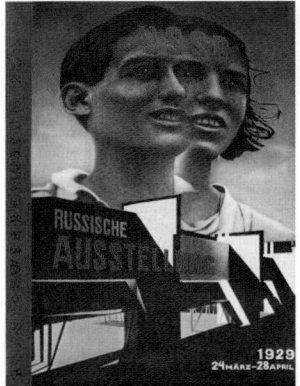

'Russische Ausstellung', by El Lissitsky, the two youths sharing a common eye, created with photomontage.

*1929*     48in (120cm) high

**$50,000-60,000**     **SWA**

One of two posters designed by Charles Loupot, this one, 'Mondriaan', paying tribute to the artist.

*c1970*

**$700-1,000 pair**    SWA

'Quinquina', designed by Charles Loupot, printed by Gaillard, Paris, for St. Raphael.

*c1955*    42.5in (106cm) high

**$3,000-5,000**    SWA

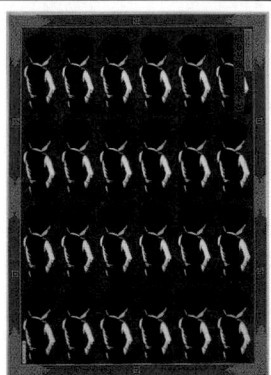

'Engelberg', designed by Herbert Matter, printed by C.J. Bucher, Luzern, depicting the immensity of the Alps.

*c1935*    39.75in (99cm) high

**$1,200-1,800**    SWA

'Jaarbeurs Utrecht', by Henri C. Pieck, advertising a fair.

*Pieck plays with industrial architecture, turning the typography into a building.*

*c1935*    39.25in (98cm) high

**$2,200-2,800**    SWA

'Addo-X', by Ladislav Sutnar, advertising an adding machine.

*c1955*    21in (52.5cm) high

**$1,200-1,800**    SWA

'Ladislav Sutnar: Visual Design in Action', by Ladislav Sutnar, to promote Sutnar's book and exhibition of the same name, with the poster mirroring the design on the cover of the book.

*1961*    24in (60cm) high

**$1,200-1,800**    SWA

'Sleeping Murderer', by Tadanori Yokoo.

*This poster was made for a poetry volume by Matsuro Takahashi, the character on the poster appears facing forward on the cover.*

*c1965*    41.75in (104cm) high

**$2,800-3,200**    SWA

'A La Maison De M. Civecawa', by Tadanori Yokoo, for the 'Aukoku Buto Ha' dance company, bearing traditional Japanese imagery, including the rising sun, the great wave and a Japanese Bullet Train.

*c1965*    40.5in (101cm) high

**$4,000-6,000**    SWA

'Hunchback in Aomori Prefecture', by Tadanori Yokoo, for the Tenjo Sajiki theater company, representing the front page of a newspaper crossed out and 'edited'.

*c1965*    40.5in (101cm) high

**$1,800-2,200**    SWA

'Kanox', by Tadanori Yokoo, advertising a film and television production company, with images of an Italian Renaissance villa and a bolt of lighting.

*c1980*    40.25in (100.5cm) high

**$1,200-1,800**    SWA

'Janie Marèse', by Jean Chassaing, the face with a dark shadow.

*This was the only poster portrait made of this actress who died in a car accident at the age of 23 shortly after filming 'La Chienne'.*

c1930                63in (160cm) high

**$7,000-10,000**                **SWA**

'La Regia', Jean Chassaing, in a caricature style with bold colors.

c1930                62in (157.5cm) high

**$800-1,200**                **SWA**

Josephine Baker, by Jean Chassaing, the actress with well stylized features.

*This is thought to be Chassaing's best image and the one of which he was most proud.*

c1930                61in (156cm) high

**$18,000-25,000**                **SWA**

A portfolio album by Paul Colin, entitled 'Le Tumulte Noir', with 42 hand-colored lithographs, one of an edition of 500, complete with double cover and insert, the first half dedicated to the black musicians of 1920s Paris, the second half a satire of Paris under the spell of the Charleston.

1927

**$28,000-35,000**                **SWA**

'Lisa Duncan', by Paul Colin, depicting the interperative dancer, the figure intwined with and framed by a grand piano.

*The influence of African art can be seen in the neo-cubist, sculptural style of the dancer's limbs.*

c1925                47in (119.5cm) high

**$28,000-35,000**                **SWA**

'Benglia', by Paul Colin, the profile of his head represented in a graphic, realistic way.

*This poster depicts the successful Algerian-born screen and stage actor.*

c1930                63in (160cm) high

**$3,000-5,000**                **SWA**

'Sylvie' (Louise Sylvain), by Paul Colin, depicting the actress, with a flat plane and a shadowy, geometric partition.

c1930                63in (160cm) high

**$1,200-1,800**                **SWA**

'Josephine Baker', by Georges de Pogedaieff, depicting the actress, the portrait of her face enclosing the text.

c1930                63.25in (160.5cm) high

**$8,000-12,000**                **SWA**

'Etoile du Nord/Pullman', by Adolphe Cassandre, with a train on a horizon.

*This image was a revolution as it depicted no landscape, no destination and no train. The low angle view of the rails is a signature technique of Cassandre's.*

c1925                    41in (104cm) high

**$15,000-20,000**                    **SWA**

'SS Côte d'Azur', by Adolphe Cassandre, depicting the boat from the side.

*This is the last of Cassandre's 'chimney series'. After this poster, his ship designs began to depict the entire ship rather than just individual design components.*

c1930                    39in (99cm) high

**$15,000-20,000**                    **SWA**

'La Route Bleue/Autocars Deluxe', by Adolphe Cassandre, the image converging to a point in the horizon where the sun is setting.

c1930                    39in (99cm) high

**$30,000-40,000**                    **SWA**

'Brillant bicycles', by Adolphe Cassandre, the composition built around the inline of the bicycle.

*This is one of Cassandre's earlier posters and represents one of his more daring attempts to stylize the human body.*

c1925                    46.25in (117.5cm) high

**$35,000-45,000**                    **SWA**

'Aubucheron', by Adolphe Cassandre, advertising a Parisian furniture store, in an unusual elongated format, with a lumberjack swinging his axe, rare.

c1925                    161in (409cm) wide

**$50,000-60,000**                    **SWA**

'Tabarin club' by Paul Colin, depicting three woman united by their dress.

*The Tabarin club opened in 1904 and made its name with the cancan.*

c1930                    63in (160cm) high

**$18,000-25,000**                    **SWA**

'Black Birds', by Paul Colin, advertising a musical revue at the Moulin Rouge by Lew Leslie, depicting three of the show's performers including Adelaide Hall in the center, unique.

c1930                    62in (157.5cm) high

**$180,000-200,000**                    **SWA**

'Bal Nègre', by Paul Colin, advertising an event at the Theater des Champs-Elysees, depicting Josephine Baker.

*Paul Colin produced his album 'Le Tumulte Noir', celebrating the 'black craze' in Paris, to be sold at this event.*

c1930                    63.25in (160.5cm) high

**$100,000-120,000**                    **SWA**

'St Jean de Luz', by Louis Floutier, with a beach in the Basque country and the Art Deco architecture of Robert Mallet-Stevens' Casino de la Pergola.

*Louis Floutier (1882-1936) was one of the major initiators of the Basque Art Deco style.*

c1930                    41in (104cm) high

**$5,000-7,000**                    **SWA**

'Sables d'Or Les Pins', by Charles Loupot, with a graceful elongated image of a couple, the sand picked out in gold ink.

c1925                    41.5in (105.5cm) high

**$8,000-12,000**                    **SWA**

## THE PAINTINGS MARKET

A single auction of American paintings raised more than $100 million last year – a total usually associated only with the Modern, Impressionist or Contemporary art markets.

Over half of that figure was realized on behalf of the estate of Rita and Daniel Fraad, who had amassed a major collection of works by the Ashcan School, including pieces by Henri, Glackens and Bellows. The market for these artists has grown rapidly as devotees of American Impressionism begin to augment their collections with Ashcan School pieces.

The Pennsylvania Impressionists, including 'secondary' artists such as Sotter, Nunamaker, Leith Ross and Meltzer, now regularly secure six figure sums at auction. Impressive results for works by Moran have highlighted growth in the Western art market.

The middle market has benefited from the 'knock on' effect of this robust growth. Specialist regional auction houses are achieving record prices on a regular basis, showing that the current boom is not confined to major urban centers. The Canadian market continued its remarkable climb, and Sotheby's in association with Ritchies enjoyed a steady series of record-breaking sales. Canadian art remains an attractive proposition for American and international buyers.

*Alasdair Nichol, Senior Vice President, Freeman's, Philadelphia*

## MALE PORTRAITS

A mid-18thC portrait of Joseph Goldthwaite (1730-1779), attributed to Joseph Badger, oil on canvas, the sitter in decorative outline against a greenish background, replaced frame.

*From 1751-1754 Joseph Badger was the only portrait painter in Boston. Only about 150 of his portraits survive.*

23.5in (59.5cm) high

**$10,000-12,000**　　　　**SK**

Rembrandt Peale, (1778-1860), 'Portrait of George Washington', oil on canvas.

*This portrait is one of the larger Patriae Pater versions of Washington, who is depicted in civilian clothes, rather than his usual military attire.*

37in (92.5cm) high

**$200,000-250,000**　　　　**RENO**

A portrait of a gentleman with landscape background, by Robert Street, oil on canvas, signed lower left with "R. Street 1843 Philadelphia".

**Provenance**: *Descended in the Bullit family to the present owner.*

1843　　　　29.5in (75cm) high

**$700-1,000**　　　　**POOK**

---

A portrait of Alexander Hamilton, attributed to William J. Weaver, (c1759-1817), oil on canvas, unsigned, framed.

*This portrait of Alexander Hamilton is one of 10 known related examples attributed to William J. Weaver, an itinerant painter of miniatures and cabinet portraits who worked from Nova Scotia to South Carolina between 1794-1817.*

c1805　　　　9.25in (23.5cm) high

**$35,000-40,000**　　　　**FRE**

Maria Howard Weeden, (1847-1905), two cards, depicting an older an older black man, signed lower left "H. Weeden", and an older black woman, inscribed in hand verso "Study of Aunt Frances Bell/Huntsville, Ala", both watercolor, unframed.

9in (22.5cm) high

**$12,000-18,000**　　　　**BRU**

An American portrait of a gentleman, oil on canvas, unframed.

c1810　　　　30in (76cm) high

**$1,200-1,800**　　　　**POOK**

**PAINTINGS**

An early 19thC half portrait, depicting a man in black coat with powdered wig, oil on canvas, with extensive hand-written label verso, possibly in French, lined, possible date 1811, modern gilt wood frame.

*26.5in (66cm) high*

**$3,000-5,000**     **BRU**

A 19thC American School portrait of a young man, oil on canvas, framed, unsigned.

**$300-500**     **FRE**

A 19thC American School small oval portrait of a gentleman, oil on paper, backed with linen, unframed, paint loss, unsigned.

*10.75in (27cm) high*

**$180-220**     **FRE**

A 19thC American School 'Portrait of a Man in Yellow Waistcoat', oil on panel, unsigned.

*27.25in (68cm) high*

**$1,200-1,800**     **FRE**

A 19thC American School 'Portrait of Benjamin Franklin', after David Martin, (1737-1797), oil on canvas, unsigned, framed, lined.

*David Martin's 1767 portrait of Franklin now hangs in the Green Room in the White House, Washington, D.C.*

*21in (53.5cm) high*

**$3,000-4,000**     **FRE**

## FEMALE PORTRAITS

A portrait of the artist's second wife Elizabeth DePeyster, by Charles Wilson Peale, (1741-1827), oil on canvas, wearing a miniature portrait of her husband.

*29.25in (74.5cm) high*

**$60,000-80,000**     **POOK**

Thomas Sulley, (1783-1872), 'Portrait of a Lady Believed to Be Marion French', oil on canvas.

*24in (61cm) high*

**$10,000-12,000**     **FRE**

A half-length portrait of a seated woman holding a book, by Martha Walter, (1875-1976), oil on canvas, signed lower right "M. Walter".

*32in (81.5cm) high*

**$4,000-6,000**     **POOK**

A 19thC American School 'Portrait of Elizabeth Fry', oil on canvas, lined, unsigned.

*14in (35cm) high*

**$600-900**     **FRE**

A 19thC American School portrait of a lady wearing a bonnet, oil on canvas, lined, unsigned.

*31.25in (78cm) wide*

**$600-900**     **FRE**

An early 19thC American portrait of Mary Margaret Green, daughter of Captain John Green, Jr., oil on canvas.

***Provenance:*** *Direct descendants of Captain John Green of Philadelphia.*

*30in (75cm) high*

**$10,000-12,000**     **POOK**

An American full-length portrait of Harriett Burr Ashton, (1817-1851), oil on canvas, original gilt frame.

*c1830*     *60.25in (150.5cm) high*

**$12,000-16,000**     **POOK**

A Western North Carolina half-length portrait of Jane Clarissa Walton, (1809-1837), holding small red book in left hand, original hand-planed yellow pine stretcher, oil on canvas, walnut cove-molded frame.

*29.75in (74cm) high*

**$20,000-25,000**     **BRU**

A 19thC American School 'Portrait of a Lady', oil on canvas, unsigned, back of canvas inscribed "Peck", framed, small tear.

*27.5in (69cm) high*

**$1,800-2,200**     **FRE**

A 19thC American School 'Portrait of a Lady', oil on canvas, lined.

*26.5in (67.5cm) high*

**$4,000-6,000**     **FRE**

## PORTRAITS OF CHILDREN

A 19thC half portrait of a young girl, attributed to David Berger, Charleston, South Carolina, oil on board, later inscription verso "Portrait study of Lora Berger by her father David J. Berger", unframed.

*23.5in (59cm) high*

**$1,200-1,800**     **BRU**

An American School full-length 'Portrait of Louise Hyde', Southern Massachusetts, oil on canvas, stenciled on the reverse "W. WA (box) ESSE (box) 208 Washington Street Boston", and "2 3/30" in pencil, unrestored.

*c1810*     *30in (75cm) high*

**$35,000-40,000**     **SK**

An American portrait of Samuel Keen Ashton, M.D., (1822-1895), oil on canvas, original gilt frame.

*c1830*     *60.25in (150.5cm) high*

**$10,000-15,000**     **POOK**

An American full-length portrait of a young girl, oil on canvas.

*c1835*     *35.5in (89cm) high*

**$14,000-18,000**     **POOK**

A mid-19thC American School 'Portrait of Three Children', oil on canvas, unsigned, original wood frame.

*c1840*     *33.25in (84.5cm) high*

**$24,000-28,000**     **SK**

An American full-length portrait of a young boy, wearing a tartan coat and black pants, oil on canvas.

*c1845*     *29.5in (74cm) high*

**$6,000-9,000**     **POOK**

A 19thC American School painting 'Portrait of the Palmer Children With Pets,' oil on canvas, framed, lined, unsigned.

*58in (145cm) wide*

**$38,000-42,000**     **FRE**

**PAINTINGS**

A mid-19thC American School oil on canvas portrait of two young girls.

*26.5in (67.5cm) high*

**$4,000-6,000** **POOK**

A 19thC American School portrait of a young girl and her cat, oil on canvas.

*30in (76cm) high*

**$2,200-2,800** **POOK**

A portrait of Achsah E. M. Connelly, oil on canvas, unsigned, in a gilt gesso frame, pencil inscription on the reverse of the frame.

*c1865* *58.5in (148.5cm) high*

**$42,000-48,000** **SK**

## SIGNED AMERICANA ARTISTS

Two mid-19thC American School portraits of a husband and wife, attributed to John James Trumbull Arnold, (1812-1865), oil on canvas.

*29in (73.5cm) wide*

**$8,000-12,000** **POOK**

A 'Portrait of the Dibble Twins', attributed to Joseph Goodhue Chandler, oil on canvas, depicting Ellen Sophia Dibble and Eliza Maria Dibble in full-length pose wearing red dresses and matching pantaloons, unsigned, replaced grain painted frame and original stretcher.

*A document attached to the reverse identifies the twins and their ages. The artist, J. G. Chandler, is recognized by his use of square-toed shoes, volumetric faces, square-fingered hands, highlighted knuckles, and accentuated mouth and brow bones. He is known for both a primitive and a more accomplished style.*

*c1840* *39.5in (100.5cm) high*

**$34,000-38,000** **SK**

A 'Portrait of a Young Girl', attributed to William W. Kennedy, oil on academy board, depicting a three-quarter length view of a girl, unsigned, reframed.

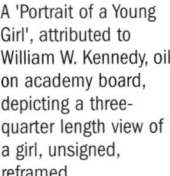

*William W. Kennedy is known to have worked as a portrait painter in New Bedford, Massachusetts, in 1845 and in Berwick, Maine in 1847. He is included in the group known as the 'Prior-Hamblin' artists because of the stylistic similarity of his portraits.*

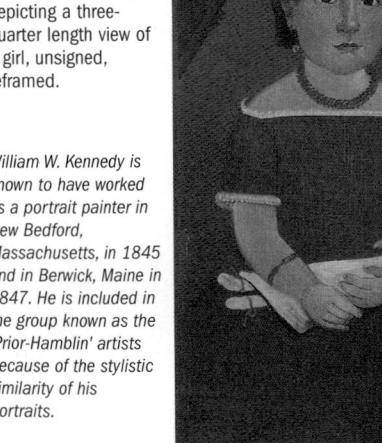

*c1840* *22in (55cm) high*

**$90,000-100,000** **SK**

'Two Young Girls Holding Hands', by Jacob Maentel, (1763-1863), watercolor on paper, walking in a hilly landscape with tree.

*8in (20cm) high*

**$15,000-20,000** **POOK**

A 19thC miniature portrait of Miss Stevens, by Edwin Plummer, unsigned, inscribed in pencil on the reverse "Stevens, lace, purple", watercolor and pencil on paper, minor foxing, color loss, later black and gilt frame.

*The Stevens family were mill owners who lived in Andover, Massachusetts, at the time the portrait was made.*

*5in (12.5cm) high*

**$22,000-28,000** **SK**

A 19thC oval portrait of a gentleman, by William Matthew Prior, (1806-1873), oil on board, inscribed verso "Robert Bruce of Rhode Island".

*11in (28cm) high*

**$1,800-2,200** **POOK**

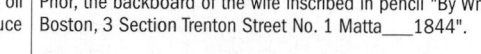

A pair of oil on panel portraits of a ship's captain and wife, by William Matthew Prior, the backboard of the wife inscribed in pencil "By Wm. M. Prior of East Boston, 3 Section Trenton Street No. 1 Matta___1844".

*1844* *13.5in (34.5cm) high*

**$12,000-18,000** **POOK**

A 'Portrait of a Girl', by William Matthew Prior, oil on academy board, period frame, which appears original, signed on the reverse in pencil.

*c1845* *13.75 (35cm) high*

**$22,000-28,000** **SK**

A 'Portrait of a Boy', by William Matthew Prior, in a period veneered frame, which appears to be original, unsigned.

*This portrait includes faintly pink cheeks, a flat style, and chubby highlighted fingers and nails, as is characteristic of William Matthew Prior's work.*

*c1845* *14in (35.5cm) high*

**$13,000-17,000** **SK**

## WILLIAM MATTHEW PRIOR

■ William Matthew Prior was born in Bath, Maine, in 1806 to Matthew Prior and Sarah Bryant Prior. In his early career it is thought that Prior was either an apprentice to the artist Charles Codman or at the very least used his shop as a studio space.

■ By 1841 Prior had married and settled in Boston, having traveled and painted in New England for a decade. Prior was skilled in both portraiture and landscape. However, he is predominantly seen as a portraitist and many of his subjects were painted onto glass.

■ Stylistically, his work tends to be quite flat, with bold lines and lacking realistic shadows. These attributes can be explained by his advertisement in the Maine Inquirer, which reads "persons who wished a flat picture can have a likeness without shade or shadow at one quarter price." Therefore, if the accuracy, complexity or realism were subordinate, Prior would price the work accordingly.

■ The artist died in 1873.

■ Prior's work is exhibited in galleries worldwide, including the National Gallery of Art, Washington, D.C. and the Fine Arts Museums of San Francisco.

A late 18th/early 19thC American portrait of a seated lady in a blue dress, watercolor, original paint-decorated frame.

*11.5in (29cm) high*

**$3,000-5,000** **PH**

A 19thC unsigned watercolor memorial picture, on paper, depicting an angel resting against an inscribed monument centered with an oval portrait of a young man, in a molded giltwood frame.

*21.5in (54.5cm) wide*

**$15,000-20,000** **SK**

## LANDSCAPES

Albert Bierstadt, (1830-1902), 'Rocky Mountains', oil on canvas, signed lower left.

*11in (28cm) wide*

**$65,000-70,000** **RENO**

Alfred Thompson Bricher, (1837-1908), 'View of Harbor With Rowboat and Sailing Vessels', watercolor on paper, gold-painted frame, signed lower right "A Bricher" with conjoined "AB", inscription verso "This belongs to Willene F. Bishop", laid down on backing board.

*20.25in (50.5cm) wide*

**$3,000-4,000** **BRU**

William Bradford, (1823-1892), 'Arctic Ice Field Under the Midnight Sun, A Sketch", oil on board, signed lower right corner "W. Bradford", in the original frame.

*This work was probably completed during the summer of 1869 during Bradford's Arctic voyage on the steam bark 'Panther'.*

21in (53.5cm) wide

**$100,000-120,000**                                    SK

Charles H. Davis, (1856-1933), 'Late Afternoon, Springtime', oil on canvas, signed and dated lower right corner "C.H. Davis 1889", framed, lined, retouch.

*1889*                        28.5in (72.5cm) wide

**$30,000-35,000**                                    SK

Alexander John Drysdale (1870-1934), 'Southern Marsh Scene', oil and kerosene on card, stained wood frame, water stain at bottom edge, signed lower left "AJ Drysdale".

30in (75cm) wide

**$2,200-2,800**                                    BRU

George Henry Durrie, (1820-1863), attributed, depicting a winter landscape with figures working around stone home, barn, and outbuilding, oil on panel.

15.5in (39.5cm) wide

**$45,000-50,000**          POOK

Thomas Griffin, (1858-1918), depicting a rolling landscape with river, distant mountains, oil on canvas, painted gilt wood frame, signed lower left "T.B. Griffin", marked verso on frame "TB Griffin".

24in (60cm) wide

**$2,200-2,800**          BRU

Arthur Hoeber, (1854-1915), 'Winter Woodland Landscape With Cottage, Pond, and Path', oil on canvas, painted wood frame, signed lower right "Arthur Hoeber".

20in (50cm) wide

**$2,200-2,800**          BRU

Thomas Harris Robinson, (1834-1888), 'The Horse Pasture', oil on canvas, signed bottom right "T. Robinson" with "Museum of the Fine Arts" stretcher label.

30in (75cm) wide

**$5,000-7,000**          FRE

Thomas Hill, (1829-1908), 'Yosemite Valley', oil on canvas, signed bottom right "T. Hill".

34.25in (87cm) high

**$150,000-180,000**                                    FRE

Christopher Shearer, (1840-1926), depicting a summer landscape with cottages, cows, and a figure by a creek, oil on canvas, signed lower right "C.H. Shearer Paris 1879".

*1879*                          *16.5in (42cm) wide*

**$3,000-5,000**                          **POOK**

Junius Brutus Stearn, (1810-1885), 'Hudson River Landscape', oil on panel, signed and dated lower right corner "J.B. Stearns NA 83", framed, retouch.

*c1883*                          *17.75in (45cm) wide*

**$7,000-10,000**                          **SK**

A 19thC American School 'Indian Encampment by a River', oil on canvas, framed, craquelure, unsigned.

*24.25in (60.5cm) wide*

**$1,800-2,200**                          **FRE**

## NINETEENTH CENTURY MARINE PAINTINGS

Thomas Birch, (1779-1851), depicting a seascape with central three-masted ship with 14 men setting the sails, watercolor on paper, signed lower right "T. Birch Phila".

*8in (20cm) wide*

**$6,000-9,000**                          **POOK**

William Bradford, (1823-1892), 'The Returning Fisherman Off Cape St. John', oil on canvas, signed "Wm. Brad" twice and inscribed "NY" in lower right corner, titled on a presentation plaque affixed to the frame, in original frame.

*24.5in (62cm) wide*

**$35,000-40,000**                          **SK**

William Hare, (1815-65), depicting a ship portrait, oil on canvas, inscribed bottom edge "Brig Sarah E. Dix of Rockland John F. Cables Master", signed lower right "W. Hare".

*26.25in (66.5cm) wide*

**$8,000-12,000**                          **POOK**

Fitz Hugh Lane, (1804-1865), 'Manchester Harbour', oil on canvas, signed, and dated "F.H. Lane 1853", original frame.

*Fitz Hugh Lane was one of the foremost American marine painters of the 19thC. As is apparent in 'Manchester Harbour', the foreground details, with its figures, piers, and spits of land, set the scale of the work while accentuating the vastness of the view and its light.*

*1853*                          *36in (90cm) wide*

**$600,000-700,000**                          **SK**

Samuel Finley Reese Morse, (1791-1872), attributed, 'USS Niagara Laying Atlantic Cable', oil on canvas, framed, some paint loss.

*The 'Niagara' carried about 1,500 miles of cable and met in the mid-Atlantic the English war steamer 'Agamemnon', carrying an equal amount of cable, and the two sections were joined.*

*30in (75cm) wide*

**$7,000-10,000**                          **FRE**

**PAINTINGS**

H. Petersen, depicting the ship 'Belle O'Brien', oil on canvas, in a gilt gesso frame, signed lower right "H. Petersen 1888".

*1888*                                                    *34in (86.5cm) wide*

**$18,000-22,000**                                                    **SK**

Percy Sanborn, mid-19thC, depicting the clipper ship 'Great Republic', oil on canvas, signed lower right corner "Percy Sanborn", framed.

*40in (100cm) wide*

**$20,000-25,000**                          **SK**

O.S. Webber, depicting a seascape with a sloop sailing off of a light ship, oil on canvas, signed lower right "O.S. Webber '77".

*1877*          *30in (75cm) wide*

**$5,000-7,000**                  **POOK**

William Trost Richards, (1833-1905), 'Sea Cliffs', watercolor on paper/board, signed and dated "Wm. T. Richards 1887" in lower left corner, framed, toning.

*c1887*                                    *32.5in (82.5cm) high*

**$8,000-12,000**                                                    **SK**

A China trade painting, depicting a three-masted sailing vessel with American flag, oil on canvas, Christie's label verso, original black-painted wood frame, lined.

*23.75in (59cm) wide*

**$12,000-18,000**                                                    **BRU**

A mid-19thC China trade harbor scene, depicting ships in Whampoa harbor, oil on canvas.

*23.5in (59.5cm) wide*

**$18,000-22,000**                                                    **POOK**

A mid-19thC American ship portrait of the 'Herbert Black', oil on paper.

*43.5in (110.5cm) wide*

**$14,000-18,000**     **POOK**

L.M. Renauli, a ship portrait 'The Valentine', oil on canvas, gilt wood cove-molded frame, one flag marked "PF", titled at bottom "Barque 'Valentine' Capne David Armaleurs Pastre Freres Marseille" and "Livourne 1869", marked at left "Fait par L.M. Renauli".

*28in (70cm) wide*

**$7,000-10,000**     **BRU**

## NINETEENTH CENTURY LITHOGRAPHS

A Nathaniel Currier hand-colored lithograph, from the 'Life of a Fireman' series, titled "The Ruins Take Up – Man Your Rope".

***Provenance:*** *Dittmar Collection.*

*1854*     *25.74in (64cm) wide*

**$1,200-1,800**     **POOK**

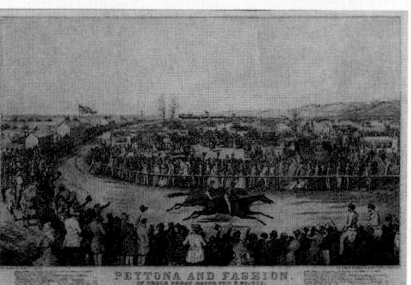

A mid-19thC lithograph, identified in the matrix as 'Peytona and Fashion. In their Great Match for $20,000', with hand-coloring on paper matted, in a molded bird's-eye maple frame.

*30in (76cm) wide*

**$6,000-9,000**     **SK**

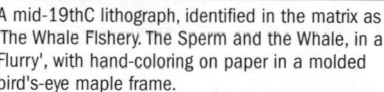

A mid-19thC lithograph, identified in the matrix as 'The Whale Flshery. The Sperm and the Whale, in a Flurry', with hand-coloring on paper in a molded bird's-eye maple frame.

*27.25in (69cm) wide*

**$10,000-12,000**     **SK**

A hand-colored lithograph, titled "The Conflagration of the Masonic Hall Chestnut Street Philadelphia", published by William Smith.

*24.5in (62cm) high*

**$700-1,000**     **POOK**

A lithograph titled "Philadelphia from Girard College 1850", inscribed lower left "J.W. Hill & Smith, Del."

*41in (104cm) wide*

**$2,200-2,800**     **POOK**

**PAINTINGS**

A mid-19thC lithograph, identified in the matrix as 'Catching A Trout', with hand-coloring on paper in a molded bird's-eye maple frame.

*28.25in (72cm) wide*

**$4,000-6,000**     **SK**

A mid-19thC lithograph, identified in the matrix as 'American Forest Scene', with hand-coloring on paper, in a molded bird's-eye maple frame.

*32in (81cm) wide*

**$22,000-28,000**     **SK**

A chromolithograph titled "Washington's Triumphant Entry into New York, Nov. 25 1783", published 1860.

*44.5in (113cm) wide*

**$4,000-6,000**     **POOK**

· THE · LIFE · OF · A · HUNTER ·

A lithograph, identified in the matrix as 'The Life of the Hunter', with hand-coloring on paper, in a molded maple frame, some damage.

*c1860*     *31.25in (79.5cm) wide*

**$45,000-50,000**     **SK**

A lithograph, identified in the matrix as 'Husking', with hand-coloring on paper, matted in a molded maple frame.

*c1860*     *31.75in (80.5cm) wide*

**$18,000-22,000**     **SK**

A lithograph, identified in the matrix as 'A Good Chance', with hand-coloring on paper in a molded maple frame, some damage, penciled inscription on lower right hand corner.

*c1865*     *31in (78cm) wide*

**$5,000-8,000**     **SK**

A lithograph, identified in the matrix as 'The Rocky Mountains. Emigrants Crossing the Plains', with hand-coloring on paper, in a molded bird's-eye maple frame.

*c1865*     *29.25in (74.5cm) wide*

**$23,000-27,000**     **SK**

Edward Clarkson, 'Two Horses', oil on canvas, framed, some inpaint, small hole, signed "E. Clarkson, Philadelphia".

Ferdinand A. Brader, an elaborate graphite on paper farm scene, entitled "Residence of Barnhard Schrader, Canal Fulton Lawrence Tp. Stark Co. Ohio 1888", signed lower left "FA Brader No 578".

| 1888 | 41.5in (104cm) wide |
|---|---|
| **$4,000-6,000** | **POOK** |

| | 24in (60cm) wide |
|---|---|
| **$2,800-3,200** | **FRE** |

William Aiken Walker, (1838-1921), woodcock and partridge suspended from cord and nail on wood panel, signed lower left "WA Walker 1860", oil on canvas, simple gilt wood frame.

| 1860 | 20.25in (50.5cm) high |
|---|---|
| **$18,000-22,000** | **BRU** |

A 19thC American School 'Masonic Tracing Board', oil on canvas, framed, unsigned.

*Provenance: Found in Michigan.*

| | 53in (132.5cm) high |
|---|---|
| **$7,000-10,000** | **FRE** |

A polychrome-stenciled centennial picture, eagle with outstretched wings grasping American flags, bannerette inscribed "Liberty and the Pursuit of Happiness", above a shield inscribed "Anniversary of the Nation's Birth", all enclosed by a border inscribed "Declaration of Independence Adopted July 4th 1776 Centennial Celebration of Independence July 4th 1876", polychrome pigments on oilcloth, framed, lined.

| 1876 | 22.5in (56cm) diam |
|---|---|
| **$2,200-2,800** | **FRE** |

Hugh H. Breckenridge, (1870-1937), "Light Study", oil on board.

*4.5in (11cm) wide*

**$6,000-9,000** FRE

Maude Drein Bryant, (1880-1946), depicting a winter scene of a home in Hendricks, Pennsylvania, oil on canvas, signed lower left "Maude Drein".

*Provenance: Descended in the family of the artist.*

*36in (90cm) high*

**$10,000-15,000** POOK

Arthur Beecher Carles, (1882-1952), entitled "Rooftops II", oil on panel.

*16in (40.5cm) wide*

**$12,000-18,000** FRE

Arthur Beecher Carles, (1882-1952), entitled "Harbor Scene", oil on board.

*c1908* *9.25in (23.5cm) wide*

**$18,000-22,000** FRE

James Hamilton, (1819-1878), 'Ships at Sunset', oil on canvas, signed, dated.

*1877* *30.25in (75.5cm) wide*

**$6,000-9,000** FRE

James Hamilton, (1819-1878), depicting a seascape of a steamboat at sunset in an elaborate carved giltwood frame, oil on canvas, signed lower right "J. Hamilton", bears Frank Schwarz label verso.

*36in (90cm) wide*

**$8,000-12,000** POOK

## A CLOSER LOOK AT A WILLIAM JAMES GLACKENS PAINTING

During his brief time at the Pennsylvania Academy of the Fine Arts, Glackens' fellow students included George Luks, John Sloan, Everett Shinn, and Robert Henri. Together with several other prominent American artists, they went on to form the celebrated group 'The Eight'. The group helped to introduce European modern art to the American public.

Glackens' early work was heavily indebted to the dark palette and fluid brushstrokes of Manet. This painting can clearly be dated as one of Glackens' later works – after 1910 – when his colors brightened and began to show the influence of the French Impressionists.

The vivid red of the poppy and the feathery brushstrokes in this still life are characteristic of the mature work of Glackens.

The characteristics of this painting are reminiscent of Pierre-Auguste Renoir, (1841-1919), an artist Glackens held in high regard.

William James Glackens, (1870-1938), entitled "Bouquet with Oriental Poppy", oil on canvas, signed bottom left, inscribed on label verso.

*This painting is accompanied by its original bill of sale.*

*17in (43cm) high*

**$85,000-90,000** FRE

Leon Kelly, (1901-1982), still life, oil on canvas, signed top left.

*31.25in (79.5cm) wide*

**$40,000-45,000** **FRE**

Edmund Darch Lewis, (1835-1910), 'Sailing Boat by a Waterfall', oil on canvas, signed and dated "Edmund D. Lewis 189*" bottom right.

*50in (125cm)*

**$8,000-12,000** **FRE**

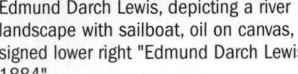

Edmund Darch Lewis, depicting a river landscape with sailboat, oil on canvas, signed lower right "Edmund Darch Lewis 1884".

*1884* *50in (125cm) wide*

**$8,000-12,000** **POOK**

Dorothy van Loan, 'Nude Bathers, Attributed to Cezanne', oil on canvas, signed "Van Loan Dorothy" verso.

*24in (60cm) wide*

**$3,000-4,000** **FRE**

Alfred Richard Mitchell, 'La Jolla', oil on board, signed "Alfred R. Mitchell" bottom right, signed, inscribed with title, and inscribed "SAN DIEGO, CAL." verso.

*10in (25cm) wide*

**$12,000-15,000** **FRE**

Hobson Pittman, 'Vase of Flowers', oil on canvas, signed "Pittman" upper left.

*20in (50cm) high*

**$5,000-8,000** **FRE**

Seymour Remenick, 'Still Life on Chair', oil on canvas, inscribed on stretcher.

*29in (72.5cm) high*

**$6,000-9,000** **FRE**

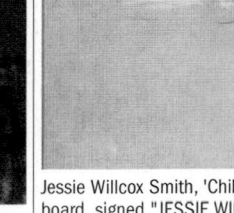

Jessie Willcox Smith, 'Children at the Beach', oil, mixed media and charcoal on board, signed "JESSIE WILLCOX SMITH" lower left.

***Provenance:*** *Collection of Margaret E. Phillips, Langhorne, Pennsylvania.*

*21in (52.5cm) high*

**$45,000-50,000** **FRE**

Walter Emerson Baum, (1884-1956), 'Harvest Web', oil on canvasboard, signed bottom right, inscribed verso.

*20in (50cm) wide*

**$7,000-10,000** **FRE**

Walter Emerson Baum, 'Pennsylvania Dutch Motif', oil on canvas, signed bottom left, signed, inscribed, and with artist's label verso.

*50in (127cm) wide*

**$35,000-40,000** **FRE**

Walter Emerson Baum, 'Pennsylvania Hills, Winter', oil on canvas, signed bottom left, inscribed verso.

*36in (90cm) wide*

**$55,000-60,000** **FRE**

Rae Sloan Bredin, (1881-1933), 'A Day on the Delaware', oil on canvas, signed bottom right, frame with incised signature "HARER" verso.

*30in (76cm) wide*

**$120,000-150,000** **FRE**

Fern Isabel Coppedge, (1888-1951), 'In Old Virginia', oil on canvas, signed bottom right, inscribed on stretcher verso.

*12in (30cm) square*

**$15,000-20,000** **FRE**

Fern Isabel Coppedge, (1883-1951), 'Marten's Creek', oil on canvas, signed bottom right, signed and inscribed on label verso.

*20in (50cm) wide*

**$45,000-50,000**     **FRE**

Fern Isabel Coppedge, 'Houses by a River', oil on canvas, signed bottom left.

*24in (60cm) square*

**$75,000-80,000**     **FRE**

John Fulton Folinsbee, (1892-1972), 'Maine Landscape', oil on canvas, inscribed "Il. Maine Landscape Estate of Ruth B. Folinsbee Dec'd Brown Brothers" verso.

*24in (60cm) wide*

**$20,000-25,000**     **FRE**

Fern Isabel Coppedge, 'Delaware Reflections', oil on canvas, signed bottom left.

*20in (50cm) wide*

**$200,000-225,000**     **FRE**

Albert Van Nesse Greene, (1887-1971), 'Snowfall at Yellow Springs', oil on board.

**Provenance:** *Purchased from the Gratz Gallery, New Hope, Pennsylvania.*

*17in (43cm) wide*

**$4,000-6,000**     **FRE**

Antonio Pietro Martino, (1902-1989), 'The Canal, New Hope', oil on canvas, signed bottom left "A. P. Martino".

*30in (76cm) wide*

**$40,000-50,000**     **FRE**

Antonio Pietro Martino, 'Houses on a River Bank', oil on canvas, signed and dated bottom right.

*1925*     *30.25in (77cm) square*

**$90,000-110,000**     **FRE**

Antonio Pietro Martino, 'Winter Landscape', oil on canvas, signed and dated bottom right.

*1926*     *32in (81cm) wide*

**$120,000-140,000**     **FRE**

A winter landscape with trees and a central red farmhouse, by Arthur Meltzer, (1893-1989), oil on canvas, signed lower left "Arthur Meltzer '30", inscribed verso "Neighborly Maples $500", retaining original painted frame.

*30in (76cm) wide*

**$70,000-80,000**     **POOK**

**PAINTINGS**

Alfred Richard Mitchell, (1888-1972), 'Manayunk', oil on board, signed bottom right, signed and inscribed verso.

*12in (30.5cm) wide*

| $5,000-8,000 | FRE |

Alfred Richard Mitchell, 'Road to New Hope', oil on board, signed bottom left, signed, dated, and inscribed with title verso.

*1927*      *20in (50cm) wide*

| $28,000-32,000 | FRE |

Lilian Amy Montague, (b. 1868), 'New Hope Bridge', oil on canvas, signed bottom right, the Raymond Vanselous frame signed with incised intitials "RV" verso.

*26in (66cm) wide*

| $27,000-30,000 | FRE |

Kenneth R. Nunamaker, (1890-1957), 'Old Home, Bucks County, PA', oil on canvas, signed bottom left, signed and inscribed "K.Nunamker, Center Bridge, PA" on stretcher verso, inscribed "Old Home Bucks County, PA. K. R. Nunamaker New Hope, PA. R. D. Center Bridge" verso.

*14in (35.6cm) square*

| $80,000-100,000 | FRE |

Kenneth R. Nunamaker, 'Winter Sunlight', oil on canvas, signed bottom right, inscribed "To our good friends Harold & Dot from the Nunny's" verso.

*36in (90cm) square*

| $130,000-140,000 | FRE |

Kenneth R. Nunamaker, 'Tony's Place', oil on canvas, signed bottom left, artist's stamp verso.

**Provenance:** *Acquired directly from the artist.*

*24in (60cm) wide*

| $125,000-130,000 | FRE |

### KENNETH R. NUNAMAKER

- Born in 1890 in Akron, Ohio, Kenneth R. Nunamaker was relatively untrained and had never been to art school. At seventeen he moved west and herded cattle for a living. In his spare time he would paint the surrounding countryside.
- Nunamaker soon became involved with the New Hope School, having befriended Daniel Garber and various other members of the group. As a New Hope Pennsylvania Impressionist, he was inspired by beautiful surroundings and, like the French impressionists, painted en plein air, with feathery brushstrokes.
- Nunamaker's work has achieved international acclaim, and his pieces have been displayed in some of the most influential institutions around the world, such as the Pennsylvania Academy of the Fine Arts, the International Gallery in Venice, the National Academy of Design in New York, and the Art Institute of Chicago. The artist died in 1957.
- The decorative landscapes by Nunamaker always demand a premium when in good condition.
- Kenneth R. Nunamaker's son Alfred Nunamaker is also a prominent American artist. He is well known as a Bucks County painter whose specialties were winter landscapes and seascapes. His interest in painting the sea was further inspired by vacations in the Virgin Islands, Alaska, Newfoundland, Cape Breton, and rock-bound Monhegan Island, Maine.

Kenneth R. Nunamaker, 'The Delaware Spring', oil on canvas, signed bottom left.

*32in (82cm) wide*

**$40,000-50,000**     **FRE**

Kenneth R. Nunamaker, 'The Laurel Road', oil on canvas, signed bottom center left, laid down on board.

*32in (81cm) wide*

**$85,000-95,000**     **FRE**

Roy C. Nuse, (1885-1975), 'Quarry: Autumn', oil on canvas, laid down on board, typewritten label verso.

**Provenance**: *Through the Nuse family, Missouri.*

*16in (40cm) wide*

**$45,000-50,000**     **FRE**

Roy C. Nuse, 'Woodhill Bridge, Autumn', oil on canvas, signed with intitials bottom left.

*24in (61cm) high*

**$85,000-95,000**     **FRE**

Roy C. Nuse, 'Three Boys at the Sheephole', oil on canvas.

*According to Robin Nuse, the artist's grand-daughter, the two figures on the left of the painting were posed for by the artist's son, Paul, the remaining figure on the right was his other son, Oliver.*

**$300,000-350,000**     **FRE**

Samuel George Phillips, (1890-1965), 'Still Life of Flowers', oil on canvas, signed bottom right "S. George Phillips".

*20in (50cm) high*

**$5,000-8,000**     **FRE**

## A CLOSER LOOK AT A PENNSYLVANIA IMPRESSIONIST PAINTING

*This painting is a fine example of Redfield's earlier period. The bravura brushwork, sumptuous impasto, and the snowy theme are the characteristics of Redfield's work that most appeal to collectors.*

*This painting with its bold verticals of the trees balanced by the horizontals of the upper part of the composition would have been completed in one go, as was Redfield's practice.*

*The tremendous freshness and appeal of this work has its roots in the dynamic approach pioneered by Impressionist Redfield, who would often paint outside deep in the snow to capture the shifting light effects.*

*Redfield is regarded nowadays as America's greatest painter of winter and snow scenes. His paintings have risen dramatically in value. Redfield's snow scenes are without doubt the most sought-after today.*

Edward Willis Redfield, 'The Briar Patch', oil on canvas, signed bottom right.

**Provenance**: *This painting is accompanied by the original bill of sale from the Panama-Pacific International Exposition and other related material including the original artist's label.*

*40in (100cm) wide*

**$550,000-650,000**                                                                 **FRE**

Samuel George Phillips, (1890-1965), 'A Covered Bridge', oil on canvas, signed bottom left "S. George Phillips".

*25in (62.5cm) high*

**$8,000-12,000**                    **FRE**

Edward Willis Redfield, 'Under the Laurel', oil on canvas, signed bottom left.

*The artist sent a letter dated 27 April 1928, to Judge H. Walton Mitchell, the original owner of the painting, which is included with the painting.*

*32in (81cm) wide*

**$250,000-350,000**                    **FRE**

Paulette Van Roekens, (1896-1988), 'Little Girl in Pink', oil on canvas, signed bottom left.

*The subject of this portrait is Phyllis Hinton.*

*20in (50cm) high*

**$12,000-15,000**                    **FRE**

**PAINTINGS**

Harry Leith-Ross, (1886-1973), 'Spring House 1938, Diabase Farm, New Hope, Pennsylvania', oil on canvas, laid on masonite, signed bottom left "Leith-Ross", titled verso.

*Provenance*: Jim's Antiques, Lambertville, New Jersey, Private Collection, Washington, D.C.

*15.75in (39cm) wide*

**$12,000-18,000**                    **FRE**

Harry Leith-Ross, 'Bucks County Landscape', oil on canvas, signed lower right "Leith-Ross".

*40in (100cm) wide*

**$135,000-140,000**                  **POOK**

Walter Elmer Schofield, (1867-1944), 'Evening Clouds, St. Ives Bay', oil on canvas, signed bottom right "Schofield", inscribed with title in pencil on stretcher verso.

*Provenance*: Collection of Margaret E. Phillips, grand-niece of the artist, Langhorne, Pennsylvania.

*27in (68.5cm) wide*

**$26,000-30,000**                    **FRE**

Walter Elmer Schofield, 'Spring Landscape', oil on canvas, signed bottom right.

Walter Elmer Schofield, 'Coast - St Ives', oil on canvas, partial signature lower left, inscribed with title on stretcher verso.

*Provenance*: Collection of Margaret E. Phillips, grand-niece of the artist, Langhorne, Pennsylvania.

*27in (68.5cm) high*

**$25,000-30,000**                    **FRE**

*Provenance*: Private collection, Illinois.

*36in (90cm) wide*

**$90,000-110,000**                   **FRE**

Walter Elmer Schofield, 'Canal, Bruges', oil on canvas, signed lower center left.

*36in (91.5cm) wide*

**$50,000-55,000**      **FRE**

Walter Elmer Schofield, 'Cottages by a Turn in the Road', oil on canvas, signed and indistinctly dated lower left.

*Provenance*: Private collection, New Hampshire.

*30in (76cm) wide*

**$55,000-65,000**      **FRE**

Walter Elmer Schofield, 'Docks, Penzance', oil on canvas, signed bottom left "Schofield".

*c1900*          *27in (67.5cm) wide*

**$25,000-30,000**                    **FRE**

Walter Elmer Schofield, 'Polperro', oil on canvas, signed bottom left "Schofield", inscribed and dated "Polperro 1912" verso.

*1912*          *36.25in (90.5cm) wide*

**$45,000-50,000**                    **FRE**

Walter Elmer Schofield, 'Sunlit Houses', oil on canvas, signed bottom left, signed and dated verso.

*1921*                    *24in (61cm) wide*

**$60,000-80,000**                    **FRE**

Henry Bayley Snell, (1858-1943), 'The Bathers', oil on board, signed bottom left.

*13.75in (35cm) wide*

**$24,000-26,000**                    **FRE**

William Francis Taylor, (1883-1970), 'Raven Rock to Lumberville', oil on canvas, signed bottom left.

*30in (76cm) wide*

**$18,000-22,000**                    **FRE**

Elizabeth F. Washington, (1871-1953), 'Farm in the Snow', oil on canvas, signed lower right "Elizabeth F. Washington", bears Newman Galleries label verso.

*24in (61cm) wide*

**$16,000-20,000**                    **POOK**

George William Sotter, (1879-1953), 'The Village Road', oil on canvas, signed and dated bottom right, signed and inscribed with title on the artist's label attached verso.

*26in (66cm) wide*

**$230,000-250,000**                    **FRE**

PAINTINGS

Charles Ephraim Burchfield, (1893-1967), watercolor landscape with rolling hills, monogrammmed lower left.

*21in (52.5cm) wide*

**$35,000-40,000**      **POOK**

Ben Foster, (1852-1926), 'On the Riverbank', oil on canvas, signed bottom left "Ben Foster".

*36in (90cm) wide*

**$5,000-7,000**      **FRE**

John Fabian Carlson, (1875-1945), entitled "Derelicts, Kingston, New York", oil on canvas, signed lower right "John F. Carlson", Belgian canvas stamp, signed, titled, and artist's stamp on the stretcher, framed.

*30in (75cm) wide*

**$30,000-35,000**      **SK**

Aaron Harry Gorson, (1872-1933), depicting an industrial landscape, oil on canvas, signed lower left "A.H. Gorson".

*44.25in (112.5cm) wide*

**$35,000-45,000**      **POOK**

William Jurian Kaula, (1871-1953), entitled "Afternoon in Mason", oil on canvas, signed "William J. Mason" in lower right corner, artist's label on the reverse, framed, repaired and retouched puncture.

*38.75in (98.5cm) wide*

**$10,000-12,000**      **SK**

An autumnal landscape with farmhouse, by Lloyd Nelson Grofe, oil on canvas, signed lower right "Nelson Grofe".

**Provenance**: *Descended in the family of the artist.*

*28in (71cm) high*

**$5,000-7,000**      **POOK**

Carl Rudolph Krafft, (1884-1938), 'Across and Beyond', oil on board, signed bottom left "CARL R. KRAFFT", inscribed verso.

*12.5in (32cm) wide*

**$6,000-9,000**     **FRE**

Max Kuehne, (1880-1968), 'House in the Snow', oil on board, signed bottom right "Kuehne", signed and indistinctly inscribed "The ***** House" verso.

*11.5in (29cm) wide*

**$4,000-6,000**     **FRE**

Julian Onderdonk, (1882-1922), 'Landscape with Lady on a Pathway and Cattle', oil on canvas, signed "Julian Onderdonk" bottom right.

*20in (50cm) wide*

**$15,000-18,000**     **FRE**

Sydney Laurence, 'Welcome Light Along the Trail', oil on canvas, signed.

**Provenance**: *C.M. Russell Auction of Original Western Art, Great Falls, Montana, 1979, The Montgomery, California, 1979, gifted to The George Montgomery Foundation of the Arts, 1988.*

*40in (100cm) wide*

**$60,000-70,000**     **RENO**

William Louis Otte, 'Eucalyptus Trees at Twilight, Santa Barbara', pastel on paper, signed bottom right "William Louis Otte", signed, inscribed, and inscribed with title verso.

**Provenance**: *Estate of Dr. E. Lee.*

*27.5in (69cm) wide*

**$8,000-12,000**     **FRE**

A summer landscape with lane leading to houses by a river, by Henry Bollar Pancoast, oil on canvas, signed lower left "H.B. Pancoast".

**Provenance**: *Descended in the artist's family to the present owner.*

*29.75in (75.5cm) wide*

**$4,000-6,000**     **POOK**

Paul Weber, (1823-1916), 'A Landscape with Cliveden in Germantown', oil on canvas, framed, signed "Paul Weber 1850".

*Born in Germany, Paul Weber came to Philadelphia in 1848. He painted, taught, and exhibited his work at the Pennsylvania Academy of the Fine Arts until 1860 when he returned to Europe.*

*15in (37.5cm) wide*

**$7,000-10,000**     **FRE**

Guy Carleton Wiggins, (1883-1962), "Spring in Essex 1950", oil on canvas, signed lower right "Guy Wiggins".

*29.5in (75cm) wide*

**$6,000-9,000**     **POOK**

Carl Wuermer, (1900-1983), 'Houses in a Valley', oil on canvas, signed bottom right "Carl Wuermer".

**Provenance**: *Galerie Spielhagen, Batman & Murphy Inc., Kansas City, Missouri.*

*36.25in (92cm) wide*

**$12,000-18,000**     **FRE**

Charles Morris Young, (1869-1964), 'Spring Landscape', oil on canvas, signed and indistinctly dated "C. Morris Young/May 189*" bottom left.

*16in (40cm) wide*

**$4,000-6,000**     **FRE**

Yarnall Abbott, (1870-1938), 'Fishing Boats in a Harbor', oil on canvas, signed bottom right "YARNALL ABBOTT".

*Partial label "JOHN WANAMAKER, New York, Philadelphia, Paris, London" attached verso.*

*24in (60cm) wide*

**$6,000-9,000**     **FRE**

### EMILE A. GRUPPE

- Emile A. Gruppe was born in 1896 in Rochester, New York, the son of landscape artist Charles P. Gruppe. He continued the family tradition, studying at the National Academy in New York, and was instructed by Charles Chapman, George Bridgeman, Richard Miller, and John F. Carlson, with whom Gruppe eventually co-founded the Gruppe Summer School in 1942.
- Gruppe is best known for his lucid land and seascapes, and his Gloucester harbor scenes and vistas around Cape Ann are especially notable.
- His fluid, modern style was heavily inspired by Claude Monet's work, in particular the Water Lily series.
- Gruppe was responsible for teaching a generation of early 20thC American artists. He died in 1978.

Arthur Clifton Goodwin, (1866-1929), 'T Wharf, Boston', oil on canvas, signed lower right corner "A.C. Goodwin", indistinctly inscribed on the reverse, framed.

*Most of Goodwin's work depict the Boston area, where he lived until 1920. His works are part of the permanent collections of the Metropolitan Museum of Art in New York, and the Museum of Fine Arts, Boston.*

*40in (100cm) wide*

**$25,000-30,000**     **SK**

Emile A. Gruppe, (1896-1978), 'A Calm Day at the Dock', oil on canvas, signed bottom right "Emile A. Gruppe".

*30in (76cm) high*

**$12,000-18,000**     **FRE**

Emile A. Gruppe, 'Low Tide at Motif 1', oil on canvas, laid down on board, signed bottom left "Emile A. Gruppe".

*20in (50cm) high*

**$30,000-35,000**     **FRE**

Antonio Nicolo Gasparo Jacobsen, (1850-1912), 'Larchmont', oil on canvas, signed and dated lower right corner "A. Jacobsen 1905", framed, lined.

*1905*     *36in (90cm) wide*

**$25,000-30,000**     **SK**

Carl Peters, (1897-1980), 'Harbor Side Shack', oil on canvas.

*24in (61cm) wide*

**$4,000-6,000**     **FRE**

Jane Peterson, (1876-1965), 'San Giorgio, Venice', oil on board.

*17in (42.5cm) wide*

**$12,000-15,000**     **FRE**

Jane Peterson, 'Venice', oil on board, signed lower left.

*17.5in (44cm) high*

**$7,000-10,000**     **S&K**

Jane Peterson, 'Venetian Sailing Boats', gouache and crayon, signed bottom left "JANE PETERSON".

*11.75in (30cm) wide*

**$6,000-9,000**     **FRE**

Mabel May Woodward, 'Rockport Harbor', oil on canvas, laid on board, signed bottom right "M. Woodward".

*13in (32.5cm) wide*

**$9,000-11,000**     **FRE**

Edward Henry Potthast, (1857-1927), 'Moonlight Scene', watercolor and crayon, signed bottom left "E. Potthast".

***Provenance:*** *Chapellier Galleries, New York City, New York.*

*28in (71cm) high*

**$14,000-16,000**     **FRE**

Frederick Stone Batcheller, (1837-1889), 'A Pause in the Day', oil on canvas, signed bottom left "Batcheller".

*20in (50cm) high*

**$5,000-7,000**    **FRE**

Edward Cucuel, (1879-1951), 'East Wind', oil on canvas, signed bottom right "Cucuel", signed twice verso, inscribed on stretcher.

*27.75in (70.5cm) high*

**$90,000-100,000**    **FRE**

Joseph Hirsch, (1910-1981), 'Wrestlers', oil on canvas, signed and dated bottom right "Joseph Hirsch - 32".

*Exhibited Whitney Museum of American Art, New York, New York. "Paintings And Prints By Philadelphia Artists" October 23 - November 22, 1934.*

*20in (50cm) wide*

**$20,000-25,000**    **FRE**

Philip Russel Goodwin, (1882-1935), 'Untitled/A Surprise Encounter', oil on canvas, signed lower right "Philip R. Goodwin", framed.

*36in (90cm) wide*

**$120,000-130,000**    **SK**

Fred Machetanz, (b.1908), 'Whaling Dance', oil on masonite, signed and dated "F. Machetanz 1962" bottom right, also inscribed "'Whaling Dance' by Fred Machetanz/High Ride - Palmer Alaska/1965" verso.

*1962*    *28in (70cm) wide*

**$8,000-12,000**    **FRE**

Pauline Palmer, (1869-1938), 'At the Easel', oil on canvas board, signed lower right corner "Pauline Palmer", framed.

*36in (90cm) high*

**$20,000-25,000**    **SK**

Arthur Watson Sparks, (1870-1919), 'Woman Sewing Under a Tree', pastel, signed and dated "A. W. Sparks 1912" bottom left.

*1912*    *22in (55cm) wide*

**$4,000-6,000**    **FRE**

William Aiken Walker, (1838-1921), 'An Old Cotton Picker', oil on board, signed bottom left "W A Walker".

*8.25in (21cm) high*

**$9,000-11,000**    **FRE**

William Acheff, 'Zuni Medicine', oil on canvas, signed lower left, dated.

*1982*        *30in (76cm) wide*

**$45,000-50,000**      **RENO**

Roy Anderson, 'This One Will Care For You', oil on canvas.

*30in (76cm) wide*

**$55,000-60,000**      **RENO**

Oscar E. Berninghaus, (1874-1952), 'Indians Following A Wagon Train', gouache, signed lower left.

*17.5in (44.5cm) wide*

**$90,000-110,000**      **RENO**

Ralph Albert Blakelock, (1847-1919), 'Indian Encampment', oil on board, signed verso.

*12in (30cm) wide*

**$32,000-38,000**      **RENO**

Edward Borein, (1872-1945), 'Charros in Mission Courtyard', watercolor, signed lower left, with letter of authenticity.

*19in (48.5cm) wide*

**$70,000-80,000**      **RENO**

Gerald Cassidy, (1879-1934), 'The Hillside', oil on canvas, signed lower left.

*20in (50cm) wide*

**$46,000-50,000**      **RENO**

John Clymer, (1907-1989), 'Home in the Clouds', oil on canvas, signed.

*40in (100cm) wide*

**$95,000-105,000**      **RENO**

John Clymer, (1907-1989), 'The Game Trail', oil on canvas, signed lower left.

*36in (90cm) square*

**$150,000-170,000**      **RENO**

**PAINTINGS**

Guy Coheleach, 'Victoria Falls, Twilight Leopard', oil on canvas, signed.

*48in (120cm) high*

**$60,000-80,000** RENO

Eanger Irving Couse, (1866-1936), 'The Moccasin Maker', oil on canvas.

*29in (73.5cm) wide*

**$170,000-200,000** ALT

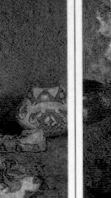

Eanger Irving Couse, 'The Tomahawk Pipe', oil on canvas.

*24in (60cm) wide*

**$120,000-130,000** ALT

## EANGER IRVING COUSE

■ Eanger Irving Couse was born in Saginaw, Michegan, in 1866, where he grew up among the Chippewa Indians. As an aspiring artist, he often made sketches of the neighboring Chippewa people.

■ Brought up in a poor family, Couse was determined to become an artist and scraped together enough money to study at the Art Institute of Chicago. After three months at the Chicago Institute, Couse furthered his studies in New York, and made a great many trips to Paris, where he took inspiration from the draftsman William Adolphe Bouguereau.

■ On a trip to Taos, New Mexico in 1902, Couse encountered the Pueblo Indians, who would become a central theme in his subsequent artwork.

■ His paintings often feature Indian males standing or squatting, overlooking waterfalls, or sitting by campfires carrying out everyday activities. His subjects are typically lit by campsite fires, or by moonlight, which highlights their physique.

■ Eanger Irving Couse died in 1936.

Eanger Irving Couse, 'The Arrow Maker', gouache over charcoal, signed lower left.

*40in (100cm) wide*

**$320,000-380,000** RENO

Catherine Critcher, (1868-1964), 'Indian Portrait', oil on canvas, laid on board, signed lower right.

*12in (30cm) high*

**$90,000-100,000** ` RENO

Maynard Dixon, (1875-1946), 'Cut Bank, Tucson', oil on board, signed and dated lower left.

*1942* *20in (50cm) high*

**$210,000-250,000** **RENO**

W. Herbert Dunton, (1978-1936), 'The Buffalo Runners', oil on canvas.

*32in (81.5cm) wide*

**$120,000-130,000** **ALT**

Robert Duncan, 'A Rough Start', oil on canvas, signed lower left.

*40in (100cm) wide*

**$35,000-40,000** **RENO**

Fremont Ellis, (1897-1985), 'El Vaquero', oil on board.

*24in (60cm) high*

**$30,000-35,000** **ALT**

Nicolai Fechin, (1881-1955), 'The Mandolin', oil on canvas.

*16in (40cm) high*

**$160,000-180,000** **ALT**

John Frost, (1890-1937), 'Live Oaks', oil on canvas, signed and dated lower right.

*1921* *40in (100cm) wide*

**$350,000-400,000** **RENO**

Elling William Gollings, (1878-1932), 'Indian Walking Through the Snow', oil on canvasboard, signed and dated lower left.

*1923* *10.5in (26.5cm) high*

**$70,000-90,000** **RENO**

Elling William Gollings, (1878-1932), 'Horses Grazing in the Snow', oil on board, signed and dated lower right.

*1923*                    *10in (25cm) wide*

**$55,000-60,000**                    **RENO**

Philip R. Goodwin, (1881-1935), 'Waiting Out the Storm', oil on canvas, signed.

*Provenance: Judy Goffman Fine Art, Blue Bell, Pennsylvania; George Montgomery, 1977, gifted to The George Montgomery Foundation of the Arts, December 15, 1988.*

*36in (90cm) high*

**$90,000-100,000**                    **RENO**

G. Harvey, 'Through Golden Aspens', oil on canvas, signed and dated lower left.

*1987*                    *30in (76cm) high*

**$40,000-50,000**                    **RENO**

E. Martin Hennings, (1886-1956), 'Taos Pueblo Indian', oil on canvas, signed lower left.

*18in (45.5cm) high*

**$40,000-50,000**                    **RENO**

Victor Higgins, (1884-1949), 'Fish Ponds', watercolor, signed lower right.

*22.25in (56.5cm) wide*

**$65,000-75,000**                    **RENO**

Frank Tenney Johnson, (1874-1939), 'Moon-Bathed Night', oil on board, signed lower right.

*'Moon-Bathed Night' was a wedding gift from the artist to Dr. and Mrs. Raymond P. Kellogg. Kellogg was Johnson's personal physician, and his father, T. Penfield Kellogg, built Johnson's studio in Alhambra, California.*

*16in (40.5cm) high*

**$200,000-220,000**                    **RENO**

William R. Leigh, (1866-1955), 'Indian Pottery', oil on canvas, signed lower right.

*10in (25cm) wide*

**$50,000-70,000**     **RENO**

Stephen Lyman, (1957-1996), 'High Creek Crossing', acrylic on board, signed.

***Provenance:*** *The Estate of Gust Hronis, West Bend, Wisconsin.*

*72in (180cm) wide*

**$35,000-40,000**     **RENO**

Grant Macdonald, (b. 1944), 'A Winter's Tale', oil on canvas.

*60in (152.5cm) wide*

**$22,000-28,000**     **ALT**

Frank C. McCarthy, (1924-2002), 'In Search of New Grass', oil on board, signed.

***Provenance:*** *The Collection of William Shay, Nevada.*

*24in (60cm) wide*

**$42,000-48,000**     **RENO**

Frank C. McCarthy, (1924-2002), 'Heading Back', oil on canvas.

*40in (100cm) wide*

**$50,000-70,000**     **ALT**

Frank C. McCarthy, (1924-2002), 'Apache Scouts', oil on canvas, signed lower left.

*40in (100cm) wide*

**$75,000-80,000**     **RENO**

Alfred Jacob Miller, (1810-1874), 'Indian Village', oil on canvas.

*Of this painting art historian Ron Tyler wrote, "The main purpose of the rendezvous was to trade pelts for supplies and to refit the trappers for the coming year, but the days were first filled with contests, gambling, and visiting, as can be seen in this painting, done several years after Miller returned from the Rockies and based on his observations and on-the-spot sketches".*

*c1850*     *48.25in (120.5cm) wide*

**$1,200,000-1,500,000**     **RENO**

Thomas Moran, (1837-1926), 'Mists in the Yellowstone', oil on canvas, signed and dated lower right.

*This painting was commissioned in 1908 by the Thomas D. Murphy Calendar Company of Red Oak, Iowa, for the express purpose of making a chromolithograph reproduction for Mr. Murphy's widely distributed art calendars.*

1908                                                             45in (114.5cm) wide

**$5,000,000-6,000,000**                                                    **RENO**

Bill Owen, (b. 1942), 'Nighthawk's Evening Song', oil on linen.

28in (71cm) high

**$28,000-32,000**                                                    **ALT**

Jim Norton, (b.1953), 'Cheyenne at Sunset', oil on canvas.

40in (100cm) wide

**$22,000-28,000**                                                    **ALT**

Edgar S. Paxson, (1852-1919), 'Scouting Party', gouache, signed and dated lower right.

1905                                                             19in (48.5cm) wide

**$45,000-50,000**                                                    **RENO**

Edgar S. Paxson, (1852-1919), 'Chief Charlo', oil on canvas, signed and dated lower right.

1910                          22in (55cm) high

**$60,000-70,000**                          **RENO**

Frederic Remington, (1861-1909), 'A Mexican Haciendero', watercolor, signed and dated lower right.

1893                     18.5in (47cm) high

**$150,000-170,000**                     **RENO**

Kenneth Riley, (b. 1919), 'The White Captive', oil on canvas.

*17in (43cm) wide*

**$25,000-35,000**     **ALT**

A Western landscape of a buffalo hunt, by Peter Rindisbacher, (1806-1834), watercolor and pen on paper, signed lower right margin "P. Rindisbacher".

*15.25in (38.5cm) wide*

**$220,000-250,000**     **POOK**

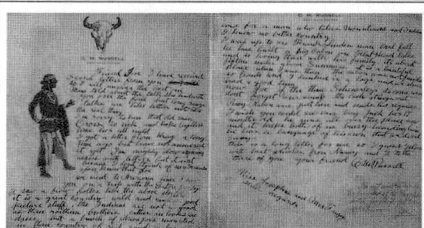

Carl Rungius, (1869-1959), 'Two Mountain Sheep', oil on canvas, signed lower right.

*30in (76cm) wide*

**$160,000-180,000**     **RENO**

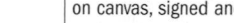

Charles Marion Russell, (1864-1926), 'Cowboy Riding His Horse Uphill', watercolor with traces of pencil, signed "C. M. Russell" and with skull device lower left.

*Provenance: The artist, Great Falls, Montana. Timothy Burns, Great Falls, Montana, believed to have been obtained directly from the above. By family descent to his son, Gregg Burns.*

*15.75in (39cm) wide*

**$70,000-80,000**     **FRE**

Charles Marion Russell, (1864-1926), 'Buck Deer', oil on canvas, signed and dated.

*1910*     *19.5in (49cm) wide*

**$150,000-170,000**     **RENO**

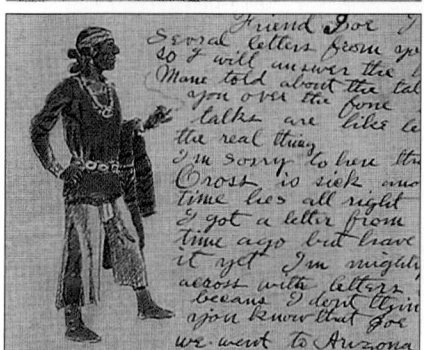

Charles Marion Russell, 'Letter to Friend Jo', watercolor, pen, and ink, signed, dated.

*Provenance: The Lola and Otha D. Wearin Collection.*

*1918*     *16.5in (41cm) wide*

**$55,000-65,000**     **RENO**

Charles Marion Russell, 'Navajo Lookout/Surveying the Plains', watercolor, signed lower left.

*c1918*     *21.5in (54.5cm) wide*

**$650,000-750,000**     **RENO**

Tom Ryan, (b.1922), 'Texas Dust', oil on board.

*22.5in (57cm) high*

**$45,000-50,000**      **ALT**

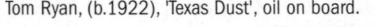

Olaf C. Seltzer, (1877-1957), 'Overlooking the Missouri', watercolor, signed.

*12in (30cm) wide*

**$45,000-50,000**      **RENO**

## OLAF C. SELTZER

- Born in Denmark 1877, Olaf Seltzer's artistic talents were realized at the early age of twelve when he was enrolled as a special student at the Danish Art School and Polytechnic Institute in Copenhagen.
- After his fathers untimely death, Seltzer and his mother emigrated to the Great Falls, Montana. He went through several jobs, including a cowboy and railroad worker, but continued to draw and sketch in his spare time.
- Seltzer was soon learning the techniques of watercolor and oil painting thanks to his mentor and friend Charles Russell, who he met at the Great Falls. After Russell's death, Seltzer moved to New York in 1926, where he studied art and carried out some important commissions.
- Seltzer is best known for illustrating the history and landscape of the west, using bold lines and true-to-life colors. His subject matter includes death, cowboys, Native Americans, and wildlife.
- The painter died in 1957.

Olaf C. Seltzer, (1877-1957), 'Swiftcurrent Lake', oil on canvas, signed lower left.

*48in (123cm) wide*

**$65,000-70,000**      **RENO**

Olaf C. Seltzer, (1877-1957), 'Blackfoot Chief', watercolor, signed lower left.

*15in (38cm) wide*

**$35,000-40,000**      **RENO**

Joseph. H. Sharp, (1859-1953), 'Winter Camp', oil on canvas, signed lower right.

*24in (61cm) wide*

**$210,000-250,000**      **RENO**

Joseph H. Sharp, (1859-1953), 'Blackfeet Teepees, Glacier Park, Montana', oil on board, signed lower right.

*13.5in (34.5cm) wide*

**$110,000-140,000**     **RENO**

Howard Terpning, 'Shoshone Visitors', oil on canvas, signed lower left.

*32in (81cm) wide*

**$230,000-250,000**     **RENO**

Joseph H. Sharp, (1859-1953), 'Squaw Winter', oil on canvas, signed lower left.

*c1910*     *30in (76cm) high*

**$1,000,000-1,500,000**     **RENO**

Howard Terpning, 'Guardians', gouache, signed lower left.

*29.5in (75cm) wide*

**$250,000-300,000**     **RENO**

Olaf Wieghorst, (1899-1988), 'Roundup Riders', oil on canvas, signed.

**Provenance:** *The Estate of Justine B. Fenton, San Diego, California.*

*38in (95cm) wide*

**$65,000-75,000**     **RENO**

Eustace Ziegler, (1881-1969), 'Three Wise Men', oil on canvas, signed lower left.

*36in (90cm) wide*

**$50,000-70,000**     **RENO**

Olaf Wieghorst, (1899-1988), 'Stolen Stock', oil on canvas.

*30in (75cm) wide*

**$26,000-30,000**     **ALT**

Robert Spear Dunning, (1829-1905), 'Still Life with Peaches and Grapes', oil on canvas, signed "R.S. Dunning" in lower right corner, framed, varnish inconsistencies.

*Dunning was one of the co-founders of the Fall River School, which focused mainly on still life. Dunning's work was exhibited at the National Academy of Design, the American Art Union, the Boston Art Club, and the Providence Art Club, and is in the collections of numerous museums including the National Museum of American Art.*

18in (47.5cm) wide

**$80,000-100,000** **SK**

John F. Francis, (1808-1886), 'Still Life With Central Bottles of Cognac and Wine', oil on canvas, signed and dated lower right "J.F Francis Pt. 1854".

*1854* 23.5in (60cm) wide

**$45,000-50,000** **POOK**

Levi Wells Prentice, 'Red Currants', oil on canvas, signed and dated "L W Prentice 1891" bottom right.

*1891* 7in (17.5cm) high

**$16,000-20,000** **FRE**

## A CLOSER LOOK AT A STILL LIFE PAINTING

*'Still Life of Apples and Nuts in a Basket,' painted in 1855 is an excellent example of Francis' work and provoked frenzied bidding when it appeared at auction in Philadelphia – the city of his birth, soaring past its pre-sale estimate of $40,000-$60,000.*

*Francis was skilled in his use of 'chiaroscuro', the use of a strong single light source, revealing his indebtedness to the great Dutch still life masters of the 17thC.*

*The randomly scattered nuts give the painting an appealing informality, while the varied surfaces and textures of the apples show the pleasure the artist took in his subject.*

*The contrast of the dark background and the white cloth combined with the play of light on the reflective surfaces and the wicker basket, contribute to the drama of this painting.*

John F. Francis, (1808-1886), 'Still Life of Apples and Nuts In a Basket', oil on canvas, signed, inscribed, and dated "J Francis Pt. 1855" bottom right.

*Originally a portrait painter, Francis turned to still life painting around 1850. He was a largely self-taught artist who helped initiate the revitalization of still life painting in America, eventually producing some of the nation's most important examples.*

*1855* 30in (76cm) wide

**$250,000-300,000** **FRE**

Milne Ramsay, (1846-1915), 'Still Life With Ewer and Fruit', oil on canvas, signed lower right "Milne Ramsey 2.72".

36in (90cm) high

**$20,000-25,000** **POOK**

Mary Russell Smith, (1842-1878), 'Three Chicks with Strawberries', oil on canvas, signed and dated "Mary Smith 1875" bottom right.

*1875* 12in (30cm) wide

**$13,000-17,000** **FRE**

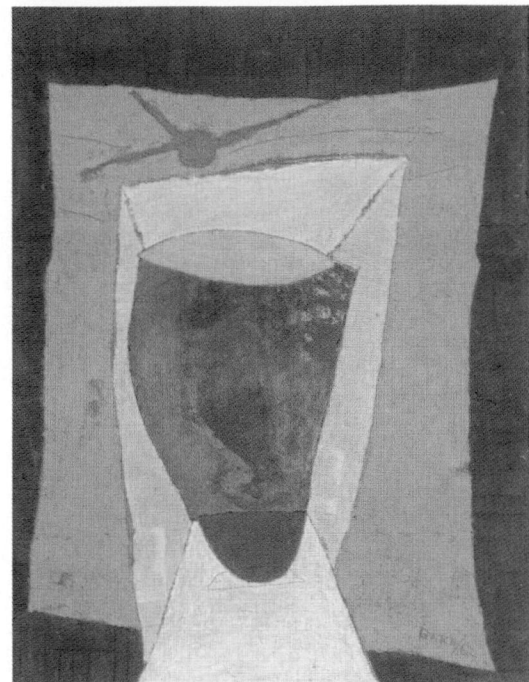

Lee Gatch, (1902-1968), 'Amphora', oil, collage, mixed media on board, signed and dated "GATCH/62" bottom right.

**Provenance**: *Staempfli Gallery, New York, New York, Mrs. Josiah Marvel, Greenville, Delaware. Dr. & Mrs. Frank A. Elliot.*

*1962*                                              *34.25in (85.5cm) high*

**$12,000-18,000**                                              **FRE**

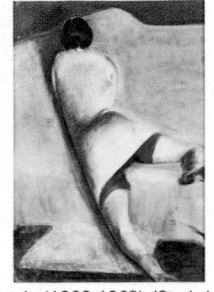

Lee Gatch, (1902-1968), 'Study in White, 1925-26', oil on canvas.

*20in (50cm) high*

**$30,000-35,000**                **FRE**

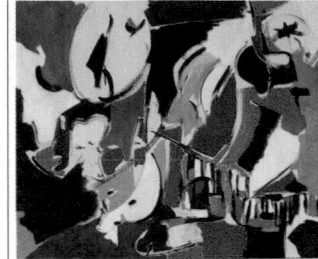

Michael Goldberg, (b.1924), untitled, oil on canvas, signed "GOLDBERG" verso.

*59in (150cm) wide*

**$15,000-18,000**                **FRE**

Hans Hofmann, (1880-1966), untitled, gouache on paper, signed bottom right, with the estate stamp and number "681" verso.

**Provenance**: *Andre Emmerich Gallery, New York, NY; Makler Gallery, Philadelphia, PA; Private Collection, Philadelphia, PA.*

*c1955*                                              *28.25in (72cm) wide*

**$55,000-65,000**                                              **FRE**

Paul Jenkins, (b.1923), 'Phenomena Forth Turn', oil on canvas, signed bottom left "Jenkins", inscribed verso.

**Provenance**: *Martha Jackson Gallery, New York, New York.*

*39.25in (99cm) square*

**$8,000-12,000**                                              **FRE**

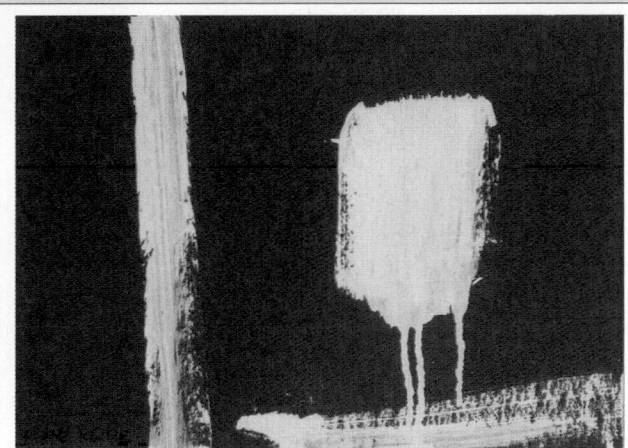

Franz Kline, (1910-1962), untitled, acrylic on board, signed bottom left "FRANZ KLINE".

*11.25in (28cm) wide*

**$25,000-28,000**                **FRE**

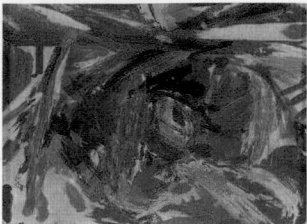

Elaine de Kooning, (1919-1989), "Redondo", acrylic on masonite, signed bottom left "E de K", with stamped dates" Nov 15 1960" and "Nov 8 1960" on stretcher verso.

*1960*                    *24in (61cm) wide*

**$12,000-15,000**                    **FRE**

Joseph Meierhans, (1890-1980), "South Seas", oil on canvas.

*40in (100cm) wide*

**$18,000-22,000**                    **AAC**

Joan Mitchell, (1926-1992), 'Drowned', pastel and typewritten text, signed bottom right and left "Joan Mitchell".

*14.25in (36cm) high*

**$12,000-18,000**                    **FRE**

Gaston Lachaise, 'Female Nude', pencil on paper, signed bottom right "G. Lachaise".

*17.25in (43cm) high*

**$4,000-6,000**                    **FRE**

Jane Piper, (1916-1991), abstract composition, oil on canvas, signed "Jane Piper" verso.

*20in (50cm) wide*

**$22,000-28,000**                    **FRE**

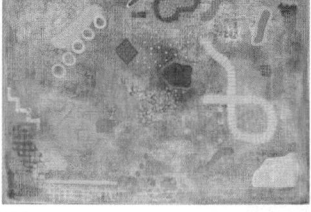

Robert Natkin, (b. 1930), untitled, acrylic on canvas, signed bottom center right "Natkin".

*60in (152.5cm) wide*

**$7,000-10,000**                    **FRE**

Gregorio Prestopino, (1907-1984), 'Nude, Late Sunday', oil on canvas, signed bottom right "Prestopino".

*53.75in (134cm) wide*

**$5,000-7,000**                    **FRE**

## CANADIAN ART

■ Canada was renowned for its steam liners and ships, which were some of the most established methods of transport in Canada, and this encouraged the successful marine painting genre.

■ The Canadian Wilderness was an accessible source of inspiration for Canadian artists. The Group of Seven, formed in 1920, was made up of several landscape painters who sought to convey the spirit of Canada, and moved away from restrictive Academic art. They used a brighter and much bolder palette. Lawren Stewart Harris was one such member, and his work became increasingly abstract over the years.

■ Canadian abstract art was developed further by The Group of Eight, which included the artist Harold Barling Town. Established in 1953, Town and his colleagues wanted to introduce abstract art to Toronto. European artists, such as Pablo Picasso and Paul Klee, inspired much of their work.

■ Canadian Art is not only popular in the Canadian market but it is becoming increasingly in demand in the US as well.

Caven Atkins, CSPWC, (1907-2000), 'Totem Poles', linocut, signed, titled, dated "31" and numbered "17/26" in the margin.

*6.25in (16cm) high*

**$600-900**     **RTC**

Leon Bellefleur, (b. 1910), 'L'Ephemere', gouache, signed, titled, and dated "'80", titled and dated gallery label verso.

*22.75in (57cm) high*

**$2,800-3,200**     **RTC**

Lawren Stewart Harris PRCA, OSA (1885-1970), 'Sketch', graphite, certified by Alfred Joseph Casson and inscribed "This drawing is by Lawren Harris".

*10.75in (27cm) wide*

**$2,800-3,200**     **RTC**

Dennis Juneau RCA, (b. 1925), 'Monement en Couleur', acrylic on canvas, signed, titled, and dated "76" verso.

*20.25in (51.5cm) square*

**$1,800-2,200**     **RTC**

Harold Barling Town RCA, OSA, CPE, (1924-1990), 'untitled (Snap)', oilprint on canvas, signed with handprint verso.

*24in (61cm) square*

**$2,200-2,800**     **RTC**

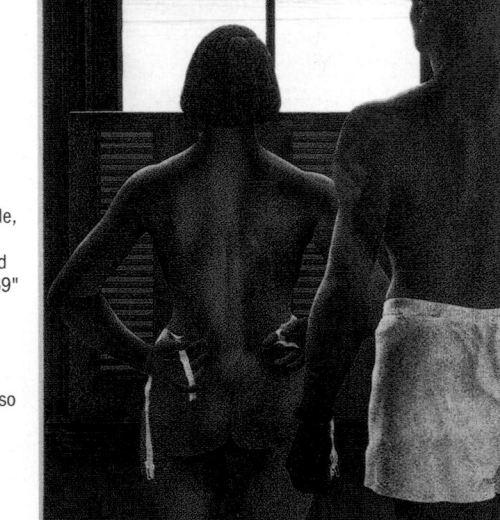

Alexander Colville, 'Snow', color serigraph, signed and dated "1969" verso and numbered "66/70" in margin, titled gallery label verso backing.

*Provenance:* Marlborough Godard Gallery, Toronto and Confederation Art Gallery & Museum, Charlottetown, Prince Edward Island Gallery labels verso backing.

*24.75in (62cm) high*

**$3,200-3,800**     **RTC**

Ernest Neuman CPE, 'Montreal Harbour', etching with drypoint, signed and titled in margin.

*plate 6.5in (16cm) wide*

**$320-380** RTC

Leonard Hutchinson RCA, OSA, CPE, 'Old Ontario Village', color block print, signed, titled, and numbered "46/50" in margin.

*31cm (12.5cm) wide*

**$500-700** RTC

Frederic Bourchier Taylor RCA, CPE, CSGA, 'Ottowa', etching with aquatint, signed and numbered "16/100".

*8in (20cm) wide*

**$600-900** RTC

C.I. Gibbons, 'Jasmine', color pencil and graphite, signed and dated, inscribed "Toronto Ont.".

**Provenance**: *Ex-collection of the former curator of the Upper Canada Marine Museum.*

*1908*      *32.5in (81cm) wide*

**$4,000-6,000** RTC

C.I. Gibbons, 'Toronto', color pencil and graphite, signed, titled, dated and inscribed "Toronto Ont."

*1905*      *37in (92.5cm) wide*

**$2,200-2,800** RTC

C.I. Gibbons, 'John Hanlan', color pencil and graphite, signed and dated, inscribed "Jan 10th 1908" verso.

**Provenance**: *Ex-collection of the former curator of the Upper Canada Marine Museum.*

*1908*      *29.5in (74cm) wide*

**$5,000-7,000** RTC

Davidialuk Alasua Amittu, (1910-1976), black stone carving of a spider, signed to the underside.

*3.5in (9cm) long*

**$1,800-2,200** **RTC**

Davidialuk Alasua Amittu, (1910-1976), black stone carving of a kneeling figure, signed to the underside.

*3.25in (8cm) high*

**$1,200-1,800** **RTC**

Ashevak Tunnillie, (b. 1956), green striated carving of a falcon with outstretched wings, signed with syllabics.

*10.5in (26.5cm) high*

**$1,800-2,200** **RTC**

Lloyd Wadhams, (b. 1938), carved cedar plaque of a salmon, signed and inscribed "Kwagiutl" verso.

*30.5in (77.5cm) long*

**$500-800** **RTC**

Sorel Etrog RCA, (b. 1933), 'Bashota (A Maquette)', bronze sculpture, stamped "ETROG" and numbered "2/10".

*13.25in (33.5cm) high*

**$2,200-2,800** **RTC**

Willia Weetaluktuk, (b. 1920), black stone carving of a young girl holding a seal, signed and with disc number to the underside.

*6.25in (16cm) high*

**$180-220** **RTC**

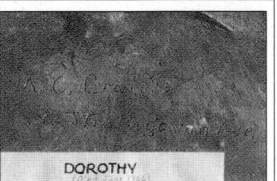

Florence Wyle RCA, (1881-1968), 'Dorothy', painted plaster, signed, title label verso.

*18in (46cm) high*

**$700-1,000** **RTC**

# KEY TO ILLUSTRATIONS

Every antique illustrated in *DK Antiques Price Guide 2006* by Judith Miller has a letter code which identifies the dealer or auction house that sold it. The list below is a key to these codes. In the list, auction houses are shown by the letter Ⓐ and dealers by the letter Ⓓ. Some items may have come from a private collection, in which case the code in the list is accompanied by the letter Ⓟ. Inclusion in this book in no way constitutes or implies a contract or a binding offer on the part of any of our contributors to supply or sell the goods illustrated, or similar items, at the prices stated.

**AA** Ⓓ
**Albert Amor** 37 Bury Street, St James's, London SW1Y 6AU, UK
Tel: 011 44 20 7930 2444
www.albertamor.co.uk

**AAC** Ⓐ
**Sanford Alderfer Auction Company**
501 Fairgrounds Road, Hatfield, PA 19440
Tel: 215 393 3000
www.alderferauction.com

**ABIJ** Ⓓ
**Aurora Bijoux**
Tel: 215 872 7808
www.aurorabijoux.com

**AD** Ⓓ
**Andrew Dando** 34 Market Street, Bradford on Avon, Wiltshire BA15 1LL, UK
Tel: 011 44 1225 865 444
www.andrewdando.co.uk

**AG** Ⓓ
**Antique Glass at Frank Dux Antiques**
33 Belvedere, Lansdown Road, Bath, Avon BA1 5HR, UK
Tel: 011 44 1225 312 367
www.antique-glass.co.uk

**AGO** Ⓓ
**Anona Gabriel** Otford Antiques Center, 26-28 High Street, Otford, Sevenoaks, Kent TN14 5PQ, UK
Tel: 011 44 1959 522 025
info@otfordantiques.co.uk

**AHL** Ⓓ
**Andrea Hall Levy** PO Box 1243, Riverdale, NY 10471
Tel: 646 441 1726
barangrill@aol.com

**AJK** Ⓓ
**Antiques by Joyce Knutsen**
Tel: 315 637 8238 (Summer)
Tel: 352 567 1699 (Winter)

**AL** Ⓓ
**Andrew Lineham Fine Glass** PO Box 465, Chichester, West Sussex PO18 8WZ, UK
Tel: 011 44 1243 576 241
www.antiquecolouredglass.info

**ALL** Ⓐ
**Allard Auctions** PO Box 1030, St. Ignatius, MT 59865
Tel: 460 745 0500
www.allardauctions.com

**ALT** Ⓐ
**Altermann Galleries** Santa Fe Galleries, 225 Canyon Road, Santa Fe, NM 87501
Tel: 505 983 1590
www.altermann.com

**ARK** Ⓓ
**Ark Antiques** PO Box 3133, New Haven, CT 06515
Tel: 203 498 8572
www.ark-antiques.com

**AS** Ⓓ
**Alistair Sampson Antiques** 120 Mount Street, London W1K 3NN, UK
Tel: 011 44 20 7409 1799

**ATL** Ⓓ
**Antique Textiles and Lighting** 34 Belvedere, Lansdown Road, Bath, Avon BA1 5HR, UK
Tel: 011 44 1225 310 795
www.antiquetextilesandlighting.co.uk

**AVW** Ⓓ
**Circa 1900** Shop 17, Georgian Village, Camden Passage, London N1 8DU, UK
Tel: 011 44 7713 709 211
www.circa1900.org

**B** Ⓐ
**Dreweatt Neate (Formerly Bracketts)**
Tunbridge Wells Saleroom, The Auction Hall, The Pantiles, Tunbridge Wells, Kent TN2 5QL, UK
Tel: 011 44 1892 544 500
www.dnfa.com/tunbridgewells

**B&H** Ⓐ
**Burstow & Hewett** Lower Lake, Battle, East Sussex TN33 0AT, UK
Tel: 011 44 1424 772 374
www.burstowandhewett.co.uk

**BAM** Ⓐ
**Bamfords Ltd** The Old Picture Palace, 133 Dale Road, Matlock, Derbyshire DE4 3LU, UK
Tel: 011 44 1629 574460

**BBI** Ⓓ
**B&B Italia - Maxalto** Strada Provinciale 32, n° 15, 22060 Novedrate (CO), Italy
Tel: 011 39 031 795 111
www.bebitalia.it

**BCAC** Ⓓ
**Bucks County Antique Center**
8 Skyline Drive, Lahaska, PA 18914
Tel: 215 794 9180

**BEA** Ⓐ
**Beaussant Lefèvre** 32 rue Drouot, 75009 Paris, France
Tel: 0011 33 147 704 000
www.beaussant-lefevre.auction.fr

**BEJ** Ⓓ
**Bébés et Jouets** c/o Lochend Post Office, 165 Restalrig Road, Edinburgh, Midlothian EH7 6HW, UK
Tel: 011 44 131 332 5650
bebesetjouets@tiscali.co.uk

**BEL** Ⓐ
**Belhorn Auction Services** PO Box 20211, Columbus, OH 43220
Tel: 614 921 9441
www.belhorn.com

**BEV** Ⓓ
**Beverley** 30 Church Street, Marylebone, London NW8 8EP, UK
Tel: 011 44 20 7262 1576

**BIB** Ⓓ
**Biblion** 1-7 Davies Mews, London W1K 5AB, UK
Tel: 011 44 20 7629 1374
www.biblion.com

**BL** Ⓓ
**Blanchard Ltd** 86-88 Pimlico Road, London SW1W 8PL, UK
Tel: 011 44 20 7823 6310
piers@jwblanchard.com

**BLA** Ⓐ
**Blanchet et Associés** 3 rue Geoffroy Marie, 75009 Paris, France
Tel: 011 33 153 341 444
blanchet.auction@wanadoo.fr

**BLO** Ⓐ
**Bloomsbury Auctions** Bloomsbury House, 24 Maddox Street, London W1S 1PP, UK
Tel: 011 44 20 7495 9494
www.bloomsburyauctions.com

**BMN** Ⓐ
**Auktionshaus Bergmann** Möhrendorfer Straße 4, 91056 Erlangen, Germany
Tel: 011 49 9131 450 666
www.auction-bergmann.de

**BO** Ⓓ
**Le Blason d'Or** 117 boulevard Stalingrad, 69100 Villeurbanne, France
Tel: 011 33 478 280 108

**BONM** Ⓐ
**Bonhams Knowle** The Old House, Station Road, Knowle, Solihull, West Midlands B93 0HT, UK
Tel: 011 44 1564 776 151
www.bonhams.com

**BOY** Ⓓ
**Boym Partners Inc** 131 Varick Street, 915, New York, NY 10013
Tel: 212 807 8210
www.boym.com

**BRB** Ⓓ
**Bauman Rare Books** 535 Madison Avenue, New York, NY 10022
Tel: 212 751 0011
www.baumanrarebooks.com

**BRU** Ⓐ
**Brunk Auctions** PO Box 2135,
Asheville, NC 28802
Tel: 828 254 6846
www.brunkauctions.com

**BP** Ⓓ
**The Blue Pump** 178 Davenport Road,
Toronto, Ontario M5R 1J2, Canada
Tel: 416 944 1673
www.thebluepump.com

**BY** Ⓓ
**Bonny Yankauer**
bonnyy@aol.com

**C** Ⓐ
**Cottees** The Market, East Street, Wareham,
Dorset BH20 4NR, UK
Tel: 011 44 1929 552 826
www.auctionsatcottees.co.uk

**CA** Ⓐ
**Chiswick Auctions** 1-5 Colville Road,
London W3 8BL, UK
Tel: 011 44 20 8992 4442
www.chiswickauctions.co.uk

**CATO** Ⓓ
**Lennox Cato Antiques** 1 The Square,
Church Street, Edenbridge, Kent TN8 5BD, UK
Tel: 011 44 1732 865 988
www.lennoxcato.com

**CGC** Ⓟ
**Cheryl Grandfield Collection**

**CGPC** Ⓟ
**Cheryl Grandfield Private Collection**

**CHA** Ⓓ
**Charlotte Marler** Booth 14,
1528 West 25th Street,
New York, NY 10010
Tel: 212 367 8808
char_marler@hotmail.com

**CHEF** Ⓐ
**Cheffins** Clifton House, 1-2 Clifton Road,
Cambridge, Cambridgeshire CB1 7EA, UK
Tel: 011 44 1223 213 343
www.cheffins.co.uk

**CHI** Ⓓ
**Chicago Silver**
www.chicagosilver.com

**CO** Ⓐ
**Cooper Owen** 74 High Street, Egham,
Surrey TW20 9LF, UK
Tel: 011 44 1784 434900
www.cooperowen.com

**CRIS** Ⓓ
**Cristobal** 26 Church Street,
London NW8 8EP, UK
Tel: 011 44 20 7724 7230
www.cristobal.co.uk

**CSA** Ⓓ
**Christopher Sykes Antiques**
The Old Parsonage, Woburn, Milton Keynes,
Buckinghamshire MK17 9QJ, UK
Tel: 011 44 1525 290 259
www.sykes-corkscrews.co.uk

**CSB** Ⓐ
**Chenu Scrive Berard** Hôtel des Ventes Lyon
Presqu'île, 6 rue Marcel Rivière,
69002 Lyon, France
Tel: 011 33 472 777 801
www.chenu-scrive.com

**D&G** Ⓓ
**Domas & Gray Gallery**
Tel: 228 467 5294
www.domasandgraygallery.com

**DJI** Ⓓ
**Deco Jewels Inc** 131 Thompson Street, NY
Tel: 212 253 1222
decojewels@earthlink.net

**DL** Ⓓ
**David Love** 10 Royal Parade,
Harrogate, North Yorkshire HG1 2SZ, UK
Tel: 011 44 1423 565 797

**DN** Ⓐ
**Dreweatt Neate** Donnington Priory Salerooms,
Donnington, Newbury, Berkshire RG14 2JE, UK
Tel: 011 44 1635 553 553
www.dnfa.com/donnington

**DOR** Ⓐ
**Dorotheum** Palais Dorotheum,
Dorotheergasse 17, A-1010 Vienna, Austria
Tel: 011 43 1 515 600
www.dorotheum.com

**DR** Ⓓ
**Derek Roberts Fine Antique Clocks &
Barometers** 25 Shipbourne Road, Tonbridge,
Kent TN10 3DN, UK
Tel: 011 44 1732 358 986
www.qualityantiqueclocks.com

**DRA** Ⓐ
**David Rago Auctions** 333 North Main Street,
Lambertville, NJ 08530
Tel: 609 397 9374
www.ragoarts.com

**EG** Ⓐ
**Edison Gallery** Susanin's,
900 South Clinton St., Chicago, Il 60607
Tel: 617 359 4678
www.edisongallery.com

**EPO** Ⓓ
**Elaine Perkins** Otford Antiques Center,
26-28 High Street, Otford, Kent TN15 9DF, UK
Tel: 011 44 1959 522 025
www.otfordantiques.co.uk

**EVE** Ⓓ
**Evergreen Antiques** 1249 Third Avenue,
New York, NY 10021
Tel: 212 744 5664
www.evergreenantiques.com

**FAN** Ⓓ
**Fantiques**
Tel: 011 44 20 8840 4761
paula.raven@ntlworld.com

**FD** Ⓓ
**Fragile Design** 8 Lakeside, The Custard Factory,
Digbeth, Birmingham,
West Midlands B9 4AA, UK
Tel: 011 44 121 693 1001
www.fragiledesign.com

**FER** Ⓓ
**Vittorio Ferro at Fratelli Pagnin**
See **VET**

**FIS** Ⓐ
**Auktionshaus Dr Fischer**
Trappensee-Schlößchen,
74074 Heilbronn, Germany
Tel: 011 49 7131 155 570
www.auctions-fischer.de

**FM** Ⓓ
**Francesca Martire** F131-137, Alfies Antique
Market, 13 Church Street, Marylebone,
London NW8 8DT, UK
Tel: 011 44 20 7724 4802

**FRE** Ⓐ
**Freeman's** 1808 Chestnut Street,
Philadelphia, PA 19103
Tel: 215 563 9275
www.freemansauction.com

**GAL** Ⓓ
**Gallery 532** 142 Duane Street,
New York, NY 10013
Tel: 212 964 1282
www.gallery532.com

**GCC** Ⓓ
**Cook's Cottage Antiques at The Ginnel**
The Ginnel Antiques Center, off Parliament
Street, Harrogate, North Yorkshire HG1 2RB, UK
Tel: 011 44 1423 508 857
www.redhouseyork.co.uk

**GCL** Ⓓ
**Claude Lee at The Ginnel** The Ginnel Antiques
Center, off Parliament Street, Harrogate,
North Yorkshire HG1 2RB, UK
Tel: 011 44 1423 508 857
www.redhouseyork.co.uk

**GIL** Ⓐ
**Gilding's Auctioneers** 64 Roman Way, Market
Harborough, Leicestershire LE16 7PQ, UK
Tel: 011 44 1858 410 414
www.gildings.co.uk

**GK** Ⓐ
**Gallerie Koller** Hardturmstrasse 102, Postfach,
8031 Zürich, Switzerland
Tel: 011 41 144 563 63
www.galeriekoller.ch

**GKA** Ⓓ
**Kismet Antiques at The Ginnel** The Ginnel
Antiques Center, off Parliament Street,
Harrogate, North Yorkshire HG1 2RB, UK
Tel: 011 44 1423 508 857
www.redhouseyork.co.uk

**GMC** Ⓓ
**Mary Cooper at The Ginnel** The Ginnel
Antiques Center, off Parliament Street,
Harrogate, North Yorkshire HG1 2RB, UK
Tel: 011 44 1423 508 857
www.redhouseyork.co.uk

**GOL** Ⓓ
**Nancy Goldsmith** New York, NY
Tel: 212 696 0831

## GORL Ⓐ
**Gorringes** 15 North Street, Lewes, East Sussex BN7 2PD, UK
Tel: 011 44 1273 472 503
www.gorringes.co.uk

## GS Ⓓ
**Goodwins Antiques** 15-16 Queensferry Street, Edinburgh, Midlothian EH2 4QW, UK
Tel: 011 44 131 225 4717

## GV Ⓓ
**Galerie Vandermeersch** Voltaire Antiquités-Vandermeersch SA, 21, quai Voltaire, 75007 Paris, France
Tel: 011 33 142 612 310

## H&L Ⓐ
**Hampton & Littlewood** The Auction Rooms, Alphin Brook Road, Alphington, Exeter, Devon EX2 8TH, UK
Tel: 011 44 1392 413 100
www.hamptonandlittlewood.co.uk

## HAMG Ⓐ
**Dreweatt Neate (Formerly Hamptons)** Baverstock House, 93 High Street, Godalming, Surrey GU7 1AL, UK
Tel: 011 44 1483 423 567
www.dnfa.com/godalming

## HBK Ⓓ
**Hall-Bakker at Heritage** Heritage, 6 Market Place, Woodstock, Oxfordshire OX20 1TA, UK
Tel: 011 44 1993 811 332

## HFG Ⓓ
**Galerie Hélène Fournier Guérin** 18 rue des Saints-Pères, 75007 Paris, France
Tel: 011 33 142 602 181

## HMN Ⓐ
**Hermann Historica OHG** Linprunstrasse 16, 80335 Munich, Germany
Tel: 011 49 895 237 296
www.hermann-historica.com

## HOL Ⓓ
**Holsten Galleries** Elm Street, Stockbridge, MA 01262
Tel: 413 298 3044
www.holstengalleries.com

## IF Ⓓ
**Madame Isabelle Franc** Cité des Antiquaires, 117, boulevard Stalingrad, 69100 Lyon-Villeurbane, France
Tel: 011 33 472 449 891

## ISA Ⓐ
**Ivey Selkirk Auctioneers** 7447 Forsyth Boulevard, Saint Louis, MI 63105
Tel: 314 726 5515
www.iveyselkirk.com

## JBB Ⓓ
**Jean-Baptiste Bacquart**
www.africanandoceanicart.com

## JBS Ⓓ
**John Bull (Antiques) Ltd.** JB Silverware, 139a New Bond Street, London W1S 2TN, UK
Tel: 011 44 20 7629 1251
www.jbsilverware.co.uk

## JDJ Ⓐ
**James D Julia Inc** PO Box 830, Fairfield, ME 04937
Tel: 207 453 7125
www.juliaauctions.com

## JES Ⓓ
**John Jesse** 160 Kensington Church Street, London W8 4BN, UK
Tel: 011 44 20 7229 0312
jj@johnjesse.com

## JH Ⓓ
**Jeanette Hayhurst Fine Glass** 32A Kensington Church Street, London W8 4HA, UK
Tel: 011 44 20 7938 1539

## JHD Ⓓ
**John Howard at Heritage** Heritage, 6 Market Place, Woodstock, Oxfordshire OX20 1TA, UK
Tel: 011 44 1993 811 332
www.antiquepottery.co.uk

## JHOR Ⓓ
**Jonathan Horne** 66c Kensington Church Street, London W8 4BY, UK
Tel: 011 44 20 7221 5658
www.jonathanhorne.co.uk

## JJ Ⓓ
**Junkyard Jeweler**
www.tias.com/stores/thejunkyardjeweler

## JK Ⓓ
**John King** 74 Pimlico Road, London SW1W 8LS, UK
Tel: 011 44 20 7730 0427
kingj896@aol.com

## JM Ⓓ
**John Makepeace** Farrs, Beaminster, Dorset DT8 3NB, UK
Tel: 011 44 1308 862 204
www.johnmakepeace.com

## JN Ⓐ
**John Nicholsons** The Auction Rooms, 'Longfield', Midhurst Road, Fernhurst, Haslemere, Surrey GU27 3HA, UK
Tel: 011 44 1428 653 727
www.johnnicholsons.com

## KAU Ⓐ
**Auktionhaus Kaup** Schloss Sulzburg, Hauptstrasse 62, 79295 Sulzburg, Germany
Tel: 011 49 763 450 380
www.kaupp.de

## KGO Ⓓ
**Pauline Guy** Otford Antiques Center, 26-28 High Street, Otford, Kent TN15 9DF, UK
Tel: 011 44 1959 522 025
www.otfordantiques.co.uk

## L&T Ⓐ
**Lyon & Turnbull Ltd** 33 Broughton Place, Edinburgh, Midlothian EH1 3RR, UK
Tel: 011 44 131 557 8844
www.lyonandturnbull.com

## LAN Ⓐ
**Lankes** Triftfeldstrasse 1, 95182 Döhlau, Germany
Tel: 011 49 928 695 050
www.lankes-auktionen.de

## LANE Ⓓ
**Eileen Lane Antiques** 150 Thompson Street, New York, NY 10012
Tel: 212 475 2988
www.eileenlaneantiques.com

## LB Ⓓ
**Linda Bee** Grays Mews Antique Market, 1-7 Davies Street, London, W1Y 2LP, UK
Tel: 011 44 20 7629 5921
www.graysantiques.com

## LC Ⓐ
**Lawrence's Fine Art Auctioneers** The Linen Yard, South Street, Crewkerne, Somerset TA18 8AB, UK
Tel: 011 44 1460 73041
www.lawrences.co.uk

## LFA Ⓐ
**Law Fine Art Ltd** Ash Cottage, Ashmore Green, Newbury, Berkshire RG18 9ER, UK
Tel: 011 44 1635 860 033
www.lawfineart.co.uk

## LM Ⓓ
**Lili Marleen**
www.lilimarleen.net

## LN Ⓓ
**Lillian Nassau Ltd,** 220 East 57th Street, New York, NY 10022
Tel: 212 759 6062
www.lilliannassau.com

## LOS Ⓓ
**Lost City Arts** 18 Cooper Square, New York, NY 10003
Tel: 212 375 0500
www.lostcityarts.com

## LPZ Ⓐ
**Lempertz** Neumarkt 3, 50667 Cologne, Germany
Tel 011 49 2219 257 290
www.lempertz.com

## LYNH Ⓓ
**Lynn & Brian Holmes**
Tel: 011 44 20 7368 6412

## M&D Ⓓ
**Myers & Duncan** 12 East 86th Street, Suite 239, New York, NY 10028
jmyersprimitives@aol.com

## MACK Ⓓ
**Macklowe Gallery** 667 Madison Avenue, New York, NY 10021
Tel: 212 644 6400
www.macklowegallery.com

## MB Ⓓ
**Mostly Boxes** 93 High Street, Eton, Windsor, Berkshire SL4 6AF, UK
Tel: 011 44 1753 858 470

## MGL Ⓓ
**Mix Gallery** 17 South Main Street, Lambertville, NJ 08530
Tel: 609 773 0777
www.mix-gallery.com

## MILLB Ⓓ
**Million Dollar Babies**
Tel: 518 885 7397

**MJM** (D)
**Marc Matz Antiques** 368 Broadway,
Cambridge, MA 02139
Tel: 617 460 6200
www.marcmatz.com

**MOD** (D)
**Moderne Gallery** 111 North Third Street,
Philadelphia, PA 19106
Tel: 215 923 8536
www.modernegallery.com

**MTZ** (A)
**Auktionshaus Metz** Friedrich-Eber-Anlage 5,
69117 Heidelberg, Germany
Tel: 011 49 622 123 571
www.Metz-Auktion.de

**MW** (D)
**Mike Weedon** 7 Camden Passage, Islington,
London N1 8EA, UK
Tel: 011 44 20 7226 5319
www.mikeweedonantiques.com

**NA** (A)
**Northeast Auctions** 93 Pleasant Street,
Portsmouth, NH 03801
Tel: 603 433 8400
www.northeastauctions.com

**NAG** (A)
**Nagel** Neckarstraße 189-191,
70190 Stuttgart, Germany
Tel: 011 49 711 649 690
www.auction.de

**NBLM** (D)
**N. Bloom & Son (1912) Ltd**
Tel: 011 44 20 7629 5060
www.nbloom.com

**NEA** (A)
**Dreweatt Neate (Formerly Neales)** The
Nottingham Salerooms, 192 Mansfield Road,
Nottingham, Nottinghamshire NG1 3HU, UK
Tel: 011 44 115 962 4141
www.dnfa.com/neales

**PC** (P)
**Private Collection**

**PER** (D)
**Perkins** 1198 Yonge Street, Toronto, Ontario
M4T 1W1, Canada
Tel: 416 925 0973
www.perkinsantiques.com

**PH** (D)
**Pantry & Hearth** 994 Main Street South,
Woodbury, CT 06798
Tel: 203 263 8555
www.nhada.org/pantryhearth.htm

**PIA** (A)
**Piasa** 5 rue Drouot, 75009 Paris, France
Tel: 011 33 153 341 010

**PIL** (A)
**Salle des Ventes Pillet** 1 rue de la Libération,
27480 Lyons la Forèt, France
Tel: 011 33 232 496 064
www.pillet.auction.fr

**POOK** (A)
**Pook & Pook** 463 East Lancaster Avenue,
Downington, PA 19335
Tel: 610 269 4040/0695
www.pookandpook.com

**PSA** (A)
**Potteries Specialist Auctions** 271 Waterloo
Road, Cobridge, Stoke-on-Trent,
Staffordshire ST6 3HR, UK
Tel: 011 44 1782 286 622
www.potteriesauctions.com

**PST** (D)
**Patricia Stauble Antiques** 180 Main Street,
PO Box 265, Wiscasset, ME 04578
Tel: 207 882 6341
pstauble@midcoast.com

**PUR** (D)
**Puritan Values** The Dome, St Edmund's Road,
Southwold, Suffolk IP18 6BZ, UK
Tel: 011 44 1502 722 211
www.puritanvalues.co.uk

**QU** (A)
**Quittenbaum Kunstauktionen München**
Hohenstaufenstraße 1, D-80801,Munich, Germany
Tel: 011 49 893 300 756
www.quittenbaum.de

**R&GM** (D)
**R & G McPherson Antiques** 40 Kensington
Church Street, London W8 4BX, UK
Tel: 011 44 20 7937 0812
www.orientalceramics.com

**RBRG** (D)
**RBR Group at Grays** 158/168, Grays Antique
Market, 58 Davies Street, London W1Y 5LP, UK
Tel: 011 44 20 7629 4769
www.graysantiques.com

**RDER** (D)
**Rogers de Rin** 76 Royal Hospital Road,
Paradise Walk, Chelsea, London SW3 4HN, UK
Tel: 011 44 20 7352 9007
www.rogersderin.co.uk

**RDL** (A)
**David Rago/Nicholas Dawes Lalique Auctions**
333 North Main Street, Lambertville, NJ 08530
Tel: 609 397 9374
www.ragoarts.com

**REL** (D)
**Relick** 8 Golborne Road, London W10 5NW, UK
Tel: 011 44 20 8962 0089

**RENO** (A)
**The Coeur d'Alene Art Auction** PO Box 310,
Hayden, ID 83835
Tel: 208 772 9009
www.cdaartauction.com

**RG** (D)
**Richard Gibbon** 34-34a Islington Green,
London N1 8DU, UK
Tel: 011 44 20 7354 2852
neljeweluk@aol.com

**RGA** (D)
**Richard Gardner Antiques** Swan House, Market
Square, Petworth, West Sussex GU28 0AN, UK
Tel: 011 44 1798 343 411
www.richardgardnerantiques.co.uk

**RITZ** (D)
**Ritzy** 7 The Mall Antiques Arcade,
359 Upper Street, London N1 0PD, UK
Tel: 011 44 20 7704 0127

**ROS** (A)
**Rosebery's** 74-76 Knight's Hill, West Norwood,
London SE27 0JD, UK
Tel: 011 44 20 8761 2522
www.roseberys.co.uk

**ROW** (A)
**Rowley Fine Arts** 8 Downham Road, Ely,
Cambridge, Cambridgeshire CB6 1AH, UK
Tel: 011 44 1353 653020
www.rowleyfineart.com

**ROX** (D)
**Roxanne Stuart** PA, USA
Tel: 215 750 8868
gemfairy@aol.com

**RSS** (A)
**Rossini SA** 7 rue Drouot, 75009 Paris, France
Tel: 011 33 153 345 500
www.rosslnl.fr

**RTC** (A)
**Ritchies Auctioneers & Appraisers** 288 King
Street East, Toronto, Ontario M5A 1KA, Canada
Tel: 416 364 1864
www.ritchies.com

**RUM** (D)
**Rumours** 4 The Mall Antiques Arcade,
359 Upper Street, London, N1 0PD, UK
Tel: 011 44 20 7704 6549

**RY** (D)
**Robert Young Antiques** 68 Battersea Bridge
Road, London SW11 3AG, UK
Tel: 011 44 20 7228 7847
www.robertyoungantiques.com

**S&K/SL** (A)
**Sloans & Kenyon** 7034 Wisconsin Avenue
Chevy Chase, MD 20815
Tel: 301 634 2330
www.sloansandkenyon.com

**SDR** (A)
**Sollo:Rago Modern Auctions** 333 North Main
Street, Lambertville, NJ 08530
Tel: 609 397 9374
www.ragoarts.com

**SF** (D)
**The Silver Fund** 1 Duke of York Street,
London SW1Y 6JP
Tel: 011 44 207 839 7664
www.thesilverfund.com

**SHF** (D)
**Steppes Hill Farm Antiques** Steppes Hill Farm,
Stockbury, Sittingbourne, Kent ME9 7RB, UK
Tel: 011 44 1795 842 205

**SK** (A)
**Skinner Inc.** The Heritage on the Garden,
63 Park Plaza, Boston MA 02116
Tel: 617 350 5400
www.skinnerinc.com

# KEY TO ILLUSTRATIONS

**KEY TO ILLUSTRATIONS**

**SSP** (D)
**Sylvie Spectrum** Stand 372, Grays Antique Market, 58 Davies Street, London W1K 5LP, UK
Tel: 011 44 20 7629 3501
spectrum@grays.clara.net

**STY** (D)
**Style Gallery** 10 Camden Passage, London N1 8ED, UK
Tel: 011 44 20 7359 7867
www.styleantiques.co.uk

**SWA** (A)
**Swann Galleries Image Library** 104 East 25th Street, New York, NY 10010
Tel: 212 254 4710
www.swanngalleries.com

**SWO** (A)
**Sworders** 14 Cambridge Road, Stansted Mountfitchet, Essex CM24 8BZ, UK
Tel: 011 44 1279 817 778
www.sworder.co.uk

**SUM** (D)
No longer trading

**TA** (A)
**333 Auctions** 333 North Main Street, Lambertville, NJ 08530
Tel: 609 397 9374
www.ragoarts.com

**TB** (D)
**Trotta-Bono American Indian Art** PO Box 34, Shrub Oak, NY 10588
Tel: 914 528 6604
tb788183@aol.com

**TCF** (D)
**Cynthia Findlay** Toronto Antiques Center, 276 King Street West, Toronto, Ontario M5V 1J2, Canada
Tel: 416 260 9057
www.cynthiafindlay.com

**TCM** (D)
**Twentieth Century Marks** Whitegates, Rectory Road, Little Burstead, Essex CM12 9TR, UK
Tel: 011 44 1268 411 000
www.20thcenturymarks.co.uk

**TCS** (D)
**The Country Seat** Huntercombe Manor Barn, nr. Henley on Thames, Oxfordshire RG9 5RY
Tel: 011 44 1491 641 349
www.thecountryseat.com

**TDG** (D)
**The Design Gallery** 5 The Green, Westerham, Kent TN16 1AS, UK
Tel: 011 44 1959 561 234
www.designgallery.co.uk

**TDO** (D)
**Tendo Mokko** 1-3-10 Midaregawa, Tendo, Japan
Tel: 011 81 23 653 3121

**TJL** (D)
**Jospehine Liss** Toronto Antiques Center, 276 King Street West, Toronto, Ontario M5V 1J2, Canada
www.ohayonantiques.com

**TO** (D)
**Titus Omega**
Tel: 011 44 20 7688 1295
www.titusomega.com

**TR** (D)
**Terry Rodgers & Melody** 1050 Second Avenue, New York, NY 10022
Tel: 212 758 3164
melodyjewelnyc@aol.com

**TRIO** (D)
**Trio** Stand L24, Grays Antique Markets, 58 Davies Street, London W1K 5LP, UK
Tel: 011 44 20 7493 2736
www.trio-london.fsnet.co.uk

**TSG** (D)
**Shand Galleries** Toronto Antiques Center, 276 King Street West, Toronto, Ontario M5V 1J2, Canada
Tel: 416 260 9056
kenshand@attcanada.ca

**VDB** (D)
**Van Den Bosch** Shop 1, Georgian Village, Camden Passage, Islington, London N1 8DU, UK
Tel: 011 44 20 7226 4550
www.vandenbosch.co.uk

**VEC** (A)
**Vectis Auctions** Fleck Way, Thornaby, Stockton on Tees, County Durham TS17 9JZ, UK
Tel: 011 44 1642 750 616
www.vectis.co.uk

**VET** (D)
**Vetro & Arte Gallery** Calle del Cappeller 3212, Dorsoduro, Venice 30123, Italy
Tel: 011 39 0415 228 525
www.venicewebgallery.com

**VS** (D)
**Von Spaeth** Willhelm-Diess-Weg 13, 81927 Munich, Germany
Tel: 011 49 892 809 132
www.glasvonspaeth.com

**VZ** (A)
**Von Zezschwitz** Friedrichstraße 1a, 80801 Munich, Germany
Tel: 011 49 893 898 930
www.von-zezschwitz.de

**W&W** (A)
**Wallis & Wallis**, West Steet Auction Galleries, Lewes, East Sussex BN7 2NJ, UK
Tel: 011 44 1273 480 208
www.wallisandwallis.co.uk

**WAD** (A)
**Waddington's Auctioneers & Appraisers** 111 Bathurst St., Toronto, Ontario M5V 2R1, Canada
Tel: 416 504 9100
www.waddingtons.ca

**WAIN** (D)
**William Wain at Antiquarius** Stand J6, Antiquarius, 135 King's Road, London SW3 4PW, UK
Tel: 011 44 20 7351 4905
w.wain@btopenworld.com

**WDL** (D)
**Kunst-Auktionshaus Martin Wendl** August-Bebel-Straße 4, 07407 Rudolstadt, Germany
Tel: 011 49 3672 424 350
www.auktionshaus-wendl.de

**WKA** (A)
**Wiener Kunst Auktionen** Palais Kinsky Freyung 4, 1010 Vienna, Austria
Tel: 011 43 153 242 00
www.palais-kinsky.com

**WW** (A)
**Woolley & Wallis** 51-61 Castle Street, Salisbury, Wiltshire SP1 3SU, UK
Tel: 011 44 1722 424 500
www.woolleyandwallis.co.uk

# NOTE

For valuations, it is advisable to contact the dealer or auction house in advance to confirm that they will perform this service and whether any charge is involved. Telephone valuations are not possible, so it will be necessary to send details, including a photograph, of the object to the dealer or auction house, along with a stamped addressed envelope for response. While most dealers will be happy to help you, do remember that they are busy people. Please mention *DK Antiques Price Guide 2006* by Judith Miller when making an enquiry.

728

# DIRECTORY OF AUCTIONEERS

THIS IS A LIST OF AUCTIONEERS that conduct regular sales. Auction houses that would like to be included in the next edition should contact us by 1 February 2006.

## Alabama

**Flomaton Antique Auction**
PO Box 1017, 320 Palafox Street,
Flomaton 36441
Tel: 251 296 3059
Fax: 251 296 1974
info@flomatonantiqueauction.com
www.flomatonantiqueauction.com

**Jim Norman Auctions**
201 East Main St, Hartselle, 35640
Tel: 205 773 6878

**Vintage Auctions**
Star Rte Box 650,
Blountsville, 35031
Tel: 205 429 2457
Fax: 205 429 2457

## Arizona

**Dan May & Associates**
4110 North Scottsdale Road,
Scottsdale, 85251
Tel: 480 941 4200

**Old World Mail Auctions**
PO Box 2224
Sedona, 86339
Tel: 928 282 3944
marti@oldworldauctions.com
www.oldworldauctions.com

**Star Auction Inc**
P. O. Box 1232, Dolan Springs,
86441-1232
Tel: 602 767 4774
Fax: 602 767 3900

## Arkansas

**Hanna-Whysel Auctioneers**
3403 Bella Vista Way,
Bella Vista, 72714
Tel: 501 855 9600

**Ponders Auctions**
1203 South College,
Stuttgart, 72160
Tel: 501 673 6551

## California

**Bonhams & Butterfields**
7601 Sunset Blvd,
Los Angeles, 90046-2714
Tel: 323 850 7500
Fax: 323 850 5843
info@butterfields.com
www.butterfields.com

**Bonhams & Butterfields**
220 San Bruno Ave,
San Francisco, 94103
Tel: 415 861 7500
Fax: 415 861 8951
info@butterfields.com
www.butterfields.com

**I.M. Chait Gallery**
9330 Civic Center Drive,
Beverly Hills, 90210
Tel: 310 285 0182
Fax: 310 285 9740
www.chait.com

**Cuschieri's Auctioneers & Appraisers**
863 Main Street,
Redwood City, 94063
Tel: 650 556 1793
info@cuschieris.com
www.cuschieris.com

**eBay, Inc**
2005 Hamilton Ave, Ste 350,
San Jose, 95125
staff@ebay.com
www.ebay.com

**San Rafael Auction Gallery**
634 Fifth Avenue, San Rafael,
San Rafael, 94901
Tel: 415 457 4488
Fax: 415 457 4899
sanrafaelauction@aol.com
www.sanrafael-auction.com

**L. H. Selman Ltd**
123 Locust St, Santa Cruz, 95060
Tel: 800 538 0766
lselman@got.net
www.paperweight.com

**Slawinski Auction Co**
PO Box 67059
Scotts Valley, 95067
antiques@slawinski.com
www.slawinski.com

## North Carolina

**Robert S. Brunk Auction Services, Inc**
P. O. Box 2135, Asheville 28802
Tel: 828 254 6846
auction@brunkauctions.com
www.brunkauctions.com

**Historical Collectible Auctions**
24 NW Court Square, Suite 201,
Graham 27253
Tel: 336 570 2803
auctions@hcaauctions.com
www.hcaauctions.com

## South Carolina

**Charlton Hall Galleries, Inc**
912 Gervais St, Columbia 29201
Tel: 803 799 5678
info@charltonhallauctions.com
www.charltonhallauctions.com

## Colorado

**Pacific Auction**
1270 Boston Ave.,
Longmont, 80501
Tel: 303 772 9401
ojpratt@pacificauction.com
www.pacificauction.com

**Pettigrew Auction Company**
1645 South Tejon Street,
Colorado Springs, 80906
Tel: 719 633 7963

**Priddy's Auction Galleries**
5411 Leetsdale Drive,
Denver, 80222
Tel: 800 380 4411

**Stanley & Co**
Auction Room, 395 Corona Street,
Denver
Tel: 303 355 0506

## Connecticut

**Norman C. Heckler & Company**
79 Bradford Corner Rd,
Woodstock Valley, 06282-2002
Tel: 860 974 1634
info@hecklerauction.com
info@hecklerauctin.com

**Lloyd Ralston Toys**
350 Long Beach Blvd,
Stratford, 06615
Tel: 203 386 9399
lrgallery@sbcglobal.net
www.lloydralstontoys.com

**Winter Associates, Inc**
Auctioneers & Appraisers, 21 Cooke
St, P. O. Box 823, Plainville, 06062
Tel: 860 793 0288

## North Dakota

**Curt D. Johnson Auction Company**
4216 Gateway Drive, Grand Forks,
58203
Tel: 701 746 1378
merfeld@rrv.net
www.curtdjohnson.com

## South Dakota

**Fischer Auction Company**
238 Haywire Ave, P. O. Box 667,
Long Lake, 57457-0667
Tel: 800 888 1766/
605 577 6600
figleo@hotmail.com
www.fischerauction.com

## Delaware

**Remember When Auctions, Inc**
42 Sea Gull Rd, Swann Estates,
Selbyville, 19975
Tel: 302-436-4979
sales@history-attic.com
www.history-attic.com

## Florida

**Auctions Neapolitan**
1100 1st Ave South.,
Naples 34102
Tel: 239 262 7333
info@autionsneapolitan.com
www.auctionsneapolitan.com

**Burchard Galleries/Auctioneers**
2528 30th Ave North,
St Petersburg, 33713
Tel: 727 821 1167
mail@burchardgalleries
www.burchardgalleries.com

**Arthur James Galleries**
615 East Atlantic Avenue,
Delray Beach
Tel: 561 278 2373
arjames@bellsouth.net
www.arthurjames.com

**Kincaid Auction Company**
3809 East Hwy 42,
Lakeland 33801
Tel: 800 970 1977
kincaid@kincaid.com
www.kincaid.com

**Albert Post Galleries**
809 Lucerne Ave,
Lake Worth, 33460
Tel: 561 582 4477
a.postgallery@juno.com
www.albertpostgallery.com

## Georgia

**Arwood Auctions**
26 Ayers Ave, Marietta, 30060
Tel: 770 423 0110

**Great Gatsby's**
5070 Peachtree Industrial Blvd,
Atlanta, GA 30341
Tel: 770 457 1903
info@gatsbys.com
info@greatgatsbys.com

**My Hart Auctions Inc**
PO Box 2511, Cumming, GA 30028
Tel: 770 888 9006
myhart@antiquefurniture.us

**Red Baron's Auction Gallery**
6450 Roswell Rd, Atlanta, 30328
Tel: 404 252 3770
rbarons@onramp.net

**Southland Auction Inc**
3350 Riverwood Parkway, Atlanta
Tel: 770 818 2418

## Idaho

**The Coeur d'Alene Art Auction**
PO Box 310, Hayden, 83835
Tel: 208 772 9009
cdaartauction@cdaartaution.com
www.cdaartauction.com

## Indiana

**Kruse International**
PO Box 190, Auburn, 46706
Tel: 219 925 5600/
800 968 4444

**Lawson Auction Service**
923 Fourth St, Columbus, 47265
Tel: 812 372 2571
dlawson@lawsonauction.com
www.lawsonauction.com

**Curran Miller Auction & Realty, Inc**
4424 Vogel Rd, Ste. 400,
Evansville, 47715
Tel: 800 264 0601
email@curranmiller.com
www.curranmiller.com

**Schrader Auction**
209 West Van Buren St,
Columbia City, 46725
Tel: 219 244 7606

**Slater's Americana**
5335 North Tacoma Ave, Suite 24,
Indianapolis, 46220
Tel: 317 257 0863

**Stout Auctions**
529 State Road East, Williamsport,
47993
Tel: 765 764 6901
info@stoutauctions.com
www.stoutauctions.com

**Strawser Auctions**
Michael G. Strawser, 200 North
Main, P. O. Box 332,
Wolcotville, IN 46795
Tel: 260 854 2859
info@strawserauctions.com
www.strawserauctions.com

## Illinois

**Butterfield & Dunning**
755 Church Rd, Elgin, 60123
Tel: 847 741 3483
info@butterfields.com
www.butterfields.com

**Hack's Auction Center**
Box 296, Pecatonica, 61063
Tel: 815 239 1436

**Hanzel Galleries**
1120 South Michigan Ave,
Chicago, 60605-2301
Tel: 312 922 6247

**Joy Luke Auction Gallery**
300 East Grove St,
Bloomington, 61701-5232
Tel: 309 828 5533
robert@joyluke.com
www.joyluke.com

**Susanin's Auction**
228 Merchandise Mart,
Chicago, 60654
Tel: 888 787 2646/
312 832 9800
info@susanins.com
www.susanins.com

## Iowa

**Jackson's Auctioneers & Appraisers**
2229 Lincoln St, P. O. Box 50613,
Cedar Falls, 50613
Tel: 319 277 2256
jacksons@jacksonsauction.com
www.jacksonsauction.com

**Tubaugh Auctions**
1702 8th Ave, Belle Plaine, 52208
Tel: 319 444 2413
www.tubaughauctions.com

## Kansas

**AAA Historical Auction Service**
P. O. Box 12214,
Kansas City, 66112
www.manions.com,

**CC Auction Gallery**
416 Court, Clay Center, 67432
Tel: 785 632 6062

**Spielman Auction**
2259 Homestead Rd, Lebo, 66856
Tel: 316 256 6558

## Kentucky

**Hays & Associates, Inc**
120 South Spring St,
Louisville, 40206-1953
Tel: 502 584 4297

**Steffen's Historical Militaria**
P. O. Box 280, Newport, 41072
Tel: 859 431 4499
www.steffensmilitaria.com

## Louisiana

**Estate Auction Gallery**
3374 Government St,
Baton Rouge, 70806
Tel: 504 383 7706

**New Orleans Auction**
Galleries, Inc, 801 Magazine St,
New Orleans, 70130
Tel: 504 566 1849
info@neworleansauction.com
www.neworleansauction.com

## Maine

**James D Julia Auctioneers Inc**
Rte 201, Skowhegan Rd, P. O. Box
830, Fairfield, ME 04937
Tel: 207 453 7125
jjulia@juliaauctions.com
www.juliaauctions.com

**Thomaston Place Auction Galleries**
P. O. Box 300, Business Rt 1,
Thomaston, ME 04861
Tel: 207 354 8141
auction@kajav.com
www.thomastonauction.com

## Maryland

**Camelot Antiques**
7871 Ocean Gateway
Easton, Maryland 21601
Tel: 410 820 4396
camelot@goeastern.net
www.about-antiques.com

**Hantman's Auctioneers & Appraisers**
P. O. Box 59366,
Potomac, 20859-9366
Tel: 301 770 3720
hantman@hantmans.com
www.hantmans.com

**Isennock Auctions & Appraisals, Inc**
4106B Norrisville Rd,
White Hall, 21161-9306,
Tel: 410 557 8052
isennock@starix.net
www.isennockauction.com

**Richard Opfer Auctioneering, Inc**
1919 Greenspring Dr, Lutherville,
Timonium, 21093-4113
Tel: 410 252 5035
info@opferauction.com
www.opferauction.com

**Sloans & Kenyon**
4605 Bradley Boulevard
Bethesda, MD 20815
Tel: 301 634-2330
Fax: 301 656-7074
www.sloansandkenyon.com

## Massachusetts

**Douglas Auctioneers**
Rte 5, South Deerfield, 01373
Tel: 413 665 2877
www.douglasauctioneers.com
info@douglasauctioneers.com

**Eldred's**
P. O. Box 796,
East Dennis, 02641-0796
Tel: 508 385 3116
info@eldreds.com
www.eldreds.com

**Grogan & Company Auctioneers**
22 Harris St, Dedham, 02026
Tel: 781 461 9500
grogans@groganco.com
www.groganco.com

**Shute Auction Gallery**
850 West Chestnut St,
Brockton, 02401
Tel: 508 588 0022/
508 588 7833

**Skinner Inc.**
63 Park Plaza, Boston,
MA 02116
Tel: 617 350 5400
info@skinnerinc.com
www.skinnerinc.com

**Skinner, Inc**
357 Main St,
Bolton, MA 01740
Tel: 978 779 6241

**Willis Henry Auctions, Inc**
22 Main St, Marshfield, 02050
Tel: 781 834 7774
wha@willishenry.com
www.willishenry.com

## Michigan

**DuMouchelle Art Galleries Co**
409 East Jefferson Ave,
Detroit, 48226
Tel: 313 963 6255
info@dumouchelles.com
www.dumouchelles.com

## Minnesota

**Buffalo Bay Auction Co**
5244 Quam Circle, Rogers, 55374
Tel: 612 428 8480
buffalobay@aol.com

**Tracy Luther Auctions**
2548 East 7th Ave, St. Paul, 55109
Tel: 612 770 6175

**Rose Auction Galleries**
3180 Country Drive, Little Canada,
55117
Tel: 612 484 1415
auctions@rosegalleries.com
www.rosegalleries.com

## Missouri

**Ivey Selkirk Auctioneers**
7447 Forsyth Blvd,
Saint Louis, 63105
Tel: 314 726 5515
www.iveyselkirk.com

**Simmons & Company Auctioneers**
40706 East 144th St,
Richmond, 64085
Tel: 816 776 2936/
800 646 2936
www.simmonsauction.com

## Montana

**Allard Auctions** PO Box 1030, St.
Ignatius, MT 59865
Tel: 460 745 0500
www.allardauctions.com

**Stan Howe & Associates**
4433 Red Fox Dr, Helena,
MT 59601
Tel: 406 443 5658/
800 443 5658

## New Hampshire

**Northeast Auctions**
694 Lafayette Rd, P. O. Box 363,
Hampton, 03483
Tel: 603 926 9800

## New Jersey

**Bertoia Auctions**
2141 Dearco Dr, Vineland, NJ
08360
Tel: 856 692 1881
toys@bertoiaauctions.com
www.bertoiaauctions.com

**Dawson & Nye**
128 American Road, Morris Plains,
NJ 07950
Tel: 973 984 8900
info@dawsonandnye.com
www.dawsonandnye.com
info@dawsons.org www.dawsons.org

**Greg Manning Auctions, Inc**
775 Passaic Ave,
West Caldwell, NJ 07006
Tel: 973 882 0004/
800 221 0243
info@gregmanning.com
www.gregmanning.com

**David Rago Modern Auctions**
333 North Main Street,
Lambertville, NJ 08530
Tel: 609 397 9374
info@ragoarts.com
www.ragoarts.com

## New Mexico

**Altermann Galleries**
Santa Fe Galleries, 203 Canyon
Road, Santa Fe, 87501
info@altermann.com
www.altermann.com

## New York

**Christie's**
502 Park Ave, New York, NY 10022
Tel: 212 546 1000
info@christies.com
www.christies.com

**Christie's East**
219 East 67th St, New York, NY
10021
Tel: 212 606 0400
info@christies.com
www.christies.com

**Samuel Cottone Auctions**
15 Genesee St,
Mount Morris, 14510
Tel: 716 658 3180

**William Doyle Galleries**
175 East 87th St,
New York, 10128-2205
Tel: 212 427 2730
info@doylegalleries.com
www.doylegalleries.com

**Framefinders**
454 East 84th Street,
New York 10028
Tel: 212 396 3896
framefinders@aol.com
www.framefinders.com

**Guernsey's Auction**
108 East 73rd St, New York, 10021
Tel: 212 794 2280
auctions@guernseys.com
www.guernseys.com

**Mapes Auction Gallery**
1729 Vestal Parkway,
West Vestal, 13850-1156
Tel: 607 754 9193
info@mapesauction.com
www.mapesauction.com

**Phillip's, De Pury & Luxemburg**
450 West 15 Street,
New York, 10011
Tel: 212 940 1200
info@phillipsdepury.com
www.phillipsdepury.com

**Sotheby's**
1334 York Ave, New York, 10021
Tel: 212 606 7000
info@sothebys.com
www.sothebys.com

**Swann Galleries, Inc**
104 East 25th St,
New York, 10010-2977
Tel: 212 254 4710
swann@swanngalleries.com
www.swanngalleries.com

## Ohio

**Belhorn Auction Services** PO Box
20211, Columbus, OH 43220
Tel: 614 921 9441
www.belhorn.com

**Cowan's Historic Americana
Auctions**
673 Wilmer Avenue,
Cincinnati, 45226
Tel: 513 871 1670
info@historicamericana.com
www.historicamericana.com

**DeFina Auctions**
1591 State Route 45,
Austinburg, 44010
Tel: 440 275 6674
info@definaauctions.com
www.definaauctions.com

**Garth's Auction, Inc**
2690 Stratford Rd, P. O. Box 369,
Delaware, 43015
Tel: 740 362 4771
info@garths.com
www.garths.com

## Pennsylvania

**Noel Barrett**
P.O. Box 300, Carversville, 18913
Tel: 215 297 5109
toys@noelbarrett.com
www.noelbarrett.com

**Dargate Auction Galleries**
5607 Baum Blvd,
Pittsburgh, 15206
Tel: 412 362 3558
dargate@dargate.com
www.dargate.com

**Freeman's**
1808 Chestnut St,
Philadelphia, 19103
Tel: 610 563 9275/
610 563 9453
info@freemansauction.com
www.freemansauction.com

**Hunt Auctions**
75E. Uwchlan Ave.
Suite 130, Exton, Pa 19341
Tel: 610 524 0822
Fax: 610 524 0826
info@huntauctions
www.huntauctions.com

**Pook & Pook, Inc**
P. O. Box 268,
Downington, 19335-0268
Tel: 610 269 0695/
610 269 4040
info@pookandpook.com
www.pookandpook.com

**Sanford Alderfer Auction Company**
501 Fairgrounds Rd, P. O. Box 640,
Hatfield, 19440-0640
Tel: 215 393 3000
info@alderfercompany.com
www.alderfercompany.com

**Skinner's Auction Company**
170 North HAmpton Street, Easton,
PA 18042
Tel: 610 330 6933

## Rhode Island

**Gustave White Auctioneers**
37 Bellevue, Newport, 02840-3207
Tel: 401 841 5780

## Tennessee

**Kimball M Sterling Inc**
125 West Market St,
Johnson City, 37601,
Tel: 423 928 1471
kimsold@tricon.net
www.sterlingsold.com

## Texas

**Austin Auctions**
8414 Anderson Mill Road,
Austin, 78729-5479
Tel: 512 258 5479
austinauction@cs.com
www.austinauction.com

## Utah

**America West Archives**
P. O. Box 100,
Cedar City, 84721
Tel: 435 586 9497
info@americawestarchives.com
www.americawestarchives.com

## Vermont

**Eaton Auction Service**
RR 1, Box 333, Fairlee, 05045
Tel: 802 333 9717
eas@sover.com
www.eatonauctionservice.com

## Virginia

**The Auction Gallery**
225 Gun Club Road,
Richmond, 23221
Tel: 804 358 0500
www.estate-services.com

**Ken Farmer Auctions & Estates**
105 Harrison Street,
Radford, 24141
Tel: 540 639 0939
info@kfauctions.com
www.kenfarmer.com

**Phoebus Auction Gallery**
14-16 East Mellen St,
Hampton, 23663
Tel: 757 722 9210
bwelch@phoebusauction.com
www.phoebusauction.com

## Washington DC

**Weschler's**
909 East St NW,
Washington, 20004-2006
Tel: 202 628 1281/
800 331 1430
www.weschlers.com

## Wisconsin

**Milwaukee Auction Galleries**
1919 North Summit Ave,
Milwaukee, 53202
Tel: 414 271 1105

**Schrager Auction Galleries, Ltd**
P. O. Box 10390,
2915 North Sherman Blvd,
Milwaukee, 53210
Tel: 414 873 3738
www.schragerauctions.com

# DIRECTORY OF CANADIAN AUCTIONEERS & SPECIALISTS

## AUCTIONEERS

### Alberta

**Arthur Clausen & Sons, Auctioneers**
11802 - 145 Street, Edmonton, Alberta, Canada, T5L 2H3
Tel: 780 451 4549
arthur.clausen@telus.net
www.clausenauction.com

**Hall's Auction Services Ltd**
5240 1A Street S.E.,
Calgary, Alberta, Canada, T2H 1J1
Tel: 403 640 1244
info@hallsauction.com
www.hodginshalls.com

**Hodgins Art Auctions Ltd**
5240 1A Street S.E.,
Calgary, Alberta, Canada, T2H 1J1
Tel: 403 640 1244
info@hallsauction.com
www.hodginshalls.com

**Lando Art Auctions**
11130-105 Avenue N.W.,
Edmonton, Alberta,
Canada, T5H 0L5
Tel: 1 780 990 1161
mail@landoartauctions.com
www.landoartauctions.com

### British Columbia

**All Nations Stamp & Coin**
Hudson's Bay Company
4th Floor, 674 Granville Street,
PO Box 54023, Vancouver, British
Columbia, Canada, V6C 3P4
Tel: 604 689 2230
collect@direct.ca
www.allnationsstampandcoin.com

**Maynards Fine Art Auction House**
415 West 2nd Avenue, Vancouver,
British Columbia, Canada, V5Y 1E3
Tel: 604 876 6787
www.maynards.com

**Robert Derot Associates**
P.O. Box 52205, Vancouver, British
Columbia, Canada, V7J 3V5
Tel: 604 649 6302
robert@robertderot.com
www.robertderot.com

**Waddington's West**
3286 Bellevue Road, Victoria,
British Columbia, Canada, V8X 1C1
Tel: 1 250 384 3737
www.waddingtonsauctions.com

## Ontario

**Empire Auctions**
165 Tycos Drive, Toronto,
Ontario, Canada, M6B 1W6
Tel: 416 784 4261
www.empireauctions.com

**Grand Valley Auctions**
154 King Street East,
Cambridge, Ontario,
Canada
Tel: 519 653 6811
www.grandvalleyauctions.ca

**A Touch of Class**
92 College Crescent, Barrie,
Ontario, Canada, L4M 5C8
Tel: 1 888 891 6591
info@atouchofclassauctions.com
www.atouchofclassauctions.com

**Estate and Antiques Sales**
2030 Eglinton Avenue West,
Toronto, Ontario, Canada,
M6E 3S4
Tel: 416 780 9101
www.estateandantiquesales.com

**Gordon's Auction Center**
1473 Princess Street,
Kingston Ontario,
Canada, K7M 3E9
Tel: 613 542 0963
mail@gordonsauction.com
www.gordonsauction.com

**Ritchies**
288 King Street East, Toronto,
Ontario, Canada, M5A 1K4
Tel: 416 364 1864
www.ritchies.com

**Waddington's**
111 Bathurst Street, Toronto,
Ontario, Canada, M5V 2R1
Tel: 416 504 9100
www.waddingtonsauctions.com

## Quebec

**Empire Auctions**
5500, rue Paré, Montréal,
Québec, Canada, H4P 2M1
Tel: 514 737 6586

**iegor - Hôtel des Encans**
872, rue Du Couvent,
Angle Saint-Antoine Ouest,
Montréal, Quebec, Canada,
H4C 2R6
Tel: 514 842 7447
information@iegor.net
www.iegor.net

**Montreal Auction House**
5778 St. Lawrent Blvd.,
Montreal, Quebec,
Canada, H2T 1S8
Tel: 514 278 0827
maison.des.encans@videotron.ca
www.pages.videotron.com

**Pinneys Auctions**
2435 Duncan Road (T.M.R.),
Montreal, Quebec,
Cananda, H4P 2A2
Tel: 514 345 0571
pinneys@ca.inter.net
www.pinneys.ca

**Ritchies**
1980, rue Sherbrooke O.
Suite 100 (Ground Floor),
Quebec, Canada, H3H 1E8
Tel: 514 934 1864
www.ritchies.com

## SPECIALISTS

**Toronto Antiques Centre**
276 King Street West, Toronto,
Ontario, Canada, M5V 1J2
Tel: 416 345 9941
www.torontoantiquectr.com

### Canadiana

**The Blue Pump**
178 Davenport Road,
Toronto, Ontario, Canada, M5R 172
Tel: 416 944 1673
john@thebluepump.com
www.thebluepump.com

**Ingram Antiques & Collectibles**
669 Mt. Pleasant Road, Toronto,
Ontario, Canada, M4S 2N2
Tel: 416 484 4601

### Ceramics

**Cynthia Findlay**
Toronto Antiques Centre, 276 King
Street West, Toronto, Ontario,
Canada, M5V 1J2
Tel: 416 260 9057
call@cynthiafindlay.com
www.cynthiafindlay.com

**Pam Ferrazzutti Antiques**
Toronto Antiques Centre, 276 King
Street West, Toronto, Ontario,
Canada, M5V 1J2
Tel: 416 260 0325
pam@pamferrazzuttiantiques.com
www.pamferrazzuttiantiques.com

**Staffordshire House**
1 Chestnut Park Road, Toronto,
Ontario, Canada, M4W 1W4
Tel: 416 929 3258
jjd@aol.com
www.staffordshirehouse.com

### Fine Art

Barbara M. Mitchell
Tel: 416 699 5582
fineartsbarbara@hotmail.com

### Furniture

**Howard & Co.**
158 Davenport Rd., Toronto,
Ontario, Canada, M5R 1J2
Tel: 416 922 7966
bhoward@on.aibn.com

**Jonny's Antiques**
21 Avenue Road, Four Season's
Hotel, Toronto, Ontario,
Canada, M5R 2G1
Tel: 416 928 0205
jonnysantiques@rogers.com

**Lorenz Antiques Ltd.**
701 Mount Pleasant Road, Toronto,
Ontario, Canada, M4S 2N4
Tel: 416 487 2066
info@lorenzantiques.com
www.lorenzantiques.com

**Maus Park Antiques**
176 Cumberland Street, Toronto,
Ontario, Canada, M5R 1A8
Tel: 416 944 9781
mauspark@bellnet.ca
www.mausparkantiques

### Jewelry

**Fraleigh Jewellers – Gemmologists**
1977 Yonge Street, Toronto, Ontario,
Canada, M4S 1Z6
Tel: 416 483 1481
rfraleigh@sympatico.ca

### Oriental

**Pao and Molkte Ltd.**
Four Seasons Hotel, 21 Avenue
Road, Toronto, Ontario, Canada,
M5R 2G1
Tel: 416 925 6197
paomoltke@mail.com

**Topper Gallery**
1111 Finch Avenue West, Toronto,
Ontario, Canada, M3J 2E5
Tel: 416 663 7554

### Silver

**Richard Flensted-Holder**
86 Gloucester Street,
Toronto, Ontario, Canada, M4Y 2S2
Tel: 416 961 3414
(by appointment only)

**Louis Wine Ltd.**
140 Yorkville Avenue, Toronto,
Ontario, Canada, M5R 1C2
Tel: 416 929 9333
louiswine@rogers.com
www.louiswine.com

# DIRECTORY OF SPECIALISTS

SPECIALISTS WHO WOULD LIKE TO BE INCLUDED in the next edition, or have a change of address or telephone number, should contact us by 1 February 2006.

Readers should contact dealers by telephone before visiting them to avoid a wasted journey.

## American Paintings

**James R Bakker Antiques Inc**
248 Bradford Street, Provincetown,
MA 02657
Tel: 508 487 9081

**Jeffrey W. Cooley**
The Cooley Gallery Inc,
25 Lyme Street, Old Lyme,
CT 06371
Tel: 860 434 8807
info@cooleygallery. com
www.cooleygallery. com

## Americana and Folk Art

**Augustus Decorative Arts Ltd**
Philadelphia
Tel: 215 587 0000
elle@portraitminatures.com

**Thomas and Julia Barringer**
26 South Main Street, Stockton,
NJ 08559
Tel: 609 397 4474
Fax: 609 397 4474
tandjb@voicenet.com

**Bucks County Antique Center**
Route 202, Lahaska, PA 18931
Tel: 215 794 9180

**J M Flanigan American Antiques**
1607 Park Avenue, Baltimore,
MD 21217
Tel: 410 225 3463
jmf745i@aol.com

**Frank Gaglio, Inc**
56 Market St., Suite B, Rhinebeck
NY 12572
Tel: 845 876 0616

**Sidney Gecker**
226 West 21st Street,
New York, NY 10011
Tel: 212 929 8769

**Pat and Rich Garthoeffner
Antiques**
122 East Main Street, Lititz,
PA 17543
Tel: 717 627 7998
Fax: 717 627 3259
patgarth@voicenet.com

**Allan Katz Americana**
25 Old Still Road, Woodbridge,
CT 06525
Tel: 203 393 9356
folkkatz@optonline.net

**Nathan Liverant and Son**
168 South Main Street, P.O. Box
103, Colchester, CT 06415
Tel: 860 537 2409
www.liverantantiques.com
mail@liverantantiques.com

**Judith and James Milne Inc**
506 East 74th Street, New York,
NY 10021
Tel: 212 472 0107
www.milneantiques.com
milneinc@aol.com

**Monkey Hill**
6465 Route 202, New Hope,
PA 18938
Tel: 215 862 0118
Fax: 215 862 3436
info@monkeyhillantiques.com

**Olde Hope Antiques Inc**
P.O. Box 718, New Hope, PA 18938
Tel: 215 297 0200
Fax: 215 297 0300
info@oldehopeantiques.com
www.oldehopeantiques.com

**Pantry & Hearth,**
994 Main Street South, Woodbury,
CT 06798
Tel: 203 263 8555
gail.lettick@prodigy.net

**Sharon Platt**
1347 Rustic View, Manchester,
MO 63011
Tel: 636 227 5304
sharonplatt@postnet.com

**Raccoon Creek Antiques**
Box 276, 208 Spangsville Road,
Oley, PA 19547
www.raccoonantiques.com

**J. B. Richardson**
6 Partrick Lane, Westport,
CT 06880
Tel: 203 226 0358

**Marion Robertshaw Antiques**
P.O. Box 435, Route 202, Lahaska,
PA 18931
Tel: 215 295 0648

**Cheryl and Paul Scott**
P.O. Box 835, 232 Bear Hill Road,
Hillsborough, NH 03244
Tel: 603 464 3617
rivrebend@mcttelecom.com

**The Splendid Peasant**
Route 23 and Sheffield Road, P. O.
Box 536, South Egremont,
MA 01258
Tel: 413 528 5755
folkart@splendidpeasant.com
www.splendidpeasant.com

**The Stradlings**
1225 Park Avenue, New York,
NY 10028
Tel: 212 534 8135

**Patricia Stauble Antiques**
180 Main Street, PO Box 265,
Wiscasset, ME 04578
Tel: 207 882 6341
pstauble@midcoast.com

**Jeffrey Tillou Antiques**
33 West Street & 7 East Street, P.O.
Box 1609, Litchfield, CT 06759
Tel: 860 567 9693
webmaster@tillouantiques.com

**Paul and Karen Wendhiser**
P.O. Box 155, Ellington, CT 06029

## Antiquities

**Frank & Barbara Pollack**
1214 Green Bay Road, Highland
Park, IL 60035
Tel: 847 433 2213
FPollack@compuserve.com

## Architectural Antiques

**Garden Antiques**
Katonah, NY 10536
Tel: 212 744 6281
gardenantiques@pipeline.com
www.bigardenantiques.com

**Cecilia B Williams**
12 West Main Street, New Market,
MD 21774
Tel: 301 865 0777

## Books

**Bauman Rare Books** 535 Madison
Avenue, New York, NY 10022
Tel: 212 751 0011
www.baumanrarebooks.com

## Canadiana

**The Blue Pump**
178 Davenport Road,
Toronto, Ontario, M5R 172, Canada
Tel: 416 944 1673
www.thebluepump.com
john@thebluepump.com

**The Canadian Antique Dealers
Association** PO Box 131
Bloor Street West, Toronto, Ontario
M5S 3L7, Canada
Tel: 416 483 1481
cada@bellnet.ca
www.cadinfo.com

## Carpets and Rugs

**John J Collins**
Jr Gallery, P.O. Box 958, 11 Market
Square, Newburyport, MA 01950
Tel: 978 462 7276
www.bijar.com
bijar@telcity.com

**Karen and Ralph Disaia**
Oriental Rugs Ltd, 23 Lyme Street,
Old Lyme, CT 06371
Tel: 860 434 1167
www.orientalrugsltd.com
info@orientalrugsltd.com

**D B Stock Antique Carpets**
464 Washington Street, Wellesley,
MA 02482
Tel: 781 237 5859
www.dbstock.com
douglas@dbstock.com

## Ceramics

**Charles & Barbara Adams**
289 Old Main St, South Yarmouth,
MA 02664
Tel: 508 760 3290
adams_2430@msn.com

**Jill Fenichell**
by appointment only
Tel: 212 980 9346
jfenichell@yahoo.com

**Mark & Marjorie Allen**
6 Highland Drive, Amherst,
NH 03031
Tel: 603 672 8989
mandmallen@antiquedelft.com
www.antiquedelft.com

**Mellin's Antiques**
P.O. Box 1115, Redding, CT 06875
Tel: 203 938 9538
rich@mellin.us

**Philip Suval, Inc**
1501 Caroline Street,
Fredericksburg, VA 22401
Tel: 540 373 9851
jphilipsuval@aol.com

## Clocks

**Kirtland H Crump**
387 Boston Post Road, Madison,
CT 06443
Tel: 203 245 7573
kirtland@sbaglobal.net
www.crumpclocks.com

## Decorative Arts

**Sumpter Priddy Inc**
323 South Washington Street,
Alexandria, VA 22314
Tel: 703 299 0800
info@sumpterpriddy.com

**Leah Gordon Antiques**
Gallery 18, Manhattan Art and
Antiques Center, 1050 Second
Avenue, New York, NY 10022
Tel: 212 872 1422

**Lillian Nassau**
220 East 57th Street New York,
NY 10022
Tel: 212 759 6062
lilnassau@aol.com
www.lilliannassau.com

**Susie Burmann**
23 Burpee Lane, New London,
NH 03257
Tel: 603 526 5934
rsburmann@tds.net

**H L Chalfant Antiques**
1352 Paoli Pike, West Chester,
PA 19380
Tel: 610 696 1862
chalfant@gateway.net

**Brian Cullity**
18 Pleasant Street, P.O. Box 595,
Sagamore, MA 02561
Tel: 508 888 8409
info@briancullity.com
www.briancullity.com

**Gordon and Marjorie Davenport Inc**
4250 Manitou Way, Madison,
WI 53711
Tel: 608 271 2348
GMDaven@aol.com

**Ron and Penny Dionne**
55 Fisher Hill Road, Willington,
CT 06279
Tel: 860 487 0741

**Peter H Eaton Antiques**
24 Parker Street, Newbury,
MA 01951
Tel: 978 465 2754
peter@petereaton.com
www.petereaton.com

**Gallery 532**
142 Duane Street, New York,
NY 10013
Tel: 212 964 1282
www.gallery532.com

**Stephen H Garner Antiques**
P.O. Box 136, Yarmouth Port,
MA 02675
Tel: 508 362 8424

**Samuel Herrup Antiques**
35 Sheffield Plain Road (Route 7),
Sheffield, MA 01257
Tel: 413 229 0424
ssher@ben.net

**R Jorgensen Antiques**
502 Post Road (US Route 1), Wells,
ME 04090
Tel: 207 646 9444
info@rjorgensen.com
www.rjorgensen.com

**Leigh Keno American Antiques**
127 East 69th Street, New York,
NY 10021
Tel: 212 734 2381
leigh@leighkeno.com
www.leighkeno.com

**Bettina Krainin**
289 Main Street, Woodbury,
CT 06798
Tel: 203 263 7669

**William E Lohrman**
248 Route 208, New Paltz,
NY 12561
Tel: 845 255 6762

**Lorraine's**
23 Battery Park Avenue
Asheville, NC 28801
Tel: 828 251 1771
Fax: 828 254 9490
lorrainesantiques@cs.com

**Gary and Martha Ludlow Inc**
5284 Golfway Lane, Lyndhurst,
OH 44124,
Tel: 440 449 3475
ludlowantiques@aol.com

**Macklowe Gallery**
667 Madison Ave., New York,
NY 10021
Tel: 212 644 6400
www.macklowegallery.com

**Milly McGehee**
P.O. Box 666, Riderwood,
MD 21139
Tel: 410 653 3977
millymcgehee@comcast.com

**Jackson Mitchell Inc**
5718 Kennett Pike, Wilmington,
DE 19807
Tel: 302 656 0110
JacMitch@aol.com

**James L Price Antiques**
831 Alexander Spring Rd, Carlisle,
PA 17013
Tel: 717 243 0501
jlpantiques@earthlink.net

**RJG Antiques**
P.O. Box 60, Rye, NH 03870
Tel: 603 433 1770
antiques@rjgantiques.com
www.rjgantiques.com

**John Keith Russell Antiques Inc**
110 Spring Street, P.O. Box 414,
South Salem, NY 10590
Tel: 914 763 8144
info@jkrantiques.com
www.jkrantiques.com

**Israel Sack**
730 Fifth Avenue, Suite 605, New
York, NY 109
Tel: 212 399 6562

**Lincoln and Jean Sander**
235 Redding Road, Redding,
CT 06896
Tel: 203 938 2981
sanderlr@aol.com

**Kathy Schoemer American Antiques**
P.O. Box 429, 12 McMorrow Lane,
North Salem, NY 10560
Tel: 603 835 2105

**Thomas Schwenke Inc**
50 Main Street North, Woodbury,
CT 06798
Tel: 203 266 0303
schwenke@schwenke.com
www.schwenke.com

**Jack and Ray Van Gelder**
Conway House, 468 Ashfield Road,
Conway, MA 01341
Tel: 413 369 4660

**Van Tassel/Baumann American Antiques**
690 Sugartown Road,
Malvern, PA 19355
Tel: 610 647 3339

## Furniture

**American Antiques**
161 Main Street, P.O. Box 368,
Thomaston, ME 04861
Tel: 207 354 6033
acm@midcoast.com

**American Spirit Antiques**
P.O. Box 11152, Shawnee Mission,
KS 66207
Tel: 913 345 9494
Tedatiii@aol.com

**Barbara Ardizone Antiques**
P.O. Box 433, 62 Main Street,
Salisbury, CT 06068
Tel: 860 435 3057

**Artemis Gallery**
Wallace Road, North Salem,
NY 10560
Tel: 914 669 5971
artemis@optonline.net
www.artemisantiques.com

**Carswell Rush Berlin, Inc**
P.O. Box 0210, Planetarium Station,
New York, NY 0024 0210
Tel: 212 721 0330
carswellberlin@msn.com
www.americanantiques.net

**Joanne and Jack Boardman**
522 Joanne Lane, DeKalb,
IL 06115
Tel: 815 756 359
boardmanantiques@aol.com

**Boym Partners Inc** 131 Varick
Street, 915, New York, NY 10013
Tel: 212 807 8210
www.boym.com

**Joan R Brownstein**
Daniel Hightower, 2068 Ellis Hollow
Road, Ithaca, NY

**Evergreen Antiques**
1249 Third Avenue,
New York, NY 10021
Tel: 212 744 5664
www.evergreenantiques.com

**Eileen Lane Antiques**
150 Thompson Street,
New York, NY 10012
Tel: 212 475 2988
www.eileenlaneantiques.com

**Lost City Arts**
18 Cooper Square,
New York, NY 10003
Tel: 212 375 0500
www.lostcityarts.com

**Lill Marleen**
www.lilimarleen.net

**Mix Gallery**
17 South Main Street,
Lambertville, NJ 08530
Tel: 609 773 0777
www.mix-gallery.com

**Moderne Gallery**
111 North 3rd Street,
Philadelphia, PA 19106
Tel: 215 923 8536
www.modernegallery.com

## Glass

**Holsten Galleries**
Elm Street, Stockbridge, MA 01262
Tel: 413 298 3044
www.holstengalleries.com

**Antiques by Joyce Knutsen**
Tel: 315 637 8238 (Summer)
Tel: 352 567 1699 (Winter)

**Lillian Nassau Ltd**
220 East 57th Street,
New York NY 10022
Tel: 212 759 6062
www.lilliannassau.com

**L.H. Selman Ltd**
123 Locust Street,
Santa Cruz, CA 95060
Tel: 800 538 0766
www.selman.com/pwauction/

**Paul Reichwein**
2321 Hershey Avenune, East
Petersburg, PA 17520
Tel: 717 569 7637

## Jewelry

**Ark Antiques**
P.O. Box 3133,
New Haven, CT 06515
Tel: 203 498 8572
www.ark-antiques.com

**Aurora Bijoux**
Tel: 215 872 7808
www.aurorabijoux.com

**Deco Jewels Inc**
131 Thompson Street, NY
Tel: 212 253 1222
decojewels@earthlink.net

**Junkyard Jeweler**
www.tias.com/stores/thejunkyard-jeweler

**Arthur Guy Kaplan**
P.O. Box 1942, Baltimore,
MD 21203
Tel: 410 752 2090

**Million Dollar Babies**
Tel: 518 885 7397

**Terry Rodgers & Melody**
1050 2nd Avenue,
New York, NY 10022
Tel: 212 758 3164
melodyjewelnyc@aol.com

**Roxanne Stuart**
PA
Tel: 215 750 8868
gemfairy@aol.com

## Marine Antiques

**Hyland Granby Antiques**
P.O. Box 457, Hyannis Port,
MA 02647
Tel: 508 771 3070
alan@hylandgranby.com
www.hylandgranby.com

## Metalware

**Wayne and Phyllis Hilt**
176 Injun Hollow Road,
Haddam Neck,
CT 06424
Tel: 860 267 2146
philt@snet.net
www.hiltpewter.com

## Oriental

**Marc Matz Antiques**
By appointment
368 Broadway,
Cambridge, MA 02139
Tel: 617 460 6200
www.marcmatz.com

## Scientific Instruments

**Edison Gallery**
Susanin's 900 S. Clinton St.,
Chicago, Il 60607
Tel: 617 359 4678
www.edisongallery.com

## Silver

**Chicago Silver**
www.chicagosilver.com

**Jonathan Trace**
P.O. Box 418, 31 Church Hill Road,
Rifton, NY 12471
Tel: 914 658 7336

**Imperial Half Bushel**
831 N Howard Street,
Baltimore, MD 21201
Tel: 410 462 1192
ihb@imperialhalfbushel.com
www.imperialhalfbushel.com

## Textiles

**Colette Donovan**
98 River Road, Merrimacport,
MA 01860
Tel: 978 346 0614
colettedonovan@adelphia.net

**M Finkel & Daughter**
936 Pine Street, Philadelphia,
PA 19107
Tel: 215 627 7797
mailbox@finkelantiques.com
www.samplings.com

**Cora Ginsburg**
19 East 74th Street New York,
NY 10021
Tel: 212 744 1352
coraginsburg@rcn.com
www.coraginsburg.com

**Nancy Goldsmith**
New York, NY
Tel: 212 696 0831

**Andrea Hall Levy**
PO Box 1243,
Riverdale, NY 10471
Tel: 646 441 1726
barangrill@aol.com

**Stephen & Carol Huber**
40 Ferry Road, Old Saybrook,
CT 06475
Tel: 860 388 6809
hubers@antiquesamplers.com
www.antiquesamplers.com

**Fayne Landes Antiques**
593 Hansell Road, Wynnewood,
PA 19096
Tel: 610 658 0566

**Charlotte Marler**
Booth 14,
1528 West 25th Street,
New York, NY 10010
Tel: 212 367 8808
char_marler@hotmail.com

## Toys

**Harper General Store**
10482 Jonestown Road, Annville,
PA 17003
Tel: 717 865 3456
lauver5@comcast.net
www.harpergeneralstore.com

## Tribal Art

**Marcy Burns American Indian Arts**
525 East 72nd Street, New York,
~NY 10021
Tel: 212 439 9257
marcy@marcyburns.com
www.marcyburns.com

**Domas & Gray Gallery**
Tel: 228 467 5294
www.domasandgraygallery.com

**Elliot & Grace Snyder**
P.O. Box 598, South Egremont,
MA 01258
Tel: 413 528 3581

**Myers & Duncan**
12 East 86th Street, Suite 239,
New York, NY 10028
Tel: 212 472 0115
jmyersprimitives@aol.com

**Trotta-Bono American Indian Art**
PO Box 34, Shrub Oak, NY 10588
Tel: 914 528 6604
tb788183@aol.com

# COLLECTING ON THE INTERNET

The internet has revolutionized the trading of both antiques and collectibles, especially for smaller pieces, such as ceramics and metalware, which are are easily defined, described and photographed. Shipping is also comparatively easy for smaller items. The Internet has provided a cost-effective way of buying and selling, away from the overheads of shops and auction rooms. Around the world, antiques are offered for sale and traded daily, with sites varying from global online marketplaces, such as eBay, to specialist dealers' websites.

When searching online, remember that some people may not know how to accurately describe their item or may use special terminology. General category searches, even though more time consuming, and even deliberately misspelling a name, can yield results. Also, if something looks too good to be true, it probably is. Using this book to get to know your market visually, so that you can tell the difference between a real bargain and something that sounds like one, is a good start.

As you will understand from buying this book, color photography is vital – look for online listings that include as many images as possible and check them carefully. Be aware that colors can appear differently, even between computer screens.

Always ask the vendor questions about the object, particularly regarding condition. If there is no image, or you want to see another aspect of the object – ask. Most sellers (private or trade) will want to realize the best price for their items so will be more than happy to help – if approached politely and sensibly.

Sellers should describe their item accurately. Include as much detail as possible including maker, size, color, any other marks, condition, and damage. Always include as many digital photographs as possible. These should be shot in focus and in clear, preferably natural, light. Try to find out likely shipping and packaging costs in advance and aim to include them on your listing, along with methods of payment you will accept. Have the item at hand and be ready to answer questions promptly from potential buyers.

As well as the 'e-hammer' price, you will probably have to pay additional transactional fees such as packing, shipping, and possibly regional or national taxes. It is always best to ask for an estimate for these additional costs before leaving a bid. This will also help you tailor your bid as you will have an idea of the maximum price the item will cost if you are successful.

As well as the well-known online auction sites, such as eBay, there is a host of other online resources for buying and selling, for example fair and auction date listings.

# INTERNET RESOURCES

**Live Auctioneers**
www.liveauctioneers.com
info@liveauctioneers.com
*A free service which allows users to search catalogs from selected auction houses in the US and Europe. Through its connection with eBay, users can bid live via the Internet into salerooms as auctions happen. Registered users can also search through an illustrated archive of past catalogs and receive a free newsletter by email.*

**invaluable.com**
www.invaluable.com
sales@invaluable.com
*A subscription service which allows users to search selected European auction house catalogs. Also offers an extensive archive for appraisal uses.*

**The Antiques Trade Gazette**
www.atg-online.com
*The online version of the UK trade newspaper, comprising British auction and fair listings, news, and events.*

**Maine Antiques Digest**
www.maineantiquesdigest.com
*The online version of America's trade newspaper including news, articles, fair and auction listings, and more.*

**La Gazette du Drouot**
www.drouot.com
*The online home of the magazine listing all auctions to be held in France at the Hotel de Drouot in Paris and beyond. An online subscription enables you to download the magazine online.*

**AuctionBytes**
www.auctionbytes.com
*Auction resource with community forum, news, events, tips, and a weekly newsletter.*

**Internet Auction List**
www.internetauctionlist.com
*Auction news, online and offline auction search engines and live chat forums.*

**Go Antiques/Antiqnet**
www.goantiques.com
www.antiqnet.com
*An online global aggregator for art, antiques and collectibles dealers who showcase their stock online, allowing users to browse and buy.*

**eBay**
www.ebay.com
*Undoubtedly the largest and most diverse of the online auction sites, allowing users to buy and sell in an online marketplace with over 52 million registered users. Collectors should also view eBay Live Auctions (www.ebayliveauctions.com) where traditional auctions are combined with realtime, online bidding allowing users to interact with the saleroom as the auction takes place.*

**Tias**
www.tias.com
*An online global aggregator for art, antiques and collectibles dealers who showcase their stock online, allowing users to browse and buy.*

**Collectors Online**
www.collectorsonline.com
*An online global aggregator for art, antiques and collectibles dealers who showcase their stock online, allowing users to browse and buy.*

**Antiques and The Arts**
www.antiquesandthearts.com
*Website of Antiques and the Arts weekly newspaper. Calendar of events, auctions, shows, and book reviews.*

**PayPal**
www.paypal.com
*An online transaction site, allowing payment to be made and accepted in a secure environment.*

**BidPay**
www.bidpay.com
*An online transaction site, allowing payment for goods by Western Union money order, sterling cheque or payment to a US bank account.*

# GLOSSARY

## A

**albarello jar** An Italian tin-glazed earthenware pharmacy jar.

**albumen print** Photographic paper that is treated with egg white (albumen) to enable it to hold light sensitive chemicals.

**ashet** A large plate or dish.

**astragal** Architectural molding with a semi-circular section.

**aventurine** A translucent glass given a sparkling appearance by the incorporation of flecks of oxidised metal. Can also be used as a glaze on ceramics.

## B

**Bakelite** An early synthetic plastic which was patented in 1907.

**balance** An escape mechanism that is used in clocks without pendulums.

**baluster** A curved form with a bulbous base and slender neck.

**Baroque** An ornate and extravagant decorative style which was popular in the 17th and 18thC.

**bergère** The French term for an upholstered armchair.

**bezel** The groove or rim on the inside of the cover or lid on vessels such as teapots.

**bianco-sopra-bianco** A technique involving painting opaque white glaze on to a grayish ground.

**boulle** A type of marquetry that includes tortoiseshell and metal.

**brassing** Wear to plating that reveals the underlying base metal.

**break-front** A term for furniture with a projecting center section.

**broderie anglaise** White thread embroidered onto white cloth, used after the 1820s.

## C

**cabochon** A protruding, polished, but not faceted, stone.

**cabriole leg** A leg with two gentle curves that create an S-shape.

**cameo** Hardstone, coral or shell that has been carved to show a design in a contrasting color.

**cameo glass** Decorative glass made from two or more layers of differently colored glass, which are then carved or etched to reveal the color beneath.

**caryatid** An architectural column in the form of a woman.

**cased glass** Glass encased with a further layer of glass.

**celadon** A distinctive gray/green or blue/green glaze.

**center seconds hand** A seconds hand that is pivoted at the center of the dial.

**chamfered** A surface that has been cut with a slanted edge.

**champlevé** A type of decoration where enamel is applied to stamped hollows in metal.

**chapter ring** The ring of hour and minute numbers on a clock dial.

**character doll** A doll with a face that resembles a real child.

**charger** A large plate or platter, used for display or serving.

**chasing** The technique of decorating the surface of silver by punching it with small tools.

**chinoiserie** Oriental-style lacquered or painted decoration featuring figures and landscapes.

**chronometer** A timekeeper used for calculating longitude at sea.

**clock garniture** A matching clock and candelabra set.

**cloisonné** A decorative technique whereby metal cells are filled with colored enamels.

**commode** A decorated low chest of drawers with a curved form.

**composition** A mixture including wood pulp, plaster and glue and used as a cheap alternative to bisque in the production of dolls.

**core forming** An early form of glass-making where molten glass is wound around a mud core.

**crackle** A deliberate crazed glaze effect used on porcelain.

**credenza** The Italian term for a side cabinet with display shelves at both ends.

**crewelwork** A wool embroidery technique used on linen.

**cricket cage** A small box designed to amplify the chirping of a cricket contained therein.

## D

**Daguerrotype** An early type of photograph, from c1839 until the 1850s.

**Davenport** A large parlor sofa. In Europe, a small writing desk.

**dentils** Small teeth-like blocks that form a border under a cornice.

**Deutsche Blumen** Floral decoration found on 18thC faience and porcelain.

**diecast** Objects made by pouring molten metal into a closed metal die or mold.

**Ding** A very small dent in metal.

**dovetailing** A method of joining two pieces of wood together by interlocking mortises and tenons.

**dump** A doorstop made from left-over glass, often with decoration.

## E

**earthenware** A type of porous pottery that requires a glaze to make it waterproof.

**ebonised** Wood that has been dyed black to resemble ebony.

**egg and dart** A classical molding that incorporates egg and 'v' shapes used to enrich Neo-classical wares.

**enamel** Colored glass paste that is applied to surfaces to create a decorative effect.

**escapement** The mechanical part of the clock or watch that regulates the transfer of energy from the weights or spring to the movement of the clock or watch.

**escutcheon** A protective plate, as for a keyhole.

## F

**faïence** Earthenware treated with an impervious tin glaze.

**fairing** A small porcelain figure made in Eastern Germany and given away as prizes or sold inexpensively at fairs.

**Fazackerly** A style of floral painting found on English delft.

**Fazackerley colors** The bright enamel colors used to decorate pieces of English delft. The name probably derives from a pair of Liverpool delft mugs, dedicated to Thomas and Catherine Fazackerley, which were destroyed in WWII.

**festoon** A decorative motif in the form of a garland or chain of fruit, flowers and ribbons suspended on a loop.

**figuring** A natural pattern created by the grain in the wood.

**finial** A decorative knob on a terminal or cover of a vessel.

**flatware** Any type of cutlery.

**free blown** Glass blown and manipulated into shape without the use of a mold.

**fretwork** Geometric pierced decoration.

**frieze** A piece of wood supporting a table top or cornice.

**frit** Powdered glass added to white clay to produce a soft-paste porcelain. Also describes impurities found in old glass.

**fusee** A grooved device found in clocks that offsets the force of the spring as it runs down.

## G

**gadroon** A decorative border of flutes or reeds.

**gesso** A paste mixture applied to timber then carved and gilded.

**gnomon** The part of a sundial which casts the shadow.

**Greek key** A Classical motif of interlocking lines.

**grosse point** A stitch that crosses two warp and two weft threads.

**guilloché** An engraved pattern of interlaced motifs, sometimes with translucent enamels.

## H

**hard-paste porcelain** Porcelain made from kaolin, petuntse and quartz.

**harlequin set** A set of ceramics or furniture, in which the pieces are similar rather than identical.

**hiramakie** A Japanese decorative technique whereby a powdered charcoal design is coated with a layer of transparent lacquer.

**honey gilding** A decorative technique using gold leaf mixed with honey for a reddish tinge.

**hotei** The Japanese god of contentment and happiness.

## I J K

**intaglio** Cut or engraved decoration on glass.

**japanning** The process of coating objects with layers of colored varnish in imitation of lacquer.

**knop** The knob on lids and covers and also the bulge on the stem of a candlestick or glass.

**kovsh** A Russian shallow drinking vessel with a handle.

**kraak ware** Late Ming Chinese blue and white porcelain exported by Dutch traders in ships known as 'carracks.'

## L

**lacquer** An oriental varnish made from tree gum with a gloss finish.

**lead glass or crystal** A particularly clear type of glass with a high lead oxide content.

**lead glaze** A clear glaze with a lead based component.

**luster** An iridescent finish found on pottery and produced using metallic oxides.

## M

**manganese** A mineral used to produce a purple glaze.

**maiolica** Italian tin-glazed earthenware produced from the 14thC.

**marqueterie sur verre** A method of decorating glass in which a hot glass shape is pressed onto the surface of a shape.

**marquetry** A decorative veneer made up from colored woods.

**married** A term uses to describe a piece that is composed of parts that were not originally together.

**Meiji** A period in Japanese history dating from c1868-1912.

**Mon** A Japanese family crest. A common example is the 16-petal chrysanthemum flower.

**movement** The entire time-keeping mechanism of a clock or watch.

## N O

**netsuke** A small toggle used to secure pouches and boxes hung on cords through the belt of a kimono.

**ogee** An S-shaped shallow curve.

**okimono** A Japanese ornamental carving.

**opalescent** An opal-like, milky glass with subtle gradations of color.

**opaline glass** A translucent white glass made with the addition of oxides and bone ash.

**ormolu** Bronze gilding used in 18thC and early 19thC France as decorative mounts.

**overglaze** Enamel or transfer-printed decoration on porcelain that is applied after firing.

**ovolo** A quarter-circle shaped molding.

## P

**parian** A semi-matt type of porcelain, made with feldspar, that does not require a glaze.

**parquetry** A variant of marquetry where veneers are applied in symmetrical designs.

**parure** A jewelry set usually comprising a matching necklace, pair of earrings, bracelet and a pin.

**paste** The mixture of ingredients that make up porcelain. Also a compound of glass used to make imitation gemstones.

**patina** A surface sheen on objects that is produced over time through polishing and handling.

**pavé setting** A method of mounting jewels so that each stone is set close to the next.

**pearlware** English earthenware with a blue tinted glaze, developed by Wedgwood.

**penwork** Indian ink decoration applied with a pen.

**petit point** Finely worked embroidery with stitches that cross one warp or weft thread.

**pinion** A small toothed gear within a clock movement.

**piqué** A decorative technique where small strips or studs of gold are inlaid onto ivory or tortoiseshell on a pattern and secured in place by heating.

**plique-à-jour** Technique where enamel is set into an openwork metal frame to create an effect similar to stained glass.

**porcelain** A mixture of china clay and china stone that becomes hard, translucent and white when fired. Hard-paste porcelain is fired at a higher temperature than soft paste.

**pounce pot** A small pot for gum dust used to prevent ink from spreading.

**press-molded** Ceramics formed by pressing clay into a mold. Pressed glass is made by pouring molten glass into a mold and pressing it with a plunger.

## Q R S

**repoussé** A French term for the raised, 'embossed', decoration on metals such as silver.

**sabot** The metal 'shoe' on the end of cabriole legs.

**saber leg** A leg shaped like the curved blade of a saber.

**scagliola** Imitation marble made with plaster.

**sgraffito** A pattern of scratched decoration that reveals a contrasting color beneath.

**slip** A mixture of clay and water used to decorate pottery and to produce slip-cast wares.

**soft-paste porcelain** Porcelain made from kaolin, powdered glass, soapstone and clay.

**splat** The central upright in a chair back.

**squab** A stuffed cushion.

**sterling silver** A standard of silver where the silver content is 92.5 per cent pure silver.

**stretchers** The bar between two legs on tables and chairs used to stabilise the structure.

**stuff-over seat** A chair with an upholstered seat rail.

## T

**tall case clock** A weight-driven, free-standing clock.

**tin-glaze** An opaque tin oxide glaze used on earthenware.

**transfer printing** A method of printing ceramics that involves transferring a design from an inked engraving to a vessel.

**transitional** The Chinese period around the transition from the Ming to the Qing dynasty.

## U V W Y

**underglaze** Decoration painted on to a biscuit body before glazing.

**veneering** A technique used in furniture making which involves using fine woods to cover or decorate the surface of less expensive woods.

**vermeil** Gold-plated silver.

**wheel engraving** A method of engraving into the surface of glass by holding a rotating wheel of stone or metal against it.

**white metal** Precious metal that is possibly silver, but not officially marked as such.

**yellow metal** Precious metal that is possibly gold, but not officially marked as such.

**INDEX**